Hispanic Writers

Hispanic Writers

SECOND EDITION

*A
Selection
of Sketches
from*
**Contemporary
Authors**

*Contains a variety of entries on
twentieth-century Hispanic writers, all originally
written or updated for this volume*

GALE GROUP

**Detroit
San Francisco
London
Boston
Woodbridge, CT**

STAFF

Scot Peacock, *Senior Editor and Project Manager*

Jerry Moore, *Project Editor*

Simone Sobel, *Assistant Project Editor*

Amy Francis, John Jorgenson, *Senior Content Editors*

Regie A. Carlton, Dwayne D. Hayes, *Content Editors*

Anja Barnard, Elizabeth A. Cranston, Thomas Wiloch,
Associate Content Editors

Kristen A. Dorsch, *Assistant Content Editor*

Susan M. Trosky, *Managing Editor*

Victoria B. Cariappa, *Research Manager*

Andrew Guy Malonis, Barbara McNeil, Gary J. Oudersluys, Maureen Richards,
Cheryl L. Warnock, *Research Specialists*

Tamara C. Nott, Tracie A. Richardson, Corrine A. Stocker, *Research Associates*

Phyllis J. Blackman, Tim Lehnerer, Patricia L. Love,
Research Assistants

Library of Congress Catalog Card Number 62-52046
ISBN 0-8103-8377-2

Printed in the United States of America

10 9 8 7 6 5 4 3 2 1

Contents

Introduction

An Important Information Source on Hispanic Literature and Culture

The first and second editions of *Hispanic Writers* cumulatively provide students, teachers, researchers, and interested readers with comprehensive and accurate biographical and bibliographical information on approximately 550 authors who are a part of twentieth-century Hispanic literature and culture in the Americas. Those covered include authors from the United States, Puerto Rico, Cuba, Mexico, the Spanish-speaking countries of Central and South America, as well as a limited number of authors from Spain who have influenced the literature of the New World. Most of the authors represented in *Hispanic Writers* are available in English translation, making this book an especially useful guide to American audiences interested in Hispanic culture.

Broad Coverage in a Single Source

Before preparing the first edition of *Hispanic Writers*, the editors of *Contemporary Authors* conducted a telephone survey of librarians and mailed a print survey to more than four thousand libraries to help determine the kind of reference source libraries wanted. The list of authors compiled was then submitted for review to an advisory board of prominent members of the Hispanic community: Oscar Hijuelos, Pulitzer-Prize-winning novelist; Nicholas Kanellos, founder and publisher of Arte Publico Press in Houston; Luis Leal, director of the Center for Chicano Studies at the University of California, Santa Barbara; Doris Meyer, professor of Hispanic studies at Connecticut College; and David Unger, co-director of the Latin American Writers Institute in New York City. The editors of the second edition of *Hispanic Writers* expanded upon the work of the first edition's advisory board to select nearly 150 new entries while revising and completely updating approximately 100 entries from the first edition.

Hispanic Writers provides single-source coverage of a diverse set of authors:

- **Major literary figures** such as Federico Garcia Lorca, Pablo Neruda, Federico Gamboa, Gabriela Mistral, Jorge Luis Borges, Gabriel Garcia Marquez, Carlos Fuentas, Oscar Hijuelos, Camilo Jose Cela, and Octavio Paz.

- **Social and political figures** including Bolivian Liberal Party leader Alcides Arguedas, Brazilian theologian Leonardo Boff, former President of the Dominican Republic Juan Bosch, and former Nicaraguan vice president Sergio Ramirez.

- **Scholars, historians, and journalists** such as Juan Estevan Arellano, Ron Arias, Roberto Arlt, Maria Teresa Babin, Jose Augustin Balseiro, Elizabeth Coonrod Martinez, Gregory Rabassa, Victor Manuel Valle, and Victor E. Villasenor.

- **Lesser-known writers not well covered in other sources,** including Lya Fett Luft, Javier Marias, Tomas Eloy Martinez, Cherrie Moraga, Achy Obejas, Milcha Sanchez-Scott, and Gloria Velasquez.

Easy Access to Information

Both the newly written and the completely updated entries in *Hispanic Writers* provide in-depth information in a format designed for ease of use. Individual paragraphs of each entry, labeled with descriptive rubrics, ensure that a reader seeking specific information can quickly focus on the pertinent portion of an entry.

Sketches in *Hispanic Writers* contain the following biographical and bibliographical information:

- **Entry heading:** the most complete form of author's name, plus any pseudonyms or name variations used for writing

- **Personal information:** author's date and place of birth, family data, ethnicity, educational background, political and religious affiliations, and hobbies and leisure interests

- **Addresses:** author's home, office, or agent's addresses, plus e-mail and fax numbers, as available

- **Career summary:** name of employer, position, and dates held for each career post; resume of other vocational achievements; military service

- **Membership information:** professional, civic, and other association memberships and any official posts held

- **Awards and honors:** military and civic citations, major prizes and nominations, fellowships, grants, and honorary degrees

- **Writings:** a comprehensive, chronological list of titles, publishers, dates of original publication and revised editions, and production information for plays, television scripts, and screenplays

- **Adaptations:** a list of films, plays, and other media which have been adapted from the author's work

- **Work in progress:** current or planned projects, with dates of completion and/or publication, and expected publisher, when known

- **Sidelights:** a biographical portrait of the author's development; information about the critical reception of the author's works; revealing comments, often by the author, on personal interests, aspirations, motivations, and thoughts on writing

- **Biographical and critical sources:** a list of books and periodicals in which additional information on an author's life and/or writings appears

Other Features

This edition of *Hispanic Writers* provides indexing to the entries in both the first and second editions and directs the reader to the most current entry.

- **Cumulative Index:** Lists the names, name variations, and pseudonyms of authors featured in both the first and second editions of *Hispanic Writers*.

- **Nationality Index:** Lists alphabetically the authors featured in both the first and second editions of *Hispanic Writers* according to country of origin and/or country of citizenship.

Suggestions Are Welcome

The editors hope that you find *Hispanic Writers* a useful reference tool and welcome comments and suggestions on any aspect of this work. Please send comments to : The Editors, *Hispanic Writers*, Gale Group, 27500 Drake Rd., Farmington Hills, MI 48331-3535; or call at 1-248-699-4253; or fax at 1-248-699-8054.

A

ACUNA, Rodolfo
  See ACUNA, Rodolfo F(rancis)

* * *

ACUNA, Rodolfo F(rancis) 1932-
  (Rodolfo Acuna, Rudy Acuna)

PERSONAL: Born May 18, 1932, in Los Angeles, CA; son of Francisco and Alicia (Elias) Acuna; married Guadalupe Compean, 1984; children: (former marriage) Frank, Walter; Angela. *Education:* California State University, Los Angeles, B.A. (social science), 1957, B.A. (general), 1958, M.A., 1962; University of Southern California, Ph.D., 1968. *Politics:* "Radical." *Religion:* Catholic.

ADDRESSES: Office—Department of Chicano Studies, California State University, Northridge, 18111 Nordhoff St., Northridge, CA 91324.

CAREER: Worked as columnist for the *Los Angeles Herald-Examiner;* California State University, Northridge, professor of Chicano studies, 1969—. Member of board of Labor/Community Strategy Center; member of Committee in Solidarity with the People of El Salvador.

AWARDS, HONORS: Community service award from Liberty Hill Foundation; Rockefeller Humanities fellowship; Ford grant; outstanding scholar awards from American Council of Learned Societies and National Association of Chicano Studies; award from University of Guadalajara/state of Jalisco (Mexico) for contributions to border research.

WRITINGS:

(Under name Rudy Acuna) *The Story of the Mexican Americans: The Men and the Land,* American Book Co. (New York City), 1969.
(With Peggy Shackelton, under name Rudy Acuna) *Cultures in Conflict: Problems of the Mexican Americans* (children's textbook), Charter School Books, 1970.
(Under name Rudy Acuna) *A Mexican-American Chronicle,* American Book Co., 1971.
(Under name Rodolfo Acuna) *Occupied America: The Chicano's Struggle toward Liberation,* Canfield Press, 1972,), 1981, 3rd edition, Harper (New York City 1987.
Sonoran Strongman: Ignacio Pesqueira and His Times, University of Arizona Press (Tucson, AZ), 1974.
A Community Under Seige: A Chronicle of Chicanos East of the Los Angeles River, 1945-1975, University of California, Los Angeles, Chicano Studies Research Center (Los Angeles, CA), 1984.
Anything but Mexican: Chicanos in Contemporary Los Angeles, Verso (New York City), 1996.
Sometimes There Is No Other Side: Chicanos and the Myth of Equality, University of Notre Dame (Notre Dame, IN), 1998.

Contributor to periodicals, including *Arizona and the West, Los Angeles Times,* and *Texas Observer,* and to the Pacific News Service.

WORK IN PROGRESS: A collection of previously published newspaper essays on Los Angeles in the 1980s; *When the Moment Comes: The Revolt of the Mexican Cotton Pickers, 1933.*

SIDELIGHTS: Professor of Chicano studies at the University of California, Northridge, Rodolfo F. Acuna is the author of several books and textbooks on Chicano and Mexican history. Acuna founded the Chicano Studies program at Northridge and has played a part in making it one of the largest departments of its kind in the United States. His own writings reveal the plight of Hispanic Americans in a racist environment, and as a person who grew up speaking Spanish as a first language, he has been a proponent of bilingual education. To quote James McCarthy in the *Dictionary of Hispanic Biography,* Acuna "has remained a controversial figure throughout his academic career, and continues to challenge American society for what he calls its 'endemic racism.'"

Born in Los Angeles in 1932, Acuna grew up with a strong sense of the unjust aspects of American life. In a *Nation* piece on bilingual education he recalled "having to sit through English-only sessions and being pinched by teachers for speaking Spanish" as a schoolboy. His firsthand experience of racism continued after he volunteered for military service during the Korean War and suffered hostile treatment by white soldiers. He has spent the rest of his career as a teacher and writer trying to draw attention to "inequity and systematic unfairness directed at racial minorities," to quote McCarthy.

Acuna earned his Ph.D. from the University of Southern California in 1968. The following year he joined the faculty of California State University at Northridge, where he created the Chicano Studies program and developed much of the curriculum for it. After being denied tenure by the institution in 1991, Acuna sued his university, claiming that he was the victim of the same sort of racism that he had been writing about. The lawsuit garnered quite a bit of media attention in California, and Acuna told the *Dictionary of Hispanic Biography* that his case "will make it easier for others to sue on the basis of discrimination."

As an author Acuna is perhaps best known for *Occupied America: The Chicano's Struggle toward Liberation,* an historical study in which he argues that the United States's acquisition of the Southwest from Mexico was an act of imperialism. Referring to the Chicano population in the United States as an "internal colony," Acuna contends that Mexican Americans continue to suffer the effects of economic exploitation and racism perpetrated upon them by an Anglo majority. "My purpose is to bring about an awareness . . . of the forces that control and manipulate seven million

people in this country," he notes in the book. "If Chicanos can become aware of *why* they are oppressed and *how* the exploitation is perpetuated, they can work more effectively toward ending their colonization." Acuna told *CA* that in later editions of *Occupied America* he "broke with the internal colonial model, giving a more materialist interpretation."

Occupied America elicited contrasting responses from reviewers. Some critics found the book lacking in objectivity, while others appreciated the study's challenge to traditional interpretations of the Chicano experience. Writing in the *Western Historical Quarterly,* Victor C. Dahl, for example, called the work "an angry polemic," and charged that it "abounds with generalizations defying either substantiation or refutation." On the other hand, Robert W. Blew's *Southern California Quarterly* review of *Occupied America* praised the study's scholarly content and found it to contain "an intimacy and vigor that is frequently lacking in secondary studies." Blew declared that Acuna "has presented a provocative, stimulating, and challenging interpretation and view of the history of the southwestern portion of the United States." Similarly impressed were Carrol Hernandez and Nathaniel N. Wagner, who concluded in the *International Migration Review* that while Acuna's perspective may be unpopular, he "is trying to rectify myths and distortions that came about as a result of the 'objective academic' writing of past American historians."

BIOGRAPHICAL/CRITICAL SOURCES:

BOOKS

Acuna, Rodolfo, *Occupied America: The Chicano's Struggle toward Liberation,* Canfield Press, 1982.
Contemporary Literary Criticism, Volume 2, Gale (Detroit, MI), 1974.
Dictionary of Hispanic Biography, Gale, 1996, pp. 3-5.

PERIODICALS

Black Issues in Higher Education, July 27, 1995, pp. 27-30.
International Migration Review, Volume 7, number 4, 1973.
Los Angeles Times Book Review, January 20, 1985.
Nation, June 29, 1998, pp. 2-3.
Southern California Quarterly, fall, 1973.
Western Historical Quarterly, July, 1973.*

ACUNA, Rudy
  See ACUNA, Rodolfo F(rancis)

*   *   *

ADOUM, Jorge Enrique 1926-

PERSONAL: Born in 1926.

ADDRESSES: Home—Paris, France.

CAREER: Writer. Worked as director of Casa de la Cultura Ecuatoriana (publishers), national director of Ecuadorian culture, and secretary of Institute of Theatre and Folklore in Ecuador.

AWARDS, HONORS: Ecuadorian National Prize for Poetry, for *El enemigo y la manana;* Poetry prize from Casa de las Americas, for *Dios trajo la sombra.*

WRITINGS:

Poderes; o, El libro que divinizia, Editorial Fernandez, 1940.
Las llaves del reino, Quito, 1942.
Ecuador amargo (verse), Casa de la Cultura Ecuatoriana, 1949.
Los cuadernos de la tierra (verse; includes "Los origenes" and "El enemigo y la manana"), Casa de la Cultura Ecuatoriana, 1952, revised edition (includes *Dios trajo la sombra* and *Eldorado y las occupaciones nocturnas*), Editorial Casa de la Cultura Ecuatoriana, 1963.
Poesia del siglo XX: Rilke, Claudel, Lubicz-Milosz, Hughes, Eliot, Nicolas, Guillen, Maiacovski, Garcia Lorca, Vallejo, Hikmet, Neruda (criticism), Editorial Casa de la Cultura Ecuatoriana, 1957.
(Editor) Jose de la Cuadra, *Obras completas,* Editorial Casa de la Cultura Ecuatoriana, 1958.
Dios trajo la sombra (verse), Casa de la Cultura Ecuatoriana, 1959.
Eldorado y las ocupaciones nocturnas (verse), Editorial Casa de la Cultura Ecuatoriana, 1961.
(Contributor) Paulo de Carvalho Neto, editor, *Folklore de Lican y Sicalpa,* Casa de la Cultura Ecuatoriana, 1962.
(Editor) Jose de la Cuadra, *Cuentos,* Casa de las Americas, 1970.
Do aprendiz e seus misterios, Editora Pensamento, 1972.

Do companheiro e seus misterios, Editora Pensamento, 1972.
Esta e a maconario, Editora Pensamento, 1972.
Informe personal sobre la situacion, J. Gimenez-Arnau, 1973.
Adonai: Novela iniciates do colegio dos magos, Editora Pensamento, 1973.
Informe personal sobre la situacion, Casa de las Americas, 1975.
As chaves do reino interno; ou, O conhecimento de si mesmo, Editora Pensamento, 1978.
Entre Marx y una mujer desnuda: Texto con personajes, Siglo Veintiuno, 1978.
No son todos los que estan, Editorial Seix Barral, 1979.
Teatro, la subida a los infiernos, 1976, Casa de la Cultura Ecuatoriana, 1981.
Ecuador, imagenes de un preterio presente, Editorial El Conejo, 1981.
La gran literatura ecuatoriana del 30, Editorial El Conejo, 1984.
Ciudad sin angel, Siglo Veintiuno, 1995.

Also author of *Yo me fui por la tierra con tu nombre* (verse), *Notas del hijo prodigo,* and *Relato del extranjero* (verse).*

*   *   *

AGUILERA, Carolina Garcia
  See GARCIA-AGUILERA, Carolina

*   *   *

AGUSTINI, Delmira 1886-1914

PERSONAL: Born October 24, 1886, in Montevideo, Uruguay; murdered, 1914; married Enrique Job Reyes, 1914.

CAREER: Poet.

WRITINGS:

El Libro Blanco (title means "The White Book"), 1907.
Cantos de la Manana (title means "Songs of Morning"), 1910.

Los Calices Vacios (title means "The Empty Chalices"), O. M. Bertani (Montevideo), 1913.

El Rosario de Eros (title means "The Rosary of Eros") M. Garcia (Montevideo), 1924.

Los Astros del Abismo (title means "Stars of the Abyss"), M. Garcia (Montevideo), 1924.

Por Campos de Ensueno, B. Bauza (Barcelona), 1927.

Obras Poeticas, Talleres Graficos de Institutos Penales (Montevideo), 1940.

Poesias completas, Editorial Losada (Buenos Aires), 1944.

Correspondencia Intima, Biblioteca Nacional, Publicaciones del Departamento de Investigaciones (Montevideo), 1969.

Antologia, edited by Esther de Caceres, Ministerio de Educacion y Cultura (Montevideo), 1986.

Poesia, Casa de Las Americas (Ciudad de la Habana), 1988.

SIDELIGHTS: Delmira Agustini was born in Montevideo, Uruguay, to an upper middle-class family. Her mother had been a teacher before marrying, and she tutored Delmira at home, supporting her prodigy daughter's writing with an atmosphere of quiet solitude. Agustini published her first book of poetry when she was twenty-one. The lawyer Vaz Ferreira, after reading *El Libro Blanco,* stated, "Considering her age and so forth, if I had to compare this book to anything, I would simply describe it as a miracle." Agustini's mother was very protective of her young daughter, whom she called "Baby," and was always at her side when she left their home.

Agustini's poetry, however, was filled with passion and symbolic sex. Lucia Fox-Lockert, writing in *Americas,* said Agustini "paid homage to Eros in her work." When the family moved to another town close by, Agustini traveled by train to Montevideo for classes in painting, French, and piano. In 1908 she met Enrique Job Reyes, a non-intellectual farm auctioneer, and a long relationship developed that led to marriage some years later. Her letters to him were childish and sometimes signed "Baby, Delmira and I." Fox-Lockert commented, "Agustini's critics have seized upon this correspondence as evidence that she had a dual personality. Some of them see in her a lifelong urge to disguise herself in order to play games with those who loved her." Fox-Lockert wrote that Agustini's dedication of her second book *Cantos de la Manana* "wholly to Eros" is reflected by the prologue and said that "the themes of love and death interweave constantly."

Agustini met and corresponded with poet Ruben Dario, finding him "a soul of depth that could understand her," wrote Fox-Lockert. One of the letters to Dario read, "I don't know whether you have seen insanity face to face and struggled with it in the anguished loneliness of a hermetic spirit. There is, there can be, no sensation more horrible."

Agustini's third book, *Los Calices Vacios,* was published in 1913, a year before her death. She commented, "While my previous books were sincere and produced with little premeditation, these calices vacios, brought forth in a beautiful moment of exalted perception, are the most sincere, the least premeditated . . . and the most beloved." Agustini married Job Reyes in 1914 and left him after less than two months of marriage on grounds of "vulgarity."

Fox-Lockert wrote of Augustini, "Traditional biographies seem to convey that she had been too spoiled by her parents to be able to accept living with a 'vulgar' man." Fox- Lockert explored the possibility that Job Reyes may have married two different women—Baby, who would have been happy in the marriage, and the poet "who needed nights for composing and for her poetic trance." Alone again, Agustini wrote *El Rosario de Eros.* Fox-Lockert wrote, "The time had come when she would be able to make herself whole, join her fantasy world to the real world."

Agustini began seeing poet Ricardo Mas de Ayala. Her husband had been seeking help from friends to intercede on his behalf, but Agustini would not return to him. Job Reyes ultimately killed Agustini, then himself, with a pistol. Fox-Lockert wrote that "Agustini exemplifies a conflict of the divided self—in her case the division was between the poet and the woman." She vacillated between being "an obedient daughter and proper young woman," and a poet with all her "rebelliousness, her passion and her desire for freedom." It was only when she tried to wed her two extremes that she had problems, and ended with her final acceptance of herself as a poet. Fox-Lockert commented that Agustini's poetry "is still read and appreciated for her robust individualism and her courage to reveal the intimate secrets of her fantasy."

BIOGRAPHICAL/CRITICAL SOURCES:

PERIODICALS

Americas, January-February, 1987, p. 38.*

ALBA, Bernardo Dominguez 1904-1994
(Rogelio Sinan, a pseudonym)

PERSONAL: Born April 25, 1904 (some sources say 1902), in Taboga, Panama; died in 1994. *Education:* National Institute of Panama, graduated with a *bachillerato* (equivalent to baccalaureate degree), 1923; attended University of Rome, 1926; attended various universities in Chile, Italy, and Mexico.

CAREER: Author and educator. Panamanian consul to Calcutta, 1938-40; director, Department of Fine Arts, government of Panama, 1941-c.53; founder Biblioteca Selecta, Panama, 1941; director, National Department of Culture, Panama Ministry of Education; Panamanian diplomat in Mexico, 1953-60, and in India; University of Panama, drama instructor, c. 1960s; National Institute of Panama, Spanish instructor, c. 1960s; instructor of literature and theatre at universities in Brazil.

AWARDS, HONORS: Inter-American Short Story Prize, *El Nacional,* 1954 for *La boina roja;* received three Ricardo Miro National Literature Prizes, government of Panama, for *Plenilunio, La isla magica,* and *Semana santa en la niebla.*

WRITINGS:

UNDER PSEUDONYM ROGELIO SINAN

Onda (title means "Wave"), Casa Edifrice (Rome), 1929.

Incendios (title means "Fires"), Mar del Sur (Panama City), 1944.

Dos aventuras en el Lejano Oriente (title means "Two Adventures in the Far East"), Biblioteca Selecta (Panama City), 1947.

Plenilunio (title means "Full Moon"), [Panama City], 1947.

Semana santa en la niebla (title means "Holy Week in the Cloud"), Ediciones del Departamento de Cultura y Publicaciones (Panama City), 1949.

La boina roja (title means "The Red Beret"), Nacional (Panama City), 1954.

Los valores humanos en la lirica de Maples Arce, Conferencia (Mexico City), 1959.

Chiquilinga, Panama (Panama City), 1961.

La poesia panamena, (Panama City), 1962.

Cuna comun, Tareas (Panama City), 1963.

A la orilla de las estatuas maduras, Secretaria de Educacion Publica, Subsecretaria de Asuntos Culturales (Mexico City), 1967.

Saloma sin salomar (title means "Saloma without Salomar"), Ministerio de Educacion (Panama City), 1969.

Cuentos de Rogelio Sinan (title means "Stories by Rogelio Sinan"), Editorial Universitaria Centroamerican (San Jose), 1971.

Teatro infantil, Geminis (Panama City), 1977.

La isla magica, Instituto Nacional de Cultura (Panama City), 1977.

Los pajaros del sueno, Casa de la Cultura Ecuatoriana (Guayaquil, Ecuador), 1978.

El candelabro de los malos ofidios y otros cuentos, Signos (Mexico City), 1982.

El conejito; El Pato Patuleco; Motivo de Rato Perez; El caballito negro; El caballito del naranjal, Editorial Universitaria Centroamericana (San Jose), 1985.

La cucarachita Mandinga (title means "Mandinga the Cockroach"), Instituto Nacional de Cultura (Panama City), 1992.

SIDELIGHTS: Considered by some literary critics as the most important Panamanian author of the twentieth century, Bernardo Dominguez Alba, who was known by his pseudonym, Rogelio Sinan, devoted his life to promoting the cause of literature in his native land. As a writer, Sinan was widely known for his works of poetry and his short stories, as well as two exceptional, award-winning novels. His countrymen also recognize him for his contributions as a public servant and an educator. In addition to having served as the director for the National Department of Culture in Panama's Ministry of Education, Sinan was also a diplomat, serving his country in both Mexico and India. In addition to these duties, Sinan taught both literature and theater at some of Brazil's distinguished universities. Sinan's writing bloomed and matured during a time when the vanguard movement was sweeping through Panamanian literary circles during the 1920s and 1930s, and its influence is evident in his work.

A world traveler, Sinan was exposed to a range of styles, including German expressionism, French cubism, and Italian futurism. Together with his deep understanding and appreciation for his Panamanian heritage, Sinan melded these traits and developed a distinct style that has profoundly influenced a new generation of writers in Panama. His unique voice became evident with the publication of *Onda* ("Wave"), his first volume of poetry, in 1929, a work that some critics point to as Panamanian literature's break with modernism. In addition to this work, some of Sinan's more renowned collections of poetry include *Incendios*

("Fires"), *Semana santa en la niebla* ("Holy Week in the Cloud"), and *Saloma sin Salomar* ("Saloma without Salomar"), all containing inventive language and creative structure. Many critics believe Sinan's prose was even more innovative, as he employed narrative techniques such as inner monologue and stream-of-consciousness, as well as creating surrealistic scenes and dream sequences, which demand much of the reader.

Born on the lush island of Taboga, which is just off of the mainland, Sinan was imbued with the importance of nature in the Panamanian psyche. His stories reflect this importance, as they are filled with vivid images of the country's physical landscape. "Rogelio Sinan," asserted *Dictionary of Literary Biography* contributor Maida Watson Espener, "has always believed that universal values in literature must spring from a thorough knowledge of the writer's own national reality. His poetry, fiction, and drama are permeated with a sense of Panama's history, landscape, and racial relations." Yet, being a diplomat who had come to know his country from both a native and foreign perspective, Sinan had a deep understanding of Panama's social and political landscapes as well. His works are especially critical of oppressive foreign influences, as well as the country's upper class, both of which he usually symbolizes as being from the white, or lighter race. The heroes of his stories are usually of a darker skin color, symbolizing the indigenous native. Though Sinan never makes specific mention of it, the island of Taboga plays a significant role in some of his works, particularly in *La isla magica,* his most praised novel. The exotic island setting, separated from the rest of the world, is an allusion to a time before colonialism and the invasion of foreign influences. A complex work, *La isla magica* is also important because it signifies Sinan's divergence into magical realism.

Sinan's peers recognized his literary achievements, as he collected a host of awards for his work. *Plenilunio, La isla magica,* and *Semana santa en la niebla* all were awarded the prestigious Ricardo Miro National Literature Prize, Panama's highest literary prize, and Sinan also won many other awards. His crowning moment may have come in 1988, when the Panamanian government bestowed upon him several medals as national homage for his fiction and his endless promotion of the art. Sinan was, according to Espener, "not only . . . an innovative writer but . . . a teacher and mentor to numerous writers during his many decades as the undisputed leader of the country's literary circles."

BIOGRAPHICAL/CRITICAL SOURCES:

BOOKS

Dictionary of Literary Biography, Volume 145: *Modern Latin-American Fiction Writers, Second Series,* edited by William Luis and Ann Gonzalez, Gale (Detroit, MI), 1994.*

* * *

ALBERTI, Rafael 1902-

PERSONAL: Born December 16, 1902, in Puerto de Santa Maria, Cadiz, Spain; immigrated to Rome, Italy; married Maria Tersa Leon (deceased); married M. A. Mateo, 1990; children: Aitana (a daughter). *Education:* Attended a Jesuit academy in Spain.

CAREER: Poet, dramatist, and painter.

AWARDS, HONORS: National Prize for Literature (Spain), 1924, for *Marinero en tierra;* Cervantes Prize, 1983.

WRITINGS:

ALL POETRY, EXCEPT AS NOTED; IN ENGLISH

Sobre los angeles (1927-1928) (also see below), Editorial Plutarco, 1924, translation by Geoffrey Connell published as *Concerning the Angels,* University of California Press, 1966.
A Spectre Is Haunting Europe: Poems of Revolutionary Spain, translation from the original Spanish manuscript by Ira Jan Wallach and Angel Flores, Critics Group (New York City), 1936.
La arboleda perdida y otras prosas (also see below), Editorial Seneca, 1942, translation by Gabriel Berns published as *The Lost Grove: Autobiography of a Spanish Poet in Exile,* University of California Press, 1976.
Rafael Alberti: Selected Poems, edited by Ben Belitt, translation by Lloyd Mallan, New Directions, 1944.
Poesias completas, Losada, 1961, translated by Mark Strand published as *The Owl's Insomnia* (text in English and Spanish), Atheneum (New York City), 1973.
Los ocho nombres de Picasso, y No digo mas que lo que no digo (1966-1970), inscribed by Pablo

Picasso, Editorial Kairos, 1970, translation published as *The Eight Names of Picasso.*

A Year of Picasso's Paintings, translation by Anthony Kerrigan, Abrams (New York City), 1971.

The Other Shore: 100 Poems, edited by Kosrof Chantikian, translated by Jose A. Elgorriaga and Martin Paul, introduction by Gabriel Berns, Kosmos (San Francisco), 1981.

El Negro, lithographs by Robert Motherwell, Tyler Graphics (Bedford, NY), 1983.

IN SPANISH

Marinero en tierra, Losada, 1924, 4th edition, 1970.

La amante canciones (also see below), Editorial Plutarco, 1925.

El alba del alheli (also see below),[Buenos Aires] 1927.

Cal y canto, Revista de Occidente, 1929.

El hombre deshabitado, Gama (Madrid), 1930.

La poesia popular en la lirica espanola contemporanea, W. Gronan, 1933.

Poesia, 1924-1930, Ediciones del arbol, 1934.

Verte y no verte: A Ignacio Sanchez Mejias, Fabula (Mexico), 1935.

Nuestra diaria palabra, [Madrid], 1936.

Trece bandas cuarenta y ocho estrellas, [Madrid], 1936.

Entre el clavel y la espada (1939-1940), illustrations by Maria Carmen, Losada, 1941.

El poeta en la Espana de 1931, [Buenos Aires], 1942.

Eh, los toros!, illustrations by Luis Seoane, Emece, 1942.

(Editor) Federico Garcia Lorca, *Antologia poetica,* Losada, 1942, revised edition, 1972.

(Compiler and author of introduction) *Eglogas y fabulas castellanas,* two volumes, Pleamar, 1944.

(Compiler and author of introduction) *Romancero general de la guerra espanola,* illustrations by Gori Munoz, Patronato Hispano Argentino de Cultura, 1944.

Pleamar (1942-1944), Losado, 1944.

A la pintura; cantata de la linea y del color, Imprenta Lopez, 1945.

Buenos Aires en tinta china, edited by Attilio Rossi, Losada, 1951.

Retornos de lo vivo lejano (1948-1952), Losada, 1952.

Ora maritima, seguido de Baladas y canciones del Parana (also see below), illustrations by Juan Batte Planas, Losada, 1953.

Maria Carmen Portela, Losada, 1956.

(Editor with Guillermo de Torre) Garcia Lorca, *Antologia poetica (1918-1936),* Losada, 1957.

(With Maria Teresa Leon; self-illustrated) *Sonrie China,* J. Muchnik, 1958.

Cal y canto, sobre los angeles, Sermones moradas, Losada, 1959.

El otono, otra vez, [Lima], 1960.

Los viejos olivos, Direccion de Cultura y Bellas Artes, Departmento de Publicaciones, 1960.

Poemas escenicos, Losada, 1962.

(Self-illustrated) *Suma taurina: Verso, prosa, teatro,* edited by Rafael Montesinos, Editorial R. M., 1963.

Diez sonetos romanos, Ediciones Galeria Bonino, 1964.

Rafael Alberti (anthology), edited by Eduardo Gonzales Lanuza, Ediciones Culturales Argentines, 1965.

(Editor and compiler) Lope Felix de Vega Carpio, *Poesias* (title means "Poetry"), Losada, 1965.

El Poeta en la calle, poesia civil, 1931-1965, compiled by Pablo Neruda, Editions de la Librairie du Globe, 1966.

(Contributor) Angel Caffarena Such, *Homenaje que ofrecen Picasso,* El Guadalhorce, 1966.

Poemas de amor, Alfaguara, 1967.

Roma, peligra para caminantes, 1964-1967, J. Mortiz, 1968.

Libro del mar, compiled by Aitaina Alberti, illustrations by F. Catal Roca, Lumen, 1968.

Poesias anteriores a marinero en tierra, 1920-1923, Ediciones V.A., 1969.

Prosas encontradas (1924-1942), compiled by Robert Marrast, Ayuso, 1970.

(Compiler and author of introduction) *Antologia poetica: Antonio Machado, Juan Ramon Jimenez, Federico Garcia Lorca,* illustrations by Jaume Pla, Nauta, 1970.

Canciones del alto valle del Aniene y otros versos y prosas, 1967-1972, Losada, 1972.

Retornos de lo vivo lejano 1948-1956, Libres de Sinera (Barcelona), 1972.

Obras completas, Aguilar, 1972.

La arboleda perdida: Libros I y II de memorias, Seix Barral, 1975.

Picasso, el rayo que no cesa, Poligrafa, 1975.

Poemas del destierro y de la espera (anthology), compiled by J. Corredor-Matheos, Espasa-Calpe (Madrid), 1976.

Alberti (anthology), Ediciones Litoral, 1976.

Coplas de Juan Panadero (1949-1977) seguida de Vida bilingue de un refugiado espanol en Francia (1939-1940), Editorial Mayoria, 1977.

Signos del dia, Seix Barral, 1978.

Los Cinco destacagados: Reparto, Calle del Aire, 1978.

Aire, que no me lleva el aire: Antologia juvenil, Labor, 1979.

Fustigada luz (1972-1978), Seix Barral, 1980.
Relatos y prosa, Bruguera, 1980.
Lo que cante y dije de Picasso, Bruguera, 1981.
Obra completa, 3 volumes, Aguilar, 1988.

Also author of *Costa sur de la muerte* (title means "The South Coast of Death"), 1936, *Cantata de los heroes y la fraternidad de los pueblos* (title means "Cantato of Heroes and the Fraternity of Peoples"), and *El burro explosivo.* Other works include: *Imagen primera de Federico Garcia (1940-1944),* Losada, 1945; (editor) *El gran amor de Gustavo Becquert,* Losada, 1946; *Raul Soldi,* Losada, 1963; *Lope de Vega y la poesia contemporanea seguita de la pajara pinta* (also see below), introduction by Marrast, Centre de recherches de l'Institut d'etudes hispaniques, 1964; and *Picasso en Avignon, commentaires a une peinture en mouvement,* translation from original Spanish manuscript by Georges Franck, Editions Cercle d'art, 1971. Also contributor to *Martin Fierro,* by Jose Hernandez Pueyrnedon, 1968. Translations include: Gloria Alcorta, *Visages (rostros),* Botella al mar, 1951; (and editor with Leon) *Doinas y baladas populares rumanas,* Losado, 1963; and *Abierto a todas horas (1960-1963),* A. Aguado, 1964. Plays include: *La pajara pinta* (title means "The Game of Forfeits"), Argentina, 1925; *De un momento a otro* (title means "From One Moment to the Next"), Editorial Bajel (Buenos Aires), 1942; *El adefesio* (three-act; title means "The Folly"; also see below), Losada, 1944, 1976; *Teatro: El hombre des habitado, El trebol florido, La gallarda* (also see below), Losada, 1950; *Noche de guerra en el Museo del Prado* (one-act), Ediciones Losange, 1956; *Teatro: El hombre des habitado, El trebol florido, El adefesio, La Gallarda,* Losada, 1959; and *Teatro: La lozana andaluza, De un momento a otro, Noche de guerra en el Museo del Prado,* Losado, 1964. Also author of *Fermin Gala.* Works included in numerous anthologies in Spanish and English.

SIDELIGHTS: Rafael Alberti and Federico Garcia Lorca are considered the most prominent twentieth-century Spanish surrealist poets. Unlike Garcia Lorca, Alberti is not well known on an international level; only a few of his books have been translated into English. Comparing Alberti to Garcia Lorca, editor Ben Belitt called Alberti "more intellectual." In *Rafael Alberti: Selected Poems,* Belitt wrote: "Alberti found his subjects more and more in himself, in his own contradictions and problems. . . . He lacked Lorca's instinctive joy and instinctive melancholy: his gifts were more varied and more conflicting." Making the same comparison, Ruth Stephan commented in

Poetry, "Those who know Spain say these two poets, one impulsive and sensuous, the other subjectively wise, are complementary components of the Spanish character."

Both Alberti and Garcia Lorca belonged to an avant garde group, the "Generation of 1929," which also included Spanish surrealist painter Salvador Dali. In his autobiographical collection, *The Lost Grove,* Alberti relates anecdotes concerning this coterie of writers and artists. *Best Sellers* called the work "a truly lovely book," in which Alberti "evokes all the joys, the sorrows, the embarrassments, and the longings of a boy growing up, and unashamedly presents all the pleasant and all the bitter reflections of the man looking back on himself as a youth."

"Alberti is so accomplished a craftsman of verse and so well trained in its different forms that he has no difficulty in finding the right measures for his different moods," said Luis Monguio in *The Poetry of Rafael Alberti: An Introduction.* In his early period of writing, Alberti wrote popular poetry such as that in *Marinero en tierra,* for which he won the National Prize for Literature. *Cal y canto* has been classified as "Gongoristic," after sixteenth-century poet Gongora, while *Sobre los angeles* is a surrealistic work. It is in this collection that "Alberti approaches nearest to pure poetry," critic Erik Proll once wrote. Alberti's later works are more spiritual in mood.

During the Spanish Civil War Alberti sympathized with the Popular Front and eventually became a self-imposed political exile in Paris, in Buenos Aires, and in Italy. He did not return to Spain until 1977, two years after the death of dictator Franciso Franco. *Sobre los angeles* reflects Alberti's strong political views. It deals with a "terrible crisis in which Alberti finds that for no explicable reason he has lost his trust in himself and his hold on existence, that things which have hitherto meant much to him and guided and sustained him have suddenly left him," and he has lost all that "gives savour and significance to life," wrote Monguio. Alberti speaks not only for himself, "who has lost a most precious possession but of a generation which fears that it has lost its way in the world," Monguio continued. Because of his ability to identify with the working class, Alberti has been called "a poet of the proletariat."

The Owl's Insomnia contains fifty selected poems from Alberti's *Poesias completas,* a work over one thousand pages in length. Reviewing the poetry in *Prairie Schooner,* Hilda Gregory remarked, "They are beautiful and strange, more moving when read in the company of their fellows than as single pieces."

BIOGRAPHICAL/CRITICAL SOURCES:

BOOKS

Contemporary Literary Criticism, Gale, Volume 7, 1977.

Dictionary of Literary Biography, Volume 108: *Twentieth-Century Spanish Poets, First Series,* Gale, 1991.

Jentsch-Grooms, Lynda, *Exile and the Process of Individuation: A Jungarian Analysis of Marine Symbolism in the Poetry of Rafael Alberti, Pablo Neruda, and Cecilia Meireles,* Albatros Ediciones (Valencia), 1983.

Jimenez-Fajardo, Salvador, *Multiple Spaces: The Poetry of Rafael Alberti,* Tamesis Books (London), 1985.

Manteiga, Robert C., *The Poetry of Rafael Alberti: A Visual Approach,* Tamesis Books, 1978.

Monguio, Luis, *The Poetry of Raphael Alberti: An Introduction,* University of California Press, 1966.

Morris, C. B., *Rafael Alberti's "Sobre los angeles": Four Major Themes,* University of Hull, 1966.

Morris, *A Generation of Spanish Poets 1920-1936,* Cambridge University Press, 1969.

Nantell, Judith, *Rafael Alberti's Poetry of the Thirties: The Poet's Public Voice,* University of Georgia Press (Athens), 1986.

Reference Guide to World Literature, second edition, St. James Press (Detroit), 1995.

Velloso, Jose Miguel, *Conversaciones con Rafael Alberti,* Sedmay Ediciones (Madrid), 1977.

Wesseling, Pieter, *Revolution and Tradition: The Poetry of Rafael Alberti,* Albatros, 1981.

PERIODICALS

American Poetry Review, November, 1976.
Best Sellers, May, 1977.
Choice, April, 1974; July/August, 1977.
Nation, May 28, 1973; January 11, 1975; April 16, 1977.
Newsweek, December 11, 1972.
Parnassus, fall/winter, 1974.
Poetry, August, 1974.
Prairie Schooner, fall, 1974.
Publishers Weekly, June 26, 1972; November 22, 1976.
Times Literary Supplement, October 15, 1971; March 11, 1994, p. 18.

Village Voice, June 20, 1974; March 16, 1993, p. 61.*

* * *

ALEGRIA, Fernando 1918-

PERSONAL: Born September 26, 1918, in Santiago, Chile; son of Santiago Alegria Toro (in business) and Julia Alfaro; married Carmen Letona Melendez, January 29, 1943; children: Carmen, Daniel, Andres, Isabel. *Education:* Bowling Green State University, M.A., 1941; University of California, Berkeley, Ph.D., 1947.

ADDRESSES: Home—55 Arlmonte Dr., Berkeley, CA 94707. *Office*—Department of Spanish and Portuguese, Stanford University, Stanford, CA 94305.

CAREER: University of Chile, Santiago, Chile, professor of Spanish, 1939; Bowling Green State University, Bowling Green, OH, Extension Division, instructor in Spanish, 1940-41; University of California, Berkeley, instructor, 1947-49, assistant professor, 1949-55, associate professor, 1955-63, professor of Spanish and Portuguese, 1964-67; Stanford University, Stanford, CA, professor of Spanish, 1967-87, professor of Portuguese, 1976-87, professor emeritus, 1987—. Consultant in Spanish–American literature, UNESCO, 1968. Cultural attache in Chilean Embassy, Washington, DC, 1970-73.

MEMBER: Instituto Internacional de Literatura Iberoamericana, American Association of Teachers of Spanish, Sociedad de Escritores (Chile).

AWARDS, HONORS: Latin American Prize of Literature, 1943, for *Lautaro: Joven libertador de Arauco;* Guggenheim fellow, 1947-48; Premio Atenea and Premio Municipal (both Chile), for *Caballo de copas.*

WRITINGS:

Recabarren, Antares, 1938.
Ideas esteticas de la poesia moderna, Multitud, 1939.
Leyenda de la ciudad perdida, Zig-Zag (Santiago, Chile), 1942.
Lautaro: Joven libertador de Arauco (juvenile fiction), Zig-Zag, 1943, 5th edition, 1965.
Ensayo sobre cinco temas de Tomas Mann, Funes, 1949.
Camaleon, Ediapsa, 1951.

La poesia chilena: Origenes y desarollo del siglo XVI al XIX, University of California Press (Berkeley), 1954.

Walt Whitman en hispanoamerica, Studium, 1954.

El poeta que se volvio gusano, Cuadernos Americanos, 1956.

Caballo de copas, Zig-Zag, 1957, 2nd edition, 1961, translated by Carlos Lozano published as *My Horse Gonzales,* Casa de las Americas, 1964.

Breve historia de la novela hispanoamericana, Studium, 1959, 2nd edition published as *Historia de la novela hispanoamericana,* De Andrea, 1965, published as *Nueva historia de la novela hispanoamericana,* Ediciones del Norte (Hanover, NH), 1985.

El cataclismo (short stories), Nascimento, 1960.

Las noches del cazador, Zig-Zag, 1961.

Las fronteras del realismo: Literatura chilena del siglo XX, Zig-Zag, 1962, 2nd edition published as *La literatura chilena del siglo XX,* 1967.

(Editor) *Novelistas contemporaneos hispanoamericanos,* Heath (New York City), 1964.

Manana los guerreros (novel), Zig-Zag, 1964.

Viva chile M!, Editorial Universitaria (Santiago), 1965.

(Editor and translator) Rene Marill, *Historia de la novela moderna,* Union Tipografica Editorial Hispano Americana, 1966.

Genio y figura de Gabriela Mistral, Editorial Universitaria de Buenos Aires (Buenos Aires, Argentina), 1966.

La novela hispanoamericana, siglo XX, Centro Editor de America Latina, 1967.

(Translator with others) Nicanor Parra, *Poems and Antipoems,* edited by Miller Williams, New Directions (New York City), 1967.

Los dias contados (novel), Siglo XXI, 1968.

Ten Pastoral Psalms (poetry; bilingual edition; English versions by Bernardo Garcia and Matthew Zion), Kayak (Santa Cruz, CA), 1968.

Como un arbol rojo, Editora Santiago, 1968.

La maraton del palomo (short stories), Centro Editor de America Latina, 1968.

Los mejores cuentos de Fernando Alegria, edited with prologue by Alfonso Calderon, Zig-Zag, 1968.

La literatura chilena contemporanea, Centro Editor de America Latina, 1969.

Instructions for Undressing the Human Race / Instrucciones para desnudar a la raza humana (poem; bilingual edition; English version by Matthew Zion and Lennart Bruce; also see below), Kayak, 1969.

Amerika (manifiestos de Vietnam), Editorial Universitaria, 1970.

(With others) *Literatura y praxis en America Latina,* Monte Avila Editores, 1974.

Retratos contemporaneos, Harcourt (New York City), 1979.

Coral de guerra, Nueva Imagen, 1979.

El paso de los gansos, Laia, 1980.

The Chilean Spring, translated by Stephen Fredman, Latin American Literary Review Press (Pittsburgh, PA), 1980.

(Contributor of poetry) Moraima de Semprun Donahue, *Figuras y contrafiguras en la poesia de Fernando Alegria,* Latin American Literary Review Press, 1981.

(Author of prologue) Pablo Neruda, *Canto general,* 2nd edition, Biblioteca Ayacucho, 1981.

(Editor and contributor) *Chilean Writers in Exile: Eight Short Novels,* Crossing Press (Trumansburg, NY), 1982.

Una especie de memoria, Editorial Nueva Imagen, 1983.

Changing Centuries: Selected Poems of Fernando Alegria (includes selections from *Instrucciones para desnudar a la raza humana*), translated by Stephen Kessler, Latin American Literary Review Press, 1984, 2nd edition, 1988.

Los trapecios, Ediciones Agua Pesada, 1985.

The Funhouse, translated by Kessler, Arte Publico (Houston, TX), 1986.

(Editor with Jorge Ruffinelli) *Paradise Lost or Gained? The Literature of Hispanic Exile,* Arte Publico, 1992.

Allende: A Novel (English translation of *Allende: Mi vecino, el presidente),* Stanford University Press (Stanford, CA), 1994.

Also author of *La venganza del general, La prensa, Literatura y revolucion,* 1970.

SIDELIGHTS: "The most distinguished Chilean writer living in the United States," reports Victor Perera in the *Nation,* "is the critic and novelist Fernando Alegria, who was [former Chilean President Salvador] Allende's cultural attache in Washington." Noted for his important critical works on Latin American literature, his poetry, and his novels, Alegria has been living in exile since a military junta overthrew Allende's government on September 11, 1973. His own experience as an expatriate—as well as his deeply felt opinions on the course of Chilean politics—have informed his writings throughout the years, particularly in the most recent decades.

A native of Santiago, Chile, Alegria was an avid reader as a child and was encouraged in his writing by his mother and grandmother. While still in high school he began to publish pieces in *La Nacion,* Santiago's daily newspaper, and by the time he was twenty he had completed his first full-length book, the biography of a Chilean labor movement leader entitled *Recabarren.* Alegria continued his studies at Bowling Green State University, majoring in literature. He put himself through graduate school by teaching Spanish and Portuguese, and after earning his Ph.D. he served as a professor at the University of California, Berkeley and at Stanford University.

Alegria made a name for himself in Chile after publishing *Caballo de copas,* an extended essay on the similarities between life among the Chilean working class and Hispanic laborers in California. The work was a bestseller in Chile, enabling Alegria to return to his homeland with a ready audience for his books. Once there, the author became actively involved in the Popular Unity Movement, led by his old friend Salvador Allende. When Allende was elected president of Chile in 1970, Alegria became the nation's cultural attache in Washington, D.C.

The high expectations attending Allende's election were dashed just three years later when a military junta overthrew the government and assassinated Allende. Alegria was in Chile at the time of the coup but managed to escape and return to the United States. He has lived in California ever since.

The Chilean Spring, Alegria's fictionalized account of a young photographer's ordeal and death at the hands of the junta, is a "tribute to a modestly heroic photographer [that] becomes a poignant elegy to a nation whose future has been taken from it," declared *New York Times Book Review* contributor Jeffrey Burke. "That Mr. Alegria accomplishes so much so effectively in so few pages," Burke continued, "is a remarkable achievement." Alegria also addressed the Allende overthrow in *Allende: A Novel,* a quasi-fictional biography of the socialist hero. "Alegria manages to provide interesting glimpses into Allende's complex personality," observed Jorge Heine in the *Journal of Latin American Studies.* "We are enriched by a book that makes one of Latin America's most significant leaders come alive in a way that only somebody who knew him so well as Alegria could have done."

His own experience as an exile led Alegria to seek out the writings of other Latin American expatriates, and the result was *Paradise Lost or Gained? The Literature of Hispanic Exile,* which he edited with Jorge

Ruffinelli. "The stories, poems and essays in this collection—some in English, some in Spanish—focus on different phases of [the exile] process," wrote Barbara Mujica in *Americas.* "Surprisingly, few of these pieces are nostalgic or angry. The best treats the dilemma of the exile with warmth and humor." Mujica concluded that Alegria and Ruffinelli "have done an excellent job of compiling material that increases our understanding of the trauma of exile. Through the intimate testimonies in *Paradise Lost or Gained?* millions of exiles who have been uprooted from their native soil cease to be faceless statistics and become flesh and blood men and women whose stories move and enlighten us."

BIOGRAPHICAL/CRITICAL SOURCES:

BOOKS

Dictionary of Hispanic Biography, Gale (Detroit, MI), 1996.

Epple, Juan Armando, *Nos reconoce el tiempo y silba su tonada* (interview), Ediciones LAR, 1987.

PERIODICALS

Americas, November/December, 1992, pp. 30-38, 39; May/June, 1993, pp. 60-61.
Books Abroad, winter, 1970.
Carleton Miscellany, number 3, 1969.
Chicago Review, number 1, 1968; January/February, 1971.
Journal of Latin American Studies, October, 1995, pp. 748-49.
Nation, February 11, 1978.
New York Times Book Review, May 11, 1980.
Poetry, March, 1970.
Publishers Weekly, April 5, 1993, pp. 66-67.*

*   *   *

ALEGRIA, Ricardo E(nrique) 1921-

PERSONAL: Born April 14, 1921, in San Juan, Puerto Rico; son of Jose S. and Celeste (Gallardo) Alegria; married Mela Pons (an artist), December 7, 1947; children: Ricardo, Jose Francisco. *Education:* University of Puerto Rico, B.A., 1943; University of Chicago, M.A., 1947; Harvard University, Ph.D., 1955. *Religion:* Roman Catholic.

ADDRESSES: Home—San Jose 101, San Juan, PR 00901. *Office*—Department of History, University of Puerto Rico, Rio Piedras, PR 00901.

CAREER: University of Puerto Rico, Rio Piedras, associate professor of history, 1947-55, director of archaeological museum and research center, 1947-55; Instituto de Cultura Puertorriquena (Institute of Puerto Rican Culture), San Juan, director, 1955-73; University of Puerto Rico, professor of anthropology and history, 1955—. Director, Office of Cultural Affairs, San Juan, 1973-76.

MEMBER: American Anthropological Association (fellow), Society for American Archaeology.

AWARDS, HONORS: Guggenheim Foundation fellow, 1953-55; Doctorate Honoris Causae, humanities, Catholic University (Puerto Rico), 1971; Doctorate Honoris Causae, law, New York University, 1971; National Trust for Historic Preservation award, 1973; Ph.D., University of Puerto Rico, 1974.

WRITINGS:

Historia de nuestros indios, illustrated by wife, Mela Pons de Alegria, Seccion de Publicaciones e Impresos, Departamento de Instruccion (San Juan, PR), 1950, 8th edition, Coleccion de Estudios Puertorriquenos (San Juan), 1972, translation by C. Virginia Matters published as *History of the Indians of Puerto Rico,* Coleccion de Estudios Puertorriquenos, 1970, 3rd edition, 1974.

La fiesta de Santiago Apostol en Loiza Aldea, prologue by Fernando Ortiz, Artes Graficas (Madrid), 1954.

El Instituto de Cultura Puertorriquena: Los primeros cinco anos, 1955-1960, Instituto de Cultura Puertorriquena, 1960.

El tema del cafe en la literature puertorriquena, Instituto de Cultura Puertorriquena, 1965.

(With others) *Cafe,* Instituto de Cultura Puertorriquena, 1967.

(Collector and editor) *Cuentos folkloricos de Puerto Rico,* Editorial El Ateneo (Buenos Aires, Argentina), 1967.

(Selector and adaptor) *The Three Wishes: A Collection of Puerto Rican Folktales,* translated by Elizabeth Culbert, illustrated by Lorenzo Homar, Harcourt (New York City), 1968.

Descubrimiento, conquista y colonizacion de Puerto Rico, 1493-1599, Coleccion de Estudios Puertorriquenos, 1969, translation published as *Dis-

covery, Conquest and Colonization of Puerto Rico, 1493-1599,* 1971.

El fuerte de San Jeronimo del Boqueron, Instituto de Cultura Puertorriquena, 1969.

A History of Our Indians, Urban Media Materials, 1970.

Apuntes en torno a la mitologia de los indios tainos de las Antillas Mayores y sus origenes suramericanos, Centro de Estudios Avanzados de Puerto Rico y el Caribe, Museo del Hombre Dominicano (Santo Domingo, Dominican Republic), 1978.

Las primeras representaciones graficas del indio americano, 1493-1523, Centro de Estudios Avanzados de Puerto Rico y el Caribe, Instituto de Cultura Puertorriquena, 1978.

El Instituto de Cultural Puertorriquena, 1955-1973: 18 anos contribuyendo a fortalecer neustra conciencia nacional, Instituto de Cultura Puertorriquena, 1978.

Fort of San Jeronimo Del Boqueron, Gordon Press (New York City), 1979.

Institute of Puerto Rican Culture, Gordon Press, 1979.

Utuado Ceremonial Park, Gordon Press, 1979.

Cristobal Colon el tesoro de los indios tainos de La Espanola, Fundacion Garcia-Arevalo (Santo Domingo), 1980.

El uso de la incrustacion en la escultura de los indios antillanos, Centro de Estudios Avanzados de Puerto Rico y el Caribe con la colaboracion de la Fundacion Garcia Arevalo, 1981.

Las primeras noticias sobre los indios Caribes, Editorial Universidad de Puerto Rico, en colaboracion con el Centro de Estudios Avanzados de Puerto Rico y el Caribe, 1981.

Ball Courts and Ceremonial Plazas in the West Indies, Yale University Publications in Anthropology (New Haven, CT), 1983.

(With Lucas Moran Arce and others) *Historia de Puerto Rico,* Librotex (San Juan), 1985, 2nd edition, 1986.

(With Irving Rouse) *Excavations at Maria de la Cruz Cave and Hacienda Grande Village Site, Loiza, Puerto Rico,* Yale University Publications in Anthropology, 1993.

(Contributor) *Taino: Pre-Columbian Art and Culture from the Caribbean,* Monacelli Press, 1998.

Also author of *Cacicazgo among the Aborigines of the West Indies,* 1947, and *La poblacion aborigen antillana y su relacion con otras areas de America,* 1948. Contributor of articles on archaeology and folklore to journals in Puerto Rico, the United States, and Mexico, including *Revista del Instituto de Lutural Puertorriquena, American Antiquity,* and *Revista Mexicana de Estudios Antropologicos.*

WORK IN PROGRESS: Writing on the folklore and history of Puerto Rico and on archaeology of the West Indies.

SIDELIGHTS: Ricardo E. Alegria is a noted Puerto Rican historian and anthropologist who, from 1955 through 1973, served as director of the prominent Instituto de Cultura Puertorriquena (Institute of Puerto Rican Culture). Alegria has also directed archaeological excavations at one of Puerto Rico's most important sites, comprising the Maria de la Cruz Cave and Hacienda Grande. At that site Alegria and his colleagues have found Archaic-age and very early Ceramic-age deposits that have broadened understanding of ancient Puerto Rican history. "Hacienda [Grande] is one of the earliest Ceramic-age sites in Puerto Rico, and is therefore of enormous importance," wrote William F. Keegan in *American Antiquity.* Keegan found Alegria's monograph *Excavations at Maria de la Cruz Cave and Hacienda Grande Village Site, Loiza, Puerto Rico* "a cogent expression of . . . senior scholars' interpretations of the earliest periods of Puerto Rican prehistory. It is essential reading for students of Caribbean archaeology."

In addition to his archaeological work, Alegria has compiled books of Puerto Rican folklore and has written histories of the European Age of Exploration. He is an authority on the Indians of Puerto Rico and has written a comprehensive summary of his native country's legacy in *Historia de Puerto Rico.*

BIOGRAPHICAL/CRITICAL SOURCES:

BOOKS

Dictionary of Hispanic Biography, Gale (Detroit, MI), 1996, pp. 13-14.

PERIODICALS

American Antiquity, October, 1993, p. 777.
Book World, August 17, 1969.
Horn Book, August, 1969.
New York Times Book Review, May 4, 1969.*

*　　　*　　　*

ALEIXANDRE, Vicente 1898-1984

PERSONAL: Born April 26, 1898, in Seville, Spain; died of kidney failure and shock from intestinal hemorrhage, December 14, 1984 (one source says December 13), in Madrid, Spain; son of Cirilo (an engineer) and Elvira (Merlo) Aleixandre. Attended University of Seville; University of Madrid, license in law and diploma in business, both 1919.

CAREER: Poet and writer, 1925-84. Central School of Commerce, Madrid, Spain, associate professor, 1919-21; Residencia de Estudiantes, Madrid, teacher of business terminology, 1921; worked for Ferrocarriles andaluces (railroad company), 1921-25. Lecturer at Oxford University and University of London, 1950, and in Morocco, 1953.

MEMBER: Real Academia Espanola, American Association of Teachers of Spanish and Portuguese (honorary fellow), Hispanic Society of America, Monde Latin Academy (Paris); corresponding member of Malaga Arts Academy, Academy of Science and Arts (Puerto Rico), and Hispanic-American Academy (Bogota).

AWARDS, HONORS: National Literary Prize (Spain), 1933, for *La destruccion o el amor;* Spanish Critics' Prize, 1963, 1969, and 1975; Nobel Prize in literature, Swedish Academy, 1977; Grand Cross of the Order of Carlos III, 1977; Gold Medal of the City of Madrid, 1984.

WRITINGS:

IN ENGLISH TRANSLATION; POEMS

La destruccion o el amor, Signo (Madrid), 1935, 2nd edition, 1967, translation by Stephen Kessler of selected poems published as *Destruction or Love,* Green Horse Three (Santa Cruz, CA), 1976.
Mundo a solas, Clan (Madrid), 1950, translation by Lewis Hyde and David Unger published as *World Alone/Mundo a solas* (bilingual edition), Penmaen Press (Great Barrington, MA), 1982.
Poems (bilingual edition), translations by Ben Belitt, Alan Brilliant, and others, Department of English, Ohio University, 1969.
Vicente Aleixandre and Luis Cernuda: Selected Poems (bilingual edition), translations by Linda Lehrer and others, Copper Beach Press (Providence, RI), 1974.
The Cave of Night: Poems (bilingual edition), translation by Jeffrey Bartman, Solo Press (San Luis Obispo, CA), 1976.
Twenty Poems, edited by Hyde, translations by Hyde and Robert Bly, Seventies Press (Madison, MN), 1977.

Poems-Poemas (bilingual edition), Unicorn Press, 1978.

A Longing for the Light: Selected Poems of Vicente Aleixandre, edited by Hyde, translations by Kessler and others, Harper (New York City), 1979.

The Crackling Sun: Selected Poems of the Nobel Prize Recipient 1977, translated and introduced by Louis Bourne, Sociedad General Espanola de la Libreria (Madrid), 1981.

A Bird of Paper: Poems of Vicente Aleixandre, translated by Willis Barnstone and David Garrison, Ohio University Press, 1982.

IN SPANISH; POEMS

Ambito, Litoral (Malaga), 1928.

Espadas como labios (title means "Swords Like Lips"; also see below), Espasa Calpe (Madrid), 1932.

Pasion de la tierra (title means "Passion of the Earth"; also see below), Fabula (Mexico), 1935, revised edition, Adonais (Madrid), 1946.

Sombra del paraiso (title means "Shadow of Paradise"; also see below), Adan (Madrid), 1944.

Poemas paradisiacos (title means "Poems of Paradise"; includes selections from *Sombra del paraiso*), [Malaga], 1952, 3rd edition, edited by Jose Luis Cano, Catedra, 1981.

Nacimiento ultimo (title means "Final Birth"), Insula (Madrid), 1953.

Historia del corazon (title means "History of the Heart"), Espasa Calpe, 1954.

Antigua casa madrilena (title means "Ancient Madrid House"; also see below), Hermanos Bedia (Santander, Spain), 1961.

Picasso (long poem), [Malaga], 1961.

En un vasto dominio (title means "In a Vast Dominion"; includes *Antigua casa madrilena*), Revista de Occidente, 1962.

Retratos con nombres (title means "Portraits with Names"), El Bardo, 1965.

Poemas de la consumacion (title means "Poems of Consummation"), Plaza y Janes (Barcelona), 1968.

Sonido de la guerra, Fomento de Cultura Ediciones (Valencia), 1972.

Dialogos del conocimiento (title means "Dialogues of Knowledge"), Plaza y Janes, 1974.

OMNIBUS VOLUMES IN SPANISH

Mis poemas mejores (title means "My Best Poems"), Gredos (Madrid), 1956, revised edition, 1976.

Espadas como labios [and] Pasion de la tierra, Losada, 1957.

Poemas amorosos: Antologia (title means "Love Poems: Anthology"), Losada, 1960.

Poesias completas (title means "Complete Poems"), introduction by Carlos Bousono, Aguilar, 1960.

Presencias (title means "Presences"; limited edition), Seix Barral (Barcelona), 1965.

Obras completas (title means "Complete Works"), introduction by Bousono, Aguilar, 1968, revised edition published in two volumes, 1977.

Poesia superrealista (title means "Surrealistic Poetry"), Barral Editores, 1971.

Antologia del mar y de la noche (title means "Anthology of the Sea and the Night"), edited by Javier Lostale, Al-Borak, 1971.

Antologia total (title means "Complete Anthology"), compiled by Pere Gimferrer, Seix Barral, 1975.

Antologia poetica (title means "Poetry Anthology"), edited by Leopoldo de Luis, Castalia, 1976.

Aleixandre para ninos (title means "Aleixandre for Children"; juvenile), Ediciones de la Torre (Madrid), 1984.

AUTHOR OF PROLOGUE IN SPANISH

Bousono, *La primavera de la muerte,* Adonais, 1946.

Gregoria Prieto, *Poesia en linea,* Adonais, 1948.

Fernando Charry Lara, *Nocturnos y otros suenos,* [Bogota], 1948.

Adonais: Segunda antologia, Rialp (Madrid), 1962.

CONTRIBUTOR TO ANTHOLOGIES

Eleanor Laurelle Turnbull, editor, *Contemporary Spanish Poetry: Selections from Ten Poets* (bilingual edition), Johns Hopkins University Press, 1945.

Penguin Book of Spanish Verse, Penguin (London), 1956.

Willis Barnstone, editor, *Modern European Poetry,* Bantam (New York City), 1966.

Hardie St. Martin, editor, *Roots and Wings, Poetry from Spain: A Bilingual Anthology,* Harper (New York City), 1976.

OTHER

Algunos caracteres de la poesia espanola contemporanea (title means "Some Characteristics of Contemporary Spanish Poetry"; criticism), Imprunta Gongora (Madrid), 1955.

Los encuentros (title means "The Meetings"; critical/biographical sketches), Guadarrama (Madrid), 1958.

(Contributor) Francisco Sabadell Lopez, *Desnudos,* [Valladolid], 1961.

(Author of epilogue) Federico Garcia Lorca, *Obras completas,* Aguilar, 1963.

(Contributor) Jose Angeles, editor, *Estudios sobre Antonio Machado,* Ariel, 1977.

Contributor of poetry and articles to Spanish journals. Co-editor, *Revista de Economia,* 1920-22; staff member, *La Semana Financiera* (financial magazine), ending 1927.

SIDELIGHTS: Poet Vicente Aleixandre was a member of Spain's Generation of 1927, which Manuel Duran described in a *World Literature Today* essay as "perhaps the brightest and most original poetic generation in twentieth-century Western Europe." Along with Aleixandre, the group included many of modern Spain's most influential writers, such as Jorge Guillen, Gerardo Diego, and Rafael Alberti. Although nearly unknown outside his native country before receiving the Nobel Prize for Literature in 1977, Aleixandre had much in common with the generation's best-known poet, Federico Garcia Lorca. The two men were from the same region in Spain—the southernmost Andalusia—and revealed the same sources of inspiration in their poetry: Spanish writing of the fifteenth and sixteenth centuries, popular folk rhythms of their native Andalusia, and surrealism. But, while Lorca's death at the hands of Franco's forces at the beginning of the Spanish Civil War catapulted him into international recognition, Aleixandre's name was known only in Spanish circles. He survived both having his house nearly destroyed in a Civil War bomb attack—an autographed book of Lorca's was one of the only items recovered from his gutted library—and having his work banned by government censors for nearly five years after the war to become one of Spain's most prominent poets.

Most critics of Aleixandre's work comment on the thematic and stylistic evolution evident in his poetry. In *Contemporary Spanish Poetry (1898-1963),* for example, Carl W. Cobb noted that in Aleixandre's early poems the poet "rejected the historical and social world around him and created from his elemental passions a vast domain of cosmic and telluric forces anterior to man himself." In contrast, Cobb described the poet's later work as being focused "directly in the historical reality of his *pueblo,* his 'people'." Other critics, such as Diana Der Hovanessian, Arthur Terry, and Kessel Schwartz, echoed Cobb's assessment. In the *Christian Science Monitor,* for instance,

Der Hovanessian noted: "Some of [Aleixandre's] early poetry might tax a reader with its mysticism and disjointed style. But Aleixandre's poetry loses much of the disconnectedness in later years, and begins to address people directly." Terry similarly stated in the *Times Literary Supplement* that while Aleixandre's early poems were "Surrealist- influenced," in later poems "emphasis shifts to the contemplation of man in his human context." Schwartz described the poet's work in *Vicente Aleixandre* as a movement from "the chaotic maelstrom" of his early work to a new poetry in which Aleixandre "became aware of historical man, the temporal man, that is, man in time and space." Dario Fernandez-Morera explained the transformation in Aleixandre's poetry in light of the dramatic change in Spanish society following the Civil War. In *Symposium* the critic stated: "Before [the war], poets had lived in an atmosphere of continuity, of relative intellectual security; therefore they could be concerned with their own psyches rather than with the world they lived in. . . . But the growing turmoil made this attitude no longer feasible."

The selection of Aleixandre as a Nobel laureate was controversial, since the complexity of his surrealistic poetry made it unintelligible to many critics and most readers. A *Washington Post* writer quoted a translated line of poetry from Aleixandre's second book, *Pasion de la tierra* ("Passion of the Earth"), as an example of what the reviewer called Aleixandre's "puzzling" verse: "To sleep when my time comes on a conscience without a pillowcase." G. G. Brown referred to the same book of poetry in *A Literary History of Spain* as "a collection of largely incomprehensible prose-poems, whose private subconscious ramblings Aleixandre tried to excuse later by calling them Freudian." And in *A Longing for the Light: Selected Poems of Vicente Aleixandre,* Lewis Hyde noted that the poems in *Pasion de la tierra* were "written in an almost hermetic dream-language."

According to Hyde, Aleixandre agreed with critics who called *Pasion de la tierra* difficult, but he nevertheless defended the book's worth. Hyde translated the poet's comments: "I have always thought I could see in its chasm-like layers the sudden start of my poetry's evolution, which, from its earliest, has been . . . a longing for the light. This book has therefore produced in me a double, complicated feeling: of aversion, because of its difficulty, which contradicts the call, the appeal it makes to basic levels, common to all of us; and of affection, for the maternal *humus* from which it grew."

Although Fernandez-Morera pointed out that "Aleixandre's surrealist phase is perhaps [his] most publicized," the poet's Nobel Prize was awarded largely for his later, more accessible, work. This was evident, Pablo Beltran de Heredia observed in the *Texas Quarterly,* "when [the Swedish Academy] stated, during the award ceremonies, that the work of this Spanish poet 'illuminates the condition of man in the cosmos and in our present-day society.'"

Cobb noted that "it is perhaps with a feeling of relief that the reader turns from the difficult and turbulent world of Aleixandre's first period . . . to the quieter and simpler but no less moving world of his second phase. . . . His major theme becomes human solidarity, with compassion toward all human beings living in time." Cobb singled out *Historia del corazon* ("History of the Heart"), published in 1954, as Aleixandre's first book of this new style of poetry. Abandoning the obscurity of his early poems, Aleixandre came to believe that poetry was essentially communication. In general, the prose-poems gave way to what a *New York Times* writer called "carefully cadenced free verse." The nightmarish images were replaced by portraits of everyday life. According to Duran, "*Historia del corazon* is basically the story of a love affair, in its daily moments of joy and anguish, and also the story of a growing awareness, a solidarity: the poet realizes that he is only one member of a vast society, the Spanish people, and that ultimately he is a part of mankind."

Beltran de Heredia pointed out that Aleixandre expressed a fondness for this simpler poetry, preferring *Historia del corazon* among his books and—from that same collection—"*Enla plaza*" ("On the Square") among his poems. Both Santiago Daydi-Tolson in *The Post-Civil War Spanish Poets* and Duran emphasized the importance of this same poem. Aleixandre "uses the image of the public square," Daydi-Tolson observed, "to represent the greatness of human solidarity." According to the critic, the plaza, the axis around which society revolves in every Spanish city, is the perfect embodiment of the essence of Spanish life. In the symbol of the public square the poet "feels and understands this essential communal quality of man's existence." Duran saw the poem as an encapsulated portrait of Aleixandre's evolution from personal to communal poet. Duran explained the imagery of the poem: "After being long confined in his room, the poet goes out into the street, to the square, in order to mingle with other human beings and be part of humanity." Duran illustrated his point with a translation from the poem: "It is a beautiful feeling, beau-tifully humble and buoyant, life-giving and deep, / to feel yourself beneath the sun among other people."

Aleixandre is important for his own poetry but also for his influence on the poetry of subsequent generations. As one of the few poets to remain in Spain during the Civil War, he was a symbol of hope to younger poets. In a *New York Times Book Review* essay, Robert Bly suggested that after the war "the younger writers felt abandoned, dead, in despair. It turned out that Aleixandre's decision to stay helped all that. He represented the wild energy still alive on Spanish soil." A London *Times* writer noted that although Aleixandre "was privately distressed at the low quality of verse of Falangist poets [members of Franco's party], . . . he encouraged them as he encouraged every other poet, seeking with a noble magnanimity of spirit to unify all factions. He worked behind the scenes . . . to obtain the release of imprisoned writers, and was more responsible than any other single person for creating the relaxed [Spanish] censorship of the middle and late 1960s, which led to better things." In Aleixandre's prologue to the second edition of *La destruccion o el amor (Destruction or Love),* the Spaniard summarized his ideas on poets and poetry. The prologue, written in 1944 shortly before the poet began work on *La historia del corazon* and translated by David Pritchard in the *Paris Review,* ends with a short explanation of Aleixandre's poetics. "Some poets . . . ," he wrote, "are poets 'of the few.' They are artists . . . who address themselves to men by attending, so they say, to exquisite and narrow obsessions. . . . Other poets . . . address themselves to what is permanent in man. Not to the details that set us apart, but to the essence that brings us together. . . . These poets are radical poets and they speak to what is primordial, to what is elemental in humanity. They cannot *feel* themselves to be poets of the few. I am one of these."

BIOGRAPHICAL/CRITICAL SOURCES:

BOOKS

Aleixandre, Vicente, *Twenty Poems,* edited by Lewis Hyde, Seventies Press, 1977.

Aleixandre, Vicente, *A Longing for the Light: Selected Poems of Vicente Aleixandre,* edited by Lewis Hyde, Copper Canyon Press, 1985.

Alonso, Damaso, *Ensayos sobre poesia espanola,* Revista de Occidente, 1946.

Bousono, Carlos, *La poesia de Vicente Aleixandre,* Insula, 1950, revised edition, 1977.

Brown, G. G., *A Literary History of Spain,* Barnes and Noble, 1972.

Cabrera, Vicente, and Harriet Boyer, editors, *Critical Views on Vicente Aleixandre's Poetry,* Society of Spanish and Spanish-American Studies (Lincoln, NE), 1979.

Cobb, Carl W., *Contemporary Spanish Poetry (1898-1963),* Twayne, 1976.

Contemporary Literary Criticism, Volume 9, Gale (Detroit), 1978.

Daydi-Tolson, Santiago, editor, *Vicente Aleixandre: A Critical Appraisal,* Bilingual Press, 1981.

Daydi-Tolson, Santiago, *The Post-Civil War Spanish Poets,* Twayne, 1983.

Jimenez, Jose Olivio, *Cinco poetas del tiempo,* Insula, 1964.

Jimenez, Jose Olivio, *Vicente Aleixandre: Una aventura hacia el conocimiento,* Ediciones Jucar (Madrid), 1982.

Ley, Charles David, *Spanish Poetry since 1939,* Catholic University of America Press, 1962.

Morris, C. B., *A Generation of Spanish Poets: 1920-1936,* Cambridge University Press, 1969.

Schwartz, Kessel, *Vicente Aleixandre,* Twayne, 1970.

PERIODICALS

Christian Science Monitor, January 2, 1980.
Hispania, May, 1967.
Hispanic Journal, fall, 1982.
Hudson Review, winter, 1978-79.
Nation, March 4, 1978.
New Republic, December 24-31, 1977.
Newsweek, October 17, 1977.
New York Times, October 7, 1977.
New York Times Book Review, October 30, 1977.
Paris Review, fall, 1978.
Parnassus, fall/winter, 1979.
Poetry, April, 1980.
Symposium, summer, 1979.
Texas Quarterly, winter, 1978.
Time, October 17, 1977.
Times Literary Supplement, May 17, 1957; November 2, 1958; July 10, 1969;

May 23, 1975.
World Literature Today, spring, 1975.

OBITUARIES:

PERIODICALS

AB Bookman's Weekly, January 21, 1985.

Chicago Tribune, December 16, 1984.
Los Angeles Times, December 16, 1984.
Time, December 24, 1984.
Times (London), December 15, 1984.
Washington Post, December 15, 1984.*

*   *   *

ALLENDE, Isabel 1942-

PERSONAL: Surname is pronounced "Ah-*yen*-day"; born August 2, 1942, in Lima, Peru; daughter of Tomas (a Chilean diplomat) and Francisca (Llona Barros) Allende; married Miguel Frias (an engineer), September 8, 1962 (divorced, 1987); married William Gordon (a lawyer), July 17, 1988; children: (first marriage) Paula (deceased), Nicolas; Scott (stepson). *Education:* Graduated from a private high school in Santiago, Chile, at age sixteen.

ADDRESSES: Home—15 Nightingale Lane, San Rafael, CA 94901. *Agent*—Carmen Balcells, Diagonal 580, Barcelona 21, Spain.

CAREER: United Nations Food and Agricultural Organization, Santiago, Chile, secretary, 1959-65; *Paula* magazine, Santiago, journalist, editor, and advice columnist, 1967-74; *Mampato* magazine, Santiago, journalist, 1969-74; television interviewer for Canal 13/Canal 7 (television station), 1970-75; worked on movie newsreels, 1973-75; *El Nacional* newspapers, Venezuela, journalist, 1975-84; Colegio Marroco, Caracas, Venezuela, administrator, 1979-82; writer. Guest teacher at Montclair State College, NJ, spring, 1985, and University of Virginia, fall, 1988; Gildersleeve Lecturer, Barnard College, spring, 1988; teacher of creative writing, University of California, Berkeley, spring, 1989.

AWARDS, HONORS: Panorama Literario Award (Chile), 1983; Grand Prix d'Evasion (France), 1984; Author of the Year and Book of the Year Awards (Germany), 1984; Point de Mire (Belgium), 1985; Colima Award for Best Novel (Mexico), 1985; Author of the Year Award (Germany), 1986; Quality Paperback Book Club New Voice Award nomination, 1986, for *The House of the Spirits; Los Angeles Times* Book Prize nomination, 1987, for *Of Love and Shadows;* XV Premio Internazionale I Migliori Dell'Anno (Italy), and Mulheres Best Foreign Novel Award (Portugal), 1987; Before Columbus Foundation Award, 1988; *Eva Luna* was named one of *Library Journal's*

Best Books of 1988; Freedom to Write Pen Club Award, 1991; XLI Bancarella Literature Award (Italy), and Brandeis University Major Book Collection Award, 1993.

WRITINGS:

Civilice a su troglodita: Los impertinentes de Isabel Allende (humor), Lord Cochran (Santiago), 1974.

La casa de los espiritus, Plaza y Janes (Barcelona), 1982, translation by Magda Bogin published as *The House of the Spirits,* Knopf (New York City), 1985.

La gorda de porcelana (juvenile; title means "The Fat Porcelain Lady"), Alfaguara (Madrid), 1984.

De amor y de sombra, Plaza y Janes, 1984, translation by Margaret Sayers Peden published as *Of Love and Shadows,* Knopf, 1987.

Eva Luna, translation by Peden published under same title, Knopf, 1988.

Cuentos de Eva Luna, Plaza y Janes, 1990, translation by Peden published as *The Stories of Eva Luna,* Atheneum (New York City), 1991.

El Plan infinito, Editorial Sudamericana, translation by Peden published as *The Infinite Plan,* Harper Collins, 1993.

Paula (autobiography), HarperCollins (New York City), 1995.

Afrodita: Recetas, cuentos y otros afrodisiacos, HarperCollins, 1997, translation by Sayers Peden, published as *Aphrodite: A Memoir of the Senses,* HarperFlamingo, 1998.

Also author of several plays and stories for children. Author of weekly newspaper column for *El Nacional* (Caracas), 1976-83. Also contributor to *Paths of Resistance: The Art and Craft of the Political Novel,* edited by William Zinsser, Houghton Mifflin, 1989, and *El Amor: Grandes escritores latinoamericanos,* Ediciones Instituto Movilizador, 1991.

ADAPTATIONS: The House of the Spirits was filmed in English by Bille August.

SIDELIGHTS: When Chilean President Salvador Allende was assassinated in 1973 as part of a military coup against his socialist government, it had a profound effect on his niece, novelist Isabel Allende. "I think I have divided my life [into] before that day and after that day," Allende told *Publishers Weekly* interviewer Amanda Smith. "In that moment, I realized that everything was possible—that violence was a dimension that was always around you." At first, Allende and her family did not believe that a dictator-

ship could last in Chile; they soon found it too dangerous to remain in the country, however, and fled to Venezuela. Although she had been a noted journalist in Chile, Allende found it difficult to get a job in Venezuela and did not write for several years; but after receiving word from her grandfather, a nearly one-hundred-year-old man who had remained in Chile, she began to write again in a letter to him. "My grandfather thought people died only when you forgot them," the author explained to Harriet Shapiro in *People.* "I wanted to prove to him that I had forgotten nothing, that his spirit was going to live with us forever." Allende never sent the letter to her grandfather, who soon died, but her memories of her family and her country became the genesis of *The House of the Spirits,* her first novel. "When you lose everything, everything that is dear to you . . . memory becomes more important," Allende commented to *Mother Jones* writer Douglas Foster. With *The House of the Spirits,* the author added, "[I achieved] the recovery of those memories that were being blown by the wind, by the wind of exile."

Following three generations of the Trueba family and their domestic and political conflicts, *The House of the Spirits* "is a novel of peace and reconciliation, in spite of the fact that it tells of bloody, tragic events," claimed *New York Times Book Review* contributor Alexander Coleman. "The author has accomplished this not only by plumbing her memory for the familial and political textures of the continent, but also by turning practically every major Latin American novel on its head," the critic continued. The patriarch of the family, Esteban Trueba, is a strict, conservative man who exploits his workers and allows his uncompromising beliefs to distance him from his wife and children, even in the face of tremendous events.

Allende's grand scope and use of fantastic elements and characters have led many critics to place *The House of the Spirits* in the tradition of the Latin American novel of "magic realism," and they compare it specifically to Nobel winner Gabriel Garcia Marquez's *One Hundred Years of Solitude.* "Allende has her own distinctive voice, however," noted a *Publishers Weekly* reviewer; "while her prose lacks the incandescent brilliance of the master's, it has a whimsical charm, besides being clearer, more accessible and more explicit about the contemporary situation in South America." In contrast, *Village Voice* contributor Enrique Fernandez believed that "only the dullest reader can fail to be distracted by the shameless cloning from *One Hundred Years of Solitude.* . . . Allende writes like one of the many earnest minor authors that began aping Gabo after his success, except she's better at it than most." Although Lori M. Carlson agreed that *The House of the Spirits* is too reminiscent of Garcia Marquez's masterpiece, she wrote in *Review* that "Allende's novel does remain compelling, nevertheless. Technique is polished, imagination full." "Isabel Allende is very much under the influence of Gabriel Garcia Marquez, but she is scarcely an imitator," remarked *Washington Post Book World* critic Jonathan Yardley, concluding that "she is most certainly a novelist in her own right and, for a first novelist, a startlingly skillful, confident one."

While *The House of the Spirits* contains some of the magic realism that is characteristic of much Latin American fiction, it is counterbalanced by the political realities that Allende recounts. *Times Literary Supplement* reviewer Antony Beevor stated that whereas the early chapters of *The House of the Spirits* seem "to belong firmly in the school of magical realism," a closer reading "suggests that Isabel Allende's tongue is lightly in her cheek. It soon becomes clear that she has taken the genre to flip it over," the critic elaborated. "The metaphorical house, the themes of time and power, the *machista* violence and the unstoppable merry-go-round of history: all of these are reworked and then examined from the other side-from a woman's perspective." Other critics, however, fault Allende for trying to combine the magical and the political. Richard Eder of the *Los Angeles Times* felt that the author "rarely manages to integrate her magic and her message," while *Nation* contributor Paul West said that the political story is "the book Allende probably wanted to write, and would have had she not felt obliged to toe the line of magical realism." But others maintain that the contrast between the fantastic and political segments is effective, as Harriet Waugh of *Spectator* explained: "[The] magic gradually dies away as a terrible political reality engulfs the people of the country. Ghosts, the gift of foretelling the future and the ability to make the pepper and salt cellars move around the dining-room table cannot survive terror, mass-murder and torture."

Although *The House of the Spirits* includes political approaches similar to other Latin American works, it also contains "an original feminist argument that suggests [a] women's monopoly on powers that oppose the violent 'paternalism' from which countries like Chile continue to suffer," according to *Chicago Tribune* contributor Bruce Allen. Alberto Manguel likewise considered important Allende's "depiction of woman as a colonial object," as he wrote in the

Toronto *Globe and Mail,* a depiction reinforced by Esteban Trueba's cruel treatment of his wife, daughter, and female workers. But despite the concentration on female characters and "the fact that Esteban rapes, pillages, kills and conspires, he never entirely loses the reader's sympathy," commented Waugh. "It is a remarkable achievement to make the old monster lovable not just to his wife, daughter, and grand-daughter, and the other women in his life, but also to the reader," Philip Howard contended in the London *Times.* "It is a fair-minded book, that pities and understands people on both sides of the politics." Allen concurred: "The most remarkable feature of this remarkable book is the way in which its strong political sentiments are made to coexist with its extravagant and fascinating narrative. . . . Despite its undeniable debt to 'One Hundred Years of Solitude,'" the critic concluded, *The House of the Spirits* "is an original and important work; along with Garcia Marquez's masterpiece, it's one of the best novels of the postwar period, and a major contribution to our understanding of societies riddled by ceaseless conflict and violent change. It is a great achievement, and it cries out to be read."

With *Of Love and Shadows,* which *Detroit Free Press* contributor Anne Janette Johnson called "a frightening, powerful work," Allende "proves her continued capacity for generating excellent fiction. She has talent, sensitivity, and a subject matter that provides both high drama and an urgent political message." The novel begins "matter-of-factly, almost humorously," with the switching of two identically named babies, as Charles R. Larson described it in the *Detroit News.* The story becomes more complex, however, when one of the babies grows up to become the focus of a journalist's investigation; after a reporter and photographer expose the political murder of the girl, they are forced to flee the country. "And so," Larson observed, "Allende begins with vignettes of magical realism, only to pull the rug out from under our feet once we have been hooked by her enchanting tale. What she does, in fact, is turn her story into a thriller." "Love and struggle a la 'Casablanca'—it's all there," Gene H. Bell-Villada likewise stated in the *New York Times Book Review.* "Ms. Allende skillfully evokes both the terrors of daily life under military rule and the subtler form of resistance in the hidden corners and 'shadows' of her title." But while political action comprises a large part of the story, "above all, this is a love story of two young people sharing the fate of their historical circumstances, meeting the challenge of discovering the truth, and determined to live their life fully, accepting their world of love and shadows," *Christian Science Monitor* reviewer Marjorie Agosin declared. With *Of Love and Shadows* "Allende has mastered the craft of being able to intertwine the turbulent political history of Latin America with the everyday lives of her fictional characters caught up in recognizable, contemporary events."

"Fears that Isabel Allende might be a 'one-book' writer, that her first success . . . would be her only one, ought to be quashed by *Eva Luna,*" asserted Abigail E. Lee in the *Times Literary Supplement.* "The eponymous protagonist and narrator of this, her third novel, has an engaging personality, a motley collection of interesting acquaintances and an interesting angle on political upheavals in the unnamed Latin American republic in which she lives." Born illegitimate and later orphaned, Eva Luna becomes a scriptwriter and storyteller who becomes involved with a filmmaker—Rolf Carle, an Austrian emigre haunted by his Nazi father—and his subjects, a troop of revolutionary guerrillas. "In *Eva Luna,* Allende moves between the personal and the political, between realism and fantasy, weaving two exotic coming-of-age stories-Eva Luna's and Rolf Carle's-into the turbulent coming of age of her unnamed South American country," Elizabeth Benedict summarized in Chicago's *Tribune Books.* Switching between the stories of the two protagonists, *Eva Luna* is "filled with a multitude of characters and tales," recounted *Washington Post Book World* contributor Alan Ryan. Allende's work is "a remarkable novel," the critic elaborated, "one in which a cascade of stories tumbles out before the reader, stories vivid and passionate and human enough to engage, in their own right, all the reader's attention and sympathy."

Perhaps due to this abundance of stories and characters, John Krich thought that "few of the cast of characters emerge as distinctive or entirely believable," as he commented in the *New York Times Book Review.* "Too often, we find Eva Luna's compatriots revealed through generalized attributions rather than their own actions. . . . Is this magic realism *a la* Garcia Marquez or Hollywood magic *a la* Judith Krantz? We can only marvel at how thin the line becomes between the two, and give Ms. Allende the benefit of the doubt." London *Times* writer Stuart Evans, however, praised Allende's "range of eccentric or idiosyncratic characters who are always credible," and added: "Packed with action, prodigal in invention, vivid in description and metaphor, this cleverly plotted novel is enhanced by its flowing prose and absolute assurance." "*Eva Luna* is a great read that *El Nobel* [Garcia Marquez] couldn't hope to

write," claimed Dan Bellm in the *Voice Literary Supplement,* for the women "get the best political debate scenes, not the men." Lee also saw a serious political side to the novel, noting "an interesting juxtaposition in *Eva Luna* of feminism and revolutionary politics. . . . In all the depictions of women and their relationships with men, though, one feels not a militant or aggressive feminism—rather a sympathetic awareness of the injustices inherent in traditional gender roles." The critic continued, remarking that *Eva Luna* "is an accomplished novel, skillfully blending humour and pathos; its woman's perspective on Latin American is a refreshing one, but it is enjoyable above all for its sensitivity and charm." "Reading this novel is like asking your favorite storyteller to tell you a story and getting a hundred stories instead of one . . . and then an explanation of how the stories were invented . . . and then hearing the storyteller's life as well," concluded Ryan. "Does it have a happy ending? What do you think?"

BIOGRAPHICAL/CRITICAL SOURCES:

BOOKS

Coddou, Marcelio, editor, *Los libros tienen sus propios espiritus: Estudios sobre Isabel Allende,* Universidad Veracruzana, 1986.
Contemporary Literary Criticism, Gale (Detroit), Volume 39, 1986, Volume 57, 1990, Volume 97, 1997.
Hart, Patricia, *Narrative Magic in the Fiction of Isabel Allende,* Fairleigh Dickinson University Press, 1989.
Rojas, Sonia Riquelme, and Edna Aguirre Rehbein, editors, *Critical Approaches to Isabel Allende's Novels,* Lang, 1991.

PERIODICALS

Americas, November-December, 1995, p. 36.
Architectural Digest, April, 1995, p. 32.
Booklist, February 1, 1998, p. 875.
Chicago Tribune, May 19, 1985.
Christian Science Monitor, June 7, 1985; May 27, 1987.
Detroit Free Press, June 7, 1987.
Detroit News, June 14, 1987.
Globe and Mail (Toronto), June 24, 1985; June 27, 1987.
Los Angeles Times, February 10, 1988.
Los Angeles Times Book Review, June 16, 1985; May 31, 1987.
Mother Jones, December, 1988.

Ms., May-June, 1995, p. 75.

Nation, July 20/27, 1985.

New Statesman, July 5, 1985.

Newsweek, May 13, 1985.

New York Review of Books, July 18, 1985.

New York Times, May 2, 1985; May 20, 1987; February 4, 1988.

New York Times Book Review, May 12, 1985; July 12, 1987; October 23, 1988; May 21, 1995, p. 11.

People, June 10, 1985; June 1, 1987; June 5, 1995, p. 34; April 20, 1998, p. 47.

Publishers Weekly, March 1, 1985; May 17, 1985; January 19, 1998, p. 360. *Review,* January-June, 1985.

Spectator, August 3, 1985.

Time, May 20, 1985.

Times (London), July 4, 1985; July 9, 1987; March 22, 1989; March 23, 1989.

Times Literary Supplement, July 5, 1985; July 10, 1987; April 7-13, 1989.

Tribune Books (Chicago), October 9, 1988.

U.S. News and World Report, November 21, 1988.

Village Voice, June 7, 1985.

Voice Literary Supplement, December, 1988.

Wall Street Journal, March 20, 1998.

Washington Post Book World, May 12, 1985; May 24, 1987; October 9, 1988.

World Press Review, April, 1995, p. 47.

*   *   *

ALMODOVAR, Pedro 1949(?)-
(Pati Difusa, Patty Diphusa)

PERSONAL: Born September 25, 1949 (one source says 1951), in Calzada de Calatrava, Spain; son of Francisca Caballero. *Education:* Educated in Caceres, Spain.

CAREER: Screenwriter and director. Telephone company worker; singer in rock band, Almodovar and McNamara; actor with independent theater troupe, Los Goliardos; writer of comic strips and columns for underground newspaper, all in Madrid, Spain, all c. 1970s.

AWARDS, HONORS: Best screenplay award, Venice International Film Festival, and best foreign film awards National Board of Review of Motion Pictures and New York Film Critics Circle, all 1988, all for *Women on the Verge of a Nervous Breakdown;* special citation for originality, National Society of Film Critics, 1988; named Man of the Year by Spanish magazine *Cambio 16,* 1989; Academy Award nomination for best foreign film, Academy of Motion Picture Arts and Sciences, 1989, for *Women on the Verge of a Nervous Breakdown.*

WRITINGS:

SCREENPLAYS; AND DIRECTOR

Pepi, Lucy, Bom y otros chicas del monton (title means "Pepi, Lucy, Bom and a Whole Lot of Other Girls"), Figaro, 1980.

Laberinto de pasiones, Musidora S.A., 1982, released in the United States as *Labyrinth of Passion,* 1990.

Entre tinieblas, Tesauro P.C., 1983, released in the United States as *Dark Habits* (also titled *Dark Hideout* and *Sisters of Darkness*), Cinevista, 1988.

Que he hecho yo para merecer esto?, Tesauro S.A./Kaktus P.C., 1984, released in the United States as *What Have I Done to Deserve This?,* Cinevista, 1985.

Matador, Iberoamericana, 1986, released in the United States under same title, Cinevista/Promovision International, 1988.

La ley del deseo, El Deseo/Laurenfilms, 1986, released in the United States as *Law of Desire,* Cinevista, 1987.

Mujeres al borde de un ataque de nervios, El Deseo/Laurenfilm, 1988, released in the United States as *Women on the Verge of a Nervous Breakdown,* Orion Classics, 1988.

Atame!, El Deseo/Laurenfilm, 1990, released in the United States as *Tie Me Up! Tie Me Down!,* Miramax, 1990.

Tacones lejanos, El Deseo, 1991, released in the United States as *High Heels,* Warner Bros., 1991.

Kika, El Deseo, 1993.

La Flor de mi secreto, El Deseo, 1995, released in the United States as *The Flower of My Secret,* Sony Pictures Classics, 1996.

Carne tremula, El Deseo, 1997, released in the United States as *Live Flesh,* MGM, 1998.

OTHER

Pati Difusa y otros textos, Editorial Anagrama (Barcelona), 1991, translation by Kirk Anderson published as *Patty Diphusa and Other Writings,* Faber (Boston, MA), 1991.

Also author of photonovella *Todo Toya*. Contributor of articles to Spanish periodicals.

WORK IN PROGRESS: More feature films.

SIDELIGHTS: A provocative figure in European cinema, Spanish screenwriter and director Pedro Almodovar rose from underground filmmaker to internationally renowned auteur during the course of the 1980s. With a distinctive blend of raw emotion and camp humor, his unconventional motion pictures defy classification and frequently incite controversy among moviegoers and critics. In an interview with Marsha Kinder for *Film Quarterly*, Almodovar explained: "My films are about pleasure, sensuality, and living—about the celebration of living," and added, "I prefer just to inspire, to suggest, not to explain." Indeed, *Film Criticism* contributor Patricia Hart observed that in his films, Almodovar "plays with a series of impossible (and for some, unspeakable) fantasies, constructing tenuous implausibilities where for a few moments on screen, if not in life, complimentary 'perversions' can be aligned, shortcomings matched with corresponding excesses, and one desiring domination can be lined up with a benevolent sexpot despot."

Frequent entries at various European and American film festivals, Almodovar's movies routinely topple traditional theories of culture and morality and consequently attract extensive criticism and analysis. The filmmaker's works embody a bold and satiric vision that allows for the satisfaction of even the most bizarre human desires and fetishes. Known for his use of stunning and intense imagery, Almodovar frequently juxtaposes fantasy and reality, creating a world on film in which the outrageous seems ordinary and individual freedom is exalted. His movies reflect the influence of diverse masters of the medium, including Alfred Hitchcock, Billy Wilder, surrealist Luis Bunuel, and several neorealist filmmakers of Italy and Spain.

Several critics have suggested that Almodovar's avant-garde motion pictures border on the grotesque and are designed primarily to jolt and disturb his viewers. But he insists that his works are merely exaggerated depictions of universal themes. In an interview with Vito Russo for *Film Comment*, Almodovar capsulized his filmmaking philosophy: "I make movies for my needs. My goal has never, never, never, been to make shocking movies."

With the end of the oppressive, authoritative rule of Spanish dictator Francisco Franco in 1975, a new wave of creativity infused the Spanish arts. Almodovar exploits this post-Franco mentality—popularly known as "la movida"—in his films, emphasizing tolerance and acceptance of individuality over the repression and divisiveness inherent in a totalitarian state. When asked by *Interview* writer David Lida for his reaction to the end of the Franco era, Almodovar recalled that he—and many other Spanish citizens "waiting for that moment to celebrate"—had been "chilling [champagne] in the Frigidaire for a week while Franco lay in agony." In the *Film Comment* interview with Russo, Almodovar asserted that while his films are not overtly political in content, they "are political in the sense that [they] always defend the autonomy and absolute freedom of the individual—which is very dangerous to some people."

Almodovar's motion pictures generally focus on the lives, loves, and desires of women. While the filmmaker, a candid homosexual, suggests that his sexuality has heightened his sensitivity, he rejects the notion that his fascination with women is rooted in his being gay. "Women are more spontaneous and more surprising as dramatic subjects," he told Marcia Pally in *Film Comment*, "and my spontaneity is easier to conduct through them."

Inspired by classic Hollywood stars, including Bette Davis and Katharine Hepburn, and films of the 1950s such as *Cat on a Hot Tin Roof*, Almodovar was attracted to the cinematic scene as a youth. Following a parochial education in a western province of Spain, he moved at age seventeen to Madrid and worked for the next decade as a typist for the telephone company. Simultaneously, he dabbled in the arts by acting with an independent theater troupe, singing in a rock band, writing articles and X-rated comics for an avant-garde newspaper, and composing the memoirs of fictitious porn queen Pati Difusa (*patidifusa* means "flabbergasted" in Spanish). By the mid-1970s, without having attended film school, he was already shooting experimental short films, which he showed at bars, parties, and small film festivals.

Almodovar completed his first full-length feature, the raunchy *Pepi, Lucy, Bom y otros chicas del monton* ("Pepi, Lucy, Bom and a Whole Lot of Other Girls"), in 1980. Eighteen months in the making, the film was shot only on weekends, because Almodovar worked at the national telephone company during the week. A movie "devoted almost exclusively to topics banned from cinema screens only a few years earlier, . . . [seeking] shamelessly to offend the sensibility of the average viewer," to quote Hart, *Pepi* was an underground hit. Its success enabled Almodovar to find funding for his next project, the equally perverse *Labyrinth of Passion,* a work that attained cult status in Spain.

The 1984 film *What Have I Done to Deserve This?*—Almodovar's fourth feature, but his first to be distributed in the United States—effectively explodes the Mediterranean myth of machismo. The story of an overworked woman's attempts to support her family, *What Have I Done to Deserve This?* offers sharp commentary on life in the crowded housing projects of Madrid. The film's heroine, Gloria, subsists mainly on amphetamines, juggling her responsibilities as a housewife with an outside job as a cleaning woman. Her unsupportive family consists of a crude and boorish taxi driver husband, two sons—the elder a drug dealer, the younger a homosexual—and a daffy mother-in-law. Sexually and emotionally unsatisfied and desperate for a change in her life, Gloria takes sudden action, killing her husband with a frozen ham and selling her younger son to a homosexual dentist. In a *New York* review, David Denby surmised, "*What Have I Done to Deserve This?* is bitterly funny, but it never feels nihilistic or merely cruel. . . . Every frame of it breathes freedom and pleasure in freedom." *Variety* correspondent Jonathan Holland called *What Have I Done to Deserve This?* "one of the most hilarious and despairing of Spanish films, establishing a delightful yet dangerous blend that would become a later [Almodovar] hallmark."

Almodovar's 1986 film *Law of Desire* became another cult classic in Madrid. Released the following year in the United States, the film concerns homosexual film director Pablo and his transsexual sibling Tina (who had undergone a sex change to more conventionally facilitate incestuous relations with her father). Tina becomes a lesbian after her father abandons her. Pablo falls in love with Juan, a bisexual, but also finds himself drawn to the obsessive Antonio. In a jealous rage, Antonio tracks and murders Juan, then holds Tina hostage in exchange for a single hour with Pablo. Moved by Antonio's uncompromising passion, Pablo consents. Remarking in *Film Comment* on the seemingly disastrous implications of the story, Almodovar reasoned, "It would have been a tragedy if [Antonio] couldn't have had that one hour."

Dark Habits, Almodovar's third film, and his first to be marketed outside Spain, was not released in the United States until 1988. *Dark Habits* begins with a nightclub singer-stripper fleeing to the safety of a convent following the drug-overdose death of her lover. The film, which takes its title from the unusual activities the nuns engage in during their spare time, then focuses on the irregularities of life inside the convent walls. Oddly named nuns—Sister Damned, Sister Sin, Sister Rat, to list a few—indulge in everything from drugs to exotic pets and thrive on saving the souls of the downtrodden. Several critics have contended that *Dark Habits* lacks the polish and bravura of Almodovar's later works, but most concede that the film served as an important step in his growth as a filmmaker.

Matador, one of the top-grossing Spanish films of 1986, also received its first American showing in 1988. A controversial story of indulgence and obsession, *Matador* was both censured as a twisted and offensive study in psychosexual brutality and celebrated as an exaggerated and outrageously lavish comedy of passion. The film centers on the warped alliance between a former matador and a murderous female lawyer, both of whom can only experience sexual fulfillment in conjunction with killing. The pair's own relationship culminates in ecstasy and death. A *Newsweek* reviewer judged *Matador* "a twisted, oddly invigorating comedy." And Pauline Kael, writing in the *New Yorker,* deemed the film "all lush, clownish excess," adding, "Everything is eroticized—the colors, the violence. It's all too much—it's sumptuously sick and funny."

In the *Advocate,* Jan Stuart wrote: "The Almodovar signature invariably signals an elaborate network of the desired and the desirous, a maze of ardor that coils back on itself in unexpected ways. His resourceful lovers seem prepared for anything, as if betrayal, revenge, and unlikely sexual encounters were their daily bread. Handguns are always within easy reach—in the drawer next to the condoms and the diaphragms, we figure—and they tend to go off in homicidal orgasms."

In his conversation with Kinder, Almodovar justified his use of violence in his oeuvre: "The moral of all my films is to get to a stage of greater freedom. . . . I have my own morality. And so do my films. If you see *Matador* through the perspective of traditional morality, it's a dangerous film because it's just a celebration of killing. *Matador* is like a legend. I don't try to be realistic; it's very abstract, so you don't feel identification with the things that are happening, but with the sensibility of this kind of romanticism."

Almodovar earned international acclaim with his next film, *Women on the Verge of a Nervous Breakdown,* which was the second largest box office draw in Spain in 1988. Winner of numerous international film awards, the fast-paced comedy-melodrama chronicles Spanish television and radio actress Pepa's attempts to contact her suave and evasive ex-lover Ivan, also an actor. Ivan leaves a message on Pepa's answering machine informing her of his decision to end their relationship. Upon discovering the farewell message, the vulnerable Pepa heaves her telephone and answering machine out her window and proceeds to contemplate her options: reconciliation, murder, or suicide (with barbiturate-laced gazpacho, which she never gets a chance to drink). *Women on the Verge* features a myriad of supporting characters, including Pepa's friend Candela, who fears arrest because of her involvement with a Shiite terrorist; Ivan's demure son, Carlos, who falls for Candela; and Carlos's overbearing fiancee, Marisa, who experiences her first orgasm in a gazpacho-induced sleep. The film culminates in Pepa and Ivan's final confrontation, following a hectic chase and gunplay.

Women on the Verge scored a resounding critical and popular success. Denby credited Almodovar with creating in Pepa "perhaps the most lovable movie heroine in years." In a *Newsweek* review, David Ansen suggested that *Women on the Verge,* probably the most mainstream of Almodovar's films, exemplifies the refinement of the filmmaker's cinematic skills: "With each film Almodovar's technical assurance grows: he makes stylized high comedy look easy, unforced. . . . Some aficionados may miss the more outrageous edges of [the filmmaker's] earlier works, but the *enfant terrible* has not gone soft; he's just in a holiday mood, and his new comic optimism is infectious." Reviewing the film for *Interview,* Luc Sante pointed to an underlying compassion in Almodovar's treatment of his characters' trials: "*Women on the Verge of a Nervous Breakdown* may be camp, but it is camp of the highest order, *haut* camp, in fact. It exaggerates, but it does not mock; its humor is a weapon used on behalf of the protagonists, not turned against them."

Almodovar followed *Women on the Verge* with *Tie Me Up! Tie Me Down!,* which *New Republic* critic Stanley Kauffmann pronounced "his pinnacle so far." Released without a rating because of allegedly objectionable sex scenes, *Tie Me Up! Tie Me Down!* turns on the abduction of a former porno film star who eventually falls in love with her kidnapper, a recently released mental patient. Though faulted by some critics for its predictability and lack of originality, *Tie Me Up! Tie Me Down!* clearly impressed several other

reviewers, including *Rolling Stone* contributor Peter Travers, who called the film "disturbing and invigorating . . . , another masterwork from Spain's most explosive talent." Addressing the supposedly objectionable theme of the movie, Hart concluded: "Viewers may share in the fantasy or not, but only the tacky would condemn a director for sharing with us in witty fashion what turns him on."

Subsequent Almodovar features have revealed a maturation and a world view that is "hopeful without being rosy-tinted," to quote Joseph Cunneen in *National Catholic Reporter.* In *The Flower of My Secret,* for instance, a disenchanted romance writer finds a degree of peace and self-respect even as her marriage disintegrates and her career unravels. In *The Flower of My Secret,* declared Stuart Klawans in *Nation,* Almodovar "has made a thoroughly heartfelt melodrama, one that revels in color and hyperbole not only for their own sake but also because they're garments that shield a human need so abashed that it dares show itself only in the gaudiest disguise." The critic concluded: "How strange that the bad boy should have turned into a benevolent god who respects his creature even though she disagrees with him. How surprising; how just."

With his 1998 comedy *Live Flesh,* Almodovar has established himself as "spiritual padre to a whole new wave of Spanish filmmakers," in Holland's view. Another study of violence, passion, and obsession, *Live Flesh*—an adaptation of a Ruth Rendell crime novel—weaves a web of intrigue and interrelationship between a hapless petty criminal named Victor, two police officers, and two women variously involved with the officers and with Victor. "Almodovar normally focuses on women on the verge, but *Live Flesh* is more about men and their mess," maintained James Greenberg in *Los Angeles Magazine.* "These guys are literally crawling at the feet of their women, struggling to find a way out of the skin they were born into." Declared Lisa Schwarzbaum in *Entertainment Weekly:* "In *Live Flesh* Almodovar is positively mature, adapting a novel by Ruth Rendell so deftly that the plot now also describes the invigorating and sometimes disorienting effects of democracy after long years of repression under the Franco regime." *Time* film critic Richard Corliss described *Live Flesh* as "sensuous [and] delirious," adding: "Obsession has seldom looked as gaudy or thrilling as here. . . . Few films these days are about sex, let alone love. Almodovar is that rare moviemaker who still thinks they are as important as a space invasion or a sinking ship."

Though generally regarded as the exemplar of modern Spanish cinema, Almodovar takes a modest view of his international renown. Reflecting on his career in the *Film Comment* interview with Russo, the filmmaker revealed: "What's wonderful is to notice that people want to see my movies. And that by the miracle of communication I am able to put my obsessions, my problems, my life on the screen and have them reach my audience. That impresses me tremendously. But curiously, it doesn't make me feel more sure of myself as an artist. Each time I start a new movie I know that I want to make that movie, but I don't know if I will know *how* to do it."

BIOGRAPHICAL/CRITICAL SOURCES:

BOOKS

Besas, Peter, *Behind the Spanish Lens: Spanish Cinema under Fascism and Democracy,* Arden Press (Denver, CO), 1985.

Cowie, Peter, editor, *International Film Guide,* Tantivy Press, *1982,* 1981, *1983,* 1982, *1984,* 1983, *1986,* 1985, *1987,* 1986, *1988,* 1987.

Dictionary of Hispanic Biography, Gale (Detroit, MI), 1996.

Hopewell, John, *Out of the Past: Spanish Cinema after Franco,* British Film Institute (London), 1986.

Smith, Paul Julian, *Desire Unlimited: The Cinema of Pedro Almodovar,* Verso (New York City), 1994.

PERIODICALS

Advocate, February 3, 1998, pp. 47, 49.

America, January 21, 1989.

American Film, March, 1988.

Entertainment Weekly, December 6, 1996, pp. 76-77; January 23, 1998, p. 41; January 30, 1998, p. 47.

Film Comment, November/December, 1988.

Film Criticism, winter, 1997, pp. 71-74.

Film Quarterly, fall, 1987.

Guardian, May 8, 1998, p. T10.

Interview, July, 1988; November, 1988.

Los Angeles Magazine, February, 1998, p. 100.

Nation, April 1, 1996, pp. 35-36.

National Catholic Reporter, April 26, 1996, p. 10.

New Republic, May 20, 1985; June 6, 1988; December 12, 1988; May 14, 1990.

Newsweek, July 18, 1988; December 5, 1988.

New York, April 29, 1985; November 21, 1988.

New Yorker, June 3, 1985; April 20, 1987; May 16, 1988.

New York Times, April 22, 1990; May 4, 1990.

People Weekly, January 26, 1998, p. 22.

Playboy, January, 1998, p. 19.

Rolling Stone, May 8, 1986; May 17, 1990.

Time, January 30, 1989; February 23, 1998, p. 90.

Variety, April 20, 1998, pp. 39-40.*

* * *

ALONSO, Damaso 1898-1990

PERSONAL: Born October 22, 1898, in Madrid, Spain; died of a respiratory ailment, January 24, 1990, in Madrid, Spain; married Eulalia Galvarriato (a writer), 1929. *Education:* Received LL.L, M.A., Ph.D. (1928), University of Madrid.

CAREER: Centro de Estudios Historicos, Madrid, Spain, professor, 1923-36; University of Valencia, Valencia, Spain, professor of Spanish language and literature, 1933-39; University of Madrid, Madrid, professor of Romance philology, 1939-68; writer. Lecturer and visiting professor at universities throughout the world, including Berlin, Cambridge, Columbia, Harvard, Johns Hopkins, London, Stanford, and Yale universities.

MEMBER: International Association of Hispanists (president), Royal Academy of the Spanish Language (president, 1968-82; director emeritus), Royal Academy of History, Higher Council for Scientific Research, American Association of Teachers of Spanish and Portuguese, Hispanic Society of America, American Philosophical Society, Modern Language Association, Modern Humanities Research Association (president).

AWARDS, HONORS: Premio Nacional de Literatura, c. 1935, for *La lengua poetica de Gongora;* award from the Royal Spanish Academy of the Language, c. 1942, for *La poesia de San Juan de la Cruz;* Premio Miguel de Cervantes from Spain's Ministerio de Cultura, 1978; numerous honorary degrees from universities, including Oxford University and the universities of Madrid, San Marcos, Bordeaux, Hamburg, Freiburg, Rome, Massachusetts, and Leeds.

WRITINGS:

NONFICTION

(Editor and author of text and notes) Luis de Gongora y Argote, *Soledads,* Revista de Occidente (Madrid), 1927.

(Editor) Desiderius Erasmus, *El Enquiridion; o, Manual del caballero cristiano,* Consejo Superior de Investigaciones Cientificas, Instituto Miguel de Cervantes (Madrid), 1932, reprinted, 1971.

La lengua poetica de Gongora, S. Aguirre (Madrid), 1935, 3rd edition, Consejo Superior de Investigaciones Cientificas, Instituto Miguel de Cervantes, 1961.

(Editor and author of prologue, notes, and vocabulary) *Poesia espanola, antologia,* (also see below) [Madrid], 1935.

(Editor) Luis Carrillo de Sotomayor, *Poesias completas,* Signo (Madrid), 1936.

(Editor) *Poesia de la edad media y poesia de tipo tradicional* (originally published as first volume of *Poesia espanola, antologia*), Losada (Buenos Aires), 1942.

La poesia de San Juan de la Cruz (desde esta ladera), Consejo Superior de Investigaciones Cientificas, Instituto Antonio de Nebrija (Madrid), 1942.

(Editor) Gil Vicente, *Tragicomedia de Don Duardos,* Consejo Superior de Investigaciones Cientificas, 1942.

Ensayos sobre poesia espanola, Revista de Occidente (Madrid), 1944.

Vida y obra de Medrano (about Francisco de Medrano), Volume 1: *Estudio,* Volume 2 (editor, with Stephen Reckert): *Edicion critica,* Consejo Superior de Investigaciones Cientificas, Instituto Miguel de Cervantes, 1948-58.

Poesia y novela de Espana: Conferencias, Departamento de Extension Cultural, Universidad Nacional Mayor de San Marcos (Lima), 1949.

Poesia espanola, ensayo de metodos y limites estilisticos: Garcilaso, fray Luis de Leon, San Juan de la Cruz, Gongora, Lope de Vega, Quevedo, Gredos, 1950.

(With Carlos Bousono) *Seis calas en la expresion literaria espanola (prosa, poesia, teatro),* Gredos, 1951, 3rd edition, 1963.

Poetas espanoles contemporaneos, Gredos, 1952, 3rd edition, 1965.

La primitiva epica francesca a la luz de una Nota Emilianense, Consejo Superior de Investigaciones Cientificas, Instituto Miguel de Cervantes, 1954.

Estudios y ensayos gongorinos, Gredos, 1955.

Menendez Pelayo, critico literario, Gredos (Madrid), 1956.

Antologia: Creacion, edited by Vicente Gaos, Escelicer (Madrid), 1956.

Antologia: Critica, edited by Gaos, Escelicer, 1956.

(Editor, with Jose M. Blecua) *Antologia de la poesia espanola: Poesia de tipo tradicional,* Gredos, 1956, 2nd edition, 1964.

En la Andalucia de la e: Dialectologia pintoresca, [Madrid], 1956.

De los siglos oscuros al de Oro: Notas y articulos a traves de 700 anos de letras espanolas, Gredos, 1958.

Dos espanoles de Siglo de Oro: Un poeta madrilensta, latinista, y francesista en la mitad del siglo XVI. El Fabio de la "Epistola moral": Su cara y cruz en Mejico y en Espana, (also see below) Real Academia de la Historia, 1959 .

Gongora y el "Polifemo," Gredos, 1960, 4th edition published in two volumes, 1961, 5th edition published in three volumes, 1967, 6th edition, 1974, 7th edition, 1985.

Primavera temprana de la literatura europea: Lirica, epica, novela, Guadarrama (Madrid), 1961.

Cuatro poetas espanoles: Garcilaso, Gongora, Maragall, Antonio Machado, Gredos, 1962.

(Editor, with wife, Eulalia Galvarriato de Alonso) *Para la biografia de Gongora: Documentos desconocidos,* Gredos, 1962.

(Editor and author of prose version) Luis de Gongora y Argote, *Romance de Angelica y Medoro,* Ediciones Acies (Madrid), 1962.

Del siglo de Oro a este siglo de siglas: Notas y articulos a traves de 350 anos de letras espanolas, Gredos, 1962.

(Author of introduction) *Antologia de poetas ingleses modernos,* Gredos, 1963.

(With others) *Homenaje a don Ramon Carande,* Sociedad de Estudios y Publicaciones, 1963.

(Editor, with Galvarriato) *Poesias completas y comentarios en prosa a los poemas mayores* (poetry of San Juan de la Cruz), Aguilar (Madrid), 1963.

(With Luis Rosales) *Pasion y muerte del Conde de Villamediana* (debate), Real Academia Espanola (Madrid), 1964.

(With Pedro Lain Entralgo) *La amistad entre el medico y el enfermo en la Edad Media* (debate), Real Academia de la Historia (Madrid), 1964.

(With Martin de Riquer) *Vida caballeresca en la Espana del siglo XV* (debate), Real Academia Espanola, 1965.

(With Galvarriato and Luis Rosales) *Primavera y flor de la literatura hispanica,* 4 volumes, Selecciones de Reader's Digest, 1966.

Cancionero y romancero espanol, Salvat (Madrid), 1969.

La novela cervantina, Universidad Internacional Menendez Pelayo (Santander), 1969.

(With others) *Homenaje a Menendez Pidal,* Prensa de la Universidad de Madrid (Madrid), 1969.

Libro de indices, Gredos, 1969.

En torno a Lope: Marino, Cervantes, Benavente, Gongora, los Cardenios, Gredos, 1972.

Obras completas, Gredos, ten volumes, 1972-93.

(Editor) *Antologia de Gongora,* Gredos, 1974.

La Epistola moral a Fabio, de Andres Fernandez de Andrada: Edicion y estudio, Gredos, 1978.

(Author of essay) Vicente Gaos, *Obra poetica completa,* Institucion Alfonso el Magnanimo, Diputacion Provincial de Valencia (Valencia), 1982.

(With others) Federico Garcia Lorca, *Llanto por Ignacio Sanchez Mejias* (critical study), Casona de Tudanca (Santander), 1982.

(With Gerardo Diego and Luis Rosales) *Antonio Machado: Conferencias pronunciadas en la Fundacion Universitaria Espanola,* Fundacion Universitaria Espanola, 1983.

Reflexiones sobre mi poesia, Universidad Autonoma de Madrid (Madrid), 1984.

Antologia de nuestro monstruoso mundo: Duda y amor sobre el Ser Supremo, edited by Margarita Smerdou Altolaguirre, Catedra (Madrid), 1985.

Also author of *El viento y el verso,* 1925, *La tragicomedia de Don Duardos* (critical study of the work by Gil Vicente), 1942, and *Un poeta madrilenista, latinista y francesista en la mitad del siglo XVI,* c. 1957; author of *La poesia del Petrarca e il petrarchismo,* Italian language edition published by L. S. Olschki, 1959.

POETRY

Poemas puros, poemillas de la ciudad, Galatea (Madrid), 1921.

Oscura noticia (also see below), Hispanica (Madrid), 1944.

Hombre y dios (also see below), [Malaga], 1955 .

Hijos de la ira: Diario intimo (originally published c. 1944), Espasa-Calpe (Buenos Aires), 1946, translation by Elias L. Rivers published in a bilingual edition as *Hijos de la ira/Children of Wrath,* Johns Hopkins University Press (Baltimore, MD), 1970.

Hombre y dios (also see below), Arroyo de los Angeles (Malaga), 1955.

Oscura noticia [and] *Hombre y dios* (first title originally published in 1944), Espasa-Calpe (Madrid), 1959.

Poemas escogidos, Gredos, 1969.

Antologia poetica, edited by Jose Luis Cano, Plaza y Janes (Esplugas de Llobregat), 1973.

Antologia poetica, edited by Philip W. Silver, Alianza, 1979.

Gozos de la vista, Espasa-Calpe (Madrid), 1981.

Vida y obra (contains *Poemas puros: Poemillas de la ciudad* and *Hombre y dios*), Caballo Griego para la Poesia (Madrid), 1984.

OTHER

Translator of works from English into Spanish, including *A Portrait of the Artist as a Young Man* and poems by James Joyce, *Marie Antoinette,* by Hilaire Belloc, and the poetry of Gerard Manley Hopkins.

SIDELIGHTS: "Damaso Alonso was one of the strongest forces in the intellectual and cultural history of twentieth-century Spain," wrote Jerry Phillips Winfield in the *Dictionary of Literary Biography.* "His contributions to literary and stylistic analysis inspired a new approach to literary criticism, particularly in poetry." Alonso was widely hailed in his native Spain for both his works of literary criticism and his poetry. As a critic, he was considered without equal in twentieth-century Spain, and as a poet he "restored the human condition as a vital theme in Spanish poetry and offered a new freedom of technique and style," to quote Winfield. In a career spanning six decades, Alonso wrote, lectured, and befriended many of the important literary voices in Spain. He was by any measure a distinguished intellectual, respected all over the world for his scholarship and verse.

Alonso was perhaps best known for his studies on the poetry of Spain's Golden Age—the sixteenth and seventeenth centuries. Alonso's edition of Luis de Gongora's poem, "Soledades," which included a prose version that explained the meaning of a poem long considered incomprehensible, rescued both Gongora and his poem from oblivion. Among the other poets that Alonso examined are Saint John of the Cross, Garcilaso, and Fray Luis de Leon. Eventually, Alonso's criticism encompassed the entire range of Spanish literature—early and modern, poetry and prose. Winfield declared the author to be "the dominant figure in literary scholarship in postwar Spain, initiating entirely new schools of criticism. He was one of the greatest intellectual influences on Spanish culture in [the twentieth] century."

As a poet Alonso was an instrumental part of the renaissance of Spanish verse that occurred in the decades after the civil war of 1936 to 1939. Alonso first began to publish his poetry during the 1920s, when he was a member of the group of poets known as the "Generation of 1927," a group that included Federico

Garcia Lorca and Rafael Alberti. It wasn't until the 1940s, however, that Alonso began to attract attention as a major poet. In his two most important collections of poetry, *Hijos de la ira* and *Oscura noticia*—both published in the mid-1940s—the author examines humanity's "search for religious and personal transcendence on the one hand, and [its] temptation to egotism, pettiness and destruction on the other," according to Andrew P. Debicki in his biography, *Damaso Alonso.*

Winfield saw several constant themes in Alonso's poetry, most notably anxiety over death, love, loneliness, and—as the poet matured—humankind's existential struggle. Particularly after the horrors of the Spanish civil war and World War II, Alonso mounted "an anguished, bitter outcry against the particular circumstances of his life and a universal protest against the injustice inherent in life," to quote Winfield. Alonso's poetry also addressed the relationship between man and God, revealing the artist to be deeply religious but still perplexed by the concept of deity. In *Duda y amor sobre el Ser Supremo,* for instance, Alonso finds "meaning in the incessant desire to know and love," in Winfield's words. The critic continued: "In the tension of the constant struggle among doubt, love, and desire, Alonso elicits the participation of the reader in order to solve a mystery of intuition, not logic. . . . The book is a tribute to human nobility in the desperate attempt to endure."

Beginning with *Hijos de la ira,* Alonso challenged the stylistic direction and aesthetics of Spanish poetry, some of which he himself had embraced in his earlier work. Winfield observed that Alonso "was influential in motivating a new and authentic voice in postwar Spain. He stretched the limits of theme and technique, [rebelling] . . . against the existing apathetic schools of surrealism and 'pure' poetry. Through free verse, multiple layers of imagery, and courageous exploration of reality, the author removed traditional boundaries and led Spanish poetry in novel directions." Winfield concluded: "The profound themes of his poetry—existence, God, and humankind's role in the universe—achieved an intensity, precision, and emotive force that was equaled by few Spanish poets of his time. His poems reflect the natural languages of the people in a desolate atmosphere of loneliness and chaos. Yet, amid guilt and injustice, and facing a silent God, Alonso found humans to be wondrous creations who were fragile yet strong in their courage to survive."

As a testament to his importance as a poet, Alonso was awarded the 1978 Miguel de Cervantes prize, Spain's highest literary honor. He was elected to the Royal Academy of the Spanish Language in 1945 and served four terms as its director. In addition to his works of poetry and criticism, he was a respected translator. His own writings have been translated into several languages, including English, German, Portuguese, and Italian. Alonso died early in 1990 after a long battle with respiratory disease.

BIOGRAPHICAL/CRITICAL SOURCES:

BOOKS

Alvarado de Ricord, Elsie, *La obra de Damaso Alonso,* Gredos (Madrid), 1968.
Contemporary Literary Criticism, Volume 14, Gale (Detroit, MI), 1980.
Debicki, Andrew P., *Damaso Alonso,* Twayne (Boston, MA), 1970.
Dictionary of Hispanic Biography, Gale, 1996.
Dictionary of Literary Biography, Volume 108: *Twentieth-Century Spanish Poets, First Series,* Gale, 1991.
Flys, Miguel Jaroslaw, *La poesia existencial de Damaso Alonso,* Gredos, 1969.
Homenaje a Damaso Alonso, El Club (Madrid), 1978.
Manach, Jorge, *Visitas espanolas,* Revista de Occidente (Madrid), 1960.
Modern Spanish and Portuguese Literatures, Continuum (New York City), 1988.
Vivanco, Luis Felipe, *Introduccion a la poesia espanola contemporanea,* Guadarrama (Madrid), 1957.

PERIODICALS

Arbor, Volume 45, number 172, 1960, pp. 38-50.
Cuadernos Hispanoamericanos, November-December, 1951, pp. 113-26.
Papeles de Son Armadans, November-December, 1958, pp. 256-300; Volume 36, 1965, pp. 167-96.
Times Literary Supplement, May 31, 1974.

OBITUARIES:

PERIODICALS

New York Times, January 27, 1990.
Times (London), January 27, 1990.
Washington Post, January 27, 1990.*

ALTOLAGUIRRE, Manuel 1905(?)-1959

PERSONAL: Born June 29, 1905 (some sources say 1904), in Malaga, Spain; immigrated to Mexico, 1944; died following an automobile accident, July 26, 1959, in Burgos, Spain; son of Manuel Altolaguirre (a lawyer, judge, and writer) and Concepcion Bolin (Gomez de Cadiz) Alvarez; married Concha Mendez (a writer), June 5, 1932 (marriage ended, c. 1946); married Maria Luisa Gomez Mena, c. 1949; children: (first marriage) Paloma. *Education:* Studied law in Granada, Spain, 1922-24.

CAREER: Writer, editor, and publisher. Worked as lawyer in Madrid, Spain, mid-1920s; cofounded Imprenta Sur (printing company), 1925; lecturer in England, mid-1930s; director of La Barraca (theatre troupe), 1936; producer and director of motion pictures in Mexico, 1950s. *Military service:* Served in Republican Army during Spanish Civil War.

AWARDS, HONORS: Scholarship from Centro de Estudios Historicos, 1933; National Prize of Literature (Spain), c. 1936, for *La lenta libertad;* National Theatre Prize (Spain), 1938, for *Ni un solo muerte.*

WRITINGS:

POETRY

Las islas invitadas y otros poemas (title means "The Invited Isle and Other Poems"; also see below), Imprenta Sur (Malaga, Spain), 1926.
Ejemplo (title means "Example"; also see below), Imprenta Sur, 1927.
Soledades juntas (title means "Joint Solitudes"; see also below), Plutarco (Madrid, Spain), 1931.
La lenta libertad (title means "The Slow Freedom"), Heroe (Madrid), 1936.
Las islas invitadas (title means "The Invited Isle"; includes poems from *Las islas invitadas y otros poemas, Ejemplo,* and *Soledades juntas*), Viriato/ Altolaguirre (Madrid), 1936, revised edition, Castalia (Madrid), 1973.
Nube temporal (title means "Temporary Clouds"), Veronica/Altolaguirre (Havana, Cuba), 1939.
Poemas de las islas invitadas (title means "Poems from the Invited Isle"), Litoral (Mexico City, Mexico), 1944.
Nuevos poemas de las islas invitadas (title means "New Poems from the Invited Isle"), Isla (Mexico City), 1946.
Fin de un amor (title means "End of a Love"), Isla, 1949.

Poemas en America, Dardo (Malaga), 1955.
Poesias completas (title means "Complete Poetry"), Tezontle (Mexico City), 1960, enlarged edition edited by Margarita Smerdou Altolaguirre and Milagros Arizmendi, Catedra (Madrid), 1982.
Vida poetica, edited by Angel Caffarena Such, Guadalhorce (Malaga), 1962.
Poema del agua (title means "Poem of the Water"), Curso Superior de Filologia de Malaga (Malaga), 1973.

Contributor of poetry to periodicals.

PLAYS

(With Jose Bergamin) *El triunfo de las germanias* (title means "The Triumph of the Brotherhood of the Guilds"), produced in Valencia, Spain, 1937.
Ni un solo muerte (title means "Not One Single Dead Man"), c. 1938.

SCREENPLAYS

(With Egon Eis) *El puerto de los siete vicios,* Posa Films, 1951.
Subida al cielo (title means "Life and Afterlife"), 1952.
Golpe de suerte, Posa Films, 1952.
Los emigrantes (adapted from a short story by Guy de Maupassant), Posa Films, c. 1952.
(With Gilberto Martinez Solares) *Vuelta al paraiso,* Posa Films, 1958.
El cantar de los cantares (title means "The Song of Songs"; derived from Fray Luis de Leon's translations of the Biblical "Song of Songs"), Posa Films, 1959.

EDITOR

Antologia de la poesia romantica espanola (title means "Anthology of Romantic Spanish Poetry"), Espasa-Calpe, 1933.
Poemas escogidos de Federico Garcia Lorca, Veronica/ Altolaguirre, 1939.
Presente de la lirica mexicana, Ciervo Herido (Mexico City), 1946.
Gerardo Diego, *Poemas,* Secretaria de Educacion Publica (Mexico City), 1948.

Co-founding editor of *Ambos,* 1923, and *Litoral,* 1926-27; founding editor of *Poesia,* 1930; co-founding editor of *Heroe,* c. 1931, and *1616,* 1934-35; editor of *Hora de Espana* in mid-1930s; co-founding editor of *Atentamente,* c. 1940, *La Veronica,* 1942,

Litoral, 1944, and *Antologia de Espana en el recuerdo* (title means "Anthology of Spain Remembered").

TRANSLATOR

Auguste-Rene de Chateaubriand, *Atala, Rene, y El ultimo Abencerraje,* Espasa-Calpe, 1932.

Victor Hugo, *Los trabajadores del mar,* Espasa-Calpe, 1932.

(With others) Jules Supervielle, *Bosque sin horas,* Plutarco, 1932.

(With O. Savich) A. S. Pushkin, *Festin durante la peste. El convidado de piedra,* Veronica/Altolaguirre, 1939.

(With Bertha Pritchard) Luigi Sturzo, *El ciclo de la creacion,* Tiempos Nuevos (Buenos Aires), 1940.

(With Bernardo Clariana) Iwan Goll, *La cancion de Juan sin Tierra,* Veronica/Altolaguirre, 1941.

(With Antonio Castro Leal) Percy Bysshe Shelly, *Adonais,* Veronica/Altolaguirre, 1941.

OTHER

Garcilaso de la Vega (biography), Espasa-Calpe (Madrid), 1933.

(Author of introduction) Jorge Manrique, *Coplas a la muerte de su padre,* Veronica/Altolaguirre, 1939.

Romancero de la guerra civil, Visor (Madrid), 1984.

Las islas invitadas y cien poemas mas, Andaluzas Unidas (Seville, Spain), 1985.

Obras completas, edited by James Valender, Istmo (Madrid), 1986.

SIDELIGHTS: Manuel Altolaguirre, a poet, editor, and publisher, is known for his devotion to the genre of poetry and to literature generally. He was born in Malaga, Spain, in 1905 and began writing poetry when he was only a child. His playmates included other future poets, including Emilio Prados, Vicente Aleixandre, and Federico Garcia Lorca. In the mid-1920s, after completing law studies in Granada, Altolaguirre co-founded the magazine *Ambos.* The publication lasted for only four issues, but those issues provided a forum for several important new poets, including Lorca. Altolaguirre then traveled to Madrid, where he worked briefly as a lawyer before returning to Malaga to start the printing shop Imprenta Sur (which means "Southern Press").

In 1926 Altolaguirre published *Las islas invitadas y otros poemas* ("The Invited Isle, and Other Poems"), which Barbro Diehl described in the *Dictionary of Literary Biography* as "a collection of twenty-four

poems about nature, solitude, and death." Diehl added, "The poems are mostly descriptive, with relatively little symbolism." That same year Altolaguirre helped found the literary periodical *Litoral,* which was regarded, according to Diehl, as "the best poetry magazine of that period in Europe." *Litoral's* features included Altolaguirre's next verse collection, *Ejemplo* ("Example"), which contains many mournful poems inspired by the death of Altolaguirre's mother the previous year. Some of the poems also show the influence of surrealism, which was developing as an influential artistic movement in Europe.

In 1930 Altolaguirre founded still another magazine, *Poesia,* which he also printed and bound. In addition, he traveled to Paris with his portable printing press and consorted with other artists and literary figures, some of whom would provide material for *Poesia.* Altolaguirre then settled in Madrid, where he produced the verse volume *Soledades juntas* ("Joint Solitudes"), which features love poems that Diehl noted for their "erotic aspect." This eroticism, Diehl conjectured, was likely the result of Altolaguirre's relationship with fellow poet Concha Mendez, whom he would marry in 1932.

With Mendez, Altolaguirre founded the publications *Heroe* and *1616,* but he also found time to write the biography *Garcilaso de la Vega,* edit *Antologia de la poesia romantica espanola* ("Anthology of Romantic Spanish Poetry") and translate works by such writers as Victor Hugo and Jules Supervielle. In 1936 he also produced another poetry collection, *La lenta libertad* ("The Slow Freedom"), in which—as was his usual habit—Altolaguirre included many poems from previous volumes. In the newer poems, Diehl observed, Altolaguirre "is primarily concerned with evil and social injustice." Diehl added, however, that "some of the poems reflect his sorrow at the loss of his son [who died at birth] in 1933."

In 1936, as Spain erupted in civil war, Altolaguirre became a member of the Alliance of Anti-Fascist Intellectuals and assumed directorship of "La Barraca," a theatre troupe, after its leader, Federico Garcia Lorca, was killed. Before the end of the year, Altolaguirre enlisted with the Republican forces, where he involved himself in printing projects.

In 1939, as defeat loomed for the Republicans, Altolaguirre suffered an emotional collapse and entered an asylum in France, the country where his wife and daughter had already settled. Later that year, the Altolaguirres traveled to Mexico, but their daughter fell ill during the journey, compelling the family to stop in Cuba. There Altolaguirre soon resumed his literary activities, founding still more magazines, *Atentamente* and *La Veronica,* and completing another volume of verse, *Nube temporal* ("Temporary Clouds"), which features poems reflecting on war and human suffering.

Altolaguirre remained in Cuba until 1944, when he moved his family to Mexico City. Two years later he completed *Nuevos poemas de las islas invitadas* ("New Poems from the Invited Isle"), which revealed his increasing interest in mysticism. A few years later, after having left his wife for another woman, he published *Fin de un amor* ("End of a Love"), which includes poems celebrating his newfound passion.

For the next several years Altolaguirre was involved in the Mexican film industry, where he supplied scripts and worked as a producer and director. In 1959 he traveled to Spain to accompany a showing of his *El cantar de los cantares* ("Song of Songs") at a film festival in San Sebastian. Shortly after the festival ended, he suffered fatal injuries in an automobile accident.

Although Altolaguirre was rather overshadowed by such poets as Lorca and Aleixandre during his lifetime, he has since become a subject of increasing interest in the literary world. Given the appearance of substantial biographical and critical studies on the poet since the 1970s, the publication of a new edition of his complete poetry in 1982, and the printing of a volume of his complete works in 1986, it is likely that such interest will continue to flourish.

BIOGRAPHICAL/CRITICAL SOURCES:

BOOKS

Alvarez Harvey, Maria Luisa, *Cielo y tierra en la poesia lirica de Manuel Altolaguirre,* University and College Press of Mississippi (Hattiesburg, MS), 1972.

Crispin, John, *Quest for Wholeness: The Personality and Works of Manuel Altolaguirre,* Albatros Hispanofila (Valencia, Spain), 1983.

Dictionary of Literary Biography, Volume 108: *Twentieth-Century Spanish Poets,* First Series, Gale, 1991.

Morris, C. B., *A Generation of Spanish Poets: 1920-1936,* Cambridge University Press (Cambridge), 1969.*

AMADO, Jorge 1912-

PERSONAL: Born August 10, 1912, Itabuna, Bahia, Brazil; son of Joao Amado de Faria (a plantation owner) and Eulalia (Leal) Amado; married Matilde Garcia Rosa, 1933 (divorced 1944); married Zelia Gattai, July 14, 1945; children: Joao Jorge, Paloma. *Education:* Federal University of Rio de Janeiro, J.D., 1935. *Avocational interests:* Reading, gardening, cats, poker.

ADDRESSES: Home and office—Rua Alagoinhas 33, Rio Vermelho-Salvador, Bahia, Brazil.

CAREER: Writer. *Diario da Bahia,* reporter, 1927. Imprisoned for political reasons, 1935, exiled, 1937, 1941-43, 1948-52. Federal deputy of Brazilian parliament, 1946-48; *Para Todos* (cultural periodical), Rio de Janeiro, Brazil, editor, 1956-59.

MEMBER: Brazilian Association of Writers, Brazilian Academy of Letters.

AWARDS, HONORS: Stalin International Peace Prize, 1951; National Literary Prize (Brazil), 1958; Calouste Gulbenkian Prize, Academie du Monde Latin, 1971; Italian-Latin American Institute Prize, 1976; Nonnino Literary Prize (Italy), 1983; candidate for Neustadt International Prize for Literature, 1984; Neruda Prize and Volterra Prize (Italy), 1989; Sino del Duca Prize (Paris) and Mediterranean Prize, 1990; Commander, Legion d'Honneur (France).

WRITINGS:

IN ENGLISH TRANSLATION

Jubiaba, J. Olympio, 1935, translation by Margaret A. Neves published under same title, Avon (New York City), 1984.

Mar morto, J. Olympio, 1936, translation by Gregory Rabassa published as *Sea of Death,* Avon, 1984.

Capitaes da areia, J. Olympio, 1937, translation by Rabassa published as *Captains of the Sands,* Avon, 1988.

Terras do sem fim, Martins, 1942, translation by Samuel Putnam published as *The Violent Land,* Knopf, 1945, revised edition, 1965.

Gabriela, cravo e canela, Martins, 1958, translation by James L. Taylor and William L. Grossman published as *Gabriela, Clove and Cinnamon,* Knopf (New York City), 1962.

Os velhos marinheiros, Martins, 1961, translation by

Harriet de Onis published as *Home Is the Sailor,* Knopf, 1964.

A morte e a morte de Quincas Berro Dagua, Sociedade dos Cem Bibliofilos do Brasil, 1962, translation by Barbara Shelby published as *The Two Deaths of Quincas Wateryell,* Knopf, 1965.

Os pastores da noite, Martins, 1964, translation by de Onis published as *Shepherds of the Night,* Knopf, 1966.

Dona Flor e seus dois maridos: Historia moral e de amor, Martins, 1966, translation by de Onis published as *Dona Flor and Her Two Husbands: A Moral and Amorous Tale,* Knopf, 1969.

Tenda dos milagres, Martins, 1969, translation by Shelby published as *Tent of Miracles,* Knopf, 1971.

Bahia (bilingual Portuguese-English edition), Graficos Brunner, 1971.

Tereza Batista cansada de guerra, Martins, 1972, translation by Shelby published as *Tereza Batista: Home from the Wars,* Knopf, 1975.

O gato malhado e a andorinha Sinha, Editora Record, 1976, translation by Barbara Shelby Merello published as *The Swallow and the Tom Cat: A Love Story,* Delacorte (New York City), 1982.

Tieta do agreste, pastora de cabras; ou, A volta da filha prodiga: Melodramatico folhetim em cinco sensacionais episodios e comovente epilogo, emocao e suspense! Editora Record, 1977, translation by Shelby Merello published as *Tieta, the Goat Girl; or, The Return of the Prodigal Daughter: Melodramatic Serial Novel in Five Sensational Episodes, with a Touching Epilogue, Thrills and Suspense!* Knopf, 1979.

Farda, fardao, camisola de dormir: Fabula para acender uma esperanca, Editora Record, 1979, translation by Helen R. Lane published as *Pen, Sword, Camisole: A Fable to Kindle a Hope,* D. R. Godine, 1985.

The Miracle of the Birds, Targ Editions, 1982.

Tocaia grande, Editora Record, 1984, translation by Rabassa published as *Showdown,* Bantam, 1988.

The Golden Harvest, translated by Clifford E. Landers, Avon, 1992.

The War of the Saints (published as *Sumico da Santa*), translated by Rabassa, Bantam, 1992.

(With Claudio Edinger, Arnaldo Jabor, and Roberto Damatta) *Carnaval,* Distributed Art Publishers, 1997.

OTHER

O pais do carnaval (title means "Carnival Land"), Schmidt, 1932.

Suor (title means "Sweat"), [Brazil], 1933, 2nd edition, J. Olympio, 1936.

Cacau (title means "Cocoa"), [Brazil], 1934, 3rd edition, J. Olympio, 1936.

A B C de Castro Alves (title means "The Life of Castro Alves"), Martins, 1941.

Vida de Luiz Carlos Prestes, o cavaleiro da esperanca (title means "The Life of Luiz Carlos Prestes"), Martins, 1942.

Sao Jorge dos Ilheus (title means "St. George of Ilheus"), Martins, 1944.

O pais do carnaval [and] *Cacau* [and] *Suor,* Martins, 1944.

Obras (collected works), seventeen volumes, Martins, beginning 1944.

Bahia de Todos os Santos: Guia das ruas e dos misterios da cidade do Salvador (title means "Bahia: A Guide to the Streets and Mysteries of Salvador"), Martins, 1945.

Seara vermelha (title means "Red Harvest"), Martins, 1946.

Homens e coisas do Partido Comunista (title means "Men and Facts of the Communist Party"), Edicoes Horizonte, 1946.

O amor de Castro Alves (title means "Castro Alves's Love"), Edicoes do Povo, 1947, published as *O amor do soldado* (title means "The Soldier's Love"), Martins, 1958.

O mundo da paz: Uniao Sovietica e democracias populares (title means "The World of Peace: The Soviet Union and Popular Democracies"), Editorial Vitoria, 1952.

Os subterraneos da liberdade (title means "The Subterraneans of Freedom"; contains *Os asperos tempos, Agonia da noite,* and *A luz no tunel*), Martins, 1954.

Jorge Amado: Trinta anos de literatura (title means "Jorge Amado: Thirty Years of Literature"), Martins, 1961.

Agonia da noite (title means "Night's Agony"), Martins, 1961.

Os asperos tempos (title means "Harsh Times"), Martins, 1963.

A luz no tunel (title means "A Light in the Tunnel"), Martins, 1963.

O poeta Ze Trindade (title means "Ze Trindade: A Poet"), J. Ozon, 1965.

Bahia boa terra Bahia (title means "Bahia Sweet Land"), Image (Rio de Janeiro), 1967.

O compadre de Ogun, Sociedade dos Cem Bibliofilos do Brasil, 1969.

Jorge Amado, povo e terra: Quarenta anos de literatura (title means "Jorge Amado, His Land and People: Forty Years of Literature"), Martins, 1972.

(With others) *Brandao entre o mar e o amor* (title means "Swinging between Love and Sea"), Martins, 1973.

(With others) *Gente boa* (title means "The Good People"), Editora Brasilial/Rio, 1975.

(With Luis Viana Filho and Jeanine Warnod) *Porto Seguro recriado por Sergio Telles* (title means "Porto Seguro in the Painting of Sergio Telles"), Bolsa de Arte do Rio de Janeiro, 1976.

Conheca o escritor brasileiro Jorge Amado: Textos para estudantes com exercicios de compreensao e dabate (title means "Know the Writer Jorge Amado: Texts for Students"), edited by Lygia Marina Moraes, Editora Record, 1977.

O menino grapiuna, Editora Record, 1981.

Jorge Amado: selecao de textos, notas, estudios historico e critico e exercicios por Alvaro Cardosa Gomes (selected works), Abril Educacao, 1981.

A bola e o goleiro, Editora Record, 1984.

Les Terres Au Bou Du Monde, French and European Publications, 1991.

Les Chemins De la Faim, French and European Publications, 1991.

Conversaciones con Alice Raillard, Emece Editores, 1992.

Navegacao de cabotagem: apontamentos para um livro de memorias que jamais escreverei, Editora Record, 1992.

Discursos, Fundacao Cassia de Jorge Amado, 1993.

A descoberta da America pelos turcos: romancinho, Editora Record, 1994.

ADAPTATIONS: Gabriela, Clove and Cinnamon was adapted to film as *Gabriela,* released by Metro-Goldwyn-Mayer/United Artists, 1984; *Dona Flor and Her Two Husbands: A Moral and Amorous Tale* was adapted to the stage and appeared on Broadway as *Sarava.*

SIDELIGHTS: Ranked by some critics as Brazil's greatest twentieth-century novelist, Jorge Amado is certainly the most widely read. His depictions of the social, political, and cultural aspects of Brazil's northwestern Bahia region have been translated into as many as fifty languages. Amado writes with the eye of a social realist. His early work was politically inflammatory and evoked a poverty-stricken land afflicted by brutal government management. In more recent novels Amado has mellowed his political approach—still depicting the underclass, but with informed compassion and humor.

Amado was born the son of immigrant farmers on a cacao plantation in Southern Bahia. When he was old enough to work, he spent his summer holidays toiling in the cacao groves with other area laborers. These early episodes among Brazil's impoverished proved an invaluable learning experience for Amado, and provided a foundation for much of his writing. In a Berta Sichel interview for *Americas,* he elaborated on the importance these people hold for him and his work: "I am a writer who basically deals with social themes, since the source material for my creation is Brazilian reality. . . . [Many of my] novels narrate the life of the people, everyday life, the struggle against extreme poverty, against hunger, the large estates, racial prejudice, backwardness, underdevelopment. The hero of my novels is the Brazilian people. My characters are the most destitute, the most needy, the most oppressed—country and city people without any power other than the strength of the mestizo people of Brazil. They say that I am a novelist of whores and vagabonds, and there is truth in that, for my characters increasingly are anti-heroes. I believe that only the people struggle selflessly and decently, without hidden motives."

Appreciating Amado's concern for social realism requires an understanding of the socio-political climate in which he first began to write. Following a global economic crisis that had shattered the coffee industry and forced an unprecedented number of Brazilians into poverty, Brazil's 1930 presidential election was rife with revolution. When the liberal challenger Getulio Vargas met with apparent defeat, he headed an armed rebellion against the state—gaining control of civilian and military establishments, dissolving the congress, and issuing a decree of absolute power for his government. Initially, the overthrow of the old order produced a renaissance of sorts among Brazil's writers. Vargas had championed achievement and reform, and the writers were quick to adopt this spirit of social renewal. The new critical literature of Brazil lay bare the squalor of its lower classes and offered solutions for a nation restless for change.

Amado's early novels, often termed works of social protest, were published amid these turbulent times. *O pais do carnaval, Suor,* and *Cacau,* all written during the early 1930s, depict a destitute and violent Brazil and offer answers to many of the prevailing social problems. For many critics though, these early works hold little literary merit. In his assessment of this first phase in Amado's literary career, Fred P. Ellison wrote in *Brazil's New Novel:* "Character, plot, and literary form are consistently neglected. . . . In fact, there is reason to believe that Amado purposely slighted artistic qualities in attempting to draft social documents."

If Amado was indeed attempting to affect social change, he was not alone. As nationwide impatience with the economic plight grew, Vargas's support waned. Several political factions—notably the Communist Party and the fascist *Integralistas*—began to exert a marked influence among Brazilians. In 1935 a short-lived rebellion broke out, and Vargas subsequently declared martial law. Communists and other labeled seditionists were hunted down relentlessly, and a censorship department was created to suppress all forms of dissent. Amado's inflammatory early novels, though given little regard by critics, attracted the suspicious eye of the Vargas regime. Amado was imprisoned as a member of the Communist Party in 1935, exiled on several later occasions, and, in 1937 following a national ban, two thousand of his books were burned in a plaza by the Brazilian military.

The Vargas crackdown did not silence the writers' call for reform so much as alter the form of protest. Starting with his 1935 book *Jubiaba,* Amado began to display a greater concern for technique, often cloaking social themes within psychological studies. This new style found its greatest success in *Terras do sem fin* (*The Violent Land*). Published in 1942, *The Violent Land* depicts the brutal land-battles that ensue when two neighboring estates rush for the last, precious cacao groves in northern Brazil.

Bertram D. Wolfe noted similarities between the Brazilian power wars Amado characterizes in *The Violent Land* and those that took place during the expansion of the American West. He wrote in the *New York Herald Tribune Weekly Book Review:* "To the raw violence and action of one of our gold-rush, claim-jumping, frontier tales, this novel adds an exuberant, tropical lyricism. . . . It is one of the most important novels to have come North in some time, and, because of its frontier character and crowded action, one of the most accessible to the American reader." Ellison termed the book "Amado's masterpiece, a story of almost epic grandeur," and attributed its success to Amado's avoidance of the propaganda in his earlier work: "*The Violent Land* shows what Amado can achieve when art is not encumbered with the millstone of political argument." Although Amado continued for several years to write novels of social realism, none ever earned the literary acclaim given *The Violent Land.*

In 1958, with the publication of *Gabriela, cravo e canela* (*Gabriela, Clove and Cinnamon*), Amado's writing took another significant shift. As in his earlier work, the underclasses of Brazil's Bahia region continued to dominate Amado's novels. Beginning with *Gabriela,* however, the examination of their afflictions gave way to romantic and humorous themes. In the *New York Times Book Review,* Juan de Onis attributed this shift in tone to Amado's alignment with the contemporary European rejection of Communism. "*Gabriela,*" he wrote, "represents undoubtedly the artistic liberation of Senhor Amado from a long period of ideological commitment to Communist orthodoxy."

The novel is named for a spirited migrant worker who is discovered by an Ilheus bar owner and elevated to social respectability. Gabriela's healthy sexual appetite is instrumental in liberating the growing Bahian town from its restrictive social values. For most critics, Amado's foray into the lighter side of Brazilian life proved highly successful. "It is in *Gabriela* that [Amado] really finds himself," wrote Harriet de Onis in *Saturday Review.* "One hardly knows what to admire most: the dexterity with which Amado can keep half a dozen plots spinning; the gossamer texture of the writing; or his humor, tenderness, and humanity." Juan de Onis described Amado's stylistic evolution thusly: "In his earlier novels on the cacao region, . . . Amado tended to paint caricatures rather than characters. . . . In striking contrast to these flat symbols, the characters in *Gabriela* are created in-the-round; they live, breathe and feel as genuine individuals— and none more so than Gabriela herself." The critic also noticed a change in the tone of Amado's writing. For example, the earlier novel *The Violent Land,* wrote Juan de Onis, "is spun out with grim, humorless indignation. In *Gabriela,* however, irony, satire and plain high spirits illuminate every page."

With the critical acclaim that Amado's new style attracted came a growing popularity. The 1960s found him enjoying best-seller status with several novels, notably *Dona Flor e seus dois maridos* (*Dona Flor and Her Two Husbands*). Like most of Amado's later novels, *Dona Flor* blends elements of burlesque with the surreal. Critic David Gallagher granted credit for the success of this strange brew to Amado's convincing characters. "*Dona Flor and Her Two Husbands* is a remarkable novel for the coolness with which the author is able to impose his extraordinary characters on us," Gallagher wrote in the *New York Times Book Review.* "Like them, we learn to take exoticism and magic in our stride."

The novel presents the life of the virtuous Dona Flor who, after her disreputable first husband dies in drunken revelry, weds an upstanding and meticulous pharmacist. When the ghost of her first husband appears—with his exceptional lovemaking skills still effective on Dona Flor—she is ambivalent about her dilemma: She appreciates the security that her new husband provides, but longs for his predecessor's passion. A *Time* magazine critic charged *Dona Flor* with overblown sentimentalism, calling the book "a love letter to Bahia." The reviewer claimed that Amado "romanticizes his Bahians into virile lovers, darkly sensual *morenas* [women], whores and neighbors, all larger than life. . . . In lavishing details of color, touch and taste, Amado so ignores the canons of construction that at times he seems embarked on little more than an engaging shaggy-dog story." Gallagher held a similar opinion of Amado's prose: "It is a pity that Amado mars his achievement by often writing flatly, without discipline or tension. His refreshing exuberance is diminished by the novel's almost aggressive repetitiveness. Cut to half its size, it would have been a better book."

Amado has continued to produce international bestsellers despite such charges of prosaic deficiency and claims that machismo elements dominate his work. (In *Myth and Ideology in Contemporary Brazilian Fiction*, Daphne Patai criticized "Amado's evident commitment to the status quo in that most fundamental of issues: men's domination of women.") His 1988 work, *Showdown*, is no exception. Tracing the lively history of a town founded on the Brazilian frontier, the novel proves to be an epic patchwork of the nation's heritage. "*Showdown* is a second look at the terrain Amado covered in *The Violent Land*," commented Pat Aufderheide in the *Washington Post Book World*. "It has the plot drive that has kept people reading the latest Amado novel all these years; it's loaded with sex and violence; and the picaresque characters all share their inner lives with the reader through Amado's omniscient narration." Paul West, writing in the *New York Times Book Review*, called *Showdown* "a vital novel, more complex than it seems at first, written in a long series of ebullient lunges, none of them stylish or notably elegant or eloquent, but in sum haunting and massive. . . . [Amado] creates something fecund and funny, tender and burly, as if his lively social conscience, under pressure, . . . yet again had to take the side of the human race."

Bahia's leading literary authority has continually painted a lyrical image of his homeland, aggrandizing Brazil's downtrodden in rollicking tales of passion and mystique. In summation of Amado's writing, Fred P. Ellison wrote: "In the works of this most controversial of modern Brazilian writers, unevenness is the salient characteristic. Amado seems to write solely by instinct. Of conscious art intellectually arrived at, the result of reflection and high craftsmanship, there is relatively little. Yet his novels have a mysterious power to sweep the reader along. Serious defects in artistry are overcome by the novelist's ability to weave a story, to construct vivid scenes, and to create fascinating characters." In an interview with Berta Sichel, Amado revealed the source of his inspiration: "I consider myself to be a writer with a commitment, a writer who is for the people and against their enemies, who develops his work around the reality of Brazil, discussing the country's problems, touching on the dramatic existence of the people and their struggle."

BIOGRAPHICAL/CRITICAL SOURCES:

BOOKS

Chamberlain, Bobby J., *Jorge Amado,* Twayne, 1990.
Contemporary Literary Criticism, Gale (Detroit), Volume 13, 1980, Volume 40, 1986, Volume 106, 1998.
Curran, Mark J., *Jorge Amado e a literature de cordel,* Fundacao Cultural do Estado da Bahia, 1981.
Dictionary of Literary Biography, Volume 113: *Modern Latin-American Fiction Writers,* Gale, 1992.
Ellison, Fred P., *Brazil's New Novel: Four Northeastern Masters,* University of California Press, 1954.
Patai, Daphne, *Myth and Ideology in Contemporary Brazilian Fiction,* Fairleigh Dickinson University Press, 1983.
Peden, Margaret Sayers, editor, *The Latin American Short Story: A Critical History,* Twayne, 1983.
Tati, Miecio, *Amado: Vida e obra,* Itatiaia, 1960.
Tavares, Paulo, *O baiano Jorge Amado e sua obra,* Record, 1985.

PERIODICALS

Americas, May-June, 1984; September-October, 1992, p. 60.
Booklist, August, 1992, 1993; September 15, 1993, p. 100.
Book World, August 24, 1969.
Hispania, May, 1968; September, 1978.
Kirkus, October 15, 1993.
Library Journal, August, 1992, p. 144; December, 1993.
Los Angeles Times Book Review, February 28, 1988; March 27, 1988.

Nation, June 5, 1967.

New York Review of Books, May 4, 1967; February 26, 1970.

New York Times, October 1, 1977; January 12, 1985; January 24, 1988.

New York Times Book Review, September 16, 1962; November 28, 1965; January 22, 1967; August 17, 1969; October 24, 1971; September 21, 1975; July 1, 1979; October 28, 1984; May 19, 1985; February 7, 1988; November 28, 1993, p. 20.

Publishers Weekly, November 21, 1980.

Saturday Review, September 15, 1962; January 8, 1966; February 4, 1967; August 16, 1969; August 28, 1971.

Times Literary Supplement, July 2, 1970; October 2, 1981; November 12, 1982; January 20-26, 1989.

Tribune Books (Chicago), September 9, 1979; January 24, 1988.

Variety, March 31, 1997, p. 56.

Washington Post, December 29, 1984.

Washington Post Book World, September 12, 1971; January 10, 1988.

* * *

ANDRADE, Mario
  See de ANDRADE, Mario

* * *

ANZALDUA, Gloria 1942-

PERSONAL: Born September 26, 1942, in Jesus Maria of the Valley, TX; daughter of Urbano (a rancher) and Amalia (Garcia) Anzaldua. *Education:* Pan-American University, B.A., 1969; University of Texas at Austin, M.A., 1973; University of California, Santa Cruz, post-graduate study.

ADDRESSES: Office—c/o Literature Board, University of Santa Cruz, Santa Cruz, CA 95064.

CAREER: Worked as teacher in Texas; San Francisco State University, San Francisco, CA, lecturer in feminist literature, 1979-80; University of California, Santa Cruz, instructor in creative writing, 1982-86; writer. Lecturer, Norwich University, 1984-86; lecturer, Georgetown University and Colorado Univer-

sity, both 1990; Distinguished Visiting Professor in Women's Studies, University of California, Santa Cruz, 1998.

AWARDS, HONORS: MacDowell Colony fellowship, 1982; American Book Award, Before Columbus Foundation, 1986, for *This Bridge Called My Back;* fiction award, National Endowment for the Arts, 1991; Sappho Award, Astraea National Lesbian Action Foundation, 1992.

WRITINGS:

(Editor with Cherrie Moraga, and contributor) *This Bridge Called My Back: Writings by Radical Women of Color,* Persephone Press (Watertown, MA), 1981.

(Contributor) Cherrie Moraga, Alma Gomez, and Mariana Romo-Carmona, editors, *Cuentos: Stories by Latinas,* Kitchen Table/Women of Color (New York City), 1983.

(With Annie Cheatham and Mary Clare Powell) *This Way Daybreak Comes* (poetry), 1986.

Borderlands/La Frontera: The New Mestiza (poetry and prose), Spinsters/Aunt Lute (San Francisco, CA), 1987.

(Editor and contributor) *Making Face, Making Soul/ Hacieno Caras: Creative and Critical Perspectives by Women of Color,* Aunt Lute, 1990.

Prietita Has a Friend—Prietita tiene un Amigo (for children), Children's Book Press (San Francisco), 1991.

Friends from the Other Side—Amigos del otra lado (for children), Children's Book Press, 1993.

Lloronas, Women Who Howl: Autohistorias—Torias and the Productions of Writing, Knowledge, and Identity, Aunt Lute, 1996.

Prietita and the Ghost Woman—Prietita y La Llorona (for children), Children's Book Press, 1996.

La Prieta (novel; title means "The Dark One"), Aunt Lute, 1997.

Work represented in anthologies. Contributor to periodicals, including *Conditions: Six, Ikon: Creativity and Change, Tejidos, Third Woman,* and *Trivia.* Contributing editor, *Sinister Wisdom,* 1984—.

SIDELIGHTS: Gloria Anzaldua is an educator and author who has proved herself an authority on feminism, particularly as it relates to Third World countries and Chicano culture. In addition, she has produced a varied canon that includes volumes of verse, children's stories, fiction, and feminist essays. In these works, Anzaldua has embraced various writing styles while inevitably addressing both Chicano culture and feminist issues. Hector A. Torres wrote in the *Dictionary of Literary Biography:* "Critics of Anzaldua's work recognize the daring and innovative aspect of her mode of writing and they describe her as a writer who has the rare ability to write in a mixture of discursive styles and aims."

Anzaldua was born in 1942 on a ranch settlement in Texas. After her father's death in the late 1950s, Anzaldua moved with her family to Arkansas, where she worked the fields with migrant Chicanos. She found Chicano society oppressive and sexist, and turned to reading as a means of both withdrawing from her surroundings and discovering other cultures. After receiving a master's degree from the University of Texas at Austin in 1973, she taught high-school English and became involved in education programs for migrants. Towards the end of the decade, she became a lecturer in feminist literature at San Francisco State University, and in the mid-1980s she taught creative writing at the University of California, Santa Cruz.

In 1981 Anzaldua collaborated with Cherrie Moraga in editing *This Bridge Called My Back: Writings by Radical Women of Color,* which included Anzaldua's controversial essay "La Prieta" (meaning "The Dark One"). Torres wrote in the *Dictionary of Literary Biography* that "La Prieta" constitutes "an autobiographical piece . . . that speaks openly of matters concerning [Anzaldua's] lesbian sexuality . . . and her vision of a political coalition of 'Third World women, lesbians, feminists, and feminist-oriented men of all colors.'" In another essay, "Speaking in Tongues: A Letter to 3rd World Women Writers," Anzaldua suggests that feminist political theory be written in a freewheeling style free of academic abstraction and dense, counter-productive convolution. Torres reports that "for Anzaldua, in the construction of a theoretical framework that would articulate the experience of the minority writer, anything is allowed."

To *Cuentos: Stories by Latinas,* a 1983 volume edited by Cherrie Moraga, Alma Gomez, and Mariana Romo-Carmona, Anzaldua contributed a story that concerns a woman who must choose between a fixed marriage and an acknowledgment of her own lesbianism. Anzaldua collaborated with Annie Cheatham and Mary Clare Powell on the 1986 poetry collection *This Way Daybreak Comes.* The following year Anzaldua completed *Borderlands/La Frontera: The New*

Mestiza, a volume comprised of both an extended, seven-part essay and a collection of poems. *Borderlands/La Frontera* focuses on various aspects of the border between the United States and Mexico. Despite the seemingly limited nature of such a subject, Anzaldua manages to probe not only historical subjects but feminist issues and even autobiographical concerns.

Borderlands/La Frontera has been recognized as a notable literary achievement. Writing in *Dictionary of Literary Biography,* Hector A. Torres called *Borderlands* Anzaldua's "major work to date," and he declared that the book is written "with the clear, crisp prose of historiography as well as with the rhythms and images of poetry." In addition, he noted that it is "a far-reaching work, shifting in and out of the traditional literary and expository genres, blending poetry and prose, switching between English and Spanish, all in order to weave an autobiography resonating with the many voices of Anzaldua's lived, imagined, and 'read' experience." A *Library Journal* reviewer, meanwhile, deemed Anzaldua's book "a rich and moving personal account."

Among Anzaldua's subsequent publications are the children's books *Prietita Has a Friend— Prietita tiene un Amigo, Friends from the Other Side—Amigos del otra lado,* and *Prietita and the Ghost Woman— Prietita y La Llorona,* and the novel *La Prieta.* In addition, she edited the 1990 volume *Making Face, Making Soul/Hacieno Caras: Creative and Critical Perspectives by Women of Color,* which includes her essay "En Rapport, in Opposition," in which she advocates greater unity within the feminist movement.

BIOGRAPHICAL/CRITICAL SOURCES:

BOOKS

Dictionary of Literary Biography, Volume 122: *Chicano Writers,* Second Series, Gale (Detroit, MI), 1992.

Keating, AnaLouise, *Women Reading and Writing: Self-Invention in Paul Gunn Allen, Gloria Anzaldua, and Audre Lorde,* Temple University Press, 1996.

PERIODICALS

Library Journal, April, 1988.
Village Voice, June 28, 1990, pp. 60, 62.*

ARELLANO, Juan Estevan 1947-

PERSONAL: Born September 17, 1947, in Embudo, NM; son of Adolfo (a farmer) and Celia (a farmer) Arellano; married Elena Martinez, 1972; children: three. *Education:* New Mexico State University, earned degree, 1970.

ADDRESSES: Office—c/o Taos News, 226 Albright St., P.O. Box U, Taos, NM 87571.

CAREER: Writer. Worked as a reporter. Co-founder of Academia de la Nueva Raza, 1970.

AWARDS, HONORS: Honorable mention in New Mexico writing competition, 1962; Washington Journalism Center fellowship, 1971.

WRITINGS:

(Editor) *Entre verde y seco,* Academia de la Nueva Raza (Dixon, NM), 1972.
(And photographer) *Palabras de la vista/Retratos de la pluma* (poetry; title means "Sight Words/Pen Portraits"), Academia (Albuquerque, NM), 1984.
Inocencio: Ni siembra, ni escarda y siempre se come el mejor elote (novel; title means "Inocencio: Neither Plant nor Dig and You'll Always Eat the Best Corn"), Grijalva (Mexico City), 1991.
Cuentos de Cafe y Tortilla, Universidad Autonoma de Ciudad Mexico (Chihuahua, Mexico), 1997.
(Author of poetry) *Low'n Slow: Lowriding in New Mexico,* photographs by Jack Parsons, text by Carmella Padilla, Museum of New Mexico Press (Santa Fe, NM), 1999.

Work represented in anthologies, including *Voces: An Anthology of Nuevo Mexicano Writers,* University of New Mexico Press, (Albuquerque), 1987. Also author of column "El Crespuscalo" (title means "The Twilight") in *Taos News.* Contributor to periodicals, including *Caracol* and *Cuaderno.* Editor of *Cuaderno;* publisher and editor of *Resolana.*

SIDELIGHTS: Juan Estevan Arellano is a writer who helped establish the Academia de la Nueva Raza ("Academy of the New People") to promote Chicano culture. Arellano was born in 1947 in Embudo, New Mexico. His parents were farmers, and according to Reynaldo Ruiz, writing in the *Dictionary of Literary Biography,* their "work ethic, along with their strong religious beliefs and their need to work and live off the land, instilled in [Arellano] a sense of reverence and respect for nature, the land, the water rights, and

the cultural traditions of his community." Allegiance to his Mexican-American culture, in turn, spurred Arellano, according to Ruiz, to become "a dedicated advocate for his people."

Arellano received his undergraduate degree from New Mexico State University in 1970, whereupon he returned to Embudo and founded the Academia de la Nueva Raza. In addition, he obtained the editorship of *Cuaderno,* a journal that furthered the Academia's aims of promoting Chicano culture and providing a forum for Chicano expression.

Arellano has distinguished himself as a writer of both fiction and poetry. In 1972 he produced the story "No nos murimos este ano," which, despite its Spanish title, is in English. This tale concerns an unemployed Vietnam veteran who grows increasingly unhappy when he fails to find work. Ruiz wrote in the *Dictionary of Literary Biography* that in this story Arellano "skillfully synthesizes a realistic picture of many maladies that the young Chicanos in northern New Mexico experience."

In two ensuing tales published in *Cuaderno,* Arellano portrays the character Innocencio, whom Ruiz describes as "a picaro who always manages to survive without working." In one tale, Innocencio enters a Catholic school, where he suffers humiliation from the nuns, and thereafter becomes a drunken bum. The tale ends several years later, with Innocencio in middle age and surviving by practicing deceit and thievery. A following tale features Innocencio as an old man recalling the humiliations of his youth and bemoaning the victimization of Chicanos by capitalist opportunists. Ruiz affirmed: "The outstanding features in these two stories . . . are the use of authentic Spanish dialect as spoken in northern New Mexico; humor that ranges from the most basic to sophisticated plays on words; and the realistic depiction of the characters." These two tales eventually served as the opening chapters of Arellano's novel *Inocencio: Ni siembra, ni escarda y siempre se come el mejor elote.* Other tales by Arellano include "Cuentos de Cafe y Tortilla," a series of three narratives on what Ruiz described as "issues of importance"; "No es hablar de su vida, sino su muerte," in which a writer reflects on the steady undoing of Chicano culture by Anglo-American values.

In addition to writing fiction, Arellano has published *Palabas de la vista/Retratos de la Pluma,* a collection of poems accompanied by his own photographs. The poems in this volume explore various aspects of

Chicano life in northern New Mexico, and they embrace such themes as the fragility of innocence, the cynicism of contemporary society, and the inspirational nature of life itself. In these and other writings, Arellano succeeds in maintaining Chicano culture, and he also manages, as Ruiz concluded, to provide "a peek into the psyche, beliefs, and socioeconomic conditions of the New Mexican Chicano."

BIOGRAPHICAL/CRITICAL SOURCES:

BOOKS

Dictionary of Literary Biography, Volume 122: *Chicano Writers,* Second Series, Gale (Detroit), 1992.*

*   *   *

ARGUEDAS, Alcides 1879-1946

PERSONAL: Born July 15, 1879, in La Paz, Bolivia; died May 6, 1946, in Chulumani, Bolivia.

CAREER: Lawyer and writer, c. 1903-34. Held diplomatic posts in Paris, France, London, England, and Bogota, Colombia; served as Bolivian senator and leader of the Bolivian Liberal Party.

WRITINGS:

(With Sabino Pinilla and Severino Campuzano) *La Creacion de Bolivia,* Editorial-America (Madrid, Spain), 1917.

Also author of *Pisagua,* 1903; *Wata wara* (novel), 1904, expanded version published as *Raza de bronce* (title means "Race of Bronze"), 1919; *Vida criolla* (novel; title means "Native Life"), 1905; *Historia de Bolivia,* four volumes, 1920-26; *Los caudillos barbaros,* 1929; *La danza de las sombras,* 1934; *Obras completas,* 1959; and *Etapas en la vida de un escritor,* 1963. Also author of the essay "Pueblo Enfermo" (title means "A Sick People"), 1909.

BIOGRAPHICAL/CRITICAL SOURCES:

BOOKS

Encyclopedia of World Literature in the Twentieth Century, St. James Press (Detroit), 1999.*

ARIAS, Ron(ald Francis) 1941-

PERSONAL: Born November 30, 1941, in Los Angeles, CA; son of Armando (an army officer) and Emma Lou (a homemaker; maiden name, Estrada) Arias; married Joan Londerman (an business executive), April 1, 1966; children: Michael. Attended Oceanside-Carlsbad College (now Mira Costa College), 1959-60, University of Barcelona, Spain, 1960, University of California, Berkeley, 1960-61, and National University, Buenos Aires, Argentina, 1962; University of California, Los Angeles, B.A., 1967, M.A., 1968. *Politics:* Independent. *Religion:* "None."

ADDRESSES: Home—283 Weed Ave., Stamford, CT 06902. *Office—People* Magazine, Time and Life Building, Rockefeller Center, New York, NY 10020. *Agent*—Reid Boates, 44 Mountain Ridge Rd., Wayne, NJ 07470.

CAREER: Buenos Aires Herald, Buenos Aires, Argentina, reporter, 1962; community development volunteer with Peace Corps in Cuzco, Peru, 1963-64; writer for Copley Newspapers and for national and international wireservices, 1960s; *Caracas Daily Journal,* Caracas, Venezuela, reporter, 1968-69; Inter-American Development Bank, Washington, DC, editor foragency publications, 1969-71; San Bernardino Valley College, San Bernardino, CA, instructor, 1971-80, associate professor of English, until 1985; Crafton Hills College, Yucaipa, CA, instructor in English and journalism, 1980-84; *People* magazine, New York City, senior writer, 1986—.

Member of the board of directors of the National Endowment for the Arts coordinating council of literary magazines, 1979-80.

MEMBER: Newspaper and Magazine Writers Guild.

AWARDS, HONORS: Scholarship to study journalism in Buenos Aires, Argentina, from Inter-American Press Association, 1962; Machris Award for journalistic excellence from Los Angeles Press Club, 1968; writer's fellowship from California Arts Commission, 1973; Chicano Literary Contest first place award in fiction from University of California, Irvine, 1975, for short story "The Wetback"; Modern Language Association fellowship, 1975; National Book Award nomination for fiction, 1976, for *The Road to Tamazunchale.*

WRITINGS:

The Road to Tamazunchale (novel), West Coast Poetry Review, 1975.
Five against the Sea (nonfiction), New American Library (New York City), 1989.
(With Mehmet Oz and Lisa Oz) *Healing from the Heart: A Leading Heart Surgeon Explores the Cutting Edge of Alternative Medicine,* Dutton (New York City), 1998.

Also author of short stories, including "El mago," 1970, "The Interview"and "Stoop Labor," both 1974, "The Wetback," "A House on the Island," and "The Story Machine" and "El senor del chivo," both 1976, "Chinches," 1977, and "The Boy Ate Himself" and "The Chamizal Express," both 1980; author of the play The *Interview*, adapted from the author's short story, 1979; author of screenplays, including *Jesus and the Three Wise Guys*; author of television scripts.

Work represented in anthologies, including *The Chicanos: Mexican-American Voices,* edited by Ed Ludwig and James Santibanez, Penguin, 1971; *First Chicano Literary Contest Winners,* edited by Juan Villegas, Spanish and Portuguese Department, University of California, 1975; and *Cuentos Chicanos: A Short Story Anthology,* edited by Rudolfo A. Anaya and Antonio Marquez, revised edition, University of New Mexico Press, 1984.

Contributor to periodicals, including the *New York Times, Quarry West, Bilingual Review/Revista Bilingue, Latin American Literary Review, Journal of Ethnic Studies, Revista Chicano-Riquena, Nuestro, Christian Science Monitor, Nation,* and *Los Angeles Times.*

WORK IN PROGRESS: Nonfiction project, tentatively titled *The Secret Man: The Search for My Real Father;* researching Latin America and Third-World situations and themes.

SIDELIGHTS: Ron Arias is a journalist and short story writer whose widely acclaimed debut novel, *The Road to Tamazunchale,* distinguished him as a leading Chicano writer of "magic realism," a literary form popularized by Gabriel Garcia Marquez that blends reality with fantasy. Influenced by Garcia Marquez's *One Hundred Years of Solitude,* Arias related to Juan Bruce-Novoa in *Chicano Authors: Inquiry by Interview* the novel's effect on him: "For me, Garcia-Marquez transformed, *deepened* reality in so many of

its aspects—tragic, humorous, adventurous, wondrous. The work was alive, entertaining at every word. There was nothing sloppy, facile, overly clever, belabored, preachy—all the things I detest in literature." Arias's own style of magic realism is a mixture of precise, journalistic descriptions and stream-of-consciousness writing which often centers on magical figures who can manipulate reality. Bruce-Novoa contended that even more important than Arias's stylistic affinities with magic realism are his achievements as "a skilled, patient craftsman, with a healthy sense of irony about himself and the world. . . . [H]e shares the current—we could say modern—sense of literature as one enormous text, interrelated and consciously self-referential."

Though he has written several short stories, Arias is best known for his novel, *The Road to Tamazunchale.* Nominated for a National Book Award, the novel is about the final days of a retired encyclopedia salesman named Fausto Tejada. In order to understand and accept his impending death Fausto makes an imaginative journey to Tamazunchale, a Mexican village which in the book symbolizes the final resting place after death. The story opens with an ailing and despondent Fausto peeling off his skin; not until his niece Carmela enters the room does the reader learn that Fausto has actually been playing with a wad of Kleenex. Still, the incident functions as the first in a series of events in which the boundaries between reality and illusion, past and present, and life and death are clouded: Fausto travels to sixteenth-century Lima; he helps an Inca shepherd move his flock off the Los Angeles freeway; he leads hundreds of men across the Mexican-American border; he finds himself in a play called "The Road to Tamazunchale"; and, finally, he joins friends and neighbors on a cosmic picnic where he is reunited with his deceased wife. The events culminate with Fausto accepting his inevitable demise, though exactly when this occurs is ambiguous. As quoted in *Chicano Literature: A Reference Guide,* Vernon Lattin explained in *American Literature* that even after Fausto apparently dies, "the novel continues for one more chapter without suggestions of distortion or logical violation. Fausto and his friends continue as in the past: there is no funeral or burial; the logic of the world and the dichotomy of life and death have been transcended, and the road to Tamazunchale has become a sacred way for Everyman to follow."

The Road to Tamazunchale earned favorable reviews. Calling Arias's novel "skillful and imaginative," *Los*

Angeles Times Book Review contributor Alejandro Morales defended the book's status as a Chicano classic because of its "magical realistic imagination, its precise crisp prose, its relationship to the 'new reality' of Spanish American fiction and its compassionate treatment of death, its central theme." Morales concluded that Arias offers "a new social reality and a new vision of the American literary mosaic in which [he himself] must now be recognized." *Chicano Literature* noted that Eliud Martinez lauded Arias in the *Latin American Literary Review* for examining universal themes and capturing distinctly Chicano speech patterns. Moreover, Martinez asserted that "no Chicano novel before *Tamazunchale* has tapped the artistic resources of the modern and contemporary novel (and the arts) in a comparable way, deliberately and intuitively." Arias commented: "My Mexican family heritage and continuing travel abroad, especially in Latin American countries for magazine story assignments, are strong inspirations for my writing. My work in the Peace Corps with the Andean poor also gave me an abiding insight into the world of basic survival, which is the theme of my own favorite writing projects."

BIOGRAPHICAL/CRITICAL SOURCES:

BOOKS

Bruce-Novoa, Juan, *Chicano Authors: Inquiry by Interview,* University of Texas Press, 1980.
Dictionary of Literary Biography, Volume 82, *Chicano Writers, First Series,* Gale, 1989.
Martinez, Julio A., and Francisco A. Lomeli, editors, *Chicano Literature: A Reference Guide,* Greenwood Press, 1985.
von Bardeleban, Renate, Dietrich Briesemeister, and Juan Bruce-Novoa, editors, *Missions in Conflict: Essays on U.S.– Mexican Relations and Chicano Culture,* Gunter Narr Verlag (Tubingen), 1986.

PERIODICALS

American Literature, number 50, 1979.
Americas Review, fall-winter, 1994, p. 114.
Latin American Literary Review, number 4, 1976; number 5, 1977.
Los Angeles Times Book Review, April 12, 1987.
New Mexico Humanities Review, Volume 3, number 1, 1980.
Revista Chicano-Riquena, Volume 5, number 4, 1977; Volume 10, number 3, 1982.

ARLT, Roberto (Godofredo Christophersen) 1900-1942

PERSONAL: Born April 4, 1900, in Buenos Aires, Argentina; died of a heart attack, July 26, 1942, in Buenos Aires, Argentina; son of Karl (a glass blower and accountant) and Catalina (a homemaker; maiden name, Iobstraibitzer) Arlt; married first wife, c. 1923 (died, c. 1929); married Elizabeth Shine, 1939; children: (first marriage) Mirta. *Education:* Self-educated; attended Naval School of Mechanics, c. 1919-20. *Avocational interests:* Inventing.

CAREER: Writer, 1914-42; *El Mundo* (daily newspaper), Buenos Aires, Argentina, columnist, 1929-42. Secretary to writer and publisher Ricardo Guiraldes, Buenos Aires, 1925-27; Arna (inventing business), Buenos Aires, founder, 1941-42. Employed as a book store clerk, apprentice to a tinsmith, painter, mechanic, vulcanizer, brick factory manager, newspaper manager, and port worker. *Military service:* Served in Argentine armed forces, c. 1919-20.

AWARDS, HONORS: The Seven Madmen won a municipal prize, 1929.

WRITINGS:

El juguete rabioso (novel; title means "The Rabid Plaything"), Editorial Latina, 1926.
Los siete locos (novel), [Buenos Aires], 1929, recent edition, with introduction by daughter, Mirta Arlt, Fabril (Buenos Aires), 1968, translation by Naomi Lindstrom published as *The Seven Madmen,* Godine (London), 1984.
Los lanzallamas (novel; title means "The Flame-throwers"), Claridad (Buenos Aires), 1931.
El amor brujo (novel; title means "Love of the Sorcerer"), [Buenos Aires], 1932, Losada, 1980.
El jorobadito (short stories; title means "The Little Hunchback"), [Buenos Aires], 1933, with introduction by M. Arlt, Fabril, 1968.
Aguafuertes portenas (newspaper columns; title means "Porteno Etchings"), [Buenos Aires], 1933, Hyspamerica, 1986.
Aguafuertes espanolas (essays; title means "Spanish Etchings"), L. J. Rosso (Buenos Aires), 1936, with introduction by M. Arlt, Fabril, 1971.
El criador de gorilas (short stories; title means "The Gorilla Breeder"), [Buenos Aires], 1941, Losada, 1982.
Nuevas aguafuertes portenas (newspaper columns; title means "New Porteno Etchings"), selected by Pedro G. Orgambide, Hachette, 1960.

Novelas completas y cuentos (complete novels and short stories), prologue by M. Arlt, three volumes, Fabril, 1963.

Saverio el cruel [and] *La isla desierta* (plays; titles mean "Saverio the Cruel" and "The Desert Island"), EUDEBA, 1965.

Teatro completo (complete plays; contains *Trescientos millones* [title means "The Three Hundred Million"; produced by El Teatro del Pueblo, 1932]; and *El fabricante de fantasmas* [title means "The Ghost Manufacturer"]), introduction by M. Arlt, two volumes, Schapire, 1968.

Un viaje terrible (novella; title means "The Terrible Journey"), originally published in journal *Nuestra Novela,* 1941, edited with an introduction by Adolfo Prieto, Tiempo Contemporaneo, 1968.

El traje del fantasma, Edicom, 1969.

Regreso (story), prologue by Alberto Vanasco, Corregidor, 1972.

Obra completa (complete works), preface by Julio Cortazar, two volumes, Lohle, 1981.

Estoy cargada de muerte y otros borradores, (stories; originally published in *Mundo Argentino* and *El Hogar,* 1926-39), Torres Aguero (Buenos Aires), 1984.

Works represented in anthologies, including *Cuatro escritores argentinos,* 1965; and *Dos panoramas del cuento,* Centro, 1972. Selected short stories appear in English-language volumes, including *Doors and Mirrors: Fiction and Poetry from Spanish America, 1920-1970,* edited by Hortense Carpenter and Janet Brof, Grossman; *The Eye of the Heart: Short Stories from Latin America,* edited by Barbara Howes, Bobbs-Merrill; and *Contemporary Latin American Short Stories,* edited by Pat M. Mancini, Fawcett. Selected works published in various collections. Contributor to periodicals, including *Mundo Argentino, Nuestra Novela,* and *El Hogar.*

SIDELIGHTS: Roberto Arlt was a prolific and versatile Argentine novelist, short story writer, playwright, and journalist. Although he wrote four novels, two collections of short stories, volumes of essays, and seven plays, only one work, his experimental and wholly original novel *Los siete locos,* has been translated into English, as *The Seven Madmen.* Arlt was condemned by many contemporary reviewers who considered his works of fiction to be vulgar. General readers, however, applauded his writings, particularly his weekly newspaper column, "Aguafuertes portenas" ("Porteno Etchings"), in which he addressed social and political issues that deeply concerned lower- and middle-class Argentineans. In an attempt to impel the

Spanish language into the modern age, Arlt consistently used slang and informal grammar in his works, and his writings influenced the trend toward the antiliterary in Hispanic literature begun in the 1960s.

Arlt was born in 1900 in Buenos Aires to German immigrants. His father had served in Bismarck's army; his mother was Italian. Neither spoke Spanish particularly well and German was spoken at home. Although he was expelled from school as "useless" at the age of eight, he read widely and published his first story at fourteen. He left home two years later and worked at odd jobs while aspiring to be a writer. While working as a secretary to the novelist Ricardo Guiraldes, he published his first novel, *El juguete rabioso* ("The Rabid Plaything"), in 1926. Although it garnered little attention from established critics, it found a youthful audience. The novel concerns a man who idolizes historical bandits; when he emulates them, however, he fails miserably, capable of only stealing canes and billiard balls from Buenos Aires cafes. Arlt was a frequent patron of these taverns, particularly the cafe La Punalada, whose seedy denizens—"outcast weirdos" according to David William Foster in *Review: Latin American Literature and Arts*—inspired characters in his works.

Arlt published his second—and most notable—novel, *The Seven Madmen,* in 1929. *The Seven Madmen* and its sequel, *Los lanzallamas* ("The Flamethrowers"), feature the neurotic antihero Erdosain, considered by some the epitome of the alienated man in twentieth-century society. After he loses his job because of petty theft and his wife leaves him for another man, Erdosain—searching for meaning to his life—joins a mysterious coterie of misfits. Led by the Astrologer, the society is plotting to take over the country and subsequently institute a utopian dictatorship that will lift the people from their economic exploitation and spiritual malaise. The scheme turns out to be only an elaborate hoax against Erdosain, and after he witnesses an execution and murders his mistress, he commits suicide.

"The reader's first reaction to [*The Seven Madmen*] is complete disorientation," Foster noted in *Currents in the Contemporary Argentine Novel,* because "the controlling consciousness of the novel [is] Erdosain's muddled perspective on reality." Arlt's confusing narrative is a deliberate manifestation of Erdosain's own bewildered involvement with the society, whose members and plotting he does not understand. In *The Seven Madmen* and *Los lanzallamas* the reader is not given any background information on Erdosain; his character is revealed only through present actions. Ironies and loose ends abound; time sequences are often unclear (sometimes the reader does not know if an event actually happened or was hallucinated); and elaborate trivial detail is presented while significant information is withheld. Finally, even seemingly straightforward storytelling passages in the books make the reader suspicious.

"The key to an understanding of [*The Seven Madmen* and *Los lanzallamas*]" according to Foster in *Currents,* "lies in the essential nature of Erdosain as one anguished soul who may well be a figure of Everyman." Arlt later commented that the characters in these novels "are tied or bound together by desperation," as quoted by Aden W. Hayes in *Romance Notes.* Arlt continued: "The desperation in them originates, more than from material poverty, from another factor: the disorientation that, after the Great War, has revolutionized the conscience of men, leaving them empty of ideals and hopes. . . . The anguish of these men is born in their internal sterility."

The Seven Madmen won a municipal award but drew the censure of critics who, failing to appreciate the novel's experimental and expressionistic tendencies, read it as a realistic book and lambasted its poor grammar, composition, and craftsmanship. "If anyone ever actually believed that this novel was realistic," Paul Gray wrote in a 1984 issue of *Time,* "then life in the Argentine capitol must once have been unimaginably weird." Arlt's subject matter and style did not fit the traditional aesthetic concept of beauty upheld by established Spanish literary critics and authors, many of whom were still extolling the virtues of cowboys on the vanishing Argentine frontier. Arlt dwelt on the least pleasant aspects of urban life: "The setting sun lit up the most revolting inner recesses of the sloping street," Gray quoted *The Seven Madmen.* According to Foster in the *Review,* his novels depict, with "appalling fidelity," the horrid conditions in which Argentineans were forced to live. In the prologue to *Los lanzallamas,* quoted by Lee Dowling in *Review,* Arlt answered and indicted his detractors, particularly the wealthy and genteel establishment writers: "It is said of me that my writing is poor. That may be . . . often I have wanted to compose a novel that would consist of panoramic scenes like Flaubert's. But today, amid the babble of an inevitably crumbling social edifice, it is impossible to linger over embroidery."

Many of Arlt's contemporary readers admired his linguistic audacity. During the 1920s and 1930s, when academics were calling for purity and uniformity in the Spanish language, Arlt, along with other avant-garde writers, proposed the "derhetoricizing" of what they considered a pompous, florid, and stodgy literary idiom that lacked the resources for innovation and invention. Thus his characters and narrators use colloquialisms common to middle- and lower-class Spanish, and he was the first novelist to consistently write with the familiar form of "you," *voseo,* rather than the acceptable literary form of "you." In "The Language of the Argentines," translated for *Review* from his collection *Aguafuertes porteñas,* Arlt condemned those demanding linguistic purity, criticizing "the absurdity of trying to straightjacket in a prescriptive grammar the constantly changing, new ideas of a people."

In 1932 Arlt published his last novel, *El amor brujo* ("Love of the Sorcerer"), about a man who attempts to inject his life with scenes duplicated from novels he read in his youth, only to be jarred by the harsh contrast between his life and his fantasies. His other fiction includes two collections of short stories, *El jorobadito* ("The Little Hunchback"), published in 1933, and *El criador de gorilas* ("The Gorilla Breeder"), published in 1941. Arlt's stories resemble his longer fiction in their confusing chronology, fragmentation, and chaos, as well as their portrayal of warped personalities in a disintegrating society.

Arlt also tried his hand at play writing, encouraged by Leonidas Barletta, director of the Teatro del Pueblo. He wrote his first play, *Los 300 Millones* ("The Three Hundred Million"), in 1932, and like many of his later dramas it explores the constant tension between the real and illusory worlds and is peopled by grotesque and surreal figures that often appear more lifelike than the principal characters. In *Los 300 Millones* a poor servant girl relieves the tedium of her life by fantasizing about what she would do if she inherited three hundred million pesos; she is brought back to reality usually by the sound of her patroness's voice. When her patroness's drunken son enters her room in an attempt to seduce her when she is about to meet her fantasy son-in-law, the shocking disparity between her daydreams and the sordidness of real life impels her to kill herself.

Arlt wrote two other plays in 1936 dealing with the interplay between fantasy and reality. In *Saverio el cruel* ("Saverio the Cruel") a group of rich young pranksters ask a timid dairyman, Saverio, to pose as a brutal colonel. They claim that one of the girls, Susana, believes herself to be a princess pursued by him and he must act out her fantasy to set her free. Although Saverio reluctantly agrees, he soon becomes immersed in his role, even buying a guillotine to eliminate his enemies. He is eventually informed of the hoax and returns to his normal self, but Susana, unable to return to reality, shoots and kills Saverio. *El fabricante de fantasmas* ("The Ghost Manufacturer") focuses on a fantasizing author who murders his wife and is condemned to the distorted, nightmarish world in his mind—peopled by a hangman, prostitute, cripple, and hunchback.

Although he tried his hand at various literary genres, Arlt's greatest popularity came through his journalism. From 1929 until his death in 1942 he wrote a column called "Porteno Etchings" for the newspaper *El Mundo.* The column provided for him a forum to express his views on society, economics, and politics and was enormously successful—the paper sold twice as many copies on the day his column appeared. Today it is considered an invaluable chronicle of a decade of Argentine life. Juan Carlos Onetti, in the preface to *Los siete locos,* translated in *Review,* explained "the journalistic triumph" of the "Porteno Etchings": "The common man, the petty and smaller-than-petty bourgeois of the streets of Buenos Aires, the office worker, the owner of a rundown business, the enormous mass of burned-out, bummed-out cases, could read their own thoughts, sorrows, their pallid hopes, intuited and stated in their everyday language."

Arlt's works influenced innovative Spanish writers such as Gabriel Garcia Marquez and Jorge Luis Borges, although they received little critical recognition during his lifetime. Since the 1960s his books have been enthusiastically accepted by Argentine writers who see in Arlt a proponent of anti-literary and anti-establishment writing. Beginning in 1968 a number of his books were reissued, many—including *El juguete rabioso, El jorobadito,* and *Aguafuertes espanolas*—with introductions by his daughter, Mirta. Complete collections of his novels, short stories, and plays have been recently published by such influential houses as Hachette and Fabril. Importantly, Lindstrom translated *The Seven Madmen* in 1984, introducing Arlt's original vision to the English-speaking world.

BIOGRAPHICAL/CRITICAL SOURCES:

BOOKS

Flint, Jack M., *The Prose Works of Roberto Arlt: A Thematic Approach,* University of Durham, 1985.

Flores, Angel, *Spanish–American Authors: The Twentieth Century,* H. W. Wilson, 1992.

Foster, David William, *Currents in the Contemporary Argentine Novel: Arlt, Mallea, Sabato, and Cortazar,* University of Missouri Press, 1975.

Hispanic Literature Criticism, Volume 1, Gale (Detroit), 1994.

Lindstrom, Naomi, *Literary Expressionism in Argentina: The Presentation of Incoherence,* Center for Latin American Studies, Arizona State University, 1977.

Martinez, Victoria Jeanne, *The Semiotics of a Bourgeois Society: An Analysis of the Aguafuertes Portenas by Roberto Arlt,* Scripta Humanistica (Potomac, MD), 1997.

Sole, Carlos A., and Maria Isabel Abreu, editors, *Latin American Writers,* Scribner's, 1989.

Twentieth-Century Literary Criticism, Volume 29, Gale, 1988.

PERIODICALS

Journal of Spanish Studies: Twentieth Century, winter, 1977.

Latin American Literary Review, spring-summer, 1976.

Review: Latin American Literature and Arts, fall, 1982.

Romance Notes, fall, 1980.

Time, August 27, 1984.*

*　　*　　*

ARMAND, Octavio Rafael 1946-

PERSONAL: Born in 1946 in Guantanamo, Cuba; immigrated to United States, c. 1960, naturalized citizen. *Education:* Rutgers University, B.A., 1968, M.A., 1972, Ph.D., 1975.

ADDRESSES: Home—Caracas, Venezuela; and Elmhurst, NY *Office*—Bennington College, Bennington, VT 05201.

CAREER: Affiliated with Bennington College, Bennington, VT; visiting professor at University of Michigan, fall, 1988.

WRITINGS:

Horizonte no es siempre lejania (poems), Las Americas, 1970.

El pajaro de lata, Editorial San Juan, 2nd edition, 1973.

Raices al viento, Editorial San Juan, 1974.

Entretes, Grafica Urex, 1974.

Piel menos mia, Escolios, 1976, 2nd edition, 1979.

Cosas pasan (1975) (poems), Monte Avila Editores, 1976.

America en su literatura, Editorial Universitaria (San Juan), 2nd edition, 1978.

Raiz y ala, Editorial San Juan, 2nd edition, 1979.

(Editor) *Mark Strand: Viente poemas* (title means "Mark Strand: Twenty Poems"), Fundarte, 1979.

Como escribir con erizo, 1976, Asociacion de Escritores de Mexico, 1979.

Superficies, Monte Avila Editores, 1980.

Razon y pasion de Sor Juana Ines de la Cruz, Editorial Porrua, 3rd edition, 1980.

Biografia para feacios, Pre-Textos, 1981.

(Editor and author of introduction) *Toward an Image of Latin American Poetry* (bilingual anthology), Logbridge-Rhodes, 1982.

El grillo grunon, Editorial Universitaria, 1984.

With Dusk, translated by Carol Maier, Logbridge-Rhodes, 1984.

Origami, Fundarte, 1987.

Refractions, translated by Carol Maiser, SITES/Lumen Books (New York City), 1994.

El Pez Volador, Casa de la Poesia (Caracas), 1997.

Also author of *Entre testigos: 1971-1973,* 1974, and *Narrativa hispanoamericana actual,* 1980. Contributor of poems and articles to literary journals in the United States and Latin America. Founder and editor of *Escandalar,* 1978—.

BIOGRAPHICAL/CRITICAL SOURCES:

PERIODICALS

World Literature Today, winter, 1986; autumn, 1988.*

*   *   *

ARREOLA, Juan Jose   1918-

PERSONAL: Born September 12, 1918, in Ciudad Guzman, Jalisco, Mexico. *Education:* Studied theater in Paris, France, 1945, and at the College of Mexico.

ADDRESSES: Agent—c/o Grijalbo, Ave. Granjas 82, Mexico 16, DF.

CAREER: Professional actor in Mexico City, Mexico; writer. Founder of literary journals; conductor of writers' workshops.

AWARDS, HONORS: First prize in INBA Drama Festival, for the play *La hora de todos.*

WRITINGS:

Gunther Stapenhorst: Vinetas de Isidoro Ocampo, [Mexico], 1946.

Varia invencion (short stories), Tezontle (Mexico), 1949.

Confabulario (short stories), Fondo de Cultura Economica, 1952, 2nd edition published with *Varia invencion* as *Confabulario y Varia invencion, 1951-1955,* 1955, 3rd edition published with *Bestiario* and *Punta de Plata* as *Confabulario total, 1941-1961,* 1962, translation by George D. Schade published as *Confabulario and Other Inventions,* University of Texas Press, 1964.

La hora de todos: Juguete comico en un acto (one-act play), Los Presentes (Mexico), 1954.

Bestiario (short stories and vignettes; title means "Bestiaries"), Universidad Nacional Autonoma de Mexico, 1958.

Punta de Plata (short stories), [Mexico], 1958.

(Editor) *Cuadernos del unicornio* (Spanish-American literature), [Mexico], 1958-60.

La feria (novel), Joaquin Mortiz (Mexico), 1963, translation by John Upton published as *The Fair,* University of Texas Press, 1977.

(Compiler) *Lectura en voz alta* (translations of literature into Spanish), Porrua (Mexico), 1968.

Antologia de Juan Jose Arreola, introduced and selected by Jorge Arturo Ojeda, Oasis (Mexico), 1969.

Cuentos (short stories), Casa de las Americas (Havana), 1969.

Palindroma (short stories, vignettes, and a one-act play; title means "Palindrome"), Joaquin Mortiz, 1971.

Mujeres, animales, y fantasias mecanicas, Tusquets (Barcelona), 1972.

La palabra educacion, Secretaria de Educacion Publica (Mexico), 1973.

(With others) *Zoo en cuarta dimension* (short stories), Samo (Mexico), 1973.

Y ahora, la mujer, Utopia (Mexico), 1975.

(Editor) Fernando Pereznieto Castro, *La ciudad de Queretaro* (in English and Spanish), Joaquin Mortiz, 1975.

Inventario, Grijalbo (Mexico), 1976.

Confabulario personal, Bruguera (Barcelona), 1980.

Estas paginas mias (anthology; includes stories originally published in *Confabulario y Varia invencion, 1951-1955*), Fondo de Cultura Economica, 1985.

Estas Paginas Mias, Fondo de Cultura, 1994.

Narrativa completa, Alfaguara (Colegio del Valle, Mexico), 1997.

Editor of literary magazines, including *Pan* and *Eos,* during the 1940s.

SIDELIGHTS: Juan Jose Arreola is "a true man of the twentieth century, an eclectic," according to *Hispania* contributor Seymour Menton, "who at will can draw upon the best of all who have preceded him in order to create truly masterful works of art which in turn will be seized upon by others." Arreola has written a novel, plays, and numerous short pieces, some of which are easily identified as short stories and others that defy strict literary definition. In those works that break with literary tradition, critics have considered the lack of such devices as conventional plots or character development not carelessness, but ingenious and essential features of Arreola's unique style. Furthermore, reviewers have noted, the numerous literary and biblical allusions found throughout Arreola's writings provide a unifying aspect to his otherwise dissimilar works. Arreola's best-known collection of short stories and sketches is probably *Confabulario,* which was first published in 1952 and, after being expanded twice, was published in English translation as *Confabulario and Other Inventions.* Selections from *Confabulario* were also included in a later Spanish collection, *Estas paginas mias,* which was published in 1985.

Among the pieces reviewers have lauded are "Verily, Verily I Say Unto You" and "The Disciple." The story "Verily, Verily I Say Unto You" alludes to the biblical warning that a camel can pass through the eye of a needle more easily than a rich person can enter heaven. In the tale a scientist devises a costly method—which would be financed by wealthy people—to disintegrate a camel and thus allow it to pass through a needle. The scientist reasons that if he and the rich people can make the camel go through the needle, they will go to heaven. In his introduction to *Confabulario and Other Inventions,* translator George D. Schade described Arreola's often cynical portrayals of human shallowness and greed, such as the one in "Verily, Verily I Say Unto You": "With mordant descriptions, pungent attacks, or sly irony, [Arreola] shows how silly mankind is, how outrageous man's behavior and antics are, how one is at the mercy of a world and society that more often seems to care for

what is trivial and ephemeral than for what is essential."

"The Disciple" reveals Arreola's artistic, rather than social, concerns; in the story, an art teacher draws an outline for his pupil and calls the outline "beauty." The teacher then creates a splendid picture by filling in the outline, but he explains that he has destroyed beauty and subsequently burns the picture. Menton considered the story a reflection of Arreola's sentiments about literature as well as other forms of art. The reviewer explained in his *Hispania* article, as quoted in *Modern Latin American Literature,* "Arreola's message is, of course, that true beauty lies in suggestion only. Once a work of art goes beyond suggesting beauty, it loses its charm." Arreola's 1963 novel *La feria* (*The Fair*) exemplifies the writer's theory of artistic and literary aesthetics. Like many of Arreola's shorter works, *The Fair* lacks the well-defined characters and plots of conventional fiction. Instead, the novel develops from related and unrelated scenes, partial conversations, and portions of letters and diaries; it suggests plot and character instead of depicting them outright. "Yet the totality of the work has body, literary development, and novelistic scope," assessed Joseph Sommers in *Books Abroad,* as quoted by *Modern Latin American Literature.* The novel's fragmented parts coalesce, Sommers explained, to portray the life cycle of a Mexican village, from its founding in colonial times to its deterioration in the present age. It concludes with a fabulous display of fireworks set off by vandals, which, instead of providing harmless entertainment, kills several onlookers. "If this symbolism implies anguish and cynicism," wrote Sommers, "these qualities are mediated by the author's understanding and sympathy for the complexity of human problems. His sensitive use of language . . . and his wry tone of bitter humor are the basis for the literary unity of this novel."

BIOGRAPHICAL/CRITICAL SOURCES:

BOOKS

Acker, Bertie, *El cuento mexicano contemporaneo:Rulfo, Arreola y Fuentes;Temas y cosmovision,* Playor, 1984.

Arreola, Juan Jose, *Confabulario and Other Inventions,* translated and introduced by George D. Schade, University of Texas Press, 1964.

Carballo, Emmanuel, *Diecinueve protagonistas de la literatura mexicana del siglo xx,* Empresas, 1968.

Dictionary of Literary Biography, Volume 131: *Modern Latin-American Fiction Writers,* First Series, Gale, 1992.

Foster, David William, and Virginia Ramos Foster, editors, *Modern Latin–American Literature,* Ungar, 1975.

Washburn, Yulan M., *Juan Jose Arreola,* Twayne, 1983.

PERIODICALS

Books Abroad, autumn, 1964.
Chasqui, May, 1989.
Hispania, September, 1959; April, 1973; December, 1988.
Hispanofila, September, 1983.
Journal of Spanish Studies: Twentieth Century, spring-fall, 1980.
Latin American Literary Review, fall-winter, 1977.
Latin American Theatre Review, 1975.
Revista de Estudios Hispanicos, May, 1974.
Studies in Short Fiction, winter, 1971.

*   *   *

ARTEAGA, Alfred 1950-

PERSONAL: Born May 2, 1950, in Los Angeles, CA; son of Alfred (a bartender) and Lillian (an insurance claims adjuster; maiden name, Frias; present surname, Wilding) Arteaga; married, December, 1972 (divorced, May, 1995); children: Marisol, Xochitl, Mireya (daughters). *Ethnicity:* "Chicano." *Education:* University of California, Santa Cruz, A.B., 1972, M.A., 1984, Ph.D., 1987; Columbia University, M.F.A., 1974. *Politics:* La Raza Unida. *Religion:* Roman Catholic. *Avocational interests:* Race cars, music, guitars, fusion.

ADDRESSES: Home—Berkeley, CA. *Office*—c/o Mercury House, 785 Market St., San Francisco, CA 94103. *E-mail*—bluebed@hotmail.com.

CAREER: San Jose City College, San Jose, CA, instructor in Mexican-American studies, 1977-87; University of Houston, Houston, TX, assistant professor of English, 1987-90; University of California, Berkeley, assistant professor of English, 1990-98.

AWARDS, HONORS: Rockefeller Foundation fellow, 1993-94; poetry fellow, National Endowment for the Arts, 1995.

WRITINGS:

Cantos (poems), Chusma House Publications (San Jose, CA), 1991.

(Editor) *An Other Tongue: Nation and Ethnicity in the Linguistic Borderlands,* Duke University Press (Durham, NC), 1994.

First Words: Origins of the European Nation, Center for German and European Studies, University of California, 1994.

House with the Blue Bed (essays), Mercury House (San Francisco, CA), 1997.

Chicano Poetics: Heterotexts and Hybridities, Cambridge University Press, 1997.

Love in the Time of Aftershocks (poems), Chusma House and Moving Parts Press, 1998.

Work represented in anthologies, including *Spivak Reader.* Contributor of essays and poems to journals, including *Stanford Humanities Review, Critical Studies, Baldus,* and *River Styx,* and to electronic journals.

WORK IN PROGRESS: Flesh and Verse, poems, essays, and criticism; *Lost Line,* poems; *Rage: The Politics of Racism in the University of California,* essays; *Lacuna,* on "the theory of time and its relation to literary genre and human subjectivity," completion expected in 1999.

SIDELIGHTS: Alfred Arteaga told *CA:* "God made me a poet, and that shapes my vision, my conception, my understanding, and my path through the world. It is a poetic means whether I write poetry, construct literary theory, or delineate my life in essay. It is a gift or a curse that took hold as I came into being in words.

"Life has it that I am Chicano, born in the center of Chicano culture in the middle of the last century of the millennium. I struggled hard to become an intellectual work and to shape my vision into the acts of language needed at this hour. My bent and my desire have me stringing together words so that they might mean, and that they might mean in ways both new and reflective of my kind. So this is what I do: in verse, in literary and cultural theory, and in personal essay.

"My art is influenced by the philosophies of time, chaos theory, and the magic of Neruda, Rimbaud, Sor Juana Ines de la Cruz, Nezahualcoyotl, the fight of hummingbirds, and driving formula cars in races.

"As for process, I observe and wait. I walk and think and let the trick of language get loose. When it seems gestated, I put the stuff onto a screen and work on paper from a printer, with pencil or ink more often. Perhaps superstitiously, I do not share a piece until it has set, seemingly then firm enough to withstand total erasure.

"I am inspired to write of only a few subjects: the possibility of love between people across the impossible break between us; the question of what next, of what follows in thought and meaning; and time, from my vantage as an achronist, who doesn't believe in the reality of time. I write across language, mostly English and Spanish, but much more. I am taken by the dynamics of mix, by the confusion and flow at the site of linguistic *xing*."

* * *

AZUELA, Arturo 1938-

PERSONAL: Born in 1938.

ADDRESSES: Office—c/o Academia Mexicana de la Lengua, Donceles 66, Centro, Delegacion Cuauhtemoc, 06010 Mexico City, Mexico.

CAREER: Writer, mathematician, and symphony violinist, c. 1973—.

MEMBER: Academia Mexicana de la Lengua.

WRITINGS:

Un Tal Jose Salome, J. Mortiz (Mexico), 1975.
Manifestacion de Silencios, J. Mortiz (Mexico), 1979, translation by Elena C. Murrary published as *Shadows of Silence,* University of Notre Dame Press (Notre Dame, IN), 1985.
El Tamano del Infierno, Casa de las Americas, 1981.
La Casa des las Mil Virgenes, Argos Vergara (Barcelona), 1983.
El Don de la Palabra, Plaza y Janes (Barcelona), 1984.
El Matematico, Plaza y Valdes (Mexico), 1988.
La Mar de Utopias, Plaza y Valdes (Mexico), 1991.*

* * *

AZUELA, Mariano 1873-1952
(Beleno)

PERSONAL: Born January 1, 1873, in Lagos de Moreno, Jalisco, Mexico; died of a heart attack, March 1, 1952, in Mexico City, Mexico; buried in the Rotonda de Hombres Illust; son of Evaristo Azuela and Paulina Gonzalez; married Carmen Rivera; children: Salvador, Mariano, Carmen, Julia, Paulina, Maria de la Luz, Augustin, Esperanza, Antonio, Enrique. *Education:* Faculty of Medicine and Pharmacy of Guadalajara, degree of doctor, 1898.

CAREER: Physician, 1898-1952; writer, 1907-52. Director of public education in Jalisco province under government of Francisco "Pancho" Villa. *Wartime service:* Physician with Villa's army during the Mexican Revolution.

AWARDS, HONORS: National Prize for Literature, 1949; *The Underdogs* won a prize for drama, 1950.

WRITINGS:

NOVELS AND NOVELLAS

Maria Luisa, [Mexico], 1907, 2nd edition, Botas, 1938.
Los fracasados (title means "The Failures"), [Mexico], 1908, 4th edition, Botas, 1939.
Mala yerba: Novela de costumbres nacionales, [Mexico], 1909, R. Terrazas, 1924, translation by Anita Brenner published as *Marcela: A Mexican Love Story,* foreword by Waldo Frank, Farrar & Rinehart, 1932.
Andres Perez, maderista, Botas, 1911, (New York City), 2nd edition, Botas, 1945.
Los de abajo: Novela de la revolucion mexicana, [Mexico], 1916, translation by E. Munguia Jr. published as *The Underdogs: A Novel of the Mexican Revolution,* preface by Carleton Beals, illustrations by J. C. Orozco, Brentano's, 1929, foreword by Harriet de Onis, illustrations by Orozco, New American Library, 1963, translation by Frances K. Hendricks and Beatrice Berler published as *The Underdogs* in *Two Novels of the Mexican Revolution: The Trials of a Respectable Family* and *The Underdogs,* Principia Press of Trinity University, 1963 (also see below).
Los caciques (also see below), [Mexico], translation by Lesley Byrd Simpson published as *The Bosses* in *Two Novels of Mexico: The Flies. The Bosses,* University of California Press, 1956.
Las moscas [and] Domitilo quiere ser diputado [and] De como al fin lloro Juan Pablo, Tip de A. Carranza e hijos, 1918, translation of *Las moscas* by Simpson published as *The Flies* in *Two Novels of Mexico: The Flies. The Bosses,* University of California Press, 1956 (also see below).

Las tribulaciones de una familia decente, [Mexico], 2nd edition, Botas, 1938, translation by Hendricks and Berler published as *The Trials of a Respectable Family* in *Two Novels of the Mexican Revolution: The Trials of a Respectable Family and The Underdogs,* Trinity University Press, 1963.

La Malhora, [Mexico], 3rd edition published with 2nd edition of *El desquite,* Botas, 1941.

El desquite, [Mexico], 2nd edition published with 3rd edition of *La Malhora,* Botas, 1941.

La luciernaga, Espasa-Calpe (Madrid), 1932, translation by Hendricks and Berler published as *The Firefly* in *Three Novels of Mariano Azuela,* Trinity University Press, 1979 (also see below).

Pedro Moreno, el insurgente: Biografia novelada, Ediciones Ercilla (Santiago, Chile), 1935.

Precursores, Ediciones Ercilla, 1935.

El camarada Pantoja, Botas, 1937.

San Gabriel de Valdivias, comunidad indigena, Ediciones Ercilla, 1938.

Regina Landa, Botas, 1939.

Avanzada, Botas, 1940.

Nueva burguesia, Club del Libro Amigos del Libro Americano (Buenos Aires), 1941, recent edition, Secretaria de Educacion Publica, Cultura, Fondo de Cultura Economica, 1985.

El padre don Agustin Rivera, Botas, 1942.

Chanta, Seminario de Cultura Mexicana, Secretaria de Educacion Publica, 1944.

La mujer domada, El Colegio Nacional, 1946.

Sendas perdidas, Botas, 1949.

La maldicion, Fondo de Cultura Economica, 1955.

Esa sangre, Fondo de Cultura Economica, 1956.

Also author of *Madero: Biografia novelada.* Author of various works under the pseudonym Beleno.

OTHER

Teatro: Los de abajo, El buho en la noche, Del llano hnos (plays), Botas, 1938.

Cien anos de novela mexicana (criticism), Botas, 1947.

Obras completas (complete works) three volumes, prologue by Francisco Monterde, Fondo de Cultura Economica, 1958-60, recent edition, 1976.

Introduccion al estudio del amparo: Lecciones, Department de Bibliotecas, Universidad de Nuevo Leon, 1968.

Epistolario archivo, compiled with notes and appendices by Berler, Centro de Estudios Literarios, Universidad Nacional Autonoma de Mexico, 1969.

SIDELIGHTS: Mariano Azuela was one of the leading writers of twentieth-century Mexico and the foremost chronicler of that country's revolution. During his forty-year literary career he wrote more than twenty novels describing the volatile Mexican political scene, including *Las tribulaciones de una familia decente* (*The Trials of a Respectable Family*), and an account of his experiences with Francisco "Pancho" Villa's army of revolutionaries, *Los de abajo* (*The Underdogs*). A physician, he dedicated his life to alleviating the suffering of the poor and oppressed, and through his novels he strove to rectify social inequality. His works, imbued with his pessimistic view of Mexico's future, expose the sources of the oppression that brought about the revolution, the false idealism and brutality of many of the politicians and military leaders during the war years, and the anarchy that pervaded postrevolutionary Mexican society.

Azuela was originally compelled to write by the desperate conditions he encountered while practicing medicine in the Mexico City slums. His first novel, *Maria Luisa,* was based on a story about a woman forced to choose between becoming a factory worker or a student's mistress. The composition of this novice work, published in 1907 when Azuela was thirty-four, displays the strengths and weaknesses of his subsequent writings. While creating vivid social and cultural scenes, he pays little attention to plot and structure. He forms his characters by concentrating on a few actions or other outstanding physical features, a technique some critics contend is dangerously close to caricature. And his characters, though well-rounded, are often stereotypical: villains are rich, conservative, and ruthless, while heroes are poor and seek only social equality. Although he wrote about both the lower and middle classes throughout Mexico, most commentators label his provincial characters—rich and poor—his most believable and interesting.

Maria Luisa also displays Azuela's hallmark use of dialogue. The author is consistently praised for mimicking speech patterns and idioms particular to specific social classes, professions, and provinces. He writes with few subordinate clauses, and his sentence structure is straightforward but lyrical, especially when describing nature and, ironically, the horrors of war. He is also noted for his concision. Jefferson Rea Spell in *Contemporary Spanish-American Fiction* assessed that it is Azuela's "mastery of the art of selection and condensation . . . whether he is describing nature, persons, or the man-made world," that distinguishes him as a literary artist. In his early novels—*Los fracasados* ("The Failures"), *Mala yerba* (*Marcela:*

A Mexican Love Story), and *Sin amor*— Azuela outlines the social and political circumstances that led to the revolution. *Los fracasados* excoriates Porfirio Diaz, Mexico's notoriously corrupt dictator who, during his thirty-five year tenure, rewarded his political allies with lands taken from the peasants. Azuela condemns the provincial landowners and the middle class—Diaz's chief supporters—by satirizing their greed and pettiness. Some critics, including Spell, however, complained that in the novel Azuela seems "less concerned with telling a story than with exposing the iniquity of certain inhabitants of Alamos." Although reviewers found the novel technically and artistically lacking, most agreed with Spell, who claimed that the work "is significant in that it portrays the intolerable conditions in a Mexican town that gave rise to the brutality of the underlings when they rose a few years later against their masters."

Azuela continued his attack on rural bourgeois society in *Marcela* and *Sin amor,* two books exploring the differences between the wealthy landowners and the wretched peasants who worked the estates. Spell noted that *Sin amor* successfully depicts "the great gulf between those that have and those that have not; the resentment of the latter toward the former; and the scorn of the wealthy for the poor."

Azuela's novels written during the Mexican Revolution unflinchingly portray war and display his growing disgust as the violence escalated. The revolution began with Diaz's overthrow by liberal leader Francisco I. Madero in 1910, and Madero's subsequent assassination by an opposing faction. During the consequent struggle for succession, which lasted seven years and embroiled the whole country, Azuela supported Villa. When the guerrilla army led by Venustiano Carranza gained the upper hand in government, however, Azuela was forced to flee with Villa's band to Texas. After the war Azuela returned to Mexico, where he practiced medicine and chronicled the revolution in five novels, *Andres Perez, Maderista, The Underdogs, Los caciques* (*The Bosses*), *Las moscas* (*The Flies*), and *The Trials of a Respectable Family.*

Andres Perez, Maderista recounts the chaos and confusion of the initial battles of the revolution and analyzes the various motives of some of Madera's followers, including an altruistic ideologist, a landowner whose property had been seized, and a political opportunist. "Ideologically, [*Andres Perez, Maderista*] is one of his most significant novels," John E. Englekirk and Lawrence B. Kiddle observed in their

introduction to Azuela's *Los de abajo.* "Conceived during those very months when Azuela already foresaw the tragic turn the revolt of the idealist Madero was soon to take, . . . it is the work of one who boldly, fearlessly, and prophetically [decried the revolution]."

The Underdogs, considered Azuela's masterwork, followed. He wrote it in 1915 while a fugitive in El Paso, Texas, with Villa's band. By presenting the experiences of a common soldier during the conflict Azuela condemned the gratuitous violence, the sociopolitical forces that drove the Mexican people into poverty, and the opportunism that contradicted the goals of the revolution. The novel follows poor country boy Demetrio Macias's rise to the rank of general in Villa's revolutionary army. Opening in a battle in Juchipila Canyon, where Demetrio's forces deftly triumph, the drama and violence escalate until Macias is killed in the same canyon. Azuela depicts him as being defeated by the same forces—corruption and greed—that were bastardizing the revolution.

Azuela's despair for the future of his country permeates *The Underdogs.* Citing the "brutality" of many of his scenes, *Bookman* contributor Carleton Beals likened Azuela's writing to that of Russian revolutionary author Maxim Gorki. The critic pointed out, however, that the Mexican shares "Gorki's terrific pessimism [but] none of [his] revolutionary optimism." Spell also remarked on *The Underdogs's* "intense and varied emotive power," extrapolating: "while the author arouses pity for the downtrodden peasants, he also horrifies the reader with the crimes that some of them, in their ignorance and bestiality, commit." Beals noted that Azuela's "language is the language of reality . . . crude, often vile, truculent, fiendish."

"*The Bosses* is a pessimistic account of life in a small western town owned and run by a family of wealthy Diaz supporters who viciously defend their privileged position by making war against the cruelty and injustice of a system," Lesley Byrd Simpson wrote in the preface to *Two Novels of Mexico,* "and uses the effective device of extreme caricature to point up his thesis." Spell agreed, noting that Azuela's apparent intention for writing *The Bosses*—to expose the oppressors—applies to all of his novels of the war in general: "Through the injustice that it lays bare, the book affords a vindication, in a measure, of those who committed the most shocking atrocities against the lives and property of the privileged classes when the Revolution broke."

Azuela continues in the same vein with *The Flies,* considered one of his finest works. The action opens as a panicked throng of middle-class merchants are crowding onto trains in a Mexico City railway station to escape imminent slaughter by guerrilla leader Alvaro Obregon's ferocious troops. Throughout the night the characters reveal their thoughts and fears, and, Simpson wrote, condemn themselves. "The choppy, fragmentary dialogue," the critic noted, "the abrupt shifts, the callousness of some, the maudlin drunkenness of others, and the prodigious silliness of the frightened mother and her gold-digging family, together give us an etching of civil war not easily forgotten."

Azuela's last war novel, *Trials of a Respectable Family,* is an uncharacteristically sensitive study of the plight of the bourgeoisie during the revolution. Some critics surmise he wrote this novel after realizing that during war "good" men are as capable of atrocities as "bad" men. When affluent provincials heard reports of slaughters and pilfering by the revolutionaries, they fled to Mexico City, where they faced hardship in a city overrun by barbarous gangs. Azuela portrays the refugees' suffering as ennobling. Today *Trials of a Respectable Family* is considered second only to *The Underdogs* in the canon of Mexican revolutionary literature, although when it was published in 1918—directly following the revolution—it was ignored by critics who were perhaps unwilling to review a book sympathetic to the bourgeoisie.

Some critics claim that Azuela next produced three experimental novels, *La Malhora, El desquite,* and *La luciernaga (The Firefly),* in response to this lack of contemporary critical attention. Published in 1923, 1925, and 1932 respectively, these novels are difficult to read due to their thick, obscure, and sometimes incomprehensible imagery, heavy symbolism, and distorted sentence structure. "Azuela's striving for inordinate effects has definitely marred the work," Englekirk and Kiddle assessed in their critique of *La Malhora.* They also complained that Azuela's continual digressions overwhelmed the main narrative threads. Other commentators noted that Azuela's dialogue was exaggerated and ill-suited to his characters.

Yet the sentiment that *La Malhora, El desquite,* and *The Firefly* purvey, critical of postrevolutionary society, is undoubtedly true to Azuela's social philosophy. According to Englekirk and Kiddle, "the picture Azuela paints for us here is a somber one indeed . . . in the sordidness and the physical and mental degeneracy it portrays." His last radical novel, *The Firefly,* is his only work that can be called a psychological study. In it he contrasts two brothers, a guilt-ridden thief and a drug addict.

Azuela abandoned his experimental style and addressed national problems clearly in his next novels, *El camarada Pantoja, San Gabriel de Valdivias, Regina Landa, Avanzada,* and *Nueva burguesia,* which are nonetheless steeped in his characteristic pessimism. In subsequent works he shifted his focus away from society to the individual, a trend foreshadowed in *The Firefly.* In these works, *La marchanta, La mujer domada, Sendas perdidas, La maldicion, Esa sangre,* and *Madero,* he forsakes his depiction of traditional provincial life for an exploration of hectic urban life.

Luis Leal suggested in *Mariano Azuela* that these latest novels are his least effective, perhaps due to Azuela's becoming "a stern critic of [the] new social order" rather than remaining "an objective recorder of social change." A probable cause for his change in style is his growing disillusionment with Mexico's notoriously corrupt government. Critics contend that Azuela's literary reputation rests not on his plots or imagery or characterization, but on his ability to analyze Mexico's changing social and political scene and its players.

BIOGRAPHICAL/CRITICAL SOURCES:

Azuela, Mariano, *Two Novels of Mexico: The Flies. The Bosses,* translated with preface by Lesley Byrd Simpson, University of California Press, 1956.

Brushwood, John S., *Mexico in Its Novel: A Nation's Search for Identity,* University of Texas Press, 1966.

Leal, Luis, *Mariano Azuela,* Twayne, 1971.

Robe, Stanley Linn, *Azuela and the Mexican Underdogs,* University of California Press, 1979.

Spell, Jefferson Rea, *Contemporary Spanish-American Fiction,* reprinted, Biblo & Tannen, 1968.

Stroup, Thomas B. and Sterling A. Stoudemire, *South Atlantic Studies for Sturgis E. Leavitt,* Scarecrow Press (Metuchen, NJ), 1953.

Twentieth-Century Literary Criticism, Volume 3, Gale (Detroit), 1980.

PERIODICALS

Bookman, May, 1929.

Books Abroad, autumn, 1953.

Forum for Modern Language Studies, January, 1979,
    pp. 14-25.
Hispania, February, 1935; February, 1952; May,
    1967; March, 1972; December, 1980.
Hispanofila, May, 1981, pp. 51-67.
Journal of Spanish Studies: Twentieth Century, fall,
    1979, pp. 207-12.
New York Times Book Review, July 21, 1985.
Philological Quarterly, January, 1972, pp. 321-28.*

B

BABIN, Maria-Teresa 1910-1989

PERSONAL: Born in 1910, in Ponce, Puerto Rico; died December 19, 1989; daughter of Emmanuel (a plantation worker) and Joaquina (Cortes) Babin; married Estevan Vicente (an artist; marriage ended); married Jose Nieto (a professor), 1964; *Education:* University of Puerto Rico, B.A., 1939, M.A., 1939; Columbia University, Ph.D., 1951.

CAREER: Worked as teacher in Puerto Rico and United States, 1932-40; University of Puerto Rico, Rio Piedras, associate professor of Spanish and chairperson of department, 1940-46; Hunter College (now of the City University of New York), New York City, instructor in Romance languages, 1946; assistant professor of Spanish at New York University's Washington Square College in 1950s; Lehman College of the City University of New York, member of faculty and founding director of Department of Puerto Rican Studies, 1969-72; City University of New York Graduate Center, professor of Spanish, 1970-78, professor emeritus, 1978; writer. Consultant.

AWARDS, HONORS: Literary prize, Instituto de Literatura Puertorriquena, 1954; literary prize, Ateneo Puertorriqueno, 1955; literary prize, Union Mujeres Americanas, 1962; Literary Prize of the Year, Instituto Puertorriqueno, 1970.

WRITINGS:

IN ENGLISH

The Puerto Ricans' Spirit: Their History, Life, and Culture, translated by Barry Luby, Collier (New York City), 1971.

(Editor with Stan Steiner) *Borinquen: An Anthology of Puerto Rican Literature,* Knopf (New York City), 1974.

(Contributor) Arturo Morales Carrion, editor, *Puerto Rico: A Political and Cultural History,* Norton (New York City), 1983.

OTHER

Introduccion a la Cultura Hispanica, 1949.
Fantasia Boricua: Estampas de mi terra, 1956.
Panorama de la cultura Puertorriquena, 1958.
La hora colmada, 1960.
La gesta de Puerto Rico, 1967.
(With Jaime Luis Rodriguez) *Antologia poetica de Evaristo Ribera Chevremont,* 1967.

Also author of *Federico Garcia Lorca y su vida, El mundo poetica de Federico Garcia Lorca, Garcia Lorca—Vida y obra, La prosa magica de Garcia Lorca, La poesia gallega de Garcia Lorca, Estudios Lorquianos,* and *Genio y figura de Nemesio R. Canales.* Contributor to *Columbia Encyclopedia.* Contributor to periodicals, including *Brujula, El mundo, El imparcial, Repertorio Americano,* and *Revista del Instituto de Cultura Puertorriquena.*

SIDELIGHTS: Maria Teresa Babin was a distinguished writer and literary critic with particular expertise in Spanish and Puerto Rican art and culture. She was born in 1910 in Ponce, Puerto Rico, and she received two degrees from the University of Puerto Rico in the late 1930s, after which she worked as a teacher in both Puerto Rico and the continental United States. During the 1940s she published articles and essays on numerous Spanish and Puerto Rican writers, including Miguel Melendez Munoz, Emilio S. Belaval, Carmelina Vizcarrondo, and Manuel Joglar Cacho. Around this time she also taught at the University of Puerto Rico and Hunter College. In 1949 she published one of her most significant works, *Introduccion a la Cultura Hispanica,* which became an essential textbook.

While in the United States Babin continued her collegiate studies, and in 1951 she received her doctorate from Columbia University. Her doctoral thesis, like her earlier master's thesis, concerned the life and writings of Spanish poet Federico Garcia Lorca. Babin eventually published several books on Garcia Lorca, including *Federico Garcia Lorca y su vida, El mundo poetica de Federico Garcia Lorca, Garcia Lorca—Vida y obra, La prosa magica de Garcia Lorca,* and *La poesia gallega de Garcia Lorca.* Upon leaving Columbia University, Babin joined the faculty of New York University's Washington Square College, where she became an assistant professor of Spanish.

During the 1950s and early 1960s Babin continued to publish prolifically. Perhaps her most notable work from this period is *Fantasia Boricua: Estampas de mi terra,* which Pam Berry, writing in *Notable Hispanic Women,* described as a volume of "fantasies and images . . . of her native land, interwoven with major events, such as the celebration of Christmas . . . , the great hurricane of 1899, and the importance of fishing and harvesting sugar cane." Other volumes from this time are *La Hora colmada,* which Berry summarized as "a theatrical fable," and *Antologia poetica de Vevaristo Ribera Chevremont,* on which Babin collaborated with Jaime Luis Rodriguez. For her 1950s publications, Babin received various honors, including literary prizes from the Instituto de Literatura Puertorriquena and the Ateneo Puertorriqueno.

In 1969 Babin left Washington Square College for Lehman College of the City University of New York, where she became founding director of the Department of Puerto Rican Studies, which was the first such department at an American university. The next year, 1970, Babin also joined the faculty of the City University of New York Graduate Center, where she would remain professor of Spanish until 1978, when she became professor emeritus. During the 1970s Babin published several more volumes, including *The Puerto Ricans' Spirit: Their History, Life, and Culture.* She also produced further Spanish-language volumes, including *Estudios Lorquianos* and *Genio y figura de Nemesio R. Canales.*

Writing and teaching, however, were not Babin's only preoccupations. As Pam Berry reported in *Notable Hispanic American Women,* "Although busy with her various full-time teaching positions and writing assignments, Babin also found time to share her extensive knowledge and love of Puerto Rican culture and literature with others by lecturing at numerous universities across the United States and consulting with various universities, organizations, and government agencies." Berry acknowledged that upon Babin's death in 1989 "literary and academic communities mourned her passing."

BIOGRAPHICAL/CRITICAL SOURCES:

BOOKS

Notable Hispanic American Women, Gale, 1993, pp. 34-35.*

*   *   *

BACA, Jimmy Santiago 1952-

PERSONAL: Born Jose Santiago Baca, January 2, 1952, in Santa Fe, NM; married wife, Beatrice (a therapist); children: Antonio, Gabriel. *Education:* Self-educated; received G.E.D.

ADDRESSES: Home—Albuquerque, NM.

CAREER: Writer.

AWARDS, HONORS: American Book Award for poetry, Before Columbus Foundation, 1988, for *Martin and Meditations on the South Valley;* National Hispanic Heritage Award, 1989; Wallace Stevens Poetry fellowship, Yale University.

WRITINGS:

Jimmy Santiago Baca (poetry), Rock Bottom (Santa Barbara, CA), 1978.
Immigrants in Our Own Land: Poems, Louisiana State University Press, 1979.
Swords of Darkness (poetry), Mango Publications, 1981.
What's Happening (poetry), Curbstone Press, 1982.
Martin and Meditations on the South Valley (poetry), introduction by Denise Levertov, New Directions (New York City), 1987.

Black Mesa Poems, New Directions, 1989.

(Author of introduction) Jim Nye, *Aftershock: Poems and Prose from the Vietnam War,* Cinco Puntos Press, 1991.

Los tres hijos de Julia (play), produced at the Los Angeles Theatre Center, 1991.

Working in the Dark: Reflections of a Poet of the Barrio (stories and essays), Red Crane Books, 1992.

In the Way of the Sun, Grove Press, 1997.

Contributor of poetry to periodicals, including *Mother Jones.*

SIDELIGHTS: Jimmy Santiago Baca, an ex-convict who taught himself to read while in prison, is a highly acclaimed poet who won the prestigious American Book Award in 1988. Admired for his use of rich imagery and lyrical language, Baca, unlike a growing number of "prison writers" who inject their works with rage and desolation, writes poems dealing with spiritual rebirth and triumph over tragedy. "You really don't have time to be angry," Baca explained his attitude to Beth Ann Krier in the *Los Angeles Times.* "If you compare a life to daytime photography, my life has been more like nighttime photography. My life as a background has had darkness; the only way to survive the darkness is to have my soul flash. I'm too busy trying to capture the aspects of myself in the dark."

Of Chicano and Apache Indian descent, Baca lived with a grandparent after his parents divorced and abandoned him at the age of two. By the time he was five, Baca's mother had been murdered by her second husband, his father was dead of alcoholism, and Baca was in a New Mexico orphanage. Fleeing the institution when he was eleven, Baca was reduced to a life on the street. He soon abused drugs and alcohol and, by age twenty, was convicted of drug possession. Sentenced to serve several years in a maximum-security prison in Arizona, Baca would ultimately spend four years in isolation and receive electric shock treatments for his combative nature.

Despite his hardship, Baca did not lose spirit. Rather, he became intellectually invigorated during his incarceration period, teaching himself to read and write. He later divulged to Krier: "[In prison], I saw all these Chicanos going out to the fields and being treated like animals. I was tired of being treated like an animal. I wanted to learn how to read and to write and to understand. . . . I wanted to know how to function in this world. Why was I so ignorant and deprived?. . . The only way of transcending was through language and understanding. Had I not found the language, I would have been a guerrilla in the mountains. It was language that saved [me]." Baca began writing poetry and, at the behest of a fellow inmate, sent his works to *Mother Jones* magazine. "I took a wild chance," he related to Krier, "I didn't even know how to put the stamp on the envelope and address it."

His determination was rewarded when poet and professor Denise Levertov, then poetry editor of *Mother Jones,* printed Baca's poems in the periodical. Judging Baca a talented writer, Levertov began corresponding with the inmate and eventually found a publisher for his first book. Baca's *Immigrants in Our Own Land* appeared in 1979. The collection of poems, highlighting the splendor of human existence amidst the desolate surroundings of prison life, met with rave reviews. A *Kliatt* critic, for example, found Baca's poems "astonishingly beautiful" for their "celebration of the human spirit in extreme situations." Writing in the *American Book Review,* Ron Arias commended the poet's skill and versatility: "At times [Baca] can be terse, narrowly focused, directly to the point. . . . Other times he can resemble an exuberant Walt Whitman in the long-lined rhythm and sweep of his emotions—expansive, wordy, even conversational." The critic concluded that Baca "is a freshly aggressive poet of many abilities. . . . His is a gifted, young vision, and judging from this collection, I get the feeling he is just warming up." Baca produced another work, the ten-poem collection *What's Happening,* in 1982.

While less well-received than his first effort, the book garnered praise for its subject matter concerning both the Chicano and prison experience. Michael Hogan writing in the *American Book Review* found Baca's focus on racial oppression, exploitation of laborers, and the horrors of state-run penitentiaries "powerful"; yet he also agreed with other reviewers, deciding that the poems showed a "tendency toward looseness and the prosaic. . . . There is entirely too much telling and too little showing." Hogan, however, praised some of the poems' "wry humor" and "disarming ingenuousness," deducting that Baca "is a gifted poet and has a natural lyricism in the best of his work." The reviewer declared: "One hopes to see the promise of his first book realized . . . in a future, better-crafted volume."

Baca's next work, 1987's *Martin and Meditations on the South Valley,* met with outstanding success, earning the him American Book Award for poetry. A semiautobiographical work that critics termed a novel in verse, the book chronicles the life of Martin, an orphaned "detribalized" Apache who sojourns across the United States in search of permanence and meaning in his life. Intended to convey the sometimes traumatic Chicano experience in America, *Martin and Meditations on the South Valley* details the protagonist's sense of abandonment and displacement. "Your departure uprooted me mother," writes Baca in the book, "Hallowed core of a child / your absence whittled down / to a broken doll / in a barn loft. The small burned area of memory, / where your face is supposed to be, / moons' rings pass through / in broken chain of events / in my dreams." Although enduring emotional pain, the narrator, by book's end, finds spiritual comfort. Critics found much to praise in *Martin and Meditations on the South Valley*. While several recognized the work as a forceful sociological and cultural document, Liam Rector in the *Hudson Review* also deemed the poetry volume "a pageturner." He explained: "It's . . . a powerful orchestration and revision of a narrative and lyrical admixture . . . with an utterly compelling dramatic form." Commending Baca's descriptions, drawn with "great telescopic accuracy and poignance," the reviewer called *Martin and Meditations on the South Valley* "a book of great complicity, maturity, and finally responsibility. . . . It is a contemporary hero tale."

The success of *Martin and Meditations on the South Valley* brought international attention to the former prison inmate, who found himself in demand for teaching positions and poetry readings; he also enjoyed the publication of another book, *Black Mesa Poems,* in 1989. Despite his impressive accomplishments, Baca claims to maintain the humble attitude he first fostered while in prison. Proclaiming to Krier that producing poetry still "comes down to my act of sitting down in my little room and writing what's in my heart," Baca elaborated: "I have been hailed by some of the most severe critics in the country. It doesn't mean anything. . . . I just try to stay within the rules of the earth, within the boundaries of dignity. I don't do anything for money. . . . I live on a day-to-day basis. . . . In prison, I didn't know if I was going to be alive from day to day."

BIOGRAPHICAL/CRITICAL SOURCES:

PERIODICALS

American Book Review, January, 1982, pp. 11-12; November, 1983, pp. 19-20.

Americas Review, fall-winter, 1988, pp. 214-31.
Commonweal, December 5, 1980.
Esquire, June, 1993, p. 48.
Hudson Review, summer, 1988, pp. 393-400.
Kliatt, spring, 1980, p. 20.
Library Journal, October 15, 1987, p. 83.
Los Angeles Times, February 15, 1989, pp. 1, 6-7.
National Catholic Reporter, May 10, 1991, p. 29.
Publishers Weekly, February 3, 1992, p. 71.*

* * *

BALSEIRO, Jose Agustin   1900-1991

PERSONAL: Born August 23, 1900, in Barceloneta, PR; died January 13, 1991; son of Rafael and Dolores (Romos-Casellas) Balseiro; married Mercedes Pedreira, March 3, 1924; children: Yolanda Buchanon, Liliana Mees. *Education:* University of Puerto Rico, LL.B., 1921.

ADDRESSES: Home—408 Valencia 4, Coral Gables, FL 33134.

CAREER: University of Illinois, Urbana, professor of romance languages, 1930-33 and 1936-38; University of Puerto Rico, Rio Piedras, visiting professor of Spanish literature, 1933-36; U.S. delegate to First International Congress on Teaching Ibero-American Literature, 1938; U.S. representative to First International American Conference on Libraries and Publications, 1939; senator-at-large to Puerto Rican senate, 1942-44; University of Miami, Coral Gables, FL, professor of Hispanic literature, 1946-67; University of Arizona, Tucson, visiting professor of Spanish literature, 1967-72. Consultant on Hispanic literature at University of Miami. Summer lecturer, Northwestern University, 1937, Duke University, 1947, 1949, and 1950, Inter-American University, Puerto Rico, 1957-63, University of Mexico, 1959, University of North Carolina at Chapel Hill, 1973, Bryn Mawr College, 1973, Yale University, 1973, and Emory University, 1975. U.S. State Department, International Educational Exchange Program, lecturer in South America, 1954, in Spain and England, 1955-56, and in Puerto Rico, 1956; member of U.S. consultative committee of UNESCO, 1957; vice president of Fourth Congress of the Academies of the Spanish Language, 1964.

MEMBER: International Institute of Ibero-American Literature (president, 1955-57), North American Academy of Spanish Languages, Modern Language

Association of America (president of contemporary Spanish literature section, 1938), National Association of Authors and Journalists (honorary member), Spanish Royal Academy of Language (corresponding member), Spanish-American Academy of Sciences and Arts, Colombian Academy of Letters (corresponding member), Instituto Sarmiento of Argentina, Puerto Rican Academy.

AWARDS, HONORS: Spanish Royal Academy prize for best collection of essays of the year, 1925, for *El vigia*, Volume 1; Litt.D., Inter-American University, 1950; Sc.D., Catholic University, Chile, 1954; L.H.D., Belmont Abbey, 1962; Litt.D., Catholic University, Puerto Rico, 1972; diploma of honor, Mexican Academy of Letters; D.H.L., Polytechnic Institute of Puerto Rico; decorated commander of the Order of Queen Isabel La Catolica, Spain; member of the Order of Vasco Nunez of Balboa, Panama.

WRITINGS:

IN ENGLISH

Eugenio Maria de Hostos: Hispanic America's Public Servant, [Coral Gables, FL], 1949.
The Americas Look at Each Other, translated by Muna Munoz Lee, University of Miami Press (Miami, FL), 1969.
(Editor) *The Hispanic Presence in Florida,* E. A. Seeman (Miami, FL), 1976.

POETRY

Flores de primavera (title means "Flowers of Spring"), [San Juan], 1919.
Las palomas de Eros (title means "The Doves of Eros"), [Madrid], 1921.
Al rumor de la fuente (title means "To the Murmur of the Fountain"), [San Juan], 1922.
La copa de Anacreonte (title means "The Crown of Anacreon"), Editorial Mundo Latino (Madrid), 1924.
Musica cordial (title means "Friendly Music"), Editorial Lex (Havana), 1926.
Sonetos (title means "Sonnets"), [San Juan], 1933.
La pureza cautiva (title means "Captive Purity"), Editorial Lex, 1946.
Saudades de Puerto Rico (title means "Homesickness for Puerto Rico"), Aguilar, 1957.
Visperas de sombras y otros poemas (title means "Eves of Shadow and Other Poems"), Ediciones de Andre (Mexico), 1959.

NOVELS

La maldecida (title means "The Cursed Woman"), [Madrid], 1922.
La ruta eterna (title means "The Eternal Way"), [Madrid], 1926.
En vela mientras el mundo duerme (title means "Vigil While the World Sleeps"), Mnemosyne Publishing, 1969.
La gratitud humana Mnemosyne Publishing, 1969.

Also author of *El sveno de Manon,* 1922.

EDITOR

Novelistas espanoles modernos (title means "Modern Spanish Novelists"), Macmillan (New York City), 1933, 8th revised and enlarged edition, University of Puerto Rico Press, 1977.
(With J. Riis Owre and others) Alejandro Casona, *La barca sin pescador* (title means "The Boat without a Fisherman"), Oxford University Press (New York City), 1955.
(With Owre) Casona, *Corona de amor y muerte* (title means "Crown of Love and Death"), Oxford University Press, 1960.
(With Eliana Suarez-Rivero) Casona, *El Cabellero de las espuelas de oro* (title means "The Cowboy of the Golden Spurs"), Oxford University Press, 1968.

OTHER

El vigia (title means "The Watchman"), Volume 1, Editorial Mundo Latino, 1925, Volume 2, [Madrid], 1926, Biblioteca de autores Puertor-riquenas, 1956, Volume 3, [San Juan], 1942.
El Quijote de la Espana contemporanea: Miguel de Unamuno (title means "The Quixote of Contemporary Spain"), E. Gimenez, 1935.
Blasco Ibanez, Unamuno, Valle Inclan y Baroja, cuatro individualistas de Espana (title means "Four Spanish Individualists"), University of North Carolina Press (Chapel Hill), 1949.
Mediciones fisicas: calculo de errores, approximaciones, metodos graficos (title means "Physical Measurements: Calculation of Errors, Approximations, Graphic Methods"), Lebreria Machette (Buenos Aires), 1956.
Expresio de Hispanoamerica (title means "Expression of Spanish America"), Instituto de Cultura Puertorriquena, Volume 1, 1960, Volume 2, 1963, 2nd edition, 1970.

Seis estudios sobre Ruben Dario (title means "Six Studies about Ruben Dario"), Editorial Gredos (Madrid), 1967.

Contributor to periodicals, including *Cuadernos Americanos, Nosotros, Hispanic Review,* and *La Torre.* Editor of numerous Spanish periodicals.

SIDELIGHTS: Jose Agustin Balseiro brought a multitude of talents to his work. He was internationally known as a writer and critic, a musician whose compositions have been performed at Carnegie Hall, and a respected lecturer on Hispanic cultures in North America. Balseiro published poetry and novels while teaching language and literature at colleges in America and abroad. As Jane Stewart Cook noted in the *Dictionary of Hispanic Biography,* Balseiro "became a kind of cultural ambassador to the world. His lectures on the arts and the role of the artist as a conduit between the Hispanic and American cultures earned him praise throughout the world, especially within the Spanish-speaking countries."

Although once invited to play professional baseball, Balseiro set out at a young age to become a writer. He was born in Puerto Rico in 1900 and educated there, gaining his bachelor's degree from the University of Puerto Rico in 1921. Balseiro studied law but also loved literature, especially poetry. Even before earning his bachelor's degree he published his first work of poetry, *Flores de primavera* ("Flowers of Spring"). After living for some time in Spain, he accepted a job at the University of Illinois, Urbana, and taught there for five years during the 1930s, spending the rest of the decade at home in Puerto Rico. His most notable career milestone was passed when he accepted a teaching position at the University of Miami in Coral Gables, Florida. He taught there from 1946 until 1967.

Balseiro was always more than a college professor. He authored novels, criticism, and more poetry. He traveled extensively, giving lectures on the connections between Hispanic and American cultures, "and set himself the goal of interpreting the spirit of each of those cultures to the other," to quote Cook. Eventually, he came to be regarded world-wide as a kind of cultural ambassador whose topics have included the philosophies and biographies of poets, public leaders, artists, and musicians.

Critics have acknowledged Balseiro's importance to people both within and without the Spanish-speaking world. One such reviewer from the *South Atlantic*

Bulletin, as quoted in the *Dictionary of Hispanic Biography,* called the author "an international scholar who knows no boundaries, and whose criterion is world literature."

During a lecture at the University of Miami in the 1950s, Balseiro explained the reason for his emphasis on internationalism. *Miami Herald* staff writer Sandy Flickner quotes the author's speech: "The nearer we approach our neighbors by the disinterested paths of art, literature, scholarship, and open-hearted friendship, the sooner will we demolish the prejudices that hamper the constructive development of human nature." In his honor, the University of Miami established the Jose A. Balseiro Award, an essay contest, in 1967.

BIOGRAPHICAL/CRITICAL SOURCES:

BOOKS

Dictionary of Hispanic Biography, Gale (Detroit, MI), 1996, pp. 94-96.
Hill, Marnesba D., and Harold B. Schleifer, *Puerto Rican Authors,* Scarecrow Press (Metuchen, NJ), 1974.

PERIODICALS

Miami Herald, April 29, 1974.*

*   *   *

BARNET, Miguel   1940-

PERSONAL: Born January 28, 1940, in Havana, Cuba. *Education:* Attended Escuela de Publicidad, Havana, Cuba.

ADDRESSES: Agent—c/o Smithsonian Institution Press, 470 L'Enfant Plaza, Room 7100, Washington, DC 20560.

CAREER: Ethnologist, poet, and novelist. Escuela de Instruciones de Arte, Havana, Cuba, professor of folklore, 1961-66. Also worked at Editorial Nacional (Cuban publishing house), c. 1960s. Researcher at the Institute of Ethnology and Folklore of the Academy of Science.

AWARDS, HONORS: La sagrada familia received an award from Casa de las Americas; *Carta de noche* received a special mention in a literary competition.

WRITINGS:

La piedra fina y el pavorreal, Union de Escritores y Artistas de Cuba (Havana), 1963.

Isla de guijes, El Puente (Havana), 1964.

Biografia de un cimarron, Instituto de Etnologia y Folklore (Havana), 1966, translated by Jocasta Innes as *The Autobiography of a Runaway Slave,* Bodley Head (London), 1966, Pantheon (New York City), 1968.

La sagrada familia (poems), Casa de las Americas (Havana), 1967.

Cancion de Rachel, Instituto del Libro (Havana), 1969, translated by W. Nick Hall as *Rachel's Song: A Novel,* Curbstone Press (Willimantic, CT), 1991.

Akeke y la jutia, Union de Escritores y Artistas de Cuba (Havana), 1978.

Orikis y otros poemas, Letras Cubanas (Havana), 1980.

Gallego, Alfaguara (Madrid), 1981.

Carta de noche, Union de Escritores y Artistas de Cuba (Havana), 1982.

La fuente viva, Letras Cubanas (Havana), 1983.

(Editor) Fernando Ortiz, *Ensayos etnograficos,* Editorial de Ciencias Sociales (Havana), 1984.

La vida real, Letras Cubanas (Havana), 1986.

Claves por Rita Montaner [Montanzas, Cuba], 1987.

Viendo mi vida pasar, Letras Cubanas (Havana), 1987.

Oficio de angel, Alfaguara (Madrid), 1989.

(With Enrique Pineda Barnet and Julio Garcia Espinosa) *La bella del Alhambra* (screenplay; directed by Enrique Pineda Barnet, produced by Humberto Hernandez), released by Instituto Cubano del Arte e Industria Cinematograficos, 1990, World Service Publications (Cuba), 1990.

(Contributor of poetry) Rene Burri, *Cuba and Cuba,* Smithsonian Institution Press (Washington, DC), 1998.

Also contributor to periodicals, including *Cuban Studies/Estudios cubanos, Latin American Literary Review, Union,* and *New Yorker.*

SIDELIGHTS: As both a Latin-American ethnologist and writer of fiction, poetry, and essays, Miguel Barnet explores cults, beliefs, and myths of Afro-Cuban folklore. He is best known for developing the *testimonio* form, a first-person narrative created from personal interviews. Barnet was born into an affluent Havana family. He attended American schools in Havana but spent his formative years in a culturally mixed neighborhood, el Vedado, where he was ex-

posed to African customs and traditions. Here he developed an avid interest in black ethnography and in Afro-Cuban studies, particularly the religious aspects of folklore. The 1959 revolution in Cuba further affected Barnet. At this time, he began writing poetry grounded in Afro-Cuban folk tales and religious beliefs. Two of his early works—*La piedra fina y el pavorreal* and *Isla de guijes*—converted such anthropological material into literary forms.

During the early 1960s Barnet became associated with El Puente, a circle of second-generation poets named for a publishing company. These poets, initially politically linked to Fidel Castro's revolution, eventually came under scrutiny for their artistic beliefs. The government sent some el Puente members to Military Units of Aid to Production, or detention camps, or otherwise prohibited the poets from artistic pursuits. This experience, and others like it, strengthened Barnet's political commitment and led to his development of a new genre—the *testimonio*—that combined his interests in ethnology and literature. "One has to go towards a fusion of the disciplines towards integration," Barnet explained in a *Caribbean Review* interview in 1980.

The *testimonio* allowed Barnet to comment on contemporary Cuban issues without offending revolutionary powers, including Castro. Barnet used this new literary form to record the legacies of the Cuban populations ignored or neglected by earlier historians, giving voice to the otherwise unheard. Barnet's most notable *testimonio* is his biography of Esteban Montejo, a former slave and an insurgent in Cuba's War of Independence during the late 1890s. Barnet interviewed Montejo in 1963, when Montejo was one hundred and five years old. Barnet tape-recorded conversations with Montejo to create a history of slavery, abolition, and independence in pre-revolutionary Cuba. The resulting book, *Biografia de un cimarron*—an account rich in African folklore, feasts, rituals, and witchcraft—profiles the life and times of a nineteenth-century black slave in Cuba. It remains one of a handful of Latin American anti-slavery novels written through an authentic nineteenth-century voice.

Barnet's biography of Montejo sold well in Cuba. In fact, this *testimonio* became the best-selling native book since the inception of the revolution. *Biografia de un cimarron,* published in English as *The Autobiography of a Runaway Slave,* was widely translated into other languages; critics abroad embraced the book, and scholars praised the work for presenting history from a new—that is, non-white—point of view. Nevertheless, Barnet remained relatively unnoticed within Cuba's literary establishment.

Barnet continued to write poetry, essays, and novels, including more testimonios. His later examples of this literary form include *Cancion de Rachel,* about a music-hall performer; *Gallego,* about a Cuban immigrant; and *La vida real,* about a Cuban emigre to New York. Despite his low profile, Barnet's contribution of the testimonio to Latin-American literature cannot be understated, for it is the one literary genre through which the silent members of his society speak.

BIOGRAPHICAL/CRITICAL SOURCES:

BOOKS

Dictionary of Literary Biography, Volume 145: *Modern Latin-American Fiction Writers, Second Series,* Gale (Detroit, MI), 1994.
Gonzalez Echevarria, Roberto, *Myth and Archive: A Theory of Latin American Narrative,* Cambridge University Press, 1990.
Gonzalez Echevarria, Roberto, *The Voice of the Masters: Writing and Authority in Modern Latin American Literature,* University of Texas Press, 1985.
Jara, Rene, and Hernan Vidal, *Testimonio y literatura,* Institute for the Study of Ideologies and Literature (Minneapolis, MN), 1986.
Luis, William, editor, *Literary Bondage: Slavery in Cuban Narrative,* University of Texas Press, 1990.
Luis, William, editor, *Voices from Under: Black Narrative in Latin America and the Caribbean,* Greenwood Press, 1984.
Rincon, Carlos, *El cambio de la nocion de la literatura,* Instituto Colombiano de Cultura (Bogota Columbia), 1978.
Sariol, Jose Prats, editor, *Nuevos criticos cubanos,* Letras Cubanas, 1983.
Sklodowska, Elzbieta, *Testimonio hispanoamericano,* Peter Lang, 1992.

PERIODICALS

Araucaria, Volume 25, 1984.
Caravelle, Volume 43, 1984.
Caribbean Review, fall, 1980.
Casa de las Americas, May-June, 1990.
Centennial Review, Volume 30, number 2, 1986.
Critica Hispanica, Volume 7, number 2, 1985.
Cuban Studies/Estudios cubanos, Volume 11, number 1, 1981.

El Urogallo, April 24, 1988.
Escritura, January-December, 1988.
Estudios del Caribe, Volume 22, numbers 1-2, 1989.
Hispamerica, Volume 10, number 9, 1981.
Inti, Volumes 29-30, 1989.
Latin American Literary Review, Volume 8, number 16, 1980.
Letras Cubanas, Volume 3, 1987.
Modern Fiction Studies, Volume 35, number 1, 1989.
Nueva Estafeta, Volume 31, 1981.
Publications of the Modern Language Association, Volume 99, number 1, 1984.
Revista Iberoamericana, July-December, 1990.
Revista/Review Interamericana, fall, 1982.
Union, Volume 4, 1966; Volume 4, 1978.
Vortice, Volume 2, numbers 2-3, 1979.*

* * *

BARRAL, Carlos   1928-1989

PERSONAL: Born June 2, 1928, in Barcelona, Spain; died of an internal hemorrhage, December 12, 1989; married Yvonne Hortet. *Education:* Received law degree from the University of Barcelona, 1950. *Politics:* Spanish Socialist Worker Party.

CAREER: Publisher, editor, and writer. Seix Barral (publishing house), Barcelona, Spain, editor, beginning 1951; founded publishing house Barral Editores, Barcelona, 1970; elected a senator from Tarragona to the Spanish National Senate as a candidate of Partido Socialista Obrero Espanol (Spanish Socialist Worker Party), 1982-88; also served as a member of the European Parliament.

WRITINGS:

Las aguas retiradas (poetry; title means "Secluded Waters"), Publicaciones de la Revista Laye (Barcelona), 1952.
Metropolitano (poetry), Cantalapiedra (Torrelavega), 1957, enlarged as *Metropolitano y poemas, 1973-1975,* Ambito (Barcelona), 1976.
Diecinueve figuras de mi historia civil (poetry; title means "Nineteen Figures of My Civil History"), Literaturasa (Barcelona), 1961.
Usuras (poetry; title means "Usuries"), Poesia para Todos (Madrid), 1965.
Figuracion y fuga (poetry; title means "Figuration and Fugue"), Seix Barral (Barcelona), 1966.

Informe personal sobre el alba y acerca de algunas auroras particulares (poetry; title means "Personal Report on Daybreak and Concerning Some Particular Dawns"), Lumen (Barcelona), 1970.

Usuras y figuraciones: Poesia 1952-1972 (poetry; title means "Usuries and Figurations"), Inventarios Provisionales (Las Palmas), 1973, enlarged edition, Lumen (Barcelona), 1979.

Anos de penetencia (memoirs; title means "Years of Penitance"), Alianza (Madrid), 1975, enlarged as *Anos de penetencia; Precedido de dos capitulos ineditos de Memorias de infancia,* Tusquets (Barcelona), 1990.

Los anos sin excusa (memoirs; title means "Years without Excuse"), Barral (Barcelona), 1978.

Memorias, Barral (Barcelona), 1978.

Pel car de fora: Catalunya des del mar (travelogue; title means "Catalonia from the Sea"), photographs by Xavier Miserachs, Ediciones 62 (Barcelona), 1982.

Penultimos castigos (novel; title means "Penultimate Punishments"), Seix Barral (Barcelona), 1983.

Diez poemas para el nieto Malcolm (poetry; title means "Ten Poems for Grandson Malcolm"), [Barcelona], 1984.

Catalunya a vol d'ocell, Ediciones 62 (Barcelona), 1985.

Roca-Sastre, Ambit (Barcelona), 1985.

Lecciones de cosas: Veinte poemas para el nieto Malcolm (poetry; title means "Lessons of Things: Twenty Poems for Grandson Malcolm"), Ediciones 62 (Barcelona), 1986.

Cuando las horas veloces (memoir; title means "When Hours Pass Swiftly"), Tusquets (Barcelona), 1988.

The Mediterranean, Lunwerg Editores (Barcelona), 1988.

Diario de "Metropolitano," edited by Luis Garcia Montero, Excma (Granada), 1989.

Antologia poetica, edited by Juan Garcia Hortelano, Alianza (Madrid), 1989.

Poesia, edited by Carmen Riera, Catedra (Madrid), 1991.

Los diarios, 1957-1989, edited by Riera, Anaya & M. Muchnik (Madrid), 1993.

Also author of "Poesia no es comunicacion" (title means "Poetry Is Not Communication"), in *Poeticas espanolas contemporaneas: La generacion del 50,* edited by Pedro Provencio, Libros Hiperion (Madrid), 1988; "Debate con Carlos Barral," translated by Yvonne Hortet, in *Revista de Occidente,* July-August 1990. Contributor to periodicals, including *Papeles de Son Armadans, Laye,* and *Cuadernos para el Dialogo.*

Also translator of poetry of Ranier Maria Rilke into Spanish.

SIDELIGHTS: Though Spanish poet and editor Carlos Barral wrote relatively few books during his lifetime, he is considered one of the leading figures in postwar Spanish literature and is particularly associated with the literary attitudes and cultural atmosphere of his native Barcelona. There Barral was part of the Escuela de Barcelona ("Barcelona School"), along with poets Jaime Gil de Biedma, Jose Agustin Goytisolo, and Jose Maria Castellet, a critic. Literary scholars also name Barral as one of the Generacion del 50, another notable assemblage of Spanish writers that put him in company of Angel Gonzalez, Jose Angel Valente, Francisco Brines, and Gloria Fuertes.

Still, Barral—who spent years as an editor and translator and was twice elected to Spain's national senate—failed to achieve any genuine literary honors during his lifetime. His poetry and single novel have been called "hermetic" for their insular, sometimes difficult texts, and Barral's three volumes of memoirs are said to be rife with factual errors. In addition to his handful of poetry collections, he also penned travelogues on his native Catalonia and numerous literary essays. Barral viewed all of his work as interconnected, and believed that his verse was further illuminated by his memoirs; he once described his writing as *una busqueda de mi mismo y de la experiencia*—"a search for myself and for experience"—explained Mary Makris in her essay on the writer for *Dictionary of Literary Biography.* "Barral believed that his life and works complemented each other: his life explained his creative works, and these works, in turn, created his life."

Barral was born in 1928 into a well-off family of Catalonian heritage in Barcelona, a city in which he would remain for his entire life. It was a place with a thriving cultural heritage and progressive attitude, and Barral would become part of its literary scene early on in his adulthood. But his childhood had been decimated by the events of the Spanish Civil War which ended with the victory of fascist dictator Francisco Franco in 1939. This initiated a period of censorship and internal repression for Spain, and young intellectuals like Barral were forced to temper their spoken and written words with a certain amount of caution. He earned a law degree from the University of Barcelona in 1950—studies completed only at the urging of his family—but had already begun writing poetry and demonstrated a tremendous lyrical vocabulary even in his exams.

Barral joined the Barcelona publishing house Seix Barral as an editor in 1951, and spent the next two decades with it. Seix Barral published a number of authors whose works were deemed too controversial by the heavy-handed Franco regime, a government that did not hesitate to seize shiploads of books before they arrived in stores. During Barral's long tenure, the firm introduced the work of Marguerite Duras, Doris Lessing, and Henry Miller to the Spanish public; Barral himself translated the works of the German poet Rainer Maria Rilke into Spanish. His first published poetry, however, did not appear until 1952 with the work "Las aguas retiradas" ("Secluded Waters"), a poem published by the influential Barcelona journal *Laye*. Later that year *Laye* issued the verse in booklet form.

Barral's reputation as an emerging literary mind was boosted with a 1953 essay he wrote for *Laye* titled "Poesia no es comunicacion" ("Poetry Is Not Communication"). It was written in response to the theories of another Spanish poet, Carlos Bousono, who had declared in his 1952 work *Teoria de la expresion poetica* ("Theory of Poetic Expression") that poetry is a form of human communication. Barral disagreed, and in his essay, noted Makris, "Barral distinguishes between pre- and postsymbolist poetry and relegates those who pretend to communicate something in poetry, either an intimate or collective message, to the realm of the superficial. Barral also outlines the basic differences between poetry as a reflection of a specific reality or experience and poetry as a kind of linguistic laboratory." Makris also noted Barral's criticism of contemporary trends in poetry, which the poet said indicated "the existence of a series of theoretical ghosts: the message, communication, the accessibility to the majority, themes of our time that limit the creative vocation."

Barral's first collection of verse, *Metropolitano*, was published in 1957. Its title refers to both the city and the subway—the same term in Spanish—and the poems about both are like dramatic monologues. "Ciudad mental" ("Mental City"), for instance, observes that the vertical lines of the city suggest its creation and aspirations, but contrast with the horizontal lines that forecast its eventual destruction. Water and its ability to distort time and place is the subject of "Portillo automatico" ("Automatic Door"). "Despite the varied thematic content of *Metropolitano* and the use of multiple speakers, Barral observes the unities of time, action, and place," noted Makris. The essayist also termed the work as exemplary of Barral's "interest in language as an element of experimentation as well as a source of ambiguity."

Barral considered *Metropolitano* a solid thematic beginning to his career as a writer, but as Makris wrote, "the poems of *Metropolitano* abound with archaisms, *cultismos* (erudite words), juristic terminology, and slang. The linguistic difficulties presented by such poetry may cause Barral's readers to make ample use of dictionaries. In light of *Metropolitano,* many viewed Barral's poetry as intellectual and baroque." His next work, 1961's *Diecinueve figuras de mi historia civil* ("Nineteen Figures of My Civil History"), was met with a more favorable reception. Drawing upon a work from 1613, Luis de Gongora's *Soledades* ("Solitudes"), Barral's poems recall the days of the Civil War and its aftermath and how the events of the time shaped the identity of the poems' speaker. "He is characterized by his guilty social conscience, eroticism that borders on the voyeuristic, and his affinity for the sea," declared Makris in her *Dictionary of Literary Biography* essay. "Given Barral's intent and the particular historical, temporal trajectory of the collection, the poems are more like short narratives than poetry."

In his next two volumes of verse, Barral returned to the earlier style of *Metropolitano* in which he freely experimented with the Spanish language and allowed a sensuality to permeate his poems. There are six poems in *Usuras* ("Usuries"), published in 1965; its title is a term that can be defined as the earning of interest, but in some Romance languages "usury" also means deterioration through use. Barral, asserted Makris, "writes for those who have been initiated, for readers who have an interest in poems filled with sensuality and intelligence. . . . Thus the underlying themes of the collection concern the erosion caused by time. These themes, along with the recurring ones of the horror of dying, the horror of decadence, and the passing of time, also permeate the other books of poetry he published between 1965 and 1970," Makris continued. *Usuras* was followed by *Figuracion y fuga* in 1966.

For *Informe personal sobre el alba y acerca de algunas auroras particulares* ("Personal Report on Daybreak and Concerning Some Particular Dawns"), published in 1970, Barral created fourteen poems that center upon an individual who is undergoing an inner crisis in an urban setting. "Clave del insomne" ("Key of the Insomniac") is one of the several poems that laments the unwelcome beginning of a new day. "The poems include sordid images, as the speaker is forced to confront himself and his daily responsibilities," wrote Makris. *Informe personal* was published with photographs of nudes by Cesar Malet.

That same year, Barral left Seix Barral and founded the publishing house Barral Editores in Barcelona. He would spend the next decade on this venture, beginning work on his memoirs as well. A volume of his complete works up to this point in his career, with the addition of some previously unpublished verse, *Usuras y figuraciones: Poesia 1952-1972* ("Usuries and Figurations"), was issued in 1973. The first volume of his memoirs, *Anos de penetencia* ("Years of Penitence"), appeared in 1975. Though Barral was a poet, the work won him great praise for his prose; more than one scholar has described it as one of the best portraits of early Franco-era Barcelona ever written. A second volume, *Los anos sin excusa* ("Years without Excuse"), was issued by his own firm in 1978. In it Barral focuses on his years at Seix Barral, postwar Spanish literary circles, and his travels. A third volume of memoirs, *Cuando las horas veloces* ("When Hours Pass Swiftly"), appeared in 1988, the year before his death. Barral had also began to write a fourth volume, and two chapters of this were included in an expanded edition of *Anos de penetencia* in 1990.

Like his fellow citizens relishing the new era of freedom after Franco's death in 1975, Barral became involved in politics during the 1980s. He was elected to represent the province of Tarragona in the national senate on the Partido Socialista Obrero Espanol (Spanish Socialist Worker Party) ticket in 1982, and was reelected in 1985. After the publication of his memoirs, he penned a travelogue of sorts in the Catalan language. *Pel car de fora: Catalunya des del mar* recounts his solitary sailboat journey, and the text is enhanced by photographs from Xavier Miserachs. The second part of title means "Catalonia from the sea," but the first part is untranslatable. As Makris explained in the *Dictionary of Literary Biography* essay, Catalan is a spoken language with no literary tradition, which makes the poet's attempt at writing in it "of extraordinary interest to scholars of Catalonian philology," Makris wrote. "Barral merely comments that he wrote the book in Catalan because of his 'motivacion de memorialista' (motivation of an amanuensis)—his need to transcribe the history and feelings of the Catalonian people."

The sole novel of Barral's career is *Penultimos castigos* ("Penultimate Punishments"), published in 1983. The author himself once called it a poem in actuality, not a novel, and stated that the inspiration for the book was the duality of two particular mythical deities, Janus and Gemini. All the characters in the book possess imaginary doppelgangers, and as a result the narrative is a dense one that is somewhat difficult to follow.

Barral had not written poetry in almost a decade, but in 1984 returned to the genre with *Diez poemas para el nieto Malcolm* ("Ten Poems for Grandson Malcolm"); this was followed two years later by *Lecciones de cosas: Veinte poemas para el nieto Malcolm* ("Lessons of Things: Twenty Poems for Grandson Malcolm"). The title of the latter work "refers to didactic illustrated books and encyclopedias that were familiar to children and adolescents of the post-Spanish Civil War generations," explained Makris. "Through the familiar images of children's books, Barral also hoped to recuperate part of a world ruined by the passing of an age."

The senator-poet-publishing executive lost his bid for reelection in 1988, and was working on his fourth volume of memoirs as well as a new volume of poetry titled *Extravios* ("Losses"), when he died of an internal hemorrhage in December of 1989. Barral had also been readying for publication the extensive creative journals that he had kept over the years. "In them Barral kept copious notes regarding the circumstances surrounding his creative efforts, including the composition of individual poems and collections," wrote Makris. Only one, *Diario de "Metropolitano"* (Diary for "Metropolitan") was published in 1989 and Makris called it "a valuable tool for understanding not only his first poetry collection but also his poetry in general." A more complete work, *Los diarios, 1957-1989,* appeared in 1993.

BIOGRAPHICAL/CRITICAL SOURCES:

BOOKS

Dictionary of Literary Biography, Volume 134: *Twentieth-Century Spanish Poets,* edited by Jerry Phillips Winfield, Gale, 1994.

Gil de Biedma, Jaime, *El pie de la letra,* Critica, 1980.

Jove, Jordi, *Carlos Barral en su poesia,* 1952-1979, Pages Editors, 1991.

Riera, Carmen, *La escuela de Barcelona: Barral, Gil de Biedma, Goytisolo: el nucleo poetico de la generacion de los 50,* Editorial Anagrama, 1988.

Riera, Carmen, *La obra poetica de Carlos Barral,* Peninsula, 1990.

Santiago, Tomas Sanchez, and Jose Manuel Diego, *Dos poetas de la generacion de los 50: Carlos Barral y Jose Angel Valente,* Ediciones A. Ubago, 1990.

PERIODICALS

Camp de l'Arpa, March, 1974, pp. 8-13.
Cuadernos Hispanoamericanos, August/September, 1970, pp. 657-61.
Insula, July/August, 1990, pp. 25-27.
Quimera, 1985, pp. 32-39.
Revista de Occidente, July/August, 1990, pp. 5-10, 21-50, 57-72, 73-78.*

*   *   *

BARRIOS, Greg 1945-

PERSONAL: Born October 31, 1945, in Victoria, TX; son of Gregorio (a photographer) and Eva (Falcon) Barrios. *Education:* University of Texas, B.A., 1968.

ADDRESSES: Agent—c/o Posada Baltazar, 1508 North Western Ave., Los Angeles, CA 90027-5620.

CAREER: Worked as teacher in Crystal City, TX, c. 1970s; writer. *Military service:* Served in U.S. Air Force.

WRITINGS:

Dale Gas Cristal (play; title means "Give It Gas, Crystal"), produced in 1977.
Puro rollo (A colores) (poetry; title means "Much Ado about Nothing [in Color]"), introduction by Tomas Rivera, Posada (Los Angeles, CA), 1982.

Contributor to periodicals, including *Film Quarterly* and *Sight and Sound.* Editor of *La Verdad.*

WORK IN PROGRESS: Birthmark, a poetry collection; a novel; plays.

SIDELIGHTS: Gregg Barrios is a Chicano writer whose publications include a poetry collection, a play, and film essays. He was born in 1945 in Victoria, Texas, and after a stint in the U.S. Air Force he graduated from the University of Texas in 1968. During his undergraduate years Barrios proved an incisive film critic, and he supplied probing commentaries to such publications as *Film Quarterly* and

England's *Sight and Sound.* At that time Barrios also became involved in political activism and Chicano culture. In 1970 he began working as a teacher in Crystal City, Texas, a city that Nuria Bustamante, writing in the *Dictionary of Literary Biography,* described as "the birthplace of the Chicano movement." In Crystal City Barrios became editor of the Chicano periodical *La Verdad.* In addition he helped stage politically provocative plays, including his own *Dale Gas Cristal* ("Give It Gas, Crystal"). He also published poems that were likewise volatile in their political slant. A decade later, Barrios produced the poetry collection *Puro rollo (A colores)* ("Much Ado about Nothing [in Color]"). According to Bustamante, the writing of *Puro rollo* was prompted by Barrios's "disillusionment with the betrayal of Chicano hopes and ideals by the leaders of the [Chicano] movement."

Puro rollo is comprised of twenty-seven poems divided into three parts, each of which is designated as a specific film reel (called a "rollo"). Each reel, in turn, consists of nine poems. The first reel, perhaps reflecting Barrios's own initial political naivete, is expressed with a tone of optimism. The second reel culminates in a sense of despair and disillusionment, while the concluding reel embodies a sense of tranquility. The poems in *Puro rollo* reveal both Barrios's passionate social activism and his keen appreciation of popular music. Bustamante noted in the *Dictionary of Literary Biography* that "*Puro rollo* deals with social protest related to Chicano issues, racial discrimination, social injustice, alienation, and cultural genocide," but she also discerned that "a strong underlying theme protests the lack of representation of Mexican-American music within the cultural mosaic in this country."

Puro rollo has been recognized as a significant achievement in Chicano literature. Tomas Rivera, in his introduction to the volume, deemed it a "spiritual history" of Chicanos. Reviewer Luis Leal, meanwhile, wrote in *La Opinion* that in *Puro rollo* Barrios succeeds in "rescuing . . . the social life and culture of the Chicano community."

BIOGRAPHICAL/CRITICAL SOURCES:

BOOKS

Dictionary of Literary Biography, Volume 122: *Chicano Writers, Second Series,* Gale (Detroit, MI), 1992.

PERIODICALS

La Opinion, December 12, 1982.*

*   *   *

BEHAR, Ruth 1956-

PERSONAL: Born November 12, 1956, in Havana, Cuba; immigrated to the United States, 1962; naturalized citizen, 1986; daughter of Alberto and Rebecca (Glinsky) Behar; married David Frye, June 6, 1982; children: Gabriel Frye-Behar. *Ethnicity:* "Latino." *Education:* Wesleyan University, B.A., 1977; Princeton University, M.A., 1981, Ph.D., 1983. *Religion:* Jewish.

ADDRESSES: Home—Ann Arbor, MI.   *Office*—c/o Department of Anthropology, University of Michigan, 1020 LSA Building, Ann Arbor, MI 48109.

CAREER: University of Michigan, Ann Arbor, assistant professor, 1986-89, associate professor, 1989-94, professor of anthropology, 1994—.

AWARDS, HONORS: MacArthur fellowship, 1988-93; Guggenheim fellowship, 1995-96.

WRITINGS:

Santa Maria del Monte: The Presence of the Past in a Spanish Village (nonfiction), Princeton University Press (Princeton, NJ), c. 1986, published as *The Presence of the Past in a Spanish Village: Santa Maria del Monte,* Princeton University Press, 1991.
Translated Woman: Crossing the Border with Esperanza's Story (nonfiction), Beacon Press (Boston, MA), 1993.
(Editor) *Bridges to Cuba/Puentes a Cuba* (literary anthology), University of Michigan Press (Ann Arbor), 1995.
Las Visiones de una Bruja Guachichil en 1599: Hacia una Perspectiva Indaigena Sobre la Conquista de San Luis Potosai, Centro de Investigaciones Histaoricas (San Luis Potosai), 1995.
(Editor with Deborah A. Gordon) *Women Writing Culture* (nonfiction), University of California Press (Berkeley), 1995.
The Vulnerable Observer: Anthropology That Breaks Your Heart (nonfiction), Beacon Press, 1996.
(Editor, with others) *The Color of Privilege: Three Blasphemies on Race and Feminism,* 1996.

Contributor of poetry to *Tikkun, Michigan Quarterly Review, Prairie Schooner, American VOICE, Bridges,* and *Witness;* contributor of articles to journals, including *Kenyon Review, Chronicle of Higher Education,* and *Natural History;* contributor to anthologies including *Little Havana Blues: A Cuban-American Literature Anthology, Cubana: Contemporary Fiction by Cuban Women,* and *Sephardic American Voices: Two Hundred Years of Literary Legacy.*

SIDELIGHTS: Educator and author Ruth Behar was born in Havana, Cuba, and raised by Eastern European and Sephardic Jewish grandparents who had immigrated there after the passage in 1924 of the Immigration and Nationality Act (through which the United States sought to limit Jewish immigration). This background led to her interest in anthropology; her academic home for the past several years has been the University of Michigan's anthropology department. Though she has also written poetry and edited a literary anthology of Cuban writers, Behar has become known for her anthropological works which blur the line between social science and personal involvement with the people she studies, including the well-received 1993 book *Translated Woman: Crossing the Border with Esperanza's Story.* Behar explained her philosophy of the "involved participant" in anthropology in her 1996 collection of personal essays *The Vulnerable Observer: Anthropology That Breaks Your Heart.*

Behar's first full-length anthropological work, however, was *Santa Maria del Monte: The Presence of the Past in a Spanish Village,* published in 1986. In this generously illustrated volume, Behar examines a Spanish village that had remained in isolation from modern Spain longer than most settlements. By the time she wrote her book, however, the village was finally becoming encroached upon by a nearby development of holiday 'chalets.' The people of the village of Santa Maria in the province of Leon, Spain, felt "the presence of the past" and had a long tradition of literacy; thus Behar was aided in her study by well-kept village records dating back to the eighteenth century. Her chronicle portrays what Sandra Ott in the *Times Literary Supplement* describes as "long term cultural continuity" rather than the more fashionable anthropological depiction of modern social and economic change, and includes the conventions of inheriting private property as well as some methods of control by the "concejo" (village council) over communal property. D. D. Caulkins, reviewing *Santa Maria del Monte* in *Choice,* noted that "this admirable work sets a high standard for historical ethnography."

Ott greeted it as "a welcome step forward in Iberian anthropology." Similarly, James S. Amelang in the *New York Times Book Review* complimented it as "an impressive foray into historical ethnography."

Translated Woman began when Behar was working on a very different project—archival records of women affected by the Mexican Inquisition. She went to a cemetery near the town of Mexquitic and attempted to photograph a Mexican-Native American woman placing flowers on the graves of her children. The woman, to whom Behar assigned the name Esperanza, questioned her about what she was doing. The two struck up an acquaintance, and Esperanza bargained with Behar. If Behar and her husband would serve as godparents to one of her living children, Esperanza would tell her story to Behar and provide the anthropologist with intimate details of the life of women in Mexquitic.

Esperanza's story appears in *Translated Woman,* and it is a tale of suffering and abuse. Her first memory is of her father beating her mother; later, she herself is battered by her own first husband. Esperanza credits the rage this produced within her with spoiling her breast milk, and thus causing several of her infant children to die of malnutrition. When her husband—who is not only abusive but an adulterer as well—is suddenly and mysteriously stricken with blindness, Esperanza is labeled a witch by the rest of her community. She is already somewhat on the outside of society because of her poverty and her Native American heritage, but the suspicion of witchcraft places her further outside the circle of community.

At the end of *Translated Woman,* Behar provides an autobiographical chapter, comparing her own life to Esperanza's and claiming outsider status as well—as a granddaughter of Jewish emigrants in Cuba, as a Cuban refugee in the United States, and as a woman difficult to classify in academia. This has proven the most controversial section of the work. Victor Perera in the *Nation* cautioned that "it is disingenuous to compare the suffering Mexican village society inflicts on Esperanza for rebelling against its strictures with the ordeal of having to accept tenure at a prominent university," while Nancy Scheper-Hughes in the *New York Times Book Review* determined that "the metaphor is contrived and the lesson is clear: the lives of anthropologists are rarely as rich and fascinating as those of their subjects." Conversely, Louise Lamphere in the *Women's Review of Books* observed that "the difficulties of articulating the connections between the American woman academic and Mexican female

street peddler, the sense of contradictions in tension, and the lack of an easy resolution are perhaps, paradoxically, the most satisfying aspects of Behar's book." Emma Perez in the *Journal of American History* observed: "Behar has offered a gift. . . . Rarely do academicians engage their contradictions so honestly."

On the value of *Translated Woman* as a whole, critics were clear. Perez predicted that "the book will become a model for ethnographers, historians, and other scholars crossing disciplines to reconstruct life histories." Lamphere held the volume up as "postmodernist writing at its best," while Scheper-Hughes offered appreciation for the fact that "Behar has broken many taboos and inhibitions in writing an experimental ethnographic text that has for its subject a poor native Mexican woman who refuses to be a pitiful victim, or a saint, or a Madonna, or a whore, or a Joan of Arc." Perera praised *Translated Woman* as "a ground-breaking Latina feminist ethnography" and a "powerful and brilliant study."

Reviewing *The Vulnerable Observer* in the electronic magazine *Salon,* Sally Eckhoff explained Behar's new method of anthropological study: "Combine traditional fieldwork with a researcher's personal experience . . . and you come up with a mode of study that informs the intellect as it grips the emotions—without smashing the delicate subject(s) flat, the way conventional research often does." Eckhoff went on to report that Behar structures *The Vulnerable Observer* in such a way as to first explain and defend her position, then illustrate its benefits with specific essays that have resulted from her method. Included in this section is a piece about studying elderly villagers in Spain while simultaneously worrying about her own elderly grandfather's decline in Miami, Florida. Diane Cole, discussing *The Vulnerable Observer* in the *New York Times Book Review,* congratulated Behar on the "insight, candor and compassion" of "her vision."

The volumes Behar has edited or co-edited have attracted critical notice as well. *Bridges to Cuba/ Puentes a Cuba* contains literary contributions both from writers living in Cuba and from writers living in exile from that nation. R. Ocasio, reviewing the anthology in *Choice,* observed that "Behar introduces readers to the diaspora of the rich literature of Cuba" and concluded by recommending the book for most libraries. *Women Writing Culture,* which Behar edited with Deborah A. Gordon, contains essays by women anthropologists and discusses important contributions to that field by women whose works have been often overlooked. Kate Gilbert, holding forth on the essay collection in the *Women's Review of Books,* protested "the way some contributors, largely successful in academic anthropology, rush to claim outsider status," but found most of the individual essays to be useful contributions to the field. C. Hendrickson in *Choice,* however, concluded that "this lively and important book . . . challenges readers to rethink ethnographic traditions in the face of experimental feminist writing."

BIOGRAPHICAL/CRITICAL SOURCES:

PERIODICALS

Belles Lettres, summer, 1993.
Bookworld, March 21, 1993.
Choice, October, 1986, p. 346; June, 1996, pp. 1649, 1690-1691.
Journal of American History, September, 1994, pp. 836-837.
Nation, September 20, 1993, pp. 290-292.
New York Times Book Review, September 28, 1986, p. 27; September 5, 1993, p. 22.
Times Literary Supplement, January 16, 1987, p. 64.
Women's Review of Books, May, 1993, p. 14; June, 1996, pp. 21-22.

OTHER

www.Salon.com, April 15, 1997.*

*   *   *

BELENO
  See AZUELA, Mariano

*   *   *

BENAVENTE (y MARTINEZ), Jacinto 1866-1954

PERSONAL: Born August 12, 1866, in Madrid, Spain; died July 14, 1954, in Madrid, Spain; son of Mariano Benavente (a pediatrician) and Venancia Martinez. Studied law at University of Madrid, 1882-85.

CAREER: Writer and actor. Founder, with Porredon, of a children's theatre, 1909; director of Teatro Espanol, beginning 1920. Actor; president of Spanish Theater Commission (advisory body of Central Theater Council), beginning 1936; lecturer.

MEMBER: Royal Spanish Academy (became honorary member, 1946).

AWARDS, HONORS: Piquer Prize, Royal Spanish Academy, 1912; Nobel Prize in literature, Swedish Academy, 1922; made honorary citizen of New York City, Columbia University and Instituto de las Americas, 1923; named Hijo Predilecto ("Favorite Son") of Madrid, 1924; awarded Grand Cross of King Alfonso XII of Spain, 1924; Mariano de Cavia Prize, 1948, for best newspaper article of 1947.

WRITINGS:

IN ENGLISH TRANSLATION

El nido ajeno (three-act play; also see below; first produced in Madrid at Teatro de la Comedia, 1894), translation published as *Another's Nest* in *Nineteenth-Century Spanish Plays,* edited by L. E. Brett, [New York], 1935.
La gobernadora (three-act play; first produced in Madrid at Teatro de la Comedia, 1901), translation by John Garrett Underhill published as *The Governor's Wife: A Comedy in Three Acts,* R. G. Badger (Boston), 1913.
La noche de sabado (five-act play; produced in Madrid at Teatro Espanol, 1903), translation by Underhill published as *Saturday Night: A Novel for the Stage, in Five Tableaux,* R. G. Badger, 1918.
No fumadores (produced in Madrid at Teatro de Lara, 1904), translation by Underhill published as *No Smoking: A Farce in One Act,* Baker, 1935.
El encanto de una hora (one-act dialogue; also see below; produced in Madrid at Teatro de la Princesa, 1905), translation by Underhill published as *The Magic of an Hour: A Comedy in One Act,* Baker, 1935.
La sonrisa de Gioconda (produced 1908), translation by John Armstrong Herman published as *The Smile of Mona Lisa: A Play in One Act,* R. G. Badger, 1915.
El marido de su viuda: Comedia en un acto (produced in Madrid at Teatro del Principe Alfonso, 1908), R. Velasco (Madrid), 1908, translation by Underhill published as *His Widow's Husband: A Comedy in One Act,* Baker, 1935.
De cerca: Comedia en un acto (produced in Madrid at Teatro de Lara, 1909), Hernando, 1909, transla-

tion by Underhill published as *At Close Range: A One-Act Play,* Samuel French, 1936.

El principe que todo lo aprendio en los libros: Comedia en dos actos y siete cuadros (children's fantasy; produced in Madrid at Teatro del Principe Alfonso, 1909), Artes Graficas Mateu, 1910, published under title *El principe que todo lo aprendio en los libros,* with notes, exercises, and vocabulary by Aurelio M. Espinosa, World, 1918, original Spanish edition translation by Underhill published as *The Prince Who Learned Everything out of Books: A Fairy Play in Three Acts and Five Scenes,* R. G. Badger, 1919.

La malquerida (three-act drama; produced in Madrid at Teatro de la Princesa, 1913, produced in English translation as *The Passionflower* in New York City, c. 1920), edited with introduction, notes, and vocabulary by Paul T. Manchester, Crofts, 1941, translation by Underhill published as *The Passionflower* in *Twenty-five Modern Plays,* edited by S. M. Tucker and A. S. Downer, 3rd edition, 1953.

Los intereses creados: Comedia de polichinelas en dos actos, tres cuadros y un prologo, (three-act play with prologue; produced in Madrid at Teatro de Lara, 1907; produced in English translation as *The Bonds of Interest,* in New York City, April 19, 1919; produced in English translation as *The Bias of the World* in London), 4th edition, Nuevo Mundo (Madrid), 1914, translation by Underhill published as *The Bonds of Interest,* Scribner, 1929, published as *The Bonds of Interest. Los intereses creados.* (bilingual edition), edited and revised by Hymen Alpern, F. Ungar, 1967.

La Verdad (dialogue; produced in Madrid at Teatro de la Comedia, 1915), translation by Underhill published as *The Truth: A Play in One Act,* Baker, 1935.

Plays (contains *His Widow's Husband, The Bonds of Interest, The Evil Doers of Good,* and *La malquerida*), edited and translated by Underhill, Scribner, 1917.

Plays: Second Series (contains *No Smoking, Princess Bebe, The Governor's Wife,* and *Autumnal Rose*), edited and translated by Underhill, Scribner, 1919.

La fuerza bruta (two-act musical comedy; produced in Madrid at Teatro de la Zarzuela, 1919), translation by Underhill published as *Brute Force: A Comedy in Two Acts,* S. French, 1935.

Plays: Third Series (contains *The Prince Who Learned Everything out of Books, Saturday Night, In the Clouds,* and *The Truth*), edited and translated by Underhill, Scribner, 1923.

Plays: Fourth Series (contains *The School of Princesses, A Lady, The Magic of an Hour,* and *Field of Ermine*), edited and translated by Underhill, Scribner, 1924.

(Contributor) Lope de Vega, *Four Plays,* translated by Underhill with a critical essay by Benavente, Scribner, 1936.

PUBLISHED PLAYS; IN SPANISH

Teatro fantastico (contains *Comedia italiana* [title means "Italian Comedy"; two scenes], *El criado de Don Juan* [title means "Don Juan's Servant"; also see below], *La senda del amor* [title means "The Path of Love"; one-act comedy for marionettes], *La blancura de Pierrot* [title means "The Whiteness of Pierrot"; one-act pantomine], *Cuento de primavera* [title means "Spring Story"; two-act], *Amor de artista* [title means "Artist's Love"; one-act], *Modernismo* [title means "Modernism"; one-act], and *El encanto de una hora* [title means "The Magic of an Hour"; also see below]), 1892, reprinted, Fortanet (Madrid), 1905.

Los malhechores del bien (two-act; produced in Madrid at Teatro de Lara, 1905), edited with introduction, notes and vocabulary by Irving A. Leonard and Robert K. Spaulding, Macmillan, 1933.

Las cigarras hormigas (title means "The Harvest Flies"; three-act; produced in Madrid at Teatro de la Comedia, December 24, 1905), edited with notes and vocabulary by University of Michigan Sociedad Hispanica, C. W. Graham, 1923.

Los buhos: Comedia en tres actos (title means "The Owls: Three-Act Play"; first produced in Madrid at Teatro de Lara, 1907), Hernando, 1908.

Hacia la verdad: Escenas de la vida moderna, en tres cuadros (title means "Toward the Truth: Scenes from Modern Life, in Three Scenes"; produced in Madrid at Teatro del Principe Alfonso, 1908), Hernando, 1909.

La escuela de las princesas: Comedia en tres actos (title means "The School of Princesses: Play in Three Acts"; produced in Madrid at Teatro de la Comedia, 1909), R. Velasco, 1910.

La senorita se aburre: Comedia en un acto, basada en una poesia de Tennyson (title means "The Princess Is Bored: One-Act Play, Based on a Poem by Tennyson"; produced in Madrid at Teatro del Principe Alfonso, 1909), R. Velasco, 1910.

La losa de los suenos: Comedia en dos actos (title means "The Graveyard of Dreams: Two-Act

Play"; produced in Madrid at Teatro de Lara, 1911), *Nuevo Mundo* (Madrid), 1911.

El collar de estrellas: Comedia en cuatro actos (title means "The Necklace of Stars: Four-Act Play"; produced in Madrid at Teatro de la Princesa, 1915), R. Velasco (Madrid), 1915.

Campo de armino: Comedia en tres actos (title means "Field of Ermine: Three-Act Play"; produced in Madrid at Teatro de la Princesa, 1916), R. Velasco and V. H. de Sanz Calleja (Madrid), 1916.

La ciudad alegre y confiada: Comedia en tres cuadros y un prologo, considerados como tres actos (title means "The Joyous and Confident City: Play in Three Scenes and A Prologue, Considered as Three Acts"; sequel to *Los intereses creados;* produced in Madrid at Teatro de Lara, 1916), R. Velasco, 1916.

Los cachorros: Comedia en tres actos (three-act; produced in Madrid at Teatro de la Princesa, 1918), V. H. de Sanz Calleja, 1918.

La fuerza bruta: Comedia en un acto y dos cuadros (one act; produced in Madrid at Teatro de Lara, 1908), Hernando, 1909.

Lecciones de buen amor: Comedia en tres actos (title means "Lessons in Good Love: Three-Act Play"; produced in Madrid at Teatro Espanol, 1924), Hernando, 1924.

La otra honra: Comedia en tres actos (title means "The Other Honor: Three-Act Play"; produced in Madrid at Teatro de Lara, 1924), Hernando, 1924.

La virtud sospechosa: Comedia en tres actos (title means "Suspect Virtue: Three-Act Play"; produced in Madrid at Teatro Fontalba, 1924), Hernando, 1924.

Alfilerazos: Comedia en tres actos (title means "Pinpricks: Comedy in Three Acts"; produced in Buenos Aires at Teatro Avenida, 1924; produced in Madrid at Teatro del Centro, 1925), Hernando, 1925.

Los nuevos yernos: Comedia en tres actos (title means "The New Sons-in-Law: Three-Act Play"; produced in Madrid at Teatro Fontalba, 1925), Hernando, 1925.

La mariposa que volo sobre el mar: Comedia en tres actos (title means "The Butterfly that Flew over the Sea: Three-Act Play"; produced in Madrid at Teatro Fontalba, 1926), Hernando, 1926.

La noche iluminada: Comedia de magia en tres actos (title means "The Illuminated Night: Three-Act Magical Comedy"; produced in Madrid at Teatro Fontalba, 1927), Hernando, 1927.

El hijo de Polichinela: Comedia en un prologo y tres actos (produced in Madrid at Teatro de Lara, 1927), Hernando, 1927.

El demonio fue antes angel: Comedia en tres actos (title means "The Devil Used to Be an Angel: Three-Act Play"; produced in Madrid at Teatro Calderon, 1928), Hernando, 1928.

No quiero, no quiero!: Comedia en tres actos (title means "I Don't Want To, I Don't Want To: Three-Act Play"; produced in Madrid at Teatro Fontalba, 1928), Hernando, 1928.

Pepa Doncel: Comedia en tres actos y dos cuadros (title means "Pepa Doncel: Play in Three Acts and Two Scenes"; produced in Madrid at Teatro Calderon, 1928), Hernando, 1928.

Para el cielo y los altares: Drama en tres actos, dividos en trece cuadros, y un epilogo (title means "For Heaven and the Altars: Three-Act Drama, Divided into Thirteen Scenes and an Epilogue"), Hernando, 1928.

Vidas cruzadas: Cinedrama en dos partes, dividida la primera en diez cuadros, y la segunda en tres y un epilogo (title means "Crossed Lives: A Screenplay in Two Parts, the First Divided into Ten Scenes, and the Second into Three and an Epilogue"; produced in Madrid at Teatro de la Reina Victoria, 1929), Hernando, 1929.

Los andrajos de la purpura: Drama en cinco actos (title means "Purple Tatters: Drama in Five Acts"; produced in Madrid at Teatro Munoz Seca, 1930), Hernando, 1930.

Literatura: Comedia en tres actos (title means "Literature: Play in Three Acts"; first produced in Madrid at Teatro Alcazar, 1931), Hernando, 1931.

De muy buena familia: Comedia en tres actos (title means "From a Very Good Family: Three-Act Play"; produced in Madrid at Teatro Munoz Seca, 1931), Hernando, 1931.

La melodia del jazz-band: Comedia en un prologo y tres actos (title means "The Jazz Band's Melody: Play with a Prologue and Three Acts"; produced in Madrid at Teatro Fontalba, 1931), Hernando, 1931.

Cuando los hijos de Eva no son los hijos de Adan: Comedia en tres actos (title means "When Eve's Sons Are Not Adam's: Three-Act Play"; based on Margaret Kennedy's novel, *The Constant Nymph;* produced in Madrid at Teatro Calderon, 1931), Hernando, 1931.

Santa Rusia, primera parte de una trilogia (title means "Holy Russia, First Part of a Trilogy"; produced in Madrid at Teatro Beatriz, 1932), Imprenta Helenica (Madrid), 1932.

La duquesa gitana: Comedia de magia en cinco actos divididos en diez cuadros (title means "The

Gypsy Duchess: Magic Comedy in Five Acts Divided in Ten Scenes"; produced in Madrid at Teatro Fontalba, 1932), Imprenta Helenica, 1932.

La moral del divorcio: Conferencia dialogada, dividida en tres partes (title means "The Moral of Divorce: Lecture in Dialogue, Divided into Three Parts"; produced in Madrid at Teatro de la Avenida, 1932), Imprenta Helenica, 1932.

La verdad inventada: Comedia en tres actos (title means "The Invented Truth: Three-Act Play"; produced in Madrid at Teatro de Lara, 1933), Artes Graficas (Madrid), 1933.

El rival de su mujer: Comedia en tres actos (title means "His Wife's Rival: Three-Act Play"; produced in Buenos Aires at Teatro Odeon, 1933), Artes Graficas, 1934.

El pan comido en la mano: Comedia en tres actos (title means "Bread Eaten from the Hand: Three-Act Play"; produced in Madrid at Teatro Fontalba, 1934), Artes Graficas, 1934.

Ni al amor ni al mar: Drama en cuatro actos y un epilogo (title means "Neither to Love nor to the Sea: Drama in Four Acts and an Epilogue"; produced in Madrid at Teatro Espanol, 1934), Artes Graficas, 1934.

Memorias de un madrileno: Puestas en accion en cinco cuadros (title means "Memories of a Man from Madrid: Performed in Five Scenes"; five-act moving tableaux; first performed in Madrid at Teatro de Lara, 1934), Artes Graficas, 1934.

La novia de nieve: Comedia en un prologo y tres actos (title means "The Snow Bride: Three-Act Play with a Prologue"; produced in Madrid at Teatro Espanol, 1934), Artes Graficas, 1934.

No jugueis con esas cosas: Comedia en tres actos (title means "Don't Play with Those Things: Three-Act Play"; produced in Madrid at Teatro Esclava, 1935), Artes Graficas, 1935.

Cualquiera lo sabe: Comedia en tres actos (title means "Anyone Knows That: Three-Act Play"; produced in Madrid at Teatro de la Comedia, 1935), Artes Graficas, 1935.

Also author of *La princesa sin corazon* [title means "The Heartless Princess" (one-act horror play)], 1908; *A ver que hace un hombre!* (title means "Let's See What a Man Does!"), 1909; *Caridad* (title means "Charity"; monologue; produced in Madrid at Teatro Real, 1911; one-act), 1918; *Si creeras tu que es por mi gusto!* (title means "If You Think I Want It This Way!"; one-act dialogue), 1925; *A las puertas del cielo* (title means "At the Gates of Heaven"; one-act dialogue), 1927; *La culpa es tuya* (title means "It's Your Fault"; three-act comedy; produced in San

Sebastian, Spain, August, 1942, produced in Madrid at Teatro de la Zarzuela, 1942), 1943; *La enlutada* (title means "The Mourner"; three-act; produced in Saragossa, Spain at Teatro Principal, 1942), 1943; *El demonio del teatro* (title means "The Demon of the Theatre"; three-act comedy; produced in Madrid at Teatro Comico, 1942), 1943; *Al servicio de su majestad imperial* (title means "In the Service of His Imperial Majesty"; one-act comedy), 1947; *La vida en verso* (title means "Life in Verse"; three-act comedy; produced in Madrid at Teatro de la Infanta Isabel, 1951), 1953; *El lebrel del cielo* (title means "The Hound of Heaven"; three-act comedy; based on Francis Thompson's poem of the same title; produced in Madrid at Teatro Calderon, 1952), 1953. Plays also published in numerous collections.

PLAY PRODUCTIONS; IN SPANISH

Gente conocida (title means "People of Importance"; four-act drama), produced in Madrid at Teatro de la Comedia, 1896.

El marido de la Tellez (title means "The Tellez Woman's Husband"; one-act), produced in Madrid at Teatro de Lara, 1897.

De alivio (title means "On Comfort"; one-act monologue), produced in Madrid at Teatro de la Comedia, 1897.

Don Juan (based on the play by Moliere; five-act), produced in Madrid at Teatro de la Princesa, 1897.

La farandula (title means "Bombastic Actors"; two-act), produced in Madrid at Teatro de Lara, 1897.

La comida de las fieras (title means "The Wild Beasts' Banquet"; three-act; also see below), produced in Madrid at Teatro de la Comedia, 1898.

Teatro feminista (title means "Feminist Theatre"; one-act), produced in Teatro de la Comedia, 1898.

(Adapter) *Cuento de amor* (title means "Love Story"; based on Shakespeare's *Twelfth Night;* three-act drama), produced in Madrid at Teatro de la Comedia, 1899.

Operacion quirugica (title means "Surgery"; one-act), produced in Madrid at Teatro de Lara, 1899.

Despedida cruel (title means "Cruel Farewell"; one-act), produced in Madrid at Teatro de Lara, 1899.

La gata de Angora (title means "The Angora Cat"; four-act), produced in Madrid at Teatro de la Comedia, 1900.

Viaje de instruccion (title means "The Journey of Instruction"; one-act musical comedy), produced in Madrid at Teatro Alhambra, 1900.

Por la herida (title means "Through Affliction"; one-act drama), produced in Madrid at Teatro de Novedades, 1900.

Modas (title means "Fashions"; one-act farce), produced in Madrid at Teatro de Lara, 1901.

Lo cursi (title means "Vulgarity"; three-act drama), produced in Madrid at Teatro de la Comedia, 1901.

Sin querer (title means "In Perfect Innocence"; one-act comic sketch), produced in Madrid at Teatro de la Comedia, 1901.

Sacrificios (title means "Sacrifices"; three-act drama), produced in Madrid at Teatro de Novedades, 1901.

El primo roman (three-act), produced in Saragossa, 1901.

Amor de amar (title means "Love of Loving"; two-act), produced in Madrid at Teatro de la Comedia, 1902.

Libertad! (title means "Liberty!"; three-act; based on a play by Santiago Rusinol y Prats), produced in Madrid at Teatro de la Comedia, 1902.

En tren de los maridos (title means "In the Husbands' Retinue"; two-act comedy), produced in Madrid at Teatro de Lara, 1902.

Alma triunfante (title means "Triumphant Soul"; three-act drama), produced in Madrid at Teatro de la Comedia, 1902.

El automovil (title means "The Automobile"; two-act), produced in Madrid at Teatro de Lara, 1902.

Los favoritos (title means "The Favorites"; one-act), produced in Seville, 1903.

El hombrecito (title means "The Manikin"; three-act), produced in Madrid at Teatro de la Comedia, 1903.

Por que se ama (title means "Why One Loves"; one-act), produced in Madrid at Teatro Espanol, 1903.

Al natural (title means "No Affectation"; two-act), produced at Madrid at Teatro de Lara, 1903.

La casa de la dicha (title means "The House of Happiness"; produced in Barcelona at Teatro Intimo, 1903.

El dragon de fuego (title means "The Fire Dragon"; three-act drama with epilogue), produced in Madrid at Teatro Espanol, 1904.

Rosas de otono (title means "Autumnal Roses"; three-act drama), produced in Madrid at Teatro Espanol, 1905.

El susto de la condesa (title means "The Countess's Terror"; one-act dialogue), produced in Madrid at Teatro Espanol, 1905.

Cuento inmoral (title means "Immoral Story"; one-act monologue), produced in Madrid at Teatro Espanol, 1905.

La sobresalienta (title means "The Understudy"; one-act lyrical farce), produced in Madrid at Teatro Espanol, 1905.

El encanto de una hora (title means "The Magic of an Hour"; dialogue), produced in Madrid at Teatro de la Princesa, 1905.

Mas fuerte que el amor (title means "Stronger than Love"; four-act drama), first produced in Madrid at Teatro Espanol, 1906.

La princesa Bebe (title means "Princess Bebe"; four-act), produced in Madrid at Teatro Espanol, 1906.

El amor asusta (title means "Love Shocks"; one-act), produced in Madrid, 1907.

Abuela y nieta (title means "Grandmother and Granddaughter"; one-act dialogue), produced in Madrid at Teatro de Lara, 1907.

La copa encantada (title means "The Enchanted Cup"; one-act musical comedy), produced in Madrid at Teatro de la Zarzuela, 1907.

Todos somos unos (title means "All Are One"; one-act lyrical farce), produced in Madrid at Teatro Esclava, 1907.

La historia de Otelo (title means "The Story of Othello"; one-act), produced in Madrid at Teatro de Apolo, 1907.

Los ojos de los muertos (title means "The Eyes of the Dead"; three-act drama), produced in Madrid at Teatro de la Princesa, 1907.

Senora Ama (three-act), produced in Madrid at Teatro de la Princesa, 1908.

De pequenas causas . . . (title means "From Small Beginnings . . ."; one-act), produced in Madrid at Teatro de la Princesa, 1908.

Por las nubes (title means "In the Clouds"; two-act; also see below), produced in Madrid at Teatro de Lara, 1909.

El ultimo minue (title means "The Last Minuet"; one-act comedy), produced in Madrid at Teatro Benavente, 1909.

Ganarse la vida (title means "Earning a Living"; one-act), produced in Madrid at Teatro del Principe Alfonso, 1909.

El nietecito (title means "The Little Grandson"; one-act), produced in Teatro del Principe Alfonso, 1910.

El criado de Don Juan (title means "Don Juan's Servant"; one-act), produced in Madrid at Teatro Espanol, 1911.

La losa de los suenos (title means "The Graveyard of Dreams"; two-act comedy), produced in Madrid at Teatro de Lara, 1911.

La propia estimacion (title means "Proper Esteem"; three-act), produced in Madrid at Teatro de la Comedia, 1915.

La mal que nos hacen (title means "The Evil Done to Us;" three-act), produced in Madrid at Teatro de la Princesa, 1917.

La Inmaculada de los Dolores (title means "Our Lady of Sorrow"; three-act dramatic novel), produced in Madrid at Teatro de Lara, 1918.

La ley de los hijos (title means "The Children's Law"; three-act drama), produced in Madrid at Teatro de la Zarzuela, 1918.

Por ser con todos leal, ser para todos traidor (title means "Loyalty to All Through Treachery to All"; three-act drama), produced in Madrid at Teatro del Centro, 1919.

La vestal de Occidente (title means "The Vestal of the West"; four-act drama), produced in Madrid at Teatro de Lara, 1919.

La honra de los hombres (title means "The Honor of Men"; two-act comedy), produced in Madrid at Teatro de Lara, 1919.

(Adaptor) *El audaz* (five-act drama; based on the novel of the same title by Benito Perez Galdos), produced in Madrid at Teatro Espanol, 1919.

La Cenicienta (title means "Cinderella"; three-act), produced in Madrid at Teatro Espanol, 1919.

Y va de cuento (title means "And Once Upon a Time"; four-act fantasy with prologue), produced in Madrid, 1919.

Una senora (title means "A Lady"; three-act dramatic novel), produced in Madrid at Teatro del Centro, 1920.

Una pobre mujer (title means "A Poor Woman"; three-act drama), produced in Madrid at Teatro de la Princesa, 1920.

Mas alla de la muerte (title means "Beyond Death"; three-act drama), produced in Buenos Aires, 1922.

Por que se quito Juan de la bebida (title means "Why Juan Quit Drinking"; monologue), produced in Montevideo, Uruguay at Teatro Soles, 1922.

Un par de botas (title means "A Pair of Boots"; one-act comedy), produced in Madrid at Teatro de la Princesa, 1924.

Nadie sabe lo que quiere; o, El bailarin y el trabajador (title means "Nobody Knows What He Wants; or, The Dancer and the Laborer"; three-act comedy), produced in Madrid at Teatro Comico, 1925.

El suicidio de Lucerito (title means "Lucerito's Suicide"; one-act comedy), produced in Madrid at Teatro Alcazar, 1925.

Los amigos del hombre (title means "Man's Friends"; four-act farce), produced in Madrid at Teatro de la Avenida, 1930.

Aves y pajaros (title means "Birds and Fowl"; two-part), produced in Madrid at Teatro de Lara, 1940.

Lo increible (title means "The Incredible"; three-act comedy), produced in Madrid at Teatro de la Comedia, 1940.

Abuelo y nieto (title means "Grandfather and Grandson"; one-act dialogue), produced in San Sebastian, Spain, at Teatro del Principe, 1941.

Y amargaba . . . (title means "And It Was Bitter . . . "; three-act comedy), produced in Madrid at Teatro de la Zarzuela, 1941.

La ultima carta (title means "The Last Letter"; three-act comedy), produced in Madrid at Teatro Alcazar, 1941.

La honradez de la cerradura (title means "The Integrity of the Lock"; three-act comedy), produced in Madrid at Teatro Espanol, 1942.

Al fin, mujer (title means "Finally, Woman"; three-act comedy), produced in San Sebastian, Spain, at Teatro del Principe, produced in Madrid at Teatro Alcazar, 1942.

Hija del alma! (title means "Daughter of My Soul!"; one-act), produced in Madrid at Teatro de Lara, 1942.

Don Magin, el de las magias (title means "Don Magin, the Magician"; three-act comedy), produced in Barcelona at Teatro Barcelona, 1944, produced in Madrid at Teatro Alcazar, 1945.

Los ninos perdidos en la selva (title means "Children Lost in the Forest"; four-act dramatic novel), produced in Madrid at Teatro de la Infanta Beatriz, 1944.

Espejo de grandes (title means "Mirror of the Great"; one-act), produced, 1944, produced in Madrid at Teatro de Lara, 1946.

Nieve en mayo (title means "Snow in May"; four-act dramatic poem), produced in Madrid at Teatro de la Zarzuela, 1945.

La ciudad doliente (title meansy "The Suffering City"; three-act comedy), produced in Madrid at Teatro de la Comedia, 1945.

Titania (three-act comedy), produced in Buenos Aires, 1945, produced in Madrid at Teatro Calderon, 1946.

La infanzona (title means "The Noblewoman"; three-act drama), produced in Buenos Aires, 1945, produced in Madrid at Teatro Calderon, 1947.

Abdicacion (title means "Abdication"; three-act comedy), produced in Madrid at Teatro de Lara, 1948.

Divorcio de almas (title means "Divorce of Souls"; three-act comedy), produced in Madrid at Teatro Fontalba, 1948.

Adoracion (title means "Adoration"; two-act dramatic comedy with prologue), produced in Madrid at Teatro Comico, 1948.

Al amor hay que mandarlo al colegio (title means "Love Should be Sent to School"; comedy with four episodes), produced in Madrid at Teatro de Lara, 1950.

Su amante esposa (title means "His Lover-Wife"; three-act comedy), produced in Madrid at Teatro de la Infanta Isabel, 1950.

Tu una vez, y el diablo diez (title means "You Once, the Devil Ten Times"; three-act comedy), produced in Valladolid, Spain at Teatro Lope de Vega, 1950, produced in Madrid at Teatro de la Infanta Isabel, 1951.

Mater imperatrix (three-act dramatic comedy), produced in Barcelona at Teatro de la Comedia, 1950, produced in Madrid at Teatro de la Comedia, 1951.

Ha llegado Don Juan (title means "Don Juan Has Arrived"; two-act comedy with prologue), produced in Barcelona at Teatro de la Comedia, 1952.

Servir (title means "To Serve"; two-act comedy with interlude), produced in Madrid at Teatro Maria Guerrero, 1953.

El alfiler en la boca (title means "A Pin in the Mouth"; three-act comedy), produced in Madrid at Teatro de la Infanta Isabel, 1953.

Almas prisioneras (title means "Imprisoned Souls"; two- act drama with prologue), produced in Madrid at Teatro Alvarez Quintero, 1953.

Caperucita asusta al lobo (title means "Little Red Riding-Hood Frightens the Wolf" three-act), produced in Madrid at Teatro de la Infanta Isabel, 1953.

Hijos padres de sus padres (title means "Sons Fathers of their Fathers"; three-act comedy), produced in Madrid at Teatro de Lara, 1954.

El marido de bronce (three-act comedy), produced in Madrid at Teatro de la Infanta Isabel, 1954.

OTHER

Cartas de mujeres (title means "Women's Letters"; fictional letters), 1893, Espasa-Calpe, 1965.

Figulinas (sketches), Fortanet, 1898.

(Translator) Alexandre Dumas, *Mademoiselle de Belle-Isle* (five-act play), produced in Valladolid, Spain, 1903.

(Translator) Edward Bulwer-Lytton, *Richelieu* (five-act drama), produced in Mexico City, 1904.

(Translator) Emile Augier, *Buena boda* (title means "A Good Marriage"; three-act), produced in Madrid at Teatro de Sociedad, 1905.

Vilanos (sketches), Fortanet, 1905.

El teatro del pueblo (title means "The People's Theatre"), F. Fe (Madrid), 1909.

(Translator) Paul Hervieu, *El destino manda* (title means "Destiny Commands"; two-act drama; translation of *Le destin est maitre*), produced in Madrid at Teatro de la Princesa, 1914.

(Translator) George C. Hazelton and Harry Benrimo, *La tunica amarilla* (title means "The Yellow Tunic"; three-act), produced in Madrid at Teatro de la Princesa, 1916.

Los ninos (title means "The Children"; anthology), Hesperia (Madrid), 1917.

La Mefistofela (title means "Mephistopheles"; three-act comic operetta), produced in Madrid at Teatro de la Reina Victoria, 1918.

Conferencias (title means "Lectures"), Hernando, 1924.

Pensamientos (title means "Thoughts"), Hernando, 1931.

De sobremesa: Cronicas (title means "After-Dinner Conversation: Chronicles"), F. Fe (Madrid), 1940.

Plan de estudios para una escuela de arte escenico, Aguilar, 1940.

Asi piensan los personajes de Benavente (title means "Benavente's Characters Think Thusly"; excerpts from his writings), edited by Jose Maria Viqueira, Aguilar, 1958.

Recuerdos y olvidos (memorias) (title means "Things Recalled and Forgotten: Memories"), Aguilar, 1959.

Las terceras de ABC (selections of contributions to *ABC*), edited by Adolfo Prego, Prensa Espanola, 1976.

Editor of *El ano germanofilo* (title means "The Germanic Year"; symposium), 1916; also author of unpublished and unproduced play, *El bufon de Hamlet* (title means "The Buffoon of Hamlet"). Also translator of *King Lear* by Shakespeare published as *El rey Lear,* 1911. Weekly columnist, *El Imparcial,* 1908-12. Contributor to *ABC* (Madrid newspaper). Editor, *La Vida Literaria* (magazine).

SIDELIGHTS: Dramatist Jacinto Benavente was the dominant force in Spanish drama during the first third of the twentieth-century. He produced nearly two hundred works for stage and in 1922 was granted the Nobel Prize for literature. Although extremely popular during the early years of his career, many critics noted a decline in Benavente's work for the stage beginning shortly before he won the highly coveted award. In a *World Literature Today* essay chronicling the Nobel prizes received by Hispanic authors throughout the history of the award, Manuel Duran seemed to summarize modern thought on the playwright when he wrote: "Another prize was squandered in 1922. The laurel went that year to playwright Jacinto Benavente, whose vast production is now mostly obsolete and was already out of phase with modern times when the medallion was conferred." However slighted by today's critics, Benavente's impact on Spanish theater and the high esteem in which he was held by the theater-going public and critics of his day cannot be denied.

Son of a well-respected pediatrician (a bust of whom can be found in Madrid's *Buen Retiro* park), Benavente showed an early interest in theater and, as a boy, he often wrote short skits to be performed for his young friends. Besides attending plays produced on the stages of Madrid, he read voraciously all the plays he could find. When as a teenager he learned several foreign languages, he began to read plays by foreign authors, especially those by William Shakespeare, in their original languages. Although he studied law for a time, Benavente's true career was in the theater and he soon became an actor with a professional company based in Madrid. (Later in life he stated on numerous occasions that he would have preferred to have been an actor rather than a playwright and often appeared in the cast of his own productions.) In the late 1880s he began to regularly submit plays to Emilio Mario, a family friend and director of Madrid's famous Teatro de la Comedia. Mario rejected nearly a dozen of the fledgling dramatist's efforts until finally consenting to produce a three-act play titled *El nido ajeno* ("Another's Nest") in 1894.

Although the work was virtually ignored by critics, Benavente's next offering, *Gente conocida* ("People of Importance") won for the playwright an adoring public. *Gente conocida* introduced to Madrid a type of theater completely different from that in vogue at the time. Spanish theater was under the spell of Spain's first Nobel Prize winner, Jose Echegaray (who won the award in 1904), a playwright whose work was characterized by exaggerated melodrama, grandiloquent verses, and artificiality. Although Benavente confessed a deep admiration for the older playwright, his own theater was in direct contrast to that of Echegaray. "Benavente's theater . . . meant a reaction against the anachronistic, turn-of-the-century Romanticism of Echegaray," wrote Marcelino C. Penuelas in *Jacinto Benavente*. "Against a background of the affected gesture, the hollow voice, the melodramatic, declamatory and solemn tone, the vio-

lence of passion and the traditional concept of honor, appear the theater of clever conversation in a confidential, ironic and satirical tone which Benavente succeeded in popularizing."

Critics John Van Horne and Walter Starkie both group Benavente's plays produced from 1894 to 1901 as the author's first period. This phase is marked by what Starkie referred to in his 1924 biography *Jacinto Benavente,* as "the Toledo blade of satire." In these plays Benavente satirized the decadent upper and middle classes of Madrid and Moraleda, the playwright's fictional version of a provincial town of the countryside surrounding the Spanish capital. Productions of this period include *La farandula,* which compares the empty speech of politicians to the meaningless line of actors; *La comida de las fieras,* which explores what happens to a wealthy family when it loses its fortune; and *La gobernadora,* which reveals the intrigue behind small town politics. In these first plays Benavente showed a tendency to imitate several French authors with whose work he was familiar, including Alfred Capus, Mauric Donnay, and Henry Lavedan, all of whom wrote satirical works about French society.

Critics who noted this influence, along with Benavente's obvious rejection of the theatrical standard established by Echegaray, accused Benavente of not being a true Spanish playwright. "Perhaps without his knowing it, he is more foreign than Spanish," commented Jose Vila Selma in his *Benavente: Fin de siglo* which Penuelas quoted in English translation. Vila Selma continued, "Whatever is new in Benavente's theater is something which singularly sets itself apart from the traditional course." In an essay included in *The Theatre, the Drama, the Girls* George Jean Nathan seemed to side with Vila Selma's assessment when he accused Benavente of copying many of his plays from a variety of Italian, French, and German sources.

Benavente's theater reflected his cosmopolitan lifestyle: He had traveled extensively through Europe and, because he was fluent in several languages, was familiar with several European literatures. Differing with Vila Selma and Nathan, some critics saw these influences in Benavente's theater as a reason to praise the playwright for bringing fresh material into the tradition-bound Spanish theater. "It was he," *Books Abroad* contributor Robert G. Sanchez pointed out, "who brought to the Spanish stage all the currents of the European theater of the first quarter of the century." Julius Brouta, and others, likened Benavente to several of the best dramatists on the European scene.

In comments published in *Drama* Brouta wrote, "Benavente is, in many respects, the Bernard Shaw of Spain. Like Shaw, he is a disciple of Ibsen; like him, an iconoclast, a reformer, a teacher, a preacher, and his dialectics are hardly less efficient or his spirit less brilliant." Elsewhere in the same essay, Brouta noted that Benavente's ironic touch was "similar to that of Anatole France." In a comparison with another European author, *Topic* contributor Alfredo Marquerie found Benavente "had much in common with Oscar Wilde."

While admitting to the European influences in Benavente's theater, other critics, including Storm Jameson and Starkie, found the playwright's work to be firmly rooted in that of the seventeenth-century Spanish playwright Lope de Vega, known as the father of Spanish drama, and who represented the very essence of *lo espanol*. Starkie noted: "Many of [Benavente's] enemies have made it an accusation against him that he introduced foreign ideals which caused the decline of true Spanish art. To those, however, who examine carefully Benavente's drama, it will become plain that foreign influences did not altogether hide the Spanish dramatist who counted back his literary descent to Lope de Vega." In a similar vein, Jameson observed in an essay in his *Modern Drama in Europe,* "The work of Jacinto Benavente is in the highest tradition of the Spanish drama. . . . The creative genius of Lope de Vega informed his vision of reality." "Cosmopolitan as he may be in theories," Van Horne wrote in his introduction to *Tres Comedias: "Sin querer," "De pequenas causas . . . ," "Los intereses creados,":* "his nature is essentially and intensely Spanish." Benavente's witty dialogue and fertile imagination won over skeptical actors, critics, and public.

The second phase of his career, which in Starkie's estimation covered the years 1901 to 1914, brought the playwright his greatest triumphs. In 1905 he was acclaimed by Madrid's theatrical community with a festival in his honor that concluded with the public reading of a tribute by the great Spanish novelist Benito Perez Galdos. Two plays from this period, *Los intereses creados ("The Bonds of Interest")* and *La malquerida ("The Passionflower"),* were successfully produced in English translation on the New York stage. These plays show Benavente's evolution from the social satire of his first period to a broader scope, including a wide variety of theatrical genres, but often focusing on comedy with a moral tone. Considered Benavente's masterpiece, *The Bonds of Interest* is a three-act comedy based on the Italian *commedia dell'arte*. This dramatic genre consisted of a improvisational skit performed by actors filling the roles of stock characters, including "the beautiful young lady," her "suitor," "the Doctor," and others. Later versions also included "Polichinelle," who survived to modern times as Punch in Punch and Judy shows, and "Harlequin," known for his unique costume. Benavente's play tells the story of the handsome Leander's attempt to dupe an entire city into thinking he is a wealthy aristocrat traveling incognito. After falling in love with the beautiful Sylvia, daughter of Polichinelle, Leander tells her of his true identity. Meanwhile, Leander's servant, Crispin, who is unaware of his master's confession, contrives to have the whole town and Sylvia turn against Polichinelle. The comedy ends happily with Crispin forced to admit his lies and Sylvia stepping forward to address the audience, declaring that although we are often selfishly ruled by "bonds of interest," the power of love is there to redeem us. Sylvia's closing statement embodies an important facet of Benavente's view of life as presented in his work: the value of love and tolerance in combating society's evils.

In his introduction to *Plays,* Benavente's chief translator John Garrett Underhill wrote, "The subject of Jacinto Benavente is the struggle of love against poverty, of obligation against desire, of imputed virtue against the consciousness of sin." Jameson commented on the same aspect of Benavente's work, noting "The other side of the dramatist's passionate indignation is love, love towards the oppressed, the thwarted and the maimed of life. . . . Men are to be pitied, but they are also to be loved. Through the dynamic force of love they will be set free, not from pain, but from despair and the isolation of defeat." "Love stands forth prominently in Benavente as the principle dynamic factor," Brouta concluded. Many of the plays of Benavente's second period explore the problems of married life.

Included in this group is *La Malquerida ("The Passionflower"),* one of the plays individually cited for merit in the Nobel prize presentation address given by the then-chairman of the Nobel Committee of the Swedish Academy, Per Hallstroem. This three-act peasant drama of provincial life focuses on the relationship between Esteban and Acacia, Esteban's wife Raimunda's daughter from her first marriage. The play ends tragically with the death of Raimunda at Esteban's hands. Such was the success of the first production of the play in 1913 that Benavente was carried home in triumph by enthusiastic theater-goers. Sanchez called it "a powerful and fascinating melo-

drama, a landmark in the modern Spanish theater."
In *The Passionflower,* as in many of his plays,
Benavente focuses his attention on his female characters. Dubbed a feminist for his portrayals of strong
females, he expressed his interest in female characterization in one of his first works, *Cartas de mujeres,*
a volume of letters purported to be written by women.
"In these letters," Starkie observed, "he tries to
plumb the depths of the Spanish woman's soul."
Unlike some Spanish dramatists who insisted in their
works on the centuries-old concepts of honor and
machismo, according to Brouta, Benavente "stoutly
espoused the rights of woman, the idea of equality of
the sexes, and pointed out the moral obligation which
matrimony imposes upon man."

He was also fond of poking fun at one of Spain's
national heroes, Don Juan, the professional se-
ducer. *Rosas de otono* and *Senora Ama,* which each
deal with how a woman married to a philandering
husband deals with his infidelity, are just two of the
works in which his interest in feminine psychology is
apparent.

At the beginning of his career Benavente was seen as
a reformer of the Spanish stage and a revealer of the
hypocrisy of Spanish society. Because of this revolutionary beginning, he is often included by many critics as a member of Spain's Generation of '98, a
loosely knit group of writers who broke with the
members of the preceding generation in hopes of
avoiding a disaster similar to the one Spain suffered
in 1898 when it lost all of its overseas empire. By the
time the playwright had entered his third period,
starting in 1914, his plays had changed so that characters, and not reform, had became their focus.
Speaking of this last phase of Benavente's career
Starkie commented, "His heroes and heroines in most
cases tend to become mere mechanical symbols of an
abstract thought. In many cases also he falls into
sentimentality, and mistakes rhetoric for art." He
seemed to be writing for that very portion of society
that he previously had so bitterly satirized.

When Benavente was awarded the Nobel Prize in
1922, members of the Generation of '98, who previously had held him in high esteem as one of their
own, protested vehemently. Penuelas explained that
although Benavente had indeed reformed Spanish theater, at least technically, "he never came to experience the artistic and human anxieties which appeared
at the turn of the century in Europe and in Spain with
the writers of the Generation of '98." Because of

Benavente's failure to continue on the path of revision
suggested by his early works, nearly all his plays
remain essentially bound to the Spanish society in
which they were originally written. As Penuelas concluded: "Although Benavente undoubtedly influenced
twentieth-century Spanish writers, the best of his followers oriented their works in other directions and
Benavente's theater was soon out of date."

BIOGRAPHICAL/CRITICAL SOURCES:

BOOKS

Benavente, Jacinto, *Plays,* edited and translated by
    John Garrett Underhill, Scribner, 1917.
Benavente, Jacinto, *Tres comedias: "Sin querer," "De
    pequenas causas . . . ," "Los intereses creados,"*
    edited by John Van Horne, Heath, 1918.
Goldberg, Isaac, *The Drama of Transition: Native and
    Exotic Playcraft,* Stewart Kidd, 1922.
Jameson, Storm, *Modern Drama in Europe,* Collins,
    1920.
Nathan, George Jean, *The Theatre, the Drama, the
    Girls,* Knopf, 1921.
Nobel Prize Library: Asturias, Benavente, Bergson,
    Helvetica Press, 1971.
Penuelas, Marcelino C., *Jacinto Benavente,* Twayne,
    1968.
Starkie, Walter, *Jacinto Benavente,* Oxford Univer-
    sity Press, 1924.
Twentieth-Century Literary Criticism, Volume 3,
    Gale, 1980.
Vila Selma, Jose, *Benavente: Fin de siglo,* Rialp,
    1952.
Warren, L. A., *Modern Spanish Literature: A Com-
    prehensive Survey of the Novelists, Poets, Drama-
    tists and Essayists from the Eighteenth Century to
    the Present Day,* Volume 2, Brentano's Ltd.,
    1929.

PERIODICALS

Bookman, May, 1921.
Books Abroad, winter, 1955.
Drama, November, 1915.
Modern Drama, May, 1961.
Modern Languages, December, 1968.
Revista de Estudios Hispanicos, May, 1974.
Romance Notes, winter, 1978.
South Atlantic Bulletin, January, 1976.
Times Literary Supplement, September 18, 1924.
Topic, spring, 1968.
World Literature Today, spring, 1988.

OBITUARIES:

PERIODICALS

Newsweek, July 26, 1954.
New York Times, July 15, 1954.
Publishers Weekly, August 7, 1954.
Time, July 26, 1954.*

*   *   *

BENEDETTI, Mario 1920-
(Damocles)

PERSONAL: Born September 14, 1920, in Paso de los Toros, Tacuarembo, Uruguay; son of Brenno Benedetti (a civil servant) and Matilde Farrugia; married Luz Lopez. *Education:* Attended the Colegio Aleman.

CAREER: Accountant in Montevideo, Uruguay; journalist for *Marcha* (weekly periodical), Montevideo; transcriber for UNESCO, Paris, 1966; Center for Literary Research of the Casa de las Americas, Havana, Cuba, organizer and director, 1969-71; exiled from Uruguay, c. 1975-85; writer.

WRITINGS:

ESSAYS AND LECTURES

Peripecia y novela, [Montevideo], 1948.
Marcel Proust y otros ensayos, Numero (Montevideo), 1951.
El pais de la cola de paja, Asir (Montevideo), 1960.
(Under pseudonym Damocles) *Mejor es meneallo,* Alfa (Montevideo), 1961.
Literatura uruguaya siglo xx, Alfa, 1963, revised 2nd edition, 1969.
(With others) *Sobre Julio Cortazar,* [Havana], 1967.
Letras del continente mestizo, Arca (Montevideo), 1967.
Sobre artes y oficios, Alfa, 1968.
Cuaderno cubano, Arca, 1969, revised 2nd edition, 1971.
(With others) *Nueve asedios a Garcia Marquez,* Universitaria (Santiago), 1969.
(With others) *Literatura y arte nuevo en Cuba,* Estela (Barcelona), 1971.
(With others) *Rodo: Parabolas y textos escogidos,* Fundacion Editorial Union del Magisterio (Montevideo), 1971.

Critica complice, Instituto Cubano del Libro (Havana), 1971.
(With Angel Rama) *Cielitos y dialogos patrioticos* (about Bartolome Hidalgo), Bibliotecade Marcha (Montevideo), 1971.
Cronicas del 71, Arca, 1972.
Los poetas comunicantes, (Montevideo), 1972.
El escritor latinoamericano y revolucion posible, Alfa Argentina (Buenos Aires), 1974.
El ejercicio del criterio: Critica literaria, 1950-1970, Nueva Imagen (Mexico City), 1981.
Escritos politicos, Arca, 1985.

FICTION

Esta manana (short stories), [Montevideo], 1949, published as *Esta manana y otros cuentos* (also see below), Arca, 1967.
El ultimo viaje y otros cuentos (short stories), Numero, 1951.
Quien de nosostros (novel), Alfa, 1953.
Montevideanos (short stories; also see below), Alfa, 1959.
La tregua (novel), Alfa, 1960, translation by Benjamin Graham published as *The Truce,* Harper (New York City), 1969.
Gracias por el fuego (novel), Alfa, 1965.
La muerte y otras sorpresas (also see below; short stories), Siglo XXI (Mexico City),1968.
(With others) *Montevideo en cuentas* (short stories), Arca, 1968.
Cuentos completos (short stories; contains *Esta manana y otros cuentos, Montevideanos,* and *La muerte y otras sorpresas*), Universitaria, 1970, expanded edition, Editorial Alfaguara (Madrid), 1995.
El cumpleanos de Juan Angel (novella in verse), Siglo XXI, 1971.
(With others) *Cuentos de la revolucion* (short stories), Giron (Montevideo), 1971.
Letras de emergencia (includes poetry), Alfa Argentina, 1973.
(With others) *Siete cuentos de hoy* (short stories), Sandino (Montevideo), 1974.
Geografias (short stories and poetry), Nueva Imagen, 1984.
El amor, las mujeres y a la vida, [Madrid], 1996.
Blood Pact and Other Stories, Curbstone Press (Willimantic, CT), 1997.
Andiamos (novel; title means "Scaffolds"), [Madrid], c. 1998.

POETRY

Poemas de la oficina (poetry), Numero, 1956.

Poemas del hoy por hoy (poetry), Alfa, 1961.

Inventario (poetry), Alfa, 1963, revised 3rd edition published as *Inventario 67,* 1967, revised 4th edition published as *Inventario 70,* 1970, revised 5th edition published as *Inventario,* Alfa Argentina, 1974.

Contra los puentes levadizos (poetry), Alfa, 1966.

Antologia natural (poetry), Alfa, 1967.

A ras de sueno (poetry), Alfa, 1967.

Poemas de otros (poetry), Alfa Argentina, 1974.

Cotidianas (poetry), Siglo XXI, 1979.

Pedro y el capitan: Pieza en cuatro partes, Nueva Imagen, 1979.

Poesia trunca: Poesia latinoamericana revolucionaria (poetry), Visor (Madrid), 1980.

Viento del exilio (poetry), Nueva Imagen, 1981.

Antologia poetica (poetry), Alianza (Madrid), 1984.

Nocion de patria: Proximo projimo (poetry), Visor, 1985.

Also author of *La vispera indeleble,* 1945, and *Solo mientras tanto,* 1950. A collection of the author's poems and short stories was recorded by Benedetti and released as the album, *Mario Benedetti: Poemas y cuentos.*

PLAYS

El reportaje (also see below), Marcha (Montevideo), 1958.

Ida y vuelta (also see below), Talia (Buenos Aires), 1963.

Dos comedias (contains *El reportaje* and *Ida y vuelta*), Alfa, 1968.

EDITOR

Narradores rumanos (Rumanian short stories), Alfa, 1965.

(And author of prologue) Ruben Dario, *Poesias* (poetry), Casa de las Americas (Havana), 1967.

(And author of prologue) *Poemas de amor hispanoamericanos* (poetry), Arca, 1969.

(With Antonio Benitez Rojo) *Quince relatos de la America Latina* (essays), Casa de las Americas, 1970.

(With Benitez) J. J. Fernandez de Lizardi and others, *Un Siglo del relato latinoamericano* (short stories), Casa de las Americas, 1976.

(And author of prologue) *Jovenes de esta America* (essays and lectures), Casa de las Americas, 1978.

Roque Dalton, *Poesia* (poetry), Casa de las Americas, 1980.

Also editor of *Naturaleza vida: Introduccion a la poesia Hispanoamericana,* translation by Darwin J. Flakoll and Claribel Alegria published as *Unstill Life: An Introduction to the Spanish Poetry of Latin America,* Harcourt, 1969.

OTHER

Genio y figura de Jose Enrique Rodo, Universitaria de Buenos Aires, 1966.

Datos para el viudo, Galerna (Buenos Aires), 1967.

Los poetas comunicantes (interviews), Biblioteca de Marcha, 1972.

(With others) *Onetti* (literary criticism), Biblioteca de Marcha, 1973.

Hasta aqui, La Linea (Buenos Aires), c. 1974.

Daniel Viglietti (musical criticism), Jucar (Madrid), 1974.

La casa y el ladrillo, Siglo XXI, 1976.

Con y sin nostalgia, Siglo XXI, 1977.

El recurso del supremo patriarca (literary criticism), Nueva Imagen, 1979.

Notas sobre algunas formas subsidiarias de la penetracion cultural, Tierra Adentro (Mexico City), 1979.

El escritor y la critica en el contexto del subdesarrollo, Universidad Nacional Autonomade Mexico (Mexico City), 1979.

Primavera con una esquina rota, Nueva Imagen, 1982.

(With Helder Camara) *Escritos sobre la teologia de la liberacion en Latinoamerica,* Instituto de Estudios Latinoamericanos (Buenos Aires), 1984.

El desexilio, y otras conjeturas, Nueva Imagen, 1985.

La cultura, ese blanco movil, Division Publicaciones y Ediciones, Universidad de la Republica (Montevideo), 1985.

Cultura entre dos fuegos, Division Publicaciones y Ediciones, Universidad de la Republica, 1986.

Preguntas al azar, Nueva Imagen, 1986.

Yesterday y manana, Arca, 1987.

Subdesarrollo y letras de osadia, Alianza, 1987.

Recuerdos olvidados, Trilce (Montevideo), 1988.

La vida ese parentesis, Visor Libros (Madrid), 1998.

Contributor to *Panorama historico-literario de nuestra America,* by America Diaz Acosta and others, Casa de las Americas, 1982. Literary, film, and theater critic for *El Diario, Tribuna Popular,* and *La Manana, Montevideo.*

SIDELIGHTS: Even in English translation, Uruguayan writer Mario Benedetti's prose has a restrained, mature strength and evenness. Using a well-defined style built solidly on a perceptive view of the myriad facets of human nature, Benedetti's work has received a positive response from critics. Hailed as one of his country's most popular and most prolific men of letters, Benedetti writes about the small but telling moments of life, weaving them into short-story collection such as 1959's *Montevideanos* and 1968's *La muerte y otras sorpresas* ("Death and Other Surprises"), as well as poetry, novels, and essays in which he condemns the imperialist tendencies of the United States with regard to Latin America. As Bart L. Lewis commented of Benedetti's work in *Chasqui*, "Activism, productive contemplation and awareness of the need for Latin American solidarity are central features of Benedetti's essays . . . while his prose fiction makes a major contribution to the luster emanating from the modern Latin American novel."

Born in the rural town of Paso de Toros, Benedetti moved to the Uruguayan capital city of Montevideo when he was a boy. Raised by educated parents, he was encouraged in his love of learning and wrote his first novel-length work by the time he was twelve. After graduating from college, he began a career as a journalist, and he contributed theater, book, and film criticism to several newspapers. After the government of Uruguay fell into moral and political decay in the 1950s, Benedetti left and traveled through Europe, eventually settling in Cuba, where he headed a literary research center under dictator Fidel Castro. Since 1971 Benedetti has devoted his full time to his writing, which continues to achieve a wide-ranging popularity throughout Latin America. He returned to Montevideo in 1985.

Compared to Irish author James Joyce's *Dubliners,* Benedetti's *Montevideanos* contains stories that reflect its author's interest in middle-class life. Many of the stories deal with morality, particularly as it plays out in the narrow world of lower-level business managers, people who settle for a lackluster, mediocre existence, and those who are trapped by tradition and the status quo. In one often-anthologized story, "The Budget," a group of bureaucrats in a tiny government department react to news of a new budget that at first promises to increase salaries but ultimately is suffocated by the legislative process, leaving several bureaucrats in debt after spending money they thought they would be receiving but did not. As Benedetti explained to *Americas* interviewer Caleb Bach, "The Budget" is more about the political process than office politics; it "deals with the solitary nature of the employee who is disconnected and deprived of knowing what's going on. In these state bureaucracies nobody knew what was going on!" Much of Benedetti's

early verse, written during the 1940s, also concentrates on the life of the bureaucrat, with its constraints, petty squabbling, and lack of change.

Other works by Benedetti include the novel *Andiamos* ("Scaffolds") and the short-story collection *Blood Pact and Other Stories,* the latter published in 1997. In *Andiamos* the experience of exile is Benedetti's subject, as he follows his main characters back to Uruguay after many years away during the country's dictatorial rule. Returning to their homeland means reconstructing not only the physical life—home, job, community—but healing the emotional trauma brought on by being torn from one's birth culture and forced by circumstance to adopt unfamiliar living habits. The stories in *Blood Pact* are drawn from Benedetti's entire oeuvre, and show the change in focus from his earlier works to the writing done during the author's own period of exile in the 1960s and 1970s while Uruguay suffered from a repressive political regime. Praising "the singular and surprising nature" of these tales, *New York Times Book Review* contributor James Polk noted that the best stories "lead relentlessly toward one apparent ending before abruptly shifting direction and winding up in a totally unexpected place." Influenced by the work of Ernest Hemingway, Chekhov, and Uruguayan writer Horacio Quiroga, Benedetti's fiction also reflects the constant political upheaval to which his country was heir. "The effect of the short story is the surprise, the astonishment, the revelation," he was quoted as writing by Bach. But, he added, "the real influence on my work was reality, that of my country and Latin America in general."

BIOGRAPHICAL/CRITICAL SOURCES:

BOOKS

Tardiff, Joseph C., and L. Mpho Mabunda, editors, *Dictionary of Hispanic Biography,* Gale (Detroit), 1996.

PERIODICALS

Americas, August, 1998, p. 38.
Books Abroad, An International Literary Quarterly, spring, 1966, pp. 145-148.
Chasqui, February-May, 1982, pp. 3-12.
Hispanofila, January, 1987, pp. 89-99.
Latin American Literary Review, fall-winter, 1980, pp. 28-36.
Library Journal, July, 1996, p. 94.

Massachusetts Review, fall-winter, 1986, pp. 511-525.
New York Times Book Review, October 19, 1969; November 9, 1969; August 17, 1997, p. 16.
Saturday Review, January 10, 1970, p. 44.
Studies in Short Fiction, summer, 1974, pp. 283-90.
Times Literary Supplement, December 7, 1967; June 20, 1968; September 18, 1970; August 6, 1976.
World Literature Today, spring, 1982, p. 310; spring, 1983, p. 251; spring, 1985, p. 245; winter, 1988, p. 95.
World Press Review, June, 1995, p. 44.*

*   *   *

BILAC, Olavo (Braz Martinos dos Guimaraes) 1865-1918

PERSONAL: Born December 16, 1865, in Rio de Janeiro, Brazil; died December 28, 1918, in Rio de Janeiro, Brazil. *Education:* Studied medicine and law.

CAREER: Poet and essayist, c. 1888-1916. Worked as a journalist in Rio de Janeiro, Brazil.

WRITINGS:

Poesias, 1888.
Cronicas e Novelas, 1894.
Critica e Fantasia, 1904.
Conferencias Literarias, 1906.
Ironia e Piedade, 1916.
Tarde, 1919.
Poesias Completas, 1929.

Work represented in anthologies, including *Diadems and Fagots,* privately printed (Santa Fe, NM), 1921.*

*   *   *

BIOY CASARES, Adolfo 1914-1984
(B. Suarez Lynch, H(onorio) Bustos Domecq, B. Lynch Davis, Javier Miranda, Martin Sacastru)

PERSONAL: Surname appears in some sources as Bioy-Casares; born September 15, 1914, in Buenos Aires, Argentina; died in 1984; son of Adolfo and Marta (Casares) Bioy; married Silvina Ocampo (a writer); children: Marta.

CAREER: Writer.

AWARDS, HONORS: Premio Municipal de la Ciudad de Buenos Aires, 1940, for *La invencion de Morel;* 2nd Premio Nacional de Literatura, 1963, for *El lado de la sombra;* 1st Premio Nacional de Literatura, 1969, for *El gran serafin;* Gran Premio de Honor, Argentine Society of Writers, 1975; Premio Mondello, 1984, for *Historias fantasticas;* Premio IILA (Rome), 1986, for *Historias fantasticas* and *Historias de amor;* Premio Cervantes, 1990; Premio Alfonso Reyes, 1991.

WRITINGS:

SHORT STORIES

(Under pseudonym Martin Sacastru) *17 disparos contra lo porvenir,* Tor (Buenos Aires), 1933.
Caos, Viau & Zona (Buenos Aires), 1934.
Luis Greve, muerto, Destiempo (Buenos Aires), 1937.
El perjurio de la nieve, Emece, 1944, translation by Ruth L. C. Simms published as *The Perjury of the Snow,* Vanishing Rotating Triangle (New York City), 1964.
La trama celeste (title means "The Celestial Plot"), Sur, 1948, translation by Simms published with her translation of *La invencion de Morel* (also see below) as *The Invention of Morel, and Other Stories from "La trama celeste,"* University of Texas Press, 1964.
Las visperas de Fausto, Arturo J. Alvarez (Buenos Aires), 1949.
Historia prodigiosa (title means "Prodigious History"), Obregon (Mexico), 1956, augmented edition, Emece, 1961.
Guirnalda con amores: cuentos (title means "A Garland of Love: Stories"), Emece, 1959.
El lado de la sombra, Emece, 1962.
El gran serafin, Emece, 1967.
Historias de amor, Emece, 1972.
Historias fantasticas, Alianza (Madrid), 1976.
El heroe de la mujeres, Emece, 1978.
Historias desaforadas, Emece, 1986.
Una muneca Rusa, Tusquets (Barcelona), 1991.
Selected Stories, translated by Suzanne Jill Levine, New Directions (New York City), 1994.

NOVELS

La nueva tormenta o La vida multiple de Juan Ruteno, published by author, 1935.
La invencion de Morel, prologue by Jorge Luis Borges, Losada (Buenos Aires), 1940, translation

by Simms published with stories from *La trama celeste* as *The Invention of Morel, and Other Stories from "La trama celeste,"* University of Texas Press, 1964.

Plan de evasion, Emece, 1945, translation by Suzanne J. Levine published as *A Plan for Escape,* Dutton, 1975.

(With wife, Silvina Ocampo) *Los que aman, odian* (title means "Those Who Love, Hate"), Emece, 1946.

El sueno de los heroes (title means "The Dream of Heroes"), Losada, 1954.

Diario de la guerra del cerdo, Emece, 1969, translation by Gregory Woodruff and Donald A. Yates published as *Diary of the War of the Pig,* McGraw, 1972.

Dormir al sol, Emece, 1973, translation by Levine published as *Asleep in the Sun,* Persea, 1975.

La aventura de un fotografo en La Plata, Emece, 1985.

Also author of *Un campeon desparejo.*

OMNIBUS VOLUMES

Adolfo Bioy Casares, edited by Ofelia Kovacci, Ediciones Culturales Argentinas, Ministerio de Educacion y Justicia, Direccion General de Cultura, 1963.

Adversos milagros, prologue by Enrique Pezzoni, Monte Avila (Caracas), 1969.

Paginas de Adolfo Bioy Casares seleccionadas por el autor, preface by Alberto Lagunas, Celtia, 1985.

WITH JORGE LUIS BORGES

(Under joint pseudonym H. Bustos Domecq) *Seis problemas para don Isidro Parodi,* Sur, 1942, translation by Norman Thomas di Giovanni published under authors' real names as *Six Problems for Don Isidro Parodi,* Dutton, 1981.

(Under joint pseudonym H. Bustos Domecq) *Dos fantasias memorables,* Oportet & Haereses, 1946, reprinted under authors' real names with notes and bibliography by Horacio Jorge Becco, Edicom (Buenos Aires), 1971.

(Under joint pseudonym B. Suarez Lynch) *Un modelo para la muerte* (novel; title means "A Model for Death"), Oportet & Haereses, 1946.

Los orilleros [and] *El paraiso de los creyentes* (screenplays; titles mean "The Hoodlums" and "The Believers' Paradise"; *Los orilleros* produced in Argentina, 1975), Losada, 1955.

Cronicas de Bustos Domecq, Losada, 1967, translation by di Giovanni published as *Chronicles of Bustos Domecq,* Dutton, 1976.

(With Hugo Santiago) *Les Autres; scenario original* (screenplay; produced in France, 1974), C. Bourgois (Paris), 1974.

Contributor with Borges, under joint pseudonym B. Lynch Davis, to *Los anales de Buenos Aires,* 1946-48.

EDITOR WITH WIFE, SILVINA OCAMPO, AND BORGES

Antologia de la literatura fantastica (title means "Anthology of Fantastic Literature"), Editorial Sudamericana, 1940.

Antologia poetica argentina (title means "Anthology of Argentine Poetry"), Editorial Sudamericana, 1941.

EDITOR OR COMPILER; WITH BORGES

(And translator with Borges) *Los mejores cuentos policiales* (title means "The Best Detective Stories"), Emece, 1943.

(And translator with Borges) *Los mejores cuentos policiales; Segunda serie,* Emece, 1951.

Cuentos breves y extraordinarios, Raigal (Buenos Aires), 1955, revised and enlarged edition, Losada, 1973, translation by Anthony Kerrigan published as *Extraordinary Tales,* Souvenir Press, 1973.

(And author of prologue, notes, and glossary with Borges) *Poesia gauchesca* (two volumes; title means "Gaucho Poetry"), Fondo de Cultura Economica, 1955.

Libro del cielo y del infierno (anthology; title means "Book of Heaven and Hell"), Sur, 1960.

Also editor, with Borges, of a series of detective novels, "The Seventh Circle," Emece, 1943-56, and of *Destiempo* (literary magazine), 1936-37.

OTHER

Prologo (miscellany), Biblos (Buenos Aires), 1929.

La estatua casera (miscellany), Jacaranda (Buenos Aires), 1936.

La otra aventura (essays), Galerna, 1968.

Memoria sobre la pampa y los gauchos (essay), Sur, 1970.

(Under pseudonym Javier Miranda) *Breve diccionario del argentino exquisito,* Barros Merino, 1971, augmented edition with new prologue, published under author's real name, Emece, 1978.

Memorias: Infancia, adolescencia y como se hace un escritor, Tusquets (Barcelona), 1994.

ADAPTATIONS: Three of the stories in *Six Problems for Don Isidro Parodi* were dramatized for radio broadcast by the British Broadcasting Corp. (BBC). Films based on Bioy Casares' work include *El crimen de Oribe,* Argentina, 1950, *L'invention de Morel,* France, 1967, *L'invenzione di Morel,* Italy, 1973, *La guerra del cerdo,* Argentina, 1975, *In memoriam,* Spain, 1977, *I problemi di don Isidro Parodi,* Italy, 1978, *El gran serafin,* Spain, 1987, *Otra esperanza,* Argentina, 1991, and *En memoria de Paulina,* Argentina, 1992.

SIDELIGHTS: A noted fiction writer in his own right in his native Argentina, Adolfo Bioy Casares was known in the United States primarily for his collaborative work with his more famous countryman Jorge Luis Borges. The two met when Bioy Casares was seventeen and Borges nearly fifteen years older. Bioy Casares had already published his *Prologo,* and their mutual interest in books led to a friendship. Within a few years of their original meeting they began writing together.

Bioy Casares recalled that their first joint effort involved creating a commercial pamphlet about yogurt, one of the products of the Casares family's large dairy ranch. In *La otra aventura,* Bioy Casares remembered this initial endeavor: "That pamphlet was a valuable lesson to me; after writing it, I was a different writer, more experienced and skillful. Any collaboration with Borges is the equivalent of years' work."

When the two worked together on their later fiction, Emir Rodriguez Monegal suggested in *Jorge Luis Borges: A Literary Biography,* "Borges and Bioy [Casares were] replaced by their own creations. A new writer had been born, a writer who ought to be called 'Biorges' because he was neither Borges nor Bioy [Casares], and because he did not stick to one pseudonym." The two authors' various joint pseudonyms—Honorio Bustos Domecq, B. Suarez Lynch and B. Lynch Davis—were produced by combining parts of the names of two of their great-grandfathers. "In a 1964 interview," remarked Donald A. Yates in the *Washington Post Book World,* "Borges offered this insight into the nature of the collaboration. 'We wrote somewhat for each other and since everything happened in a joking mood, the stories turned out so involved, so baroque, that it was difficult to understand them. At first we made jokes, and in the end

jokes on jokes. It was a kind of algebraic contest: jokes squared, jokes cubed.'"

In their work, Bioy Casares and Borges focused on social criticism of their homeland, primarily through the use of humor. Their complex exaggerations of the tragically funny Argentine society—a society in which the Peron government "elevated" an author of Borges's stature from his library position to inspector of chickens and rabbits—deal with false appearances and their acceptance in Argentina. They painted a social order which *Time*'s Paul Gray described as "invariably monstrous: [full of] novels and poems that cannot be read, art that cannot be seen, architecture—freed from the 'demands of inhabitability'—that cannot be used."

In *Six Problems for Don Isidro Parodi,* six people visit a barber, Don Isidro Parodi, and ask for solutions to their problems. Ironically, Don Isidro himself is in jail, serving time for a murder he didn't commit; the real murderer has escaped prosecution because of his connections with the authorities. Each story defines and ridicules a particular type of Argentine personality, including what Yates identifies as "the foppish journalist" and members of the Argentine Academy of Letters. *Chronicles of Bustos Domecq* offers a collection of tongue-in-cheek sketches of characters from Argentine literary and artistic circles. One piece deals with the poet F. J. C. Loomis who, because of his dislike of metaphors, begins writing poems containing only one word. Domecq explained that the poor reception of Loomis's poem "Beret" stems from "the demands it makes on the reader of having to learn French," Gray reported. Other writers and artists Domecq praised include Adalberto Vilaseco, who repeatedly publishes the same poem with a different title each time, and artist Antarctic A. Garay, who sets up pieces of junk and invites onlookers to admire the spaces between the works—a concept he labels "concave sculpture." Gray described Domecq as "the pure incarnation of the middleman between a world gone culturally haywire and the uncomprehending mass of mankind. . . . This inept critic is a figure of Chaplinesque pathos: a tastemaker totally lacking in taste, a perpetual target of the avant-garde's custard pies."

Initially the fruits of Borges's and Casares's collaboration were not received enthusiastically in Argentina. When Victoria Ocampo, whose magazine *Sur* published the first of the stories in 1942, realized that it was a collaborative work, she was appalled that it had appeared in her serious literary journal. Rodriguez

Monegal suggested that the two authors' use of humor was lost on their original audience: "The readers [of the original works] did not realize that a joke could be serious, and that irony and parody are among the deadliest forms of criticism. The gap between readers and authors was unbridgeable. Not until Bustos Domecq's first book was reissued a quarter of a century later would it be read by readers who could see its point."

Both *Six Problems for Don Isidro Parodi* and *Chronicles of Bustos Domecq* have been well received by U.S. reviewers. Some critics applaud the books' humor; others mention the validity of the authors' social criticism. Denis Lynn Heyck asserted in the *Chicago Tribune Book World* that *Six Problems* "is an extremely funny book. . . . [It] mercilessly exposes Argentine pretentiousness, pseudo-cosmopolitanism, and shallow nativism. . . . And it caricatures those Argentines, and others, who live life as if it were bad literature." In the *New Republic*, Clarence Brown noted the "sheer nonsensical hilarity" of *Chronicles,* while *Atlantic* reviewer Phoebe-Lou Adam found the same book "hilariously awful and a great creation."

Plot complexity, humor, and the contradictions between appearance and reality mark the works solely written by Bioy Casares as well as his work written with Borges. *A Plan for Escape,* Robert M. Adams observed in *Review,* is "beset with complexities and ambiguities which render practically everything said in [it] subject to question." Writing in the same journal, Rodriguez Monegal refered to "the almost unbearable complexity of *A Plan for Escape* and the stories of *The Celestial Plot."* Bizarre plots are found in others of Bioy Casares's books, as well. The narrator of *The Invention of Morel,* shipwrecked on a desert island, discovers that several people meet regularly on the island, including a woman named Faustine with whom he falls in love. Eventually he learns that the group exists merely as images projected by a machine. Propelled by love for Faustine, he attempts to become part of the film the machine is projecting. *Asleep in the Sun* tells the story of Bordenave, who sends his neurotic wife to a clinic only to have her return "inhabited" by someone else's personality.

Some critics believe these complicated plots add an element of absurd humor to Bioy Casares's work. In the *Bulletin of Hispanic Studies,* D. P. Gallagher refered to Bioy Casares's novels and short stories as "comic masterpieces whose fundamental joke is the gap that separates what his characters know from

what is going on." In the *Nation,* Richard Kostelanetz labeled *The Invention of Morel* "marvelously comic" because of the narrator's repeated attempts to get close to a woman who does not exist. In *Asleep in the Sun,* Bordenave's efforts to remove his wife from the clinic are humorous because he succeeds in recovering her body but not her spirit.

The humor of Bioy Casares's solo work, like the parody of his works with Borges, is a double-edged humor that mixes bitterness with laughter. The bitterness is particularly evident in the theme of false appearances or perception that Rodriguez Monegal, in his *Review* article, saw as unifying Bioy Casares's oeuvre. As well as pointing out the obvious role of false appearances in *The Invention of Morel* and *Asleep in the Sun,* the critic described less obvious occurrences of the theme. In *Diary of the War of the Pig,* for instance, in which the young people of Buenos Aires begin killing off the older people, "a political fiction masks the allegory of the corruption of the body."

The complex satire of the absurd tales written by Bioy Casares alone and in collaboration with Jorge Luis Borges exposed the senseless contradictions between reality, perception, and social acceptance in their native Argentina and in modern society in general. Commented Deborah Weinberger in *Review,* "Everything [Bioy Casares] writes offers a world or postulates the possibility of worlds different from the one we inhabit, or think we inhabit." Nathan Rosenstein concluded in the *Village Voice,* "Perhaps the most powerful theme at work . . . is the implicit and telling contrast of the intellect's great potential and the petty pursuits and intrigues of mankind."

A Russian Doll and Other Stories explores reality and fantasy and their combined effects on the human mind. The stories also expose foibles of the human personality in male-female relationships, business dealings, and other situations. According to Evelio Echevarria in *Studies in Short Fiction,* "The great vital conflicts that characterize Spanish-American literature are not here. But these stories are not dull."

Fantasy, love, powerful forces, and wry humor permeate the collection of stories Bioy Casares wrote between 1959 and 1986 and gathered into a volume titled *Selected Stories.* "All the entries are solidly made and the frequently quirky people in them, despite their considerable fumbling and stumbling, manage to make it from here to there without disrupting the plot line," maintained James Polk in the *New York Times Book Review.*

Bioy Casares related selected incidents in his childhood and formative years in *Memoirs: Infancia, adolescencia y como se hace un escritor.* In *World Literature Today* Melvin S. Arrington, Jr. stated: "Stylistically, the volume resembles a collection of short stories: the narrator switches topics erratically; chapters are brief and episodic; not all the narratives appear significant or even interesting. Aptly titled, these vignettes and accompanying photos offer an intimate portrait of a man whose life has been intertwined with Argentine literary activity for over a half-century."

BIOGRAPHICAL/CRITICAL SOURCES:

BOOKS

Bioy Casares, Adolfo, *The Invention of Morel, and Other Stories from "La trama celeste,"* prologue by Jorge Luis Borges, translated by Ruth L. C. Simms, University of Texas Press, 1964.

Bioy Casares, Adolfo, *La otra aventura* (essays), Galerna, 1968.

Borinsky, Alicia, *Intersticios,* Universidad Veracruzana, 1987.

Camurati, Mireya, *Bioy Casares y el alegre trabajo de la inteligencia,* Corregidor (Buenos Aires), 1990.

Contemporary Literary Criticism, Gale (Detroit), Volume 4, 1975; Volume 8, 1978; Volume 13, 1980; Volume 88, 1995.

Dictionary of Literary Biography, Volume 113: *Modern Latin-American Fiction Writers, First Series,* Gale, 1992.

Gallagher, D. P., *Modern Latin American Literature,* Oxford University Press, 1973.

Hernandez Martin, Jorge, *Readers and Labyrinths: Detective Fiction in Borges, Bustos Domecq, and Eco,* Garland Publishers (New York City), 1995.

Hispanic Writers, Gale, 1991.

MacAdam, Alfred J., *Modern Latin American Narratives,* University of Chicago Press, 1977.

Martino, Daniel, *ABC de Adolfo Bioy Casares,* Emece, 1989.

Martino, editor, *Adolfo Bioy Casares,* Ministerio de Cultura (Madrid), 1991.

Rodriguez Monegal, Emir, *Jorge Luis Borges: A Literary Biography,* Dutton (New York City), 1978.

Schwartz, Kessel, *A New History of Spanish American Fiction,* Volume 2, University of Miami Press, 1971.

Villordo, Oscar Hermes, *Genio y figura de Adolfo Bioy Casares,* Editorial Universitaria de Buenos Aires, 1983.

PERIODICALS

Atlantic, April, 1976; January, 1979; April, 1981.

Booklist, October 15, 1994, p. 400; April 15, 1995, p. 1485.

Bulletin of Hispanic Studies, July, 1975.

Chicago Tribune Book World, April 19, 1981.

Hudson Review, summer, 1973.

Library Journal, October 1, 1994, p. 117.

Los Angeles Times, May 5, 1981.

Nation, October 11, 1965.

New Republic, June 5, 1976.

Newsweek, November 27, 1978.

New Yorker, September 19, 1970; May 25, 1981.

New York Review of Books, April 19, 1973.

New York Times Book Review, January 28, 1973; March 29, 1981; November 29, 1992, p. 15; November 6, 1994, p. 37.

Paris Review, winter-spring, 1967.

Publishers Weekly, September 5, 1994, p. 90.

Review, fall, 1975.

Studies in Short Fiction, winter, 1994, p. 126.

Time, March 29, 1976.

Times Literary Supplement, June 12, 1981; August 27, 1982.

Village Voice, November 3, 1975.

Washington Post Book World, April 19, 1981.

World Literature Today, winter, 1980; winter, 1995, p. 109.*

*   *   *

BLADES, Ruben 1948-

PERSONAL: Born July 16, 1948, in Panama City, Panama; son of Ruben Dario (a police detective) and Anoland Benita (an actress and singer; maiden name, Bellido de Luna) Blades; married Lisa A. Lebenzon (an actress), December 13, 1986. *Education:* Instituto Nacional, Panama, B.A., 1966; University of Panama, lic. in law and political science, 1973; Harvard University, LL.M., 1985. *Religion:* Roman Catholic. *Avocational interests:* Baseball, soccer, boxing, dominoes, collecting toy soldiers, old books, reading.

ADDRESSES: Office—c/o David Maldonado Management, 1674 Broadway, Ste. 703, New York, NY 10019. *Agent*—Paul Schwartman, International Creative Management, 8899 Beverly Hills Blvd., Los Angeles, CA 90048.

CAREER: Composer, singer, actor, and writer. Banco Nacional, Panama City, Panama, member of legal staff, 1973-74; Fania Records, New York City, recording artist and legal advisor, 1973-83; Elektra Records, New York City, recording artist, 1984—. Songwriter and performer with Pete Rodriguez, with the Willie Colon Combo, and as solo artist; composer of music for films, including *Q & A,* 1990. Actor in films, including *Crossover Dreams,* 1985, *The Milagro Beanfield War,* 1988, and *The Two Jakes,* 1990.

MEMBER: American Society of Composers, Authors, and Publishers (ASCAP), National Academy of Recording Arts and Sciences, Screen Actors Guild, American Federation of Television and Radio Artists, Harvard Law School Association (vice president, 1984-85), Colegio Nacional de Abogados (Panamanian law association).

AWARDS, HONORS: Named honorary citizen, City of Chicago, 1984; *Time* magazine "Top Ten Albums of the Year" list, 1984, for *Buscando America,* and 1985, for *Escenas;* New York Award, 1985, for *Buscando America,* and 1986, for *Escenas;* New York Music Awards for Best Ethnic/International Act and Best Latin Act, *New York Post,* 1986; Grammy Award for Best Tropical Latin Performance, National Academy of Recording Arts and Sciences, 1986, for *Escenas.*

WRITINGS:

RECORDINGS; SONGWRITER

(With the Willie Colon Combo) *The Good, the Bad, the Ugly,* Fania, 1975.
(With the Willie Colon Combo) *Metiendo Mano,* Fania, 1976.
(With the Willie Colon Combo) *Siembra,* Fania, 1977.
Bohemio y Poeta, Fania, 1979.
(With the Willie Colon Combo) *Canciones del Solar de los Aburridos,* Fania, 1982.
The Last Fight, Fania, 1982.
Maestra Vida, Fania, c. 1982.
El Que la Hace la Paga, Fania, 1983.
Buscando America, Elektra, 1984.
Escenas, Elektra, 1985.
Move On, Elektra, 1985.
Crossover Dreams, Elektra, 1986.

Agua de Luna, Elektra, 1987.
Ruben Blades with Strings, Fania, 1988.
Nothing but the Truth, Elektra, 1988.
Caminando, Discos International, 1991.
The Best, Globo Records, 1992.
Mucho Mejor, West Wind Latina, 1993.
Poeta Latino, Charly Latin, 1993.

OTHER

(With Leon Ichaso and Manuel Arce) *Crossover Dreams* (screenplay), Miramax, 1985.
(With Sergio Santana) *Yo, Ruben Blades: Confessiones de un Relator de Barrio,* Ediciones Salsa y Cultura, 1997.

Contributor of book reviews and articles to periodicals, including *Village Voice;* author of political columns for Panamanian newspapers, including *La Estrella de Panama.*

WORK IN PROGRESS: Three more recordings for Elektra.

SIDELIGHTS: Ever since he started writing and recording songs in the late sixties, Ruben Blades has been an innovator in the Latino music world. "An intellectual who maintains passionate ties to street-level Latino culture, Mr. Blades has been compared to such thoughtful pop-rock composers as Bruce Springsteen, Jackson Browne, and Paul Simon," Stephen Holden of the *New York Times* reports. At a time when salsa musicians mostly sung of dancing and good times, "Blades made the argument for a change in subject matter as a means of changing the stereotypes [of Latin Americans]," Pete Hamill relates in a *New York* article. Blades's lyrics are literate—the 1987 album *Agua de Luna* was inspired by the stories of Nobel winner Gabriel Garcia Marquez—and deal with political and social concerns and everyday life in the barrio. Indeed, the artist feels so strongly about his lyrics being understood that he has translations included with his albums. The quality of his writing, along with his transforming of salsa "into what he terms an 'urban sound,' with instrumental trappings borrowed from rock and jazz," writes Anthony DePalma in the *New York Times,* has brought Blades popularity with critics and fans, Latinos and Anglos alike.

While Blades appreciates the success he has enjoyed outside the Latino community, he hasn't made a concerted attempt to cross over into mainstream popularity. "I find the whole idea of crossover dangerous, because it implies the abandonment of one base for another," he told Holden. Blades elaborated, saying that most crossover attempts fail because "they were either seeking to escape their own backgrounds or trying to cash in," he continued. "The attempts have been forced, rather than natural, and when the elements don't match, you have performers who end up looking like fools."

This concern about forsaking one's heritage became the genesis for the 1985 film *Crossover Dreams,* which Blades co-wrote and starred in. The movie follows the attempts of salsa singer Rudy Veloz to break into the mainstream music scene; in the process of pursuing stardom, however, Rudy abandons his friends and subsequently has no one to support him when he fails. While the plot of the story is "one of the hoariest cliches—the artist struggling for recognition and success," as *Washington Post* writer Richard Harrington observes, the film is "a big-hearted snapshot of life in East Harlem and its vibrant musical subculture."

Chicago Tribune movie critic Gene Siskel likewise states that "even though 'Crossover Dreams' treads familiar territory in its dramatic structure, the specific Latino terrain is as fresh as is [Blades,] its genuinely charismatic star." "As in pop songs, familiarity can give the artist an emotional edge, can be a tool for greater economy," explains *Los Angeles Times* reviewer Michael Wilmington. The film "might have had a better, subtler, fresher script, with somewhat deeper characterizations—but it doesn't necessarily need it. There are too many elements that keep it fresh . . . most of all, the wizardly economy of the storytelling." Wilmington concludes that the film "is hot, lyrical, spicy and soulful. . . . Anyone who passes it up is missing a rich, body- and heart-satisfying treat."

With his increased visibility as an actor and the recording of his first album in English, Blades has been the target of accusations that he is forsaking his Latino origins. In answer to these criticisms, Blades told *Time* writer Bill Barol: "You don't have to leave your background behind in order to see what's on the other side. The proposition is simple: let's talk. Let's meet in the middle someplace, and then we'll walk together." Blades views *Nothing but the Truth* as an attempt to allow Anglo audiences to share in his native music and culture; as DePalma quoted him as saying in concert: "I'm going to speak in English . . . , but don't accuse me of selling out or anything. These people [Anglos]

came here to share our culture with us, and this will help them understand what we're trying to do."

In addition, Blades has frequently commented that English is also a part of the Latino tradition, whether it comes from the Afro-Cuban calypso music he heard as a child or the American rock 'n' roll popular in Panama when he was teenager. "I want people to acknowledge the possibilities of a Latin artist fully—meaning we can do English, too," Blades told *Rolling Stone* writer David Fricke. He accepts, however, that his unconventional career moves might cost him. As he explained to *Time*'s Guy D. Garcia, "I will never be a superstar. My role is to be different, to do what others won't do, and, as a result, my fortunes will always fluctuate. I will always be viewed with suspicion by some, though not by all, because I move against the current."

"I've always believed that music can do more than offer escape—it can help bring people together to change their lives," the singer remarked to Holden. Blades also hopes someday to express his concerns through political action in addition to his music. "Eventually I'll return to Panama and the odds are good I'll run for office," he told Barol. "I'll participate in some way. There's a need there for figures people can trust." Blades believes his experience in law (he is a member of the Panamanian bar and has a degree from Harvard) and his regular political commentaries (published in Panamanian newspapers) provide him with a legitimate background for public office. And he realizes that his singing can only do so much, as he noted to DePalma: "I made a foundation of talking and singing about people's lives. I'm proud of that and proud of my singing. But I can't sing forever with the world exploding around me."

BIOGRAPHICAL/CRITICAL SOURCES:

BOOKS

Contemporary Musicians, Volume 2, Gale, 1990.

PERIODICALS

Chicago Tribune, October 4, 1985.
Los Angeles Times, October 2, 1985.
Newsweek, September 9, 1985.
New York, August 19, 1985.
New York Times, August 18, 1985; June 21, 1987.
Rolling Stone, April 23, 1987.
Time, July 11, 1988; January 29, 1990.

Village Voice, March 5, 1985.
Washington Post, October 11, 1985.*

*   *   *

BLASCO IBANEZ, Vicente 1867-1928

PERSONAL: Born January 29, 1867, in Valencia, Spain; died January 28, 1928, in Menton, France; originally buried in France, reinterred in 1933 in Valencia, Spain; son of Gaspar Blasco Teruel and Ramona Ibanez Martinez; married Maria Blasco del Cacho, November 8, 1891 (died, January, 1925); married Elena Ortuzar Bulnes, October, 1925; children: (first marriage) Mario, Libertad, Julio Cesar, Sigfriedo. University of Valencia, licentiate in civil and canonical law, 1888.

CAREER: Writer. Secretary to novelist Manuel Fernandez y Gonzalez, Madrid, Spain, beginning 1883. Legislative delegate for six terms; founder of Blasquista party.

AWARDS, HONORS: Honorary degree from George Washington University, Washington, DC, 1920; Legion d'Honneur (France).

WRITINGS:

NOVELS

Viva la republica! (Romeu el guerrillero), Volume 1: *En el crater del volcan,* Volume 2: *La hermosa Liejesa,* Volume 3: *La explosion,* Volume 4: *Guerra sin cuartel,* Sempere, 1892.

Arroz y tartana (also see below), Sempere, 1894, translation by Stuart Edgar Gummon published as *The Three Roses,* Dutton (New York City), 1932.

Flor de mayo (includes four stories published in *Cuentos valencianos;* also see below), Sempere, 1896, translation by Arthur Livingston published as *The Mayflower: A Tale of the Valencian Seashore,* Dutton, 1921.

La barraca: Novela (also see below), Sempere, 1898, edited with introduction, notes, and vocabulary by Hayward Keniston, Holt (New York City), 1910, translation by Francis Haffkin Snow and Beatrice M. Mekota of original Spanish edition published as *The Cabin,* Knopf, 1917, translation published with a new introduction by John Garrett Underhill, 1938, reprinted, Fertig, 1975.

Entre naranjos (title means "Among the Orange Trees"), Prometeo, 1900, translation by Isaac Goldberg and Arthur Livingston published as *The Torrent,* Dutton, 1921.

Sonnica la cortesana, Sempere, 1901, translation by Frances Douglas published as *Sonnica,* Duffield, 1912.

Canas y barro (also see below), Prometeo, 1902, translation by Issac Goldberg published as *Reeds and Mud,* Dutton, 1928, translation by Lester Beberfall published as *Reeds and Mud,* Branden Press (Boston), 1966.

La catedral, Prometeo, 1903, translation by Mrs. W. A. Gillespie published as *The Shadow of the Cathedral,* Constable (London), 1909, Dutton, 1919.

El intruso, Prometeo, 1904, translation by Mrs. W. A. Gillespie published as *The Intruder,* Dutton, 1928.

La voluntad de vivir (title means "The Will to Live"), Prometeo, 1904.

La bodega, Sempere, 1905, translation by Goldberg published as *The Fruit of the Vine,* Dutton, 1919.

La horda, Sempere, 1905, translation by Mariano Joaquin Lorente published as *The Mob,* Dutton, 1927.

La maja desnuda (title means "The Nude Maja"), Prometeo, 1906, translation by Hayward Keniston published as *Woman Triumphant,* with an introductory note by the author, Dutton, 1920, translation by Frances Partridge published as *The Naked Lady,* Elek (London), 1969.

Sangre y arena (also see below), Sempere, 1908, translation by Frances Douglas published as *The Blood of the Arena,* A. C. McClurg (Chicago), 1911, translation by Mrs. W. A. Gillespie published as *Blood and Sand,* Simpkin, Marshall & Co., 1913, Dutton, 1919, published as *The Matador,* Nelson, 1918, edition based on Mrs. Gillespie's translation published as *Blood and Sand: The Life and Loves of a Bullfighter, A New English Version of the Novel,* Dell, 1951, translation by Frances Partridge published as *Blood and Sand,* Ungar, 1958.

Los muertos mandan, Prometeo, 1909, translation by Frances Douglas published as *The Dead Command,* Duffield, 1919, abridged Spanish edition edited by Frederick Augustus Grant Cowper and John Thomas Lister, Harper, 1934.

Luna Benamor (includes "El ultimo leon and other stories"; also see below), Prometeo, 1909, translation by Isaac Goldberg published under same title, J. W. Luce (Boston), 1919.

Los Argonautas: Novela, Prometeo, 1914.

Los cuatro jinetes del Apocalipsis, Prometeo, 1916, translation by Charlotte Brewster Jordan published as *The Four Horsemen of the Apocalypse,* Dutton, 1918.

Mare Nostrum, Prometeo, 1918, translation by Jordan published as *Our Sea,* Dutton, 1919.

Los enemigos de la mujer, Prometeo, 1919, translation by Irving Brown published as *The Enemies of Women,* Dutton, 1920.

La tierra de todos (title means "Everyone's Land"), Prometeo, 1921, translation by Leo Ongley published as *The Temptress,* Dutton, 1923.

El paraiso de las mujeres (title means "The Paradise of Women"), Prometeo, 1922.

El comediante Fonseca, Rivadeneyra (Madrid), 1923.

La reina Calafia, Prometeo, 1923, translation published as *Queen Calafia,* Dutton, 1924.

El Papa del mar (also see below), Prometeo, 1925, translation by Arthur Livingston published as *The Pope of the Sea: An Historical Medley,* Dutton, 1927.

A los pies de Venus (los Borgia): Novela (sequel to *El Papa del mar*), Prometeo, 1926, translation by Livingston published as *The Borgias; or, At the Feet of Venus,* Dutton, 1930.

Mademoiselle Norma, [Madrid], 1927.

El conde Garci-Fernandez, Cosmopolis, c. 1928.

En busca del Gran Kan (Cristobal Colon) (title means "In Search of the Great Khan [Christopher Columbus]"), Prometeo (Valencia), 1929, translation by Livingston published as *Unknown Lands: The Story of Columbus,* Dutton, 1929.

El caballero de la Virgen (Alonso de Ojeda), Prometeo, 1929, translation by Livingston published as *Knight of the Virgin,* Dutton, 1930.

El fantasma de las alas de oro, Prometeo, 1930, translation by Livingston published as *The Phantom with Wings of Gold,* Dutton, 1931.

COLLECTIONS

Fantasias (leyendas y tradiciones) (title means "Fantasies [Legends and Traditions]"; short stories), Prometeo, 1887.

El adios de Schubert (title means "Schubert's Goodbye"; short stories), Prometeo, 1888.

Cuentos valencianos (title means "Valencian Tales"), Prometeo, 1896.

La condenada (cuentos) (title means "The Condemned Woman [Stories]"; includes "En el mar and Other Stories"), Prometeo, 1900, published as *La condenada y otros cuentos,* Espasa-Calpe, 1960.

The Last Lion and Other Tales (translation of stories included in *Luna Benamor*), Four Seas (Boston), 1919.

El prestamo de la difunta (title means "The Loan of the Dead Woman"; stories; also see below), Prometeo, 1920, edited with introduction, notes, and vocabulary by George Baer Fundenburg and John F. Klein, Century, 1925.

Novelas de la costa azul (title means "Novellas of the Blue Coast"), Prometeo, 1924.

The Old Woman of the Movies, and Other Stories (translation of stories included in *El prestamo de la difunta*), Dutton, 1925.

Obras completas (complete works), eleven volumes, Prometeo, 1925-34, expanded edition published in three volumes, Aguilar, 1946.

Siete cuentos de Vicente Blasco Ibanez, edited with introduction, notes, and vocabulary by Sturgis E. Leavitt, Holt, 1926.

The Mad Virgins, and Other Stories (translation of stories from *El prestamo de la difunta* and other collections), Butterworth, 1926.

Novelas de amor y de muerte (title means "Novellas of Love and Death"), Prometeo, 1927.

La arana negra (title means "The Black Spider"), eleven volumes, Cosmopolis (Madrid), 1928, published in two volumes, A. T. E. (Barcelona), 1975.

Cuentos escogidos (title means "Selected Stories"), edited by J. Bayard Morris, Dent, 1932.

Tres novelas valencianas: Arroz y tartana, La barraca, Canas y barro, Plenitud (Madrid), 1958.

OTHER

Historia de la revolucion espanola (desde la guerra de la independencia a la restauracion en Sagunto) 1808-1874 (title means "History of the Spanish Revolution [from the War of Independence to the Restauration in Sagunto] 1808-1874)," three volumes, Enciclopedia Democratica (Barcelona), 1892.

Paris, impresiones de un emigrado (title means "Paris, An Emmigrant's Impressions"), Prometeo, 1893.

El juez (title means "The Judge"; play), Ripolles, 1894.

En el pais del arte (tres meses en Italia) (travel), Pellicers (Valencia), 1896, translation by Douglas published as *In the Land of Art,* Dutton, 1923.

(Translator from the French and author of preface) Onesime Reclus and J. J. E. Reclus, *Novisima geografia universal,* six volumes, La Novela Ilustrada (Madrid), 1906-07.

Oriente (title means "East"; travel), Prometeo, 1907.

(Translator from the French) Ernesto Laviss and Alfredo Rambaud, *Novisima historia univeral, dirigida a partir del siglo IV,* fifteen volumes, Prometeo, 1908-30.

Argentina y sus grandezas (title means "Argentina and Her Grandeurs"; travel), Espanola Americana (Madrid), 1910.

Historia de la guerra europea de 1914 (title means "History of the European War of 1914"), Prometeo, thirteen volumes, 1914-19.

(Translator from the French) J. C. Mardrus, *El libro de los mil y una noches,* twenty-three volumes, Prometeo, 1915.

The Bull-Fight (Spanish and English text; extract from *Sangre y arena*), translation by C. D. Campbell, Harrap, 1919.

El militarismo mejicano: Estudios publicados en los principales diarios de los Estados Unidos (contains articles originally published in U.S. newspapers), Prometeo, 1920, translation by Jose Padin and Arthur Livingston published as *Mexico in Revolution,* Dutton, 1920.

Vistas sudamericanas (title means "South American Views"; excerpts), edited by Carolina Marcial Dorado, Ginn, 1920.

Una nacion secuestrada (El terror militarista en Espana), J. Dura (Paris), 1924, translation by Leo Ongley published as *Alfonso XIII Unmasked: The Military Terror of Spain,* Dutton, 1924.

Blasco Ibanez: Paisajista (title means "Blasco Ibanez: Landscape Artist"), edited by Camille Pitollet, Vuibert (Paris), 1924.

La vuelta al mundo de un novelista (memoirs), three volumes, Prometeo, 1924-25, translation by Leo Ongley and Arthur Livingston published as *A Novelist's Tour of the World,* Dutton, 1926.

Lo que sera la republica espanola: Al pais y al ejercito (title means "What the Spanish Republic Will Become; To the Country and to the Army"), La Gutenberg (Valencia), 1925.

Por Espana y contra el rey, Excelsior (Paris), 1925.

Estudios literarios (title means "Literary Studies"; essays chiefly on French authors), Prometeo, 1933.

Discursos literarios (title means "Literary Lectures"), Prometeo, 1966.

Cronicas de viaje (title means "Travel Chronicles"), Prometeo, 1967.

Contra la Restauracion: Periodismo politico, 1895-1904 (articles previously published in *El Pueblo*), compiled by P. Smith, Nuestra Cultura (Madrid), 1978.

Founding editor, *El Pueblo* (Valencian newspaper), beginning 1891.

ADAPTATIONS: La tierra de todos was adapted for a stage production by L. Linares Becerra, 1927; *Blood and Sand* and *The Four Horsemen of the Apocalypse* were made into films of the same titles starring Rudolph Valentino, produced by Paramount Pictures; *The Four Horsemen of the Apocalypse* was made into a film starring Glenn Ford and Charles Boyer, 1961; four other novels were also made into U.S. films.

SIDELIGHTS: A novelist, politician, and adventurer who enjoyed worldwide fame during the first part of the twentieth century, Vicente Blasco Ibanez remains a controversial figure in Spanish literature. Blasco Ibanez was a nonconformist committed to political and social action and to the toppling of the Spanish monarchy that ruled Spain during his lifetime; he pursued these goals both directly as a political activist and indirectly through several of his novels.

In his youth his rebellious spirit caused his expulsion from school, and as Ricardo Landeira has pointed out in *The Modern Spanish Novel, 1898-1936,* "this incident of rebelliousness marks the beginning of a chronicled biography that reads like an adventure story worthy of Blasco [Ibanez] the novelist." Repeatedly in his early adulthood he was incarcerated for his outspoken criticism of the government. By the author's own account, his stays in Spanish jails numbered as many as thirty.

No less evident than his nonconformist spirit was Blasco Ibanez's strong literary and journalistic inclination. As a young student, he compiled short stories and news items for circulation among his classmates and wrote an original short story for submission to a literary competition. Blasco Ibanez later founded *El Pueblo,* a liberal newspaper that served as a vehicle for his political ideas and in which he also published short stories and novels in serialized form. Yet throughout his young adult years he compromised his reputation as a writer by moving farther and farther into the realm of political and social activism, a fact that at least partially explains Blasco Ibanez's often unfavorable treatment in Spanish literary histories. In many ways he represented a new literary phenomenon: he shattered the traditional model of the passive intellectual who did not take sides. Blasco Ibanez's early novels and short stories, all set in his native Valencia, stand as highly original and significant artistic contributions to modern Spanish literature.

In his early works, Blasco Ibanez proved himself a natural storyteller and a master of descriptive technique in the Naturalistic and Impressionistic modes. Often referred to as his "Valencian cycle" or "regional works," the novels included in this group are *Arroz y tartana* (*The Three Roses,* 1894), *Flor de mayo* (*The Mayflower,* 1896), *La barraca* (*The Cabin,* 1898), *Entre naranjos* (*The Torrent,* 1900), and *Canas y barro* (*Reeds and Mud,* 1902). Also belonging to this group are such short story collections as *Cuentos valencianos* ("Valencian Tales," 1896) and *La condenada y otros cuentos* ("The Condemned Woman, and Other Stories," 1900). In these early works Blasco Ibanez treated subjects and settings with which he had had direct contact and revealed an acute understanding of regional social problems. Elements of Naturalism—deterministic themes (such as the human being's subjugation to the natural elements), a focus on the common individual and his struggle for survival in a hostile or uncaring society, and an essential note of pessimism—color these works. But what often separates them from conventional Naturalistic narratives is the quality of the struggle depicted.

Blasco Ibanez's characters often take on heroic proportions; they are rarely Naturalism's sickly, feeble men and women, predisposed to failure because of their physical makeup or their heredity. In his regional works Blasco Ibanez created an artistic canvas that captured the quintessential aspects of the people of Valencia as they lived and worked at the turn of the century. *The Three Roses* portrays the materialistic aspirations of the bourgeoisie; *The Mayflower* and *Reeds and Mud* depict the lives of the people associated with the fishing industry so important to the region; *The Cabin* vividly recreates the hardships of the farmer; and *The Torrent,* which uses the Valencian orange groves as a poetic backdrop, addresses the conflict between materialistic or political aspirations and the desire for purity and beauty. These novels represent significant contributions to Spanish Naturalism and Realism for several reasons.

Blasco Ibanez surpassed many of his contemporaries such as Jose Maria Pereda and Pedro Antonio de Alarcon who, in keeping with the *costumbrista* mode of literature with its focus on customs, types, and characteristic scenes of a particular region, created a rather superficial, romantic image of society. Although Blasco Ibanez did make extensive use of local color and picturesque details, these features never constituted the final objective of his writing. In *Historia social de la literatura espanola,* Carlos Blanco Aguinaga comments on this dimension of Blasco Ibanez's works, stating that "the characteristic Spanish *costumbrista* novel . . . never offers a real-

istic critical analysis of social conflicts nor a progressive interpretation of those conflicts that one finds in these works of Blasco Ibanez." *The Mayflower* illustrates Blasco Ibanez's combining of local color and realistic social analysis. In this novel the *costumbrista* stamp appears in the extensive references to and description of local customs (for example, religious processions and the practice of inaugurating new boats) and in the vision of the fishermen's and fisherwomen's everyday dealings at sea and in the fish market. But the overriding theme of the novel concerns the tremendous danger to which the fishermen must expose themselves and the small compensation they receive from society.

In the final episode of the novel, the village witnesses the destruction of a fishing boat during a terrifying storm, and Tia Picores, a wise elder of the town and in many ways a living monument of the region's psychological and spiritual makeup—stoic, proud, hardworking, moral, and peace-loving—conveys Blasco Ibanez's theme. When the boat has finally crashed against the rocks, and hope has faded for a possible sole survivor (a young child who has been equipped with a life preserver and thrown from the ship), Tia Picores turns away to face the city and cries out: "And after this they'll come to the Fishmarket, the harlots, and beat you down, and beat you down! And still they'll say fish comes high, the scullions! And cheap 't would be at fifty, yes, at seventy-five a pound!"

Along with this thematic consideration Blasco Ibanez's early works embody a stylistic feature that also proves original to fiction in the Naturalistic mode: the use of simile and metaphor to create a dramatic tension between the character and his environment. *The Cabin* is exemplary in this respect. In an article appearing in *Hispania,* Douglas Rogers summarizes this technique: "The suggestive power of the similes rings so emphatically throughout the novel that the 'as if' situations are as though converted into effective power, and the sense of a huge, all-controlling destiny, where there once were Greek and Roman Gods, swallows up the smaller intellectual concept of sociopolitical determinism." Blasco Ibanez records and dramatically evokes vivid sensations. In so doing, he imbues nature with an often very poetic sense of mystery and power.

This quality in Blasco Ibanez's works is often obscured by Naturalistic features, such as determinism and a belief in the destructive power of man's base instincts, which, to be sure, are present in Blasco

Ibanez's works. But the poetic quality is just as important since the sea, the earth, and the other natural elements described in the fiction are intrinsically poetic. Nature is a cruel, destructive force; it is also something marvelous and beautiful. Thematically, the presentation of nature in these terms emphasizes the tragic dimension of the works since the characters are victims of their own courses of action and not mere toys of impersonal, destructive, deterministic forces. Blasco Ibanez's characters are strong-willed and healthy individuals, who in refusing to accept their human limitations and to pay heed to warnings ultimately bring about their own downfall.

In *The Mayflower,* for example, the protagonist decides to set sail in the storm, knowing that he is placing himself and his crew in great danger. When he realizes his mistake, he relies upon his abilities as a seaman and makes a desperate but failing attempt to defy the elements. A variation on this theme appears in one of Blasco Ibanez's most famous short stories, "En el mar" ("At sea"). Here, the protagonist sets out to catch a huge tuna, and when a storm threatens, the character blindly but boldly moves forward, venturing far out into the sea. After a preliminary encounter with the fish, which nearly results in his boat being capsized, a clear warning to the would-be hero, the protagonist is even more determined to catch his prey. He finally succeeds, though at a terrible price: his young son is thrown from the boat during the violent struggle with the fish and is given up for dead.

Yet another example of this bold behavior appears in *The Cabin* as a newly arrived farmer decides to cultivate a parcel of land that all the other farmers of the region, joined together in a spirit of solidarity, have sworn to abandon in protest of the unjust treatment and death of the farmer who previously occupied that land. As in the previous narratives, the protagonist is given several warnings but nevertheless persists in his endeavour, even if it means placing his family in great danger. When his cabin is finally burned down, he is forced to leave. Bernardo Suarez in a *Cuadernos hispanoamericanos* essay states that "nature as it is presented in *The Cabin* . . . is a favorable agent . . . a type of paradise."

The notion of paradise helps define man's relationship to nature, a subject that manifests itself repeatedly in Blasco Ibanez's regional novels and short stories. These works artistically convey man as a primitive being exiled from a mythic paradise; providing a chronicle of the social and historical changes that

were taking place in Spain at the turn of the century, the regional fiction depicts the lives of individuals caught between present and past, between, on the one hand, the realities of a mechanized economy, government intervention, and a social gospel of "progress" and, on the other, the futile yearning to regain harmony with nature.

In terms of narration, Blasco Ibanez wrote in an objective omniscient mode, often relying on dialogue and indirect discourse to maintain his distance from the work and thereby producing, as Sherman H. Eoff declares in *The Modern Spanish Novel,* "an unusually strong singleness of narrative effect." In adopting the omniscient voice Blasco Ibanez remained faithful to Naturalism, which in theory sought to emulate the laboratory setting of the scientist to insure objectivity and to obtain a "truer" sense of reality. But he rarely made use of Naturalism's encyclopedic descriptive approach, where even the most minute detail is recorded. And in spite of his predominantly objective tone, Blasco Ibanez often playfully interacted with his characters by adding a humorous comment or juxtaposing images that end an ironic quality to his prose. He did not make extensive use of irony, especially as a narrative framework, but it does appear in several novels and short stories; for example, in "El ultimo leon" ("The Last Lion"), a masterful sketch portraying an anachronistic Valencian artisan who champions the cause of tradition (dressing like a legendary lion in a religious procession) in a world which has long since disassociated itself from its noble, legendary past. In such instances the reader encounters compassion, admiration, and humor in the narrator's characterization, but there is no romantic idealization or nostalgic appeal as in the typical *costumbrista* writer.

After the regional works, Blasco Ibanez wrote a series of novels which are commonly referred to as his "thesis cycle." Each of these novels bore a specific ideological orientation and sought to denounce a particular aspect of Spanish society. Much more political than the preceding works, these novels are generally considered artistically inferior to the Valencian cycle. If the early works present a realistic image of society in its many aspects, the thesis cycle addresses specific problems articulated through the struggle of the worker (the proletariat) for economic and political emancipation. *La catedral* (*In the Shadow of the Cathedral,* 1903) seeks to unveil the retrogressive effect of the Catholic Church on the Spaniard; *El intruso* (*The Intruder,* 1904) deals with the problems of the mine workers in northern Spain; *La horda* (*The Mob,* 1905) focuses on the conditions of the inhabitants of

Madrid's ghettos; and *La bodega* (*The Fruit of the Vine,* 1905) is an expose of southern Spain's sherry industry, which on the one hand exploits Spanish workers and on the other produces the widely consumed alcohol that ultimately enslaves them by inhibiting their intellectual growth.

Other novels can also be loosely classified within this group: *La maja desnuda* (*Woman Triumphant,* 1906) examines the manner in which artistic talent is stifled by capitalistic influences, and *Sangre y arena* (*Blood and Sand,* 1908), the best novel of this group, portrays the bullfighter as a victim of society and tradition. Using as a setting the Balearic Islands, *Los muertos mandan* (*The Dead Command,* 1909) addresses the problem of social barriers and racial prejudices, a theme that reappears in *Luna Benamor* (1909). Although these works risk being viewed as nothing more than propagandistic documents, they also significantly contribute to modern Spanish literature. Examined in the specific historical context from which they were conceived, they represent an important development in what would later become the contemporary novel of Social Realism. Transitional works, they break with the Naturalistic model by replacing the unique protagonist with the collective protagonist and by discarding the individual focus on a particular scene or situation for a larger historical vision of the worker's universal struggle for equality and justice through socialism.

In the novels of the thesis cycle, actual events and social movements are recognizable; for example, the 1892 peasant uprising in southern Spain is incorporated into *The Fruit of the Vine.* One might even say that through his creation of this group of novels Blasco Ibanez could be considered the father of the modern Spanish novel. This opinion is advanced by Raphael Bosch who declares in *La novela espanola del siglo XX* that Blasco Ibanez helped inaugurate "an open novel, attentive to the immediate reality, urgent, common, in opposition to the closed action and the more or less explored characters, all as protagonists, characteristic in the nineteenth century." The cycle of thesis novels might also be considered important for the light it casts on Blasco Ibanez's relationship with the universally acclaimed group of Spanish writers known as the Generation of 1898, a group to which he technically belonged by virtue of his birthdate. This group included such prominent philosophical and literary figures as Miguel de Unamuno and Pio Baroja, but critics have commonly excluded Blasco Ibanez from this circle on aesthetic grounds: the Generation

of 1898 espoused an innovative and experimental style of writing whereas Blasco Ibanez continued to pursue the traditional, realistic manner.

All of these writers, however, including Blasco Ibanez, were deeply concerned with the fate of Spain; they saw the once vast and mighty Spanish empire quickly decline when, defeated by the United States in the Spanish-American War of 1898, it lost its last territorial possessions and whatever remained of its world power. Both Blasco Ibanez and the members of this group wanted to remedy the ills of Spain by introducing national reforms. To this end, Blasco Ibanez proposed the formation of an Academy of Arts and Letters similar to that in France. Initially, the response of the Generation of 1898 was positive, and the Academy was in fact formed, if only in theory. Eduardo Betoret-Paris has observed in an article published in *Hispania* that "not only [was] there a lot in common between the concerns of Blasco [Ibanez] and those of the most distinguished components of the Generation of 1898, but these members also [accepted] Blasco [Ibanez]'s leadership in these enterprises, perhaps because they [knew] that Blasco [Ibanez did] not suffer from the so often referred to *abulia* (apathy)," a common symptom experienced by these writers.

If in his thesis novels Blasco Ibanez was primarily concerned with criticizing contemporary society, in most of his subsequent novels his goal was quite different: he conceived a monumental work of several volumes in which he would present to the world an account of Spain's glorious past, focusing on figures and events that were not well known. This phase of historical vindication might well have represented a desire on Blasco Ibanez's part to balance the negative image of Spain elaborated in his previous novels. On the other hand, the historical framework also allowed him to incorporate his life experiences outside of Spain, especially since many of the themes he treated dealt with voyages, conquest, and discovery. Blasco Ibanez had traveled extensively, giving speeches wherever he went, often about Spain. In many ways he himself was both the Columbus protagonist of *En busca del Gran Kan* (*Unknown Lands: The Story of Columbus,* 1929) and the character Alonso de Ojeda, one of Columbus's ship commanders during his second voyage to the Americas, in *El caballero de la Virgen* (*The Knight of the Virgin,* 1929). Like them, he was engaged in a "mission"; he was spreading Spanish culture throughout the Spanish-speaking Americas and the United States as well. Other characters presented in these works are less convincing as historical figures: the Spanish Benedict XIII, Avignon pope during the Church schism in *El papa del mar* (*The Pope of the Sea,* 1925), and the Borgias, also Spanish popes, in *A los pies de Venus (los Borgias)* (*The Borgias; or, At the Feet of Venus,* 1926).

Blasco Ibanez was at the pinnacle of his success during this later period of his life, having a sure platform and an international audience, but this position of renown ultimately proved detrimental to the artistic quality of these works. In most of these writings, his artistry gave way to a formulaic approach to literature in which he wrote to a thesis or endeavored to produce best-sellers. His later books are often marred by incongruous and extraneous elements of romance and intrigue, unrealistic descriptions, and anachronisms. Such works pleased the uncritical reader of commercial fiction but did little to enhance Blasco Ibanez's reputation in literary circles. His early, regional works, however, continue to be held in great esteem by readers throughout the world.

BIOGRAPHICAL/CRITICAL SOURCES:

BOOKS

Bell, Aubrey F. G., *Contemporary Spanish Literature,* Knopf (New York City), 1925.

Blanco Aguinaga, Carlos, and others, *Historia social de la literatura espanola,* Castalia, 1978.

Bosch, Rafael, *La novela espanola del siglo XX,* Volume 1, Las Americas, 1970.

Cejador y Frauca, Julio, *Historia de la lengua y literatura castellana,* Volume 9, Revista de Archivos, Biliotecas y Museos, 1918.

Day, A. Grove, and Edgar C. Knowlton, *Vicente Blasco Ibanez,* Twayne, 1972.

Eoff, Sherman H., *The Modern Spanish Novel: Comparative Essays Examining the Philosophical Impact of Science on Fiction,* New York University Press, 1961.

Landeira, Ricardo, *The Modern Spanish Novel, 1898-1936,* Twayne, 1985.

Twentieth-Century Literary Criticism, Volume 12, Gale, 1984.

PERIODICALS

Cuadernos hispanoamericanos, May, 1981.

Hispania, Volume 53, number 1, 1969; Volume 53, number 4, 1970.

BOFF, Leonardo (Genezio Darci) 1938-

PERSONAL: Born December 14, 1938, in Concordia, Santa Catarina, Brazil; son of Mansueto (a teacher) and Regina (a farmer; maiden name, Fontana) Boff. Attended the Institute Teologico Franciscano; attended the National University of Rio de Janeiro, 1959-65; attended the University of Wurzburg; attended the Catholic University of Louvain; attended Oxford University; University of Munich, Ph.D., 1972. *Politics:* "Democracy with full participation." *Religion:* Roman Catholic. *Avocational interests:* Gardening, social work, child minding.

ADDRESSES: Home—Pr. Martins Leao 12/204, Alto Vale Encantado, 20531-350 Rio de Janeiro, Brazil.

CAREER: Ordained a priest of the Franciscan order in 1964. Roman Catholic priest, Petropolis, Brazil, 1964-92; Institute Teologico Franciscano, Petropolis, professor of systematic theology, Franciscan spirituality, and theology of liberation, 1971-92; University of Rio de Janeiro, Rio de Janeiro, Brazil, professor of theology, 1992—. Adviser to Latin American Conference of religions, and National Conference of Brazilian Bishops, 1971-80. Member of editorial board for *Revista Eclesiastica Brasileira,* and member of the board of directors, Vozes publishing house, 1971-92.

AWARDS, HONORS: Paz y Justicia Award, from Barcelona; Menschenrechte in der Kirche Award from the Herbert Haag Foundation of the Federal Republics of Germany and Switzerland; Catholic Book Award, 1987, for *Passion of Christ, Passion of the World.*

WRITINGS:

O Evangelho do Cristo cosmico: A Realidade de um mito e o mito de uma realidade, Vozes (Petropolis, Brazil), 1971.

The Question of Faith in the Resurrection of Jesus, Franciscan Herald Press (Chicago, IL), 1971.

Vida Religiosa e secularizacao, Conferencia dos Religiosos do Brasil (Rio de Janeiro), 1971.

(With others) *A Oracao no mundo secular: Desafio e chance,* Vozes, 1971.

Die Kirche als Sakrament im Horizont der Welterfahrung: Versuch einer Legitimation und einer struktur-funktionalistischen Grundlegung der Kirche im Anschluss an das II. Vatikanische Konzil, Verlag Bonifacius-Druckerei (Paderborn, West Germany), 1972.

Jesus Cristo libertador: Ensaio de cristologia critica para o nosso tempo, Vozes, 1972, translated by Patrick Hughes as *Jesus Christ Liberator: A Critical Christology for Our Times,* Orbis Books (Maryknoll, NY), 1978.

A Ressurreicao de Cristo e a nossa na morte: A Dimensao antropologica da esperanca crista, Vozes, 1972.

(With others) *Credo para amamha,* Vozes, 1972.

O Destino do homem e do mundo, Vozes, 1973.

A Atualidade da experiencia de Deus, Conferencia dos Religiosos do Brasil, 1973.

Vida para alem da morte: O Futuro, a festa e a contestacao do presente, Vozes, 1974.

(With others) *Experimentar Deus hoje,* Vozes, 1974.

Minima Sacramentalia: Os Sacramentos da vida e a vida dos sacramentos, Vozes, 1975.

A Vida religiosa e a Igreja no processo de libertacao, Vozes, 1975.

Teologia desde el cautiverio, Indo American Press Service (Bogota, Colombia), 1975.

Pobreza, obediencia, realizacion personal en la vida religiosa, CLAR (Bogota, Colombia), 1975.

(With others) *A Mulher na Igreja: Presenca e acao hoje,* Vozes, 1975.

(With others) *Nosso Irmao Francisco de Assis,* Vozes, 1975.

(With others) *Quem e Jesus Cristo no Brasil,* ASTE (Sao Paulo), 1975.

Teologia da libertacao e do cativeiro, Multinova (Lisboa), 1976.

A Graca libertadora no mundo, Vozes, 1976, translated by John Drury as *Liberating Grace,* Orbis, 1979.

Paixao de Cristo—paixao do mundo: Os Fatos as interpretacoes e o significado ontem e hoje, Vozes, 1976, translated by Robert R. Barr as *Passion of Christ, Passion of the World: The Facts, Their Interpretation, and Their Meaning Yesterday and Today,* Orbis, 1987.

Encarnacao: A Humanidade e a jovialidade de nosso Deus, Vozes, 1976.

Testigos de Dios en el corazon del mundo, Instituto Teologico de Vida Religiosa (Madrid), 1977.

Eclesiogenese: As Comunidades eclesiais de base reinventam a Igreja, Vozes, 1977, translated by Barr as *Ecclesiogenesis: The Base Communities Reinvent the Church,* Orbis Books, 1986.

Que es hacer teologia desde Amreica Latina, MIEC-JECI, 1977.

A Fe na periferia do mundo, Vozes, 1978.

Via—sacra da justica, Vozes, 1978, translated by Drury as *Way of the Cross—Way of Justice,* Orbis, 1980.

(With others) *Die lateinamerikanische Befreiungstheologie,* Suhrkamp, 1978.

(With others) *Religiosita popolare e cammino di liberazione,* Edizioni Dehoniane (Bologna), 1978.

(With others) *Jesucristo: Fe y historia,* Ediciones de Cristiandad (Madrid), 1978.

(With others) *Responsabilidades eclesiales y sociales de los religiosos,* Instituto Teologico de Vida Religiosa, 1978.

(With others) *Renovacao carismatica catolica,* Vozes, 1978.

O Rosto materno de Deus: Ensaio interdisciplinar sobre o feminino e suas formas religiosas, Vozes, 1979, translated by Barr and John W. Diercksmeier as *The Maternal Face of God: The Feminine and Its Religious Expressions,* Harper (San Francisco, CA), 1987.

O Pai-nosso: A Oracao de libertacao integral, Vozes, 1979, translated by Theodore Morrow as *The Lord's Prayer: The Prayer of Integral Liberation,* Orbis, 1983.

Die Anliegen der Befreiungstheologie, Benzinger Verlag (Einsiedeln, Switzerland), 1979.

(With others) *Da libertacao: O Teologico das libertacoes socio-historicas,* Vozes, 1979.

Pueblas Herausforderung an die Franziskaner (Berichte, Dokumente, Kommentare), Missionszentrale der Franziskaner (Bonn-Badgodesberg), 1979.

(With others) *Frontiers of Theology in Latin America,* Orbis, 1979.

(With others) *Roberto Burle Marx: Homenagem a natureza,* Vozes, 1979.

Em Preparo: O Homem, o nao-homem, o homem novo: Ensaio de antropologia a partir do oprimido, Vozes, 1980.

Em Preparo: A Ave-Maria, o espirito santo e o feminino, Vozes, 1980.

O caminhar da Igreja com os oprimidos: Do Vale de lagrimas a terra prometida, CODECRI (Rio de Janeiro), 1980.

Igreja, carisma e poder, Vozes, 1981, translated by Diercksmeier as *Church: Charism and Power: Liberation Theology and the Institutional Church,* Crossroad, 1985.

Vida segundo o espirito, Vozes, 1982.

Saint Francis: A Model for Human Liberation, Crossroad, 1982.

(With Clodovis Boff) *Salvation and Liberation,* Orbis, 1984.

(With Peter Eicher) *Theologie der Befreiung im Gesprach,* Kosel-Verlag (Munich), 1985.

(With Clodovis Boff) *Bedrohte Befreiung,* Schauble Verlag (Rheinfelden, Switzerland), 1985.

Francisco de Assis: Homem do paraiso, illustrated by Porto, Vozes, 1985.

(With Clodovis Boff) *Teologia da libertacao no debate atual,* Vozes, 1985.

Como pregar a cruz hoje numa sociedade de crucificados?, Vozes, 1986.

(Editor with Virgil Elizondo and Marcus Lefebure) *The People of God Amidst the Poor,* T. & T. Clark (Edinburgh), 1986.

(Editor with Elizondo and Lefebure) *Option for the Poor: Challenge to the Rich Countries,* T. & T. Clark, 1986.

(With others) *Teologos de la liberacion hablan sobre la mujer,* Editorial Dei (San Jose, Costa Rica), 1986.

A Trindade, a sociedade e a libertacao, Vozes, 1986, translated by Paul Burns as *Trinity and Society,* Orbis, 1988.

E a Igreja se fez povo: Eclesiogenese a Igreja que nasce de fe do povo, Vozes, 1986.

(With Clodovis Boff) *Como fazer teologia da libertacao,* Vozes, 1986, translated by Burns as *Introducing Liberation Theology,* Orbis, 1987.

(With Clodovis Boff) *Liberation Theology: From Dialogue to Confrontation,* translated by Barr, Harper, 1986.

(With Bruno Kern and Andreas Muller) *Werkbuch Theologie der Befreiung: Anliegen, Streitpunkte, Personen: Materialien, und Texte,* Patmos (Dusseldorf), 1988.

(Editor with Elizondo and James Aitken Gardiner) *Convergences and Differences,* T. & T. Clark, 1988.

When Theology Listens to the Poor, translated by Barr, Harper, 1988.

Faith on the Edge: Religion and Marginalized Existence, selections from Boff's works translated by Barr, Harper, 1989.

(Editor with Elizondo) *1492-1992: The Voice of the Victims,* Trinity Press International (Philadelphia), 1990.

Nova evangelizacao: Perspectiva dos oprimidos, Vozes, 1990, translated by Barr as *New Evangelization: Good News to the Poor,* Orbis, 1991.

(With others) *Direitos humanos, direitos dos pobres,* Vozes, 1991.

(With others) *Sobre la opcion por los pobres,* Ediciones Nicarao (Managua), 1991.

America Latina: Da Conquista a nova evangelizacao, Editora Atica (Sao Paulo), 1992.

Ecologia, mundializacao, espiritualidade, a emergencia de um novo paradigma, Editora Atica, 1993, translated as *Ecology and Liberation: A New Paradigm,* Orbis, 1995.

(Editor with Elizondo) *Is There Room for Christ in Asia?,* Orbis, 1993.

The Path to Hope: Fragments from a Theologian's Journey, translated by Philip Berryman, Orbis, 1993.

(Editor with Virgil Elizando) *Poverty and Ecology,* Orbis, 1995.

Ecologia, translated by Philip Berryman and published as *Cry of the Earth, Cry of the Poor,* Orbis (Maryknoll, NY), 1997.

Contributor to *Hans Kung: Church and Faith in an Ecumenical World,* Continuum, 1993. Contributor of articles to periodicals, including *Revista Eclesiastica Brasileira, Vozes, Convergencia, Vida en Fraternidad, Nuevo Mundo, Atualizacao, Grande Sinal, Concilium, Vida Espiritual, Lumiere et Vie, Seleciones de Teologia, Mision Abierta, Relief, Encontros com a Civilizacao brasileira, Verdad y Vida, Haversack, SEDOC,* and *Puebla.*

SIDELIGHTS: A former Catholic priest, Brazilian theologian Leonardo Boff is one of the chief proponents of liberation theology, a school of thought that holds that the purpose of Christianity is to take the part of the poor and to improve their worldly condition. Alone and with others—including his brother, Clodovis—Boff has written many books on liberation theology, several of which have been translated into English. Perhaps his most controversial work is *Church: Charism and Power: Liberation Theology and the Institutional Church.* The contents of this volume had consequences for its author. Boff was officially barred from writing or public speaking by the Catholic Church for almost a year. A second disciplinary action in 1991 led to his resignation from the priesthood.

Boff was born in 1938 in Concordia, Brazil. He was ordained a priest of the Franciscan order in 1964 and continued academic study of theology, earning a doctorate from the University of Munich in 1972. He returned to Brazil to teach theology at the Institute Teologico Franciscano in Petropolis. In addition Boff became the editor of Brazil's foremost theological journal, the *Revista Eclesiastica Brasileira.* Boff's first work, *O Evangelho do Cristo cosmico: A Realidade de um mito e o mito de uma realidade,* was published in Brazil in 1971. He attracted attention in the English-speaking world with *Jesus Christ Liberator: A Critical Christology for Our Times,* first published in Brazil in 1972, then translated to English in 1978. In this volume Boff applied liberation theology to the theological subgenre of Christology. *Teilhard*

Review contributor Anthony Dyson hailed *Jesus Christ Liberator* as a "theological and human challenge to the affluent, complacent, and de facto domineering parts of the world to undergo a massive personal and corporate act of repentance and reorientation."

Boff became widely known, however, with *Church: Charism and Power.* Most works of liberation theology owe at least a small debt to Marxism, but in *Church: Charism and Power,* Boff used Marxism to critique the hierarchy of the Catholic Church, putting forth the idea that the Church controlled divine grace in the same manner that capitalists controlled the means of production. Church officials were notably displeased with Boff's assertions. In 1984 he was called to the Vatican to discuss the book with Joseph Cardinal Ratzinger, head of the Church's Sacred Congregation. After a lengthy interview the Vatican continued to condemn the ideas expressed in *Church: Charism and Power* while Boff refused to recant. According to the *Washington Post,* Cardinal Ratzinger found that the book showed "a profound misunderstanding of the Catholic faith as regards the church of God in the world" and declared that "to interpret the reality of the sacraments, of the hierarchy, of the word and of all the life of the church in terms of production and consumption, of monopoly, expropriation, of conflict with the ruling block . . . is equal to a subversion of religious reality."

The controversy surrounding Boff brought his ideas even wider exposure. He was invited to speak in many places, including the United States, but he refused to leave Brazil, where he believed the poor people needed his help and ministry. At about the same time that the Catholic Church decreed Boff was to refrain from publishing and lecturing for an indefinite period, *Church: Charism and Power* saw print in an English-language edition. Peter Hebblethwaite, critiquing the volume in the *Times Literary Supplement,* observed that it "is difficult for a reviewer to ignore the silencing of Boff and to treat the book as what it really is: a useful but unremarkable contribution to post-conciliar ecclesiology." Marianne Sawicki in the *Los Angeles Times Book Review* asserted that *Church: Charism and Power* mainly dealt with conditions between the Brazilian poor and the Church as it was manifested in that country, and that therefore it might seem strange to readers in the United States. Nevertheless, she praised Boff's effort as "a gold mine of information," and explained that the theologian "describes the Latin American grass-roots movement to reorganize the church" and "explores the theoretical foundations of liberation theology itself."

Boff accepted the Catholic Church's decree of silence, and, in response, church officials seemed to soften both toward Boff and toward liberation theology in general. The Church lifted the silence it had imposed on the priest earlier than was expected. At about the same time the Sacred Congregation issued a new document, that, while continuing to warn of the dangers of Marxism, praised the grass-roots movements within the church that Boff had long advocated.

In addition to economic theories involving redistribution of wealth, liberation theology embraces other modern ideas in conflict with the more conservative leadership of the Catholic Church, such as greater equality for women. One of Boff's works, *The Maternal Face of God: The Feminine and Its Religious Expressions,* wrestled with this issue and saw English-language publication in 1987. A long-time advocate of the ordination of women as priests, Boff "looks back over the long centuries in which women have been silenced in the Church, and he feels uncomfortable and embarrassed," according to Monica Furlong, reviewing *The Maternal Face of God* in the *Times Literary Supplement.* "He also explicitly rejects the Augustinian view that only in the male is human nature fully realized, with its corollary that realization for the female is only a function of her relation to the male." Furlong faulted Boff, however, for pointing to the Virgin Mary as an ideal for women, concluding that "the image of femininity as one of unremitting self-sacrifice has often been a crippling one."

Boff again elicited the displeasure of Church officials in 1991 when he published a series of articles calling for acceptance of married clergy. When his next manuscript was denied approval for publication by church officials, Boff resigned from the priesthood. In an open letter to his followers, published in the *National Catholic Reporter,* he wrote: "I am leaving the priestly ministry but not the church. I am leaving the Franciscan Order but not putting aside the tender and fraternal dream of St. Francis of Assisi. I continue to be and will always be a theologian in the Catholic and ecumenical mold, fighting with the poor against their poverty and in favor of their liberation."

BIOGRAPHICAL/CRITICAL SOURCES:

BOOKS

Nordstokke, Kjell, *Council and Context in Leonardo Boff's Ecclesiology: The Rebirth of the Church*

Among the Poor, E. Mellen Press (Lewiston, NY), 1996.

PERIODICALS

Los Angeles Times Book Review, May 5, 1985, p. 6.
National Catholic Reporter, July 17, 1992, p. 12.
Publishers Weekly, August 14, 1987, p. 73.
Teilhard Review, summer, 1980.
Times Literary Supplement, September 6, 1985, p. 986; November 6, 1987, p. 1232.
Washington Post, March 30, 1985.*

* * *

BONALD, Jose Manuel Caballero 1926-

PERSONAL: Born November 11, 1926, in Jerez e la Frontera, Spain; son of Placido Caballero and Julia de Bonald; married Maria Josefa Rramis Cabot, January, 1960; children: Rafael, Jose Manuel, Miguel, Maria Julia, Alejandro.

ADDRESSES: Agent—c/o Plaza y Janes, Enrique Granados 86-88, 08008 Barcelona, Spain.

CAREER: Universidad Nacional, Bogota, Colombia, professor of Spanish literature, c. 1960; Royal Academy, worked in lexicography, c. 1975; record producer in 1970s; writer.

MEMBER: PEN (Spain; president, 1977-80).

AWARDS, HONORS: Boscan Poetry Prize, and Critica, 1960, both for *Las horas muerta;* Critica, 1969, for *Archivo del cante flamenco,* and 1978, for *Descredito del heroe;* Ateneo de Sevilla, 1981, for *Toda la noche oyeron pasar los pajaros;* Premio Internacional de Novela Plaza y Janes, 1988, for *En la casa del padre.*

WRITINGS:

IN ENGLISH TRANSLATION

El Baile Andaluz, Editorial Noguer (Barcelona), 1957, translation by Charles David Ley published as *Andalusian Dances* (poetry), Noguer, 1957.
Cadiz, Jerez, and Los Puertos (travel), translated by Doireann MacDermott, Noguer, 1963.
Botero, the Bullfight, translated by Jan Foley, with photography by Dirk Reinartz, Rizzoli (New York City), 1990.

Espana, Fiestas y Ritos, photography by Cristina Garcia Rodero, Lunwerg (Barcelona), 1992, translation published as *Festivals and Rituals of Spain,* edited by Wayne Finkel, Abrams (New York City), 1994.

OTHER

Las adivinaciones (poetry; title means "The Prophecies"), Rialp/Adonais (Madrid, Spain), 1952.
Memorias de poco tiempo (poetry; title means "Small-Time Memories"), Cultura hispanica (Madrid), 1954.
Anteo (poetry; title means "Spectacle"), Papeles de Son Armadans (Palma de Mallorca, Spain), 1956.
Isabel Santalo, o "La moral construida," Ateneo (Madrid), 1958.
(Translator) Michel Butor, *El empleo del tiempo,* Seix Barral (Barcelona), 1958.
Las horas muertas (poetry; title means "The Dead Hours"), Instituto de estudios Hispanicos (Barcelona, Spain), 1959.
El papel del coro (poetry; title means "The Paper of the Heart"), Mito (Bogota, Colombia), 1961.
Dos dias de setiembre (novel; title means "Two Days in September"), Seix Barral, 1962.
Pliegos de cordel (poetry; title means "Sheets of String"), Literaturasa/Colliure (Barcelona), 1963.
(Author of introduction) Jose Ortega, *Les moissonneurs: Dessins et temperas,* Ebro/Libraire du Globe (Paris, France), 1966.
Lo que sabemos del vino, Gregorio Del Toro (Madrid), 1967.
(Editor) *Narrativa cubana de la Revolucion* (anthology; title means "The Cuban Story of the Revolution"), Alianza (Madrid), 1968.
Vivir para contarlo (poetry; title means "To Live to Tell about It"), Seix Barral, 1969.
(Editor with Darie Novaceanu) *Antologia de la piesia rumana contemporanea* (title means "Anthology of Contemporary Rumanian Poetry"), Jucar (Barcelona), 1972.
Agata, ojo de gato (novel; title means "Agata, Eye of the Cat"), Barral (Barcelona), 1974.
Luces y sombras del flamenco, Lumen (Barcelona), 1975.
Cuixart, Rauela (Madrid), 1977.
Descredito del heroe (poetry; title means "Discrediting of the Hero"), Lumen, 1977.
Abre el ojo (play; title means "Open Your Eyes;" adapted from Rojas Zorrilla's play), produced in 1978.
Poesia, 1951-1977 (poetry), Plaza y Janes (Barcelona), 1979.

Dos Dias de Setiembre, Editorial A. Vergara (Barcelona), 1979.

Breviario del vino (title means "Wildness of the Winds"), Esteban (Madrid), 1980.

Toda la noche oyeron pasar pajaros (novel; title means "All Night They Watch the Birds Fly"), Planeta (Barcelona), 1981.

(Author of introduction) Luis de Gongora, *Poesia: Soledades, Fabula de Polifemo y Galatea, Panegirico al Duque de Lerma y Otros Poemas,* Taurus (Madrid), 1981.

(Editor) *Luis de Gongora: Poesia,* Taurus (Madrid), 1982.

Seleccion natural (title means "Natural Selection"), Catedra (Madrid), 1983.

El laberinto de fortuna (title means "The Labyrinth of Fortune"), Laia (Barcelona), 1984.

(Author of introductory essay) Alfonso Gross, *El capirote,* Espasa-Calpe (Madrid), 1984.

Los personajes de Fajardo, Cabildo Insular de Tenerife (Santa Cruz de Tenerife, Spain), 1986.

En las casa del padre (novel; title means "In the House of the Father"), Plaza y Janes, 1988.

Luces y Sombra del Flamenco, Algaida (Seville), 1988.

Doble Vida: Antologia Poetica, prologue by Pere Gimferrer, Alianza Editorial (Madrid), 1989.

Sevilla en Tiempos de Cervantes, Planeta (Barcelona), 1991.

Campo de Agramante, Editorial Anagrama (Barcelona), 1992.

Tiempo de Guerras Perdidas: La Novela de la Memoria, I, Editorial Anagrama (Barcelona), 1995.

El Imposible Oficio de Escribir: Antologia, Prensa Universitaria (Barcelona), 1997.

Diario de Argonida, Tusquets (Barcelona), 1997.

Copias del Natural, Alfaguara (Madrid), 1999.

Also contributor to periodicals, including *Mito, Papeles de Son Armadans,* and *Poesia de Espana.* Contributor to *Archivo del cante flamenco* (recordings), six volumes, edited by Ariola-Vergara, 1969. Literary editor of *Ediciones Jucar* in 1970s.

SIDELIGHTS: Jose Manuel Caballero Bonald is a versatile, prolific writer whose works are typified by the union of expression and experience. Bonald was born in 1926 in Spain, and he was only nine years old when the nation erupted into civil war, a conflict that would later influence his writings. Maria del Carmen Caballero reflected in the *Dictionary of Literary Biography* that in "some of his works, the ones in which he turns to his childhood, one sees the uncertainty, the anxiety to comprehend war seen through the eyes

of a child, to absorb the wartime visions of a boy who could take no other part than that of a mute, fascinated witness." Bonald began writing poems in the late 1940s, when he was in his early twenties, and he published his first verse collection, *Las adivinaciones,* when he was twenty six years old. This often-autobiographical volume reveals Bonald's interest in linguistic form and his appreciation for other poets. As Caballero reported, "A curiosity for examining the language, due to his readings of the modernist, symbolist, surrealist, and baroque poets, made . . . *Las adivinaciones* . . . somewhat a product of all those readings, especially the baroque."

Bonald's next two poetry collections, *Memorias de poco tiempo* and *Anteo,* include autobiographical evocations of childhood. *Anteo* also serves as evidence of Bonald's continued exploration of linguistic experimentation and his search for a means of expression that precisely indicates the quality of his recollected experiences. The remainder of the 1950s proved a particularly fruitful period for Bonald. Notable among his works from this time are *Andalusian Dances,* which appeared in 1957 in multiple translations, and *Las horas muertas,* a prize-winning collection in which he maintains his radical approach to language but also enters into the social and political aspects of actions and experiences.

In 1962, while teaching Spanish literature at the Universidad Nacional in Bogota, Colombia, Bonald produced his first novel, *Dos dias de septiembre.* Caballero wrote in the *Dictionary of Literary Biography* that in this tale Bonald "wields daring descriptions and accurate literary techniques through a rich and innovative vocabulary." She added that in the novel "one finds human authenticity in an objective and smooth narration." Bonald followed *Dos dias de septiembre* with *Pliegos de cordel,* a verse volume constituting a relatively objective psychological self-portrait. He then produced *Cadiz, Jerez, and Los Puertos,* which serves as both a geographical and a historical/culture guidebook. Among his other achievements from this decade is the editing of *Narrativa cubana de la Revolucion,* a formidable anthology of post-revolution Cuban literature. In addition, Bonaldo organized the flamenco music compiled by Ariola-Vergara in the six-disc compilation *Archivo de cante flamenco.* In the 1970s Bonald continued to write prolifically, but he also traveled extensively. He produced another novel, *Agata, ojo de gato,* which depicts the colonization of a territory in Spain, and the masterful verse volume *Descredito del heroe,* wherein he advocates greater moral accountability and constructiveness, and he participated in literary functions in the Netherlands and Rumania.

Bonald continued to publish impressive works in the ensuing years. He completed the novels *Toda la noche oyeron pasar los pajaros,* which received the Ateneo de Sevilla, and *En la casa del padre,* which earned the Premio Internacional de Novela Plaza y Janes, produced an edition of Luis de Gongora's poetry, and issued the key poetry collection, *El laberinto de fortuna,* which Caballero acknowledged in the *Dictionary of Literary Biography* as a volume "opening new dimensions." She observed: "With every poem, Bonald entangles the expressive techniques of an articulated language with an unusual rhythmic structure, investing it with the power of a new style of poetic prose."

According to Caballero, Bonald's synthesis of life and art has resulted in writings "that have erased the boundaries among the man, the poet, the novelist." She added: "His art is a consequence of living, an art that pleases the artist in its process, the essential equilibrium of artistic elaboration being enjoyable and being later shared by the reader. Thus, his work is doubtless the result of his joy of life."

BIOGRAPHICAL/CRITICAL SOURCES:

BOOKS

Dictionary of Literary Biography, Volume 108: *Twentieth-Century Spanish Poets, First Series,* Gale (Detroit, MI), 1991.

PERIODICALS

Ateneo, May, 1955.
Espectador, April, 1980.
Insula, April, 1978.
Pueblo, June 8, 1978.
World Literature Today, July, 1978.*

*   *   *

BORGES, Jorge Luis 1899-1986
(Francisco Bustos, H. Bustos Domecq, B. Lynch Davis, B. Suarez Lynch)

PERSONAL: Born August 24, 1899, in Buenos Aires, Argentina; died of liver cancer, June 14, 1986, Geneva, Switzerland; buried in Plainpalais, Geneva, Switzerland; son of Jorge Guillermo Borges (a lawyer, teacher, and writer) and Leonor Acevedo Suarez (a translator); married Elsa Astete Millan, September 21, 1967 (divorced, 1970); married Maria Kodama, April 26, 1986. *Education:* Attended College Calvin, Geneva, Switzerland, 1914-18; also studied in Cambridge, England and Buenos Aires, Argentina.

CAREER: Writer. Miguel Cane branch library, Buenos Aires, Argentina, municipal librarian, 1937-46; teacher of English literature at several private institutions and lecturer in Argentina and Uruguay, 1946-55; National Library, Buenos Aires, director, 1955-73; University of Buenos Aires, Buenos Aires, professor of English and U.S. literature, beginning in 1956. Visiting professor or guest lecturer at numerous universities in the United States and throughout the world, including University of Texas, 1961-62, University of Oklahoma, 1969, University of New Hampshire, 1972, and Dickinson College, 1983; Charles Eliot Norton Professor of Poetry, Harvard University, 1967-68.

MEMBER: Argentine Academy of Letters, Argentine Writers Society (president, 1950-53), Modern Language Association of America (honorary fellow, 1961-86), American Association of Teachers of Spanish and Portuguese (honorary fellow, 1965-86).

AWARDS, HONORS: Buenos Aires Municipal Literary Prize, 1928, for *El idioma de los argentinos;* Gran Premio de Honor, Argentine Writers Society, 1945, for *Ficciones, 1935-1944;* Gran Premio Nacional de la Literatura (Argentina), 1957, for *El Aleph;* Premio de Honor and Prix Formentor, International Congress of Publishers (shared with Samuel Beckett), 1961; Commandeur de l'Ordre des Lettres et des Arts (France), 1962; Fondo de les Artes, 1963; Ingram Merrill Foundation Award, 1966; Matarazzo Sobrinho Inter-American Literary Prize, Bienal Foundation, 1970; nominated for Neustadt International Prize for Literature, *World Literature Today* and University of Oklahoma, 1970, 1984, and 1986; Jerusalem Prize, 1971; Alfonso Reyes Prize (Mexico), 1973; Gran Cruz del Orden al merito Bernando O'Higgins, Government of Chile, 1976; Gold Medal, French Academy, Order of Merit, Federal Republic of Germany, and Icelandic Falcon Cross, all 1979; Miguel de Cervantes Award (Spain) and Balzan Prize (Italy), both 1980; Ollin Yoliztli Prize (Mexico), 1981; T. S. Eliot Award for Creative Writing, Ingersoll Foundation and Rockford Institute, 1983; Gold Medal of Menendez Pelayo University (Spain), La Gran Cruz de la Orden Alfonso X, el Sabio (Spain), and Legion d'Honneur (France), all

1983; Knight of the British Empire. Recipient of honorary degrees from numerous colleges and universities, including University of Cuyo (Argentina), 1956, University of the Andes (Colombia), 1963, Oxford University, 1970, University of Jerusalem, 1971, Columbia University, 1971, and Michigan State University, 1972.

WRITINGS:

POETRY

Fervor de Buenos Aires (title means "Passion for Buenos Aires"), Serantes (Buenos Aires), 1923, revised edition, Emece, 1969.

Luna de enfrente (title means "Moon across the Way"), Proa (Buenos Aires), 1925.

Cuaderno San Martin (title means "San Martin Copybook"), Proa, 1929.

Poemas, 1923-1943, Losada, 1943, 3rd enlarged edition published as *Obra poetica, 1923-1964,* 1964, translation published as *Selected Poems, 1923-1967* (bilingual edition; also includes prose), edited, with an introduction and notes, by Norman Thomas di Giovanni, Delacorte (New York City), 1972.

Seis poemas escandinavos (title means "Six Scandinavian Poems"), privately printed, 1966.

Siete poemas (title means "Seven Poems"), privately printed, 1967.

El otro, el mismo (title means "The Other, the Same"), Emece, 1969.

Elogio de la sombra, Emece, 1969, translation by di Giovanni published as *In Praise of Darkness* (bilingual edition), Dutton, 1974.

El oro de los tigres (also see below; title means "The Gold of Tigers"), Emece, 1972.

Siete poemas sajones/Seven Saxon Poems, Plain Wrapper Press, 1974.

La rosa profunda (also see below; title means "The Unending Rose"), Emece, 1975.

La moneda de hierro (title means "The Iron Coin"), Emece, 1976.

Historia de la noche (title means "History of Night"), Emece, 1977.

The Gold of Tigers: Selected Later Poems (contains translations of *El oro de los tigres* and *La rosa profunda*), translated by Alastair Reid, Dutton, 1977.

La cifra, Emece, 1981.

Also author of *Los conjurados* (title means "The Conspirators"), 1985.

ESSAYS

Inquisiciones (title means "Inquisitions"), Proa, 1925.

El tamano de mi esperanza (title means "The Measure of My Hope"), Proa, 1926.

El idioma de los argentinos (title means "The Language of the Argentines"), M. Gleizer (Buenos Aires), 1928, 3rd edition (includes three essays by Borges and three by Jose Edmundo Clemente), Emece, 1968.

Figari, privately printed, 1930.

Las Kennigar, Colombo (Buenos Aires), 1933.

Historia de la eternidad (title means "History of Eternity"), Viau y Zona (Buenos Aires), 1936, revised edition published as *Obras completas,* Volume 1, Emece, 1953.

Nueva refutacion del tiempo (title means "New Refutation of Time"), Oportet y Haereses, 1947.

Aspectos de la literatura gauchesca, Numero (Montevideo), 1950.

(With Delia Ingenieros) *Antiguas literaturas germanicas,* Fondo de Cultura Economica (Mexico), 1951, revised edition with Maria Esther Vazquez published as *Literaturas germanicas medievales,* Falbo, 1966.

Otras inquisiciones, Sur (Buenos Aires), 1952, published as *Obras completas,* Volume 8, Emece, 1960, translation by Ruth L. C. Simms published as *Other Inquisitions, 1937-1952,* University of Texas Press, 1964.

(With Margarita Guerrero) *El "Martin Fierro,"* Columba, 1953.

(With Bettina Edelberg) *Leopoldo Lugones,* Troquel (Buenos Aires), 1955.

(With Guerrero) *Manual de zoologia fantastica,* Fondo de Cultura Economica, 1957, translation published as *The Imaginary Zoo,* University of California Press, 1969, revised Spanish edition published as *El libro de los seres imaginarios,* Kier (Buenos Aires), 1967, translation and revision by di Giovanni and Borges published as *The Book of Imaginary Beings,* Dutton, 1969.

La poesia gauchesca (title means *Gaucho Poetry*), Centro de Estudios Brasileiros, 1960.

(With Vazquez) *Introduccion a la literatura inglesa,* Columba, 1965, translation by L. Clark Keating and Robert O. Evans published as *An Introduction to English Literature,* University Press of Kentucky, 1974.

(With Esther Zemborain de Torres) *Introduccion a la literatura norteamericana,* Columba, 1967, translation by Keating and Evans published as *An Introduction to American Literature,* University of Kentucky Press, 1971.

(With Alicia Jurado) *Que es el budismo?* (title means "What Is Buddhism?"), Columba, 1976.

Nuevos ensayos dantescos (title means "New Dante Essays"), Espasa-Calpe, 1982.

SHORT STORIES

Historia universal de la infamia, Tor (Buenos Aires), 1935, revised edition published as *Obras completas,* Volume 3, Emece, 1964, translation by di Giovanni published as *A Universal History of Infamy,* Dutton, 1972.

El jardin de senderos que se bifurcan (also see below; title means *Garden of the Forking Paths*), Sur, 1941.

(With Adolfo Bioy Casares, under joint pseudonym H. Bustos Domecq) *Seis problemas para Isidro Parodi,* Sur, 1942, translation by di Giovanni published under authors' real names as *Six Problems for Don Isidro Parodi,* Dutton, 1983.

Ficciones, 1935-1944 (includes *El jardin de senderos que se bifurcan*), Sur, 1944, revised edition published as *Obras completas,* Volume 5, Emece, 1956, with English introduction and notes by Gordon Brotherson and Peter Hulme, Harrap, 1976, translation by Anthony Kerrigan and others published as *Ficciones,* edited and with an introduction by Kerrigan, Grove, 1962, published in England as *Fictions,* John Calder, 1965.

(With Bioy Casares, under joint pseudonym H. Bustos Domecq) *Dos fantasias memorables,* Oportet & Haereses, 1946, reprinted under authors' real names with notes and bibliography by Horacio Jorge Becco, Edicom (Buenos Aires), 1971.

El Aleph, Losada, 1949, revised edition, 1952, published as *Obras completas,* Volume 7, Emece, 1956, translation and revision by di Giovanni in collaboration with Borges published as *The Aleph and Other Stories, 1933-1969,* Dutton, 1970.

(With Luisa Mercedes Levinson) *La hermana de Eloisa* (title means "Eloisa's Sister"), Ene (Buenos Aires), 1955.

(With Bioy Casares) *Cronicas de Bustos Domecq,* Losada, 1967, translation by di Giovanni published as *Chronicles of Bustos Domecq,* Dutton, 1976.

El informe de Brodie, Emece, 1970, translation by di Giovanni in collaboration with Borges published as *Dr. Brodie's Report,* Dutton, 1971.

El matrero, Edicom, 1970.

El congreso, El Archibrazo, 1971, translation by di Giovanni in collaboration with Borges published as *The Congress* (also see below), Enitharmon Press, 1974, translation by Alberto Manguel pub-

lished as *The Congress of the World,* F. M. Ricci (Milan), 1981.

El libro de arena, Emece, 1975, translation by di Giovanni published with *The Congress* as *The Book of Sand,* Dutton, 1977.

(With Bioy Casares) *Nuevos cuentos de Bustos Domecq,* Libreria de la Cuidad, 1977.

Rosa y azul (contains *La rosa de Paracelso* and *Tigres azules*), Sedmay (Madrid), 1977.

Veinticinco agosto 1983 y otros cuentos de Jorges Luis Borges (includes interview with Borges), Siruela, 1983.

OMNIBUS VOLUMES

La muerte y la brujula (stories; title means "Death and the Compass"), Emece, 1951.

Obras completas, ten volumes, Emece, 1953-67, in one volume, 1974.

Cuentos (title means "Stories"), Monticello College Press, 1958.

Antologia personal (prose and poetry), Sur, 1961, translation published as *A Personal Anthology,* edited and with foreword by Kerrigan, Grove Press, 1967.

Labyrinths: Selected Stories and Other Writings, edited by Donald A. Yates and James E. Irby, preface by Andre Maurois, New Directions, 1962, augmented edition, 1964.

Nueva antologia personal, Emece, 1968.

Prologos (title means "Prologues"), Torres Aguero (Buenos Aires), 1975.

(With others) *Obras completas en colaboracion* (title means "Complete Works in Collaboration"), Emece, 1979.

Narraciones (stories), edited by Marcos Ricardo Bamatan, Catedra, 1980.

Borges: A Reader (prose and poetry), edited by Emir Rodriguez Monegal and Reid, Dutton, 1981.

Ficcionario: Una antologia de sus textos, edited by Rodriguez Monegal, Fondo de Cultura Economica, 1985.

Textos cautivos: Ensayos y resenas en 'El Hogar'[1936-1939] (title means "Captured Texts: Essays and Reviews in 'El Hogar'"), edited by Rodriguez Monegal and Enrique Sacerio-Gari, Tusquets, 1986.

El aleph borgiano, edited by Juan Gustavo Cobo Borda and Martha Kovasics de Cubides, Biblioteca Luis-Angel Arango (Bogota), 1987.

Biblioteca personal: Prologos, Alianza, 1988.

Collected Fictions, edited and translated by Andrew Hurley, Viking Press, 1998.

OTHER

(Author of afterword) Ildefonso Pereda Valdes, *Antologia de la moderna poesia uruguaya,* El Ateneo (Buenos Aires), 1927.

Evaristo Carriego (biography), M. Gleizer (Buenos Aires), 1930, revised edition published as *Obras completas,* Volume 4, Emece (Buenos Aires), 1955, translation by di Giovanni published as *Evaristo Carriego: A Book about Old-Time Buenos Aires,* Dutton, 1984.

(Translator) Virginia Woolf, *Orlando,* Sur, 1937.

(Editor with Pedro Henriquez Urena) *Antologia clasica de la literatura argentina* (title means "Anthology of Argentine Literature"), Kapelusz (Buenos Aires), 1937.

(Translator and author of prologue) Franz Kafka, *La metamorfosis,* [Buenos Aires], 1938.

(Editor with Bioy Casares and Silvina Ocampo) *Antologia de la literatura fantastica* (title means "Anthology of Fantastic Literature"), with foreword by Bioy Casares, Sudamericana, 1940, enlarged edition with postscript by Bioy Casares, 1965, translation of revised version published as *The Book of Fantasy,* with introduction by Ursula K. Le Guin, Viking (New York City), 1988.

(Author of prologue) Bioy Casares, *La invencion de Morel,* Losada, 1940, translation by Simms published as *The Invention of Morel and Other Stories,* University of Texas Press, 1964.

(Editor with Bioy Casares and Ocampo and author of prologue) *Antologia poetica argentina* (title means "Anthology of Argentine Poetry"), Sudamericana, 1941.

(Translator) Henri Michaux, *Un barbaro en Asia,* Sur, 1941.

(Compiler and translator with Bioy Casares) *Los mejores cuentos policiales* (title means "The Best Detective Stories"), Emece, 1943.

(Translator and author of prologue) Herman Melville, *Bartleby, el escribiente,* Emece, 1943.

(Editor with Silvina Bullrich) *El compadrito: Su destino, sus barrios, su musica* (title means "The Buenos Aires Hoodlum: His Destiny, His Neighborhoods, His Music"), Emece, 1945, 2nd edition, Fabril, 1968.

(With Bioy Casares, under joint pseudonym B. Suarez Lynch) *Un modelo para la muerte* (novel; title means "A Model for Death"), Oportet & Haereses, 1946.

(Compiler and translator with Bioy Casares) *Los mejores cuentos policiales: Segunda serie,* Emece, 1951.

(Editor and translator with Bioy Casares) *Cuentos breves y extraordinarios: Antologia,* Raigal (Buenos Aires), 1955, revised and enlarged edition, Losada, 1973, translation by Kerrigan published as *Extraordinary Tales,* Souvenir Press, 1973.

(With Bioy Casares) *Los orilleros* [and] *El paraiso de los creyentes* (screenplays; titles mean "The Hoodlums" and "The Believers' Paradise"; *Los orilleros* produced by Argentine director Ricardo Luna, 1975), Losada, 1955.

(Editor and author of prologue, notes, and glossary with Bioy Casares) *Poesia gauchesca* (title means "Gaucho Poetry"), two volumes, Fondo de Cultura Economica, 1955.

(Translator) William Faulkner, *Las palmeras salvajes,* Sudamericana, 1956.

(Editor with Bioy Casares) *Libro del cielo y del infierno* (anthology; title means Book of "Heaven and Hell"), Sur, 1960.

El hacedor (prose and poetry; Volume 9 of *Obras completas;* title means "The Maker"), Emece, 1960, translation by Mildred Boyer and Harold Morland published as *Dreamtigers,* University of Texas Press, 1964.

(Editor and author of prologue) *Macedonio Fernandez,* Culturales Argentinas, Ministerio de Educacion y Justicia, 1961.

Para las seis cuerdas: Milongas (song lyrics; title means "For the Six Strings: Milongas"), Emece, 1965.

Dialogo con Borges, edited by Victoria Ocampo, Sur, 1969.

(Translator, editor, and author of prologue) Walt Whitman, *Hojas de hierba,* Juarez (Buenos Aires), 1969.

(Compiler and author of prologue) Evaristo Carriego, *Versos,* Universitaria de Buenos Aires, 1972.

Borges on Writing (lectures), edited by di Giovanni, Daniel Halpern, and Frank MacShane, Dutton, 1973.

(With Bioy Casares and Hugo Santiago) *Les Autres: Escenario original* (screenplay; produced in France and directed by Santiago, 1974), C. Bourgois (Paris), 1974.

(Author of prologue) Carlos Zubillaga, *Carlos Gardel,* Jucar (Madrid), 1976.

Cosmogonias, Libreria de la Ciudad, 1976.

Libro de suenos (transcripts of Borges's and others'dreams; title means "Book of Dreams"), Torres Aguero, 1976.

(Author of prologue) Santiago Dabove, *La muerte y su traje,* Calicanto, 1976.

Borges-Imagenes, memorias, dialogos, edited by Vazquez, Monte Avila, 1977.

Adrogue (prose and poetry), privately printed, 1977.

(Editor with Maria Kodoma) *Breve antologia anglo-sajona,* Emece, 1979.

Borges oral (lectures), edited by Martin Mueller, Emece, 1979.

Siete noches (lectures), Fondo de Cultura Economica, 1980, translation by Weinberger published as *Seven Nights,* New Directions (New York City), 1984.

(Compiler) Paul Groussac, *Jorge Luis Borges selecciona lo mejor de Paul Groussac,* Fraterna (Buenos Aires), 1981.

(Compiler and author of prologue) Francisco de Quevedo, *Antologia poetica,* Alianza, 1982.

(Compiler and author of introduction) Leopoldo Lugones, *Antologia poetica,* Alianza, 1982.

(Compiler and author of prologue) Pedro Antonio de Alarcon, *El amigo de la muerte,* Siruela (Madrid), 1984.

(With Maria Kodama) *Atlas* (prose and poetry), Sudamericana, 1984, translation by Kerrigan published as *Atlas,* Dutton, 1985.

En voz de Borges (interviews), Offset, 1986.

Libro de dialogos (interviews), edited by Osvaldo Ferrari, Sudamericana, 1986, published as *Dialogos ultimos,* 1987.

(Editor with James F. Lawrence), *Testimony to the Invisible: Essays on Swedenborg,* Chrysalis Books (West Chester, PA), 1995.

Editor, with Bioy Casares, of series of detective novels, "The Seventh Circle," for Emece, 1943-56. Contributor, under pseudonym F. Bustos, to *Critica* (Buenos Aires), 1933. Contributor, with Bioy Casares, under joint pseudonym B. Lynch Davis, to *Los anales de Buenos Aires,* 1946-48. Founding editor of *Prisma* (mural magazine), 1921; founding editor of *Proa* (Buenos Aires literary revue), 1921 and, with Ricardo Guiraldes and Pablo Rojas Paz, 1924-26; literary editor of weekly arts supplement of *Critica,* beginning 1933; editor of biweekly "Foreign Books and Authors" section of *El Hogar* (magazine), 1936-39; co-editor, with Bioy Casares, of *Destiempo* (literary magazine), 1936; editor of *Los anales de Buenos Aires* (literary journal), 1946-48.

ADAPTATIONS: "Emma Zunz," a short story, was made into the movie *Dias de odio (Days of Wrath)* by Argentine director Leopoldo Torre Nilsson, 1954, a French television movie directed by Alain Magrou, 1969, and a film called *Splits* by U.S. director Leonard Katz, 1978; "Hombre de la esquina rosada," a short story, was made into an Argentine movie of the same title directed by Rene Mugica, 1961; Bernardo Bertolucci based his *La strategia de la ragna (The Spider's Stratagem),* a movie made for Italian televi-

sion, on Borges's short story, "El tema del traidor y del heroe," 1970; Hector Olivera, in collaboration with Juan Carlos Onetti, adapted Borges's story "El muerto" for the Argentine movie of the same name, 1975; Borges's short story "La intrusa" was made into a Brazilian film directed by Carlos Hugo Christensen, 1978; three of the stories in *Six Problems for Don Isidro Parodi* were dramatized for radio broadcast by the British Broadcasting Corporation.

SIDELIGHTS: "Jorge Luis Borges [was] a great writer," noted French author Andre Maurois in his preface to the Argentine poet, essayist, and short story writer's *Labyrinths: Selected Stories and Other Writings,* "who . . . composed only little essays or short narratives. Yet they suffice for us to call him great because of their wonderful intelligence, their wealth of invention, and their tight, almost mathematical style. Argentine by birth and temperament, but nurtured on universal literature, Borges [had] no spiritual homeland."

Borges was nearly unknown in most of the world until 1961 when, in his early sixties, he was awarded the Prix Formentor—the International Publishers Prize—an honor he shared with Irish playwright Samuel Beckett. Before winning the award, according to Gene H. Bell-Villada in *Borges and His Fiction: A Guide to His Mind and Art,* "Borges had been writing in relative obscurity in Buenos Aires, his fiction and poetry read by his compatriots, who were slow in perceiving his worth or even knowing him." The award made Borges internationally famous: a collection of his short stories, *Ficciones,* was simultaneously published in six different countries, and he was invited by the University of Texas to come to the United States to lecture, the first of many international lecture tours.

Borges's international appeal was partly a result of his enormous erudition which becomes immediately apparent to the reader in the multitude of literary allusions from cultures from around the globe contained in his writing. "The work of Jorge Luis Borges," Anthony Kerrigan wrote in his introduction to the English translation of *Ficciones,* "is a species of international literary metaphor. He knowledgeably makes a transfer of inherited meanings from Spanish and English, French and German, and sums up a series of analogies, of confrontations, of appositions in other nations' literatures. His Argentinians act out Parisian dramas, his Central European Jews are wise in the ways of the Amazon, his Babylonians are fluent in the paradigms of Babel." In *National Review* Peter

Witonski commented: "Borges' grasp of world literature is one of the fundamental elements of his art."

The familiarity with world literature evident in Borges's work was initiated at an early age, nurtured by a love of reading. His paternal grandmother was English, and, since she lived with the Borgeses, English and Spanish were spoken in the family home. Jorge Guillermo Borges, Borges's father, had a large library of English and Spanish books in which his son, whose frail constitution made it impossible to participate in more strenuous activities, spent many hours. "If I were asked to name the chief event in my life," Borges stated in "An Autobiographical Essay" which originally appeared in the *New Yorker* and was later included in *The Aleph and Other Stories, 1933-1969,* "I should say my father's library."

Under his grandmother's tutelage, Borges learned to read English before he could read Spanish. Among the first books he read were works—in English—by Twain, Poe, Longfellow, Stevenson, and Wells. In Borges's autobiographical essay he recalled reading even the great Spanish masterpiece, Cervantes's *Don Quixote,* in English before reading it in Spanish. Borges's father encouraged writing as well as reading: Borges wrote his first story at age seven, and, at nine, saw his Spanish translation of Oscar Wilde's "The Happy Prince" published in a Buenos Aires newspaper. "From the time I was a boy. . . ," Borges noted, "it was tacitly understood that I had to fulfill the literary destiny that circumstances had denied my father. This was something that was taken for granted. . . . I was expected to be a writer."

Borges became a writer whose works were compared to those of many others, Franz Kafka and James Joyce in particular, but whose style was unique. Critics were forced to coin a new word—Borgesian—to capture the magical world invented by the Argentine master. As Jaime Alazraki noted in *Jorge Luis Borges,* "As with Joyce, Kafka, or Faulkner, the name of Borges has become an accepted concept; his creations have generated a dimension that we designate' Borgesian.'" And, in *Atlantic,* Keith Botsford declared: "Borges is . . . an international phenomenon, . . . a man of letters whose mode of writing and turn of mind are so distinctively his, yet so much a revealed part of our world, that 'Borgesian' has become as commonplace a neologism as the adjectives 'Sartrean' or 'Kafkaesque.'"

U.S. writers did not escape Borges's influence. "The impact of Borges on the United States writing scene,"

commented Bell-Villada, "may be almost as great as was his earlier influence on Latin America. The Argentine reawakened for us the possibilities of far-fetched fancy, of formal exploration, of parody, intellectuality, and wit." Bell-Villada specifically noted Borges's presence in works by Robert Coover, Donald Barthelme, and John Gardner. Another important novelist, John Barth, confessed Borges's influence in his own novels. Bell-Villada concluded that Borges's work paved "the way for numerous literary trends on both American continents, determining the shape of much fiction to come. By rejecting realism and naturalism, he . . . opened up to our Northern writers a virgin field, led them to a wealth of new subjects and procedures."

The foundation of Borges's literary future was laid in 1914 when the Borgeses took an ill-timed trip to Europe. There, the outbreak of World War I stranded them temporarily in Switzerland where Borges studied French and Latin in school, taught himself German, and began reading the works of German philosophers and expressionist poets. He was also introduced to the poetry of Walt Whitman in German translation and soon began writing poetry imitative of Whitman's style. "For some time," Emir Rodriguez Monegal wrote in *Borges: A Reader,* "the young man believed Whitman was poetry itself."

After the war the Borgeses settled in Spain for a few years. During this extended stay Borges published reviews, articles, and poetry and became associated with a group of avant-garde poets called Ultraists (named after the magazine, *Ultra,* to which they contributed). Upon Borges's return to Argentina, in 1921, he introduced the tenets of the movement—they believed, for example, in the supremacy of the metaphor—to the Argentine literary scene. His first collection of poems, *Fervor de Buenos Aires,* was written under the spell of this new poetic movement. Although in his autobiographical essay he expressed regret for his "early Ultraist excesses" and in later editions of *Fervor de Buenos Aires* eliminated more than a dozen poems from the text and considerably altered many of the remaining poems, Borges still saw some value in the work. In his autobiographical essay he noted, "I think I have never strayed beyond that book. I feel that all my subsequent writing has only developed themes first taken up there; I feel that all during my lifetime I have been rewriting that one book."

One poem from the volume, "El truco" (named after a card game), for example, seems to testify to the truth of Borges's statement. In the piece he introduced two themes that appear over and over again in his later writing: circular time and the idea that all people are but one person. "The permutations of the cards," Rodriguez Monegal observed in *Jorge Luis Borges: A Literary Biography,* "although innumerable in limited human experience, are not infinite: given enough time, they will come back again and again. Thus the cardplayers not only are repeating hands that have already come up in the past. In a sense, they are repeating the former players as well: they are the former players."

Illusion is an important part of Borges's fictional world. In *Borges: The Labyrinth Maker,* Ana Maria Barrenechea called it "his resplendent world of shadows." But illusion is present in his manner of writing as well the fictional world he describes. In *World Literature Today,* William Riggan quoted Icelandic author Sigurdur Magnusson's thoughts on this aspect of Borges's work. "With the possible exception of Kafka. . . ," Magnusson stated, "no other writer that I know manages, with such relentless logic, to turn language upon itself to reverse himself time after time with a sentence or a paragraph, and effortlessly, so it seems, come upon surprising yet inevitable conclusions."

Borges expertly blended the traditional boundaries between fact and fiction and between essay and short story and he was similarly adept at obliterating the border between other genres as well. In a tribute to Borges that appeared in the *New Yorker* after the Argentine's death in 1986, Mexican poet and essayist Octavio Paz wrote: "He cultivated three genres: the essay, the poem, and the short story. The division is arbitrary. His essays read like stories, his stories are poems; and his poems make us think, as though they were essays." In *Review,* Ambrose Gordon, Jr., similarly noted, "His essays are like poems in their almost musical development of themes, his stories are remarkably like his essays, and his poems are often little stories." Borges's "Conjectural Poem," for example, is very much like a short story in that it is an account of the death of one of his ancestors, Francisco Narciso de Laprida. Another poem, "The Golem," is a short narrative relating how Rabbi Low of Prague created an artificial man.

To deal with the problem of actually determining to which genre a prose piece by Borges might belong, Martin S. Stabb proposed in *Jorge Luis Borges,* his book-length study of the author, that the usual manner of grouping all of Borges's short fiction as short sto-

ries was invalid. Stabb instead divided the Argentine's prose fiction into three categories which took into account Borges's tendency to blur genres: "'essayistic' fiction," "difficult-to-classify' intermediate' fiction," and those pieces deemed "conventional short stories." Other reviewers saw a comparable division in Borges's fiction but chose to emphasize the chronological development of his work, noting that his first stories grew out of his essays, his "middle period" stories were more realistic, while his later stories were marked by a return to fantastic themes.

"Funes the Memorious," listed in Richard Burgin's *Conversations with Jorge Luis Borges* as one of the Argentine's favorite stories, is about Ireneo Funes, a young man who cannot forget anything. His memory is so keen that he is surprised by how different he looks each time he sees himself in a mirror because, unlike the rest of us, he can see the subtle changes that have taken place in his body since the last time he saw his reflection. The story is filled with characteristic Borgesian detail. Funes's memory, for instance, becomes excessive as a result of an accidental fall from a horse. In Borges an accident is a reminder that man is unable to order his existence because the world has a hidden order of its own. Alazraki saw this Borgesian theme as "the tragic contrast between a man who believes himself to be the master and maker of his fate and a text or divine plan in which his fortune has already been written." The deliberately vague quality of the adjectives Borges typically uses in his sparse descriptive passages is also apparent: Funes's features are never clearly distinguished because he lives in a darkened room, he was thrown from his horse on a dark "rainy afternoon," and the horse itself is described as "blue-gray"—neither one color or the other. "This dominant chiaroscuro imagery," commented Bell-Villada, "is further reinforced by Funes's name, a word strongly suggestive of certain Spanish words variously meaning 'funereal,' 'ill-fated,' and 'dark.'" The ambiguity of Borges's descriptions lends a subtle, otherworldly air to this and other examples of his fiction.

In "Partial Magic in the *Quixote*" (also translated as "Partial Enchantments of the *Quixote*") Borges describes several occasions in world literature when a character reads about himself or sees himself in a play, including episodes from Shakespeare's plays, an epic poem of India, Cervantes's *Don Quixote,* and *The One Thousand and One Nights.* "Why does it disquiet us to know," Borges asked in the essay, "that Don *Quixote* is a reader of the *Quixote,* and Hamlet is a spectator of *Hamlet?* I believe I have found the answer: those inversions suggest that if the characters in a story can be readers or spectators, then we, their readers, can be fictitious."

With his analysis of this literary device Borges offered his own interpretation of what John Barth referred to in the *Atlantic* as "one of Borges' cardinal themes." Barrenechea explained Borges's technique, noting: "To readers and spectators who consider themselves real beings, these works suggest their possible existence as imaginary entities. In that context lies the key to Borges' work. Relentlessly pursued by a world that is too real and at the same time lacking meaning, he tries to free himself from its obsessions by creating a world of such coherent phantasmagorias that the reader doubts the very reality on which he leans."

For example, in one of Borges's variations on "the work within a work," Jaromir Hladik, the protagonist of Borges's story "The Secret Miracle," appears in a footnote to another of Borges's stories, "Three Versions of Judas." The note refers the reader to the "Vindication of Eternity" a work said to be written by Hladik. In this instance, Borges used a fictional work written by one of his fictional characters to lend an air of erudition to another fictional work about the works of another fictional author.

These intrusions of reality on the fictional world are characteristic of Borges's work. He also uses a device, which he calls "the contamination of reality by dream," that produces the same effect of uneasiness in the reader as "the work within the work" but through directly opposite means. Two examples of stories using this technique are "Tlon, Uqbar, Orbis Tertius" and "The Circular Ruins." The first, which Stabb included in his "difficult-to-classify' intermediate' fiction," is one of Borges's most discussed works. It tells the story, according to Barrenechea, "of an attempt of a group of men to create a world of their own until, by the sheer weight of concentration, the fantastic creation acquires consistency and some of its objects—a compass, a metallic cone—which are composed of strange matter begin to appear on earth." By the end of the story, the world as we know it is slowly turning into the invented world of Tlon. Stabb called the work "difficult-to-classify" because, he commented, "the excruciating amount of documentary detail (half real, half fictitious) . . . make[s] the piece seem more like an essay" than a short story. There are, in addition, footnotes and a postscript to the story as well as an appearance by Borges himself and references to several other well-known Latin-American literary figures, including Borges's friend, Bioy Casares.

"The Circular Ruins," which Stabb considered a "conventional short story," describes a very unconventional situation. (The story is conventional, however, in that there are no footnotes or real people intruding on the fictive nature of the piece.) In the story a man decides to dream about a son until the son becomes real. Later, after the man accomplishes his goal, much to his astonishment, he discovers that he in turn is being dreamt by someone else. "The Circular Ruins" includes several themes seen throughout Borges's work, including man's attempt to establish order in a chaotic universe, the infinite regression, the symbol of the labyrinth, and the idea of all men being one.

The futility of any attempt to order the universe, seen in "Funes the Memorious" and in "The Circular Ruins," is also found in "The Library of Babel" where, according to Alazraki, "Borges presents the world as a library of chaotic books which its librarians cannot read but which they interpret incessantly." The library was one of Borges's favorite images, often repeated in his fiction. In another work, Borges uses the image of a chessboard, however, to elaborate the same theme. In his poem "Chess," he speaks of the king, bishop, and queen who "seek out and begin their armed campaign." But, just as the dreamer dreams a man and causes him to act in a certain way, the campaign is actually being planned by someone other than the members of royalty. "They do not know it is the player's hand," the poem continues, "that dominates and guides their destiny." In the last stanza of the poem Borges uses the same images to suggest the infinite regression: "God moves the player, he in turn, the piece. / But what god beyond God begins the round / of dust and time and sleep and agonies?" Another poem, "The Golem," which tells the story of an artificial man created by a rabbi in Prague, ends in a similar fashion: "At the hour of anguish and vague light, / He would rest his eyes on his Golem. / Who can tell us what God felt, / As he gazed on His rabbi in Prague?" Just as there is a dreamer dreaming a man, and beyond that a dreamer dreaming the dreamer who dreamt the man, then, too, there must be another dreamer beyond that in an infinite succession of dreamers.

The title of the story "The Circular Ruins" suggests a labyrinth. In another story, "The Babylon Lottery," Stabb commented, "an ironically detached narrator depicts life as a labyrinth through which man wanders under the absurd illusion of having understood a cha-otic, meaningless world." Labyrinths or references to labyrinths are found in nearly all of Borges's fiction. The labyrinthine form is often present in his poems, too, especially in Borges's early poetry filled with remembrances of wandering the labyrinth-like streets of old Buenos Aires.

In *The Circular Ruins* Borges's returns to another favorite theme: circular time. This theme embraces another device mentioned by Borges as typical of fantastic literature: time travel. Borges's characters, however, do not travel through time in machines; their travel is more on a metaphysical, mythical level. Circular time—a concept also favored by Nietzsche, one of the German philosophers Borges discovered as a boy—is apparent in many of Borges's stories, including "Three Versions of Judas," "The Garden of the Forking Paths," "Tlon, Uqbar, Orbis Tertius," "The Library of Babel," and "The Immortal." It is also found in another of Borges's favorite stories, "Death and the Compass," in which the reader en-counters not only a labyrinth but a double as well. Stabb offered the story as a good example of Borges's "conventional short stories."

"Death and the Compass" is a detective story. Erik Lonnrot, the story's detective, commits the fatal error of believing there is an order in the universe that he can understand. When Marcel Yarmolinsky is mur-dered, Lonnrot refuses to believe it was just an acci-dent; he looks for clues to the murderer's identity in Yarmolinsky's library. Red Scharlach, whose brother Lonnrot had sent to jail, reads about the detective's efforts to solve the murder in the local newspaper and contrives a plot to ambush him. The plan works be-cause Lonnrot, overlooking numerous clues, blindly follows the false trail Scharlach leaves for him.

The final sentences—in which Lonnrot is murdered—change the whole meaning of the narrative, illustrate many of Borges's favorite themes, and crystalize for the reader Borges's thinking on the problem of time. Lonnrot says to Scharlach: "'I know of one Greek labyrinth which is a single straight line. Along that line so many philosophers have lost themselves that a mere detective might well do so, too. Scharlach, when in some other incarnation you hunt me, pretend to commit (or do commit) a crime at A, then a second crime at B. . . , then a third crime at C. . . . Wait for me afterwards at D. . . . Kill me at D as you now are going to kill me at Triste-le-Roy. "The next time I kill you,' said Scharlach, 'I promise you that laby-rinth, consisting of a single line which is invisible and

unceasing. 'He moved back a few steps. Then, very carefully, he fired.'"

"Death and the Compass" is in many ways a typical detective story, but this last paragraph takes the story far beyond that popular genre. Lonnrot and Scharlach are doubles (Borges gives us a clue in their names: rot means red and scharlach means scarlet in German) caught in an infinite cycle of pursuing and being pursued. "Their antithetical natures, or inverted mir-ror images," George R. McMurray observed, "are demonstrated by their roles as detective/criminal and pursuer/pursued roles that become ironically re-versed." Rodriguez Monegal concluded: "The con-cept of the eternal return . . . adds an extra dimension to the story. It changes Scharlach and Lonnrot into characters in a myth: Abel and Cain endlessly per-forming the killing."

Doubles, which Bell-Villada defined as "any blurring or any seeming multiplication of character identity," are found in many of Borges's works, including "The Waiting," "The Theologians," "The South," "The Shape of the Sword," "Three Versions of Judas," and "Story of the Warrior and the Captive." Borges's explanation of the story "The Theologians" (included in his collection, *The Aleph and Other Stories, 1933-1969*) reveals how a typical Borgesian plot involving doubles works: "In *The Theologians* you have two enemies," Borges told Burgin in an interview, "and one of them sends the other to the stake. And then they find out somehow they're the same man." In a *Studies in Short Fiction* essay Robert Magliola no-ticed, "Almost every story in *Dr. Brodie's Report* is about two people fixed in some sort of dramatic op-position to each other." In two pieces, "Borges and I" (also translated as "Borges and Myself") and "The Other," Borges appears as a character along with his double. In the former, Borges, the retiring Argentine librarian, contemplates Borges, the world-famous writer. It concludes with one of Borges's most-ana-lyzed sentences: "Which of us is writing this page, I don't know."

Some critics saw Borges's use of the double as an attempt to deal with the duality in his own personal-ity: the struggle between his native Argentine roots and the strong European influence on his writing. They also pointed out what seemed to be an attempt by the author to reconcile through his fiction the re-ality of his sedentary life of an almost-blind scholar with the longed for adventurous life of his dreams based on that led by his famous ancestors who ac-tively participated in Argentina's wars for independence. This latter tendency is especially evident in "The South," a largely autobiographical story about a library worker who, Bell-Villada noted, like Borges, "is painfully aware of the discordant strains in his ancestry."

The idea that all men are one, which Anderson-Imbert observed calls for the "obliteration of the I," is perhaps Borges's farthest step towards a literature devoid of realism. In this theme we see, according to Ronald Christ, "the direction in Borges' stories away from individual psychology toward a universal mythology." This explains why so few of Borges's characters show any psychological development; instead of being interested in his characters as individuals, Borges typically uses them only to further his philosophical beliefs.

All of the characteristics of Borges's work, his blending of genres, confusion of the real and the fictive, his favorite themes and symbols, seem to come together in one of his most quoted passages, the final paragraph of his essay "A New Refutation of Time." While in *Borges: A Reader* Rodriguez Monegal called the essay Borges's "most elaborate attempt to organize a personal system of metaphysics in which he denies time, space, and the individual 'I,'" Alazraki noted that it contains a summation of Borges's belief in "the heroic and tragic condition of man as dream and dreamer."

"Our destiny . . . ," wrote Borges in the essay, "is not horrible because of its unreality; it is horrible because it is irreversible and ironbound. Time is the substance I am made of. Time is a river that carries me away, but I am the river; it is a tiger that mangles me, but I am the tiger; it is a fire that consumes me, but I am the fire. The world, alas, is real; I, alas, am Borges."

BIOGRAPHICAL/CRITICAL SOURCES:

BOOKS

Alazraki, Jaime, *Jorge Luis Borges,* Columbia University Press, 1971.

Barrenechea, Ana Maria, *Borges: The Labyrinth Maker,* translated by Robert Lima, New York University Press (New York City), 1965.

Bell-Villada, Gene H., *Borges and His Fiction: A Guide to His Mind and Art,* University of North Carolina Press (Chapel Hill), 1981.

Burgin, Richard, *Conversations with Jorge Luis Borges,* Holt (New York City), 1969.

Christ, Ronald J., *The Narrow Act: Borges' Art of Illusion,* New York University Press, 1969.

Contemporary Literary Criticism, Gale (Detroit), Volume 1, 1973; Volume 2, 1974; Volume 3, 1975; Volume 4, 1975; Volume 6, 1976; Volume 8, 1978; Volume 9, 1978; Volume 10, 1979; Volume 13, 1980; Volume 19, 1981; Volume 44, 1987; Volume 48, 1988.

Cottom, Daniel, *Ravishing Tradition: Cultural Forces and Literary History,* Cornell University Press (Ithaca, NY), 1996.

Dictionary of Literary Biography: Yearbook, 1986, Gale, 1987.

Hernandez Martin, Jorge, *Readers and Labyrinths: Detective Fiction in Borges, Bustos Domecqu, and Eco,* Garland Publishers (New York City), 1995.

Irwin, John T., *The Mystery to a Solution: Poe, Borges, and the Analytic Detective Story,* Johns Hopkins University Press (Baltimore), 1994.

Maier, Linda S., *Borges and the European Avant-Garde,* P. Lang (New York City), 1996.

McMurray, George R., *Jorge Luis Borges,* Ungar, 1980.

Molloy, Sylvia, and Oscar Montero, *Signs of Borges,* Duke University Press (Durham, NC), 1994.

Rodriguez Monegal, Emir, *Jorge Luis Borges: A Literary Biography,* Dutton, 1978.

Stabb, Martin S., *Jorge Luis Borges,* Twayne, 1970.

Woodall, James, *Borges: A Life,* Basic Books, 1997.

PERIODICALS

Atlantic Monthly, January, 1967; August, 1967; February, 1972; April, 1981.

Detroit News, June 15, 1986; June 22, 1986.

Los Angeles Times, June 15, 1986.

Nation, December 29, 1969; August 3, 1970; March 1, 1971; February 21, 1972; October 16, 1972; February 21, 1976; June 28, 1986.

National Review, March 2, 1973.

New Republic, November 3, 1986.

New Yorker, July 7, 1986.

New York Review of Books, August 14, 1986.

New York Times, June 15, 1986.

Publishers Weekly, July 4, 1986.

Review, spring, 1972; spring, 1975; winter, 1976; January-April, 1981; September-December, 1981.

Studies in Short Fiction, spring, 1974; winter, 1978.

Time, June 23, 1986.

USA Today, June 16, 1986.

Washington Post, June 15, 1986.

World Literature Today, autumn, 1977; winter, 1984.

Yale Review, October, 1969; autumn, 1974.*

BORTNIK, Aida (Beatriz) 1938-

PERSONAL: Born January 7, 1938, in Buenos Aires, Argentina; daughter of Aron and Celia (Federovsky) Bortnik. *Education:* Attended University of Buenos Aires, 1956-58, 1961-64; also attended schools of theater and film.

ADDRESSES: Home—595 Salta St., Buenos Aires 1074, Argentina.

CAREER: Playwright, short-story writer, art critic, and journalist.

MEMBER: General Association of Authors of Argentina.

AWARDS, HONORS: (With Luis Puenzo) Academy Award nomination for best screenplay written directly for the screen, 1986, for *La Historia oficial.*

WRITINGS:

SCREENPLAYS

La Tregua (title means "The Truce"), 1974.
Una Mujer, 1975.
Crecer de Golpe, 1976.
La Isla, 1979.
Volver, 1983.
No habra mas penas ni olvido (title means "Funny Dirty Little War"), c. 1984.
(With Luis Puenzo) *La Historia oficial,* 1985.
Pobre mariposa (title means "Poor Butterfly"), 1986.
Old Gringo, 1989.
(With Marcelo Pineyro) *Tango feroz: la leyenda de Tanguito* (title means "Wild Tango"), produced by Claudio Pustelnik and Katrina Bayonas, 1993.
Caballos salvajes (title means "Wild Horses"), 1995.

Also author of stage plays, including *Doldados y Soldaditos,* 1972; *Tres por Chejov,* 1974; *Dale Nomas,* 1975; and *Papa Querido* and *Domesticados,* both 1981. Author of television plays.

OTHER

Guiones cinematograficos, selection and prologue by Jorge Miguel Couselo, Centro Editor de America Latin (Buenos Aires), 1981.
Primaveras, Teatro Municipal General San Martin (Buenos Aires), 1985.

Also author of art criticism and short stories for the magazine *Humor.*

SIDELIGHTS: Although not a household name in the United States, Aida Bortnik is often considered "Argentina's best scriptwriter," in the opinion of critic John Mosier in *Americas.* She has been nominated, with director and co-writer Luis Puenzo, for an Oscar in the category of best screenplay written directly for the screen, for their widely acclaimed 1985 movie *La Historia oficial* ("The Official Story"). That movie, which, according to *New York* contributor David Denby, "sent shock waves through Argentina," deals with the tragedy of Argentina's post-1974 military dictatorship by focusing on one possible domestic repercussion. The time is 1983, shortly after Argentina lost the Falklands war against Great Britain, and shortly before the demise of its ruling dictatorship. Alicia, a high school teacher and the wife of a businessman, is a complacent, constitutionally conservative bourgeois woman who, more or less accidentally, learns that her five-year-old adopted daughter may have been the child of leftists who were tortured and killed by the regime. *Los desaparecidos,* "the disappeared," is the common name for such victims of the dictatorship.

Although far from a model of anti-militaristic virtue, Alicia's suspicions are aroused; she investigates the matter indefatigably, with results that shock her and cause lasting damage to her marriage and herself. As Denby observed, "As she falls into knowledge—and therefore into misery—she achieves greatness." A "WONDERFUL" film, in Denby's opinion, *La Historia oficial* "has the passionate sternness of a Greek tragedy." The key to the Bortnik-penned film, as Denby sees it, is the character of Alicia, both as written by Bortnik and as acted by Norma Aleandro. Alicia is "neither patronize[d] nor mythicize[d]" in the film, for the character, with all her flaws, "has been created in such depth that we accept her nature and her peculiar fate as ineluctable elements in a tragic conception of life. . . . A whole society's complicity in terror is encapsulated in the lie that Alicia has lived by. . . . Yet Alicia is never merely defined by her problem; she is always something greater. In the end, she's one of the few genuine dramatic creations in recent movies."

Bortnik's ability to create a rounded, dramatic heroine was presaged by her several plays for the Argentine stage, as well as by her previous work for the screen. That ability continued to be displayed in her next screenplay, for the film *Pobre mariposa* ("Poor Butterfly"), which became the 1986 Argentine entry at the prestigious Cannes Film Festival. The "butterfly" of the title is Clara, an Argentine radio star of the 1940s as well as a social butterfly and the wife of a surgeon. Set in 1945, the film depicts the effects on Clara of her gradual realization that her recently deceased father was Jewish. Confronted with her father's Yiddish-speaking, argumentative family, Clara is confused; yet she is no longer quite at ease with her emotionally repressed husband, either. "One of the strengths here is that [the film] isn't afraid to deal in cultural stereotypes," opined Mosier in a review of *Pobre mariposa*. Mosier also described the film's 1940s atmosphere, with its recreations of old radio shows, as "some of the best period work around." Mosier praised the characterization of Clara for its realistic consistency-within-inconsistency as she progresses toward an emotional breakdown; he also praised the rather offbeat, almost casually violent ending, calling it "a curiously fitting testimony." All in all, the critic declared, though not an overwhelming film experience, *Pobre mariposa*'s "virtues definitely grow on you. . . . Technically, this is by far the best Argentine film [yet] made."

A third Bortnik screenplay to reach American screens was 1993's *Tango Feroz: La leyenda de Tanguito*. The film uses the rise and fall of an Argentine rock star to dramatize the ideals and disillusions of the generation that grew up during the 1960s only to see its hopes—and often its lives—cut short by the military regime. "Tango" is the rock star's stage name; his real name is revealed only near the end of the movie. Using *rock nacional*—Argentine pop music— to emblematize the spirit of youthful Argentina, the movie shows Tango becoming a star, being thrust into conflict about American influences on his music, and later coming into conflict with the police. A dark-skinned victim of racial prejudice as well, Tango is ultimately placed in an asylum, where he commits suicide. His death, reflected David Sheinin in *American Historical Review,* symbolizes the destruction of the freedom and innocence of Argentine youth by the military dictatorship. "The film's message is poignant and effectively delivered," writes Sheinen, and although *Tango Feroz*' portrayal of the pre-dictatorship Argentina may be somewhat sentimental, that fact in itself "reminds viewers that romancing the past is intrinsic to Argentine popular culture."

BIOGRAPHICAL/CRITICAL SOURCES:

PERIODICALS

American Historical Review, October 1996, pp. 1164-1165.

Americas, November-December 1986, pp. 55-56.
New York, November 18, 1985, pp. 88-89.

OTHER

Internet Movie Database, http://us.imdb.com, 1997.*

*   *   *

BOSCH (GAVINO), Juan 1909-

PERSONAL: Born in 1909, in the Dominican Republic. *Education:* Attended school in La Vega and Santo Domingo, Dominican Republic.

ADDRESSES: Agent—c/o Alfa y Omega, M Cabral 11, Santo Domingo, Dominican Republic.

CAREER: Writer and politician. Founder and president of Partido Revolucionario Dominicano, 1939-1966. President of Dominican Republic, February-September, 1963 (deposed in military coup). Professor at Institute of Political Science of Costa Rica.

AWARDS, HONORS: Short story award, FNAC Foundation (France), 1988.

WRITINGS:

FICTION

La manosa: Novela de las revoluciones (novel), El Diario (Santiago, Dominican Republic), 1936.
Camino real (short stories), El Diario, 1937.
Dos pesos de agua (short stories), privately printed (Havana), 1941.
Ocho cuentos (short stories), [Havana], 1947.
La muchacha de La Guaira (short stories), Nascimento (Santiago, Chile), 1955.
Cuento de Navidad, Ercilla (Santiago, Chile), 1956.
Cuentos escritos en el exilio y apuntes sobre el arte de escribir cuentos (short stories), Libreria Dominicana (Santo Domingo), 1962.
Mas cuentos escritos en el exilio (short stories), Libreria Dominicana, 1964.
Cuentos escritos ante del exilio (short stories), Edicion Especial (Santo Domingo), 1974.
El oro y la paz (novel), [Santo Domingo], 1977.
Cuentos (short stories), Casa de Las Americas (Havana), 1983.

NONFICTION

Indios: Apuntes historicos y leyendas, La Nacion (Santo Domingo), 1935.

Mujeres en la vida de Hostos, conferencia, Asociacion de Mujeres Graduadas de la Universidad de Puerto Rico (San Juan), 1938.

Cuba: La isla fascinante, Universitaria (Santiago, Chile), 1955.

Trujillo: Causas de una tirania sin ejemplo, Las Novedades (Caracas), 1959.

Apuntes para una interpretacion de la historia costarricense, Eloy Morua Carrillo (San Jose, Costa Rica), 1963, reprinted as *Una interpretacion de la historia costarricense,* Juricentro (San Jose), 1980.

(With Adolfo Lopez Mateos) *Un nuevo planteamiento de las relaciones entre Mexico y la Republica Dominicana,* La Justicia (Mexico City), 1963.

Crisis de la democracia de America en la Republica ominicana, Centro de Estudios y Documentacion Sociales (Guadalquivir), 1964, translation published as *The Unfinished Experiment: Democracy in the Dominican Republic,* Praeger, 1965.

Tres articulos sobre la Revolucion Dominicana, Partido Revolucionario Dominicano (Mexico City), 1965.

Paginas para la historia, Libreria Dominicana, 1965.

Bolivar y la guerra social, Jorge Alvarez (Buenos Aires), 1966.

Teoria del cuento: Tres ensayos (essays), Universidad de los Andes, Facultad de Humanidades y Educacion, Escuela de Letras, Centro de Investigaciones Literarias (Merida, Venezuela), 1967.

El pentagonismo: Sustituto del imperialismo, Publicaciones Ahora (Santo Domingo), 1967, translation by Helen R. Lane published as *Pentagonism: A Substitute for Imperialism,* Grove Press, 1968.

Composicion social dominicana: Historia e interpretacion, [Santo Domingo], 1970.

De Cristobal Colon a Fidel Castro: El Caribe, frontera imperial, Alfaguara (Madrid), 1970.

El proximo paso: Dictadura con respaldo popular, Impresora Arte y Cine (Santo Domingo), 1970.

Breve historia de la oligarquia, Impresora Arte y Cine, 1971.

Tres conferencias sobre el feudalismo, Talleres Graficos (Santo Domingo), 1971.

(Author of prologue) Federico Garcia Godoy, *El derrumbe,* La Universidad Autonoma de Santo Domingo, 1975.

Viaje a los antipodas, Alfa y Omega (Santo Domingo), 1978.

Articulos y conferencias, Alfa y Omega, 1980.

(With others) *Abril* (essays), Alfa y Omega, 1980.

(With others) *Coronel Fernandez Dominguez: Fundador del movimiento militar constitucionalista* (essays), Cosmos (Santo Domingo), 1981.

La Revolucion de Abril (essays; first published in periodical *Vanguardia del Pueblo,* 1979), Impresora Mercedes (Santo Domingo), 1981.

Clases sociales en la Republica Dominicana (essays; first published in periodicals *Vanguardia del Pueblo* and *Politica—Teoria y Accion,* beginning in 1974), Corripio (Santo Domingo), 1982.

La guerra y la restauracion, Corripio, 1982.

El partido: Concepcion, organizacion y desarrollo (essays), Alfa y Omega, 1983.

Capitalismo, democracia y liberacion nacional (essays; first published in periodical *Vanguardia del Pueblo,* 1978-83), Alfa y Omega, 1983.

(With Narciso Isa Conde) *El problema de las alianzas* (essays; first published in periodicals *Vanguardia del Pueblo* and *Hablan los Comunistas,* 1983), Ediciones de Taller (Santo Domingo), 1983.

La fortuna de Trujillo (excerpts from *Trujillo: Causas de una tirania sin ejemplo*), Alfa y Omega, 1985.

La pequena burguesia en la historia de la Republica Dominicana (essays; first published in periodical *Vanguardia del Pueblo,* 1984-85), Alfa y Omega, 1985.

Capitalismo tardio en la Republica Dominicana, Alfa y Omega, 1986.

Las dictaduras dominicanas, Alfa y Omega, 1988.

(With Avelino Stanley Rondon) *Antologia Personal,* University of Puerto Rico Press, 1998.

BIOGRAPHY

Hostos, el sembrador, Tropico (Havana), 1939.

Simon Bolivar: Biografia para escolares, Escolar (Caracas), 1960.

David: Biografia de un rey, Libreria Dominicana, 1963, translation by John Marks published as *David: The Biography of a King,* Hawthorn Books, 1966.

El Napoleon de las guerrillas, Alfa y Omega, 1977.

Judas Iscariote: El calumniado, Alfa y Omega, 1978.

(With Luis Cordero Velasquez) *Juan Vicente Gomez: Camino del poder,* Humboldt (Caracas), 1982.

Maximo Gomez: De Monte Cristi a la gloria; tres anos de guerra en Cuba (includes *El Napoleon de las guerrillas*), Alfa y Omega, 1986.

SIDELIGHTS: Juan Bosch has written a multitude of fictional and non-fictional works in Spanish, but he is best known in the English-speaking world for his short-lived career as the President of the Dominican

Republic, and as the author of three books translated into English during the 1960s. Bosch was born in Dominica in 1909, and attended school in Santo Domingo. By the age of thirty he was both an artist and a political leader. He founded the Partido Revolucionario Dominicano in 1939 and served as its president until 1966. He also founded the literary group, Las Cuevas ("The Caves"). Between 1937 and 1961 Bosch travelled throughout Latin America. Bosch returned to the Dominican Republic and was elected as the country's first constitutional President in thirty-eight years. Bosch served for approximately seven months during 1963. A military coup deposed Bosch and sent him into exile. He relocated to Costa Rica, where he became a professor at the Institute of Political Science. Bosch continued to express a strong interest in regaining his presidency. In 1989, at the age of eighty, Bosch ran for re-election, only to lose the 1990 election to Joaquin Balaguer.

Bosch's writings published shortly after he was first deposed were calls for political reform. *The Unfinished Experiment: Democracy in the Dominican Republic,* published in 1965, *David: The Biography of a King,* published in 1966, and *Pentagonism: A Substitute for Imperialism,* published in 1968, are often considered valuable by critics more for their first-hand commentary on Latin American political issues rather than their literary value. Nevertheless, Bosch's Spanish works have been compared to those of Ernest Hemingway. Bosch's literary accomplishments include a number of studies and biographies that serve as standard texts in some Latin American schools. Bosch has been praised for his transformation of David into a contemporary figure and his comparison of the Dominican Republic to Israel without its David was received with interest by students of Latin American politics. Bosch's insider's experience within the tumult of Latin American politics has been appreciated as an unusual source of informed commentary.

BIOGRAPHICAL/CRITICAL SOURCES:

BOOKS

Garcia Cuevas, Eugenio de J., *Jual Bosch: Novela, Historia, y Sociedad,* Isla Negra, 1995.

PERIODICALS

America, May 3, 1969, p. 546.
Booklist, January 15, 1967, p. 498.
Economist, August 26, 1989, p. 30.
Journal of Politics, August, 1965, pp. 671-673.
New Republic, February 8, 1969, pp. 20-22.
New Statesman, June 10, 1966, pp. 849-850.
New York Times Book Review, January 9, 1966, p. 28.
New York Times Magazine, August 6, 1989, p. 24.
Saturday Review, November 27, 1965, p. 36.
Time, May 28, 1990, p. 39.
Washington Post Book World, January 12, 1969, p. 7.*

*   *   *

BOUSONO, Carlos 1923-

PERSONAL: Born May 9, 1923, in Boal, Spain; son of Luis Bousono (in business) and Margarita Prieto (a teacher; maiden name, Fernandez de la Llana) Canocera; married Ruth Crespo, November 15, 1975; children: Carlos Alberto. *Education:* Attended University of Madrid.

ADDRESSES: Home—Majorca, Spain. *Office*—University of Madrid, Madrid, Spain. *Agent*—c/o Visor Libros, Isaac Peral, 18, 28015 Madrid, Spain.

CAREER: Poet and critic, 1945—. Visiting instructor at Wellesley College, 1947-48; member of faculty at University of Madrid, beginning 1951. Lecturer at various institutions, including Harvard University. *Military service:* Spanish military, 1949-50.

MEMBER: Spanish Royal Academy.

AWARDS, HONORS: Premio Nacional de Literature, 1978, for *El irracionalismo poetico.*

WRITINGS:

Subida al amor (poetry; title means "Ascent to Love"), Hispanica (Madrid, Spain), 1945.
Primavera de la muerte (poetry; title means "Springtime of Death"), prologue by Vicente Aleixandre, Hispanica, 1946.
La poesia de Vicente Aleixandre: Imagen, estilo, mundo poetico (criticism; title means "The Poetry of Vicente Aleixandre: Image, Style, Poetic World"), Insula (Madrid), 1950, 4th revised and enlarged edition, Gredos (Madrid), 1977.
(With Damaso Alonso) *Seis calas en la expresion literaria espanola* (criticism; title means "Six Samples of Spanish Literary Expression"), Gredos, 1951.

Hacia otra luz (poetry; title means "Toward Another Light"), Insula, 1952.

Teoria de la expresion poetica (literary theory; title means "Theory of Poetic Expression"), Gredos, 1952, revised and enlarged edition, two volumes, 1970, 6th edition, 1976.

Noche del sentido (poetry; title means "Night of the Senses"), Insula, 1957.

Poesias completas (title means "Complete Poems"), Giner (Madrid), 1960.

Invasion de la realidad (poetry; title means "Invasion of Reality"), Espasa-Calpe (Madrid), 1962.

Oda en la ceniza (poetry; title means "Ode in the Ashes"), Ciencia Nueva (Madrid), 1967.

Antologia de textos criticos (criticism; title means "Anthology of Critical Texts"), edited by Julio Garcia Morejon, Universidade de Sao Paulo (Sao Paulo, Brazil), 1969.

Al mismo tiempo que la noche, Anticuaria El Guadalhorce (Malaga, Spain), 1971.

La busqueda, Fomento de Cultura, Valencia (Spain), 1971.

Las monedas contra la losa (poetry; title means "Coins against the Stone"), Corazon (Madrid), 1973.

Antologia poetica (title means "Poetry Anthology"), Plaza & Janes (Madrid), 1976.

El irracionalismo poetico (criticism; title means "Poetic Irrationalism"), Gredos, 1977.

Superrealismo poetico y simbolizacion (criticism; title means "Surrealistic Poetry and Symbolism"), Gredos (Madrid), 1979.

Sentido de la evolucion de la poesia contemporanea en Juan Ramon Jiminez, Real Academia Espanola, 1980.

Epocas literarias y evolucion (criticism; title means "Literary Epochs and Evolution"), Gredos, 1981.

Seleccion de mis versos (poetry; title means "Selection of My Verse"), Catedra (Madrid), 1982.

Poesia poscontemporanea, Jucar (Madrid), 1985.

Metaforca del desafuero, Visor (Madrid), 1988.

SIDELIGHTS: Carlos Bousono is a prominent Spanish poet and literary theorist. C. Christopher Soufas, Jr., writing in the *Dictionary of Literary Biography,* described Bousono as "an important figure in the history of twentieth-century Spanish letters" and added that he stands "as perhaps the best poet" among the early post-civil war generation in Spain. Soufas also considered Bousono "the finest Spanish literary theorist of the last forty years."

Bousono was born in 1923 in Boal, Spain. His father worked in business, and his mother maintained a ca-

reer as a teacher. After his mother died unexpectedly and his father and brother relocated to Mexico, ten-year-old Bousono moved into the home of an aunt who showed little tolerance for children. He stayed with his aunt for the next nine years, a period he later recalled as one of suffering and unhappiness. Soufas found this period to be pivotal to the development of Bousono's general outlook on life as later expressed in his poetry. According to Soufas, in his writing Bousono "constantly confronts objects and people he invests with love and in which he places his hope only to find that this love, if not misplaced, will never receive a definitive reply."

In the mid-1940s, after leaving his aunt, Bousono distinguished himself at the University of Madrid, where he studied literature. During this time Bousono published his first poetry collection, *Subida al amor* ("Ascent to Love"), which includes "Recuerdo de infancia" ("Memory of Childhood"), wherein he recalls the unhappy period he spent with his affectionless aunt. The general tone of the collection, however, is one of religious ecstasy, for Bousono's poems continually represent the Christian deity in terms of profound love. Soufas traces Bousono's Christian faith to the desire for self-affirmation and reciprocated love and declares that the poet "is demanding a form of love that can only be satisfied by the direct experience of the divine."

Bousono's next volume, *Primavera de la muerte* ("Springtime of Death"), is a far more pessimistic collection, one that considers death as the one inevitable aspect of life. In the title poem, Bousono acknowledges the relatively swift passing of life, while in "Primavera sin tiempo" ("Springtime without Time") he contrast his earlier sense of spiritual eternity with his growing realization of life as fleeting and, thus, profoundly saddening.

In the early 1950s Bousono began teaching at the University of Madrid. Around this time he established himself as a significant literary critic and theorist by publishing *Seis calas en la expresion literaria espanola* ("Six Samples of Spanish Literary Expression"), written with Damaso Alonso, and *Teoria de la expresion poetica* ("Theories of Poetic Expression"). Soufas deemed the former volume "one of the first works of Spanish criticism to study poetry . . . according to a standard of scientificity with regard to explanation and classification of literary phenomena." Soufas accorded even greater significance to *Teoria de la expresion poetica,* which he called "one of the monumental studies in the history of Spanish criticism" and the work that "marks Bousono . . . as one of the greatest Spanish literary critics of the twentieth century." This study, wherein Bousono distinguishes the language of poetry from that of conventional expression and, furthermore, analyzes irrational poetic modes, has exerted considerable influence in Spanish academic and literary circles.

In 1952, the same year that he published *Teoria de la expresion poetica,* Bousono also produced *Hacia otra luz* ("Toward Another Light"), a poetry collection that marks his transition from the youthful fervor of both the ecstatic *Subida al amor* and the pessimistic *Primavera de la muerte* to more contemplative considerations, as evidenced also in his later works *Noche del sentido* ("Night of the Senses") and *Invasion de la realidad* ("Invasion of Reality"). These volumes reflect a view that life, however insignificant on the cosmic scale, nonetheless constitutes a privileged experience. In *Hacia otra luz,* poems such as "El apostol" reveal Bousono's spiritual restlessness, his inability to either secure a replacement for the Christian deity that inspired *Subida al amor* or fill the void that is acknowledged in *Primavera de la muerte.*

But by the time of *Noche del sentido,* which appeared in 1957, Bousono had resumed his quest for an alternative to the Christian deity, and with *Invasion de la realidad,* which Bousono published in 1962, he concedes the likelihood of alternatives to Christianity, and he comes to believe that perception, itself and an act of faith, leads to apprehension of reality as divine truth. Soufas notes that "Mi Verdad" ("My Truth"), exemplifies Bousono's newfound understanding with such verses as: "Terrible world. Breathed out world. / You, my solitary truth. / My lone faith, my lone profound love; / my sole light." In the concluding poem, "Salvacion de la vida" ("Salvation of Life"), Bousono contends that human efforts fill the emptiness left by the absence of a god, and that enterprise is, thus, the alternative to despair before the spiritual void.

In the collections *Oda en la ceniza* (1967; "Ode in the Ashes") and *Las monedas contra la losa* (1973; "Coins against the Stone"), Bousono continued to reflect on the validity of human existence while simultaneously refuting the likelihood of spiritual salvation. In *Oda en la ceniza,* he lauds the creative act as a means of thwarting despair before the spiritual void, while in *Las monedas contra la losa* he expresses the notion of pain and pleasure as experiences that intensify the substantiality of a reality that lacks a conventional spiritual dimension. With these collections,

which some critics rank as the poet's greatest achievements, Bousono seems to have come to terms with his own despair.

BIOGRAPHICAL/CRITICAL SOURCES:

BOOKS

Dictionary of Literary Biography, Volume 108: *Twentieth-Century Spanish Poets, First Series,* Gale (Detroit), 1991.

PERIODICALS

Modern Language Notes, March, 1974.*

*   *   *

BRYCE ECHENIQUE, Alfredo 1939-

PERSONAL: Born February 19, 1939, in Lima, Peru; son of Francisco (a banker) and Elena Bryce Echenique.

ADDRESSES: Agent—c/o Plaza y Janes, Virgen de Guadelup 12-33, 08950 Esplugas de Llubregat, Barcelona, Spain.

CAREER: Writer and novelist, 1965—.

WRITINGS:

Huerto cerrado, Casa de las Americas (Havana), 1968.
Un mundo para Julius, Barral (Barcelona), 1970, translation by Dick Gerdes published as *A World for Julius,* University of Texas Press (Austin), 1992.
Muerte de Sevilla en Madrid; Antes de la cita con los Linares, Mosca Azul (Lima), 1972.
La felicidad, ja, ja, Barral, 1974.
La Pasion segun San Pedro Balbuena que fue tantas veces Pedro y que nunca pudo negar a nadie, Libre-1 (Lima), 1977.
Avuelo de buen cubero y otras cronicas, Anagrama (Barcelona), 1977.
Todos los cuentos (title means "Short Stories"), Mosca Azul, 1979.
Cuentos completos, Alianza (Madrid), 1981.
La vida exagerada de Martin Romana, Argos Vergara (Barcelona), 1981.
El hombre que hablaba de Octavia de Cadiz, Plaza y Janes (Barcelona), 1985.

Magdalena peruana y otros cuentos, Plaza y Janes, 1986.

Goig, Debate (Madrid), 1987.

Tantas veces pedro, Plaza y Janes (Barcelona), 1987.

La ultima mudanza de Felipe Carrilo, Plaza y Janes, 1988.

Cronicas personales, Editorial Anagrama (Barcelona), 1988.

Dos senoras conversan; Un sapo el desierto; Los grandes hombres son asi, y tambien asa, Plaza y Janes, 1990.

Permiso para vivir: antimemorias, Anagrama (Barcelona), 1993.

Antologia personal, Editorial de la Universidad de Puerto Rico (San Juan), 1995.

No me esperen en abril, Anagrama (Barcelona), 1995.

Para que duela menos, Espasa Calpe (Madrid), 1995.

A trancas y barrancas, Espasa (Madrid), 1996.

15 cuentos de amor y humor, PEISA (Lima, Peru), 1996.

La Amigdalitis de Tarzan, Alfaguara (Lima, Peru), 1998.

Guia triste de Paris, PEISA, 1999.

Reo de nocturnidad, Editorial Anagrama (Barcelona), 1997.

SIDELIGHTS: Although Alfredo Bryce Echenique has been widely read in Europe and Latin America and is considered a leading novelist of Peru, he is less well known in the United States. During his career Bryce Echenique has authored five novels, three collections of short stories, novellas, and several collections of journalism. Echenique's writing is characterized by its readable tone and its humor. He has created characters who are often underdogs and has written about the experience of exile from a Latin American perspective.

The author was born in Peru, where he attended exclusive schools prior to college. He was exposed to writing and reading at an early age, as his mother was an admirer of French literature. Though Bryce Echenique wanted to pursue a literature degree in college, he made law school a priority at the wish of his father. Nonetheless, he also earned a literature degree in 1964, and his thesis addressed Hemingway. Bryce Echenique won a scholarship to study in Paris and happened to arrive there as a Latin American literary movement was growing in the city. Paris was later to influence his writing. He published his first book in 1965—a collection of short stories titled *Closed Garden (Huerto cerrado).* The collection later won an award and remained significant because it identified a number of themes that Bryce Echenique

continued to write about in later works. *Closed Garden* was also influenced by Ernest Hemingway, whom Bryce Echenique greatly admired.

One of the stories in *Closed Garden* (titled "With Jimmy, in Paracas") was considered significant by the author because it identified a narrative style that he later used repeatedly. According to a profile of Bryce Echenique by Cesar Ferreira in *Dictionary of Literary Biography,* this style was characterized by a "confessional tone," usually narrated by "protagonists who are losers and emotionally incapable of asserting themselves in the world." These characters were usually sentimental and also quite aware of their shortcomings.

Bryce Echenique later used this narrative device in his 1970 novel *A World for Julius (Un Mundo para Julius),* which put the author in the forefront of Latin American writers. *A World for Julius,* like the preceding short story, explores the chasm between rich and poor in Peru. According to Ferreira, *A World for Julius* effectively uses language by subtly shifting between a variety of narrative viewpoints. Bryce Echenique continued to write about the Peruvian upper class in *Happiness, Ha, Ha (La felicidad, ja, ja),* published in 1974. In this work, according to Ferreira, Bryce Echenique "insists that the happiness of the wealthy is frivolous and illusory," as well as morally bankrupt.

Death of Sevilla in Madrid (Muerte de Sevilla en Madrid; Antes de la cita con los Linares), which appeared in 1972, again uses an underdog protagonist—a bureaucrat with little self-confidence or zest for life. When the character unexpectedly wins a trip to Spain as part of a promotion, the experience is too much for him and he commits suicide. Ferreira said that the story is narrated with humor but that the tone turns gradually dark and "grotesque." Bryce Echenique takes an outsider's look at United States locations in the 1977 work *Wayward Journeys and Other Chronicles (Avuelo de buen cubero y otras cronicas).* Focusing mainly on the South, the author attempts to dispel some of the myths of North America that have been promulgated by American cinema. Ferreira noted the influence of Faulkner in *Journeys,* particularly Bryce Echenique's depiction of more "marginal" American characters in places like New Orleans or Memphis.

Bryce Echenique produced a number of other works, many of which were influenced by his life as an outsider in Europe. He also captured a sense of his homeland—Ferreira called him "an outstanding chronicler of contemporary Peruvian society with its numerous contradictions." Many of Bryce Echenique's characters suffer inwardly but are also searching for meaning in themselves and in the world around them. Ferreira gives Bryce Echenique credit for bringing a renewed sense of the cosmopolitan to modern Peruvian writing.

BIOGRAPHICAL/CRITICAL SOURCES:

BOOKS

Dictionary of Literary Biography, Volume 145: *Modern Latin-American Fiction Writers, Second Series,* Gale (Detroit), 1994.*

*   *   *

BUENAVENTURA, Enrique 1925-

PERSONAL: Born August 23, 1925, in Cali, Colombia; son of Cornelio Buenaventura and Julia Emma Alder; married Jacqueline Vidal, 1961; children: one son.

ADDRESSES: Office—Teatro Experimental de Cali, Calle 7, Numero 8-63, Apt. Aereo 5838, Cali, Colombia. *Agent*—c/o Casa de las Americas, Calle 3a y G Vedaldo, Havana, Cuba.

CAREER: Worked as manual laborer, sailor, literature teacher, and journalist, before 1955; Experimental Theater of Cali, Cali, Colombia, founder and leader, 1955—; affiliated with Cali School of Fine Arts, until 1969.

AWARDS, HONORS: UNESCO Prize, 1965, for *La tragedia del rey Christophe;* prize for drama, Casa de las Americas, 1980, for *Historia de una bala de plata.*

WRITINGS:

PLAYS; SEPARATE WORKS OR PRODUCTIONS

En la diestra de Dios Padre (title means "In the Right Hand of God the Father"; based on Tomas Carrasquilla's retelling of a folktale; also see below), produced in 1960.
La tragedia del rey Christophe (title means "The Tragedy of King Christophe"; also see below), produced in 1963.

Un requiem por el Padre Las Casas (title means "Requiem for Father Las Casas"; also see below), produced in 1963.
La trampa (title means "The Trap"; also see below), produced in 1966.
Los papeles del infierno (title means "Documents from Hell"; assembly of various shorter works, at various times including *La maestra* ["The Schoolteacher"], *La autopsia* ["The Autopsy"], *La requisa, La tortura* ["Torture"], *El entierro, La orgia* ["The Orgy"], *El menu,* and *El sueno* ["The Dream"]; also see below), produced in 1968.
Tirano Banderas (title means "Tyrant Banderas"; based on the novel of the same title by Ramon Valle-Inclan), produced in 1969.
Historia de una bala de plata (title means "Tale of a Silver Bullet"), Casa de las Americas (Havana, Cuba), 1980.

Author or co-author of additional plays and play adaptations. Author of adaptation of Sophocles' *Oedipus Rex* and of *El fantoche lusitano,* based on a work by Peter Weiss.

PLAYS IN OMNIBUS VOLUMES

Teatro (includes *Un requiem por el Padre Las Casas, La tragedia del rey Christophe,* and *En la diestra de Dios Padre*), Tercer Mundo (Bogota, Colombia), 1963.
(With others) *Voices of Change in the Spanish American Theater* (includes *In the Right Hand of God the Father*), edited by William I. Oliver, University of Texas Press, 1971.
(With others) *The Orgy: Modern One-Act Plays from Latin America* (includes *The Orgy* and *The Schoolteacher*), edited and translated by Gerardo Luzuriaga and Robert S. Rudder, University of California, Los Angeles, Latin American Center, 1974.
Teatro (includes *Los papeles del infierno, El menu, La orgia, Soldados,* and *En la diestra de Dios Padre*), introduction by Carlos Jose Reyes, Instituto Colombiano de Cultura (Bogota), 1977.
Teatro (includes *En la diestra de Dios Padre, Los papeles del infierno, La maestra, La tortura, La audiencia, La autopsia, La orgia, El menu,* and *Vida y muerte del Fantoche Lusitano*), Casa de las Americas, 1980.
Teatro inedito, Presidencia de la Republica, 1997.

SIDELIGHTS: Colombian dramatist Enrique Buenaventura is well known in the Latin American theater world as an advocate of innovative drama which encourages social change. Deeply concerned that the United States exercises undue influence over the culture of his region, he has sought to bring a distinctively Latin American content to his works. His plays often dramatize events in the political history of Latin America and attack the failures of its traditional oligarchical regimes.

After holding a wide variety of jobs during his twenties, Buenaventura founded the Experimental Theater in his hometown of Cali in 1955. The next few years saw production of is first major play, *En la diestra de Dios Padre* (title means "In the Right Hand of God the Father"). Based on Tomas Carrasquilla's retelling of a folktale, the work centers on Peralta, a warm-hearted common man who receives five wishes from God and tries to use them to solve the world's problems. When Peralta abolishes poverty, sickness, and death, however, new troubles arise. "The [play's] irony," wrote George McMurray in *Spanish American Writing since 1941: A Critical Survey,* "stems from the inability of God, who naively allied himself with the all-too-human Peralta, to perfect his flawed universe." "In the Right Hand of God the Father" was brought to Europe by Colombian actors and staged in Paris and other cities to great acclaim.

Soon thereafter Buenaventura wrote two of his best-known historical dramas. *Un requiem por el Padre Las Casas* ("Requiem for Father Las Casas") shows the ill-fated efforts of a priest to intercede with Spanish colonists on behalf of the Indians. *La tragedia del rey Christophe* ("The Tragedy of King Christophe") shows the downfall of Henri Christophe, a Haitian revolutionary hero of the early 1800s. After gaining renown as a fighter for Haitian independence, Christophe betrays his own ideals by proclaiming himself king and emulating the decadence of French royalty. The play received the UNESCO Prize for drama in 1965. During the late 1960s Buenaventura's work became more iconoclastic, as he experimented with theatrical styles and became openly critical of the society around him. His 1966 drama *La trampa* ("The Trap"), for example, is outwardly a portrait of the regime of Guatemalan dictator Jorge Ubico. By implication, however, as McMurray suggested, the play is also a portrait of some Colombian leaders. In 1967 Buenaventura released a group of short plays, known collectively as *Los papeles del infierno* ("Documents from Hell"), that forthrightly condemned the state of contemporary Colombian society. As the author wrote in a preface to the work, quoted in *Latin American Theatre Review,* the plays comprise

"a testimony of twenty years of violence and undeclared civil war" that plagued Colombia during *la violencia,* a period of political turmoil that lasted from the 1940s to the 1960s. To strengthen his message, observers suggest, Buenaventura employed the deliberately shocking "theater of cruelty" style advocated by French drama theorist Antonin Artaud. Among the plays considered part of *Las papeles del infierno* are *La maestra* ("The Schoolteacher"), in which a teacher testifies from beyond the grave about how she was raped by government soldiers and lost the will to live; *La tortura,* in which a government torturer makes brutality a part of his marriage; and *La autopsia,* in which a coroner who signs false autopsies to hide state-sponsored terrorism must inspect the corpse of his own son.

In *La orgia* ("The Orgy"), one of the culminating works of the collection, an old woman offers food and money to beggars if they will entertain her by impersonating her past lovers. As the beggars appear in borrowed finery, they parody four leading components of Colombia's longstanding oligarchy: the aristocracy, the politicians, the military, and the Catholic church. As the result of political controversy, by 1969 the Experimental Theater had been stripped of its government subsidy; Buenaventura and his followers were expelled from the local School of Fine Arts by order of the government of Cali and the Cuaca Valley. But under Buenaventura's leadership, the Experimental Theater continued successfully as an independent organization. It has since become known as a pioneer in collective production, in which the traditional hierarchy of the theater is de-emphasized and directors, actors, playwrights, and technicians work together to create their plays.

Two of the company's productions, each scripted and directed by Buenaventura, received high praise from Wolfgang Luchting in *Latin American Theatre Review.* Both productions were marked by heavy political exhortation, Luchting noted, but in each case the work was done "intelligently and *professionally.*" "Buenaventura is, I think, a very great director," the reviewer observed. "With a minimum of props and costumes he devises [stage] effects that are astounding." In keeping with such a highly visual style, the actors vividly physicalized their roles, displaying an aptitude for such skills as mime and even acrobatics. Luchting continued: "What they offer and how they perform and make use of the public's receptivity, for politics or for simple entertainment, is so engaging, so well orchestrated . . . that even the 'esthetes' cannot really criticize it; at least not the *theatricality* of it." The skill and self-assurance of both the actors and the director, the reviewer declared, placed them on a level of accomplishment far above the norm for experimental theaters in Latin America.

In a 1980 interview for *Theater,* Buenaventura looked back on the changing goals of Latin American playwrights such as himself, who wanted to foster a socially relevant alternative to commercial theater. "At first, we sought audiences made up of workers, of what is generally considered a popular audience," he recalled. However, he said, "experience has taught us that we can't base all our efforts on getting the working masses to go to the theater because they don't go"—whether in the Third World, in the West, or in Marxist Cuba. "Yet, this isn't new," he continued, adding, "Marx knew he had to write for the workers but, did they read him? Of course not." Accordingly, Buenaventura observed, "Our relationship with the viewing public has become rather 'polemic.' We now seek to engage the audience in the fundamental problems of our countries."

As the 1980s began, Buenaventura was at work on a new trilogy of historical dramas, according to Ana Maria Hernandez of *World Literature Today.* The first play in the series was the prize-winning *Historia de una bala de plata* ("Tale of a Silver Bullet"). Here the author returned to the early years of Haitian independence, showing the difficulties that plagued its original slave revolt, from American intruders to feuding revolutionaries. According to Hernandez, Buenaventura planned to cap the trilogy with a drama of the Cuban Revolution.

BIOGRAPHICAL/CRITICAL SOURCES:

PERIODICALS

Latin American Theatre Review, fall, 1975; spring, 1976; spring, 1979.
Revista-Chicano-Riquena, spring, 1983.
Theater, fall/winter, 1980.
World Literature Today, summer, 1981.*

*   *   *

BUNGE, Mario 1919-

PERSONAL: Born September 21, 1919, in Buenos Aires, Argentina; son of Augusto (a physician) and Marie (a nurse; maiden name, Mueser) Bunge; married Juluia D. Molina y Vedia (marriage ended); married Marta Cavallo (a professor of mathematics), 1959; children: Carlos, Mario A. J., Eric, Silvia. *Education:* Universidad Nacional de la Plata, Ph.D., 1952. *Politics:* Liberal. *Avocational interests:* Science and philosophy.

ADDRESSES: Office—Department of Philosophy, McGill University, Montreal, Quebec, Canada.

CAREER: Universidad de Buenos Aires, Buenos Aires, Argentina, professor of philosophy and physics, 1956-63; McGill University, Montreal, Quebec, professor of philosophy, 1966—. Universidad de la Plata, professor of physics, 1956-59; visiting professor at University of Pennsylvania, University of Texas, Temple University, University of Delaware, University of Freiburg, University of Aarhus, University of Zurich, Universite de Geneva, Universita di Genova, and Universidad Nacional Autonoma de Mexico.

MEMBER: Institut International de Philosophie, Academie Internationale de Philosophie des Sciences, Royal Society of Canada, American Association for the Advancement of Science (fellow).

AWARDS, HONORS: Guggenhiem fellow, 1972-73; Principe de Astudias Prize, 1982.

WRITINGS:

Causality, Harvard University Press (Cambridge, MA), 1959.
Treatise on Basic Philosophy, eight volumes, D. Reidel, 1974-89.
Finding Philosophy in Social Science, Yale University Press (New Haven, CT), 1996.
Social Science under Debate, University of Toronto Press (Toronto, Ontario), 1998.
Philosophy of Science, two volumes, Transaction Books (New Brunswick, NJ), 1998.

WORK IN PROGRESS: A manuscript on social dynamics.

*   *   *

BUSTOS, Francisco
See BORGES, Jorge Luis

C

CABEZA de BACA, Manuel 1853-1915

PERSONAL: Born in 1853; died in 1915; son of Tomas Cabeza de Baca and Estefanita Delgado. *Politics:* Republican.

CAREER: Lawyer for Atchison, Topeka & Sante Fe Railway; editor of the newspapers *El Sol de Mayo* and *El Independiente;* probate judge of San Miguel County, NM, 1889-90; superintendent of instruction in New Mexico, c. 1900; writer.

WRITINGS:

Historia de Vicente Silva, sus cuarenta bandidos, sus crimenes y retribuciones, Voz del Pueblo (Las Vegas, New Mexico), 1896, corrected and augmented by Francisco L. Lopez, Spanish-American Publishing (Las Vegas, New Mexico), c. 1900, translated by Lane Kauffmann as *Vicente Silva and His 40 Bandits,* McLean (Washington, DC), 1947.

Contributor of the poem "Duerme La Justica" ("Justice Sleeps") in *El Sol de Mayo,* 1891.

SIDELIGHTS: Writer Manuel Cabeza de Baca grew up in northern New Mexico and saw first hand the breakup of community property ownership that was the topic of his only book. Cabeza de Baca was the son of wealthy landholders and his grandfather was actually one of the first settlers of the Las Vegas land grant in 1821. Cabeza de Baca adopted the conservative beliefs of the elite to which he belonged and became active in Republican politics in the northern New Mexico county of San Miguel. In addition to practicing law, the author also served as a probate judge, superintendent of instruction, and newspaper editor.

Cabeza de Baca's book *Historia de Vicente Silva, sus cuarenta bandidos, sus crimenes y retribuciones* is the author's perspective of the nineteenth-century attempt to upset the status quo and transfer communal land holdings into the hands of wealthy northern New Mexicans such as the author's family. During this time, masked riders known as the White Caps (or *Gorras Blancas*) attempted to fight this land grab by raiding crops, buildings, and other property of the wealthy. Many in the region supported the White Caps, including the people on the settlements who had lost land to the wealthy. The White Caps were therefore often not punished for their actions.

From Cabeza de Baca's perspective, bandits such as the White Caps were responsible for the deterioration of Hispanic society in this region of New Mexico. The author uses the example of a real criminal and suspected White Cap—Vicente Silva—to illustrate that point. Silva carried out a number of crimes aimed at protesting the land-grabbing of the elite. The author covers the life of Silva, who gathered a band of criminals around him in the mid-1800s. Silva eventually killed his wife in 1893 and was murdered himself after a bounty of $3,000 had been placed on his head. According to essayist Ramon Sanchez in *Dictionary of Literary Biography,* "Silva is a real life symbol not only for Hispanic criminals but also cultural renegades." Sanchez remarked that the main thrust of Cabeza de Baca's work is to demonstrate how Silva (and others performing similar actions) "dishonored the community." In this way, the author gives voice to the conservative Hispanic opinions of the time. Cabeza de Baca accomplishes this with a mixture of journalistic facts, research, and literary devices. Sanchez pointed out that it appears that the book's narrator is "ringing the bell of alarm and that his sense of history is colored by the perception of community betrayal." As an example of this tone Sanchez quotes the following lines from the introduction to *Historia de Vicente Silva:* " . . . we want to demonstrate how and in what manner a gang of thieves, who after having laughed at society for years, have decayed and fallen apart one by one." Nonetheless, Sanchez pointed out that Cabeza de Baca falls short of giving the reader an explanation of how the region could have created and fostered a criminal such as Silva. In cases where the author lacked the research to explain the motives of his historical characters, he was forced to create dramatic enactments. These scenes, according to Sanchez, give the work (which could have been a strictly journalistic endeavor) a more literary feel. Sanchez concluded that the author's use of scenes, different voices, and symbolism make his work "more than a historical piece."

BIOGRAPHICAL/CRITICAL SOURCES:

BOOKS

Lomeli, Francisco A., and Carl R. Shirley, editors, *Dictionary of Literary Biography,* Volume 122: *Chicano Writers,* Second Series, Gale (Detroit), 1992.*

*   *   *

CABEZAS (LACAYO), Omar 1951(?)-

PERSONAL: Born c. 1951 in Nicaragua.

CAREER: Worked for Nicaraguan Government as chief of Council of Higher Education, as chief of Office of National Security, and as vice-minister of Office of Interior, beginning in 1979. Member of Sandinista National Liberation Front, beginning in 1968.

AWARDS, HONORS: Prose award from Casa de las Americas for *La montana es algo mas que una inmensa estepa verde.*

WRITINGS:

La montana es algo mas que una inmensa estepa verde (autobiography), Siglo Veintiuno (Mexico City), 1982, translation by Kathleen Weaver published as *Fire from the Mountain: The Making of a Sandinista,* introduction by Carlos Fuentes, Crown, 1985.

(With Dora Maria Tellez) *La insurreccion de las paredes: Pintas y graffiti de Nicaragua,* Editorial Nueva Nicaragua, 1984.

Cancion de amor para los hombres, Editorial Nueva Nicaragua (Managua, Nicaragua), 1988.

SIDELIGHTS: In *La montana es algo mas que una inmensa estepa verde* (*Fire from the Mountain: The Making of a Sandinista*), Nicaraguan official Omar Cabezas describes his early years as a member of the Sandinista National Liberation Front (FSLN). In 1968, when Cabezas joined the organization, the FSLN was a small, leftist movement committed to overthrowing the existing Nicaraguan government—long controlled by the Somoza family and supported by the United States. Within a decade, the FSLN—named after the famous Nicaraguan guerrilla Augusto Cesar Sandino—joined with other opposition elements in Nicaragua and toppled the Somoza regime. The Sandinistas, emerging from the revolution as the most powerful of the opposition groups, gained control of the new Nicaraguan government. During the 1980s Cabezas was appointed to several government posts and was awarded the rank of *comandante,* the highest in the Sandinista military.

Before the success of the revolution, though, the FSLN was barely able to survive as an opponent of the Somoza government. After Cabezas became a member in 1968, he spent the next several years as a student activist, recruiting members at the university in Leon, Nicaragua. This task proved extremely difficult, since the students knew that to criticize the Somoza government could mean imprisonment and death. In 1974 Cabezas decided to join a small group of Sandinistas living in the mountains of Nicaragua. Although the FSLN hoped to launch guerrilla attacks against the Nicaraguan army, the group remained too small to make an impact on the army. Since the army was unwilling to seriously pursue the Sandinistas, Cabezas and his fellow fighters never engaged in direct combat with the army during the year that the author spent in the mountains. Instead of fighting government soldiers, the Sandinistas fought disease and desertion. In his book, Cabezas reveals how difficult that struggle was, and highlights the precariousness of the FSLN's existence. The author notes, however, that after surviving their exile in the mountains, the Sandinistas forged a stronger cohesiveness and a more intense commitment to their cause.

Because *Fire from the Mountain* is in large part a political document, reviewers tended to focus less on the book's literary merits than on its political content. Some critics expressed their opposition to the U.S. government, which during the 1980s openly supported an armed rebellion against the Sandinistas simply because of the latter's leftist ideology. Accordingly, such reviewers commended Cabezas for revealing the Sandinistas as decent people committed only to improving the living conditions of their fellow Nicaraguans. Writing in the *Los Angeles Times Book Review,* Ariel Dorfman commented that "though Sandinistas like [Cabezas] have been branded the enemy by the President of the United States, Americans who read his story with an open mind may find it difficult to say, after finishing it, 'This man is my enemy. This man must be eliminated.'" Critics of different political persuasions reacted differently to the book. For example, in a review for *New Republic,* former Sandinista Xavier Arguello wrote of his opposition to the cause to which the book is devoted. Questioning Cabezas's respect for "liberty and democracy," Arguello noted that "a truly democratic socialism, creative and free, which the Sandinistas once promised, exists only as a myth for the consumption of . . . foreigners who after brief visits to Nicaragua return to their own countries to defend a system they do not truly know and would never themselves accept if by some misfortune they were forced to endure it."

Regardless of their political opinions, though, reviewers reacted favorably to the book's literary qualities. Some critics praised the chatty, informal tone of writing that Cabezas uses, achieved in part because the author dictated most of the text to a tape recorder. Others noted the tension and drama that he is able to create. Arguello, for his part, conceded that *Fire from the Mountain* is both interesting and largely accurate. "With a sense of humor all his own, and at times a distinctly poetic quality," stated Arguello, "Cabezas portrays the Sandinista forces very much as they really were in their early years, during their long physical and emotional struggle to survive as a small guerrilla army in the northern mountains of Somoza's Nicaragua." Similarly, Dorfman praised "the author's extraordinary sense of humor, the irreverence and earthiness of his language, [and] the sensuality of his imagery" and commented that "even for those who disagree with the author's politics . . . his story is fascinating."

BIOGRAPHICAL/CRITICAL SOURCES:

BOOKS

Cabezas, Omar, *Fire from the Mountain: The Making of a Sandinista,* Crown, 1985.

PERIODICALS

Los Angeles Times Book Review, June 16, 1985.
Nation, May 10, 1986.
New Republic, February 24, 1986.
New York Times Book Review, June 30, 1985.
Times Literary Supplement, October 25, 1985.
Washington Post Book World, July 14, 1985.*

*   *   *

CABRERA INFANTE, G(uillermo) 1929-
(G. Cain, Guillermo Cain)

PERSONAL: Born April 22, 1929, in Gibara, Cuba; immigrated to London, England, 1966; naturalized British citizen; son of Guillermo Cabrera Lopez (a journalist) and Zoila Infante; married Marta Calvo, August 18, 1953 (divorced, October, 1961); married Miriam Gomez, December 9, 1961; children: (first marriage) Ana, Carola. *Education:* Graduated from University of Havana, Cuba, 1956. *Politics:* "Reactionary on the left." *Religion:* Catholic. *Avocational interests:* Birdwatching, old movies.

ADDRESSES: Home—53 Gloucester Rd., London SW7, England. *Agent*—Carmen Balcells, Diagonal 580, Barcelona, 21, Spain.

CAREER: Writer. School of Journalism, Havana, Cuba, professor of English literature, 1960-61; Government of Cuba, Cuban embassy, Brussels, Belgium, cultural attache, 1962-64, charge d'affairs, 1964-65; scriptwriter for Twentieth-Century Fox and Cupid Productions, 1967-72. Visiting professor, University of Virginia, spring, 1982.

MEMBER: Writers Guild of Great Britain.

AWARDS, HONORS: Asi en paz como en la guerra was nominated for Prix International de Literature (France), 1962; unpublished manuscript version of *Tres tristes tigres* won Biblioteca Breve Prize (Spain), 1964, and was nominated for Prix Formentor—International Publishers Prize, 1965; Guggenheim fellowship for creative writing, 1970; Prix du Meilleur Livre Etranger (France), 1971, *Tres tristes tigres.*

WRITINGS:

FICTION

Asi en la paz como en la guerra: Cuentos (title means "In Peace as in War: Stories"), Revolucion (Havana), 1960, also published as *Writes of Passage,* translation by John Brookesmith, Peggy Boyers, and Cabrera Infante, Faber and Faber (London and Boston), 1993.

Vista del amanacer en el tropico, Seix Barral (Barcelona, Spain), 1965, translation by Suzanne Jill Levine published as *View of Dawn in the Tropics,* Harper, 1978.

Tres tristes tigres, Seix Barral, 1967, translation by Donald Gardner, Levine, and the author published as *Three Trapped Tigers,* Harper, 1971.

La Habana para un infante difunto, Seix Barral, 1979, translation by Levine and the author published as *Infante's Inferno,* Harper, 1984.

FILM CRITICISM

(Under pseudonym G. Cain) *Un oficio del siglo veinte* (film reviews originally published in magazine, *Carteles;* also see below), Revolucion, 1963, translation by Kenneth Hall and Cabrera Infante published as *A Twentieth-Century Job,* Faber, 1991.

Arcadia todas las noches (title means "Arcadia Every Night"), Seix Barral, 1978.

Cine o sardina, Santillana (Madrid), 1997.

OTHER

(Editor) *Mensajes de libertad: La Espana rebelde—Ensayos selectos,* Movimiento Universitario Revolucionario (Lima, Peru), 1961.

Vanishing Point (screenplay), Twentieth-Century Fox, 1970.

(Translator into Spanish) James Joyce, *Dublineses* (*Dubliners*), Lumen (Barcelona), 1972.

O (essays), Seix Barral, 1975.

Exorcismos del esti(l)o (title means "Summer Exorcisms" and "Exorcising Style"; English, French, and Spanish text), Seix Barral, 1976.

Cuban Writer Guillermo Cabrera Infante Reading from His Work (sound recording; recorded February 26, 1982, for the Archive of Hispanic Literature on Tape), Library of Congress (Washington, DC), 1982.

Holy Smoke (nonfiction; English text), Harper, 1985.

(Author of introduction) Virgilio Pianera, *Cold Tales,* translation by Mark Schafer, revised by Thomas Christensen, Eridanos Press (New York City), 1988.

(With others) *Diablesas y diosas: 14 perversas para 15 autores,* Editorial Laertes (Barcelona), 1990.

Mea Cuba (collection of writings on Cuba), Plaza & Janes (Barcelona), 1992, translation by Kenneth Hall with the author published as *Mea Cuba,* Farrar, Straus, & Giroux (New York City), 1994.

(Author of prologue) *La fiesta innombrable: trece poetas cubanos,* Ediciones el Tucan de Virginia (Mexico, DF), 1992.

Vaya papaya!: Ramon Alejandro (exhibition catalog), Le Polygraphe (Paris), 1992.

(Author of prologue) Jose Luis Guarner, *Autoretrato del cronista,* Anagrama (Barcelona), 1994.

Delito por bailar el chachacha, Santillana (Madrid), 1995.

(Contributor) *The Borges Tradition,* Constable (London), 1995.

Mi musica extremada, Espasa Calpe (Madrid), 1996.

Ella cantaba boleros, Santillana (Madrid), 1996.

(Author of prologue) Augusto M. Torres, *Diccionario Espasa cine,* Espasa (Madrid), 1996.

Also author of screenplay, *Wonderwall,* 1968, and of unfilmed screenplay, *Under the Volcano,* based on Malcolm Lowry's novel of the same title. Also translator of stories by Mark Twain, Ambrose Bierce, Sherwood Anderson, Ernest Hemingway, William Faulkner, Dashiell Hammett, J. D. Salinger, Vladimir Nabokov, and others. Work is represented in many anthologies. Contributor to periodicals, including *New Yorker, New Republic, El Pais* (Spain), and *Plural* (Mexico). *Carteles* (Cuban magazine), film reviewer under pseudonym G. Cain, 1954-60, fiction editor, 1957-60; editor of *Lunes* (weekly literary supplement of Cuban newspaper, *Revolucion*), 1959-61.

SIDELIGHTS: Talking about his award-winning first novel *Tres tristes tigres,* translated as *Three Trapped Tigers,* Cuban-born writer Guillermo Cabrera Infante told Rita Guibert in *Seven Voices:* "I would prefer everyone to consider the book solely as a joke lasting about five hundred pages. Latin American literature errs on the side of excessive seriousness, sometimes solemnity. It is like a mask of solemn words, which writers and readers put up with by mutual consent."

As Alastair Reid points out in the *New York Review of Books,* Cabrera Infante is a contemporary of Castro; his parents were founding members of the

Cuban Communist Party. Following Castro's rise to power, Cabrera Infante was appointed editor of *Lunes de Revolucion,* the literary supplement to the new regime's mouthpiece, *Revolucion.* In this role, he also provided support to his brother's development of a documentary on night-life in Havana. The documentary was subsequently banned by authorities as counter-revolutionary. Cabrera Infante protested the banning via *Lunes* but was rebuked publicly on his "duties to the Revolution" by Castro in a trial, and *Lunes* was closed down. Notes Reid, "Cabrera Infante found himself in the kind of limbo many Cuban writers of his generation were to inhabit in succeeding years, forbidden to publish. 'Within the Revolution, everything! Against the Revolution, nothing!' as Fidel 'thundered like a thousand Zeuses.'" He was assigned to Brussels as a cultural attache and returned to Cuba for his mother's funeral in 1965, but faced "the precariousness of any continuing Cuban existence under an imposed silence . . . he accepted the inevitability of exile," concludes Reid. He was expelled from the Union of Writers and Artists of Cuba as a traitor in 1968, following the publishing of *Three Trapped Tigers,* and began to write and speak publicly on Cuba.

In *Three Trapped Tigers,* we hear the voices of a group of friends as they take part in the nightlife of pre-Castro Havana. The friends take turns narrating the story using the colloquial speech of the lower-class inhabitants of that city. Told from many perspectives and using the language of a small population group, the narrative is not always easy to follow. Elias L. Rivers explains in *Modern Language Notes:* "While some passages are readily accessible to any reader, others are obscured by Cuban vernaculars in phonetic transcription and by word-plays and allusions of many different kinds. A multiplicity of 'voices' engage in narrative, dialogue and soliloquy. [The novel] is a test which fascinates as it eludes and frustrates; the over-all narrative sense is by no-means obvious."

The importance of spoken language in *Three Trapped Tigers* is apparent even in the book's title, which in its English version repeats only the alliteration found in the Spanish title and not the title's actual meaning. Inside the book, the emphasis on sound continues as the characters pun relentlessly. There are so many puns in the book that *New Republic* contributor Gregory Rabassa maintains that in it Cabrera Infante "established himself as the punmaster of Spanish-American literature." Appearing most often are literary puns, including such examples as "Shame's Choice" used to refer to James Joyce, "Scotch

Fizzgerald" for Scott Fitzgerald and "Somersault Mom" for Somerset Maugham. In another example, a bongo player—a member of the group of friends whose exploits are followed in the novel—is called "Vincent Bon Gogh."

If the emphasis on spoken rather than written language makes complete understanding of the novel difficult, it has made translating nearly impossible. Comparison of the Spanish, English, and French editions of the book prove that readers of each language are not reading the same text. "What Cabrera [Infante] has really done," comments Roger Sale in the *New York Review of Books,* "is to write, presumably with the help of his translators, three similar but different novels." Because of the word play, Sale continues, "quite obviously no translation can work if it attempts word-for-word equivalents."

Playing with words is also an important part of Cabrera Infante's next novel, *Infante's Inferno,* and his nonfiction work, *Holy Smoke.* The latter—Cabrera Infante's first book written originally in English—tells the history of the cigar and describes famous smoking scenes from literature and film. Unlike the nearly universal acclaim received for *Three Trapped Tigers,* critics were unable to reach a consensus on these two works. While some praised Cabrera Infante's continued use of puns as innovative, other had grown tired of the Cuban's verbal contortions.

Commenting on *Infante's Inferno* in the *New York Review of Books* Michael Wood complains that Cabrera Infante's relentless punning "unrepentedly mangles language and hops from one tongue to another like a frog released from the throat. Some of the jokes are . . . terrible. . . . Others are so cumbersome, so fiendishly worked for, that the noise of grinding machinery deafens all the chance of laughter." *New York Review of Books* contributor Josh Rubins has similar problems with *Holy Smoke.* He comments, "In *Holy Smoke* . . . the surfeit of puns seems to arise not from mania. . . , but from mere tic. Or, worse yet, from a computer program."

Other reviewers are not so harsh in their criticism. In Enrique Fernandez's *Voice Literary Supplement* review of *Infante's Inferno,* for example, the critic observes that the novel is written in "an everyday Cuban voice, unaffected, untrammeled [and], authentic." John Gross of the *New York Times* hails Cabrera Infante as a master in the use of language. Commenting on *Holy Smoke,* he claims: "Conrad and Nabokov apart, no other writer for whom English is a second language can ever have used it with more virtuousity. He is a master of idiomatic echoes and glancing allusions; he keeps up a constant barrage of wordplay, which is often outrageous, but no more outrageous than he intends it to be."

Cabrera Infante's *Mea Cuba* is a collection of his writings on Cuba produced after he left the country. Given the nature of his departure, *Mea Cuba* "as opposed to its gleeful predecessors . . . is in a sense a reluctant book, one that he would hardly have chosen to write had it not more or less accrued through time," comments Reid. Critics, while recognizing the inherent value of the work, were mixed in their reactions. "For all its essential rectifications, *Mea Cuba* is so overstated, so patently inflamed by spite and thwarted ambition, that it forfeits its place in the rational, non-polarised debate about Cuba that is needed at this time," declares Lorna Scott Fox in the *London Review of Books*. Alma Guillermopriet, commenting in the *New York Times Book Review*, concludes, "Despite the dazzling writing . . . the style sometimes overwhelms the chronicle, and one finds oneself wishing for a respite from the shrill delivery and the endless petty settling of accounts. . . . At his worst, the bombastic punster's salvos are not meaningful but mean. At his best, he provides a moving chronicle of love and despair for the country he lost to Castro." Will H. Corral, writing for *World Literature Today*, finds academic significance as well as entertainment in Cabrera Infante's writings, noting "his texts read as the ideal format for what is bandied about the United States as cultural studies. Despite one's differences with his politics, Cabrera Infante's knowledge of Cuban literariness is the broadest, liveliest, and nastiest to date."

Three Trapped Tigers established Cabrera Infante's reputation as a writer of innovative fiction, a reputation that some critics find justified by his later work. Cabrera Infante once described his literary beginnings to *CA*: "It all began with parody. If it were not for a parody I wrote on a Latin American writer who was later to win the Nobel Prize, I wouldn't have become a professional writer and I wouldn't qualify to be here at all. My parents wanted me to go to University and I would have liked to become a doctor. But somehow that dreadful novel crossed my path. After reading a few pages (I just couldn't stomach it all, of course) and being only seventeen at the time, I said to myself, 'Why, if that's what writing is all about—*anch'io sono scrittore* [I am also a writer]!' To prove I too was a writer I wrote a parody of the pages I had read. It was a dreadfully serious parody and unfortunately

the short story I wrote was taken by what was then the most widely read publication in Latin America, the Cuban magazine, *Bohemia*. They paid me what at the time I considered a fortune and I was hooked: probably hooked by fortune, probably hooked by fame but certainly hooked by writing."

BIOGRAPHICAL/CRITICAL SOURCES:

BOOKS

Alvarez-Borland, Isabel, *Discontinuidad y ruptura en Guillermo Cabrera Infante*, Hispanamerica, 1982.

Contemporary Literary Criticism, Gale, Volume 5, 1976, Volume 25, 1983, Volume 45, 1987.

Diaz Ruiz, Ignacio, *Cabrera Infante y otros escritores latinoamericanos*, Universidad Nacional Autonoma de Mexico (Mexico), 1992.

Dictionary of Literary Biography, Volume 113: *Modern Latin-American Fiction Writers*, First Series, Gale, 1992.

Feal, Rosemary Geisdorfer, *Novel Lives: The Fictional Autobiographies of Guillermo Cabrera Infante and Mario Vargas Llosa*, University of North Carolina Press (Chapel Hill), 1986.

Gallagher, David Patrick, *Modern Latin-American Literature*, Oxford University Press, 1973.

Gil Lopez, Ernesto, *Guillermo Cabrera Infante: La Habana, el lenguaje y la cinematografia*, ACT, Cabildo Insular de Tenerife (Tenerife), 1991.

Guibert, Rita, *Seven Voices*, Knopf, 1973.

Hernandez-Lima, Dinorah, *Versiones y re-versiones historicas en la obra de Cabrera Infante*, Pliegos (Madrid), 1990.

Jimenez, Reynaldo L., *Guillermo Cabrera Infante y Tres tristes tigres*, Ediciones Universal (Miami, FL), 1976.

Machover, Jacobo, *El heraldo de las malas noticias: Guillermo Cabrera Infante: ensayo a dos voces*, Ediciones Universal, 1996.

Nelson, Ardis L., *Cabrera Infante in the Menippean Tradition*, with prologue by Cabrera Infante, Juan de la Cuesta (Newark, Delaware), 1983.

Pereda, Rosa Maria, *Guillermo Cabrera Infante*, Edaf, D.L. (Madrid), 1979.

Souza, Raymond D., *Major Cuban Novelists: Innovation and Tradition*, University of Missouri Press, 1976.

Souza, Raymond D., *Guillermo Cabrera Infante: Two Islands, Many Worlds*, University of Texas Press (Austin), 1996.

Tittler, Jonathan, *Narrative Irony in the Contemporary Spanish-American Novel*, Cornell University Press, 1984.

Volek, Emil, *Cuatro claves para la modernidad: Aleixandre, Borges, Carpentier, Cabrera Infante,* Gredos (Madrid), 1984.

PERIODICALS

Americas, July-August, 1995, p. 24.
Booklist, November 1, 1994, p. 475.
Book World, October 3, 1971.
Commonweal, November 12, 1971.
Library Journal, November 1, 1994, p. 93.
London Review of Books, October 4-17, 1984; February 6, 1986; November 24, 1994, p. 22.
Los Angeles Times, June 6, 1984.
Modern Language Notes, March, 1977.
Nation, November 4, 1978.
New Republic, July 9, 1984.
Newsweek, October 25, 1971.
New Yorker, September 19, 1977.
New York Review of Books, December 16, 1971; June 28, 1984; May 8, 1986; February 2, 1995.
New York Times Book Review, October 17, 1971; May 6, 1984; March 2, 1986.
Observer (London), September 2, 1984; October 13, 1985; December 21, 1986.
Paris Review, spring, 1983.
Review, January 10, 1972.
Time, January 10, 1972.
Times Literary Supplement, April 18, 1968; October 12, 1984; August 26, 1986.
Village Voice, March 25, 1986.
Voice Literary Supplement, April 18, 1968; October 12, 1984; August 29, 1986.
Washington Post Book World, January 28, 1979; May 27, 1984.
World Literature Today, spring, 1977; summer, 1981.*

* * *

CAIN, G.
See CABRERA INFANTE, G(uillermo)

* * *

CAIN, Guillermo
See CABRERA INFANTE, G(uillermo)

CANDELARIA, Nash 1928-

PERSONAL: Born May 7, 1928, in Los Angeles, CA; son of Ignacio N. (a railway mail clerk) and Flora (Rivera) Candelaria; married Doranne Godwin (a fashion designer), November 27, 1955; children: David, Alex. *Education:* University of California, Los Angeles, B.S., 1948. *Politics:* "I usually seem to vote for the person who doesn't get elected." *Religion:* "Non-church-going monotheistic and cultural Christian." *Avocational interests:* The arts and family, reading, and the stock market.

ADDRESSES: Home—1295 Wilson St., Palo Alto, CA 94301.

CAREER: Don Baxter, Inc. (pharmaceutical firm), Glendale, CA, chemist, 1948-52; Atomics International, Downey, CA, technical editor, 1953-54; Beckman Instruments, Fullerton, CA, promotion supervisor, 1954-59; Northrup-Nortronics, Anaheim, CA, in marketing communications, 1959-65; Hixon & Jorgensen Advertising, Los Angeles, CA, account executive, 1965-67; Varian Associates, Inc. (in scientific instruments), Palo Alto, CA, advertising manager, 1967-82; freelance writer, 1982-85; Daisy Systems Corp., Mountain View, CA, marketing writer, 1985-87; Hewlett-Packard Co., Palo Alto, marketing writer, 1987—. *Military service:* U.S. Air Force, 1952-53; became second lieutenant.

AWARDS, HONORS: Not by the Sword was a finalist in the Western Writers of America Spur Award competition, 1982, and received the Before Columbus Foundation American Book Award, 1983.

WRITINGS:

Memories of the Alhambra (novel), Cibola Press (Palo Alto, CA), 1977.
(Contributor) Gary D. Keller and Francisco Jimenez, editors, *Hispanics in the United States: An Anthology of Creative Literature,* Bilingual Press (Ypsilanti, MI), Volume 1, 1980, Volume 2, 1982.
Not by the Sword (novel), Bilingual Press, 1982.
(Contributor) Nicholas Kanellos, editor, *A Decade of Hispanic Literature: An Anniversary Anthology* Arte Publico, 1982.
Inheritance of Strangers (novel), Bilingual Press (Binghampton, NY), 1984.
The Day the Cisco Kid Shot John Wayne (short stories), Bilingual Press (Tempe, AZ), 1988.
Leonor Park (novel), Bilingual Press, 1991.

Uncivil Rights, and Other Stories, Bilingual Press (Tempe, AZ), 1998.

Contributor of short stories to *Bilingual Review;* contributor to *Science.* Editor, *VIA.*

SIDELIGHTS: Nash Candelaria is an historical novelist who writes about the Hispanic people of New Mexico. Himself a descendent of one of the founders of Albuquerque, Candelaria "explores the relationship between historical incident and individual destiny," to quote *Dictionary of Literary Biography* correspondent Paula W. Shirley. Candelaria's works—written in English—have reached a readership beyond the Chicano community in which he was raised, helping to increase awareness of the cultural conflicts and nuances of assimilation among Hispanic Americans.

Although he was born and raised in Los Angeles, Candelaria spent many of his summers in New Mexico with his extended, Spanish-speaking family. These summertime experiences helped him to forge an awareness of the unique aspects of New Mexican Chicano culture—and his immersion in Anglo life gave him a broader perspective on how his family's culture was changing in modern times. According to Shirley, "Participation in Anglo and Hispanic life made [Candelaria] feel part of both cultures yet gave him a certain objectivity that has to a great extent determined the course of his writing." These impulses would simmer many years while the author earned a college degree in chemistry and embarked on a long and fruitful career of science writing, science advertising, and sales promotions.

During his tour of duty in the Korean War, Candelaria began to spend his spare time writing fiction. He continued when he returned to civilian life, and by his own estimate he penned seven novels that never saw print before finally embarking on the project that would become *Memories of the Alhambra* in 1977.

Memories of the Alhambra is the first novel in a tetralogy that explores the links between family and history in New Mexico. The saga that unfolds in *Memories of the Alhambra* is enriched in the subsequent titles, *Not by the Sword, The Inheritance of Strangers,* and *Leonor Park.* All of the works follow the various vicissitudes of the Rafa family, small landowners in the vicinity of Albuquerque. Candelaria was quoted in the *Dictionary of Hispanic Biography* as having said that his Rafa series grew from a desire to reveal to his sons "something of their Hispano-

Indian background" as his own pride in his heritage grew.

In *Memories of the Alhambra,* the foundation for the tetralogy is laid in the depiction of "the contemporary conflict of the Hispanic New Mexican who identifies with the Spanish and European past more than with his Indian and mestizo heritage," to quote Shirley. The central character, Jose Rafa, leaves his home and family in search of his genealogical ties to European conquistadors, in a psychological attempt to free himself from what he perceives as an inferior Mexican ancestry. Rafa's travels only serve to illustrate that European and Native American are inexorably tied in Mexico, and he dies disappointed with the discovery. In a review of the book in *De Colores,* Vernon E. Lattin wrote: "Candelaria adds a new page to the Chicano novel, testifying to the fact that Chicano fiction is not limited to certain ideological themes or certain stock answers to questions of identity and ethnicity."

The issues of history, genealogy, and myth are further explored in the subsequent Rafa novels, two of which are set in the nineteenth century in the years encompassing the Mexican War of 1846 to 1848. Shirley declared that the books are concerned with "tradition and the continuing struggle to preserve it," as Yankees overrun New Mexico and proceed to influence its Spanish-speaking inhabitants. "Candelaria's Rafa [tetralogy] is a novelistic representation of his view of culture as steadily evolving," observed Shirley. "Through his work he rejects the notion 'that there is a fixed Chicano culture that we can go back to, like Eden, when in reality it is changing all the time.' This appears to be a repudiation of the myth of Aztlan in favor of acceptance of the inevitability of radical change and assimilation." Despite his assimilationist view, however, Candelaria "vividly depicts the present in which his characters live and their natural resistance to change," noted Shirley. The critic concluded that, as a historical novelist, Candelaria "contributes a view of historical reality which enhances the reader's understanding of the Chicano experience."

Candelaria once told *CA:* "*Memories of the Alhambra* is about the Chicano heritage myth of being descendants of conquistadors, the unsolvable dilemma of Hispanics from the state of New Mexico who acknowledge their European heritage and may not accept their American Indian heritage. . . . *Not by the Sword* is a look at the Mexican War (1846-48) from the point of view of New Mexicans, who became

Americans by conquest. *Inheritance of Strangers,* a sequel to *Not by the Sword,* looks at the aftermath of the Mexican War forty years later, and the problems of assimilation; it focuses on the futility of revenge and the difficulty of forgiveness by a conquered people. *The Day the Cisco Kid Shot John Wayne* is a collection of twelve stories that give insight into and understanding of the Hispanic experience in the United States and its interface with the dominant Anglo culture.

"I am a descendant of one of the founding families of Albuquerque, New Mexico, and an ancestor, Juan, authored a history of New Mexico in 1776. Although I was born in California, I consider myself a New Mexican by heritage and sympathy. My writing is primarily about Hispanic Americans, trying, through fictIon, to present some of their stories to a wider audience that may only be aware of them as a 'silent minority.'"

BIOGRAPHICAL/CRITICAL SOURCES:

BOOKS

Dictionary of Hispanic Biography, Gale (Detroit, MI), 1996, pp. 159-161.
Dictionary of Literary Biography, Volume 82: *Chicano Writers, First Series,* Gale, 1989, pp. 68-73.
Martinez, Julio A., and Francisco A. Lomeli, editors, *Chicano Literature: A Reference Guide,* Greenwood Press (Westport, CT), 1985.
Meier, Matt S., *Mexican American Biographies: A Historical Dictionary, 1836-1987,* Greenwood Press, 1988.

PERIODICALS

Best Sellers, August, 1977; May, 1983.
Carta Abierta, number 9, 1977.
De Colores, September, 1980, pp. 102-14, 115-29.
La Opinion, March 31, 1985, pp. 6-7.
New Mexico Magazine, September, 1977.
Western American Literature, summer, 1978, p. 191; spring, 1984.

*   *   *

CANTU, Norma Elia 1947-

PERSONAL: Born January 3, 1947, in Nuevo Laredo, Tamaulipas, Mexico; immigrated to the United States, 1948; naturalized citizen, 1968; daughter of Florentino and Virginia (Ramon) Cantu. *Ethnicity:* "Chicana." *Education:* Texas A & I, Laredo, B.S., 1973; Texas A & I, Kingsville, M.S., 1975; University of Nebraska, Ph.D., 1982; attending Georgetown University. *Avocational interests:* Human rights and environmental issues.

ADDRESSES: Email—necantu@tamiu.edu.

CAREER: Texas A & M International University, Laredo, TX, professor of English, 1980—. Visiting professor at Georgetown University School for Continuing Education, 1994-95; has read poetry, given lectures, and presented papers in locations throughout the United States, Mexico, and Paris, France. Has served as an editor or consultant for the University of New Mexico Press, Texas A & M University Press, and *Chicana/Latina Studies Journal;* produced and moderated *Fiesta Latina,* a weekly public service radio program on KRNU; past director of Teatro Chicano/a at the University of Nebraska; past translator at the Development Center for Hispanic Affairs in Lincoln, NE; has served on several other community projects.

MEMBER: Amnesty International, Modern Languages Association, American Association of University Women, National Women's Studies Association, National Association of Chicano/Chicana Studies, Mujeres Activas en Letras y Cambio Social, Feministas Unidas, South Central Modern Languages Association, Texas Council of Teachers of English, Laredo Philosophical Society, Literacy Volunteer of America.

AWARDS, HONORS: Rotary International Scholarship, 1965-66; Ford Foundation Graduate Fellow, 1977-78, 1978-79; Fulbright-Hays Research Fellow to Spain, 1979-80; Ford Foundation Chicano Dissertation Completion Grant, 1982; U.S.-Spanish Joint Committee Post Doctoral Research Fellowship, 1985; research grant from Texas Folklife Resources, 1987-88; elected to Laredo Women's Hall of Fame, 1995.

WRITINGS:

Canicula: Snapshots of a Girlhood en la frontera, University of New Mexico Press (Albuquerque), 1995.

Also author of *Papeles de mujer;* contributor of articles, stories, poems, and reviews to periodicals, including *LareDOS, Nebraska Humanist, Prairie Schooner, Texas Humanist, Huehuetitlan, Washington*

Post Book World, Western Historical Quarterly, Journal of Popular Culture, La Red/The Net, English in Texas, Si Laredo, and *ERIC.*

Contributor to books, including *Para Ninos from Two Cultures,* Texas A & I University at Laredo (Laredo, TX), 1973; *New Chicano/a Literature* (short stories), University of Arizona Press (Tucson, AZ), 1992; *Mito y Leyenda* (nonfiction; title means "Myth and Legend"), Colegio de la Frontera Norte (Tijuana, Mexico), 1992; *Hecho en Texas* (nonfiction; title means "Made in Texas"), University of North Texas Press (Denton, TX), 1992; *Program Book for the Festival of American Folklife,* Smithsonian Institution (Washington, DC), 1993; *Feasts and Celebrations in U.S. Ethnic Communities* (nonfiction), edited by Ramon Gutierrez, University of New Mexico Press, 1995; and *In Short* (short stories), edited by Judith Kitchen and Mary Paumier Jones, Norton (New York City), 1996.

WORK IN PROGRESS: Soldiers of the Cross: Matachines of Laredo Texas, for Texas A & M Press; a volume of poetry, *Shadow of Smoke;* a novel, *Cabanuelas.*

SIDELIGHTS: Educator and author Norma Elia Cantu has spent much of her life in Laredo, Texas, just across the border from Nuevo Laredo, Mexico, where she was born. She immigrated to the United States with her parents when she was a small child, and received much of her education—even at the college level—in and around Laredo. Cantu earned her doctorate, however, in Nebraska, but returned to her long-time home to teach at Texas A & M International University, where she has remained since 1980. She has been active in promoting Chicano/Chicana culture both as an educator and in academic and community organizations.

Cantu has written in several genres, ranging from short stories and poetry to academic articles and book chapters. She has also penned a book of her own. One of the best known of these works is 1995's *Canicula: Snapshots of a Girlhood en la frontera.* "Canicula," explained Sara Castro-Klaren in the *Washington Post Book World,* "is Spanish for the dog days, the hottest days of summer, those idle days when the mind wanders in reverie." As the Spanish of the secondary title implies, Cantu's knowledge of growing up along the U.S.-Mexican border informs the volume. "What may appear to be autobiographical," Cantu declares in *Canicula,* "is not always so." The author instead of-

fers the label "fictional autobioethnography" for the book.

Canicula is narrated by Nena, whose recounted memories are sparked by the family photographs she finds in a cardboard box. Cantu has included photographs of her own family, often placed at the head of the various stories Nena relates to the reader. In addition to Nena herself, these tales—eighty-six in all—focus on her mother, father, and grandmother, as well as her siblings and friends. Ana Maria Juarez in *Southwestern American Literature* praised Cantu's ability to richly portray characters of many different sexes, races, and economic states. She also lauded the genre multiplicity of the book as a whole: "By drawing on the innovative and interdisciplinary nature of cultural studies, along with her personal and cultural experiences, Cantu's new genre represents the South Texas border better than depictions that are strictly wedded to official disciplinary borders or to objectivist and positivist notions of truth. . . . Furthermore, it is such a pleasure to read." Similarly, Castro-Klaren hailed *Canicula* as "a joy to read and a nice addition to the growing body of distinguished Chicano literature."

Claire Joysmith, reviewing *Canicula* in *Voices of Mexico,* revealed that Cantu wrote the work during the season for which she named it. To Joysmith, "*Canicula* smells of musty, parchment-like, sepia-tinted pictures that live suspended in time inside an old shoebox tied with faded ribbon, enclosed in near-oblivion until the miracle of sight, memory and articulated words restore them to life—to a life of their own." The critic also discussed the author's multiple use of the border concept within the work. Besides the border between the United States and Mexico, for instance, there is also the border which Nena crosses from girlhood into womanhood. Joysmith concluded that "Cantu points to the ambiguous relationship Chicanas and Chicanos have with their past, and to the imperative need *not* to forget that past, even when it is painful."

Cantu told *CA:* "As a daughter of the U.S.-Mexico borderlands, I am fluent in two languages and multiple cultures; this gives me an edge as a writer. I write in Spanish, in English, and in the language of the border depending on whether I am writing poetry, criticism, or fiction.

"Writing is an extension of my work as a Chicana activist. When I work with the local literacy program or work with the community women's group, *Las mujeres (The Women),* I am also creating and impacting the world.

"A writer owes allegiance to herself first and foremost, and in honoring her truth all else falls into place. I love books, and I know the power of words to inspire and to incite, but I also know that writing can obfuscate and distort truth. Writers follow a path, although they don't always know where it leads, and discover truths not always pleasant but critical."

BIOGRAPHICAL/CRITICAL SOURCES:

PERIODICALS

Southwestern American Literature, spring, 1995, pp. 110-112.
Voices of Mexico, January-March, 1996, pp. 107-109.
Washington Post Book World, August 20, 1995, p. 8.

*   *   *

CARBAJAL, Xavier Joseph 1958-

PERSONAL: Born September 22, 1958, in Camp LeJeune, NC; son of Henry and June (Stinson) Carbajal; married Sherry Lynn Jodway (a publisher). *Ethnicity:* "Hispanic/Irish American." *Education:* Attended Schoolcraft Community College and Michigan State University, 1976-81, and University of Michigan, 1981-88. *Politics:* Republican. *Religion:* "Roman Catholic/Jewish." *Avocational interests:* Writing screenplays, mass media, publishing, archival research.

ADDRESSES: Office—New Future Publishing, Inc., 2222 Fuller Court, Suite 505A, Ann Arbor, MI 48105.

CAREER: New Future Publishing, Inc., Ann Arbor, MI, staff member, c. 1995—.

AWARDS, HONORS: MacClean Hunter Cable Awards, 1987, 1988; award for volunteer work, American Red Cross, 1990-91.

WRITINGS:

Captain Nemo (science fiction/fantasy), New Future Publishing (Ann Arbor, MI), 1996.
Lady President (political suspense novel), New Future Publishing, 1997.

WORK IN PROGRESS: Captain Nemo: Rise of the Empire, publication by New Future Publishing expected in 1999; research on environmental issues, international affairs, politics, oceanography, computer science, medical research, naval and navigational research, and space sciences.

SIDELIGHTS: Xavier Joseph Carbajal told *CA:* "I enjoy protagonists in conflicts that seem impossible to resolve or survive. I also enjoy pursuing subjects that involve challenging research and detail."

*   *   *

CARDENAL, Ernesto 1925-

PERSONAL: Born January 20, 1925, in Granada, Nicaragua; son of Rodolfo and Esmerelda (Martinez) Cardenal. *Education:* Attended University of Mexico, 1944-48, and Columbia University, 1948-49. *Politics:* Christian-Marxist.

ADDRESSES: Home—Carretera a Masaya Km. 9 1/2, Apt. A-252, Managua, Nicaragua.

CAREER: Ordained Roman Catholic priest, 1965. Poet, and author; formerly Minister of Culture in Nicaragua.

AWARDS, HONORS: Christopher Book Award, 1972, for *The Psalms of Struggle and Liberation;* Premio de la Paz grant, Libreros de la Republica Federal de Alemania, 1980.

WRITINGS:

Ansias lengua de la poesia nueva nicaraguense (poems), [Nicaragua], 1948.
Gethsemani, Ky. (poems), Ecuador 0 Degrees 0' 0", 1960, 2nd edition, with foreword by Thomas Merton, Ediciones La Tertulia (Medellin, Colombia), 1965.
Hora 0 (poems), Revista Mexicano de Literatura, 1960.
Epigramas: Poemas, Universidad Nacional Autonoma de Mexico, 1961.
(Translator with Jose Coronel Urtecho) *Antologia de la poesia Norteamericana,* Aguilar (Madrid), 1963, Alianza (Madrid), 1979.
(Translator and editor-at-large with Jorge Montoya Toro) *Literatura indigena americana: Antologia,*

Editorial Universidad de Antioquia (Medellin), 1964.

Oracion por Marilyn Monroe, y otros poemas, Ediciones La Tertulia, 1965, reprinted, Editorial Nueva Nicaragua-Ediciones Monimbo, 1985, translation by Robert Pring-Mill published as *Marilyn Monroe and Other Poems,* Search Press, 1975.

El estrecho dudoso (poems), Ediciones Cultura Hispanica (Madrid), 1966, Editorial Nueva Nicaragua-Ediciones Monimbo, 1985, translation by Tamara R. Williams published as *The Doubtful Strait,* Indiana University Press (Bloomington), 1995.

Antologia de Ernesto Cardenal (poems), Editora Santiago (Santiago, Chile), 1967.

Poemas de Ernesto Cardenal, Casa de las Americas (Havana), 1967.

Salmos (poems), Institucion Gran Duque de Alba (Avila, Spain), 1967, Ediciones El Pez y la Serpiente (Managua, Nicaragua), 1975, translation by Emile G. McAnany published as *The Psalms of Struggle and Liberation,* Herder & Herder, 1971, translation from the sixth edition of 1974 by Thomas Blackburn and others published as *Psalms,* Crossroad Publishing, 1981.

Mayapan (poem), Editorial Alemana (Managua, Nicaragua), 1968.

Homenaje a los indios americanos (poems), Universidad Nacional Autonoma de Nicaragua, 1969, Laia (Madrid), 1983, translation by Carlos Altschul and Monique Altschul published as *Homage to the American Indians,* Johns Hopkins University Press, 1974.

Vida en el Amor (meditations; with foreword by Thomas Merton), Lohle (Buenos Aires), 1970, translation by Kurt Reinhardt published as *To Live Is to Love,* Herder & Herder, 1972, published in England as *Love,* Search Press, 1974, translation by Dinah Livingstone published as *Love,* Crossroad Publishing, 1981, translation by Mev Puleo published as *Abide in Love,* Orbis Books (Maryknoll, NY), 1995.

La hora cero y otros poemas, Ediciones Saturno, 1971, translation by Paul W. Borgeson and Jonathan Cohen published as *Zero Hour and Other Documentary Poems,* edited by Donald D. Walsh, New Directions, 1980.

Antologia: Ernesto Cardenal, edited by Pablo Antonio Cuadra, Lohle, 1971, 2nd edition, Universidad Centroamericana, 1975.

Poemas, Editorial Leibres de Sinera, 1971.

Poemas reunidos, 1949-1969, Direccion de Cultura, Universidad de Carabobo, 1972.

(And translator) *Epigramas* (with translations from Catullus and Martial), Lohle, 1972.

En Cuba, Lohle, 1972, translation published as *In Cuba,* New Directions, 1974.

Canto nacional, Siglo Veintiuno (Mexico), 1973.

Oraculo sobre Managua, Lohle, 1973.

(Compiler and author of introduction) *Poesia nicaraguense,* Casa de las Americas, 1973, 4th edition, Editorial Nueva Nicaragua, 1981.

Cardenal en Valencia, Ediciones de la Direccion de Cultura, Universidad de Carabobo (Venezuela), 1974.

El Evangelio en Solentiname (also see below), Ediciones Sigueme, 1975, Editorial Nueva Nicaragua-Ediciones Monimbo, 1983, translation by Donald D. Walsh published as *The Gospel in Solentiname,* Orbis Books, 1976, published in England as *Love in Practice: The Gospel in Solentiname,* Search Press, 1977, reprinted in four volumes, Orbis Books, 1982.

Poesia escogida, Barral Editores, 1975.

La santidad de la revolucion (title means "The Sanctity of the Revolution"), Ediciones Sigueme, 1976.

Poesia cubana de la revolucion, Extemporaneos, 1976.

Apocalypse, and Other Poems, translation by Thomas Merton, Kenneth Rexroth, Mireya Jaimes-Freyre, and others, New Directions, 1977.

Antologia, Laia (Barcelona, Spain), 1978.

Epigramas, Tusquets (Barcelona), 1978.

Catulo-Marcial en version de Ernesto Cardenal, Laia, 1978.

Canto a un pais que nace Universidad Autonoma de Puebla, 1978.

Antologia de poesia primitiva, Alianza, 1979.

Nueva antologia poetica, Siglo Veintiuno, 1979.

La paz mundial y la Revolucion de Nicaragua, Ministerio de Cultura, 1981.

Tocar el cielo, Loguez, 1981.

(With Richard Cross) *Nicaraugua: La Guerra de liberacion/der Befreiungskrieg,* Ministerio de Cultura de Nicaragua, c. 1982.

Los campesinos de Solentiname pintan el evangelio, Monimbo, c. 1982.

(Translator from the German) Ursula Schulz, *Tu paz es mi paz,* Editorial Nueva Nicaragua-Ediciones Monimbo, 1982.

(Contributor) *Entrustet Euch!: Fur Frieden und volkerverstandigung; Katholiken gegen Faschismus und Krieg* (essays on nuclear disarmament), Rdrberg, 1982.

La democratizacion de la cultura, Ministerio de Cultura, 1982.

Nostalgia del futuro: Pintura y buena noticia en Solentiname, Editorial Nueva Nicaragua, 1982.

Evangelio, pueblo, y arte (selections from *El Evengelio en Solentiname*), Loguez, 1983.

Waslala: Poems, translated by Fidel Lopez-Criado and R. A. Kerr, Chase Avenue Press, 1983.

Antologia: Ernesto Cardenal, Editorial Nueva Nicaragua-Ediciones Monimbo, 1983.

Poesia de la nueva Nicaragua, Siglo Veintiuno, 1983.

The Gospel in Art by the Peasants of Solentiname (translated from *Bauern von Solentiname malen des Evangelium,* selections from *Evangelio en Solentiname*), edited by Philip and Sally Sharper, Orbis Books, 1984.

Vuelos de Victoria, Visor (Madrid), 1984, Editorial Universitaria, (Leon, Nicaragua), 1987, translation by Marc Zimmerman published as *Flights of Victory: Songs in Celebration of the Nicaraguan Revolution,* Orbis Books, 1985.

(Contributor) Teofilo Cabestrero, *Ministros de Dios, ministros del pueblo: Testimonio de tres sacerdotes en el Gobierno Revolucionario de Nicaragua, Ernesto Cardenal, Fernando Cardenal, Miguel d'Escoto,* Ministerio de Cultura, 1985.

Quetzalcoatal, Editorial Nueva Nicaragua-Ediciones Monimbo, 1985.

Nuevo cielo y tierra nueva, Editorial Nueva Nicaragua-Ediciones Monimbo, 1985.

With Walker in Nicaragua and Other Early Poems, 1949-1954, translated by Cohen, Wesleyan University Press, 1985.

(Compiler and author of introduction) *Antologia: Azarias H. Pallais,* Nueva Nicaragua, 1986.

From Nicaragua with Love: Poems 1979-1986, translated by Cohen, City Lights Press, 1986.

Golden UFOs: The Indian Poems/Los Ovnis de oro: poemas indios, translated by Carlos and Monique Altschul, Indiana University Press, 1992.

Cosmic canticle, translated by Jonathan Lyons, Curbstone Press, 1993.

Telescopio en la noche oscura, Editorial Trotta, 1993.

El rio San Juan; estrecho dudoso en el centro de American, Latino Editores, 1993.

Contributor to *Christianismo y revolucion,* Editorial Quetzal (Buenos Aires), and *La Batalla de Nicaragua,* Bruguera Mexicana de Ediciones (Mexico).

SIDELIGHTS: Ernesto Cardenal is a major poet of the Spanish language well known in the United States as a spokesman for justice and self-determination in Latin America. Cardenal, who recognizes that poetry and art are closely tied to politics, used his poetry to protest the encroachments of outsiders in Nicaragua and supported the revolution that overthrew Somoza in 1979. Once the cultural minister of his homeland, Cardenal spends much of his time as "a kind of international ambassador," notes Richard Elman in the *Nation.*

Victor M. Valle, writing in the *Los Angeles Times Calendar,* cites Cardenal's statement, "There has been a great cultural rebirth in Nicaragua since the triumph of the revolution. A saving of all of our culture, that which represents our national identity, especially our folklore." Literacy and poetry workshops established throughout the "nation of poets," as it has been known since the early twentieth century, are well attended by people whose concerns had been previously unheard. Most workshops are led by government-paid instructors in cultural centers, while others convene in police stations, army barracks, and workplaces such as sugar mills, Valle reports. In these sessions, Romantic and Modern poetry is considered below standard; Cardenal also denigrates socialist realism, which he says "comes from the Stalinist times that required that art be purely political propaganda." The "greatest virtue" of Cardenal's own poems, says a *Times Literary Supplement* reviewer, "is the indirectness of Cardenal's social criticism, which keeps stridency consistently at bay." In addition, says the reviewer, Cardenal's poems "are memorable and important both for their innovations in technique and for their attitudes." In this way they are like the works of Ezra Pound, whose aesthetic standards Cardenal promotes.

Review contributor Isabel Fraire demonstrates that there are many similarities between Cardenal's poetry and Pound's. Like Pound, Cardenal borrows the short, epigrammatic form from the masters of Latin poetry Catullus and Martial, whose works he has translated. Cardenal also borrows the canto form invented by Pound to bring "history into poetry" in a manner that preserves the flavor of the original sources—a technique Pablo Neruda employed with success. Cardenal's use of the canto form "is much more *cantabile*" than Pound's *Cantos,* says Fraire. "We get passages of a sustained, descriptive lyricism . . . where the intense beauty and harmony of nature or of a certain social order or life style are presented." Pound and Cardenal develop similar themes: "the corrupting effect of moneymaking as the overriding value in a society; the importance of precision and truthfulness in language; the degradation of human values in the world which surrounds us; [and] the search through the past (or, in Cardenal's poetry, in more 'primitive' societies, a kind of contemporary past) for better world-models." Fraire also points out an important difference between the two: "Cardenal is rooted in a wider cultural conscience. Where Pound seems to spring up disconnected from his own contemporary cultural scene and to be working against it, Cardenal is born into a ready-made cultural context and shared political conscience. Cardenal's past is common to all Latin Americans. His present is likewise common to all Latin Americans. He speaks to those who are ready and willing to hear him and are likely to agree on a great many points."

Cardenal's early lyrics express feelings of love, social criticism, political passion, and the quest for a transcendent spiritual life. Following his conversion to Christianity in 1956, Cardenal studied to become a priest in Gethsemani, Kentucky, with Thomas Merton, the scholar, poet, and Trappist monk. While studying with Merton, Cardenal committed himself to the practice of nonviolence. He was not allowed to write secular poetry during this period, but kept notes in a journal that later became the poems in *Gethsemani, Ky.* and the spiritual diary in prose, *Vida en el amor.* Cardenal's stay in Kentucky was troubled by illness; he finished his studies in Cuernevaca, Mexico, where he was ordained in 1965. While there, he wrote *El estrecho dudoso* and other epic poems that discuss Central America's history.

Poems collected in *With Walker in Nicaragua and Other Early Poems, 1949-1954* look at the history of Nicaragua which touches upon the poet's ancestry. During the 1800s, the William Walker expedition from the United States tried to make Nicaragua subservient to the Southern Confederacy. According to legend, a defector from that expedition married into Cardenal's family line. Incorporating details from Ephraim George Squier's chronicles of that period, Cardenal's poem "With Walker in Nicaragua" "is tender toward the invaders without being sentimental," Elman observes. "This is political poetry not because it has a particular rhetorical stance but because it evokes the distant as well as the more recent historical roots of the conflict in Central America," Harris Schiff relates in the *American Book Review.* The poet identifies with a survivor of the ill-fated expedition in order to express the contrast between the violent attitudes of the outsiders and the beauty of the tropical land they hoped to conquer. "The theme of the gringo in a strange land," as Elman puts it, an essentially political topic, is developed frequently in Cardenal's work.

Later poems become increasingly explicit regarding Cardenal's political sympathies. "Zero Hour," for example, is his "single greatest historical poem about gringoism, a patriotic epic of sorts," says Elman. The poem's subject is the assassination of revolutionary leader Cesar Augusto Sandino, who used guerilla tactics against the United States Marines to force them to leave Nicaragua in 1933. "It's a poem of heroic evocation in which the death of a hero is also seen as the rebirth of nationhood: when the hero dies, green herbs rise where he has fallen. It makes innovative use of English and Spanglais and is therefore hard to translate, but . . . it is very much a work of national consciousness and unique poetic expression," Elman relates.

Moving further back in time to reclaim a common heritage for his countrymen, Cardenal recaptures the quality of pre-Columbian life in *Homage to the American Indians.* These descriptions of Mayan, Incan and Nahuatl ways of life present their attractiveness in comparison to the social organization of the present. In these well-crafted and musical poems written at the end of the 1960s, the poet praises "a way of life which celebrates peace above war and spiritual strength above personal wealth. One has a strong sense when reading Cardenal that he is using the American Indian as a vehicle to celebrate those values which are most important to him as a well-educated Trappist monk who has dedicated himself to a life of spiritual retreat," F. Whitney Jones remarks in the *Southern Humanities Review.* That the poems are didactic in no way impedes their effectiveness, say reviewers, who credit the power of the verses to Cardenal's mastery of poetic technique.

The use of Biblical rhetoric and prosody energizes much of Cardenal's poetry. *El estrecho dudoso,* like the Bible, "seeks to convince men that history contains lessons which have a transcendent significance," James J. Alstrum maintains in *Journal of Spanish Studies: Twentieth Century.* Poems in *Salmos,* written in the 1960s, translated and published as *The Psalms of Struggle,* echo the forms and the content of the Old Testament psalms. Cardenal's psalms are updated to speak to the concerns of the oppressed in the twentieth century. "The vocabulary is contemporary but the . . . sheer wonder at the workings of the world, is biblical," Jack Riemer observes in *Commonweal.* "Equally memorable are those Psalms in which Cardenal expresses his horror at the cruelty and the brutality of human life. His anguished outcries over the rapaciousness of the greedy and the viciousness of the dictators are the work of a man who has lived through some of the atrocities of this century."

As the conflict between the Nicaraguan people and the Somoza government escalated, Cardenal became convinced that without violence, the revolution would not succeed. "In 1970 he visited Cuba and experienced what he described as 'a second conversion' which led him to formulate his own philosophy of Christian Marxism. In 1977 the younger Somoza destroyed the community at Solentiname and Cardenal became the field chaplain for the Sandinista National Liberation Front," reports Robert Hass in the *Washington Post Book World*. Poems Cardenal wrote during that "very difficult time in his country"—collected in *Zero Hour and Other Documentary Poems*—are less successful than the earlier and later work, says Hass, since "there is a tendency in them to make of the revolution a symbol that answers all questions." Some reviewers have found the resulting combination of Biblical rhetoric and Marxist revolutionary zeal intimidating. For example, Jascha Kessler, speaking on KUSC-FM radio in Los Angeles, California in 1981, commented, "It is clearly handy to be a trained priest, and to have available for one's poetry the voices of Amos, Isaiah, Hosea and Jeremiah, and to mix prophetic vision with the perspectives of violent revolutionary Marxist ideology. It makes for an incendiary brew indeed. It is not nice; it is not civilized; it is not humane or sceptical or reasonable. But it is all part of the terrible heritage of Central Latin America." Also commenting on *Zero Hour and Other Documentary Poems, American Book Review* contributor Harold Jaffe suggests, "Although the manifest reality of Cardenal's Central America is grim, its future—which to Cardenal is as 'real' as its present—appears eminently hopeful. Furious or revolted as Cardenal is over this or that dreadful inequity, he never loses hope. His love, his faith in the disadvantaged, his great good humor, his enduring belief that communism and Christ's communion are at root the same—these extraordinary convictions resound throughout the volume."

"Though Cardenal sees no opposition between Marxism and the radical gospel, neither is he a Moscow-line communist," Mary Anne Rygiel explains in *Southern Humanities Review*. Rygiel cites the poem "Las tortugas" (title means "The Turtles") to demonstrate that Cardenal's reference to "communism" as the order of nature might better be understood as "communalism," a social organization of harmonious interdependence founded on spiritual unity. The poet-priest's social vision stems from his understanding of "the kingdom of God," Lawrence Ferlinghetti notes in *Seven Days in Nicaragua Libre*. "And with [Cardenal's] vision of a primitive Christianity, it was logical for him to add that in his view the Revolution

would not have succeeded until there were no more masters and no more slaves. 'The Gospels,' he said, 'foresee a classless society. They foresee also *the withering away of the state*' [Ferlinghetti's emphasis]."

In the 1980s, Pope John Paul II reprimanded Cardenal for promoting a liberation theology that the prelate found divergent from Roman Catholicism. Alstrum notes, however, that *El estrecho dudoso* "reaffirms the Judeo-Christian belief that there is an inexorable progression of historical events which point toward the ultimate consummation of the Divine Word. Cardenal himself views his poetry as merely the medium for his hopeful message of the transformation of the old order into a new and more just society in which the utopian dreams and Christian values of men . . . can finally be realized." Cardenal founded the Christian commune Solentiname on an island in Lake Nicaragua near the Costa Rican border to put that dream into practice.

Cardenal's work of several decades reaches its zenith in two collections focusing on his primary subjects: American Indians and Christian Marxism. *Golden UFOs: The Indian Poems/Los onis de oro: Poemas indios* gathers Cardenal's poetry on North, South, and Central American Indians placed against the background of his Christian-Marxist viewpoint. This reveals "nothing less than an original mythology closely tied to a modern poetics," as Terry O. Taylor notes in *World Literature Today*. *Cosmic Canticle* unifies Cardenal's cantos written over three decades into a modern epic poem. It covers Nicaraguan and world history from the "Big Bang" through the present-day as Cardenal contemplates political leaders, oppressed peoples, capitalism, and the Nicaraguan Revolution, among other topics.

Some critics feel that the political nature of Cardenal's poetry precludes its appreciation by a sophisticated literary audience. Reviewers responded to the 1966 volume *El estrecho dudoso,* for example, as an attack on the Somoza dynasty while neglecting "the intricate artistry with which Cardenal has intertwined the past and present through myth and history while employing both modern and narrative techniques in his poem," asserts Alstrum. Others point out that Cardenal's work gains importance to the extent that it provides valuable insights into the thinking of his countrymen. Cardenal's poetry, which he read to audiences in the United States during the seventies, was perhaps more informative and accessible than other reports from that region, Kessler concluded in 1981, soon after

Nicaraguan revolutionaries ousted the Somoza regime. "It may well be that Cardenal's poems offer us a very clear entrance into the mentality of the men we are facing in the . . . bloody guerilla warfare of Central America," Kessler suggested. More recently, a *New Pages* reviewer comments, "We can learn some contemporary history, [and] discover the feelings and thoughts of the people who were involved in Nicaragua's revolution by reading Cardenal's poems. And once we know what the revolution 'felt' like, we'll be a lot smarter, I believe, than most . . . who . . . make pronouncements about Nicaragua's threat to the free world."

BIOGRAPHICAL/CRITICAL SOURCES:

BOOKS

Bhalla, Alok, *Latin American Writers: A Bibliography with Critical Biographical Introductions,* Envoy Press, 1987.

Brotherston, Gordon, *Latin American Poetry: Origins and Presence,* Cambridge University Press, 1975.

Cardenal, Ernesto, *Zero Hour and Other Documentary Poems,* edited by Donald D. Walsh, New Directions, 1980.

Contemporary Literary Criticism, Volume 31, Gale (Detroit), 1985.

Ferlinghetti, Lawrence, *Seven Days in Nicaragua Libre,* City Lights Books, 1984.

PERIODICALS

America, November 6, 1976.

American Book Review, summer, 1978; January, 1982; January-February, 1982; September, 1985.

Booklist, April 1, 1992, p. 1425; December 1, 1993, p. 671; October 15, 1994, p. 394.

Choice, July/August, 1994, p. 1727; October, 1995, p. 299.

Commonweal, September 17, 1971.

Journal of Spanish Studies: Twentieth Century, spring & fall, 1980.

Library Journal, March 15, 1992, p. 91; January, 1994, p. 119.

Los Angeles Times Calendar, January 8, 1984.

Nation, March 30, 1985, p. 372.

National Catholic Reporter, May 27, 1994, p. 28.

New Leader, May 4, 1981.

New Pages, Volume 10, 1986.

New Republic, October 19, 1974; April 9, 1977.

Parnassus, spring-summer, 1976.

Publishers Weekly, November 8, 1993, p. 60; October 31, 1994, p. 54.

Review, fall, 1976.

Small Press, October, 1989, p. 83.

Southern Humanities Review, winter, 1976; winter, 1988.

Stand, autumn, 1991, p. 18.

Times Literary Supplement, July 12, 1974; August 6, 1976; July 14, 1989, p. 779.

Voice Literary Supplement, September, 1982.

Washington Post Book World, June 23, 1985.

World Literature Today, spring, 1983; winter, 1990, p. 80; autumn, 1995, p. 772.

OTHER

Kessler, Jascha, "Ernesto Cardenal: 'Zero Hour and Other Documentary Poems'" (radio broadcast), KUSC-FM, Los Angeles, CA, April 15, 1981.*

*   *   *

CARDOSO, Lucio 1913-1968

PERSONAL: Born in 1913, in Brazil; died in 1968.

CAREER: Novelist and poet, c. 1934-59.

WRITINGS:

Maleita (title means "Malaria"), 1934.

Historias da Lagoa Grande, 1939.

O Desconhecido (novel), J. Olympio (Rio de Janeiro, Brazil), 1940.

Inacio, 1944.

Angelica, 1950.

O Enfeiticado, 1954.

Cronica da Casa Assassinada (novel; title means "Chronicle of the Assassinated House"), 1959.

Poemas Ineditos, 1982.*

*   *   *

**CARPENTIER (y VALMONT), Alejo 1904-1980
(Jacqueline, a pseudonym)**

PERSONAL: Born December 26, 1904, in Havana, Cuba; died of cancer, April 24, 1980, in Paris, France; son of Jorge Julian Carpentier y Valmont (an architect; also known as Georges); married Lilia Esteban Hierro. *Education:* Attended Universidad de Habana.

CAREER: Journalist, editor, educator, musicologist, and author. Worked as a commercial journalist in Havana, Cuba, 1921-24; *Cartels* (magazine), Havana, editor-in-chief, 1924-28; Foniric Studios, Paris, France, director and producer of spoken arts programs and recordings, 1928-39; CMZ radio, Havana, writer and producer, 1939-41; Conservatorio Nacional, Havana, professor of history of music, 1941-43; traveled in Haiti, Europe, the United States and South America in self-imposed exile from Cuba, 1943-59; Cuban Publishing House, Havana, director, 1960-67; Embassy of Cuba, Paris, cultural attache, 1966-80.

AWARDS, HONORS: Prix du Meilleur Livre Etranger (France), 1956, for *The Lost Steps* (*Los pasos perdidos*); Cino del duca Prize, 1975; Prix Medici, 1979.

WRITINGS:

FICTION

Ecue-yambo-o! (title means "Praised Be the Lord!"), Espana, 1933.

Viaje a la semilla (title means "Journey to the Seed"), Ucar & Garcia, 1944; translation published as *Journey Back to the Source,* 1970.

El reino de este mundo, Ibero Americana, 1949, translation by Harriet de Onis published as *The Kingdom of This World,* Knopf (New York City), 1957.

Los pasos perdidos, Ibero Americana (Mexico City), 1953, enlarged edition, Editorial de Arte y Literatura (Havana), 1976, translation by de Onis published as *The Lost Steps,* Knopf, 1956, new edition with introduction by J. B. Priestly, Knopf, 1967.

El acoso, Losada (Buenos Aires), 1956, new edition with introduction by Mercedes Rein, Biblioteca de Marcha (Montevideo), 1972; translation published as *Manhunt* in *Noonday,* Volume 2, 1959, translation by Alfred MacAdam published as *The Chase,* Farrar, Straus (New York City), 1990.

Guerra del tiempo: Tres Relatos y una novela (contains "El camino de Santiago" [title means "Highroad of St. James"; also see below], "Viaje a la semilla," "Semejante a la noche" [title means "Like the Night"], and *El acoso*), General (Mexico City), 1958, translation by Frances Partridge published as *The War of Time,* Knopf, 1970.

El siglo de las luces, General, 1962, translation by John Sturrock published as *Explosion in a Cathedral,* Little, Brown (Boston, MA), 1963.

El camino de Santiago (short story), Galerna (Buenos Aires), 1967.

(With others) *Cuentos cubanos de lo fantastico y lo extraordinario,* UNEAC (Havana), 1968, published as *Cuentos cubanos,* Laia (Barcelona), 1974.

"Viaje a la semilla" y otros relatos (short stories), Editorial Nascimento (Santiago), 1971.

Concierto barroco: Novela (title means "Baroque Concert"), Siglo XXI (Mexico City), 1974, reprinted, Editorial de la Universidad de Puerto Rico (San Juan), 1994.

El recurso del metodo: Novela, Editorial Arte y Literatura (Havana), 1974, translation by Partridge published as *Reasons of State,* Knopf, 1976.

Dos novelas (contains *El reino de este mundo* and *El acoso*), Editorial Arte y Literatura, 1976.

Cuentos, Arte y Literatura, 1977.

La consagracion de la primavera: Novela (title means "The Consecration of Spring"), Siglo Veintiuno, 1979.

El arpa y la sombra (title means "The Harp and the Shadow"), Siglo Veintiuno, 1979, reprinted, Ediciones de la Universidad de Alcala, 1994.

Cuentos completos, French & European Publications, 1980.

Los confines del hombre, edited by Felix Baez-Jorge, Siglo Veintiuno Editores (Mexico), 1994.

El amor a la ciudad, Santillana (Madrid), 1996.

OTHER

Poemes des Antilles (poetry), [Paris], 1929.

Dos poemas afro-cubanos (deux poemes afro-cubains), Senart, 1930.

La musica en Cuba (music history; title means "Music in Cuba"), Fondo de cultura economica (Mexico), 1946.

Tristan y Isolda en Tierra Firme, Nacional, 1949.

El derecho de asilo, illustrations by Marcel Berges, General, 1962.

Tientos y diferencias (essays; title means "Probes and Differences"), Universidad Nacional Autonoma (Mexico City), 1964, 3rd enlarged edition, Arca (Montevideo), 1973.

Literatura y conciencia politica en America Latina (essays), Corazon, 1969.

Papel social del novelista, Hombre Nuevo (Buenos Aires), 1969.

(Author of text) *La ciudad de las columnas* (architectural study of Havana), photographs by Paolo Gasparini, Lumen (Barcelona), 1970.

Los convidados de plata, Sandino (Montevideo), 1972.

Novelas y relatos, Union de Escritores y Artistas de Cuba (Havana), 1974.

America Latina en su musica, UNESCO (Havana), 1975.

Letra y solfa, edited by Alexis Marquez Rodriguez, Sintesis Dosmil (Caracas), 1975, reprinted, Editorial Letras Cubanas (Havana), 1993.

El acoso [and] El derecho de asilo (collection), Editora Latina (Buenos Aires), 1975.

Cronicas (collection of articles), Arte y Literatura, 1975.

El periodista: Un cronista de su tiempo, Granma (Havana), 1975.

Razon de ser: Conferencias, Rectorado (Caracas), 1976.

Vision de America (essays), Nemont (Buenos Aires), 1976.

Afirmacion literaria americanista, Universidad Central (Caracas), 1978.

Bajo el signo de La Cibeles: Cronicas sobre Espana y los espanols, 1925-1937, edited by Julio Rodrigeuz Puertolas, Nuestra Cultura (Madrid), 1979.

El adjetivo y sus arrugas, Galerna, 1980.

Ese musico que llevo dentro, three volumes, edited by Zoila Gomez Garcia, Letras Cubanas (Havana), 1980.

La novela latinoamericana en visperas de un nuevo siglo y otros ensayos (essays), Siglo Veintiuno, 1981.

Obras completas, nine volumes, Siglo Veintiuno, 1983-86.

Ensayos, Letras Cubanas, 1984.

Historia y ficcion en la narrativa hispanoamericana, Monte Avila (Caracas), 1984.

Conferencias, Letras Cubanas, 1987.

Tientos, diferencias y otros ensayos, Plaza & Janes (Barcelona), 1987.

Author of oratorio, *La Passion noire,* first performed in Paris, c. 1920s. Also author of libretti; author of two sound recordings, both produced by Casa de las americas, *Alejo Carpentier narraciones* (cassette), and *Alejo Carpentier lee sus narraciones.* Former columnist for *El Nationale* (Caracas). Contributor of articles on politics, literature, and musicology to numerous publications, including *Revolutions Surrealist.* Former editor, under pseudonym "Jacqueline," of fashion section of Havana publication; former editor, *Iman* (Paris).

SIDELIGHTS: Although considered a major literary force in his native Latin America, Cuban Alejo Carpentier did not achieve widespread recognition with the U.S. reading public. His prose examines historico-political factors as they relate to Latin American life and cultural development. In his writing, "Carpentier searches for the marvelous buried beneath the surface of Latin American consciousness, where African drums still beat and Indian amulets rule; in depths where Europe is only a vague memory of a future still to come," asserted Roberto Gonzalez-Echevarria in his *Alejo Carpentier: The Pilgrim at Home.* Gonzalez-Echevarria continued: "On the one hand, Carpentier maintains that the baroque nature of Latin American literature stems from the necessity to name for the first time realities that are outside the mainstream of Western culture. On the other, he states that what characterizes Latin American reality is its stylelessness, which results from its being an amalgam of styles from many cultural traditions and epochs: Indian, African, European, Neoclassical, Modern, etc."

Saturday Review contributor G. R. McMurray praised Carpentier as "a mature, imaginative artist, one of the first to universalize in fiction the Latin American experience." Indeed, Carpentier is said to have had an influence on such other notable Latin American authors as Gabriel Garcia Marquez and Carlos Fuentes. To quote Gonzalez-Echevarria in the *Dictionary of Literary Biography,* Carpentier's works provide "a model of how to write fiction in Latin America that is based on the history of the New World."

Born in Cuba in 1904, Carpentier was the son of a French father and a Russian mother who had only recently arrived on the island. His family was affluent, and he grew up immersed in his father's library, speaking French at home and Spanish in the streets with his friends. His association with Cubans of African, Indian, and Spanish origin influenced Carpentier profoundly as he sought to combine the European and American worlds of his childhood. Gonzalez-Echevarria wrote in the *Dictionary of Literary Biography:* "Carpentier never succeeded in synthesizing the mixture of cultures from which he sprang, and perhaps it is to this failure that one can attribute the tension behind his creative impulse."

After spending part of his teen years touring France and Russia—and attending a prestigious private school in Paris—Carpentier returned to Cuba to enroll at the University of Havana, where he planned to study music and architecture. His education ended abruptly when his father deserted the family in 1922. Forced by economic necessity to find a job, Carpentier became a journalist, and in only two years he had become editor-in-chief of *Carteles,* an avant-garde weekly magazine.

As political tensions escalated in the 1920s, Carpentier joined the student movement to oust dictator Gerardo Machado y Morales. His literary and political efforts led to his arrest and forty-day imprisonment, and upon his release he discovered that he was blacklisted and still under suspicion. A French poet, Robert Desnos, helped Carpentier escape to France, and the author spent eleven years in Paris, immersing himself in the study of American history and culture. Carpentier was quoted in the *Dictionary of Hispanic Biography* as saying of this period: "America was seen as an enormous nebula that I tried to understand, because I felt vaguely that my work originated there, that it was going to be profoundly American." Gonzalez-Echevarria observed in the *Dictionary of Literary Biography:* "Years later Carpentier would attempt to substitute the Spanish America that he discovered in book in Paris for another experienced firsthand. This effort was, perhaps, together with his attempt to define himself culturally, the essence of Carpentier's spiritual and artistic life."

Active in the French avant-garde, Carpentier continued to contribute to Cuban periodicals, and it was while he was in Paris that he published his first novel, *Ecue-yamba-o!* The book did not fare well with critics, and it would be more than a decade before Carpentier tried again to publish fiction. In the meantime he enjoyed a comfortable existence as a journalist, lecturer, and radio writer.

In 1939 Carpentier returned to Havana, and it was there—as well as in another self-imposed exile in Venezuela—that he began to create the important works of his career. His triumphant re-entry into Cuba in 1959 as a supporter of Fidel Castro brought him a controversial position of privilege within that regime. To quote Gonzalez-Echevarria in the *Dictionary of Literary Biography:* "Carpentier probably saw in the Cuban revolution the culmination of a kind of theodicy similar to the one present in many of his books, a synthesis of politics and art, the unity of a desire for a utopia and its realization in history. Inspired perhaps by the feeling that life ultimately imitates art, Carpentier did not care to test too severely the connection of such lofty ideals with the practice of politics, and he looked the other way."

Carpentier's relative obscurity in the United States may have been related to his position in Cuba, or else

to the broad spectrum of knowledge he displayed in his writing. Commented Gene H. Bell in the *New Boston Review:* "Out of a dozen or so major [South American] authors (Borges and Garcia Marquez are the best-known here), Alejo Carpentier remains the one least recognized in these parts. . . . Some readers may be put off by Carpentier's displays of learning, an encyclopedism that ranges over anthropology, history, geography, botany, zoology, music, folk and classical, the arts, visual and culinary, and countless forgotten novels and verse—in all an erudition easily rivaling that of Borges." Yet despite Carpentier's immense scholarship, Bell perceived a universal quality in the author's writing, noting, "Precisely because of . . . national differences, however, Carpentier's novel[s] (like those of Fuentes or Garcia Marquez) can furnish already interested Americans more insight into the social dislocations of the Southern continent than many a Yankee Poli Sci professor could."

Most critics familiar with Carpentier's work applauded the scholarly qualities that Bell enumerated, yet others criticized these very elements. The *New York Times Book Review*'s Alexander Coleman commented that Carpentier's early books were "often pretty heavy going, what with their tiresome philosophizing and heavily laid-on historical panoplies." Alan Cheuse concurred in *Review,* observing that some "readers may have decided that indeed the reasons for Carpentier's failure to capture an audience here are the same reasons put forth by the earliest reviewers: that his fiction is too 'erudite,' that he is more a 'cultural historian' than a novelist, . . . or that he is a 'tiresome philosophizer.'" However, Paul West remarked, also in *Review,* that "Carpentier is a master of both detail and mass, of both fixity and flux." West continued, "He can not only describe: he can describe what no-one has seen; and, best, he seems to have the hypothetical gift of suggesting, as he describes."

Carpentier's writing encompasses numerous styles and techniques. The *New York Review of Book*'s Michael Wood remarked that Carpentier "is interested not in myth but in history, and his method is to plunge us circumstantially into an earlier period, before, during, and after the First World War." Cheuse noted: "Intelligence and erudition are certainly present . . . in Carpentier's fiction. But so are sex, violence, political uproar, war, revolution, voyages of exploration, naturalist extravaganzas, settings ranging from ancient Greece to contemporary New York City, and characters running the gamut from the simple Haitian protagonist of *The Kingdom of This World* to the worldly wise, word-weary Head of State [in *Reasons of State*], . . . all of this comprising a complex but highly variegated and appealing fictional matrix."

Carpentier's themes often illustrate an awareness of broad social issues. Bell noted in the *New Boston Review* that "Carpentier's fiction regularly depicts individuals swept—often against their wishes—into the larger social struggle; they thereby become participants in history and embody the conflicts of their times." Gonzalez-Echevarria asserted in *Alejo Carpentier: The Pilgrim at Home* that "the plot in Carpentier's stories always moves from exile and fragmentation toward return and restoration, and the overall movement of each text is away from literature into immediacy." Gonzalez-Echevarria further explained the historical relevance of Carpentier's themes: "The persistence of the structure and thematics of fall and redemption, of exile and return, of individual consciousness and collective conscience, stems from a constant return to the source of modern Latin American self-awareness."

Many critics found *Reasons of State* and *The Lost Steps* among Carpentier's best efforts. *Reasons of State (El recurso del metodo)* deals with a Francophile South American dictator attempting to rule the fictitious Nueva Cordoba from his Paris home, periodically returning to his country to control revolutionary outbreaks. Bell stated: "This is no drama of the individual soul, but an imaginative evocation of the material and cultural forces of history." He added: "*Reasons of State* is not a psychological study in tyranny. . . . Carpentier rather places the Dictator (who is actually something of a cultural-historical caricature) within a broader global process, shows how the petty brutalities of South American politics ultimately interlock with European and, later, U.S. interests."

Reviewers saw *Reasons of State* as a departure in style from earlier Carpentier books. The *New York Times Book Review*'s Coleman commented: "*Reasons of State* is something different—a jocular view of imaginative idealism, repressive power and burgeoning revolution, all done with breezy panache. Once again Carpentier has shown how canny and adept a practitioner he can be in mediating between the many realms which his own life has touched upon." Bell concurred, noting that the novel "exhibits a new lightness of touch, a wry and rollicking humor."

Carpentier's *The Lost Steps (Los pasos perdidos)* "is considered his masterpiece," wrote Ruth Mathewson in the *New Leader*. The novel, which contains auto-

biographical elements, "represents an attempt at unification and synthesis, if only because it is centered on a continuous and reflexive narrative presence," suggested Gonzalez-Echevarria in *Alejo Carpentier: The Pilgrim at Home*. Like his other novels which deal with historical analysis, *The Lost Steps* also exhibits historical aspects. Gregory Rabassa observed in the *Saturday Review* that "Carpentier digs into the past: it almost seems as if he cannot get away from it, even in his novel *The Lost Steps,* which is contemporary in time but is really a search for origins—the origin first of music and then of the whole concept of civilization."

In an overall summation of Carpentier's work presented in *Alejo Carpentier: The Pilgrim at Home,* Gonzalez-Echevarria stated: "History is the main topic in Carpentier's fiction, and the history he deals with—the history of the Caribbean—is one of beginnings or foundations." Gonzalez-Echevarria concluded in his book-length work that, "in a sense, as in *The Lost Steps,* Carpentier's entire literary enterprise issues from the desire to seize upon that moment of origination from which history and the history of the self begin simultaneously—a moment from which both language and history will start, thus the foundation of a symbolic code devoid of temporal or spatial gaps."

Carpentier was serving as Cuba's cultural attache to France—and had just finished the first novel of a planned trilogy—when he succumbed to cancer at his home in Paris on April 24, 1980. He was buried in Cuba at the Necropolis de Colon.

BIOGRAPHICAL/CRITICAL SOURCES:

BOOKS

Acosta, Leonardo, *Musica y epica en la novela de Alejo Carpentier,* Letras Cubanas (Havana), 1981.
Chao, Ramon, *Palabras en el tiempo de Alejo Carpentier,* Argos Vergara (Barcelona), 1984.
Contemporary Literary Criticism, Gale (Detroit, MI), Volume 8, 1978; Volume 11, 1979; Volume 38, 1986.
Dictionary of Hispanic Biography, Gale, 1996, pp. 177-80.
Dictionary of Literary Biography, Volume 113: *Modern Latin American Fiction Writers, First Series,* Gale, 1992, pp. 96-109.
Flores, Angel, *Spanish American Authors: The Twentieth Century,* H. W. Wilson (New York City), 1992, pp. 168-72.

Garcia-Carranza, Araceli, *Biobibliografia de Alejo Carpentier,* Letras Cubanas, 1984.

Giacoman, Helmy F., editor, *Homenaje a Alejo Carpentier,* Las Americas, 1970.

Gonzalez, Eduardo, *Alejo Carpentier: El tiempo del hombre,* Monte Avila (Caracas, Venezuela), 1978.

Gonzalez Echevarria, Roberto, *Alejo Carpentier: The Pilgrim at Home,* Cornell University Press (Ithaca, NY), 1977.

Gonzalez Echevarria and Klaus Mueller-Bergh, *Alejo Carpentier: Bibliographical Guide,* Greenwood Press (Westport, CT), 1983.

Harss, Luis, and Barbara Dohmann, *Into the Mainstream,* Harper (New York City), 1967.

Hispanic Literature Criticism, Gale, 1994.

Janny, Frank, *Alejo Carpentier and His Early Works,* Tamesis (London), 1981.

King, Lloyd, *Alejo Carpentier, Caribbean Writer,* University of the West Indies Press (St. Augustine, Trinidad), 1977.

Marques Rodriguez, Alexis, *La obra narrativa de Alejo Carpentier,* Universidad Central (Caracas), 1970.

Marques Rodriguez, *El barroco y lo real maravilloso en la obra de Alejo Carpentier,* Siglo XXI (Mexico City), 1982.

Mazziotti, Nora, editor, *Historia y mito en la obra de Alejo Carpentier,* Garcia Cambeiro (Buenos Aires, Argentina), 1972.

Mueller-Bergh, Klaus, editor, *Asedios a Carpentier,* Universitaria (Santiago, Chile), 1972.

Rodriguez Monegal, E., *Narradores de esta America,* Alfa (Montevideo), 1963.

Sentata aniversario de Alejo Carpentier, La Habana, 1975.

Shaw, Donald L., *Alejo Carpentier,* Twayne (Boston, MA), 1985.

Speratti-Pinero, Emma S., *Pasos hallados en El reino de este mundo,* Colegio de Mexico (Mexico City), 1981.

Vila Selma, Jose, *El "ultimo" Carpentier,* Mancomunicadad del Cabildo, 1978.

PERIODICALS

Books Abroad, spring, 1959.
Bulletin of Hispanic Studies, Volume 57, 1980, pp. 55-66.
Casa de las Americas, Volume 131, 1982, pp. 117-22.
Cuba, Volume 3, number 24, 1964, pp. 30-33.
Hispanic Review, summer, 1981, pp. 297-316.
Latin American Research Review, Volume 16, number 2, 1981, pp. 224-45.

Modern Language Notes, March, 1979, pp. 386-93.
New Boston Review, fall, 1976.
New Leader, July 5, 1976.
New Statesman, May 28, 1976.
New York Review of Books, December 9, 1976.
New York Times Book Review, May 2, 1976.
PMLA, spring, 1963; September, 1963, pp. 440-48.
Review, fall, 1976.
Revista Iberoamericana, Volume 40, number 86, 1974, pp. 65-86; Volume 41, numbers 92-93, 1975, pp. 297-442; January-June, 1981, pp. 95-128; April-September, 1983, pp. 293-322; Volume 154, 1991, pp. 151-60.
Saturday Review, March 21, 1970, p. 42; May 29, 1976.
Studies in Short Fiction, winter, 1971.
Times Literary Supplement, January 8, 1970, p. 39.
UNESCO Courier, January, 1972; June, 1973.

OBITUARIES:

PERIODICALS

New York Times, April 26, 1980.
Times (London), April 26, 1980.*

*   *   *

CARRILLO, Adolfo 1855-1926

PERSONAL: Born July, 1855, in Sayula, Jalisco, Mexico; died August 24, 1926, in Los Angeles, CA; married, 1897; children: a daughter. *Education:* Attended Seminario de Guadalajara; studied law at the Sorbonne, c. 1890s.

CAREER: Publisher, journalist, and writer. Publisher, *La Picota,* Guadalajara, Mexico, beginning 1877; publisher, *La Union Mercantil,* Guadalajara, beginning 1878; editor of *El Correo de los Lunes* Mexico City, Mexico, c. 1885; print shop owner, San Francisco, CA, beginning 1897; press agent for Mexican revolutionary movement, c. 1910s; director of economic affairs, Los Angeles Mexican consulate, beginning 1914; publisher, *Mexico Libre,* beginning c. 1914.

WRITINGS:

(With Sebastian Lerdo de Tejada) *Memorias Ineditas del Lic. Don Sebastian Lerdo de Tejada* (title means "Unpublished Memoirs of Mr. Sebastian

Lerdo de Tejada, Attorney at Law"), [Browns-
ville, TX], 1889.
(Published anonymously; attributed to Carrillo) *Mem-
orias del Marques de San Basilisco,* International
(San Francisco), 1897.
Cuentos californianos (short stories; title means
"Californian Tales") [Los Angeles], c. 1922.

Also contributor to periodicals including *Revista Azul*
and *Dos Republicas.*

SIDELIGHTS: Mexican writer Adolfo Carrillo was
known not only as a journalist, but as a person unafraid to voice his political opinion. His outspoken-
ness against the Mexican government influenced at
least one of his written works and caused him to be
exiled from his native Mexico.

Carrillo was born in central Mexico in 1855. He studied journalism in Guadalajara, and went on to publish
two newspapers. Carrillo voiced critical opinions of
the local government beginning in 1878, using his
newspaper as a vehicle. Persecuted for his criticisms,
he moved to Mexico City where he continued to criticize the government—particularly the regime of General Porfirio Diaz, who had assumed power in 1876.
Carrillo was arrested, tried, and sentenced to prison
in Mexico. After he served his sentence, he was exiled to Cuba and later moved to New York.

Carrillo became good friends in New York with
Sebastian Lerdo de Tejada, a previous Mexican ruler
who had been ousted by Diaz. Carrillo's work
*Memorias Ineditas del Lic. Don Sebastian Lerdo de
Tejada* is the summary of his visits with Lerdo and
the political secrets that Lerdo shared. The book was
immensely popular, reprinted several times, and used
as a tool by those who opposed the Diaz regime and
supported Lerdo.

When Lerdo died, Carrillo moved to several locations
in Europe. The Mexican government continued to
follow his movements and at one point pressured him
into moving out of Spain. Eventually Carrillo was
forced to move back to the United States. He set up
a print shop in San Francisco and anonymously published *Memorias del Marques de San Basilisco* in
1897. Copies of the novel are extremely rare and its
existence was not discovered by critics until 1928.
The story portrays the life of a Mexican who drifts
through several jobs, serves as a soldier, and has a
difficult time adjusting to hard work in America.
Eventually the character takes up with a rich woman
in France who helps him earn the title of Marquis of

San Basilio. Ortiz de Montellano, a critic of the time
quoted by Luis Leal in *Dictionary of Literary Biography,* commented that the memoir stood out because of
its "sincerity and purity, characteristics that [one]
does not find in the average romantic novel."

Carrillo's third and last published work consisted of a
collection of short stories. The stories take place in
various California locations (including San Francisco)
and some of them utilize the legends of the old missions of California. In *Dictionary of Literary Biography* Leal described the collection as similar to the
work of other Mexican writers of Carrillo's time who
were living in the United States. Leal noted that these
similarities included a large use of the Spanish language and Mexican characters with a sense of cultural
displacement. According to Leal, this type of literature (including Carrillo's work) featured characters
that were caricatures rather than well-developed characters.

Carrillo was respected by many as a journalist of
honesty and integrity. When he died in 1926, a Arizona newspaper obituary, as quoted by Leal, commented that Carrillo was "a good man-of-letters . . .
He was irreproachably honest, and every time he was
approached by the followers of Don Porfirio [Diaz] to
join them he refused."

BIOGRAPHICAL/CRITICAL SOURCES:

BOOKS

Lomela, Francisco A., and Carl R. Shirley, editors,
Dictionary of Literary Biography, Volume 122:
Chicano Writers, Gale (Detroit), 1992.*

*   *   *

CARVALHO, Ronald de
  See de CARVALHO, Ronald

*   *   *

**CASTANEDA, Carlos (Cesar Aranha) 1931(?)-
1998**

PERSONAL: Born, according to author, December
25, 1931 (immigration records list 1925 as birth year;
other sources list birth years from 1925 through the

1930s), in Sao Paulo, Brazil (immigration records list Cajmarcs, Peru as birthplace); immigrated to U.S., 1951; died in 1998; son of C. N. and Susana (Aranha). *Education:* University of California, Los Angeles, B.A., 1962, M.A., 1964, Ph.D., 1970.

CAREER: Writer. Apprentice to a Yaqui Indian sorcerer, Mexico, five years. Anthropologist.

WRITINGS:

The Teachings of Don Juan: A Yaqui Way of Knowledge, University of California Press (Berkeley), 1968.

A Separate Reality: Further Conversations with Don Juan, Simon & Schuster (New York City), 1971.

Journey to Ixtlan: The Lessons of Don Juan, Simon & Schuster, 1972.

Tales of Power, Simon & Schuster, 1974.

Trilogy (three volumes), Simon & Schuster, 1974.

Don Juan Quartet (boxed set; includes *The Teachings of Don Juan: A Yaqui Way of Knowledge, A Separate Reality: Further Conversations with Don Juan, Journey to Ixtlan: The Lessons of Don Juan,* and *Tales of Power*), Simon & Schuster, 1975.

The Second Ring of Power, Simon & Schuster, 1977.

The Eagle's Gift, Simon & Schuster, 1981.

The Fire from Within, Simon & Schuster, 1984.

The Power of Silence: Further Lessons of Don Juan, Simon & Schuster, 1987.

El Arte de Ensonar (title means "The Art of Dreaming"), HarperLibros (New York City), 1995.

SIDELIGHTS: Carlos Castaneda's recorded experiences as an apprentice to Don Juan, a Yaqui Indian *brujo,* or sorcerer, are detailed in his many books, all of which deal with becoming a Yaqui "man of knowledge." According to Castaneda, Don Juan sensed in the younger man "the possibility of a disciple and proceeded to introduce him, by way of rigorous curriculum, into realms of esoteric experience which clash disconcertingly with our prevailing scientific conception of reality," wrote *Nation* contributor Theodore Roszak in a review of the author's first book, *The Teachings of Don Juan: A Yaqui Way of Knowledge.* The world through which Don Juan wished to lead Castaneda initially included using hallucinogenic drugs in order to attain certain experiences, although as the books progress, other means are used to reach different levels of consciousness.

A Separate Reality: Further Conversations with Don Juan records Castaneda's subsequent visits with Don Juan and his continuing visits to other phases of the intangible world. *Natural History* contributors William and Claudia Madsen felt the book's strength lies in its presentation of sorcery: "In his haunting story, [Castaneda] draws you into the weird world of witches—a world you will never be able to explain or forget. . . . Castaneda's work is unique because it reveals an inside view of how witchcraft works." However, *New York Times Book Review* contributor William Irwin Thompson thought that by concentrating on the narrative instead of striving for an anthropological report, Castaneda's style becomes more readable. Throughout his books, the author shows himself as an occasional bungler and reports his teacher's often harsh criticism of his mistakes. Thompson noted this and remarked that Castaneda "can parody himself and mock his own ignorance without ever tilting the balance away from Don Juan toward himself. The tone is . . . perfect for the book."

Journey to Ixtlan: The Lessons of Don Juan concentrates on how a sorcerer becomes a "man of power" through "seeing" instead of using the ordinary means of perception, "looking." In *Book World,* Barry Corbet noted: "*Ixtlan* marks an enormous change in Castaneda. . . . His reporting is warm, human and perceptive. The extraordinary thing is that the book represents very little new teaching from Don Juan, but is the result of Castaneda's new ability to discern the best of the earlier teachings. This is a book of rejects, all the field notes he previously considered irrelevant. And it is this material which makes *Ixtlan* such staggeringly beautiful reading. . . . *Journey to Ixtlan* is one of the important statements of our time." A *Times Literary Supplement* contributor, however, felt that Castaneda drew too close to his subject, and "rejected the objective and scientific approach to [his] subject-matter in favour of an extravagant empathy with the human object of [his] studies." While a *Time* contributor, like many other critics, found Don Juan himself puzzling, he appreciated the *Journey to Ixtlan:* "Indeed, though [Don Juan] is an enigma wrapped in mystery wrapped in a tortilla, [Castaneda's books are] beautifully lucid. [His] story unfolds with a narrative power unmatched in other anthropological studies. . . . In detail, it is as thoroughly articulated a world as, say, Faulkner's Yoknapatawpha County. In all the books, but especially in *Journey to Ixtlan,* Castaneda makes the reader experience the pressure of mysterious winds and the shiver of leaves at twilight, the hunter's peculiar alertness to sound and smell."

Tales of Power continues with Castaneda's mysterious experiences, although this book centers more on the pupil's dealings with the unseen than with the lessons of his master. Michael Mason, however, wrote in the *New Statesman* that Castaneda's ideas may not be as unusual as they seem: "Ideas from European existentialism pervade the book more than Castaneda's admirers might care to recognise," Mason claimed. He added: "*Tales of Power* is not a work of mysticism." Mason also voiced an objection to seeing Castaneda as a student of Yaqui spiritism: "The awkwardness arises of how Castaneda can be achieving enlightenment if he is such a spiritual clodhopper." *New York Times Book Review* contributor Elsa First found the tale more convincing, however: "This is a splendid book, for all that it may seem ungainly, at times ponderous, at others overwrought. . . . [*Tales of Power*] could well be read as a farcical picaresque epic of altered states of consciousness. . . . One of the finest things in [*Tales of Power*], however stylized or fictional it may be, is the convincing portrait of a spiritual teacher working away at his student's tendency to 'indulge' in self-dramatization and self-pity."

Castaneda's *The Art of Dreaming* describes his ability to gain control over his dreams, based on Don Juan's teachings. In the process of doing so, he meets up with inorganic beings who test his abilities. While some critics praised the book, others noted that Castaneda's themes have lost their sparkle as the series has progressed, giving support to the possibility of their fictitious nature. A *Kirkus Reviews* contributor commented, "this lackluster entry . . . adds fuel to the argument that the Don Juan books are fiction and that their author has passed his creative prime."

The debate of whether Don Juan really exists, despite the factual presentation of Castaneda's books, has been taken up by many critics. *New York Times Book Review* Paul Riesman saw them as scholarly works: "Taken together—and they should be read in the order they were written—[Carlos Castaneda's books] form a work which is among the best that the science of anthropology has produced." In another *New York Times Book Review* article, however, Joyce Carol Oates stated another view: "I realize that everyone accepts them as anthropological studies, yet they seem to me remarkable works of art, on the Hesse-like theme of a young man's initiation into 'another way' of reality." And Dudley Young, also writing in the *New York Times Book Review*, questioned Don Juan's credibility: "Since we are given virtually no information about the Don's credentials as a sorcerer (or indeed about his family or friends) it is very difficult to decide whether his symbology has genuine ethnic

roots in Yaqui culture, whether he is just a more or less harmless crank, or whether he was seeking a corrupting kind of power over his disciple. . . . But Mr. Castaneda nowhere considers this possibility." Other reviewers, however, dismissed the question of Don Juan's origins as irrelevant. According to *Washington Post* contributor Joseph McLellan: "The material in Castaneda's books is probably rooted in some sort of objective or hallucinatory experience—not cynically invented. If he had made it all up, as some observers have suggested, he could surely have produced something more interesting and coherent; something in which he is not seen so constantly as a dimwitted blunderer. Seen in context with other mystical writings, Castaneda's work seems less eccentric and its authenticity seems less dubious. . . . But by the same token, his work becomes less interesting—simply an exotic variant on fairly well-known themes."

Other critics voiced different objections to Castaneda's writings. Weston LaBarre, in *Seeing Castaneda: Reactions to the "Don Juan" Writings of Carlos Castaneda,* questioned the disciple's memory: "The long disquisition of Don Juan and the detailing of each confused emotional reaction of the author, . . . imply either total recall, novelistic talent, or a tape recorder." And in *Horizon,* Richard de Mille brought up what he considers important inconsistencies: "First, the so-called field reports contradict each other. Carlos meets a certain witch named La Catalina for the first time in 1962 and *again* for the first time in 1965. . . . A second kind of proof arises from absence of convincing detail and presence of implausible detail. . . . A third kind of proof is found in [Don] Juan's teachings, which combine American Indian folklore, oriental mysticism, and European philosophy. Indignantly dismissing such a proof, [Don] Juan's followers declare that enlightened minds think alike in all times and places, but there is more to the proof than similar ideas; there are similar words." But according to Joshua Gilder in his *Saturday Review* article on *The Eagle's Gift:* "It isn't necessary to believe to get swept up in Castaneda's other-worldly narrative; like myth it works a strange and beautiful magic beyond the realm of belief. . . . Sometimes, admittedly, one gets the impression of a con artist simply glorifying in the game—even so, it is a con touched by genius."

BIOGRAPHICAL/CRITICAL SOURCES:

BOOKS

Contemporary Literary Criticism, Volume 12, Gale (Detroit), 1980.

De Mille, Richard, *The Don Juan Papers: Further Castaneda Controversies,* Wadsworth (Belmont, CA), 1990.

Fort, Carmina, *Conversations with Carlos Castaneda,* [United States,] 1994.

LaBarre, Weston, *Seeing Castaneda: Reactions to the "Don Juan" Writings of Carlos Castaneda,* edited by Daniel C. Noel, Putnam, 1976.

Sanchez, Victor and Robert Nelson, *The Teachings of Don Carlos: Practical Applications of the Works of Carlos Castaneda,* Bear & Co. (Santa Fe, NM), 1995.

Tomas, *Creative Victory: Reflections on the Process of Power from the Collected Works of Carlos Castaneda,* S. Weiser (York Beach, ME), 1995.

PERIODICALS

American Anthropologist, Volume 71, number 2, 1969.

Booklist, July, 1993, p. 1914.

Book World, October 22, 1972; November 17, 1974.

Horizon, April, 1979.

Kirkus Reviews, June 15, 1993, p. 761.

Los Angeles Magazine, May, 1996, p. 84.

Nation, February 10, 1969.

Natural History, June, 1971.

New Statesman, June 27, 1975.

New York Times Book Review, September 29, 1968; February 13, 1972; October 22, 1972; November 26, 1972; October 27, 1974; January 22, 1978.

Psychology Today, December, 1977; March-April, 1996, p. 30.

Publishers Weekly, June 14, 1993, p. 55.

Saturday Review, May, 1981.

Time, November 6, 1972; March 5, 1973.

Times Literary Supplement, June 15, 1973.

Washington Post, December 18, 1987.*

*   *   *

CASTELLANO, Olivia Guerrero 1944-

PERSONAL: Born July 25, 1944, in Del Rio, TX; daughter of Secundino Pena and Cruz Guerrero Castellano. *Education:* California State University, Sacramento, B.A. (French and English), 1966, M.A. (social anthropology), 1970; Stanford University, Ph.D. (Modern Thought and Literature), 1976. *Politics:* Democrat.

ADDRESSES: Office—California State University, 6000 J St., Sacramento, CA 95819-2605.

CAREER: San Juan Unified School District, Sacramento, CA, high school teacher, 1967-69; Sacramento City College, CA, instructor of Mexican-American studies, 1969-72; California State University, Sacramento, professor of English, 1972—; Alameda School District, Oakland, CA, consultant, 1980-85; Sacramento College, Sacramento, consultant, 1969-85. Community organizer, Sacramento Concilio, 1969-80; Mexican American Experienced Teachers, 1969-70.

MEMBER: Modern Language Association.

AWARDS, HONORS: Ford Foundation fellow, 1976.

WRITINGS:

POETRY

Blue Mandolin, Yellow Field, Tonatiuh-Quinto Sol International (Berkeley, CA), 1980.

Blue Horse of Madness, Crystal Clear (Sacramento, CA), 1983.

Spaces That Time Missed, Crystal Clear, 1986.

Contributor to anthologies, including *Landing Signals,* edited by B.L. Kennedy, Anne Menebroker, and Kevin Dobbs, Sacramento Poetry Center, 1986; and *Beginnings in Literature,* edited by Alan Madsen, Sarah Durand Wood, and Phillip M. Connors, Scott, Foresman (Glenview, IL), 1987. Contributor to periodicals, including *Tejidos, Colores, Hard-Pressed Magazine, Montoya Poetry Review, Grito del Sol, Imagine, Literati Chicago, Women's Review of Books,* and *Blue Mesa Review.*

SIDELIGHTS: Olivia Castellano's childhood roots of poverty in Texas were to influence much of her later work in poetry and prose. The author was the second of five children of parents who had never been educated beyond the fifth grade. When Castellano was in her teens, her father relocated the family to California; according to a sketch of Castellano by Tiffany Ana Lopez in *Dictionary of Literary Biography,* she recalls later in one of her writings that he was "tired of seeing his days fade into each other without promise."

Castellano knew early in life that she had a love of words and language. She gravitated particularly toward the French language as well as English, considering them more learned languages than her native Spanish. Castellano received no support for her efforts at home, and her family worried that she would go crazy reading her many books and would never have time to get married. The author's childhood frustrations were the source of the anger that infused much of her work, once she learned to express her voice in words. She was also discouraged by a high school teacher, who advised Castellano that she would never be a poet and that she should stick to essay writing. According to Lopez in the *Dictionary of Literary Biography* profile, Castellano reflected on these influences in later writing and remarked, "When nothing on either side of the two cultures, Mexican or Anglo-American, affirms your existence, that is how rage is shaped."

Castellano originally went to college with the goal of teaching French, in part because of her previous bad experience at the hands of English literature teachers. But when the author went on to pursue a master's degree in teaching, she discovered a group of understanding Chicano and Caucasian professors. Castellano felt that for the first time, she had permission to express her anger and that she had role models worthy of emulating. In her own words, according to Lopez, she "vowed to do for other students what these people had done for me."

Castellano's poetry is filled with the images and mythology of her early Texas roots, Lopez asserted. The author uses the colors blue and yellow to represent the large Texas sky and the parched soil. Lopez points out that Castellano easily blends the language styles of both Spanish and English and uses symbolism from both cultures in her poetry. A prose poem titled "The Renaissance" (from *Blue Mandolin, Yellow Field*) blends an everyday scene with symbolism that suggests a larger meaning: "But even after the earth and the sun and fields had arched their backs completely . . . even after all that, they continued on their trek to clarity and compassion. Thus they remained suspended throughout time: two little men forever smiling, and walking perfectly straight." According to Lopez, the poem suggests the larger symbolism of the ability of these men to "feed the families of the world." The symbolism of horses is present in many of Castellano's poems, and, Lopez said, is representative of imagination. Similarly, the "Blue Mandolin" of Castellano's title is symbolic of the muse within the poet.

According to Lopez, Castellano's poetry gradually evolved from anger to mature reflection. As her writing progressed, the author mined the creative possibilities of her Chicano roots. She also began to delve into genres such as novels and short stories. Castellano purposefully decided to self-publish her last two books of poetry, in order not to be motivated by profit and marketing. While the author's work can be difficult to find, a few critics have studied her work.

BIOGRAPHICAL/CRITICAL SOURCES:

BOOKS

Dictionary of Literary Biography, Volume 122: *Chicano Writers, Second Series,* Gale (Detroit, MI), 1992.

PERIODICALS

Third Woman, volume 2, number 1, pp. 83-192.*

*   *   *

CASTRO (RUZ), Fidel 1926(?)

PERSONAL: Born August 13, 1926 (some sources say 1927), in Mayari, Oriente Province, Cuba; son of Angel Castro y Argiz (a sugar cane planter) and Lina Ruz Gonzalez de Castro (a homemaker); married Mirta Diaz Bilart (some sources spell surname Balart), October 12, (some sources say November), 1948 (divorced, 1955); children: (first marriage) Fidel, Jr. *Education:* Colegio Belen, Havana, bachelor's degree, 1945; University of Havana, doctor of laws, 1950. *Avocational interests:* Reading, cooking, fishing, skindiving.

ADDRESSES: Office—Office of the President, Palacio del Gobierno, Havana, Cuba.

CAREER: Student leader at University of Havana, 1945-50; founding member, Partido del Pueblo Cubano (Ortodoxos), Havana, 1947; private practice of law in Havana, 1950-53; participated in revolutionary movement in the Dominican Republic; initiated armed rebellion against the Fulgencio Batista dictatorship by leading attack on Moncada army barracks in Santiago de Cuba, July 26, 1953; imprisoned in Santiago de Cuba, 1953-55; exiled to Mexico and New York, 1955-56; organized Cuban rebel force in Mexico, 1955-56, and landed force in Cuba, December, 1956; commander-in-chief of the 26th of July Movement rebel army, Cuba, 1956-76; prime minister of Cuba, 1959-76; appointed first secretary of the

Cuban Communist Party, 1965—; head of state and President of Council of State and Council of Ministers of Cuba, 1976—; head of National Defense Council, 1992—.

MEMBER: Agrarian Reform Institution (chair, 1965—).

AWARDS, HONORS: Lenin Peace Prize, 1961, Hero of the Soviet Union award, 1963, Order of Lenin, 1972, and Order of the October Revolution, 1976, all from the Union of Soviet Socialist Republics (U.S.S.R.); Somali Order (first class), 1977; Order of Jamaica, 1977; Dimitrov Prize, People's Republic of Bulgaria, 1980; Gold Star, Socialist Republic of Vietnam, 1982.

WRITINGS:

SPEECHES AND INTERVIEWS IN ENGLISH TRANSLATION

History Will Absolve Me, Liberty Press, 1959, Lyle Stuart, 1961, new translation by Robert Taber, 1984.

Fidel Castro: Major Speeches, Stage 1 (London), 1968.

Fidel Castro Speaks, edited by Martin Kenner and James Petras, Grove, 1969.

Revolutionary Struggle, 1947-1958, edited by Rolando E. Bonachea and Nelson P. Valdes, MIT Press, 1972.

The Speeches of Fidel in Chile, Editions Latin America (Montreal), 1972.

Fidel in Chile: A Symbolic Meeting between Two Historical Processes, International Publishers, 1972.

Education in Revolution, Instituto Cubano del Libro (Havana), 1975.

Current Problems of Underdeveloped Countries: A Selection of Speeches, Oficina de Publicaciones del Consejo de Estado (Havana), 1979.

Fidel Castro Speeches, Pathfinder Press, Volume I: *Cuba's Internationalist Foreign Policy, 1975-80,* 1981, Volume II: *Our Power Is That of the Working People,* translated and edited by Michael Taber, 1983, Volume III: *War and Crisis in the Americas, 1984-85,* translated by Taber, 1985.

(With Vilma Espin and others) *Women and the Cuban Revolution: Speeches and Documents,* edited by Elizabeth Stone and translated by M. Taber, Pathfinder (New York City), 1981.

Fidel Castro in Chile, Pathfinder, 1982.

The World Economic and Social Crisis, Publicaciones del Consejo de Estado, 1983.

Fidel Castro: Nothing Can Stop the Course of History, edited by Jeffrey M. Elliot and Mervyn M. Dymally, Pathfinder, 1986.

Fidel and Religion: Castro Talks on Revolution and Religion with Frei Betto, Simon & Schuster (New York City), 1987.

(With Mary-Alice Waters) *In Defense of Socialism: Four Speeches on the Thirtieth Anniversary of the Cuban Revolution,* Pathfinder, 1989.

Loyalty to Principles, Editora Politica (La Habana), 1989.

(With David Deutschmann, Deborah Shnookal, and Osvaldo Salas) *The Right to Dignity: Fidel Castro and the Nonaligned Movement,* Ocean Press (Melbourne, Australia), 1989.

Socialism or Death, Jose Marti Publishing (Havana), 1989.

(With Ricardo Alarcon) *U.S. Hands Off the Mideast!: Cuba Speaks Out at the United Nations,* Pathfinder, 1990.

(With Nelson Mandela) *How Far We Slaves Have Come!: South Africa and Cuba in Today's World,* Pathfinder, 1991.

(With Ernesto Guevara) *To Speak the Truth: Why Washington's "Cold War" against Cuba Doesn't End,* Pathfinder, 1992.

The Second Declaration of Havana: With the First Declaration of Havana: Cuba's 1962 Manifesto of Revolutionary Struggle in the Americas, Pathfinder, 1994.

Also author of numerous political pamphlets and collections of speeches published in Havana.

OTHER

My Early Years, Ocean Press (New York City), 1998.

SIDELIGHTS: A master of the spoken word, Cuban President Fidel Castro has written relatively little in the course of his long political career. But the controversial Communist leader has spawned a vast literature about himself and his regime, and many collections of his speeches and interviews have been published. Probably no other living political figure has been as thoroughly documented, analyzed, praised, and vilified in print as Castro, a testimony to the Cuban leader's forceful political personality and the intense passions he arouses as the figure associated with the introduction of communism to the Americas.

Castro was born the illegitimate son of a poor Spanish immigrant who became a wealthy sugar cane planter in Cuba's eastern province, Oriente. Fidel's mother, whom his father later married, was the family cook; she was also of Spanish extraction. Fidel, described as a strong-willed, active, and tempestuous boy, once threatened to burn the house down unless his parents sent him to school. He was duly educated at Jesuit institutions in the provincial capital of Santiago de Oriente and in Havana, and he later credited the Jesuits with helping him to understand the value of discipline, self-sacrifice, and hard work. But Castro also chafed under the Jesuits' authoritarianism and never really acquired a religious faith. Energetic, charismatic, and already a powerful orator, he distinguished himself academically and was also voted one of Cuba's outstanding high school athlete.

Castro started his political career when he entered the University of Havana to study law in 1945. At that time, the University bore more resemblance to a lawless frontier town than an ivory tower. A tumultuous period in Cuban democracy due to its occurrence between two dictatorships, the mid-1940s saw the formation of violent political "action groups" that sought control of the country's civil institutions. University leadership was regarded as a major political prize, and these intellectual gangs—composed largely of outsiders—fought gun battles with each other to establish domination over the students, faculty, and administration. Determined to become a student leader, Castro found himself obliged to join one of these groups—the left-populist Union Insurreccional Revolucionaria—to pursue his political ambitions. Packing a pistol and eluding several assassination attempts (he later described his university years as more dangerous than all the time he spent as a guerrilla commander), Castro managed to win the leadership of the law students' federation. His magnetic personality and powerful oratory made him a popular figure on campus and helped launch him into national politics as a founding member of Eduardo Chibas's liberal reformist Partido del Pueblo Cubano, or Ortodoxo party, in 1947. While taking part in such international political adventures as a 1948 popular uprising in Bogota, Columbia, and an aborted invasion of the Dominican Republic to oust dictator Rafael Trujillo, Castro still managed to earn top marks at law school.

Several of Castro's speeches and manifestos from his university days would later be collected in *Revolutionary Struggle, 1947-1958,* which also includes a detailed introduction to the complex Cuban politics of the 1940s. After taking his law degree in 1950 Castro set up a private practice in Havana, where he often represented workers and the poor for no fee. He ran

for Congress in 1952 on the Ortodoxo ticket, but found his political ambitions frustrated when Fulgencio Batista took power in a military coup that year and canceled the elections. The young lawyer promptly filed a court petition to have the coup declared unconstitutional, but Cuba's authorities ruled against him. After several other unsuccessful attempts to have the dictator removed through institutional means, Castro organized an armed force of some 165 rebels and launched a bold night attack on the Moncada military barracks in Santiago de Cuba in July 26, 1953. The attack was quickly repulsed and failed to spark the civil insurrection the rebels had hoped for, but Castro's extraordinary daring made him famous throughout Cuba. Captured right after the assault, Castro was spared the summary execution meted out to scores of his comrades when his arresting officer turned out to be an old university acquaintance who protected him.

The insurgent leader conducted his own defense at his secret trial and delivered an impassioned speech on the right of a people to rebel against tyranny. Later circulated clandestinely under the title *History Will Absolve Me,* the speech helped build support for the revolutionary movement. Castro, his brother Raul, and other insurgent leaders were released from the Isle of Pines prison under a general political amnesty in May, 1955, after serving two years of their fifteen-year sentences. Finding Batista still intent on keeping power, and the prospects for peaceful change closed, the Castro brothers and their supporters soon left for Mexico to organize a new revolutionary armed force. Taking the name "26th of July Movement" to commemorate the Moncada assault, the insurgents obtained financial support from exiled Cuban president Carlos Prio Socarras and received intensive training in guerrilla warfare from an exiled Spanish Civil War veteran. A force of eighty-two lightly equipped Cubans, joined by an Argentine doctor named Ernesto ("Che") Guevara, embarked for Cuba aboard the small yacht *Granma* in December, 1956. All but thirty of the rebels were killed by the Cuban army shortly after landing on the north coast of the Oriente province, but the survivors—including the Castros and Guevara—managed to reach the rugged Sierra Maestra mountains, where they launched their guerrilla insurgency.

Several conditions in Cuba favored the success of the 26th of July Movement. Oriente province had a long tradition of peasant rebellion and the insurgents enjoyed the confidence of some influential peasant leaders. Castro deepened this local support and won peasant recruits for his guerrilla army by expropriating and redistributing land in the insurgent zones of control. The guerrillas also forged a strategic alliance with underground anti-Batista forces in the cities who supported the insurgents by organizing civil disruption and sabotage operations. The monumentally corrupt and repressive Batista regime, moreover, was widely despised, while Cubans of all classes stirred to Castro's daring rebellion and his program of democratic and populist reforms. The guerrillas' bold military tactics—Castro himself usually fought at the front—demoralized Batista's ill-trained conscript army, and the United States refused to come to the dictator's aid. Supported by a general strike wave in the cities, Castro's eight hundred insurgents mounted a multi-front offensive in mid-1958 that defeated Batista's thirty-thousand-strong army and drove the dictator into exile on January 1, 1959.

Castro's record as a guerrilla leader can be studied in *Revolutionary Struggle, 1947-1958,* which includes some of the rebel commander's most important field orders, letters, proclamations, and decrees. After the revolutionary victory Castro briefly cooperated with moderate liberals in a provisional government and was named prime minister of Cuba. The rebel commander's popularity and control of the armed forces gave him almost total power, however, and he swiftly steered the Cuban Revolution sharply to the left. Historians have long debated the question of whether Castro might have been a "secret Marxist" before the revolution or whether he was radicalized by a series of confrontations with the United States in the early 1960s. The United States had treated Cuba as a virtual colony for most of the century and reacted to Castro's early reforms—including an extensive agrarian redistribution and the nationalization of some foreign-owned industries—as a threat to U.S. political and economic interests. Castro's refusal to hold early elections and his deepening friendship with the Soviet Union also upset the U.S. government, which broke off diplomatic relations with Cuba in January, 1961.

The U.S.-sponsored Bay of Pigs invasion, in which fifteen hundred CIA-trained Cuban exiles attempted unsuccessfully to overthrow Castro's government, and Castro's declaration of the "Marxist-Leninist" character of the revolution later that year sealed the nations' enmity. While later evidence would suggest that the United States's aggressive stance hastened the consolidation of a leftist regime in Cuba, socialism had long been Castro's ultimate political objective. The Cuban leader told interviewer Frei Betto in *Fidel and Religion* that he had "a Marxist-Leninist, Socialist

concept of political struggle several years before 1951," but adopted a nationalist and populist program to ensure the broadest popular support for the revolution. "I believe my contribution to the Cuban Revolution consists of having synthesized [Cuban independence leader Jose] Marti's ideas and those of Marxism-Leninism and having applied them consistently in our struggle," Castro observed in the 1986 interview.

The political ferment and bold social experimentation of the Cuban Revolution's early years is well documented in *Fidel Castro Speaks,* the first volume of speeches by the Cuban leader to be published in the United States. A voluble but seldom boring orator, Castro often made important policy pronouncements and addressed specific problems in public speeches lasting up to four hours and longer. Cuban policy in the mid-1960s was characterized by a strong effort to develop revolutionary consciousness and cooperative social relations among the Cuban people and by material and political support for revolutionary movements abroad, particularly in Latin America. Influenced by Che Guevara, Castro stressed moral over material incentives in building Cuba's new socialist economy and criticized the Soviet Union for failing to aid Third World revolutionary movements.

Fidel Castro Speaks includes the famous "Second Declaration of Havana" that Castro delivered after Cuba's expulsion from the Organization of American States in 1962. In this speech, the Cuban leader denounced U.S. imperialism in Latin America and defiantly pledged to assist leftist rebellions in the region. Castro's militant stance earned him great prestige among leftists all over the world but strained his relations with the U.S.S.R., on which Cuba depended for vital economic and military support. It would be this growing dependence—along with severe economic problems and the collapse of the Latin American guerrilla movements after the death of Che Guevara during an insurgency in Bolivia in 1967—that prompted Castro to adopt more conservative policies in the 1970s.

The first volume of *Fidel Castro Speeches,* published in 1981, covers the period between 1975 and 1980 and details this new foreign policy, which centered on military support to such established Third World leftist states as Ethiopia, Angola, and Nicaragua; extensive material aid programs that sent Cuban doctors, teachers, technicians, and construction workers to many corners of the globe; and leadership of the Non-Aligned Movement of nations. A second volume of *Fidel Castro Speeches,* subtitled *Our Power Is That of the Working People,* focuses on Cuban politics and government and attempts to meet criticism of Castro's regime as personalistic and authoritarian. Among other topics, the Cuban leader discusses the "People's Power" system of popular input in political and economic decision-making. Castro would also defend Cuba's government at some length in *Fidel and Religion,* insisting that "our system is a thousand times more democratic than the capitalist, imperialist system of the developed capitalist countries" because it defends basic class interests of the majority workers and allows active participation in local government administration.

While acknowledging that he enjoys great personal authority and influence as the leader of the Cuban Revolution, Castro has insisted that a collective leadership determines government and Communist party policy in Cuba. Independent observers of Cuban politics have found that the system permits some genuine—if limited—grassroots initiative and criticism of the leadership within the parameters of support for the basic revolutionary changes. But the unrelenting hostility of the nearby United States produced a siege mentality among Cuba's leaders that has identified the revolution with the regime and refuses to countenance any organized political opposition, even one committed to socialism.

The Cuban Communist party, led by Castro since 1965, remains the country's sole political party and the Cuban press is among the most tightly controlled of any Communist state. The Castro regime also holds several hundred political prisoners, two hundred of whom were released in a major amnesty in 1988. Castro's speeches amply document the Cuban Revolution's tremendous social achievements and modest economic successes in a country once noted for its poverty and corruption. Gains made since 1959 included all but wiping out illiteracy and raising educational and health standards to levels that rivaled and often exceeded those prevalent in developed countries. Unemployment was abolished in Cuba, rents were held to ten percent of a tenant's salary, and all Cubans were guaranteed a basic diet through a rationing system. However, Castro's policies have not been without their detractors within Cuba; many residents have fled the country for permanent exile in the southeastern United States (particularly the Miami, Florida, area), awaiting the overthrow of the communist dictator, some funding terrorist activities within Cuba's borders.

The fall of the Soviet Empire would have a devastating effect on such gains. Despite strenuous efforts to develop a tourist industry, Castro was unable to diversify the Cuban economy; its dependence upon sugar exports—most of which were purchased by the Soviet Union at prices well above the world market rate—and the importation of twelve million tons of Soviet petroleum each year caused an aftershock in the Cuban economy that resulted in stringent standard-of-living cutbacks and a reevaluation of that government's international policies. Since the collapse of its former economic and political ally in the early 1990s—at one point in the late 1980s the U.S.S.R. was subsidizing the Cuban economy to the tune of $6 billion per year—Cuba has been forced to woo the governments of capitalist nations to enter into trade agreements. Deprived of access to the U.S. market by a longstanding economic embargo, the Cuban leader began to make overtures to U.S. policymakers beginning in the early 1990s, visiting Cuba's neighbor to the north and negotiating possible changes in drug interdiction and immigration policies as a first step in opening economic markets between the two countries. However, Castro remained adamant in his refusal to succumb to capitalism; despite Cuba's plight, he continued to show little interest in decentralizing the economy or promoting domestic *laissez faire* market mechanisms. Some economic liberalization—including a free market for farmers and greater local input in economic planning—was permitted beginning in the late 1970s, but the Cuban economy remains highly centralized, its leader continuing to favor moral over material production incentives.

Despite the economic setbacks of the 1990s and conjecture by analysts in the United States over his ability to survive politically, Castro continues to be a popular and heroic figure among poor and working-class Cubans, who appreciate the revolution's social welfare measures and take pride in their leader's continued defiance of capitalist superpowers and his stature as a world leader. Castro's moderating foreign policy and curtailment of direct support to insurgent movements have also earned him increasing respect among mainstream statesmen in Latin America and elsewhere, although U.S. policymakers continue to view him with a suspicion shadowed by the Cold War.

BIOGRAPHICAL/CRITICAL SOURCES:

BOOKS

Bender, Lynn Darrell, *Politics of Hostility: Castro's Revolution and United States Policy,* Inter-American University Press, 1975.

Bentley, Judith, *Fidel Castro of Cuba,* J. Messner (Englewood Cliffs, NJ), 1991.

Beyer, Don E., *Castro!,* F. Watts (New York City), 1993.

Bourne, Peter G., *Fidel: A Biography of Fidel Castro,* Dodd, 1986.

Brennan, Ray, *Castro, Cuba, and Justice,* Doubleday, 1959.

Brown, Warren, *Fidel Castro: Cuban Revolutionary,* Millbrook Press (Brookfield, CT), 1994.

Casuso, Teresa, *Cuba and Castro,* translated from the Spanish by Elmer Grossberg, Random House, 1961.

Cuban American National Foundation, *Castro's "Special Period in a Time of Peace": Proceedings from a Conference Sponsored by the Cuban American National Foundation, October 11, 1990, The Four Seasons Hotel,* The Foundation (Washington, DC), 1990.

Draper, Theodore, *Castro's Revolution: Myths and Realities,* Praeger, 1962.

Draper, Theodore, *Castroism: Theory and Practice,* Praeger, 1965.

Dubois, Jules, *Fidel Castro: Rebel, Liberator, or Dictator?,* Bobbs-Merrill, 1959.

Elliot, Jeffrey M., and Mervyn M. Dymally, *Fidel by Fidel: A New Interview with Dr. Fidel Castro Ruz, President of the Republic of Cuba,* Borgo Press (San Bernadino, CA), 1989.

Fernandez Revuelta, Alina, *Castro's Daughter: An Exile's Memoir of Cuba,* St. Martin's Press, 1998.

Franqui, Carolos, *Family Portrait with Fidel: A Memoir,* translated from the Spanish by Alfred MacAdam, Random House, 1984.

Garcia-Calzadilla, Miguel A., *The Fidel Castro I Knew,* Vantage, 1971.

Halperin, Maurice, *The Rise and Decline of Fidel Castro: An Essay in Contemporary History,* University of California Press, 1972.

Halperin, Maurice, *The Taming of Fidel Castro,* University of California Press, 1981.

Hinckle, Warren, and William W. Turner, *Deadly Secrets: The CIA-Mafia War against Castro and the Assassination of JFK,* Thunder's Mouth Press (New York City), 1992.

Karol, K. S., *Guerrillas in Power,* Hill & Wang, 1970.

Liss, Sheldon B., *Fidel! Castro's Political and Social Thought,* Westview Press (Boulder, CO), 1994.

Lockwood, Lee, *Castro's Cuba, Cuba's Fidel: An American Journalist's Look at Today's Cuba in Text and Picture,* Macmillan, 1967, revised edition, Westview Press, 1990.

Lopez-Fresquet, Rufo, *My Fourteen Months with Castro,* World Publishing, 1966.

Lorenz, Marita, and Ted Schwarz, *Marita: One Woman's Extraordinary Tale of Love and Espionage from Castro to Kennedy,* Thunder's Mouth Press, 1993.

Luque Escalona, Roberto, *The Tiger and the Children: Fidel Castro and the Judgement of History,* Transaction (New Brunswick), 1992.

Madden, Paul, *Fidel Castro,* Rourke (Vero Beach, FL), 1993.

Mallin, Jay, *Covering Castro: Rise and Decline of Cuba's Communist Dictator,* Transaction, 1994.

Mankiewicz, Frank, and Kirby Jones, *With Fidel: A Portrait of Castro and Cuba,* Playboy Press, 1975.

Martin, Lionel, *Early Fidel: Roots of Castro's Communism,* Lyle Stuart, 1978.

Matthews, Herbert L., *Fidel Castro: A Political Biography,* Simon & Schuster, 1969.

Meneses, Enrique, *Fidel Castro,* translated from the Spanish by J. Halcro Ferguson, Taplinger, 1966.

Mina, Gianni, and Gabriel Garcia Marquez, *An Encounter with Fidel: An Interview,* Ocean Press (New York City), 1991.

Montaner, Carlos Alberto, *Fidel Castro and the Cuban Revolution: Age, Position, Character, Destiny, Personality, and Ambition,* Transaction, 1989.

Oppenheimer, Andres, *Castro's Final Hour: The Secret Story behind the Coming Downfall of Communist Cuba,* Simon & Schuster, 1992, updated edition, 1993.

Paterson , Thomas G., *Contesting Castro: The United States and the Triumph of the Cuban Revolution,* Oxford University Press (New York City), 1994.

Quirk, Robert E., *Fidel Castro,* Norton (New York City), 1993.

Rice, Donald E., *The Rhetorical Uses of the Authorizing Figure: Fidel Castro and Jose Marti,* Praeger (New York City), 1992.

Rice, Earle, *The Cuban Revolution,* Lucent Books (San Diego, CA), 1995.

Sebastian, Balfour, *Castro,* Longman (New York City), 1990, second edition, 1995.

Selsdon, Esther, *The Life and Times of Fidel Castro,* Chelsea House, 1997.

Stein, Edwin C., *Cuba, Castro, and Communism,* Macfadden, 1962.

Suchilicki, Jaime, editor, *Cuba, Castro, and Revolution,* University of Miami Press, 1972.

Szulc, Tad, *Fidel: A Critical Portrait,* Morrow, 1986.

PERIODICALS

American Heritage, November, 1991, p. 90.

American Legion, June, 1990, p. 26.
Atlantic Monthly, June, 1990, p. 34.
Christian Science Monitor, March, 1991, p. 24.
Current History, March, 1985; February, 1992, p. 59.
Economist, March 6, 1993, p. 45; April 6, 1996, p. SC4.
Esquire, March, 1992, p. 102.
Foreign Policy, fall, 1982.
Harper's, January, 1996, p. 58.
History Today, May, 1981.
Life, January 19, 1959; August 28, 1964.
Mother Jones, July-August, 1989, p. 20.
Nation, October 24, 1988; January 1, 1990, p. 4.
National Review, March 5, 1990, p. 29; December 28, 1992, p. 33.
New Leader, January 8, 1990, p. 10.
New Republic, January 19, 1987; September 12, 1994, p. 11; October 3, 1994, p. 15.
New Statesman & Society, May 11, 1990, p. 29.
Newsweek, January 19, 1959.
New York Review of Books, May 31, 1990, p. 12; March 26, 1992, p. 22; October 6, 1994, p. 45.
New York Times Magazine, March 8, 1959; November 1, 1959; December 31, 1961; March 13, 1977; November 18, 1979.
People, January 10, 1994, p. 72.
Progressive, August, 1992, p. 17.
Reader's Digest (Canadian), September, 1989, p. 61; July, 1991, p. 97.
Society, September-October, 1992, p. 53; July-August, 1994, p. 66.
Time, January 26, 1959; March 8, 1993, p. 18; February 20, 1995, p. 57.
U.S. News & World Report, January 9, 1989, p. 37; August 6, 1990, p. 11; September 26, 1994, p. 56; May 15, 1995, p. 48.
Vanity Fair, November, 1993, p. 80; March, 1994, p. 128.*

*   *   *

CATACALOS, Rosemary 1944-

PERSONAL: Born March 18, 1944, in San Antonio, TX (one source says St. Petersburg, FL); daughter of Demetres Stratos Catacalos and Beatrice (Penaloza) Catacalos.

ADDRESSES: Home—2817 Belvoir Dr., San Antonio, TX 78230.

CAREER: Poet. Leader of poetry workshops in Arizona, Arkansas, and Texas, 1974-85; Guadalupe Cultural Arts Center, San Antonio, TX, literature program director, 1986-89; San Francisco State University, San Francisco, CA, director of poetry center; Stanford University, Stanford, CA, affiliated scholar at Institute for Research on Women and Gender; has also worked as a copywriter, arts publicist, newspaper reporter, producer of cable TV arts programs, and educator in San Antonio schools. Visiting scholar at University of Texas at Austin, 1986; founder and organizer of San Antonio Inter-American Book Fair, 1987. Co-chair of City of San Antonio Fine Arts and Cultural Advisory Committee, 1985; has served as co-chair of Texas and Arizona arts commissions; has served as literature panelist for the National Endowment for the Arts.

MEMBER: Texas Institute of Letters (counselor, 1988-89; chair, poetry judging panel, 1988), American Literary Translators Association.

AWARDS, HONORS: Creative writing fellowship, National Endowment for the Arts, 1985; annual poetry award, Texas Institute of Letters, 1985, for *Again for the First Time;* Dobie Paisano fellowship, University of Texas at Austin and Texas Institute of Letters, 1986; Wallace E. Stegner writing fellowship, Stanford University, 1989-91.

WRITINGS:

Again for the First Time (poetry), Tooth of Time Books (Santa Fe, NM), 1984.
As Long as It Takes (poetry), Iguana Books (Springfield, MO), 1984.

WORK IN PROGRESS: A new book of poems; a series of interviews with Mexican immigrant women.

SIDELIGHTS: Rosemary Catacalos's poetry is unique in that it blends elements from both her Greek and Hispanic ancestry. While Catacalos prefers to write in the English language, she incorporates elements of the lyricism of the Spanish language in her writings. Much of the author's work is not widely known as she has purposefully avoided the "poetry scene" and believes that her work stands on its own. Nonetheless, she has been active as an arts administrator and has been awarded several literary prizes.

Catacalos was born into a poor family of mixed Hispanic and Greek heritage. In a *Dictionary of Literary Biography* essay, Merrihelen Ponce quoted Catacalos, who recalled her youth as "difficult," but "complicated and gloriously rich in grounding." She had early Hispanic and Greek influences, which were later to appear in her writing. Catacalos was, for example, familiar with Greek mythology before she knew she'd been exposed to the classics, because these tales were the basis for her family's nightly storytelling. She also enjoyed studying and reading books from an early age.

The author has been involved with community arts organizing for much of her career. Catacalos taught bilingual poetry workshops in the 1970s and 1980s, as well as producing cable television programs on the arts. In the late 1980s, the author directed a literature program for a Latino arts group in San Antonio. She was also responsible for organizing the first Inter-American Bookfair in San Antonio in 1987, which included an exchange program featuring noted writers like Isabel Allende and Alice Walker.

Much of Catacalos's poetry is bilingual, and it particularly makes use of the sounds of the barrio where she was raised. According to Ponce in the *Dictionary of Literary Biography,* the author's work is "based in the community and expresses the human condition of Mexicans and Chicanos living a marginal existence." Ponce cited the poem "From Home," from the collection *Again for the First Time,* as an example of a poem that captures the sense of the barrio: "The mornings become brittle and cool / with their sound. Camarada [comrade] / the moon is on the rise, / dogs howl through the night, / and it is September." Ponce noted that the author incorporates figures from Mexican folklore and Greek mythology into her poetry. For example, the poem "A Vision of La Llorona" captures the Mexican story of La Llorona, the woman who wailed while searching for her children after she had killed them. Catacalos also touches upon Greek mythology with the poem "Ariadne to Dionysios," which, in the words of Ponce, "melds myth to reality." Ponce commented that Catacalos often portrays sensuality in her poetry, but from the viewpoint of women who are waiting for love rather than being fulfilled with it. Much of the author's poetry is, according to Ponce, infused with loneliness and pain.

BIOGRAPHICAL/CRITICAL SOURCES:

BOOKS

Dictionary of Literary Biography, Volume 122: *Chicano Writers, Second Series,* Gale (Detroit, MI), 1992.*

CELAYA, Gabriel 1911-1991
(Rafael Mugica, Juan de Leceta, pseudonyms)

PERSONAL: Born Rafael Gabriel Juan Mugica Celaya Leceta, March 18, 1911, in Spain; died April 18, 1991; son of Luis Mugica Leceta and Ignacia Celaya Cendoya; married, 1938; companion of Amparo Gaston, beginning 1946. *Education:* Studied engineering at University of Madrid.

CAREER: Poet, sometimes under the names Rafael Mugica and Juan de Leceta.

AWARDS, HONORS: Becquer Centennial, 1936, for *La soledad cerrada;* Critic's Poetry Prize, c. 1956, for *De claro en claro;* Premio Nacional de las Letras Espanolas (National Prize for Spanish Letters), 1986.

WRITINGS:

Marea del silencio (poetry; title means "Tide of Silence"), Itxaropena (Zarauz, Spain), 1935.
Tentativas (memoirs), Adan (Madrid), 1946.
La soledad cerrada (poetry; title means "Enclosed Solitude"), Norte (San Sebastian), 1947.
Movimientos elementales (title means, "Elementary Movements"), Norte, 1947.
(As Juan de Leceta) *Tranquilamente Hablando* (poetry; title means "Calmly Speaking"), Norte, 1947.
Objetos poeticos, Halcon (Valladolid, Spain), 1948.
Lazaro calla (novel; title means "Lazarus Becomes Silent"), S.G.E. de L. (Madrid), 1949.
El principio sin fin (poetry, title means "The Beginning without End"), Cantico (Cordoba), 1949.
Se parece al amor, Arca (Las Palmas, Canary Isles), 1949.
Las cosas como son, Isla de los Ratones (Santander, Spain), 1949.
Deriva, Ifach (Alicante, Spain), 1950.
El arte como lenguaje, Ediciones de Conferencias y Ensayos (Bilbao), 1951.
Las cartas boca arriba (poetry; title means "The Cards Face Up"), Rialp/Adonais (Madrid), 1951.
Lo demas es silencio (poetry; title means "The Rest Is Silence"), Furest/Cucuyo (Barcelona), 1952.
(With Amparo Gaston) *Ciento volando,* Nebli (Madrid), 1953.
Paz y concierto (poetry; title means "Peace and Agreement"), Pajaro de Paja (Madrid), 1953.
Via muerta, Alcor (Barcelona), 1954.
(With Amparo Gaston) *Coser y cantar,* Dona Endrina (Guadalajara, Spain), 1955.

Cantos iberos (poetry; title means "Iberian Songs"), Verbo (Alicante, Spain), 1955.

De claro en claro (poetry; "From Time to Time"), Rialp/Adonais (Madrid), 1956.

Pequena antologia poetica, Cigarra (Santander, Spain), 1957.

Entreacto (poetry; title means "Intermission"), Agora (Madrid), 1957.

Las resistencias del diamante (poetry; title means "The Endurance of the Diamond"), Luciernaga (Mexico City), 1957.

(With Amparo Gaston) *Musica celestial,* Baladre (Cartagena), 1958.

Cantata en Aleixandre (poetry; title means "Cantata on Aleixandre"), Papeles de Son Armadans (Madrid), 1959.

El corazon en su sitio, Lirica Hispana (Caracas), 1959.

Poesia y verdad (title means "Poetry and Truth"), Litoral (Pontevedra, Spain), 1959.

(Editor, with Phyllis Turnbull) *Castilla, A Cultural Reader,* Appleton-Century-Crofts (New York City), 1960.

Para vosotros dos (poetry; title means "For Both of You"), Alrededor de la Mesa (Bilbao, Spain), 1960.

Penultimas tentativas, Arion (Madrid), 1960.

Poesia urgente (poetry; title means "Urgent Poetry"), Losada (Buenos Aires), 1960.

Homenatge a todo, Horta (Barcelona), 1961.

La buena vida, Isla de los Ratones, 1961.

Los poemas de Juan de Leceta, Literaturasa/Colliure (Barcelona), 1961.

L'Espagne en marche, Seghers (Paris), 1961.

Rapsodia euskara, Biblioteca Vascogada de los Amigos del Pais (San Sebastian), 1961.

Lo uno y lo otro, Seix Barral (Barcelona), 1962.

Poesia (1934-61), Giner (Madrid), 1962.

Episodios nacionales (poetry; title means "National Episodes"), Ruedo Iberico (Paris), 1962.

Mazorcas, Rocamador (Palencia, Spain), 1962.

El relevo (play), Gora (San Sebastian), 1963.

Versos de otono, Grupo Atalaya/Venencia (Jerez, Spain), 1963.

Dos cantatas, Revista de Occidente (Madrid), 1964.

Exploracion de la poesia, Seix Barral (Barcelona), 1964.

La linterna sorda, Bardo (Barcelona), 1964.

Baladas y decires vascos, Bardo, 1965.

Los buenos negocios, Seix Barral, 1965.

Lo que faltaba, Bardo, 1967.

Poemas de Rafael Mugica, Comunicacion Literaria de Autores (Bilbao, Spain), 1967.

Los espelos transparentes (poetry; title means "Transparent Mirrors"), Bardo, 1968.

Canto en lo mio, Ciencia Nueva/Bardo (Madrid), 1968.

Poesias completas, Aguilar (Madrid), 1969.

Lirica de camara (poetry; title means "Poetic Operations"), Bardo, 1969.

Operaciones poeticas, Corazon/Visor (Madrid), 1971.

Cien poemas de amor, Plaza y Janes (Barcelona), 1971.

Campos semanticos (title means "Semantic Fields"), Javalambre/Fuendetodos (Zaragoza, Spain), 1971.

Inquisicion de la poesia, Taurus (Madrid), 1972.

La voz de los ninos, Laia (Barcelona), 1972.

Gustavo Adolfo Becquer, Jucar (Madrid), 1972.

Direccion prohibida, Losada (Buenos Aires), 1973.

Funcion de uno, equis, ene (title means "Function of 1, X, N"), Javalambre/Fuendetodos, 1973.

El derecho y el reves, Sinera/Ocnos (Barcelona), 1973.

Los espacios de Chillida, Poligrafa (Barcelona), 1974.

Itinerario poetico (title means "Poetic Itinerary"), Catedra (Madrid), 1975.

La higa de Arbigorriya (poetry; title means "The Fig Tree of Arbigorriya"), Visor (Madrid), 1975.

Buenos dias, buenas noches (poetry; title means "Good Morning, Good Night"), Hiperion (Madrid), 1976.

Poesia abierta, Doncel (Madrid), 1976.

El hilo rojo, Visor, 1977.

Parte de guerra, Laia (Barcelona), 1977.

Poesia, edited by Angel Gonzalez, Alianza (Madrid), 1977.

Poesias completas, edited by Jose Maria Valverde, Laia, 1977-80.

Iberia sumergida, Peralta/Hiperion (Pamplona), 1978.

Memorias inmemoriales (title means "Unforgettable Memories"), Catedra (Madrid), 1980.

Penultimos poemas, Seix Barral, 1982.

Cantos y mitos, Visor, 1984.

The Poetry of Gabriel Celaya, translated by Betty Jean Craige, Bucknell University Press (Lewisburg, PA), 1984.

Trilogia vasca, Guipuzcoa (San Sebastian), 1984.

El mundo abierto, Hiperion (Madrid), 1986.

Ritos y farsas: La obra teatral completa, Txertoa (San Sebastian), 1989.

TRANSLATIONS

Rainer Maria Rilke, *Cincuenta poemas franceses,* Norte, 1947.

William Blake, *El libro de Urizen,* Norte, 1947.

Arthur Rimbaud, *Una temporada en el infierno,* Norte, 1947.

Paul Eluard, *Quince poemas,* Dona Endrina (Guadalajara, Spain), 1954.

SIDELIGHTS: The Spanish poet Gabriel Celaya played a large part in defining the direction of Spanish poetry after the Spanish Civil War (1936-1938). Celaya particularly influenced the advent of social poetry in Spain and gave voice to the growing disaffection of some citizens with the new fascist political regime in Spain.

Celaya was born Rafael Gabriel Juan Mugica Celaya Leceta in the Basque region of Spain. The early influences in his life were varied—his mother's upbringing represented wealth while his father came from poorer origins but was progressive politically. It was assumed that Celaya would follow his father and manage the family factory business after he received education in engineering. But Celaya developed an early love for poetry which never quite died out, even though his family considered this quirk in his personality an embarrassment. The young student was further influenced during his time in college, where he met and was inspired by literary figures such as Pablo Neruda and Juan Ramon Jimenez. In the late 1920s Celaya also became familiar with the French classics and further broadened his base of literary knowledge.

Celaya returned to run the family business in 1935 and wrote two books of poetry; the second, *La soledad cerrada,* won a literary prize. Essayist Shirley Mangini, writing in the *Dictionary of Literary Biography,* noted that this collection, compared to his first set of poems, revealed "a more individualistic voice and marked the colloquial fluidity that was to characterize [Celaya's] later social poetry." Mangini commented that the collection also illustrated the poet's characteristic oscillating moods.

But the poet's literary progress was interrupted by the Spanish Civil War, which also bought cultural growth in the country to a standstill. After the war and until 1946, Celaya published nothing. According to Mangini, many artists remained silent during this time (particularly those who opposed the new regime, such as Celaya) or created works that focused on themes such as love and religion rather than politics.

After a period of depression, in 1946 Celaya met Amparo Gaston, a woman who became his life com-

panion. The partnership seemed to restart Celaya's career and he wrote prolifically into the 1950s. The couple also founded Norte, a press that published Celaya's work, the work of other poets that had been silent since the war, and the work of foreign authors. Mangini noted that this was a significant point in Celaya's life, as it established him as "one of the most active cultural agents among dissident intellectuals."

According to Mangini, the poet's publication of *Tranquilamente Hablando* in 1947 marked the end of Celaya's first period of poetry—it was also representative of the style that was to follow with Celaya's social poetry and his use of "long, rambling, conversational, rhymeless verses." Celaya also changed the tone of his poetry and moved from surrealistic influences to a "jocular and often ironic voice." The second period of Celaya's poetry began in 1947 and marked the birth of his protest poetry. The poet was considered highly influential among opponents of the political regime of that time. Celaya published prolifically during this period, writing eight books of poetry between 1947 and 1950. In 1951 Celaya's role solidified further into a true motivating force among dissidents and a voice for social change. One of his most famous protest poems is "La poesia es un arma cargada de futuro" ("Poetry Is a Weapon Filled with Future"), a work that appeared in his 1955 collection *Cantos iberios* ("Iberian Songs"). In this poem he writes: "I curse the poetry which is conceived as a / cultural luxury by the neutral ones, / those who by washing their hands, pretend not to understand and flee. / I curse the poetry that doesn't take a stand to the point of staining itself." According to Mangini, Celaya is specifically referring to regime-sanctioned poetry, which had preceded the social poetry in Spain that Celaya had a hand in launching.

Celaya remained active and influential in the intellectual sector of the clandestine communist movement during the 1950s and early 1960s. In *Itinerario poetico* (1975) he described this period as a time when social poetry was at its peak and a time that inspired nostalgia for him personally—because "then it seemed that one served a purpose." When this period of rebellion began to wane in Spain, Celaya eventually turned to other styles of poetry, some of which were similar to the experimentalism of his early works.

Celaya struggled with the downturn of activism and according to Mangini, the poet "groped for a way to resolve his distance from social realism." An example of Celaya's work from this period is *Poemas de Rafael Mugica,* a book "in which Celaya describes his existential thoughts by means of surrealist imagery," stated Mangini. But Mangini noted that critics and readers did not receive Celaya's work well during this time, and perhaps his most important contributions of this era were his numerous essays and works of literary criticism.

According to Mangini, Celaya used diverse styles in the late 1960s and 1970s, and his poetry often displayed an underlying "political and personal disillusionment, and a kind of literary bewilderment." Mangini noted that many critics consider one of the best works of this period to be the 1976 publication *Buenos dias, buenas noches,* which seems to represent a mature acceptance of life. One poem in the collection, "The Breeze," exemplifies this sentiment: "When it seems that nothing means anything anymore/we are left with one happiness/senselessness:/the breeze."

The poet remained active in political interests until he died. In 1971 he unsuccessfully ran as a candidate for the Basque communist party. The campaign was motivated by a desire to attract attention to the party, and Celaya had no serious intentions of winning, according to Mangini. One of Celaya's last works was *Memorias inmemoriales,* a recap of the poet's life using a stream-of-consciousness monologue that Mangini felt "marked [Celaya's] total release from the confines of realism."

Celaya died a poor man in 1991 after a lengthy bout with depression. The poet is remembered as one of the prime influences during the Spanish post-civil war period and as a catalyst among Spanish artists and intellectuals for social change. He worked to revitalize art and cultural pursuits in Spain, even when faced with the constraints of an oppressive government.

BIOGRAPHICAL/CRITICAL SOURCES:

BOOKS

Brooks, Zelda Irene, *The Poetry of Gabriel Celaya: A Thematic Study,* Scripta Humanistica (Potomac, MD), 1986.
Perna, Michael L., editor, *Dictionary of Literary Biography,* Volume 108: *Twentieth Century Spanish Poets,* First Series, Gale (Detroit), 1991.
Uglade, Sharon Keefe, *Gabriel Celaya,* Twayne (Boston), c. 1978.*

CHAMICO
See NALE ROXLO, Conrado

*   *   *

CHARLES, RuPaul Andre 1960-
(RuPaul)

PERSONAL: Born November 14, 1960, in San Diego, CA.

ADDRESSES: Agent—c/o Hyperion Press, 47 Riverside Ave., Westport, CT 06880.

CAREER: Performer and writer, as RuPaul. Program host of *RuPaul Show* on VH1-TV, 1996—; radio host on WKTU, c. 1997—. Spokesperson and model for M.A.C. Cosmetics. Co-chair of M.A.C. AIDS Fund. Actor in motion pictures, including *Mahogany II, Wigstock: The Movie, Blue in the Face, The Brady Bunch Movie,* and *A Very Brady Sequel.* Performer on recording *Supermodels of the World.*

WRITINGS:

(As RuPaul) *Lettin' It All Hang Out* (autobiography), Hyperion (Westport, CT), 1995.

Co-writer and performer of songs on recording *Foxy Lady,* Rhino Records, 1996. Compiler of *Go-Go Box Classics* recording.

SIDELIGHTS: RuPaul Andre Charles, better know simply as RuPaul, is a flamboyant cross-dressing performer who has distinguished himself as a television and radio personality, singer, actor, and writer. In *Interview,* he was described as "America's most telegenic, tell-'em-baby talk-show host, recording artist, radio personality, pinup, and general all-round breath of fresh air." But in that same publication, he told interviewer Liz Smith that his considerable success had not come without adversity. "I've been challenged at every turn," he observed. "Drag is still very taboo in our culture because it's associated with sexuality, and we don't like to talk about sex." He added, "I think I've been able to slip through . . . because I've taken some of the sexuality out."

In the 1990s, RuPaul has triumphed in seemingly every medium in which he has ventured an enterprise. As a singer, he has realized a hit song, "Supermodel," and has released such collections as *Supermodels of the World* and *Foxy Lady*. An *Entertainment Weekly* reviewer of *Foxy Lady* acknowledged that RuPaul invests the dance-music genre with "a much-needed infusion of personality." RuPaul also compiled *Go-Go Box Classics,* a collection of dance-music songs such as Natalie Cole's "Party Lights" and Nicole's "Don't You Want My Love." *Advocate* reviewer Barry Walters noted that *Go-Go Box Classics* includes "quirky groove morsels that have been played on the radio but not to death." He added, "These are the records that—like RuPaul herself—walk that fine line between freaky and funky, mainstream and mad."

On television and radio, RuPaul has also been a memorable presence. He has hosted his own program, the *RuPaul Show,* on the VH1 music video network, and he has also served as a broadcaster on WKTU radio. RuPaul told Liz Smith, in *Interview,* that both shows afford him the opportunity to promote his optimistic perspective. "We wake people up and tell them, 'You're beautiful. You're gorgeous. You can make it happen,'" he said. "People want to hear that kind of thing. I know I do."

As an actor, meanwhile, RuPaul has appeared in a range of motion pictures, from the low-budget *Mahogany II* to the mainstream Hollywood productions *The Brady Bunch Movie* and *A Very Brady Sequel.* In addition, he appears briefly in director Wayne Wang's *Blue in the Face,* a sequel to the lauded independent film *Smoke.* Among his other notable screen credits is a performance as himself in *Wigstock: The Movie,* a film about cross-dressers. *Entertainment Weekly* reviewer Lisa Schwarzbaum deemed this film "a sweet . . . celebratory movie."

RuPaul's other activities include serving as a model and spokesperson for M.A.C. Cosmetics. The company's founder, Frank Toskan, refuted the notion that only women could endorse cosmetics, asking an *Entertainment Weekly* interviewer, "Who better than RuPaul to show what makeup can do?" RuPaul also serves as co-chair of the M.A.C. AIDS Fund, which supports various AIDS foundations. Regarding his fundraising activities on behalf of the M.A.C. AIDS Fund, RuPaul told Liz Smith in a 1997 *Interview:* "I make personal appearances—in full drag, of course—and, most importantly, I appear in their Viva Glam lipstick adds. So far, they've raised $5.5 million just through Viva Glam."

RuPaul wrote about his life and achievements in *Lettin' It All Hang Out,* a 1995 autobiography. Alex Tresniosky, writing in *People,* asserted: "RuPaul's touch-ing account of his journey from drugged-out go-go dancer to pop-culture icon is a captivating drag-to-riches story that celebrates perseverance and press-on nails." *Booklist* reviewer Mike Tribby was likewise impressed, deeming RuPaul's autobiography "wholly entertaining."

BIOGRAPHICAL/CRITICAL SOURCES:

PERIODICALS

Advocate, April 28, 1998, p. 80.
Booklist, May 15, 1995, p. 1619.
Entertainment Weekly, March 10, 1995, p. 13; June 23, 1995, p. 38; November 29, 1996, p. 92.
Essence, August, 1995, p. 59.
Harper's Bazaar, February, 1996.
Interview, January, 1997.
Maclean's, October 16, 1995, p. 83.
People, June 12, 1995, p. 18; July 10, 1995; September 23, 1996, p. 148; October 14, 1996, p. 20.
Playboy, July, 1995, p. 20.
Publishers Weekly, April 24, 1995, p. 52.

OTHER

Official RuPaul Website, http://www.rupaul.net (July 22, 1999).
SonicNet Artist Info, http://www.sonicnet.com/artists/ai_singlestory.jhtml?id=1876&ai_id=13946 (July 15, 1999).*

* * *

CHAVEZ, Denise (Elia) 1948-

PERSONAL: Born August 15, 1948, in Las Cruces, NM; daughter of Ernesto E. (an attorney) and Delfina (a teacher; maiden name, Rede) Chavez; married Daniel Zolinsky (a photographer and sculptor), December 29, 1984. *Education:* New Mexico State University, B.A., 1971; Trinity University, San Antonio, TX, M.F.A., 1974; University of New Mexico, M.A., 1982. *Politics:* Democrat. *Religion:* Roman Catholic. *Avocation:* Swimming, bowling, movies.

ADDRESSES: Home—80 La Colonia, Las Cruces, NM 88005.

CAREER: Northern New Mexico Community College, Espanola, instructor in English, 1975-77, professor of English and Theatre, 1977-80; playwright, 1977—; New Mexico Arts Division, Santa Fe, artist in the schools, 1977-83; University of Houston, Houston, TX, visiting scholar, 1988, assistant professor of drama, 1988-91; New Mexico State University, Las Cruces, assistant professor of creative writing, playwrighting, and Chicano literature, 1996—. Instructor at American School of Paris, 1975-77; visiting professor of creative writing at New Mexico State University, 1992-93 and 1995-96; artistic director of the Border Book Festival, 1994—; past member of faculty at College of Santa Fe; teacher at Radium Springs Center for Women (medium-security prison); gives lectures, readings, and workshops throughout the United States and Europe; has given performances of the one-woman show *Women in the State of Grace* throughout the United States. Writer-in-residence at La Compania de Teatro, Albuquerque, NM, and Theatre-in-the-Red, Santa Fe, NM; artist-in-residence at Arts with Elders Program, Santa Fe and Las Cruces; co-director of senior citizen workshop in creative writing and puppetry at Community Action Agency, Las Cruces, 1986-89.

MEMBER: National Institute of Chicana Writers (founding member), PEN USA West, Author's Guild, Western Writers of America, Women Writing the West, Santa Fe Writers Cooperative.

AWARDS, HONORS: Best Play Award, New Mexico State University, 1970, for *The Wait;* grants from New Mexico Arts Division, 1979-80, 1981, and 1988; award for citizen advocacy, Dona Ana County Human Services Consortium, 1981; grants from National Endowment for the Arts, 1981 and 1982, Rockefeller Foundation, 1984, and University of Houston, 1989; creative writing fellowship, University of New Mexico, 1982; Steele Jones Fiction Award, New Mexico State University, 1986, for short story "The Last of the Menu Girls"; Puerto del Sol Fiction award, 1986, for *The Last of the Menu Girls;* creative artist fellowship, Cultural Arts Council of Houston, 1990; Favorite Teacher Award, University of Houston, 1991; Premio Aztlan Award, American Book Award, and Mesilla Valley Writer of the Year Award, all 1995, all for *Face of an Angel;* New Mexico Governor's Award in literature and *El Paso Herald Post* Writers of the Pass distinction, both 1995; Luminaria Award for Community Service, New Mexico Community Foundation, 1996.

WRITINGS:

PLAYS

The Wait (one-act), 1970, also produced as *Novitiates,* Dallas Theater Center, Dallas, TX, 1971.

Elevators (one-act), produced in Santa Fe, NM, 1972.

The Flying Tortilla Man (one-act), produced in Espanola, NM, 1975.

The Mask of November (one-act), produced in Espanola, NM, 1977.

Nacimiento (one-act; title means "Birth"), produced in Albuquerque, NM, 1979.

The Adobe Rabbit (one-act), produced in Taos, NM, 1979.

Santa Fe Charm (one-act), produced in Santa Fe, NM, 1980.

Si, hay posada (one-act; title means "Yes, There Is Shelter"), produced in Albuquerque, NM, 1980.

El santero de Cordova (one-act; title means "The Woodcarver of Cordova"), produced in Albuquerque, NM, 1981.

How Junior Got Throwed in the Joint (one-act), produced in Santa Fe at Penitentiary of New Mexico, 1981.

(With Nita Luna) *Hecho en Mexico* (one-act; title means "Made in Mexico"), produced in Santa Fe, NM, 1982.

The Green Madonna (one-act), produced in Santa Fe, NM, 1982.

La morenita (one-act; title means "The Dark Virgin"), produced in Las Cruces, NM, 1983.

Francis! (one-act), produced in Las Cruces, NM, 1983.

El mas pequeno de mis hijos (one-act; title means "The Smallest of My Children"), produced in Albuquerque, NM, 1983.

Plaza (one-act), produced in Albuquerque, NM, 1984, also produced in Edinburgh, Scotland, and at the Festival Latino, New York City.

Plague-Time, 1985.

Novena narrativas (one-woman show; title means "The Novena Narratives"), produced in Taos, NM, 1986.

The Step (one-act), produced in Houston at Museum of Fine Arts, 1987.

Language of Vision (one-act), produced in Albuquerque, NM, 1987.

Women in the State of Grace (one-woman show), produced in Grinnell, IA, 1989; produced nationally since 1993.

The Last of the Menu Girls (one-act; adapted from Chavez's short story of the same title), produced in Houston, TX, 1990.

Author of unproduced plays *Mario and the Room Maria,* 1974, *Rainy Day Waterloo,* 1976, *The Third Door* (trilogy), 1979, and *Cruz Blanca, Story of a Town.*

OTHER

(Editor) *Life Is a Two-Way Street* (poetry anthology), Rosetta Press (Las Cruces, NM), 1980.

The Last of the Menu Girls (stories), Arte Publico (Houston, TX), 1986.

The Woman Who Knew the Language of Animals (juvenile), Houghton (Boston), 1992.

(Selector) *Shattering the Myth: Plays by Hispanic Women,* edited by Linda Feyder, Arte Publico, 1992.

Face of an Angel (novel), Farrar, Straus (New York City), 1994.

(Author of essays) *Writing Down the River: Into the Heart of the Grand Canyon,* photographed and produced by Kathleen Jo Ryan, foreword by Gretel Ehrlich, Northland (Flagstaff, AZ), 1998.

Work represented in numerous anthologies, including *An Anthology of Southwestern Literature,* University of New Mexico Press, 1977; *An Anthology: The Indian Rio Grande,* San Marcos Press, 1977; *Voces: An Anthology of Nuevo Mexicano Writers,* El Norte Publications, 1987; *Iguana Dreams: New Latino Fiction,* Harper Collins, 1992; *Mirrors Beneath the Earth,* Curbstone Press, 1992; *Growing Up Latino: Memories and Stories,* Houghton, 1993; *New Mexico Poetry Renaissance,* Red Crane Books, 1994; *Modern Fiction about Schoolteaching,* Allyn & Bacon, 1996; *Mother of the America,* Riverhead Books, 1996; *Chicana Creativity and Criticism: New Frontiers in American Literature,* edited by Maraia Herrera-Sobek and Helena Maraia Viramontes, University of New Mexico Press, 1996; and *Walking the Twilight II: Women Writers of the Southwest,* edited by Kathryn Wilder, Northland, 1996. Contributor to periodicals, including *Americas Review, New Mexico, Journal of Ethnic Studies,* and *Revista Chicano-Riquena.*

SIDELIGHTS: Denise Chavez is widely regarded as one of the leading Chicana playwrights and novelists of the U.S. Southwest. She has written and produced numerous one-act plays since the 1970s; however, she is best known for her fiction, including *The Last of the Menu Girls,* a poignant and sensitive short story collection about an adolescent girl's passage into womanhood, and *Face of an Angel,* an exploration of a woman's life in a small New Mexico town. With the publication of *Face of an Angel*—and its selection as a Book-of-the-Month Club title in 1994—Chavez gained a national readership for her portraits of Chicanos living in the Mexican-American borderlands.

Born in Las Cruces, New Mexico, Chavez was reared in a family that particularly valued education and self-improvement. The divorce of her father, an attorney, and her mother, a teacher, when Chavez was ten was a painful experience. She spent the rest of her childhood in a household of women that included her mother, a sister, and a half-sister, and has acknowledged that the dominant influences in her life—as well as in her work—have been female. From an early age Chavez was an avid reader and writer. She kept a diary in which she recorded her observations on life and the personal fluctuations in her own life. During high school she became interested in drama and performed in productions. Chavez recalled her discovery of the theater to *Journal North* interviewer Jim Sagel as a revelation: "I can extend myself, be more than myself." She wrote her first play while a senior in college at New Mexico State University: originally titled *The Wait,* it was renamed *Novitiates* when it was produced in 1971. A story about several persons in transitional periods in their lives, her play won a prize in a New Mexico literary contest.

Critics have noted that Chavez's plays typically focus on the characters' self-revelation and developing sense of their personal place within their community. *Mario and the Room Maria,* for example, is a play about personal growth: its protagonist, Mundo Reyes, is unable to develop emotionally due to his refusal to confront painful experiences from his past. Likewise, *Si, hay posada* depicts the agony of Johnny Briones, whose rejection of love during the Christmas season is the result of emotional difficulties experienced as a child. While Chavez's plays often concentrate on her characters' inner lives, some deal with external and cultural elements that impede social interaction. Set in Santa Fe, New Mexico, her well-known 1984 play *Plaza* contrasts characters who have different impressions of life in the town square. According to *Dictionary of Literary Biography* contributor Rowena A. Rivera, the theme of *Plaza* "emphasizes the importance of family and friendship bonds as a means by which individuals can recover their personal and cultural heritage."

Many of the themes within Chavez's plays are echoed and drawn together in her short story collection *The Last of the Menu Girls.* Composed of seven related stories, the work explores the coming of age of Rocio Esquibel through high school and college. In the opening story, Rocio goes to work handing out menus in a hospital, where she is exposed to many different people and experiences. Her impressions are shaped, in large part, by the ordinary individuals whom she daily encounters: the local repairman, the grandmother, and the hospital staff, among others.

Reviewers have argued that Chavez interweaves the seven stories that comprise *The Last of the Menu Girls* in order to emphasize the human need for *comunidad,* or community. Although some scholars find her style to be disjointed and flawed, many laud her lively dialogue, revealing characterization, and ability to write with insight. Chavez does not look upon *The Last of the Menu Girls* as a novel, but as a series of dramatic vignettes that explore the mysteries of womanhood. In fact, she envisions all her work as a chronicle of the changing relationships between men and women as women continue to avow their independence. This assertion has led to the creation of nonstereotypical Chicana heroines like Rocio, who *Women's Studies Review* contributor Maria C. Gonzalez described as "an individual who fights the traditional boundaries of identity that society has set up and expects her to follow."

Chavez's ambitious first novel, *Face of an Angel,* centers on the life of Soveida Dosamantes and her relations with her family, coworkers, former husbands, and lovers in the small New Mexico town of Agua Oscura. Soveida has worked as a waitress for more than thirty years and is deeply involved in preparing a handbook, *The Book of Service,* that she hopes will aid other would-be waitresses. *Face of an Angel* received far wide attention for a first novel; it was chosen as a Book-of-the-Month Club selection and slated as a major paperback release as well. Groundbreaking in the Chicana fiction genre due to its nontraditional heroines and frank discussion of sexual matters, the book was generally hailed as the debut of an important new voice in Hispanic American letters. *Belles Lettres* correspondent Irene Campos Carr called *Face of an Angel* "engrossing, amusing, and definitely one to be savored," adding: "The author's mordant wit is pervasive, the language is pithy, blunt, and explicit." Campos Carr concluded: "Chavez has become a fine writer and a great storyteller. With *Face of an Angel,* her second book, her name can be added to the growing list of Chicana authors making their mark in contemporary American fiction."

Chavez once told *CA:* "I consider myself a performance writer. My training in theater has helped me to write roles that I myself would enjoy acting. My characters are survivors, and many of them are women. I feel, as a Chicana writer, that I am capturing the voice of so many who have been voiceless for years. I write about the neighborhood handymen, the waitresses, the bag ladies, the elevator operators. They all have something in common: they know what it is to love and to be merciful. My work as a playwright is to capture as best as I can the small gestures of the forgotten people, the old men sitting on park benches, the lonely spinsters inside their corner store. My work is rooted in the Southwest, in heat and dust, and reflects a world where love is as real as the land. In this dry and seemingly harsh and empty world there is much beauty to be found. That hope of the heart is what feeds me, my characters."

BIOGRAPHICAL/CRITICAL SOURCES:

BOOKS

Balassi, William, John Crawford, and Annie Eysturoy, editors, *This Is about Vision: Interviews with Southwestern Writers,* University of New Mexico Press (Albuquerque), 1990.

Dictionary of Literary Biography, Volume 122: *Chicano Writers, Second Series,* Gale (Detroit), 1992, pp. 70-6.

Kester-Shelton, Pamela, editor, *Feminist Writers,* St. James Press (Detroit), 1996, pp. 94-6.

Saldivar, Jose-David and Rolando Hinojosa, editors, *Criticism in the Borderlands: Studies in Chicano Literature, Culture, and Ideology,* Duke University Press (Durham, NC), 1991.

PERIODICALS

American Studies International, April, 1990, p. 48.
Americas Review, Volume 16, number 2, 1988.
Belles Lettres, spring 1995, p. 35.
Bloomsbury Review, September/October 1993; May/June 1995.
Boston Globe, September 30, 1994, p. 61.
Journal North, August 14, 1982, p. E4.
Journal of Semiotic and Cultural Studies, 1991, pp. 29-43.
Los Angeles Times, November 9, 1994, pp. E1, E4.
New York Times Book Review, October 12, 1986, p. 28; September 25, 1994, p. 20.
Performance, April 8, 1983, p. 6.
Publishers Weekly, August 15, 1994, pp. 77-8.
Village Voice, November 8, 1994, p. 18.
Women's Studies Review, September/October, 1986.
World Literature Today, autumn, 1995, p. 792.

CISNEROS, Antonio 1942-1989

PERSONAL: Born December 27, 1942, in Lima, Peru; died in 1989. *Education:* Attended Catholic University, Lima; National University of San Marcos, Ph.D., 1974.

CAREER: Poet and essayist. Teacher of literature at University of Huamanga, Ayacucho, Peru, 1965, University of Southampton, Southampton, England, 1967-70, University of Nice, Nice, France, 1970-72, and University of San Marcos, Lima, Peru, beginning 1972; University of Budapest, Budapest, Hungary, exchange professor, 1974-75.

AWARDS, HONORS: Peruvian National Poetry Prize, 1965, for *Comentarios reales;* Cuban Casa de las Americas prize, 1968, for *Canto ceremonial contra un oso hormiguero.*

WRITINGS:

POETRY

Destierro, [Lima, Peru], 1961.
David, El Timonel (Lima), 1962.
Comentarios reales (title means "Royal Commentaries"; also see below), Ediciones de la Rama Florida and Ediciones de la Biblioteca Universitaria, 1964.
Canto ceremonial contra un oso hormiguero (title means "Ceremonial Song Against the Anteater"; also see below), Casa de las Americas (Havana), 1968.
The Spider Hangs Too Far from the Ground (contains selections from *Comentarios reales* and *Canto ceremonial contra un oso hormiguero*), translated by Maureen Ahern, William Rowe, and David Tipton, Cape Goliard (London), 1970.
Agua que no has de beber (also see below), CMB Ediciones (Barcelona), 1971.
Como higuera en un campo de golf (also see below), Instituto Nacional de Cultura (Lima), 1972.
El libro de Dios y los hungaros (also see below), illustrations by David Herskovitz, Libra-1 (Lima), 1978.
(Contributor) *Cuatro poetas: Victor Garcia Robles, Antonio Cisneros, Pedro Shimose, Armando Tejada Gomez,* Casa de las Americas, 1979.
At Night the Cats (bilingual text; contains selections from *Comentarios reales, Canto ceremonial contra un oso hormiguero, Agua que no has de beber, Como higuera en un campo de golf, El libro de Dios y los hungaros,* and *La cronica del Nino Jesus;* also see below), edited and translated by Ahern, Rowe, and Tipton, Red Dust (New York City), 1985.
Monologo de la casta Susana y otros poemas, Instituto Nacional de Cultura (Peru), 1986.

Also author of *La cronica del Nino Jesus,* 1981. Contributor to anthologies.

WORK IN PROGRESS: Los hijos de Albion, a collection of essays on British poetry.

SIDELIGHTS: An award-winning Peruvian poet, the late Antonio Cisneros was internationally acclaimed for his satirical works challenging the established values and conventions of his native country. The author first attracted literary attention with the poetry volumes *Comentarios reales* and *Canto ceremonial contra un oso hormiguero,* works exploring alternative interpretations of history and myth. Proceeding to produce such collections as *Agua que no has de beber, Como higuera en un campo de golf,* and *At Night the Cats,* Cisneros consistently won critical approval for his precise language, evocative imagery, and irreverent and ironic humor. Deeming the author "the most distinguished poet now writing in Peru," Jack Schmitt in the *Los Angeles Times Book Review* further proclaimed: "Cisneros . . . is today one of the major poets of all Spanish America."

Born in Lima, Peru, in 1942, Cisneros grew up with an avid interest in poetry. He studied literature at the Catholic University in Lima, and much later—after having published and taught for years—received a doctorate degree from the National University of San Marcos. He sought to broaden his experiences through travel and, in addition to teaching literature in his native Peru, taught at foreign universities in England, France, and Hungary.

Many critics have attributed Cisneros' fresh perspective on his own country to his multi-cultural experiences. "Cisneros is the product of over ten years of travel between London, Nice and Budapest; the political unrest of the 1960s in his own country and abroad; and a keen sense of literary technique," explained Gloria F. Waldman in *Hispania.* "He brings his own ironic, gently critical voice to the exotic settings he evokes." In the *Dictionary of Hispanic Biography,* James McCarthy noted: "By living in . . . European countries—with their own decidedly different historical perspectives on colonialism—Cisneros came to see those countries and Peru more clearly. His time abroad gave him a sharpened perspective on the world around him as well as a keener view of his own Peruvian culture."

Cisneros produced the poetry collections *Destierro* and *David* in the early 1960s, but it was not until the appearance of *Comentarios reales* that the poet earned international recognition. Published when Cisneros was twenty-two years old, the work offers sardonic views of Peruvian history. In doing so, *Comentarios reales* was considered significant for its departure from traditionally repressive twentieth-century Peruvian poetry, and the work garnered Peru's National Poetry Prize in 1965. Reviewing the poems of *Comentarios reales* when many of them appeared in a 1970 volume titled *The Spider Hangs Too Far from the Ground*, a *Times Literary Supplement* writer thought the pieces "terse and irreverent." The reviewer extolled, for example, such poems as "Dead Conquerors" for not mythologizing past warriors, quoting: "Shat upon by scorpions & spiders few / survived their horses." "As for the nineteenth century," the critic continued, "all that remains are a few grotesque monuments and allegories. . . . Ants, vultures, rocks, red cactus are the elements of [a] pitiless landscape in which neither history nor environment can offer shelter." McCarthy observed of *Comentarios:* "While critics appreciated [Cisneros's] boldness, they perceived that [his] wit served not simply to degrade his nation but to hold it up to gentle, but insistent, scrutiny." McCarthy concluded that the work "established Cisneros as a permanent poetic voice in his nation."

Cisneros enjoyed continued success with his next volume, *Canto ceremonial contra un oso hormiguero,* winner of the Cuban Casa de las Americas prize in 1968. While this volume branches out to embrace Cisneros' remembrances of travels and experiences in Ayacucho and England, it nonetheless casts a critical eye on culture and history. Discussing the poems of *Canto ceremonial* (some of which also appeared in *The Spider Hangs Too Far from the Ground*), the *Times Literary Supplement* critic considered "Chronicle of Lima" one of the volume's finest offerings; in it, "history and organic growth have been halted and distorted. The poet's Lima is a place of accidental, historical fragments, of absurd superimposed modernity, 'the jungle of cars, a sexless snake of no known species'—a city whose seasons have been altered by the cutting down of forests, where the sea is only visible in rust, where rivers have dried up and 'a white furry veil protects you from the open sky.'"

Cisneros' subsequent poetry volumes further destroy myth, legend, history, and culture through his hallmark satirical voice. *Agua que no has de beber,* containing twenty-two poems written between the years 1964 and 1966, was published in 1971, and the poet's *Como higuera en un campo de golf* appeared in 1972. Selections from these two volumes, as well as those from *Comentarios reales* and *Canto ceremonial* and Cisneros' more recent productions, 1978's *El libro de Dios y los hungaros* and 1981's *La cronica del Nino Jesus,* all appear in *At Night the Cats;* this bilingual anthology containing seventy-six poems was published in 1985.

"For those not previously familiar with Antonio Cisneros' original voice, . . . *At Night the Cats* is an excellent introduction," wrote Waldman. Widely praised for its excellent translation and its choice selections that capture the essence of Cisneros' voice and style, the book gave critics another opportunity to extol Cisneros' craftsmanship. "His early poems, characterized by their epigrammatic brevity, are lean and taut, precise in language and ironic in tone," declared Schmitt. Discussing Cisneros' later works, the reviewer praised the author's "intensely poetic imagination; his stunning images and metaphors, often surreal; his incisive irony and droll humor, sometimes wistful, often self-mocking; his personal, confessional tone; his decorum and reserve, so typical of Peruvians, and also his passion and tenderness." Waldman concurred and compared Cisneros to such famed twentieth-century Hispanic poets as the irreverent Nicanor Parra, the historically astute Pablo Neruda, and the melancholic Cesar Vallejo. Waldman concluded by deeming *At Night the Cats* a "highly valuable volume . . . that will surely make new and old readers smile, and sometimes even laugh out loud, cause indignation at ancient and present injustices, and delight, as good poetry does."

Cisneros' poetry has appeared in numerous anthologies in such languages as French, German, Russian, Danish, and Ukrainian. He also wrote a number of scholarly essays for periodicals and anthologies. Cisneros died in 1989.

BIOGRAPHICAL/CRITICAL SOURCES:

BOOKS

Cisneros, Antonio, *The Spider Hangs Too Far from the Ground,* Cape Goliard (London), 1970.
Dictionary of Hispanic Biography, Gale (Detroit, MI), 1996, pp. 225-27.

PERIODICALS

Hispania, September, 1987.
Los Angeles Times Book Review, October 27, 1985.
Times Literary Supplement, August 21, 1970.*

*   *   *

CISNEROS, Sandra 1954-

PERSONAL: Born December 20, 1954, Chicago IL.
Education: Loyola University, B.A., 1976; University
of Iowa Writers' Workshop, M.F.A., 1978.

ADDRESSES: Office—Alfred A. Knopf Books, 201
E. 50th St., New York, NY, 10022. *Agent*—Susan
Bergholz Literary Services, 17 West 10th St. #5, New
York, NY 10011.

CAREER: Writer. Latino Youth Alternative High
School, Chicago IL, teacher, 1978-80; Loyala Uni-
versity of Chicago, Chicago, IL, college recruiter and
counselor for minority students, 1981-82; Foundation
Michael Karolyi, Vence, France, artist-in-residence,
1983; Guadalupe Cultural Arts Center, San Antonio,
TX, literature director, 1984-85; guest professor,
California State University, Chico, 1987-88, Univer-
sity of California, Berkeley, 1988, University of
California, Irvine, 1990, University of Michigan,
Ann Arbor, 1990, and the University of New Mexico,
Albuquerque, 1991.

MEMBER: PEN, Mujeres por la paz (member and
organizer; a women's peace group).

AWARDS, HONORS: National Endowment for the
Arts fellow, 1982, 1988; American Book Award from
Before Columbus Foundation, 1985, for *The House
on Mango Street;* Paisano Dobie Fellowship, 1986.
First and second prize in Segundo Concurso Nacional
del Cuento Chicano, sponsored by University of Arizona; Lannan Foundation Literary Award, 1991;
H.D.L, State University of New York at Purchase,
1993; MacArthur fellow, 1995.

WRITINGS:

Bad Boys (poems), Mango Publications, 1980.
The House on Mango Street, Arte Publico, 1984.
My Wicked, Wicked Ways, (poems), Third Woman
   Press, 1987.

Woman Hollering Creek and Other Stories, (stories),
   Random House, 1991.
Hairs: Pelitos (juvenile; bilingual), illustrated by
   Terry Ybanez, Knopf, 1994.
Loose Woman (poems), Knopf, 1994.

Contributor to various periodicals, including *Imagine,
Contact II, Glamour, New York Times, Los Angeles
Times, Village Voice* and *Revista Chicano-Riquena.*

SIDELIGHTS: With only a handful of poetry and
short story collections, Sandra Cisneros has garnered
wide critical acclaim as well as popular success.
Drawing heavily upon her childhood experiences and
ethnic heritage as the daughter of a Mexican father
and Chicana mother, Cisneros addresses poverty,
cultural suppression, self-identity, and gender roles in
her fiction and poetry. She creates characters who are
distinctly Latina/o and often isolated from mainstream
American culture by emphasizing dialogue and sensory imagery over traditional narrative structures.
Best known for *The House on Mango Street,* a volume
of loosely structured vignettes that has been classified
as both a short story collection and a series of prose
poems, Cisneros seeks to create an idiom that integrates both prosaic and poetic syntax. "Cisneros is a
quintessentially American writer, unafraid of the
sentimental; avoiding the cliches of magical realism, her work bridges the gap between Anglo and
Hispanic," remarked Aamer Hussein in the *Times
Literary Supplement.*

Born in Chicago, Cisneros was the only daughter
among seven children. Concerning her childhood,
Cisneros recalled that because her brothers attempted
to control her and expected her to assume a traditional
female role, she often felt like she had "seven fathers." The family frequently moved between the
United States and Mexico because of her father's
homesickness for his native country and his devotion
to his mother who lived there. Consequently, Cisneros
often felt homeless and displaced. She began to read
extensively, finding comfort in such works as Virginia Lee Burton's *The Little House* and Lewis
Carroll's *Alice's Adventures in Wonderland.* Cisneros
periodically wrote poems and stories throughout her
childhood and adolescence, but it was not until she
attended the University of Iowa's Writers Workshop
in the late 1970s that she realized her experiences as
a Latina woman were unique and outside the realm of
dominant American culture.

Following this realization, Cisneros decided to write
about conflicts directly related to her upbringing, in-

cluding divided cultural loyalties, feelings of alienation, and degradation associated with poverty. Incorporating these concerns into *The House on Mango Street,* a work that took nearly five years to complete, Cisneros created the character Esperanza, a poor, Latina adolescent who longs for a room of her own and a house of which she can be proud. Esperanza ponders the disadvantages of choosing marriage over education, the importance of writing as an emotional release, and the sense of confusion associated with growing up. In the story *"Hips,"* for example, Esperanza agonizes over the repercussions of her body's physical changes: "One day you wake up and there they are. Ready and waiting like a new Buick with the key in the ignition. Ready to take you where?" Written in what *Booklist* contributor Penelope Mesic called "a loose and deliberately simple style, halfway between a prose poem and the awkwardness of semiliteracy," the pieces in *The House on Mango Street* won praise for their lyrical narratives, vivid dialogue, and powerful descriptions.

Woman Hollering Creek and Other Stories is a collection of twenty-two narratives revolving around numerous Mexican-American characters living near San Antonio, Texas. Ranging from a few paragraphs to several pages, the stories in this volume contain the interior monologues of individuals who have been assimilated into American culture despite their sense of loyalty to Mexico. In "Never Marry a Mexican," for example, a young Latina begins to feel contempt for her white lover because of her emerging feelings of inadequacy and cultural guilt. And in the title story, a Mexican woman deluded by fantasies of a life similar to that of American soap operas ventures into Texas to marry an American. When she discovers that her husband and marriage share little in common with her TV dreams, she is forced to reappraise her life.

Reviewers praised the author's vivid characters and distinctive prose. Noting Cisneros's background as a poet, *Los Angeles Times Book Review* contributor Barbara Kingsolver remarked that "Cisneros has added length and dialogue and a hint of plot to her poems and published them in a stunning collection." Writing in the *Nation,* Patricia Hart exclaimed, "Cisneros breathes narrative life into her adroit, poetic descriptions, making them mature, fully formed works of fiction." Hart also commended Cisneros's "range of characters" as "broad and lively." *Time* reviewers Peter S. Prescott and Karen Springen averred, "Noisily, wittily, always compassionately, Cisneros surveys woman's condition—a condition that

is both precisely Latina and general to women everywhere." Kingsolver, who stated that "nearly every sentence contains an explosive sensory image," concluded that Cisneros "takes no prisoners and has not made a single compromise in her language." Similarly, Bebe Moore Campbell, discussing the work in the *New York Times Book Review,* felt that "the author seduces with precise, spare prose and creates unforgettable characters we want to lift off the page and hang out with for a little while." Prescott and Springen agreed that *Woman Hollering Creek* "should make Cisneros's reputation as a major author."

Although Cisneros is noted primarily for her fiction, her poetry has also garnered attention. In *My Wicked Wicked Ways,* published in 1987, Cisneros writes about her native Chicago, her travels in Europe, and, as reflected in the title, sexual guilt resulting from her strict Catholic upbringing. A collection of sixty poems, each of which resemble a short story, this work further evidences Cisneros's penchant for merging various genres. *Bloomsbury Review* critic Gary Soto explained: "Cisneros's poems are intrinsically narrative, but not large, meandering paragraphs. She writes deftly with skill and idea, in the 'show-me-don't-tell-me' vein, and her points leave valuable impressions." Writing in *Belles Lettres,* Andrea Lockett commented, "Particularly alluring here are the daring, perceptive, and sometimes rough-hewn expressions about being a modern woman." In her 1994 poetry collection, *Loose Woman,* Cisneros offers a portrait of a fiercely proud, independent woman of Mexican heritage. "Cisneros probes the extremes of perceptions and negotiates the boundary regions that define the self," remarked Susan Smith Nash in a *World Literature Today* review of the collection. Discussing her poetry with David Mehegan of the *Boston Globe,* Cisneros stated that her poetry "is almost a journal of daily life as woman and writer. I'm always aware of being on the frontier. Even if I'm writing about Paris or Sarajevo, I'm still writing about it from this border position that I was raised in."

In her poetry, as in all her works, Cisneros incorporates Latino dialect, impressionistic metaphors, and social commentary in ways that reveal the fears and doubts unique to Latinas and women in general. She told Mary B. W. Tabor in a *New York Times* interview: "I am a woman and I am a Latina. Those are the things that make my writing distinctive. Those are the things that give my writing power. They are the things that give it sabor [flavor], the things that give it picante [spice]."

BIOGRAPHICAL/CRITICAL SOURCES:

BOOKS

Chesla, Elizabeth L., *Sandra Cisneros' "The House on Mango Street,"* Research & Education Association (Piscataway, NJ), 1996.
Contemporary Literary Criticism, Volume 69, Gale, 1992.
Dictionary of Literary Biography, Volume 152: *American Novelists since World War II, Fourth Series,* Gale, 1995.
Mirriam-Goldberg, Caryn, *Sandra Cisneros: Latina Writer and Activist,* Enslow (Springfield, NJ), 1998.

PERIODICALS

America, July 18, 1992, p. 39.
Americas Review, spring, 1987, pp. 69-76.
Belles Lettres, summer, 1993, p. 51; spring, 1995, p. 62.
Bloomsbury Review, July-August, 1988, p. 21.
Boston Globe, May 17, 1994, p. 73.
Chicago Tribune, November 19, 1992, section 5, p. 8; December 20, 1992, section 2, p. 1.
Chicano-Riquena, fall-winter, 1985, pp. 109-19.
Christian Science Monitor, March 12, 1993, p. 12.
Glamour, November, 1990, pp. 256-57.
Horn Book, November-December, 1994, p. 716.
Library Journal, May 15, 1994, p. 76.
Los Angeles Times, May 7, 1991, p. F1.
Los Angeles Times Book Review, April 28, 1991, p. 3.
Mirabella, April, 1991, p. 46.
Nation, May 6, 1991, p. 597.
Newsweek, June 3, 1991, p. 60.
New York Times, January 7, 1993, p. C10.
New York Times Book Review, May 26, 1991, p. 6.
Publishers Weekly, March 29, 1991, pp. 74-75; April 25, 1994, p. 61.
Quill & Quire, May, 1991, p. 30.
School Library Journal, August, 1994, p. 181.
Times Literary Supplement, August 13, 1993, p. 18.
Washington Post Book World, June 9, 1991, p. 3.
World Literature Today, winter, 1995, p. 145.*

*   *   *

COELHO NETO, Henrique 1864-1934

PERSONAL: Born in 1864; died in 1934; son of a Portuguese merchant; married, 1890. *Education:* Studied medicine and law.

CAREER: Writer, c. 1891-1929. Also worked as journalist and teacher. Served three terms as a federal deputy; also served as diplomat and government official.

MEMBER: Brazilian Academy of Letters (president, 1926-34).

AWARDS, HONORS: Named "prince of Brazilian prose writers," 1928; Nobel Prize nomination, 1932.

WRITINGS:

Rapsodias, 1891.
A Capital Federal (novel; title means "The Federal Capital"), 1893.
Fruto Proibido, 1895.
Sertao, 1896.
A Conquista, 1898.
A Bico da Pena, 1904.
Turbilhao (novel; title means "Crowd"), 1906.
Esfinge, 1908.
Vida Mundana, 1909.
O Rei Negro (novel; title means "The Black King"), 1914.
Brazilian Tales, edited and translated by Isaac Goldberg, Four Seas (Boston, MA), 1921.
A Cidade Maravilhosa, 1928.
Fogo-Fatuo, 1929.
A Arvore da Vida, 1929.*

*   *   *

COFER, Judith Ortiz 1952-

PERSONAL: Born February 24, 1952, in Hormigueros, Puerto Rico; immigrated to the United States, 1956; daughter of J. M. (in U.S. Navy) and Fanny (Morot) Ortiz; married Charles John Cofer (in business), November 13, 1971; children: Tanya. *Education:* Augusta College, B.A., 1974; Florida Atlantic University, M.A., 1977; attended Oxford University, 1977.

ADDRESSES: Home—P.O. Box 938, Louisville, GA 30434. *Office*—Department of English and Creative Writing, University of Georgia, Athens, GA 30602. *Agent*—Berenice Hoffman Literary Agency, 215 West 75th St., New York, NY 10023.

CAREER: Bilingual teacher at public schools in Palm Beach County, FL, 1974-75; Broward Community

College, Fort Lauderdale, FL, adjunct instructor in English, 1978-80, instructor in Spanish, 1979; University of Miami, Coral Gables, FL, lecturer in English, 1980-84; University of Georgia, Athens, instructor in English, 1984-87, Georgia Center for Continuing Education, instructor in English, 1987-88; Macon College, instructor in English, 1988-89; Mercer University College, Forsyth, GA, special programs coordinator, 1990; University of Georgia, Athens, associate professor of English and Creative Writing, 1992—. Adjunct instructor at Palm Beach Junior College, 1978-80. Visiting professor at numerous colleges and universities, including University of Michigan, Arizona University, and University of Minnesota, Duluth. Conducts poetry workshops and gives poetry readings. Member of regular staff of International Conference on the Fantastic in Literature, 1979-82; member of literature panel of Fine Arts Council of Florida, 1982; member of administrative staff of Bread Loaf Writers' Conference, 1983 and 1984.

MEMBER: Poetry Society of America, Poets and Writers, Associated Writing Programs.

AWARDS, HONORS: Scholar of English Speaking Union at Oxford University, 1977; fellow of Fine Arts Council of Florida, 1980; Bread Loaf Writers' Conference, scholar, 1981, John Atherton Scholar in Poetry, 1982; grant from Witter Bynner Foundation for Poetry, 1988, for *Letters from a Caribbean Island;* National Endowment for the Arts fellowship in poetry, 1989; Pulitzer Prize nomination, 1989, for *The Line of the Sun;* Pushcart Prize for nonfiction, 1990; O. Henry Prize for short story, 1994; Anisfield Wolf Award in Race Relations, 1994, for *The Latin Deli.*

WRITINGS:

Latin Women Pray (chapbook), Florida Arts Gazette Press, 1980.
The Native Dancer (chapbook), Pteranodon Press, 1981.
Among the Ancestors (chapbook), Louisville News Press, 1981.
Latin Women Pray (three-act play), first produced in Atlanta at Georgia State University, June, 1984.
Peregrina (poems), Riverstone Press (Golden, CO), 1986.
Terms of Survival (poems), Arte Publico (Houston, TX), 1987.
(Contributor) *Triple Crown: Chicano, Puerto Rican and Cuban American Poetry* (trilogy; contains

Cofer's poetry collection *Reaching for the Mainland*), Bilingual Press (Ypsilanti, MI), 1987.
The Line of the Sun (novel), University of Georgia Press (Athens, GA), 1989.
Silent Dancing: A Partial Remembrance of a Puerto Rican Childhood (personal essays), Arte Publico, 1990.
The Latin Deli, University of Georgia Press, 1993.
An Island like You: Stories of the Barrio (young adult), Orchard Books (New York City), 1995.
The Year of Our Revolution: New and Selected Stories and Poems, Arte Publico, 1998.

Also author of the poetry collection *Letters from a Caribbean Island.*

OTHER

Contributor to anthologies, including *Hispanics in the U.S.,* Bilingual Review/Press (Tempe, AZ), 1982; *Woman of Her Word,* Arte Publico, 1983; *The Heath Anthology of Modern American Literature,* Heath (Boston, MA), 1990; *Pushcart Prize XV Anthology,* Pushcart Press (Atlanta, GA), 1990; *Puerto Rican Writers at Home in the U.S.A.,* Open Hand (New York City), 1991; and *Literature: Reading, Reacting, Writing,* Holt (New York City), 1991.

Contributor of poems to magazines, including *Southern Humanities Review, Poem, Prairie Schooner, Apalachee Quarterly, Kansas Quarterly,* and *Kalliope.* Poetry editor of *Florida Arts Gazette,* 1978-81; member of editorial board of *Waves.*

SIDELIGHTS: Judith Ortiz Cofer is a highly regarded poet, essayist, and novelist who has written extensively on the experience of being a Puerto Rican in the United States. Cofer was born in Hormigueros, Puerto Rico, but raised and educated primarily in New Jersey. She grew up attempting to reconcile her parents' traditional values with her experiences stateside, eventually producing work that "focuses on the effect on Puerto Rican Americans of living in a world split between the island culture of their homeland and the teeming tenement life of the United States," to quote Marian C. Gonsior in the *Dictionary of Hispanic Biography.*

Cofer left Puerto Rico as a young child, when her father joined the U.S. Navy and was assigned to a post in the Brooklyn Naval Yard. The family lived in Paterson, New Jersey, but undertook extensive visits back to Puerto Rico whenever the father was sent to sea. Back in New Jersey, it was Cofer who learned English in order to help her Spanish-speaking mother run the household and make important decisions. In an interview for *Melus,* the author spoke of reconciling the contradictions in her cultural identity: "I write in English, yet I write obsessively about my Puerto Rican experience. . . . That is how my psyche works. I am a composite of two worlds. . . . I lived with . . . conflictive expectations: the pressures from my father to become very well versed in the English language and the Anglo customs, and from my mother not to forget where we came from. That is something that I deal with in my work all the time."

Trained to be a teacher, Cofer came to creative writing as a graduate student, when she began to craft poems in English about Latina women and their concerns. Her work began to appear in literary periodicals as well as chapbooks and collections by small presses. "I think poetry has made me more disciplined," Cofer observed in *Melus.* "It taught me how to write, because to write a poem takes so much skill. . . . Poetry contains the essence of language. Every word weighs a ton. . . . Poetry taught me about economizing in language and about the power of language. So I will never stop writing poetry."

Branching out from poetry in the late 1980s, Cofer published a well-received novel, *The Line of the Sun,* in 1989, and an essay collection, *Silent Dancing,* in 1990. *The Line of the Sun* was applauded by *New York Times Book Review* contributor Roberto Marquez for the "vigorous elegance" of its language. Marquez called Cofer "a prose writer of evocatively lyrical authority, a novelist of historical compass and sensitivity." The first half of *The Line of the Sun* depicts the poor village of Salud, Puerto Rico, and introduces the characters Rafael Vivente and his wild brother-in-law, Guzman. *Los Angeles Times Book Review* contributor Sonja Bolle noted that the author's eye for detail "brings alive the stifling and magical world of village life." The second part of the novel follows Rafael to Paterson, New Jersey, where his daughter Marisol, the story's narrator, grows up. Marisol's father encourages her to become wholly American, but her mother advises her to adopt the customs and values of Puerto Rico. Marisol learns about her heritage mainly through the stories told by her family, which often focus on her Uncle Guzman, the "demon child"; his arrival at her New Jersey home helps Marisol to balance the American and Puerto Rican aspects of her identity. Though Marquez criticized parts of the plot as contrived, he proclaimed Cofer as

"a writer of authentic gifts, with a genuine and important story to tell." *The Line of the Sun* was nominated for a Pulitzer Prize in 1989.

The title of *Silent Dancing* is derived from a home movie of Cofer's parents in their youth. The scene is a New Year's Eve party, and the revelers form a conga line in which each gets a moment of personal attention from the camera. The author uses the film clip as a launching place for a discussion of how her parents' generation—and hers—has responded to the challenge of living between cultures, not wholly comfortable in either.

This theme has been extended into Cofer's volume for young adults, *An Island like You: Stories of the Barrio.* Set in Paterson, New Jersey, the collection consists of stories about young expatriate Puerto Ricans who live in a tenement building. *Horn Book* contributor Nancy Vasilakis deemed the book "a milestone in multicultural publishing for children," noting: "The Caribbean flavor of the tales gives them their color and freshness, but the narratives have universal resonance in the vitality, the brashness, the self-centered hopefulness, and the angst expressed by the teens as they tell of friendships formed, romances failed, and worries over work, family, and school." In a different *Horn Book* review, Rudine Sims Bishop wrote of *An Island like You:* "There is humor, and poignancy as well. The voices in these stories ring true, as do the stories themselves. I hope Cofer continues to write for young people." A *Publishers Weekly* reviewer concluded: "This fine collection may draw special attention for its depictions of an ethnic group underserved by YA writers, but Cofer's strong writing warrants a close look no matter what the topic."

Cofer told *CA:* "The 'infinite variety' and power of language interest me. I never cease to experiment with it. As a native Puerto Rican, my first language was Spanish. It was a challenge, not only to learn English, but to master it enough to teach it and—the ultimate goal—to write poetry in it.

"My family is one of the main topics of my poetry; the ones left behind on the island of Puerto Rico, and the ones who came to the United States. In tracing their lives, I discover more about mine. The place of birth itself becomes a metaphor for the things we all must leave behind; the assimilation of a new culture is the coming into maturity by accepting the terms necessary for survival. My poetry is a study of this process of change, assimilation, and transformation."

BIOGRAPHICAL/CRITICAL SOURCES:

BOOKS

Cofer, Judith Ortiz, *Silent Dancing: A Partial Remembrance of a Puerto Rican Childhood,* Arte Publico (Houston, TX), 1990.
Dictionary of Hispanic Biography, Gale (Detroit, MI), 1996, pp. 235-36.

PERIODICALS

Booklist, February 15, 1995, p. 1082.
Georgia Review, spring/summer, 1990, pp. 51-59.
Horn Book Magazine, July-August, 1995, pp. 464-65; September-October, 1995, pp. 581-83.
Library Journal, July, 1998, p. 76.
Los Angeles Times Book Review, August 6, 1989, p. 6.
Melus, fall, 1993, pp. 83-97; fall, 1997, pp. 206-08.
New York Times Book Review, September 24, 1989, pp. 46-47.
Publishers Weekly, April 17, 1995, p. 61; July 27, 1998, p. 78.
Women's Review of Books, December, 1990, p. 9.

*   *   *

COLLIGNON, Rick 1948-

PERSONAL: Born in 1948.

ADDRESSES: Home—Questa, NM. *Agent*—c/o Mac-Murray & Beck, 1649 Downing St., Denver, CO 80218.

CAREER: Novelist. Worked as a roofer for twenty years.

WRITINGS:

The Journal of Antonio Montoya: A Novel, Mac-Murray & Beck (Denver, CO), 1996.
Perdido: A Novel, MacMurray & Beck (Denver, CO), 1997.

SIDELIGHTS: Rick Collignon burst upon the literary scene with the widely reviewed and well-received novel titled *The Journal of Antonio Montoya.* The novel concerns a series of supernatural events occurring in the town of Guadeloupe, New Mexico, after an accident that leaves a young boy orphaned. Cus-

tody of Jose Montoya is left to his father's brother, but after the funeral the boy's dead mother rises in her coffin to request a change: she asks Ramona Montoya, her husband's unmarried sister, to take the boy in. On Ramona's return home with the boy, she is awaited by her long-dead grandparents, who between fixing dinner and running errands in her car bequeath to her the journal of her great-uncle, her grandfather's cousin. Ramona reads the journal, which is spliced into the action of the novel. Like Ramona, who has given years of her life to try to establish a career in painting, Antonio Montoya was an artist, a sculptor of santos (small figures of the saints). The novel weaves parallels between Antonio's and Ramona's lives, and between all the living and the dead.

A number of critics, including Lawrence Olszewski, reviewing the novel for *Library Journal,* linked Collignon's surreal situations to the writing of Gabriel Garcia Marquez, the renowned South American writer. But critics were mixed in their appreciation for the novel as a whole. Olszewski called the book an "enchanting work," and Wendy Cavenett of *Between the Lines* declared that "in *The Journal of Antonio Montoya,* Collignon beckons us to drink from the cup of divine omniscience, to believe that the world is a vast realm of the improbable and that life, in its many guises, exists concurrently, each effecting the other." She also called the book "an astonishing debut, one that heralds a clear, imaginative voice from the contemporary chasm of post-modernism." Others, however, though finding much to like in the novel, had criticisms as well. A *Publishers Weekly* reviewer praised Collignon's "spare style" and "bracingly fresh descriptions," but requested more plot line. Andy Solomon, writing for the *New York Times Book Review,* commented that "the problem . . . is less that the novel's dead characters are still living than that its living ones are half dead."

Though his first novel was published only after working as a roofer for twenty years, Collignon's next novel, *Perdido,* was published only a year after *The Journal of Antonio Montoya.* This second novel is also set in Guadeloupe, New Mexico, and inhabited almost exclusively by Mexican Americans. The protagonist is Will Sawyer, an Anglo who drifted into Guadeloupe nearly twenty years prior to the beginning of the novel and decided to hang around. His sense of belonging in the community is challenged, however, after he discovers that a mysterious death has occurred—the hanging of a young Anglo woman at a bridge—not long before his arrival to town. When he starts asking questions, it isn't long before tensions bloom into violence, revealing just how tentatively accepted Will is in the town.

Nancy Pearl of *Booklist* expressed enjoyment of *Perdido*. Although she thought some readers might be distracted by the author's habit of "dropping the reader into the middle of the story," she admired the novel's style and its "simple and direct narrative." Faye A. Chadwell, writing for the *Library Journal*, appreciated Collignon's ability to explore the connections between ethnic and racial groups "while delving into the concept of identity." An *Atlantic Monthly* reviewer applauded Collignon for having "created a distinct and meaningful world." *New York Times Book Review* critic Denise Gess said, "driven by Collignon's decisive prose, his strong characters and his deep knowledge of New Mexico folklore, *Perdido* is a one-sitting read, a novel that captivates and surprises all the way to its chilling end."

BIOGRAPHICAL/CRITICAL SOURCES:

PERIODICALS

Atlantic Monthly, August 1997, p. 98.
Booklist, July 1997, p. 1794.
Library Journal, May 1, 1996, p. 129; June 15, 1997, p. 94.
New York Times Book Review, August 25, 1996, p. 19.
Publishers Weekly, April 29, 1996, p. 53.
Western American Literature, spring, 1997, p. 88.

OTHER

Between the Lines, http://www.thei.aust.com/isite/btl/btlrvmontoya.html (1998).
MacMurray & Beck, http://www.macmurraybeck.com (1998).*

* * *

CONDE (ABELLAN), Carmen 1901-1996
(Florentina del Mar, Magdalena Noguera)

PERSONAL: Born August 15, 1901 (some sources say 1907), in Cartagena, Spain; died in 1996; daughter of Luis Conde Parreno and Maria de la Paz Abellan; married Antonio Oliver Belmas (a poet), 1931 (died, 1968). *Education:* Escuela Normal, Albacete, pedagogy degree.

CAREER: Writer. Co-founder of *El Gallo Crisis* magazine.

MEMBER: Spanish Royal Academy.

AWARDS, HONORS: Elisendo de Montcadda prize, 1953; Simon Bolivar international poetry prize, 1954; Primo de Rivera, 1967; Seville Athenaeum prize, 1980, for *Soy la madre;* National prize for children's and teenage literature in Spain, 1987, for *Canciones de nana y desvelo.*

WRITINGS:

POETRY

Brocal, Cuadernos Literarios (Madrid), 1929.
Jubilos, Sudeste (Murcia), 1934.
Pasion del verbo, Marsiega (Madrid), 1944.
Honda memoria de mi, Romo (Madrid), 1944.
Ansia de la gracia, Adonais (Madrid), 1945.
Mujer sin Eden, Jura (Madrid), 1947, translation by Alexis Levitin and Jose R. de Armas published as *Woman without Eden,* Universal (Miami, FL), 1986.
Sea la luz (title means "Let There Be Light"), Mensaje (Madrid), 1947.
Mi fin en el viento (title means "My Destiny in the Wind"), Adonais (Madrid), 1947.
Iluminada tierra (title means "Lighted Land"), privately printed, 1951.
Vivientes de los siglos, privately printed, 1954.
Los monologos de la hija, privately printed, 1959.
En un mundo de fugitivos (title means "In a World of Fugitives"), Losada (Buenos Aires), 1960.
Derribado Arcangel (title means "Fallen Archangel"), Revista de Occidente (Madrid), 1960.
En la tierra de nadie, Laurel del Sureste (Madrid), 1960.
Los poemas del Mar Menor, Catedra Savedra Fajardo/Universidad de Murcia (Murcia), 1962.
Su voz le doy a la noche, privately printed, 1962.
Obra poetica de Carmen Conde, 1929-1966, Biblioteca Nueva (Madrid), 1967.
A este lado de la eternidad ("This Side of Eternity"), Biblioteca Nueva (Madrid), 1970.
Corrosion, Biblioteca Nueva (Madrid), 1975.
Cita con la vida, Biblioteca Nueva (Madrid), 1976.
Dias por la tierra: antologia incompleta, Nacional (Madrid), 1977.
El tiempo es un rio lentisimo de fuego, Ediciones 29 (Barcelona), 1978.
La noche oscura del cuerpo, Biblioteca Nueva (Madrid), 1980.

Desda nunca, Rio Nuevo (Barcelona), 1982.

Derramen su sangre las sombras, Torremozas (Madrid), 1983.

Del obligado dolor, Almarabu (Madrid), 1984.

Brocal, y Poemas a Maria, edited by Rosario Hiriart, Biblioteca Nueva (Madrid), 1984.

La calle de los balcones azules, Plaza y Janes (Barcelona), 1985.

Crater, Biblioteca Nueva (Madrid), 1985.

Hermosos dias en China, Torremozas (Madrid), 1985.

Antologia poetica, edited by Rosario Hiriart, Espasa-Calpe (Madrid), 1985.

Canciones de nana y desvelo, Minon (Valladolid), 1985.

Memoria puesta en olvido: antologia personal, Torremozas (Madrid), 1987.

Una palabra tuya, Torremozas (Madrid), 1988.

FOR CHILDREN

Dona Cenenioto, gato savaje, Alhambra (Madrid), 1943.

El caballito y la luna, CVS (Madrid), 1974.

Zoquetin y Martina, Ediciones 29 (Barcelona), 1979.

EDITOR

Poesia feminina espanola viviente, Anroflo (Madrid), 1955.

Once grandes poetisas americohispanas, Cultura Hispanica (Madrid), 1967.

Poesia feminia espanola, 1939-1950, Bruguera (Barcelona), 1967.

Antologia de poesia amoroa contemporanea, Bruguera (Barcelona), 1969.

Memoria puesta en el olvido, Torremozas (Madrid), 1987.

FICTION

En manos del silencio, Plaza y Janes (Barcelona), 1950.

Mientra los hombres mueren (title means "While Men Die"), Cisalpino (Milan), 1953.

Cobre, Grifon (Madrid), 1954.

Las oscuras raices, Garbo (Barcelona), 1954.

La rambla, Magisterio Espanol/Novelas y Cuentos (Madrid), 1977.

Crecio espesa la yerba, Planeta (Barcelona), 1979.

Soy la madre, Planeta (Barcelona), 1980.

MEMIOR

Por el camino, viendo sus orillas, three volumes, Plaza y Janes (Barcelona), 1986.

PLAYS

Belen, ENAG (Madrid), 1953.

(With Antonio Oliver) *A la estrella por la cometa,* Doncel (Madrid), 1961.

OTHER

Por la escuela renovada, Embajador Vich (Valencia), 1931.

Dios en la poesia espanola, Alhambra (Madrid), 1944.

La poesia ante la eternidad, Alhambra (Madrid), 1944.

Don Alvaro de Luna, Hesperia (Madrid), 1945.

Empezando la vida: memorias de una infancia en Marruecos, 1914-1920, al-Motamid (Tetuan, Morocco), 1955.

Jaguar puro immarhito, privately printed, 1963.

Acompanando a Francisca Sanchez: resumen de una vida junto a Ruben Dario, Union (Managua), 1964.

Un pueblo que lucha y canta, Nacional (Madrid), 1967.

Menendez Pidal, Union (Madrid), 1969.

Gabriela Mistral, Union (Madrid), 1970.

Cancionera de la enamorada, Torro de Granito (Avila), 1971.

Al encuertro de Santa Teresa, Belmar, 1978.

Poesia ante el tiempo y la inmortalidad, Real Academia (Madrid), 1979.

Una nina oye su voz, Escuela Espanola (Madrid), 1979.

Un conejo sonador rompe conla tradicion, Escuela Espanola (Madrid), 1979.

El mundo empieza fuera del mundo, Escuela Espanola (Madrid), 1979.

El Conde Sol, Escuela Espanola (Madrid), 1979.

El monje y el pajarillo, Escuela Espanola (Madrid), 1980.

Cuentos para ninos de buena fe, Escuela Espanola (Madrid), 1982.

Centenito, Escuela Espanola (Madrid), 1987.

Cuentos del romancero, Escuela Espanola (Madrid), 1987.

Cantando al amanecer, Escuela Espanola (Madrid), 1987.

AS FLORENTINA DEL MAR

Los ernredos de Chismecita (for children), Alhambra (Madrid), 1943.

Don Juan de Austria, Hesperia (Madrid), 1943.

La amistad en la literatura espanola, Alhambra (Madrid), 1944.

Soplo que va y no vuelve (fiction), Alhambra (Madrid), 1944.

Vidas contra su espejo (fiction), Alhambra (Madrid), 1944.

Aladino (play), Hesperia (Madrid), 1945.

Juan Ramon Jimenez, Conferencias y Ensayos (Bilbao), 1952.

Viejo venis y florido (poetry), Caja de Ahorros del Sureste (Alicante), 1963.

AS MAGDALENA NOGUERA

El Cristo de Medinaceli, Alhambra (Madrid), 1944.

En santuario del Pilar, Alhambra (Madrid), 1945.

Cartas a Katherine Mansfield, Doncel (Zaragoza), 1948.

El escorial: una meditacion mas, Riaz (Madrid), 1948.

Mi libro de El Escorial, Coegio Mayor Universitario de Santa Cruz (Valladolid), 1949.

Obras escogidas, Plenitud (Madrid), 1949.

SIDELIGHTS: Spanish writer Carmen Conde wrote in a number of genres, but is best known for her contributions to poetry. Much of her poetry elaborated on the role of women in the world, or denounced human suffering. Conde incorporated elements of nature into her poetry. Her husband played a large part in the development of some of her work, serving as one of her closest critics. Conde's poetry and other literary works were affected by events in her life. As Pilar Martin commented in *Dictionary of Literary Biography,* "to ignore any part of Conde's life would be ignoring also the evolution of her writings."

Conde spent the early part of her life in Morocco, a country which made an impression on her and which was reflected in one of her earlier works, 1934's *Jubilos.* She began writing as a teenager, showing a particular interest in poetry and prose. At this point in Conde's writing, nature was a large influence and the presence of the sea was particularly apparent. *Brocal,* which was published in 1929, reflects the presence of nature and also the deep love that Conde had for her future husband, Oliver Belmas. Conde considers the publication of *Brocal,* along with earlier publications of pieces in periodicals, to comprise what she calls her first period of writing.

Conde's second period of writing began after her marriage in 1931 and is characterized by a major emphasis on poetry. Essayist Paul Vincent of *Contem-*

porary Writers called *Jubilos* a classic representation of this period of her writing. The work, according to Vincent, uses "traces of ultraism and surrealist touches." During this period of Conde's developing literary career, the poet and her husband also opened the Public University of Cartegena. The impetus for creating the university was, in essayist Martin's words, Conde's "interest in the diffusion of culture."

Conde's world changed dramatically with the advent of the Spanish Civil War in 1936. Suddenly the poet was aware of the enormous suffering that war could cause. As she stated in her 1945 volume *Ansia de la gracia:* "The land covered with corpses presented to my eyes an incredible and astonishing landscape." According to Martin, Conde's third period of literary development was instigated with the start of the war and is characterized by her realization that the "presence of suffering would walk hand in hand with her longing for truth and light." Conde summed up her evolving realizations in her memoir, *Por el camino,* which was published in 1986: "Our war made me lose faith in humanity . . . if the truth changes from moment to moment, what are we to believe in? Honesty, Courage, responsibility, and nothing else." Though many intellectuals fled Spain during the war, Conde and her husband remained and were forced to use pseudonyms to continue publishing work. Conde published prolifically during the 1930s and 1940s and her work included the children's biographies *Don Juan de Austria*—published in 1943—and 1945's *Don Alvaro de Luna.* Conde later wrote about the war, and captured her husband's impressions as a soldier on the front. The 1953 volume *Mientra los hombres mueren* ("While Men Die") expresses Conde's feelings about the war: "All suffering is useless, I found out then and I know it better now. And, nevertheless to say aloud how much one is suffering for the insoluble seems to erase all the boundaries that separate us from others."

The poet's writing during this period went onto cover more than her feelings about war. Love and destiny are the topics of *Ansia de la gracia,* according to Martin. Martin noted that Conde writes about "a love for life and fellow creatures, and sorrow for the presence of mediocrity and lack of beauty in the world." According to Martin, 1947's *Mujer sin Eden*—translated as *Woman without Eden* in 1986—is one of the hallmarks of this period of Conde's writing. The theme of oppressed womanhood is apparent throughout the work, which takes its basis from scripture and is collected as a series of poems. In a last poem titled "The Woman's Final Supplication," Conde's speaker implores for death by the flaming sword of Eden, so that "she will no longer bear babies who become men who hate." The role of woman in the world was just as important to Conde as the rest of her universal themes, and the poet claimed that her works that addressed women were "not a matter of writing strictly feminine poetry, but to enrich the common cultural inheritance." Conde also hoped to bring understanding to the field of women's poetry. Janet Perez, in *Contemporary World Writers,* called *Mujer sin Eden* "one of Conde's most significant and controversial works, a feminist rewriting of the biblical myth of the Fall from Grace in which Eve's side of the story is privileged and the image of oppressed women throughout history reappears in each of the five cantos."

Conde also published *Sea la luz* ("Let There Be Light") and *Mi fin en el viento* ("My Destiny in the Wind") in 1947. The first title explores topics of death, remembrance, and destiny. According to Martin, Conde muses about destiny in these lines: "Always measuring the immeasurable, / the paradox. Yes. no; or yes, not yet . . . / Or not, but still yes . . . light and shadow, / death or resurrection." The latter title explores the human connection with nature, According to Perez, Conde expressed her relationship with nature as a "soulful identification, whereby body and spirit are detached and expressed through a favorite Conde image, the archangels." Spiritual references to nature continued to influence some of the poet's later works, including *Iluminada tierra* ("Lighted Land"). Conde also wrote about the struggle between good and evil in *Derribado Arcangel* ("Fallen Archangel") and *En un mundo de fugitivao* ("In a World of Fugitives"), which Perez maintained "expresses the poet's sense of identification with the losers."

Conde's later poetry fell into the realm of social poetry, or poetry that opposed the Spanish governmental regime. Vincent points out that Conde's work in this area focused on injustices but that "personal and religious concerns prevented complete engagement." When the poet's husband died in 1968, her intense grieving found its way into subsequent work, which dealt with life and death and manifested itself in titles including 1970's *A esto lado de la eternidad* ("This Side of Eternity") and 1975's *Corrosion.* According to essayist Martin, the latter title is characterized by the presence of "material substances such as marble and magma, [and] nature expresses human feelings." Martin points out that a poem in the collection—"A Miguel"—focuses on the paradox of human life: "I do not know; I do not know. / But there is

darkness. / An immense unstable oppressing / darkness. / Yes, I know. There is darkness."

Conde continued to publish poetry and prose into the 1980s; she died in 1996. Martin called her voice "one of the strongest in Spanish poetry" and claimed that "her work has been the basis for that of many current women poets in Spain."

BIOGRAPHICAL/CRITICAL SOURCES:

BOOKS

Contemporary World Writers, edited by Tracy Chevalier, St. James Press, 1993.
Dictionary of Literary Biography, Volume 108: *Twentieth-Century Spanish Poets, First Series,* edited by Michael L. Perna, Gale (Detroit), 1991.*

*   *   *

CONTI, Haroldo   1925-1976(?)

PERSONAL: Born May 25, 1925, in Chacabuco, Argentina; disappeared May 5, 1976 (presumed killed); son of a shopkeeper and provincial leader; married. *Education:* Attended Seminario de los Salesianos and Colegio Metropolitano Conciliar; studied philosophy and letters at a university.

CAREER: Writer and filmmaker, c. 1962-76. Worked as a Latin teacher, bank employee, operator of a transport business, airline pilot, and fisherman.

AWARDS, HONORS: Grants from Gente de Cine, 1952; OLAT Prize, 1956, for *Examinado; Life* Magazine Prize, 1960, for the story "La Causa"; Premio Fabril, 1962, for *Sudeste;* Premio Municipal, for *Todos los Veranos;* Premio Universidad Veracruzana, for *Alrededor de la Jaula;* winner of Barral competition, 1971, with *En Vida Gana;* first prize, Casa de las Americas, Havana, Cuba, 1975, for *Mascaro, el Cazador Americano.*

WRITINGS:

Sudeste (novel), Fabril (Buenos Aires, Argentina), 1962.
Todos los Veranos (stories), Nueve 64 (Buenos Aires), 1964.
Alrededor de la Jaula (novel), Universidad Veracruzana (Xalapa, Mexico), 1966.

Con Otra Gente (stories), CEDAL (Buenos Aires), 1967.

En Vida Gana, Barral (Barcelona, Spain), 1971.

La Balada del Alamo Carolina (stories), Corregidor (Buenos Aires), 1975.

Mascaro, el Cazador Americano (novel), Crisis (Buenos Aires), 1975.

Cuentos y Relatos de Haroldo Conti, Kapelusz (Buenos Aires), 1976.

Author of *Examinado* (one-act play), 1956, and *La Muerte de Sebastian Arache y su Pobre Entierro* (screenplay), 1974. Work represented in anthologies.

BIOGRAPHICAL/CRITICAL SOURCES:

BOOKS

Chamberlain, B. J., editor, *The City in the Latin American Novel,* Michigan State University (East Lansing, MI), 1980, pp. 14-28.*

*   *   *

CORPI, Lucha 1945-

PERSONAL: Born April 13, 1945, in Jaltipan, Veracruz, Mexico; immigrated to the United States; married. *Education:* University of California, Berkeley, B.A., 1975; San Francisco State University, M.A. (comparative literature), 1979.

ADDRESSES: Home—Oakland, CA. *Office*—Clinton Park Adult School, 655 East 14th St., Oakland, CA 94606.

CAREER: University of California, Berkeley, vice-chair of Chicano Studies executive committee, 1970-71, coordinator of Chicano Studies Library, 1970-72; Oakland Public Neighborhood Centers, Oakland, CA, teacher of English as a second language, 1973—; writer. Founding member of Aztlan Cultural, 1971, and Centro Chicano de Escritores, 1980; member of Oakland Museum and Latin American Commission.

MEMBER: California Association of Teachers of English as a Second Language.

AWARDS, HONORS: Fellow of National Endowment for the Arts, 1979-80; winner of *Palabra nueva* literary contest, 1983, for short story "Los cristos del alma" ("The Martyrs of the Soul"); first place in the tenth Chicano Literary Contest, University of California, Irvine, 1984, for short story "Shadows on Ebbing Water."

WRITINGS:

POETRY

(With Elsie Alvarado de Ricord and Concha Michel) *Fireflight: Three Latin-American Poets,* translation from Spanish by Catherine Rodriguez-Nieto, Oyez (Berkeley, CA), 1976.

Palabras de mediodia: Noon Words (text in English and Spanish), translation from Spanish by Catherine Rodriguez-Nieto, El Fuego de Aztlan (Oakland), 1980.

Variaciones sobre una Tempestad / Variations on a Storm, English translation by Catherine Rodriguez-Nieto, Third Woman Press (Berkeley, CA), 1990.

Work represented in anthologies, including *The Other Voice: Twentieth-Century Women's Poetry in Translation,* translation by Corpi and Catherine Rodriguez-Nieto, edited by Joanna Bankier and others, Norton (New York City), 1976; *Contemporary Women Poets: An Anthology of California Poets,* translated by Catherine Rodriguez-Nieto, edited by Jennifer McDowell and M. Loventhal, Merlin (San Jose), 1977; *Chicanos: Antologia historica y literaria,* edited by Tino Villanueva, Fondo de Cultura Economica (Mexico City), 1980; *A Decade of Hispanic Literature: An Anniversary Anthology,* edited by Nicolas Kanellos, Revista Chicano-Riquena (Houston), 1982; *Women Poets of the World,* edited by Joanna Bankier, Dierdre Lashgari, and Doris Earnshaw, Macmillan (New York City), 1983; and *Palabra nueva: Cuentos chicanos,* edited by Ricardo Aguilar and others, Texas Western Press (El Paso), 1984. Contributor of poems and stories to periodicals, including *Prisma, Semana de Bella Artes, Imagine, Poetry San Francisco, Boston Review, De colores* and *El Fuego de Aztlan.*

NOVELS

Delia's Song, Arte Publico (Houston), 1989.

Eulogy for a Brown Angel (mystery), Arte Publico, 1992.

Cactus Blood (mystery), Arte Publico, 1995.

OTHER

Where Fireflies Dance (for children; autobiographical), illustrated by Mira Reisberg, Children's Book Press (San Francisco), 1997.

(Editor) *Mascaras,* Third Woman Press, 1997.

Also author of short stories, including "Los cristos del alma."

SIDELIGHTS: "The work of [Lucha] Corpi is distinguished," lauded Barbara Brinson Curiel in the *Dictionary of Literary Biography:* "Accomplished and recognized as a prose writer and as a poet, she has used discernible thematic patterns. Two particularly prominent concerns are women cornered by the circumstances of their lives and a notion that fate is inescapable. She speaks for the powerless unable to speak for themselves." When she was nineteen years old, the Mexican-born author immigrated to the United States with her new husband. The author's identity as a female Latina artist living in the United States is reflected in her career, not only through writing, but also in her founding two Chicano arts organizations and coordinating the Chicano Studies Library at the University of California, Berkeley. In her autobiographical work for children, *Where Fireflies Dance,* Corpi relates anecdotes of her small-town Mexican childhood in an "unusually sophisticated (though still accessible) text," indicated *Booklist*'s Susan Dove Lempke. For her 1997 work *Mascaras,* Corpi edited a volume of essays written by fifteen contemporary women authors who were Americans as well as Latinas or Chicanas. The "authors expose the many cultural, political, and linguistic barriers to their success," related Rebecca Martin in a *Library Journal* review recommending the work.

"Corpi's poetry is . . . rooted in the reality of her own life, the short lines of clear and simple language-building as they express the poet's emotions and concerns," described Denise Wiloch in *Contemporary Women Poets.* "Her poetry, produced mainly in Spanish and published with translations . . . is characterized by an imaginistic lyricism combined with a controlled and direct use of language. Thematically, her work examines love, feelings of isolation and loneliness, and social topics, especially the role of women in the home and in society, political commitment, and the experiences of the marginalized," summarized Curiel. "Her bilingual collection *Palabras de mediodia / Noon Woods* gathers together for English readers many of her early poems, while the much-anthologized four-poem series 'The Marina Poems' draws on historical events at the time of the Spanish conquest of Mexico," related Wiloch. *Palabras de mediodia / Noon Words* describes and contrasts three places familiar to Corpi—Jaltipan, the sunny, friendly coastal town where she was born, the less genial San Luis

Potosi, a town in central Mexico where she moved at the age of nine, and the United States. The poems set in the United States often feature homey scenes of domestic activities such as ironing and cleaning.

"Corpi is recognized primarily for her work as a poet, although in recent years she has also been recognized as an accomplished prose writer," noted Curiel. "One of Corpi's early works of short fiction, "Tres mujere" (*Three Women,* 1977) . . . which Corpi describes as both 'autobiographical and allegorical,' is about a young woman with a son who takes a trip looking for her destiny," recounted Curiel. *Delia's Song,* Corpi's first novel, has some parallels to the author's own experiences; its main character chooses to part from her family in order to attend college in California, and ultimately decides to become a writer. "Corpi's recent fiction," remarked Curiel in 1989, "is characterized by it portraits of women in untenable situations who choose a course of action and who follow it, often with tragic consequences."

In 1992 and 1995, Corpi published her first fiction in a slightly different domain—mystery. The detective in both *Eulogy for a Brown Angel* and *Cactus Blood* is Gloria Damasco, a Chicana. In *Cactus Blood,* Damasco investigates victims who in years past were all actively involved with the United Farmworkers Strike and 1973's grape boycott. A *Publishers Weekly* critic presented a mixed assessment, stating that the plot is "mildly suspenseful" and elements of characterization are done well, but the narrative is sometimes "slow" due to "many moments of harking-back and a rash of coincidences."

BIOGRAPHICAL/CRITICAL SOURCES:

BOOKS

Contemporary Women Poets, St. James Press (Detroit), 1997.
Dictionary of Literary Biography, Volume 82: *Chicano Writers, First Series,* Gale, 1989.
Notable Hispanic American Women, 1st edition, Gale, 1993.
Sanchez, Marta Ester, *Contemporary Chicano Poetry: A Critical Approach to an Emerging Literature,* University of California Press, 1985.

PERIODICALS

Booklist, January 1, 1998.
Hispanic, January-February, 1996.

Library Journal, March 1, 1995; January, 1998.
National Catholic Reporter, May 22, 1998.
Prisma, Volume 1, number 1, 1979.
Publishers Weekly, February 6, 1995.
School Library Journal, December, 1997.*

*   *   *

CORTAZAR, Julio 1914-1984
(Julio Denis)

PERSONAL: Born August 26, 1914, in Brussels, Belgium; held dual citizenship in Argentina and (beginning 1981) France; died of a heart attack February 12, 1984, in Paris, France; son of Julio Jose and Maria Herminia (Descotte) Cortazar; married Aurora Bernardez, August 23, 1953 (marriage ended). *Education:* Received degrees in teaching and public translating; attended Buenos Aires University. *Avocational interests:* Jazz, movies.

CAREER: Writer. High school teacher in Bolivar and Chivilcoy, both in Argentina, 1937-44; teacher of French literature, University of Cuyo, Mendoza, Argentina, 1944-45; manager, Argentine Publishing Association (Camara Argentina del Libro), Buenos Aires, Argentina, 1946-48; public translator in Argentina, 1948-51; freelance translator for UNESCO, Paris, 1952-84. Member of jury, Casa de las Americas Award.

AWARDS, HONORS: Prix Medicis, 1974, for *Libro de Manuel;* Ruben Dario Order of Cultural Independence awarded by Government of Nicaragua, 1983.

WRITINGS:

FICTION

Bestiario (short stories; also see below), Sudamericana (Buenos Aires), 1951, reprinted, 1983.
Final del juego (short stories; also see below), Los Presentes (Mexico), 1956, expanded edition, Sudamericana, 1964, reprinted, 1983.
Las armas secretas (short stories; title means "The Secret Weapons"; also see below), Sudamericana, 1959, reprinted, Catedra (Madrid), 1983.
Los premios (novel), Sudamericana, 1960, reprinted, Ediciones B, 1987, translation by Elaine Kerrigan published as *The Winners,* Pantheon, 1965, reprinted, 1984.

Historias de cronopios y de famas (novel), Minotauro (Buenos Aires), 1962, reprinted, Alfaguara, 1984, translation by Paul Blackburn published as *Cronopios and Famas,* Pantheon, 1969.
Rayuela (novel), Sudamericana, 1963, reprinted, 1984, translation by Gregory Rabassa published as *Hopscotch,* Pantheon, 1966, reprinted, 1987.
Cuentos (collection), Casa de las Americas (Havana), 1964.
Todos los fuegos el fuego (short stories), Sudamericana, 1966, reprinted, 1981, translation by Suzanne Jill Levine published as *All Fires the Fire, and Other Stories,* Pantheon, 1973, reprinted, 1988.
La vuelta al dia en ochenta mundos (essays, poetry, and short stories), Siglo Veintiuno (Mexico), 1967, reprinted, 1984, translation by Thomas Christensen published as *Around the Day in Eighty Worlds,* North Point Press, 1986.
El perseguidor y otros cuentos (short stories), Centro Editor para America Latina (Buenos Aires), 1967, reprinted, Bruguera, 1983.
End of the Game, and Other Stories, translated by Blackburn (includes stories from *Final del juego, Bestiario,* and *Las armas secretas*), Pantheon, 1967, published as *Blow-Up, and Other Stories,* Collier, 1968, reprinted, Pantheon, 1985.
Ceremonias (collection), Seix Barral, 1968, reprinted, 1983.
62: Modelo para armar (novel), Sudamericana, 1968, translation by Rabassa published as *62: A Model Kit,* Pantheon, 1972.
Ultimo round (essays, poetry, and stories; title means "Last Round"), Siglo Veintiuno, 1969, reprinted, 1984.
Relatos (collection), Sudamericana, 1970.
La isla a mediodia y otros relatos (contains twelve previously published stories), Salvat, 1971.
Libro de Manuel (novel), Sudamericana, 1973, translation by Rabassa published as *A Manual for Manuel,* Pantheon, 1978.
Octaedro (stories; title means "Octahedron"; also see below), Sudamericana, 1974.
Antologia (collection), La Libreria, 1975.
Fantomas contra los vampiros multinacionales (title means "Fantomas Takes on the Multinational Vampires"), Excelsior (Mexico), 1975.
Los relatos (collection), four volumes, Alianza, 1976-1985.
Alguien que anda por ahi y otros relatos (short stories), Alfaguara (Madrid), 1977, translation by Rabassa published as *A Change of Light, and Other Stories* (includes *Octaedro;* also see below), Knopf, 1980.
Territorios, Siglo Veintiuno, 1978.

Un tal Lucas, Alfaguara, 1979, translation by Rabassa published as *A Certain Lucas,* Knopf, 1984.

Queremos tanto a Glenda, Alfaguara, 1980, translation by Rabassa published as *We Love Glenda So Much, and Other Tales* (also see below), Knopf, 1983.

Deshoras (short stories), Alfaguara, 1982, translation by Alberto Manguel published as *Unreasonable Hours,* Coach House Press (Toronto), 1995.

We Love Glenda So Much and *A Change of Light,* Vintage, 1984.

Salvo el Crepusculo, translated by Stephen Kessler, published as *Save Twilight,* City Lights Books (San Francisco, CA), 1997.

Julio Cortazar: New Readings, edited by Carlos J. Alonso, Cambridge University Press (New York City), 1998.

TRANSLATOR

Alfred Stern, *Filosofia de la risa y del llanto,* Iman (Buenos Aires), 1950.

Lord Houghton, *Vida y cartas de John Keats,* Iman, 1955.

Marguerite Yourcenar, *Memorias de Adriano,* Sudamericana, 1955.

Edgar Allan Poe, *Obras en prosa,* two volumes, Revista de Occidente, 1956.

Poe, *Cuentos,* Editorial Nacional de Cuba, 1963.

Poe, *Aventuras de Arthur Gordon Pym,* Instituto del Libro (Havana), 1968.

Poe, *Eureka,* Alianza (Madrid), 1972.

Daniel Defoe, *Robinson Crusoe,* Bruguera, 1981.

Also translator of works by G. K. Chesterton, Andre Gide, and Jean Giono, published in Argentina between 1948 and 1951.

OTHER

(Under pseudonym Julio Denis) *Presencia* (poems; title means "Presence"), El Bibliofilo (Buenos Aires), 1938.

Los reyes (play; title means "The Monarchs"), Gulab y Aldabahor (Buenos Aires), 1949, reprinted, Alfaguara, 1982.

(Contributor) *Buenos Aires de la fundacion a la angustia,* Edi-ciones de la Flor (Buenos Aires), 1967.

(With others) *Cuba por argentinos,* Merlin (Buenos Aires), 1968.

Buenos Aires, Buenos Aires (includes French and English translations), Sudamericana, 1968.

Viaje alrededor de una mesa (title means "Trip around a Table"), Cuadernos de Rayuela (Buenos Aires), 1970.

(With Oscar Collazos and Mario Vargas Llosa) *Literatura en la revolucion y revolucion en la literatura,* Siglo Veintiuno, 1970.

(Contributor) *Literatura y arte nuevo en Cuba,* Estela (Barcelona), 1971.

Pameos y meopas (poetry), Editorial Libre de Sivera (Barcelona), 1971.

Prosa del observatorio, Lumen (Barcelona), 1972.

La casilla de los Morelli (essays), edited by Jose Julio Ortega, Tusquets, 1973.

Convergencias, divergencias, incidencias, edited by Ortega, Tusquets, 1973.

(Author of text) *Humanario,* La Azotea (Buenos Aires), 1976.

(Author of text) *Paris: Ritmos de una ciudad,* Edhasa (Barcelona), 1981.

Paris: The Essence of an Image, Norton, 1981.

(With Carol Dunlop) *Los autonautas de la cosmopista,* Muchnik (Buenos Aires), 1983.

Nicaragua tan violentamente dulce (essays), Nueva Nicaragua, 1983.

Argentina: Anos de almabradas culturales (essays), edited by Saul Yurkievich, Muchnik, 1984.

Nada a pehuajo: Un acto; Adios, Robinson (plays), Katun, 1984.

Salvo el crepusculo (poems), Nueva Imagen, 1984.

Textos politicos, Plaza y Janes, 1985.

Divertimento, Sudamericana/Planeta, 1986.

El examen, Sudamericana/Planeta, 1986.

Nicaraguan Sketches, Norton, 1989.

Contributor to numerous periodicals, including *Revista Iberoamericana, Cuadernos Hispanoamericanos, Books Abroad,* and *Casa de las Americas.*

ADAPTATIONS: The story "Las babas del diablo," from the collection *Las armas secretas* was the basis for Michaelangelo Antonioni's 1966 film *Blow Up.*

SIDELIGHTS: Argentine author Julio Cortazar was "one of the world's greatest writers," according to novelist Stephen Dobyns. "His range of styles," Dobyns wrote in the *Washington Post Book World,* "his ability to paint a scene, his humor, his endlessly peculiar mind makes many of his stories wonderful. His novel *Hopscotch* is considered one of the best novels written by a South American." A popular as well as a critical success, *Hopscotch* not only established Cortazar's reputation as a novelist of international merit but also, according to David W. Foster in *Currents in the Contemporary Argentine Novel,* prompted wider acceptance in the United States of novels written by other Latin Americans. For this reason many critics, such as Jaime Alazraki in *The Final Island,* viewed the book as "a turning point for Latin American literature." A *Times Literary Supplement* reviewer, for example, called *Hopscotch* "the first great novel of Spanish America."

Still other critics, including novelists Jose Donoso and C. D. B. Bryan, saw the novel in the context of world literature. Donoso, in his *The Boom in Spanish American Literature: A Personal History,* claimed that *Hopscotch* "humanized the novel." Cortazar was a writer, Donoso continued, "who [dared] to be discursive and whose pages [were] sprinkled with names of musicians, painters, art galleries, . . . movie directors, [and] all this had an undisguised place within his novel, something which I would never have dared to presume to be right for the Latin American novel, since it was fine for [German novelist] Thomas Mann but not for us." In the *New York Times Book Review,* Bryan stated: "I think *Hopscotch* is the most magnificent book I have ever read. No novel has so satisfactorily and completely and beautifully explored man's compulsion to explore life, to search for its meaning, to challenge its mysteries. Nor has any novel in recent memory lavished such love and attention upon the full spectrum of the writer's craft."

Cortazar attempted to perfect his craft by constant experimentation. In his longer fiction he pursued, as Leo Bersani observed in the *New York Times Book Review,* both "subversion and renewal of novelistic form." This subversion and renewal was of such importance to Cortazar that often the form of his novels overshadowed the action that they described. Through the form of his fiction Cortazar invited the reader to participate in the writer's craft and to share in the creation of the novel. *Hopscotch* is one such novel. In *Into the Mainstream: Conversations with Latin-America Writers,* Luis Harss and Barbara Dohmann wrote that *Hopscotch* "is the first Latin American novel which takes itself as its own central topic or, in other words, is essentially about the writing of itself. It lives in constant metamorphoses, as an unfinished process that invents itself as it goes, involving the reader in such a way to make him part of the creative impulse."

Thus, *Hopscotch* begins with a "Table of Instructions" that tells the reader that there are at least two ways to read the novel. The first is reading chapters one to fifty-six in numerical order. When the reader finishes chapter fifty-six he can, according to the in-

structions, stop reading and "ignore what follows [nearly one hundred more short chapters] with a clean conscience." The other way of reading suggested by the instructions is to start with chapter seventy-two and then skip from chapter to chapter (hence, the title of the book), following the sequence indicated at the end of each chapter by a number which tells the reader which chapter is next. Read the second way, the reader finds that chapter 131 refers him to chapter fifty-eight, and chapter fifty-eight to chapter 131, so that he is confronted with a novel that has no end. With his "Table of Instructions" Cortazar forces the reader to write the novel while he is reading it.

Cortazar's other experimental works include *62: A Model Kit* (considered a sequel to *Hopscotch*), *A Manual for Manuel, Ultimo round* ("Last Round"), and *Fantomas contra los vampiros multinacionales* (*"Fantomas Takes on the Multinational Vampires"*). *62: A Model Kit* is based on chapter sixty-two of *Hopscotch* in which a character, Morelli, expresses his desire to write a new type of novel. "If I were to write this book," Morelli states, "standard behavior would be inexplicable by means of current instrumental psychology. Everything would be a kind of disquiet, a continuous uprooting, a territory where psychological causality would yield disconcertedly." In *62: A Model Kit* Cortazar attempted to put these ideas into action. Time and space have no meaning in the novel: although it takes place in Paris, London, and Vienna, the characters move and interact as if they are in one single space. The characters themselves are sketchily presented in fragments that must be assembled by the readers; chapters are replaced by short scenes separated by blank spaces on the pages of the novel. Cortazar noted in the book's introduction that once again the reader must help create the novel: "The reader's option, his personal montage of the elements in the tale, will in each case be the book he has chosen to read."

A Manual for Manuel continues in the experimental vein. Megan Marshall described the book in *New Republic* as "a novel that merges story and history, a supposed scrapbook of news clippings, journal entries, diagrams, transcripts of conversations, and much more." The book, about the kidnapping of a Latin American diplomat by a group of guerillas in Paris, is told from the double perspective of an unnamed member of the group, who takes notes on the plans for the kidnapping, and a nonmember of the group, Andres, who reads the notes. Periodically, these two narrations are interrupted by the inclusion of English-, French-, and Spanish-language texts reproduced in the pages of the novel. These texts, actual articles collected by Cortazar from various sources, form part of a scrapbook being assembled for Manuel, the child of two of the members of the group. On one page, for example, Cortazar reprinted a statistical table originally published in 1969 by the U.S. Department of Defense that shows how many Latin Americans have received military training in the United States. The reader reads about the compilation of the scrapbook for Manuel, while at the same time reading the scrapbook and reacting to the historical truth it contains.

Other such experimentation is found in *Ultimo round,* a collection of essays, stories, and poetry. William L. Siemens noted in the *International Fiction Review* that this book, like *Hopscotch* and *62: A Model Kit,* "is a good example of audience-participation art." In *Ultimo round,* he declared, "it is impossible for the reader to proceed in a conventional manner. Upon opening the book the reader notes that there are two sets of pages within the binding, and he must immediately decide which of them to read first, and even whether he will go through by reading the top and then the bottom of page one, and so on."

Cortazar's brief narrative *Fantomas contra los vampiros multinacionales* is yet another experiment with new forms of fiction. It presents, in comic book form, the story of a "superhero," Fantomas, who gathers together "the greatest contemporary writers" to fight the destructive powers of the multinational corporations. Chilean Octavio Paz, Italian Alberto Moravia, and American Susan Sontag, along with Cortazar himself, appear as characters in the comic book. Although short, the work embodies several constants in Cortazar's fiction: the comic (the comic book form itself), the interplay of fantasy and reality (the appearance of historical figures in a fictional work), and a commitment to social activism (the portrayal of the writer as a politically involved individual). These three elements, together with Cortazar's experiments with the novelistic form, are the basic components of his fiction.

Cortazar explained how these elements function together in his essay *"Algunos aspectos del cuento"* (*"Some Aspects of the Story"*), which Alazraki quoted in *The Final Island.* His work, Cortazar claimed, was "an alternative to that false realism which assumed that everything can be neatly described as was upheld by the philosophic and scientific optimism of the eighteenth century, that is, within a world ruled more or less harmoniously by a system of laws, of principles, of causal relations, of well defined psychologies, of well mapped geographies. . . . In my case, the suspicion of another order, more secret and less communicable [was one of the principles guiding] my personal search for a literature beyond overly naive forms of realism." Whatever the method, whether new narrative forms, unexpected humor, incursions into fantasy, or pleas for a more humane society, Cortazar strove to shake the reader out of traditional ways of thinking and seeing the world and to replace them with new and more viable models. Dobyn explained in the *Washington Post Book World,* "Cortazar wants to jolt people out of their self-complacency, to make them doubt their own definition of the world."

Cortazar's last full-length work of fiction, *A Certain Lucas,* for example, "is a kind of sampler of narrative ideas, a playful anthology of form, including everything from parables to parodies, folk tales to metafictions," as Robert Coover describes it in the *New York Times Book Review.* Including chapters with such titles as "Lucas, His Shopping," "Lucas, His Battles with the Hydra," and "Lucas, His Pianists," the book "builds a portrait, montage-like, through a succession of short sketches (humorous set-pieces, really) full of outrageous inventions, leaping and dream-like associations and funny turns of phrase," states *Los Angeles Times Book Review* critic Charles Champlin. "Lucas is not Cortazar," Dobyns suggests in the *Washington Post Book World,* "but occasionally he seems to stand for him and so the book takes on an autobiographical quality as we read about Lucas' friends, his struggles with himself, his dreams, his tastes, his view of writing." The result, writes Champlin, might appear to be "no more than a series of extravagant jokes, [and] it would be an exceptional passing entertainment but no more than that. Yet under the cover of raillery, self-indicting foolishness and extremely tall tales," the critic continues, "Cortazar is discovered to be a thoughtful, deep-feeling man, impassioned, sentimental, angry, complicated, a philosopher exploring appearances vs. realities is the way of philosophers ever." "What we see in Lucas and in much of Cortazar's work is a fierce love of this earth, despite the awfulness, and a fierce respect for life's ridiculousness," concludes Dobyns. "And in the midst of this ridiculousness, Cortazar dances . . . and that dance comforts and eases our own course through the world."

This ridiculousness, or humor, in Cortazar's work often derived from what a *Time* reviewer referred to as the author's "ability to present common objects from strange perspectives as if he had just invented them." Cortazar, declared Tom Bishop in *Saturday Review,* was "an intellectual humorist. . . . [He had] a rare gift for isolating the absurd in everyday life [and] for depicting the foibles in human behavior with an unerring thrust that [was] satiric yet compassionate." *Hopscotch* is filled with humorous elements, some of which Saul Yurkievich listed in *The Final Island.* He included "references to the ridiculous, . . . recourse to the outlandish, . . . absurd associations, . . . juxtaposition of the majestic with the popular or vulgar," as well as "puns, . . . [and] polyglot insults." *New York Times* writer John Leonard called absurdity "obligatory" in a work by Cortazar and gave examples of the absurd found in *A Manual for Manuel,* such as "a turquoise penguin [is] flown by jet to Argentina; the stealing of 9,000 wigs . . . and obsessive puns."

In an interview with Evelyn Picon Garfield, quoted in *Books Abroad,* Cortazar called *Cronopios and Famas* his "most playful book." It is, he continued, "really a game, a very fascinating game, lots of fun, almost like a tennis match." This book of short, story-like narratives deals with two groups of creatures described by Arthur Curley in *Library Journal* as the "warm life-loving cronopios and practical, conventional famas . . . imaginary but typical personages between whom communication is usually impossible and always ridiculous." One portion of the book, called "The Instruction Manual," contains detailed explanations of various everyday activities, including how to climb stairs, how to wind a clock, and how to cry. In order to cry correctly, the author suggested thinking of a duck covered with ants. With these satiric instructions Cortazar, according to Paul West in *Book World,* "cleanses the doors of perception and mounts a subtle, bland assault on the mental rigidities we hold most dear." By forcing us to think about everyday occurrences in a new way, Cortazar, Malva E. Filer noted in *Books Abroad,* "expresses his rebellion against objects and persons that make up our everyday life and the mechanical ways by which we relate to them." Filer continued: "In Cortazar's fictional world [a] routine life is the great scandal against which every individual must rebel with all his strength. And if he is not willing to do so, extraordinary elements are usually summoned to force him out of this despicable and abject comfort." These "extraordinary elements" enter into the lives of Cortazar's characters in the form of fantastic episodes which interrupt their otherwise normal existences.

Alexander Coleman observed in *Cinco maestros: Cuentos modernos de Hispanoamerica (Five Masters:*

Modern Spanish-American Stories): "Cortazar's stories start in a disarmingly conversational way, with plenty of local touches. But something always seems to go awry just when we least expect it." "Axolotl," a short story described by novelist Joyce Carol Oates in the *New York Times Book Review* as her favorite Cortazar tale, begins innocently: a man describes his trips to the Parisian botanical gardens to watch a certain type of salamander called an axolotl. But the serenity ends when the narrator admits, "Now I am an axolotl." In another story, a woman has a dream about a beggar who lives in Budapest (a city the woman has never visited). The woman ends up actually going to Budapest where she finds herself walking across a bridge as the beggar woman from her dream approaches from the opposite side. The two women embrace in the middle of the bridge and the first woman is transformed into the beggar woman—she can feel the snow seeping through the holes in her shoes—while she sees her former self walk away. In yet another story, a motorcyclist is involved in a minor traffic accident and suddenly finds himself thrown back in time where he becomes the victim of Aztec ritual sacrifice. Daniel Stern noted in *Nation* that with these stories and others like them "it is as if Cortazar is showing us that it is essential for us to reimagine the reality in which we live and which we can no longer take for granted."

Although during the last years of his life Cortazar was so involved with political activism that Jason Weiss described him in the *Los Angeles Times* as a writer with hardly any time to write, the Argentine had early in his career been criticized "for his apparent indifference to the brutish situation" of his fellow Latin Americans, according to Leonard. Evidence of his growing political preoccupation is found in his later stories and novels. Leonard observed, for instance, that *A Manual for Manuel* "is a primer on the necessity of revolutionary action," and William Kennedy in the *Washington Post Book World* noted that the newspaper clippings included in the novel "touch[ed] the open nerve of political oppression in Latin America." Many of the narratives in *A Change of Light, and Other Stories* are also politically oriented. Oates described the impact of one story in the *New York Times Book Review.* In "Apocalypse at Solentiname," a photographer develops his vacation photographs of happy, smiling people only to discover pictures of people being tortured. Oates commented, "The narrator . . . contemplates in despair the impotence of art to deal with in any significant way, the 'life of permanent uncertainty . . . [in] almost all of Latin America, a life surrounded by fear and death.'"

Cortazar's fictional world, according to Alazraki in *The Final Island,"* represents a challenge to culture." This challenge is embedded in the author's belief in a reality that reaches beyond our everyday existence. Alazraki noted that Cortazar once declared, "Our daily reality masks a second reality which is neither mysterious nor theological, but profoundly human. Yet, due to a long series of mistakes, it has remained concealed under a reality prefabricated by many centuries of culture, a culture in which there are great achievements but also profound aberrations, profound distortions." Bryan further explained these ideas in the *New York Times Book Review:* Cortazar's "surrealistic treatment of the most pedestrian acts suggest[ed] that one way to combat alienation is to return to the original receptiveness of childhood, to recapture this original innocence, by returning to the concept of life as a game."

Cortazar confronted his reader with unexpected forms, with humor, fantasy, and unseemly reality in order to challenge him to live a more meaningful life. He summarized his theory of fiction (and of life) in an essay, "The Present State of Fiction in Latin America," which appeared in *Books Abroad.* The Argentine concluded: "The fantastic is something that one must never say good-bye to lightly. The man of the future . . . will have to find the bases of a reality which is truly his and, at the same time, maintain the capacity of dreaming and playing which I have tried to show you . . . , since it is through those doors that the Other, the fantastic dimension, and the unexpected will always slip, as will all that will save us from that obedient robot into which so many technocrats would like to convert us and which we will not accept—ever."

BIOGRAPHICAL/CRITICAL SOURCES:

BOOKS

Alazraki, Jaime, and Ivar Ivask, editors, *The Final Island: The Fiction of Julio Cortazar,* University of Oklahoma Press, 1978.

Boldy, Steven, *The Novels of Cortazar,* Cambridge University Press, 1980.

Colas, Santiago, *Postmodernity in Latin America: The Argentine Paradigm,* Duke University Press (Durham, NC), 1994.

Coleman, Alexander, editor, *Cinco maestros: Cuentos modernos de Hispanoamerica,* Harcourt, Brace & World, 1969.

Contemporary Literary Criticism, Gale, Volume 2, 1974, Volume 3, 1975, Volume 5, 1976, Volume 10, 1979, Volume 13, 1980, Volume 15, 1980, Volume 33, 1985, Volume 34, 1985.

Donoso, Jose, *Historia personal del "boom,"* Anagrama (Barcelona), 1972, translation by Gregory Kolovakos published as *The Boom in Spanish American Literature: A Personal History,* Columbia University Press, 1977.

Foster, David W., *Currents in the Contemporary Argentine Novel,* University of Missouri Press, 1975.

Garfield, Evelyn Picon, *Julio Cortazar,* Ungar, 1975.

Garfield, *Cortazar por Cortazar* (interviews), Universidad Veracruzana, 1981.

Giacoman, Helmy F., editor, *Homenaje a Julio Cortazar,* Anaya, 1972.

Goloboff, Gerardo Mario, *Julio Cortazar: la biografia,* Seix Barral (Buenos Aires), 1998.

Harss, Luis and Barbara Dohmann, *Into the Mainstream: Conversations with Latin-American Writers,* Harper, 1967.

Legaz, Maria Elena, and others, *Un Tal Julio: Cortazar, otras lecturas,* Alcion (Cordoba, Argentina), 1998.

Prego, Omar, *La fascinacion de las palabras* (interviews), Muchnik, 1985.

Ramirez, Sergio, *Hatful of Tigers: Reflections on Art, Culture, and Politics,* Curbstone Press (Willimantic, CT), 1995.

Stavans, Ilan, *Julio Cortazar: A Study of the Short Fiction,* Twayne (New York City), 1996.

Vasquez Amaral, Jose, *The Contemporary Latin American Narrative,* Las Americas, 1970.

PERIODICALS

America, April 17, 1965; July 9, 1966; December 22, 1973.

Atlantic, June, 1969; October, 1973.

Books Abroad, fall, 1965; winter, 1968; summer, 1969; winter, 1970; summer, 1976.

Book World, August 17, 1969.

Casa de las Americas, numbers 15-16, 1962.

Chicago Tribune, September 24, 1978; February 14, 1984.

Chicago Tribune Book World, November 16, 1980; May 8, 1983.

Christian Science Monitor, August 15, 1967; July 3, 1969; December 4, 1978; July 17, 1984, p. 24.

Commentary, October, 1966.

El Pais, April 19, 1981.

Globe and Mail (Toronto), February 18, 1984.

Hispania, December, 1973.

Hispanic Journal, spring, 1984, pp. 172-73.

Hudson Review, spring, 1974; autumn, 1983, pp. 549-62.

International Fiction Review, January, 1974; January, 1975.

Library Journal, July, 1967; September, 1969; September 15, 1980.

Listener, December 20, 1979.

Los Angeles Times, August 28, 1983; February 14, 1984.

Los Angeles Times Book Review, December 28, 1980; June 12, 1983; May 27, 1984; June 24, 1984, pp. 4, 14.

Nation, September 18, 1967.

National Review, July 25, 1967.

New Republic, April 23, 1966; July 15, 1967; October 21, 1978; October 25, 1980.

Newsweek, September 17, 1984, p. 82.

New Yorker, May 18, 1965; February 25, 1974.

New York Review of Books, March 25, 1965; April 28, 1966; April 19, 1973; October 12, 1978.

New York Times, November 13, 1978; March 24, 1983; February 13, 1984.

New York Times Book Review, March 21, 1965; April 10, 1966; June 15, 1969; November 26, 1972; September 9, 1973; November 19, 1978; November 9, 1980; March 27, 1983, pp. 1, 37-38; March 4, 1984; May 20, 1984.

Novel: A Forum on Fiction, fall, 1967.

Review of Contemporary Fiction (special Cortazar issue), fall, 1983.

Revista Iberoamericana, July-December, 1973.

Saturday Review, March 27, 1965; April 9, 1966.

Symposium, spring, 1983, pp. 17-47.

Time, April 29, 1966; June 13, 1969; October 1, 1973.

Times (London), February 14, 1984.

Times Literary Supplement, October 12, 1973; December 7, 1979.

Virginia Quarterly Review, spring, 1973.

Voice Literary Supplement, March, 1984.

Washington Post, February 13, 1984.

Washington Post Book World, November 18, 1973; November 5, 1978; November 23, 1980; May 1, 1983; June 24, 1984.

World Literature Today, winter, 1977; winter, 1980.*

CAREER: Worked for the foreign affairs branch of the Nicaraguan government under the Sandinistas, 1978-82; worked as political adviser for Contra movement in Washington, DC, beginning in 1982; writer.

WRITINGS:

Nicaragua's Continuing Struggle: In Search of Democracy, edited by James Finn, Freedom House, 1988.
Memoirs of a Counterrevolutionary, Doubleday, 1989.

SIDELIGHTS: Arturo Cruz, Jr., has written two books about the political struggles in Nicaragua. After studying at England's Institute of Developmental Studies and at Johns Hopkins University, he returned to his country in 1978 to support the newly installed communist Sandinista government. Cruz became disillusioned by the Sandinistas, however, when he determined that the new regime was more concerned with establishing military power and alliances with other communist countries than with instituting social and economic reforms. Consequently, he joined his father, also a former Sandinista, in working for the Contras, a counterrevolutionary faction attempting to oust the Sandinistas. Cruz later resigned from the Contra movement as well; he recounts his experiences in *Memoirs of a Counterrevolutionary* and presents his views on Nicaraguan politics in *Nicaragua's Continuing Struggle.*

BIOGRAPHICAL/CRITICAL SOURCES:

BOOKS

Cruz, Arturo, Jr., *Memoirs of a Counterrevolutionary,* Doubleday, 1989.

PERIODICALS

Los Angeles Times Magazine, April 19, 1987.
New York Times Book Review, October 15, 1989.*

*   *   *

CRUZ, Arturo, Jr. 1954(?)-

PERSONAL: Born c. 1954 in Nicaragua; son of Arturo Cruz, Sr. (a banker and political leader). *Education:* Attended Institute of Development Studies, Sussex, England, and Johns Hopkins University.

*   *   *

CRUZ, Ricardo Cortez 1964-

PERSONAL: Born August 10, 1964, in Decatur, IL; son of Theodore and Carol M. (Belue) Cruz; married Carol M. Milling, 1994; children: Ricardo Cortez, II. *Ethnicity:* "Black-Hispanic." *Education:* Richland

Community College, A.A.; Illinois State University, B.S. (English), completed coursework towards Doctor of Philosophy in English. *Politics:* "Democratic, liberal." *Religion:* "Belief in God and the importance of spirituality." *Avocational interests:* Stereo mixing, film, basketball.

ADDRESSES: Home—Bloomington, IL. *Office*—Department of English, Stevenson Hall, Campus Box 4240, Illinois State University, Normal, IL 61790-4240. *E-mail*—rccruz@ilstu.edu.

CAREER: Herald & Review, Decatur, IL, sportswriter, intern, and clerk, 1982-88; *Pantagraph,* Bloomington, IL, sportswriter and clerk, 1988-89; Heartland Community College, Bloomington, IL, English instructor, 1992-93; Southern Illinois University, Carbondale, assistant and associate professor, 1993-98; Illinois State University, Normal, IL, guest and assistant professor, 1998—.

AWARDS, HONORS: Charles H. and N. Mildred Nilon Excellence in Minority Fiction Award, for *Straight Outta Compton;* Distinguished Alumnus Award, Illinois Community College, 1996.

WRITINGS:

NOVELS

Straight Outta Compton: A Dive into Living Large, a Work Where Characters Trip, Talk Out the Side of Their Neck, and Cuss Like It Was Nothing, Fiction Collective Two (Normal, IL), 1992.
Five Days of Bleeding, Fiction Collective Two/Black Ice, 1992.

Also contributor to literary journals, including the *Kenyon Review, Iowa Review, Postmodern Culture,* and the *African-American Review.*

WORK IN PROGRESS: Premature Autopsies, a novel.

SIDELIGHTS: Ricardo Cortez Cruz writes about the lives of African Americans in a fast, gritty style. His first novel, *Straight Outta Compton,* which borrows from the rap music genre, is considered to be the first notable rap novel published. Cruz worked as a sportswriter and intern at several publications before publishing the novel. He then went on to teach English at the college level. Cruz has contributed to many literary journals.

The author's second work, *Five Days of Bleeding,* takes its title from a reggae song. The story takes place in modern-day Harlem and involves a homeless woman named Zu-Zu and a narrator who has fallen in love with her. A *Publishers Weekly* review noted that much of the story consists of transcribed song lyrics from rap, reggae, and other popular music. The critic claimed that Cruz's narrative style "entirely overwhelms the characterizations" and that some readers will have difficulty understanding the language and life in the modern urban setting. Cruz should have developed the plot more fully, and leaned less on song sketches to hold the plot up, claimed the *Publishers Weekly* reviewer. Nonetheless, the critic gave Cruz credit for "the innovative way in which he describes his city scenarios."

Cruz told *CA:* "I write (s)language, creating dark, urban landscapes replete with hard cadences, riffs, muted voices, magic realism, black comedy, sampling, postmodern conditions, rap, madness and violence, raging energy, asides, pop culture references, and characters talking smack out the side of the necks. My hope is to represent. And, I recommend fiction(s) for the study of sociolinguistics. My heroes livin in/for the city. My villains are people who might have been heroes under different circumstances.

"I am a 'cultural worker.' My goal is to move the crowd."

BIOGRAPHICAL/CRITICAL SOURCES:

BOOKS

The Schomburg Center Guide to Black Literature, Gale Research (Detroit, MI), 1996.

PERIODICALS

Publishers Weekly, July 31, 1995, p. 77.

*   *   *

CRUZ, Victor Hernandez 1949-

PERSONAL: Born February 6, 1949, in Aguas Buenas, Puerto Rico; immigrated to the U.S., 1954; son of Severo and Rosa (Hernandez) Cruz; divorced; children: Vitin Ajani, Rosa Luz. *Education:* Attended high school in New York, NY.

ADDRESSES: Office—P.O. Box 40148, San Francisco, CA 94140; P.O. Box 1047, Aguas Buenas, PR 00607.

CAREER: Poet. East Harlen Gut Theatre, New York City, co-founder, 1968; University of California, Berkeley, guest lecturer, 1970; San Francisco State University, San Francisco, CA, instructor, beginning 1973. Also associated with the San Francisco Art Commission; co-founder, Before Columbus Foundation.

AWARDS, HONORS: Creative Artists public service award, 1974, for *Tropicalization;* National Endowment for the Arts fellow, 1980.

WRITINGS:

Papo Got His Gun! and Other Poems, Calle Once Publications, 1966.
Doing Poetry, Other Ways, 1968.
Snaps (poems), Random House, 1969.
(Editor with Herbert Kohl) *Stuff: A Collection of Poems, Visions, and Imaginative Happenings from Young Writers in Schools—Open and Closed,* Collins & World, 1970.
Mainland (poems), Random House, 1973.
Tropicalization (poems and prose), Reed, Canon, 1976.
The Low Writings, Lee/Lucas Press, 1980.
By Lingual Wholes, Momo's Press, 1982.
Rhythm, Content and Flavor: New and Selected Poems, Arte Publico Press, 1989.
Red Beans, Coffee House Press, 1991.
(Editor with Leroy V. Quintana and Virgil Suarez) *Paper Dance: Fifty-four Latino Poets,* Persea Books, 1994.
Panaramas, Coffee House Press, 1997.

Cruz's work has been included in anthologies, including *An Anthology of Afro-American Writing,* Morrow, 1968, and *Giant Talk: An Anthology of Third World Writings,* Random House, 1975. Contributor to *Evergreen Review, New York Review of Books, Ramparts, Down Here,* and *Revista del Instituto de Estudios Puertorriquenos.* Editor, *Umbra* magazine, 1967-69.

SIDELIGHTS: Victor Hernandez Cruz wrote: "My family life was full of music, guitars and conga drums, maracas and songs. My mother sang songs. Even when it was five below zero in New York she sang warm tropical ballads." He continued: "My work is on the border of a new language, because I create out of a consciousness steeped in two of the important world languages, Spanish and English. A piece written totally in English could have a Spanish spirit. Another strong concern in my work is the difference between a tropical village, such as Aguas Buenas, Puerto Rico, where I was born, and an immensity such as New York City, where I was raised. I compare smells and sounds, I explore the differences, I write from the center of a culture which is not on its native soil, a culture in flight, living half the time on memories, becoming something totally new and unique, while at the same time it helps to shape and inform the new environment. I write about the city with an agonizing memory of a lush tropical silence. This contrast between landscape and language creates an intensity in my work."

In a *New York Times Book Review* of *By Lingual Wholes,* Richard Elman remarks: "Cruz writes poems about his native Puerto Rico and elsewhere which often speak to us with a forked tongue, sometimes in a highly literate Spanglish. . . . He's a funny, hard-edged poet, declining always into mother wit and pathos: 'So you see, all life is a holy hole. Bet hard on that.'" And Nancy Sullivan reflects in *Poetry* magazine: "Cruz allows the staccato crackle of English half-learned, so characteristic of his people, to enrich the poems through its touching dictional inadequacy. If poetry is arching toward the condition of silence as John Cage and Susan Sontag suggest, perhaps this mode of inarticulateness is a bend on the curve. . . . I think that Cruz is writing necessary poems in a period when many poems seem unnecessary."

Cruz's 1991 work *Red Beans,* the title of which is a play on the words "red beings," referring to Puerto Ricans, has also received critical attention. Reviewers have characterized the volume as a highly imaginative exploration of Puerto Rican history as well as the Puerto Rican's history in America. In a review for the *San Francisco Review of Books,* Jose Amaya assessed, "Cruz experiments with the vast linguistic and cultural possibilities of 'indo-afro-hispano' poetry and comes up with a strong vision of American unity." Commenting on the development of Cruz's style, Amaya noted that "Cruz is at his best in *Red Beans* when he portrays . . . the distinct sounds and voices of Caribbean life which crash into his poetic consciousness like a wild ocean surf." Calling Cruz a "vigorous bilingual Latino troubadour," Frank Allen in *Library Journal* declared the book is "a dance on the edges."

BIOGRAPHICAL/CRITICAL SOURCES:

PERIODICALS

Bilingual Review, Volume 1, 1974, pp. 312-19.
Library Journal, October 1, 1997.
MELUS, spring, 1989-90, pp. 43-58.
New York Times Book Review, September 18, 1983.
Poetry, May, 1970.
Publishers Weekly, September 22, 1997.*

*   *   *

CUMPIAN, Carlos

PERSONAL: Male.

ADDRESSES: Office—Department of English, Columbia College, 600 South Michigan Ave., Chicago, IL 60605-1996. *Agent*—c/o March, Inc., P.O. Box 2890, Chicago, IL 60690; fax: (773) 539-0013.

CAREER: Poet. Columbia College, Chicago, IL, part-time instructor of poetry writing; also works as a high school English teacher; gives workshops; has given readings at Museum of Contemporary Art, Chicago, 1996, DePaul University, 1997, and Earlham College, 1997. Guadalajara International Book Fair, cultural exchange guest.

AWARDS, HONORS: Community Arts Assistance grants, Chicago Department of Cultural Affairs; honored by Illinois State Library.

WRITINGS:

Emergency Tacos, March/Abrazo (Chicago, IL), 1989.
Coyote Sun, March/Abrazo (Chicago, IL), 1990.
Latino Rainbow: Poems about Latino Americans, illustrated by Richard Leonard, Childrens Press (Chicago, IL), 1994.
Armadillo Charm, Tia Chucha Press (Chicago, IL), 1996.
Real Things: An Anthology of Popular Culture in America, Indiana University Press (Bloomington), 1998.
Astillas de Luz/Shards of Light, Tia Chucha Press (Chicago, IL), 1998.

Work represented in anthologies, including *Third World: Anthology*, Pig Iron (Youngstown, OH), 1989; *Scars: American Poetry in the Face of Violence*, University of Alabama Press (University, AL), 1995; *El Coro: A Chorus of Latino and Latina Poetry*, University of Massachusetts Press (Amherst, MA), 1997; *Literatura Chicana: An Anthology in Spanish, English, and Calo*, Garland Publishing (New York City), 1997; and *Telling Stories: An Anthology for Writers*, edited by Joyce Carol Oates, Norton (New York City), 1998.

Contributor to periodicals, including *Spoon River Quarterly, Exquisite Corpse,* and *Another Chicago.*

BIOGRAPHICAL/CRITICAL SOURCES:

PERIODICALS

School Library Journal, March, 1995, p. 209.

OTHER

Illinois Writers Directory, http://www.litline.org/IWD/cumpian.html (July 15, 1999).*

D

DALTON, Roque 1935-1975(?)

PERSONAL: Born in 1935, in El Salvador; lived in exile in Mexico and Cuba; murdered in 1975 (one source says 1973). *Politics:* Communist.

CAREER: Writer. *Military service:* Fought as a guerrilla in the El Salvadoran revolution.

WRITINGS:

Los pequenos infiernos, Libres de Sinera (Barcelona, Spain), 1970.

Historias prohibidas del pulgracito, Siglo Veintiuno Editores (Mexico), 1974.

Pobrecito poeta que era yo, Editorial Universitaria Centroamericana (Costa Rica), 1976.

El Salvador: Monografia, Curbstone Press (Willimantic, CT), 1979.

(With Peperuiz) *Los helicopteros: Pieza teatral en varias escenas,* Editorial Universitaria de El Salvador (San Salvador, El Salvador), 1980.

Poesia, Casa de las Americas (Havana, Cuba), 1980.

Poemas clandestinos, Editorial Universitaria Centroamericana, 1980, translated by Jack Hirschman and published as *Clandestine Poems—Poemas clandestinos: Bilingual Edition,* introduction by Margaret Randall, Solidarity Publications (San Francisco, CA), 1984, published as *Clandestine Poems,* Curbstone Press, 1990.

(With Eduardo Baehr) *Guerra a la guerra,* prologue by Juan Antonio Medina Duron, Universidad Nacional Autonoma de Honduras (Tegucigalpa, Honduras), 1981.

Las ensenanzas de Vietnam: Apuntes, [California], 1981.

Poesia elegida, Editorial Guaymuras (Tegucigalpa, Honduras), 1981.

Poetry and Militancy in Latin America, translated by Arlene Scully and James Scully, Curbstone Press, 1981.

Taberna y otros lugares, Ediciones de Taller (Santo Domingo, Dominican Republic), 1983.

Poesia escogida, prologue by Manilo Argueta, Editorial Universitaria Centroamericana, 1983, translated by Richard Schaaf and published as *Poems,* Curbstone Press, 1984.

Miguel Marmol: Los sucesos de 1932 en El Salvador, Casa de las Americas, 1983, translated by Kathleen Ross and Richard Schaaf and published as *Miguel Marmol,* preface by Margaret Randall, introduction by Manlio Argueta, Curbstone Press, 1987.

Un libro rojo para Lenin, Editorial Nueva Nicaragua (Managua, Nicaragua), 1986.

Con manos de fantasma: Antologia, Editorial Nueva America (Buenos Aires, Argentina), 1987.

Un libro levemente odioso, prologue by Elena Poniatowska, UCA Editores (San Salvador, El Salvador), 1989.

En la humedad del secreto: Antologia poetica, selections, introduction, and bibliography by Rafael Lara Martinez, Direccion de Publicaciones e Impresos (San Salvador, El Salvador), 1994.

Roque Dalton: Antologia, selected by Juan Carlos Berrio, Txalaparta (Tafalla, Navarra, Spain), 1995.

La ventana en el rostro, Consejo Nacional para la Cultura y el Arte (San Salvador, El Salvador), 1996.

Small Hours of the Night: Selected Poems of Roque Dalton, translated by Jonathan Cohen and others, edited by Hardie St. Martin, Curbstone Press, 1996.

For the Record: Selected Poems, translated by Richard Schaaf, Azul Editions, 1999.

With others, wrote *Roque y David,* Universidad Tecnologica (El Salvador). Contributor of poems to books, including *El Salvador at War: A Collage Epic,* edited by Marc Zimmerman, MEP Publications (Minneapolis, MN), 1988; and *Leonel/Roque,* Coteau Books (Regina, Saskatchewan, Canada), 1998. Dalton's work has been translated into other languages, including English and German.

SIDELIGHTS: Roque Dalton is among the most famous writers produced by El Salvador. In his short life he produced several poems as well as unique histories of El Salvador and its people. His major works include the poetry collection *Poesia escogida,* the biographical and historical document *Miguel Marmol: Los sucesos de 1932 en El Salvador,* and the humorous chronicle *Historias prohibidas del pulgracito.* Known for his criticism of all ideological stances, Dalton spent much of his life in exile. He later joined El Salvador's revolutionary movement but was murdered by his associates.

BIOGRAPHICAL/CRITICAL SOURCES:

PERIODICALS

Library Journal, July, 1996, p. 120.
Publishers Weekly, July 22, 1996, p. 236.*

*   *   *

DAMOCLES
See BENEDETTI, Mario

*   *   *

DARIO, Ruben 1867-1916

PERSONAL: Name originally Felix Ruben Garcia y Sarmiento; born January 18, 1867, in Metapa, Nicaragua; died February 6, 1916, in Leon, Nicaragua; married Rafaela Contrera, 1890 (died, 1892); married Francisca Sanchez; children: two sons (one from each marriage). *Education:* Attended a Jesuit school.

CAREER: Writer and poet. Began work as a journalist for newspapers in Santiago and Valparaiso, Chile, and Buenos Aires, Argentina, c. 1881. Became correspondent for *La Nacion,* Buenos Aires, and other Latin American papers in Latin America; Paris, France; and Madrid, Spain. Founder, with Gilberto Freyre, of *Revista de America,* 1896. Also served in various diplomatic and representative posts for Colombia and Nicaragua.

WRITINGS:

Primeras notas (title means "First Notes"), Tipografia Nacional, 1888.
Azul (poetry and short prose; title means "Blue"), [Chile], 1888, reprinted, Espasa-Calpe (Madrid), 1984 (also see below).
Los raros (literary biography and critical essays; title means "The Rare Ones"), 1893, reprinted, Universidad Autonoma Metropolitana (Mexico), 1985 (also see below).
Prosas profanas (title means "Profane Prose"), 1896, reprinted, introduction and notes by Ignacio M. Zuleta, Castalia (Madrid), 1983 (also see below).
Castelar, B. R. Serra (Madrid), 1899.
Espana contemporanea (title means "Contemporary Spain"), Garnier (Paris), 1901, reprinted, Lumen, 1987 (also see below).
Cantos de vida y esperanza, Los cisnes, y otros poemas (title means "Songs of Life and Hope, The Swans, and Other Poems"), [Madrid], 1905, reprinted, Nacional (Mexico), 1957 (also see below).
El canto errante (poetry; title means "The Wandering Song"), M. Perez Villavicencio (Madrid), 1907, reprinted, Espasa-Calpe, 1965 (also see below).
El viaje a Nicaragua; e, Intermezzo tropical (travel writings), Biblioteca Ateneo (Madrid), 1909, reprinted, Ministerio de Cultura, 1982 (also see below).
Poema del otono y otros poemas (title means "Poem of Autumn and Other Poems"), Biblioteca Ateneo, 1910, Espasa-Calpe, 1973 (also see below).
Muy antiguo y muy moderno (poetry; title means "Very Old and Very Modern"), Biblioteca Corona (Madrid), 1915.
El mundo de los suenos: Prosas postumas (title means "The World of Dreams: Posthumous Prose"), Libreria de la Viuda de Pueyo (Madrid), 1917.
Sol del domingo (title means "Sunday Sun"), Sucesores de Hernando (Madrid), 1917.
Alfonso XIII y sus primeras notas (addresses, essays, lectures and biographical text; title means "Alfonso the Thirteenth and His Principal Notes"), R. Dario Sanchez (Madrid), 1921.

Baladas y canciones (title means "Ballads and Songs"), prologue by Andres Gonzalez-Blanco, Biblioteca Ruben Dario Hijo (Madrid), 1923.

Sonetos (title means "Sonnets"), Biblioteca Ruben Dario (Madrid), 1929.

En busca del alba (poetry; title means "In Search of Dawn"), Aristides Quillet (Buenos Aires), 1941.

Brumas y luces (poetry; title means "Fogs and Lights"), Ediciones Argentinas S.I.A., 1943.

Wakonda: Poemas, Guillermo Kraft (Buenos Aires), 1944.

El ruisenor azul: Poemas ineditos y poemas olvidados (title means "The Blue Nightingale: Unpublished and Forgotten Poems"), prologue by Alberto Ghiraldo, Talleres Graficos Casa Nacional del Nino, c. 1945.

Quince poesias (title means "Fifteen Poems"), illustrated by Mallol Suazo, Argos (Barcelona), 1946.

Cerebros y corazones (biographical sketches; title means "Minds and Hearts"), Nova (Buenos Aires), 1948.

La amargura de la Patagonia (novella; title means "The Grief of Patagonia"), Nova (Buenos Aires), 1950.

El manto de nangasasu (novella; title means "The Cloak of Nangasasu"), S.A.C.D.I.C., 1958.

El sapo de oro (novella; title means "The Golden Toad"), G. Kraft (Buenos Aires), 1962.

Also author of *Epistolas y poemas* (title means "Epistles and Poems"), 1885; *Abrojos* (poetry; title means "Thorns"), 1887; *Canto epico a las glorias de Chile* (poetry; title means "Epic Song to the Glories of Chile"), 1887; *Emelina* (novel), with Eduardo Poirier, 1887; *Las rosas andinas: Rimas y contra-rimas* (title means "Andean Roses: Rhymes and Counter-Rhymes"), with Ruben Rubi, 1888; *Rimas* (title means "Poems"), 1888; *Peregrinaciones* (travel writings; title means "Journeys"), 1901 (also see below); *Oda a Mitre* (poetry; title means "Ode to Mitre"), 1906 (also see below); *Canto a la Argentina y otros poemas* (title means "Song to Argentina and Other Poems"), c. 1910 (also see below); *Historia de mis libros* (title means "The Story of My Books"), 1912; *Caras y caretas* (title means "Faces and Masks"), 1912; *Vida de Ruben Dario, escrita por el mismo* (title means "The Life of Ruben Dario, Written By Himself"), 1916; *Edelmira* (fiction), edited by Francisco Contreras, c. 1926; and *El hombre de oro* (title means "The Golden Man"), Zig-Zag.

Fiction and verse also published in numerous anthologies and collections.

Eleven Poems, introduction by Pedro Henriquez Urena, translation by Thomas Walsh and Salomon de la Selva, Putnam, 1916, revised edition published as *Eleven Poems of Ruben Dario: Bilingual Edition,* Gordon, 1977.

Selected Poems of Ruben Dario, introduction by Octavio Paz, translated by Lysander Kemp, University of Texas Press, 1965, reprinted, 1988.

Obras completas (title means "Complete Works"), twenty-two volumes, edited by author's son, Ruben Dario Sanchez, illustrations by Enrique Ochoa, Mundo Latino (Madrid), Volume 1: *La caravana pasa* (poetry; title means "The Caravan Passes"), prologue by Ghiraldo, 1917; Volume 2: *Prosas profanas,* 1917; Volume 3: *Tierras solares* (travel writings; title means "Lands of the Sun"), 1917; Volume 4: *Azul,* 1917; Volume 5: *Parisiana,* 1917; Volume 6: *Los raros,* 1918; Volume 7: *Cantos de vida y esperanza, Los cisnes, y otros poemas,* 1920; Volume 8: *Letras* (addresses, essays, lectures), 1918; Volume 9: *Canto a la Argentina, Oda a Mitre, y otros poemas,* 1918; Volume 10: *Opiniones,* 1918; Volume 11: *Poema del otono y otros poemas,* 1918; Volume 12: *Peregrinaciones,* 1918; Volume 13: *Prosas politicas: Las republicas americanas* (title means "Political Prose: The American Republics"), 1918; Volume 14: *Cuentos y cronicas* (title means "Stories and Chronicles"), 1918; Volume 15: *Autobiografia,* 1918; Volume 16: *El canto errante,* 1918; Volume 17: *El viaje a Nicaragua, e historia de mis libros* (title means "The Trip to Nicaragua and the Story of My Books"), 1919; Volume 18: *Todo al vuelo* (title means "All On the Fly"), 1919; Volume 19: *Espana contemporanea,* 1919; Volume 20: *Prosa dispersa* (title means "Random Prose"), 1919; Volume 21: *Lira postuma* (title means "Posthumous Verse"), 1919; Volume 22: *Cabezas: Pensadores y artistas, politicos* (biographical essays; title means "Heads: Thinkers, Artists, Politicians"), 1919.

Obras poeticas completas (title means "Complete Poetic Works"), twenty-one volumes, edited by Ghiraldo and Gonzalez-Blanco, [Madrid], 1923-29, new edition edited by A. Mendez Plancarte, [Madrid], 1952.

Cuentos completos (title means "Complete Stories"), edited with notes by Ernesto Mejia Sanchez, preliminary study by Raimundo Lida, Fondo de

Cultura Economica (Mexico), 1950, reprinted, 1983.

Poesias completas (title means "Complete Poems"), two volumes, edited by Alfonso Mendez Plancarte, 1952, revised edition edited by Antonio Oliver Belmas, 1967.

Poesia erotica, Hiperion (Madrid), 1997.

Several volumes of Dario's *Obras completas* were reissued separately during the 1980s. Works collected in other volumes, including *Obra poetica* (title means "Poetic Works"), four volumes, 1914-1916; *Textos socio-politicos,* [Managua], 1980; *Poesias escogidas,* 1982; and *Cuentos fantasticos,* Alianza (Madrid), 1982.

SIDELIGHTS: Nicaraguan writer Ruben Dario ranks among the most esteemed and enduring figures in South American literature. A journalist, critic, poet and author of short stories, he is credited with both founding and leading the *modernista* literary movement, which ended a period of creative latency among Spanish-language writers. Dario is probably best remembered for his innovative poetry, noted for its blending of experimental rhymes and meters with elements of French and Italian culture, classical literature, and mythology.

A bright and inquisitive child, Dario displayed a propensity for poetry while he was still quite young. His aunt, who raised him after the separation of his parents, nurtured his literary aspirations, and his early interest in journalism led to his association with members of the European and South American intelligentsia. By the turn of the twentieth century, Dario had taken his place among the literary and cultural elite and, as a foreign correspondent and diplomat, had become a symbol of a new bohemianism in Latin America. Stephen Kinzer, writing in the *New York Times,* summarized the author's career as that of a "vagabond poet who . . . influence[d] Latin American and Spanish literature forever and dazzle[d] Europe as no provincial ever had."

Though generally dismissed by critics as an uninspired and predictable contribution to the romance genre, *Emelina*—one of Dario's earliest writings and his only novel—offers a glimpse at the artistry that the poet would perfect in his 1888 volume *Azul ("Blue"),* a work that revolutionized Spanish letters. The poetry and short prose in *Azul* marks a deliberate break with the conventions of Romanticism, a bold experimentation with line and metre construction, and an introduction to Dario's celebration of literature as an *alcazar interior* ("tower of ivory"), a dreamlike shelter dedicated to pure art.

Another collection, *Prosas profanas ("Profane Prose"),* first published in 1896, is a masterful, melodic display of the poet's fascination with Symbolism. The 1905 volume *Cantos de vida y esperanza ("Songs of Life and Hope"),* however, reveals a change in Dario's orientation as an artist—a move away from the idealistic "ivory tower" toward the global concerns of political and humanistic unity and nationalism among Hispanics. In *Studies in Spanish-American Literature,* Isaac Goldberg asserted: "*Cantos de vida y esperanza* is the keystone of Dario's poetical arch. It most exemplifies the man that wrote it; it most reveals his dual nature, his inner sincerity, his complete psychology; it is the artist at maturity."

Dario remains largely unknown among English-speaking readers, mainly because of the difficulty in translating his poetry while preserving the unique rhythms and linguistic nuances that the works possess in their original form. However, two volumes of the author's poems are available in English, and several critics have noted that the universality of Dario's themes precludes the problem of accessibility. Commenting on Dario's widespread appeal, Goldberg rated the poet among "the consecrated few who belong to no nation because they belong to all." And S. Griswold Morley, writing in *Dial,* concluded: "What cannot be denied is that Dario, single-handed, initiated a movement in Spain that affects today nearly every branch of literary art; that he renovated the technique of both poetry and prose; that he made his own many diverse styles; and that his verse is often so inevitable as to touch the finality of art."

BIOGRAPHICAL/CRITICAL SOURCES:

BOOKS

Dario, Ruben, *Eleven Poems of Ruben Dario,* introduction by Pedro Henriquez Urena, translated by Thomas Walsh and Salomon de la Selva, Putnam, 1916. Dario, Ruben, *Selected Poems of Ruben Dario,* introduction by Octavio Paz, translated by Lysander Kemp, University of Texas Press, 1965.

Ellis, Keith, *Critical Approaches to Ruben Dario,* University of Toronto Press, 1974.

Fiore, Dolores Ackel, *Ruben Dario in Search of Inspiration: Greco-Roman Mythology in His Stories and Poetry,* Las Americas Publishing Co., 1963.

Fitzmaurice-Kelly, James, *Some Masters of Spanish Verse,* Oxford University Press, 1924.

Goldberg, Isaac, *Studies in Spanish-American Literature,* Brentano's, 1920.

Peers, E. Allison, *A Critical Anthology of Spanish Verse,* University of California Press, 1949.

Twentieth-Century Literary Criticism, Volume 4, Gale, 1981.

Watland, Charles D., *Poet-Errant: A Biography of Ruben Dario,* Philosophical Library, 1965.

PERIODICALS

Dial, June 14, 1917.

Hispania, March, 1919; May, 1966.

Latin American Literary Review, spring, 1973.

New York Times, January 18, 1987.

Poetry, July, 1916.*

* * *

DAVIS, B.Lynch
See Borges, Jorge Luis

* * *

de ANDRADE, Mario 1892-1945

PERSONAL: Born October 9, 1892, in Sao Paulo, Brazil; died February 25, 1945, in Sao Paulo, Brazil. *Education:* Attended Conservatory of Drama and Music, Sao Paulo, Brazil.

CAREER: Journalist, novelist, poet, and critic, 1928-41. Conservatory of Drama and Music, Sao Paulo, Brazil, professor of musicology and aesthetics, beginning in 1922; University of the Federal District, Rio de Janeiro, Brazil, head of department of art history and director of Art Institute, beginning in 1938. Sao Paulo Department of Culture, cofounder and director, beginning in 1934.

MEMBER: Brazilian Society of Ethnography and Folklore (founder, 1937, and president).

WRITINGS:

Macunaima (novel; originally published, 1928, translated by E. A. Goodland, Random House (New York City), 1984.

A Musica e a Cancao Populares no Brasil, Ministerio das Relacoes Exteriores, Divisao de Cooperacao Intelectual, 1936.

Musica do Brasil: Desenho de Portinari, Editora Guaira Limitada (Sao Paulo, Brazil), 1941.

O Padre Jesuino do Monte Carmelo (originally published, 1946), reprinted, Libraria Martins (Sao Paulo), 1963.

Contos Novos (title means "New Stories"; originally published, 1947), reprinted, edited by Maria Celia de Almeida Paulillo, Editora Itatiaia (Belo Horizonte, Brazil), 1983.

Poesias Completas (originally published, 1955), reprinted, Livraria Martins, 1980.

(With Oneyda Alvarenga) *Cartas* (title means "Letters"; originally published, 1958), reprinted, Livraria Duas Cidades (Sao Paulo), 1983.

Dancas Dramaticas do Brasil, Livraria Martins, 1959.

Hallucinated City, translation by Jack E. Tomlins, Vanderbilt University Press (Nashville, TN), 1968.

(With Manuel Bandeira) *Itinerarios: Cartas a Alphonsus de Guimaraens Filho,* Libraria Duas Cidades, 1974.

O Banquete, Livraria Duas Cidades, 1977.

Obra Escogida: Novela, Cuento, Ensayo, Epistolario, edited by Gilda de Mello e Souza, Biblioteca Ayacucho (Caracas, Venezuela), 1979.

Cartas a um Jovem Escritor: de Mario de Andrade a Fernando Sabino, Editora Record (Rio de Janeiro, Brazil), 1981.

Mario de Andrade, Cartas de Trabalho: Correspondencia com Rodrigo Mello France de Andrade, Ministerio da Educacao e Cultura, Secretaria do Patrimonio Historico e Artistico Nacional (Brasilia, Brazil), 1981.

Correspondente Contumaz: Cartas a Pedro Nava, 1925-1944, edited by Fernando da Rocha Peres, Editora Nova Fronteira (Rio de Janeiro), 1982.

A Licao do Amigo: Cartas de Mario de Andrade a Carlos Drummond de Andrade, Anotadas pelo Destinario, Livraria Jose Olympio Editora (Rio de Janeiro), 1982.

Cartas de Mario de Andrade a Alvaro Lins, Livraria Jose Olympio Editora, 1983.

Quatro Pessoas: Romance, Editora Itatiaia, 1985.

Cartas de Mario de Andrade a Prudente de Moraes, Neto, 1924/36, edited by Georgina Koifman, Editora Nova Fronteira, 1985.

Mario de Andrade: Castas a Anita Malfatti, edited by Marta Rossetti Batista, Forense Universitaria (Rio de Janeiro), 1989.

Querida Henriqueta: Cartas de Mario de Andrade a Henriqueta Lisboa, edited by Lauro Palu, Livraria Jose Olympio Editora, 1990.

Aspectos da Musica Brasileira, Villa Rica (Belo Horizonte), 1991.

Cartas de Mario de Andrade a Luis da Camara Cascudo, introduction by Verissimo de Melo, Villa Rica, 1991.

Mario de Andrade e Campos dos Goitacazes: Cartas de Mario de Andrade a Alberto Lamego, 1935-1938, Editora Universitaria Universidade Federal Fluminense (Rio de Janeiro), 1992.

"Eu Sou Trezentos, Sou Trezentos-e-Cincoenta": Uma "Autobiografia" de Mario de Andrade, Instituto de Estudos Brasileiros, Universidade de Sao Paulo (Sao Paulo), 1992.

A Arte Religiosa no Brasil: Cronicas Publicadas na Revista do Brasil em 1920, edited by Claudete Kronbauer, Editora Giordano (Sao Paulo), 1993.

Musica e Jornalismo: Diario de S. Paulo, edited by Paulo Castagna, Editora HUCITEC (Sao Paulo), 1993.

O Modernismo no Museu de Arte Brasileira: Pintura, Fundacao Armando Alvares Penteado (Sao Paulo), 1993.

Introducao a Estetica Musical, edited by Flavia Camargo Toni, Editora HUCITEC, 1995.

Mario e o Pirotecnico Aprendiz: Cartas de Mario de Andrade e Murilo Rubiao, edited by Marcos Antonio de Moraes, Editora Giordano, 1995.

Portinari, Amico Mio: Cartas de Mario de Andrade a Candido Portinari, edited by Annateresa Fabris, Projeto Portinari (Rio de Janeiro), 1995.

Other books include *Ha Uma Gota de Sangue em Cada Poema,* 1927; *A Escrava Que Nao e Isaura* (title means "The Slave Who Is Not Isaura"), 1925; *Primeiro Andar* (stories; title means "First Floor"), 1926; *Losango Caqui,* 1926; *Amar, Verbo Intransitivo: Idilio* (novel), 1927; *Cla Do Jabuti,* 1927; *Ensaio sobre a Musica Brasileira,* 1928; *Compendio de Historia da Musica,* 1929; *Remate de Males,* 1930; *Modinhas Imperiais,* 1930; *Musica, Doce Musica,* 1933; *Belazarte* (stories), 1934; *O Aleijadinho e Alvares de Azevedo,* 1935; *Namoros com a Medicina,* 1939; *Poesias,* 1941; *O Movimento Modernista,* 1942; *Aspectos da Literatura Brasileira* (title means "Aspects of Brazilian Literature"), 1943; *O Baile das Quatro Artes,* 1943; *Os Filhos de Candinha,* 1943; *O Empalhador de Passarinho* (title means "The Stuffer of Birds"), 1944; *Obras Completas,* twenty vols., beginning in 1944; *Lira Paulistana* (poems; title means "The Sao Paulo Lyre"), 1946; and *Musica de Feiticaria,* 1963.

Contributor to magazines and newspapers.

BIOGRAPHICAL/CRITICAL SOURCES:

BOOKS

Encyclopedia of World Literature in the Twentieth Century, Volume I: *A-D,* St. James Press (Detroit, MI), 1999, p. 92.*

*   *   *

de ANDRADE, Oswald   1890-1954

PERSONAL: Born in 1890; died in 1954; married Tarsila do Amaral (a painter).

CAREER: Writer.

WRITINGS:

Serafim Ponte Grande/Seraphim Grosse Pointe, translated by Kenneth D. Jackson and Albert Bork, New Latin Quarter Editions (Austin, TX), 1979.

Work represented in anthologies, including *An Anthology of Twentieth-Century Brazilian Poetry,* edited by Elizabeth Bishop and Emanuel Brasil, Wesleyan University Press (Middletown, CT), 1972. Author of novels, plays, and poems, including the epic "Poesia Pau-Brasil" (title means "Brazil-Wood Poetry"), during the 1920s.*

*   *   *

de BURGOS, Julia   1914-1953

PERSONAL: Born February 17, 1914, in Santa Cruz, Carolina, Puerto Rico; died July 6, 1953, in New York, NY; daughter of Francisco Burgos Hans and Paula Garcia de Burgos; married Ruben Rodriguez Beauchamp, 1934 (divorced, 1937); married Armando Marin, c. 1943. *Education:* University of Puerto Rico, teaching certificate, 1933, summer study, 1935.

CAREER: Puerto Rican poet. Puerto Rico Economic Reconstruction Administration, day care worker, 1934; teacher, Naranjito, Puerto Rico, 1935; participated in the publication of the periodical *Pueblos Hispanicos,* New York City, c. 1940s.

AWARDS, HONORS: Award recipient, Institute of Puerto Rican Literature, for *Cancion de la verdad sencilla.*

WRITINGS:

POETRY

Poemas exactos a mi misma (title means "Exact Poems to Myself"), privately printed, Puerto Rico, 1937.

Poema en veinte surcos (title means "Poem in Twenty Furrows"), [Puerto Rico], 1938, Ediciones Huracan (Rio Piedras, Puerto Rico), 1982.

Cancion de la verdad sencilla (title means "Song of the Simple Truth"), [Puerto Rico], 1939, Ediciones Huracan, 1982.

El mar y tu, y otros poemas, 1954, Ediciones Huracan, 1981.

POETRY COLLECTIONS

Obra poetica, 1961.

Antologia poetica, Editorial Coqui (San Juan, Puerto Rico), 1967.

Julia de Burgos: yo misma fui mi ruta, edited by Maria M. Sola, Ediciones Huracan, 1986.

Julia de Burgos (selections of poems and letters), edited by Manuel de la Puebla, Ediciones Mairena (Rio Piedras, Puerto Rico), 1986.

Julia de Burgos (selections), Instituto de Cultura Puertorriquena (San Juan, Puerto Rico), 1990.

Roses in the Mirror (selections; bilingual edition), translated and edited by Carmen D. Lucca, Ediciones Mairena, 1992.

Julia de Burgos: amor y soledad (selections), edited by Manuel de la Puebla, Ediciones Torremozas (Madrid, Spain), 1994.

Song of the Simple Truth (complete poems; bilingual edition), translated and with an introduction by Jack Agueros, Curbstone Press (Willimantic, CT), 1995.

SIDELIGHTS: Julia de Burgos has been proclaimed "Puerto Rico's greatest poet" by her translator, Jack Agueros, as reported by Anne-Marie Cusac in the *Progressive.* She has also been called "the most important Puerto Rican woman poet of the century" by Patricia Monaghan in *Booklist,* and "almost legendary" by Lawrence Olszewski in *Library Journal.* According to a *Publishers Weekly* reviewer, de Burgos "looms larger than life in the literary psyche of Puerto Rico." Yet this poet had not been fully appreciated in the United States until the 1990's, when the bilingual edition of her complete poems appeared under the title *Song of the Simple Truth.*

De Burgos was born in a rural barrio in Carolina, Puerto Rico, in 1914, the eldest of many children. Her family moved to the city of Rio Piedras in 1928, and she enrolled first at the University of Puerto Rico High School, and later at the university itself, from which she earned a teaching certificate in 1933 after two years of study. Financially unable to continue working toward a degree, she got married in 1934 and worked in a publicly funded day care center, as well as teaching in rural schools.

De Burgos divorced in 1937, the same year she published her first volume of poems, *Poemas exactos a mi misma.* Privately printed, it reflects the revolutionary patriotism of the Nationalist Party in Puerto Rico, for de Burgos was a longtime activist for Puerto Rican independence. Unhappy with that first collection, de Burgos tried to have the work suppressed.

De Burgos went on to publish her 1938 volume, *Poema en veinte surcos.* The book's title, which means "Poem in Twenty Furrows," expresses Burgos' deep attachment to her native land, as does its most famous single poem, "Rio Grande de Loiza," an ode to the river by the side of which she spent much of her childhood. This river, according to Amiris Perez-Guntin in *American Women Writers,* recurs as an image throughout much of Burgos' poetry, as do themes of disappointed love, the search for the true self, the fight for social improvement, and the liberating power of art.

An outspoken feminist, opponent of dictators, and striver for personal as well as political independence, de Burgos moved to New York and then Cuba in 1940 in her search for freedom. A meeting with the Chilean poet Pablo Neruda in Havana in 1940 deepened the profound influence of that poet upon de Burgos' work. De Burgos' traveling companion to New York and Cuba was a man for whom she had written many love poems. However, in 1942 she suffered a traumatic disappointment in love, which scarred the remaining eleven years of her life and prompted her to flee Cuba for New York, where she remarried in the early 1940's. Her remaining years were plagued by alcoholism; although she continued to write, she spent a good deal of time in hospitals, and finally collapsed, unrecognized, on a Harlem street in 1953. She was buried near the Rio Grande de Loiza in Puerto Rico.

Since her death, de Burgos has become increasingly renowned on her home island and beyond. A posthumous volume, *El mar y tu, y otros poemas,* was published in 1954, and a collection, *Obra Poetica,* in 1961. Her last poems, gathered in *El Mar y tu,* are in many cases love poems about her great but disappointing romance, and, in Perez-Guntin's words, portray "her disillusionment and final disintegration."

A bilingual selection of Burgos' work, *Roses in the Mirror,* was published in Puerto Rico in 1992, and in 1995 came the complete bilingual collection, *Song of the Simple Truth.* Reviewing it in the *Progressive,* Cusac saw "a poet of physical celebration" expressing "active and happy female sexuality," but also at times "horror." The *Publishers Weekly* reviewer found de Burgos to be "ahead of her time in grasping connections between history, the body, politics, love, self-negation and feminism that would later prove to be the foundations for writers like [Adrienne] Rich and [Sylvia] Plath."

Monaghan, the reviewer for *Booklist,* praised de Burgos as "a woman of fire and blood. . . . feminist, revolutionary, patriotic," who wrote in a "sibylline voice, full of expansive power." For Olszewski, writing in *Library Journal,* the poems "speak for themselves" on "timeless themes." Perez-Guntin, pointing out that Burgos gave priority to message rather than technique and cared more for social justice than for aesthetics, declared that what might seem to be "imperfections" in the eyes of some critics were actually a "revelation of the essence of the poet," making Burgo's work "strikingly unique."

BIOGRAPHICAL/CRITICAL SOURCES:

BOOKS

Gonzalez, Jose E., *La Poesia Contemporanea de Puerto Rico, 1930-1960,* 1972.
Green, Carol Hurd, and Mason, Mary Grimley, editors, *American Women Writers, Volume 5: Supplement,* Continuum Publishing Co. (New York), 1994, pp. 94-96.
Jimenez de Baez, Lvette, *Julia de Burgos: Vida y Poesia,* 1966.
Manrique Cabrera, Francisco, *Historia de la Literatura Puertoriquena,* 1971.
Puerto Rican Authors: A Biobibliographic Handbook, 1974.

PERIODICALS

Booklist, February 15, 1997, p. 996.
La Torre, September-December, 1965.
Library Journal, March 1, 1997, p. 80.
National Catholic Reporter, July 1, 1994, p. 3.
Progressive, January, 1998, p. 38.
Publishers Weekly, February 24, 1997, p. 85.
Sin Nombre, October-December, 1976.*

*   *   *

de CARVALHO, Ronald 1893-1935

PERSONAL: Born in 1893; died in 1935. *Education:* Studied law.

CAREER: Diplomat, beginning in 1914; poet and literary critic. Week of Modern Art, lecturer. *Orpheu* (literary review), cofounder, 1915.

WRITINGS:

Luz Gloriosa (verse; title means "Glorious Light"), 1913.
Pequena Historia da Literatura Brasileira (title means "A Short History of Brazilian Literature"), 1919.
Estudios Brasileiros, 1924.
Jogos Pueris, 1926.
Toda a America verse; title means "All the Americas"), 1926.

Contributor to periodicals, including *Inter-America.*

BIOGRAPHICAL/CRITICAL SOURCES:

PERIODICALS

University of Kansas City Review, spring, 1953, pp. 163-168.*

*   *   *

De JENKINS, Lyll Becerra 1925-1997

PERSONAL: Born November 14, 1925, in San Gil, Colombia; died on May 7, 1997, in Fripp Island, SC; daughter of Luis Becerra Lopez and Teresa Breton de Becerra; married John Jenkins; children: Francesca,

Marcela, Alexandra Jenkins Reed, John, Jr., William. *Religion:* Catholic.

ADDRESSES: Office—c/o Rosemary Brosnan, Executive Editor, Morrow Junior Books, 1350 Avenue of the Americas, New York, NY 10019.

CAREER: Writer; served 14 years as adjunct professor of English at Fairfield University, Fairfield, CT.

AWARDS, HONORS: Scott O'Dell Award for Historical Fiction, Scott O'Dell Foundation, 1988, for *The Honorable Prison.*

WRITINGS:

The Honorable Prison, Dutton/Lodestar, 1988.
Celebrating the Hero, Dutton/Lodestar, 1993.
So Loud a Silence, Dutton/Lodestar, 1996.

Also author of short stories appearing in periodicals, including *The New Yorker, New York Times,* and *Boston Globe.*

SIDELIGHTS: A novelist and professor, Lyll Becerra de Jenkins skillfully intertwined the personal with the political in both her life and her life's work. As an author of short stories and novels for young adults, de Jenkins intended "to awaken a political conscience in young people," as she once told *Publishers Weekly.* Contributing to de Jenkins' own political awareness was her father—a politically outspoken judge and journalist in his native country of Colombia.

Growing up in Colombia, de Jenkins did not understood the political battles that her father fought with such graveness. Her move to the United States, however, clarified de Jenkins' memories of her father's activism. The relocation, after thirty-seven years in Colombia, provided de Jenkins with distance and room to be critical, allowing the writer to recognize that her political beliefs conflicted with those of the Colombian oligarchy. In a *Booklist* interview with her editor, Rosemary Brosnan, de Jenkins commented on the impact that living in the United States had had on her writing: "I not only think that I would write differently, but I probably would never have written at all. It is precisely being in this country . . . see[ing] the contrasts between the U.S. and Colombia. . . . I understood with a new perspective the meaning of injustice and the meaning of political abuse—particularly the abuse of power." Her learned passion for politics, a respect for human rights, and love of the English language took de Jenkins on a journey from

a girl who told exaggerated and theatrical true stories to a writer of political fiction based on personal truth.

De Jenkins' writing career began with short stories. One of these stories, published in the *New Yorker,* evolved into the first of her three novels, *The Honorable Prison,* for which she received the Scott O'Dell Award for Historical Fiction. All three of de Jenkins' young adult books—*The Honorable Prison, Celebrating the Hero,* and *So Loud a Silence*—address issues of Colombian politics and social injustice; just as the author told Brosnan that she grew to see "with clarity the true colors and the true dimensions of the Colombian political situation," so, too, do her main characters.

It is perhaps Marta Maldonado, protagonist of *The Honorable Prison,* who is most like the author herself. Marta, the teenaged daughter of a journalist who uses his editorials to attack the military dictator of his South American homeland, is imprisoned in the mountains with her family and kept under military surveillance. Many external dangers threaten Marta and her family, including the military, the elements, illness, and starvation. Internally, Marta struggles to gain strength, freedom, and independence. At times, she must examine the conflict between her own desires and those of her family. Decisions are difficult—is friendship with a handsome young teacher daring and defiant, or life-threatening? Turmoil and despair thunder over the entire country, but when the political storm dies down, the government is overthrown, and—according to a *Publishers Weekly* reviewer—"Marta has grown from a protected girl into a politically astute and sensitive young woman." *Horn Book* reviewer Mary M. Burns called the characters of *The Honorable Prison* "unique and unforgettable," noting that "the book achieves its stunning effects not through sensationalism but through control." Recognizing this controlled quality, Gerry Larson remarked in *School Library Journal* that the "understated narrative gives dramatic emphasis" to a "vivid and troubling portrayal of the ongoing struggle for human rights."

Celebrating the Hero, de Jenkins' second novel, also has as its protagonist an increasingly self-aware young woman. Camila Draper, a seventeen-year-old from Connecticut, is invited to a small town in Colombia for the unveiling of a memorial dedicated to the town's benefactor—her grandfather. Her mother having recently died, Camila accepts the invitation in order to learn all she can about her maternal grandparents. Camila's journey to unveil the truth about the ominous shadows of her grandfather's past—the truth she had not dared to ask her mother—begins. Exposed over the course of Camila's journey are her grandfather's secrets, her feelings of alienation from both of her homelands, and her awareness of oppression. "With sudden insight," wrote *New York Times Book Review* critic Caitlin Francke, "Camila comes to a more profound understanding not only of herself and her two worlds, but also of the bittersweet nature of forgiveness." Francke suggests that de Jenkins's "eloquent contribution to . . . literature dealing with issues of dislocation and displacement" would be "especially affecting for first-generation American teenagers searching for their identity." *Kliatt* reviewer Barbara Shepp, who particularly enjoyed the way de Jenkins "captures beautifully the details of how a Latin American town can feel, look, smell, sound and taste," praised *Celebrating the Hero* as a "sophisticated book . . . recommended for all its features, but especially for this atmospheric aspect."

BIOGRAPHICAL/CRITICAL SOURCES:

PERIODICALS

Booklist, September 1, 1997, pp. 10-11.
Bulletin of the Center for Children's Books, January, 1997, p. 175.
Horn Book, July/August, 1988, pp. 501-2.
Kirkus Reviews, August 15, 1996, p. 1236.
Kliatt, March, 1996, p. 8.
New York Times Book Review, January 2, 1994, p. 16.
Publishers Weekly, December 11, 1987, p. 67; December 23, 1988, pp. 29-30.
School Library Journal, February, 1988, p. 84.
Voice of Youth Advocates, February, 1997, p. 328.*

*   *   *

de la PARRA, (Ana) Teresa (Sonojo) 1890(?)-1936

PERSONAL: Born October 5, 1890 (some sources say 1889), in Paris, France; died of tuberculosis, April 23, 1936, in Madrid, Spain. *Education:* Attended school in Valencia, Spain.

CAREER: Writer. Lecturer on Simon Bolivar and on feminist issues.

AWARDS, HONORS: Winner of a newspaper contest, 1922, with the story "La Mama X;" winner of literary competition, Instituto Hispanoamericano de la Cultura Francesa, Paris, for the novel *Ifigenia.*

WRITINGS:

Ifigenia: Diario de una senorita que escribo porque se fastidiaba (novel), Franco-Ibero-Americana (Paris, France), 1924, translation by Bertie Acker published as *Iphigenia: The Diary of a Young Lady Who Wrote Because She Was Bored,* University of Texas Press (Austin, TX), 1993.
Las Memorias de Mama Blanca (novel), Livre Libre (Paris), 1929, version edited by C. Garcia Prada and C. M. Wilson, Macmillan (New York City), 1932, translation by Harriet de Onis published as *Mama Blanca's Souvenirs,* Pan American Union (Washington, DC), 1959, revised edition by Frederick H. Fornoff, University of Pittsburgh Press (Pittsburgh, PA), 1993.
Blanca nieves y compania, edited by Prada, Heath (Boston, MA), 1946.
Cartas, Cruz del Sur (Caracas, Venezuela), 1951.
Epistolario intimo, Linea Aeropostal Venezolana (Caracas), 1953.
Teresa de la Parra a traves de sus cartas, Garrido (Caracas), 1954.
Cartas a Rafael Carias, edited by Carias, Penitenciarios, 1957.
Tres Conferencias, Garrido, 1961.
Obras Completas, edited by Prada, Editorial Arte (Caracas), 1965.
Obra: Narrativa, ensayos, cartas, edited by Velia Bosch, Biblioteca Ayacucho (Caracas), 1982.
Cartas a Lydia Cabrera: Correspondencia inedita de Gabriela Mistral y Teresa de la Parra, edited by Rosario Hiriart, Torremozas (Madrid, Spain), 1988.
Influencia de las mujeres en la formacion del alma Americana, Fundarte (Caracas), 1991.
Obra Escogida, Monte Avila Latinoamericana (Caracas), 1992.

Work represented in anthologies, including *Lectura Semanal,* edited by Jose Rafael Pocaterra. Contributor of stories to newspapers.*

*   *   *

de las CASAS, Walter 1947-

PERSONAL: Born February 3, 1947, in Havana, Cuba; naturalized U.S. citizen; son of Mario and

Aracelia (Vivo) de las Casas. *Ethnicity:* "Hispanic." *Education:* Iona College, B.A. (cum laude), 1970; Hunter College of the City University of New York, M.A., 1977; doctoral study at City University of New York, 1987-94. *Politics:* Liberal Democrat.

ADDRESSES: Home—323 Dahill Rd., Apt. 1A, Brooklyn, NY 11218-3848.

CAREER: High school Spanish teacher in Brooklyn, NY, 1978-94; Science Skill Center High School, Brooklyn, teacher of Spanish language and literature, 1994-96.

MEMBER: American Association of Teachers of Spanish and Portuguese.

WRITINGS:

La Ninez Que Dilata (poems), Editorial Catoblepas, 1986.
Libido (poems in Spanish), Linden Lane Press, 1989.
Tributes (poems in English), E. Press, 1993.

WORK IN PROGRESS: Discourse, in English; *Human,* in English; *Hojas Dispersas,* in Spanish.

SIDELIGHTS: Walter de las Casas told *CA:* "Poetry is the lyrical expression of my intimate, interior, psychological life and of human relationships. It is also the lyrical expression of knowledge. Poetry should be transparent, a clean windowpane through which living feeling shines."

*   *   *

de LECETA, Juan
   See CELAYA, Gabriel

*   *   *

de LEON, Nephtali 1945-

PERSONAL: Born May 9, 1945, in Laredo, TX; son of Francisco De Leon Cordero (a migrant worker) and Maria Guadalupe De Leon-Gonzalez (a migrant worker); children: Aide (deceased). *Education:* Attended Texas Technological University, Our Lady of the Lake University of San Antonio, Instituto de Alianza Francesa, and University of Mexico City.

ADDRESSES: Home—411 Betty Dr., San Antonio, TX 78224.

CAREER: La Voz de los Llanos (bilingual weekly journal; title means "The Voice of the Plains"), Lubbock, TX, editor, 1968-73; freelance poet, writer, painter, and sculptor, c. 1973—. President of Le Cercle Francais; director of Teatro Chicano del Barrio; vice chair of American Civil Liberties Union, and Ciudadanos Pro Justicia Social. Has given poetry readings on television. *Military service:* U.S. Army.

MEMBER: Hispanic Writers Guild, Revolucion Artistica y Accion Social, Royal Chicano Air Force (affiliate), Congreso de Artistas Cosmicos de Aztlan (affiliate).

AWARDS, HONORS: Ford fellowship, 1975; award from Canto Al Pueblo Commission, 1976; award from National Hispanic Writers Guild, 1977; first place award from Le Cercle Francais.

WRITINGS:

(And illustrator) *Chicanos: Our Background and Our Pride* (essays), Trucha Publications (Lubbock, TX), 1972.
Five Plays (contains *The Death of Ernesto Nerios* [first produced in San Antonio, TX, at San Pedro Playhouse, 1978], *Chicanos! The Living and the Dead* [first produced in Hagerman, NM, 1974], *Play Number Nine* [first produced in Boulder, CO, at University of Colorado, 1976], *The Judging of Man,* and *The Flies* [first produced in El Paso, TX, at University of Texas at El Paso, 1973]), Totinem Publications (Denver, CO), 1972.
(And illustrator) *Chicano Poet: With Images and Visions of the Poet* (poetry; includes "Coca Cola Dream" [also see below]), Trucha Publications, 1973.
(And illustrator) *I Will Catch the Sun* (for children; first produced in San Antonio, TX, at Our Lady of the Lake University's Thiry Auditorium, 1979), Trucha Publications, 1973.
(And illustrator) *Coca Cola Dream* (poetry), Trucha Publications, 1973, 2nd edition, 1976.
I Color My Garden (for children), Tri-County Housing (Shallowater, TX), 1973.
Hey, Mr. President, Man!: On the Eve of the Bicentennial, Trucha Publications, 1975.
El tesoro de Pancho Villa (play), first produced in Lubbock, TX, 1977.
Tequila Mockingbird; or, The Ghost of Unemployment (play), Trucha Publications, 1979.

(With Carlos Gonzalez and Alfredo Aleman) *El Segundo de Febrero* (historical play for children), Centro Cultural Aztlan (San Antonio, TX), 1983.

Guadalupe Blues (poetry), privately printed, 1985.

Sparky y su Gang (for children), Nosotros (San Antonio, TX), 1985.

Artemia: La Loca del River Walk: An Allegory of the Arts in San Antonio, Educators' Roundtable (San Antonio, TX), 1986.

El pollito amarillo: Baby Chick Yellow, Educators' Roundtable, 1987.

Chicano Popcorn: Poetry: A Trilingual Publication, Educators' Roundtable (San Antonio, TX), 1990.

Also author of *Poems by Nephtali,* 1977, and *Getting It Together,* 1980. Contributor to anthologies, including *We Are Chicanos: An Anthology of Mexican-American Literature,* edited by Philip D. Ortego, Washington Square Press (New York City), 1973; *Floricanto,* edited by Mary Ann Pacheco, University of California, Los Angeles, 1974; *Floricanto II,* University of Texas, Austin, 1975; and *El Quetzal Emplumece,* edited by Carmela Montalvo and others, Mexican-American Cultural Center (San Antonio, TX), 1976. Contributor of articles and poems to periodicals, including *Texas Observer, Reverberations, American Dawn, La Luz, Noticias, New Blood, Grito del Sol, New Morning, El Regional, El Sol of Houston, La Voz de Texas, Floricante, Caracol, El Tecolote, La Guardia, Tiempo,* and *Canto Al Pueblo.*

SIDELIGHTS: Nephtali De Leon is a Chicano writer of poems, plays, essays, and children's stories. A sculptor and painter, he has also illustrated many of his books. Although these diverse artistic activities keep him busy, De Leon nonetheless considers himself a Chicano activist first. "De Leon writes mainly to express the dreams, desires, and aspirations of the Chicano people," noted Jean S. Chittenden in *Dictionary of Literary Biography.* "His motivation in writing is to give an honest and truthful representation of the plight of the Chicano, which he sees as the result of a historical process. His inspiration, as he described it in an unpublished interview granted in 1985, comes from the realization that Chicanos have been held in a "psychological and spiritual bondage,' that they are "cultural and intellectual hostages' in American society."

His passion for justice and equality for his people formed during childhood when, as a migrant worker in Texas, he witnessed the cruel treatment of illegal aliens by American border patrolmen. As an adult activist, De Leon has primarily focused his efforts on improving the quality of education for young Chicanos by writing books for them and by working with school systems in the Southwest. In addition, De Leon has supported Chicanos by helping establish Trucha Publications, a small press founded in 1970 by barrio residents of Lubbock, Texas, for the purpose of supporting emerging Chicano writers. Trucha published many of De Leon's early books, most of which center on the author's interest in promoting equal opportunity for Chicanos.

Whether based on historical events or his own musings, De Leon's writings advocate Chicano liberation from all forms of repression. His play *Chicanos! The Living and the Dead,* for instance, involves Chicano protestors rallying against the abuses of Americans and their system of government; *Play Number Nine* compares the mythological Prometheus, who is seeking physical freedom, with the Chicanos seeking cultural freedom through improved education; and *The Flies* equates downtrodden Chicanos with squashed flies. That drama was written one night after he killed several flies, then began musing on how easily and thoughtlessly he had brought about their deaths. Chittenden quoted De Leon as saying about this work: "I am asked if it is a comedy. Everyone roars with laughter each time it is performed. I remain silent and grim." Chittenden added, "The dialogue is witty, but there is a deep compassion for society's victims which underlies the humor."

De Leon's call for liberation continues in his poetry, where his imaginative works typically promote a world of peace and happiness beyond the life of injustice and discrimination Chicanos often experience in America. One of his more notable poems, *Coca Cola Dream,* attacks American materialism for preventing humans from achieving Christian kindness and a full understanding of each other. Discussing the verses collected in *Chicano Poet,* Chittenden commented, "In this poetry De Leon gives free reign to his imagination to create a world full of plastic, sometimes sensuous, imagery."

The education of Chicano children is a key concern for De Leon. He has made his own contribution to a better understanding between cultures by publishing many of his works in bilingual and bicultural editions, including the children's book *I Color My Garden,* which is used in many schools. According to the author, it can be used for teaching a variety of skills, including art, science, spelling, numbers, reading, and writing. Included in the book are seventeen poems, each printed in Spanish and English; cultural information; and coloring pages. *Sparky y Su Gang* is similar in format.

De Leon suffered a great personal loss in 1985 when his ten-year-old daughter, Aide, died from leukemia. Her tragic illness and death "profoundly affected" the author, wrote Chittenden. His literary output dwindled, although he did continue to write, paint, and lecture. Chittenden concluded, "[De Leon] sees the Chicano literature as a nascent one but believes that it can grow and survive. As he continues to write, he will no doubt contribute even more to that literature."

BIOGRAPHICAL/CRITICAL SOURCES:

BOOKS

Dictionary of Literary Biography, Volume 82: *Chicano Writers, First Series,* Gale, 1989.

PERIODICALS

Caracol, May, 1979, pp. 12-13, 19.
El Bravo, December 15, 1985, Section II, pp. 1, 4.
El Visitante Dominical, August 5, 1979.
Texas Circuit Newsletter, February-March, 1982.
Viaztlan, summer, 1985, pp. 7-8.*

*   *   *

DELGADO, Abelardo B(arrientos) 1931-

PERSONAL: Born November 27, 1931, in La Boquilla de Conchos, Chihuahua, Mexico; immigrated to United States, 1943; naturalized citizen, 1954; son of Vicente Delgado (a rancher and cattleman) and Guadalupe Barrientos; married Dolores Estrada, October 11, 1953; children: Ana, Alicia, Arturo, Alfredo, Angela, Amelia, Abbie, Andie. *Education:* University of Texas at El Paso, B.S., 1962; graduate study at University of Texas at El Paso, 1972, and at University of Utah, Salt Lake City, 1974- 77.

ADDRESSES: Office—6538 Eaton St., Arvada, CO 80003; Bueno Center for Multicultural Education, School of Education, Campus Box 249, University of Colorado, Boulder, CO 80309-0249; and Aims Community College, South Campus, 260 College Ave., Fort Lupton, CO 80621.

CAREER: Held various positions in construction and restaurant work, 1950-55; Our Lady's Youth Center,

El Paso, TX, special activities and employment director, 1955-64; Colorado Migrant Council, Denver, executive director, 1969-71; University of Texas at El Paso, Special Services Program, executive director and faculty member, 1971-72; Northwest Chicano Health Task Force, Seattle, Wash., executive director, 1973-74; University of Utah, Salt Lake City, instructor, 1974-77; Colorado Migrant Council, Farmerworker Data Network, Wheat Ridge, CO, project director, 1977-81; Colorado Migrant Council, Henderson, CO, special services/parent involvement coordinator, 1981-84, executive director, 1985; House of Neighborly Services, Inc., Brighton, CO, adult basic education director, 1986-88; Aims Community College, South Campus, Fort Lupton, CO, instructor, 1986—; St. Thomas Seminary, Denver, instructor, 1986—; Denver Metro State College, Denver, instructor, 1986—; University of Colorado, Bueno Center for Multicultural Education, Boulder, instructor and curriculum specialist, 1986—. Consultant to Interstate Research Associates, Washington, D.C., 1973, and Adrienne Hynes Associates, Denver, 1988—. Former area education director of New Mexico's state-wide migrant program. Has given numerous poetry readings. Founder and president of Barrio Publications, 1970—.

AWARDS, HONORS: Tonatiuh Prize for literature, 1978, for *Letters to Louise;* Mayor's Award for Literature, Denver, CO, 1988; first prize for poetry from *El Paseno* (newspaper), El Paso, TX, 1988.

WRITINGS:

Chicano: Twenty-five Pieces of a Chicano Mind (poetry), Barrio (Denver), 1969.
The Chicano Movement: Some Not Too Objective Observations (essays), Colorado Migrant Council (Denver), 1971.
(Editor with Ricardo Sanchez and contributor) *Los cuatro: Abelardo Delgado, Reymundo "Tigre" Perez, Ricardo Sanchez, Juan Valdez (Magdaleno Avila)—Poemas y reflecciones de cuatro chicanos* (poetry), Barrio, 1971.
Mortal Sin Kit (chapbook), Idaho Migrant Council, 1973.
Bajo el sol de Aztlan: Veinticinco soles de Abelardo (title means "Under the Sun of Aztlan: Twenty-five Suns of Abelardo;" poetry), Barrio, 1973.
It's Cold: Fifty-two Cold-Thought Poems of Abelardo, Barrio (Salt Lake City), 1974.
A Thermos Bottle Full of Self-Pity: Twenty-five Bottles of Abelardo (poetry), Barrio (Arvada, CO), c. 1975.

Reflexiones: Sixteen Reflections of Abelardo (poetry and short stories), Barrio (Salt Lake City), 1976.

Here Lies Lalo: Twenty-five Deaths of Abelardo (poetry), Barrio (Salt Lake City), 1977, revised edition, Barrio (Arvada), 1979.

Under the Skirt of Lady Justice: Forty-three Skirts of Abelardo (poetry), Barrio (Denver), 1978.

Siete de Abelardo, Barrio (Arvada), 1979.

Totoncaxihuitl, a Laxative: Twenty-five Laxatives of Abelardo (poetry and fiction), Barrio (Arvada), 1981.

Letters to Louise (novel), Tonatiuh-Quinto Sol International, 1982.

Unos perros con metralla (Some Dogs with a Machine-gun): Twenty-five Dogs of Abelardo (poetry), Barrio, 1982.

Also author of *A Quilt of Words: Twenty-five Quilts of Abelardo,* c. 1976, *Seven Abelardos,* and of plays. Contributor to numerous anthologies, including *Canto al Pueblo: Antologia,* Arizona Canto al Pueblo IV, Comite Editorial, 1980, and *Chicanos: Antologia historica y literaria,* Fondo de Cultura Economica, 1980. Contributor to periodicals. Founder and editor of *La Onda Campesina* (newsletter) and *Farmworker Journal,* both Denver; editor-at-large, *La Luz* (magazine), Denver.

SIDELIGHTS: Although the author of several of Chicano literature's most popular poems, including *"Stupid America," "La Causa,"* and *"The Organizer,"* Abelardo B. Delgado's books are not widely known or reviewed largely due to nearly all of them being published on a small-scale by the author's own Barrio Publications. Undaunted by a lack of approval from mainstream publishers, Delgado (known to his friends as "Lalo") has established his reputation on the strength of numerous personal appearances throughout the United States. While his dramatic poetry readings help to increase Delgado's popularity, they also enable him to spread his message of social justice for Mexican-Americans and other minority groups.

The desire to promote social reform has been a major theme in Delgado's poetry since 1969 when his first collection, *Chicano: Twenty-five Pieces of a Chicano Mind,* appeared during the height of the Chicano Movement. In this work Delgado explores the many concepts that define Mexican-American culture, such as *chicanismo, carnalismo* (brotherhood), and machismo, while examining the impact on Chicano society of the migrant, the undocumented worker, and living in the barrio. Writing about the collection in a *Dictionary of Literary Biography* essay, Donaldo W.

Urioste claims, "Delgado is at his best when he advocates social justice, human dignity, and equality for Chicanos, and when he angrily condemns those forces—be they social or cultural, Anglo or Chicano—that work against these ideals." Urioste quotes from Delgado's *"Stupid America"* as an example of the poet's socially motivated work. The poem begins: "stupid america, see that chicano / with a big knife / on his steady hand / he doesn't want to knife you / he wants to sit on a bench / and carve Christfigures."

One of the many difficulties associated with the Chicano culture about which Delgado writes is the use of Spanish in a nation where the majority speak only English. Delgado himself writes in a combination of Spanish and English typical of many Mexican-American authors. In an interview with Juan David Bruce-Novoa appearing in *Chicano Authors: Inquiry by Interview,* Delgado calls bilingualism a "trademark" of Chicano expression. "Chicano literature's main characteristic," the poet observes, "is that it is a literature that is naturally at ease in the way that Chicanos express themselves, and that is a natural bilingualism, with the influence of English naturally predominant, as that is the language in which all Chicanos are educated. . . . To write using natural bilingual style is a very vivid affirmation that we are here, that we are alive and well, thinking and writing in both idiomas [languages]."

Delgado's papers are part of the Nettie Lee Benson Collection in the Latin American Collection of the University of Texas at Austin.

BIOGRAPHICAL/CRITICAL SOURCES:

BOOKS

Bruce-Novoa, Juan David, *Chicano Authors: Inquiry by Interview,* University of Texas Press, 1980.

Dictionary of Literary Biography, Volume 82: *Chicano Writers, First Series,* Gale, 1989.

Martinez, Julio A. and Francisco A. Lomeli, editors, *Chicano Literature: A Reference Guide,* Greenwood Press, 1985.

Steiner, Stan, *La Raza: The Mexican Americans,* Harper & Row, 1970.*

*   *   *

DEL MAR, Florentina
See CONDE, Carmen

DENIS, Julio
  See CORTAZAR, Julio

*   *   *

DeSENA, Carmine 1957-

PERSONAL: Born December 31, 1957, in New York; son of Vincent (in sales) and Angelina (a hotel manager; maiden name, Risi) DeSena. *Education:* Queens College of the City University of New York, B.A., 1979; studied playwriting at HB Studios. *Politics:* Liberal Democrat. *Religion:* Roman Catholic. *Avocational interests:* Theater, film, reading, exercise, art.

ADDRESSES: Home—320 East 42nd St., Apt. 1308, New York, NY 10017. *Agent*—Barbara Zitwer, Barbara Zitwer Agency, 525 West End Ave., Apt. 29E, New York, NY 10024.

CAREER: Vocational Rehab Services, Bayside, NY, supervisor of intensive psychological rehabilitation treatment program, 1979—. Cofounder of comedy troupe OK, So We Lied.

MEMBER: Certified Rehabilitation Counselors Association.

WRITINGS:

Lies: The Whole Truth (humor), Perigee Books (New York City), 1993.
(With Gil C. Alicea) *The Air Down Here: True Tales from a South Bronx Boyhood,* photographs by Alicea, Chronicle Books (San Francisco), 1995.
The Comedy Market: A Writer's Guide to Making Money Being Funny (writers' handbook), Berkley (New York City), 1996.
Satan's Little Instruction Book (humor), Doubleday (New York City), 1996.

Contributor to magazines and newspapers, including *Us, Theater Week,* and *Country Life.*

ADAPTATIONS: Tommy Boy Records optioned the film writes to *The Air Down Here: True Tales from a South Bronx Boyhood.*

WORK IN PROGRESS: A novel, *The Bad Movie Club;* a play, *Our Daily Bread.*

SIDELIGHTS: After befriending Gil C. Alicea, a Puerto Rican teenager living with his dad in the South Bronx, Carmine DeSena began recording what would become *The Air Down Here: True Tales from a South Bronx Boyhood*—115 "short-attention-span observations of a teenager growing up in the hood," according to a *Publishers Weekly* reviewer who felt the collection may appeal to its juvenile audience but that it tells less about "ghetto teens" than other similar works. Merri Monks's *Booklist* review more positively lauds the book as an "authentic and truthful self-portrait," claiming adolescents both native to and foreign to "urban neighborhoods" may "enjoy the book."

"Writing was never something I planned," DeSena once told *CA.* "It began innocently in high school and evolved into a major facet of my life. After college graduation I worked as a reporter for a local newspaper, doing reviews, news articles, and human interest stories. My experience in the human services helped me branch out as a freelancer, working on science, medical, and service pieces. After a busy two years I felt the need to be on the creative end.

"I began to study playwriting, improvisation, and acting. For the next five years I wrote and performed with the comedy troupe OK, So We Lied, at New York clubs, parties, conferences, and colleges. Although it was a wonderful learning experience, the performance aspect limited my writing. I left the group and began writing comedy for NBC-Radio. Two years later I published my first humor work. Finally I feel I have found my niche. I plan to continue to work on humor and socially relevant issues.

"My strength as a writer is my ability to create from the world around me. Often I find myself creating pieces or solidifying book ideas based on my own experiences, as well as those of the people around me. I am influenced by the arts, with a strong attraction to theater. I am what you would consider a culture junkie. I imbibe plays, novels, nonfiction, short stories, films, museums, television, and music.

"My creativity and love of the arts is my process. I don't quite understand how it works, but I have never experienced writer's block. My mind weaves ideas into writing, based on what I observe and the inspiration I get from the arts. My concern for the human condition defines my subjects. I want people to laugh, to be able to identify themselves with others to see that they are not alone, and to convince people that change is possible. I want to offer solutions. Positivism remains a constant focus.

"Writing has been a journey of self-discovery. It has helped me define who I am, my values, and the lifestyle I lead. For the last seventeen years I have felt privileged to reach out to others as a writer and rehabilitation counselor. I hope to maintain my positive quality."

BIOGRAPHICAL/CRITICAL SOURCES:

PERIODICALS

Booklist, October 15, 1995, p. 393.
Library Journal, October 1, 1995, p. 106; August, 1996, p. 84.
Publishers Weekly, August 21, 1995, p. 54; October 23, 1995, p. 22.
School Library Journal, March, 1996, p. 222.*

*   *   *

DIFUSA, Pati
   See ALMODOVAR, Pedro

*   *   *

DIPHUSA, Patty
   See ALMODOVAR, Pedro

*   *   *

DOMECQ, H(onorio) Bustos
   See BIOY CASARES, Adolfo

*   *   *

DOMECQ, H. Bustos
   See BORGES, Jorge Luis

DONOSO, Jose 1924-1996
(Jose Donoso Yanez)

PERSONAL: Born October 5, 1924, in Santiago, Chile; died of cancer, December, 1996, in Santiago, Chile; son of Jose Donoso (a physician) and Alicia Yanez; married Maria del Pilar Serrano (a translator), 1961. *Education:* Attended University of Chile, beginning in 1947; Princeton University, A.B., 1951.

CAREER: Writer, journalist, and translator. Shepherd in southern Chile, 1945-46; dockhand in Buenos Aires, Argentina, c. 1946; Kent School, Santiago, Chile, English teacher, c. 1953; Catholic University of Chile, Santiago, professor of conversational English, beginning in 1954; worked in Buenos Aires, 1958-60; *Ercilla* (weekly newsmagazine), Santiago, journalist with assignments in Europe, beginning in 1960, editor and literary critic, beginning in 1962; University of Chile, Santiago, lecturer at school of journalism, beginning in 1962; *Siempre* (periodical), Mexico City, Mexico, literary critic, 1965; University of Iowa, Dubuque, teacher of writing and modern Spanish American literature at Writers' Workshop, 1965-67; Colorado State University, Fort Collins, teacher, 1969.

AWARDS, HONORS: Santiago Municipal Short Story Prize, 1955, for *Veraneo y otros cuentos;* Chile-Italia Prize for journalism, 1960; William Faulkner Foundation Prize, 1962, for *Coronacion;* Guggenheim awards, 1968 and 1973; Critics Award for best novel in Spanish, 1979, for *Casa de campo;* National Literature Prize, Chile, 1990; Woodrow Wilson Fellow, 1992.

WRITINGS:

Veraneo y otros cuentos (title means "Summertime and Other Stories", privately printed (Santiago, Chile), 1955.
Dos cuentos (title means "Two Stories"), Guardia Vieja (Santiago, Chile), 1956.
Coronacion (novel), Nascimento (Santiago), 1957, Seix Barral (Barcelona), 1981, translation by Jocasta Goodwin published as *Coronation,* Knopf (New York City), 1965.
El charleston (short stories; title means "The Charleston"), Nascimento, 1960.
Los mejores cuentos de Jose Donoso (short stories; title means" The Best Stories of Jose Donoso"), Zig-Zag (Santiago), 1965.
Este domingo (novel), Zig-Zag, 1965, translation by Lorraine O'Grady Freeman published as *This Sunday,* Knopf, 1967.

El lugar sin limites (novella; title means "The Place Without Limits"), J. Moritz (Mexico), 1966; translation by Suzanne Jill Levine and Hallie D. Taylor published as *Hell Has No Limits* in *Triple Cross,* Dutton (New York City), 1972.

(Editor with William A. Henkin and others) *The Tri-Quarterly Anthology of Contemporary Latin American Literature,* Dutton, 1969.

El obsceno pajaro de la noche (novel), Seix Barral, 1970, translation by Hardie St. Martin and Leonard Mades published as *The Obscene Bird of Night,* Knopf, 1973.

Cuentos (title means "Stories"), Seix Barral, 1971, translation by Andree Conrad published as *Charleston and Other Stories,* David Godine (Boston, MA), 1977.

Historia personal del "boom" (memoir), Anagrama (Barcelona), 1972, translation by Gregory Kolovakos published as *The Boom in Spanish American Literature: A Personal History,* Columbia University Press (New York City), 1977.

Tres novelitas burguesas (title means "Three Bourgeois Novellas "), Seix Barral, 1973, translation by Andree Conrad published as *Sacred Families: Three Novellas,* Knopf, 1977.

Casa de campo (novel), Seix Barral, 1978, translation by David Pritchard and Suzanne Jill Levine published as *A House in the Country,* Knopf, 1984.

El jardin de al lado (novel), Seix Barral, 1981, translation by Hardie St. Martin published as *The Garden Next Door,* Grove (New York City), 1994.

La misteriosa desparicion de la Marquesita de Loria (novel; title means "The Mysterious Disappearance of the Young Marchioness of Loria "), Seix Barral, 1981.

Poemas de un novelista (poems), Ganymedes (Santiago), 1981.

Cuatro para Delfina (novellas; title means "Four for Delfina"), Seix Barral, 1982.

Suenos de mala muerte (play; first produced in Santiago, Chile by ICTUS, November, 1982), Universitaria (Santiago), 1985.

Seis cuentos para ganar, Cochrane-Planeta/Teleduc (Santiago), 1985.

La desesperanza (novel; title means "Despair"), Seix Barral, 1986, translation by Alfred MacAdam published as *Curfew,* Weidenfeld & Nicolson (London), 1988.

(Contributor) Doris Meyer, editor, *Lives on the Line: The Testimony of Contemporary Latin American Authors,* University of California Press, 1988.

(With Carlos Cerda) *Este domingo: Version teatral de la novela homonima,* Bello (Santiago), 1990.

Taratuta; Naturaleza muerta con cachimba (novellas), Mondadori (Madrid), 1990; translation by Gregory Rabassa published as *Taratuta; and, Still Life with Pipe: Two Novellas,* W.W. Norton (New York City), 1993.

El Mocho, Santanilla Publishing Co., 1998.

Translator into Spanish of numerous works, including *The Life of Sir Arthur Conan Doyle* by John Dickson Carr and *Last Tales* by Isak Dinesen, and, with wife, Maria del Pilar Serrano, of *The Scarlet Letter* by Nathaniel Hawthorne and *Les Personnages* by Francoise Malet-Joris. Contributor of articles and short stories to periodicals, including *Americas, mss.* (Princeton University), *Epoca,* and *Review.*

SIDELIGHTS: "I fear simplification more than anything," said Chilean novelist Jose Donoso in *Partisan Review.* Donoso's novels, noted for their complexity and insistent pessimism, seem to embody his observation that life, society, and writing are each an "adventure into [a] mad, dark thing." Donoso has often been ranked among the finest Latin American authors of the twentieth century, and many critics consider him the best Chilean novelist of modern times. "He is an extraordinarily sophisticated writer," wrote *Newsweek*'s Walter Clemons, "in perfect control of time dissolves, contradictory voices, gritty realism and hallucinatory fugues." *Dictionary of Literary Biography* contributor Ricardo Gutierrez Mouat declared that Donoso "powerfully ushered in the modern Chilean novel, a form Donoso used to explore the relationships and identity of the dominant classes."

Observers suggest that Donoso's concern with the complexity of life is particularly appropriate to the situation in his homeland. Chile, which appeared to be a moderate, stable democracy for most of the twentieth century, erupted in violent political conflict in the 1970s. The country lurched abruptly from the Marxist government of Salvador Allende to the brutal conservative dictatorship of General Augusto Pinochet. From the time his first novels appeared in the 1950s, Donoso was praised for his sense of the strained relations between rich and poor that underlay Chilean society. The author was reluctant, however, to be viewed as a social commentator: he seemed determined, in both his life and his work, to avoid the didacticism he witnessed in politics. "Ideologies and cosmogonies are alien to me," he stated in *Lives on the Line.* "Their life is too short and they are too soon proved wrong, their place immediately taken by another explanation of the world." Accordingly, as Donoso observed in *Review,* "I'm not interested in the novels of ideas. . . . If I write a novel, it won't be to express an idea I saw in an essay."

Writers of the Chilean left, Donoso suggested, have repeatedly challenged his political standoffishness; sometimes, he observed in *Nation,* he has been "denounced . . . as decadent bourgeois." But Donoso's many admirers suggested that his pessimistic outlook, even his refusal to offer a solution to the problems that he surveyed in his work, reflected an acute awareness of the breadth and depth of human suffering. As Z. Nelly Martinez explained in *Books Abroad:* "Beyond the social reality and its multiple stratification, Donoso probes into life's duality of good and evil, order and chaos, life and death, and examines man's inability to reconcile both sides of existence. Therein lies the tragedy; for, despite man's effort to build an illusion of order, life's anarchy eventually overcomes him." In much of the author's work, as Martinez observed, "madness, abdication to chaos, becomes the only alternative." Against such all-encompassing pain, Donoso seems to offer hope primarily in the form of intellectual understanding. "Kicking people in the shins gets you nowhere," he said in the *New York Times Book Review.* "Understanding gets you much farther."

Indeed, while not excluding political repression as a theme, Donoso pursued a wide variety of deep issues in his fiction, from existential crises and madness to the relationship between an artist and his creations. His fascination with the form and functions of fiction led some to label him a postmodernist, especially in reference to his later work. In *MLN,* Rosemary Geisdorfer Feal observed: "Donoso constantly questions the ontological status of fiction and challenges its traditional mimetic function. This questioning informs his conception of reality as incapable of allowing for true insight and of power as the main obstacle to genuine human interaction. The obsession with power, inauthenticity, masquerade, irrationality, and the fragmentary makes for a persistent and painful exploration of the dark side of human existence. The language, which is equal to the large purpose assigned to it, is the final mark of Donoso's mastery and of his commitment to the excesses and obliquities of the carnivalesque."

Donoso was born into a family that kept a tenuous foothold in Chile's respectable upper middle class. His father "was a young physician more addicted to horse racing and to playing cards than to his profession," the author recalled in *Review.* His mother, who "somehow coped," came from "the ne'er-do-well branch of a *nouveau riche* family." The father used family connections to get a newspaper job, but he was fired; thereafter he became house physician to three decrepit great-aunts whose fortunes he hoped to inherit. When the aunts died the Donosos inherited nothing, but soon they were sheltering other relatives, including an irresponsible uncle and Donoso's grandmother, who lived with the family for ten years while slowly succumbing to insanity. "The gradual process of [my grandmother's] deterioration, intertwined with lightning flashes of memory and family lore . . . is one of the episodes that has most marked my life," Donoso declared, "not because I loved this old woman but because her madness brought the ironies of family life and the horrors of aging and dying so cruelly into focus." He became a high-school truant and then a dropout, associating with bums and spending a year as a shepherd in the remote grasslands of southern Chile. In his early twenties he returned home and resumed his education, rejecting the traditional careers open to "an upper middle-class boy" by becoming an undergraduate English major.

Donoso described his literary development in the memoir *Historia personal del "boom"* (*The Boom in Spanish American Literature: A Personal History*). The book introduces readers to one of the most renowned periods in Spanish American Literature—the "Boom," a flowering of literary activity during the 1960s—by showing its relationship to Donoso's own life. As an aspiring author in the 1950s, Donoso relates in his memoir, he shared with other young writers throughout Latin America the sense of being "asphyxiated" by the provincial cultural environment of his native land. Great authors of the past such as Mexico's Manuel Azuela, who saw the novel as a practical way to discuss contemporary social problems, seemed to members of Donoso's generation like "statues in a park." The earnest, simple style that such "grandfathers" had made popular seemed to rob the novel of creativity and expressiveness. The region's publishers, too poor to take risks on new talent, preferred to reprint literary classics and popular foreign works; accordingly, Donoso and his peers had difficulty getting published, often had to sell copies of their books on their own, and found it difficult to obtain each others' work in print. For role models, Donoso declares, writers of his generation looked beyond the Hispanic world. Some authors he mentions, including William Faulkner and Henry James, were subtle stylists who experimented with the conventions of the novel, showing, for instance, how a character's point of view could affect his perception of reality. Others, including Franz Kafka and Albert

Camus, were critics of human nature who seemed to have little hope of reform: their works showed isolated individuals grappling with an uncaring and fundamentally absurd society. By the late 1950s and early 1960s, Donoso began to see such innovative writing in novels by his peers, notably Cuba's Alejo Carpentier and Mexico's Carlos Fuentes. Such works, Donoso recalls, were "a spur to my envy, to my need to emulate," and they confirmed his sense that "the baroque, the distorted, the excessive could all increase the possibilities of the novel."

In his first novel, *Coronacion* (*Coronation*), Donoso combined traditional realism with the more complex personal vision that would emerge in his later works. The book's main character is an affluent old woman who lives with her servants in a mansion; her vivid delusions and curses frighten her grandson, a repressed middle-aged bachelor. The old woman, Donoso admitted, is a portrait of his insane grandmother, and some relatives were indignant at the resemblance. Reviewers in Chile praised *Coronation* as a realistic depiction of that country's society, especially, recalled Donoso in *The Boom,* "the decadence of the upper class." Wishing to transcend realism, Donoso found such praise frustrating. The resolution of the novel, he suggested, was designed to challenge traditional literary style. The book's climax largely abandons the restraints of realism by dwelling on madness and the grotesque. The old woman, costumed and crowned by her maids during a drunken prank, dies convinced she has already gone to heaven. The grandson, confronting his mortality and his unfulfilling life, concludes that God himself must have been mad to create such a world and then follows his grandmother into insanity. *Coronation* brought Donoso an international reputation and won the 1962 William Faulkner Foundation Prize, established in Faulkner's will to encourage the translation of outstanding Latin American fiction into English.

Donoso's second novel, *Este domingo* (*This Sunday*), with its themes of upper-class decay and incipient chaos, has often been likened to *Coronation.* Many reviewers considered the later work a significant advance for Donoso, showing greater subtlety, impact, and stylistic sophistication. "As Donoso sees it," wrote Alexander Coleman in the *New York Times Book Review,* "the rich are different because they cannot live without the underworld of the poor to exploit and command." Don Alvaro is an affluent, middle-aged professional who has grown up weak and ineffective, but has kept a sense of virility by making a chambermaid his mistress. His wife Chepa, who has

an obsessive need to minister to others, becomes the domineering patroness to a paroled murderer still drawn toward a life of crime. The novel's climax occurs when Chepa, unhappy with the parolee's conduct, seeks him out in the slum where he lives; she is hounded by poor neighborhood children and collapses on a trash heap. Throughout the book Donoso experiments with differing points of view, showing parts of the story through the eyes of its obsessive participants, and part through the eyes of a young relative of Alvaro, too naive to understand the underlying brutality of the world around him. Noting Donoso's "cool and biting intelligence," Coleman praised the author's "perfect balance between compulsion and control as he exorcises his infernally driven characters."

Donoso delved much further into obsession and fantasy with his novella *El lugar sin limites* (*Hell Has No Limits*), written at about the same time as *This Sunday.* The work is set in an isolated small town owned by Don Alejo, a powerful, all-knowing, selfish aristocrat whom many reviewers saw as the satirical embodiment of an unfeeling God. The main character is Manuela, whose delusions about being a lithe, young female dancer are lavishly echoed by the story's narration; in fact, however, Manuela is an aging male transvestite who works as a dancer in his daughter's bordello and uses fantasy to transcend his absurd existence. The story culminates in violence when Pancho, a virile male truck driver attracted to Manuela, lashes out against his own underlying homosexuality by savagely assaulting the transvestite. Biographer George McMurray considered *Hell Has No Limits* a powerful comment on the futility of human aspirations, so pessimistic as to approach nihilism. The author's intentions, McMurray explained, "are to undermine traditional values, reveal the bankruptcy of reason, and jar the reader onto new levels of awareness by exposing the other side of reality." McMurray found the story one of Donoso's most accomplished works.

During the 1960s Donoso moved beyond the intellectual confines of Chile to become part of a growing international community of Latin American writers— major figures of the Boom—who knew each other as friends and colleagues and shared moral support, ideas, and interesting books. At a 1962 conference of such writers he became close friends with Carlos Fuentes; after attending another conference in Mexico two years later, Donoso began more than a dozen years of voluntary exile from his homeland. He wrote *Hell Has No Limits* while renting a house from

Fuentes in Mexico, taught for two years at the University of Iowa's prestigious Writers Workshop, then settled in Spain. Meanwhile he went through numerous drafts of a novel far more lengthy, intricate, and allusive than his previous efforts. Its title came from a letter that young Henry James received from his father Henry Sr., warning about life's underlying chaos. "Life is no farce," the letter advised: "the natural inheritance of everyone who is capable of spiritual life is an unsubdued forest where the wolf howls and the obscene bird of night chatters."

When *El obsceno pajaro de la noche* (*The Obscene Bird of Night*) finally emerged in 1970, reviewers found it both masterful and indescribable—"How do you review a dream?" asked Wolfgang Luchtig in *Books Abroad*. The novel is narrated by Humberto, an unsuccessful writer who becomes the retainer to a decaying aristocratic family and the tutor of their only son and heir. The child, monstrously deformed, is seen by his father as an emblem of chaos and is surrounded by freaks so that he will seem "normal." Eventually Humberto apparently flees to one of the family's charitable ventures—a decrepit convent that houses some of society's castoff women, ranging from the elderly to young orphans. Throughout the novel past and present are confusingly intermingled, and characters undergo bizarre transformations, sometimes melting into one another. Humberto appears as a deaf-mute servant in the convent; is apparently transformed into a baby by the old women, who often seem to be witches; and is finally sealed in a bundle of rags and thrown onto a fire, where he turns to ashes as the book ends.

Observers such as McMurray suggested that the novel should not be viewed as a "story" in the conventional sense, but as an outpouring of the deranged mind of its narrator, Humberto. According to such a view, Humberto is a schizophrenic, driven mad, perhaps, by his lack of success; his narration is disordered because he freely mixes reality with his fantasies, fears, and resentments of the world. Humberto's many transformations reflect his disintegrating personality, as he picks up and discards various identities in an effort to define himself; his bizarre demise, in which he is cut off from the world and then destroyed, represents the madman's final withdrawal from reality. In *Review* Donoso said that while the narrator is hardly autobiographical in a literal sense, "he is the autobiography of my fears, of my fantasies"; interestingly, the author finished his book while recovering from an episode of near-madness, brought on by a traumatic ulcer operation and the administration of pain-killing drugs. "Basically I don't know what my novel is about," Donoso also observed. "It's something that has happened to me rather than something I've written." "Donoso does not offer us . . . a novel simply to read," explained *Review* correspondent John J. Hassett, "but one to experience in which we are continuously called upon to give the text some order by discovering its unities and its repetitions." Many commentators ranked *The Obscene Bird of Night* among the best novels of the Boom era, which ended in the early 1970s, and quite a few have styled the work Donoso's "masterpiece."

Until the 1980s Donoso continued to reside primarily in Spain. After he finished *The Obscene Bird of Night,* his writing began to change: his style became less hallucinatory and his narratives were less concerned with the Chilean aristocracy. Some of his work was set in Spain, including *Tres novelitas burguesas* (*Sacred Families*), novellas that portray that country's upper middle class with a blend of fantasy and social satire, and *El jardin de al lado* (*The Garden Next Door*), which features a novelist-in-exile who is haunted by his past. Throughout his years in Spain, Donoso reported in *Lives on the Line,* he found it impossible to cut his emotional ties to Chile. He did not feel nostalgia, he continued, but rather "the *guilt of absence*" or the "guilt of not being connected with action." His dilemma was heightened because he remained abroad by choice while Pinochet established his dictatorship. "All of us who lived abroad during that period who didn't have to," he explained in *Vogue,* "have a terrible feeling of guilt" because "we didn't share in the history of Chile during a very important time."

In the mid-1970s Donoso resolved to discuss Chile's turmoil in a novel, which became *Casa de campo* (*A House in the Country*). Aware that he was cut off from the daily life of Chileans—including the way they spoke—he wrote about them indirectly, creating what reviewers called a political allegory. Once more Donoso set his book in an aristocratic household. When the estate's owners leave on an excursion, their children (perhaps representing the middle class) and exploited Indians from the surrounding area (perhaps the working class) take over and wreak havoc. They are led by an aristocratic uncle (Salvador Allende?) who may be insane or may be the victim of injustice at the hands of his relatives. When the owners return, they use servants to ruthlessly re-establish order and then proclaim—despite all the bitterness they have engendered—that nothing has changed since they first left. Though some reviewers faulted the novel for being too intellectual and emotionally detached, others found it highly relevant and involving. "The combination of literary grace, political urgency and a fierce and untethered imagination," wrote Charles Champlin in the *Los Angeles Times Book Review,* "give Donoso and *A House in the Country* the power of an aimed projectile."

By the mid-1980s Donoso had resettled in Chile, and in 1986 he produced a more direct study of life under Pinochet in the novel *La desesperanza (Curfew).* Though the book describes both Pinochet's torturers and the dispossessed poor, its principal focus is the country's well-educated, dispirited political left. The two main characters—a onetime revolutionary and a political folksinger who fled to Paris—share deep feelings of guilt because they were not punished as much by the regime as were other leftists. Their old comrades, meanwhile, seem paralyzed by infighting, didacticism, and bitterness. The book was highly praised by prominent American critics and, notably, by Jacobo Timerman, an Argentine journalist respected worldwide as an eloquent victim of political oppression. "Donoso is a moderate who has written a revolutionary novel," Timerman observed in *Vogue;* in *New Yorker* he wrote that "it is a relief, finally, to read a work of Chilean literature in which none of the characters are above history or appear to dominate it." *Curfew,* reviewers suggested, displays the deep personal flaws of leftists and rightists alike: by avoiding simple conclusions, the novel makes plain that Chile abounds in uncertainty and despair. In contrast to its reception abroad, *Curfew* was viewed rather coolly by many Chilean intellectuals. "The book doesn't flag-wave" or "present an alternative," Donoso explained in *Vogue,* and "people would respect me much more if it did." However, he observed, "I'm not a crusader. I'm not a hero. I'm just a man who is very hurt, and who wants change."

The two novellas in Donoso's *Taratuta; and, Still Life with Pipe* "immerse readers in the intriguing interplay between art and reality," noted Larsen Olszewski in *Library Journal.* In "Taratuta" the narrator, a novelist, seeks to learn more about Lenin by tracing an obscure Russian revolutionary named "Taratuta." But the quest remains uncompleted when Taratuta's descendent, whom the narrator hopes will shed light on the revolutionary, mysteriously disappears. In "Still Life with Pipe" a young man becomes obsessed with a forgotten Chilean artist and wrecks his own life in the in the pursuit of so-called high culture. "From these modest starting points, Donoso attempts nothing less than a meditation on the power of the word and

the role of fantasy in everyday reality, the renewing energy of art," noted Fernando Gonzalez in the *Boston Globe.* In the *Washington Post,* James Polk likewise maintained that the two novellas reveal Donoso's preoccupation with "the nature of inspiration and the ambivalent relationship between the artist and his art." The reviewer concluded that the works "show the author at his near best, challenging, provoking, forcing reexamination. Both are complex but intensely readable, told with generous amounts of irony and wit. All of this may or may not be postmodern, but it certainly is striking."

In 1990 Donoso received the highest literary award his country bestows, the Chilean National Literature Prize. He joked of the award: "It's as if somebody had driven a nail into the wall to hang my posthumous portrait." In fact it was a rather eerie coincidence that his health—never very good—began to fail in the mid-1990s. He died of cancer in December of 1996 at his home in Santiago. In an interview he gave to *Americas* magazine late in his life, Donoso declared: "A writer is a very confused person. . . . A novel happens to him. We are not very rational people. A novelist is a man who is involved with words and words that lead to words, which leads him to some memory, which he thought was forgotten. The words and sentences and the rhythm of what he is saying stem from a dark world, rains of many seasons, many streams. You want to make something out of clay, but you are not really sure what it is."

BIOGRAPHICAL/CRITICAL SOURCES:

BOOKS

Bacarisse, Salvador, editor, *Contemporary Latin American Fiction,* Scottish Academic Press (Edinburgh), 1980, pp. 18-33.

Contemporary Literary Criticism, Gale (Detroit, MI), Volume 4, 1975; Volume 8, 1978; Volume 11, 1979; Volume 32, 1985; Volume 99, 1996, pp. 215-78.

Dictionary of Hispanic Biography, Gale, 1996.

Dictionary of Literary Biography, Volume 113: *Modern Latin-American Fiction Writers, First Series,* Gale, 1992, pp. 134-48.

Donoso, Jose, *The Boom in Spanish American Literature: A Personal History,* Columbia University Press (New York City), 1977.

Forster, Merlin H., editor, *Tradition and Renewal: Essays on Twentieth-Century Latin American Literature and Culture,* University of Illinois Press (Champaign, IL), 1975.

Gutierrez Mouat, Ricardo, *Jose Donoso: Impostura e impostacion,* Hispamerica (Gaithersburg, MD), 1983.

Hispanic Literature Criticism, Gale, Volume 1, 1994.

MacAdam, Alfred J., *Modern Latin American Narratives: The Dreams of Reason,* University of Chicago Press (Chicago, IL), 1977.

McMurray, George R., *Jose Donoso,* Twayne (Boston, MA), 1979.

Meyer, Doris, editor, *Lives on the Line: The Testimony of Contemporary Latin American Authors,* University of California Press (Berkeley, CA), 1988.

Schwartz, Ronald, *Nomads, Exiles, and Emigres: The Rebirth of the Latin American Narrative, 1960-80,* Scarecrow Press (Metuchen, NJ), 1980.

PERIODICALS

Americas, June 9, 1984; November/December, 1987, pp. 8-13.
Book Forum, summer, 1977.
Booklist, December 15, 1992, p. 714.
Books Abroad, winter, 1968; winter, 1972; spring, 1972; spring, 1975.
Boston Globe, January 5, 1993, p. 65.
Christian Science Monitor, June 27, 1973; June 2, 1988, p. 20.
Commonweal, September 21, 1973; May 18, 1984.
Comparative Literature, spring, 1988, pp. 150-71.
Contemporary Literature, winter, 1987, pp. 520-29.
Essays in Literature, spring, 1975.
Hispania, May, 1972.
Hudson Review, winter, 1978; winter, 1989.
Journal of Spanish Studies: Twentieth Century, winter, 1973.
Kirkus Reviews, November 15, 1992, p. 1393.
Library Journal, January, 1993, p. 168.
London Review of Books, December 6, 1990, pp. 24-26.
Los Angeles Times Book Review, February 5, 1984; May 15, 1988, pp. 3, 13; September 10, 1989, p. 15; November 29, 1992, p. 7; February 14, 1993, p. 6.
MLN, March, 1988, pp. 398-418.
Modern Fiction Studies, winter, 1978.
Mundo Nuevo, June, 1967, pp. 77-85.
Nation, March 11, 1968; June 11, 1973; February 11, 1978.
New Leader, October 1, 1973; January 23, 1989, pp. 21-22.
New Statesman, June 18, 1965; March 1, 1974.
New Statesman & Society, October 19, 1990, p. 34.
Newsweek, June 4, 1973.
New Yorker, June 16, 1973; April 30, 1984; November 2, 1987; June 13, 1988, pp. 112-14; August 16, 1993, pp. 86-89.
New York Review of Books, April 19, 1973; December 13, 1973; August 4, 1977; July 18, 1985.
New York Times Book Review, March 14, 1965; November 26, 1967; December 24, 1972; June 17, 1973; June 26, 1977; February 26, 1984; May 29, 1988, p. 9; August 14, 1988, pp. 1, 22-23; January 10, 1993, p. 11.
Partisan Review, fall, 1974; number 1, 1982; number 2, 1986.
PMLA, January, 1978; January, 1991, pp. 60-70.
Publishers Weekly, November 30, 1992, p. 30.
Punch, April 18, 1984.
Review, fall, 1973, pp. 31-33; January-May, 1984.
Review of Contemporary Fiction, fall, 1988, pp. 16-24; summer, 1992, pp. 11-17, 50-55, 70-76, 77-79.
Revista de Estudios Hispanicos, January, 1975.
Revista Iberoamericana, April-September, 1983, pp. 449-467.
Salmagundi, spring/summer, 1989, pp. 258-68.
Saturday Review, March 13, 1965; December 9, 1967; January 23, 1971; July 9, 1977.
Spectator, June 18, 1965.
Studies in Short Fiction, winter, 1971.
Symposium, summer, 1976; fall, 1987, pp. 200-13.
Time, April 23, 1965; July 30, 1973; June 27, 1977; February 20, 1984.
Times Literary Supplement, July 1, 1965; October 12, 1967; February 22, 1968; July 2, 1971; February 10, 1978; April 6, 1984; January 4, 1991, p. 16.
UNESCO Courier, July-August, 1994, p. 4.
Village Voice, March 27, 1984.
Vogue, May, 1988.
Washington Post, December 22, 1992, p. C2; April 8, 1993, p. D2.
Washington Post Book World, May 27, 1973; August 14, 1977; February 26, 1984; May 22, 1988, p. 7.
World Literature Today, autumn, 1977; spring, 1981; summer, 1982; winter, 1983.

OBITUARIES:

PERIODICALS

New York Times, December 9, 1996, p. B13.*

*   *   *

do REGO, Jose Lins 1901-1957

PERSONAL: Born June 3, 1901, in Pilar, Brazil; died

September 12, 1957, in Rio de Janeiro, Brazil. *Education:* Studied law in Pernambuco, Brazil.

CAREER: Writer. Worked as a district attorney and as a bank inspector, Maceio, Brazil.

WRITINGS:

"SUGARCANE CYCLE"; NOVELS

O Moleque Ricardo (title means "Black Boy Ricardo"), 1935.
Usina (title means "Sugar Refinery"), 1936.
Fogo Morto (title means "Dead Fire"), 1943, translation published by HarperCollins (New York), 1991.
Menino de Engenho, 1932, translated as *Plantation Boy,* 1966.
Doidinho (novel, also see below), 1933.
Bangue (novel, also see below), 1934.
Plantation Boy (includes *Menino de Engenho, Doidinho,* and *Bangue*), translation by Emmi Baum, Knopf (New York City), 1966.

OTHER

Historias da Velha Totonia, 1936.
Pureza, 1937.
Pedra Bonita (novel), 1938.
Riacho Doce, 1939.
Agua-Mae, 1941.
Gordos e Magros, 1942.
Pedro Americo, 1943.
Poesia e Vida, 1945.
Conferencias no Prata, 1946.
Euridice, 1947.
Bota da Sete Leguas, 1951.
Homens, Seres, e Coisas, 1952.
Cangaceiros (novel; title means "Backlands Bandits"), 1953.
A Casa e o Homem, 1954.
Roteiro de Israel, 1955.
Meus Verdes Anos, 1956.
Presenca do Nordeste na Literatura Brasileira, 1957.
Gregos e Troianos, 1957.
O Vulcao e a Fonte, 1958.
Dias Idos e Vivados: Antologia, 1981.

Contributor to Brazilian periodicals.

BIOGRAPHICAL/CRITICAL SOURCES:

BOOKS

Ellison, Fred P., *Brazil's New Novel: Four Northeastern Masters, Jose Lins do Rego, Jorge Amado,* *Graciliano Ramos, Rachel de Queiroz,* Greenwood Press (Westport, CT), 1979.
Encyclopedia of World Literature in the Twentieth Century, St. James Press (Detroit, MI), 1999, p. 644.*

* * *

DORFMAN, Ariel 1942-

PERSONAL: Born May 6, 1942, in Buenos Aires, Argentina; naturalized Chilean citizen, 1967; son of Adolfo (an economist, engineer, and adviser to the government of Argentina) and Fanny (a Spanish literature teacher; maiden name, Zelicovich) Dorfman; married Maria Angelica Malinarich (an English teacher and social worker), January 7, 1966; children: Rodrigo, Joaquin. *Education:* University of Chile, Licenciado en filosofia con mencion en literatura general (summa cum laude), 1967.

ADDRESSES: Home—Durham, NC; and Santiago, Chile. *Office*—Center for International Studies, 2122 Campus Dr., Box 90404, Duke University, Durham, NC 27708-0404. *Agent*—Andrew Wylie, 250 West 57th St., Suite 2106, New York, NY 10017.

CAREER: University of California, Berkeley, research scholar, 1968-69; University of Chile, Santiago, Chile, professor of Spanish-American studies, 1970-73; exiled from Chile, 1973; Sorbonne, University of Paris, Paris, France, maitre des conferences reemplacant of Spanish-American literature, 1975-76; University of Amsterdam, Amsterdam, Holland, chief research scholar at Spaans Seminarium, 1976-80; Woodrow Wilson Center for International Scholars, Washington, DC, fellow, 1980-81; Institute for Policy Studies, Washington, DC, visiting fellow, 1981-84; Duke University, Durham, NC, visiting professor during fall semesters, 1984-89, research professor of literature and Latin American studies, 1989-96, Walter Hines Page research professor of literature and Latin American studies, 1996—. Visiting professor at University of Maryland, College Park, 1983. Coproducer of film *Death and the Maiden,* Canal Productions/Fine Line Features, 1994. Guest on television and radio news programs, including *All Things Considered, Nightline, This Week with David Brinkley, Crossfire, This Morning, Nightwatch,* and *Larry King Live;* lecturer.

MEMBER: International PEN, National Writers' Union, Sociedad de Escritores Chilenos, Drama Guild,

Academie Universelle des Cultures, Academic Freedom Committee Human Rights Watch.

AWARDS, HONORS: Award for best screenplay, Chile Films, 1972, for unproduced film *Balmaceda;* Premio Ampliado Sudamericana, *La Opinion* (Buenos Aires newspaper), 1973, for *Moros en la costa;* New American Plays award, Kennedy Center-American Express, 1988, for *Widows;* Roger L. Stevens Award, 1991, for extraordinary playwrighting; Sir Laurence Olivier Award for best play in London, 1992; Dong Award for best play of the season, 1992-93, for *Death and the Maiden;* named Literary Lion, New York Public Library, 1992; honorary degrees: L.H.D., Illinois Wesleyan University, 1989, Litt.D., Wooster College, 1991, L.H.D., Bradford College, 1993.

WRITINGS:

NOVELS

Moros en la costa (title means "The Coast Is Not Clear in Chile"), Sudamericana, 1973, translation by George R. Shivers published as *Hard Rain,* Readers International, 1990.
Viudas (also see below), Siglo XXI, 1981, translation by Stephen Kessler published as *Widows,* Pantheon Books, 1983.
La ultima cancion de Manuel Sendero, Siglo XXI, 1983, translation by Dorfman and Shivers published as *The Last Song of Manuel Sendero,* Viking, 1987.
Mascara, Viking, 1988.
Konfidenz, Planeta (Buenos Aires), 1994, English edition, Farrar, Straus (New York City), 1995.
The Nanny and the Iceberg, Farrar, Straus, 1999.

OTHER

El absurdo entre cuatro paredes: El teatro de Harold Pinter (criticism; title means "Enclosures at the Absurd: Harold Pinter's Theatre"), Universitaria, 1968.
Imaginacion y violencia en America (essays; title means "Imagination and Violence in Latin America"), Universitaria, 1970.
(With Armand Mattelart) *Para leer al Pato Donald,* Siglo Vientiuno Argentina, 1972, translation by David Kunzle published as *How to Read Donald Duck: Imperialist Ideology in the Disney Comic,* International General, 1975, 2nd edition, 1984.
Ensayos quemados en Chile: Inocencia y neocolonialismo (essays; title means "Essays Burnt in Chile: Innocence and Neocolonialism"), Ediciones de la Flor, 1974.
(With Manuel Jofre) *Superman y sus amigos del alma* (essays; title means "Superman and His Cronies"), Galerna, 1974.
Culture et resistance au Chili (essays; title means "Culture and Resistance in Chile"), Institut d'Action Culturelle, 1978.
La ultima aventura del Llanero Solitario (essays; title means " The Last Adventure of the Lone Ranger"), Universitaria Centroamericana (Costa Rica), 1979.
Cria Ojos (short stories; also see below), Nueva Imagen, 1979, translation by Dorfman and Shivers published as *My House Is on Fire* (includes "Reader"), Viking, 1990.
(Contributor) *El intelectual y el estado, Venezuela-Chile* (essays; title means "The Intellectual and the State, Venezuela-Chile"), University of Maryland, 1980.
Pruebas al canto (poems; title means "Soft Evidence"), Nueva Imagen, 1980.
Reader's nuestro que estas en la tierra: Ensayos sobre el imperialismo cultural (essays; title means "Our Readers That Art on Earth"), Nueva Imagen, 1980, translation by Clark Hansen published as *The Empire's Old Clothes: What the Lone Ranger, Babar, and Other Innocent Heroes Do to Our Minds* (includes three previously unpublished essays in English), Pantheon, 1983.
Missing (poems), translated by Edie Grossman, Amnesty International British Section, 1982.
Hacia liberacion del lector latinoamericano (essays), Ediciones del Norte, 1984.
Patos, elefantes y heroes: La infancia como subdesarrollo (essays; title means "On Ducks, Elephants, and Heroes"), Ediciones de la Flor, 1985, revised edition, Planeta, 1997.
Dorando la pildora (stories; title means "The Medicine Goes Down"), Ediciones del Ornitorrinco, 1985.
Los suenos nucleares de Reagan (nonfiction), Editorial Legasa, 1986.
Pastel de choclo (poetry), Sinfronteras, 1986, translation by Dorfman and Grossman published as *Last Waltz in Santiago and Other Poems of Exile and Disappearance* (includes selected poems originally published in *Missing*), Penguin, 1988.
Widows (two-act play based on Dorfman's novel of the same name; produced in Williamstown, MA, at the Williamstown Theatre Festival, 1988; revised version, cowritten with Tony Kushner, produced in 1991), Nick Hern Books, 1996.
Some Write to the Future: Essays on Contemporary Latin American Fiction (criticism), translated by

Dorfman and George Shivers, Duke University Press, 1991.

Cuentos casi completos (short stories), Ediciones Letra Buena (Buenos Aires), 1991.

Death and the Maiden (drama), Viking, 1992.

La obra de Ariel Dorfman: ficcion y critica, (collection), Editorial Pliegos (Madrid), 1992.

Teatro (play collection), Ediciones de la Flor (Buenos Aires), 1992.

Traverse Theatre Presents the World Premier of Reader (play; based on Dorfman's short story of the same title), Nick Hern Books (London), 1995.

(With son, Rodrigo Dorfman) *Prisoners in Time* (teleplay), British Broadcasting Corporation, 1995.

The Resistance Trilogy, Nick Hern Books, 1998.

Heading South, Looking North: A Bilingual Journey (nonfiction; biographies of exiled Chilean writers), Farrar, Straus and Giroux, 1998.

Author of plays, with son Rodrigo Dorfman, *Mascara* (based on Ariel Dorfman's novel of the same name), staged in both Germany and the United States, 1998, and *Who's Who,* staged in Germany, 1998. Also author and director, with son, Rodrigo Dorfman, of film short *My House Is on Fire,* 1997; also author of unproduced screenplay *Balmaceda,* 1972. Contributor of articles, stories, and editorials to periodicals, including *Harper's, Nation, New York Times, Los Angeles Times, Village Voice, Washington Post,* and *New York Times Sunday Magazine.*

WORK IN PROGRESS: A second part of *Heading South, Looking North,* to be titled *Heading North, Looking South;* a novella, *Therapy.*

ADAPTATIONS: Death and the Maiden was adapted as a motion picture, written by Dorfman and Rafael Yglesias, directed by Roman Polanski, starring Sigourney Weaver and Ben Kingsley, Canal Productions/Fine Line Features, 1994.

SIDELIGHTS: Argentinean-born author, journalist, and scholar Ariel Dorfman is best known for his opposition to political oppression in Chile. Since his 1973 expulsion from his adopted country for his outspoken resistance to the harsh policies of dictator Augusto Pinochet, Dorfman has produced poetry, nonfiction, short stories, and three acclaimed novels that probe the terror of dictatorship and the despair of exile. According to Robert Atwan in the *New York Times Book Review,* Dorfman's fiction displays his "ability to create methods of storytelling that enact, not merely record, a political vision, [and] that fuse both the political and the literary imaginations."

Dorfman was born in Argentina in 1942 to a family well acquainted with the pain of exile: his Jewish grandparents had escaped the pogroms in Eastern Europe, and his father, an economist, fled Argentina and took a job in New York City at the United Nations when Dorfman was two years old. Dorfman and his family spent ten years in the United States before they returned to South America, settling in Chile in 1954. Although initially averse to leaving New York, Dorfman grew to love his new country; he completed his education, married, and in 1967 became a naturalized Chilean citizen.

Dorfman established himself in Chile as a writer, publishing his first novel, *Moros en la costa,* and several nonfiction studies. These included a critical analysis of the works of English playwright Harold Pinter, a book of essays on the Latin American novel, and a 1972 collaboration with Armand Mattelart titled *Para leer al Pato Donald,* which was widely reviewed in English. Translated as *How to Read Donald Duck: Imperialist Ideology in the Disney Comic,* the book is an examination of the ways Donald Duck and other Disney characters subtly transmit capitalist ideology to their Latin American audiences, with whom the cartoons are extremely popular. A later study translated as *The Empire's Old Clothes: What the Lone Ranger, Babar, and Other Innocent Heroes Do to Our Minds* presents Dorfman's analysis of how American children's literature and popular culture also project dominant values.

Dorfman worked as an activist, journalist, and writer in Chile until 1973, when Salvador Allende's democratically elected Marxist government was overthrown by Pinochet in a U.S.-supported coup, resulting in Allende's death and the expulsion of thousands of intellectuals, writers, clergymen, and politicians from the country. After receiving death threats and witnessing the burning of his books in Santiago, Dorfman was expelled from Chile. Devastated by the loss of his citizenship and appalled by the intimidation and violence perpetrated on his countrymen by the Pinochet regime, Dorfman, after a brief stay in Argentina, settled in France. There he worked for the Chilean resistance movement in Paris and later taught Spanish-American literature at the Sorbonne.

After a period of two years during which his distress over his country's turmoil blocked his creativity and left him unable to write, Dorfman composed a group of poems expressing his thoughts about the atrocities—which included torture, murder, and abductions—he knew were still occurring in his homeland.

The poems, which were published in an English collection titled *Missing* in 1982, center on *desaparecidos,* people deemed subversive by the Chilean government and abducted ("disappeared") by secret agents. In the collection Dorfman describes the effects this practice has upon the families of the disappeared; one poem conveys the conflicting emotions of parents who receive word from a prison camp veteran that their son—whom they feared dead—is still alive but being tortured. "I discovered a way in which I could become a meeting ground of the living and the dead—a way to give voice to the missing, which was also a metaphor for the whole country and what had been irretrievably lost," Dorfman later told Leslie Bennetts of the *New York Times*. "All of my poems are ways of giving voices to those who have disappeared and those who are left behind; I am a bridge between them. Words become a way of returning to your country—a cemetery, but also a resurrection ground."

Dorfman left France in 1976 for a position as chief research scholar at the University of Amsterdam, remaining there until 1980, when he accepted a Woodrow Wilson fellowship in Washington, D.C. He returned to fiction writing, voicing his deep concern for the disappeared in a second novel, *Viudas* (*Widows*). Knowing that its highly sensitive subject would probably prevent the book's publication in Chile, he devised an elaborate scheme to have *Viudas* printed first in Europe. Using the pseudonym Eric Lohmann, Dorfman included in the manuscript a foreword—which claimed to be written by Lohmann's son—explaining that the book's author was a World War II Danish resistance fighter who had set the story in Greece in order to have it safely published in his homeland. *Viudas*'s foreword also stated that Lohmann had been killed by the Nazi secret police just days after the book's completion, and that Lohmann's son had only recently found and published the manuscript. Dorfman then planned to have the novel published first in Danish, French, or German and subsequently issued at home as a Spanish translation of the European novel. "That double distancing—of mediation through an author who was not me and a country which was not my own—allowed me to write an allegory which is simultaneously realistic, [and] a literary solution to the problem of how to write about overwhelming horror and sorrow," the author explained in an interview with Peggy Boyers and Juan Carlos Lertora in *Salmagundi*. At the last minute, however, Dorfman's Spanish-language publisher backed out; the novel was ultimately released, under Dorfman's real name, by the Mexican firm Siglo XXI in 1981. Translated in 1983, *Widows* is set in a Greek village

under the control of Nazi soldiers during World War II and centers on Sofia Angelos, a village peasant woman whose husband, father, and son have been disappeared by the military regime. Given no information about their menfolk's safety or whereabouts, Sofia and the other peasant women—whose male relatives have also been abducted—rise in opposition to the soldiers when Sofia claims an unidentifiable corpse that has washed up on the river bank is her father and demands the right to bury him.

Widows was acclaimed for its political relevance as well as for its powerful portrayal of the grief and emotional strain that disappearances put on the families of the missing. Alan Cheuse, for example, in his *New York Times Book Review* critique, compared the book's intensity and scope to that of such Greek tragedies as *Antigone* and *The Trojan Women,* and praised *Widows*'s "emotional amplitude and political resonance." Noting especially its "sharply observed details of the bereaved . . . who suffer . . . painfully," Cheuse asserted that the reader "moves [through the novel] as if in a dream of outrage among its tombs of love." *Times Literary Supplement* contributor Nicholas Rankin also admired Dorfman's work, applauding the way the author bypassed the "realist clutter of local detail" in order to create "a tragedy of universal application."

Dorfman followed *Widows* with the 1983 *La ultima cancion de Manuel Sendero,* a lengthy novel that explores the larger implications of repression and exile through several complexly interwoven narratives. "There's fantasy," Dorfman said of the book in an interview with Richard J. Meislin in the *New York Times Book Review,* "but also the very harsh terror of reality. Writers of Latin American literature, especially my generation, are constantly being pulled between two poles: what you would call the dictatorship of everyday life and the imagination of things that might come and might be." Translated as *The Last Song of Manuel Sendero,* the work unfolds through several perspectives, mainly that of unborn fetuses who have been organized into a revolt—in the form of a mass refusal to emerge from their mothers' wombs. Much of the novel contains the generation's discussions about whether it is better to shun a world full of violence and fear, or to risk birth in order to solve human problems. The babies, according to Dorfman, also serve as the book's principal metaphor. "They are the utopia that are inside each of us," the author affirmed in a *Los Angeles Times* interview with Mona Gable. "There are millions of people who are born and never born—they don't leave any change in the world. To read the novel means I want people to come away with a sense of what is unborn inside them." Other narratives in *The Last Song of Manuel Sendero* include the realistic dialogue between David and Felipe, exiled Chilean cartoonists living in Mexico and collaborating on a comic strip for their fellow expatriates; the lives of characters within David and Felipe's comic strip; and notes and scholarly commentary from a course in "Prehistoric Amerspanish III," given thirty thousand years in the future.

Critical response to *The Last Song of Manuel Sendero* was generally favorable, with reviewers commenting both on the book's complexity and on Dorfman's success in blending his political and artistic concerns. Judith Freeman, for example, in the *Los Angeles Times Book Review,* stated: "This is a demanding book, but for those who make the effort it requires, the result is a ride on a parabolic roller coaster of timely and humanitarian thought." Earl Shorris's *New York Times Book Review* critique expressed a similar assessment, noting that "after the complications of plot and puzzle have done their work, the richness of invention breaks through." Concluded Pat Aufderheide in the *Boston Review:* "every page, every insistent act of imagination is an act of resistance against the death-in-life of political oppression and the life-on-hold of exile."

In 1983, ten years after Dorfman was forced to leave Chile, Pinochet's government softened its attitude somewhat towards many of the nation's exiles, and Dorfman was allowed to return to the country temporarily; he began to split his time between living in Santiago and teaching as a visiting professor at North Carolina's Duke University. He persisted, however, in voicing his criticism of Pinochet's dictatorial policies during the next five years, both in articles and editorials in American and international publications as well as during appearances on American news programs. Although Dorfman has been given permission to return to Chile, unsettling incidents (such as Chilean news reports announcing Dorfman's death and Dorfman's unexplained detention and expulsion from the Santiago airport after which he was temporarily refused entry into the country in 1987) have made his full-time residence there unlikely as long as Pinochet remains in power.

In the late 1980s Dorfman published another volume of poetry titled *Last Waltz in Santiago and Other Poems of Exile and Disappearance* and *My House Is on Fire,* a translation of earlier short stories. He also completed the thriller *Mascara* in 1988. Written in

English and considered the least overtly political of Dorfman's novels, the story centers on personal identity as it is created, controlled, changed, and escaped by three characters—an anonymous loner who works as a photographer for an obscure government agency, an amnesiac woman with multiple personalities, and a manipulative plastic surgeon—whose monologues form the book's three sections. *Mascara* was well received by critics, who admired its compelling narration, suspenseful plot, and ambiguous ending, and compared it to the fiction of German novelists Guenter Grass and Franz Kafka. *Mascara,* noted Atwan, "is an intricately layered book [that] can be read as an ominous fairy tale, a literary horror story, a post-modern version of Jekyll and Hyde. But the book is also a parable of human identity and paranoia engendered by authoritarian politics."

Dorfman's *Some Write to the Future,* published in 1991, is a collection of his essays (some previously published) on contemporary Latin American fiction. His prose themes of violence and repression surface within critical reviews of the works of writers such as Garcia Marquez, Borges, and Arguedas. Mark I. Millington, writing for the *Modern Language Review,* found the essays "constrained" both "by their not having been revised"so as to take advantage of more current thinking, as well as Dorfman's own tendency "to work *with* the grain of the texts under analysis, so that there is a slight lack of critical edge." However, the "sense of [Dorfman's] emotional and ideological involvement. . .makes for enjoyable reading." Other critics, such as D. A. N. Jones in the *London Review of Books,* reviewed *Some Write to the Future* with an eye to this emotional involvement of Dorfman's rather than as a critical work. Commenting on his interpretation of Garcia Marquez's *Chronicle of a Death Foretold* Jones noted, "The sombre Dorfman does try to offer an optimism of the will, as well as a pessimism of the intellect."

Dorfman returned to playwriting in 1992 with his critically acclaimed piece, *Death and the Maiden.* A powerful story centered on three characters, the drama takes place in a country recently returned to a democratic government after an era of fearsome repression. Paulina is the wife of a lawyer asked to serve on a commission investigating the crimes under the previous government, including her own brutal rape by a doctor. Through her husband, she meets the man she believes raped her. She kidnaps him and decides to place him on trail for his crimes in her own home. The play, which was staged in London and New York, was later produced as a film by Roman

Polanski. The story's juxtaposition of politics and ethics was hailed by critics. John Butt in the *Times Literary Supplement* noted that "More than one critic has commented on . . . the way it unwinds with a remorseless inevitability that recalls the finest classical tragedy" and concluded "Such praise hardly seems exaggerated." Ilan Stavans, writing for *World Literature Today,* mirrored Butt's comments, finding *Death and the Maiden* to have "the taste of a tautly constructed classic."

Konfidenz, Dorfman's 1994 novel, is a story told almost entirely through dialogue. As a result, it "reveals some of the possibilities as well as some of the hazards of the mode," remarked Sven Birkert in the *New York Times Book Review.* The conversation is between Barbara and Leon/Max. Barbara has come to Paris believing that her lover Martin, who is engaged in the resistance movement, is in danger. Leon/Max identifies himself as a political friend of Martin's but seems to know the intimate details of Barbara's life. As their conversation and relationship deepen, they elaborate on Dorfman's themes of identity and trust.

Critics noted that while the tightly woven tale engages readers initially, the suspense fades as the novel progresses. Michael Kerrigan stated in the *Times Literary Supplement,* "Instead of building on the complex and dramatic situation with which he began, Dorfman unpacks it piece by piece, rendering it less complex, less dramatic with each chapter." Birkert continued, "We begin to feel the law of diminishing returns assert itself. We listen less intently and let our attention begin to drift." Kate Kellaway, writing for *The Observer,* commented, "The novel aims for the menace of Genet, but keeps being brought down by something cheaper and more ordinary, a touch of Francois Sagan or of Marguerite Duras on a bad day." Still, Dorfman's attempts at something out of the ordinary were appreciated. "The originality of Dorfman's technique is welcome proof that the experimental nature of contemporary Latin American fiction is not on the wane," declared Marie Arana-Ward in the *Washington Post Book World.* "With [this novel] Dorfman steps confidently from the realm of Latin American storyteller into the arena of a world novelist of the first category."

Despite the uncertainty about his permanent return to Chile, Dorfman continues to protest—through his writing and in person—repression and brutality in his homeland and elsewhere. Denouncing violence and offering hope through his writing that the situation in Chile will improve, Dorfman remains optimistic. "My

literature *should* be the literature of despair," Dorfman concluded to Geoffrey Stokes in the *Voice Literary Supplement,* "but always, not because I desire it, but because it comes out, I find myself telling the story of human beings who have managed to rescue dignity from the midst of terror."

Dorfman once explained "My writing has been haunted, ever since I can remember, by twin obsessions, a central paradox that I cannot be rid of: on the one hand, the glorious potential and need of human beings to tell stories; and, on the other, the brutal fact that in today's world, most of the lives that should be telling these stories are generally ignored, ravaged and silenced.

"My life has been fortunate, inasmuch as I have been able to dedicate my existence to reaching others through my imagination; and unfortunate because a great part of that life, like the life of so many others in the twentieth century of ours, has been spent under the shadow of innumerable tyrannies that thrive by denying people the possibility of communicating with each other.

"And yet, as of late, I have come to the conclusion that my writing may not be determined exclusively by the exploration, at the personal and the historical levels, of the two opposite experiences of liberation and domination, but that there is another struggle going on simultaneously in my life and in my work: the attempt to overcome distance, question its corrosion, defeat it. Wondering, all these years, how to achieve closeness. Even while recognizing that too much closeness can also be dangerous. Embraces can smother: being too near anybody, anything, too deep inside a community. We may lose ourselves in closeness—just like in distance. So that I have had to learn to use distance, use exile, use the perspective of the uprooted, to understand what otherwise I would perhaps not even have been able to see, let alone deal with.

"The struggle with distance must have begun at my birth, but as I don't remember that initial leap into life, it is with banishment that this story really starts: when, hardly more than two years old, I left my native Argentina to go to the United States in 1945. I adopted my new country as a foster homeland and its language, English, as my protector; but distance was following me, it lay in wait, and ten years later, when my father had to flee McCarthy and go to Chile, I found myself suddenly returned to Spanish and Latin America, with literature as my one secure ally against the currents and outrages of geography and death, my connection to a community that had been marginalized from history and power. Seduced by Chile and its language and by an upcoming revolution, I eventually disowned English and the United States, hoping that I could will myself into becoming monolingual, intact, immobile, hoping that distance would leave me alone. It did not: the democratically elected government of Salvador Allende was overthrown in 1973 and, like my father before me, I had to escape a dictatorship. I had to accept that I would not be able to live and die in one land forever, accept, in fact, that the word 'forever' was not meant for me: except inasmuch as I marked a page with words that could withstand the vagaries and ambiguities of a body that can be expelled one day, arrested another, welcomed on yet a different day, literature as a home in the midst of migration. The migration of words through a text bridging that other distance, with other members of this errant humanity, bringing me closer to them, allowing me to persist inside heads and hearts that I suspect exist, out there, in here, waiting to create a community of interconnected language and imagination. Political distance defeated by closeness; closeness facilitated by aesthetic distance.

"Divided and joined by politics and literature: like my work itself, my books, my plays, my films, my poems. Trying to go back home in the only way I now know, in a way that I carry with me every place I travel, in the disturbances and joyful turbulence I create in others, returning to men and women what they unknowingly have offered me, the nearby voices beyond frontiers they have loaned to my distance all these years.

"The culmination of this search has probably been *Heading South, Looking North: A Bilingual Journey.* By writing a memoir and figuring out how my life had ended up being so different from what I had planned, trying to come to terms with how and why I had survived the 1973 military takeover that fractured my existence and tore my country asunder, by looking at my two languages and cultures and continents, I feel that I have liberated myself to write in a different way, though probably always obsessed by the same themes of memory and justice, duality and resistance."

BIOGRAPHICAL/CRITICAL SOURCES:

BOOKS

Contemporary Literary Criticism, Gale (Detroit), Volume 48, 1988, Volume 77, 1993.
Hispanic Literature Criticism, Volume 1, Gale, 1994.

PERIODICALS

Booklist, April 15, 1992, p. 1496.
Books Abroad, June 27, 1978.
Boston Review, April, 1987.
Chasqui XX, May, 1991.
Chicago Tribune, March 18, 1987.
Globe and Mail (Toronto), March 4, 1989.
Harper's, December, 1989.
Index on Censorship, June, 1991.
Library Journal, April 15, 1992, p. 89.
London Review of Books, November 5, 1992, p. 30.
Los Angeles Magazine, March, 1994.
Los Angeles Times, August 7, 1987; August 16, 1987; September 16, 1987.
Los Angeles Times Book Review, June 12, 1983; April 5, 1987; October 30, 1988; January 28, 1990, pp. 3, 10.
Modern Language Review, April, 1993, p. 501.
Nation, February 11, 1978; September 24, 1983; October 18, 1986.
New Republic, May 11, 1992.
New Statesman and Society, July 10, 1992, p. 40.
New Yorker, March 30, 1992, p. 69.
New York Times, February 17, 1987; April 14, 1988; October 8, 1988.
New York Times Book Review, May 8, 1983; July 24, 1983; February 15, 1987; November 6, 1988; December 31, 1989; August 11, 1991, p. 20; December 25, 1994, p. 10.
Observer (London), June 28, 1992, p. 66; February 19, 1995, p. 19.
Publishers Weekly, October 21, 1988, pp. 39-40.
Salmagundi, spring/summer, 1989.
Spectator, July 26, 1975.
Times Literary Supplement, June 11, 1971; December 9, 1983; February 28, 1992, p. 22; June 26, 1992, p. 22; February 24, 1995, p. 20.
Tribune Books, (Chicago), July 17, 1983.
Voice Literary Supplement, September, 1982; April, 1987.
Washington Post, August 25, 1988.
Washington Post Book World, June 12, 1983; April 5, 1987; January 21, 1990; February 19, 1995.
World Literature Today, summer, 1993, p. 596.

*   *   *

DOURADO, (Waldomiro Freitas) Autran 1926-

PERSONAL: Born January 18, 1926, in Patos de Minas, Minas Gerais, Brazil; son of Telemacos (a judge) and Alice Freitas Autra Dourado. *Education:* University of Minas Law School in Belo Horizonte.

CAREER: Writer. Press secretary for Brazilian President Juscelino Kubitschek de Oliveira, 1954-59; worked for Ministry of Justice, beginning 1959.

AWARDS, HONORS: Mario Sette Prize, 1950, for *Sombra e Exilio;* Artur Azevado prize, Instituto Nacional do Livro, 1957, for *Nove historia em grupo de tres;* Brazilian Union of Writers' Fernando Chinaglia Prize, 1961, for *A barca dos homens.*

WRITINGS:

Teia, Edificio (Belo Horizonte, Brazil), 1947.
Sombre e exilio, Joao Calazans (Belo Horizonte, Brazil), 1950.
Tempo de amar, Jose Olympio (Rio de Janeiro), 1952.
Tres historias na praia, Ministerio da Educacao e Cultura, Servico de Documentatacao (Rio de Janeiro), 1955.
Nove historias em grupos de tres, Jose Olympio (Rio de Janeiro), 1957.
A barca dos homens, Editora do Autor (Rio de Janeiro), 1961.
Uma vida em segredo, Civilizacao Brasileira (Rio de Janeiro), 1964, translated by Edgar M. Miller Jr. as *A Hidden Life,* Knopf (New York City), 1969.
Opera dos mortes, Civilizacao Brasileira (Rio de Janeiro), translated by John M. Parker as *The Voices of the Dead: A Novel,* Taplinger Publishing Co. (New York City), 1981.
O risco de bordado, Expressao e Cultura (Rio de Janeiro), 1970, translated by John M. Parker as *Pattern for a Tapestry: A Novel,* P. Owen (London), 1984.
Solidao solitude, Civilizacao Brasileira (Rio de Janeiro), 1972.
Uma poetica de romance-Materia de carpinteria, Editora Perspectiva (Sao Paolo, Brazil), 1973.
Os sinos da agonia, Expressao e Cultura (Rio de Janeiro), 1974, translated by John M. Parker as *The Bells of Agony,* P. Owen (London), 1989.
Novelaria de Donga Novais, Difel (Rio de Janeiro), 1976.
Armas e coracoes, Difel (Rio de Janeiro), 1978.
Tres historias no internato: Conto, Editora Nacional (Sao Paolo), 1978.
Novelas de aprendizado, Nova Fronteira (Rio de Janeiro), 1980.
As imaginacoes pecaminosas, Record (Rio de Janeiro), 1981.

O meu mestre imaginario, Record (Rio de Janeiro), 1982.
A servico de-Rei, Record (Rio de Janeiro), 1984.
Lucas Procopio, Record (Rio de Janeiro), 1984.
Violetas e caracois, Guanabara (Rio de Janeiro), 1987.
Um artista aprendiz, Jose Olympio (Rio de Janeiro), 1989.
Monte da Alegria, Francisco Alves (Rio de Janeiro), 1990.
Um cavalheiro de antigamente, Siciliano (Rio de Janeiro), 1992.
Opera dos fantoches, Francisco Alves (Rio de Janeiro), 1995.
Confissoes de Narciso, Francisco Alves (Rio de Janeiro), 1997.

SIDELIGHTS: Brazilian author Autran Dourado has written thirteen novels, seven story collections, and critical essays, several of which are considered masterpieces. He has received international critical acclaim and has won major literary awards. As M. Angelica Lopez wrote in *Modern Latin-American Fiction Writers,* he lists Gustave Flaubert, Henry James, Franz Kafka, William Faulkner, and Joaquim Maria Machado de Assis as his literary forebears, and "presents himself as both the heir of and speaker for the golden ear of his native region, the eighteenth century, whose complexity and abundance he shares."

Dourado was born in 1926 in Patos de Minas, Minas Gerais, Brazil, the son of Telemaco Autran Dourado, a judge, and Alice Frietas Autran Dourado. From an early age, he was interested in literature, and when he attended the University of Minas Law School in Belo Horizonte, he met many other young writers. The group included Fernando Sabino, Paulo Mendes Campos, Otto Lara Resende, and film critic Savato Magaldi. Together, the group of friends began publishing a literary magazine, *Edificio* ("Building"), which only produced four issues but which also published Dourado's first major piece of writing, a novella titled *Teia* ("Web"). He had considered publishing a collection of his stories, but his friend, novelist Godofredo Rangel, had advised against it, saying that Dourado, though talented, needed to improve his technique before publishing.

Teia, according to M. Angelica Lopez in *Dictionary of Literary Biography* is "a somber book that has both the virtues and defects of 1940s and 1950s Brazilian fiction. Well constructed, with Dourado's excellent command of literary Portuguese, it presents situations and characters closer to allegory than to fiction. . . .

Like much of his later fiction, this early novella includes secrets gnawing away at family members, mystery, and a dark, oppressive atmosphere created by the dysfunctional family and reinforced by dangerous gossip."

The publication of this book was financed by Dourado's mother, as was his second book, *Sombra e exilio* ("Shadow and Exile"). As in *Teia,* the main character is a discontented young man who is tormented by his relationship with his weak mother and deceased, evil father, who still haunts him. Lopez noted that this book contains a device Dourado used in *Teia,* which would become characteristic of his fiction: "gossip as a means of thickening both plot and atmosphere. Evil characters spread gossip and reveal secrets about people they dislike, often ruining their lives."

Many critics consider *Tempo de amar* to be Dourado's first important work. Like his previous two novels, it features an intellectual but unmotivated and unchallenged son, growing up in a small, repressive town. Like other writers of his time, in this book Dourado deals with morals, sexual desires, and conflicts between generations, told from the point of view of an introverted, intellectual protagonist.

In 1954 Dourado became the press secretary for the President of Brazil, Juscelino Kubitschek de Oliveira. He held this position until 1959, when Kubitschek's term ended. At that time, he began working for the Ministry of Justice.

Dourado's novel *A barco dos homens* ("The Ship of People") was his first widely popular book. Its success led to success for the rest of his books. The book has a maritime setting, and is based on late medieval and Renaissance Portuguese writings, including sixteenth-century stories of shipwrecks. Lopez wrote, "The novel's solidity, brilliance, and pathos firmly established Dourado as a major contemporary Brazilian novelist. It includes his usual combination—love and innocence, lust, distrust, anguish, and madness—in a plot loaded with mythical and religious connections in a realistically drawn Brazilian setting, an island off the Atlantic coast."

His next book, *Um vida em segredo* ("A Hidden Life") sold better than any of his other books, and according to Dourado, was written in one month. In *Opera dos mortes* ("Voices of the Dead"), Dourado introduces the Cota family, who would appear in several more of his novels. Like Faulkner, he explores this family and their home and presents psychologically complex situations involving generations.

In 1976 Dourado published *Uma poetica de romance-Materia de carpinteria,* which is a discussion of his beliefs and methods about the construction of fiction. According to Lopez, he believes that "As both a technical construction and a mysterious constellation of metaphors, the fictional text is woven, a pattern to be deciphered, an embroidery to be read."

Dourado has since written many more novels and story collections, and continued to experiment with new techniques and challenges. Lopez, remarking on this, wrote that "Autran Dourado's opus is marked by talent, discipline, and experimentation soundly based on literary research. His awards have acted as incentives; Dourado has chosen not to rest on his brilliance or his laurels, but has instead always sought newer paths as he continued to perfect ones he had already chosen."

BIOGRAPHICAL/CRITICAL SOURCES:

BOOKS

Dictionary of Literary Biography, Volume 145: *Modern Latin-American Fiction Writers,* Gale (Detroit), 1994.*

* * *

DURAN, Roberto (Tinoco) 1953-

PERSONAL: Born May 13, 1953, in Bakersfield, CA; son of Pedro H. (a farm labor contractor) and Guadalupe Tinoco (a cannery worker) Duran; married Anna Hough, February, 1982 (separated, 1988); children: Deserie, Marcella. *Education:* Attended San Jose City College, 1972-74; San Jose State University, B.S.W., 1985. *Politics:* Democrat. *Religion:* Catholic.

ADDRESSES: Home and office—2212 Quimby Rd., San Jose, CA 95122.

CAREER: Poet. Barrio Leadership Training Program, San Jose, CA, youth supervisor, summer, 1982; Mosquitos Boys Club, San Jose, recreation manager, summer, 1985; Western Homes for Youth, San Martin, CA, house counselor, summer, 1987; Vida Nueva, San Jose, program attendant, summers, 1989—. Consultant for Mid-Peninsula Conversion Project, 1983; liaison for East San Jose jobs in energy. Secretary for Alcoholics Anonymous. Active in United Farmworkers Organization. Gives poetry readings.

AWARDS, HONORS: Received first place in contest sponsored by El Tecolote Literary Review for Poetry, San Francisco, CA, 1982.

WRITINGS:

A Friend of Sorrow, privately printed, 1980.
(With Judith Ortiz Cofer and Gustavo Perez Firmat) *Triple Crown: Chicano, Puerto Rican, and Cuban-American Poetry* (poetry anthology), Bilingual Press, 1987.
Reality Ribs, Bilingual Press (Tempe, AZ), 1993.

Contributor of poems to periodicals, including *Quarry West* and *Traces.*

WORK IN PROGRESS: A poetry collection tentatively titled *Up and Down the New Downtown;* a series of essays and short stories about the judicial system and drug abuse in certain communities.

SIDELIGHTS: Roberto Duran is a Chicano poet who wrote *Triple Crown* with fellow poets Judith Ortiz Cofer and Gustavo Perez Firmat. Writing from the perspective of a Chicano farmworker, Duran was praised for employing in the book strong metaphor and highly charged emotions. Reviewers generally found *Triple Crown* to be a valuable collection relating the hispanic experience.

Duran has also earned acclaim for his many poetry readings. "Though my poetry is my personal perception, I like to share it with others," the author told John Ramos in *El Observador*. Duran, who writes of such topics as drug abuse, police brutality, immigration, discrimination, and the justice system, related to Ramos, "I can't change things, but I can be vocal about the truth." Critics praise his readings for relating serious topics with a measure of hope.

Duran once noted of his ongoing work: "My current manuscript deals with issues and social economic realities as they affect the plight of the homeless, working poor, etcetera, of Santa Clara, California. I take a humorous yet serious look at the diversity of the Santa Clara Valley—its impact on its residents, their interaction (or non-interaction, as the case may be)—and issues of crime and punishment, especially as they relate to minorities."

BIOGRAPHICAL/CRITICAL SOURCES:

PERIODICALS

El Observador, July 30, 1986.

*   *   *

DUVALL, Aimee
  See THURLO, Aimee

E

EDWARDS BELLO, Joaquin 1886(?)-1968

PERSONAL: Born in 1886 (some sources say 1887), in Valparaiso (some sources say Santiago), Chile; died February 23, 1968. *Education:* Attended English School, Valparaiso, Chile; also educated in Europe.

CAREER: Novelist and essayist, c. 1910-35.

WRITINGS:

El inutil (novel), 1910.
Tres meses en Rio de Janeiro, 1911.
El monstruo (novel), 1912.
La tragedia del "Titanic," 1912, revised edition published as *La muerte de Vanderbilt,* 1922.
La cuna de Esmeraldo, [Paris, France], 1918.
El roto, 1920.
El Chileno en Madrid (novel), 1928.
Cap Polonio, 1929.
Valparaiso: La ciudad del viento, 1931, revised edition published as *En el viejo Almendral,* 1943.
Criollos en Paris, 1933.
La chica del Crillon, 1935.*

* * *

ELIZONDO, Salvador 1932-

PERSONAL: Born December 19, 1932, in Mexico City, Mexico; son of Salvador Elizondo Pani (a businessman) and Josefina Alcalde y Gonzalez Martinez; married Michele Alban; married Paulina Lavista (a photographer); children: (with Alban) Mariana, Pia; (with Lavista) Pablo. *Education:* Elizondo's education was fragmented and wandering; he attended the Colegio Aleman (German School) in Mexico City; later attended a private school in California and did college-prep work at the University of Ottawa in Canada; received a certificate of proficiency in English from the University of Cambridge, and traveled in Italy, France, and England, where he studied various subjects, including architecture and cinematography; later studied literature at the Universidad Nacional Autonoma de Mexico.

CAREER: Writer. Professor of literature, National University in Mexico City.

AWARDS, HONORS: Scholarships from the Centro Mexicano de Escritoires (Mexican Center for Writers), 1963-64, 1967-68.

WRITINGS:

Poemas, privately printed (Mexico City), 1960.
Luchino Visconti, Universidad Nacional Autonoma de Mexico (Mexico City), 1963.
Farabeuf, o La cronica de un instante, Joaquin Mortiz (Mexico City), 1963.
Narda o el verano, Era (Mexico City), 1966.
Salvador Elizondo, Empresas Editorials (Mexico City), 1966.
Eli Hipogee Secreto, Universidad de Guanajuato (Guanajuato, Mexico), 1969.
Cuaderno de escritura, Universidad de Guanajuato (Guanajuato, Mexico), 1969.
El retrato do Zoe y otras mentiras, Joaquin Mortiz (Mexico City), 1969.
El grafografo, Joaquin Mortiz (Mexico City), 1972.
Contextos, Secretaria de Educacion Publica (Mexico City), 1973.

Antologia personal, Fondo de Cultura Economica (Mexico City), 1974.

(Editor) *Museo poetica,* Universidad Nacional Autonoma de Mexico (Mexico City), 1974.

Miscast, o, Ha llegenda la senora Marquesa: Comedia opaca en tres actos, Oasis (Mexico City), 1981.

Regreso a casa, Universidad Nacional Autonoma de Mexico (Mexico City), 1982.

(Translator) Paul Valery, *Paul Valery,* Sepsetentas Diana (Mexico City), 1982.

Camera lucida, Joaquin Mortiz (Mexico City), 1983.

La luz que regresa, Fondo de Cultura Economica (Mexico City), 1985.

Elsinore: Un cuaderno, Ediciones del Equilibrista (Mexico City), 1988.

Teoria del infierno y otros ensayos, El Colegia Nacional/Ediciones del Equilibrista (Mexico City), 1992.

SIDELIGHTS: Stephen M. Bell, in *Modern Latin American Fiction Writers,* wrote, "to read Salvador Elizondo Alcalde is to enter a dark, difficult, seemingly private realm that does not easily yield its secrets. The author is a stubbornly idiosyncratic and disruptive figure in Mexican and Latin-American literature. . . . His works . . . are like a stage upon which he reenacts some of the more radical fictional experiments in the Western tradition, or an operating table upon which he dissects philosophical issues such as pleasure versus pain, nature versus culture, and existence in life and in writing." Elizondo has produced experimental films, written several books, and contributed to numerous literary journals; he is now a professor of literature at the National University in Mexico City. Although he is a respected literary figure in Mexico, Bell remarked that Elizondo is well known largely for his "works largely inaccessible and even threatening to the general reading public, and he remains better known as an eccentric figure than as a writer."

Elizondo was born on December 19, 1932, the only child of wealthy parents. He was taught by tutors and nannies, and attended private schools, and his education was a combination of indulgence and anarchy: he continually became interested in new areas, grew bored with them, and dropped them in favor of something else, which he would grow tired of in turn. This pattern of interest, followed by disillusionment or boredom, can be seen in his works, which, Bell remarked, "have the air of stemming from impetuous sparks of intense but short-lived inspiration."

His family encouraged his interest in art, and his uncle was Enrique Gonzalez Martinez, a well-known Mexican poet. Even when he was ten years old,

Elizondo dreamed of being a writer someday, but it would be many years before he realized this goal.

Elizondo lived with his family in Berlin from 1936 to 1929, and when they returned to Mexico City, he attended the Colegio Aleman (German School). He later attended a private school in Californa and did college-prep work at the University of Ottawa in Canada. Eventually, he received a certificate of proficiency in English from the University of Cambridge, and also traveled in Italy, France, and England, where he studied various subjects, including architecture and cinematography. Later, he studied literature at the Universidad Nacional Autonoma de Mexico.

Although in childhood he had planned to be a writer, he undertook his studies in Europe with the thought that he would become a painter. Later he became interested in film, but found that there was not much opportunity for filmmakers in Mexico, and turned his attention to writing. His writing is strongly visual, an indication of his interest in the visual arts.

As he notes in his autobiography, *Salvadore Elizondo,* he found it difficult to enter the Mexican literary scene, perhaps because he was so often far from Mexico, and perhaps because of his unsettled personality. The 1950s and 1960s were difficutl times for him, although his most productive; he lived the life of the struggling artist (although as Bell noted, this poverty-stricken life was perhaps "a role taken on more by choice than from necessity"). During this time he also and married his first wife, Michele Alban; they had two daughters, and later divorced.

In 1963-64 and in 1967-68, Elizondo received scholarships from the Centro Mexicano de Escritoires (Mexican Center for Writers). These scholarships financed the writing of his two novels. He first gained public attention with his novel *Farabeuf; o, La cronica de un instante* (*Farabeuf, or the Account of One Instant*), a novel about a nineteenth-century French anatomist, Dr. Farabeuf, and his mistress, whom he is plotting to dissect while she is still living. The book's erotic and sadistic themes are heightened by Elizondo's use of a surrealistic kaleidoscope of images, rather than a traditional cause-and-effect plot. Bell called the book "difficult and disquieting," and noted that "through repetition and variation, the novel fuses and confuses a series of scenes and motifs seemingly distant in time and space."

El hipogeo secreto ("The Secret Hypogeum") is based on the linguistic theories of philosopher Ludwig

Wittgenstein, who stated that anything that cannot be expressed in words, cannot exist, and that therefore, language cannot be used to discuss metaphysics. Like *Farabeuf*, this novel does not have a plot, but is a series of poetic images that convey how an author feels as he creates his work of art. The primary tension in the book is derived from the unbridgeable distance between the author's ideal vision of the finished work and the actual work, which falls short, indicating that perfection and absolute truth are unattainable goals.

In *El grafografo*, Elizondo presents several short texts that Bell described as "arguably the most representative of Elizondo's works." Difficult to categorize, these experimental pieces shade from essay to short story to prose poem, and as Bell wrote, they "can easily seem pointless or unbearably self-satisfied." Writing is the topic of these pieces, and many of them are self-referential or paradoxical: as Bell remarked, "they mean just what they say, but what they say seems to mean nothing." The pieces comment on themselves, short-circuiting the links between the writer, reader, and literary critic: an example is "Mnemothrepos," which presents several variations of one passage, with commentaries critiquing each one in detail. Interestingly, Elizondo's commentaries on his own writing are typically harsh.

Narda; o, El Verano ("Narda; or, Summertime") is a collection of short stories whose styles reveal the authors who influenced Elizondo, particularly Edgar Allen Poe and Jorge Luis Borges. *Elsinore: Un cuaderno* ("Elsinore: A Notebook") is Elizondo's most recent fictional work. A combination of novella and memoir, it describes the author's adolescent experiences at a private military academy in California during World War II. The narrator, son of a wealthy Mexican family, meets immigrant laborers from Mexico who have been drafted to serve in the war, and has to confront the distance he feels from them as a result of his wealth and privilege. The book is more traditionally structured and conventional than his previous works, although it treats some of the same themes, including the search for meaning in life; the connection between writing and life; authority and rebellion; and the accidents of fate and class.

In recent years, Elizondo has not written as much, but his reputation is undiminished. Despite his unconventional education and youth, Elizondo has settled down to a more stable life with his second wife, photographer Paulina Lavista, and their son in Coyoacan, Mexico. He writes, teaches part-time, speaks, and is a member of several editorial boards and honor societies. He is proud of the acceptance he has gained among academics. As Bell noted, "In these appointments perhaps he has found some measure of vindication for having dared to be different, for confronting the darker side of our existence in his writing, or for his early struggles and general isolation in Mexican culture."

BIOGRAPHICAL/CRITICAL SOURCES:

BOOKS

Dictionary of Literary Biography, Volume 145: *Modern Latin-American Fiction Writers*, Gale (Detroit), 1994.
Klein, Leonard S., editor, *Encyclopedia of World Literature in the Twentieth Century*, Continuum (New York City), 1993.*

*   *   *

ENRIQUEZ de SALAMANCA, Cristina 1952-

PERSONAL: Born March 8, 1952, in Madrid, Spain; daughter of Fernaudo Enriquez de Salamanca (a plastic surgeon) and Pilar Celada (a homemaker); married Steve L. Etteuheim (marriage ended); married Carlos Pedros Alio, July 26, 1995. *Education:* Universidad Autonoma de Madrid, law degree, 1976; University of Minnesota, M.A., 1990, Ph.D., 1994.

ADDRESSES: Home—Barcelona, Spain.

CAREER: Law office of Rafael Burgos, Madrid, Spain, associate, 1976-77; law office of Jaime Miralles and Manuel Miralles, Madrid, Spain, partner, 1978-79; U.S. Federal Government, Fort Macoy, WI, bilingual interpreter, 1980; Hata Reservations, Inc., Madison, WI, bilingual interpreter, 1980-82; Institutos Eurocentres Barcelona, Barcelona, Spain, teacher of Spanish as a second language, 1983, 1984, 1992-94; Universidad Autonoma de Barcelona, Barcelona, independent research associate at Women's Studies Center, 1984-88; Sanyo Spain, Spain, teacher of Spanish for foreign employees, 1984-85; Yale University, New Haven, CT, visiting assistant professor of Spanish and Portuguese, 1995-96; Middlebury College, Middlebury, VT, professor of Spanish, 1996; University of California, San Diego, lecturer in Spanish literature, 1996—.

MEMBER: American Association of Teachers of Spanish and Portuguese, Feministas Unidas, International Federation of University Women, Midwest Modern Language Association, Modern Language Association of America, North American Catalan Society.

AWARDS, HONORS: Grant, Instituto de la Mujer, Ministerio de Cultura, 1984; grant, Diputacio de Barcelona, 1986; block grants, Department of Spanish and Portuguese committee on graduate studies, two in 1988, one in 1989; international fellow, American Association of University Women Educational Foundation, 1990; grants, Program for Cultural Cooperation, Spain-U.S.A., two in 1990.

WRITINGS:

(Editor with Kathleen McNerney) *Double Minorities of Spain: A Bio-Bibliographical Guide to Women Writers of Catalonia, Galicia, and the Basque Country,* Modern Language Association of America (New York City), 1994.

(Contributor and editor with Catherine Jagoe and Alda Blanco) *La mujer en los discursos de genero del siglo XIX: Textos y contextos,* Editorial Siglo XXI (Madrid, Spain), 1997.

Contributor to books, including *Dictionary of the Literature of the Iberian Peninsula,* edited by German Bleiberg, Maureen Ihrie, and Janet Perez, Greenwood Press (London), 1993; *Spanish Women Writers: A Bio-Bibliographical Sourcebook,* edited by Gloria Walman, Ellen Engelson, and Linda Levine, Greenwood Press, 1993; and *Maria de Zayas: The Dynamics of Discourse,* edited by A. R. Williamsen and J. A. Whitenak, Associated University Presses (Cranbury, NJ), 1995.

Contributor of articles and reviews to periodicals, including *Chasqui, El Pais, Hispania, Letras Peninsulares, Monographic Review/Revista Monografica, Revista Canadiense de Estudios Hispanicos, Revista de Estudios Hispanicos,* and *World Literature Today.*

Translator of books from English into Spanish, including *Early Life,* by L. Margulis and *Molecular Biology,* by M. Freifelder.

WORK IN PROGRESS: Under the Mother's Gaze, on domesticity in nineteenth-century Spain.

ESCOTO, Julio 1944-

PERSONAL: Born February 28, 1944, in San Pedro Sula, Cortes, Honduras; son of Pedro Escoto Lopez (a newspaper publisher) and Concepcion Borjas de Escoto; married Nohemi Cordova Santos, 1964 (divorced, 1975); married Gypsy Silverthorne Turcios, c. 1976 (died, 1990); children: (first marriage) Julio Guillermo, Carlos Adolfo, Jorge Enrique. *Education:* Received teaching degree from La Escuela Superior del Profesorado, 1964; University of Florida at Gainesville, B.A., 1971; participant in International Writing Program, University of Iowa, 1975; Universidad de Costa Rica, magister literarum degree (with honors), 1984.

ADDRESSES: Home—San Pedro Sula, Honduras. *Agent*—c/o Editorial Guaymuras, Calle Adolfo Zuniga No. 1227, Apdo 1843, Teguecigalpa, Honduras.

CAREER: High school Spanish teacher in Honduras, 1965-69; Escuela Superior del Profesorado, Tegucigalpa, Honduras, professor of grammar, 1972; Banco Central de Honduras (Central Bank of Honduras), director of publications, early 1970s; Universidad Nacional Autonoma de Honduras (UNAH), professor of Spanish, Latin-American and Honduran literature, 1972-76, and chair of department of languages and literature, 1974-76; CSUCA (Council of Universities of Central America), San Jose, Costa Rica, director of cultural development, 1976; EDUCA (Editorial Universitaria Centroamericana), San Jose, director, 1977-80; Instituto Interamericano de Cooperacion Agricola (Inter-American Institute of Agricultural Cooperation), Coronado, Costa Rica, various positions, including director of the editorial board, 1980-86; founder of the publishing house Centro Editorial, San Pedro Sula, 1987, and director, 1987—; founder of literary review *Imaginacion,* 1989. Also served as editor of the reviews *Turrialba* and *Desarrollo Rural de Centro America* ("Rural Development in Central America"), in the 1980s. Organizer of workshops on cultural identity in Honduras in the 1990s.

AWARDS, HONORS: Second prize, Froylan Turcios competition, Escuela Superior del Profesorado, 1967, for *Los guerreros de Hibueras;* Premio Nacional de Literatura del Estado de Honduras (Honduran National Literary Prize), 1974; Gabriel Miro Prize, Spain, 1983, for the short story "Abril antes del mediodia"; presented with a plaque by President Rafael Leonardo Callejas of Honduras, c. 1992, for

El general Morazan marcha a batallar desde la muerte.

WRITINGS:

Los guerreros de Hibueras (novel; title means "The Warriors of Hibueras"), Lopez (Tegucigalpa, Honduras), 1967.

La balada del herido pajaro y otros relatos, Universidad Nacional Autonoma de Honduras, (Tegucigalpa), 1968.

El arbol de los panuelos (novel; title means "The Tree of Handkerchiefs"), Editorial Universitaria Centroamericana (San Jose, Costa Rica), 1972.

(Editor) *Antologia de la poesia amorosa en Honduras* (title means "Honduran Love Poetry: An Anthology"), Banco Central de Honduras (Tegucigalpa), 1974.

Casa del agua (essays; title means "House of Water"), Banco Central de Honduras (Tegucigalpa), 1975.

(With Gypsy Silverthorne Turcios) *Descubrimiento y conquista para ninos,* Editorial Universitaria Centroamericana (San Jose), 1979.

(With Gypsy Silverthorne Turcios) *Los Mayas* (nonfiction), Editorial Universitaria Centroamericana (San Jose), 1979.

Dias de ventisca, noches de huracan (novel; title means "Days of Wind, Nights of Hurricane"), Nueva Decada (San Jose), 1980.

Bajo el almendro . . . junto al volcan (novel; title means "Under the Almond Tree . . . Next to the Volcano"), Centro Editorial (San Pedro Sula, Honduras), 1988.

Jose Cecilio del Valle: Una etica contemporanea (nonfiction; title means "Jose Cecilio del Valle: A Contemporary Ethic"), Fundacion para el Museo del Hombre Hondureno (Tegucigalpa), 1990.

El ojo santo: La ideologia en las religiones y la television (nonfiction; title means "The Holy Eye: Ideology in Religion and Television"), Universidad Nacional Autonoma de Honduras (Tegucigalpa), 1990.

El general Morazan marcha a batallar desde la muerte (title means "General Morazan Comes Back to Fight from His Death"; novel), Centro Editorial (San Pedro Sula), 1992.

Rey del albor: Madrugada (title means "King of the Dawn: Madrugada"; novel) Centro Editorial (San Pedro Sula), 1993.

Also author of "Resistir. No resistir. La resistencia. Por que la resistencia?," in *Antologia del cuento hondureno,* edited by Oscar Acosta and Roberto Sosa, Universidad Nacional Autonoma de Honduras, 1968; and "Relato primero del fotografo loco," in *Antologia del cuento centroamericano,* edited by Sergio Ramirez, Editorial Universitaria Centroamericana, 1973. Author of preface to *Tierras, mares y cielos,* by Juan Ramon Molina, Editorial Universitaria Centroamericana, 1976.

Escoto's piece "Abril antes del mediodia," originally published in *Premio "Gabriel Miro"* in Spain in 1983, and included in the author's story collection *La balada del herido pajara* ("Dance of the Wounded Bird), 1985, was translated by Alberto Huerta and published as "High Noon in April" in *Clamor of Innocence: Stories from Central America,* edited by Barbara Paschke and David Volpendesta, City Lights Books (San Francisco), 1988, and also translated by Gregory Rabassa as "April in the Forenoon" in *And We Sold the Rain: Contemporary Fiction from Central America,* edited by Rosario Santos, Four Walls Eight Windows (New York City), 1988.

SIDELIGHTS: Honduran academic Julio Escoto is the acclaimed author of several works of both fiction and nonfiction that address his country's historical, political, and social legacies and currents. In 1974, after just a few published titles, Escoto won the Premio Nacional de Literatura del Estado de Honduras, or Honduran National Literary Prize, marking him as one of Latin America's new generation of rising literary talents. Almost none of Escoto's work has been translated into English, however, with the exception of the 1983 short story "Abril antes del mediodia," published in two 1988 anthologies.

Escoto was born in 1944 in San Pedro Sula, Honduras, one of eight children in a middle-class family. His father, who published a local newspaper for a time, had been a revolutionary soldier against a despotic government in Honduras in the 1920s. Both this and his father's Lenca Indian heritage would provide rich inspiration for Escoto early in his career as a novelist. He penned his first short story for a high school magazine after fearing that he had run over a child one evening when he first learned how to drive, and the piece won praise from his peers and teachers alike. Encouraged, Escoto wrote and published a second short story before he even arrived at college.

Escoto attended a teachers' training college in Tegucigalpa, the Honduran capital, receiving his degree in 1964. Between the years 1965 and 1969 he taught high school Spanish and began a family with his first wife, whom he had married in 1964. His first novel, *Los guerreros de Hibueras,* was published in 1967 after he submitted it to a national competition and it took second prize. "The Warriors of Hibueras" were men like his father who fought as guerrillas in the 1920s, and their brutal and bloody experiences are related in the spent narrative voices of the book, illustrating the ultimately dehumanizing aspects of war on individuals. "Even though the characters in *Los guerreros de Hibueras* are trying to achieve a social change that would bring better times for them and their families, their efforts are enormously destructive," explained *Dictionary of Literary Biography* essayist Amanda Castro-Mitchell. "These warriors have developed a strong sense of solidarity among themselves but at the same time are unaffected by the smell of their enemies' burning corpses."

Escoto's second novel, *El arbol de los panuelos* ("The Tree of Handkerchiefs"), appeared in 1972 at a time when he was beginning a new dual career—as director of publications for Central Bank of Honduras and as a professor at the Universidad Nacional Autonoma de Honduras—and while continuing to write fiction. The work was inspired by a trip he took to a noted mystical Honduran village, Ilama, also the birthplace of his Lenca grandmother. The novel addresses the struggle for a Honduran identity through the fictional portrayal of an actual nineteenth-century independence fighter named Balam Cano. The hero believes his father was a *brujo,* or witch, and attempts to merge both sides of his heritage—the rational and dogmatic Spanish with the mysticism of the Mayan indigenous peoples. Through his hero's conflicts Escoto addresses the plight of the *mestizo,* as Hondurans of mixed Indian and Spanish ancestry like himself are called. Mayan spirituality, which allows for moral dualism, contrasted with the Roman Catholicism imposed by the Spaniards, is another significant issue addressed in the novel; a Catholic priest is depicted as notably brutal and hypocritical.

After the outbreak of war between El Salvador and Honduras in 1969, Escoto moved to the United States and earned a degree from the University of Florida, then returned to Tegucigalpa's Universidad Nacional. In 1974 he edited the first anthology of love poetry from Honduran writers, *Antologia de la poesia amorosa en Honduras.* A collection of his essays, *Casa del agua* ("House of Water"), was published in 1975. Around this same time Escoto was invited to take part in the International Writing Program at the University of Iowa, then returned once more to Tegucigalpa in 1975. Shortly afterward he divorced

his first wife and married Gypsy Silverthorne Turcios, with whom he would co-edit a number of nonfiction titles, such as the 1979 work *Los Mayas.*

Mid-career as both a writer and leading Latin American intellectual figure, Escoto became engaged in many projects and professional activities. He chaired the department of languages and literature at the Universidad Nacional Autonoma de Honduras until 1976, then moved to Costa Rica for a decade as a result of Honduras's conflicts with El Salvador and later Nicaragua. In the Costa Rican capital of San Jose, Escoto served as director of a consortium of Central America's university presses, the Editorial Universitaria Centroamericana, an important institution in region's contemporary literary scene. After 1980 he worked for the Costa Rican-based Inter-American Institute of Agricultural Cooperation.

In 1980 his first novel in several years, *Dias de ventisca, noches de huracan* ("Days of Wind, Nights of Hurricane"), appeared in Costa Rica. Its publication was censored in Honduras because of the highly critical stance it takes toward the left-wing movement in both Honduras and the entire Latin American region. Escoto's time in Costa Rica, and his wide range of contacts with other Latin American writers and activists, had given him a considerably less nationalistic perspective on the politics of the region. "Escoto's broader vision gave him the ability to see what was really happening inside the Honduran left-wing movement, where factional leaders squandered their time criticizing other left-wing groups," wrote Castro-Mitchell in her essay in *Dictionary of Literary Biography.* "Living outside Honduras, Escoto could see the artificiality of the leftist movements of Honduras, and he attempted to portray this vision in *Dias de ventisca, noches de huracan.*"

Another work of Escoto's that dealt with the destruction that war wreaks upon the human spirit was the 1983 short story "Abril antes del mediodia," which was awarded Spain's Gabriel Miro Prize. Translated into English in two versions—"High Noon in April" and "April in the Forenoon"—it was published in the United States, respectively, in two 1988 collections, *Clamor of Innocence: Stories from Central America* and *And We Sold the Rain: Contemporary Fiction from Central America.*

A parliamentary democracy returned to Escoto's homeland in 1982, and with the realization that his teenage sons were rapidly losing their sense of Honduran heritage, the writer and Silverthorne Turcios returned in 1986. They settled in Escoto's hometown of San Pedro Sula, and he launched an editorial house the following year. Renewed, he also returned to writing fiction. The terrifying experiences of the summer of 1969, when he, his first wife, and three young sons were living in a residential area of Tegucigalpa that came under fire, would provide the basis for his 1988 novel *Bajo el almendro . . . junto al volcan* ("Under the Almond Tree . . . Next to the Volcano").

Bajo el almendro opens with Centella, an aging veteran of the 1920s strife, preparing a peasant militia as war between Honduras and El Salvador looms in 1969. A town mayor, Centella is fanatically prepared to die to defend his country once more, a sentiment the safely-ensconced political leaders know they can exploit. The peasants are depicted as decent Honduran citizens opposed to killing on simple moral grounds. At one point Centella and his men nearly kill their town's tailor—a Salvadoran who has lived there for several years—for mistaking the clicks of his sewing machine for a spy's telegraph device. The novel, wrote Castro-Mitchell, "is probably Escoto's most merciless social criticism; moral, religious, and ideological conventions of Honduran society are examined ironically and sarcastically and by juxtaposing differing concepts of nationalism, honesty, decency, and democracy." Centella sees the real horror of war when the achievements he could once boast of as mayor are handily destroyed by the Honduran army itself; in the end he and his wife join the newer generation in their attempt to wage *la guerra de la paz,* or "the war of peace."

After publishing two works of nonfiction in 1990—*El ojo santo: La ideologia en las religiones y la television* ("The Holy Eye: Ideology in Religion and Television") and *Jose Cecilio del Valle: Una etica contemporanea* ("Jose Cecilio del Valle: A Contemporary Ethic")—Escoto wrote what would become the most important book of his career to date. The 1992 novel *El general Morazan marcha a batallar desde la muerte* ("General Morazan Comes Back to Fight from His Death") is based upon an actual historical figure who led Honduras to independence from Spain in 1821 and created a solid, seventeen-year Central American Federation. Escoto's book quickly became a sensation in Honduras and sold ten thousand copies in just three months.

El general Morazan begins with the hero's execution and then recounts his life story from the other side of this experience. "Although the reader receives an enormous quantity of historical data, it is presented by Morazan in such a manner that the reader is drawn as much to Morazan's own views of the battles as to the historical events," wrote Castro-Mitchell in the *Dictionary of Literary Biography* essay. Castro-Mitchell also explained that the 1990 death of Escoto's second wife awakened in him a deeper sense of the spiritual, in particular each individual's mission in life. As his hero Morazan remarks, "death . . . does not exist; it is only a step taken by our imperfect qualities into the place where truth resides. . . . We swim in a cosmic emptiness where love surrounds us and gives us essence made transparent by the light."

Honduras's president, Rafael Leonardo Callejas, conferred upon Escoto a plaque honoring the author and his *El general Morazan* for reawakening interest in this period of Central American history. Escoto remains head of his own publishing house, Centro Editorial, in San Pedro Sula, and is involved in the children's cultural foundation and community center that Silverthorne Turcios established before her death. Escoto's 1993 novel, *Rey del albor: Madrugada* ("King of the Dawn: Madrugada") addresses Honduran cultural identity as well as the wider Central American sense of alliance.

BIOGRAPHICAL/CRITICAL SOURCES:

BOOKS

Dictionary of Literary Biography, Volume 145: *Modern Latin-American Fiction Writers,* Gale (Detroit), 1994.*

*   *   *

ESPAILLAT, Rhina P. 1932-

PERSONAL: Born January 20, 1932, in Santo Domingo, Dominican Republic; naturalized U.S. citizen; daughter of Homero and Dulce Maria (Batista) Espaillat; married Alfred Moskowitz, June 28, 1952; children: Philip Elias, Warren Paul; foster-children: Gaston W. Dubois. *Ethnicity:* "Hispanic." *Education:* Hunter College, B.A., 1953; Queens College, M.S.E., 1964. *Avocational interests:* Drawing, gardening, needlework.

ADDRESSES: E-mail—espmosk@juno.com.

CAREER: Teacher and poet. New York City public schools, teacher, 1953-54; Jamaica High School, Jamaica, NY, teacher, 1965-80; New York City Board of Education, consultant, 1984-89.

MEMBER: Academy of American Poets, Women Poets of New York, Poets & Writers, Fresh Meadows Poets, Poetry Society of America, Powow River Poets, New England Poetry Club, Newburyport Art Association.

AWARDS, HONORS: Gustav Davidson Memorial Award, Poetry Society of America, 1986 and 1989; Croton Review Annual Award, 1987; T. S. Eliot Prize, 1998, for *Where Horizons Go; Sparrow* Sonnet Award, 1997; Howard Nemerov Sonnet Award, 1998; also recipient of awards from *Orbis, Lyric, Amelia,* and The World Order of Narrative and Formalist Poets.

WRITINGS:

Lapsing to Grace: Poems and Drawings, Bennett & Kitchel (East Lansing, MI), 1992.
Where Horizons Go, Thomas Jefferson University Press (Kirksville, MO), 1998.

Contributor of poetry to anthologies and textbooks, including *Looking for Home: Women Writing about Exile,* Milkweed Editions, 1990; *In Other Words: Literature by Latinas of the United States,* Arte Publico Press, 1994; *A Formal Feeling Comes: Poems in Form by Contemporary Women,* Story Line Press, 1994; *Patchwork of Dreams: Voices from the Heart of the New America,* The Spirit That Moves Us Press, 1996; *Anthology of Magazine Verse & Yearbook of American Poetry,* Monitor Book Co., 1997; and *The Muse Strikes Back: A Poetic Response by Women to Men,* Story Line Press, 1997.

Contributor of poetry to numerous periodicals and journals, including *American Scholar, Commonwealth, Ekphrasis, Formalist, Hellas, Ladies' Home Journal, Lyric, Manhattan Poetry Review, New York Times, Orbis, Piedmont Literary Review, Pivot, Plains Poetry Journal, Poet Lore, Poetry,* and *Voices International.*

ADAPTATIONS: Various poems have been set to music and used as part of visual art works.

WORK IN PROGRESS: Seeking publication for four completed manuscripts; contributing twenty poems to the collection *Landscapes with Women: Four American Poets,* for Singular Speech Press.

SIDELIGHTS: "I began writing at the age of six, in Spanish," explained Dominican-born poet Rhina P. Espaillat, "inspired by my paternal grandmother, who loved—and wrote—poetry, but never published any. At seven, as the daughter of political exiles in the United States, I learned English and by eight had begun to write in my second and now dominant language, but have retained fluency in Spanish and publish poems in both languages.

"Early and enduring influences on my English-language poetry include the Elizabethans, the Metaphysical poets of the seventeenth century, Emily Dickinson, Thomas Hardy, A. E. Houseman, Charlotte Mew, and such twentieth-century poets as Robert Frost, W. B. Yeats, W. H. Auden, Edna St. Vincent Millay, Sara Teasdale, Elinor Wylie and Stanley Kunitz.

"While there are many individual poems in free or experimental forms that I love, the poems that I return to with the greatest satisfaction tend to be formal, metrical and consciously musical. I've never believed that strict form hampers communication, but feel, in fact, that formal constraints serve to stimulate the imagination, liberate it from the commonplace, and heighten the exressivity of language by subjecting it to tension that charges and enriches it. I am heartened and delighted to note that formal verse has begun to come back into favor as one of the legitimate choices available to the poet.

"When I advise young poets, as I do often as teacher and workshop leader, my advice is always the same: read a great deal, roam the centuries in your reading, be aware of how language is used in what you read, write for the ear as well as the mind and heart, and revise your work as if it were not yours."

F

FELICIANO, Hector 1952(?)-

PERSONAL: Born c. 1952, in Puerto Rico; son of a doctor and a homemaker. *Education:* Brandeis University, degree in history, 1974; three literature degrees from the University of Paris.

ADDRESSES: Agent—c/o Basic Books, 10 East 53rd St., New York, NY 10022.

CAREER: Journalist. World Media Network (newspaper syndicate), New York City, editor–in–chief; worked for the City of Paris Cultural Affairs Bureau, Paris, France; journalist for the *Washington Post,* Washington, DC, and the *Los Angeles Times,* Los Angeles, CA; also worked as an investigator of stolen art and a lecturer.

WRITINGS:

NONFICTION

(With Didier Senecal and others) *A New York* (guide book in the Guides Bleus Visa Series), Hachette (Paris, France), 1988.

Musee disparu, [Paris, France], 1995, translated by the author and published in English as *The Lost Museum: The Nazi Conspiracy to Steal the World's Greatest Works of Art,* Basic Books (New York City), 1997.

Contributor to periodicals, including *Le Monde* and the *New York Times.*

WORK IN PROGRESS: A follow-up to *The Lost Museum: The Nazi Conspiracy to Steal the World's Greatest Works of Art.*

SIDELIGHTS: A former journalist, Hector Feliciano researched the Nazi confiscation of art owned by European Jews and wrote *The Lost Museum: The Nazi Conspiracy to Steal the World's Greatest Works of Art,* first published in France as *Musee disparu* in 1995, and published in the United States in 1997. *The Lost Museum* focuses on five prominent Jewish families in France who had valuable art stolen by the Nazis and their collaborators.

Feliciano asserts that the Nazis had help confiscating the works of art. In the beginning of *The Lost Museum,* he states that the Nazis were assisted "by an intricate network of collaborators, moving companies, neighbors, and house servants who informed them." Crucial collaborators included French art dealers and Swiss government officials. In the case of one Jewish family's collection, two Parisian antique dealers agreed to reveal to the Nazis the location of that family's collection of nineteenth-century art if the Nazis paid them ten percent of the net worth of the collection. Feliciano also attempts to track where the art was taken and found that much of it initially ended up in the Jeu de Paume, a small museum that also served as a Nazi administration building and as the site of many art transactions. One art dealer with German citizenship purchased quite a few paintings and sold them to several buyers, making them difficult to trace after World War II.

Feliciano also focuses on prominent Nazi politician Hermann Goering's famous appetite for fine art at any expense. According to the author, Goering would interrupt or reschedule official Nazi business to travel and purchase confiscated art, often using his official train for the purpose. During the war many Germans who could afford to purchase these valuable works of art had ample opportunity to do so.

Feliciano also outlines the role of the Swiss government in facilitating the stealing and reselling of the confiscated art. According to the author, the Swiss government ignored the large amount of confiscated art entering the country. Swiss citizens who purchased the stolen art were protected under Swiss law, as Swiss political neutrality prevented postwar investigators from prosecuting many of these buyers. Switzerland's justice system found Swiss art collector Emil G. Buehrle guilty of buying art stolen from dealer Paul Rosenberg, but Buehrle was able to keep other art obtained through questionable means, such as works he acquired from the collection of another French Jew, Alphonse Kann.

When *Lost Museum* was first published in France in 1995, it prompted a number of family descendants to pursue claims for stolen art. While many of these families suspected that their art might be on display in a number of museums, lawsuits were tougher and more turbulent when the art was found to have ended up in the ownership of a private individual. Many of the lawsuits were still in litigation in the late 1990's.

A *Publishers Weekly* reviewer found Feliciano's style in *The Lost Museum* somewhat "self-aggrandizing," as if he didn't realize the importance of his topic, yet the same reviewer had also noted that Feliciano "has certainly done his legwork" in researching the stolen art. Gordon A. Craig, writing in the *New York Review of Books,* noted that the book "has some of the elements of a good detective story," while *Art in America* contributor Michael FitzGerald noted that "Feliciano's real contribution is his dogged pursuit of the trail of lost art works."

BIOGRAPHICAL/CRITICAL SOURCES:

BOOKS

The Lost Museum: The Nazi Conspiracy to Steal the World's Greatest Works of Art, Basic Books, 1997.

PERIODICALS

Art in America, February, 1998, pp. 33, 35.
Booklist, June 1, 1997, pp. 1639-1640.
Library Journal, August, 1997, p. 105.
Milwaukee Journal Sentinel, September 23, 1998.
New York Review of Books, October 9, 1997, pp. 27-29.

New York Times, June 18, 1997, p. C17; November 4, 1997.
Publishers Weekly, April 28, 1997, p. 59.*

*   *   *

FELIPE, Leon   1884-1968

PERSONAL: Original name, Leon Felipe Camino Galicia; born April 11, 1884, in Tabara, Spain; died September 18, 1968, in Mexico City, Mexico; married Berta Gamboa (a professor), 1925 (died, c. 1958). *Education:* Institute of Santander, Spain, earned bachelor's degree; earned advanced degree in Madrid, Spain, c. 1908; attended Columbia University in mid-1920s.

CAREER: Writer. Worked as pharmacist in Spain in 1910s; member of theatre companies in the 1910s; hospital administrator on Fernando Po Island, 1920-22; Berlitz School, New York City, Spanish teacher, c. 1925; Cornell University, Ithaca, NY, lecturer in Spanish language and literature, 1925-29; New Mexico Highlands University, Las Vegas, teacher, 1933; National University, Mexico City, Mexico, teacher, c. 1934; cultural attache for Spanish Embassy and professor at a university in Panama, 1936; Casa de Espana (became Colegio de Mexico), Mexico City, teacher, c. 1939-45. Director of radio acting troupe for Office of Public Education in Mexico, c. 1933; co-founded the journal *Cuadernos Americanos,* c. 1941.

WRITINGS:

FICTION AND VERSE

Versos y oraciones de caminante (poetry; title means "Poems and Prayers of a Traveler"), Volume 1, Torres (Madrid), 1920, Volume 2, Instituto de las Espanas (New York City), 1930.
Drop a Star: Poema (poetry), Ortega (Mexico City, Mexico), 1933.
Vendra una espada de luz, published anonymously, [Veracruz, Mexico], 1933.
Antologia (poetry; title means "Anthology"), Espasa-Calpe (Madrid), 1935.
La insignia: Alocucion poematica (poetry), Tipografia Moderna (Valencia), 1937.
Poesia revolucionaria, Oficinas de propaganda (Barcelona), 1937.
El payaso de las bofetadas y el pescador de cana: Poema tragico espanol (poetry; title means "The

Battered Clown and Cane-Pole Fisherman: Tragic Spanish Poems"), Fondo de Cultura Economica (Mexico City), 1938.

El hacha: Elegia espanola (poetry; title means "The Axe: Spanish Elegies"), Letras de Mexico (Mexico City), 1939.

Espanol del exodo y del llanto: Doctrina, elegias y canciones (title means "The Spaniard of the Exodus and the Flood of Tears"), Casa de Espana (Mexico City), 1939.

El gran responsable: Grito y salmo (title means "The Great Responsible One"), Tezontle (Mexico City), 1940.

Los lagartos (title means "The Lizards"), Editorial Huh (Merida de Yucatan, Mexico), 1941.

Ganaras la luz: Biografia, poesia y destino (poetry; title means "You Will Win the Light"), Cuadernos Americanos (Mexico City), 1943.

Antologia rota (poetry; title means "Fragmented Anthology"), Pleamar (Buenos Aires, Argentina), 1947, revised edition, Losada (Buenos Aires), 1957, revised edition published as *Nueva antologia rota,* Finisterre (Mexico City), 1974.

Llamadme publicano (poetry; title means "Call Me a Publican"), Almendros (Mexico City), 1950.

La manzana (play; title means "The Apple"), Tezontle, 1951.

El asesino del sueno (play; adaptation of *Macbeth* by William Shakespeare; title means "The Dream Murderer"), Finisterre, 1954.

No es cordero . . . que es cordera (play; adaptation of *Twelfth Night* by William Shakespeare; title means "Not a Ram . . . but a Ewe"; produced in 1953), Cuadernos Americanos, 1955.

El ciervo: Poema (poetry; title means "The Stag"), Grijalbo (Mexico City), 1958.

Dos obras: La mordida y Tristan e Isolda (title means "Two Plays: A Piece of the Action and Tristan and Isolde"), Coleccion Teatro de Bolsillo (Mexico City), 1958.

Cuatro poemas con epigrafe y colofon (title means "Four Poems with an Epigraph and a Colophon"), Papeles de Son Armadans (Madrid), 1958.

El Juglaron (plays and comic sketches; title means "The Teller of Tall Tales"; includes *Dos obras: La mordida y Tristan e Isolda*), Ecuador (Mexico City), 1961.

Dire como murio, Ediciones 5 Regimiento (San Salvador, El Salvador), 1961.

Que se hizo el Rey Don Juan?, Ecuador, 1962.

Obras completas, Losada, 1963.

Oh, este viejo y roto violin! (poetry; title means "Oh, This Old and Broken Violin!"), Tezontle, 1966.

Antologia y homenaje, Finisterre, c. 1967.

Biblioteca Leon Felipe, eight volumes, Malaga (Mexico City), 1967-74.

Rocinante, Finisterre, 1969.

Oh, el barro, el barro!, Finisterre, 1970.

Israel, Finisterre, 1970.

The Living Voice of Leon Felipe (selected poetry), translated by Dorothy Prats, D. Prats (Cuernavaca, Mexico), 1973.

Versos del mercolico o del sacamuelas, Finisterre, 1974.

Obra poetica escogida (title means "Selected Poetry"), edited by Gerardo Diego, Espasa-Calpe, 1977.

Contributor to periodicals, including *Espana*.

TRANSLATOR

Marie Louise Antoinette de Regnier, *El seductor,* Estrella (Madrid), 1921.

Waldo David Frank, *America hispana,* Espasa-Calpe, 1932.

Waldo David Frank, *Espana virgen,* Espasa-Calpe, 1937.

Walt Whitman, *Canto a mi mismo,* Losada, 1941.

Benjamin Franklin, *Autobiografia y otros escritos,* edited by Mark Van Doren, Nuevo Mundo (Mexico City), 1942.

Willa Cather, *Una dama perdida,* Nuevo Mundo, 1942.

SIDELIGHTS: Leon Felipe was an important Spanish poet known for his humanist verses. Felipe was born in 1884 in Tabara, Spain. He trained as a pharmacist and worked in that occupation in the 1910s. In 1920 he produced his first poetry collection, *Versos y oraciones de caminante* ("Poems and Prayers of a Traveler"), which revealed Felipe's keen interest in the timeless struggle between good and evil. With the backing of such literary notables as Salvador de Madariaga and Enrique Diez-Canedo, Felipe won praise as a promising new poet. In avant-garde circles, however, he was decried as a conventional, even derivative poet, one who favored the outmoded lyric genre over newer, more radical forms.

Felipe traveled throughout much of his life. In the early 1920s he worked as a hospital administrator on an island near the African coast. He then sailed to Mexico, where he eventually befriended such artists and intellectuals as the painter Diego Rivera and the philosopher Antonio Caso. He also made the acquaintance of professor Berta Gamboa, whom he married in 1925. That same year the couple found work at Cornell University in the United States, where Felipe lectured in Spanish language and literature. Felipe and his wife remained at Cornell for four years. During that time Felipe published the second volume of *Versos y oraciones de caminante,* which E. T. Aylward described in the *Dictionary of Literary Biography* as a book showing "a spiritual kinship with Walt Whitman."

In the mid-1930s, when Spain erupted in civil war, Felipe supported the Republican cause. He returned to Spain and lived in Madrid during the harrowing bombings of late 1936. He left Spain when Barcelona fell under heaving bombing in 1938. After stopping in Havana, Cuba, he returned to Mexico, where he obtained employment at a university in Mexico City. Felipe remained in Mexico for the next several years, during which time he published several books, including the celebrated 1943 poetry collection *Ganaras la luz: Biografia, poesia y destino* ("You Will Win the Light"), a series of hopeful contemplations on humanity. Aylward deemed *Ganaras la luz* "the greatest articulation of [Felipe's] feelings of pain and protest." Aylward added: "Rather than be narrowly political, Felipe attempts to be visionary, utopian, even quixotic in his search for justice. His subject is humankind . . . and the misery people must endure."

Felipe resumed traveling in 1945. He toured Central and South America, where—according to Aylward— he "played the role of the bearded pilgrim from Spain, his native land's authentic messenger in exile who had come to stir his listeners with his religious fervor." Felipe returned to Mexico in 1947, and he continued to live there for the remainder of his life.

In the 1950s Felipe diversified as a writer. He continued to publish poetry collections, notably *Llamadme publicano* ("Call Me a Publican"), which includes a portion dedicated to the medieval Spanish poet Juan Ruiz. But he also produced stage productions, including *La manzana* ("The Apple"), a drama about Paris and Helen of Troy, and *No es cordero . . . que es cordera* ("Not a Ram . . . but a Ewe"), which is derived from William Shakespeare's *Twelfth Night.* Felipe also published *Dos obras: La mordida y Tristan y Isolde* ("Two Plays: A Piece of the Action and Tristan and Isolde") and *El Juglaron* ("The Teller of Tall Tales"), two volumes containing comic sketches that he had written for Mexican television.

Felipe's prolific rate of writing diminished considerably in the last decade of his life. In 1958 he pub-

lished *El ciervo* ("The Stag"), a collection of uncharacteristically gloomy and self-mocking poems. Eight years then passed before he produced another significant collection, *Oh, este viejo y roto violin!* ("Oh, This Old and Broken Violin!") But since his death in 1968, many collections of his writings have appeared, and these works have served to maintain Felipe's stature as a significant figure in the field of Spanish poetry.

BIOGRAPHICAL/CRITICAL SOURCES:

BOOKS

Dictionary of Literary Biography, Volume 108: *Twentieth-Century Spanish Poets,* First Series, Gale, 1991.*

                                    *   *   *

FERNANDEZ, Roberto G. 1951-

PERSONAL: Born September 24, 1951, in Sagua la Grande, Cuba; immigrated to United States, 1961; naturalized citizen, 1972; son of Jose Antonio (a certified public accountant) and Nelia G. (a homemaker; maiden name, Lopez) Fernandez; married Elena Reyes (a psychologist), July 7, 1978 (divorced, April 26, 1983; remarried Elena Reyes, 1990); children: Tatiana. *Education:* Florida Atlantic University, B.A., 1970, M.A., 1973; Florida State University, Ph.D., 1977. *Religion:* Roman Catholic.

ADDRESSES: Home—Tallahassee, FL. *Office*—Department of Modern Languages, Florida State University, Tallahassee, FL 32306.

CAREER: Florida State University, Tallahassee, instructor of Spanish literature, 1975-78; University of South Alabama, Mobile, assistant professor of Spanish, 1978-80; Florida State University, associate professor of Spanish and Spanish literature, 1980—.

MEMBER: American Association of Teachers of Spanish and Portuguese, Modern Language Association of America, Associated Writing Programs, Florida Arts Council.

AWARDS, HONORS: Florida Artist fellowship and Cintas fellowship, both 1986-87, for fiction-writing; writer-in-residence at University of Texas at El Paso, 1989; King-Chavez-Parks Visiting Professorship at

Western Michigan University, 1990.

WRITINGS:

Cuentos sin rumbos (short stories), Ediciones Universal (Miami), 1975.

El jardin de la luna (short stories), Ediciones Universal, 1976.

La vida es un special .75 (novel), Ediciones Universal, 1981.

(With Jose B. Fernandez) *Indice bibliografico de autores cubanos (Diaspora, 1959-1979): literatura* (nonfiction), Ediciones Universal, 1983.

La montana rusa (novel), Arte Publico (Houston), 1985.

Raining Backwards (novel), Arte Publico, 1988.

Holy Radishes!, Arte Publico, 1995.

Contributor to periodicals, including *Apalachee Quarterly, Florida Review, Linden Lane,* and *West Branch.*

SIDELIGHTS: Roberto Fernandez has published several novels and short story collections in his native Spanish since the mid-1970s, but it is his first English-language novel, *Raining Backwards* (1988), that has earned him attention from critics. Praised for its humor and affectionate tone, *Raining Backwards* challenges notions of cultural assimilation and identity among Cuban exiles in Miami. Fernandez' ability to satirize both the immigrant community and the reluctance of the American majority to accept minority cultures gives his narrative a foundation of realism and strong social commentary under the hyperbolic, humorous behavior of his characters. The novel was praised as an important contribution to the development of the North American Latino voice, which has lagged behind the development of South American literature.

Fernandez was born on September 24, 1951 in Sagua la Grande, Cuba, the son of an accountant and a homemaker. In 1961 Fernandez immigrated to the United States, becoming a naturalized citizen in 1972. He attended Florida Atlantic University for undergraduate and graduate work, and earned a Ph.D. at Florida State University in 1977. Fernandez published two collections of short stories, *Cuentos sin rumbos* (1975) and *El jardin de la luna* (1976), while earning his doctorate and teaching Spanish Literature. In 1978, he married Elena Reyes, a psychologist; they divorced five years later, only to remarry in 1990. Fernandez published two Spanish-language novels in the early eighties, *La vida es un special .75* (1981) and *La montana rusa* (1985). In 1988 *Raining Back-*

wards brought Fernandez an expanded audience and favorable critical reception. He has received the Florida Artists fellowship and Cintas fellowship for fiction writing (1986-87), and has been the writer-in-residence at the University of Texas at El Paso and a visiting professor at Western Michigan University. Today, Fernandez continues to teach Spanish and Spanish Literature at Florida State University while contributing to publications and writing novels.

Fernandez' early stories and novels chronicled the Cuban community in Miami with humor, satire, and a lively use of colloquial language and colorful characters. In the struggle to assimilate into the American mainstream while retaining an unique cultural identity, Fernandez' characters often yearn for an idealized Cuba. Mary Vasquez writes of his early work, "Beneath the carnivalesque vibrance and color, the entrepreneurial successes and the outrageous humor, the effort to preserve a heritage and the sometimes equally fervent attempt to embrace another, is heard a long and deep lament for an uprooted people." These themes are echoed and developed in *Raining Backwards,* in which every aspect of the exile experience is parodied, sometimes to outrageous proportions. The novel is populated with characters on the fringe of sanity and normalcy: a drug dealer who forms a guerilla unit in the Everglades, a woman who makes her fortune selling guava pastries, an old maid who seduces a young boy and pines for the diamond dusted beaches of her native Cuba. Fernandez' narration relies on shifting points of view, letters, and telephone calls. The prevailing tone of the novel is one of restless transition, of desiring acceptance and success while clinging to a homeland elevated to mythical status.

Critics consider Fernandez' early works to be blueprints for themes more thoroughly and successfully developed in *Raining Backwards.* Some commentators criticized the narrative style of *Raining Backwards,* contending that it renders the plot confusing at times, and some found the colloquial language less vibrant than in earlier works. However, most critics lauded Fernandez' lively characters and vivid portrayal of the struggle for identity among Cuban exiles in their attempts to transcend their community while retaining their heritage.

Fernandez followed *Raining Backwards* with *Holy Radishes!* As with the author's previous efforts, the novel is set in South Florida—this time in the Everglades community of Belle Glade. The satiric plot concerns the lives of former aristocrats now working at a radish-processing plant. Fernandez again uses shifting narrative and exuberant dialogue. While some critics felt that the author's attempt at satire failed, others praised the novel for its intriguing mix of characters and colorful plot.

BIOGRAPHICAL/CRITICAL SOURCES:

PERIODICALS

Americas Review, spring-summer, 1994, p. 106.
Booklist, October 1, 1995, p. 252.
Confluencia, Fall, 1990.
Hispanic, March, 1989.
Kirkus Reviews, August 1, 1995, p. 1043.
New York Times Book Review, August 14, 1988.
Philadelphia Inquirer, December 6, 1988.
San Francisco Chronicle, April 14, 1988.
USA Today, January 3, 1989.
Vista, September 3, 1988.*

*   *   *

FERRE, Rosario 1942-

PERSONAL: Born July 28, 1942, in Ponce, Puerto Rico; daughter of Luis A. (an engineer and governor of Puerto Rico from 1968 to 1972) and Lorenza Ramirez Ferre; married Benigno Trigo (a merchant), 1960 (divorced); children: Rosario, Benigno, Luis. *Education:* University of Puerto Rico, M.A.; University of Maryland, Ph.D., 1986. *Religion:* Catholic.

ADDRESSES: Agent—Tomas Colchie, 5 rue de la Villette, Paris, France 75019.

CAREER: Writer. Founder and director of *Zona de carga y descarga,* a Latin American journal devoted to new Puerto Rican literature.

AWARDS, HONORS: National Book Award nomination, 1996, for *The House on the Lagoon.*

WRITINGS:

Papeles de Pandora (title means "Pandora's Roles"), Joaquin Mortiz (Mexico City), 1976, translation by the author published as *The Youngest Doll,* University of Nebraska Press (Lincoln), 1991.
El medio pollito: Siete cuentos infantiles (title means "The Half Chicken"; children's stories), Ediciones Huracan (Rio Piedras), 1976.

La muneca menor/The Youngest Doll (bilingual edition), illustrations by Antonio Martorell, Ediciones Huracan, 1980.
Sitio a Eros: Trece ensayos literarios (title means "Eros Besieged"), Joaquin Mortiz, 1980, translation by Ferre and Diana L. Velez published as "The Writer's Kitchen" in *Lives on the Line: The Testimony of Contemporary Latin American Authors,* edited by Doris Meyer, University of California Press (Berkeley, CA), 1988.
Los cuentos de Juan Bobo (title means "The Tales of Juan Bobo"; children's stories), Ediciones Huracan, 1980.
La mona que le pisaron la cola (title means "The Monkey Whose Tail Got Stepped On"; children's stories), Ediciones Huracan, 1981.
Fabulas de la garza desangrada (title means "Fables of a Bleeding Crane"), Joaquin Mortiz, 1982.
La caja de cristal, La Maquina de Escribir (Mexico), 1982.
Maldito amor (title means "Cursed Love"), Joaquin Mortiz, 1986, revised and translated by Ferre and published as *Sweet Diamond Dust* (see also below), Ballantine (New York City), 1988.
El acomodor: Una lectura fantastica de Felisberto Hernandez, Fondo de Cultura Economica, 1986.
Sonatinas, Ediciones Huracan, 1989.
El arbol y sus sombras, Fondo de Cultura (Mexico), 1989.
El coloquio de las perras, Cultural (San Juan), 1990, selections translated by the author and published as "On Destiny, Language, and Translation; or, Ophelia Adrift in the C & O Canal," in *The Youngest Doll,* 1991.
El cucarachita Martina, Ediciones Huracan, 1990.
Cortazar, Literal (Washington, DC), 1991.
Las dos Venecias (title means "The Two Venices"), Joaquin Mortiz, 1992.
Memorias de Ponce: Autobiografia de Luis A. Ferre, Editorial Norma (Barcelona, Spain), 1992.
La batalla de las virgenes, Editorial de la Universidad de Puerto Rico, (San Juan, Puerto Rico), 1993.
The House on the Lagoon, Farrar, Straus (New York City), 1995.
Sweet Diamond Dust and Other Stories, Plume (New York City), 1996.
El Sombrero Magico (title means "The Magical Hat"), Santillana Publishing Company, 1997.
La Casa de la Laguna, Vintage, 1997.
La Sapita Sabia y Otros Cuentos (title means "The Smart Frog and Other Stories"), Santillana Publishing Company, 1997.
Pico Rico Mandorico y Otros Cuentos, Santillana Publishing Company, 1997.

Eccentric Neighborhoods, Farrar Straus (New York City), 1998.

(Translator) *Vecindarios Eccentricos,* Vintage, 1999.

CONTRIBUTOR

Teresa Mindez-Faith, editor, *Contextos: Literarios hispanoamericanos,* Holt (New York City), 1985.

Anthology of Contemporary Latin American Literature, 1960-1984, Farleigh Dickinson University Press, 1986.

Reclaiming Medusa: Short Stories by Contemporary Puerto Rican Women, Spinsters Aunt Lute (San Francisco, CA), 1988.

Marie-Lisa Gazarian Gautier, editor, *Interviews with Latin American Writers,* Dalkey Archive Press, 1989.

Some of Ferre's writings have also been anthologized in *Ritos de iniciacion: Tres novelas cortas de Hispanoamerica,* a textbook for intermediate and advanced students of college Spanish, by Grinor Rojo, and *Anthology of Women Poets.*

SIDELIGHTS: "Rosario Ferre," writes *Dictionary of Literary Biography* contributor Carmen S. Rivera, "has become the 'translator' of the reality of Puerto Rican women, opening the doors for the feminist movement on the island. By combining classical mythology with indigenous folktales that usurp the traditional actions of female characters, Ferre has interpreted, translated, and rewritten a more active and satisfying myth of Puerto Rican women." Ferre—the daughter of a former governor of Puerto Rico—writes about politics (she favors Puerto Rican independence), about literature, and about the status of women in modern Puerto Rican society. A former student of Angel Rama and Mario Vargas Llosa, she often utilizes magic realist techniques to communicate her points. "Many critics believe that with the publication of her first book," Rivera continues, "Ferre began the feminist movement in Puerto Rico and became, if not its only voice, one of its most resonant and forceful spokespersons."

Chronologically, Ferre's first work was the short story collection *Papeles de Pandora.* Its original Spanish-language version was published in Mexico in 1976, but it was not until 1991 that an English-language translation by the author became available. "Defiant magic feminism challenges all our conventional notions of time, place, matter and identity in Rosario Ferre's spectacular new book, *The Youngest Doll,*" declares Patricia Hart in the *Nation. New York*

Times Book Review contributor Cathy A. Colman states, "Ms. Ferre . . . writes with an irony that cloaks anger about the oppression and danger inherent in being either a protected upper-class woman or a marginalized working-class women caught in Puerto Rico's patriarchal society." In "Sleeping Beauty," for example, a young woman's desire to become a dancer is railroaded by her family, who wants her to marry an aristocratic young man. The protagonist of "The Poisoned Story" starts out as a Cinderella figure (she marries a sugarcane planter) but ends up playing the role of a wicked stepmother to his daughter. "From beginning to end . . . whether she is conceiving stories, translating them or providing commentary," Hart concludes, "Rosario Ferre shines, and it is high time for English-speaking readers to bask in her light."

Ferre's first work to be translated into English was *Sweet Diamond Dust,* a short novel telling the stories of influential Puerto Rican women in different time periods. "Ferre parodies novels about the land, a popular genre during the first half of the century, as she sets out to rewrite Puerto Rican history from a woman's perspective," Rivera declares. "She describes how the island (*isla* is a female noun in Spanish) is oppressed by the government and American businesses—both of which are rendered as masculine in Spanish—while drawing parallels to the situation of women." Reviewer Alan Cheuse, writing in the *Chicago Tribune,* called Ferre "one of the most engaging young Latin American fiction writers at work today," and added, "Ferre shows off her linguistic talent as well as her inventiveness by giving us her own English version of the book."

The House on the Lagoon was Ferre's first work composed in English and was nominated for the National Book Award in 1996. "Most of this novel," declares a *Publishers Weekly* reviewer, "is comprised of . . . semi-fictionalized family history." The book tells of a Puerto Rican couple, Quintin Mendizabal and Isabel Monfort, who come into conflict over politics (she favors independence for the island, he favors close ties with the United States), their attitudes (he believes in traditional women's roles, she favors feminism) and the history she is writing, which includes stories about her husband's family. The family's black servant Petra Aviles also plays a role in the family dynamic. "The novel's conclusion affirms in the strongest terms the necessity of interracial alliances, both sexual and familial, to the future of a Puerto Rican community," writes Judith Grossman in the *Women's Review of Books.* "Ferre dramatizes the issue of who gets to write history," states the *Publishers Weekly* contributor, "gracefully incorporating it into a compelling panorama of Puerto Rican experience that is rich in history, drama and memorable characters." "*The House on the Lagoon,*" Grossman concludes, "gives us a performance of great accomplishment and wit, and the sense of a world held in measured but deeply affectionate memory."

BIOGRAPHICAL/CRITICAL SOURCES:

PERIODICALS

Chicago Tribune, January 13, 1989.
Library Journal, August, 1995, p. 115.
Nation, May 6, 1991, pp. 597-98.
New York Times Book Review, March 24, 1991, p. 24.
Publishers Weekly, July 3, 1995, p. 47.
Woman's Review of Books, February, 1996, p. 5.*

*   *   *

FIGUERA, Angela   1902-1984

PERSONAL: Born Angela Figuera Aymerich, October 30, 1902, in Bilbao, Spain; died April 2, 1984; daughter of an industrial engineer and a teacher; married Julio Figuera (a civil servant), c. 1934; children: Juan Ramon. *Education:* Attended University of Valladolid, mid-1920s; earned degree from the University of Madrid, c. 1928. *Politics:* Spanish Republican. *Religion:* Roman Catholic.

CAREER: Poet. School teacher and private tutor in Madrid, Spain, 1930-33, in Huelva, Spain, 1933-36, and in Murcia, Spain, c. 1938; employed with Spanish National Library, Madrid, beginning c. 1948; freelance translator.

WRITINGS:

Mujer de barro (poetry; title means "Clay Woman"), SAETA (Madrid, Spain), 1948.
Soria pura (poetry; title means "Pure Soria"), Jura (Madrid), 1949.
Vencida por el angel (poetry; title means "Overcome by the Angel"), Verbo (Alicante, Spain), 1950.
El grito inutil (poetry; title means "The Futile Cry"), Such & Serra (Alicante), 1952.
Vispera de la vida (poetry; title means "Vespers of Life"), Nebli (Madrid), 1953.

Los dias duros (poetry; title means "Difficult Days"), Aguado (Madrid), 1953.
Belleza cruel (poetry; title means "Cruel Beauty"), General de Ediciones (Mexico City, Mexico), 1958.
Primera antologia, Lirica Hispana (Caracas, Venezuela), 1961.
Toco la tierra: Letanias (poetry; title means "I Touch the Earth: Litanies"), Rialp/Adonais (Madrid), 1962.
Antologia, edited by Alfredo Gracia Vicente, Sierra Madre (Monterrey, Mexico), 1969.
Antologia total, edited by Julian Marcos, Videosistemas (Madrid), 1973.
Cuentos tontos para ninos listos (children's book; title means "Stupid Tales for Clever Children"), Sierra Madre, 1979.
Canciones para todo el ano (children's book; title means "Year-Round Songs"), Trillas (Monterrey), 1984.
Obras completas (poetry), edited by Julio Figuera, Hiperion (Madrid), 1986.

SIDELIGHTS: As a poet, Angela Figuera is not widely known outside her native Spain, but her work is considered fully representative of the writers known as the Generation of 1927, which included Federico Garcia Lorca, Vicente Aleixandre, Rafael Alberti, and Luis Cernuda, among many others. But Figuera did not publish her first volume of verse until 1948, after much had changed in Spain, and during her most productive period in the 1950s her work took on a decidedly progressive tone. Yet in nearly all of her writing is a concern for the traditional values of motherhood and family, as well as the decidedly independent streak that reflects her Basque heritage. "Rather than a feminist, Figuera is feminine in her poetry, with her early books celebrating motherhood, marriage, conjugal love, and domestic life," wrote Janet Perez in her essay on Figuera in *Dictionary of Literary Biography.* "Her 'social' poetry, part of the larger literature of engagement in postwar Europe, likewise has an unmistakably feminine and personal viewpoint, although the testimonial thematics and denunciation of injustice and oppression coincide in other ways with the social poetry authored by men," noted Perez.

Figuera was born Angela Figuera Aymerich on October 30, 1902, in Bilbao, a major city in northern Spain and home to many of Basque origin like herself. Her father was an industrial engineer, but her mother—a former teacher—suffered from health problems. As the eldest of their nine children, Figuera spent much of her youth looking after her younger siblings. These formative circumstances would later infuse her poetry with a quintessentially sympathetic maternal strain.

Figuera began writing short stories and poems as a child, but saved almost nothing. After graduating from high school in Bilbao in 1924, she planned to study literature; her father, however, deemed this an impractical aspiration, and pushed her toward a career in teaching. After two years, the determined Figuera successfully passed the University of Valladolid's exams for its literature course and began study on her own. When her father died in 1927, her uncle began supporting her—and her many siblings as well—and sent her to Madrid to finish her degree instead. After university, much of the financial responsibility then fell to her, and she became a teacher and private tutor in Madrid in the early 1930s. She then took a formal examination to receive a secondary-school teaching certificate and with it was hired as a teacher in the Andalusian town of Huelva in 1933.

During this period, Figuera married her cousin, Julio Figuera, and suffered the loss of her first child during labor. By 1936 she was pregnant again and studying in Madrid when the recently elected leftist government was overthrown by a coalition that included the Spanish army, supporters of the deposed royal family, and Roman Catholic clergy. Full-scale civil war broke out that summer, and Julio Figuera left to serve in the leftist Republican army. Their son was born in December, and Figuera spent time in Valencia and later near Murcia, where she again taught school. But with the victory of the fascist forces of Generalissimo Francisco Franco, Figuera lost her teaching job because of her and her husband's Republican sympathies. She spent the next decade as a wife, mother, and writer.

Figuera's first book of poetry was published in 1948 when she was already forty-six years old. *Mujer de barro* ("Clay Woman") offers poems about marriage and motherhood—such as verses that commemorate her son's birthdays, his first day of school, and his play activities and natural curiosity—in the section "Poemas de mi hijo y yo" ("Poems of My Child and Me"); another part, "El fruto redondo" ("The Round Fruit"), features verse that sings the praises of nature and the changing seasons and also addresses slightly more prosaic concerns such as insomnia and writer's block. "*Mujer de barro* contains a joyful affirmation of motherhood as the vehicle for the perpetuation of

the species, a positive acceptance of womanhood as defined by patriarchal society," wrote Perez in *Dictionary of Literary Biography*. "Reflecting the intimacy of a happy marriage and fulfilling life, the poems reveal Figuera's subjectivity as well as including some sensual erotic lyrics that blend traditional themes with then-popular forms."

Around this time Figuera began working as a librarian in Madrid's National Library; and also found work as a freelance translator. She and her family had been spending summers in a pastoral area called Soria, and her love of the countryside there inspired her next collection of poems, *Soria pura* ("Pure Soria"), published in 1949. In it are guarded hints of the social concerns she would express in later verse, especially in her observations about the hard life of the rural area's inhabitants. The book's title and a quintet of its poems pay tribute to the Spanish poet Antonio Machado.

The postwar years were a time of great repression and censorship in Spain under Franco, and like other writers of the day, Figuera began cautiously pushing her writing a toward a criticism of the regime. A heightened caution was necessary in her case, however, since her Republican sympathies during the Civil War made her "suspect" as someone who might be a subversive. But Figuera's work took on a new direction after her contact with a work by Basque poet Gabriel Celaya; his *Las cosas como son* ("Things as They Are"), published in 1950, impacted her own work decisively. "From this point onward her poetry acquires more aggressive, rebellious notes and becomes less personal and less affirmative, more critical and denunciatory," wrote Perez in the *Dictionary of Literary Biography* essay, citing her subsequent title as a prime example of this shift. "In some poetry of *Vencida por el angel,* her next collection, she adopts an attitude of self-criticism, as the 'new' Figuera denounces the egotism of the old for having sequestered herself in domestic tranquillity, ignoring the world's ugliness and problems," noted Perez.

Like other Spanish poets of the era, Figuera became skilled at skirting the suspicions of government censors by various means. One method was to use a voice that addressed God, as she does in poems in *El grito inutil* ("The Futile Cry"), published in 1952. *Vispera de la vida* ("Vespers of Life"), which appeared the following year, also utilizes this subterfuge; one of its poems chronicles the anguish of childbirth, contrasting it with miserable plight of the people on the street below. Perez, critiquing the verse in these two titles, found that "death, collective guilt, social responsibility, an idealization of labor and the working man, poverty, silence, imprisonment, exile, unemployment, and emigration are among her themes."

Figuera's sixth volume of poetry, *Los dias duros* ("Difficult Days"), appeared in 1953. It features many earlier pieces that had been written around 1950 and reflect the direction her poetry would soon take. "The previously unpublished poems are more aggressive and strident than anything by Figuera that had appeared earlier," explained Perez, "and the posture adopted is one of solidarity with other mothers the world over; at the same time, she begins to expose contradictions between, on the one hand, the cult of the Virgin and the idealization of mothers, and, on the other hand, the disempowerment of women."

During this period Figuera was writing even more vociferously critical verse, but kept it on her desk at home, fearing she might lose her job, or worse. In 1957 she obtained a study grant for Paris and managed to smuggle some of her work outside the country on her trip. From France the writings were mailed to a friend of hers in Mexico and then entered in a literary contest sponsored by a group of exiled Spanish writers. The end result was the 1958 publication in Mexico City of Figuera's *Belleza cruel* ("Cruel Beauty"), a title that would not appear in Spain until twenty years later. "*Belleza cruel* reflects more clearly than any other of Figuera's books her reaction to the misery and injustice of postwar Spain," declared Perez.

The volume is considered a significant event in the literature of post-Civil War Spain: many of the writers in exile had assumed that contemporary poetry had decayed immeasurably inside Franco's Spain, but Figuera's poems showed instead that it was alive and thriving—and critical of the regime. Commenting upon some of the poems of *Belleza cruel,* Perez found that "in 'Si no has muerto un instante' ('If You Haven't Died for an Instant') Figuera proclaims that those who do not suffer and die a little with each human injustice and grief would be better buried for they are already dead, while 'Libertad' ('Liberty') contrasts approved behavior and conventional pastimes with the risk of thinking, dreaming, speaking of freedom."

Figuera lived in Madrid until 1961, when she moved to the provincial city of Aviles, where her husband, a civil servant, had been working for the past two years. *Toco la tierra: Letanias* ("I Touch the Earth:

Litanies") was published in 1962 and was her last volume of original poetry. "Isolation from literary circles, loss of contact with other writers, and, perhaps, age combined to halt her activities in the forefront of combative poetry," noted Perez in *Dictionary of Literary Biography*. Figuera returned to Madrid in 1971, and anthologies of her work were published in the 1970s. A granddaughter's love of her stories led Figuera to author two children's books. *Cuentos tontos para ninos listos* ("Stupid Tales for Clever Children") appeared in 1979; in typically subversive fashion, the book's "Silly Tale of the Little Witch Who Couldn't Get Her Identity Card" features a sorceress so exhausted by government travel restrictions that she abandons her vocation. Another work for children, *Canciones para todo el ano* ("Year-Round Songs"), was published in 1984, the year of Figuera's death. A complete anthology of her poetry, *Obras completas,* was published in 1986.

BIOGRAPHICAL/CRITICAL SOURCES:

BOOKS

Dictionary of Literary Biography, Volume 108: *Twentieth-Century Spanish Poets,* First Series, edited by Michael L. Perna, Gale, 1991.*

* * *

FILHO, Adonias   1915-1990

PERSONAL: Born November 27, 1915, in Ilheus, Brazil; died August 2, 1990, in Itajuape, Brazil; son of Adonias (a cacao plantation owner) and Rachel Bastos; married Rosita Galiano, 1944; children: Rachel, Adonias. *Education:* Faculdade de Direito do Distrito Federal (Federal Law School), Rio de Janeiro, LL.B., 1942. *Religion:* Catholic.

CAREER: Writer, 1946-87. Reporter, *Correio da Manha* and *O Jornal,* beginning 1936; translator and literary critic for newspapers and literary journals; director of the newspaper *A Noite,* 1946-50; director; Service Nacional de Teatro (National Theater Service), beginning 1954; interim director, Instituto Nacional do Livro (National Book Institute), beginning 1955; director, National Library, 1961-71; director, National Information Agency, 1961-64.

AWARDS, HONORS: Member, Academia Brasileira de Letras, 1965.

WRITINGS:

Os servos da morte, Jose Olympio (Rio de Janeiro), 1946.

Memorias de Lazaro, O Cruzeiro (Rio de Janeiro), 1952, translation by Fred P. Ellison published as *Memories of Lazarus,* University of Texas Press (Austin, TX), 1969.

Journal de um escritor, Ministerio de Educacao e Cultura (Rio de Janeiro), 1954.

Modernos ficcionistas Brasileiros, O Cruzeiro, 1958.

Cornelia Peno, Agir (Rio de Janeiro), 1960.

Corpo vivo, Civilizacao Brasileira (Rio de Janeiro), 1962.

O bloqueio cultural: O intelectual, a liberdade, a receptividade, Livraria Martins (Sao Paulo), 1964.

O Forte, Civilizacao Brasileira, 1965.

Modernas ficcionistas Brasileiros, Tempo Brasileiro (Rio de Janeiro), 1965.

(With Jorge Amado) *A nacao grapiuna: Adonias Filho na Academia,* Tempo Brasileiro, 1965.

Leguas de promissao, Civilizacao Brasileira, 1968.

O romance brasileiro de trinta, Bloch (Rio de Janeiro), 1969.

Luanda, Beira Bahia, Civilizacao Brasileira, 1971.

(With Octales Gonzales) *Volta Redonda: O processo brasileiro de mudanca,* Image (Rio de Janeiro), 1972, translation by Richard J. Spock published as *Volta Redonda: The Brazilian Process of Change,* 1972.

Uma nota de cem, Ouro (Rio de Janeiro), 1973.

As velhas, Civilizacao Brasileira, 1975.

Sul de bahia, chao de cacau: Uma civilizacao regional, Civilizacao Brasileira, 1976.

Fora da pista, Civilizacao Brasileira, 1978.

O Auto dos Ilheus, Civilizacao Brasileira, 1981.

O Largo da Palma, Civilizacao Brasileira, 1981.

Noite sem madrugada, Difel (Sao Paulo), 1983.

O Homem de branco, Bertrand Brasil (Rio de Janeiro), 1987.

SIDELIGHTS: Novelist and reporter Adonias Filho was born in 1915 on his family's cacao plantation in the Brazilian municipality of Ilheus. Filho attended primary school in Ilheus, and when he was thirteen was sent to the Ginasio Ipiranga in Salvador, the state capital of Bahia. At the school he began a lifelong friendship with Jorge Amado, who was also from Ilheus, and who would eventually become Brazil's most successful novelist. When he was nineteen, Filho completed his education and began working in journalism, along with writing his own literary work. In 1936 he moved to Rio de Janeiro, the capital of Brazil, and began writing for the papers *Correio da Manha* and *O Jornal,* and in 1938 he began translating European literature and writing literary criticism for both newspapers and literary journals. In 1942 he received a bachelor of law degree from the Faculdade de Direito do Distrito Federal (Federal Law School) in Rio de Janeiro, and in 1944 he married Rosita Galiano, who was from Rio. They would eventually have a daughter, Rachel, and a son, Adonias.

By the time he was twenty-one, Filho had already completed a novel, *Cachuca* ("Rum"). No one ever saw this novel, however, and it was eventually destroyed. In *Dictionary of Literary Biography,* Fred P. Ellison speculated that "Perhaps it was a regional social novel of the type then widely successful, especially as practiced by his lifelong friend Rachel de Quiroz." Filho's first published novel, *Os servos da morte* ("Servants of Death"), established him as an innovative and important writer. The novel, set in the cacao-growing region of his childhood, featured a brutal cacao planter, Paulino Duarte, his wife Elisa, their five sons, one son's wife, and several servants and relatives. The youngest child, and the most vicious, was not Paulino's son at all, but the result of Elisa's vengeful affair with another landowner. Most of the novel's brutal and decadent characters become involved in a holocaust by the time the book ends.

The novel's style and focus was reminiscent of that of William Faulkner, who was one of Filho's inspirations; the author was a keen student of Faulkner, analyzing his work and writing notes about it in his journal. Like Faulkner, Filho explored the complex inner states of uneducated rural people, presenting existential tragedy in a rough setting. Of this kinship, Ellison wrote, "In *Os servos da morte* the central characters are in constant psychological turmoil. Some have inherited insanity; others are driven mad in this environment of hatred, brutality, revenge, sexual violence, murder, mutilation, and degradation. The overarching theme is the struggle of evil with good, the novel suggesting that evil inevitably—at least at present and in the setting of the cacao zone—will prevail."

Filho announced that this book would be the first of a trilogy set in the cacao region, and in 1952 the second volume, *Memorias de Lazarus* ("Memories of Lazarus") was published. Set in the arid, forbidding Ouro Valley of Bahia, the book presented this region as hellish, emphasizing its mud, dust, heat, and blackened sky. The narrator, Alexandre, told his story to Jeronimo, who lived deep in a cave. The tale involved his childhood, his brutal courtship of a farm girl, Rosalia, who was either killed or who killed herself; his murder of her brother, who might or might not be the father of the child she was pregnant with; Alexandre's escape from the people who want to hang him for the murder; and his wandering through the region, seeking peace but never finding it. The book ended with Alexandre back in the valley of Jeronimo's cavern, where he killed himself. Ellison remarked that Filho "implies that people, not only of this region but everywhere, are like their literary symbol, the Ouro Valley—forbidding, unforgiving, uncivilized, and inhuman."

In 1962 the third volume of the cacao trilogy, *Corpo vivo,* was published. It was the most successful of his works, and was widely translated. Based on sketches dating back to 1938, the book, whose title means "living body" or "body alive," began with a massacre. Cajango, a boy living on a cacao plantation, escaped the marauders who kill his family so they can take over the land. He was taken in by his father's half-brother, Inuri, who is partly white but lives like an Indian. Inuri taught him the skills of the jungle and hunting, and also taught him that he must avenge the deaths of his family. When Cajango began to take his revenge, however, he met a woman named Malva, fell in love with her, and fled with her to the mountains and a new life with her-but not before he killed Inuri, who came to represent the incarnation of vengeance.

In this book Filho's language is lyrical, and the atmosphere was strange is filled with mystery. Ellison noted that the book's poetic language and mysterious setting lend it to mythic interpretation. "As an example," he wrote, "Cajango and Malva are reminiscent of Adam and Even, mythical hero and heroine escaping into the 'sacred' space of forest and mountain, with the implicit promise of a rebirth of the Brazilian race."

O Forte ("the Fort") was set in the state capital, Salvador, in Fort Sao Paolo. Covering 400 years, the book was narrated by Olegario, a black murderer, now dead, who was imprisoned in the fort. Telling the stories of loves, partings, and historical events, the book was more an extended metaphor based on the fort than a love story. Ellison wrote, "Adding to the value of the book as an epic re-creation of history is its musicality, which in the simple poetic prose of *O Forte* rises to perhaps the highest level of intensity to be found anywhere in Adonias's oeuvre. . . . *O Forte* is considered by critics to be one of his best."

Filho began writing shorter pieces after the publication of *O Forte,* many of them set in the rural, lawless region of Itajuape, where he was born. The stories, like his novels, are filled with barbarism and aggression, but also include hints of hope, progress, and redemption. He also wrote several more novels, also regionally based, with his characteristically rhythmic language and emphasis on common people. According to Ellison, Filho was once asked to what extent a writer should participate in the public life of his country. Filho replied that "what is important is that, rising above fanaticisms and idological dogmas, the writer be a logical thinker in the service of the values of life and of culture, for example liberty."

BIOGRAPHICAL/CRITICAL SOURCES:

BOOKS

Dictionary of Literary Biography, Volume 145: *Modern Latin-American Fiction Writers,* Gale (Detroit, MI), 1994.*

*   *   *

FORNES, Maria Irene 1930-

PERSONAL: Born May 14, 1930, in Havana, Cuba; immigrated to the United States, 1945; naturalized U.S. citizen, 1951; daughter of Carlos Luis (a public servant) and Carmen Hismenia (Collado) Fornes. Attended public schools in Havana, Cuba. *Politics:* Democrat. *Religion:* Catholic.

ADDRESSES: Home—One Sheridan Sq., New York, NY 10014. *Agent*—Helen Merrill, 435 West 23rd St. #1A, New York, NY 10011.

CAREER: Playwright, 1960—. Painter in Europe, 1954-57; textile designer in New York City, 1957-60. Director of her plays, including *Tango Palace, The Successful Life of 3, The Annunciation, Molly's Dream, Aurora, Cap-a-Pie, Fefu and Her Friends, Washing, Eyes on the Harem, Evelyn Brown (A Diary), Life Is Dream, A Visit, The Danube, Abingdon Square, Sarita, Mud, Cold Air, The Conduct of Life, A Matter of Faith,* and *Lovers and Keepers.* Founding member and president, New York Theatre Strategy, 1973-78. Teacher with Theatre for the New City, New York City, 1972-73, Padua Hills Festival, Claremont, CA, 1978—, INTAR (International Arts

Relations), New York City, 1981—, and at numerous universities and theater festivals in the United States.

MEMBER: Dramatists Guild, ASCAP, League of Professional Theatre Women, Society of Stage Directors and Choreographers.

AWARDS, HONORS: John Hay Whitney Foundation fellowship, 1961; Centro Mexicano de Escritores fellowship, 1962; Obie Award (Off-Broadway theatre award) for distinguished playwriting (and direction), 1965, for *Promenade* and *The Successful Life of 3,* 1977, for *Fefu and Her Friends,* 1984, for *The Danube, Mud,* and *Sarita,* and 1988, for *Abingdon Square;* Yale University fellowships, 1967, 1968; Cintas Foundation fellowship, 1967; Boston University-Tanglewood fellowship, 1968; Rockefeller Foundation grant, 1971, 1984; Guggenheim fellowship, 1972; Creative Artist Public Service grants, 1972, 1975; National Endowment for the Arts grants, 1974, 1984, and 1985; Obie Award for distinguished direction, 1979, for *Eyes on the Harem;* Obie Award for sustained achievement, 1982; Obie Award for best new play, 1985, for *The Conduct of Life;* American Academy and Institute of Arts and Letters Award in Literature, 1985; Playwrights U.S.A. Award, 1986, for translation of *Cold Air.*

WRITINGS:

PLAYS

The Widow (published as *La Viuda* in *Cuatro Autores Cubanos*), Casa de las Americas (Havana), 1961.
There! You Died (also see below; later produced as *Tango Palace*), produced in San Francisco at Actor's Workshop, 1963; produced in New York City at Theatre Genesis, 1973.
The Successful Life of 3 (also see below), produced with *Tango Palace* at Firehouse Theatre, 1965; produced Off-Broadway at Sheridan Square Playhouse Theatre, 1965.
Promenade (musical; also see below), music by Al Carmines, produced Off-Off-Broadway at Judson Poets' Theatre, April 9, 1965; produced Off-Broadway at Promenade Theatre, June 4, 1969.
The Office (produced on Broadway at Henry Miller's Theatre, 1966 preview performances; never officially opened), Establishment Theatre Co., 1965.
A Vietnamese Wedding (also see below), produced in New York City at Washington Square Methodist Church, 1967; produced Off-Broadway at La Mama Experimental Theatre, 1969.

The Annunciation, produced with *The Successful Life of 3* at Judson Poets' Theater.
Dr. Kheal (also see below), produced at Judson Poets' Theater, 1968; produced in London, 1969.
The Red Burning Light: or Mission XQ3 (also see below), produced in Zurich, Switzerland, for Open Theatre European Tour, 1968; produced at La Mama Experimental Theatre, 1969.
Molly's Dream (also see below), music by Cosmos Savage, first produced Off-Off-Broadway at New York Theatre Strategy, 1968.
Promenade and Other Plays (includes *Tango Palace, The Successful Life of 3, Promenade, A Vietnamese Wedding, Dr. Kheal, The Red Burning Light: or Mission XQ3,* and *Molly's Dream*), Winter House, 1971.
The Curse of the Langston House, produced in Cincinnati at Playhouse in the Park, 1972.
Aurora, produced at New York Theatre Strategy, 1974.
Cap-a-Pie, music by Jose Raul Bernardo, produced Off-Off-Broadway at INTAR (International Arts Relations), 1975.
Washing, produced Off-Off-Broadway at the Theatre for the New City, 1976.
Lolita in the Garden, produced at INTAR, 1977.
Fefu and Her Friends, produced at New York Theatre Strategy, 1977; produced Off-Broadway at the American Place Theater, 1978; published in *Wordplays 1,* PAJ Publications, 1981.
In Service, produced in Claremont, CA, at the Padua Hills Festival, 1978.
Eyes on the Harem, produced at INTAR, 1979.
Evelyn Brown (A Diary), produced at Theatre for the New City, 1980.
(Adaptor) Federico Garcia Lorca, *Blood Wedding,* produced at INTAR, 1980.
(Adaptor) Pedro Calderon de la Barca, *Life Is Dream,* produced at INTAR, 1981.
A Visit, produced at the Padua Hills Festival, 1981; produced at Theatre for the New City, 1981.
The Danube (also see below), produced at the Padua Hills Festival, 1982; produced at Theatre for the New City, 1983; produced at the American Place Theater, 1984.
Mud (also see below), produced at the Padua Hills Festival, 1983; produced at Theatre for the New City, 1983.
Sarita (musical; also see below), music by Leon Odenz, produced at INTAR, 1984.
No Time, produced at the Padua Hills Festival, 1984.
The Conduct of Life (also see below), produced at Theatre for the New City, 1985.

(Adaptor and translator) Virgilio Pinera, *Cold Air* (produced at INTAR, 1985), Theatre Communications Group, 1985.

Maria Irene Fornes: Plays (includes *Mud, The Danube, Sarita,* and *The Conduct of Life*), preface by Susan Sontag, PAJ Publications, 1986.

A Matter of Faith, produced at Theatre for the New City, 1986.

Lovers and Keepers (three one-act musicals; produced at INTAR, 1986), music by Tito Puente and Fernando Rivas, Theatre Communications Group, 1987.

Drowning (one-act; adapted from Anton Chekhov's story of the same title; produced with six other one-act plays under collective title *Orchards*; produced Off-Broadway at Lucille Lortel Theater, 1986), published in *Orchards,* Knopf, 1986.

Art, produced at Theatre for the New City, 1986.

The Mothers (also see below), produced at the Padua Hills Festival, 1986.

Abingdon Square, produced the American Place Theater, 1987.

(Adaptor) Chekhov, *Uncle Vanya,* produced Off-Broadway at the Classic Stage Company, 1987.

Hunger (also see below), produced Off-Off-Broadway by En Garde Productions, 1989.

And What of the Night (includes *Hunger, Springtime, Lust,* and *Charlie* previously *The Mothers*), produced in Milwaukee, WI, at Milwaukee Repe

Also author of *The Anatomy of Inspiration* and *La Plaza Chica.*

SIDELIGHTS: "One would almost think," writes *Chicago Tribune* contributor Sid Smith, that playwright and director Maria Irene Fornes "was a hot young New York experimentalist—indeed, in a sense, she is and always will be. Her work spans decades, but she endures as a refreshing influence." Smith comments that although Fornes has won six "Obie" awards for her plays produced Off-Broadway, she is "one of the art form's most cherished secrets. Ask playgoers about her, and they are apt to answer with a blank look. Mention Fornes to those who work in the theater, and their faces light up." As Wynn Handman of the American Place Theatre told *New York's* Ross Wetzsteon, "She's clearly among the top five playwrights in America today. But playwrights like Irene, whose work haunts and resonates rather than spelling everything out, almost never receive immediate recognition." Although they frequently deal with human and even "political" issues, "Fornes's plays are whimsical, gentle and bittersweet, and informed with her individualistic intelligence," states

Bonnie Marranca in *American Playwrights: A Critical Survey.* "Virtually all of them have a characteristic delicacy, lightness of spirit, and economy of style. Fornes has always been interested in the emotional lives of her characters, so human relationships play a significant part in the plays." The critic adds that Fornes "apparently likes her characters, and often depicts them as innocent, pure spirits afloat in a corrupt world which is almost absurd rather than realistic. . . . Political consciousness is present in a refined way."

It is not Fornes's subjects, however, that make her work unconventional; as the playwright told Kathleen Betsko and Rachel Koenig in *Interviews with Contemporary Women Playwrights,* "I realized that what makes my plays unacceptable to people is the form more than the content. My content is usually not outrageous. . . . What makes people vicious must be the form." This form is influenced by diverse factors, "neither theatre nor literature but certain styles of painting and the movies," notes Susan Sontag in her preface to *Maria Irene Fornes: Plays.* "But unlike similarly influenced New York dramatists, her work did not eventually become parasitic on literature (or opera, or movies). It was never a revolt against theatre, or a theatre recycling fantasies encoded in other genres." The critic continues by remarking that "Fornes is neither literary nor anti-literary. These are not cerebral exercises or puzzles but the real questions."

Fornes's first major critical success was *Promenade,* a musical that first debuted in 1965 and contributed to her first Obie Award. "The play mixes wit and compassion, humor and tenderness, zaniness and social satire as prisoners named 105 and 106 journey from prison out into the world and back again," describes Phyllis Mael in a *Dictionary of Literary Biography* essay. While much of the play's action concerns the comic conflict between the prisoners and the rich and powerful people they meet, it is Fornes's lyrics that "comment on unrequited love, the abuse of power, the injustice of those who are supposed to uphold the law, and the illogical and random nature of life," adds Mael. "In a work that is really more a choreographed oratorio than a conventional musical," comments Stephen Holden in the *New York Times,* "the music and language are reduced to artful basics, as in the Virgil Thomson-Gertrude Stein operas." Because of this lack of conventional plot, "there may be those who will question the slightness of the story line," maintains *New York Times* critic Clive Barnes, "but there will be more, many, many more who will glory in the show's dexterity, wit and compassion. Miss Fornes's lyrics, like her book, seem to have a sweetly irrelevant relevance." Marranca similarly observes that "*Promenade* has the joie de vivre, the disregard for external logic and spatial convention, the crazy-quilt characters that one associates with the plays of Gertrude Stein. . . . The satire seems almost effortless because the playwright's touch is so playful and laid back. Yet Fornes makes her point, and there's no confusion as to whose side she is on in this comedy of manners." As Barnes concludes in his review: "One definition of 'Promenade' might be that it is a protest musical for people too sophisticated to protest."

Fefu and Her Friends, Fornes's next major success, ventures even farther into new dramatic forms. Set in one house where eight women are meeting, "the play has no plot in the conventional sense, and the characters are presented as fragments," remarks Marranca. "Though there is much about them that Fornes keeps hidden, the play—seeming at first like realism—is purposely set in the realm of the mysterious and abstract. By setting the play in a home, and then offering a narrative that subverts realistic conventions, Fornes plays ironically with domestic space, and the notion of domestic drama." The playwright presents a further innovation by having the audience separate and move out of the main theatre to view four separate scenes in different areas of the house. "But the conceit is more than just a gimmick," writes David Richards in the *Washington Post.* "Fornes, you see, is literally asking her audience to 'track down' her characters. . . . Theater-goers are being transformed into sleuths." The result of this fragmentation, claims Richard Eder in the *New York Times,* is that "'Fefu' is the dramatic equivalent of a collection of poems. Each conversation, each brief scene tries to capture an aspect of the central, anguished vision."

This reformation of traditional staging has disturbed some critics, however. Walter Kerr believes that there is too much emphasis on the structure of the play; he states in the *New York Times* that while "everyone finally gets to see every scene, though not in the same sequence . . . this does not matter for the play is not going anywhere; *you* are." The critic also comments that "if I lasted as long as I did, it was because I kept hoping during my constant journeyings that I *might* find a play in the very next room." But others, such as *Washington Post* contributor Lloyd Grove, find that this complicated staging is effective: "You're close enough to touch the characters in action, and suddenly on intimate-enough terms with them to grasp what they're about." Mael similarly

believes that "these close-ups (another example of Fornes's use of cinematic style) enable members of the audience to experience the women's relationship in a more intimate manner than would be possible on a proscenium stage." And Richards feels that "the strength of this production is that it has you thinking, 'If only I could look into one more room, catch one more exchange, come back a minute later.' In short, it lures you into a labyrinth of the mind." "*Fefu and Her Friends* has the delicacy of tone and economical style of Fornes's earlier plays," concludes Marranca. "But what makes this play stand apart—and ahead—of the others is, more than the inclusiveness of the experiment in text and performance, the embodiment of a deeply personal vision."

"Ever since *Fefu and Her Friends* Maria Irene Fornes has been writing the finest realistic plays in this country," asserts Marranca in *Performing Arts Journal.* "In fact, one could say that *Fefu* and the plays that followed it . . . have paved the way for a new language of dramatic realism, and a way of directing it." The critic explains: "Fornes brings a much needed intimacy to drama, and her economy of approach suggests another vision of theatricality, more stylized for its lack of exhibitionism." Calling Fornes "America's truest poet of the theatre," a *Village Voice* critic observes that in the 1985 Obie-winner *The Conduct of Life,* the author "takes on a subject so close to the bones of our times you'd think it unapproachable." *The Conduct of Life* follows the family life of a torturer who works for a fascist Latin American government. Although "we don't think of the fascist classes in Latin America bothering with disgust or introspection or moral concern," remarks Paul Berman in the *Nation,* "of course they do, and no doubt they ask questions much the way Fornes shows this officer's unhappy wife asking in *The Conduct of Life,* with agonies of soul and eventually with a gun. And what is this, by the way, if not the spirit of our time?"

In presenting the internal and external conflicts of these characters, Fornes uses "a dozen or so vignettes, some lasting only a moment or two, that are punctuated by lighting that fades slowly," describes Herbert Mitgang of the *New York Times.* The critic adds that "these theatrical punctuation marks are the equivalent of the ellipses that some poets and novelists use, and abuse, to tell the reader: At this point it's time to think about the wisdom of what is being said." Thus "the play conjures a lot of tension, mostly by keeping the scenes tight and disciplined and unsettlingly short," states Berman. "The dialogue and staging seem almost to have been cropped too close

. . . but sometimes the cropping pares away everything but the musing of a single voice, and these monologues are the most effective aspect of all." Although he finds some faults with the play, Berman concludes that "*The Conduct of Life* is incomparably more serious than any of the new plays on Broadway and will surely stand out in memory as a bright spot of the season." And another *Village Voice* critic presents a comparable assessment, calling Fornes's work "as important and as entertaining as any you're likely to see this year."

"Fornes's work goes to the core of character," writes Marranca. "Instead of the usual situation in which a character uses dialogue or action to explain what he or she is doing and why, her characters exist in the world by their very act of trying to understand it. In other words, it is the characters themselves who appear to be thinking, not the author having thought." Sontag also praises the playwright, commenting that "Fornes's work has always been intelligent, often funny, never vulgar or cynical; both delicate and visceral. Now it is something more. . . . The plays have always been about wisdom: what it means to be wise. They are getting wiser." "Working for more than thirty years in Off-Broadway's unheralded spaces," declares Marranca, "Fornes is an exemplary artist who through her writing and teaching has created a life in the theatre away from the crass hype that attends so many lesser beings. How has she managed that rare accomplishment in this country's theatre—a career?" Explains the critic: "What is admirable about Fornes is that she is one of the last real bohemians among the writers who came to prominence in the sixties. She never changed to fit her style to fashion. She has simply been writing, experimenting, thinking. Writers still have to catch up to her." The critic concludes that "if there were a dozen writers in our theatre with Fornes's wisdom and graciousness it would be enough for a country, and yet even one of her is sometimes all that is needed to feel the worth of the enormous effort it takes to live a life in the American theatre."

A manuscript collection of Fornes's work is located at the Lincoln Center Library of the Performing Arts in New York City.

BIOGRAPHICAL/CRITICAL SOURCES:

BOOKS

Betsko, Kathleen, and Rachel Koenig, *Interviews with Contemporary Women Playwrights,* Beech Tree Books, 1987.

Contemporary Literary Criticism, Volume 39, Gale (Detroit), 1986.

Dictionary of Literary Biography, Volume 7: *Twentieth-Century American Dramatists,* Gale, 1981.

Fornes, Maria Irene, *Maria Irene Fornes: Plays,* PAJ Publications, 1986.

Kent, Assunta Bartolomucci, *Maria Irene Fornes and Her Critics,* Greenwood Press (Westport, CT), 1996.

Marranca, Bonnie, and Gautam Dasgupta, *American Playwrights: A Critical Survey,* Volume 1, Drama Books Specialists, 1981.

Moroff, Diane Lynn, *Fornes: Theater in the Present Tense,* University of Michigan Press (Ann Arbor), 1996.

PERIODICALS

Chicago, April, 1990, p. 89.

Chicago Tribune, June 14, 1969; February 8, 1988.

Hispanic, July, 1988.

Los Angeles Times, July 9, 1987.

Nation, April 6, 1985.

Newsweek, June 4, 1969.

New York, June 23, 1969; March 18, 1985.

New York Times, April 17, 1968; June 5, 1969; June 6, 1969; February 22, 1972; January 14, 1978; January 22, 1978; April 25, 1979; December 30, 1981; October 25, 1983; March 13, 1984; March 20, 1985; April 17, 1986; April 23, 1986; October 17, 1987; December 15, 1987.

Performing Arts Journal, Number 1, 1984.

Variety, February 24, 1992, p. 257; March 23, 1992, p. 113.

Village Voice, April 21, 1966; April 17, 1969; March 19, 1985; March 26, 1985.

Washington Post, July 9, 1983; July 15, 1983.*

*   *   *

FROHOCK, Fred M(anuel) 1937-

PERSONAL: Born February 7, 1937, in Perry, FL; son of Fred C. (a civil engineer) and Marie A. (a homemaker; maiden name, Domenech) Frohock; married Val Jean Derrick, September 7, 1963; children: Katherine Renee, Christina Marie. *Education:* University of Florida, B.A., 1960, M.A., 1961; University of North Carolina at Chapel Hill, Ph.D. (political theory), 1966. *Politics:* Democrat. *Religion:* Catholic. *Avocational interests:* Tennis, golf, running, watching baseball.

ADDRESSES: Home—4448 Kasson Rd., Syrause, NY 13215. *Office*—Syracuse University, Maxwell School of Citizenship and Public Affairs, Political Science Dept., Syracuse, NY 13244. *E-mail*—ffrohock@syr. edu.

CAREER: Educator and writer. Dade Junior College, Miami, FL, instructor, 1961-62; Syracuse University, Syracuse, NY, assistant professor of methodology and political theory, 1965-69, associate professor of political philosophy, 1969-74, professor of political science, 1974—, chair of political science department, 1985-89. Professor in Syracuse University's Florence program, Florence, Italy, 1969-70, the Madrid program, Madrid, Spain, 1972-74, and chair of the London Politics Seminar, 1984—. Lecturer and guest speaker at colleges and conferences, including Dallas, TX; Denver, CO; Tallahassee, FL; Salt Lake City, UT; Houston, TX; Norwalk, CT; Chicago, IL; Savannah, GA; Gainesville, FL; and Tempe, AZ.

MEMBER: American Political Science Association, Southern Political Science Association, Society for the Study of Narrative Literature.

AWARDS, HONORS: University of North Carolina Departmental Teaching fellowship, 1964-65; Social Science Research Council fellowship, 1964-65; training fellowship to study analytic philosophy and its relevance to political theory in London, England, 1968-69; *Abortion: A Case Study in Law and Morals* was selected as an Outstanding Academic Book, *Choice,* 1984; National Endowment for the Humanities summer fellowship.

WRITINGS:

NONFICTION

The Nature of Political Inquiry, Dorsey (Homewood, IL), 1967.
Normative Political Theory, Prentice-Hall (Englewood Cliffs, NJ), 1974.
(Contributor) *An Introduction to the Science of Politics,* edited by Donald Freeman, Free Press (New York City), 1978.
(Contributor) *Through the Looking Glass: Epistemology and the Conduct of Inquiry—An Anthology,* edited by Maria Falco, University Press (San Francisco, CA), 1979.
Public Policy: Scope and Logic, Prentice-Hall, 1979.
Abortion: A Case Study in Law and Morals, Greenwood Press (Westport, CT), 1983.

Special Care: Medical Decisions at the Beginning of Life, University of Chicago Press (Chicago, IL), 1986.
Rational Association, Syracuse University Press (Syracuse, NY), 1987.
Healing Powers: Alternative Medicine, Spiritual Communities, and the State, University of Chicago Press, 1992.
Public Reason: Mediated Authority in the Liberal State, Cornell University Press (Ithaca, NY), 1999.

Also contributor of articles and reviews to periodicals, including *Hartford Courant, St. Louis Post Dispatch, Syracuse Scholar, Political Studies, American Political Science Review, Social Theory and Practice, Journal of Politics, Polity, Journal of Church and State, Contemporary Sociology, Ethics, USA Today, Medical Ethics for the Physician, Hastings Center Report, Bucknell Review, Philadelphia Inquirer,* and *Annals of the Association of American Geographers.*

WORK IN PROGRESS: Public Reason: Mediated Authority in the Liberal State; Lives of the Psychics: Human Experiences with the Supernatural.

SIDELIGHTS: Fred M. Frohock has had a distinguished academic career in political science, and has taught at Syracuse University in New York for over thirty years. He has penned several books, including 1967's *The Nature of Political Inquiry.* Frohock's later titles, however, have tended towards ethical issues in medical matters, as with 1983's *Abortion: A Case Study in Law and Morals,* 1986's *Special Care: Medical Decisions at the Beginning of Life,* and 1992's *Healing Powers: Alternative Medicine, Spiritual Communities, and the State.*

In *The Nature of Political Inquiry,* Frohock provides readers with an examination of the theoretical categories in use during the 1960s to facilitate political analysis. He discusses both rationalism and empiricism, and asserts a belief in the impracticality of the fact-value distinction for analytical purposes. A *Choice* reviewer gave high praise to *The Nature of Political Inquiry,* hailing it as a "meaty, candid, and courageous effort to say what the theoretical state of the discipline is."

Abortion: A Case Study in Law and Morals was named an outstanding academic book by *Choice* in 1984. Within this work, Frohock presents arguments both for and against legalized abortion, often in the words of contemporary leaders of the respective groups of activists. The author also gives readers some of his own opinions as well, arguing for legalization of abortion on the basis of female equality rather than the privacy argument upon which the U.S. Supreme Court decision *Roe vs. Wade* rests. He also urges that a compromise between anti-abortion and pro-choice forces be found and agreed upon before the fight between them becomes too bitter. "The cleanest compromise," Frohock states in *Abortion,* "is a social practice that permits abortions early in term, [and] prohibits middle- and late-term abortions." Dinesh D'Souza, discussing *Abortion* in *National Review,* remarked: "I find, in this book, the most forceful cases stated in behalf of both the pro-life and pro-choice positions, with original arguments posted for both sides." D'Souza, did, however, feel that "after an impressive plunge into the legal and moral issues that affect the abortion debate . . . Frohock splashes disappointingly to the surface." A *Choice* magazine critic reviewed the book more positively, declaring Frohock's writing to be "extremely clear and concise" and hailing *Abortion* as an "excellent reference work for both a philosophical and an empirical inquiry into abortion . . . accessible to both general readers and undergraduates."

From the topic of abortion, Frohock moved to that of the legal and ethical questions surrounding the treatment of severely handicapped and/or extremely premature babies in hospital neonatal units. His *Special Care: Medical Decisions at the Beginning of Life* was written partially in response to the 1983 "Baby Jane Doe" case of a female baby born with spina bifida, excess fluid in the brain, and an abnormally small head. As Jonathan Bor reported in the *Syracuse Post-Standard,* "without surgery, her doctors said, Jane would die within two years. With surgery, she could survive into her twenties but would be severely retarded and bedridden." Bor went on to explain that the parents, after discussing the matter with others, made the decision not to pursue surgery. Their decision was opposed, however, by a right-to-life attorney who decided to sue the hospital to take corrective measures and keep Jane alive. The case eventually went to the U.S. Supreme Court, which decided in favor of the parents.

To make his points in *Special Care,* Frohock spent four months interviewing doctors, nurses, and the parents of patients in a neonatal intensive care unit of a hospital to which he gave the protective name of Northeastern General. Frohock filled *Special Care* with individual cases—one of a child born without a brain but merely a brain stem. "The possibility ex-

isted," the author explains, "for a 'viable' child without a brain living for months, perhaps years, as a vegetable." Frohock goes on to discuss the ways the various physicians in this particular case discussed whether to deprive the child of intravenous nourishment, which would hasten his death even more than not putting him on a ventilator. Some felt that the lack of nourishment too cruel; the parents decided not to use the ventilator, and the baby died in two days. Frohock also gives examples, however, of miraculous recovery on the part of some of these very fragile infants. He describes a "favorite story" of the nursing staff in which surgeons gave up on a child suffering from the advanced stages of a disease that killed sections of her bowel. He decided that the case had progressed to the point that the girl would never be able to digest her own food and ended the surgical procedure he was performing on her half-way through. Instead of dying, however, the girl went on to thrive and became "a happy, vigorous child." Though Frohock presents many different cases with many different outcomes, and admits the complexity of the moral issues surrounding the treatment of severely damaged or premature infants, in Bor's judgment he "is concerned that the right-to-life movement, in its zest to protect the lives of those who can't speak for themselves, has missed the shades of gray that complicate the real-world business of decision-making." Frohock himself described his position in *Special Care* to Bor: "I argue that the proper instrument or vehicle for making these decisions is some group consisting of the parents, the family and the doctors—the physicians of the child."

Reviewers of *Special Care* were generally positive. Paula J. Adams Hillard asserted in the *New York Times Book Review* that Frohock "argues" his various points in the volume "cogently." A *Booklist* critic hailed *Special Care* as "a sensitive gathering of medical facts and anecdotes," while D. R. Shanklin in *Choice* affirmed that it "represents the best treatment on this subject so far available."

Frohock's 1992 effort, *Healing Powers: Alternative Medicine, Spiritual Communities, and the State,* considers the legal and ethical questions surrounding the use of alternative medical treatments, or, in some cases, purely spiritual methods of coping with illness and disease. As in his other books concerning ethical matters, Frohock presents cases and individuals that endorse both sides of the debate; between presentation of actual cases, Frohock weaves the fictional voice of Luke, a young man whose childhood was spent battling a deadly leukemia. He overcame the disease with both conventional medical treatment and the prayer support of an African-American minister named Faith. In this manner Frohock seems to illustrate his compromise position—in his belief, healing is best effected through a combination of conventional and alternative methods, and both sides must be more open to the benefits of the other.

Arthur W. Frank, reviewing *Healing Powers* in the *Christian Century,* observed: "This book is a valuable resource for clergy who advise the ill on whether and how to seek alternative therapy. Those already engaged in healing ministries," he continued, "will discover a broader context for these activities. Others will find provocative insights into the varieties and possibilities of such ministries. None will find easy answers." Marshall B. Kapp, writing for the *New England Journal of Medicine,* praised the case studies in *Healing Powers* as "fascinating," and declared that the volume "contains a storehouse of valuable information about the historical, philosophical, and psychological bases of alternative approaches to healing."

Frohock once explained that his "early experiences include a childhood in Key West, Florida, where one's senses seemed always (and gratefully so) overloaded with physical beauty—sun, water, foliage (no doubt creating my constant and nonsatiable needs for natural surroundings and possibly leading to later infatuations with the ancient Greek philosopher Plato's 'form of the good' which he made analogous to the sun)—and where a Catholic instruction on the Trinity, transubstantiation, sin, grace, etc., left the usual metaphysical marks. Memories also include frequent and continuous encounters with my father's orderly intellect—disagreement on virtually everything (especially politics) from the beginning, but the heat and light of this continuous exchange of ideas have surely helped crystallize my commitment to dialogue as a means for reaching collective outcomes. Also, membership in two cultures (Anglo and Hispanic) allowed me to share a temperament at odds with many analytic perspectives—an observation that readers of my work strangely dismiss.

"Intellectual experiences include the conventional and unconventional in literature, which I began reading on my own in the Miami Public Library while in high school. I also wrote a lot of fiction, and still do. In college, it was engineering studies combined with political science, the latter finally winning out in a package with philosophy—consisting, at that time, of existentialism and Cartesian thought. My graduate years in Chapel Hill, North Carolina, were the deci-

sive times, both because of the setting and the decade of the 1960s. The civil rights and anti-war movements were especially important. The assassination of President Kennedy was a catalyst, causing me and many others to re-think the ordinary language philosophy and non-cognitive value theory we were studying. Thus the importance to me of the revival of naturalism in recent philosophy—that of Foot and Searle in moral philosophy, and Kripke in epistemology. Finally, my rich personal life has been an influence, but its richness is in part a function of its undocumented and spontaneous nature, and thus it is inappropriate for mention here.

"The connections between this brief catalog of experiences and my work is difficult to know. I think I see certain continuities. At a very early age I started working summers in a variety of jobs, at my father's insistence. One summer in high school, for example, my brother and I were day laborers at a construction site where our father was project engineer. This varied work—as laborer, clerk, salesman, repairman, mechanic, etc.—put me in the company of people I wouldn't ordinarily have met. I always talked at length with my co-workers and formed early the conviction that everyone has a story to tell that makes their life intelligible and justifiable. To get at these stories is easy: shut up and listen to the person. This internal world that individuals create and occupy, I have always believed, is the origin of social life—a belief I developed and extended through studies in phenomenology with Natanson at Chapel Hill, primarily of the theory of Husserl and Schutz. The social world, however, can fail individual expectations. I still vividly recall driving in a pickup truck on many early mornings with the foremen of my laboring crew to hire additional construction workers. We would drive to Coconut Grove on South Dixie Highway where one encountered, at 7:00 am, hundreds of black males with lunch buckets waiting for some job. They would crowd around the truck and the foreman would say, 'You, you, and you,' pointing to two or three who would then jump into the truck. We would drive off, and those left behind, if not selected by others—and most were not—would then drift through the day. It is an easy matter while growing up and observing life to see that inequity and irrationality are assignable to the social system even when all of the members of the society have good intentions and reasons for their actions—which, for the record, they often do not.

"My work in the last several years has been in bioethics. I am particularly interested in the moral dilemmas created by medical technology. In *Special Care* I argue that our ability to maintain life today has compromised and even made unintelligible the use of right-to-life vocabularies in intensive care medicine. The good intentions of medical practitioners lead to bad and contradictory outcomes *because* medicine is so effective. Again, institutions compromise the efforts of decent individuals to realize their basic values. These contradictions between individuals and institutions are disclosed in the open-ended Terkelian interviews introduced in *Special Care*. Physicians, nurses, parents—all relate stories that exhibit the anomalous fit between our legal/moral languages and the world of modern medicine.

"All of the work I do from now on will have the kind of strong narrative frame found in *Special Care*. I also intend to work closer to the thin line separating reality—whatever that means—from fiction. The various grids of concepts and categories we all use to make our lives intelligible seem to me to move more easily between fact and fiction than is commonly acknowledged. One hopes that the blurring of such conventional distinctions is a sign of more innovative work in the future, not an indication of some lively mental disorder."

BIOGRAPHICAL/CRITICAL SOURCES:

BOOKS

Frohock, Fred M., *Special Care: Medical Decisions at the Beginning of Life,* University of Chicago Press, 1986.

PERIODICALS

American Academy of Political and Social Science Annals, September, 1984, p. 211; January, 1988, p. 191.
American Political Science Review, September, 1968, p. 870; December, 1984, p. 1099.
American Scientist, July, 1994, p. 385.
Bloomsbury Review, January, 1993, p. 13.
Booklist, August, 1986, p. 1646; September 1, 1992, p. 16.
Choice, September, 1968, p. 870; June, 1974, p. 668; November, 1979, p. 1231; March, 1984, p. 1018; January, 1987, p. 784; January, 1993, p. 830.
Christian Century, November 18, 1992, pp. 1063-67.
Contemporary Sociology, September, 1987, p. 746; September, 1993, p. 385.
Ethics, January, 1985, p. 375; January, 1988, p. 405.
Journal of Church and State, autumn, 1984, p. 550.

Journal of Politics, May, 1968, p. 582; February, 1981, p. 233; May, 1995, p. 580.
Kirkus Reviews, October 1, 1986, p. 1504; July 15, 1992, p. 895.
Library Journal, July, 1986, p. 98.
Medical Humanities Review, fall, 1993, p. 39.
National Review, January 27, 1984, pp. 52, 54.
New England Journal of Medicine, January 21, 1993, pp. 216-17.
New York Times Book Review, October 5, 1986, p. 54.
Reference and Research Book News, September, 1993, p. 48.
Religious Studies Review, July, 1988, p. 242; July, 1994, p. 219.
Science Books and Films, May, 1987, p. 290.
SciTech Book News, December, 1986, p. 27; January, 1993, p. 19.
Social Forces, June, 1993, p. 1111.
Syracuse Post-Standard, March 6, 1986.

*   *   *

FUENTES, Carlos 1928-

PERSONAL: Born November 11, 1928, in Panama City, Panama; Mexican citizen; son of Rafael Fuentes Boettiger (a career diplomat) and Berta Macias Rivas; married Rita Macedo (a movie actress), 1959 (divorced, 1969); married Sylvia Lemus (a television journalist), 1973; children: (first marriage) Cecilia; (second marriage) Carlos Rafael, Natasha. *Education:* National University of Mexico, LL.B., 1948; graduate study, Institute des Hautes Etudes, Geneva, Switzerland. *Politics:* Independent leftist. *Avocational interests:* Reading, travel, swimming, visiting art galleries, listening to classical and rock music, motion pictures, the theater.

ADDRESSES: Home—716 Watchung Rd., Bound Brook, NJ 08805. *Office*—401 Boylston Hall, Harvard University, Cambridge, MA 02138.

CAREER: Writer. International Labor Organization, Geneva, Switzerland, began as member, became secretary of the Mexican delegation, 1950-52; Ministry of Foreign Affairs, Mexico City, Mexico, assistant chief of press section, 1954; National University of Mexico, Mexico City, secretary and assistant director of cultural dissemination, 1955-56, head of department of cultural relations, 1957-59; Mexico's ambassador to France, 1975-77; Cambridge University,

Norman Maccoll Lecturer, 1977, Simon Bolivar professor, 1986-87; Barnard College, New York City, Virginia Gildersleeve Professor, 1977; Columbia University, New York City, Henry L. Tinker Lecturer, 1978; Harvard University, Cambridge, MA, Robert F. Kennedy Professor of Latin American studies, 1987—. Fellow at Woodrow Wilson International Center for Scholars, 1974; Lecturer or visiting professor at University of Mexico, University of California at San Diego, University of Oklahoma, University of Concepcion in Chile, University of Paris, University of Pennsylvania, and George Mason University; Modern Humanities Research Association, president, 1989—; member of Mexican National Commission on Human Rights.

MEMBER: American Academy and Institute of Arts and Letters (honorary).

AWARDS, HONORS: Centro Mexicano de Escritores fellowship, 1956-57; Biblioteca Breve Prize from Seix Barral (publishing house; Barcelona), 1967, for *Cambio de piel;* Xavier Villaurrutia Prize (Mexico), 1975; Romulo Gallegos Prize (Venezuela), 1977, for *Terra Nostra;* Alfonso Reyes Prize (Mexico), 1979, for body of work; National Award for Literature (Mexico), 1984, for "Orchids in the Moonlight"; nominated for *Los Angeles Times* Book Award in fiction, 1986, for *The Old Gringo;* Miguel de Cervantes Prize from Spanish Ministry of Culture, 1987; Ruben Dario Order of Cultural Independence (Nicaragua) and literary prize of Italo-Latino Americano Institute, both 1988, for *The Old Gringo;* Medal of Honor for Literature, National Arts Club, New York City, 1988; Rector's Medal, University of Chile, 1991; Casita Maria Medal, 1991; Order of Merit (Chile), 1992; French Legion of Honor, 1992; Menedez Pelayo International Award, University of Santander, 1992; named honorary citizen of Santiago de Chile, Buenos Aires, and Veracruz, 1993; Principe de Asturias Prize, 1994; Premiio Grinzane-Cavour, 1994; candidate for Neustadt International Prize for Literature, 1996; honorary degrees from Bard College, Cambridge University, Columbia College, Chicago State University, Dartmouth College, Essex University, Georgetown University, Harvard University, and Washington University.

WRITINGS:

NOVELS

La region mas transparente, Fondo de Cultura Economica, 1958, translation by Sam Hileman pub-

lished as *Where the Air Is Clear,* Ivan Obolensky, 1960.
Las buenas consciencias, Fondo de Cultura Economica, 1959, translation published as *The Good Conscience,* Ivan Oblensky, 1961.
La muerte de Artemio Cruz, Fondo de Cultura Economica, 1962, translation by Hileman published as *The Death of Artemio Cruz,* Farrar, Straus (New York City), 1964.
Aura (also see below), Era, 1962, reprinted, 1982, translation by Lysander Kemp, Farrar, Straus, 1965.
Zona sagrada, Siglo XXI, 1967, translation by Suzanne Jill Levine published as *Holy Place* (also see below), Dutton (New York City), 1972.
Cambio de piel, Mortiz, 1967, translation by Hileman published as *A Change of Skin,* Farrar, Straus, 1968.
Cumpleanos, Mortiz, 1969, translation published as *Birthday* (also see below).
Terra Nostra (also see below), Seix Barral, 1975, translation by Levine, afterword by Milan Kundera, Farrar, Straus, 1976.
La cabeza de hidra, Mortiz, 1978, translation by Margaret Sayers Peden published as *Hydra Head,* Farrar, Straus, 1978.
Una familia lejana, Era, 1980, translation by Peden published as *Distant Relations,* Farrar, Straus, 1982.
El gringo viejo, Fondo de Cultura Economica, 1985, translation by Peden and Fuentes published as *The Old Gringo,* Farrar, Straus, 1985.
Christopher Unborn (translation of *Cristobal Nonato*), Farrar, Straus, 1989.

Also author of *Holy Place & Birthday: Two Novellas,* Farrar, Straus.

SHORT STORIES

Los dias enmascarados (also see below), Los Presentes, 1954.
Cantar de ciegos (also see below), Mortiz, 1964.
Dos cuentos mexicanos (title means "Two Mexican Stories"; previously published in *Cantar de ciegos*), Instituto de Cultura Hispanica de Sao Paulo, Universidade de Sao Paulo, 1969.
Poemas de amor: Cuentos del alma, Imp. E. Cruces (Madrid), 1971.
Chac Mool y otros cuentos, Salvat, 1973.
Agua quemada (anthology), Fondo de Cultura Economica, 1981, translation by Peden published as *Burnt Water,* Farrar, Straus, 1980.

Constancia and Other Stories for Virgins, Farrar, Straus, 1989.

Diana, the Goddess Who Hunts Alone, introduction by Alfred J. Mac Adam, Farrar, Straus, (New York City), 1995.

PLAYS

Todos los gatos son pardos (also see below), Siglo XXI, 1970.

El tuerto es rey (also see below; produced in French in 1970, Mortiz, 1970.

Los reinos originarios (contains *Todos los gatos son pardos* and *El tuerto es rey*), Seix Barral, 1971.

Orquideas a la luz de la luna (produced in English as *Orchids in the Moonlight* at American Repertory Theater in Cambridge, MA, 1982), Seix Barral, 1982.

NONFICTION

The Argument of Latin America: Words for North Americans, Radical Education Project, 1963.

(Contributor) *Whither Latin America?* (political articles), Monthly Review Press, 1963.

Paris: La revolucion de mayo, Era, 1968.

La nueva novela hispanoamericana, Mortiz, 1969.

(Contributor) *El mundo de Jose Luis Cuevas,* Tudor (Mexico City), 1969.

Casa con dos puertas (title means "House with Two Doors"), Mortiz, 1970.

Tiempo mexicano (title means "Mexican Time"), Mortiz, 1971.

Cervantes; o, La critica de la lectura, Mortiz, 1976, translation published as *Don Quixote; or, The Critique of Reading* Institute of Latin American Studies, University of Texas at Austin, 1976.

On Human Rights: A Speech, Somesuch Press (Dallas), 1984.

Latin America: At War with the Past, CBC Enterprises, 1985.

Myself with Others: Selected Essays, Farrar, Straus, 1988.

A New Time for Mexico, Farrar, Straus, 1996.

OTHER

(Editor and author of prologue) Octavio Paz, *Los signos en rotacion, y otros ensayos,* Alianza, 1971.

Cuerpos y ofrendas (anthology; includes selections from *Los dias enmascarados, Cantar de ciegos, Aura,* and *Terra Nostra,*) introduction by Octavio Paz, Alianza, 1972.

(Author of introduction) Milan Kundera, *La vida esta en otra parte* (Spanish translation of *Life Is Elsewhere*), Seix Barral, 1977.

(Author of introduction) Omar Cabezas, *Fire from the Mountain,* Crown, 1988.

Valiente Mundo Nuevo, Fondo de Cultura Economica (Mexico City), 1990.

The Campaign, Farrar, Straus, 1991.

Buried Mirror: Reflections on Spain in the New World, Houghton (Boston), 1992.

Geografia de la novela, Fondo de Cultura Economica (Mexico City), 1993.

El naranjo, o los circulos del tiempo, Alfaguara, Mexico, 1993.

The Orange Tree, introduction by Mac Adam, Farrar, Straus, 1994.

La frontera de cristal, Alfaguara, Mexico, 1995.

The Writings of Carlos Fuentes, edited by Raymond L. Williams, University of Texas Press (Austin), 1996.

Collaborator on several film scripts, including *Pedro Paramo,* 1966, *Tiempo de morir,* 1966, and *Los caifanes,* 1967. Work represented in numerous anthologies, including *Antologia de cuentos hispanoamericanos,* Nueva Decada (Costa Rica), 1985. Contributor to periodicals in the United States, Mexico, and France, including *New York Times, Washington Post,* and *Los Angeles Times.* Founding editor, *Revista Mexicana de Literatura,* 1954-58; coeditor, *El Espectador,* 1959-61, *Siempre,* 1960, and *Politica,* 1960.

ADAPTATIONS: Two short stories from *Cantar de ciegos* were made into films in the mid-1960s; *The Old Gringo* was adapted into a film of the same title by Fonda Films, 1989.

WORK IN PROGRESS: A novel about the assassination of Emiliano Zapata.

SIDELIGHTS: "Carlos Fuentes," states Robert Maurer in *Saturday Review,* is "without doubt one of Mexico's two or three greatest novelists." He is part of a group of Latin American writers whose writings, according to Alistair Reid's *New Yorker* essay, "formed the background of the Boom," a literary phenomenon Reid describes as a period in the 1960s when "a sudden surge of hitherto unheard-of writers from Latin America began to be felt among [U.S.] readers." Fuentes, however, is singled out from among the other writers of the Boom in Jose Donoso's autobiographical account, *The Boom in Spanish American Literature: A Personal History,* in which the Chilean novelist calls Fuentes "the first active and conscious agent of the internationalization of the Spanish American novel." And since the 1960s, Fuentes has continued his international influence in the literary world: his 1985 novel, *The Old Gringo,* for example, was the first written by a Mexican to ever appear on the *New York Times* best-seller list.

Although, as Donoso observes, early worldwide acceptance of Fuentes's novels contributed to the internationalization of Latin American literature, his work is an exploration of the culture and history of one nation, his native Mexico. Critics note the thematic presence of Mexico in nearly all Fuentes's writing. Robert Coover comments in the *New York Times Book Review* that in *The Death of Artemio Cruz,* for instance, Fuentes delineates "in the retrospective details of one man's life the essence of the post-Revolutionary history of all Mexico." Mexico is also present in Fuentes's novel *Terra Nostra,* in which, according to *Washington Post Book World* contributor Larry Rohter, "Fuentes probes more deeply into the origins of Mexico—and what it means to be a Mexican—than ever before." Fuentes's *Old Gringo*—published more than twenty years after *The Death of Artemio Cruz*—returns to the same theme as it explores Mexico's relationship with its northern neighbor, the United States.

Fuentes explained his preoccupation with Mexico, and particularly with Mexican history, in a *Paris Review* interview. "Pablo Neruda used to say," he told Alfred MacAdam and Charles Ruas, "that every Latin American writer goes around dragging a heavy body, the body of his people, of his past, of his national history. We have to assimilate the enormous weight of our past so that we will not forget what gives us life. If you forget your past, you die." Fuentes also noted that the development of the same theme in his novels unifies them so that they may be considered part of the same work. The author observed in the same interview, "In a sense my novels are one book with many chapters: *Where the Air Is Clear* is the biography of Mexico City; *The Death of Artemio Cruz* deals with an individual in that city; [and] *A Change of Skin* is that city, that society, facing the world, coming to grips with the fact that it is part of civilization and that there is a world outside that intrudes into Mexico."

Along with thematic unity, another characteristic of Fuentes's work is his innovative narrative style. In a *New Yorker* review, Anthony West compares the novelist's technique to "a rapid cinematic movement that cuts nervously from one character to another." Evan Connell states in the *New York Times Book Review* that Fuentes's "narrative style—with few exceptions—relies on the interruption and juxtaposition of different kinds of awareness." Reviewers Donald Yates and Karen Hardy also comment on Fuentes's experimental style. In the *Washington Post Book World* Yates calls Fuentes "a tireless experimenter with narrative techniques and points of view," while in *Hispania* Hardy notes that in Fuentes's work "the complexities of a human or national personality are evoked through . . . elaborate narrative devices."

Fuentes's novels *The Death of Artemio Cruz* and *Terra Nostra* are especially good examples of his experimental techniques. The first narrative deals with a corrupt Mexican millionaire who on his deathbed relives his life in a series of flashbacks. In the novel Fuentes uses three separate narrations to tell the story, and for each of these narrations he uses a different narrative person. *New York Review of Books* contributor A. Alvarez explains the three-part narration of the novel: "Cruz's story is told in three persons. 'I' is the old man dying on his bed; 'you' is a slightly vatic, 'experimental' projection of his potentialities into an unspecified future . . . ; 'he' is the real hero, the man whose history emerges bit by bit from incidents shuffled around from his seventy-one years." In John S. Brushwood's *Mexico in Its Novel: A Nation's Search for Identity,* the critic praises Fuentes's technique, commenting: "The changing narrative viewpoint is extremely effective, providing a clarity that could not have been accomplished any other way. I doubt that there is anywhere in fiction a character whose wholeness is more apparent than in the case of Artemio Cruz."

Coover observes that in *Terra Nostra* Fuentes once again uses a variety of narrators to tell his story. Commenting favorably on Fuentes's use of the "you" narrative voice in the novel, Coover writes: "Fuentes's second person [narration] is not one overheard on a stage: the book itself, rather than the author or a character, becomes the speaker, the reader or listener a character, or several characters in succession." Spanish novelist Juan Goytisolo similarly states in *Review:* "One of the most striking and most successful devices [in *Terra Nostra*] is the abrupt shift in narrative point of view (at times without the unwary reader's even noticing), passing from first-person narration to second, . . . and simultaneously rendering objective and subjective reality in one and the same passage with patent scorn for the rules of discourse that ordinarily govern expository prose." In the *Paris Review* Fuentes comments on his use of the second person narrative, calling it "the voice poets have always used and that novelists also have a right to use."

Fuentes's use of the second person narrative and other experimental techniques makes his novels extremely complex. The author's remarks in a *New York Times Book Review* interview with Frank MacShane concerning the structure of *Terra Nostra* describe the intricacy of the work: "My chief stylistic device in 'Terra Nostra' is to follow every statement by a counter statement and every image by its opposite." This deliberate duplicity by the author, along with the extensive scope of the novel, causes some reviewers to criticize *Terra Nostra* for being unaccessible to the average reader. Maurer, for instance, calls the novel "a huge, sprawling, exuberant, mysterious, almost unimaginably dense work of 800 pages, covering events on three continents from the creation of man in Genesis to the dawn of the twenty-first century," and adds that "*Terra Nostra* presents a common reader with enormous problems simply of understanding what is going on." *Newsweek*'s Peter S. Prescott notes: "To talk about [*Terra Nostra*] at all we must return constantly to five words: excess, surreal, baroque, masterpiece, [and] unreadable."

Other critics, however, have written more positive reviews, seeing *Terra Nostra* and other Fuentes works as necessarily complex. *Village Voice* contributor Jonah Raskin finds Fuentes is at his best when the novelist can "plunge readers into the hidden recesses of his characters' minds and at the same time allow language to pile up around their heads in thick drifts, until they feel lost in a blizzard of words that enables them to see, to feel, in a revolutionary way." Fuentes also defends the difficulty of his works in a *Washington Post* interview with Charles Truehart. Recalling the conversation with the Mexican author, Truehart quotes Fuentes as saying: "I believe in books that do not go to a ready-made public. . . . I'm looking for readers I would like to *make*. . . . To *win* them, . . . to *create* readers rather than to give something that readers are expecting. That would bore me to death."

In 1992 Fuentes produced, *The Buried Mirror: Reflections on Spain in the New World,* a historical work that discusses the formation and development of the Latin American world. The title refers to polished rocks found in the tombs of ancient Mediterranean and Amerindian peoples, presaging, in Fuentes's view, the convergence of these distant cultures. Fuentes writes that his book is "dedicated to a search

for the cultural continuity that can inform and transcend the economic and political destiny and fragmentation of the Hispanic world." Attempting to disentangle the complex legacy of Spanish settlement in the New World, Fuentes first addresses the mixed ethnicity of the Spanish conquerors, whose progeny include Celts, Phoenicians, Greeks, Romans, Arabs, and Jews, and the consequent diversity produced in Latin America through war, colonization, and miscegenation.

Praising Fuentes's intriguing though broad subject, Nicolas Shumway writes in the *New York Times Book Review,* "The range of the book is both its principal defect and its chief virtue. Beginning with the prehistoric cave paintings at Altamira in Spain and ending with contemporary street art in East Los Angeles, Mr. Fuentes seeks to cover all of Spanish and Spanish-American history, with frequent digressions on a particular artist, political figure, novel or painting." *The Buried Mirror,* according to David Ewing Duncan in a *Washington Post Book World* review, is "invigorated by the novelist's sense of irony, paradox and sensuality. Here is a civilization, he says, that defies whatever stereotypes we may hold, a society at once erotic and puritanical, cruel and humane, legalistic and corrupt, energetic and sad." Guy Garcia notes in *Time* that the book "represents an intellectual homecoming for Fuentes, who conceived of the project as 'a fantastic opportunity to write my own cultural biography.'"

Four years later Fuentes followed with *A New Time for Mexico,* a collection of essays on the internal injustice and international indignity suffered by Mexico. Viewed as a sequel to his 1971 publication *Tiempo mexicano,* translated as "Mexican Time," Fuentes addresses current events in his native country, including political reform, the Chiapas rebellion, social inequities, and the significance of the North American Free Trade Agreement (NAFTA) for Mexico and its perception in the United States. Though noting the bias of Fuentes's strong nationalism, Roderic A. Camp maintains in *Library Journal* that his "brief cultural vignettes" are "appealing and insightful." A *Publishers Weekly* reviewer commends Fuentes's "lapidary, lyrical meditations on Mexico as a land of continual metamorphosis."

In *The Orange Tree* Fuentes offers five novellas whose subjects span several centuries, each connected by the image of the orange and its perennial source. For Fuentes the orange tree signifies the possibilities of beauty, sustenance, transplantation, and rejuvenation, as its seeds were introduced to Spain through Roman and Moorish invaders, reached the New World with the conquistadors, and have flourished since. Fuentes illustrates various manifestations of violence, deception, and suffering by recounting episodes from the conquest of Roman Iberia and Mexico, a contemporary corporate takeover, and the death wish of an American actor.

"In all this intercourse between Old World and New, Rome and Africa and Spain, past and present," Alan Cheuse writes in Chicago *Tribune Books,* "Fuentes makes the older material resonate with all of the exotic and yet familiar attraction of compelling human behavior." Michael Kerrigan praises the work in a *Times Supplement Review,* noting that "The challenge and opportunity *The Orange Tree* presents its reader are those of escaping from 'a more or less protected individuality' into a wider existence of multiple possibility and a cyclical history which holds past and present in simultaneity and in ceaseless renewal." Kerrigan concludes, "What strikes the reader first in Fuentes' work may be his erudition and intellectual rigour, but what remains in the mind is his sympathy, his concern to commemorate the countless lives sacrificed in pain and obscurity so that we might live."

In 1995 Fuentes published *Diana, the Goddess Who Hunts Alone,* a semi-autobiographical novel that follows a love affair between an unnamed, married Mexican novelist and an American film actress, Diana Soren. The fictional romance, however, contains obvious parallels to the author's real-life affair with film actress Jean Seberg. Mirroring actual events surrounding the liaison between Fuentes and Seberg, the writer meets Soren at a New Year's Eve party in 1969 and follows her to a Santiago film location where they enjoy a passionate, albeit brief, relationship. After several months of literary conversation and tenuous intimacy, the self-absorbed writer is abandoned by the unstable actress who maintains a second relationship via telephone with a Black Panther and keeps a photograph of her last lover, Clint Eastwood, by her bed.

Though the book received mixed reviews, Rosanne Daryl Thomas observes in Chicago's *Tribune Books* that the novel reveals "the tensions between imagination, language and reality, between generosity born of love and the profound selfishness often found in artists." Thomas concludes, "Carlos Fuentes takes off the mask of literary creation and reveals a man nakedly possessed by a desperate passion. Then he raises the mask to his face and tells a fascinating, frightening tale of heartbreak."

While Fuentes's innovative use of theme and structure has gained the author an international reputation as a novelist, he believes that only since *Terra Nostra* has he perfected his craft. "I feel I'm beginning to write the novels I've always wanted to write and didn't know how to write before," he explained to Philip Bennett in a *Boston Globe Magazine* interview. "There were the novels of youth based on energy, and conceptions derived from energy. Now I have the conceptions I had as a young man, but I can develop them and give them their full value."

BIOGRAPHICAL/CRITICAL SOURCES:

BOOKS

Authors in the News, Volume 2, Gale (Detroit), 1976.
Brushwood, John S., *Mexico in Its Novel: A Nation's Search for Identity,* University of Texas Press, 1966.
Contemporary Literary Criticism, Gale (Detroit), Volume 3, 1975, Volume 8, 1978, Volume 10, 1979, Volume 13, 1980, Volume 22, 1982, Volume 41, 1987, Volume 60, 1991.
Dictionary of Literary Biography, Volume 113: *Modern Latin American Fiction Writers, First Series,* Gale, 1992.
Donoso, Jose, *The Boom in Spanish American Literature: A Personal History,* Columbia University Press (New York City), 1977.
Hispanic Literature Criticism, Gale, 1994.
Plimpton, George, editor, *Writers at Work: The Paris Review Interviews, Sixth Series,* Penguin, 1984.
Short Story Criticism, Volume 24, Gale, 1997.
World Literature Criticism, Gale, 1992.

PERIODICALS

Boston Globe Magazine, September 9, 1984.
Hispania, May, 1978.
Kirkus Reviews, April 15, 1996, p. 575.
Library Journal, January, 1994, p. 96; January, 1995, p. 77; January, 1996, p. 81; May 1, 1996, p. 112.
London Review of Books, May 10, 1990, p. 26.
Los Angeles Times Book Review, April 10, 1994, p. 6.
Nation, February 17, 1992, p. 205.
New Perspectives, spring, 1994, p. 54.
New Statesman, August 26, 1994, p. 37; September 29, 1995, p. 57.

Newsweek, November 1, 1976.

New Yorker, March 4, 1961; January 26, 1981; February 24, 1986.

New York Review of Books, June 11, 1964.

New York Times Book Review, November 7, 1976; October 19, 1980; October 6, 1991, p. 3; April 26, 1992, p. 9; October 22, 1995, p. 12.

Observer (London), April 1, 1990, p. 67.

Paris Review, winter, 1981.

Publishers Weekly, April 15, 1996, p. 55.

Review, winter, 1976.

Saturday Review, October 30, 1976.

Time, June 29, 1992, p. 78.

Times Literary Supplement, June 10, 1994, p. 23; September 29, 1995, p. 27.

Tribune Books (Chicago), April 19, 1992; April 11, 1994, p. 6; December 17, 1995, p. 3.

Village Voice, January 28, 1981; April 1, 1986.

Washington Post, May 5, 1988.

Washington Post Book World, October 26, 1976; January 14, 1979; March 29, 1992.

World Literature Today, autumn, 1994, p. 794.*

*   *   *

FUERTES, Gloria   1918-

PERSONAL: Born July 28, 1918, in Madrid, Spain; daughter of a concierge. *Education:* Attended trade school; studied library science, c. 1955-60.

ADDRESSES: Agent—c/o University Press of New England, 23 South Main St., Hanover, NH 03755.

CAREER: Writer, c. 1950—. Worked as an editor in 1940s; librarian, beginning 1960; instructor at Bucknell University, 1961-64; teacher in Madrid c. early 1970s.

AWARDS, HONORS: Honorable mention, Concurso Internacional de Poesia Lirica Hispana, for *Todo asusta;* Fulbright fellowship, 1961; Guipuzcoa poetry prize, for *Ni tiro, ni veneno, ni navaja;* Premio Viczaya, for *Como atar los bigotes al tigre;* prize for *Cangura para todo.*

WRITINGS:

Isla ignorada (poetry; title means "Unknown Island"), Musa Nueva (Madrid), 1950.

Canciones para ninos, Escuela Espanola (Madrid), 1952.

Antologia y poemas del suburbio (title means "Anthology and Poems of the Urban Poor"), Lirica Hispana (Caracas, Venezuela), 1954.

Aconsejo beber hilo (poetry; title means "I Advise Drinking Thread"), Arquero (Madrid), 1954.

Villancicos, Magisterio Espanol (Madrid), 1954.

Piruli, Escuela Espanola, 1955.

Todo asusta (poetry; title means "Everything Is Frightening"), Lirica Hispana, 1958.

Que estas en la tierra (poetry; title means "Who Art on Earth"), Literaturasa (Barcelona), 1962.

Ni tiro, ni veneno, ni navaja (poetry; title means "Not by Gunshot, Nor by Poison, Nor by Razor"), Bardo (Barcelona), 1966.

Cangura para todo (children's book; title means "Kangaroo at Your Service"), Lumen (Barcelona), 1967.

Poeta de guardia (poetry; title means "Poet on Call"), Ciencia Nueva (Madrid), 1968.

Como atar los bigotes al tigre (poetry; title means "How to Tie the Tiger's Whiskers"), Bardo, 1969.

Antologia poetica (1950-1969), edited by Francisco Ynduran, Plaza & Janes (Barcelona), 1970.

Don Pato y Don Pito, Escuela Espanola, 1970.

Aurora, Brigida y Carlos, Lumen, 1971.

La pajara pinta, Alcala (Madrid), 1972.

Cuando amas aprendes geografia (poetry; title means "When You Love You Learn Geography"), Curso Superior de Filologia (Malaga), 1973.

Sola en la sala (poetry; title means "Alone in the Living Room"), Javalambre (Zaragoza, Spain), 1973.

El camello-auto de las reyes magos, Igreca (Madrid), 1973.

El hada acaramelada, Igreca, 1973.

La gata Chundarata y otros cuentos, Videosistemas, 1974.

Obras incompletas, Catedra (Madrid), 1975.

Miguel: Un cuento muy moral en cinco capitulos y un prologo, Alfaguara (Madrid), 1977.

El libro de los derechos del nino, Nebrija (Leon, Spain), 1978.

Las tres reinas magas: Cuento teatro, Escuela Espanola, 1979.

Historia de Gloria (Amor, humor y desamor) (poetry; title means "Gloria's Story"), Catedra (Madrid), 1980.

La ardilla y su pandilla, Escuela Espanola, 1981.

Coleta, la poeta, Minon (Valladolid, Spain), 1982.

El dragon tragon, Escuela Espanola, 1982.

El abecedario de don Hilario, Minon, 1982.

Asi soy yo, Emiliano Escolar (Madrid), 1982.

Plumilindo: El cisne que queria ser pato, Escuela Espanola, 1983.

Piopcio Lope, el pollito miope, Escuela Espanola, 1983.

La momia tiene catarro, Escuela Espanola, 1983.

Coleta payasa, que pasa?, Minon, 1983.

La oca loca, Escuela Espanola, 1983.

Yo contento, tu contenta, que bien me sale la cuenta: La tabla en verso, Escuela Espanola, 1984.

El domador mordio al leon, Escuela Espanola, 1984.

El libro loco de todo un poco: Libro primero (cuentos, versos, aventuras, historietas, fantasias, chistes, acertijos, poesias, botijos, etc.), Escuela Espanola, 1984.

Off the Map: Selected Poems, edited and translated by Philip Levine and Ada Long, Wesleyan University Press (Middleton, CT), 1984.

Pecabamos como angeles: gloripoemas de amor, Ediciones Torremozas (Madrid), 1997.

Contributor of stories to children's magazines *Maravilla* and *Pelayo.* Associated with literary magazine *Arquero,* 1952-55.

SIDELIGHTS: Gloria Fuertes is an important Spanish writer who is known for her exuberant, remarkably accessible poetry. Martha LaFollette Miller wrote in the *Dictionary of Literary Biography,* "Although [Fuertes] has never sought the acclaim of a literary elite, instead striving simply to communicate her own reality to readers from all classes of society, and to promote peace, justice, and love, she nevertheless has begun to receive serious critical attention for the poetic vitality of her forthright, energetic verse."

Fuertes was born in 1918 in Madrid, Spain, and she was raised in working-class areas of the city. Although she began writing poetry when she was still a child, she did not publish her first collection, *Isla ignorada* ("Unknown Island"), until she was in her early thirties. Before making her literary debut, she worked as an editor and supplied stories to children's magazines, including *Maravilla* and *Pelayo.* Her circumstances scarcely changed with the appearance of either *Isla ignorada,* which earned little attention from Spanish critics, or *Antologia y poemas del suburbio* ("Anthology and Poems of the Urban Poor"), which received scant distribution. But *Antologia y poemas del suburbio,* although an early work, bears Fuertes's poetic trademarks, which Miller summarized as "her use of free verse, her deliberate avoidance of polish, her use of phonetically based wordplay—alliteration, puns, echoes—and her strongly autobiographical bent." In 1954, the same year that she produced *Antologia y poemas del suburbio,* Fuertes also published *Aconsejo beber hilo* ("I Advise Drink-

ing Thread"), wherein she again showed herself to be a master of straightforward, animated expression and candid autobiography. But this book, while establishing Fuertes as what Miller called an "original lyric voice," failed to realize significant monetary success. Fuertes thereupon determined to train for a career in library science, and for a five-year period, from 1955 to 1960, she studied even as she continued to hold her office job and write.

In 1960, after completing her studies, Fuertes managed to find work in the library field. By this time, however, she had also published *Todo asusta* ("Everything Is Frightening"), which brought her increasing recognition as an accomplished poet. The collection received honorable mention at the Concurso Internacional de Poesia Lirica Hispana, a poetry competition, and it proved an apt showcase for Fuertes's humanist concerns. Among the poems in this volume are "Tener un hijo hoy" ("To Have a Child Today"), in which she favors childlessness to providing the state with future soldiers, and "Tu parcela tendras" ("You'll Have Your Plot of Land"), wherein she sympathizes with the poor and acknowledges that the property that they will someday obtain is that of the burial plot.

Fuertes won even greater recognition with *Que estas en la tierra* ("Who Art on Earth"), a compilation of her previously published poems. But instead of capitalizing on her increasing fame and following quickly with another volume, Fuertes allowed several years to elapse. During much of the early 1960s, she taught at Bucknell University. When she finally produced another new collection, *Ni tiro, ni veneno, ni navaja* ("Not by Gunshot, Nor by Poison, Nor by Razor"), she affirmed her reputation as a poet capable of lyric verses at once compelling and comprehendible. This collection, which received a prestigious poetry prize in Spain, was readily followed by *Poeta de guardia* ("Poet on Call"), and *Como atar los bigotes al tigre* ("How to Tie the Tiger's Whiskers"). The latter volume secured the Premio Vizcaya, another literary prize, and it served to represent Fuertes's continued evolution as a poet. Miller wrote in the *Dictionary of Literary Biography* that the collection "continues the trend toward a greater acceptance of human limitations, or at least toward the defusing of the tragic through humor," and she added that it evinces Fuertes's shift "from the purely personal to that of common humanity."

In the ensuing decades, Fuertes has continued to produce poetry, notably the 1980 publication *Historia de*

Gloria (Amor, humor y desamor) ("Gloria's Story"), a substantial collection of poems derived from her private diary. In this work, according to Miller, Fuertes "adopts a more mature perspective than before." In addition to her poetry collections, Fuertes has published several children's books.

BIOGRAPHICAL/CRITICAL SOURCES:

BOOKS

Debicki, Andrew P., *Poetry of Discovery: The Spanish Generation of 1956-1971,* University Press of Kentucky, 1982, pp. 81-101.
Dictionary of Literary Biography, Volume 108: *Twentieth-Century Spanish Poets, First Series,* Gale (Detroit, MI), 1991.

PERIODICALS

Hispania, May, 1989, pp. 247-55.
Revista/Review Interamericana, spring, 1982, pp. 125-132.*

G

GALINDO, P.
See HINOJOSA(-SMITH), Rolando (R.)

*   *   *

GAMBOA, Federico 1864-1939

PERSONAL: Born December 22, 1864, in Mexico City, Mexico; died in 1939; son of Manuel Gamboa (a military general and governor of Jalisco); married; children: one son. *Religion:* Catholic.

CAREER: Writer. Mexican foreign service, second secretary to Guatemala legation, beginning 1888, acting ambassador to Washington DC, 1905, minister to Guatemala, 1905-08, vice minister of foreign affairs, 1908-10, minister to Belgium and Holland, 1910-13, minister of foreign affairs, 1913; worked as a translator in Galveston and San Antonio, TX, c. 1914-15; worked as a journalist and teacher of literature in Mexico, beginning 1919; Academia Mexicana, Mexico, director and teacher of literature, c. 1920-39. Ran as vice-presidential candidate for Mexican Catholic party, 1913.

WRITINGS:

NOVELS

Del natural: Esbozos contemporaneos, E. Gomez de la Puente (Mexico City), 1889.
Apariencias, [Buenos Aires, 1892.
Suprema ley, Vda. de C. Bouret (Mexico City), 1896.
Metamorfosis, Centro mercantil (Mexico), 1899.

Santa, [Barcelona], 1903, E. Gomez de la Puente (Mexico City), c. 1920, new edition, 1960.
Reconquista, E. Gomez de la Puente (Mexico City), 1908.
La llaga, E. Gomez de la Puente (Mexico City), 1913.

PLAYS

La ultima campana, [Guatemala City], 1900.
La venganza de la gleba, [Guatemala City], 1907.
Entre hermanos, [Mexico City], 1944.

MEMOIRS

Impresiones y recuerdos, E. Gomez de la Puente (Mexico City), 1893, new editon, 1922.
Mi diario, series 1, part 1: 1892-96, [Guadalajara], 1908; series 1, part 2 (1897-1900), [Mexico City, Mexico], 1910; series 1, part 3 (1901-04), [Mexico City, Mexico], 1920; series 2, part 1 (1905-08), [Mexico City, Mexico], 1934; series 2, part 2 (1909-11), [Mexico City, Mexico], 1938.

OTHER

La novela mexicana (essays), E. Gomez de la Puente (Mexico City), 1914.
Diario de Federico Gamboa, 1892-1939, prologue, selection, and notes by Jose Emilio Pacheco, Siglo Veintiuno Editores (Mexico City), 1977.

SIDELIGHTS: Referred to as "the patriarch of Mexican letters," Federico Gamboa is best known for naturalistic novels in which he explored the problems of his country's middle and lower classes. Gamboa's subject matter and approach were influenced by Emile

Zola, the principal theorist of literary naturalism, who viewed the novel as an illustration of how human behavior is determined by various social, psychological, and hereditary forces. In his later works, Gamboa attempted to transcend the deterministic aspect of naturalism with a more idealistic philosophy. In addition to his novels, Gamboa's extensive memoirs are also highly valued, their clear rationality and balanced assessments providing unique insight into Mexican political and literary life of the late nineteenth and early twentieth centuries.

Gamboa was born in 1864 in Mexico City. Beginning his career as a court clerk and journalist, he was appointed in 1888 to a diplomatic post, serving as undersecretary in Mexican legations in Guatemala, Argentina, Brazil, and the United States, and later as Minister Plenipotentiary in several European nations. He published his first book, the short story collection *Del natural,* in 1889 and continued to write works of fiction and drama throughout his career in the diplomatic service. In 1901 a gambling problem resulted in what Gamboa referred to in his diary as "a psychological crisis." He credited his recovery to his return to the Catholic church, and critics attribute the idealism of his later works to this renewed faith. In 1913 Gamboa was forced into exile after running as the vice presidential candidate for the Catholic party, which lost the election to the dictator Victoriano Huerta. When Gamboa returned to Mexico, he resumed his career in journalism, began teaching Mexican literature at the Academia Mexicana, and worked on his memoirs until his death in 1939.

In his novels, Gamboa described the plight of individuals manipulated by psychological and social forces beyond their control. He used this naturalistic approach to portray such subjects as corrupt courts, adultery, and prostitution, connecting these to the more fundamental problems of poverty and class oppression. For example, in his depiction of the Mexican prison system in his 1896 work, *Suprema ley,* Gamboa criticized society for concerning itself with the poverty-stricken only when they have committed a crime. His best known novel, 1903's *Santa,* explores the life of a young country girl who turns to prostitution to support herself after she is deserted by her lover and disowned by her family. Arthur Wallace Woolsey, in an essay in the *Modern Language Journal,* praised Gamboa's forceful use of naturalistic techniques to present her life: "At times he is almost photographic in his description of some of the more sordid scenes. He presents his 'slices of life' in a powerful and effective manner, and the reader does

not soon forget the poverty, the squalor, and the oppression found in the lives and places which are presented to him."

Some critics have contended that while Gamboa treated themes common to Naturalism in his novels, he cannot be classified as a Naturalist writer. Instead, they characterize him as a simple observer of details rather than one who organized these materials to reveal a pattern of scientific laws, concluding that his moral judgments and explicit didacticism do not conform to the Naturalist goal of objectivity. *PMLA* contributor Robert J. Niess, remarked: "Although Federico Gamboa is often called the leading exponent of literary naturalism in Mexico and as such was inevitably a follower of Zola, it is difficult to demonstrate that he borrowed heavily or continuously from the French master. His work provides only scattered examples of direct appropriation from Zola and the latter's influence on him was rather general than specific, bearing mainly on his choice of subject-matter, method of treatment and overall social outlook."

Nevertheless, Niess conceded that only one of Gamboa's works, his 1908 novel *Reconquista,* demonstrates "evidence of an attempt on Gamboa's part not only to imitate Zola but to take a form already developed by his predecessor and to turn it to his own philosophic and artistic ends." Other critics, however, have assessed Gamboa's moralizing as resulting from his return to Catholicism and have contended that his earlier works, such as *Santa,* do represent a Naturalist philosophy.

Although not as widely known as his novels, Gamboa's extensive memoirs—*Impresiones y recuerdos,* published in 1893, and *Mi diario,* published in several volumes between 1907 and 1938—are considered important documentation of Mexican politics in the late nineteenth and early twentieth centuries, providing not only a first-hand report on the dictatorships of the period, but also information on Mexican and U.S. activities in Central America. Gamboa's recollections of the major literary figures in Mexico, Spain, and Central and South America are also considered valuable documents of literary history. Ernest R. Moore, writing in *Books Abroad* in 1940, summarized Gamboa's achievements in his memoirs by declaring: "In *Impresiones y recuerdos* and *Mi diario* [Gamboa] leaves an exciting record of his career which will be much consulted by literary and political historians in the future. The historical value of these works lies in his intimate and accurate observations on Mexican and American activities in Central America, on the Diaz and Huerta dictatorships, and on

American intervention in Mexico during the early days of the Revolution. His story vies with Jose Vasconcelos' in scope and surpasses it in unimpassioned, balanced judgments. . . . Because of his close friendship with all Mexican writers of importance during his long directorship of the Academia Mexicana . . . his comments on the intellectual and artistic life in Mexico represents the best single literary history of the last five decades which has yet been published in Mexico."

BIOGRAPHICAL/CRITICAL SOURCES:

BOOKS

Apstein, Theodore, *A Modern Mexican Playwright: Jose Joaquin Gamboa,* University of Texas Press (Austin, TX), 1940.
Behind Spanish American Footlights, University of Texas Press (Austin, TX), 1966.
Brushwood, John S., *Mexico in Its Novel: A Nation's Search for Identity,* University of Texas Press, 1966.
History of Mexican Literature, Southern Methodist University Press (Dallas, TX), 1968.

PERIODICALS

Books Abroad, autumn, 1940, pp. 364-67.
Hispanic Review, October, 1945, pp. 346-351.
Modern Language Journal, April, 1950, pp. 294-97.
PMLA, June, 1946, pp. 577-83.*

*   *   *

GAMBOA, Harry (T., Jr.) 1951-

PERSONAL: Born November 1, 1951, in Angeles, CA; son of Harry T. and Carmen Gamboa; married Barbara Carrasco (an artist); children: Diego.

ADDRESSES: Home—P.O. Box 862015, Los Angeles, CA 90086-2015.

CAREER: Visual artist and writer, Los Angeles, CA. Asco (performance art group), founding member, 1982-87; Los Angeles Contemporary Exhibitions, founding member.

AWARDS, HONORS: Photography fellow, Mexican American Legal Defense and Educational Fund, 1974; fellow of National Endowment for the Arts, 1980 and 1987; Ford Foundation playwriting commission, 1989; artist fellow, J. Paul Getty Trust Fund for the Visual Arts, 1990; Premio Mesquite, best experimental video, San Antonio CineFestival, 1992, for *Vis a Vid.*

WRITINGS:

PLAYS

Shadow Solo, produced in Santa Cruz, CA, at University of California, 1983.
Jetter's Jinx, produced in Los Angeles, CA, at Los Angeles Theater Center, 1985.
Ignore the Dents, produced in Los Angeles, at Los Angeles Festival, 1990.
Vex Requien, produced at Los Angeles Theater Center, 1990.

OTHER

Club Limbo (intermedia performance), performed in Irvine, CA, at Concert Hall, University of California, 1989.
Rush Hour (fiction), Museum of Contemporary Art (Los Angeles, CA), 1992.
La Familia (videotape), Museum of Modern Art (New York City), 1993.
Chicano Male Unbonded (documentary photography series), Phoenix Art Museum (Phoenix, AZ), 1993.

Creator of the experimental video *Vis a Vid,* 1992.

BIOGRAPHICAL/CRITICAL SOURCES:

BOOKS

Shorris, Earl, *Latinos—A Biography of the People,* Avon (New York City), 1992.

PERIODICALS

Wall Street Journal, October 17, 1986.*

*   *   *

GAMBOA, Reymundo 1948-

PERSONAL: Born February 2, 1948, in Anthony, NM; son of Jose Leonardo (a farm worker) and Maria (a farm worker; maiden name, Torres) Gamboa; married Josefina Ramos, August 23, 1970; children: Adrian, Alejandro Rey, Miguel Alonzo. *Ethnicity:* Chicano. *Education:* Fresno State College, B.A., 1970; Pepperdine University, M.A., 1978; attended University of California, Santa Barbara. *Politics:* Independent/Local, Democrat/National. *Religion:* Catholic. *Avocational interests:* Animal observation.

ADDRESSES: Home—408 Chaparral Street, Santa Maria, CA 93454. *E-mail*—Reymundo@aol.com.

CAREER: Santa Maria Joint Union High School District, Santa Maria, CA, director of bilingual-bicultural education; writer.

AWARDS, HONORS: Achievement Award, Bank of America, 1966; third prize, Annual Chicano Literary Contest, Bakersfield College, 1976; second place, Annual Chicano Literary Prize, University of California, 1979, for "Your Disdain"; fellow, Script Writing Institute, University of California, for "Living Alone", 1984; first prize, Short Story, Thirteenth Chicano Literary Prize, University of California, for "Fifty-Fifty Chance".

WRITINGS:

(With Ernesto Padilla) *The Baby Chook and Other Remnants* (poetry), introduction by Frank Voci, Other Voices (Tempe, AZ), 1976.
Madrugada del '56/Morning of '56 (poetry), introduction by Ernesto Padilla, Lalo (La Jolla, CA), 1978.

Work represented in anthologies, including *New Voices in American Poetry,* edited by Norman Denison, Vantage (New York City), 1972; *From Three Sides: Readings for Writers,* edited by Joseph Maiolo and Barbara Brentley, Prentice-Hall (Englewood Cliffs, CA), 1976; *Calafia: The California Poetry,* edited by Ishmael Reed, Y'Bird (Berkeley, CA), 1979; and *Chicanos: Antologia historica y literaria,* edited by Tino Villanueva, Fondo de Cultura Economica, 1980. Contributor to periodicals, including *California State Poetry Quarterly, Cafe Solo, Caracol, Denver Quarterly, El Grito, La Luz,* and *Out of Sight.*

WORK IN PROGRESS: Baltazar's Tunnel: Short Stories for Teenagers, HarperCollins.

SIDELIGHTS: Reymundo Gamboa is an accomplished writer who has won recognition for his self-reflective poetry and often autobiographical prose. Salvador

Guerena, writing in the *Dictionary of Literary Biography,* observed: "Gamboa classifies his writing as ethnographic fiction. He writes from a very personal frame of reference which reflects the cultural fluidity of the Chicano, Mexican, and Anglo experiences and influences upon his life."

Gamboa was born in 1948 in Anthony, New Mexico, but he grew up in California, where his parents found work on farms in the San Joaquin Valley. Gamboa attended various universities, including Fresno State College, from which he received his undergraduate degree in 1970, and Pepperdine University, where he earned a master's degree in 1978. After further study at the University of California, Santa Barbara, Gamboa became director of bilingual-bicultural education for the Santa Maria Joint Union High School District.

In 1976 Gamboa and Ernesto Padilla published the verse collection *The Baby Chook and Other Remnants.* Gamboa followed *The Baby Chook and Other Remnants* with another poetry collection, *Madrugada del '56/Morning of '56.* This succeeding volume is notable for its thematic introspection and technical precision. Among the critics who responded favorably to *Madrugada del '56/Morning of '56* was *Rayas* reviewer and editor Cecilio Garcia-Camarillo, who described Gamboa's poems as "perceptions of the poet sensing, conversing, observing himself." Notable among Gamboa's individual poems is "Quiero creer en Dios" (title means "I Wish to Believe in God"). In *Cafe Solo,* Robert Lint—whom Salvador Guerena acknowledged in the *Dictionary of Literary Biography* as having "probably written the most favorable criticism of Gamboa's poetry"—affirmed that in this poem Gamboa "skillfully employs the suave deceptions of language to hold the poem's movement under the smooth surface direction."

Among Gamboa's most celebrated prose writings is the short story "Your Disdain," which earned second prize at the Annual Chicano Literary Prize contest conducted at the University of California, Irvine. "Your Disdain" concerns a father and son who are wrestling with personal problems that undermine their ability to express love to each other. Guerena, in a more general consideration of Gamboa's fiction, stated that the writer "has shown flexibility and proven his adeptness in short stories . . . and more are certainly expected." Guerena added that Gamboa's "ethnographic fiction is bound to continue its intense introspective tendencies."

In describing his writing, Gamboa once explained "The Chinese, Mayan, and Egyptian civilizations tell their story with characters or pictographs. William S. Burroughs developed the cut-up method to tell his trilogy of the 1960s. Jack Kerouac developed automatic writing in order to tell. My challenge is to create my narrative and poems from nurtured alphabet mutations into English and Spanish, not becoming artifice, but keeping it basic, because telling is important. I present an original and energetic voice appropriate for the character and situation. At times, the latter requires that they parade invented language."

BIOGRAPHICAL/CRITICAL SOURCES:

BOOKS

Dictionary of Literary Biography, Volume 122: *Chicano Writers, Second Series,* Gale (Detroit, MI), 1992, pp. 103-106.

PERIODICALS

Cafe Solo, spring, 1974.
Rayas, May-June, 1978.

*   *   *

GARCIA, Cristina 1958-

PERSONAL: Born July 4, 1958, in Havana, Cuba; immigrated to the United States, c. 1960; daughter of Frank M. and Hope Lois Garcia; married Scott Brown, December 8, 1990; children: Pilar Akiko. *Education:* Barnard College, B.A., 1979; Johns Hopkins University, M.A., 1981. *Politics:* "Registered Democrat." *Avocational interests:* Contemporary dance, music, travel, foreign languages.

ADDRESSES: Agent—Ellen Levine, 15 East 26th St., No. 1801, New York, NY 10010.

CAREER: Journalist and author. *Time* (magazine), reporter and researcher, 1983-85, correspondent, 1985-90, bureau chief in Miami, FL, 1987-88.

MEMBER: PEN American Center, Amnesty International.

AWARDS, HONORS: National Book Award finalist, National Book Foundation, 1992, for *Dreaming in Cuban;* Hodder fellowship, Princeton University,

1992-93; Cintas fellowship, 1992-93; Whiting Writers Award, 1996.

WRITINGS:

Dreaming in Cuban (novel), Knopf (New York City), 1992.
Cars of Cuba (essay), created by D. D. Allen, photographs by Joshua Greene, Abrams (New York City), 1995.
The Aguero Sisters (novel), Knopf, 1997.

WORK IN PROGRESS: Poems and novels.

SIDELIGHTS: A reporter and correspondent for *Time* magazine during the 1980s, Cristina Garcia published her first novel, *Dreaming in Cuban,* in 1992. Inspired by Garcia's Cuban heritage, the book was highly acclaimed and became a finalist for the National Book Award. Reviewer Michiko Kakutani had this praise for the book in the *New York Times:* "Fierce, visionary, and at the same time oddly beguiling and funny, *Dreaming in Cuban* is a completely original novel. It announces the debut of a writer, blessed with a poet's ear for language, a historian's fascination with the past and a musician's intuitive understanding of the ebb and flow of emotion."

Dreaming in Cuban chronicles three generations of a Cuban family. The matriarch, Celia, falls in love with a married Spaniard and writes him letters for twenty-five years. Despite this long-distance affair, Celia marries a man she does not love, and the couple has two daughters, Lourdes and Felicia, and a son, Javier. Celia also becomes enamored of the Cuban Revolution and its leader, Fidel Castro. Lourdes, however, is raped by a revolutionary, and carries her hatred of the revolution with her when she moves to New York with her husband and opens two successful bakeries. Felicia stays in Cuba with her mother, but she marries a sailor who gives her syphilis, and she eventually meets a tragic end. Javier becomes a scientist and immigrates to Czechoslovakia, only to return a bitter alcoholic. As for the next generation, Thulani Davis explained in the *New York Times Book Review:* "Celia's grandchildren can only be described as lost and abandoned by the obsessions of the parents. Of these, Lourdes's daughter, Pilar Puente del Pino, a would-be painter and student in New York, becomes the secret sharer, a distant repository of the family's stories and some of its demons." Pilar is also the one who reunites the family, dragging her mother along with her on a trip to Cuba to see her grandmother. In detailing this family history, Alan West observed in *Washington Post Book World,* "Garcia deftly shifts the narrative from third to first person, mixing in a series of Celia's letters to her long-lost Spanish lover, Gustavo. Likewise, she shifts from the past to the present, from Brooklyn to Havana, from character to character caught in the web that blood and history have set up for them, often with cruel irony." Richard Eder, writing in the *Los Angeles Times,* called *Dreaming in Cuban* "poignant and perceptive," noting that "the realism is exquisite." Davis concluded in the *New York Times Book Review:* "I have no complaints to make. Cristina Garcia has written a jewel of a first novel."

Garcia's second novel, *The Aguero Sisters,* tells of two Cuban sisters, Constancia and Reina, who have been separated for thirty years. Constancia and her husband, recently retired from his cigar business, have moved from New York to Key Biscayne, Florida, and she has become a successful businesswoman and entrepreneur, with her own line of homemade, natural body and face creams made from such ingredients as overripe peaches and avocado pits. These beauty aids "embody the exalted image Cuban women have of themselves: as passionate, self-sacrificing, and deserving of every luxury." Heberto, though, disappears from the main plot as he embarks on a new career as a counterrevolutionary, embroiled in a Bay of Pigs-like plot to overthrow the Cuban government.

Reina still lives in Cuba, is a skilled, travelling electrician, and has been nicknamed "Companera Amazonas" for her voluptuousness and for her free-spirited sexuality. While Constancia is somewhat prudish and has only had two lovers in her entire life—her two husbands—the uninhibited libertine Reina relishes the pleasure men provide her. As Garcia describes, "Often, Reina selects the smallest, shiest electrician in a given town for her special favors, leaving him weak and inconsolable for months. After she departs, black owls are frequently sighted in the Ceiba trees." *Washington Post Book World* editor Nina King noted, "The sudden appearance of those ominous black owls is typical of Garcia's stylistic shifts from reality to myth to the heightened reality of 'magic realism.'"

According to *Time* reviewer Pico Iyer, "both Aguero sisters share something deep as blood: a matter-of-fact commitment to the magic of their island of honey and rum. Constancia makes spells for women in the form of the 'luscious unguents' she markets; Reina casts spells over men." This is typical of a mystical parallelism that runs throughout the novel; for ex-

ample, at approximately the same time Constancia elects cosmetic surgery that inadvertently leaves her with her mother's face, Reina is struck by lightning and must undergo experimental skin grafts—her skin becomes a patchwork contributed by friends and family.

As Kakutani commented in a *New York Times* review, "In Cristina Garcia's haunting new novel, 'The Aguero Sisters', a strange scar is handed down generation to generation. Bianca Aguero, the clan's ill-fated matriarch, receives the mysterious mark on her heel while swimming in Las Casas river during her honeymoon. Years later, while escaping from Cuba to the United States, Bianca's daughter Constancia leaves a similar mark on the foot of *her* daughter, Isabel, while trying to revive her from heatstroke. Isabel, in turn, eventually has a boy named Raku, who is born with a red birthmark on his foot in the same place as his mother's wound."

When the two sisters are reunited in Miami, they work to strip away the lies that constitute their lives. By the novel's denouement, their respective daughters, the artist, Isabel, and former volleyball coach-turned-prostitute, Dulce, are united, as well. The primary element that connects all four women, aside from their kinship per se, is the quest to learn the truth about the death of Constancia and Reina's mother, Blanca Mestre de Auguero. Blanca and her husband were both ornithologists, documenting the endangered wildlife of Cuba when her estranged husband, Ignacio, brutally murdered her. The reader is told, early on, the nature of her fate, but the protagonists must untwist truth from lies.

Ruth Behar of the *Chicago Tribune* noted that "Garcia offers an even more gorgeously written, even more flamboyant feminist vision of Cuban and American history, women's lives, memory and desire" than her previous novel, *Dreaming in Cuban.* The critic added, "Constancia and Reina, the feisty and rebellious Aguero sisters, are strong female protagonists whose meditations on men, sex, power and longing are among the great joys of Garcia's novel." Kakutani noted "the force of Ms. Garcia's powerfully imagined characters" and "the magic of her prose." In *Nation,* Ilan Stavans mentioned Garcia's "astonishing literary style and dazzling attention to telling detail," and deems her "an immensely talented writer, whose work . . . is renewing American fiction." And, describing Garcia as "A wise and generous storyteller," Iyer praised the novelist. "Garcia has crafted a beautifully rounded work of art," the reviewer noted, "as warm and wry and sensuous as the island she clearly loves."

BIOGRAPHICAL/CRITICAL SOURCES:

BOOKS

Contemporary Literary Criticism, Volume 76, Gale (Detroit), 1993.
Notable Hispanic American Women, Gale, 1993.

PERIODICALS

Boston Globe, May 25, 1997, p. N15.
Entertainment Weekly, March 27, 1992, p. 68; March 26, 1993, p. 74.
Globe and Mail (Toronto), March 21, 1992, p. C9.
Los Angeles Times, March 12, 1992, p. E10.
Los Angeles Times Book Review, November 19, 1995, p. 11; June 8, 1997, p. 8.
Nation, May 19, 1997, p. 32.
Newsweek, April 20, 1992, p. 78-79; April 28, 1997, p. 79.
New Yorker, June 1, 1992, p. 86.
New York Times, February 25, 1992, p. C17; May 27, 1997, p. C16.
New York Times Book Review, May 17, 1992, p. 14; June 15, 1997, section 7, p. 38.
Observer, August 10, 1997, p. 15.
Time, March 23, 1992, p. 67; May 12, 1997, p. 88.
Tribune Books (Chicago), June 8, 1997, section 14, p. 1.
Washington Post Book World, March 1, 1992, p. 9; July 13, 1997, p. 1.

* * *

GARCIA, Guy D. 1955-

PERSONAL: Born July 16, 1955, in Los Angeles, CA; married. *Education:* University of California, Berkeley, B.S.; Columbia University, M.S.

ADDRESSES: Office—*Time,* 1271 Avenue of the Americas, New York, NY 10020.

CAREER: Time, New York City, staff writer.

WRITINGS:

Skin Deep (novel), Farrar, Straus (New York City), 1988.
Obsidian Sky (novel), Simon and Schuster (New York City), 1994.

Spirit of the Maya: A Boy Explores His People's Mysterious Past (juvenile), photographs by Ted Wood, Walker and Co. (New York City), 1995.

Contributor to periodicals, including *Rolling Stone, Elle,* and *Interview.*

BIOGRAPHICAL/CRITICAL SOURCES:

PERIODICALS

Booklist, October 1, 1995, p. 306.
Publishers Weekly, November 20, 1995, p. 78.
School Library Journal, January, 1996, p. 118.*

*   *   *

GARCIA, Richard A(mado) 1941-

PERSONAL: Born December 24, 1941, in El Paso, TX; son of Amado and Alma Garcia; divorced; children: Nicholas Garcia-Mason, Kristofer Garcia-Mason, John Lane, Misty Lane-Gibler. *Education:* University of Texas at El Paso, B.A., 1964, M.A. (education), 1968, M.A. (political science), 1970; University of California, Irvine, M.A. (history), 1976, Ph.D., 1980.

ADDRESSES: Office—Department of Ethnic Studies, California State University, Hayward, CA.

CAREER: University of Colorado, Boulder, professor of history, 1980-81; University of California, visiting professor of history, 1981-82—; Santa Monica College, Santa Monica, CA, professor of history, 1982; Santa Clara University, Santa Clara, CA, visiting scholar, 1989-90; California State University, visiting professor, 1990-91; California State University, Hayward, professor of ethnic studies.

MEMBER: American Historical Association, Organization of American Historians, National Association of Chicano Studies.

AWARDS, HONORS: Grant from National Endowment for the Humanities, 1981.

WRITINGS:

(Coeditor) *Bibliografia de Aztlan,* Centro Chicano Publications, 1971.
Selected Poetry, Quinto Sol, 1973.

Political Ideology: A Comparative Study of Three Chicano Youth Organizations, R & E Research Associates (San Francisco, CA), 1977.

(Editor) *The Chicanos in America, 1540-1974: A Chronology and Fact Book,* Oceana (Dobbs Ferry, NY), 1977.

My Aunt Otilia's Spirits/Los Espiritus de Mi Tia Otilia, Spanish translation by Jesus Guerrero Rea, illustrated by Robin Cherin and Roger I. Reyes, Children's Book Press (San Francisco), 1978.

The Rise of the Mexican American Middle Class: San Antonio, 1929-1941, Texas A&M University Press (College Station, TX), 1991.

(With Richard Griswold del Castillo) *Cesar Chavez: A Triumph of Spirit,* University of Oklahoma Press (Norman, OK), 1995.

(With Matt S. Meier and Conchita Franco Serri) *Notable Latino Americans: A Biographical Dictionary,* Greenwood Press (Westport, CT), 1997.

BIOGRAPHICAL/CRITICAL SOURCES:

PERIODICALS

Booklist, September 1, 1997, p. 161.
Journal of American History, December, 1996, p. 1093.
Library Journal, September 1, 1995, p. 185.
School Library Journal, November, 1997, p. 142.*

*   *   *

GARCIA-AGUILERA, Carolina 1949-
(Carolina Garcia Aguilera)

PERSONAL: Born July 13, 1949, in Havana, Cuba; daughter of Carlos Garcia-Beltran (an agricultural engineer) and Lourdes Aguilera de Garcia; married Robert K. Hamshaw (a financial administrator); children: Sarah Almeria Wright, Carolina Antonia Wright, Gabriella von Rosen. *Ethnicity:* "Hispanic (Cuban)." *Education:* Rollins College, B.A. (history and political science), 1971; attended Georgetown University, 1971; University of South Florida, M.B.A. (finance), 1983. *Religion:* Roman Catholic. *Avocational interests:* Helping dissident writers in Cuba.

ADDRESSES: Home—1030 14th St., Miami Beach, FL 33139. *Agent*—Elizabeth Ziemska, c/o Nicholas Ellison, Inc., 55 Fifth Ave., New York, NY 10003. *E-mail*—4cubans@bellsouth.net.

CAREER: C & J Investigations (private investigative firm), Miami, FL, president, 1986—; novelist, 1995—.

MEMBER: International Association of Crime Writers, PEN American Center, Mystery Writers of America, Private-Eye Writers of America, Sisters in Crime, Author's Guild.

WRITINGS:

LUPE SOLANO MYSTERY NOVELS

Bloody Waters, Putnam (New York City), 1996.
Bloody Shame, Putnam (New York City), 1997.
Bloody Secrets, Putnam (New York City), 1998.
Miracle in Paradise, Putnam (New York City), 1999.

Contributor to an anthology of Florida mystery writers, 1999.

WORK IN PROGRESS: A fifth book in the "Lupe Solano" series, publication by Avon Twilight expected in October, 2000.

SIDELIGHTS: Born in Cuba, novelist Carolina Garcia-Aguilera and her family imigrated to the United States in 1959, one year after Fidel Castro gained power over their homeland. The family lived in Palm Beach, Florida, for two years before finally settling in New York City. Early on in her life, Garcia-Aguilera was fascinated by detective literature, beginning with Nancy Drew novels she read as a child, and dreamed of one day writing her own mystery stories.

Garcia-Aguilera made a serious step towards making her dream a reality when, having moved to Miami, she applied for a State of Florida license to start a detective agency. After ten years as a private investigator there, Garcia-Aguilera had gained invaluable experience and rich knowledge of the field, but decided that she would rather *write* detective adventures than live them. Thus, in 1996 Garcia published *Bloody Waters,* the first in her series of novels featuring Cuban-American detective Lupe Solano.

Set in Miami, *Bloody Waters* finds Lupe Solano investigating an illegal adoption business in which Cuban-born children are placed with Cuban families in Miami. Garcia-Aguilera's premier novel received favorable reviews, with most critics mentioning that the author's experience in investigative work and first-hand knowledge of Cuba and Cubans lends authenticity to the book. Writing in the *Christian Science Monitor,* for example, Amelia Newcomb deemed

Bloody Waters a "lively and engaging read," and observed that "Garcia-Aguilera's experience gives *Bloody Waters* its air of authenticity." In another account, Catherine Crohan, writing in *Multicultural Review,* remarked that "Cuba becomes as much of a character as any of the people," and assessed *Bloody Waters* "a well-written detective novel."

Published in 1997, Garcia-Aguilera's second Lupe Solano novel, *Bloody Shame,* was also well received. In this novel, Lupe is working to clear her client, a jeweler who has been charged with second-degree murder in the death of a man, Gustav Gaston. The jeweler, Alonso Arango, insists he killed the man in self defense, but his story is uncorroborated by the evidence the police have gathered. While investigating the incident, Lupe experiences her own tragedy—her best friend is killed in a car accident. As Lupe digs deeper into the jeweler's case, however, she realizes there is a connection between Gaston's murder and her friend's death. Lupe then works to uncover the truth. *Bloody Shame* was applauded by reviewers, among them Harriet Klausner, who wrote in *Armchair Detective:* "With this second book the author goes one step further by giving her mystery a literary framework. This makes for a much more exciting and entertaining whodunit which provides a first-hand, insider look into the Cuban-American South Florida culture."

Garcia-Aguilera issued the third Lupe Solano mystery, *Bloody Secrets,* in 1998. Again set in Miami, the story concerns Lupe's investigation of the prominent and respected de la Torre family, at the request of a Cuban refugee, Luis Delgado. Delgado claims the de la Torres grew rich in America with money that belonged to Delgado's father. Critics again praised Garcia-Aguilera's ability to spin a mystery story, among them a *Publishers Weekly* critic who opined: "With sharp-edged characters and some profound probing of moral ambiguities, the latest Lupe Solano tale is suspenseful, provocative and satisfying."

BIOGRAPHICAL/CRITICAL SOURCES:

PERIODICALS

Armchair Detective, spring, 1997, pp. 239-240.
Christian Science Monitor, July 25, 1996.
Multicultural Review, December, 1996.
Publishers Weekly, December 30, 1996, p. 58; December 8, 1997, p. 58.
Tribune Books (Chicago), February 2, 1997, p. 4.

GARCIA LORCA, Federico 1898-1936

PERSONAL: Surname sometimes rendered as Lorca; born June 5, 1898, in Fuentevaqueros, Granada, Spain; executed August 19, 1936, in Viznar, Granada, Spain; son of Federico Garcia Rodriguez (a landowner) and Vicenta Lorca (a teacher). *Education:* Attended University of Granada, 1914-19; received law degree from University of Madrid, 1923; attended Columbia University, 1929.

CAREER: Writer. Artistic director, serving as director and producer of plays, for University Theater (state-sponsored traveling theater group, known as *La Barraca* ["The Hut"]), 1932-35. Director of additional plays, including *Blood Wedding,* 1933. Lecturer; illustrator, with work represented in exhibitions; musician, serving as arranger and pianist for recordings of Spanish folk songs, 1931. Helped to organize Festival of *Cante Jondo* (Granada, Spain), 1922.

WRITINGS:

POETRY

Libro de poemas (title means "Book of Poems"), Maroto (Madrid), 1921 (also see below).
Canciones (1921-1924), [Malaga, Spain], 1927, translation by Phillip Cummings published as *Songs,* Duquesne University Press, 1976 (also see below).
Primer romancero gitano (1924-1927), (contains poem Romance de la guardia civil espanola), Revista de Occidente (Madrid), 1928, 2nd edition (and most later editions) published as *Romancero gitano,* 1929, translation by Langston Hughes published as *Gypsy Ballads,* Beloit College, 1951, translation by Rolfe Humphries published as *The Gypsy Ballads, With Three Historical Ballads,* Indiana University Press, 1953, translation by Michael Hartnett published as *Gipsy Ballads,* Goldsmith Press (Dublin), 1973, translation and commentary by Carl W. Cobb published as *Lorca's "Romancero gitano": A Ballad Translation and Critical Study,* University Press of Mississippi, 1983 (also see below).
Poema del cante jondo, Ulises (Madrid), 1931, translation by Carlos Bauer published as *Poem of the Deep Song/Poema del cante jondo* (bilingual edition), City Lights Books, 1987 (also see below).
Oda a Walt Whitman (title means "Ode to Walt Whitman"), Alcancia, 1933, translation by Bauer published in *"Ode to Walt Whitman" and Other Poems,* City Lights, 1988.

Llanto por Ignacio Sanchez Mejias (title means "Lament for Ignacio Sanchez Mejias"; commonly known as "Lament for the Death of a Bullfighter"), Arbol, 1935 (also see below).

Seis poemas galegos (title means "Six Galician Poems"; written in Galician with assistance from others), Nos (Santiago de Compostela), 1935 (also see below).

Primeras canciones (title means "First Songs"), Heroe (Madrid), 1936.

Lament for the Death of a Bullfighter, and Other Poems (bilingual edition), translation by A. L. Loyd, Oxford University Press, 1937.

Poems, translation by Stephen Spender and J. L. Gili, Oxford University Press, 1939.

Poeta en Nueva York, Seneca (Mexico), 1940, translations published as *Poet in New York,* (bilingual edition) by Ben Belitt, introduction by Angel del Rio, Grove Press, 1955, by Stephen Fredman, Fog Horn Press, 1975, by Greg Simon and Steven F. White, Farrar, Straus, 1988 (also see below).

The Poet in New York, and Other Poems (includes "Gypsy Ballads"), translation by Rolfe Humphries, introduction by J. Bergamin, Norton, 1940.

Selected Poems of Federico Garcia Lorca, translation by Stephen Spender and J. L. Gili, Hogarth Press (London), 1943, Transatlantic Arts (New York), 1947.

Poemas postumos, Canciones musicales, Divan del Tamarit, Mexicanas (Mexico), 1945.

Siete poemas y dos dibujos ineditos, edited by Luis Rosales, Cultura Hispanica, 1949.

The Selected Poems of Federico Garcia Lorca (bilingual edition), edited by Francisco Garcia Lorca and Donald M. Allen, introduction by Francisco Garcia Lorca, New Directions, 1955.

Lorca, translation and introduction by J. L. Gili, Penguin, 1960-65.

(With Juan Ramon Jimenez) *Lorca and Jimenez: Selected Poems,* translation by Robert Bly, Sixties Press, 1967.

Divan and Other Writings (includes *Divan del Tamarit* [title means "Divan of the Tamarit]"), translation by Edwin Honig, Bonewhistle Press, 1974.

Lorca/Blackburn: Poems, translation by Paul Blackburn, Momo's Press, 1979.

The Cricket Sings: Poems and Songs for Children (bilingual edition), translation by Will Kirkland, New Directions, 1980.

Suites (reconstruction of a collection planned by Lorca), edited by Andre Belamich, Ariel (Barcelona), 1983.

Ineditos de Federico Garcia Lorca: Sonetos del amor oscuro, 1935-1936, (title means "Unpublished Works of Federico Garcia Lorca: Sonnets of the Dark Love, 1935-1936"), compiled by Marta Teresa Casteros, Instituto de Estudios de Literatura Latinoamericana (Buenos Aires), c. 1984.

Sonnets of Love Forbidden, translation by David K. Loughran, Windson, 1989.

The Poetical Works of Federico Garcia Lorca, two volumes, edited by Maurer, Farrar, Straus, 1988-91.

At Five in the Afternoon, translated by Francisco Aragon, Vintage Books, 1997.

Robert Bly, editor and translator, *Lorca and Jimenez: Selected Poems,* Beacon Press, 1997.

Poems represented in numerous collections and anthologies.

PLAYS

El maleficio de la mariposa (two-act; title means "The Butterfly's Evil Spell"), first produced in Madrid at Teatro Eslava, 1920.

Mariana Pineda: Romance popular en tres estampas (three-act; first produced in Barcelona at Teatro Goya, 1927; first published as *Romance de la muerte de Torrijos* in *El Dia Grafico,* June 25, 1927), Rivadeneyra (Madrid), 1928, translation by James Graham-Lujan published as *Mariana Pineda: A Popular Ballad in Three Prints* in *Tulane Drama Review,* winter, 1962, translation by Robert G. Havard published as *Mariana Pineda: A Popular Ballad in Three Engravings,* Aris & Phillips, 1987 (also see below).

La zapatera prodigiosa: Farsa violenta (two-act; title means "The Shoemaker's Prodigious Wife"), first produced in Madrid at Teatro Espanol, 1930.

El publico (title means "The Public", one scene apparently missing; produced in San Juan, Puerto Rico, 1978), excerpts published in *Los Cuatro Vientos,* 1933; enlarged version published in *El publico: Amor, teatro, y caballos en la obra de Federico Garcia Lorca,* edited by R. Martinez Nadal, Dolphin (Oxford), 1970, revised edition published as *El publico: Amor y muerte en la obra de Federico Garcia Lorca,* J. Moritz (Mexico), 1974, translation published as *Lorca's "The Public": A Study of an Unfinished Play and of Love and Death in Lorca's Work,* Schocken, 1974; Lorca's manuscript published by Dolphin, 1976 (also see below).

Bodas de sangre: Tragedia (three-act; first produced in Madrid at Teatro Beatriz, 1933), Arbol, 1935, translation by Jose A. Weissberger produced as *Bitter Oleander* in New York City, 1935, translation by Gilbert Neiman published as *Blood Wedding,* New Directions, 1939 (also see below).

Amor de Don Perlimplin con Belisa en su jardin (title means "The Love of Don Perlimplin with Belisa, in His Garden"), first produced in Madrid on April 5, 1933.

Yerma: Poema tragico (three-act; first produced in Madrid on December 29, 1934), Anaconda (Buenos Aires), 1937, translation by Ian Macpherson and Jaqueline Minett published as *Yerma: A Tragic Poem* (bilingual edition), general introduction by John Lyon, Aris & Phillips, 1987 (also see below).

Retablillo de Don Cristobal (puppet play; title means "Don Cristobal's Puppet Show"; first produced in Buenos Aires, Argentina, at Teatro Avenida, March, 1934; revised version produced in Madrid at Feria del Libro, May 12, 1935), Subcomisariado de Propaganda del Comisariado General de Guerra (Valencia), 1938 (also see below).

Dona Rosita la soltera; o, El lenguaje de las flores: Poema granadino del novecientos, (three-act; title means "Dona Rosita the Spinster; or, The Language of Flowers: Poem of Granada in the Nineteenth Century"), first produced in Barcelona, at the Principal Palace, December, 1935.

Los titeres de Cachiporra: Tragecomedia de Don Cristobal y la sena Rosita: Farsa (puppet play; title means "The Billy-Club Puppets: Tragicomedy of Don Cristobal and Mam'selle Rosita: Farce"; first produced in Madrid at Zarzuela Theater, December, 1937), Losange, 1953.

From Lorca's Theater: Five Plays (contains *The Shoemaker's Prodigious Wife, The Love of Don Perlimplin with Belisa, in His Garden, Dona Rosita the Spinster, Yerma,* and *When Five Years Pass* [produced as *Asi que pasen cinco anos* in Madrid, 1978]), translation by Richard L. O'Connell and James Graham-Lujan, intro-duction by Stark Young, Scribner, 1941.

La casa de Bernarda Alba: Drama de mujeres en los pueblos de Espana (three-act; title means "The House of Bernarda Alba: Drama of Women in the Villages of Spain"; first produced in Buenos Aires at Teatro Avenida, March 8, 1945), Losada, 1944 (also see below).

Three Tragedies (contains *Blood Wedding, Yerma,* and *The House of Bernarda Alba*), translation by Richard L. O'Connell and James Graham-Lujan, introduction by Francisco Garcia Lorca, New Di-rections, 1947, Greenwood Press, 1977, transla-tion by Sue Bradbury, Folio Society (London), 1977.

Cinco forsas breves; seguidas de "Asi que pasen cinco anos, Losange, 1953.

Comedies (contains *The Butterfly's Evil Spell, The Shoemaker's Prodigious Wife, The Love of Don Perlimplin with Belisa, in His Garden,Dona Rosita the Spinster*), translation by Richard L. O'Connell and James Graham-Lujan, introduction by Francisco Garcia Lorca, New Directions, 1954, enlarged edition published as *Five Plays: Comedies and Tragicomedies* (includes *The Billy-Club Puppets*), 1963, Penguin, 1987.

Comedia sin titulo (one act of an incomplete play; title means "Play without a Title"; also known as "El sueno de la vida" ["The Dream of Life"]), first produced in Madrid, 1989.

El publico [and] Comedia sin titulo: Dos obras postumas, edited by R. Martinez Nadal and M. Laffranque, Seix Barral, 1978, translation by Carlos Bauer published as *The Public [and] Play Without a Title: Two Posthumous Plays,* New Directions, 1983.

Teatro inconcluso, edited by Laffranque, Universidad de Granada, 1986.

The Rural Trilogy: Blood Wedding [and] Yerma [and] The House of Bernarda Alba, translation by Michael Dewell and Carmen Zapata, introduction by Douglas Day, Bantam, 1987.

Three Plays (contains *Blood Wedding, Dona Rosita the Spinster,* and *Yerma*), translation by Gwynne Edwards and Peter Luke, introduction by Edwards, Methuen, 1987.

Once Five Years Pass, and Other Dramatic Works, translation by William B. Logan and Angel G. Orrios, Station Hill Press, 1989.

Two Plays of Misalliance: The Love of Don Perlimplin [and] The Prodigious Cobbler's Wife, Aris & Phillips, 1989.

Barbarous Nights: Legends and Plays from the Little Theater, translation by Christopher Sawyer-Laucanno, City Lights, 1991.

Blood Wedding; and Yerma, introduction by W. S. Merwin, Theatre Communications Group, 1994.

Four Major Plays (includes *Blood Wedding, Yerma, The House of Bernarda Alba,* and *Dona Rosita the Spinster*), translated by John Edmunds, Ox-ford University Pres, 1997.

Also author of short dramatic sketches, including "La donacella, el marinero, y el estudiante" (title means "The Maiden, the Sailor, and the Student") and "El paseo de Buster Keaton" (title means "Buster Keaton's Stroll"), both 1928, and "Quimera" (title means "Chimera").

Adapter of numerous plays, including *La dama boba* and *Fuente Ovejuna,* both by Lope de Vega. Plays represented in collections and anthologies.

OMNIBUS VOLUMES

Obras completas, (title means "Complete Works;" includes *Asi que pasen cinco anos* and "Divan of the Tamarit"), edited by Guillermo de Torre, Losada (Buenos Aires), 1938-46.

Obras completas (title means "Complete Works;" includes "The Butterfly's Evil Spell"), edited with commentary by Arturo de Hoyo, introductions by Jorge Guillen and Vicente Aleixandre, Aguilar, 1954.

Obras (title means "Works"), edited with commentary by Mario Hernandez, several volumes, Alianza, 1981—, 2nd edition, revised, 1983—.

Epistolario completo, Catedra (Madrid), 1997.

OTHER

Impresiones y paisajes (travelogue), P. V. Traveset (Granada), 1918, translation by Lawrence H. Klibbe published as *Impressions and Landscapes,* University Press of America, 1987.

Federico Garcia Lorca: Cartas a sus amigos (letters), edited by Sebastian Gasch, Cobalto (Barcelona), 1950.

Conferencias y charlas, Consejo Nacional de Cultura, 1961.

Garcia Lorca: Cartas, postales, poemas, y dibujos (includes letters and poems), edited by Antonio Gallego Morell, Monedo y Credito (Madrid), 1968.

Casidas, Arte y Bibliofilia, 1969.

Prosa, Alianza, 1969.

Granada, paraiso cerrado y otras paginas granadinas (also see below), Sanchez, 1971.

Autografos, edited by Rafael Martinez Nadal, Dolphin, Volume 1, 1975, Volume 2, 1976, Volume 3, 1979.

Deep Song, and Other Prose, translation by Christopher Maurer, New Directions, 1980.

Viaje a la luna (filmscript; translation by Richard Diers published as *Trip to the Moon* in *Windmill,* spring, 1963), edited by Laffranque, Braad, 1980.

From the Havana Lectures, 1928: "Theory and Play of the Duende" and "Imagination, Inspiration, Evasion" (lectures; bilingual edition), translation by Stella Rodriguez, preface by Randolph Severson, introduction by Rafael Lopez Pedraza, Kanathos (Dallas, TX), 1981.

Lola, la comedianta, edited by Piero Menarini, Alianza, 1981.

Epistolario, two volumes, edited by Maurer, Alianza, 1983, parts translated by David Gershator as *Selected Letters,* New Directions, 1983.

Conferencias, two volumes, edited by Maurer, Alianza, 1984.

How a City Sings from November to November (lecture; bilingual edition), translation by Maurer, Cadmus Editions, 1984.

Alocuciones argentinas, edited by Mario Hernandez, Fundacion Federico Garcia Lorca/Crotalon, 1985.

Tres dialogos, Universidad de Granada/Junta de Andalucia, 1985.

Alocucion al pueblo de Fuentevaqueros, Comision del Cincuecentenario, 1986.

Treinta entrevistas a Federico Garcia Lorca, edited by Andres Soria Olmedo, Aguilar, 1989.

Line of Light and Shadow: The Drawings of Federico Garcia Lorca (previously published as *Dibujos,* 1987), edited by Mario Hernandez, translation by Maurer, Duke University Press/Duke University Museum of Art, 1991.

Selected Verse, introductions by Christopher Maurer and Francisco Aragon, Farrar, Straus, & Giroux (New York City), 1995.

A Season in Granada: Uncollected Poems and Prose (contains *Granada, paraiso cerrado y otras paginas granadinas*), edited by Christopher Maurer, Anvil Press Poetry, 1998.

Illustrator of several books, including *El fin del viaje* by Pablo Neruda; drawings represented in collections, including *Federico Garcia Lorca: Dibujos,* Ministerio de Cultura (Granada), 1986, and Helen Oppenheimer, *Lorca—The Drawings: Their Relation to the Poet's Life and Work,* F. Watts, 1987. Co-editor of *gallo* (Granada literary magazine; title means "rooster"), 1928. Garcia Lorca's manuscripts are housed at Fundacion Garcia Lorca, Consejo Superior de Investigaciones Cientificas, Madrid.

ADAPTATIONS: Several of Lorca's plays have been adapted for opera and ballet, including *Blood Wedding, Yerma,* and *The Love of Don Perlimplin with Belisa, in His Garden. Blood Wedding* was adapted by Antonio Gades for a ballet, which was in turn adapted by Carlos Saura for a film of the same title, 1981.

SIDELIGHTS: Federico Garcia Lorca was "a child of genius beyond question," declared Jorge Guillen in *Language and Poetry.* A Spanish poet and dramatist, Garcia Lorca was at the height of his fame in 1936 when he was executed by fascist rebels at the age of thirty-eight; in the years thereafter, Guillen suggested, the writer's prominence in European culture matched that of his countryman Pablo Picasso. Garcia

Lorca's work has been treasured by a broad spectrum of the reading public throughout the world. His complete works have been reprinted in Spain almost every year since the 1950s, and observers believe he is more widely recognized in the English-speaking world than any Spanish writer except Miguel de Cervantes, author of *Don Quixote.*

Garcia Lorca was familiar with the artistic innovators of his time, and his work shares with theirs a sense of sophistication, awareness of human psychology, and overall pessimism. But while his contemporaries often preferred to appeal to the intellect, Garcia Lorca gained wide popularity by addressing basic human emotions. He possessed an engaging personality and a dynamic speaking style, and he imbued his writing with a wide range of human feeling, including awe, lust, nostalgia, and despair. "Those who knew him," wrote his brother Francisco in a foreword to *Three Tragedies,* "will not forget his gift . . . of enlivening things by his presence, of making them more intense." The public image of Garcia Lorca has varied greatly since he became famous in the 1920s. Known primarily for works about peasants and gypsies, he was quickly labeled a simple poet of rural life—an image he felt oversimplified his art. His death enraged democratic and socialist intellectuals, who called him a political martyr; but while Garcia Lorca sympathized with leftist causes, he avoided direct involvement in politics. In the years since Garcia Lorca died, his literary biographers have grown more sophisticated, revealing his complexity both as a person and as an artist.

To biographer Carl Cobb, for instance, Garcia Lorca's "life and his work" display a "basic duality." Despite friends and fame Garcia Lorca struggled with depression, concerned that his homosexuality, which he hid from the public, condemned him to live as a social outcast. While deeply attached to Spain and its rural life, he came to reject his country's social conservatism, which disdained his sexuality. Arguably, Garcia Lorca's popularity grew from his conscious effort to transform his personal concerns into comments on life in general, allowing him to reach a wide audience. During his youth Garcia Lorca experienced both Spain's traditional rural life and its entry into the modern world.

Born in 1898, he grew up in a village in Andalusia—the southernmost region of Spain, then largely untouched by the modern world. Such areas were generally dominated by the traditional powers of Spanish society, including political conservatism, the Catholic church, and affluent landowners. Garcia Lorca's father, a landowning liberal, confounded his wealthy peers by marrying a village schoolteacher and by paying his workers generously. Though Garcia Lorca was a privileged child he knew his home village well, attending school with its children, observing its poverty, and absorbing the vivid speech and folktales of its peasants. "I have a huge storehouse of childhood recollections in which I can hear the people speaking," Garcia Lorca once observed, according to biographer Ian Gibson. "This is poetic memory, and I trust it implicitly." The sense of lost innocence that recurs in Garcia Lorca's writings, Gibson averred, focuses on his early rural years, probably the happiest of his life.

But once Garcia Lorca moved with his parents to the Andalusian city of Granada in 1909, many forces propelled him into the modern world. Spain was undergoing a lengthy crisis of confidence, spurred by the country's defeat by the United States in the War of 1898. Some Spaniards wished to strengthen traditional values and revive past glory, but others hoped their country would moderate its conservatism, foster intellectual inquiry, and learn from more modernized countries. With his parents' encouragement Garcia Lorca encountered Spain's progressives through his schooling, first at an innovative, nonreligious secondary school, and then at the University of Granada, where he became a protege of such intellectual reformers as Fernando de los Rios and Martin Dominguez Berrueta. By his late teens Garcia Lorca was already known as a multi-talented artist—his first book, the travelogue *Impresiones y paisajes* (*Impressions and Landscapes*), appeared before he was twenty—but he was also a poor student. Skilled as a pianist and singer, he would probably have become a musician if his parents had not compelled him to stay in school and study law. "I am a great Romantic," he wrote to a friend at the time, according to Gibson. "In a century of Zeppelins and idiotic deaths, I weep at my piano dreaming of the Handelian mist."

In 1919 Garcia Lorca's parents let him transfer to the University of Madrid, where he ignored classes in favor of socializing and cultural life. The move helped Garcia Lorca's development as a writer, however, for some of the major trends of modern European culture were just beginning to reach Spain through Madrid's intellectual community. As Western writers began to experiment with language, Madrid became a center of ultraism, which sought to change the nature of poetry by abandoning sentiment and moral rhetoric in favor of "pure poetry"—new and startling images and metaphors. Surrealism, aided by Sigmund Freud's studies of psychology, tried to dispense with social convention and express the hidden desires and fears of the subconscious mind. New ideas surrounded Garcia Lorca even in his dormitory—an idealistic private foundation, the Residencia de Estudiantes, which tried to re-create in Spain the lively intellectual atmosphere found in the residence halls of England's elite universities. At the Residencia Garcia Lorca met such talented students as Luis Bunuel and Salvador Dali, who soon became prominent in the surrealist movement. The friendship between Garcia Lorca and Dali became particularly close, and at times painful to both. Dali, somewhat withdrawn in his youth, resisted becoming Garcia Lorca's lover but was clearly drawn to the writer's ebullient personality. Garcia Lorca, who came to view Dali with feelings of unrequited love, was impressed by his friend's audacity as a social critic and as a painter. "You are a Christian tempest," Dali told Garcia Lorca, according to Gibson, "and you need my paganism." Garcia Lorca's early poems, Carl Cobb suggested, show his "search . . . for a permanent manner of expression"; the results are promising but sometimes awkward. He quickly showed a gift for imagery and dramatic imagination, adeptly describing, for instance, the experience of a bird being shot down by a hunter.

But he had to struggle to shed the vague, overemotional style of romanticism—a difficult task because he often seemed to be making veiled comments about his unhappiness as a homosexual. For example, Garcia Lorca's poem about the doomed love of a cockroach for a butterfly became an artistic disaster when it was presented in 1920 as the play *El maleficio de la mariposa* "The Butterfly's Evil Spell". Lorca's Madrid audience derided the play, and even when he became a successful dramatist he avoided discussing the experience. A more successful poem, which Gibson called "one of Garcia Lorca's most moving," is "Encuentro" ("Meeting"), in which the poet speaks with the loving wife he might have known as a heterosexual. (At his death Garcia Lorca left behind many unpublished works—generally dominated by frustration or sadness—on homosexual themes, apparently presuming that the general public would not accept the subject matter.) Lorca tried many poetic forms, particularly in *Canciones* (*Songs*), which contains poems written between 1921 and 1924. He wrote several extended odes, including the "Ode to Salvador Dali," which was widely praised as a defense of modern art although it can also be read as a love poem.

The form and rhythm of music inspired a group of poems titled *Suites,* which were not published as a unified collection until 1983. Eventually Garcia Lorca achieved great success as a poet by describing the traditional world of his childhood with a blend of very old and very contemporary writing techniques. The impetus came from his friendship with Manuel de Falla, a renowned composer who moved to Granada to savor the exotic music of Andalusia's gypsies and peasants. The two men rediscovered the gypsies' *cante jondo* or "deep song," a simple but deeply felt form of folk music that laments the struggles of everyday life. For Garcia Lorca, the ancient *cante jondo* became a model for innovative poetry: it expressed human feeling in broad terms while avoiding the rhetorical excess of romanticism. While helping Falla to organize a 1922 *cante jondo* festival that drew folk singers from throughout Spain, Garcia Lorca wrote a poetry collection titled *Poema del cante jondo* (*Poem of the Deep Song*). In these verses, Gibson observed, Garcia Lorca tried to convey the emotional atmosphere of the folk songs while avoiding the awkward pretense that he was an uneducated gypsy. Thereafter Garcia Lorca discovered that he could increase the dramatic impact of his folk-inspired poetry by using the narrative form of old Spanish ballads to tell poetic stories about gypsies and other characters; the poems could retain a twentieth-century outlook by using innovative language and a sophisticated understanding of the human mind. The resulting work, *Romancero gitano* (*Gypsy Ballads*), appeared in 1928 and soon made Garcia Lorca famous throughout the Hispanic world.

Gypsy Ballads shows Garcia Lorca at the height of his skill as a poet, in full control of language, imagery, and emotional suggestion. The characters inhabit a world of intense, sometimes mysterious, emotional experience. In the opening ballad a gypsy boy taunts the moon, which appears before him as a sexually attractive woman; suddenly the moon returns to the sky and takes the child with her, while other gypsies wail. Observers have tried to explain the ballad as everything from a comment on Garcia Lorca's sense of being sexually "different" to a metaphor for death. Some of the ballads appear to celebrate sexual vitality. In an unusually delicate poem, Garcia Lorca describes a gypsy nun who is fleetingly aroused by the sound of men on horseback outside her convent; in another a gypsy man describes his nighttime tryst with a woman by a riverbank. Much of the book conveys menace and violence: a girl runs through the night, her fear of being attacked embodied by the wind, which clutches at her dress; a gypsy is murdered by others who envy his good looks; in the final ballad, derived from the Bible, a prince rapes his sister. In his lecture "On the Gypsy Ballads," reprinted in *Deep Song, and Other Prose,* Garcia Lorca suggests that the ballads are not really about gypsies but about pain—"the struggle of the loving intelligence with the incomprehensible mystery that surrounds it." "Lorca is not deliberately inflicting pain on the reader in order to shock or annoy him," wrote Roy Campbell in *Lorca,* but the poet "feels so poignantly that he has to share this feeling with others." Observers suggest that the collection describes the force of human life itself—a source of both energy and destructiveness. The intensity of *Gypsy Ballads* is heightened by Garcia Lorca's mastery of the language of poetry. "Over the years," observed Cobb in his translation of the work, "it has become possible to speak of the 'Lorquian' metaphor or image, which [the poet] brought to fruition" in this volume. When Garcia Lorca says a gypsy woman bathes "with water of skylarks," Cobb explained, the poet has created a stunning new image out of two different words that describe something "soothing."

Sometimes Garcia Lorca's metaphors boldly draw upon two different senses: he refers to a "horizon of barking dogs," for instance, when dogs are barking in the distance at night and the horizon is invisible. Such metaphors seem to surpass those of typical avant-garde poets, who often combined words arbitrarily, without concern for actual human experience. Garcia Lorca said his poetic language was inspired by Spanish peasants, for whom a seemingly poetic phrase such as "oxen of the waters" was an ordinary term for the strong, slow current of a river. Campbell stressed that Garcia Lorca was unusually sensitive to "the *sound* of words," both their musical beauty and their ability to reinforce the meaning of a poem. Such skills, practiced by Spain's folksingers, made Garcia Lorca a "musician" among poets, Campbell averred; interestingly, Garcia Lorca greatly enjoyed reading his work aloud before audiences and also presented Spanish folk songs at the piano. Reviewers often lament that Garcia Lorca's ear for language is impossible to reproduce in translation.

Garcia Lorca's new-found popularity did not prevent him from entering an unusually deep depression by 1929. Its causes, left vague by early biographers, seem to have been the breakup of his intense relationship with a manipulative lover and the end of his friendship with Dali. At Bunuel's urging, Dali had moved to Paris, where the two men created a bizarre surrealist film titled *Un Chien andalou* ("An Andalusian Dog"). Garcia Lorca was convinced that the film,

which supposedly had no meaning at all, was actually a sly effort to ridicule him. The poet, who knew no English and had never left Spain, opted for a radical change of scene by enrolling to study English at New York City's Columbia University. In New York Garcia Lorca's lively and personable manner charmed the Spanish-speaking intellectual community, but some have surmised that inwardly he was close to suicide. Forsaking his classes Garcia Lorca roamed the city, cut off from its citizens by the language barrier. He found most New Yorkers cold and inhuman, preferring instead the emotional warmth he felt among the city's black minority, whom he saw as fellow outcasts. Meanwhile he struggled to come to terms with his unhappiness and his sexuality.

The first product of Garcia Lorca's turmoil was the poetry collection *Poeta en Nueva York* (*Poet in New York*). In the book, Cobb observed, New York's social problems mirror Garcia Lorca's personal despair. The work opens as the poet reaches town, already deeply unhappy; he surveys both New York's troubles and his own; finally, after verging on hopelessness, he regathers his strength and tries to resolve the problems he has described. *Poet in New York* is far more grim and difficult than *Gypsy Ballads,* as Garcia Lorca apparently tries to heighten the reader's sense of alienation. The liveliness of the earlier volume gives way to pessimism; the verse is unrhymed; and, instead of using vivid metaphors about the natural world, Garcia Lorca imitates the surrealists by using symbols that are strange and difficult to understand. In poems about American society Garcia Lorca shows a horror of urban crowds, which he compares to animals, but he also shows sympathy for the poor. Unlike many white writers of his time, he is notably eloquent in describing the oppression of black Americans, particularly in his image of an uncrowned "King of Harlem"—a strong-willed black man humiliated by his menial job. Near the end of the collection he predicts a general uprising in favor of economic equality and challenges Christianity to ease the pain of the modern world.

In more personal poems Garcia Lorca contrasts the innocent world of his childhood with his later unhappiness, alludes to his disappointments in love, and rails at the decadence he sees among urban homosexuals. He seems to portray a positive role model in his "Ode to Walt Whitman," dedicated to a nineteenth-century American poet—also a homosexual—who attempted to celebrate common people and the realities of everyday life. Garcia Lorca's final poem is a song about his departure from New York for Cuba, which he found much more hospitable than the United States. Commentators disagreed greatly about the merits of *Poet in New York,* which was not published in its entirety until after Garcia Lorca's death. Many reviewers, disappointed by the book's obscure language and grim tone, dismissed it as a failed experiment or an aberration. By contrast, Cobb declared that "with the impetus given by modern critical studies and translations, *Poet in New York* has become the other book which sustains Lorca's reputation as a poet." Before Garcia Lorca returned to Spain in 1930, he had largely completed what many observers would call his first mature play, *El publico (The Public).* Written in a disconcerting, surrealist style comparable to *Poet in New York,* the play confronts such controversial themes as the need for truth in the theater and for truth about homosexuality, in addition to showing the destruction of human love by selfishness and death.

After his disastrous experience with "The Butterfly's Evil Spell," Garcia Lorca had spent the 1920s gradually mastering the techniques of drama, beginning with the light, formulaic Spanish genres of farce and puppet plays. From puppet theater, observers have suggested, Lorca learned to draw characters rapidly and decisively; in farces for human actors, he developed the skills required to sustain a full-length play. For instance, the farce *La zapatera prodigiosa(The Shoemaker's Prodigious Wife),* begun in the mid-1920s, shows the poet's growing ease with extended dialogue and complex action. In *Amor de Don Perlimplin con Belisa en su jardin (The Love of Don Perlimplin with Belisa, in His Garden),* begun shortly thereafter, Garcia Lorca toys with the conventions of farce, as the play's object of ridicule—an old man with a lively young wife—unexpectedly becomes a figure of pity. By 1927 Garcia Lorca gained modest commercial success with his second professional production, *Mariana Pineda.* The heroine of this historical melodrama meets death rather than forsake her lover, a rebel on behalf of democracy. By the time the play was staged, however, Garcia Lorca said he had outgrown its "romantic" style. Accordingly, in *The Public* Garcia Lorca proposed a new theater that would confront its audience with uncomfortable truths. As the play opens, a nameless Director of popular plays receives three visitors, who challenge him to present the "theater beneath the sand"—drama that goes beneath life's pleasing surface. The three men and the Director rapidly change costumes, apparently revealing themselves as unhappy homosexuals, locked in relationships of betrayal and mistrust. The Director then shows his audience a play about "the truth of the

tombs," dramatizing Garcia Lorca's pessimistic belief that the finality of death overwhelms the power of love. Apparently the Director reshapes William Shakespeare's *Romeo and Juliet*, in which young lovers die rather than live apart from each other. In *The Public* Juliet appears on stage after her love-inspired suicide, realizing that her death is meaningless and that she will now remain alone for eternity. The Director's audience riots when faced with such ideas, but some theater students, perhaps representing the future of drama, are intrigued. Back in Spain Garcia Lorca read *The Public* to friends, who were deeply shocked and advised him that the play was too controversial and surrealistic for an audience to accept. Lorca apparently agreed: he did not release the work and, according to biographer Reed Anderson, dismissed it in interviews as "a poem to be booed at." Nonetheless, Garcia Lorca observed, it reflected his "true intention."

Garcia Lorca remained determined to write plays rather than poetry, but he reached what some have called an unspoken compromise with his audience, presenting innovative theater that would not provoke general outrage. He became artistic director of the University Theater, a state-supported group of traveling players known by its Spanish nickname, *La barraca* ("The Hut"). The troupe, which presented plays from the "Golden Age" of Spanish drama in the seventeenth century, was welcomed by small villages throughout Spain that had never seen a stage performance. Garcia Lorca, who gained invaluable experience in theater by directing and producing the programs, decided that an untapped audience for challenging drama existed among Spain's common people. In a manner reminiscent of the *Gypsy Ballads,* he wrote a series of plays set among the common people of Spain, discussing such serious themes as human passion, unrequited love, social repression, the passing of time, and the power of death.

Rather than shock by discussing homosexuality as in *The Public,* he focused on the frustrations of Spain's women. As the plays emerged, Garcia Lorca spoke of bringing "poetry" to the theater. But his characters often speak prose, and observers suggest he was speaking somewhat metaphorically. Like other playwrights of his time, Garcia Lorca seems to have felt that nineteenth-century dramatists' emphasis on realism—accurate settings, everyday events—distracted writers from deeper, emotional truths about human experience. To make theater more imaginative and involving, Garcia Lorca used a variety of effects: vivid language, visually striking stage settings, and heightened emotions ranging from confrontation to tension and repression. By adding such "poetry" to scenes of everyday Spanish life, he could show audiences the underlying sorrows and desires of their own lives.

In accord with such aims, Garcia Lorca's four best-known plays from the 1930s— *Dona Rosita la soltera* (*Dona Rosita the Spinster*), *Bodas de sangre* (*Blood Wedding*), *Yerma,* and *La casa de Bernarda Alba* (*The House of Bernarda Alba*)—show notable similarities. All are set in Spain during Garcia Lorca's lifetime; all spotlight ordinary women struggling with the impositions of Spanish society. *Dona Rosita* is set in the Granada middle class that Garcia Lorca knew as a teenager. In three acts set from 1885 to 1911, Garcia Lorca first revels in nostalgia for turn-of-the-century Spain, then shows Rosita's growing despair as she waits helplessly for a man to marry her. By the play's end, as Rosita faces old age as an unwanted, unmarried woman, her passivity seems as outdated as the characters' costumes. The three remaining plays, called the "Rural Trilogy," are set in isolated villages of Garcia Lorca's Spain. *Yerma*'s title character is a woman whose name means "barren land." She dutifully allows relatives to arrange her marriage, then gradually realizes, to her dismay, that her husband does not want children. Torn between her desire for a baby and her belief in the sanctity of marriage, Yerma resorts to prayer and sorcery in a futile effort to become a mother. Finally she strangles her husband in a burst of uncontrollable frustration.

In *The House of Bernarda Alba,* the repressive forces of society are personified by the play's title character, a conservative matriarch who tries to confine her unmarried daughters to the family homestead for eight years of mourning after the death of her husband. The daughters grow increasingly frustrated and hostile until the youngest and most rebellious commits suicide rather than be separated from her illicit lover. *Blood Wedding* is probably Garcia Lorca's most successful play with both critics and the public. A man and woman who are passionately attracted to each other enter loveless marriages out of duty to their relatives, but at the woman's wedding feast the lovers elope. In one of the most evocative and unconventional scenes of all Garcia Lorca's plays, two characters representing the Moon and Death follow the lovers to a dark and menacing forest, declaring that the couple will meet a disastrous fate. The woman's vengeful husband appears and the two men kill each other. The play ends back at the village where the woman, who has lost both her husband and her lover,

joins other villagers in grieving but is isolated from them by mutual hatred. In each of the four plays, an individual's desires are overborne by the demands of society, with disastrous results.

After *Blood Wedding* premiered in 1933, Garcia Lorca's fame as a dramatist quickly matched his fame as a poet, both in his homeland and in the rest of the Hispanic world. A short lecture tour of Argentina and Uruguay stretched into six months, as was greeted as a celebrity and his plays were performed for enthusiastic crowds. He was warmly received by such major Latin American writers as Chile's Pablo Neruda and Mexico's Alfonso Reyes. Neruda, who later won the Nobel Prize for his poetry, called Garcia Lorca's visit "the greatest triumph ever achieved by a writer of our race." Notably, while Garcia Lorca's most popular plays have achieved great commercial success with Spanish-speaking audiences, they have been respected, but not adulated, by the English-speaking public. Some observers suggested that the strength of the plays is limited to their language, which is lost in translation. But others, including Spaniard Angel del Rio and American Reed Anderson, have surveyed Garcia Lorca's stagecraft with admiration. In the opening scenes of *Blood Wedding,* for instance, Garcia Lorca skillfully contrasts the festive mood of the villagers with the fierce passions of the unwilling bride; in *Yerma* he confronts his heroine with a shepherd whose love for children subtly embodies her dreams of an ideal husband. In an article that appeared in *Lorca: A Collection of Critical Essays,* del Rio wondered if the plays were too steeped in Hispanic culture for other audiences to easily appreciate.

Garcia Lorca's triumphs as a playwright were marred by growing troubles in Spain, which became divided between hostile factions on the political left and right. Though Garcia Lorca steadily resisted efforts to recruit him for the Communist party, his social conscience led him to strongly criticize Spanish conservatives, some of whom may have yearned for revenge. Meanwhile he seemed plagued by a sense of foreboding and imminent death. He was shocked when an old friend, retired bullfighter Ignacio Sanchez Mejias, was killed by a bull while attempting to revive his career in the ring. Garcia Lorca's elegy—*Llanto por Ignacio Sanchez Mejias* (*Lament for the Death of a Bullfighter*)—has often been called his best poem, endowing the matador with heroic stature as he confronts his fate. Later, friends recalled Garcia Lorca's melodramatic remark that the bullfighter's death was a rehearsal for his own.

In 1936 civil war broke out in Spain as conservative army officers under General Francisco Franco revolted against the liberal government. Garcia Lorca, who was living in Madrid, made the worst possible decision by electing to wait out the impending conflict at his parents' home in Granada, a city filled with rebel sympathizers. Granada quickly fell to rebel forces, who executed many liberal politicians and intellectuals. One was Garcia Lorca, who was arrested, shot outside town, and buried in an unmarked grave. Franco's regime, which controlled all of Spain by 1939, never accepted responsibility for the writer's death. But Garcia Lorca remained a forbidden subject in Spain for many years: "We knew there had been a great poet called Garcia Lorca," recalled film director Carlos Saura in the *New York Times,* "but we couldn't read him, we couldn't study him." By the 1950s Garcia Lorca's work was again available in Spain, but it was still difficult to research either his life or his death. Those who knew him avoided discussing his sexuality or releasing his more controversial work; residents of Granada who knew about his execution were afraid to speak. Gradually there emerged a new willingness to understand Garcia Lorca on his own terms, and after Franco died in 1975, Garcia Lorca could be openly admired in his homeland as one of the century's greatest poets—a status he had never lost elsewhere. His legacy endures as a unique genius whose personal unhappiness enabled him to see deeply into the human heart. "When I met him for the first time, he astonished me," Guillen recalled, according to Anderson. "I've never recovered from that astonishment."

BIOGRAPHICAL/CRITICAL SOURCES:

BOOKS

Adams, Mildred, *Garcia Lorca: Playwright and Poet,* Braziller, 1977.

Allen, Rupert C., *The Symbolic World of Garcia Lorca,* University of New Mexico Press, 1972.

Anderson, Andrew A., *Lorca's Late Poetry: A Critical Study,* Francis Cairns, 1990.

Anderson, Reed, *Federico Garcia Lorca,* Grove, 1984.

Berea, Arturo, *Lorca: The Poet and His People,* translation by Ilsa Berea, Harcourt, 1949.

Bowra, C. M., *The Creative Experiment,* Macmillan, 1949.

Byrd, Suzanne Wade, *Garcia Lorca, La Barraca, and the Spanish National Theater,* Abra, 1975.

Campbell, Roy, *Lorca: An Appreciation of His Poetry,* Yale University Press, 1952.

Cavanaugh, Cecelia J., *Lorca's Drawings and Poems: Forming the Eye of the Reader,* Bucknell University Press (Lewisburg, PA), 1995.

Cobb, Carl W., *Federico Garcia Lorca,* Twayne, 1967.

Cobb, *Contemporary Spanish Poetry (1898-1963),* Twayne, 1976.

Colecchia, Francesca, editor, *Garcia Lorca: A Selectively Annotated Bibliography of Criticism,* Garland Publishing, 1979.

Colecchia, editor, *Garcia Lorca: An Annotated Primary Bibliography,* Garland Publishing, 1982.

Dictionary of Literary Biography, Volume 108: *Twentieth-Century Spanish Poets,* Gale, 1991, pp. 136-60.

Drama Criticism, Volume 2, Gale, 1992.

Duran, Manuel, editor, *Lorca: A Collection of Critical Essays,* Prentice-Hall, 1962.

Edwards, Gwynne, *Lorca: The Theatre Beneath the Sand,* Boyars, 1980.

Garcia Lorca, Federico, *Three Tragedies,* translation by Richard L. O'Connell and James Graham-Lujan, introduction by Francisco Garcia Lorca, New Directions, 1947.

Garcia Lorca, Federico *Five Plays: Comedies and Tragicomedies,* translation by Richard L. O'Connell and James Graham-Lujan, introduction by Francisco Garcia Lorca, New Directions, 1963.

Garcia Lorca, Federico *Deep Song, and Other Prose,* translation by Christopher Maurer, New Directions, 1980.

Garcia Lorca, Federico *Lorca's "Romancero gitano": A Ballad Translation and Critical Study,* translation and commentary by Carl W. Cobb, University Press of Mississippi, 1983.

Garcia Lorca, Federico *Poet in New York,* translation by Greg Simon and Steven F. White, edited with an introduction by Maurer, Farrar, Straus, 1988.

Garcia Lorca, Francisco, *In the Green Morning: Memories of Federico,* translation by Maurer, New Directions, 1986.

Gibson, Ian, *The Assassination of Federico Garcia Lorca,* W. H. Allen, 1979.

Gibson, Ian *Federico Garcia Lorca: A Life,* Pantheon, 1989.

Guillen, Jorge, *Language and Poetry: Some Poets of Spain,* Harvard University Press, 1961.

Hispanic Literature Criticism, Gale, 1994.

Honig, Edwin, *Garcia Lorca,* New Directions, 1944.

Laurenti, Joseph L. and Joseph Siracusa, *Federico Garcia Lorca y su mundo: Ensayo de una bibliografia general/The World of Federico Garcia Lorca: A General Bibliographic Survey,* Scarecrow Press, 1974.

Lima, Robert, *The Theatre of Garcia Lorca,* Las Americas, 1963.

Londre, Felicia Hardison, *Federico Garcia Lorca,* Ungar, 1984.

Loughran, David K., *Federico Garcia Lorca: The Poetry of Limits,* Tamesis, 1978.

Morris, C. B., *A Generation of Spanish Poets, 1920-1936,* Cambridge University Press, 1969.

Morris, C. Brian, *Son of Andalusia: The Lyrical Landscapes of Federico Garcia Lorca,* Vanderbilt University Press, 1997.

Newton, Candelas, *Understanding Federico Garcia Lorca,* University of South Carolina Press (Columbia), 1995.

Poetry Criticism, Volume 3, Gale, 1991.

Pollin, Alice M. and Philip H. Smith, editors, *A Concordance to the Plays and Poems of Federico Garcia Lorca,* Cornell University Press, 1975.

Smith, Paul Julian, *The Theatre of Garcia Lorca: Text, Performance, Psychoanalysis,* Cambridge University Press, 1998.

Soufas, C. Christopher, *Audience and Authority in the Modernist Theater of Federico Garcia Lorca,* University of Alabama (Tuscaloosa), 1996.

Stanton, Edward F., *The Tragic Myth: Lorca and Cante Jondo,* University Press of Kentucky, 1978.

Trend, J. B., *Lorca and the Spanish Poetic Tradition,* Russell & Russell, 1971.

Twentieth-Century Literary Criticism, Gale, Volume 1, 1978, Volume 7, 1982, Volume 49, 1994.

World Literature Criticism, Gale, 1992.

Young, Howard T., *The Victorious Expression: A Study of Four Contemporary Spanish Poets,* University of Wisconsin Press, 1966.

PERIODICALS

Commonweal, November 3, 1939; April 20, 1945; August 12, 1955; September 2, 1955; October 21, 1955.

Kenyon Review, summer, 1955.

Nation, September 18, 1937; November 1, 1941; December 27, 1947.

New Republic, February 27, 1935; November 10, 1937; October 11, 1939; September 2, 1940; October 13, 1941.

New York Times, October 19, 1980; July 5, 1989.

New York Times Book Review, September 3, 1939; June 14, 1953; October 9, 1955; November 20, 1988; October 8, 1989.

Parnassus, spring, 1981.

Poetry, December, 1937; September, 1940.

Saturday Review, October 2, 1937; August 26, 1939; January 13, 1940; November 26, 1960.

Time, December 22, 1947; April 17, 1964.

Times Literary Supplement, October 16, 1937; May 27, 1939; September 2, 1965; September 2, 1977; November 21, 1980; August 2, 1984.*

* * *

GARCIA MARQUEZ, Gabriel (Jose) 1928-

PERSONAL: Born March 6, 1928, Aracataca, Colombia; son of Gabriel Eligio Garcia (a telegraph operator) and Luisa Santiaga Marquez Iguaran; married Mercedes Barcha, March, 1958; children: Rodrigo, Gonzalo. *Education:* Attended Universidad Nacional de Colombia, 1947-48, and Universidad de Cartagena, 1948-49.

ADDRESSES: Home—P.O. Box 20736, Mexico City D.F., Mexico. *Agent*—Agencia Literaria Carmen Balcells, Diagonal 580, Barcelona 08021, Spain.

CAREER: Novelist and author of nonfiction. Began career as a journalist, 1947; reporter for *Universal,* Cartegena, Colombia, late 1940s, *El heraldo,* Baranquilla, Colombia, 1950-52, and *El espectador,* Bogota, Colombia, until 1955; freelance journalist in Paris, London, and Caracas, Venezuela, 1956-58; worked for *Momento* magazine, Caracas, 1958-59; helped form Prensa Latina news agency, Bogota, 1959, and worked as its correspondent in Havana, Cuba, and New York City, 1961; writer, 1965—. Fundacion Habeas, founder, 1979, president, 1979—.

MEMBER: American Academy of Arts and Letters (honorary fellow).

AWARDS, HONORS: Colombian Association of Writers and Artists Award, 1954, for story "Un dia despues del sabado"; Premio Literario Esso (Colombia), 1961, for *La mala hora;* Chianciano Award (Italy), 1969, Prix de Meilleur Livre Etranger (France), 1969, and Romulo Gallegos prize (Venezuela), 1971, all for *Cien anos de soledad;* LL.D., Columbia University, 1971; Books Abroad/Neustadt International Prize for Literature, 1972; Nobel Prize for literature, 1982; *Los Angeles Times* Book Prize nomination for fiction, 1983, for *Chronicle of a Death Foretold; Los Angeles Times* Book Prize for fiction, 1988, for *Love in the Time of Cholera;* Serfin Prize, 1989.

WRITINGS:

FICTION

La hojarasca (novella; title means "Leaf Storm"; also see below), Ediciones Sipa (Bogota), 1955, reprinted, Bruguera (Barcelona), 1983.

El coronel no tiene quien le escriba (novella; title means "No One Writes to the Colonel"; also see below), Aguirre Editor (Medellin, Colombia), 1961, reprinted, Bruguera, 1983.

La mala hora (novel; also see below), Talleres de Graficas "Luis Perez" (Madrid), 1961, reprinted, Bruguera, 1982, English translation by Gregory Rabassa published as *In Evil Hour,* Harper, 1979.

Los funerales de la Mama Grande (short stories; title means "Big Mama's Funeral"; also see below), Editorial Universidad Veracruzana (Mexico), 1962, reprinted, Bruguera, 1983.

Cien anos de soledad (novel), Editorial Sudamericana (Buenos Aires), 1967, reprinted, Catedra, 1984, English translation by Rabassa published as *One Hundred Years of Solitude,* Harper, 1970, with a new foreword by Rabassa, Knopf, 1995.

Isabel viendo llover en Macondo (novella; title means "Isabel Watching It Rain in Macondo"; also see below), Editorial Estuario (Buenos Aires), 1967.

No One Writes to the Colonel and Other Stories (includes "No One Writes to the Colonel," and stories from *Los Funerales de la Mama Grande*), translated by J. S. Bernstein, Harper, 1968.

La increible y triste historia de la candida Erendira y su abuela desalmada (short stories; also see below), Barral Editores, 1972.

El negro que hizo esperar a los angeles (short stories), Ediciones Alfil (Montevideo), 1972.

Ojos de perro azul (short stories; also see below), Equisditorial (Argentina), 1972.

Leaf Storm and Other Stories (includes "Leaf Storm," and "Isabel Watching It Rain in Macondo"), translated by Rabassa, Harper, 1972.

El otono del patriarca (novel), Plaza y Janes (Barcelona), 1975, translation by Rabassa published as *The Autumn of the Patriarch,* Harper, 1976.

Todos los cuentos de Gabriel Garcia Marquez: 1947-1972 (title means "All the Stories of Gabriel Garcia Marquez: 1947-1972"), Plaza y Janes, 1975.

Innocent Erendira and Other Stories (includes "Innocent Erendira and Her Heartless Grandmother" and stories from *Ojos de perro azul*), translated by Rabassa, Harper, 1978.

Dos novelas de Macondo (contains *La hojarasca* and *La mala hora*), Casa de las Americas (Havana), 1980.

Cronica de una muerte anunciada (novel), La Oveja Negra (Bogota), 1981, translation by Rabassa published as *Chronicle of a Death Foretold,* J. Cape (London), 1982, Knopf (New York City), 1983.

Viva Sandino (play), Editorial Nueva Nicaragua, 1982, 2nd edition published as *El asalto: el operativo con que el FSLN se lanzo al mundo,* 1983.

El rastro de tu sangre en la nieve: El verano feliz de la senora Forbes, W. Dampier (Bogota), 1982.

El secuestro: Guion cinematografico (unfilmed screenplay), Oveja Negra (Bogota), 1982.

Erendira (filmscript; adapted from his novella *La increible y triste historia de la candida Erendira y su abuela desalmada*), Les Films du Triangle, 1983.

Collected Stories, translated by Rabassa and Bernstein, Harper, 1984.

El amor en los tiempos del colera, Oveja Negra, 1985, English translation by Edith Grossman published as *Love in the Time of Cholera,* Knopf, 1988.

A Time to Die (filmscript), ICA Cinema, 1988.

Diatribe of Love against a Seated Man (play; first produced at Cervantes Theater, Buenos Aires, 1988), Arango Editores (Santafe de Bogota), 1994.

El general en su labertino, Mondadori (Madrid), 1989, English translation by Grossman published as *The General in His Labyrinth,* Knopf, 1990.

Collected Novellas, HarperCollins (New York City), 1990.

Doce cuentos peregrinos, Mondadori (Madrid), 1992, English translation by Grossman published as *Strange Pilgrims: Twelve Stories,* Knopf, 1993.

The Handsomest Drowned Man in the World: A Tale for Children, translated by Rabazza, Creative Education (Mankato, MN), 1993.

Del amor y otros demonios, Mondadori (Barcelona), 1994, English translation by Grossman published as *Of Love and Other Demons,* Knopf, 1995.

NONFICTION

(With Mario Vargas Llosa) *La novela en America Latina: Dialogo,* Carlos Milla Batres (Lima), 1968.

Relato de un naufrago (journalistic pieces), Tusquets Editor (Barcelona), 1970, English translation by Randolph Hogan published as *The Story of a Shipwrecked Sailor,* Knopf, 1986.

Cuando era feliz e indocumentado (journalistic pieces), Ediciones El Ojo de Camello (Caracas), 1973.

Cronicas y reportajes (journalistic pieces), Oveja Negra, 1978.

Periodismo militante (journalistic pieces), Son de Maquina (Bogota), 1978.

De viaje por los paises socialistas: 90 dias en la "Cortina de hierro" (journalistic pieces), Ediciones Macondo (Colombia), 1978.

(Contributor) *Los sandanistas,* Oveja Negra, 1979.

(Contributor) Soledad Mendoza, editor, *Asi es Caracas,* Editorial Ateneo de Caracas, 1980.

Obra periodistica (journalistic pieces), edited by Jacques Gilard, Bruguera, Volume 1: *Textos constenos,* 1981, Volumes 2-3: *Entre cachacos,* 1982, Volume 4: *De Europa y America (1955-1960),* 1983.

El olor de la guayaba: Conversaciones con Plinio Apuleyo Mendoza (interviews), Oveja Negra, 1982, English translation by Ann Wright published as *The Fragrance of Guava,* Verso, 1983.

(With Guillermo Nolasco-Juarez) *Persecucion y muerte de minorias: dos perspectivas,* Juarez Editor (Buenos Aires), 1984.

(Contributor) *La Democracia y la paz en America Latina,* Editorial El Buho (Bogota), 1986.

La aventura de Miguel Littin, clandestino en Chile: Un reportaje, Editorial Sudamericana, 1986, English translation by Asa Zatz published as *Clandestine in Chile: The Adventures of Miguel Littin,* Holt, 1987.

Primeros reportajes, Consorcio de Ediciones Capriles (Caracas), 1990.

(Author of introduction) Mina, Gianni, *An Encounter with Fidel: An Interview,* translated by Mary Todd, Ocean Press (Melbourne), 1991.

Notas de prensa, 1980-1984, Mondadori (Madrid), 1991.

Elogio de la utopia: Una entrevista de Nahuel Maciel, Cronista Ediciones (Buenos Aires), 1992.

News of a Kidnapping, translated from the Spanish by Edith Grossman, Knopf (New York City), 1997.

ADAPTATIONS: A play, *Blood and Champagne,* has been based on Garcia Marquez's *One Hundred Years of Solitude.*

SIDELIGHTS: Winner of the 1982 Nobel Prize for literature, Gabriel Garcia Marquez "is one of the small number of contemporary writers from Latin America who have given to its literature a maturity and dignity it never had before," asserted John Sturrock in the *New York Times Book Review.* "More than any other writer in the world," declared David Streitfeld in the *Washington Post,* "Gabriel Garcia Marquez combines both respect (bordering on adulation) and mass popularity (also bordering on adulation)." *One Hundred Years of Solitude* is perhaps Garcia Marquez's best-known contribution to the awakening of interest in Latin American literature. It has sold more than twenty million copies and has been translated into over thirty languages. According to an *Antioch Review* critic, the popularity and acclaim for *One Hundred Years of Solitude* signaled that "Latin American literature will change from being the exotic interest of a few to essential reading and that Latin America itself will be looked on less as a crazy subculture and more as a fruitful, alternative way of life." So great was the novel's initial popularity, notes Mario Vargas Llosa in *Garcia Marquez: Historia de un deicido,* that not only was the first Spanish printing of the book sold out within one week, but for months afterwards Latin American readers alone exhausted each successive printing. Translations of the novel similarly elicited enthusiastic responses from critics and readers around the world.

In this outpouring of critical opinion, which *Books Abroad* contributor Klaus Muller-Bergh called "an earthquake, a maelstrom," various reviewers termed *One Hundred Years of Solitude* a masterpiece of modern fiction. For example, Chilean poet Pablo Neruda, himself a Nobel laureate, was quoted in *Time* as calling the book "the greatest revelation in the Spanish language since the *Don Quixote* of Cervantes." Similarly enthusiastic was William Kennedy, who wrote in the *National Observer* that " *One Hundred Years of Solitude* is the first piece of literature since the Book of Genesis that should be required reading for the entire human race." And Regina Janes, in her study *Gabriel Garcia Marquez: Revolutions in Wonderland,* described the book as "a 'total novel' that [treats] Latin America socially, historically, politically, mythically, and epically," adding that *One Hundred Years of Solitude* is also "at once accessible and intricate, lifelike and self-consciously, self-referentially fictive."

The novel is set in the imaginary community of Macondo, a village on the Colombian coast, and follows the lives of several generations of the Buendia family. Chief among these characters are Colonel Aureliano Buendia, perpetrator of thirty-two rebellions and father of seventeen illegitimate sons, and Ursula Buendia, the clan's matriarch and witness to its eventual decline. Besides following the complicated relationships of the Buendia family, *One Hundred Years of Solitude* also reflects the political, social, and economic troubles of South America. Many critics have found the novel, with its complex family relationships and extraordinary events, to be a microcosm of Latin America itself.

The mixture of historical and fictitious elements that appears in *One Hundred Years of Solitude* places the novel within that genre of Latin American fiction that critics have termed magical realism. Janes attributed the birth of this style of writing to Alejo Carpentier, a Cuban novelist and short story writer, and concluded that Garcia Marquez's fiction follows ideas originally formulated by the Cuban author. The critic noted that Carpentier "discovered the duplicities of history and elaborated the critical concept of 'lo maravilloso americano' the 'marvelous real,' arguing that geographically, historically, and essentially, Latin America was a space marvelous and fantastic . . . and to render that reality was to render marvels." Garcia Marquez presented a similar view of Latin America in his *Paris Review* interview with Peter H. Stone: "It always amuses me that the biggest praise for my work comes for the imagination while the truth is that there's not a single line in all my work that does not have a basis in reality." The author further explained in his *Playboy* interview with Claudia Dreifus: "Clearly, the Latin American environment is marvelous. Particularly the Caribbean. . . . The coastal people were descendants of pirates and smugglers, with a mixture of black slaves. To grow up in such an environment is to have fantastic resources for poetry. Also, in the Caribbean, we are capable of believing anything, because we have the influences of all those different cultures, mixed in with Catholicism and our own local beliefs. I think that gives us an open-mindedness to look beyond apparent reality."

In *The Autumn of the Patriarch* Garcia Marquez uses a more openly political tone in relating the story of a dictator who has reigned for so long that no one can remember any other ruler. Elaborating on the kind of solitude experienced by Colonel Aureliano Buendia in *One Hundred Years,* Garcia Marquez explores the isolation of a political tyrant. "In this fabulous, dream-like account of the reign of a nameless dictator of a fantastic Caribbean realm, solitude is linked with the possession of absolute power," described Ronald De Feo in *National Review.* Rather than relating a straightforward account of the general's life, *The Autumn of the Patriarch* skips from one episode to another using detailed descriptions. *Times Literary Supplement* contributor John Sturrock found this approach appropriate to the author's subject, calling the work "the desperate, richly sustained hallucination of

a man rightly bitter about the present state of so much of Latin America." Sturrock noted that "Garcia Marquez's novel is sophisticated and its language is luxuriant to a degree. Style and subject are at odds because Garcia Marquez is committed to showing that our first freedom—and one which all too many Latin American countries have lost—is of the full resources of our language." *Time* writer R. Z. Sheppard similarly commented on Garcia Marquez's elaborate style, observing that "the theme is artfully insinuated, an atmosphere instantly evoked like a puff of stage smoke, and all conveyed in language that generates a charge of expectancy." The critic concluded: "Garcia Marquez writes with what could be called a stream-of-consciousness technique, but the result is much more like a whirlpool."

Some critics, however, found both the theme and technique of *The Autumn of the Patriarch* lacking. J. D. O'Hara, for example, wrote in the *Washington Post Book World* that for all his "magical realism," Garcia Marquez "can only remind us of real-life parallels; he cannot exaggerate them." "For the same reason," the critic added, "although he can turn into grisly cartoons the squalor and paranoia of actual dictatorships, he can scarcely parody them; reality has anticipated him again." *Newsweek* contributor Walter Clemons found the novel somewhat disappointing: "After the narrative vivacity and intricate characterization of the earlier book [*The Autumn of the Patriarch*] seems both oversumptuous and underpopulated. It is—deadliest of compliments—an extended piece of magnificent writing."

"With its run-on, seemingly free-associative sentences, its constant flow of images and color, Gabriel Garcia Marquez's last novel, *The Autumn of the Patriarch,* was such a dazzling technical achievement that it left the pleasurably exhausted reader wondering what the author would do next," commented De Feo in the *Nation.* This next work, *Chronicle of a Death Foretold* "is, in miniature, a virtuoso performance," stated Jonathan Yardley of the *Washington Post Book World.* In contrast with the author's "two masterworks, *One Hundred Years of Solitude* and *The Autumn of the Patriarch,*" continued the critic, "it is slight . . . its action is tightly concentrated on a single event. But in this small space Garcia Marquez works small miracles; *Chronicle of a Death Foretold* is ingeniously, impeccably constructed, and it provides a sobering, devastating perspective on the system of male 'honor.'" In the novella, described Douglas Hill in the Toronto *Globe and Mail,* Garcia Marquez "has cut out an apparently uncomplicated, larger-than-life jigsaw puzzle of passion and crime, then demonstrated, with laconic diligence and a sort of concerned amusement, how extraordinarily difficult the task of assembling the pieces can be." The story is based on a historical incident in which a young woman is returned after her wedding night for not being a virgin and her brothers set out to avenge the stain on the family honor by murdering the man she names as her "perpetrator." The death is "foretold" in that the brothers announce their intentions to the entire town, but circumstances conspire to keep Santiago Nasar, the condemned man, from this knowledge, and he is brutally murdered.

"In telling this story, which is as much about the townspeople and their reactions as it is about the key players, Garcia Marquez might simply have remained omniscient," observed De Feo. But instead "he places himself in the action, assuming the role of a former citizen who returns home to reconstruct the events of the tragic day—a day he himself lived through." This narrative maneuvering, claimed the critic, "adds another layer to the book, for the narrator, who is visible one moment, invisible the next, could very well ask himself the same question he is intent on asking others, and his own role, his own failure to act in the affair contributes to the book's odd, haunting ambiguity."

In approaching the story from this re-creative standpoint, Garcia Marquez once again utilizes journalistic techniques. As Chicago's *Tribune Books* critic John Blades maintained, "Garcia Marquez tells this grisly little fable in what often appears to be a straight-faced parody of conventional journalism, with its dependence on 'he-she-they told me' narrative techniques, its reliance on the distorted, contradictory and dreamlike memories of 'eyewitnesses.'" Blades added, however, that "at the same time, this is precision-tooled fiction; the author subtly but skillfully manipulates his chronology for dramatic impact." The *New York Times*'s Christopher Lehmann-Haupt similarly noted a departure from the author's previous style: "I cannot be absolutely certain whether in *Chronicle* Gabriel Garcia Marquez has come closer to conventional storytelling than in his previous work, or whether I have simply grown accustomed to his imagination." The critic added that "whatever the case, I found *Chronicle of a Death Foretold* by far the author's most absorbing work to date. I read it through in a flash, and it made the back of my neck prickle." "It is interesting," remarked *Times Literary Supplement* contributor Bill Buford, that Garcia Marquez chose to handle "a fictional episode with the methods of a journalist. In doing so he has written an unusual and

original work: a simple narrative so charged with irony that it has the authority of political fable." Buford concluded: "If it is not an example of the socialist realism [Garcia] Marquez may claim it to be elsewhere, *Chronicle of a Death Foretold* is in any case a mesmerizing work that clearly establishes [Garcia] Marquez as one of the most accomplished, and the most 'magical' of political novelists writing today."

Despite this journalistic approach to the story, *Chronicle of a Death Foretold* does contain some of the "magical" elements that characterize Garcia Marquez's fiction. As Robert M. Adams observed in the *New York Review of Books,* there is a "combination of detailed factual particularity, usually on irrelevant points, with vagueness, confusion, or indifference on matters of more importance." The result, Adams suggested, is that "the investigation of an ancient murder takes on the quality of a hallucinatory exploration, a deep groping search into the gathering darkness for a truth that continually slithers away."

Another blending of fable and fact, based in part on Garcia Marquez's recollections of his parents' marriage, *Love in the Time of Cholera* "is an amazing celebration of the many kinds of love between men and women," according to Elaine Feinstein of the London *Times.* "In part it is a brilliantly witty account of the tussles in a long marriage, whose details are curiously moving; elsewhere it is a fantastic tale of love finding erotic fulfilment in ageing bodies." The novel begins with the death of Dr. Juvenal Urbino, whose attempt to rescue a parrot from a tree leaves his wife of fifty years, Fermina Daza, a widow. Soon after Urbino's death, however, Florentino Ariza appears on Fermina Daza's doorstep. The rest of the novel recounts Florentino's determination to resume the passionate courtship of a woman who had given him up over half a century ago. In relating both the story of Fermina Daza's marriage and her later courtship, *Love in the Time of Cholera* "is a novel about commitment and fidelity under circumstances which seem to render such virtues absurd," recounted *Times Literary Supplement* contributor S. M. J. Minta. "[It is] about a refusal to grow old gracefully and respectably, about the triumph sentiment can still win over reason, and above all, perhaps, about Latin America, about keeping faith with where, for better or worse, you started out from."

Although the basic plot of *Love in the Time of Cholera* is fairly simple, some critics have accused Garcia Marquez of over-embellishing his story. Calling the plot a" boy-meets-girl" story, Chicago *Tribune Books* contributor Michael Dorris remarked that "it takes a while to realize this core [plot], for every aspect of the book is attenuated, exaggerated, overstated." The critic also argued that "while a Harlequin Romance might balk at stretching this plot for more than a year or two of fictional time, Garcia Marquez nurses it over five decades," adding that the "prose [is] laden with hyperbolic excess." Some critics have claimed that instead of revealing the romantic side of love, *Love in the Time of Cholera* "seems to deal more with libido and self-deceit than with desire and mortality," as Angela Carter termed it in the *Washington Post Book World*. Dorris expressed a similar opinion, writing that while the novel's "first 50 pages are brilliant, provocative, . . . they are [an] overture to a discordant symphony" which portrays an "anachronistic" world of machismo and misogyny. In contrast, Toronto *Globe and Mail* contributor Ronald Wright believed that the novel works as a satire of this same kind of "hypocrisy, provincialism and irresponsibility of the main characters' social milieu." Wright concluded: "*Love in the Time of Cholera* is a complex and subtle book; its greatest achievement is not to tell a love story, but to meditate on the equivocal nature of romanticism and romantic love."

For his next novel, *The General in His Labyrinth*, Garcia Marquez chose another type of story. His protagonist, the General, is Simon Bolivar. Known as "the Liberator," Bolivar is remembered as a controversial and influential historical figure. His revolutionary activities during the early-nineteenth century helped free South America from Spanish control. The labyrinth evoked in the title consists of what John Butt described in the *Times Literary Supplement* as "the web of slanders and intrigues that surrounded [Bolivar's] decline." The book focuses on Bolivar's last months, once the leader had renounced the Colombian presidency and embarked on a long journey that ended when he died near the Caribbean coast on December 17, 1830. Even as he neared death, Bolivar staged one final, failed attempt to reassert leadership in the face of anarchy. In the *New York Times Book Review* author Margaret Atwood declared: "Had Bolivar not existed, Mr. Garcia Marquez would have had to invent him." Atwood called the novel "a fascinating literary tour de force and a moving tribute to an extraordinary man," as well as "a sad commentary on the ruthlessness of the political process."

The political process is, indeed, an integral aspect of *The General in His Labyrinth*. "Latin American politicians and intellectuals have long relied on a more saintly image of Bolivar to make up for the region's often sordid history," Tim Padgett wrote in *Newsweek*. Although Garcia Marquez presents a pro-Bolivar viewpoint in his novel, the book was greeted with controversy. Butt observed that Garcia Marquez had "managed to offend all sides. . . . From the point of view of some pious Latin Americans he blasphemes a local deity by having him utter the occasional obscenity and by showing him as a relentless womanizer, which he was. Others have detected the author's alleged 'Caribbean' tropical and lowland dislike of *cachacos*or upland and *bogotano* Colombians." The harshest criticism, Butt asserted, emanated from some Colombian historians "who claim that the novel impugns the basis of their country's independence by siding too openly with the Liberator" to the detriment of some of Bolivar's political contemporaries. Garcia Marquez earned wide praise for the quality of documentary research that contributed to the novel, although Butt, for one, lamented that the book "leaves much unexplained about the mental processes of the Liberator." He elaborated: "We learn far more about Bolivar's appearance, sex-life, surroundings and public actions than about his thoughts and motives."

In the works, off and on, for nearly two decades, *Strange Pilgrims: Twelve Stories* marked the writer's return to the short story collection. Garcia Marquez's pilgrims are Latin American characters placed in various European settings, many of them in southern Italy. "Thematically, these dozen stories explore familiar Marquesan territory: human solitude and quiet desperation, unexpected love (among older people, between generations), the bizarre turns of fate, the intertwining of passion and death," Michael Dirda asserted in the *Washington Post Book World*. At each story's core, however, "lies a variant of that great transatlantic theme—the failure of people of different cultures, ages or political convictions to communicate with each other." In *Strange Pilgrims,* Margaret Sayers Peden asserted in the *Chicago Tribune,* "Latins do not fare well in their separation from native soil." In "The Saint," for example, an old Colombian man has brought the intact corpse of his young daughter to Rome. For decades he journeys through the Vatican bureaucracy, trying to get his child canonized. "Absurd and oddly serene," Richard Eder wrote in the *Los Angeles Times Book Review,* "['The Saint'] says a great deal about Latin American boundlessness in a bounded Europe." In another story, "I Only Came to Use the Phone," a Mexican woman is mistakenly identified as a mental patient and is trapped in a Spanish insane asylum—no one heeds her cry that she only entered the building to place a telephone call.

Garcia Marquez returned to his Maconderos in his next novel, *Of Love and Other Demons.* The story stems from an event the author witnessed early in his journalistic career. As a reporter in Cartagena in 1949, he was assigned to watch while a convent's tomb was opened to transfer burial remains—the convent was being destroyed to clear space for a hotel. There soon emerged twenty-two meters of vibrant human hair, attached to the skull of a young girl who had been buried for two centuries. Remembering his grandparents' stories about a twelve-year-old aristocrat who had died of rabies, Garcia Marquez began to reconstruct the life and death of a character named Sierva Maria. Jonathan Yardley remarked in the *Washington Post Book World* that the author's mood in this novel "is almost entirely melancholy and his manner is, by contrast with his characteristic ebullience, decidedly restrained." In the *Los Angeles Times Book Review,* Eder judged the novel to be "a good one though not quite among [Garcia Marquez's] best."

As the daughter of wealthy but uninterested parents, Sierva Maria grows up with the African slaves on her family's plantation. When she is bitten by a rabid dog, a local bishop determines that she requires exorcism. The girl is taken to the Convent of Santa Clara, where the bishop's pious delegate, Father Cayetano Delaura, is charged with her case. But Delaura himself is soon possessed, by the demon of love, a forbidden love for the young woman. Yardley wrote: "Here most certainly we are in the world of Gabriel Garcia Marquez, where religious faith and human love collide in agony and passion." In *Time* magazine R. Z. Sheppard asserted that in telling "a story of forbidden love," Garcia Marquez "demonstrates once again the vigor of his own passion: the daring and irresistible coupling of history and imagination." Yardley warned, however, that "readers hoping to re-experience 'magical realism' at the level attained in the author's masterpieces will be disappointed." In the *Nation,* John Leonard stated: "My only complaint about this marvelous novella is its rush toward the end. Suddenly, [the author is] in a hurry . . . when we want to spend more time" with his characters.

Garcia Marquez again drew upon his experience as a journalist to write a nonfiction account of a bizarre episode in the history of twentieth-century Colombia in *News of a Kidnapping,* published in 1997. Set in 1992, this work recounts the abduction of ten prominent Colombians, mostly journalists, by thugs attached to the powerful Medellin drug cartel. The kidnapping and holding of hostages was ordered by Pablo Escobar, the drug cartel's kingpin, who sought to arrange some sort of deal with Colombian authorities which would lessen the chances of his being arrested and extradited to the United States, where he would face a trial and near-certain life imprisonment. As days passed, hostages were gradually released, and Garcia Marquez seized upon one hostage's story to buttress his own investigative findings and write of what he calls "the biblical holocaust that has been consuming Colombia for more than twenty years." In *Booklist,* Bonnie Smothers writes, "Garcia Marquez is dealing with reality, and at times his tone is that of the journalist reporting a newsworthy event; but his material involves intrigue, victims in hideaways, captors in hoods, incandescent meetings between negotiators from all sides, and the tyranny of fate. A complex situation but just the sort of human snakepit that Garcia Marquez finds a home in." *Kirkus Reviews* hailed *News of a Kidnapping* as "a tale featuring real-life heroes, almost comically absurd events, endless terror, and a satisfyingly dramatic ending," while Robert Stone, writing in the *New York Times Book Review,* praised the author's "quick eye for the illuminating detail and a capacity for assembling fact."

Because of this history of political involvement, Garcia Marquez has often been accused of allowing his politics to overshadow his work, and has also encountered problems entering the United States. When asked by the *New York Times Book Review*'s Marlise Simons why he is so insistent on becoming involved in political issues, the author replied that "If I were not a Latin American, maybe I wouldn't [become involved]. But underdevelopment is total, integral, it affects every part of our lives. The problems of our societies are mainly political." The Colombian further explained that "the commitment of a writer is with the reality of all of society, not just with a small part of it. If not, he is as bad as the politicians who disregard a large part of our reality. That is why authors, painters, writers in Latin America get politically involved."

BIOGRAPHICAL/CRITICAL SOURCES:

BOOKS

Bell, Michael, *Gabriel Garcia Marquez: Solitude and Solidarity,* St. Martin's Press (New York City), 1993.

Bell-Villada, Gene H., *Garcia Marquez: The Man and His Work,* University of North Carolina Press (Chapel Hill), 1990.

Brotherson, Gordon, *The Emergence of the Latin American Novel,* Cambridge University Press, 1979.

Contemporary Literary Criticism, Gale (Detroit), Volume 2, 1974; Volume 3, 1975; Volume 8, 1978; Volume 10, 1979; Volume 15, 1980; Volume 27, 1984; Volume 47, 1988; Volume 55, 1989.

Dictionary of Literary Biography Yearbook: 1982, Gale, 1983.

Dictionary of Literary Biography, Volume 113: *Modern Latin-American Fiction Writers,* Gale, 1992.

Dolan, Sean, *Gabriel Garcia Marquez,* Chelsea House (New York City), 1994.

Fiddian, Robin W., *Garcia Marquez,* Longman (New York), 1995.

Gabriel Garcia Marquez, nuestro premio Nobel, La Secretaria de Informacion y Prensa de la Presidencia de la Nacion (Bogota), 1983.

Gonzalez, Nelly S., *Bibliographic Guide to Gabriel Garcia Marquez, 1986-1992,* Greenwood Press (Westport, CT), 1994.

Janes, Regina, *Gabriel Garcia Marquez: Revolutions in Wonderland,* University of Missouri Press (Columbia), 1981.

McGuirk, Bernard, and Richard Cardwell, editors, *Gabriel Garcia Marquez: New Readings,* Cambridge University Press, 1988.

Pritchett, V. S., *The Myth Makers,* Random House (New York City), 1979.

Vargas Llosa, Mario, *Garcia Marquez: Historia de un deicido,* Barral Editores, 1971.

Wood, Michael, *Gabriel Garcia Marquez: One Hundred Years of Solitude,* Cambridge University Press (Cambridge, England), 1990.

PERIODICALS

Antioch Review, winter, 1991, p. 154.

Booklist, May 1, 1997, p. 1458.

Books Abroad, winter, 1973; summer, 1973; spring, 1976.

Chicago Tribune, March 6, 1983; October 31, 1993.

Detroit News, October 27, 1982; December 16, 1984.

Globe and Mail (Toronto), April 7, 1984; September 19, 1987; May 21, 1988.

Hispania, September, 1976; September, 1993, pp. 439-45; March, 1994, pp. 80-81.

Kirkus Reviews, May 1, 1997, p. 693.

London Magazine, April/May, 1973; November, 1979.

Los Angeles Times, October 22, 1982; January 25, 1987; August 24, 1988; June 1, 1997.

Los Angeles Times Book Review, April 10, 1983; November 13, 1983; December 16, 1984; April 27, 1986; June 7, 1987; April 17, 1988; October 24, 1993, pp. 3, 10; May 14, 1995, pp. 3, 5.

Maclean's, July 24, 1995, p. 50.

Nation, December 2, 1968; May 15, 1972; May 14, 1983; June 12, 1995, pp. 836-40; June 16, 1997.

National Observer, April 20, 1970.

National Review, May 27, 1977; June 10, 1983.

New Republic, April 9, 1977; October 27, 1979; May 2, 1983.

New Statesman, June 26, 1970; May 18, 1979; February 15, 1980; September 3, 1982.

Newsweek, March 2, 1970; November 8, 1976; July 3, 1978; December 3, 1979; November 1, 1982; October 8, 1990, p. 70.

New York Review of Books, March 26, 1970; January 24, 1980; April 14, 1983; January 11, 1996, p. 37.

New York Times, July 11, 1978; November 6, 1979; October 22, 1982; March 25, 1983; December 7, 1985; April 26, 1986; June 4, 1986; April 6, 1988.

New York Times Book Review, September 29, 1968; March 8, 1970; February 20, 1972; October 31, 1976; July 16, 1978; September 16, 1978; November 11, 1979; November 16, 1980; December 5, 1982; March 27, 1983; April 7, 1985; April 27, 1986; August 9, 1987; April 10, 1988; September 16, 1990, pp. 1, 30; May 28, 1995, p. 8; June 15, 1997, p. 16.

Paris Review, winter, 1981.

People Weekly, July 24, 1995, p. 26.

Playboy, February, 1983.

Publishers Weekly, May 13, 1974; December 16, 1983; March 27, 1995, pp. 72-73; June 10, 1996, p. 45.

Review, number 24, 1979; September/December, 1981.

Spectator, October 16, 1993, pp. 40-41.

Time, March 16, 1970; November 1, 1976; July 10, 1978; November 1, 1982; March 7, 1983; December 31, 1984; April 14, 1986; May 22, 1995; June 2, 1997.

Times (London), November 13, 1986; June 30, 1988.

Times Literary Supplement, April 15, 1977; February 1, 1980; September 10, 1982; July 1, 1988; July 14-20, 1989, p. 781; July 7, 1995; July 11, 1997.

Tribune Books (Chicago), November 11, 1979; November 7, 1982; April 3, 1983; November 18, 1984; April 27, 1986. June 28, 1987; April 17, 1988; June 29, 1997.

UNESCO Courier, February, 1996, p. 4.

Variety, March 25, 1996, p. 55.

Washington Post, October 22, 1982; April 10, 1994, p. F1.

Washington Post Book World, November 14, 1976; November 25, 1979; November 7, 1982; March 27, 1983; November 18, 1984; July 19, 1987; April 24, 1988; October 31, 1993, p. 7; May 14, 1995, p. 3.

World Literature Today, winter, 1982; winter, 1991, p. 85; autumn, 1993, pp. 782-83.

World Press Review, April, 1982.

World Research INK, September, 1977.*

*   *   *

GARDEA, Jesus   1939-

PERSONAL: Born July 2, 1939, in Dalicias, Chihuahua, Mexico; son of Vicente Gardea (in business); mother in business; married in May, 1968; children: Jacobo, Ivan. *Education:* Universidad Autonoma de Guadalajara, degree in odontology, 1966.

ADDRESSES: Office—Universidad Autonoma de Ciudad Juarez, Avenue Adolfo Lopez Mateos No.   20, Apartado Postal 1594-D, Ciudad Juarez, Chihuahua, Mexico.

CAREER: Author of novels, short stories, and poetry. Worked as a dentist, c. 1966-82; Universidad Autonoma de Ciudad Juarez, Chihuahua, Mexico, professor of dentistry, c. 1982—.

AWARDS, HONORS: Xavier Villarrutia Prize, Mexico, for *Septiembre y los otros dias,* 1980.

WRITINGS:

NOVELS

El sol que estas mirando (title means "The Sun You Look At"), Fondo de Cultura Econaomica (Mexico), 1981.

La cancion de la mulas muertas (title means "The Dead Mules' Song"), Editorial Oasis (Mexico), 1981.

El Tornavoz (title means "The Sounding Board"), Editorial Joaquin Mortiz (Mexico), 1983.

Soanar la guerra (title means "Dreaming the War"), Editorial Oasis, 1984.

Los musicos y el fuego (title means "The Musicians and the Fire"), Ediciones Oceano (Mexico), 1985.

Saobol, Grijalbo (Mexico), 1985.

El Diablo en el ojo (title means "The Devil in the Eye"), Editora y Distribuidora Leega (Mexico), 1989.

POETRY

Canciones para una sola cuerda (title means "Songs for a Single String"), Universidad Autonoma del Estado de Mexico (Toluca, Mexico), 1982.

COLLECTIONS AND SHORT STORIES

Los Viernes de Lautaro (title means "Lautaro's Fridays"), Siglo Veintiuno Editores, 1979.

Septiembre y los otros dias (title means "September and the Other Days"), Editorial Joaquin Mortiz, 1980.

De alba sombria (title means "Of Somber Dawn"), Editorial del Norte (New Hampshire), 1984.

Las luces del mundo (title means "The Lights of the World"), Universidad Veracruzana Editorial (Xalapa, Mexico), 1986.

OTHER

Antologai de cuentos (title means "Anthology of Stories"), compiled by Mario Lugo, Centro Editoral Universitario (Juarez, Mexico), 1989.

El agua de la esferas, Leega (Mexico), 1992.

La ventana hundida, Editorial Joaquin Mortiz, 1992.

Diifaicil de atrapar: Cuentos, Editorial Joaquin Mortiz, 1995.

Juegan los Commensales, Editoral Aldus (Mexico), 1998.

Also contributor of fiction to *Tri-Quarterly* and to many Mexican journals and newspapers.

SIDELIGHTS: Jesus Gardea did not publish any work until he turned forty, but quickly became one of Mexico's most prolific writers. In a period of over ten years beginning in 1979 he produced seven books, four short story collections, and one collection of poetry. His work, according to Alina Camacho-Gingerich and Eladio Cortes in *Dictionary of Mexican Literature,* focuses on creating a particular ambiance that reflects the hot Mexican desert locale in which Gardea spent his childhood. The sun is a major force in this author's writing.

It was while he was in school that Gardea discovered for the first time in his life a love of reading. Finally friends inspired him in 1977 to enter a national short story contest, in which he took second place. In 1980,

Gardea won the Mexican Xavier Villaurrutia prize for his writing. Gardea was born in 1939 in the Chihuahua desert area of Mexico. Though he originally planned to pursue odontology and earned a degree in it, he left that profession after several years in 1982 and began a career teaching odontology at the Universidad Autonoma de Ciudad Juarez in Chihuahua.

Gardea's work usually features an imaginary hot Mexican place and the effects of the land on the characters. For example, *Los Viernes de Lautaro* ("Lautaro's Fridays") takes place in a desert town where things rarely change and lonely characters pursue fatalistic ways of thinking. *El Sol que estas mirando* ("The Sun You Look At") is the story of another oppressively hot town told through the voice of a young boy. Gardea uses descriptions like "The daily heat was killing me. I was walking in a dream and spinning around an oven." Camacho-Gingerich and Cortes note that Gardea's writing focuses more on setting a mood rather than developing a plot.

Gardea's work has quickly established him as an important Mexican writer. One critic, writing in *Spanish American Authors: The Twentieth Century,* praised Gardea's *La cancion de la mulas muertas* ("The Dead Mules' Song") as "destined to rank among the greatest narratives in modern Mexican literature." This critic noted the elements of philosophy, fate, and false victory that Gardea molds into the story. *Sabado* contributor Vincente F. Torres noted that Gardea's *Saobol* captures the "asphyxiating geography of the north" and that pleasure could be taken from reading the "unfolding of images in the chiseled sentences."

Several reviewers commented on Gardea's works in *World Literature Today.* G. R. McMurray said of Gardea's award-winning collection of short stories *Septiembre y los otros dias* ("September and the Other Days") that they "universalize the Mexican experience" with the use of simple but poetic language. One of the stories is narrated by a person visiting a city who is arrested, beaten, and then returned to his hotel without explanation. Another story juxtaposes an old man's current life with his younger days while he goes through the dying process. McMurray called the collection "finely wrought" and particularly strong in its "depiction of alienation and violence." Reviewer Sonja Karsen commented on another short story collection, *De alba sombria* ("Of Somber Dawn"). Karsen applauded Gardea's insights into his poor and often troubled characters, enhanced by "carefully

chosen words." According to Karsen, Gardea has "a masterly manner and deserves to be better known outside of Mexico."

BIOGRAPHICAL/CRITICAL SOURCES:

BOOKS

Cortes, Eladio, editor, *Dictionary of Mexican Literature,* Greenwood Press (Westport, CT), 1992.

Minc, Rose, S., *Literatures in Transition: The Many Voices of the Caribbean Area,* Hispamerica (Upper Montclair, NJ), 1982.

Flores, Angel, *Spanish American Authors: The Twentieth Century,* H. W. Wilson (New York), 1992.

PERIODICALS

Sabado, January 4, 1986.
TriQuarterly, spring-summer, 1997, p. 92.
World Literature Today, autumn, 1981, p. 648; autumn, 1985, pp. 572-573; winter, 1994, p. 89.*

*   *   *

GASSET, Jose Ortega y
  See ORTEGA y GASSET, Jose

*   *   *

GILBERT, Fabiola Cabeza de Baca   1898-

PERSONAL: Born May 16, 1898, in La Liendre, NM. *Education:* New Mexico Normal (later Highlands) University, B.A. (pedagogy), 1921; studied in Spain, c. 1922; New Mexico State University, Las Cruces, B.A. (home economics), 1929.

ADDRESSES: Agent—c/o University of New Mexico Press, 1720 Lomas Blvd. NE, Albuquerque, NM 87131-1591.

CAREER: Writer. Domestic science teacher, New Mexico public schools, c. 1922-29; New Mexico State Extension Service, Las Cruces, home demonstration agent, 1929-59; UNESCO, Mexico, established home economics program among Tarascan Indians and instructed Latin Americans in cooking and preservation techniques, 1951; Peace Corps, trainer of volunteers, during the 1960s.

MEMBER: UNESCO.

AWARDS, HONORS: U.S. Department of Agriculture, Superior Service Award, 1959.

WRITINGS:

Los Alimentos y su Preparacion, New Mexico State University Extension Service (Las Cruces), 1934.

Boletin de Conservar, New Mexico State University Extension Service (Las Cruces), 1935.

Historic Cookery, New Mexico State University Extension Service (Las Cruces), 1939.

The Good Life, San Vincente Foundation (Santa Fe, NM), 1949.

We Fed Them Cactus, University of New Mexico Press (Albuquerque), 1954.

SIDELIGHTS: Fabiola Cabeza de Baca Gilbert is well known throughout New Mexico for her interest in original New Mexican food and her efforts to teach rural communities about nutrition and food preservation. Gilbert's work with Hispanic and Indian communities as a home economist not only introduced new food processing technologies, but exposed the rest of the world to these ethnic foods. Gilbert was born into a privileged family in New Mexico and become fluent in Spanish, English, and two native dialects when she was quite young; her language ability served her well later in her career. Her mother died when Gilbert was four and the author was raised by her grandmother.

Gilbert first earned a teaching degree in 1921 and spent the next several years traveling through New Mexico and teaching in rural schools. After earning a second degree in home economics in 1929, Gilbert worked for the New Mexico State Extension Service and traveled to many Hispanic and Indian communities throughout the state in order to teach residents how to can food and explore alternative food preservation methods. Gilbert also taught nutrition and helped the villagers market their products. She published her first book, *Historic Cookery,* in 1939, and it proved to be immensely popular. It initially sold over 100,000 copies and has been reprinted several times. The book presented recipes that Gilbert had learned about in her travels as an extension agent.

Gilbert continued to remain active in food and nutrition endeavors, while also developing a passion for folklore. She wrote newspaper columns and broadcast a weekly radio show on nutrition. In 1949 her second book, *The Good Life,* described the yearly cycle of food gathering, preparation, and festivals in a ficti-

tious New Mexican village. According to Enrique Lamadrid in *Dictionary of Literary Biography,* the book is significant in that it presents rural living in a realistic, rather than romanticized way. Lamadrid also pointed out that the book lends insight to the fact that the villagers actually consider themselves culturally wealthy, even though an outsider would consider the village poverty stricken. Gilbert later developed an interest in history and wrote the 1954 volume *We Fed Them Cactus,* which delineates plains history and the lives of early settlers.

Gilbert continued to educate people on methods of food preparation. She took part in a UNESCO program beginning in 1951 in which she traveled to Mexico and taught home economics techniques to Indian and Latin American communities. In the 1960s Gilbert trained Peace Corps volunteers in her home economics methods. Personal hardships in Gilbert's life—including a divorce and the loss of one leg—did not slow her down but only seemed to make her more determined to pursue her interests in home economics, folklore, and history. Her legacy as an educator continues to be remembered by people who still comment that Gilbert "first taught them that beans and tortillas are not just 'poor people's food' but the proud, ancient, and nutritional staples of the New World."

BIOGRAPHICAL/CRITICAL SOURCES:

BOOKS

Dictionary of Literary Biography, Volume 122: *Chicano Writers, Second Series,* edited by Francisco A. Lomeli and Carl R. Shirley, Gale (Detroit, MI), 1992.

Notable Hispanic American Women, first edition, Gale (Detroit), 1993.*

*   *   *

GIL de BIEDMA, Jaime   1929-1990

PERSONAL: Born November 13, 1929, in Barcelona, Spain; died of complications from acquired immune deficiency syndrome, January 8, 1990. *Education:* Studied law at the University of Barcelona, 1946-50; studied English literature at Oxford University, 1953.

CAREER: Poet. Affiliated with the Compania General de Tabacos de Filipinas (Philippines General Tobacco

Company), Barcelona, Spain, after 1955. *Military service:* Served in the Spanish army, late 1940s.

WRITINGS:

Segun sentencia del tiempo (poetry; title means "According to the Sentence of Time"), Laye (Barcelona, Spain), 1953.

(Translator)T. S. Eliot, *Funcion de la poesia y funcion de la critica,* Seix Barral (Barcelona), 1955.

Companeros de viaje (poetry; title means "Fellow Travelers"), Horta (Barcelona), 1959.

Cantico: El mundo y la poesia de Jorge Guillen (literary criticism), Seix Barral (Barcelona), 1960.

En favor de Venus (poetry; title means "In Favor of Venus"), Literaturasa/Co liure (Barcelona), 1965.

Moralidades, 1959-1964 (poetry; title means "Moralities"), Mortiz (Mexico), 1966.

Christopher Isherwood, *Adios a Berlin,* Seix Barral (Barcelona), 1967.

Poemas postumos (1965-1967) (poetry; title means "Posthumous Poems"), Poesia para Todos (Madrid, Spain), 1968.

Coleccion particular (1955-1967) (poetry; title means "Private Collection"), Seix Barral (Barcelona), 1969.

Diario del artista seriamente enfermo (memoir; title means "Diary of a Seriously Ill Artist"), Lumen (Barcelona), 1974.

Las personas del verbo (poetry; title means "The Persons of the Verb"), Barral (Barcelona), 1975, translated by James Nolan as *Longing: Selected Poems,* City Lights (San Francisco, CA), 1993.

El pie de la letra. Ensayos 1955-1979 (title means "Literally Speaking: Essays"), Critica (Barcelona), 1980.

Gil de Biedma, edited by Shirley Mangini Gonzalez, Jucar (Madrid), 1980.

Antologia poetica, edited by Gonzalez and Javier Alfaya, Alianza (Madrid), 1981.

Volver, edited by Dionisio Canas, Catedra (Madrid), 1989.

Retrato del artista en 1956, Lumen (Barcelona), 1991.

Contributor to the journal *Laye.*

SIDELIGHTS: Jaime Gil de Biedma belonged to a generation of writers and poets whose work addressed the malaise of a postwar Spain controlled by an oppressive right-wing dictatorship. His creative output managed to skirt official censorship though various means, but nonetheless conveyed an atmosphere of disillusionment. Unlike his colleagues, however, Gil

de Biedma was also keenly interested in contemporary currents in French and English literature and infused elements from abroad into his work. His later verse is pervaded by a bitter sense of irony; he was also one of the few of his generation to write erotic poetry. "Like his contemporaries, Gil de Biedma became more conscious of style and started experimenting with less prosaic poetic forms," wrote Shirley Mangini in an essay on the poet for *Dictionary of Literary Biography.* "Nevertheless, he differs from his group because of his educational background and experience. His knowledge of French and English and his analysis of diverse critical theories have influenced his work greatly. Because of his poetic sophistication, many of Spain's younger poets regard Gil de Biedma as the best of his generation."

Gil de Biedma was born in Barcelona in 1929, one of eight children from a family of well-to-do business owners. His early life was dramatically disrupted by the Spanish Civil War, which began when he was about seven. The large family fled to their country home in Nava de la Asuncion in Segovia; after the war's end, the teenaged Gil de Biedma alternated his time between Barcelona and the estate in Segovia. In 1946 he took up the study of law at the University of Barcelona and served in the military for a time as well. Contact with these two institutions—the intellectual atmosphere of the university, contrasted with the harshness of an army of a fascist dictatorship—caused Gil de Biedma to become disillusioned with yet a third, even more pervasive force in Spanish society, the Catholic church.

Some of the like-minded individuals that Gil de Biedma befriended during his student days in Barcelona included poets Carlos Barral and Alfonso Costafreda and the novelist Juan Goytisolo. He began to write himself around the age of twenty. In 1951 he officially became a lawyer, but at this time he also began contributing to the literary journal *Laye,* published under the auspices of the University of Barcelona. *Laye* became an integral part of a new movement that was stirring Barcelona's young writers, and Gil de Biedma became intensely devoted to literary pursuits. Instead of reading law journals, he spent much of his time engrossed in literature from abroad—including works by the French Symbolist poets and the English-language authors W. H. Auden and T. S. Eliot—as well as the writings of progressive Spanish poets of the 1920s.

In 1953 Gil de Biedma traveled to England to study literature at Oxford University. That same year, his first volume of verse, containing poems written between 1950 and 1951, was published by Laye as *Segun sentencia del tiempo* ("According to the Sentence of Time"). "In his early poems one can observe Gil de Biedma's obsession with the passage of time and his desire to recapture and preserve past moments," noted Mangini. "This poetry, influenced by his readings, is obviously more abstract than his later work, which is more concrete, heavily anecdotal, and historically descriptive."

After returning to Spain, Gil de Biedma considered a career as a diplomat, but failed the official examinations. He left again for a time, living and working in Paris and translating T. S. Eliot's *The Use of Poetry and the Use of Criticism.* In 1955 he took a job with a tobacco company, but soon was diagnosed with tuberculosis and spent the next few years recuperating at his family's Segovia estate. There he began *Cantico: El mundo y la poesia de Jorge Guillen,* published in 1960, a critical study one of the poets categorized as part of the Generation of 1927. Some of Gil de Biedma's own writings from this period of confinement were published in 1974 as *Diario del artista seriamente enfermo* ("Diary of a Seriously Ill Artist").

Around 1957 Gil de Biedma began working on poems that would become "Por vivir aqui" ("In Order to Live Here"), the initial section for his second volume of poetry, the 1959 work *Companeros de viaje* ("Fellow Travelers"). "The poems of 'Por vivir aqui,'" remarked Mangini, "illustrate the qualities that were to distinguish Gil de Biedma from his contemporaries. The first poem of the grouping, 'Arte poetica' (Poetic Art), is extremely important for understanding his work. He discusses the passage of time, the desire for communication with others, and the fear of non-comunication." Mangini further asserted that this first section of *Companeros de viaje* features poems that "mark some moment of the past that Gil de Biedma seeks to preserve by means of the written word, and he weaves a dreamlike atmosphere when referring to his memories of the past. His original hope of detaining the passage of time would later produce an obsessive anxiety in him, since, according to his later work, time could only result in old age, disillusionment, and death."

The second section of *Companeros de viaje,* "La historia para todos" ("History for Everyone"), features poems of a more political nature. During the late 1950s there arose increasing dissatisfaction and a push toward reform from among Spain's intellectuals,

in reaction to the conservative, censorious regime of Francisco Franco. The year 1959 was one during which Gil de Biedma and many other left-leaning Spaniards held out hope that a new, less restrictive era was on its way. Like that of his contemporaries, Gil de Biedma's verse incorporated guardedly critical sentiments. Even the term "companero de viaje"—"fellow traveler"—had leftist overtones.

In 1959 Gil de Biedma became involved in the group "Conversaciones Poeticas," a spirited crowd of writers who gathered on the island of Majorca. This and other literary events of political significance that occurred during these years were chronicled in his 1966 book of poems, *Moralidades, 1959-1964* ("Moralities"), termed by Mangini as "undoubtedly Gil de Biedma's most important book." She further opined in her *Dictionary of Literary Biography* essay, "Its collage of styles and themes show his best work. He continues to recall lost moments in *Moralidades,* especially those of his childhood during the civil war." *Moralidades* also contains erotic poetry that had previously been published in his 1965 volume *En favor de Venus* ("In Favor of Venus").

In 1965 Gil de Biedma suffered from what Mangini terms a "mental crisis" and from that experience emerged *Poemas postumos (1965-1967)* ("Posthumous Poems"), published in 1968. Nearing forty, the poet commemorated and mourned the end of his youth and offered critiques of his own work in sometimes harsh terms. Some of the verse even eulogizes the poet Jaime Gil de Biedma in the third person. "It is a book of disillusionment in the face of lost youth and lost loves," explained Mangini, "a desperate declaration concerning the search for happiness and its difficulties, and a shameless cry of jealousy in the face of those still young."

Significantly, Gil de Biedma wrote far less poetry after this point, though he continued to endure as a respected member of Spain's generation of postwar intellectuals. The bulk of his poetry was collected and published by the Barcelona house Seix Barral in 1969 under the title *Coleccion particular (1955-1967)* ("Private Collection"), but government censors destroyed nearly all copies before they could be delivered to bookstores. Six years later—the year that Franco died—a truncated version of this title appeared in Spain as *Las personas del verbo* ("The Persons of the Verb"). This was also the first of Gil de Biedma's volumes to reach English readers through a 1993 translation by James Nolan, *Longing: Selected Poems.*

During his middle age Gil de Biedma continued to write, but he did not publish his verse. He did pen a number of well-regarded essays published in the 1980 collection *El pie de la letra. Ensayos 1955-1979* ("Literally Speaking: Essays"). He alternated time between a country home outside of Barcelona, his family's Segovia estate, and the Philippines. After a long illness resulting from contracting the acquired immune deficiency syndrome (AIDS) virus, Gil de Biedma died in early 1990. A member of Spain's younger generation of progressive poets, Manuel Vazquez Montalban, penned Gil de Biedma's *El Pais* obituary. "I consider his poetry the most fundamental of the postwar period," wrote Vazquez Montalban as translated by Mangini, "because he taught later poets how to position themselves before the poetic material and to narrate nostalgia according to a poetic rhythm."

BIOGRAPHICAL/CRITICAL SOURCES:

BOOKS

Dictionary of Literary Biography, Volume 108: *Twentieth-Century Spanish Poets,* First Series, edited by Michael L. Perna, Gale, 1991, pp. 161-167.*

*   *   *

GIL-MONTERO, Martha 1940-

PERSONAL: Born September 27, 1940, in Cordoba, Argentina; immigrated to U.S., 1976, naturalized U.S. citizen, 1989; daughter of Rosendo (a civil engineer) and Beatriz Eugenia (Premoli) Gil-Montero; married Joseph A. Page (a law professor and writer), May 18, 1984. *Education:* Escuela Normal de Professores Alejandro Carbo, Cordobo, maestra normal, 1958; Cambridge University, lower certificate in English, 1959, certificate of proficiency in English, 1964; Goethe Institut, Radolfzell, West Germany (now Germany), zeugnis, 1963; Alliance Francaise, Cordoba, diploma de capacidad in French, 1965; attended Universidad Autonoma de Mexico, 1966, and Georgetown University, 1985. *Politics:* Democrat. *Religion:* Roman Catholic.

ADDRESSES: Agent—Karl D. Brandt, 1501 Broadway, New York, NY 10036.

CAREER: Author, editor, researcher, and lecturer, 1960—; Embassy of Argentina, Mexico City, Mexico, translator and interpreter, 1966; Embassy of Argentina, Washington, DC, assistant to the cultural attache, 1967-69, affiliated with Press and Cultural Office, 1979-80; head of Department of International Relations of the National Council of Science and Technology of Argentina, 1969-78. Translator and interpreter for Universidad Nacional de Cordoba, 1960-63, Industrias Kayser Argentina, 1961-63, and Editorial de la Universidad de Buenos Aires, 1969-70.

WRITINGS:

Mundomujer (poetry), Fulgor (Buenos Aires), 1970.
(Translator) Herbert Matthews, *Fidel Castro,* Cuarto Poder, 1971.
(Translator) Joseph A. Page, *Peron,* Vergara, 1984.
(Translator) James A. Whelan, *Out of the Ashes,* [Chile], 1989.
Brazilian Bombshell: The Biography of Carmen Miranda, Donald I. Fine, 1989.

Also author of several monographs on international science policy for National Council of Science and Technology of Argentina, 1969-78.

WORK IN PROGRESS: "An erotic-feminist-historical biography."

SIDELIGHTS: Argentine-born American Martha Gil-Montero is a former Argentine government official who wrote about Latin–American show business legend Carmen Miranda in *Brazilian Bombshell: The Biography of Carmen Miranda.* A singer of Brazilian samba music, Miranda was famous for her provocative dancing style and exotic costumes, which featured large, elaborately decorated hats. Gil-Montero's book records Miranda's ascent to stardom in Brazil before she moved to the United States in 1939 to appear in such Hollywood films as *That Night in Rio* and *The Gang's All Here.* Though the move boosted Miranda's career and brought her tremendous financial success, she often suffered from depression and became dependent on pills. Miranda's career waned during the late 1940s, and she died of a heart attack in 1955 at age forty-six. Gil-Montero's *Brazilian Bombshell,* however, emphasizes the positive aspects of the singer's life: "The most important part of the book is my real admiration for her music, mainly the Brazilian songs. I think that has to come back and that Americans should know about them," Gil-Montero told Rod Granger of *Inside Books.* Reviewers generally praised the biography as an important, well-researched book. Alan Ryan's comments in the *Wash-*

ington Post were typical: "Martha Gil-Montero's *Brazilian Bombshell* is just the sort of biography Carmen Miranda deserves: affectionate and generous, yet honest and realistic."

BIOGRAPHICAL/CRITICAL SOURCES:

PERIODICALS

Chicago Tribune, June 20, 1989.
City Paper, August 4, 1989.
Inside Books, July-August, 1989.
Voice Literary Supplement, August, 1989.
Washington Post, May 29, 1989.*

* * *

GODOY ALCAYAGA, Lucila 1889-1957
(Gabriela Mistral)

PERSONAL: Born April 7, 1889, in Vicuna, Chile; died in 1957 in Hempstead, New York, United States; daughter of Jeronimo Godoy Villanueva (a schoolteacher and minstrel) and Petronila Alcayaga; children: Yin Yin (adopted; deceased). *Education:* Attended Pedagogical College, Santiago, Chile.

CAREER: Poet and author. Primary and secondary school teacher and administrator in Chile, including position as principal of Liceo de Senoritas, Santiago, 1910-22; advisor to Mexican minister of education Jose Vasconcelos, 1922; visiting professor at Barnard and Middlebury colleges and the University of Puerto Rico. League of Nations, Chilean delegate to Institute of Intellectual Cooperation, member of Committee of Arts and Letters; consul in Italy, Spain, Portugal, Brazil, and the United States.

AWARDS, HONORS: Juegos Florales laurel crown and gold medal from the city of Santiago, Chile, 1914, for *Sonetos de la muerte;* Nobel Prize for literature from the Swedish Academy, 1945; honorary degree from the University of Chile.

WRITINGS:

UNDER PSEUDONYM GABRIELA MISTRAL

Desolacion (poetry and prose; title means "Desolation"), preliminary notes by Instituto de las Espanas, Instituto de las Espanas en los Estados Unidos (New York), 1922, 2nd edition augmented by Mistral, additional prologue by Pedro Prado, Nascimento, 1923, 3rd edition, prologues by Prado and Hernan Diaz Arrieta (under pseudonym Alone), 1926, new edition with prologue by Roque Esteban Scarpa, Bello, 1979 (variations in content among these and other editions).

(Editor and contributor) *Lecturas para mujeres* (essays; also see below), introduction by Mistral, Secretaria de Educacion (Mexico), 1923, 4th edition, edited with an apology by Palma Guillen de Nicolau, Porrua (Mexico), 1967.

Ternura: Canciones de ninos (title means "Tenderness"), Saturnino Calleja (Madrid), 1924, enlarged edition, Espasa Calpe, 1945, 8th edition, 1965.

Nubes blancas (poesias), y la oracion de la maestra (poetry and prose; includes selections from *Desolacion* and *Ternura* and complete text of Oracion de la maestra), B. Bauza (Barcelona), 1925.

Poesias, Cervantes (Barcelona), c. 1936.

Tala (poetry; title means "Felling"; also see below), Sur (Buenos Aires), 1938, abridged edition, Losada, 1946, reprinted with introduction by Alfonso Calderon, Bello, 1979.

Antologia: Seleccion de la autora (includes selections from *Desolacion, Tala,* and *Ternura*), selected by Mistral, prologue by Ismael Edwards Matte, ZigZag, 1941, 3rd edition published as *Antologia,* prologue by Alone, 1953.

Pequena antologia (selected poetry and prose), Escuela Nacional de Artes Graficas, 1950.

Poemas de las madres, epilogue by Antonio R. Romero, illustrations by Andre Racz, Pacifico, 1950.

Lagar (poetry; title means "Wine Press"), Pacifico, 1954.

Obras selectas, Pacifico, 1954.

Los mejores versos, prologue by Simon Latino, Nuestra America (Buenos Aires), 1957.

Canto a San Francisco, El Eco Franciscano, 1957.

Epistolario, introduction by Raul Silva Castro, Anales de la Universidad de Chile, 1957.

Mexico maravilloso (essays and poetry originally published in *Lecturas para mujeres* and periodical *El Maestro*), selected with an introduction by Andres Henestrosa, Stylo (Mexico), 1957.

Produccion de Gabriela Mistral de 1912 a 1918 (poetry, prose, and letters, most previously unpublished), edited by Silva Castro, Anales de la Universidad de Chile, 1957.

Recados: Contando a Chile, selected with prologue by Alfonso M. Escudero, Pacifico, 1957.

Selected Poems of Gabriela Mistral, translated by
    Langston Hughes, Indiana University Press, 1957.
Croquis mexicanos: Gabriela Mistral en Mexico (con-
    tains prose selections from *Lecturas para mujeres,*
    poetry, and a pedagogical lecture titled "Imagen
    y palabra en la educacion"), B. Costa-Amic
    (Mexico), c. 1957, reprinted, Nascimento, 1978.
Poesias completas, edited by Margaret Bates, prologues
    by Julio Saavedra Molina and Dulce Maria Loynaz,
    Aguilar (Madrid), 1958, 3rd edition, introduction
    by Esther de Caceres, 1966.
Poema de Chile, revisions by Doris Dana, Pomaire,
    1967.
Antologia de Gabriela Mistral, selected with prologue
    by Emma Godoy, B. Costa-Amic, 1967.
Poesias, edited with a prologue by Eliseo Diego, Casa
    de las Americas, 1967.
Homenaje a Gabriela Mistral, Orfeo, 1967.
Selected Poems of Gabriela Mistral, translated by Dana,
    Johns Hopkins Press, 1971.
Todas ibamos a ser reinas, Quimantu, 1971.
Antologia general de Gabriela Mistral (poems, essays,
    and letters; portions originally published in periodi-
    cal *Orfeo,* 1969), Comite de Homenaje a Gabriela
    Mistral, 1973.
Antologia poetica de Gabriela Mistral, selected with a
    prologue by Calderon, Universitaria, 1974.
Cartas de amor de Gabriela Mistral, Bello, 1978.
Prosa religiosa de Gabriela Mistral, notes and introduc-
    tion by Luis Vargas Saavedra, Bello, 1978.
Gabriela presente, selected by Ines Moreno, Literatura
    Americana Reunida, 1987.
Poesia Infantil/Children's Poetry, Andres Bello, 1998.

Also author of *Sonetos de la muerte,* 1914, and "An
Appeal to World Conscience: The Genocide Conven-
tion," 1956. Author of fables, including *Grillos y
ranas,* translation by Dana published as *Crickets and
Frogs,* Atheneum, 1972, and *Elefante y su secreto,*
adaptation and translation by Dana published as *The
Elephant and His Secret,* Atheneum, 1974. Poetry for
children published as *El nino en la poesia de Gabriela
Mistral,*1978. Correspondence between Mistral and
Matilde Ladron de Guevara published as *Gabriela
Mistral, "rebelde magnifica,"* 1957.

Contributor to numerous periodicals, including *Bulletin, Commonweal, Living Age,* and *Poetry.*

SIDELIGHTS: Nobel laureate Gabriela Mistral—
whose actual name was Lucila Godoy Alcayaga—was
a prominent Latin American poet, educator, and diplomat. A Chilean native of Spanish, Basque, and Indian descent, she was raised in a northern rural farm-

ing community. Following the example of her father,
Mistral initially pursued a career in education, beginning as a primary school teacher at the age of fifteen.
Over the next decade, she went on to become a secondary school professor, inspector general, and ultimately a school director. A leading authority on rural
education, Mistral served as an adviser to Mexican
minister of education Jose Vasconcelos in the early
1920s. Her background in teaching and value as an
educational consultant led to her active service in the
Chilean government. Mistral is probably best known,
however, for her brand of rich but unpretentious lyrical poetry. The tragic suicide of her fiance in the
early 1900s prompted Mistral to compose her first
lines of melancholy verse. Within several years she
completed a small body of poetry that she would later
publish under the Mistral pseudonym (which is said to
be either a tribute to poets Gabriele D'Annunzio and
Frederic Mistral or a combined reference to the archangel Gabriel and the brutal northerly wind, or "mistral," of southern France).

Having entered her *Sonetos de la muerte* ("*Sonnets on
Death*") in a Santiago writing contest in 1914, she
earned first prize and instant fame, developing in
ensuing years a reputation as one of Latin America's
most gifted poets. Critics have noted the joint influences of biblical verse and the works of Hindu poet
Rabindranath Tagore and Nicaraguan poet Ruben
Dario on the literary development of Mistral. She frequently expressed through her verse an urgent concern for outcasts, underprivileged or otherwise impoverished people, and ancestors—the poet donated
profits from her third book to Basque children orphaned in the Spanish Civil War. Her simple, un-
adorned writings evoke a sense of mystery and isolation, centering on themes of love, death, childhood,
maternity, and religion. Mistral had turned to religion
for solace in her despair over the loss of her intended
husband. Her first volume of poetry, *Desolacion*
("*Desolation*"), is imbued with the spirit of an
individual's struggle to reconcile personal fulfillment
with the will of God. In expressing her grief and
anguish throughout the collection with characteristic
passion and honesty, Mistral "talks to Christ as freely
as to a child," commented Mildred Adams in *Nation.*

Several critics of the work of Mistral, including Adams,
have suggested that both her lover's death and her failure to bear his child inspired in the poet a fervent dedication to children. *Ternura* ("*Tenderness*"), her 1924
volume of children's poetry, is a celebration of the
joys of birth and motherhood. While *Desolacion* reflects the pain of a lost love and an obsession with

death, *Ternura* is generally considered a work of renewed hope and understanding. Infused with a decidedly Christian temper, the poems in the latter collection are among the most sentimental written by Mistral, and they evoke the poet's overriding desire to attain harmony and peace in her life. Correlating Mistral's treatment of the love theme with her frequent depiction of mother and child, Sidonia Carmen Rosenbaum theorized in *Modern Women Poets of Spanish America:* "Her conception of love is . . . profoundly religious and pure. Its purpose is not to appease desire, to satisfy carnal appetites, but soberly to give thought to the richest, the most precious, the most sacred heritage of woman: maternity." *Saturday Review* contributor Edwin Honig expressed a similar view, noting that for Mistral, "Childbearing . . . approximates a mystic condition: it is like finding union with God. . . . The experience of gestating another life inside oneself is the supreme act of creation."

Though consistently stark, simple, and direct, Mistral's later verse is marked by a growing maturity and sense of redemption and deliverance. The 1938 collection *Tala* ("Felling"), according to Rosenbaum, possesses "a serenity that reveals an emotion more contained (whose key note is hope) and . . . an expression less tortured" than the early works and therefore continues Mistral's path toward renewal. The poet achieved a greater objectivity in both this work and her final volume of poetry, *Lagar* ("Wine Press"), which was published in 1954. Through pure and succinct language, *Lagar* conveys Mistral's acceptance of death and marks her growing freedom from bitterness. Several critics have implied that this collection—the culmination of her literary career—is both a refinement of her simple and skillful writing style and a testament to her strengthened faith and ultimate understanding of God. As Fernando Alegria explained in *Las fronteras del realismo*, "Here we have the secret dynamism [of the poet's verse]; it contains a salvation." In *Gabriela Mistral: The Poet and Her Work*, Margot Arce de Vazquez concluded: "[Mistral's] poetry possesses the merit of consummate originality, of a voice of its own, authentic and consciously realized. The affirmation within this poetry of the intimate 'I,' removed from everything foreign to it, makes it profoundly human, and it is this human quality that gives it its universal value."

BIOGRAPHICAL/CRITICAL SOURCES:

BOOKS

Alegria, Fernando, *Las fronteras del realismo: Literatura chilena del siglo XX,* ZigZag, 1962.

de Vazquez, Margot Arce, *Gabriela Mistral: The Poet and Her Work,* translated by Helene Masslo Anderson, New York University Press, 1964.

Foster, David William and Virginia Ramos Foster, editors, *Modern Latin American Literature,* Volume 2, Ungar, 1975.

Horan, Elizabeth, *Gabriela Mistral: An Artist and Her People,* Organization of American States (Washington, DC), 1994.

Mistral, Gabriela, *Selected Poems of Gabriela Mistral,* translated by Doris Dana, Johns Hopkins Press, 1971.

Rosenbaum, Sidonia Carmen, *Modern Women Poets of Spanish America: The Precursors, Delmira Agustini, Gabriela Mistral, Alfonsina Storni, Juana de Ibarbourou,* Hispanic Institute in the United States, 1945.

Szmulewicz, Efraim, *Gabriela Mistral: Biografia emotiva,* Sol de Septiembre, 1967.

Taylor, Martin C., *Gabriela Mistral's Religious Sensibility,* University of California Press, 1968.

Twentieth-Century Literary Criticism, Volume 2, Gale, 1979.

Vargas Saavedra, Luis, editor, *El otro suicida de Gabriela Mistral,* Universidad Catolica de Chile, 1985.

PERIDOCIALS

Cuadernos Americanos, September-October, 1962.
Living Age, November 29, 1924.
Nation, December 29, 1945.
Poet Lore, winter, 1940.
Saturday Review, March 22, 1958; July 17, 1971.*

*   *   *

GOMEZ DE LA SERNA, Ramon 1888-1963 (Tristan)

PERSONAL: Born on July 3 (one source says July 6), 1888, in Madrid, Spain; died on January 12, 1963, in Buenos Aires, Argentina; buried in Madrid's Panteon de Hombres Ilustres; son of Javier Gomez de la Serna y Laguna (an author and magazine editor) and Josefa Puig Coronado. *Education:* University of Madrid Law School, graduated, 1908.

CAREER: Writer. Held political post in Paris, France, 1909-11. Host of series of radio programs, Madrid, beginning 1930.

AWARDS, HONORS: Juan Paloma Award for literature, 1960; "Special" March Award, official March Award, awards from the Spanish provinces of Galicia and Catalonia, and lifetime monthly pension from Argentine Parliament in recognition of literary achievements, all 1962.

WRITINGS:

IN ENGLISH TRANSLATION

Cinelandia, Sempere (Valencia), 1923, reprinted, Nostromo, 1974, translation by Angel Flores published as *Movieland,* Macauley (New York), 1930.

Some greguerias (selections from *Greguerias* and *Flor de greguerias*), translation by Helen Granville- Barker, W. E. Rudge's Sons (New York), 1944.

Dali, Espasa-Calpe, 1977, translation by Nicholas Fry and Elizabeth Evans published under same title, Morrow, 1979.

Total de Greguerias, translated by Miguel Gonzalez-Gerth, Latin American Literary Press (Pittsburgh, PA), 1989.

Contributor of stories and *greguerias* in English translation to journals, including *Broom,* May, 1922, *Criterion,* January, 1923, *Bookman,* June, 1928, *Alhambra,* June, 1929. Also contributor in English translation to anthologies, including *The Best Continental Short Stories of 1927,* edited by R. Eaton, *Great Spanish Short Stories,* edited by J. G. Gorkin, and *The European Caravan,* edited by S. Putnam.

IN SPANISH

Entrando en el fuego (title means "Entering the Fray"), Imprenta del Diario de Avisos (Segovia), 1905.

Morbideces, El Trabajo (Madrid), 1908.

Cuento de Calleja (play), Sociedad de Autores Espanoles (Madrid), 1909.

Ex-votos: Dramas (play collection), Aurora (Madrid), 1910.

La bailarina (title means "The Ballerina"), Aurora-Sociedad de Autores Espanoles, 1911.

El doctor inverosimil (title means "The Unlikely Doctor"; novel), La Novela de Bolsillo (Madrid), 1914, reprinted, Destino, 1981.

El Rastro (novel), Prometeo, 1915, reprinted, La Nave, 1931.

La viuda blanca y negra (title means "The Black and White Widow"; novel), Biblioteca Nueva, 1917, reprinted, Poseidon, 1943.

El circo (title means "The Circus"), Latina (Madrid), 1917, reprinted, Plaza & Janes, 1987.

Senos (title means "Bosoms"), Latina, 1917, AHR (Barcelona), 1968.

Greguerias, Prometeo (Valencia), 1917, enlarged edition published as *Greguerias, 1940-1945,* Espasa-Calpe (Buenos Aires), 1945, enlarged edition published as *Greguerias, seleccion 1910-1960,* Espasa-Calpe (Madrid), 1960.

(Editor, contributor, and author of epilogue) Silverio Lanza, *Paginas escogidas e ineditas de Silverio Lanza,* Biblioteca Nueva, 1918.

Pombo, Meson de Panos (Madrid), 1918, published as *Pombo: Biografia del celebre cafe y de otros cafes famosos,* Juventud (Buenos Aires), 1941, abridged edition, Juventud (Barcelona), 1960.

Muestrarios (title means "Samplings"), Biblioteca Nueva, 1918.

El alba y las cosas (title means "The Dawn and Things"), Saturnino Calleja (Madrid), 1918.

Toda la historia de la Puerta del Sol (title means "The Complete History of the Puerta del Sol"), La Tribuna, 1920.

Variaciones (title means "Variations"), La Tribuna, 1920.

Virguerias (title means "Virginal Glimpses"), self-published (Madrid), 1920.

El libro nuevo (title means "The New Book"), Meson de Panos, 1920.

Edgar Poe, Biblioteca Nueva (Madrid), 1920, revised edition published as *Edgar Poe, genio de America,* Losada, 1953.

Disparates (title means "Absurdities"), Calpe (Madrid), 1921.

Oscar Wilde, Biblioteca Nueva, 1921, reprinted, Poseidon, 1944.

El secreto del acueducto (title means "The Secret of the Aqueduct"), Biblioteca Nueva, 1922, EDHASA (Barcelona), 1962.

El incongruente: Novela grande, Calpe, 1922, reprinted, Picazo (Barcelona), 1972.

Leopoldo y Teresa, La Novela Corta (Madrid), 1922.

El gran hotel (title means "Grand Hotel"), America (Madrid), 1922.

Ramonismo (title means "Ramonism"), self-illustrated, Calpe, 1923.

El chalet de las rosas, Sempere (Valencia), 1923, reprinted, Centro (Madrid), 1975.

La quinta de Palmyra (title means "Palmyra's Country Villa"), Biblioteca Nueva, 1923, reprinted, Espasa-Calpe (Madrid), 1982.

El novelista (novela grande), Sempere, 1923, reprinted, Espasa-Calpe, 1973.

Azorin (biography), La Nave (Madrid), 1923, reprinted, Losada, 1957.

La sagrada cripta del Pombo (title means "Pombo, The Sacred Crypt"), Meson de Panos, 1924.

La malicia de las acacias: Novelas (novel collection), Sempere, 1924.

Cuentos para ninos (title means "Stories for Children"), Calpe, 1924.

Caprichos (title means "Caprices"; short sketches), La Lectura (Madrid), 1925, reprinted, Espasa-Calpe (Madrid), 1962.

El Prado, Libreria (Madrid), 1925.

El drama del palacio deshabitado: Dramas (contains title play and "La utopia", "Beatriz," "La corona de hierro," and "El lunatico"), America (Madrid), 1926.

Gollerias (title means "Tidbits"), self-illustrated, Sempere, 1926, expanded edition (also includes *Ramonismo* and *Variaciones*), Losada, 1946.

El torero Caracho (novel), Agencia Mundial de Libreria (Madrid), 1926, reprinted, Espasa-Calpe (Madrid), 1969.

La mujer de ambar (title means "The Amber Woman"), Biblioteca Nueva, 1927, reprinted, Espasa-Calpe (Madrid), 1968.

Seis falsas novelas (title means "Six False Novels"), Mundial (Paris), 1927, reprinted, Mondadori (Madrid), 1989.

El caballero del hongo gris: Novela humoristica (title means "The Gentleman in the Grey Top Hat"; novel), Agencia Mundial de Libreria, 1928, reprinted, Salvat (Madrid), 1970.

El dueno del atomo: Novelas (title means "The Master of the Atom: Novels"; collection), Historia Nueva (Madrid), 1928, reprinted, Losada, 1945.

Goya (biography), La Nave, 1928, reprinted, Consejo Nacional de Cultura (Havana), 1963.

Efigies, (biographical sketches), Oriente (Madrid), 1929, reprinted, Aguilar, 1944.

Los medios seres (title means "The Half-Beings"; play; first produced in Madrid, 1929), Prensa Moderna (Madrid), 1929.

Novisimas greguerias, 1929, E. Gimenez (Madrid), 1929.

La nardo (novela grande), Ulises (Madrid), 1930, reprinted, Bruguera, 1981.

Ismos (criticism), Biblioteca Nueva (Madrid), 1931, enlarged edition, Poseidon, 1943, reprinted, Brujula (Buenos Aires), 1968.

Elucidario de Madrid, Renacimiento, 1931, 2nd edition, Artes Graficas Municipales (Madrid), 1957.

Policefalo y senora (title means "Polycephalous and Wife"; novel), Espasa-Calpe (Madrid), 1932.

Chao: Novela, [Barcelona], 1933.

La hiperestetica (El regalo del doctor, La roja, El vegetariano): Novelas, Ulises, 1934.

Flor de greguerias, Espasa-Calpe (Madrid), 1935, expanded edition published as *Flor de greguerias, 1910- 1958,* Losada, 1958.

El Greco: El visionario de la pintura, Nuestra Raza (Madrid), 1935, reprinted, Losada, 1950.

Las escaleras, Cruz y Raya (Madrid), 1935.

Los muertos y las muertas, y otras fantasmagorias (title means "Dead Men and Dead Women, and Other Phantasmagories"), Arbol (Madrid), 1935, corrected and enlarged edition, Espasa-Calpe (Madrid), 1961.

El colera azul, Sur (Buenos Aires), 1937.

Rebeca!: Novela inedita, Ercilla (Santiago de Chile), 1937, reprinted, Espasa-Calpe (Madrid), 1974.

Retratos contemporaneos (title means "Contemporary Portraits"), Sudamericana, 1941.

Don Francisco de Goya y Lucientes (biography), Poseidon, 1942.

Mi tia Carolina Coronado, Emece (Buenos Aires), 1942.

Lo cursi, y otros ensayos, Sudamericana, 1943.

El turco de los nardos, La Novela Actual (Madrid), 1943.

Don Diego de Velazquez, Poseidon (Buenos Aires), 1943.

Jose Gutierrez Solana, Poseidon, 1944, reprinted, Picazo, 1972.

Don Ramon Maria de Valle-Inclan (biography), Espasa-Calpe (Buenos Aires), 1944, reprinted, Espasa-Calpe (Madrid), 1969.

Dona Juana la loca y otras (seis novelas super-historicas), Clydoc (Buenos Aires), 1944.

Lope de Vega, La Universidad (Buenos Aires), 1945, published as *Lope viviente* (title means "Living Lope"), Espasa-Calpe (Buenos Aires), 1954.

Nuevos retratos contemporaneos (title means "New Contemporary Portraits"), Sudamericana, 1945.

Norah Borges (monograph), Losada (Buenos Aires), 1945.

El hombre perdido (title means "The Lost Man"), Poseidon, 1947, reprinted, Espasa-Calpe (Madrid), 1962.

Trampantojos (title means "Tricks of Whimsy"), La Cuerda Floja (Buenos Aires), 1947.

Cuentos del fin del ano (title means "Stories for the End of the Year"), Clan (Madrid), 1947.

Greguerias completas, Lauro (Barcelona), 1947, published as *Total de greguerias,* self-illustrated, Aguilar, 1955.

Obras selectas, ten volumes, Plenitud (Madrid), 1947, published in one volume, with prologue by Pablo Neruda, AHR, 1971.

Explicacion de Buenos Aires, Prologo (Madrid), 1948.

Automoribundia, 1888-1948 (autobiography), Sudamericana, 1948, reprinted, Guadarrama (Madrid), 1974.

Cartas a las golondrinas (title means "Letters to the Swallows"), Juventud, 1949.

Las tres gracias (novela madrilena de invierno), Perseo (Madrid), 1949.

Interpretacion del tango, Ultreya, 1949, reprinted, Albino y Asociados (Buenos Aires), 1979.

Quevedo (biography), Espasa-Calpe (Buenos Aires), 1953.

Antologia: Cincuenta anos de literatura, edited by Guillermo de Torre, Losada, 1955.

Cartas a mi mismo (title means "Letters to Myself"), AHR, 1956.

Nostalgias de Madrid (title means "Nostalgias of Madrid"), El Grifon de Plata (Madrid), 1956.

Obras completas (title means "Complete Works"), two volumes, AHR, 1956-57.

Mis mejores paginas literarias (title means "My Best Pages of Literature"), Gredos, 1957.

Nuevas paginas de mi vida: Lo que no dije en mi Automoribundia (autobiography), Marfil, 1957, reprinted, Alianza, 1970.

Biografias completas (title means "Complete Biographies"; collection), Aguilar, 1959.

Piso bajo: Novela (title means "Ground Floor: Novel"), Espasa-Calpe (Madrid), 1961.

Retratos completos (title means "Complete Portraits"; collection), Aguilar, 1961.

Guia del Rastro (title means "Guide to the Rastro"), with photographs by Carlos Saura, Taurus (Madrid), 1961.

Cartas a las golondrinas. Cartas a mi mismo, Espasa-Calpe, 1962.

Ensayo sobre lo cursi. Escaleras: Drama en tres actos, Cruz del Sur (Santiago de Chile), 1963.

Greguerias: Seleccion, introduction and selection by Gaspar Gomez de la Serna, Anaya (Salamanca), 1963.

Ramon Gomez de la Serna (selections), edited by Luisa Sofovich, [Buenos Aires], 1963.

(Editor) Ramon de Mesonero y Romanos, *Escenas matritenses* (title means "Scenes of Madrid"), Espasa-Calpe (Madrid), 1964.

Retratos contemporaneos escogidos, Sudamericana, 1968.

Caprichos postumos, La Esquina, 1969.

Diario postumo, Plaza y Janes, 1972.

Descubrimiento de Madrid, Catedra (Madrid), 1974.

Also author of *El miedo al mar,* 1921; *La hija del verano,* 1922; *La gangosa,* 1922; *Por los tejados,* 1924; *En el bazar mas suntuoso del mundo,* 1924; *Aquella novela,* 1924; *La funebre falsa,* 1925; *Hay que matar el Morse,* 1925; *El hijo del millionario,* 1927; *Siluetas y sombras,* 1934; *Ruskin, el apasionado,* 1943; and *Ventura Garcia Calderon,* 1946. Also author of prologue to Carmen de Burgos's Spanish translation of John Ruskin's *Stones of Venice.* Columnist, *El Liberal* (Madrid newspaper), 1918-23, *El Sol,* 1923-1933, and *La Nacion* (Buenos Aires newspaper), beginning 1928. Contributor, occasionally under pseudonym Tristan, to periodicals, including *La Tribuna* (Madrid daily), *Revista de Occidente* (literary journal) and *Arriba* (newspaper). Editor, *Prometeo,* beginning 1912.

SIDELIGHTS: Spanish humorist, short story writer, playwright and novelist Ramon Gomez de la Serna's literary career began while he was still in his teens. The elder Gomez de la Serna financed the publication of young Ramon's first book, *Entrando en el fuego* ("Entering the Fray"; published when he was just sixteen), used his influence to obtain a political post in Paris for his son so he could live in the city where authors such as Guillaume Apollinaire, Marcel Proust, Colette and others were writing, and later founded the literary magazine *Prometeo* and appointed Ramon its editor. Before the boy turned twenty, he had been honored at a literary banquet in his honor and had established himself as an innovative thinker. To many critics his subsequent work—spanning a period of nearly six decades—proved his early reputation to be justified and constituted a major contribution to Spanish letters.

One of the highlights of Gomez de la Serna's career was his invention of the *gregueria* in 1911. A chance glance out of his balcony window in Madrid recalled to the writer a similar view out of a balcony on the Arno River in Florence, Italy. As he longingly tried to recreate the scene in his mind, the idea struck him that maybe the river wished it could be in another location too or that the far bank of the river might want to exchange places with the near bank. Enchanted by the humor of his thoughts, Gomez de la Serna decided to name the concept *gregueria,* a Spanish word meaning a "confused hubbub of voices." In *The Literature of the Spanish People: From Roman Times to the Present* Gerald Brenan offered several examples of *greguerias* in English translation, including: "Stale bread is like a newly formed fossil" and "The seagulls were born from the handkerchiefs that wave goodbye in ports." Included in Rita Mazzetti Gardiol's *Ramon Gomez de la Serna* is the equation the writer used as his own definition of the term: "Humor + metaphor=*gregueria.*" These semi-aphoristic pieces, which often convey brilliant poetic images, have been seen by critics as precursors to several of the vanguardist schools of thought popular in Europe during the early years of the twentieth century.

The absurd humor of some of the greguerias, for example, brings to mind the writing of the surrealists who reveled in many things that would shock traditionalists. Gomez de la Serna attempted to do the same in his work nearly a decade before French writer Andre Breton's first surrealist manifesto. According to *Modern Fiction Studies* contributor Richard L. Jackson: "The power to startle consistently with surprising analogies is one of the major artistic achievements of the gregueria. The expression of this surprise, shock, and astonishment is one of the main objectives of this literary 'invention.'" Brenan wrote of the *greguerias:* "The best of them reveal the secret correspondences of things, employing for this a peculiar sort of poetic intuition. This kind of writing is of course surrealism, born long before that term was invented."

Other works that demonstrated Gomez de la Serna's surrealistic tendencies include the two early volumes, *Senos* ("Bosoms") and *El circo* ("The Circus"), published in 1917, the same year in which his first collection of greguerias was published. Both *Senos* and *El circo* can be considered collections, too, for they each contain long lists of images associated with the theme referred to in the book's title. In the former, Gomez de la Serna describes bosoms in chapters titled, for instance, "Bosoms in Art" and "Andalusian Bosoms."*El circo* focuses on the exciting and colorful world of the circus. This work was to provide its author with several opportunities to live out his surrealistic tendencies: once, when honored in Madrid for the book by a traveling circus, Gomez de la Serna chose to deliver a responding lecture entitled "The Complex Beauty of the Circus" from a circus trapeze. On the occasion of a similar tribute at the Cirque d'Hiver in Paris, he spoke about elephants while perched on the back of one.

In his listing of things or sensations associated with the circus, his listing of bosoms, and his listings of images in his gregueria collections, Gomez de la Serna revealed his love of looking for the logic behind what might at first glance appear to be a seemingly unconnected series of ideas or things. He gathered what appeared to be a confused jumble of thoughts and hoped, on completion of his work, to produce an understandable whole. Gardiol considered this characteristic of Gomez de la Serna's work an echo of a

similar inclination towards enumeration in the writings of Spanish essayist Jose Martinez Ruiz (known by his pseudonym Azorin). But while Azorin merely offered detailed descriptions of things, Gomez de la Serna granted human qualities to the objects. In *El Rastro* (which included a dedication to Azorin) Gomez de la Serna describes the sights of Madrid's lively outdoor flea market of the same name where second-hand odds and ends spread out on blankets or stretch for miles in booths. In Gomez de la Serna's hands the sea of discards takes on a life of its own, each item has a story to tell. His love of things, which might typically be construed as a characteristic of the writing of a realist, was used by the author in a vanguardist manner. "Never is Ramon more Ramon—and less a realist—then when he seems to enjoy, to take delight in things," commented Spanish philosopher and essayist Julian Marias in an *Insula* article quoted in English translation by Gardiol.

Marias greatly admired Gomez de la Serna's work and, according to Jackson, "maintained that in Ramon's generation only three men reached the stature of genius: Ortega [y Gasset] in philosophy, Picasso in art, and Ramon in literature." All three men excelled in looking at their world in ways that upset traditional modes of thought. Gomez de la Serna, in fact, was influenced by Ortega y Gasset's views, including his theory advocating the dehumanization of art (the title of his most famous work) and his emphasis on the microstructure—those seemingly unimportant events— of life. Gomez de la Serna dedicated his novel *El secreto del acueducto* ("The Secret of the Aqueduct") to Ortega y Gasset and the work's structure reveals his indebtedness to the philosopher's thinking: Human characters diminish in importance, as in most of Gomez de la Serna's novels, while things, in this case the great Roman aqueduct of Segovia, gain in significance. The aqueduct becomes the focus of the author's attention and, at times, he even stops his narrative to admire its beauty. Other Gomez de la Serna works, such as *Ramonismo* ("Ramonism"), *Caprichos* ("Caprices"), and *Gollerias* ("Tidbits"), celebrate Ortega y Gasset's idea of the microstructure by emphasizing minute details.

Ramonismo, the word the author used to describe his attitude toward art and life, serves as the title to a collection of random thoughts on a variety of topics, including polka dot blouses, parrots, and awnings. In *The Generation of 1898 and After* Beatrice Patt and Martin Nozick described ramonismo as "an outrageously unconventional and purely arbitrary vision of facts and things." The gregueria is perhaps the best expression of ramonismo and Gomez de la Serna's most enduring contribution to Spanish literature. "He proved that literary language could be richer if it used images," wrote Spanish critic Arturo Barea in *Books Abroad,* "with the same freedom as did the symbol-studded talk of the Andalusian peasants and gypsies." The "symbol-studded" speech of Andalusian country folk was what was to similarly inspire the innovative use of metaphors found in the work of Garcia Lorca (whose first book of poetry was published a decade after Gomez de la Serna's creation of the gregueria) and other writers of his generation and after. As Gardiol noted, "Because [Gomez de la Serna's] creative innovations succeeded in expanding the expressive powers of the image, he has been recognized as a major influence on the Spanish poets of the Generation of '25 and one of the precursors of the 'new' Spanish literature."

The Town Hall of the City of Madrid houses a museum of Gomez de la Serna memorabilia.

BIOGRAPHICAL/CRITICAL SOURCES:

PERIODICALS

Books Abroad, spring, 1953.
Insula, February 15, 1957.
Modern Fiction Studies, summer, 1976.*

* * *

GOMEZ ROSA, Alexis 1950-

PERSONAL: Born September 2, 1950, in Santo Domingo, Dominican Republic; son of Juan Francisco Gomez (a certified public accountant) and Altagracia de la Rosa de Gomez; married Barbara Garcia Jimenez (in psychology), February 12, 1976; children: Berenice, Yelida, Adrian. *Education:* Attended Universidad Autonoma de Santo Domingo, 1970-74, and University of Massachusetts—Boston, 1983-85; State University of New York, Empire State College, B.A., 1988.

ADDRESSES: Office—Spanish Dept., New York University, 19 University Place, 4th floor, New York, NY 10003.

CAREER: Colegio Onesimo Jimenez (high school), Dominican Republic, teacher, 1972-74; copywriter for Young & Rubicam advertising agency, 1974;

copywriter for RETHO advertising agency, 1975; teacher at Padre Billini High School, 1975-77; Dominican Export Promotion Center, publicist, 1978-83; Noticias del Mundo, publicist, 1983-90; poetry instructor in the public schools of Boston and Dorchester, MA, 1984-85; Northern Manhattan Coalition for Immigrants Rights, New York City, community liaison, 1987-88; New York University, Spanish instructor, c.1988—Journalist. Social worker with organizations and clubs of Washington Heights.

AWARDS, HONORS: First Prize for Poetry, Casa de Teatro, 1990; National Prize for Poetry, Salome Urena de Henriquez, 1991.

WRITINGS:

POETRY

Oficio de post-muerte, Williamsburg Print Shop, 1973.
(Contributor) *Los paraguas amarillos,* Ediciones del Norte, 1983.
High Quality, Ltd., Luna Cabeza Caliente (Santo Domingo, Dominican Republic), 1985.
(Contributor) *La poesia bisona,* Associated University Presses, 1986.
(Contributor) *Poesia dominicana de post-guerra,* Associated University Presses, 1986.
(Contributor) *Anthology of Contemporary Latin American Literature,* Associated University Presses, 1986.
(Contributor) *Antologia de la poesia hispanoamericana actual,* Siglo Veintiuno (Mexico), 1987.
Tiza & Tinta, Lluvia Editores (Lima, Peru), 1990.

Also author of *Pluroscopo* (Santo Domingo).

* * *

GONZALES, Rebecca 1946-

PERSONAL: Born December 24, 1946, in Laredo, TX; daughter of Jesus Flores; divorced; children: Monica, Ileana. *Education:* Attended Laredo Junior College; Texas A & I University, B.S., 1969; attended Lamar University, 1975.

ADDRESSES: Home—6616 Sherwood, Groves, TX 77619.

CAREER: Poet and writer.

WRITINGS:

Slow Work to the Rhythm of Cicada, Prickly Pear Press, 1985.

Work represented in anthologies, including *America in Poetry,* edited by Charles Sullivan, Abrams (New York City), 1988. Contributor to periodicals, including *New Mexico Humanities Review, Texas Observer,* and *Pawn Review.*

BIOGRAPHICAL/CRITICAL SOURCES:

PERIODICALS

Touchstone, volume XII, number 1, 1987.*

* * *

GONZALEZ, Alexander G. 1952-

PERSONAL: Born May 29, 1952, in the United Kingdom; naturalized U.S. citizen. *Ethnicity:* "Hispanic." *Education:* Queens College of the City University of New York, B.A. (magna cum laude), 1976; University of Oregon, M.A., 1978, Ph.D., 1982.

ADDRESSES: Home—1870 Gee Hill Rd., Dryden, NY 13053. *Office*—Department of English, State University of New York College at Cortland, P.O. Box 2000, Cortland, NY 13045.

CAREER: Queens College of the City University of New York, Flushing, NY, team teacher of English composition, 1975-76; University of Oregon, Eugene, director of writing laboratory, 1978-79; University of California, Santa Barbara, visiting lecturer in English, 1980-81; University of Oregon, instructor in writing and composition, 1982-83; Ohio State University, Columbus, assistant professor of English, 1983-88; State University of New York College at Cortland, assistant professor, 1988-91, associate professor, 1991-94, professor of English, 1994—. Pennsylvania State University, guest lecturer and distinguished scholar–in–residence, 1991. Central New York Conference on Language and Literature, director, 1995—; member of James Joyce Foundation and Irish-American Cultural Institute.

MEMBER: International Association for the Study of Anglo-Irish Literature, Modern Language Association of America, National Council of Teachers of English, Conference on College Composition and Communication, American Conference for Irish Studies, South Atlantic Modern Language Association.

AWARDS, HONORS: PDQWL grants, 1991, 1994, 1995, and 1998; grant from New York State Council on the Arts, 1995.

WRITINGS:

Darrell Figgis: A Study of His Novels, Modern Irish Literature Monograph Series, 1992.
Short Stories from the Irish Renaissance: An Anthology, Whitston (Troy, NY), 1993.
(Editor) *Assessing the Achievement of J. M. Synge,* Greenwood Press (Westport, CT), 1996.
Peadar O'Donnell: A Reader's Guide, Dufour (Chester Springs, PA), 1997.
Modern Irish Writers: A Bio-Critical Sourcebook, Greenwood Press, 1997.
(Contributor) *That Other World: The Fantastic and the Supernatural in Irish Literature,* Colin Smythe (Gerrards Cross, England), 1998.
Contemporary Irish Women Poets: Some Male Perspectives, Greenwood Press, 1999.

Contributor of numerous, poems, stories, and reviews to periodicals, including *Journal of Irish Literature, Eire-Ireland, South Atlantic Review, Abiko Literary Quarterly, Canadian Journal of Irish Studies,* and *Confluence.* Member of editorial board, *Mid-Hudson Language Studies,* 1984-90.

WORK IN PROGRESS: A "nonfiction novel," *Highway '74; The Adult Sentence Workbook; Brinsley MacNamara: A Critical Survey of His Fiction; Daniel Corkery: A Study of His Fiction;* editing *Etched in Moonlight,* by James Stephens.

* * *

GONZALEZ (MANDRI), Flora (Maria) 1948- (Flora Werner)

PERSONAL: Born October 16, 1948, in Havana, Cuba. *Ethnicity:* "Latina" *Education:* California State University, Northridge, B.A., 1969; Pennsylvania State University, M.A., 1974; Yale University, Ph.D., 1982; attended University of Miami, Coral Gables, FL, 1995.

ADDRESSES: Office—Division of Humanities and Social Sciences, Emerson College, 100 Beacon St., Boston, MA 02116; fax 617-824-7857.

CAREER: Dartmouth College, Hanover, NH, lecturer, 1974-76, visiting assistant professor of Spanish and Portuguese, 1982-83; University of Chicago, Chicago, IL, assistant professor of Romance languages, 1983-86; Emerson College, Boston, MA, assistant professor, 1986-91, associate professor of humanities and social sciences, 1991—, acting dean of graduate studies, 1994-95, director of Honors Program, 1995-96. Middlebury College, assistant professor, summers, 1984-89, associate professor, summer, 1993; lecturer at Calvin College, Yale University, Tufts University, University of Michigan, and Florida International University; guest on television programs; consultant to Amigos de las Americas.

MEMBER: Instituto Internacional de Literatura Iberoamericana, Modern Language Association of America, American Association of Teachers of Spanish and Portuguese, American Association of University Professors, Association of American Colleges, Latin American Studies Association, Northeast Modern Language Association, Southern New England Consortium on Race and Ethnicity.

AWARDS, HONORS: Tinker grant for Chile, 1985; three grants from Artists Foundation, Boston, 1987-89.

WRITINGS:

Jose Donoso's House of Fiction: A Dramatic Construction of Time and Place, Wayne State University Press (Detroit, MI), 1995.

Contributor to books, including *Silent Parenting in the Academy,* edited by Constance Coiner and Diana Hume George, University of Illinois Press (Urbana, IL), 1996; and *The Cuban-American Family Album,* edited by Dorothy Hoobler and Thomas Hoobler, Oxford University Press (New York City), 1996. Contributor of articles and reviews to periodicals, including *Michigan Quarterly Review, Americas Review, Hispania, Critica,* and *Anthropos.* Some writings appear under the name Flora Werner.

WORK IN PROGRESS: Una casa que rueda sus arenas: Memorias.

GONZALEZ, Genaro   1949-

PERSONAL: Born December 28, 1949, in McAllen, TX; son of Leonel Gonzalez (a migrant farmworker) and Dolores Portales Guerra (a migrant farmworker); married Elena Maria Bastida; children: Carlos Gabriel, Claudia Daniela, Mariella Elena. *Education:* Attended Pan American University, 1968-70; Pomona College, B.A., 1973; graduate study at University of California at Riverside, 1973-74; University of California at Santa Cruz, M.S., 1979, Ph.D., 1982.

ADDRESSES: Office—Psychology Department, University of Texas at Pan American, Edinburg, TX 78539.

CAREER: Writer and educator. Pan American University, Edinburg, TX, instructor in psychology, 1979-82; University of the Americas, Puebla, Mexico, associate professor of psychology, 1983-85; Texas Governor's School, University of Texas, Austin, TX, instructor, 1986; Wichita State University, Wichita, KS, assistant professor of minority studies, 1986-88; University of Texas at Pan American, Edinburgh, TX, associate professor in psychology, 1988—.

MEMBER: National Hispanic Council of Aging, Southwestern Social Science Association.

AWARDS, HONORS: Seminars Abroad (American University, Cairo, Egypt) Fulbright Fellowship, 1988; Critic's Choice Selection, *Los Angeles Times Book Review,* 1988, and American Book Award nomination, both for *Rainbow's End;* Creative Writing Fellowship, National Endowment for the Arts, 1990; Summer Seminar (University of Virginia), National Endowment for the Humanities, 1990; Dubic-Paisano Fellowship, Texas Institute of Letters, University of Texas at Austin, 1990.

WRITINGS:

Rainbow's End (novel), Arte Publico Press (Houston, TX), 1988.
Only Sons (short story collection), Arte Publico Press, 1991.
The Quixote Cult, Arete Publico Press (Houston, TX), 1998.

Contributor of short stories to anthologies, including *The Chicano: From Caricature to Self-Portrait,* edited by Edward Simmen, New American Library (New York City), 1971; *Quilt 1,* edited by Ishmael Reed and Al Young, Quilt, 1981; and *A Texas Christmas,*

Volume 2, edited by John Edward Weems, Pressworks (Dallas), 1986. Contributor of short stories to periodicals, including *Nuestro, Riversedge,* and *Denver Quarterly: Journal of Modern Culture.* Contributor of scholarly articles to periodicals, including *Hispanic Elderly,* and *La Causa Latina.*

SIDELIGHTS: "A large wall mirror faces him. He tries to look at the mirror with detached inspection, but his gaze immediately locks him into the mirror," Genaro Gonzalez writes in his short story "Un hijo del sol." "Adan stared. . . . Two pairs of eyes—those of himself and of his reflection—mesmerized each other and met at some distance between the mirror and Adan. He felt himself as being some place outside his body. Where am I? he thought. Space. Spaced out. Estoy afuera. Yo soy . . . Adan nada. . . ."

Just as his character Adan struggles to find himself and understand his heritage in "Un hijo del sol," Gonzalez grapples with the feelings of alienation and despair that so many young Chicanos experienced at the time of its writing. Besides entertaining readers, Gonzalez' fictional explorations of Chicano angst have contributed to the definition of Chicano identity. Scholars of Chicano literature, such as Charles M. Tatum in *The Identification and Analysis of Chicano Literature* and Ramon Saldivar in *Chicano Narrative: The Dialectics of Difference,* count Gonzalez among the most influential writers in the development of Chicano literature. In fact, authors like Gonzalez, who write "mainly from personal experience . . . create a group consciousness, a Chicano consciousness," according to Tatum.

Gonzalez was born in McAllen, Texas, to migrant farmworkers. His mother's family were all from Texas; his father believed himself to be a United States citizen, only to discover when he enlisted for service in World War II that he was an undocumented alien. The relationship between Gonzalez's parents was stormy, and he was still very young when they divorced. Gonzalez then went with his mother to live with her family. There was trouble between Gonzalez and his maternal grandmother and he was not happy in the home. His mother remarried when he was nine, moving away from the grandmother's house, but the new family only brought new problems. Financial difficulties forced the boy to work packing produce alongside his mother. It was not long before she was diagnosed with tuberculosis and sent to a state hospital. Despite this painful situation, the child refused to return to life with his father.

Gonzalez did not let his family problems or the fact that he had to work stop him from excelling in school. His dedication and talent in high school earned him an honors scholarship to Pan American University. At Pan American, Gonzalez distinguished himself academically and voiced his opinions through political activism as well as his writing. Gonzalez's first short story, "Un hijo del sol" ("A Son of the Sun"), was published in an anthology of Chicano works in 1971, during his sophomore year. According to Manuel M. Martin-Rodriguez in *Dictionary of Literary Biography,* "This story, which marks the beginning of Gonzalez's dedication to the writing of short fiction, establishes him as a new voice in expressing questions that were crucial at that time. . . . 'Un hijo del sol' delves in the existential angst felt by many young Chicanos at the time. Thus Adan's discovery of his identity conveys to the reader a message of hope. It reveals itself as a starting point for a new life that transcends the isolation of the individuals into a collective struggle."

"Un hijo del sol" consists of five sections. Adan (the Spanish equivalent of "Adam") is tormented by the knowledge that he does not really know himself or understand his heritage. In the passage quoted above, for example, Adan describes how he feels *afuera* (outside) himself and decides that he is empty, or *nada* (nothing). When Adan realizes that his quest for understanding cannot be meaningful unless he travels to Mexico, the home of his recent and ancient ancestors, he begins to make progress. In the last section of "Un hijo del sol," a fight breaks out among Chicanos and Anglos in a bar. Adan joins the Chicanos in the struggle and makes a choice that brings him the self-definition he has been searching for: "Adan suspends the knife in final decision, weighing the victim versus the act. . . . An obsidian blade traces a quick arc of instinct—somewhere in time an angry comet flares, a sleeping mountain erupts, an Aztec sun explodes in birth." The killing is "narrated in highly symbolic terms that suggest the reconciliation of Adan's roots, his inner life, and his new participation in social action," according to Martin-Rodriguez. "Adan's discovery of his identity conveys to the reader a message of hope. It reveals itself as a starting point for a new life that transcends the isolation of the individuals into a collective struggle."

"Un hijo del sol" and the message it carries brought the young writer immediate critical attention. Yet the work was not embraced by all who reviewed it. Several scholars disapproved of the imagery in the story—including Adan's own name, which, when reversed to "nada," means "nothing" in Spanish. According to these critics, the merits of the story were undermined by such negative symbolism. But even though some commentators decried what they saw as a socially unproductive message, Gonzalez nevertheless won a spot in the history of the development of Chicano literature. Juan Rodriguez, writing in *The Identification and Analysis of Chicano Literature,* calls the story "the best of all until now," and claims that it "is the only one in all Chicano literature which offers a search for and an encounter of identity in positive and viable terms."

While Gonzalez's work seemed to be a hit with literary critics, his political activities were not appreciated by college officials. Upon learning that his affiliation to Chicano organizations was being investigated by Pan American University, Gonzalez left the school and Texas and transferred to Pompano College in California. At Pompano, Gonzalez became an active member of La Raza Unida and contributed his efforts to the campaign to elect Ramsey Muniz as governor of Texas. In 1973, however, he became discouraged with La Raza Unida and left the party.

Gonzalez began graduate studies at the University of California at Riverside and then earned an M.S. and Ph.D. from the University of California at Santa Cruz. He began work as an instructor in psychology at Pan American University in 1979. During graduate school and his years at Pan American, Gonzalez continued to write. Most of the short stories Gonzalez produced during this time "revolved around isolation versus integration," Martin-Rodriguez states in *Dictionary of Literary Biography.* "Soil from the Homeland" (1978), "A Simple Question of $200 a Month" (1980), and "A Bad Back" (1981) were later integrated into the novel *Rainbow's End,* published in 1988.

Gonzalez's short story "The Heart of the Beast" (1980) tells the story of a boy who suffers from ill health. Taunted by children and even his grandfather for his sickliness, Arturo is reluctant to disclose any new information about his condition. The situation deteriorates to the point that, although he believes he has been bitten by a rabid dog, Arturo cannot bring himself to tell his family. His emotional isolation, however, bears fruit when he begins to appreciate himself. In "Too Much His Father's Son" (1981), a boy must deal with the confusion and pain generated by his parents' frequent arguments and his own difficult relationship with his father. In this work, "Gonzalez's psychological characterization is at its best," according to Martin-Rodriguez. "Real Life" (1982) features orphaned Ernesto, who has been

raised by his aunt and uncle and must help them make a difficult choice. His aunt is dying, and his uncle calls upon him to help decide whether to let her die naturally or support her artificially. When his uncle telephones Ernesto to inform him of his decision, Ernesto finds that he cannot answer the phone.

By 1982, when Pan American declined to offer him tenure and he left the university, Gonzalez devoted most of his time to writing. He was finally ready to begin a project he had put off—writing a novel intended for publication by Grove Press. He wrote a long first draft and then left the United States for Mexico. Gonzalez continued to write and taught at the University of the Americas in Puebla from 1983 to 1985. Arte Publico decided to publish a revised and shortened draft of Gonzalez's novel as *Rainbow's End,* and he returned to the United States. Gonzalez taught at Texas Governor's School at the University of Texas at Austin in 1986, and began a stint as an assistant professor of minority studies at Wichita State University.

It was during this time that his story "Home of the Brave" was first published in an anthology. In this short story, a Vietnam veteran becomes frustrated with the war and confronts his family with his decision to desert the army. While his family objects to the plan, an uncle who survived the Korean war advises the young man to flee to Mexico. According to Martin-Rodriguez, this story "depicts army life as a false hope for eventual social integration."

Two triumphs mark the year 1988 for Gonzalez: he was hired as an associate professor in psychology at the University of Texas at Pan American, and *Rainbow's End* was published. *Rainbow's End* begins in the 1930s, as Don Heraclio Cavazos stands at the threshold of his future life in the United States. He is just about to cross the Rio Grande for the first time by swimming through the swollen water when he thinks he sees a bridge joining Mexico and the United States. While the bridge Cavazos imagines is really a rainbow, no pot of gold lies on the U.S. side of the river. Cavazos soon finds that he must earn his living with tedious, back-breaking labor: years after his arrival in the United States he and his family are still cheated by the "gringo" farm owners for whom they toil. Martin-Rodriguez asserts that "the pot at the end of the rainbow, although never mentioned explicitly, provides the basis for the pervasive irony of the work. Gonzalez's novel is, in this way, connected to the satirical tradition of Chicano literature that demythologizes the popular belief of quick riches in the United States." Once Gonzalez establishes the symbolism of the rainbow, his novel flows along, telling the story of three generations with flashbacks. The reader learns how, as a young man, Cavazos lives in Dona Zoila's rooming house with migrant workers nicknamed Tomcat, Rooster, Elephant, Greased Pig, Frog Prince, Love Bandit, and El Bruto. He leaves the rooming house to marry Chaca, and they have two children together. When Chaca dies, Cavazos raises his offspring with the help of Chaca's family. During Cavazos's last years, he stubbornly refutes the superficial reality imposed upon him by reminding those around him of disagreeable facts and events. For example, he greets neighbors by remarking, "They shot Kennedy." And when he stands before an official to receive U.S. citizenship, to the question "Who discovered America?" Cavazos replies, "Los indios" (the Indians). Cavazos refuses to respond to the injustice that pervades his life with anything less than pride and dignity.

While Cavazos is not happy with the lifestyles that his children and grandchildren choose as they are assimilated into American society, he cannot persuade them to live as he has taught them. Cavazos's son earns his money illicitly, and other members of his family are involved in the drug trade. His daughter and her husband embrace popular culture. One of Cavazos's grandsons, a Vietnam veteran, cannot recover from the psychological trauma of war. Hope remains in the fact that one of Cavazos's grandsons journeys to Mexico and begins to understand himself and his grandfather, and optimism is manifested when Cavazos's sister-in-law Fela (a sorceress who has never married) decides to give her knowledge to an eager young apprentice so that it does not die with her.

Critics have appreciated various scenes in *Rainbow's End*. Tom Miller of the *Los Angeles Times Book Review,* for example, calls the scene in which a girl excites the barrio with the news that she has seen the devil (who has to dance on a hoof and a rooster foot instead of human feet) at the Saturday night dance "wonderfully comic." Miller also described a scene in which Cavazos goes to the mall to shop for a new hat as "poignant and comical." Stuart Klawans of the *Nation* praises a scene from *Rainbow's End* that "happens almost entirely in Don Heraclio's mind." In the scene, Cavazos is working in the tomato field when his nose begins to bleed. Just as he leans his head back to stop the bleeding, he gets a glimpse of his wife and his oldest friend, whose deaths he has been mourning. It is all Cavazos can do to keep from lowering his head and confirming what he has seen. A storm brings him back to reality with a rush of color, and he realizes that the figures he saw were not those

of the departed: "Suddenly sporadic patches of the world caught color all around. A pair of dungy objects in a nearby field combusted into twin calico cows with huge rust freckles, grazing without a care on the good, green earth. Even the fire ants under his feet seemed to ignite in redness." Klawans claims that when "Gonzalez writes at this level, the creatures of his imagination combust into their own living, full-color reality."

Rainbow's End has elicited some enthusiastic reviews from critics. Miller writes that Gonzalez' "bilingual puns enrich" *Rainbow's End,* and that the work "captures the *ambiente* of the life of a borderland household as well as any book I've ever read." Klawans said that the novel would make a good movie, but claimed that what "can't be transferred to film is Gonzalez's writing, which at its best deals in epiphanies." *Rainbow's End* was a *Los Angeles Times Book Review* Critic's Choice selection, and was nominated for the American Book Award. Gonzalez also received several awards that indicate his talent as a writer. These include a prestigious Fulbright Fellowship and a Creative Writing Fellowship from the National Endowment for the Arts.

Like *Rainbow's End,* the stories in the collection *Only Sons* (1991) are set in a Texas border town. Readers of Gonzalez' first novel and this collection will recognize similar themes and even characters. For example, in both works a tension between Chicanos of different generations is prominent. The problem of justice, observes Jim Christie of *Hispanic,* also appears in both books. In one story, a judge must deal with the son of a campaign contributor who is accused of raping his family's maid. Gonzalez's character tries to justify his actions: "'She's also a wetback,' said the son. 'Twice! From some country I never even heard of.' He looked at her and smiled, satisfied that his revenge had thwarted his case. Don Benito covered his eyes as the last glimmer of justice seemed to dim from the world."

In another story, an old man whose hand was mangled during his work as a farmhand tries to find the Anglo employer who paid him to keep quiet about the accident. When Vincente finds him in a trailer park, he slowly removes the glove from his hand to the horror of his former employer. By contrast, Elena, the woman Vincente had asked to accompany him because of her educated dislike of Anglos, cannot find the courage to confront them. In the opinion of Christie, Gonzalez "loves to play with anxiety and ambiguity; *Only Sons* seems to have been an exercise in refining and adapting those emotions over and over again in many different settings."

Gonzalez, who is the father of three children, continues to write fiction and conduct research in cross-cultural psychology at Pan American University. According to Martin-Rodriguez, Gonzalez's "mature style holds great promise for his future literary contributions to Chicano letters."

BIOGRAPHICAL/CRITICAL SOURCES:

BOOKS

Dictionary of Literary Biography, Volume 122, *Chicano Writers,* Gale (Detroit), 1991, pp. 115-118.

Gonzalez, Genaro, *Only Sons,* Arte Publico Press, 1991.

Gonzalez, Genaro, *Rainbow's End,* Arte Publico Press, 1988.

Simmen, Edward, editor, *The Chicano: From Caricature to Self-Portrait,* New American Library, 1971, pp. 308-317.

Jimenez, Francisco, editor, *The Identification and Analysis of Chicano Literature,* Francisco Bilingual Press, 1979, pp. 47-57, 170-178.

Saldivar, Ramon, *Chicano Narrative: The Dialectics of Difference,* University of Wisconsin Press (Madison, WI), 1990.

PERIODICALS

Book Watch, November, 1991, p. 9.
Children's Book Watch, November, 1991, p. 9.
Hispanic, May, 1992, p. 56.
Los Angeles Times Book Review, March 13, 1988, p. 8.
Multi-Cultural Review, January, 1992, p. 46.
Nation, November 14, 1988, p. 502.
Palabra, fall, 1979, pp. 3-16.

*   *   *

GONZALEZ, Ray 1952-

PERSONAL: Born September 20, 1952, in El Paso, TX. *Education:* University of Texas, El Paso, B.A. (creative writing), 1975.

ADDRESSES: Office—Guadalupe Cultural Arts Center, 1300 Guadalupe St., San Antonio, TX 78207-5514.

CAREER: Poet, editor and educator. Guadalupe Cultural Arts Center, San Antonio, TX, director, 1989—. Poet-in-residence, Woodinville, WA public schools, 1987. Also taught writing to juvenile offenders at the Emerson House Detention Center, Denver, CO.

AWARDS, HONORS: Four Corners Book Award for Poetry, for *Twilight and Chants,* 1988; Colorado Governor's Award for Excellence in the Arts, 1988.

WRITINGS:

From the Restless Roots, Arte Publico Press (Houston, TX), 1986.
Twilights and Chants: Poems, J. Andrews (Golden, CO), 1987.
(Editor) *Without Discovery: A Native Response to Columbus,* Broken Moon Press (Seattle, WA), 1992.
(Editor) *After Aztlan: Latino Poets of the Nineties,* D. R. Godine (Boston, MA), 1992.
(Editor) *Mirrors Beneath the Earth: Short Fiction by Chicano Writers,* Curbstone Press (Willimantic, CT), 1992.
Memory Fever: A Journey Beyond El Paso del Norte, Broken Moon Press (Seattle, WA), 1993.
(Editor) *Currents from the Dancing River: Contemporary Latino Fiction, Nonfiction, and Poetry,* Harcourt Brace (New York City), 1994.
(Editor) *Under the Pomegranate Tree: The Best New Latino Erotica,* Washington Square Press (New York City), 1996.
(Editor) *Inheritance of Light,* University of North Texas Press (Denton), 1996.
(Editor) *Muy Macho: Latino Men Confront Their Manhood,* Anchor (New York City), 1996.
The Heat of Arrivals, BOA Editions (Brockport, NY), 1996.
(Editor) *Touching the Fire: Fifteen Poets of Today's Latino Renaissance,* Anchor (New York City), 1998.
Cabato Sentora, BOA Editions (Brockport, NY), 1998.

Editor-in-chief, *La Voz,* 1981-82; poetry editor, *Bloomsbury Review,* 1982-89.

SIDELIGHTS: The work of award-winning poet and editor Ray Gonzalez is inextricably linked to his Mexican ancestry and his American southwestern upbringing. Born and raised in El Paso, Texas, Gonzalez has employed Chicano imagery in his poetry, oftentimes alluding to America's indigenous past, and particularly to the southwestern desert cultures. In all, Gonzalez has published five collections of his poetry, including *Twilights and Chants* (1987), which earned him the Four Corners Book Award for Poetry in 1988.

Gonzalez, who has been the director of the Guadalupe Cultural Arts Center in San Antonio, Texas since 1989, has also been a prolific editor, producing several anthologies of writings, most of which emphasize the contributions of Chicano authors to the literary scene. These anthologies, including 1998's *Touching the Fire: Fifteen Poets of Today's Latino Renaissance,* have provided a badly needed medium for many up-and-coming Latino writers to get their work to the public. Another of his anthologies, *Without Discovery: A Native Response to Columbus,* included essays by a host of indigenous writers who refuted the notion that Christopher Columbus was the discoverer of the New World.

Although he hasn't received widespread critical notice, Gonzalez has definitely made a mark for himself in the publishing community. After studying creative writing and ultimately attaining his B.A. from the University of Texas in El Paso, Gonzalez moved north to Denver, Colorado, where he spent the better part of a decade immersing himself in the literary and arts communities. Initially he taught writing classes for juvenile delinquents at the Emerson House Detention Center, before becoming the editor-in-chief of *La Voz,* the Latino newspaper of Colorado. Working for *La Voz* was a unique experience for Gonzalez because it is one of the oldest and longest-running publications of its kind in America. In 1982, after a two-year stint at the newspaper, Gonzalez moved on to become the poetry editor for *Bloomsbury Review,* a literary journal also based in Colorado. Working with many local and national writers, Gonzalez developed a better understanding of the publishing industry, both on a technical and promotional basis. In fact, he became so comfortable with it that he created his own press, which he called Mesilla. With Mesilla, Gonzalez began to publish the works of many poets, particularly from the Denver area, a fact that solidified his place in the city's literary community, as well as earning him the prestigious Colorado Governor's Award for Excellence in the Arts in 1988. The Colorado Council on the Arts also recognized Gonzalez's contributions, awarding him several publishing and writing grants.

Gonzalez has acknowledged that, at a young age, he was influenced by the poets Pablo Neruda and Robert Bly, and critics such as Bradley have commented that those influences are evident in his poetry. His poems contain lines that provide a window into his yearning to be free of social constraints. "I live like a follower, / a noise in the trees no one can claim," Gonzalez writes in the title poem of *From the Restless Roots,* which was published in 1986. Still, Gonzalez's southwestern imagery is the overriding element in his poetry. Snakes, scorpions, and lizards often appear, as do Indians and Mexicans. Poverty and other harsh realities of Mexican life also play a part in some of his work. In the poem "Blind House," publishedo in *From the Restless Roots* is one example: "[F]ootprints of a departing family. / They tremble in love / as they cross the border," Gonzalez writes. Critic John Repp praised Gonzalez for the way he "movingly" deals "with the past—his own, his family's, and his culture's." Gonzalez' fourth collection of poetry, the 1996 volume titled *The Heat of Arrivals,* is an ongoing examination of his Latino identity. He conjures up images of dead relatives, and ancient figures from America's past. He also looks into his own past, such as in "The Snake Poems," a sequence that pivots on his recollection of an incident during his childhood in which he came face to face with a rattlesnake.

The book's final section, a sequence titled "Praise the Tortilla, Praise Menudo, Praise Chorizo," moves away from Gonzalez's typical desert scenery, entering instead an urban setting. In this section, the author also experiments with his language. A contributor for *Publishers Weekly* particularly commended the book's final sequence, "Praise the Tortilla, Praise Menudo, Praise Chorizo." "This vibrant poem suggests the arrival of a new, unpredictable stage in Gonzalez' career," the contributor wrote. Gonzalez' 1998 collection of poetry, *Cabato Sentora,* presents a border world, filled with religious imagery, but apocalyptic in nature. "The blood Christ on the wall is folding his hands," Gonzalez writes in one of the poems. The collection also contains poems with titles such as "The Angels of Juarez, Mexico" and "The Poor Angel." Obviously, Gonzalez relates with this constructed world, mixed with hope and despair. "I can't speak without removing the blue throat from my body, / can't introduce you to Llaga without asking you to remove / your voice so I can examine it," he writes in another poem. A contributor for *Publishers Weekly* called the work an "impassioned collection."

Touching the Fire is indicative of the type of anthology that Gonzalez has organized. The work highlights the work of fifteen Latino writers, each of whom contributes ten poems to the collection. Though only Latinos are featured, both male and female writers are equally represented, providing a fuller perspective of the Latino existence and experience. Some of the collection's most noted pieces include Juan Felipe Herrera's "When He Believed Himself to Be a Young Girl Lifting the Skin of the Water" and Gloria Vando's "Father's Day," a poem that explores the relationship between a boy and his father. In addition to Judith Ortiz Cofer's "The Lesson of the Teeth," which she wrote in honor of her Aunt Clotilde's magnificent beauty, the book also includes writers such as Victor Hernandez Cruz and Silvia Curbelo. While some of the included poems are more traditional, there are others that are more experimental, particularly Herrera's "When He Believed Himself to Be a Young Girl Lifting the Skin of the Water," an example of surrealism. Calling *Touching the Fire* "distinctive," critic Donna Seaman of *Booklist* maintained that the volume contained a "wealth of poems" written by "new voices." Jack Shreve of *Library Journal* asserted that the poems collectively replicated "the rhythms of American daily life."

BIOGRAPHICAL/CRITICAL SOURCES:

BOOKS

Gonzales, Ray, *From the Restless Roots,* Arte Publico Press, 1986.
Gonzales, Ray, *Cabato Sentora,* BOA Editions, 1998.
Dictionary of Literary Biography, Volume 122: *Chicano Writers, Second Series,* Gale Research (Detroit, MI), 1992.

PERIODICALS

Booklist, February 15, 1998, p. 971.
Library Journal, June 15, 1996, p. 82; January, 1998, p. 104.
Publishers Weekly, September 30, 1996, p. 83; December 21, 1998, p. 64.*

*   *   *

GONZALEZ, Victor Hugo 1953-

PERSONAL: Born November 19, 1953, in Mexico; son of Pedro and Sara (Franco) Gonzalez. *Ethnicity:* "Mexican." *Education:* Rio Hondo Community College, A.A., 1976; Whittier College, B.A., 1979; California State University, graduate study, 1984. *Religion:* Roman Catholic.

ADDRESSES: Home—9622 Rex Rd., Pico Rivera, CA 90660.

CAREER: Instituto Tecnologico Superior, Mexico, professor of English and French, summer, 1985; Kendall Industries, Mexico, documentation translator, 1986; Century 21 (real estate company), Whittier, CA, salesperson, 1986-88.

WRITINGS:

Boundless Journal: The Stranger (novel), 1stBooks Library (Bloomington, IN), 1998.

WORK IN PROGRESS: Surreal Adventures and *Conde.*

SIDELIGHTS: Mexican-born novelist and educator Victor Hugo Gonzalez explained of his novel *Boundless Journal:* "Since the 1980s many music recording companies have produced songs about an unknown man, known only as 'the stranger.' In my novel, Alberto dreams about writing a book of his own adventures. Soon he forgets about his dream. For years later, he causes an involuntary disturbance at the Playboy Club in Los Angeles, where he acquires a nickname, 'the stranger.' Gossip about him reaches beyond the club's walls. Rock songs about a mysterious stranger begin to be heard on the radio. Alberto thinks about the book he wanted to write and decides to take his own challenge. He has to lead a double life, with a double identity, and he develops an alter ego. The stranger takes control of Alberto and makes a name in rock music. After fourteen years of songs about the stranger, Alberto annuls the stranger to write his book."

*   *   *

GONZALEZ-CRUSSI, F(rank) 1936-

PERSONAL: Born October 4, 1936, in Mexico City, Mexico; immigrated to United States, 1973; naturalized citizen, 1987; son of Pablo (a pharmacist) and Maria (a pharmacist; maiden name, Crussi) Gonzalez; married Ana Luz, December 22, 1961 (divorced, 1974); married Wei Hsueh (a research pathologist), October 7, 1978; children: (first marriage) Daniel, Francis Xavier, Juliana. *Education:* Universidad Nacional Autonoma de Mexico, B.A., 1954, M.D., 1961.

ADDRESSES: Office—Department of Pathology, Childrens Memorial Hospital, 2300 Childrens Plaza, Chicago, IL 60614.

CAREER: Writer and educator. Licensed to practice medicine in Indiana, Illinois, and Ontario; certified by American Board of Pathology, 1967, Canada Register, Ontario, 1970. Penrose Hospital, Colorado Springs, CO, intern, 1962; St. Lawrence Hospital, Lansing, MI, and Shands Teaching Hospital at the University of Florida, Gainesville, FL, resident in pathology, 1963-67; Queens University, Kingston, Ontario, assistant professor of pathology, 1967-73; Purdue University at Indianapolis, IN, associate professor of pathology, 1973-78; Northwestern University, Chicago, IL, professor of pathology, 1978—. Writer. Head of laboratories at Childrens Memorial Hospital, Chicago.

MEMBER: International Academy of Pathology, Society for Pediatric Pathology, American Society of Clinical Pathologists, Authors Guild, Authors League of America, Royal College of Physicians and Surgeons of Canada, Chicago Pathology Society, Society of Midland Authors.

AWARDS, HONORS: Best Nonfiction Award from the Society of Midland Authors, 1985, for *Notes of an Anatomist.*

WRITINGS:

Extragonadal Teratomas, Armed Forces Institute of Pathology (Washington, DC), 1982.
(Editor) *Wilms Tumor (Nephroblastoma) and Related Renal Neoplasms of Childhood,* CRC Press (Boca Raton, FL), 1983.
Notes of an Anatomist (essays), Harcourt (New York City), 1985.
Three Forms of Sudden Death; and Other Reflections on the Grandeur and Misery of the Body (essays; includes "Some Expressions of the Body [in Four Movements]"), Harper (New York City), 1986.
On the Nature of Things Erotic (essays), Harcourt, 1988.
The Five Senses, Harcourt, 1989.
The Day of the Dead and Other Mortal Reflections, Harcourt, 1993.
Suspended Animation: Six Essays on the Preservation of Bodily Parts, photographs by Rosamond Purcell, Harcourt, 1995.
Partir es morir un poco, prologue by Ruy Perez Tamayo, Universidad Nacional Autonoma de Mexico, 1996.
There Is a World Elsewhere: Autobiographical Pages, Riverhead Books (New York City), 1998.

Also author of a medical book titled *Extragonadal Teratomas.* Contributor to numerous medical journals.

ADAPTATIONS: The works of Gonzalez-Crussi were adapted for the stage by the Live Bait Theatrical Co. of Chicago in January, 1995, in a play titled *Memento Mori,* by Sharon Evans (director) and Valerie Olney.

SIDELIGHTS: Pathologist F. Gonzalez-Crussi established himself as a noteworthy author with the publication of three nontechnical essay collections. Described as "witty" and "well-read" by Brett Singer in the *Los Angeles Times Book Review,* Gonzalez-Crussi colors his informal writings with the insight he has gained from three decades of practicing medicine. Critics credit him with renewing the essay as a viable literary form in the twentieth century and liken his style to that of classic writers, such as Herman Melville, Michel Eyquem Montaigne, and Charles Lamb.

Gonzalez-Crussi's first collection of essays, titled *Notes of an Anatomist,* deals with a vast array of subjects, including corpses, ancient embalming techniques, the phenomenon of multiple births, bodily appendages, and natural monstrosities from a pathologist's perspective. Many critics considered the volume to be a rich and thought-provoking first effort that artfully blends the author's personal experience and wry humor with mythic and literary references. Gonzalez-Crussi spices his essays with historical asides. His use of allusions, ranging from the mention of sixteenth-century French king Henry IV's venereal diseases and Spanish painter El Greco's astigmatism to the style of a Federico Fellini film, prompted critic Dennis Drabelle to call him a "skilled wielder of literary references" in a review for *Washington Post Book World.*

John Gross, writing for the *New York Times,* suggested that *Notes of an Anatomist* "could also have been titled 'A Pathologist's Apology'," as it attempts to purge doctors who perform autopsies of their presumed callousness. Gonzalez-Crussi asserted the nobility of pathologists in "The Dead as a Living," an essay from the volume that was cited in part in *Washington Post Book World:* physicians who search for the cause of their patients deaths, explained the author, are unequaled in their "interest in the dead as dead persons, rather than abstractions." In the same excerpt, the doctor went on to argue that pathologists regard a corpse as a unique repository of clues capable of disclosing the cause of an individual human beings death. Ironically, however, the highly personal postmortem examination also reveals man's sameness in what Gonzalez-Crussi, quoted by Edward Schneidman for the *Los Angeles Times Book Review,* calls "a most brutal way." The author reminds us, wrote Bruce Hepburn in an article for *New Statesman,* of the disturbing but undeniable fact that "decomposition of one sort or other is our universal fate and that it is salutary for us all to keep our latter end in mind."

Critics applauded Gonzalez-Crussi's literary debut for both its form and content. D. J. Enright wrote in the *New York Times Book Review* that the essays "mix fact with speculation and gravity with humor, are rich in apposite and astounding anecdote and are elegant in expression." Schneidman echoed Enright's praise and expressed the consensus of the critics when he called the essays the "marvelously original and provocative" products of a "gifted" writer. *Notes of an Anatomist* earned Gonzalez-Crussi the Best Nonfiction Award from the Society of Midland Authors in 1985.

The author's follow-up volume of essays, *Three Forms of Sudden Death; and Other Reflections on the Grandeur and Misery of the Body,* centers on issues of aging and death. Allan J. Tobin, commenting on the doctor's treatment of a seemingly somber topic, wrote in the *Los Angeles Times Book Review:* "Gonzalez-Crussi deals less with the gloom of death than with the joy of life, especially of a life devoted to inquiry." Tobin suggested that just as the doctor examines physiological abnormalities in an effort to better understand normal life processes, he writes his essays in an attempt to explore timeless human mysteries: "There are only two themes worth writing . . . about," Gonzalez-Crussi stated according to Tobin, "love and death, *eros* and *thanatos.*"

The title *Three Forms of Sudden Death* refers to death by lightning, asphyxiation, and unknown causes, topics Gonzalez-Crussi discusses in the book along with thoughts on cannibalism, the female breast, and human emotions in what several critics have referred to as "pithy" and "engaging" essays. Gonzalez-Crussi's third publication, *On the Nature of Things Erotic,* marks a departure from the scientifically inspired writings that dominate the author's earlier collections. The essays deal with love, desire, and seduction, achieving "something that it is not too much to call wisdom," stated John Gross in the *New York Times.* Some reviewers expressed a desire for the author to offer his own theories on the subjects he addresses, rather than compile the thoughts of others, but most enjoyed his accounts of ancient Greek love diagnoses,

medieval Chinese seduction, and the classical view of homosexuality as a sign of high culture.

While Gonzalez-Crussi has gained both critical and popular success as a writer, he remains a practicing pathologist and a professor at Northwestern University in Chicago, Illinois. As an author, he is the practitioner of a long-ignored art, "a true essayist," wrote Gross in an article for the *New York Times.* By following the paths of his imagination, Gonzalez-Crussi has touched upon what critics consider to be universal themes in essays of universal appeal.

Gonzalez-Crussi once explained of his work: "In my books, I have attempted to join science and the humanities. I would like to produce works of literature inspired on medical and biological subjects—not scientific divulgation. *Notes of an Anatomist* originated from a desire to reflect on the personal experience of a pathologist. *Three Forms of Sudden Death* attempts to be a personal statement of perplexity at the limitations and strengths of the human body."

BIOGRAPHICAL/CRITICAL SOURCES:

PERIODICALS

Los Angeles Times Book Review, July 7, 1985; December 7, 1986; March 27, 1988.
New Statesman, April 11, 1986.
New York Times, May 14, 1985; April 15, 1988.
New York Times Book Review, July 7, 1985; April 9, 1989; November 12, 1995, p. 8.
Observer (London), April 13, 1986.
Vista, November 26, 1989.
Washington Post, July 5, 1985.
Washington Post Book World, April 9, 1989.

*   *   *

GONZALEZ MARTINEZ, Enrique 1871-1952

PERSONAL: Born April 13, 1871, in Guadalajara, Jalisco, Mexico; died February 19, 1952; son of Jose Maria (a teacher) and Feliciana Martinez de Gonzales; married Luisa Rojo y Fonseca. *Education:* Doctor of Medicine, 1886.

CAREER: Physician, poet, translator, editor, teacher, government official, ambassador to Chile, Argentina, Spain, Portugal.

MEMBER: Mexican Academy, Colegio Nacional, Congreso Continental Americano de Paz.

AWARDS, HONORS: Manuel Avila Camacho literary prize, 1944.

WRITINGS:

Los Senderos Ocultos, Porrua Hermanos (Mexico), 1915.
Jardines de Francia, Porrua Hermanos (Mexico), 1915.
La Muerte del Cisne, Porrua Hermanos (Mexico), 1915.
La Hora Inutil, Ediciones Porrua (Mexico), 1916.
Poemas Escogidos, Maucci (Barcelona), 1918.
La Palabra del Viento, Ediciones Mexico Moderno (Mexico), 1921.
El Romero Alucinado (1920-22). Editorial Babel (Buenos Aires), 1923.
Las Senales Furtivas: 1923-24, Editorial S. Calleja (Madrid), 1925.
Poemas de Ayer y de Hoy, A. Botas e hijo (Mexico), 1926.
Silentes, Porrua Hermanos (Mexico), 1926.
Poesia, 1909-29, Espasa-Calpe (Madrid), c. 1930.
Algunos Aspectos de la Lirica Mexicana, Editorial Cultura (Mexico), 1932.
Poemas Truncos, Imprenta Mundial (Mexico), 1935.
Ausencia y Canto, Taller Poetico, 1937.
Poesia, 1898-1938, Editorial "Polis" (Mexico), 1939.
Poemas: 1939-40, Nuova Voz (Mexico), 1940.
Bajo el Signo Mortal, Companis Editora y Librera (Mexico), 1942.
Antologia Poetica, Espasa-Calpe (Buenos Aires), 1943, fifth edition, 1965.
El Hombre del Buho, Miserio de Una Vocacion, Cuadernos Americanos (Mexico), 1944, Editorial Cultura (Mexico), 1944, Departamento de Bellas Artes del Gobierno del Estado (Gudalajara), 1973.
Poesias Completas, Asociacion de Libreres y Editores Mexicanos (Mexico), 1944.
Segundo Despertar, y Otros Poemas, Editorial Stylo (Mexico), 1945.
(Editor) *Poesia Espanola,* Editorial Signo (Mexico), 1945.
Vilano al Viento: Poemas, Editorial Stylo (Mexico), 1948.
Babel, Revista de Literature Mexicana (Mexico), 1949.
La Apacible Locura, Segunda Parte de "El Hombre del Buho, Misterio de una Vocacion," Cuadernos Americanos (Mexico), 1951.
El Nuevo Narciso, y Otras Poemas, Fondo de Cultura Economica (Mexico), 1952, 1971.
Cuentos y Otras Paginas, Libro-Mex Editores (Mexico), 1955.

Los Mejores Versos de Gonzales Martinez, Editorial Nuestra America (Buenos Aires), 1957.
Enrique Gonzales Martinez: Homenaje Antologica, Sociedad de Amigos del Libro Mexicano (Mexico), 1964.
Los Cien Mejors Poemas, Aguilar, 1970.
Enrique Gonzales Martinez: Antologia de Su Obra Poetico, Fondo de Cultura Economica (Mexico), 1971.

Also author of *Preludios,* 1903; *Lirismos,* 1907; *Silenter,* 1909; *Parabolas y Otras Poemas,* 1918; *Tuercele el Cuello al Cisne* (Mexico), 1951; and *Obras Completas,* (Mexico), 1971.

SIDELIGHTS: Enrique Gonzalez Martinez became serious about his poetry after his obituary appeared in a Guadalajara newspaper in 1900. He was twenty-nine at the time and very much alive. A practicing physician, Gonzalez Martinez had begun publishing poems in local periodicals when he was fifteen, but considered himself an "amateur." The post-obituary praise his poems received motivated him less than the thought that if he had in fact died, someone else would have collected and published his work. He decided to do it himself instead. For the next fifty years, Gonzalez Martinez produced a large body of work and established a reputation according to John S. Brushwood in *Enrique Gonzales Martinez* as "one of the masters of twentieth-century Hispanic poetry." Critic G. Dundas Craig in *The Modernist Trend in Spanish-American Poetry* said that Gonzalez Martinez's most important contribution to poetry was to model the necessity "for simplicity and directness of expression."

Gonzalez Martinez's first volume of poetry, *Preludio* (1903), reflects the influence of Mexican poets, while his second, *Lirismos* (1907), more strongly shows his preoccupations with French poets. With his third volume, *Silenter* (1909), according to Craig, Gonzalez Martinez comes into his own voice: "he is much more attentive to the poetic inclinations that were peculiarly his own," agreed Brushwood, and he also calls for a new poetic attitude and viewpoint. As Brushwood wrote, in "'Dioses Muertos' (title means 'Dead Gods'), Gonzalez Martinez seems to regret not being able to stay on the same path with those who had inspired him; in 'Como la Barca Es Mia' (title means 'Since the Boat Is Mine') he declares that the poet will go wherever he wishes. Gonzalez Martinez believes that truth must be sought in life as each person knows it rather than, as with earlier poets, in the form of the poem itself." To Craig, *Silenter* marks the end of one period and the beginning of another: "poets [must] listen for and interpret to men the voice of Nature." The central poem in this collection is "You Will Pass over the Life of Things," with the lines (as translated by Brushwood): "May you love yourself within yourself, your / being synthesizing heavens and abyss, so that / without ceasing to look at yourself, / your eyes may contemplate everything."

Commentaries on Gonzalez Martinez tend to grapple with the problem of classification—was he an opponent of the so-called modernismo movement (Modernism), or an exemplar? For a number of years, Gonzalez Martinez was, according to Octavio Paz in *Hispanic Writers,* "considered the first Spanish-American poet to break with Modernism." The "Parnassian" and "Symbolist" components of Modernism-the one concerned with the form of writing, the other with the idea to be conveyed—had as their motto "Art for Art's sake," according to Craig who declared that both had "Beauty as the object of their striving." While Gonzalez Martinez's early work is a reflection of modernism, according to Brushwood, his 1915 poem "Wring the Neck of the Swan" (in *La Muerte del Cisne; The Death of the Swan*), written against Ruben Dario, the leader of modernism, is regarded as a turning away. "Wring the neck of the lying feathered swan/ That gives a white note to the azure fountain!/ It glides in grace, but never thinks upon/ The soul of things, the voice from out the mountain./ Flee from every form and every fashion/ Through which life's latent rhythm does not roll;/ Only life itself adore with passion,/ And let life know this homage of your soul." Years later, in 1932, Gonzalez Martinez said, as quoted by Brushwood, that efforts to establish a poetic doctrine in his work was contrary to the nature of poetry itself: poetry "did not illustrate a belief, but was in itself the creative act that discovered truth."

BIOGRAPHICAL/CRITICAL SOURCES:

BOOKS

Anderson, Robert Roland, *Spanish American Modernism: A Selected Bibliography,* University of Arizona Press (Tucson, AZ), 1970.

Brushwood, John S., *Enrique Gonzales,* Twayne (New York City), 1969.

Craig, G. Dundas, *The Modernist Trend in Spanish-American Poetry,* University of California Press (Berkeley, CA), 1934.

Goldberg, Isaac, *Studies in Spanish-American Literature,* Brentano's, 1920.

Martinez, Jose Luis, editor, *The Modern Mexican Essay,* University of Toronto Press (Toronto, Ontario), 1965.

Torres-Rioseco, Arturo, *The Epic of Latin American Literature,* Oxford University Press (New York City), 1942.

PERIODICALS

Hispanic Writers, vol. 29, 1946, p. 155.

Journal of Spanish Studies, April, 1976, pp. 29-46.*

*   *   *

GOYTISOLO, Juan 1931-

PERSONAL: Born January 5, 1931, in Barcelona, Spain; immigrated to France, 1957. *Education:* Attended University of Barcelona and University of Madrid, 1948-52.

CAREER: Writer. Worked as reporter in Cuba, 1965; associated with Gallimard Publishing Co., France. Visiting professor at universities in the United States.

AWARDS, HONORS: Received numerous awards for *Juegos de Manos;* Premio Europalia, 1985.

WRITINGS:

NOVELS

Juegos de manos, Destino, 1954, recent edition, 1975, translation by John Rust published as *The Young Assassins,* Knopf, 1959.

Duelo en el paraiso, Planeta, 1955, Destino, 1981, translation by Christine Brooke-Rose published as *Children of Chaos,* Macgibbon & Kee, 1958.

El circo (title means "The Circus"), Destino, 1957, recent edition, 1982.

Fiestas, Emece, 1958, Destino, 1981, translation by Herbert Weinstock published as *Fiestas,* Knopf, 1960.

La resaca (title means "The Undertow"), Club del Libro Espanol, 1958, J. Mortiz, 1977.

La isla, Seix Barral, 1961, reprinted, 1982, translation by Jose Yglesias published as *Island of Women,* Knopf, 1962 (published in England as *Sands of Torremolinos,* J. Cape, 1962).

Senas de identidad, J. Mortiz, 1966, translation by Gregory Rabassa published as *Marks of Identity,* Grove, 1969.

Reivindicacion del Conde don Julian, J. Mortiz, 1970, Catedra, 1985, translation by Helen R. Lane published as *Count Julian,* Viking, 1974.

Juan sin tierra, Seix Barral, 1975, translation by Lane published as *Juan the Landless,* Viking, 1977.

Makbara, Seix Barral, 1980, translation by Lane published as *Makbara,* Seaver Books, 1981.

Paisajes despues de la batalla, Montesinos, 1982, translation by Lane published as *Landscapes after the Battle,* Seaver Books, 1987.

Quarantine, translated by Peter Bush, Dalkey Archive Press, 1994.

Also author of novels *Las virtudes del parajo solitario,* 1988, published as *The Virtues of the Solitary Bird,* 1993; and *La cuarentena,* 1991.

SHORT STORIES

Para vivir aqui (title means "To Live Here"), Sur, 1960, Bruguera, 1983.

Fin de fiesta: Tentativas de interpretacion de una historia amorosa, Seix Barral, 1962, translation by Yglesias published as *The Party's Over: Four Attempts to Define a Love Story,* Weidenfeld & Nicolson, 1966, Grove, 1967.

TRAVEL NARRATIVES

Campos de Nijar, Seix Barral, 1960, Grant & Cutler, 1984, translation by Luigi Luccarelli published as *The Countryside of Nijar* in *The Countryside of Nijar* [and] *La chanca,* Alembic Press, 1987.

La Chanca, Libreria Espanola, 1962, Seix Barral, 1983, translation by Luccarelli published in *The Countryside of Nijar* [and] *La chanca,* Alembic Press, 1987.

Pueblo en marcha: Instantaneas de un viaje a Cuba (title means "People on the March: Snapshots of a Trip to Cuba"), Libreria Espanola, 1963.

Cronicas sarracinas (title means "Saracen Chronicles"), Iberica, 1982.

OTHER

Problemas de la novela (literary criticism; title means "Problems of the Novel"), Seix Barral, 1959.

Las mismas palabras, Seix Barral, 1963.

Plume d'hier: Espagne d'aujourd'hui, compiled by Mariano Jose de Larra, Editeurs francais reunis, 1965.

El furgon de cola (critical essays; title means "The Caboose"), Ruedo Iberico, 1967, Seix Barral, 1982.

Spanien und die Spanien, M. Bucher, 1969.

(Author of prologue) Jose Maria Blanco White, *Obra inglesa,* Formentor, 1972.

Obras completas (title means "Complete Works"), Aguilar, 1977.

Libertad, libertad, libertad (essays and speeches), Anagrama, 1978.

(Author of introduction) Chukri, Mohamed, *El pan desnudo* (title means "For Bread Alone"), translation from Arabic by Abdellah Djibilou, Montesinos, 1982.

Coto vedado (autobiography), Seix Barral, 1985, translation by Peter Bush published as *Forbidden Territory: The Memoirs of Juan Goytisolo,* North Point Press, 1989.

(Author of commentary) Omar Khayyam, *Estances,* translation into Catalan by Ramon Vives Pastor, del Mall, 1985.

Contracorrientes, Montesinos, 1985.

En los reinos de taifa (autobiography; title means "Realms of Strife: The Memoirs of Juan Goytisolo, 1956-1982"), Seix Barral, 1986.

Space in Motion (essays), translation by Lane, Lumen Books, 1987.

De la Ceca a la Meca, Alfaguara (Madrid), 1997.

Cartas de Americo Castro a Juan Goytisolo, 1968-1972: el epistolario, Pre-Textos, 1997.

Also author of *Disidencias* (essays), 1977. Work represented in collections and anthologies, including *Juan Goytisolo,* Ministerio de Cultura, Direccion General de Promocion del Libro y la Cinematografia, 1982. Contributor to periodicals.

SIDELIGHTS: "Juan Goytisolo is the best living Spanish novelist," wrote John Butt in the *Times Literary Supplement.* The author, as Butt observed, became renowned as a "pitiless satirist" of Spanish society during the dictatorship of Francisco Franco, who imposed his version of conservative religious values on the country from the late 1930s until his death in 1975. Goytisolo, whose youth coincided with the rise of Franco, had a variety of compelling reasons to feel alienated from his own country. He was a small child when his mother was killed in a bombing raid, a casualty of the civil war Franco instigated to seize power from a democratically elected government. The author then grew up as a bisexual in a country dominated, in Butt's words, by "frantic machismo." Eventually, said Goytisolo in his memoir *Coto Vedado* (*Forbidden Territory*), he became "that strange species of writer claimed by none and alien and hostile to groups and categories." In the late 1950s, when his writing career began to flourish, he left Spain for Paris and remained in self-imposed exile until after Franco died.

The literary world was greatly impressed when Goytisolo's first novel, *Juegos de manos* (*The Young Assassins*), was published in 1954. David Dempsey found that it "begins where the novels of a writer like Jack Kerouac leave off." Goytisolo was identified as a member of the Spanish "restless generation" but his first novel seemed as much akin to Fedor Dostoevski as it did to Kerouac. The plot is similar to Dostoevski's *The Possessed:* a group of students plot the murder of a politician but end up murdering the fellow student chosen to kill the politician. Dempsey wrote, "Apparently, he is concerned with showing us how self-destructive and yet how inevitable this hedonism becomes in a society dominated by the smug and self-righteous."

Duelo en el paraiso (*Children of Chaos*) was seen as a violent extension of *The Young Assassins*. Like Anthony Burgess's *A Clockwork Orange* and William Golding's *Lord of the Flies, Children of Chaos* focuses on the terror wrought by adolescents. The children have taken over a small town after the end of the Spanish Civil War causes a breakdown of order.

Fiestas begins a trilogy referred to as "The Ephemeral Morrow" (after a famous poem by Antonio Machado). Considered the best volume of the trilogy, it follows four characters as they try to escape life in Spain by chasing their dreams. Each character meets with disappointment in the novel's end. Ramon Sender called *Fiestas* "a brilliant projection of the contrast between Spanish official and real life," and concluded that Goytisolo "is without doubt the best of the young Spanish writers."

El circo, the second book in "The Ephemeral Morrow," was too blatantly ironic to succeed as a follow-up to *Fiestas*. It is the story of a painter who manages a fraud before being punished for a murder he didn't commit. The third book, *La resaca,* was also a disappointment. The novel's style was considered too realistic to function as a fitting conclusion to "The Ephemeral Morrow."

After writing two politically oriented travelogues, *Campos de Nijar* (*The Countryside of Nijar*) and *La Chanca,* Goytisolo returned to fiction and the overt realism he'd begun in *La resaca*. Unfortunately, crit-

ics implied that both *La isla* (*Island of Women*) and *Fin de Fiesta* (*The Party's Over*) suffered because they ultimately resembled their subject matter. *The Party's Over* contains four stories about the problems of marriage. Although Alexander Coleman found that the "stories are more meditative than the full-length novels," he also observed, "But it is, in the end, a small world, limited by the overwhelming ennui of everything and everyone in it." Similarly, Honor Tracy noted, "Every gesture of theirs reveals the essence of the world, they're absolutely necessary, says another: we intellectuals operate in a vacuum. . . . Everything ends in their all being fed up."

Goytisolo abandoned his realist style after *The Party's Over*. In *Senas de identidad* (*Marks of Identity*), wrote Barbara Probst Solomon, "Goytisolo begins to do a variety of things. Obvious political statement, he feels, is not enough for a novel; he starts to break with form—using a variety of first, second and third persons, he is looking and listening to the breaks in language and . . . he begins to break with form—in the attempt to describe what he is really seeing and feeling, his work becomes less abstract." Robert J. Clements called *Marks of Identity* "probably his most personal novel," but also felt that the "most inevitable theme is of course the police state of Spain." Fusing experimentation with a firm political stance, Goytisolo reminded some critics of James Joyce while others saw him elaborating his realist style to further embellish his own sense of politics.

Reivindicacion del Conde don Julian (*Count Julian*), Goytisolo's next novel, is widely considered to be his masterpiece. In it, he uses techniques borrowed from Joyce, Celine, Jean Genet, filmmaker Luis Bunuel, and Pablo Picasso. Solomon remarked that, while some of these techniques proved less than effective in many of the French novels of the 1960s, "in the hands of this Spanish novelist, raging against Spain, the results are explosive." *Count Julian* is named for a legendary Spanish nobleman who betrayed his country to Arab invaders in the Middle Ages. In the shocking fantasies of the novel's narrator, a modern Spaniard living as an outcast in Africa, Julian returns to punish Spain for its cruelty and hypocrisy. Over the course of the narration, the Spanish language itself gradually transforms into Arabic. Writing in the *New York Times Book Review,* Carlos Fuentes called *Count Julian* "an adventure of language, a critical battle against the language appropriated by power in Spain. It is also a search for a new/old language that would offer an alternative for the future."

With the publication of *Juan sin tierra* (*Juan the Landless*), critics began to see Goytisolo's previous two novels as part of a second trilogy. However, reviews were generally less favorable than those for either *Marks of Identity* or *Count Julian*. Anatole Broyard, calling attention to Goytisolo's obsession with sadistic sex and defecation, remarked, "Don Quixote no longer tilts at windmills, but toilets." A writer for *Atlantic* suggested that the uninformed reader begin elsewhere with Goytisolo.

Even after the oppressive Franco regime was dismantled in the late 1970s, Goytisolo continued to write novels that expressed deep alienation by displaying an unconventional, disorienting view of human society. *Makbara,* for example, is named for the cemeteries of North Africa where lovers meet for late-night trysts. "What a poignant central image it is," wrote Paul West in *Washington Post Book World,* "not only as an emblem of life in death . . . but also as a vantage point from which to review the human antic in general, which includes all those who go about their daily chores with their minds below their belts." "The people [Goytisolo] feels at home with," West declared, "are the drop-outs and the ne'er do wells, the outcasts and the misfits." In *Paisajes despues de la batalla* (*Landscapes after the Battle*), the author moved his vision of alienation to Paris, where he had long remained in exile. This short novel, made up of seventy-eight nonsequential chapters, displays the chaotic mix of people—from French nationalists to Arab immigrants—who uneasily coexist in the city. "The Paris metro map which the protagonist contemplates . . . for all its innumerable permutations of routes," wrote Abigail Lee in the *Times Literary Supplement,* "provides an apt image for the text itself." *Landscapes* "looked like another repudiation, this time of Paris," Butt wrote. "One wondered what Goytisolo would destroy next."

Accordingly, Butt was surprised to find that the author's memoir of his youth, published in 1985, had a markedly warmer tone than the novels that had preceded it. "Far from being a new repudiation," Butt observed, *Forbidden Territory* "is really an essay in acceptance and understanding. . . . Gone, almost, are the tortuous language, the lurid fantasies, the dreams of violation and abuse. Instead, we are given a moving, confessional account of a difficult childhood and adolescence." Goytisolo's recollections, the reviewer concluded, constitute "a moving and sympathetic story of how one courageous victim of the Franco regime fought his way out of a cultural and intellectual wasteland, educated himself, and went on to inflict a brilliant revenge on the social system which so isolated and insulted him."

In *The Virtues of the Solitary Bird* Goytisolo explores the Christian, Jewish, and Moorish heritage of Spain and the hybrid mysticism that emerged from the intermingling of the three religions, particularly as expressed in the writings of Saint John of the Cross and Arabian poet Ibn al Farid. Goytisolo juxtaposes the persecution of Saint John with a contemporary narrator who entertains imaginary conversations with the sixteenth century saint while living in exile and suffering from AIDS. Mirroring the author's own political oppression and departure from Franco's Spain, the book "is also the story of the independent thinker throughout history, flushed out by those fearful of 'contaminating ideas,'" observed a *Publishers Weekly* reviewer. Jack Byrne noted in the *Review of Contemporary Fiction* that Goytisolo's version of the martyred saint's verse "modernize[s], while not sanitizing, the horror of heresy—theological, political, social, moral—wherever and whenever it appears." Amanda Hopkinson wrote in the *Times Literary Supplement,* "Goytisolo expects to be read as a parable of our time, with all its complexities and obscurities. This is not prose, at least as conventionally punctuated, it is poetry full of rhapsodic psalms and oriental mysticism."

Quarantine, another complex, experimental novel, follows the spiritual wandering of a recently deceased female writer whose soul, according to Islamic tradition, must embark on a forty–day journey to eternal rest. Through an unnamed narrator, Goytisolo likens the spiritual quarantine to the creative writing process, whereby an author remains in isolation for a time to summon memory and the imagination. In effect, the fictional author's meditations on death and writing become the story itself as he imagines his own death, encounters the soul of his dead friend among angels and a Sufi mystic, and considers parallels to Dante's *Divine Comedy*. Jack Shreve noted in a *Library Journal* review that Goytisolo "multiplies levels of interpretation in order to 'destabilize' the reader." Goytisolo also interjects a strong antiwar theme through surreal news reports that describe the carnage of the Persian Gulf War.

BIOGRAPHICAL/CRITICAL SOURCES:

BOOKS

Amell, Samuel, editor, *Literature, the Arts, and Democracy: Spain in the Eighties,* Fairleigh Dickinson University Press, 1990.

Contemporary Literary Criticism, Gale, Volume 5, 1976, Volume 10, 1979, Volume 23, 1983.

Epps, Bradley S., *Significant Violence: Oppression and Resistance in the Later Narrative of Juan Goytisolo,* Clarendon (New York City), 1996.

Gazarian Gautier, Marie-Lise, *Interviews with Spanish Writers,* Dalkey Archive Press, 1991.

Goytisolo, Juan, *Forbidden Territory,* translation by Peter Bush, North Point Press, 1989.

Pope, Randolph D., *Understanding Juan Goytisolo,* University of South Carolina Press (Columbia), 1995.

Schwartz, Kessel, *Juan Goytisolo,* Twayne, 1970.

Schwartz, Ronald, *Spain's New Wave Novelists 1950- 1974: Studies in Spanish Realism,* Scarecrow Press, 1976.

PERIODICALS

Atlantic, August, 1977.

Best Sellers, June 15, 1974.

Journal of Spanish Studies, winter, 1979, pp. 353- 364.

Kirkus Reviews, March 1, 1994, p. 234.

Lettres Peninsulares, fall-winter, 1990, pp. 259-278.

Library Journal, October 1, 1990, p. 89; March 1, 1994, p. 117.

Los Angeles Times Book Review, January 22, 1989.

Nation, March 1, 1975.

New Republic, January 31, 1967.

New Statesman, July 19, 1991, p. 38; December 17, 1993, p. 46.

New York Times Book Review, January 22, 1967; May 5, 1974; September 18, 1977; June 14, 1987; July 3, 1988; February 12, 1989.

Publishers Weekly, November 30, 1992, p. 48; March 7, 1994, p. 55.

Review of Contemporary Fiction, fall, 1993, p. 213.

Saturday Review, February 14, 1959; June 11, 1960; June 28, 1969.

Texas Quarterly, spring, 1975.

Times Literary Supplement, May 31, 1985; September 9, 1988; May 19, 1989; November 17, 1989; July 12, 1991, p. 18.

Washington Post Book World, January 17, 1982; June 14, 1987.

World Press Review, April, 1994. p. 51.*

*　　*　　*

GRACIA, Jorge J(esus) E(miliano) 1942-

PERSONAL: Born July 18, 1942, in Camaguey, Cuba; naturalized Canadian citizen, 1971; naturalized U.S. citizen; son of Ignacio Jesus Loreto (a pharmacist and landowner) and Leonila (a poet; maiden name, Otero) Gracia; married Norma Elida Silva (a vice president of a corporation); children: Leticia Isabel, Clarisa Raquel. *Ethnicity:* "Hispanic." *Education:* Wheaton College, B.A., 1965; University of Chicago, M.A., 1966; Pontifical Institute of Mediaeval Studies, M.S.L., 1970; University of Toronto, Ph.D., 1971.

ADDRESSES: Email—gracia@acsu.buffalo.edu.

CAREER: State University of New York at Buffalo, assistant professor, 1971-76, associate professor, 1976-80, professor of philosophy, 1980-85, chair of department, 1980-85, 1989-90, distinguished professor, 1995—. Visiting professor at University of Puerto Rico, 1972-73. Magister, Schola Lullistica Maioricensis, Palma de Mallorca, 1976-95.

MEMBER: Societe internationale pour l'etude de la philosophie medievale (member of organizing committee for ninth international congress, 1992, and tenth international congress, 1995-96), International Federation of Latin American and Caribbean Studies (president, 1987-79), American Philosophical Association (member of committee on international cooperation, 1981-84; member of advisory committee to program committee, 1990-93; chair of committee for Hispanics in philosophy, 1991-95; chair of program committee, 1993; member of executive committee, 1996—), Metaphysical Society of America (member of program committee, 1992-93; chair of John N. Findlay Prize committee, 1995; councillor, 1995—), Society for Medieval and Renaissance Philosophy (member of executive committee, 1986—; chair of program committee, 1989-91; vice president, 1989-91; president, 1991-93; chair of nominating committee, 1993-95), Society for Iberian and Latin American Thought (member of executive committee, 1982-95; vice president, 1984-86; president, 1986-88), American Catholic Philosophical Association (member of executive council, 1983- 86; chair of program committee, 1987; vice president, 1996-97; president, 1997-98), Sociedad Filosofica Ibero-Americana (member of executive council, 1985—), International Federation of Philosophical Societies (member of program committee for twentieth world congress, 1994-98).

AWARDS, HONORS: Grants from Canada Council, 1968-71, American Council of Learned Societies, 1977, National Endowment for the Humanities, 1981- 82, Academia Nacional Argentina de Ciencias and Goethe Institute, both 1983, and New York Council for the Humanities, 1987; Metaphysical Society of America, John N. Findlay Prize in metaphysics, 1992, for *Individuality: An Essay on the Foundations of Metaphysics.*

WRITINGS:

(Editor and co-author of introduction) *El hombre y los valores en la filosofia latinoamericana del siglo veinte* (title means "Man and Values in Twentieth-Century Latin American Philosophy"), Fondo de Cultura Economica, 1975, 2nd edition, 1981.

(Editor and author of introduction) Francesc Eiximenis, *Com usar be de beure e menjar* (title means "How to Drink and Eat Well"), Curial, 1977.

(Editor and author of introduction) *Man and His Conduct: Philosophical Essays in Honor of Risieri Frondizi,* University of Puerto Rico Press (Rio Piedras), 1980.

(Translator and author of introduction) Francisco Suarez, *Suarez on Individuation,* Marquette University Press (Milwaukee), 1982.

Introduction to the Problem of Individuation in the Early Middle Ages, Catholic University of America Press (Washington, DC), 1984, revised, 2nd edition, Philosophia Press, 1988.

(Editor with others, and author of introduction) *Philosophical Analysis in Latin America,* Reidel, 1984.

(Editor and author of introduction) *Ensayos filosoficos de Risieri Frondizi,* Fondo de Cultura Economica, 1986.

(Editor and author of introduction) *Latin American Philosophy in the Twentieth Century: Man, Value, and the Search for Philosophical Identity,* Prometheus Books (Buffalo, NY), 1986.

(Editor and coauthor of introduction) *Filosofia e identidad cultural en America Latina* (title means "Philosophy and Cultural Identity in Latin America"), Monte Avila, 1988.

Individuality: An Essay on the Foundations of Metaphysics, State University of New York Press (Albany), 1988.

(Translator and author of introduction, with Douglas Davis) *The Metaphysics of Good and Evil According to Suarez,* Philosophia Verlag, 1988.

(Editor) *Directory of Latin American Philosophers,* Society for Iberian and Latin American Thought, 1988.

(Editor and author of introduction, with M. Camurati) *Philosophy and Literature in Latin America,* State University of New York Press, 1989.

(Editor with others) *Social Sciences in Latin America,* UB Council for International Studies and Programs, 1989.

Philosophy and Its History: Issues in Philosophical Historiography, State University of New York Press, 1992.

(Editor and author of introduction) *Individuation in Scholasticism: The Later Middle Ages and the Counter-Reformation,* State University of New York Press, 1994.

(Editor with K. Barber) *Individuation and Identity in Early Modern Philosophy,* State University of New York Press, 1994.

A Theory of Textuality: The Logic and Epistemology, State University of New York Press, 1995.

Texts: Ontological Status, Identity, Author, Audience, State University of New York Press, 1996.

(Editor and author of introduction) *Concepciones de la Metafisica* (title means "Conceptions of Metaphysics"), Editorial Trotta (Madrid)

Metaphysics and Its Task: The Search for the Categorical Foundation of Knowledge, State University of New York (Albany, NY), 1999.

Hispanic/Latino Identity: A Philosophical Perspective, Blackwell (Malden, MA), 1999.

Contributor of articles to periodicals, including *Review of Metaphysics, Journal of the History of Philosophy, New Scholasticism, Journal of the History of Ideas, Philosophy and Phenomenological Research,* and *American Philosophical Quarterly.* Member of numerous editorial boards.

WORK IN PROGRESS: Tradition: The Past vs. the Future.

SIDELIGHTS: Cuban-born philosopher and educator Jorge J. E. Gracia once explained of his work: "My research and writing have centered on five subject areas: the Middle Ages, Latin America, metaphysics, philosophical historiography, and, more recently, texts and textuality. I was trained as a medievalist in Toronto, and therefore a great part of my work is concerned with the history of medieval thought. Most of this is technical and deals with such topics as the views of individuality developed during the period. In *Introduction to the Problem of Individuation in the Early Middle Ages,* I argue, for example, that the basic problems related to individuality, its causes and its nature, are raised for the first time in an explicit way in the early middle ages. The book on Francis Suarez [a Spanish philosopher of the 1500s], which contains a translation of his treatise on this topic as well as an extensive glossary of technical terms, argues that Suarez's views on individuality are the most sophisticated and developed to come out of the middle ages and that Suarez provides one of the most clear and systematic treatments of the topic to date.

"I have also worked on the theories of good and evil in late scholasticism, particularly on the views of Suarez. In the book I published with Davis on good and evil in Suarez, we present the key texts on this topic and argue that Suarez gives a credible defense of the traditional scholastic interpretation of evil as privation by introducing the concept of evil as a kind of disagreeability. Likewise, we find much merit in the view of good as a kind of agreeability. But we also argue that neither theory goes far enough, since neither of them develops sufficiently the relational character of value.

"After coming to Buffalo and visiting Puerto Rico for a year, I became interested in the thought and philosophy of Latin America, both because I was asked to teach a course on the subject and because I have never forgotten my ethnic background. Given the scarcity of sources available, I decided, with the help of my good friend, the late Risieri Frondizi, to put together a collection of readings from Latin–American philosophers centered on the themes of man and values. These themes are the areas where Latin–American philosophy had made its most important contributions in the first half of this century.

"Another area of my research related to Latin America has been concerned with the impact that philosophical analysis, as practiced in the Anglo-American tradition, has had on it. I have also worked on the crisis of philosophical identity which Latin America is undergoing. One of the most discussed issues in this geographical area for the past thirty years has been the question of whether there is such a thing as a Latin–American philosophy that may be idiosyncratically unique and authentic. In my book on the subject, I point out that the source of the question is a misunderstanding about the very nature of philosophy and philosophical method and that once a proper understanding of these is achieved, the problem dissolves.

"In the area of metaphysics, my main concern has been with the so-called problem of universals and individuals—the ontological categorization of two of our most basic notions. In the book on individuality I present my view that individuality has to do primarily with non-instantiability, while universality has to do with instantiability. I argue, moreover, that much of the concern with individuals and universals in the course of the history of philosophy is a result of a lack of understanding this fact as well as a lack of understanding and distinguishing the various issues involved in the notions of individuality and universality. These are the faults that flaw the work of most philosophers concerned with these issues, from Plato to Strawson.

"More recently I have been reflecting on the historical work I have carried out for the past twenty years. This has raised questions in my mind about the nature of historical knowledge, the proper methodology in historical investigation, and the difficulties involved in the interpretation of texts. The result was a book which argues for a philosophical approach to the history of philosophy which I characterize as the framework approach. It involves looking at the past as viable player in the current philosophical game and from a definite conceptual perspective that has become explicit.

"From the interest in historiography I naturally moved to an interest in texts, the subject matter of my two latest books. In *A Theory of Textuality* I present systematically a theory of textuality. I try to show, moreover, that the widespread confusion surrounding textuality is the result of three factors: a too-narrow understanding of the category; a lack of a proper distinction between logical, epistemological, and metaphysical issues; and a lack of proper grounding of epistemological and metaphysical questions on logical analyses. *Texts* completes the theory, raising and answering questions concerning the ontology and identity of texts and the relation of texts to their authors and audiences.

"At present, two other projects occupy my attention. One is an extension of my previous concern with texts: the relation of tradition to textual interpretations. The second picks up some of my earlier metaphysical interests: the definitions of metaphysics."

H-K

HERNANDEZ-AVILA, Ines 1947-

PERSONAL: Born February 28, 1947, in Galveston, TX; daughter of Rodolfo and Janice Tzilimamuh (Andrews) Hernandez; married. *Education:* University of Houston, B.A., 1970, M.A., 1972, Ph.D. (English), 1984. *Ethnicity:* "Native American and Chicana."

ADDRESSES: Office—Native American Studies, 2415 Hart Hall, University of California, Davis, Davis, CA 95616; fax: (916) 752-7097. *E-mail*—ighernandez@uc davis.edu.

CAREER: Writer. French teacher, La Marque High School, 1970-71; University of California, Davis, assistant professor in Native American Studies and Chicano Studies, became chair of department of Native American Studies.

AWARDS, HONORS: Ford Foundation Doctoral Fellowship for American Indians, 1971-76.

WRITINGS:

Con razon, corazon, Caracol (San Antonio, TX), 1977, enlarged edition, M & A (San Antonio, TX), 1987.
El dia de Guadelupe (play), produced at California State University, Fresno, December 12, 1984.

Also contributor of numerous poems to anthologies and literary journals.

SIDELIGHTS: Ines Hernandez-Avila was born in Galveston, Texas, the daughter of Janice Tzilimamuh Andrews Hernandez and Rodolfo Hernandez. Her mother was a member of the Nimipuh (Nez Perce) tribe, and her father was of Mexican descent; Hernandez-Avila is an enrolled member of the Colville Confederated Tribes of Nespalem, Washington, and also considers herself to be Chicana. Hernandez-Avila is active in the Chicano movement, and has worked with many groups, such as the Mexican-American Youth Organization, La Raza Unida (The United People's Party), Chicanos Artistas Sirviendo a Aztlan (Chicano Artists Serving Aztlan), and the Committee In Support of the People of El Salvador. However, she is also known for her critiques of the Chicano movement and the limitations that sexism and sexual politics in Chicano culture place on the contributions of women in that culture.

Con razon, corazon is a collection of Hernandez-Avila's early poems. In it, she presents her genealogy, her Native American and Hispanic roots, and her family history, and passes on her feminist values to her daughter. The poems examine her diverse roles as a mother, daughter, activist, lover, and friend. Some are in Spanish, some are in English, and others use "code-switching," a mixture of the two languages. She also occasionally uses Native American phrases to express her meaning.

Hernandez-Avila has been praised by critics for her clear voice in Chicano and Native American literature, and for her down-to-earth portrayal of her heritage. Her poetry, unlike the writing of some other authors, is accessible to Chicano readers because of its clear, honest nature, and its use of Spanish. In *Chicano Writers,* Laura Gutierrez Spencer wrote, "Hernandez's poetry expresses the convictions of a woman entering maturity with the confidence of one who, having struggled against a sexist/racist society, has found her way by discovering her own voice."

BIOGRAPHICAL/CRITICAL SOURCES:

BOOKS

Dictionary of Literary Biography, Volume 122: *Chicano Writers, Second Series,* edited by Francisco A. Lomeli and Carl R. Shirley, Gale (Detroit, MI), 1992.*

*   *   *

HIJUELOS, Oscar 1951-

PERSONAL: Surname is pronounced "E-way-los"; born August 24, 1951, in New York, NY; son of Pascual (a hotel worker) and Magdalena (a homemaker; maiden name, Torrens) Hijuelos; divorced. *Education:* City College of the City University of New York, B.A., 1975, M.A., 1976. *Religion:* Catholic. *Avocational interests:* Pen-and-ink drawing, old maps, turn of the century books and graphics, playing musical instruments, jazz ("I absolutely despise modern rock and roll").

ADDRESSES: Home—211 West 106th St., New York, NY 10025. *Agent*—Harriet Wasserman Literary Agency, 137 East 36th St., New York, NY 10016. *Office*—Hofstra University, English Department, 1000 Fulton Ave., Hempstead, NY 11550.

CAREER: Transportation Display, Inc., Winston Network, New York City, advertising media traffic manager, 1977-84; writer, 1984—; Hofstra University, Hempstead, NY, professor of English, 1989—.

MEMBER: International PEN.

AWARDS, HONORS: Received "outstanding writer" citation from Pushcart Press, 1978, for the story "Columbus Discovering America"; Oscar Cintas fiction writing grant, 1978-79; Bread Loaf Writers Conference scholarship, 1980; fiction writing grant from Creative Artists Programs Service, 1982, and from Ingram Merrill Foundation, 1983; Fellowship for Creative Writers award from National Endowment for the Arts, and American Academy in Rome Fellowship in Literature from American Academy and Institute of Arts and Letters, both 1985, both for *Our House in the Last World;* National Book Award nomination, National Book Critics Circle Prize nomination and Pulitzer Prize for fiction, all 1990, all for *The Mambo Kings Play Songs of Love.*

WRITINGS:

Our House in the Last World, Persea Books (New York City), 1983.
The Mambo Kings Play Songs of Love, Farrar, Straus (New York City), 1989.
The Fourteen Sisters of Emilio Montez O'Brien, Farrar, Straus, 1993.
Cool Salsa: Bilingual Poems on Growing up Latino in the United States, edited by Lori M. Calson, Holt, 1994.
Mr. Ives' Christmas, HarperCollins (New York City), 1995.
The Cuban American Family Album, Oxford University Press, 1996.
Empress of the Splendid Season (novel), HarperCollins, 1999.

Work represented in anthology *Best of Pushcart Press III,* Pushcart, 1978.

ADAPTATIONS: The Mambo Kings Play Songs of Love was adapted for film as *The Mambo Kings* in 1992.

SIDELIGHTS: Award-winning novelist Oscar Hijuelos turns the characters and experiences of his Cuban-American heritage into fictional works that have won both critical and popular praise. As Marie Arana-Ward explains in the *Washington Post Book World,* "once in a great while a novelist emerges who is remarkable not for the particulars of his prose but for the breadth of his soul, the depth of his humanity, and for the precision of his gauge on the rising sensibilities of his time. . . . Oscar Hijuelos is one of these."

Hijuelos explains to *CA* that his first novel, *Our House in the Last World,* "traces the lives of a Cuban family who came to the United States in the 1940s and follows them to the death of the father and subsequent near collapse of the family. In many ways a realistic novel, *Our House in the Last World* also reflects certain Latin attributes that are usually termed 'surreal' or 'magical.' Although I am quite Americanized, my book focuses on many of my feelings about identity and my 'Cubanness.' I intended for my book to commemorate at least a few aspects of the Cuban psyche (as I know it)."

Reviewing *Our House in the Last World* for the *New York Times Book Review,* Edith Milton affirms that Hijuelos is concerned "with questions of identity and perspective," especially those concerning family. Hijuelos is "especially eloquent," lauds *Cleveland Plain Dealer* critic Bob Halliday, "in describing the emotional storms" that transform the Santinio family of his novel as they "try to assimilate the rough realities of Spanish Harlem in terms of the values and personal identities they have inherited from their homeland." There is a "central tension," Milton explains, between the "lost, misremembered Eden [Cuba]" and the increasing squalor of the family's new life in their "last world"—New York. "Opportunity seems pure luck" to these well-intentioned immigrants, observes *Chicago Tribune Book World* reviewer Pat Aufderheide, and, in the absence of hope, each ultimately succumbs to the pressures that "work against the [American] dream of upward mobility." Hijuelos' "elegantly accessible style," Aufderheide states, "combines innocence and insight" in creating the individual voices of his characters. Beyond that, notes the reviewer, there is a "feel for the way fear . . . pervades" the Santinios' lives. The characters and the "sheer energy" of the narrative are the book's strengths, Milton concludes, adding that Hijuelos "never loses the syntax of magic, which transforms even the unspeakable into a sort of beauty." Critic Roy Hoffman in the *Philadelphia Inquirer* calls *Our House in the Last World* a "vibrant, bitter and successful" story and compares Hijuelos to an "urban poet" who creates a "colorful clarity of life." Halliday likewise deems the book to be a "wonderfully vivid and compassionate" first novel.

But it was Hijuelos' Pulitzer Prize-winning second novel, *The Mambo Kings Play Songs of Love,* that moved him to the first rank of American novelists. Telling the story of two brothers, Cesar and Nestor Castillo, who leave their native Cuba and make careers as singers in the Spanish Harlem of the 1950s, the novel traces their rise to an appearance on *The I Love Lucy Show* before fading away from public attention again, like the mambo dance their band played.

The Mambo Kings, Cathleen McGuigan explains in *Newsweek,* "isn't conventionally plotted; it slides back and forth in time and meanders into dreams and fantasies." The novel is comprised of the dreams and fantasies of Cesar Castillo at the end of his career when he lives in a run-down hotel called the Splendour and drinks away his days. McGuigan notes that Cesar "is a classic portrait of machismo: he's in closest touch with his feelings when they originate below the waist." But she acknowledges that "Hijuelos has a tender touch with his characters, and Cesar is more than a stereotype." Despite the novel's flaws, McGuigan finds *The Mambo Kings Play Songs of Love* to be a "vibrant tragicomic novel." Joseph Coates of *Tribune Books* finds echoes of magical realism in the novel and feels that it "achieves the long backward look" of novels such as *One Hundred Years of Solitude,* "dealing as fully with the old worlds the migrants left as with the new ones they find." Writing in the *Washington Post Book World,* novelist Bob Shacochis also remarks upon Hijuelos' skilled contrasts between Cuban and American life, observing that "his *cu-bop* music scene gathers credibility as a grand metaphor for the splitting of a national family that took place [with the Cuban revolution] in 1959." Finally, Margo Jefferson of *the New York Times Book Review* observes that Hijuelos alternates "crisp narrative with opulent musings," achieving a "music of the heart."

Hijuelos' 1993 novel, *The Fourteen Sisters of Emilio Montez O'Brien,* takes a very different tack from its predecessor. Whereas *The Mambo Kings Play Songs of Love* is told by one male narrator, *The Fourteen Sisters of Emilio Montez O'Brien* is told from a number of female viewpoints and spans several generations in the life of a Cuban-Irish family in Pennsylvania. Writing in *Time,* Janice E. Simpson praises the novel's warmth, suggesting that reading it "is like leafing through the pages of a treasured family album," but laments that "the fate of the sisters is determined and defined by their relationships with men." Jane Mendelsohn, writing in the *London Review of Books,* generally admires the way Hijuelos characterizes his female characters, observing that "the novel skillfully chronicles the lives" of all the sisters and that Margarita, in particular, is an embodiment of the "women's movement . . . in the 20th century." At the same time, Mendelsohn faults the novel for its sentimentality and concluded that there is "nothing of the glorious flame which set *The Mambo Kings* on fire." Nick Hornby of the *Times Literary Supplement* calls the novel "at all times readable and diverting" but finds that its many characters bog down its pacing. Even so, Arana-Ward praises the story for its celebration of "human diversity and its promise of vitality," and for its compelling characters, who "hold us captive until the very last page of this generous novel."

BIOGRAPHICAL/CRITICAL SOURCES:

BOOKS

Contemporary Literary Criticism, Gale, Volume 65, 1990.
Dictionary of Literary Biography, Volume 145: *Modern Latin-American Fiction Writers, Second Series,* Gale, 1994.

PERIODICALS

Americas Review, Volume 22, number 1-2, pp. 274-276.
Bloomsbury Review, May, 1990, p. 5.
Boston Globe, November 18, 1990, p. 21.
Chicago Tribune, August 9, 1990, p. 1; January 3, 1993; May 30, 1993, Section 6, p. 5; December 24, 1996.
Chicago Tribune Book World, July 17, 1983.
Christian Century, May 22, 1996, p. 581.
Cleveland Plain Dealer, July 17, 1983.
Cosmopolitan, March, 1993, p. 16.
Entertainment Weekly, March 19, 1993, p. 57.
Horn Book, May-June, 1995, p. 316.
Insight on the News, October 23, 1989, p. 56.
London Review of Books, September 23, 1993, p. 23.
Los Angeles Times, April 16, 1990, p. 1.
Los Angeles Times Book Review, September 3, 1989, p. 1; March 14, 1993, pp. 3, 8.
Los Angeles Times Magazine, April 18, 1993, pp. 22-28, 54.
New Republic, March 22, 1993, pp. 38-41.
New Statesman, December 15, 1995, p. 64.
New York, March 1, 1993, p. 46.
New Yorker, March 29, 1993, p. 107; August 21, 1995, pp. 126-127.
New York Times, September 11, 1989, p. C17; April 1, 1993, p. C17.
New York Times Book Review, May 15, 1983; August 27, 1989, pp. 1, 30; March 7, 1993, p. 6; December 3, 1995, p. 9.
Newsweek, August 21, 1989, p. 60.
Observer (London), July 25, 1993, p. 53.
People Weekly, April 5, 1993, p. 26.
Philadelphia Inquirer, July 17, 1983.
Publishers Weekly, July 21, 1989, pp. 42, 44.
Time, August 14, 1989, p. 68; March 29, 1993, pp. 63, 65.
Times Literary Supplement, August 6, 1993, p. 19.
Tribune Books (Chicago), August 13, 1989, p. 6; January 3, 1993, p. 6.
U. S. Catholic, May, 1996, p. 46.
Village Voice, May 1, 1990, p. 85.

Washington Post Book World, August 20, 1989; March 14, 1993, pp. 1, 10.
World Literature Today, winter, 1994, p. 127.*

*			*			*

HINOJOSA, Gilberto Miguel 1942-

PERSONAL: Born May 29, 1942; son of Jose H. (an owner of a retail dry goods store) and Concepcion (an owner of a retail dry goods store; maiden name, Gonzalez) Hinojosa; married Gloria Cordero, June 5, 1971; children: MariCarmen, Teresita. *Education:* College of Our Lady of the Snows, B.A., 1965; graduate study at Oblate College of the Southwest, 1966-68; St. Mary's University of San Antonio, M.A., 1970; University of Texas at Austin, Ph.D., 1979. *Politics:* Democrat. *Religion:* Roman Catholic.

ADDRESSES: Office—School of Humanities and Fine Arts, Incarnate Word College, 4301 Broadway, San Antonio, TX 78209.

CAREER: History teacher at Lowell Junior High School in San Antonio, TX, 1969-70; Laredo Junior College, Laredo, TX, instructor, 1970-71; Pan American University, Edinburg, TX, assistant instructor, 1974; University of Texas at Austin, assistant instructor, 1975-76; University of Texas at San Antonio, instructor, 1976-79, assistant professor, 1979-84, associate professor of history, 1984-93, assistant vice-president for academic affairs, 1988-90, discipline coordinator for history in Division of Behavioral and Cultural Sciences, 1992-93; Incarnate Word College, San Antonio, associate professor, 1993-95, professor of history, 1995—, dean of humanities and fine arts, 1993—. Juarez-Lincoln University, adjunct faculty member, 1976-78; Institute of Texan Cultures, lecturer, 1979—; University of Texas at Austin, adjunct faculty member, Mexican American Cultural Center, 1980—; Universidad Autonoma de Nuevo Leon, Fulbright professor, 1981-82. Bexar County Archives, assistant archivist, 1968-69; Yturria Papers Collection, archivist, 1986—; United States-Mexico Institute, member of planning board, 1987—; Texas-Coahuila Historical Commission, member, 1988. Crane Publishing, associate editor, 981—; KWEX-TX, program director for *Voces del Seminario,* 1967-68.

MEMBER: Texas Catholic Historical Society (president, 1991, 1992-94).

AWARDS, HONORS: Fulbright scholar in Mexico, 1981-82; Presidio La Bahia Awards, 1983, for *A Borderlands Town in Transition: Laredo, 1755-1870,* and 1988, for an essay on borderlands historiography; grants from Texas Catholic Historical Society, 1984, and Texas Committee for the Humanities, 1986-87; La Bahia Award, 1991, for *Tejano Origins in Eighteenth-Century San Antonio.*

WRITINGS:

A Borderlands Town in Transition: Laredo, 1755-1870, Texas A & M University Press (College Station, TX)), 1983.
(With Mary Ann Bruni) *Viva la Virgen de Guadalupe! A History of Our Lady of Guadalupe Parish,* Texas Monthly (Austin, TX), 1988.
(Editor with Gerald E. Poyo, and contributor) *Tejano Origins in Eighteenth-Century San Antonio,* University of Texas Press (Austin), 1991.
(Co-editor and contributor) *Mexican Americans and the Catholic Church, 1900-1965,* University of Notre Dame Press (Notre Dame, IN), 1994.

Contributor to books, including *Natives and Newcomers: Challenges to the Encounter,* Cabrillo Historical Society (San Diego, CA), 1993. Author of a biweekly column about culture and history, *San Antonio Express News.* Contributor of articles and reviews to periodicals, including *Texas Humanist, U.S. Catholic Historian, Journal of Texas Catholic History and Culture,* and *Journal of American History.*

WORK IN PROGRESS: Gonzales: Neighborhood, Town, and Region; editing and translating *"Dn. Francisco Yturria, Dear Sir": Letters From South Texas and Mexico.*

*   *   *

HINOJOSA(-SMITH), Rolando (R.) 1929-
(P. Galindo, Rolando Hinojosa-Smith)

PERSONAL: Born January 21, 1929, in Mercedes, TX; son of Manuel Guzman (a farmer) and Carrie Effie (a homemaker; maiden name, Smith) Hinojosa; married Patricia Mandley, September 1, 1963 (divorced, 1989); children: Clarissa Elizabeth, Karen Louise. *Education:* University of Texas at Austin, B.S., 1953; New Mexico Highlands University, M.A., 1963; University of Illinois, Ph.D., 1969. *Politics:* Democrat. *Religion:* Catholic.

ADDRESSES: Office—Department of English, University of Texas at Austin, Austin, TX 78712.

CAREER: High school teacher in Brownsville, TX, 1954-56; Trinity University, San Antonio, TX, assistant professor of modern languages, 1968-70; Texas A & I University, Kingsville, associate professor of Spanish and chair of modern language department, 1970-74, dean of College of Arts and Sciences, 1974-76, vice president for academic affairs, 1976-77; University of Minnesota—Minneapolis, chair of department of Chicano studies, 1977-80, professor of Chicano studies and American studies, 1980-81; University of Texas at Austin, professor of English, 1981-85, E. C. Garwood Professor, 1985—, Mari Sabusawa Michener Chair, 1989-93. Consultant to Minneapolis Education Association, 1978-80, to U.S. Information Agency, 1980 and 1989, and to Texas Commission for the Arts and Humanities, 1981-82. Texas Center for Writers, University of Texas, Austin, 1989-93. *Military service:* U.S. Army Reserves, 1956-63; became second lieutenant.

MEMBER: Modern Language Association (chair of Commission on Languages and Literature in Ethnic Studies, 1978-80), PEN, Academia de la Lengua Espanola en Norteamerica, Hispanic Society, Fellow Society of Spanish and Spanish American Studies (fellow), Texas Institute of Letters.

AWARDS, HONORS: Best in West Award for foreign language radio programming from the state of California, 1970-71; Quinto Sol Literary Award for best novel, 1972, for *Estampas del valle y otras obras;* Casa de las Americas award for best novel, 1976, for *Klail City y sus alrededores;* Southwest Studies on Latin America award for best writing in the humanities, 1981, for *Mi querido Rafa;* distinguished alumnus award from University of Illinois College of Liberal Arts, 1988.

WRITINGS:

NOVELS

Estampas del valle y otras obras (first novel in "Klail City Death Trip" series), Quinto Sol, 1972, bilingual edition with translation by Gustavo Valadez and Jose Reyna published as *Sketches of the Valley and Other Works,* Justa Publications, 1980, revised English language edition published as *The Valley,* Bilingual Press (Ypsilanti, MI), 1983.

Klail City y sus alrededores (second novel in "Klail City Death Trip" series), bilingual edition with translation by Rosaura Sanchez, Casa de las Americas, 1976, published under name Rolando R. Hinojosa-S. as *Generaciones y semblanzas* (title means "Biographies and Lineages"), Justa Publications, 1977, translation by Hinojosa published as *Klail City,* Arte Publico Press (Houston, TX), 1987.

Korean Love Songs from Klail City Death Trip (novel in verse form; third in "Klail City Death Trip" series), illustrations by Rene Castro, Justa Publications, 1978.

Claros varones de Belken (fourth novel in "Klail City Death Trip" series), Justa Publications, 1981, bilingual edition with translation by Julia Cruz published as *Fair Gentlemen of Belken County,* Bilingual Press, 1987.

Mi querido Rafa (fifth novel in "Klail City Death Trip" series), Arte Publico Press, 1981, translation by Hinojosa published as *Dear Rafe,* 1985.

Rites and Witnesses (sixth novel in "Klail City Death Trip" series), Arte Publico Press, 1982.

Partners in Crime, Arte Publico Press, 1985.

Los amigos de Becky (seventh novel in "Klail City Death Trip" series), Arte Publico Press, 1990, translation published as *Becky and Her Friends,* 1990.

The Useless Servants (eighth novel in "Klail City Death Trip" series), Arte Publico Press, 1993.

Ask a Policeman, Arte Publico Press (Houston), 1998.

OTHER

Generaciones, notas, y brechas/Generations, Notes, and Trails, (nonfiction; bilingual edition), translation by Fausto Avendano, Casa, 1978.

(Author of introduction) Carmen Tafolla, *Curandera,* M & A Editions, 1983.

(Contributor under name Rolando Hinojosa-Smith) Alan Pogue, *Agricultural Workers of the Rio Grande and Rio Bravo Valleys,* Center for Mexican American Studies, University of Texas at Austin, 1984.

(Translator from the Spanish) Tomas Rivera, *This Migrant Earth,* Arte Publico Press, 1985.

(Contributor) Jose David Saldivar, editor, *The Rolando Hinojosa Reader: Essays Historical and Critical,* Arte Publico Press, 1985.

Valley: A Re-Creation in Narrative Prose of a Portfolio of Etchings, Engravings, Sketches, and Silhouettes by Various Artists in Various Styles, Bilingual Review Press, 1994.

Also author, under pseudonym P. Galindo, of *Mexican American Devil's Dictionary.* Work represented in anthologies, including *Festival de flor y canto: An Anthology of Chicano Literature,* edited by F. A. Cervantes, Juan Gomez-Quinones, and others, University of Southern California Press, 1976. Contributor of short stories, articles, and reviews to periodicals, including *Texas Monthly, Texas Humanist, Los Angeles Times,* and *Dallas Morning News.*

SIDELIGHTS: The first Chicano author to receive a major international literary award, Rolando Hinojosa won the prestigious Premio Casa de las Americas for *Klail City y sus alrededores* (*Klail City*), part of a series of novels known to English-speaking readers as "The Klail City Death Trip." Hinojosa's fiction, often infused with satire or subtle humor, is widely admired for its blending of diverse plot lines and narrative styles. The individual perspectives of many characters come together in his works to form a unique collective voice representative of the Chicano people. Hinojosa has also produced essays, poetry, and a detective novel titled *Partners in Crime.*

Hinojosa was born in the Lower Rio Grande Valley in Texas to a family with strong Mexican and American roots: his father fought in the Mexican Revolution while his mother maintained the family north of the border. An avid reader during childhood, Hinojosa was raised speaking Spanish until he attended junior high school, where English was the primary spoken language. Like his grandmother, mother, and three of his four siblings, Hinojosa became a teacher; he has held several professorial posts and has also been active in academic administration and consulting work. Although he prefers to write in Spanish, Hinojosa has also translated his own books and written others in English.

Hinojosa entered the literary scene with the 1973 *Estampas del valle y otras obras,* which was translated as *Sketches of the Valley and Other Works.* The four-part novel consists of loosely connected sketches, narratives, monologues, and dialogues, offering a composite picture of Chicano life in the fictitious Belken County town of Klail City, Texas. The first part of *Estampas* introduces Jehu Malacara, a nine-year-old boy who is left to live with exploitative relatives after the deaths of his parents. Hinojosa synthesizes the portrait of Jehu's life through comic and satiric sketches and narratives of incidents and characters surrounding him. The second section is a collection of pieces about a murder, presented through newspaper accounts, court documents, and testimonials from the defendant's relatives. A third segment, narrated by an omniscient storyteller, is a selection of sketches depicting people from various social groups in Klail City, while the fourth section introduces the series' other main character, Jehu's cousin Rafa Buenrostro. Also orphaned during childhood, Rafa narrates a succession of experiences and recollections of his life. Hinojosa later rewrote *Estampas del valle y otras obras* in English, publishing it as *The Valley* in 1983.

Hinojosa's aggregate portrait of the Spanish southwest continues in *Klail City y sus alredededores,* published in English as *Klail City.* Like its predecessor, *Klail City* is composed of interwoven narratives, conversations, and anecdotes that portray fifty years in the town's collective life. Winner of the 1976 Premio Casa de las Americas, the book was cited for its "richness of imagery, the sensitive creation of dialogues, the collage-like structure based on a pattern of converging individual destinies, the masterful control of the temporal element and its testimonial value," according to Charles M. Tatum in *World Literature Today.* Introducing more than one hundred characters and developing further the portraits of Rafa and Jehu, *Klail City* prompted *Western American Literature* writer Lourdes Torres to praise Hinojosa for his "unusual talent for capturing the language and spirit of his subject matter."

Korean Love Songs from Klail City Death Trip and *Claros varones de Belken* are Hinojosa's third and fourth installments in the series. A novel comprised of several long poems originally written in English and published in 1978, *Korean Love Songs* presents protagonist Rafa Buenrostro's narration of his experiences as a soldier in the Korean War. In poems such as "Friendly Fire" and "Rafe," Hinojosa explores army life, grief, male friendships, discrimination, and the reality of death presented through dispassionate, often ironic descriptions of the atrocity of war. *Claros varones de Belken (Fair Gentlemen of Belken County),* released three years later, follows Jehu and Rafa as they narrate accounts of their experiences serving in the Korean War, attending the University of Texas at Austin, and beginning careers as high school teachers in Klail City. The book also includes the narratives of two more major characters, writer P. Galindo and local historian Esteban Echevarria, who comment on their own and others' circumstances. Writing about *Fair Gentlemen of Belken County,* Tatum commented that Hinojosa's "creative strength and major characteristic is his ability to render this fictional reality utilizing a collective voice deeply rooted in the His-

panic tradition of the Texas-Mexico border." Also expressing a favorable opinion of the book was *Los Angeles Times Book Review* writer Alejandro Morales, who concluded that "the scores of names and multiple narrators at first pose a challenge, but quickly the imagery, language and subtle folk humor of Belken County win the reader's favor."

Hinojosa continued the "Klail City Death Trip" series with *Mi querido Rafa.* Translated as *Dear Rafe,* the novel is divided into two parts and consists of letters and interviews. The first half of the work is written in epistolary style, containing only letters from Jehu— now a successful bank officer—to his cousin Rafa. Between the novel's two parts, however, Jehu suddenly leaves his important position at the Klail City First National Bank, and in the second section Galindo interviews twenty-one community members about possible reasons for Jehu's resignation. The two major characters are depicted through dialogue going on around and about them; the reader obtains a glimpse of Rafa's personality through Jehu's letters, and Jehu's life is sketched through the opinions of the townspeople. *San Francisco Review of Books* writer Arnold Williams compared the power of Hinojosa's fictional milieu, striking even in translation, to that of twentieth-century Jewish writer Isaac Bashevis Singer, noting that "Hinojosa is such a master of English that he captures the same intimacy and idiomatic word play in his re-creations."

After writing *Rites and Witnesses,* the sixth novel in the "Klail City Death Trip" series, Hinojosa turned to a conventional form of the novel with the 1985 *Partners in Crime,* a detective thriller about the murder of a Belken County district attorney and several Mexican nationals in a local bar. Detective squads from both sides of the border are called to investigate the case; clues lead to an established and powerful cocaine smuggling ring. Jehu and Rafa reappear in the novel as minor characters who nevertheless play important parts in the mystery's development. "Those who might mourn the ending of the ['Klail City Death Trip' series] and their narrative experimentation and look askance at Hinojosa's attempting such a predictable and recipe-oriented genre as the murder mystery need not worry," concluded Williams. "He can weave a social fabric that is interesting, surprising, realistic and still entertaining."

In *Becky and Her Friends* Hinojosa continues his attempt to capture the many voices of the Hispanic community. Twenty-six characters from previous novels in the "Klail City Death Trip" series (including Becky) are each given a chapter here to discuss Becky's divorce from Ira Escobar and her subsequent marriage to Jehu Malacara. The novel has been praised for its evocation of the American-Hispanic ethos, one that is simultaneously deeply traditional, Catholic, and superstitious. However, writing in *Western American Literature,* R. L. Streng noted that "the characters' voices are difficult to differentiate one from another, and since each character falls into a camp for or against Becky and her escapades, there is very little difference between what we hear from Lionel Villa and Viola Barragan in one camp or Elvira Navarrete and Ira Escobar in the other." Streng concluded that *Becky and Her Friends* "fails in its attempt to corral a variety of characters and establish a lively vocal forum. Instead, the novel is tedious and requires readers to wade through extensive and unnecessary redundancies."

More recently, Hinojosa has extended the "Klail City Death Trip" series with *The Useless Servants,* a novel—unlike many others in the series—with only one narrative voice. A kind of novelization of his previous book of poems *Korean Love Songs from Klail City Death Trip, The Useless Servants* is the diary kept by Rafe Buenrostro when he was an infantryman in the U. S. Army during the Korean war. It is written very much in the manner of personal diaries, employing clipped phrases, few pronouns, and little explanation of the objects in the writer's daily routine—in this case, military jargon, acronyms, etc. Thematically, the book presents Rafe's experience of warfare and army life as a Hispanic-American. Critical reaction to the novel has been mixed. B. Adler, writing in *Choice,* felt that the work "is curious in the lack of insight it demonstrates, its flatness overall, with no reaching toward even stylistic significance." Dismayed by Rafe's apparent detachment from his own experiences, Adler concluded: "Perhaps Hinojosa is trying to make a point about the essentially boring nature of the average human being, even when placed in an extraordinary situation such as war. The dilemma is how realistic to make dullness. Hinojosa is too successful here." On the other hand, while William Anthony Nericcio in *World Literature Toady* also found Hinojosa's use of military jargon and acronyms rather unrelenting, he lauded the author's allusions to Plato's *Republic,* stating that "Plato's cave fire and the Korean battlefield illuminate each other nicely." Nericcio also noted that *The Useless Servants* further enriches the thematic texture of its series, writing: "The studied effort at intertextual dialectics set up between volumes in the Klail City Death Trip Series is as dense and electric as some to be found in Faulkner's oeuvre."

Hinojosa told *CA:* "I enjoy writing, of course, but I enjoy the re-writing even more: four or five rewritings are not uncommon. Once finished, though, it's on to something else. At this date, every work done in Spanish has also been done in English with the exception of *Claros varones de Belken,* although I did work quite closely on the idiomatic expressions which I found to be at the heart of the telling of the story.

"I usually don't read reviews; articles by learned scholars, however, are something else. They've devoted much time and thought to their work, and it is only fair I read them and take them seriously. The articles come from France, Germany, Spain, and so on, as well as from the United States. I find them not only interesting but, at times, revelatory. I don't know how much I am influenced by them, but I'm sure I am, as much as I am influenced by a lifetime of reading. Scholars do keep one on one's toes, but not, obviously, at their mercy. Writing has allowed me to meet writers as diverse as Julio Cortazar, Ishmael Reed, Elena Poniatowski and George Lamming.

"My goal is to set down in fiction the history of the Lower Rio Grande Valley. . . . A German scholar, Wolfgang Karrer, from Osnabrueck University has a census of my characters; they number some one thousand. That makes me an Abraham of some sort.

"Personally and professionally, my life as a professor and as a writer inseparably combines vocation with avocation. My ability in both languages is most helpful, and thanks for this goes to my parents and to the place where I was raised."

BIOGRAPHICAL/CRITICAL SOURCES:

BOOKS

Bruce-Novoa, Juan, *Chicano Authors: Inquiry by Interview,* University of Texas Press, 1980.
Dictionary of Literary Biography, Volume 82: *Chicano Writers,* First Series, Gale, 1989.
Lee, Joyce Glover, *Rolando Hinojosa and the American Dream,* University of North Texas Press, 1997.
Saldivar, Jose David, editor, *The Rolando Hinojosa Reader: Essays Historical and Critical,* Arte Publico Press, 1985.

PERIODICALS

Choice, December, 1993.
Hispania, September, 1986.

Hispanic, September, 1990, p. 48.

Los Angeles Times Book Review, April 12, 1987; October 10, 1993.

Publishers Weekly, November 28, 1986; July 12, 1993, p. 69.

San Francisco Review of Books, spring, 1985; fall/winter, 1985.

Western American Literature, fall, 1988; summer, 1991.

World Literature Today, summer, 1977; summer 1986; winter, 1995.*

* * *

HINOJOSA-SMITH, Rolando
See HINOJOSA(-SMITH), Rolando (R.)

* * *

JACQUELINE
See CARPENTIER (Y VALMONT), Alejo

* * *

KAHLO, Frida 1907-1954

PERSONAL: Full name, Magdalena Carmen Frida Kahlo y Calderon; born in 1907, in Coyoacan, Mexico; died, 1954; daughter of a photographer; married Diego Rivera (an artist), 1929 (marriage ended; later remarried Rivera). *Ethnicity:* "Hispanic."

CAREER: Artist.

WRITINGS:

The Diary of Frida Kahlo: An Intimate Self-Portrait, with an introduction by Carlos Fuentes and essay and commentaries by Sarah M. Lowe, Abrams (New York), 1995.

The Letters of Frida Kahlo: Cartas Apasionadas, selected and edited by Martha Zamora, Chronicle Books (San Francisco), 1995.

SIDELIGHTS: Four decades after her death in 1954, the art of Mexican painter Frida Kahlo experienced a resurgence in critical and commercial popularity. Kahlo, who was married to the artist Diego Rivera, is best known for her unusual paintings—many of them self-portraits—that blend European influences such as surrealism with distinctly Latin American iconography. Despite the success she achieved as an artist, and her acquaintance with many notable figures of her day—including Leon Trotsky—Kahlo suffered immense psychological and physical pain for much of her life. The artist, who was stricken with polio at the age of six, also experienced continual back pain and underwent several operations as a result of injuries sustained in a bus accident when she was a teenager. Often, she was forced to paint while lying on her back.

By the 1990s numerous books had been published on Kahlo as a result of the renewed interest in her work, and gallery and museum exhibitions brought her art to a wider audience while prices of her auctioned works rose. A film biography was even planned. In 1995 two more books were published in conjunction with this rediscovery of Kahlo. The first was her long-secreted diary, which had been stored in a bank vault in Mexico City for several years. Administrators of the Rivera estate had previously allowed only a select few, such as Kahlo's biographers, limited access to her writings. In 1994, however, the estate put the diary up for auction, and the art-book publisher Abrams was the highest bidder for these pages that Kahlo wrote during the last ten years of her life. The diary was reproduced in the 1995 book *The Diary of Frida Kahlo: An Intimate Self-Portrait.* Kahlo's sketches, often accompanied by captions and her written musings on a variety of introspective topics, form the book's core; it also contains an introductory chapter by Mexican critic and poet Carlos Fuentes, and an essay and commentaries by Kahlo biographer Sarah M. Lowe. Deborah Solomon, reviewing *The Diary of Frida Kahlo* for the *New York Times Book Review,* noted that it "is less pure diary than a hybrid creature mixing drawings and watercolors with casual prose-poems," and remarked that Kahlo's art seems to yield more clues to the artist herself than does the journal. Donna Seaman in *Booklist,* however, had a more favorable reaction to the diary, calling it "a remarkable and precious book."

Seaman and Solomon also reviewed *The Letters of Frida Kahlo: Cartas Apasionadas,* also published in 1995. The eighty letters chosen by Martha Zamora, one of Kahlo's biographers, include letters that the artist wrote as a teenager to her first boyfriend, as well as later missives that she sent to family, friends, and even her doctors. The documents provide a portrait of a woman who was perhaps not as dark and brooding as her paintings may have suggested; critics note that in many of them Kahlo writes profusely and affectionately of Rivera. Still, Solomon found something lacking. "All in all, Kahlo's letters and diaries are most revealing in their very lack of revelation," she observed in her *New York Times Book Review* piece. "They have the odd effect of dulling the edge of her originality, allowing her to command center stage while providing no hint of how or why she got there." Seaman in *Booklist,* however, found that Kahlo's "frank, affectionate and energetic letters play in revealing counterpoint to her wrenching mythic paintings."

BIOGRAPHICAL/CRITICAL SOURCES:

PERIODICALS

Booklist, October 1, 1995, p. 244.
Library Journal, May 15, 1994, p. 72.
New York Times, August 10, 1994, p. C9.
New York Times Book Review, November 19, 1995, p. 12.
Publishers Weekly, October 9, 1995, p. 72.*

L

LEGUIZAMO, John 1965-

PERSONAL: Born July 22, 1965, in Bogota, Columbia; moved to America when he was four; son of Alberto (a waiter and landlord) and Luz Leguizamo; *Education:* Studied at the Strasberg Theater Institute and H. B. Studio; attended New York University.

ADDRESSES: Agent—Don Buchwald and Associates, 10 East 44th St., New York, NY 10017.

CAREER: Writer, actor, comedian. Actor in plays, including: *A Midsummer Night's Dream; La Puta Vida Trilogy* (title means *This Bitch of a Life*), The Public, New York City, 1987; *Parting Gestures,* INTAR Theatre, New York City, 1987; *She First Met Her Parents on the Subway,* Pearl Theatre, New York City, 1990; *Mambo Mouth* (solo show), SubPlot, American Place Theatre, New York City, 1991; *Spic-O-Rama* (solo show) Goodman and Briar Street Theaters, Chicago, 1992; *Freak: A Semi-Demi-Quasi-Pseudo Autobiography,* Broadway, 1997.

Actor in movies: *Mixed Blood,* Cinevista, 1985; *That Burning Question,* 1988; *Casualties of War,* Columbia Tristar, 1989; *Street Hunter,* RCA/Columbia Pictures, 1990; *Gentile alouette,* 1990; *Die Hard 2: Die Harder,* 20th Century-Fox, 1990; *Revenge,* Columbia/New World, 1990; *Out for Justice,* Warner Bros., 1991; *Hangin' With the Homeboys,* New Line Cinema, 1991; *Regarding Henry,* Paramount, 1991; *The Puerto Rican Mambo,* Stardance Entertainment, 1992; *Time Expired,* Zeitgeist Films, 1992; *Whispers in the Dark,* Malofilm Group, 1992; *Night Owl,* Franco Productions, 1993; *Carlito's Way,* Universal Studios, 1993; *Super Mario Brothers,* Buena Vista, 1993; *A Pyromaniac's Love Story,* Buena Vista, 1995; *To Wong Foo, Thanks for Everything! Julie Newmar,* Universal Studios, 1995; *Executive Decision,* Warner Bros., 1996; *The Fan,* TriStar Pictures, 1996; *Romeo + Juliet,* 20th Century-Fox, 1996; *A Brother's Kiss,* First Look Pictures Releasing, 1997; *The Pest,* TriStar Pictures, 1997; *Dr. Doolittle,* Fox, 1998; *Spawn,* New Line Cinema, 1997; *Frogs for Snakes,* The Shooting Gallery International, 1998; *The Split,* Polygram, 1998; *Summer of Sam,* 1999; *King of the Jungle,* Rosefunk Pictures/Bombo Sports, forthcoming; *Joe the King,* forthcoming. Actor on television: *Miami Vice,* 1984; *The Talent Pool; N.Y.P.D. Mounted* (movie), 1991; *Puerto Rican Mambo (Not a Musical),* 1993; *Spic-O-Rama,* 1993; *House of Buggin',* Fox, 1995; *Freak,* 1998.

Producer of films: *House of Buggin* (TV), Fox, 1995; *The Pest,* TriStar Pictures, 1997; *Freak* (TV), 1998; *King of the Jungle,* Rosefunk Pictures/Bombo Sports, forthcoming; *Joe the King,* forthcoming.

AWARDS, HONORS: Obie Award for performance, Outer Critics Circle Award for outstanding achievement, CableACE Award, HBO, and Vanguardin Award, for writing and performance, all 1991, all for *Mambo Mouth;* CableACE Award, for Comedy Central's *The Talent Pool,* 1991; Hull-Warrior Award for best American play, Dramatists' Guild, Lucille Lortel Outstanding Achievement Award for best Broadway performance, and Drama Desk Award for best solo performance, all 1992, all for *Spic-O-Rama;* Theatre World Award for outstanding new talent, and four CableACE Awards, 1993, for *Spic-O-Rama;* two Emmy Award nominations, 1995, for *House of Buggin';* DESHI Entertainment Award for diverse excellence in Hispanic sounds and images, 1996; Golden Globe nomination, 1996, for *To Wong Foo, Thanks for Ev-*

erything! Julie Newmar; Nosotros Golden Eagle Award, 1996; Blockbuster Entertainment Award nomination, 1997, for *Executive Decision;* Tony Award nominations for best actor and best play, 1998, for *Freak.*

WRITINGS:

PLAYS

Mambo Mouth (solo show; produced in New York City, 1991), published as *Mambo Mouth: A Savage Comedy,* Bantam Books (New York City), 1993.

Spic-O-Rama (solo show; produced in Chicago, 1992), published as *Spic-O-Rama: A Dysfunctional Comedy,* Bantam Books (New York City), 1994.

(With David Bar Katz) *Freak: A Semi-Demi-Quasi-Pseudo Autobiography* (produced on Broadway, 1997), Riverhead Books (New York City), 1997.

SCREENPLAYS

Mambo Mouth (TV), HBO, 1991.
Spic-O-Rama (TV), HBO, 1993.
(Story) *The Pest,* 1997.
Freak (TV), 1998.

SIDELIGHTS: John Leguizamo was born in Colombia and moved to New York City with his family at the age of four. He discovered his power to entertain while in high school, where his clowning often earned him a detention. He was advised by a perceptive math teacher to take acting lessons as a creative outlet. Leguizamo chose Sylvia Leigh's Showcase Theater from the yellow pages and paid for his lessons with money he earned himself. After graduating from high school, he auditioned at Juilliard, was rejected, but later received a telephone call from one of the Juilliard judges, encouraging him to continue with his acting career.

His first break came when Bonnie Timmerman, casting director for the television series *Miami Vice,* saw Leguizamo in a New York University student film. "We liked John so much that we killed him off once or twice and still found ways to bring him back," said Timmerman. "He's a beautiful, wonderful actor." Leguizamo had parts in independent films and played Puck in Shakespeare's *A Midsummer Night's Dream.* He did standup at New York comedy clubs during much of the 1980s. After returning from Thailand and the set of *Casualties of War,* he began writing and performing his own material. Director Peter Askin

saw him and worked with him on *Mambo Mouth,* which was performed in the Subplot, a space in the American Place Theatre in New York City. "What stood out first, second, and third of all was his acting," Askin told Chris Smith in *New York* magazine. "Plus he was Hispanic and dealing with what that meant, through original material." "Rave reviews in the *New Times* and the *Voice* packed the seventy-four-seat space, and soon Leguizamo moved into the theater's one-hundred-and-ninety-nine-seat mainstage," wrote Smith.

Leguizamo was inspired to write because of the absence of parts for Hispanics, but his characters in *Mambo Mouth* were viewed as stereotypes by some in the Hispanic community. Smith said, "Leguizamo didn't set out to write a Latino Manifesto, but he has, in fact, thought a great deal about the political nature of *Mambo Mouth.*" "Don't they see this show is an exorcism, a purge, of all the media images of Latinos?" asked Leguizamo. The seven characters of *Mambo Mouth* include macho talk–show host, Agamemnon, who gives advice on sex; Loco Louie, who carries a boom box and brags about his experience at a brothel; Pepe, who tries to convince the immigration man not to send him back; transvestite Manny the Fanny; and the Crossover King, who uses slides and lectures fellow Hispanics on how to skip Americanization and go straight to being Japanese businessmen.

Gerald Weales wrote in *Commonweal* that the night he saw the show Leguizamo delighted the Hispanics in the audience "who respond to familiar gestures, intonations, words, and have the added advantage of Spanish throwaway lines which, I gather, were sometimes jokes about the more obtuse 'white' playgoers, to use his designation." Weales called the show "a fine showcase for Leguizamo's versatility as a performer and his talent as a writer."

Mambo Mouth garnered many awards, as did Leguizamo's next one-man show, *Spic-O-Rama.* Both were adapted for television and later published. In *Spic-O-Rama* Leguizamo plays both female and male members of the Gigante family. "The results are unceasingly funny even though the humor, as if filtered through ground glass, draws blood," wrote Jeremy Gerard in *Variety.* The sketches center on the marriage of Krazy Willie, a Desert Storm veteran. Other family members include aspiring actor Raffi, who bleaches his hair with the "holy water of St. Clorox" and believes he is the love child of Laurence Olivier; a mother who feeds Diet Coke to her baby; an alcoholic father; and nine-year-old Miggy, who prays for a new family. Gerard felt Leguizamo's greatest accomplishment "is that these family members, while unmistakably rooted in Latin life, are recognizable to everyone." "Leguizamo turns the Gigantes into a one-man *Long Day's Journey into la Noche*," wrote Jack Kroll in *Newsweek*. "He's not as tragic as O'Neill but he's funnier, and every laugh he gets is booby-trapped with pain and pathos. . . . Leguizamo makes comedy a fun-house mirror that magically reflects social reality. . . . *Spic-O-Rama* has made Leguizamo as hot as a jalapeno pepper."

Leguizamo's *Freak: A Semi-Demi-Quasi-Pseudo Autobiography* opened on Broadway and was published simultaneously. Written with David Bar Katz, the show is about Leguizamo's childhood and young adult years in Queens. Lisa N. Johnston wrote in *Library Journal* that he uses Spanish and street slang in relating family anecdotes, "always emphasizing the struggles and emotions of an immigrant Latino family." Johnston called the result "entertaining and poignant."

Leguizamo appeared in many films and received acclaim for several roles. Randy Pitman, writing in *Library Journal*, called *Hangin' with the Homeboys* "a film with heart and more than a little insight into the human condition." It is the story of four friends— two Puerto Rican, two black—cruising on a Friday night. *Nation* reviewer Stuart Klawans said that, "like the most appealing of its characters, the picture is good-natured, unpretentious, a little naive." Klawans said that Leguizamo portrayed Johnny "with remarkable sweetness and ease."

Whispers in the Dark is a psycho-sexual thriller in which Leguizamo plays a painter who puts fantasies on canvas. "The film drags through its subplots and then shoves the viewer through its erratic pace whenever the director decides it needs a little more sex or violence," wrote Margarita Gomez in *Hispanic*. "Viewers are asked to bear with the inadequacies of the film if only to see what could be a strong follow-up for Leguizamo's already successful career as a comedian and his budding acting career."

In *Carlito's Way*, Leguizamo plays Benny Blanco, a drug dealer in East Harlem who has succeeded Carlito (Al Pacino) while Carlito served time in jail. Brian De Palma directed this film as well as *Casualties of War*, in which Leguizamo also had a part. Terrence Rafferty wrote in the *New Yorker* that *Carlito's Way* "isn't in the same class as De Palma's masterpieces, *Blow Out* and *Casualties of War*," but the film "has

a handful of brilliant, unnervingly powerful sequences that seem to detach themselves from the whole." In another film, *Super Mario Brothers*, based on the video game, Leguizamo and Bob Hoskins play the Brooklyn plumbers. The film, according to Ralph Novak in *People Weekly*, had "none of the game's hidden pleasures."

Joe Leydon's review in *Variety* said that *A Pyromaniac's Love Story* "is a modern-day fairy tale with a bemused appreciation of romantic love, blazing passions and other human follies." Leguizamo plays Sergio, a pastry chef who takes the blame for a fire that destroys the business to save his elderly employer who he suspects set the blaze to avoid bankruptcy. Leydon said, "Leguizamo hasn't been so appealing, or cast so effectively, since *Hangin' with the Homeboys*."

Following *A Pyromaniac's Love Story*, Leguizamo appeared as female impersonator Chi Chi Rodriguez in *To Wong Foo, Thanks for Everything! Julie Newmar*. Chi Chi, Vida Boheme (Patrick Swayze) and Noxeema Jackson (Wesley Snipes) are on a cross-country ride to California and the national Drag Queen of the Year competition. "All three evince a casual comic mastery of the finger-snapping, eye-rolling, hip-swiveling elan of the modern male bitch princess," wrote Owen Gleiberman in *Entertainment Weekly*. Their Cadillac convertible breaks down in Snydersville, "where all the men are brutes or louts, and all the women worn out trying to survive," wrote Richard Corliss in *Time*. The residents do not suspect that the queens are actually men, and one of the town boys falls for Chi Chi. Ralph Novak wrote in *People Weekly* that "with his slight build and soft features, Leguizamo makes the most convincing ersatz female." He was nominated for a Golden Globe for the film.

Leguizamo next played a special forces officer in *Executive Decision*, an agent in *The Fan*, and Tybalt in *Romeo + Juliet*. *Rolling Stone* reviewer Peter Travers called Leguizamo's performance in the updated Shakespeare film "excellent" as "a volatile Latino who's in a gang" that accessorizes "with pearl-handle guns and silver boot heels." "The bad news is that . . . Tybalt, as in all R & J's, gets killed off early," wrote Melanie Cole in *Hispanic*.

In *The Pest* Leguizamo plays Pestario Vargas, a small-time Miami con artist "evidencing all the restraint of a Ritalin-deprived class clown who's just O.D.'d on sugar sandwiches," according to Joe Leydon in *Variety*. Pest evades mobsters and becomes the target of a German businessman who likes to hunt humans. There is a chase through Little Havana that ends on a cargo ship. "Along the way, Pest pretends to be an Orthodox rabbi, a Japanese businessman and an African-garbed black firebrand," wrote Leydon. "John Leguizamo tears through *The Pest* like something newly unleashed from the inkwell of a demented cartoonist."

Leguizamo plays Clown in *Spawn,* the film version of the comic book. "The story of Spawn reflects the ageless battle of good vs. evil, but told in a darker, more violent way than most comics," wrote David A. Kaplan in *Newsweek.* Leguizamo added business to his writing and acting interests when he and David Bar Katz formed Lower East Side Films in the late 1990s.

BIOGRAPHICAL/CRITICAL SOURCES:

BOOKS

Contemporary Theatre, Film, and Television, Gale (Detroit, MI), 1994.
Dictionary of Hispanic Biography, Gale (Detroit, MI), 1996.

PERIODICALS

Commonweal, September 27, 1991, pp. 549-550.
Cosmopolitan, July, 1996, p. 88.
Entertainment Weekly, May 15, 1992, p. 68; June 18, 1993, p. 12; March 18, 1994, p. 94; January 13, 1995, p. 26; May 12, 1995, p. 44; September 8, 1995, pp. 49-51; October 6, 1995, p. 14; December 27, 1996, p. 66; August 15, 1997, p. 46; December 19, 1997, p. 81.
Hispanic, October, 1992, p. 82; August, 1993, p. 64; October, 1996, p. 84; November, 1997, p. 78.
Hispanic Business, July, 1995, p. 22.
Interview, May, 1991, p. 36; September, 1995, p. 78.
Library Journal, May 15, 1992, p. 136; August, 1993, p. 104; March 1, 1994, p. 88; October 15, 1997, p. 63.
Nation, June 24, 1991, p. 863.
New Leader, March 11, 1991, p. 23; November 2, 1992, p. 22.
New Republic, December 7, 1992, p. 34.
Newsweek, December 14, 1992, p. 87; November 15, 1993, p. 89; August 4, 1997, pp. 68-69.
New York, June 10, 1991, p. 44-48; November 30, 1992, p. 126.
New Yorker, December 7, 1987, p. 165; November 9, 1992, p. 142; November 22, 1993, pp. 117-120.

New York Times, November 20, 1994, p. 124.
People Weekly, July 8, 1991, p. 14; November 11, 1991, p. 148; June 21, 1993, p. 16; November 15, 1993, p. 17; January 23, 1995, pp. 13-14; September 11, 1995, p. 106; September 25, 1995, pp. 21-22; October 9, 1995, p. 99; August 18, 1997, p. 21.
Playboy, June, 1991, p. 25; May, 1992, p. 126; October, 1995, p. 22.
Premier, August, 1992, p. 49; October, 1995, p. 28.
Publishers Weekly, July 12, 1993, p. 76.
Rolling Stone, September 3, 1992, p. 72; July 8, 1993, p. 121; March 23, 1995, p. 132; September 21, 1995, p. 87; November 14, 1996, pp. 123-124.
Seventeen, July, 1993, p. 68.
Time, October 28, 1991, p. 85; November 9, 1992; July 18, 1994, p. 61; September 18, 1995, p. 108.
TV Guide, August 3, 1991, p. 10; May 15, 1993, p. 34; December 11, 1993, p. 38.
Variety, January 28, 1991, p. 70; November 2, 1992, p. 93; May 10, 1993, p. 241; June 7, 1993, p. 38; May 1-7, 1995, p. 36; September 4, 1995, p. 71; February 10, 1997, p. 64; June 2, 1997, p. 65.
Video Magazine, June, 1992, p. 64.
Vogue, April, 1993, p. 242; September, 1995, p. 331.*

*   *   *

LEZAMA LIMA, Jose 1910-1976

PERSONAL: Born December 19, 1910, in Campamento Militar de Columbia, Cuba; died suddenly from pneumonia, August 9, 1976, in Havana, Cuba; son of Jose Maria Lezama y Rodda (a military officer) and Rosa Lima y Rosado; married Maria Luisa Bautista Trevino, December 5, 1964. *Education:* Earned law degree from University of Havana.

CAREER: Poet, essayist, and novelist. In private law practice in Cuba, 1938-40; worked for various government agencies in Cuba, 1940-59; Ediciones Origenes (publishing house), co-founder and editor, 1945-56; National Council of Culture, Havana, director of the department of literature and publications, beginning 1959; Cuban Writers and Artists Union, one of six presidents, beginning 1961; Cuban Center for Literary Research, advisor, beginning 1962.

WRITINGS:

Muerte de Narciso (title means "The Death of Narcissus"), Ucar, Garcia (Havana, Cuba), 1937.

Enemigo rumor (poems; title means "Hostile Murmur"), Ucar, Garcia, 1941.

Aventuras sigilosas (title means "Secret Adventures"), Origenes (Havana, Cuba), 1945.

La fijeza (poems; title means "Persistence"), Origenes, 1949.

Analecta del reloj (essays; title means "Analects of the Clock"), Origenes, 1953.

El padre Gaztelu en la poesia, Origenes, 1955.

(Author of introduction) Angel Gaztelu, *Gradual de laudes,* Origenes, 1955.

La expresion Americana (essays and lectures), Ministerio de Educacion, 1957, enlarged edition ARCA (Montevideo), 1969.

Tratados en la Habana, Universidad Central de Las Villas (Havana, Cuba), 1958.

Dador (poems), Ucar, Garcia, 1960.

Antologia de la poesia cubana, Consejo Nacional de Cultura, 1965.

(Selector and author of introduction) *Juan Clemente Zenea: Posia,* Academia de Ciencias de Cuba (Havana, Cuba), 1966.

Orbita de Lezama Lima (edited by Armando Alvarez Bravo), Union Nacional de Escritores y Artistas (Havana, Cuba), 1966.

Paradiso (novel), Union de Escritores y Artistas de Cuba, 1966, revised edition (with illustrations by Rene Portocarrero), [Mexico City], 1966, translation by Gregory Rabassa published as *Paradise,* Farrar, Straus (New York City), 1974.

Lezama Lima (anthology), J. Alvarez, 1968.

Los grandes todos, ARCA, 1968, published as *Lezama Lima,* Alvarez (Buenos Aires, Argentina), 1968.

Posible imagen de Jose Lezama Lima (poems), Llibres de Sinera (Barcelona, Spain), 1969.

Esferaimagen: Sierpe de don Luis de Gongora; Las imagenes posibles, Tusquets Editor (Barcelona, Spain), 1970.

La cantidad hechizada (essays; title means "The Magic Quantity"), Union de Escritores y Artistas de Cuba, 1970.

Poesia completa (poems; includes "Inicio y escape" [title means "Beginning and Escape"]), Instituto del Libro (Havana, Cuba), 1970, enlarged edition, Letras Cubanas (Havana, Cuba), 1985.

Algunos tratados en La Habana, Editorial Anagrama, 1971.

Introduccion a los vasos orficos (essays; title means "Introduction to the Orphic Vessels"), Barral Editores (Barcelona, Spain), 1971.

Las eras imaginarias, Editorial Fundamentos (Madrid, Spain), 1971.

Obras completas (edited by Cintio Vitier), two volumes, Aguilar (Mexico City, Mexico), 1975, 1977.

Cangrejos, golondrinas, Calicanto (Buenos Aires, Argentina), 1977.

Fragmentos a su iman (poems), Arte & Literatura (Havana, Cuba), 1977.

Oppiano Licario (novel; sequel to *Paradiso*) Arte & Literatura, 1977.

Cartas (title means "Letters", edited by Eloisa lezama Lima), Origenes (Madrid), 1979.

Imagen y posibilidad (essays, edited by Ciro Bianchi Ross), Letras Cubanas, 1981.

El reino de la imagen, Ayacucho (Caracas, Venezuela), 1981.

Juego de las decapitaciones, Montesinos (Barcelona, Spain), 1982.

Cuentos, Letras Cubanas, 1987.

Relatos, Alianza (Madrid), 1987.

Confluencias, Letras Cubanas, 1988.

Also author of *Aristides Fernandez,* 1950.

EDITOR

Antologia de la poesia cubana, three volumes, Consejo Nacional de Cultura (Havana, Cuba), 1965.

Also co-founder, with Rene Villarnovo, of *Verbum* (literary review), Havana, June-November, 1937; cofounder, with others, of *Espuela de Plata* (literary review), Havana, 1939-41; co-founder and contributor, *Origenes: Revista de Arte y Literatura* (literary review), Havana, 1944-56. Also editor of, and contributor to, *Nadie parecia* (literary review), 1942-44.

SIDELIGHTS: Jose Lezama Lima was a Cuban poet, essayist, and novelist who gained a place in the history of Latin American literature with intricately composed, highly original works. Lezama Lima's relations within the Cuban intellectual and literary world evolved into his co-founding several literary review journals. Most notable was *Origenes: Revista de Arte y Literatura,* a journal that he edited and contributed to, and which, according to J. C. Ulloa and L. A. de Ulloa indicated in the *Dictionary of Literary Biography,* became one of the primary vehicles to his "powerful literary influence" within his country. "If international fame had not reached him because of his poems and erudite essays, the publication of *Paradiso* [at the age of fifty-six] served as a bridge between the imaginary world he had forged and the public outside his limited circle of friends," wrote Ulloa and de Ulloa.

"After [*Paradiso*'s] publication," the critics continued, "Lezama Lima emerged as a writer of astounding imagination capable of creating the most intricate and allusive metaphors. He was proclaimed [by critics as] . . . one of the most brilliant and complex authors of the latter half of the twentieth century." According to a contributor to *Publishers Weekly,* the publication of *Paradiso* "prompted critics to refer to Lezama Lima as 'the [Marcel] Proust of the Caribbean.'" The novel was released in the United States, France, Italy, and several Latin American countries, where it received important critical attention. Emerging as a controversial novel, some critics took note particularly because *Paradiso,* which describes homosexual relationships, was published in Cuba during Castro's active campaign against homosexuality.

For Lezama Lima, writing was a creative act by which an alternative universe came into being. The culmination of the exaggerated pride and self-confidence characteristic of literary modernism, *Paradiso* aims "to defy the gods by fashioning a cosmos that is impregnable and humanistically divine," Enrique Fernandez commented in a *Village Voice* article. Furthermore, Lezama Lima built his novel universe "while ignoring virtually all of modernism's tricks: cool narrative strategies, hip tones, jazzy dissonances, authorial detachment, alienation. And he roots his experiment in his native Cuban reality—including the famous dialectics of tobacco and sugar." Therefore, Fernandez concluded, "Lezama [Lima]'s work is not only an artistic feat. It is a virtual proclamation of Latin American literary independence."

Paradiso records the journey of young Jose Cemi from childhood into sexual and intellectual maturity. Cemi's quest for a spiritual mentor is as well "a search for the lost father and for a literary vocation. And the journey is strictly homosexual," Fernandez related. The commitment to language, knowledge, and philosophy among Cemi's role models in his quest supersedes the sexual activity in the novel, which Fernandez saw, by comparison, as "extreme male bonding." Though there is more thought than action in the long novel, he added, "there is passion. Sexual passion but, most important, intellectual and aesthetic passion, passion for a key concept in Lezama: culture." *Nation* contributor Peter Moscoso-Gongora concurred: "Sensuality and intellectual puzzles, char-

acter and incident, the real and the imagined whirl away in the rush of a verbal storm that wishes to concentrate on itself."

Considered a "difficult" novel for its complex uses of language, *Paradiso* is as metaphysical as Lezama Lima's poetry, which also stretches the limits of language to create unorthodox possibilities of expression. "The structure of the novel," concluded Ulloa and de Ulloa, "is a product of Lezama [Lima]'s poetical conceptions. The work can be divided into four extensive planes with marked exterior differences: 1) the familiar . . . 2) a world alien to the familiar one . . . 3) one for events that occur without apparent causality, thereby destroying the temporal dimension; and 4) the one that contains the final encounter between Cemi and . . . his poetic and intellectual mentor." "Lezama [Lima]'s force of poetic causality," the critics stated, "prevents the reader from perceiving any sequential link between the different planes, and it is for this reason that some critics initially saw the novel as a discordant medley."

"*Paradiso* and its sequel, *Oppiano Licario* (1977) [an unfinished work due to Lezama Lima's unexpected death], gather themes, preoccupations, and dialogues initiated years earlier and bring them to full development," remarked Ulloa and de Ulloa. They went on to explain that father's death when Lezama Lima was nine "created within the young Lezama an anxiety that moved him to meditate intensely upon death. In fact, the feeling of unreality that characterizes his poetry has its provenance in this youthful search for answers to the unknown. The desire to give meaning to absence and the unexplored is the most representative paradigmatic aspect of his work. But in his work one does not perceive any desperation, because he found in the image of resurrection a justification for the unknown of death."

With an overall theme of death and the unknown, "*Enemigo rumor,*" recognized Ulloa and de Ulloa, "is the book of poems that definitively classified Lezama [Lima] as a poet." The critics explained: "The collection contains daring, carefully written poems of great metric, thematic, and conceptual variety. The difficulty in comprehension is due to the original use of metaphor and arbitrary and abstruse syntactical constructions. The poems present varying levels of difficulty as well as different levels of experimentation, since fragments alluding to classical literature, mythology and religion are embedded in a bold, original style." Lezama Lima's later poetry "show[s] a more marked religious sentiment," noted Ulloa and de Ulloa. Lezama Lima's journal *Origenes,* "the most important of all Lezama [Lima's] publications" according to Ulloa and de Ulloa, started its own independent publishing house, Ediciones Origenes, the year after the journal first saw publication. And, as Ulloa and de Ulloa stated, "Through the issues of the review and the books published by Ediciones Origenes, . . . the group [who ran the journal] succeeded in making visible and accessible to Cuban and foreign readers their poetic efforts." In fact, Lezama Lima, who "undoubtedly . . . was the most prominent figure of the Origenes group," had several titles published by Ediciones Origenes, noted Ulloa and de Ulloa. They also pointed out that Lezama Lima's "search for the unknown, a characteristic that strongly marks [his] work and is repeated throughout it, also came to be a leading objective of [the literary journal, *Origenes.*]"

"*Origenes,* which began to circulate in the spring of 1944 with the subtitle *Revista de Arte y Literatura,*" reported Ulloa and de Ulloa, "welcomed not only various poets, musicians, and painters who had collaborated on former reviews edited by Lezama [Lima], but also new members who came to fill the ranks. For several years it published writings by Cuban authors; made accessible to the public previously unpublished translations of well-known foreign authors; reviewed art exhibitions; and furnished information on concerts and musical events. It was the most intense and influential literary organ of the era."

BIOGRAPHICAL/CRITICAL SOURCES:

BOOKS

Bejel, Emilio, *Jose Lezama Lima: Poet of the Image,* illustrations by Vicente Dopico, University of Florida Press (Gainesville, FL), 1990.
Contemporary Literary Criticism, Gale (Detroit, MI), Volume 4, 1975, Volume 10, 1979.
Dictionary of Literary Biography, Volume 113: *Modern Latin-American Fiction Writers,* First Series, Gale, 1992.
Heller, Ben A., *Assimilation/Generation/Resurrection: Contrapuntal Readings in the Poetry of Jose Lezama Lima,* Bucknell University Press (Lewis-burg, PA), 1997.
Levinson, Brett, *Secondary Moderns: Mimesis, History, and Revolution in Lezama Lima's "American Expression",* Bucknell University Press, 1996.

Pellon, Gustavo, *Jose Lezama Lima's Joyful Vision: A Study of Paradiso and Other Prose Works,* University of Texas Press (Austin), 1989.

PERIODICALS

New Republic, June 15, 1974.
New York Review of Books, April 18, 1974.
New York Times Book Review, April 21, 1974.
Village Voice, April 25, 1974.
Washington Post, April 14, 1974.

OBITUARIES:

PERIODICALS

New York Times, August 10, 1976.
Publishers Weekly, August 23, 1976.*

* * *

LIMA, Jose Lezama
   See LEZAMA LIMA, Jose

* * *

LISBOA, Maria Manuel 1963-

PERSONAL: Born November 17, 1963, in Mozambique; Portuguese citizen; daughter of Eugnio and Maria Antonieta (Gabao) Lisboa; married Michael Brick (a painter), May 11, 1993; children: Laura Caroline. *Education:* University of London, B.Sc., 1985; University of Nottingham, M.A., Ph.D., 1988.

ADDRESSES: Office—St. John's College, Cambridge University, Cambridge CB2 1TP, England; fax 022-333-7720. *E-mail*—MMGL100@cam.ac.uk.

CAREER: University of Newcastle upon Tyne, Newcastle upon Tyne, England, lecturer in Portuguese and Brazilian literature, 1988-93; Cambridge University, St. John's College, Cambridge, England, lecturer in Portuguese, Brazilian, and African (Lusopaone) literature, 1993—. Guest lecturer at University of Leeds, University of St. Andrews, University of Hamburg, Institute of Romance Studies, London, and University of Reading.

WRITINGS:

(Contributor) Jon Davies, editor, *Ritual and Remembrance: Responses to Death in Human Societies,* Sheffield University Press (Sheffield, England), 1994.

(Contributor) Sarah M. Hall, editor, *Reference Guide to World Literature,* Gale (London, England), 1995.

Machado de Assis and Feminism: Re-Reading the Heart of the Companion, Edwin Mellen (Lewiston, NY), 1996.

(Contributor) Georgiana Colville, editor, *Other Women's Voices/Other Americas,* Edwin Mellen, 1996.

(Contributor) Naomi Segal and Nicholas White, editors, *Scarlet Letters: Fictions of Adultery from Antiquity to the 1990s,* Macmillan (Basingstoke, England), 1997.

Contributor of stories, translations, articles, and reviews to periodicals, including *Portuguese Studies, Letras e Letras, Journal of the Institute of Romance Studies, Journal of Hispanic Research,* and *Revista Arca.*

WORK IN PROGRESS: A book of essays on themes of national identity and origin in Portugal from the nineteenth century to the present; a book of essays on Brazilian romanticism, examining both colonial and post-colonial themes.

*   *   *

LISPECTOR, Clarice 1925(?)-1977

PERSONAL: Born December 10, 1925 (various sources say 1921, 1922, and 1924), in Tchetchelnik, Ukraine; immigrated to Brazil shortly after birth; died of cancer, December 9, 1977, in Rio de Janeiro, Brazil; daughter of Pedro and Marian (Krimgold) Lispector; married Mauro Gurgel Valente (a diplomat), January 23, 1943 (divorced July, 1959); children: Pedro, Paulo. *Education:* National Faculty of Law, Rio de Janeiro, B.L., 1944 (some sources say 1943).

CAREER: Writer. Editor for the news agency Agencia Nacional and the newspaper *A noite* until 1943.

AWARDS, HONORS: Graca Aranha Prize, Brazilian PEN Club, for *Perto do coracao selvagem;* Jabuti Prize, Camara Brasileira do Livro, for *Lacos de.*

WRITINGS:

NOVELS

Perto do coracao selvagem (title means "Close to the Savage Heart"), Noite (Rio de Janeiro, Brazil), c. 1944, translation with an afterword by Giovanni Pontiero published as *Near to the Wild Heart,* New Directions (New York City), 1990.

O lustre (title means "The Chandelier"), Artes Graficas Industrias Reunidas (Rio de Janeiro, Brazil), 1946.

A cidade sitiada (title means "The Besieged City"), Noite, c. 1949, revised edition, Alvaro (Rio de Janeiro, Brazil), 1964.

A maca no escuro, Alves (Rio de Janeiro, Brazil), 1961, translation with an introduction by Gregory Rabassa published as *The Apple in the Dark,* Knopf (New York City), 1967.

A paixao segundo G. H., Autor (Rio de Janeiro, Brazil), 1964, translation by Ronald W. Sousa published as *The Passion According to G. H.,* University of Minnesota Press (Minneapolis), 1988.

Uma aprendizagem; ou, O livro dos prazeres, Sabia (Rio de Janeiro, Brazil), 1969, translation by Richard A. Mazzara and Lorri A. Parris published as *An Apprenticeship; or, The Book of Delights,* University of Texas Press (Austin), 1986.

Agua viva (title means "Sparkling Water"), Artenova (Rio de Janeiro, Brazil), 1973, translation by Earl E. Fitz and Elizabeth Lowe published as *The Stream of Life,* University of Minnesota Press, 1989.

A hora da estrela, Olympio (Rio de Janeiro, Brazil), 1977, translation with an afterword by Pontiero published as *The Hour of the Star,* Carcanet (Manchester, England), 1986.

SHORT STORY COLLECTIONS

Alguns contos (title means "Some Stories"), Ministerio de Educacao e Saude, Servico de Documentacao (Rio de Janeiro, Brazil), 1952.

Lacos de familia, Alves (Sao Paulo), 1960, translation with an introduction by Pontiero published as *Family Ties* (includes "Love," "The Imitation of the Rose," "The Smallest Woman in the World," "Preciousness," "Family Ties," and "The Crime of the Mathematics Professor"), University of Texas Press, 1972.

Felicidade clandestina (title means "Secret Happiness"), Sabia, 1971.

A imitacao da rosa, Artenova, 1973.

A via crucis do corpo (title means "The Cross Way of the Flesh"), Artenova, 1974, translation by Alexis Levitin published in *Soulstorm,* New Directions, 1989.

Onde estivestes de noite? (title means "Where Were You at Night?"), Artenova, 1974, translation by Levitin published in *Soulstorm,* New Directions, 1989.

Soulstorm: Stories (includes *A via crucis do corpo* and *Onde estivestes de noite?*), translation with an afterword by Alexis Levitin, introduction by Grace Paley, New Directions, 1989.

Selected Cronicas, translated by Pontiero, New Directions, 1996.

CHILDREN'S BOOKS

O misterio do coelho pensante (uma estoria policial para criancas) (title means "The Mystery of the Thinking Rabbit"), Alvaro, 1967.

A mulher que matou os peixes (translation by Fitz published as *The Woman Who Killed the Fish, Latin American Literary Review,* 11 (Fall-Winter 1982), pp. 89-101), Sabia, 1968.

OTHER

A legiao estrangeira (stories and nonfiction), Autor, 1964, translation with an afterword by Pontiero published as *The Foreign Legion: Stories and Chronicles* (includes "Friendship," "The Journey to Petropolis," and "Misfortunes of Sofia"), Center for Inter-American Relations (New York City), 1979.

A vida intima de Laura, Olympio, 1974.

(Translator) Oscar Wilde, *O retrato de Dorian Gray,* Ouro (Rio de Janeiro, Brazil), 1974.

De corpo inteiro, Reis Velloso, Ney Braga, Dr. J. D. Azulay, Nelida Pinon, Jorge Amado . . . (chronicles and profiles; title means "Sound of Body"), Artenova, 1975.

Seleta de Clarice Lispector (collection), edited by Renato Cordeiro Gomes, Olympio, 1975.

Visao do esplendor: Impressoes leves (chronicles and profiles; title means "Vision of Splendor"), Alves, 1975.

Para nao esquecer, Atica (Sao Paulo), 1978.

Quase de verdade, illustrations by Cecilia Juca, Rocco (Rio de Janeiro, Brazil), 1978.

Um sopro de vida: Pulsacoes (title means "A Breath of Life"), Nova Fronteira (Rio de Janeiro, Brazil), 1978.

A bela e a fera, Nova Fronteira, 1979.

A descoberta do mundo, Nova Fronteira, 1984.

Discovering the World, Carcanet (Manchester, England), 1992.

Works represented in anthologies, including *Contos,* Alves, 1974; and have been translated into French, German, and Spanish.

ADAPTATIONS: A hora da estrela was adapted for film by Suzana Amaral and Alfredo Oroz and released as *The Hour of the Star* by Kino International, 1986.

SIDELIGHTS: Clarice Lispector, one of the major Latin American writers of the twentieth century, was described by Marie-Lise Gazarian-Gautier in the *San Francisco Review of Books* as an author who "wants to annihilate herself, tear herself apart and understand what she is, who she is in relation to time, space, the now and the thereafter." Lispector composed her modernist narratives, which often examine the link between literature and philosophy, in a stream-of-consciousness, interior-monologue style. Acknowledged as one of the premiere writers of experimental fiction in the 1960s, Lispector wrote poetic prose obsessively concerned with capturing the perfectly nuanced word and with expanding the possibilities and range of language, often through paradox. "She holds a word tight in her hands, as if it were a fruit," wrote Gazarian-Gautier, "and squeezes the juice out of it to extract the essential meaning of things." Lispector's textual concern is echoed in her thematic emphasis on the connection between life and language, on how identity relates to the manner in which it is verbally expressed, and on how language governs who people are. Because of Lispector's substantial influence, Brazilian fiction began to consider psychology and aestheticism and to shift its focus from regional concerns to universal ones suggested by the local and particular.

Lispector was born in a small village in the Ukraine just before her family immigrated to Brazil. Demonstrating an early interest in writing, she created her first stories when she was only six years old. About 1944 she married Mauro Gurgel Valente, a diplomat, and graduated from the National Faculty of Law in Rio de Janeiro. After graduation she worked as an editor at both a news agency and a newspaper. Her husband's work required him to take his family abroad, and for eight years they lived in the United States. When Lispector and her husband separated in 1959, she returned to Rio de Janeiro with her two sons and stayed until her death in 1977.

Lispector's first novel, *Perto do coracao selvagem* (*Near to the Wild Heart*) was published in 1944, "in the midst of a literature still dominated by the social realisms of the 1930s," noted *Dictionary of Literary Biography* essayist Earl E. Fitz. For its title, Lispector selected a phrase from *Portrait of the Artist as a Young Man,* the first novel by influential Irish writer James Joyce; and *Near to the Wild Heart* would spur new critical and artistic thinking about the Latin American novel much as *Portrait of the Artist* had about English literature. Fitz wrote: "A richly symbolic work[,] . . . [*Near to the Wild*] dramatically altered the way Brazilian critics and writers would think of the novel genre. . . . [It] was a stunning breakthrough for its fledgling author. Critics applauded its poetic language and its probing treatment of a woman's psychological growth and development." It showed, Fitz continued, how Brazilian narrative "could benefit from such staples of modern fiction as the interior monologue; temporal dislocation; rejection of external orientation; structural fragmentation; and an emphasis on the ebb and flow of psychological, rather than chronological, time." In the book, Lispector emphasizes the conflict between the inner and outer worlds, a tension mirrored in the language of the text itself, by juxtaposing the interior life of her protagonist, Joana, with the external world Joana experiences. Joana reacts to the baseness of everyday existence by attempting to better know and express her sense of self, the only way she can impose form on chaotic reality. Her struggle symbolizes an attempt to conjoin the private with what is timelessly universal.

Lispector continued to stress the interior lives of her characters in the short story collection *Lacos de familia* (*Family Ties*). These stories are recognized for revolutionizing the Latin American short story form in the same way Lispector's novels incited reconsideration of the novel genre. The work won for her comparisons to Albert Camus and Jean-Paul Sartre because of the existentialist orientation of many of the stories. *Family Ties* also gained her widespread recognition, especially for the story "Amor" ("Love"), which delineates the confusion a middle-class woman living in Rio de Janeiro experiences when she sees a blind man out of the window of a tram on which she is riding. Anna becomes so fixated on the blind man that she cries out and dumps her bag of groceries onto the floor. This awkward moment is a crisis for Anna, and for the rest of the story she struggles with why the blind man chewing gum so jarred her.

"Citing the dramatic intensity, the economy of expression, and the internalized conflicts of her short fiction," Fitz stated, "many critics believe she is a better story writer than she is a novelist." The stories in *Family Ties,* as much of Lispector's fiction, are notable for the way in which plot is subordinated to the interior lives of her isolated, sensitive characters. Critics again mentioned Sartre when writing of the nauseated emotional response many of Lispector's characters have when confronted with raw existence. In *Luso-Brazilian Review,* Rita Herman designated the collection "a personal interpretation of some of the most pressing psychological problems of man in the contemporary western world. Liberty, despair, solitude, the incapacity to communicate, are the main themes that unite the separate stories into a definite configuration of the author's pessimistic perception of life."

A year after *Lacos de familia* appeared in 1960, Lispector published *A maca no escuro* (*The Apple in the Dark*), which became her first novel to be translated into English. A lengthy, difficult narrative, it tells the story of Martim, a man who mistakenly believes he has killed his wife in a moment of fury and flees to the countryside. In the *New York Times Book Review,* C. D. B. Bryan quoted Lispector's description of the impact the crime has on Martim: "In one fell swoop he was no longer a collaborator with other people, and in one fell swoop he had ceased to collaborate with himself." Again, Lispector eschews plot in favor of internal events, the main action of the novel taking place in the minds of Martim and two cousins, Victoria and Ermelinda, who live on a remote farm and take in Martim. Bryan summarized, "Martim's quest for his own place in the universe provokes Victoria and attracts Ermelinda, forcing a confrontation between the 'afraid to live' Victoria, 'afraid to die' Ermelinda, and 'afraid to be afraid' Martim, as he characterizes himself and the others. The ultimate confrontation however, is that of each character with himself or herself." Life is viewed as hopeless and futile, as explained by the metaphor which gives the novel its title: though an apple can be recognized in the dark by its shape and form, its color or ripeness cannot be discerned—it is not fully knowable. Lispector suggests it is best to leave the apple in the dark with its incomprehensibilities than to attempt to illuminate it in order to know it more completely, better to firmly grasp what one's ignorance of the world allows than to uselessly search for explanations.

Some critics lamented that *The Apple in the Dark* is too detailed and philosophical, judging that the very thing that makes the novel so strong—its language and philosophical basis—at times feels overdone and demands too much from the reader. However, few question the value of the novel and its importance to the field of literature. Gregory Rabassa, in his introduction to *The Apple in the Dark,* wrote, "Lispector [marshals] the syntax in a new way that is closer perhaps to original thought patterns than the language had ever managed to approach before." Many writers are cited as antecedents to Lispector, yet critics maintain at the same time that she is original and her style, brilliant. The novel, Richard Franko Goldman observed in *Saturday Review,* "is fascinating simply because Miss Lispector is a superb writer, an artist of vivid imagination and sensitivity, with a glorious feeling for language and its uses. She employs words playfully, meaningfully, deceptively, and of course seriously, not necessarily as a poet does but as few novelists do."

Lispector followed *The Apple in the Dark* with several other well-received novels, including *A paixao segundo G. H.* (*The Passion according to G. H.*), *Agua viva* (*The Stream of Life*), and *A hora da estrela* (*The Hour of the Star*), which was released the year Lispector died and is considered perhaps her most engaging novel. In *The Hour of the Star,* Lispector deliberately throws light on the creative act of fiction–writing by making its plot the writing of a text. Rodrigo S. M., the narrator, tells the story of Macabea, whom he paints as a veritable nobody who works as a secretary and has trivial conversations with her boyfriend. Rodrigo relates Macabea's story in the third person, speaks to the reader directly in the second person, and refers to himself in the first person, drawing the reader into the text and making him or her a participant in the dramatic action the novel creates. Critics praised the carefully controlled perspective admirably maintained throughout the novel, and noted the skill with which Lispector uses her construction to comment upon attempts to control language.

Rodrigo, who falsely thinks he can harness language and thereby create Macabea, is mocked. "The writer who thinks *he* controls [language] is mistaken, because, like the repressed, language always returns to overpower the author," wrote Alfred J. MacAdam in the *New York Times Book Review.* "But the author must delude himself into thinking he can be the master." With this novel, Lispector began "to deal with the delicate though critical relationship between narrator, author, and reader, or, to express it more precisely, between the real author, the implied author, the other characters, and the reader," Earl E. Fitz wrote in the *Luso-Brazilian Review.* He contin-

ued, "Given the vigor and innovativeness of what we see here, one must wonder about the wonderful stories we could have expected from Clarice Lispector had she not died so prematurely. With her untimely passing, one of Latin America's most original and powerful voices has been stilled."

"Since the 1960s," summarized Fitz in his *Dictionary of Literary Biography* essay, "critics have tended to see Lispector's contribution to Brazilian literature as occurring in three primary areas: Helping to revolutionize Brazilian narrative by turning it inward; urbanizing it; and giving it a female (if not necessarily 'feminist') orientation. Very much ahead of their time in the 1940s, her enigmatic, often mystical texts continue to exert a profound influence on Brazilian literature." Fitz explained: "Always concerned with the problems of identity, communication, language and being, Lispector would continue [from her debut novel] to be a highly complex and iconoclastic writer through her novels, short stories, children's books, translations, and nonfiction pieces. . . . Embodying many of the philosophical and literary problems associated with post-structuralism Lispector's fluid, poetic, and mythic texts have won a large and devoted following, both nationally and internationally."

BIOGRAPHICAL/CRITICAL SOURCES:

BOOKS

Abel, Elizabeth, Marianne Hirsch, and Elizabeth Longland, editors, *The Voyage In: Fictions of Female Development,* University Press of New England (Hanover, NH), 1983, pp. 287-303.

Barbosa, Maria Jose Somerlate, *Clarice Lispector: Spinning the Webs of Passion,* University Press of the South (New Orleans, LA), 1997.

Cixous, Helene, *Reading with Clarice Lispector,* edited, translated, and introduced by Verena Andermatt Conley, University of Minnesota Press, 1990.

Contemporary Literary Criticism, Volume 43, Gale (Detroit, MI), 1987.

Fitz, Earl E., *Clarice Lispector,* Twayne (Boston), 1985.

Dictionary of Literary Biography, Volume 113: *Modern Latin-American Fiction Writers, First Series,* Gale, 1992.

Marting, Diane E., *Clarice Lispector: A Bio-Bibliography,* Greenwood Press (Westport, CT), 1993.

Peixoto, Marta, *Passionate Fictions: Gender, Narrative, and Violence in Clarice Lispector,* University of Minnesota Press, 1994.

Peyre, Henri, editor, *Fiction in Several Languages,* Beacon Press (Boston), 1969, pp. 1-18. Lispector, Clarice, *The Apple in the Dark,* translated by Gregory Rabassa, Knopf, 1967.

PERIODICALS

American Book Review, April-May, 1991, p. 20.
Best Sellers, June 15, 1967.
Chicago Tribune, September 12, 1986.
Christian Science Monitor, August 23, 1967, p. 9; October 5, 1984, p. B11; December 19, 1986, p. 24; June 25, 1987, p. 22.
Listener, March 14, 1985, p. 27.
London Review of Books, February 21, 1985, pp. 20-21.
Los Angeles Times, June 23, 1989.
Luso-Brazilian Review, June, 1967, pp. 69-70; winter, 1982, pp. 195-208.
Lyra, vol. 1, no. 3, 1988, pp. 26-31.
New Statesman, January 18, 1985, pp. 29-30.
New York Times Book Review, September 3, 1967, pp. 22-23; May 18, 1986, p. 27; January 8, 1989, pp. 12-13.
Review, June, 1979, pp. 34-37.
San Francisco Review of Books, winter, 1989-90, pp. 36-38.
Saturday Review, August 19, 1967, pp. 33, 48.
Times Literary Supplement, January 25, 1985, p. 86; May 30, 1986, p. 587.
Washington Post Book World, January 21, 1990, p. 9.
Women's Review of Books, July-August, 1987, pp. 30-31.*

*   *   *

LIZARDI, Joseph 1941-

PERSONAL: Born February 12, 1941, in Caguas, Puerto Rico; immigrated to United States, 1954, naturalized U.S. citizen; son of Jose (a factory worker) and Ana (a factory worker; maiden name, Medina) Lizardi; married wife, Linda (a secretary), July 14, 1972; children: Michael Joseph. *Education:* Bronx Community College, A.A.S., 1972; Bernard M. Baruch College of the City University of New York, M.B.A., 1977. *Politics:* Democrat. *Religion:* Roman Catholic.

ADDRESSES: Home—5 Ontario Ave., Plainview, NY 11803. *Agent*—Bertha Klausner, 71 Park Ave., New York, NY 10016.

CAREER: Daily News, New York, NY, guard, 1964-66; Seven-Up Bottling Co., New York City, filler operator, 1966—. Arena Players Repertory Theater, Farmingdale, NY, playwright in residence, 1980—. *Military service:* U.S. Marine Corps, 1960-64.

MEMBER: Dramatists Guild.

AWARDS, HONORS: The Powderroom was chosen as a finalist in the Actors Theater of Louisville's Great American Play Contest, 1980.

WRITINGS:

PLAYS

The Agreement, first produced Off-Off Broadway at Carnegie Repertory Theater, 1970.
The Contract, first produced Off-Off Broadway at Carnegie Repertory Theater, 1971.
The Commitment, first produced Off-Off Broadway at Henry Street Playhouse, 1972.
Summerville, first produced Off-Off Broadway at West Side Community Theater, 1972.
The Block Party, first produced Off-Off Broadway at Henry Street Playhouse, 1974.
El Macho, first produced Off-Off Broadway at Firehouse Theater, 1977.
The Powderroom, first produced Off-Off Broadway at Arena Players Repertory Theater, 1980.
Reunion, first produced Off-Off Broadway at Arena Players Repertory Theater, 1980.
Blue Collars, first produced Off-Off Broadway at Arena Players Repertory Theater, 1980.
Love's Comedy (adapted from Henrik Ibsen's *La Comedia del Amor*), first produced Off-Off Broadway at Arena Players Repertory Theater, 1981.
December in New York (full-length), first produced Off-Off Broadway at Arena Players Repertory Theater, 1982.
Blind Dates, first produced in Plainview, NY, at Old-Bethpage Library, 1982.
Three on the Run, first produced Off-Off Broadway at Arena Players Repertory Theater, 1982.
Sea-Waves Inn: A One-Act Play, Samuel French (New York City), 1989.

Also author of the plays *Joggers, Love's Last Gasp, The Family Room, The Pretenders* (an adaptation of an Ibsen play), *The Runaway, Save the Children,"* and *Couples,* and the screenplays *The Dope War* and *Spanish Harlem.*

WORK IN PROGRESS: Then Came the Stranger and *A Place along the Highway,* two dramas.

SIDELIGHTS: Joseph Lizardi once explained of his work that "It has always been my desire to learn and perfect my craft. Knowing that it was going to take a long time, I decided to hold a job which did not require my full devotion to it. That is the reason I have been a blue-collar worker for most of my working life. I do not regret the decision, for I have been able to compile a treasury of fascinating characters for all the plays I have written so far."

Born in Puerto Rico, Lizardi came to the United States at fourteen, taught himself English, and became a notable New York playwright. His plays, such as *El Macho, Block Party,* and *Blue Collars,* explore the lives of factory workers, the ambience of the Puerto Rican neighborhoods in which he has lived, and the ethnic experience in general. His writings, described by *Newsday* critic Leo Seligsohn as "a combination of naturalism and farce," are often compared to television situation comedies; yet reviewers have heard a somber echo behind the laughter. Critic Alvin Klein explained to readers of the *New York Times:* "Mr. Lizardi builds comic momentum right up to the point of tragedy." The playwright's characters spring from the crumbling world of his youth, wherein, as Klein wrote, "disasters . . . were a way of life and humor was the handiest survival mechanism."

BIOGRAPHICAL/CRITICAL SOURCES:

PERIODICALS

Daily News (New York), November 16, 1980.
Newsday, April 25, 1980; May 9, 1980; November 5, 1980; February 3, 1982.
New York Post, May 25, 1979.
New York Times, April 13, 1980; April 27, 1980; August 24, 1980; November 16, 1980; August 30, 1981; April 4, 1982.

*　　*　　*

LoMONACO, Palmyra 1932-

PERSONAL: Born August 1, 1932, in Chicago, IL; daughter of Anthony (an insurance agent) and Palmyra (an accountant; maiden name, Casaleggi) LoMonaco; married Wayne Andrews, June 26, 1954 (divorced, February 24, 1980); married Robert Friedman (a federal administrator), December 13, 1983; stepchildren: John, Katherine, Margaret Hvartin, Elizabeth. *Education:* National College of Education (now National Louis University), B.A.; University of Illinois at Urbana-Champaign, M.A. *Politics:* Registered Democrat. *Avocational interests:* Jazz music, crafts (especially collages of found objects).

ADDRESSES: Home—4100 Five Oaks Dr., No. 41, Durham, NC 27707.

CAREER: Teacher and writer in Durham, NC, 1954-84. New Mexico Department of Human Services, child care specialist; Bernalillo County Mental Health-Mental Retardation Center, Albuquerque, NM, child care trainer; Albuquerque-Bernalillo County Economic Opportunity Board, director of child development and child care centers; University of New Mexico, adjunct instructor in on-site programs for Navajo and Apache early childhood education; University of Albuquerque, adjunct assistant professor of education; Duke University, play therapist in Department of Pediatrics; Durham Technical Community College, program director and instructor in Early Childhood Associate Program. Past member of board of directors, Durham Nursery and Pre-School, Inc., Carolina Wren, and Lollipop Press; consultant to early childhood education programs.

MEMBER: National Association for the Education of Young Children, Society of Children's Book Writers and Illustrators, North Carolina Writers' Network, Readers' Theater.

WRITINGS:

Music and Motion: The Rhythmic Language of Children, National Association for the Education of Young Children, 1976.
Up from the Classroom, Barnell Loft, 1977.
Halloween: Its Place in the Curriculum, Human Sciences, 1988.
Joey's Blanket, Human Sciences, 1994.
Night Letters, illustrated by Normand Chartier, Dutton, 1996.

Contributor to magazines, including *Teacher, Instructor, Day Care and Early Childhood Education,* and *Young Children.*

WORK IN PROGRESS: How to Get Mama to Listen and *Tumbleweed Chaser.*

SIDELIGHTS: Teacher and writer Palmyra LoMonaco asked: "What do a young child's weekly excursions with her aunt to the neighborhood library in the park, a bookshelf bulging from the weight of children's picture books (with a special section for the works of Byrd Baylor and Maurice Sendak), and young children's magical observations of their natural world have in common? Each experience connected me to the writing life and to my desire to write books for young children. Each experience led me, in diverse ways, to *Night Letters,* my first published children's book.

"One day, when I was teaching in a preschool in Albuquerque, New Mexico, a child handed me a piece of construction paper left overnight in the rain. She pointed to the rain-streaked lines and curves made on the paper and asked, 'What does this say?' She thought, in the magical way a young child thinks, that the rain had written her a message. Thus Lily was born. Lily is the young girl of *Night Letters,* who sets out to read the messages left in the tracks of ants, the markings on a hawk moth's wings, and the blinking lights of fireflies."

According to an article in *New Advocate,* students at a young people's writing workshop commented that Lily would make a great workshop leader herself. One child pointed out: "She pays attention to things, has a great imagination, and she loves to write." A further discovery for the students was the fact that Lily did not do this once but night after night, impressing on the students the importance of stick-to-itiveness.

"The natural world provides the foil for the two stories I am currently writing, *How to Get Mama to Listen* and *Tumbleweed Chaser,*" LoMonaco commented. "I see how intimately young children are connected to their environment and how keen are their observations. I respect young children's world view, as well as their thought process, finding there a poetry and wonder that I try to capture in my work.

"While visiting schools to read *Night Letters* and to discuss the writing process, I am frequently asked about my writing habits. I realize that I do as much re-writing as writing, and I think of revisions when I am in motion; that is, walking or bicycling, more so than when I am still. The teacher in me delights in the night letters sent to me by children who have read the book. One child wrote: 'It's going to be a butterfly day for fun Lily.' I treasure his words and have adopted them as my writing creed."

BIOGRAPHICAL/CRITICAL SOURCES:

PERIODICALS

Booklist, May 15, 1996, p. 1592.
Horn Book Guide, fall, 1996, p. 265.
Kirkus Reviews, December 1, 1995, pp. 1703-1704.
New Advocate, fall, 1996, p. 335.
Raleigh News & Observer, March 10, 1996.
School Library Journal, March, 1996, p. 178.
Yellow Brick Road, March/April, 1996.

*   *   *

LOPES, Dominic (M. McIver) 1964-

PERSONAL: Born July 3, 1964, in England; son of Anthony D. (a physician) and Anita C. (a writer; maiden name, Macfarlane) Lopes; married Anne M. Blackburn, August, 1988 (divorced, 1995). *Ethnicity:* "South Asian, British, and Hispanic." *Education:* McGill University, B.A. (with honors), 1986; Oxford University, D.Phil., 1992.

ADDRESSES: Office—Department of Philosophy, Indiana University at Kokomo, 2300 South Washington St., Kokomo, IN 46904-9003; fax 765-455-9528. *E-mail*—dlopes@indiana.edu.

CAREER: Indiana University at Kokomo, associate professor of philosophy, 1992—.

MEMBER: American Philosophical Association, American Society for Aesthetics, British Society of Aesthetics.

WRITINGS:

Understanding Pictures, Clarendon Press (New York City), 1996.
(Editor with Damian Lopes) *A Handful of Grams: Goan Proverbs,* Caju Press (Toronto, Ontario), 1996.

Editor, *American Society for Aesthetics Newsletter.*

WORK IN PROGRESS: Getting in Touch with Pictures: Pictures and the Blind, completion expected in 1999.

LOPEZ, Diana 1948-
(Isabella Rios)

PERSONAL: Born March 16, 1948, in Los Angeles, CA; daughter of Louis H. (a contracting business owner) and Valentine (a homemaker; maiden name, Ballesteros) Lopez; children: Jason Ho. *Education:* San Francisco State University, B.A., 1967, M.A., 1969; Nova University, Ed.D., 1979.

ADDRESSES: Office—Department of Language Arts, Moorpark College, 7075 Campus Rd., Moorpark, CA 93021.

CAREER: Moorpark College, Moorpark, CA, English instructor, 1970—, assisted in establishing and taught in Bilingual Center and tutorial program for minority students; writer.

MEMBER: Ventura Writers' Club.

WRITINGS:

UNDER PSEUDONYM ISABELLA RIOS

Victuum, Diana-Etna (Ventura, CA), 1976.
A Dance with the Eucalyptus, Whale Watch (Maui, HI), 1995.

Contributor of poems and short stories to periodicals.

WORK IN PROGRESS: A revision of *Victuum,* and a sequel; a book of poetry.

SIDELIGHTS: Diana Lopez, who writes under the pseudonym Isabella Rios, will be remembered in Hispanic literature as the author of the first Chicana *bildungsroman, Victuum.* The story of a Hispanic woman's coming of age and discovery of her psychic ability, *Victuum* also offers insight into the social and cultural changes Californian Chicano society underwent during the twentieth century. The book is based on the life and experiences of one of Rios's female relatives, whom Rios interviewed extensively for two years; woven into her story are bits of Lopez family history and Hispanic folklore.

Victuum begins with protagonist Valentina Ballesternos still in the womb, lamenting that once she is born she will not remember any of what she has learned in her past lives. As Rios follows her through birth and adolescence to marriage and motherhood she writes of the Chicano experience during the Prohibition era, the Depression, and World War II as Valentina lived it.

Valentina's psychic powers manifest themselves as she matures, and when describing her later years *Victuum* becomes her spiritual biography. Eventually the narrative becomes dominated by Valentina's psychic experiences—visions and dreams peopled by such diverse figures as poet William Wordsworth, the prophet Isaiah, and Pope Eusebius. Thus Rios recreates the mystical landscape of Valentina's mind, raising questions about the very nature of reality.

BIOGRAPHICAL/CRITICAL SOURCES:

PERIODICALS

Minority Voices, spring, 1980.

*   *   *

LUFT, Lya Fett 1938-

PERSONAL: Born September 15, 1938, in Santa Cruz do Sul, Brazil; daughter of Arthur Germano (an attorney) and Wally (Neumann) Fett; married Celso Pedro Luft, 1963; children: three. *Education:* Catholic University, M.A., 1975, Federal University of Rio Grande do Sul, M.A., 1978.

ADDRESSES: Agent—c/o Carcanet Press, Fourth Floor, Conavon Ct., Blackfriars St., Manchester M3 5BQ, UK.

CAREER: Translator, poet, essayist, novelist, and teacher, 1964—.

AWARDS, HONORS: Instituto Estadual lo Livro literary prize, 1962; Fundacion Givre's Alfonsi Storni Poetry Prize, 1978; House of Representatives' Erico Verissimo Prize for Literature, 1982.

WRITINGS:

POETRY AND ESSAYS

Cancoes de limiar, Instituto Estadual do Livro (Porto Alegre, Brazil), 1964.
Flauta doce: Tema e variacoes, Sulina (Porto Alegre, Brazil), 1972.
Materia do cotidiano, Instituto Estadual do Livro, 1978.
Mulher no palco, Salamandra (Rio de Janeiro), 1984.
O lado fatal, Rocco (Rio de Janeiro), 1988.

NOVELS

As parceiras, Instituto Estadual do Livro, 1980.
A asa esquerda do anjo, Instituto Estadual do Livro, 1981.
Reuniad do familia, Instituto Estadual do Livro, 1982.
O quarto fechado, Instituto Estadual do Livro, 1984, translation by Carmen Chaves McClendon and Betty Jean Craige published as *The Island of the Dead,* University of Georgia Press, (Athens, GA), 1986.
Exilio, Guanabars (Rio de Janeiro), 1987, translation by Giovami Pontiero published as *The Red House,* Carcanet Press (Manchester), 1994.

OTHER

A Sentinela, Editora Sciliano (Sao Paulo), 1994.
O Rio do Meio, Editora Mandarim (Sao Paulo), 1996.
Secred Mirada, Editora Mandarim (Sao Paulo), 1997.

Also translator of some fifty German- and English-language works of fiction into Portuguese.

ADAPTATIONS: Reuniad do familia was adapted for the theater by Gaio Fernando Abreu, 1984; *Mulher no palco* was adapted for a reader's theater by Luciano Alabarse, c. 1984.

SIDELIGHTS: Lya Fett Luft has been called one of the most important Brazilian writers of the 1980s, and she certainly was one of the most productive. In the decade ending in 1988, she published a collection of essays, two books of poetry, and five novels. By the time her first novel was published, Luft was already well known in Brazilian literary circles for having translated some fifty German- and English-language works of fiction into Portuguese; she was known in her home town as well for the essays and poetry she published in newspapers and literary magazines.

When Luft was forty-two, her writing changed course with the publication of her first novel. Her poems and essays up to that point had been concerned with the world of appearances, with acceptable middle-class values seen through rose-colored classes. Literature was easy for her, and so were languages: As a youngster she made good use of her father's large personal library, and German was frequently the language of choice at home. But Luft's busy and stable life as wife, mother, and literary translator almost ended in 1977 due to an automobile accident; after recovering, she turned from easy themes to darker ones involving the meaning of life, the meaning of death, and the search for identity.

All of Luft's novels share certain thematic and structural characteristics. They take place in small spaces, or small time frames—a house, a graveyard, a locked room; twenty-four hours, a weekend, a week. The characters are always immediate family members or relatives, and there is always an "other" presence—a ghost, a grandmother in the attic, a dwarf gnome—significant to the story but without a point of view. There are multiple levels of reality, open-ended endings, or circular ones, searches for meaning and questions unanswered. The last line of Luft's first novel is "We descended holding hands"; readers are uncertain about the identity of the narrator's companion and uncertain about where they descended to. The first novel, "The Players" takes up the meaningless life of Anelise, whose seven days of solitude are in effect a meditation on the theme of death. Searching for meaning, Anelise compares herself to her German grandmother who had been isolated for years in the attic of the family home. Two "partners" are playing a board game, perhaps between life and death, and there is a mysterious woman in white. The narrative is written like a diary which unfolds into a shadowy and moldy atmosphere—and then Anelise and the woman in white meet and go down from the cliffs. Luft further explores an immigrant German family in her second novel, "The Angel's Left Wing". The setting is a house and a graveyard, and the grandmother here must be exorcised, in effect, before the female protagonist can become her own person.

In "Family Gathering," two sisters and their brother, two spouses, their father, and a maid—as family members, all uncommunicative—spend a weekend unearthing buried secrets and buried emotions. In the process, each person's solid persona begins to crack, much like the large cracked mirror in front of which it all takes place. According to Carmen Chaves Tesser's profile of Luft in the *Dictionary of Literary Biography,* the circularity here is "unusual and ambiguous"—but in part because of the ambiguity, an adaptation of the novel staged in 1984 played to packed houses and earned high critical praise.

O Quarto Fechado, (The Island of the Dead) 1984), Luft's fourth novel, is a twenty–four hour wake for an eighteen year old who has killed himself. The point of view shifts from one character's thoughts about the boy's life to another's and shifts again. Characters whose points of view are expressed are his mother, who abandoned her career as a concert pianist; his father; his maiden aunt; his foster grandmother; and his twin sister. Even Camilo himself speaks, in sections prefaced with the phrase "If he could speak, the dead boy would say. . . ." The "other" character in this novel, again with no point of view of her own and no voice, turns out to be the mother's illegitimate daughter Ella, who has been kept in a locked room for thirty years, paralyzed, the victim of a long-ago accident.

Luft wrote her fifth novel in Rio de Janiero, where she spent two years living with a well-known psychoanalyst and journalist named Helio Pellegrino. It appeared in 1987 under the title *Exilio (The Red House)*. This time, the tight space is a closed boardinghouse. The characters are puppetlike caricatures, known only as "the brunette," "the blonde," "the fat one," "the mother," and "the house" (even the house is a character). As in the previous novels, there is an "other"—this time, an ever present and ever-elusive dwarf gnome—but unlike the plot of the earlier books, the searches end with answers. As Tesser put it, "The exile is present in everyone's lives whether or not they connect with anything or anyone."

Luft's brief relationship with Pellegrino was ended by his fatal heart attack, and according to Tesser, writing *O lado fatal* in 1988 provided her with some comfort. A collection of poems dedicated to her life with Pelligrino, *O lado fatal* became an instant bestseller.

BIOGRAPHICAL/CRITICAL SOURCES:

BOOKS

Dictionary of Literary Biography, Volume 145: *Modern Latin-American Fiction Writers, Second Series,* Gale (Detroit, MI), 1994.*

*   *   *

LUIS, William 1948-

PERSONAL: Born July 12, 1948, in New York, NY; son of Domingo (a radio and television technician) and Petra (a community worker; maiden name, Liduvina; present surname, Santos) Luis; married Linda Garceau, January 1, 1984; children: Tammie Luis Durham, Gabriel, Diego, Stephanie Luis Wallace. *Education:* State University of New York at Bing-hamton, B.A., 1971; attended Hunter College of the City University of New York and St. Francis College, New York City, both 1972; University of Wisconsin—Madison, M.A., 1973; Cornell University, M.A., 1979, Ph.D., 1980. *Politics:* Independent. *Religion:* Episcopalian.

ADDRESSES: Home—2112 Piccadilly Pl., Nashville, TN 37215. *Office*—Department of Spanish and Portuguese, 302 Furman Hall, Vanderbilt University, Nashville, TN 37235. *E-mail*—william.luis@vanderbilt.edu.

CAREER: Dartmouth College, Hanover, NH, lecturer, 1979-80, assistant professor, 1980-85, associate professor, 1985-88; State University of New York at Binghamton, associate professor, 1988-91, acting director of Latin American and Caribbean Area Studies Program, 1988-89, director, 1989-90; Vanderbilt University, Nashville, TN, member of Latin American and Iberian Studies Program, 1991—, associate professor, 1991-96, professor, 1996—. Washington University, St. Louis, MO, visiting associate professor, 1988; Yale University, visiting professor, 1998. Human Relations Commission, member, 1997—.

MEMBER: Modern Language Association of America, Latin–American Studies Association, Afro-Latin/American Research Association.

WRITINGS:

(Editor with Edmundo Desnoes) *Los Dispositivos en la Flor,* Ediciones del Norte (Hanover, NH), 1981.
(Editor and contributor) *Voices from Under: Black Narrative in Latin America and the Caribbean,* Greenwood Press (Westport, CT), 1984.
Literary Bondage: Slavery in Cuban Narrative, University of Texas Press (Austin, TX), 1990.
(Editor with Julio Rodriguez-Luis, and contributor) *Translating Latin America: Culture as Text,* State University of New York at Binghamton, 1991.
(Editor) *Dictionary of Literary Biography,* Volume 113: *Modern Latin American Fiction Writers, First Series,* Gale (Detroit, MI), 1992.
(Editor with Ann Gonzalez) *Dictionary of Literary Biography,* Volume 145: *Modern Latin American Fiction Writers, Second Series,* Gale, 1994.
(Contributor) James Arnold, editor, *A Literary History of Literature in the Caribbean,* John Benjamins (Philadelphia, PA), 1994.
(Contributor) Fernando de Toro and Alfonse de Toro, editors, *Borders and Margins: Post-Colonialism and Post-Modernism,* Iberoamericana (Vervuert), 1995.
(Contributor) Roberto Gonzalez Echevarria and Enrique Pupo-Walker, editors, *The Cambridge History of Latin American Literature,* Cambridge University Press (Cambridge, England), 1996.
Dance between Two Cultures: Latino-Caribbean Literature Written in the United States, Vanderbilt University Press (Nashville, TN), 1997.

Culture in Modern Cuba, Greenwood Press, 1998.
(Contributor) Ardis Nelson, editor, *Guillermo Cabrera Infante: Assays, Essays, and Other Arts,* Twayne (New York City), 1999.

Contributor of numerous articles and reviews to professional journals, including *Afro-Hispanic Review, Hispanic Journal, Modern Language Notes, Cuban Studies/Estudios Cubanos,* and *Journal of Caribbean Studies.* Editor, *Boletin de la Fundacion Federico Garcia Lorca,* 1995.

WORK IN PROGRESS: Autobiografia del Esclavo Juan Francisco Manzano y Otros Escritos; Anthology of Latino-U.S. Literature; Autopsia de "Lunes de Revolucion;" Cesar Leante: The Politics of Fiction; The Multiple Sphere: Ethnic Literatures of Spanish American and U.S. Latino Literatures.

SIDELIGHTS: Educator and author William Luis explained: "My primary motivation for writing is to explore knowledge and ideas and further our understanding of the issues at hand. I am a specialist in Latin American literature and have written about nineteenth- and twentieth-century Spanish-American, Caribbean, and Afro-Hispanic literatures. Most recently I have broken new ground with *Dance between Two Cultures: Latino Caribbean Literature Written in the United States.* With this book I look at Latino literature as a new field of study that is interdisciplinary in nature and brings together Spanish-American and U.S. cultures. Whereas some critics have considered the literature as an isolated expression of one particular group, I study the combined literature production, as each expression relates to the others and as a response to similar realities.

"I also write out of an obligation to break stereotypes and prove that we should not judge people on the basis of their origins or ethnicity or socio-economic backgrounds, but on an individual basis. Having lived on the lower east side of Manhattan, in New York City, and been raised by a single parent, I was not supposed to be successful in my career. However, through much dedication, hard work, and support from family and friends, I have proven that I can be as successful or more successful than many scholars from privileged backgrounds. Although I am interested in helping all students, I think that members of minorities, like myself, have the added obligation of assisting other minority members, so that they do not have to fight the same battles we have.

"I write about topics that have not been explored or have not been fully explored. I attempt to create a body of knowledge where it does not presently exist. For me writing is somewhat automatic. I start with an idea about literature or a particular concern, and I continue to elaborate on it until I observe that I have said all I can say at that moment about that particular issue. I try not to work from an outline because I consider it too restrictive. I believe that I need to let my mind explore subjects that may not be included in an outline. Ultimately, logic and analysis are what dictate the outcome of my writings. If the process of writing is somewhat automatic, rewriting is a labor of love. Expressing abstract ideas so that they are accessible to the average reader is what I consider to be the most challenging.

"I owe my present success to my education, in particular at the graduate levels. The courses I took at Cornell, especially those in literary criticism and theory, have helped me raise questions which address the broader picture. The single most important person in my career is Professor Roberto Gonzalez Echevarria, the Sterling Professor at Yale University. He is as demanding with his students as he is with himself. Consequently I have learned to be very demanding of myself. My family has also been a very important part of my success. In this regard, my mother deserves all the credit. A Cuban immigrant who never learned to speak English fluently, she was a woman of courage who believed in herself. She was a woman who strove for perfection and instilled the same ideals in her children. We paid very little attention to the harsh socio-political reality that was a part of our lives; rather, we focused more closely on the goals of that reality. Last but not least, I have to thank my wife and my children for helping me carry out what I consider to be my contribution to the profession and society. It has been their understanding that has allowed me to go forward."

*   *   *

LYNCH, B. Suarez
See Borges, Jorge Luis

*   *   *

LYNCH DAVIS, B.
See BIOY CASARES, Adolfo

M-N

MACHADO (y RUIZ), Antonio 1875-1939

PERSONAL: Born July 26, 1875, in Palacio de las Duenas, near Seville, Spain; died of pneumonia, February 22, 1939, in Coullioure, France; son of Antonio Machado (a lawyer) and Ana Ruiz (Hernandez) Alvarez; married Leonor Izquierdo, July, 1909 (died August 1, 1912). *Education:* University of Madrid, earned degree, 1918. *Politics:* Spanish Republican.

CAREER: Poet, playwright, and educator. Garnier (publishing), Paris, France, translator, early 1900s; teacher in Soria, Spain, late 1900s; teacher in Baeza, Spain, early 1910s; teacher in Segovia, Spain, beginning 1919; Instituto Calderon de la Barca, Madrid, Spain, professor, early 1930s.

MEMBER: Spanish Royal Academy.

WRITINGS:

IN ENGLISH TRANSLATION

Soledades: Poesias (poetry), Alvarez (Madrid, Spain), 1903, translations by Robert Bly published as *Times Alone: Selected Poems of Antonio Machado,* Wesleyan University Press (Middletown, CT), 1983, and *Times Alone: Twelve Poems from Soledades,* Graywolf (Port Townsend, WA), 1983.

Soledades, galerias y otros poemas (poetry), Pueyo (Madrid), 1907, revised edition, Calpe (Madrid), 1919, translation by Richard L. Predmore published as *Solitudes, Galleries, and Other Poems,* Duke University Press (Durham, NC), 1987.

Campos de Castilla (poetry), Renacimiento (Madrid), 1912, translation by J. C. R. Green published as *The Castilian Camp,* Aquila/Phaethon (Portree, Isle of Skye, United Kingdom), 1982.

La tierra de Alvar Gonzalez y Canciones del Alto Duero, Nuestro Pueblo (Barcelona, Spain), 1938, translation of *La tierra* by Denis Dole published as *The Legend of Alvar Gonzalez,* North Light (Harrow, Middlesex, United Kingdom), 1982.

Canciones, Aguado (Madrid), 1949, translated by Robert Bly, Toothpaste Press (West Branch, IA), 1980.

Eighty Poems of Antonio Machado, translated by Willis Barnstone, Americas (New York City), 1959.

Castilian Ilexes, translated by Charles Tomlinson and Henry Gifford, Oxford University Press (New York City), 1963.

Del camino, translated by Michael Smith, Gallery Press (Dublin), 1974.

Selected Poems of Antonio Machado, translated by Betty Jean Craige, Louisiana State University Press (Baton Rouge), 1978.

I Never Wanted Fame: Ten Poems and Proverbs, translated by Robert Bly, Ally Press (St. Paul, MN), 1979.

The Dream below the Sun: Selected Poems, translated by Willis Barnstone, Crossing (Trumansburg, NY), 1981.

Twenty Proverbs, translated by Robert Bly and Don Olsen, Ox Head (Marshall, MN), 1981.

Selected Poems, translated by Alan S. Trueblood, Harvard University Press (Cambridge, MA), 1982.

Selected Poems and Prose, edited by Dennis Maloney, translated by Robert Bly and others, White Pine (Buffalo, NY), 1983.

The Landscape of Soria, translated by Dennis Maloney, White Pine, 1985.

Roads Dreamed Clear Afternoons: An Anthology of the Poetry of Antonio Machado, translated by Carl W. Cobb, Spanish Literature (York, SC), 1994.

Works also published in other collections.

PLAYS; WITH MANUEL MACHADO

Desdichas de la fortuna, o Julianillo Valcarcel (produced in Madrid, 1926), Fernando Fe (Madrid), 1926.
Juan de Manara (produced in Madrid, 1927), Espasa-Calpe, 1927.
Las adelfas (produced in Madrid, 1928), Farsa (Madrid), 1928.
La Lola se va a los puertos (produced in Madrid, 1929; title means "La Lola Goes Off to Sea"), Farsa, 1929.
La duquesa de Benameji (produced in Madrid, 1932), Farsa, 1932.
Teatro completo, two volumes, C.I.A.P. (Madrid), 1932.
La duquesa de Benameji, La prima Fernanda, y Juan de Manara (*La prima Fernanda* produced in Madrid, 1931), Espasa-Calpe (Buenos Aires, Argentina), 1942 (also see above).
Las adelfas, y El hombre que murio en la guerra (*El hombre que murio de la guerra* produced in Madrid, 1941), Espasa-Calpe (Buenos Aires), 1947 (also see above).
Obras completas, Plenitud (Madrid), 1947.

OTHER

Paginas escogidas, Calleja (Madrid), 1917, revised and enlarged edition, 1925.
Poesias completas (poetry), Residencia de Estudiantes (Madrid), 1917, revised and enlarged edition, Espasa-Calpe (Madrid), 1928, new revised and enlarged edition, 1933, new enlarged edition, 1936, new enlarged edition, 1965, new enlarged edition, 1970.
Nuevas canciones (poetry; title means "New Songs"), Mundo Latino (Madrid), 1924.
De un cancionero apocrifo (poetry; title means "From an Apocryphal Songbook"), Revista de Occidente (Madrid), 1926.
Juan de Mairena: Sentencias, donaires, apuntes y recuerdos de un professor apocrifo (title means "Juan de Mairena: Maxims, Witticisms, Notes, and Remembrances of an Apocryphal Professor"), Espasa-Calpe, 1936, enlarged edition, two volumes, Losada (Buenos Aires), 1943.
La guerra, Espasa-Calpe, 1937.

Obras, Seneca (Mexico City, Mexico), 1940.
Abel Martin: Cancionero de Juan de Mairena. Poesias varias, Losada (Buenos Aires), 1943.
Anthologia de guerra, [Havana, Cuba], 1944.
Obra poetica, Pleamar (Buenos Aires), 1944.
Poesias escogidas, Aguilar (Madrid), 1947, revised and enlarged edition, 1958.
Los complementarios, y otras prosas postumas, edited by Guillermo de Torre, Losada, 1957.
Poesie de Antonio Machado, edited by Oreste Macri, Balcone (Milan), 1959.
Obras, poesia y prosa, edited by Guillermo de Torre and Auroro de Albornoz, Losada, 1964.
Antonio Machado: Antologia de su prosa, four volumes, edited by Auroro de Albornoz, Cuadernos para el Dialogo (Madrid), 1970-72.
Yo voy sonando caminos, Labor (Barcelona), 1981.
Proyecto del discurso de ingreso en la Real Academia de la Lengua, Observatorio (Madrid), 1986.

Contributor to periodicals, including *Hora de Espana* and *La Caricatura.*

SIDELIGHTS: Antonio Machado ranks among Spain's greatest twentieth-century poets. He was born in 1875 in Palacio de las Duenas on his family's country estate. When he was still a child, Machado moved with his family to Madrid, where his father had obtained a professorship. After Machado's father died suddenly in 1893, the family fell from financial security. Machado and his brother Manuel turned to writing and acting and circulated among fellow bohemians, including poets Ruben Dario and Juan Ramon Jiminez. In 1899 the brothers traveled to Paris and found work as translators at Garnier publishers. While in Paris Machado met the Irish writer Oscar Wilde.

By the early 1900s Machado had begun writing poetry. In 1902 he collected his verse in *Soledades: Poesias,* which reveals his inclination for the reflective and the spiritual. Five years later Machado published an enlarged version, *Soledades, galerias y otros poemas* (published in English as *Solitudes, Galleries, and Other Poems*). This collection features more poems that Carl W. Cobb, writing in the *Dictionary of Literary Biography,* described as having "spiritual and ethical emphasis." Cobb added that in these poems "Machado establishes himself as . . . a poet of temporality" and "a poet of time and memory." Notable among these poems are "Anoche cuando dormia" ("Last Night as I Lay Sleeping"), a mystical work replete with symbolism and Christian imagery, and the self-reflective "Leyendo un claro dia" ("Reading a Clear Day"), wherein he relates the discovery of his true destiny as a poet. Cobb wrote: "In these symbols of his soul he discovers the value of moral labor and the inevitability of human pain. Now he will dedicate himself to labor rather than mere song; he will work with the old griefs. First he must descend into the darkness of the soul, then he must emphasize his ethical and spiritual nature."

After completing the *Soledades* volumes, Machado assumed a teaching position in Soria, Spain, where he eventually married. He taught there until 1911, when he received a fellowship enabling him to study in Paris. While traveling, Machado's wife fell ill with tuberculosis and died. Machado thereupon returned to Spain and obtained a teaching post in Andalusia.

In 1912 Machado published another major poetry collection, *Campos de Castilla* (published in English as *The Castilian Camp*), in which he considers the fate of Spain and contemplates his late wife. As Cobb noted, "All the poems in *Campos de Castilla* look outward, toward the history and landscape of Spain, literary friends, and Machado's wife." The volume divides into three sections: the first portion regards the Spanish land and people; the central section recalls Soria, where he had met his wife; the concluding portion expresses his love for his late wife. Cobb observed in the *Dictionary of Literary Biography* that "*Campos de Castilla* has become a minor classic that expresses the hard and bitter aspects of the Spanish land and character and yet somehow suggests an enduring hope."

Machado continued to develop as a poet while he belatedly pursued collegiate study in Madrid. After graduating from the university there in 1918, he found work as a teacher in nearby Segovia. By this time Machado was actually considered a poet who was in decline, but in 1924 he produced the personal, yet philosophical, collection *Nuevas canciones* ("New Songs"), where he again recalls his late wife. This volume, however, also includes a section in which Machado expresses his love for another woman. These passionate poems signify that Machado was not yet a spent artist.

During the 1920s Machado also became involved with the theatre, and he collaborated with his brother on several works that realized production in Madrid. In addition, he published another verse collection, *De un cancionero apocrifo* ("From an Apocryphal Songbook"), wherein he proclaims his rejuvenation and passion through various guises, including both a philosopher and the philosopher's biographer. Writing in

Antonio Machado, Cobb explained, "Machado's reasons for creating this profusion of *personae* are fairly clear. He showed reluctance when it came to presenting philosophy under his own name, since he lacked systematic training in this discipline."

Machado revived Juan de Mairena, the biographer from *De un cancionero apocrifo,* in *Juan de Mairena: Sentencias, donaires, apuntes y recuerdos de un professor apocrifo* ("Juan de Mairena: Maxims, Witticisms, Notes, and Remembrances of an Apocryphal Professor"), a 1936 publication—posthumously reprinted as two volumes in 1943—in which Machado considers various elements of Spanish culture. Mairena is portrayed as an inspiring teacher who conducts freewheeling examinations of subjects ranging from Kantian philosophy to bullfighting, and from poetry to communism. As Kessel Schwartz acknowledged in the *Encyclopedia of World Literature in the Twentieth Century,* Mairena "examines the problems of existence and death" and explores "literature, truth, liberty, politics, language and philosophic works."

When Spain erupted in civil war in 1936, Machado initially remained in Madrid. But in 1939, as the country further degenerated into violence, Machado fled with his mother to Paris. During the journey, however, he developed pneumonia, and he died in Collioure, a fishing village on the coast of the Mediterranean Sea.

BIOGRAPHICAL/CRITICAL SOURCES:

BOOKS

Cobb, Carl W., *Antonio Machado,* Twayne, 1971.
Dictionary of Literary Biography, Volume 108: *Twentieth-Century Spanish Poets,* First Series, Gale, 1991, pp. 223-241.
Encyclopedia of World Literature in the Twentieth Century, third edition, Volume 3: *L-R,* St. James Press, 1999, pp. 146-147.
Hutman, Norma L., *Machado: A Dialogue with Time,* University of New Mexico Press, 1969.
Trend, J. B., *Antonio Machado,* Dolphin, 1953.
Young, Howard T., *The Victorious Expression: A Study of Four Contemporary Spanish Poets,* University of Wisconsin Press, 1964, pp. 33-73.

PERIODICALS

Hispania, May, 1965, pp. 247-254.
Poetry, February, 1963, pp. 343-345.
Romance Notes, spring, 1961, pp. 149-153.
Symposium, summer, 1965, pp. 162-170.

MARIAS, Javier 1951-

PERSONAL: Born in 1951, in Madrid, Spain.

ADDRESSES: Agent—c/o Harcourt Brace and Co., 525 B St., Suite 1900, San Diego, CA 92101-4495; c/o Harvill, HarperCollins, 10 East 53rd St., New York, NY 10022-5299.

CAREER: Writer and translator.

AWARDS, HONORS: National Translation Prize, Spain, 1979, for the translation of Laurence Sterne's *Tristram Shandy;* Herralde Prize for fiction, 1986, for *El Hombre Sentimental;* IX Premio Internacional De Novela Romulo Gallagos, 1995, for *Manana en la Batalla Piensa en Mi;* Prix Femina du Meilleur Livre Etranger for best foreign book (France), 1996, for *Tomorrow in the Battle Think on Me;* IMPAC Dublin Literary Award, 1997, for *A Heart So White.*

WRITINGS:

Los Dominios del Lobo, 1971.
Travesia del Horizonte, 1973, Editorial Anagrama (Barcelona), 1988.
(With Felix de Azua and Vicente Molina-Foix) *Tres Cuentos Didacticos* (short stories), La Gaya Ciencia (Barcelona), 1975.
El Monarca del Tiempo, Alfaguara (Madrid), 1978.
El Siglo, Seix Barral (Barcelona), 1983.
El Hombre Sentimental, Editorial Anagrama (Barcelona), 1986.
Todas las Almas, Anagrama (Barcelona), 1989, translation by Margaret Jull Costa published as *All Souls,* HarperCollins (New York City), 1992, Harvill (New York City/London), 1996.
Mientras Ellas Duermen, Anagrama (Barcelona), 1990.
Pasiones Pasadas, Editorial Anagrama (Barcelona), 1991.
Corazon Tan Blanco, Editorial Anagrama (Barcelona), 1992, translation by Margaret Jull Costa published as *A Heart So White,* Harvill, 1995 (New York City/London), VHPS, 1997.
Vidas Escritas, Ediciones Siruela (Madrid), 1992.
Vida del Fantasma: Entusiasmos, Bromas, Reminiscencias y Canones Recortados, El Pais/Aguilar (Madrid), 1995.
Literatura y Fantasma, Ediciones Siruela (Madrid), 1993.
Manana en la Batalla Piensa en Mi, Anagrama (Barcelona), 1994, translation by Margaret Jull Costa published as *Tomorrow in the Battle Think on Me,* Harcourt Brace (San Diego, CA), 1997.

Also translator of classic English novels into Spanish, including works by Laurence Stern, Joseph Conrad, Robert Louis Stevenson, Thomas Hardy, and W. B. Yeats.

SIDELIGHTS: Javier Marias began writing fiction in 1971 at age twenty. In addition, he has translated many English classics into Spanish, including the works of Thomas Hardy, Robert Louis Stevenson, Joseph Conrad, W. B. Yeats, and Laurence Sterne. One of his earlier novels, *El siglo,* is a story about destiny in which a father tells his son, Casaldaliga, to seek his own destiny, but the boy learns that his father has not followed his own advice. James H. Abbott, writing in *World Literature Today,* compared the "theme of chance or coincidence," which he said was "treated capriciously" in Marias's 1971 novel, *Los dominios del lobo,* to the more "analytical perspective" of *El siglo.* Rather than follow the events of Casaldaliga's life as they occur, Marias "chooses instead the development of the protagonist's character . . . [and] search for personal destiny." The question is whether choice of destiny is possible. Abbott commented that the author "structures *El siglo* with perfect balance. . . . lyrical passages. . . . [and] A sense of passing time related to *El Siglo* which becomes not only Casaldaliga's time but life and the world in which the reader also lives."

Ignacio-Javier Lopez, writing in *World Literature Today,* noted that Marias was one of the young Spanish novelists who followed the lead of Juan Benet, who refused to use his work as a forum for political or social commentary. Instead the new writers focus on topics not covered in recent decades, notably the topic of love. Lopez said that Marias' *El hombre sentimental* is an example of "love viewed ironically and without taking the characters' passionate declarations seriously."

Todas las almas (*All Souls*) is a novel based on Marias' two and a half years as a lecturer in Spanish literature at Oxford University and his romance with a married colleague. The characters include professors, whom Michael Kerrigan, reviewing the translated version of the novel in *Times Literary Supplement,* calls "Perfect, idealized forms in their university setting . . . haunted by the prospect of decay. . . . Uncomfortably aware of their own insignificance. . . . Authors immortal yet unread . . . mute testimony to the provisional nature of literary distinction." Juan J. Liebana, in *World Literature Today,* called Marias's novel "a book of memories, or perhaps a belated journal. . . . A stage of his life in which he rather felt alienated from his surroundings, more the observer than the participant." Liebana wrote that *Todas las almas* is "a unique book in many ways and is full of pleasant surprises that confirm Marias's literary craft." Guy Mannes-Abbot, writing in *New Statesman,* called *All Souls* a "circuitous encounter with the English, their language and their quintessential institution. . . . Narrator and reader become engaged in metaphorical detective work to uncover a culture. . . . There is a swirl of masterfully choreographed narrative leaps."

Corazon tan blanco (A Heart So White) is a story narrated in the first person. Juan, newly married at thirty-four, is fearful for his marriage because of the circumstances of the death of his father's first wife, also his mother's sister. At the outset of the novel his aunt Teresa commits suicide after one week of marriage to his father Ranz, and Juan feels a sense of impending doom. His wife Luisa elicits the truth about the suicide from Ranz, and Juan finds parallels between the events of the past and scenes he has observed in his own life. These include the blackmail of a married man by his lover while Juan is in Havana and a crippled woman who looks to personal ads for companionship while in New York City. A reviewer for *Kirkus Reviews* noted that the title and epigraph "allude openly to Macbeth's murder of Duncan, and its sinister burden of simultaneous cumulative revelation and deepening mystery. . . . The flawed, truncated nature of all human contact and efforts to reach it has rarely been given such remorseless stress." A reviewer for *Publishers Weekly* characterized the novel's tone as similar to foreplay and said that Marias' characters "tease each other—as the author teases the reader—with nibbles of information, half-divulged stories . . . to arouse a reader's curiosity the way an interrupted caress can awaken a lover's desire." Ricardo Landeira, in *World Literature Today,* called the book "truly original, intriguing, and elegantly written."

Marias' novel *Manana en la batalla piensa en mi* (*Tomorrow in the Battle Think on Me*) received the 1995 Romulo Gallagos Award, the Hispanic-American equivalent of the Nobel Prize for Literature. Judge Julio Ortega of Peru said the novel had won the award "for its philosophical concept and great narrative spirit, with innovative language which does not make the writing heavy-handed." In this story, Victor, a scriptwriter in Madrid, is having an affair with Marta, a married woman. While they are together, she dies, and Victor is faced with associated problems. A reviewer for *Kirkus Reviews* said the novel

"spins off into amusingly unpredictable directions." "Sometimes he strikes a note of genuine pathos, but just as often his musings, with their repetitions and long, long run-on sentences, become tiresome," wrote a reviewer in *Publishers Weekly.* Lisa Rohrbaugh commented in *Library Journal,* "Eventually, Victor and Marta's husband share their secrets of dealing with wives and lovers in a climactic ending."

BIOGRAPHICAL/CRITICAL SOURCES:

PERIODICALS

Booklist, November 1, 1996, p. 482; October 15, 1997, p. 389.
Hispania, summer, 1993, p. 492; March, 1996, p. 84.
Kirkus Reviews, January 1, 1996, p. 18; November 1, 1996, p. 1558; September 1, 1997, p. 1332.
Library Journal, August, 1997, p. 132.
London Review of Books, April 24, 1997, p. 13.
New Yorker, April 15, 1996, p. 92.
New Statesman & Society, October 9, 1992, p. 35; July 28, 1995, p. 38.
Observer, November 1, 1992, p. 62; November 15, 1992, p. 64; November 10, 1996, p. 18.
Publishers Weekly, January 8, 1996, p. 59; July 21, 1997, p. 180.
Times Literary Supplement, October 6, 1989, p. 19; November 6, 1992, p. 21; November 15, 1996, p. 24.
Tribune Books (Chicago), January 12, 1997, p. 2.
Washington Post Book World, July 7, 1996, p. 6.
World Literature Today, spring, 1984, p. 242; autumn, 1988, p. 635; winter, 1991, p. 86; autumn, 1993, p. 783.

OTHER

Amazon.com, http://www.amazon.com (1998).
Barnes and Noble, http://www.barnesandnoble.com (1998).
International IMPAC Dublin Literary Award 1997, http://ireland.iol.ie/dubcitylib/win97.htm (1998).*

* * *

MARQUES, Rene 1919-1979

PERSONAL: Born October 4, 1919, in Arecibo, Puerto Rico; died March 22, 1979, in San Juan, Puerto Rico; son of Juan and Pura (Garcia) Marques;

married Serena Velasco (divorced, 1957); children: Raul Ferando, Brunhilda Maria, Rene Francisco. *Education:* Graduated from College of Agriculture and Mechanical Arts; attended Columbia University.

CAREER: Writer. Agronomist for Department of Agriculture, 1943-46; manager of department store, 1946-49; *Diario de Puerto Rico* (newspaper), San Juan, Puerto Rico, journalist, 1949-50; chief of editorial section of Division of Community Education for Puerto Rico, 1950-69. Visiting instructor at University of Puerto Rico.

AWARDS, HONORS: Guggenheim scholarship; grant from Rockefeller Foundation; Ateneo awards, 1949, 1958, and 1962; prize from Puerto Rican Atheneum, 1952, for story "The Fear"; Iberian-American prize from the William Faulkner Foundation, 1962, for *La vispera del hombre;* honorable mention in Casa de las Americas literary contest, 1962, for drama *Carnaval afuera, carnaval adentro;* Diplo Trophy, 1970; diploma of honor from Institute of Puerto Rican Culture, 1979, for contribution to Puerto Rican culture.

WRITINGS:

Peregrinacion (verse), Arecibo, 1944.

Otro dia nuestro (story), [Puerto Rico], 1955.

Juan Bobo y la dama de occidente: Pantomina puertorriquena para un ballet occidental, Los Presentes, 1956, 2nd edition, Editorial Antillana, 1971.

(Editor and author of introduction) *Cuentoe puertorriquenos de hoy* (short stories), Club del libro de Puerto Rico, 1959, 3rd edition, Editorial Cultural, 1971.

La vispera del hombre (novel), Club del libro de Puerto Rico, 1959, 3rd edition, Editorial Cultural, 1972.

Teatro (plays; contains *Los soles truncos, Un nino azul para esa sombra,* and *La muerte no entrara en palacio*), Arrecife, 1959.

En una ciudad llamada San Juan, [Puerto Rico], 1960, 3rd edition, 1970.

La carreta (three-act play), Editorial Cultural, 1961, 5th edition, 1969, translation by Charles Pilditch published as *The Ox Cart,* Scribner (New York City), 1969.

La casa sin reloj: Comedia antipoetica en dos absurdos y un final razonable, Universidad Veracruzana, 1962.

Purification en la Calle del Cristo [and] *Los soles truncos* (the latter a two-act comedy), Editorial Cultural, 1963.

Mariana; o, El alba (three-act play), [Puerto Rico], 1965.

Al apartamiento (two-act play), Rumbos, 1966.

Ensayos, 1953-1966 (essays), Editorial Antillana, 1966, 2nd edition, 1972, translation by Barbara B. Aponte published as *The Docile Puerto Rican,* Temple University Press (Philadelphia), 1976.

El puertorriqueno docil, Editorial Antillana, 1967.

Sacrificio en el Monte Moriah (drama), Editorial Antillana, 1969.

David y Jonaton, Tito y Bernice: Dos dramas de amor, poder y desamor, Editorial Antillana, 1970.

Un nino azul para esa sombra (play), Editorial Cultural, 1970.

La muerte no entrara en palacio (two-act tragedy), Editorial Cultural, 1970.

Carnaval afuera, carnaval adentro, Editorial Antillana, 1971.

El hombre y sus suenos (play), Editorial Cultural, 1971.

El sol y los Mac Donald (play), Editorial Cultural, 1971.

Via crucis del hombre puertorriqueno (oratorio), Editorial Antillana, 1971.

Ese mosaico fresco sobre aquel mosaico antiguo, Editorial Cultural, 1975.

La mirada (novel), Editorial Antillana, 1975, translation by Charles Pilditch published as *The Look,* Senda Nueva de Ediciones (New York City), 1983.

Immersos en el silencio, Editorial Antillana, 1976.

Author of numerous dramas, including *Palm Sunday,* 1949, and *Los inocentes y la huida a Egipto,* 1956. Contributor to anthologies, including *Three Contemporary Latin-American Plays: Rene Marques, Egon Wolff, Emilio Carballido,* Xerox College Pub. (Waltham, MA), 1971.

EDITOR

Los derechos del hombre, Division de Educacion de la Communidad, 1957.

Ma mujer y sus derechos, Division de Educacion de la Communidad, 1957.

Juventud, Division de Educacion de la Communidad, 1958.

Cuatro cuentos de mujeres, Division de Educacion de la Communidad, 1959.

El cooperativismo y tu, Division de Educacion de la Communidad, 1960.

Las manos y el ingenio del hombre, Division de Educacion de la Communidad, 1966.

SIDELIGHTS: A prolific writer proficient in a variety of genres, Rene Marques was generally regarded as Puerto Rico's most prominent literary figure. He was associated with the Generation of the Forties, a group of distinguished Latin-American authors concerned with national aspirations. Although Marques wrote poetry, novels, essays, and several collections of short stories, he is best remembered for his signature dramas—*La carreta* (1953; English translation titled *The Ox Cart*), *Los soles truncos* (1958), and *Un nino azul para esa sombra* (1960), among others—in which he explored his native country's political and social problems. A technically accomplished playwright, Marques has also been noted for his stylistic excellence and psychological study of character. As Anibal Gonzalez has stated, "Marques raised the technical standards of each of the genres he cultivated, and he set the tone for much of the prose writing of his generation." His innovations and enthusiasm are seen by many commentators as a key force in the revitalization of Puerto Rican theater.

Born in Arecibo, Puerto Rico, Marques earned a college degree in agriculture and mechanical arts in 1942. Two years later he published *Peregrinacion,* a collection of poems that discusses a wide range of subjects including love, war, patriotism, and illusion versus reality. In 1944 Marques traveled to Madrid, where he studied Spanish literature and contemporary theater; while there, he also wrote his first play, *El hombre y sus suenos,* an allegorical work often compared to those of Golden Age dramatist Calderon de la Barca. When Marques returned to Puerto Rico in 1947 he founded the theater group Teatro Nuestro while working as a literary and drama critic for various newspapers and periodicals. The following year Marques was awarded a fellowship to study dramaturgy in the United States, touring experimental theaters in New York City, Washington, D.C., and Cleveland. Upon his return to San Juan in 1950, Marques established the Experimental Theater of the Atheneum, for which he produced his play *El sol y los MacDonald* (1950).

The 1950s proved to be a fruitful decade for Marques. In 1951 he wrote *La caretta,* which would prove to be his most popular work. The drama gained international critical recognition in 1953 when it premiered in Spanish in both New York City and San Juan. *La caretta* tells of a peasant family's migration from the Puerto Rican countryside, first to San Juan, then to the slums of New York City, searching for a better life they cannot find. Finally, the disillusioned group returns to their homeland. The drama reflected its author's deep concern about the effects of a government program called Operation Bootstrap, which he believed failed to consider the true needs of Puerto Rico and its people. During the 1950s Marques also wrote several other works that took a hard look at the suppression of Puerto Rican culture, in which he strongly endorsed political autonomy for the island. *Juan Bob y la Dama de Occident, Otro dia nuetro,* and *La muerte no entrara en palacio* all belong to this group.

After publishing his first collection of short stories, *Otro dia nuestro,* in 1955, Marques relocated to New York City and began the novel *La vispera del hombre,* a "coming of age" narrative set in Puerto Rico during the late 1930s. Marques eventually moved back to San Juan, where he accepted a position as a writer for a local radio station. During this time he composed several essays, notably *Pesimismo literario y optimismo politico: Su coexistencia en el Puerto Rico actual* (1959), in which he lamented the process of transculturation and called for the preservation of a distinctive Puerto Rican cultural identity. For the next two decades Marques continued to compose numerous award-winning plays, essays, and works of fiction. A lifelong supporter of Puerto Rican independence, he died in San Juan in 1979.

The most common theme in Marques's body of work is the search for Puerto Rican identity, and the cultural and political domination of Puerto Rico by its powerful protector, the United States. As Eleanor Martin wrote in her book *Rene Marques,* the author's "work is a mirror of his time; it is particularly a reflection of United States intervention in Puerto Rico's economy, culture, and politics since the turn of the century." The writer passionately believed that through his dramas and fiction, he could affect politics by raising public awareness and inciting the people to action. *Palm Sunday* (1956), for example, is a realistic presentation of tragic events which took place on Palm Sunday in 1937, when nationalists were massacred while demonstrating for Puerto Rican independence. Similarly, in *La muerta no entrara en palacio* (1959), Marques exposes the false claims and promises of Puerto Rican revolutionary leaders who, in his opinion, betrayed Puerto Rico to the United States and industrialization. *Los soles truncos,* like *La carreta,* examines the clash between the heritage of the past and the reality of the present as two wealthy sisters commit suicide rather than face a changing society, forfeiture of their ancestral home, and their younger sister's death. Widely regarded as Marques's finest play, *Un nino azul para esa sombra* draws attention to the precarious line between fantasy and reality. Here, an idealistic boy named Michelin, the son of a nationalistic Puerto Rican father and a materialistic, Americanized mother, grows progressively despondent and eventually kills himself, distraught over his inability to reconcile his parents' conflicting values. As Frank Dauster has explained, Michelin "is a symbol of a dying culture, of a people sacrificed to a civilization which is not their own, but he never ceases to be a particularly appealing figure, doubly so in his mixture of childish innocence and lost naivete."

Critics have described Marques's dramatic technique as sensationalistic and highly symbolic, especially in his handling of space and time. Each play's setting reflects the protagonist's state of mind. For example, in *Los soles truncos,* the dramatic action takes place in the Burkhart sisters' decaying family home: the dwelling—while serving as a shield from a materialistic society—simultaneously functions as a prison that prevents the siblings from realizing their creative potential. Space is equally important in *La carreta.* Here, Marques accentuates a family crisis by contrasting the integrated, tranquil life of the country—represented by the sound of an oxcart—with the fragmented, agitated existence of the city—symbolized by the roaring of a jackhammer.

Time also figures prominently in several of Marques's plays. In *El sol y los MacDonald,* for instance, the dramatist shows how the bigotry, prejudice, and degeneracy of past generations coincides with a family's present incestuous dilemma. Similarly, in *Un nino azul para esa sombra,* Marques makes extensive use of flashback and daydream sequences, effectively demonstrating how past, present, and future coexist within the human mind. The chopping down of an old tree also becomes a complex metaphor in the play: its demise represents Puerto Rico's social decline which, in Marques's opinion, resulted from the nation's abandonment of its cultural identity.

Until the 1960s Marques was virtually unknown outside of Puerto Rico; since then, his plays have been produced throughout North America and Europe and his work has engendered considerable critical discussion. In 1976 Charles Pilditch published *Rene Marques: A Study of His Fiction,* the first full-length discussion of the author's theater, novels, and short stories. Following his lead, recent commentators, like Eleanor J. Martin and Bonnie Hildebrand Reynolds, have explored a wide range of issues, including Marques's

impact on the political and social conscience of Puerto Rico, his experimentation with space and time, and his preoccupation with the themes of guilt and sacrifice. Many have also drawn attention to his technical innovations like the use of the flashback, integrated offstage machinations, and extensive reliance on lighting for dramatic purposes. While some scholars have criticized Marques's plays for being somewhat melodramatic and too symbolically complex and have found his agrarian and patriarchal ideology outdated, they universally praise Marques's use of the theater as a forum for giving immediate and striking voice to the concerns of the Puerto Rican community.

BIOGRAPHICAL/CRITICAL SOURCES:

BOOKS

Contemporary Literary Criticism, Volume 96, Gale (Detroit), 1997.
International Dictionary of the Theatre, Volume 2: *Playwrights,* St. James Press (Detroit), 1994.
Lyday, Leon F., and George W. Woodyard, editors, *Dramatists in Revolt: The New Latin American Theater,* University of Texas Press (Austin), 1976.
Martin, Eleanor J., *Rene Marques,* Twayne (Boston), 1979.
Pilditch, C. R., *Rene Marques: A Study of His Fiction,* Plus Ultra Educational, 1977.
Reynolds, Bonnie Hildebrand, *Space, Times, and Crisis: The Theatre of Rene Marques,* Spanish Literature Pub. (York, SC), 1988.

PERIODICALS

Critica hispanica, Volume VII, number 1, 1985, pp. 75-83.
Hispania, September, 1960, pp. 451-452; May, 1982, pp. 187-193.
Latin American Literary Review, spring-summer, 1980, pp. 196-212; fall, 1983, pp. 37-45.
Latin American Theatre Review, fall, 1968, pp. 31-38; 7, 1974; spring, 1976, pp. 21-30; fall, 1992, pp. 43-53.
Nation, December 25, 1976, pp. 696-698.
New York Times, March 25, 1979, p. 34; May 26, 1983.
Revista Chicano-Riquena, fall-winter, 1983, pp. 169-176.
Symposium, spring, 1964, pp. 35-45.
Theater, summer, 1978, pp. 75-81.
World Literature Today, winter, 1977, p. 72.

OBITUARIES:

PERIODICALS

New York Times, March 25, 1979.*

*   *   *

MARTELL, Aimee
  See THURLO, Aimee

*   *   *

MARTI (y PEREZ), Jose (Julian) 1853-1895

PERSONAL: Born January 28, 1853, in Havana, Cuba; died in battle on May 19, 1895, in Dos Rios, Oriente Province, Cuba; son of Don Mariano Marti y Navarro; married Carmen Zayas Bazan; children: a son. *Education:* Received bachelor's degrees in philosophy and law from University of Zaragoza, Spain, 1874.

CAREER: Essayist, poet, and patriot, leader of the Cuban independence movement. *Military service:* Led the struggle for Cuban independence in the late 1800s.

WRITINGS:

El presidio politico en Cuba (title means "Political Prison in Cuba"), Ramon Ramirez, 1871.
Ismaelillo (poems; title means "Little Ismael"), Farrar, Straus & Giroux (New York City), 1882.
Edad de oro (title means "Golden Age"), privately printed, 1889.
Versos sencillos (poems; title means "Plain Verses"), Farrar, Straus & Giroux, 1891, translation by Manuel Tellechea, Arte Publico (Houston, TX), 1997.
Obras Completas (title means "Complete Works"), Editorial Nacional de Cuba, 1963.
Our America: Writings on Latin American and the Struggle for Independence, Monthly Review Press (New York City), 1977.

Also author of *Nuestra America,* 1891; *Simon Bolivar,* 1893; *Versos libres* (poems), 1913; and *Diario de Cabo Haitiano a Dos Rios,* 1941.

SIDELIGHTS: Considered one of the greatest writers of Spanish America, and a leader of the Cuban struggle for independence from Spain, Jose Marti was as well known for his writing as for his political activism, and often one of these interests fueled the other. A prolific writer, he produced many essays and poems on current events in Cuba, such as the conditions in Cuban jails, the state of the movement against Spain, and conditions in other Latin-American countries. His essays and speeches motivated many to take part in Cuba's successful rebellion against Spain in the late 1800s, earning him both international acclaim and a position as a revered leader in Cuban history.

Marti was born in Havana, Cuba, on January 28, 1853. His father, Don Mariano Marti y Navarro, had recently immigrated to Cuba from Spain, and although he had worked for the Royal Artillery Corps in Spain, he had difficulty finding work in Cuba. As a young boy, Marti worked to help provide for his mother and five sisters. A mentor, Rafael Mari de Mendive, sent Marti to school at the Instituto de Segunda Ensenanza de la Havana. At school, Marti became aware that Cuba was divided by class and by political alliances; the rich, who benefited from Spanish rule, did not want Cuba to become independent, whereas the poor, as well as the intellectuals, were in favor of Cuba becoming a separate country.

When Marti was sixteen, his first published poem appeared in the newspaper *La Patria Libre* (The Free Fatherland). The poem was a patriotic story of a man who dies defending his country, and its nationalism proved to readers that Marti was a young, bold separatist. Marti and a classmate, Fermin Valdez Dominguez, were arrested and found with separatist writings on their persons, were tried for being separatists. As the trial began, Marti stated that Cuba had a right to its own government and sovereignty, and that it should be independent from Spain. For this, he was sentenced to six years in prison. He served at hard labor for a year, and then, after his parents begged the authorities for leniency, was exiled to Spain.

After arriving in Spain in 1871, Marti attended to the University of Zaragoza, and earned bachelor's degrees in philosophy and law in 1874. While at the university, he published excerpts from his first book, *El presidio politico en Cuba,* a testimony about political prison in Cuba. The book revealed his intense belief in the independence of Cuba, as well as his vivid imagery and flowing style. In 1875 Marti went to Mexico and was reunited with his family. By this time, he was well known as a strong voice in favor of Cuban freedom, and while in Mexico, he wrote for *Revista Universal* ("Universal Magazine"), a liberal publication, and participated in gatherings of intellectuals. However, his movement in Mexican society was cut short when dictator Porfirio Diaz overthrew the liberal government of Sebastian Lerdo de Tejada. The new regime was not friendly to intellectuals, so in 1877 Marti left Mexico and went to Guatemala. He then returned briefly to Cuba, then to Mexico, and then went back to Guatemala. While in Mexico, he had met and married Carmen Zayas Bazan, who was also a Cuban exile. Marti found enthusiastic followers in Guatemala, where the poor people were especially receptive to his causes, such as abolition of slavery and equal representation for all. But just as in Cuba, the ruling classes were threatened by him, and in 1878 he was forced to leave.

After wandering in Europe for the next several years, Marti went to New York City in 1881. From New York, he worked for Cuban resistance, wrote essays on the future of the Americas, and refined the political views that would shape the Partido Revolucionario Cubano or Cuban Revolutionary Party, which eventually would make Cuba an independent country. In 1890 Marti and Rafael Serra, also an exile, founded La Liga ("the League") in New York City. Members of this party were generally poor, black exiles from Cuba, since Marti believed that the poor should lead the revolution. In addition, the League held classes, workshops, and lectures intended to give members a sense of their Cuban identity and to educate them about the struggle for independence.

In 1881 Marti spoke to exiles in Florida and earned an even stronger following there. In November of 1881, he wrote the Tampa Resolutions, a plan for the rebellion that began three years later. There were four main points in the Resolutions: first, that all Cuban exiles should unite; second, that the goal of rebellion should be the installation of a popular government that was chosen by popular vote; third, that the revolution was intended to express the views and answer the needs of the majority, and that the new republic of Cuba would serve the majority of the people, not a minority; and fourth, that the revolutionary party would respect the mandates and sovereignty of the exile organizations. Marti, through his skill as an orator and writer, built a coalition of all the exile organizations, and in 1892, El Partido Revolucionario Cubano was formed. Two views that helped Marti create the coalition were his anti-racist stand (since one-third of Cubans were of African descent) and his warnings not to succumb to imperialism by the United States. Although he admired the United States, he was fearful of its power and influence on the smaller and poorer Latin American countries. Marti envisioned reforms that would help keep Cuba independent, such as diversifying its economy, land reform, redistribution of wealthy, and avoiding the danger of substituting American rule for Spanish rule.

In 1892 Marti returned to New York City to undertake the same coalition-building he had undertaken in Florida. His work there was successful, and by 1894 he was ready to begin the revolution. Fighters gathered and set out in three boats toward Cuba, but unfortunately were intercepted by U.S. authorities before they reached shore. Undaunted, Marti simply set another day for the transport, and arranged for forces in Cuba to start the revolution on February 24, 1895. On April 20, Marti and his insurgents joined the war in Cuba, and he died in battle against Spanish soldiers on May 19, 1895, in Dos Rios, Oriente Province, after disregarding General Maximo Gomez's order to retreat. His work and legacy lived on, however, and in September of that year the successful revolutionaries met to set up a provisional government for a new, free, and democratic Cuba.

BIOGRAPHICAL/CRITICAL SOURCES:

BOOKS

Adams, Jerome R., *Liberators and Patriots of Latin America,* McFarland, 1991.

Perez, Louis A., Jr., *Cuba Between Reform and Revolution,* Oxford University Press (New York City), 1988.

Perez, Louis A., Jr., *Cuba and the United States: Ties of Singular Intimacy,* University of Georgia Press, 1990.

PERIODICALS

Americas Review, spring-summer, 1994, p. 148.

School Library Journal, February, 1994, p. 130; November, 1997, p. 137.*

*   *   *

MARTINEZ, Elizabeth Coonrod 1954-

PERSONAL: Born June 3, 1954, in Austin, TX; daughter of Holmes T. "Bill" Coonrod and Phyllis

Berry Gaxiola. *Education:* Portland State University, B.A. (English), 1983; New York University, M.A. (Hispanic civilization), 1991; University of New Mexico, Ph.D. (Latin America literature), 1995.

ADDRESSES: Office—Department of Foreign Languages, Sonoma State University, 1810 East Cotati St., Rohnert Park, CA 94928.

CAREER: Woodburn Independent, Journalist. Woodburn, OR, reporter and photographer, 1983-84; *The Oregonian,* Portland, OR, general assignment reporter, 1984-86; *New Haven Independent,* New Haven, CT, reporter and assistant editor, 1986-89; *Albuquerque Monthly Magazine,* Albuquerque, NM, managing editor, 1989; KLUZ-TV (Univision), Albuquerque, news director and anchor, 1989-91; University of New Mexico, Albuquerque, teaching associate, 1991-93, journalism instructor and workshop coordinator, 1992-94, instructor in Spanish, 1993-95, assistant director and instructor for study abroad program in Xalapa, Mexico, 1993; executive director for the American Library Association, 1994-1997; Sonoma State University, Rohnert Park, CA, assistant professor of foreign languages, 1995—. Member and chair of media committee, HIV-Prevention Community Awareness Task Force, University of New Mexico Hospital, Albuquerque, 1990-91; member, Centennial Celebrations Public Relations Committee, University of New Mexico, 1991; member of conferences and committees at University of New Mexico; panelist at workshops. Former leader of the Student Nonviolent Coordinating Committee (SNCC).

MEMBER: Modern Language Association of America, American Association of University Women, American Association of Teachers of Spanish and Portuguese, Latin American Studies Association, Rocky Mountain Modern Languages Association, Southwest Writers Workshop, New Mexico Organization of Language Educators.

AWARDS, HONORS: Sammy Award, *The Portland Oregonian,* 1986, for news story; "Best Editorial Column" and "News Feature" awards, Connecticut Sigma Delta Chi Press Association, both 1986; Connecticut Public Service Award nomination, 1987; "Investigative Journalism" award, New England Press Association, 1987; first place opinion column, Connecticut Sigma Delta Chi Press Association, 1988; "Best Documentary" and "Best Newscast," KLUZ-TV (Albuquerque, NM), both 1989, and "Best Newscast," KLUZ-TV, 1990, all Associated Press Annual Broadcasting Awards; recipient of numerous educational

awards, fellowships, and grants, including a 1993-94 Challenge Assistantship fellowship from the University of New Mexico, a 1993 Latin America travel research grantee from University of New Mexico's Latin America Institute, and a 1995 teaching fellowship from the Poynter Institute.

WRITINGS:

"HISPANIC HERITAGE" SERIES; NONFICTION

Henry Cisneros: Mexican-American Leader, Millbrook Press (Brookfield, CT), 1993.
Edward James Olmos: Mexican-American Actor, Millbrook Press, 1994.
Sor Juana: A Trailblazing Thinker, Millbrook Press, 1994.

"COMING TO AMERICA" SERIES; NONFICTION

The Mexican American Experience, Millbrook Press, 1995.

TRANSLATOR

Clipper, Bolivar, and *Soliman* (three plays by Isaac Chocron), produced by Experimental Theatre Group, Department of Theatre and Arts, University of New Mexico, 1992.

Also translator of "Llanto," by Carmen Boullosa, in *Contemporary Mexican Short Stories: Writing for the Future,* University of New Mexico Press; *Lilus Kikus,* a novel by Elena Poniatowska, 1991; and essays in *The Origins of the Bolero School/Studies in Dance History,* and *On Faulkner,* an unpublished work.

OTHER

DeColores Means All of US: Latina Views for a Multi-Colored Century (essays), foreword by Angela Davis, South End Press, 1999.

Editor of *500 Years of Chicano History/500 Anos del Pueblo Chicano* (textbook). Contributor of essays to *Nuestras Mujeres: Hispanas of New Mexico, Their Images and Their Lives, 1582-1992,* El Norte Publications/Academia, 1993, and *Society for the Interdisciplinary Study of Social Imagery: Selected Papers,* University of Southern Colorado, 1994. Contributor of essays to periodicals, including *Christian Science Monitor* and *New York Times.* Contributor of scholarly articles to journals, including *Anuario de cine y literatura* and *Hispania.* Featured in the television series *Chicano! The History of the Mexican American Civil Rights Movement*'s first episode "The Search for a Homeland," broadcast on PBS.

WORK IN PROGRESS: A translation of a contemporary Mexican author's book; a book on the Latin American novel during the 1920s.

SIDELIGHTS: Elizabeth Coonrod Martinez—a journalist, university professor, and former executive director of the American Library Association—has a history of promoting the accomplishments and rights of minorities, particularly Chicanos and women. In *DeColores Means All of US: Latina Views for a Multi-Colored Century,* for example, Martinez "examines the consequences of a strictly black-white analysis of racism," according to *Progressive* contributor Demetria Martinez. Addressing the fact that Latinos—their struggles, activities, and impact on society—have been almost entirely excluded from American media coverage, even though as a minority group their numbers in the United States will soon surpass African Americans, "Martinez makes it clear that the future for progressives lies in forging coalitions across colors and causes," said the *Progressive* contributor. "Her straight talk, sharp humor, and formidable historical sensibilities are the lifeblood of this book," maintained the critic, proclaiming "I am hopeful . . . that minds might open with the publication of [this] marvelous collection of essays."

Martinez, herself a women of color, received considerable media attention for her three-year role as executive director of the American Library Association (ALA). Her term as executive director was uneasy; after her first twenty-three months she announced her resignation, then withdrew it, then left her position about a year later. In an interview printed in the September, 1997, issue of *American Libraries,* Martinez explained that as ALA executive director she accomplished what she had planned to, despite her shortened term. "I was asked by the search committee and the Executive Board to develop a national agenda and a national presence, to place ALA at the national information policy "table' to influence legislation, and to provide leadership and direction for the Association as it prepares for the 21st century. The record of my accomplishments will show that I exceeded expectations and fulfilled my duties as executive director exceedingly well, and in less than three years," stated Martinez. Her desire to leave her position was a result of many factors, including what Martinez described as "personal attacks . . . gossip . . . innuen-

does" and controversy over her compensation, which included a hundred thousand dollar retention bonus following her initial resignation. "I chose to leave ALA and continue my professional journey working with people and issues where I could make a positive contribution and enjoy support and success."

Martinez once noted: "I feel that my journalism and academic careers merge perfectly, for they are about writing, writing that will hopefully move at least one reader to new insights and reactions. Having grown up in Mexican culture, then transferring to U.S. culture as a teenager, made me acutely aware of differences in people that are fascinating but often unknown and misunderstood. I have sought to broaden awareness by my writing and publishing, whether as a newspaper reporter or more recently, in children's books on great Hispanic Latino historical figures. For example, how often can a Latina youngster read about great intellectual women of the seventeenth century? My book on Mexican poet Sor Juana [Ines de la Cruz] tells how a little girl's urge to read and know everything took her beyond the experiences of most women forbidden in their society to obtain a college education.

"In my academic work, again I seek to portray cultural identity, to open new avenues for those teaching Spanish. In my teaching, students enjoy learning about the dances, food items, politics, and news reports of the various Latin American regions and Spain. For example, stuffed corn dumplings are called *tamales* in Mexico, *pasteles* in Puerto Rico, and *arepas* in Colombia. And what do the different ways of holding a fan mean for the Spaniard? I plan to prepare a textbook that integrates these cultural items in an intermediate study of the Spanish language so that students can learn how life is *lived* by the various Spanish-speakers of the world."

BIOGRAPHICAL/CRITICAL SOURCES:

PERIODICALS

American Libraries, January, 1995, p. 17; August, 1996, p. 44; September, 1997, p. 66.
Booklist, January 1, 1995, p. 819.
Kirkus Reviews, November 1, 1993, p. 1394.
Library Journal, October 1, 1995, p. 38; August, 1996, p. 34; March 15, 1997, p. 14.
Progressive, May, 1997, p. 15; March, 1999, p. 44.
School Library Journal, April, 1994; January, 1995, p. 128; August, 1996, p. 27.*

MARTINEZ, Tomas Eloy

PERSONAL: Born in Argentina; immigrated to United States, 1975.

ADDRESSES: Office—105 George St., Douglass Campus, Rutgers University, New Brunswick, NJ 08903.

CAREER: Worked as professor of Latin–American literature at University of Maryland, College Park; journalist; writer; currently director of Latin–American program, Rutgers University.

WRITINGS:

La obra de Ayala y Torre Nilsson en las estructuras del cine argentino, Culturales Argentinas, Ministerio de Educacion y Justicia, Direccion General de Cultura, 1961.
Sagrado, Sudamericana, 1969.
La pasion segun Trelew, Granica, 1973.
Los testigos de afuera, M. Neumann, 1978.
Lugar comun la muerte, Monte Avila (Caracas), 1979.
(With Julio Aray and others) *Sadismo en la ensenanza,* Monte Avila, 1979.
La novela de Peron, translation by Asa Zatz published as *The Peron Novel,* Pantheon (New York City), 1987, translation by Helen Lane published as *The Peron Novel,* Vintage International (New York City), 1999.
La mano del amo, Planeta (Buenos Aires), 1991.
Santa Evita, English translation by Helen Lane, Knopf (New York City), 1996.
Las Memorias del General, Planeta (Buenos Aires), 1996.
La Pasion Segun Trelew, Planeta (Buenos Aires), 1997.

SIDELIGHTS: Argentine writer Tomas Eloy Martinez is the acclaimed author of *The Peron Novel,* a provocative blend of fact and fiction centering on Argentina's turbulent political history under the leadership of President Juan Domingo Peron. Peron rose to power in 1946, three years after the military overthrow of the Argentine government. But economic troubles led to his 1955 exile to Madrid and the restoration of civilian rule in Argentina. A decade later, however, the military government was reinstated, and in 1973, Peron reassumed power. Through a series of flashbacks comprising *The Peron Novel,* Martinez offers three varying perspectives on Peron: the president's own cloudy memoirs, his secretary Jose Lopez Rega's tainted version of events, and a journalist's report—based on interviews—spanning the president's childhood, his early career as an army officer, and his eventual fall from power. Furthermore, Martinez illuminates Peron's ambiguous nature: appealing to the conflicting political ideals of both right- and left-wing forces, the president fostered discord among his people and, after his death in 1974, left a legacy of violence and disorder in Argentina. Critics generally applauded *The Peron Novel* as a sharp and stunning portrait of an enigmatic man. Jay Cantor, writing in the *New York Times Book Review,* deemed the book "a brilliant image of a national psychosis."

Martinez continued his exploration of the Peron myth with *Santa Evita,* in which he mingled fact and fiction about Eva Peron, the wife of the Argentine dictator. Evita, as she was known, was arguably the most powerful woman in the world during her term as first lady. The illegitimate daughter of a provincial politician and a servant woman, she traveled to Buenos Aires as a teenager and pulled herself up by her bootstraps, becoming first a radio actress, then a minor screen star, and finally, as Peron's wife, a figure adored and reviled by various factions of the Argentine citizenry. She was notable for her fanatical speaking style, her childish grasp of politics, her insatiable hunger for power, and her erratic displays of generosity toward the lowest social classes. After her death from cancer at the age of thirty–three, she became a mythical figure to many Argentineans. Her impeccably embalmed body—along with several decoy copies of it—was shuffled around Argentina and even to Europe and back.

Santa Evita is really the story of Eva Peron's body—its indestructible nature, unbelievable journeys, and the powerful effect it had on the people who searched for and hid it. The book begins during the last days of Evita's life, then focuses on a military colonel's mission to find the real corpse and destroy it so that it can never be used as a rallying point by the remaining Peronists. "In the process, he and his men become obsessed by the body's magically hypnotic qualities, and their lives are unalterably changed. It is all a long way from the easy sentimentality of the Broadway musical. . . . This is . . . a captivating study of how magic and politics sometimes surrealistically merge," stated Sybil Steinberg of *Publishers Weekly.* Brad Hooper, a writer for *Booklist,* described *Santa Evita* as "a complex, challenging novel that lovers of Latin American fiction will applaud."

Not all reviewers were so enthusiastic. "It's a pity the novel isn't better," complained Michiko Kakutani in the *New York Times.* "Although Mr. Martinez's narrative is enlivened by some magical and highly perverse set pieces, though it possesses moments that genuinely illuminate the bizarre intersection of history, gossip and legend, the novel as a whole feels leaden and earthbound. In the end, it gives the reader neither a visceral sense of Evita's life nor an understanding of the powerful hold she has exerted on her country's imagination." Yet a *New York Times Book Review* contributor, Nicolas Shumway, extolled *Santa Evita* as "brilliant," and Martinez's insight as "bold and troubling." He found the books to be "a profound meditation on the nature and meaning of memory, the relationship between authors and subjects, and the anarchic drive of popular mythology. . . . A superb craftsman, Mr. Martinez moves through stories of Evita's life and death—and the peregrinations of her body—with a dazzling array of literary devices, including imagined interviews and memoirs, even fake screenplays. He himself plays a central role in the novel, as the obvious narrator and as a character who scrutinizes himself as he grapples with what it means to have come of age under Peronism."

Shumway concluded that Martinez's fictions of the Perons had earned him a prominent place in the literary world. "In recent years, few Latin American writers have confronted their countries' past with the wit, style and candor that Mr. Martinez shows in *Santa Evita* and its earlier companion piece, *The Peron Novel.* With these two books, he affirms his place among Latin America's best writers."

BIOGRAPHICAL/CRITICAL SOURCES:

PERIODICALS

Atlanta Journal-Constitution, October 27, 1996, p. L11.
Booklist, August, 1996, p. 1855.
Chicago Tribune, November 3, 1996, section 14, p. 3.
Christian Science Monitor, May 6, 1988, p. 20.
Hispania, March, 1971.
Library Journal, August, 1996, p. 113.
Nation, August 27, 1988, p. 173; October 28, 1996, pp. 50-52.
New York Times, September 20, 1996, p. C31.
New York Times Book Review, April 15, 1988; May 22, 1988, p. 16; July 30, 1995, section 1, p. 3; September 29, 1996, p. 27.
Publishers Weekly, July 29, 1996, pp. 70-71.
Village Voice, April 26, 1988, pp. 54, 56.
Wall Street Journal, November 14, 1996.
Washington Post, September 27, 1996, p. D2.*

MARTINEZ-FERNANDEZ, Luis 1960-

PERSONAL: Born January 14, 1960, in Havana, Cuba; son of Celestino Martinez (a photographer and retired executive) and Luisa Fernandez; married Margaret A. (a professor), 1984; children: Luis, Alberto, Andres. *Ethnicity:* "Hispanic." *Education:* University of Puerto Rico, B.A. (history; high honors), 1982; M.A. (history), 1985; Duke University, Ph.D. (history), 1990. *Politics:* Independent. *Religion:* Protestant. *Avocational interests:* Travel, reading.

ADDRESSES: Office—Department of Puerto Rican and Hispanic Caribbean Studies, Rutgers University, 235 Tillett Hall, 53 Ave. E, Piscataway, NJ 08854-8040. *E-mail*—lumartin@rci.rutgers.edu.

CAREER: Historian and writer. Augusta State University, Augusta, GA, assistant professor of Latin American, Caribbean, and United States history, 1990-92; Colgate University, Hamilton, NY, assistant professor of Latin American and Caribbean history, 1992-94; Rutgers University, Department of Puerto Rican and Hispanic Caribbean Studies, and Department of History, assistant professor, 1994-97, associate professor, 1997—, Department of Hispanic Caribbean and Latin American History, acting department chair, 1997-98, department chair, 1998—.

MEMBER: American Historical Association, Association of Caribbean Historians, Conference on Latin American History, Caribbean Studies Association, The Historical Society, Latin American Studies Association.

AWARDS, HONORS: J. B. Duke Fellowship, 1986-1988; Tinker Foundation International Travel Grant, 1987; American Historical Association Beveridge Travel Grant, 1988; National Hispanic Scholar, 1987, 1988; National Endowment for the Humanities Travel to Collections Grant, 1993; Colgate University Research Council Major Grant, 1993; Pew Evangelical Scholars Program Fellowship, 1994-95; Rutgers University Minority Faculty Development Grant, 1996-97; Rutgers University Research Council Grant, 1996-97; Rutgers University Board of Trustees Fellowship for Scholarly Excellence, 1997-98; has also received other awards, grants, and fellowships.

WRITINGS:

Torn Between Empires: Economy, Society, and Patterns of Political Thought in the Hispanic Caribbean, 1840-1878, University of Georgia Press (Athens), 1994.

Fighting Slavery in the Caribbean: The Life and Times of a British Family in Nineteenth-Century Havana, M. E. Sharpe (Armonk, NY), 1998.

Contributor of articles to periodicals, including *Magazine of History, Latin American Research Review, Caribbean Studies, Diplomatic History, New West Indian Guide, The Americas, Revista/Review Interamericana,* and *Cuban Studies, Slavery and Abolition,* as well as various anthologies.

WORK IN PROGRESS: Work on a book about religion and politics in the nineteenth–century Hispanic Caribbean; co-editing *Cuba: An Illustrated Encyclopedia,* for Oryx Press.

SIDELIGHTS: Luis Martinez-Fernandez has had a lifelong interest in the Hispanic countries of the Caribbean. He has researched and written extensively on the histories of Cuba, Puerto Rico, and the Dominican Republic, with emphasis on the nineteenth and twentieth centuries. He has also lived throughout Latin America; when he was two years old, he and his family left Havana, Cuba, as refugees fleeing from the communist regime of Fidel Castro, and came to the United States. They did not stay long; when Martinez-Fernandez's father accepted a management job with International Harvester in Peru, the family moved to Lima. In 1968 a military coup led them to move again, this time to San Juan, Puerto Rico. After completing his undergraduate education and receiving a masters degree in history at the University of Puerto Rico, he moved to the United States to pursue a Ph.D. in history at Duke University.

Published in 1994, *Torn between Empires: Economy, Society, and Patterns of Political Thought in the Hispanic Caribbean, 1840-1878* is a comparative study of the economy, society, and political culture of Cuba, Puerto Rico, and the Dominican Republic in the mid-nineteenth century. Martinez-Fernandez discusses changes in each country's balance of power and its relationship to changes in the countries' heritage of insularity, colonialism, and slavery. The book covers the years between 1840, when British consul and abolitionist David Turnbull arrived in Havana, to 1878, when the first Cuban war of independence from Spain ended. Avi Chomsky, reviewing *Torn between Empires* for *Americas,* remarked: "What is new in Martinez-Fernandez's account is the way he focuses his lens, moving easily from internal events in the United States to events in the three country/colonies of the Hispanic Caribbean . . . , to Spain, to Great Britain, and back again, showing the intricate links

between local and international events and ideas." *Journal of Latin American Studies* contributor Jean Stubbs responded favorably to *Torn Between Empires,* asserting: "For guiding us through the terrain of imperial rivalries still with us today, as well as on its own intrinsic merit, this is a book that should be on every Caribbean history reading list."

Martinez-Fernandez's 1998 book *Fighting Slavery in the Caribbean: The Life and Times of a British Family in Nineteenth-Century Havana* draws on diaries, letters, and other papers to tell the story of George and Grace Backhouse, a British couple who went to Cuba in the mid-1800s to serve on the Anglo-Spanish Havana Mixed Commission for the Suppression of the Slave Trade. Fighting slavery was an uphill battle at the time: most influential people in Cuba were strongly pro-slavery because the island's economy relied on slave labor. In addition to the difficulties of their anti-slavery struggle, the Backhouses were immersed in an unfamiliar culture and were often isolated and lonely. Through their story, the book shows the Cuban slave trade, its role in the sugar industry, and relations between races and genders on the island. Martinez-Fernandez told Michelle Adam in *Hispanic Outlook,* "I began to read [George and Grace Backhouse's] diaries, and I fell in love with this family. They had children like me. They faced a lot of the same issues." Later, he said, "His diary came to an end, and I opened an envelope. There were newspaper notices of his death. He had been killed in Cuba. From that day on, I knew I had to tell his story." Martinez-Fernandez also wrote the book because he is fascinated with Cuba's history. "I am convinced," he told Adam, "that in order to understand the current political situation of Cuba, you need to understand the nineteenth century when the political climate crystallized." And, he told Alberto Alvarez in the *Daily Targum,* "The lives of the Backhouses are like a window to the way life was lived in Cuba." Thomas Davis, in his review of *Fighting Slavery in the Caribbean* for *Library Journal,* called the volume an "elegant narrative" and a "fascinating peek into mid-19th-century Cuba." In a blurb for the cover of the book, Antonio Benitez-Rojo commented: "Martinez-Fernandez has the rare virtue of reconciling both the analytical incisiveness of a mature historian and the sweeping breath of an impassioned storyteller. His book is an indispensable source for readers interested in Carribean issues."

Martinez-Fernandez's research for the book helped him not only to understand the history of Cuba, but also to understand his own roots and personal history.

When he was thirty-four, he returned to Cuba for the first time to do research for the book. He told Adam, "I felt uncannily at home. The smells, people's accents, the skies, the architecture. It was almost as if I had never left." He visited his grandfather, and heard his entire family history for the first time. It was not until he went to Cuba, he told Adam, that he realized he was truly Cuban. Before then, the experience of emigration had marked him and his family with a sense of exile and rootlessness. "The experience of emigration becomes internalized within families," he told Adam. "It becomes a family pattern, which is painful in many ways."

Martinez-Fernandez once commented: "As is the case with most authors, I find pleasure in learning that readers enjoy my work and find it useful. Although I write about serious subjects, some of the most rewarding praise that my work has received is that it reflects a sense of humor. That is my advice to my students: 'Keep a sense of humor and enjoy what you do.'"

BIOGRAPHICAL/CRITICAL SOURCES:

PERIODICALS

Americas, July, 1996, pp. 174-175.
Daily Targum, April 24, 1998
Hispanic Outlook, October 9, 1998, p. 14.
Journal of Latin American Studies, February, 1996, pp. 266-270.
Library Journal, March 15, 1998, p. 82.
Rutgers Focus, February 13, 1998, p. 4.

*   *   *

MARZAN, Julio 1946-

PERSONAL: Born February 22, 1946, in Puerto Rico.

ADDRESSES: Home—175-20 Wexford Terrace, Jamaica Estates, NY 11432.

CAREER: Educator and author of nonfiction. Teacher of Spanish language and literature at New York University; State University of New York, State University College at Old Westbury; and Fordham University. Writer.

WRITINGS:

(Editor and author of introduction) *Inventing a Word: An Anthology of Twentieth-Century Puerto Rican Poetry,* Columbia University Press, 1980.
Translations Without Originals, I. Reed Books, 1986.
The Spanish American Roots of William Carlos Williams, foreword by David Ingatow, University of Texas Press (Austin, TX), 1994.
The Numinous Site: The Poetry of Luis Pales Matos, Fairleigh Dickinson University (Madison, NJ), 1995.
Puerta de tierra, Editorial de la Universidad de Puerto Rico (San Juan), 1998.

Also author of a play titled *When Is a Pigeon a Dove?*

BIOGRAPHICAL/CRITICAL SOURCES:

PERIODICALS

World Literature Today, spring, 1981.

*   *   *

MAYOR, Federico 1934-

PERSONAL: Born January 27, 1934, in Barcelona, Spain; married; children: three. *Education:* Complutense University of Madrid, Graduate in Pharmacy, 1956, Ph.D., 1958.

ADDRESSES: Agent—c/o Librairie Ernest Flammarion, 26 rue Racine, F-75278, Paris cedex 06, France.

CAREER: University of Granada, Granada, Spain, professor of biochemistry, 1963-73, director of Department of Pharmacy, 1967-68, rector, 1968-72, honorary rector, 1972—; Autonomous University of Madrid, Madrid, Spain, professor of biochemistry, 1973, founder of Severo Ochoa Molecular Biology Center, director, 1974-78; UNESCO, member of advisory committee for scientific research and human needs, Moscow, 1976, and Paris, 1977, member of advisory committee, European Center for Higher Education, Bucharest, Romania, 1976-78, representative of the director-general on the board of United Nations University, Tokyo, Japan, 1980-81; Spanish minister for education and science, 1981-82; Institute of the Sciences of Man, Madrid, director, 1983-87; UNESCO, director-general, 1987—. Oxford University, visiting professor and senior fellow of Trinity

College, 1966-67; Autonomous University of Madrid, scientific chairperson of Severo Ochoa Molecular Biology Center, 1983-87. Spanish Ministry for Education, under-secretary, 1974-75; Office of the Spanish Prime Minister, chairperson of Advisory Committee for Scientific and Technical Research, 1974-78; Royal Foundation of Spain for Special Education, member, 1976-78; Spanish Parliament, member of parliament and chairperson of Parliamentary Commission for Education and Science, 1977-78; European Parliament, member, 1987. Ramon Areces Foundation, vice chair of scientific committee, 1982—. Issyk-Kul Forum (Frunze, Kirghiz Republic), founding member, 1986—.

MEMBER: International Brain Research Organization, International Cell Research Organization, World Academy of Art and Science, World Science Institute, European Academy of Arts, Sciences, and Literature (founding member), Academia Europaea, Spanish Society of Biochemistry (chairperson, 1970-74), Spanish Royal Academy of Pharmacy, Royal Academy of Fine Arts of San Fernando, American Chemical Society, American Association for the Advancement of Science, American Academy of Microbiology, Biochemical Society (England), Royal Society of Chemistry (England), French Society of Biological Chemistry, French Academy of Pharmacy (corresponding member), Ateneo Veneto, Philippine Academy of Language, National Academy of Science of Bolivia, Argentinian Academy of Pharmacy and Biochemistry, Bulgarian Academy of Sciences, Chinese Academy of Sciences, Rumanian Academy, Club of Rome.

AWARDS, HONORS: Honorary doctorates.

WRITINGS:

(Translator) Strohecker and Henning, *Vitamin Assay,* Paz Montalvo, 1967.
(Editor with S. Grisolia and R. Baguena) *The Urea Cycle,* Wiley (New York), 1977.
(Editor) *Scientific Research and Goals: Towards a New Development Model,* Pergamon (Oxford, England), 1982.
(Editor) *La lucha contra la enfermedad,* Lilly (Madrid, Spain), 1986.
Manana siempre es tarde (essay), Espasa Calpe (Madrid), 1987, published as *Tomorrow Is Always Too Late,* Stamford Publishing (Singapore, China), 1992.
(Editor with Severo Ochoa and M. Barbacid) *Oncogenes y Patologia Molecular,* CEURA (Madrid), 1987.
Poeme, Editur Fundatiei Cultuale Romane, 1992.

Aguafuertes (poems), Litoral (Malaga, Spain), 1991, published as *Patterns,* Forest Books (London, England), 1994.
(Co-author) *The New Page* (essay), Dartmouth Publishing (Brookfield, VT), 1994.
La memoire de l'avenir (essay), UNESCO Publishers (Paris, France), 1994, published as *Memory of the Future,* 1995.
La Paix, Demain? (essay), Flammarion (Paris), 1995.
(With Augusto Forti) *Science and Power,* edited by Nigel Hawkes, preface by Ilya Prigogine, UNESCO (Paris), 1995.
(With Selma Tanguiane) *UNESCO—An Ideal in Action: The Continuing Relevance of a Visionary Text,* UNESCO (Paris), 1997.
Terral: 1990-1997, Circulo de Lectores (Barcelona), 1997.

Contributor to books, including *Reflections on Biochemistry,* edited by A. Kornberg, B. L. Horecker, and others, Pergamon, 1976. Contributor of more than eighty articles to scientific journals.

*   *   *

MEDINA, Pablo 1948-

PERSONAL: Born in 1948, in Cuba.

ADDRESSES: Office—Graduate Writing Program, New School for Social Research, New York, NY 10011.

CAREER: New School for Social Research, New York City, faculty member in Graduate Writing Program.

WRITINGS:

Pork Rind and Cuban Songs, Nuclassics and Science Publishing (Washington, DC), 1975.
Exiled Memories: A Cuban Childhood, University of Texas Press (Austin, TX), 1990.
Arching into the Afterlife, Bilingual Press (Tempe, AZ), 1991.
The Marks of Birth, Farrar, Straus (New York City), 1994.
The Floating Island, White Pine Press (Buffalo, NY), 1999.

Contributor to periodicals, including *Antioch Review, Pivot,* and *Poetry.**

MEJIA VALLEJO, Manuel 1923-

PERSONAL: Born April 23, 1923, in Jerico, Antioquia, Colombia; son of Manuel Mejia (a landowner) and Roxana Vallejo (a ceramic artist); married Dora Luz Echeverria Ramirez, January 31, 1975. *Education:* Universidad de Boliviariana, early 1940s; studied art at Escuela de Bellas Artes, 1944.

ADDRESSES: Agent—c/o Editorial Norma S.A., Avenue El Dorado No. 90-10, Apdo Aereo 53550, Santafe de Bogota, Cundinamarca.

CAREER: Writer, c. 1945—. Worked for a newspaper in Medellin, Colombia, early 1940s; worked as a journalist in Venezuela and Central America in the 1950s, primarily affiliated with the Colombian newspaper *El Espectador;* Imprenta Departamental (a publishing house), Medellin, director, 1958-early 1960s; involved in the literary group "Papel Sobrante" (Extra Paper), mid-1960s; Universidad Nacional de Medellin, instructor of literature, early 1970s.

AWARDS, HONORS: "El milagro" (title means "The Miracle") was named among the best stories of 1951 in a national short-story contest sponsored by the Venezuelan newspaper the *Nacional;* first prize, *Nacional* contest, 1951, for "La guitarra" (title means "The Guitar"); "Tiempo de sequia" won a national short story contest in Mexico, 1955; prize from Buenos Aires publisher, for *Al pie de la ciudad;* Premio Nadal (Spain), c. 1964, for *El dia senalado;* Premio Vivencias (Colombia), c. 1973, for *Aire de tango.*

WRITINGS:

La tierra eramos nosotros (novel; title means "We Were the Land"), Alvarez (Medellin, Colombia), 1945.

Tiempo de sequia (short stories; title means "Time of Drought"), Alvarez (Medellin), 1957.

Al pie de la ciudad (novel; title means "At the Foot of the City"), Losada (Buenos Aires), 1958.

Cielo cerrado, Tertulia (Medellin), 1963.

El dia senalado (novel; title means "The Special Day"), Destino (Barcelona), 1964.

Cuentos de la zona torrida (short stories; title means "Tales of the Torrid Zone"), Carpel-Antorcha (Medellin), 1967.

Aire de tango (novel), Bedout (Medellin), 1973.

Las noches de la vigilia (title means "Vigilant Nights"), Instituto Colombiano de Cultura (Bogota, Colombia), 1975.

Practicas para el olvido (poetry; title means "Practices for Oblivion"), Publicaciones Tecnicas (Medellin), 1977.

Las muertes ajenas (novel; title means "Foreign Deaths"), Plaza & Janes (Bogota), 1979.

Tarde de verano (novel; title means "Summer Afternoon"), Plaza & Janes (Bogota), 1980.

El viento lo dijo, Universidad de Antioquia (Medellin), 1981.

Y el mundo sigue andando (novel; title means "And the World Follows Walking"), Planeta (Bogota), 1984.

El hombre que parecia un fantasma, Biblioteca Publica (Medellin), 1984.

Maria, mas alla del paraiso, Quijada (Cali, Colombia), 1984.

Hojas de papel, Universidad Nacional (Bogota), 1985.

La sombra de tu paso (novel; title means "The Ghost of Your Step"), Planeta (Bogota), 1987.

La casa de las dos palmas (novel; title means "The House of Two Palms"), Planeta (Bogota), 1988.

Colombia campesina, Villegas (Bogota), 1989.

Manuel Mejia Vallejo (collected works), Procultura (Bogota), 1989.

Otras historias de Balandu, Intermedio (Bogota), 1990.

Memoria de olvido, Universidad de Antioquia (Medellin), 1990.

Los abuelos de cara blanca, Planeta (Bogota), 1991.

Cuentos contra el muro, Coordinacion de Difusion Cultural, Direccion de Literatura, UNAM (Mexico City), 1994.

SIDELIGHTS: Manuel Mejia Vallejo is one of Colombia's most respected literary names, with over four decades of critically acclaimed work to his credit. Since the publication of his first novel in 1945 at the age of just twenty-one, Mejia Vallejo and his literary efforts have survived political crises, peer-fomented controversy, and the impact of Latin American magical realist literature. As both a writer and a publishing-industry heavyweight, Mejia Vallejo has championed the works of his native region, the Colombian province known as Antioquia, of which Medellin is the capital. From Antioquia, long isolated as a valley surrounded by forbidding peaks, arose a sense of separate culture and a rich oral tradition; the area is also the birthplace of several other notable figures in Colombian literary history. Many of Mejia Vallejo's novels and short stories pay homage to Antioquia's rural culture of decades past.

Mejia Vallejo was born in 1923 into a landowning family in Jerico. As a child he attended a school his father funded, located on the family's estate; he was then sent to Medellin for high school. For a time he attended the Universidad de Boliviariana, but his father suffered some financial setbacks and Mejia Vallejo then dropped out of school. One day, after a visit to the cinema, he bought a notebook and began writing *La tierra eramos nosotros* ("We Were the Land"). The work is deeply evocative of the Antioquia of his childhood, the pastoral estate life that had only recently come to an end for his family. It tracks the visit of a man returning to his former home in the country and contrasts it with his life in the city; nearly all of the names used actually belonged to the people who worked for Mejia Vallejo's father.

Mejia Vallejo's mother, a gifted ceramic artist, was firmly convinced of her son's literary talents and paid the costs for the 1945 publication of *La tierra eramos nosotros*. Remarkably, although the 229-page novel was literally the first thing Mejia Vallejo had ever written, it caused a sensation. He was praised as an outstanding new voice in Colombian literature. But the country itself was experiencing political and economic crises at the time, and the 1948 assassination of a presidential candidate caused massive riots in Bogota and launched a decade of civil war in which as many as 200,000 Colombians lost their lives. During this dismal period, called La Violencia ("The Violence"), many writers, artists, and intellectuals fled the country. A military dictatorship from 1953 to 1957 imposed a regime of harsh reprisals and censorship.

During these years Mejia Vallejo worked in Venezuela as a newspaper reporter; he also claimed to have survived on his poker winnings for a time. In the city of Maracaibo he began writing short stories, and in 1951 earned honors in a Venezuelan national short-story contest for "El Milagro" ("The Miracle") and "La guitarra" ("The Guitar"). He continued to write when he moved to Costa Rica in 1952 and then to Guatemala a year or so later. The fall of Colombia's military dictatorship in 1957 opened new doors for Mejia Vallejo and other exiled writers, and he made plans to return. That same year his collection of short stories, *Tiempo de sequia* ("Time of Drought"), was published and earned him critical accolades. Many of its stories are concerned with rural Colombian life, and its title story deals with a segment of the population who live in abject poverty. Another *Tiempo de sequia* piece, "Al pie de la ciudad," soon evolved into a 1958 novel of the same title; its characters live in the Los Barrancos neighborhood of Medellin, at the "foot" of the city.

Tiempo de sequia marked Mejia Vallejo's beginning as a serious participant in the Colombian literary scene, though its publication had come a dozen years after *La tierra eramos nosotros*. His second full-length novel, *Al pie de la ciudad,* won the contest of a renowned Buenos Aires publisher and was met with critical acclaim soon afterward. First told from viewpoint of young boy growing up in this barrio of Medellin, *Al pie de la ciudad* charts the history and changes of the unique neighborhood of Los Barrancos; an affluent doctor is the main figure in its second part, but the third section fuses both narrative focal points.

Upon returning to Colombia around 1958, Mejia Vallejo was offered a post as director of Imprenta Departamental, an important publishing house in Medellin. From this position he launched the series "Coleccion de Autores Antioquenos," featuring writers from his native region; the selection became rather controversial among the greater Colombian literary establishment and debates raged in the press regarding the editors' choice of writers.

Raymond Leslie Williams, writing in *Dictionary of Literary Biography,* termed both *Al pie de la ciudad* and Mejia Vallejo's next work, *El dia senalado* ("The Special Day"), "early contributions to the modern novel in Spanish America. . . . His modern narrative techniques involve the innovative use of narrators and structures." Published in 1964, *El dia senalado* was a great commercial and critical success for the writer. Set in the isolated town of Tambo in Antioquia between 1936 and 1960, the story is told from two different perspectives—that of a young boy growing up in the region and that of a grown man returning to extract revenge upon his long-lost father—but their stories later merge. The horrors of *La Violencia* figure largely in the narrative, and the character of the village priest, a simple and good man with great faith in humanity, also plays an important role. In the end, the son discovers that his father is the leader of the guerrilla group battling the Colombian army and does not kill him; by this time the younger man has already fathered a child with a prostitute and then left it behind as his progenitor had done.

By the mid-1960s Mejia Vallejo had abandoned his publishing job and began a venture with other writers to promote Antioquian literature. They called their group Papel Sobrante ("Extra Paper"), and sold surplus paper to fund their own publishing ventures. The group included Oscar Hernandez Monsalve, Dario Ruiz Gomez, Dora Ramirez, Antonio Osorio Diaz,

John Alvarez Garcia, and Mejia Vallejo. The last of the eight volumes Papel Sobrante issued came in 1967 with Mejia Vallejo's *Cuentos de la zona torrida* ("Tales of the Torrid Zone").

But 1967 was also an important year for Latin American letters because of the publication of Gabriel Garcia Marquez's *Cien anos de soledad* (*One Hundred Years of Solitude*). Hailed as the most important and influential writer Colombia has ever produced, Garcia Marquez used a style that came to be known as magical realism and was soon widely imitated. Mejia Vallejo wrote little over the next few years. "Garcia Marquez's shadow was an insurmountable factor for all other Colombian writers, including Mejia Vallejo," noted Williams in the *Dictionary of Literary Biography* essay. "He spent his time teaching literature classes at the Universidad Nacional de Medellin and writing on his farm outside the city."

That estate, called Ziruma, which means "heaven" in the indigenous language of Antioquia, was purchased with the savings from his first early successes as a writer. There Mejia Vallejo wrote his next novel, *Aire de tango,* published in 1973. A homage to the cult of the tango and one of its leading champions, the work is set in the rougher Guayaquil barrio of Medellin. Its hero is the real-life figure of Carlos Gardel, the dancer who made Medellin a leading site for the dance, its music, and its cult of popularity before his murder in 1935. "The story is told in an oral style in which the narrator answers a series of questions, even though neither the listener nor his questions ever appear in the text," explained Williams. "It is as if the speaker were in a bar in the Barrio Guayaquil, telling stories among friends."

Aire de tango won a major literary prize in Colombia, the Premio Vivencias, and marked Mejia Vallejo's entry into a canon of seasoned Colombian writers and intellectuals. His next work, *Las noches de la vigilia* ("Vigilant Nights"), explored new structural territory: the work is a collection of over five dozen brief narratives all set in the small town of Balandu. Two years later Mejia Vallejo published a volume of short love poems, *Practicas para el olvido;* he then again turned to addressing the wrongs committed in recent Colombian history with the 1979 novel *Las muertes ajenas* ("Foreign Deaths"). The story centers on a young man falsely imprisoned for six years and his attempt to avenge the deed. "As in much of his work, Mejia Vallejo laments the loss of traditional human values in the new, modern Antioquia," remarked *Dictionary of Literary Biography* writer Williams. "As one of the characters poignantly states in the last chapter, 'Es

una verguenza la humanidad' (Humanity is a shame). The novel's denouement, with images of human corpses, certainly underlines this negative vision."

In *Tarde de verano* ("Summer Afternoon"), Mejia Vallejo's 1980 novel, he borrows a bit from other contemporary Latin American writers. The work, told in a traditional narrative voice, recounts the nevertheless otherworldly occurrences that begin to plague the life of an ordinary couple. In his 1987 work *La sombra de tu paso* ("The Ghost of Your Step"), he revisits the heady days of new intellectual freedom in Colombia and especially Medellin in the early 1960s. A love story, its narrator recounts his relationship with a woman named Claudia in flashback to those days; many leading Colombian literary figures appear in the anecdotes. "A subtle subtext is the story of the protagonist becoming a writer," noted Williams in the *Dictionary of Literary Biography*. "The formative years narrated in this novel are, in fact, the years during which Mejia Vallejo matured as a writer." Mejia Vallejo's 1988 novel, *La casa de las dos palmas* ("The House of Two Palms"), again revisited his fictional sleepy town of Balandu, this time in the early years of the twentieth century.

An esteemed figure in Colombian letters, Mejia Vallejo was invited to the presidential palace to speak on the occasion of his sixtieth birthday in 1983. In a *Spanish American Authors* essay, Mejia Vallejo recalled his mother's early belief in his abilities as a writer; one day, in her eighties, she reread *La tierra eramos nosotros* and remarked that he would someday be awarded the Nobel Prize. "She said that because I was the black sheep of the family and she wanted to make it up to me. . . . She had a lot of faith in me," said Mejia Vallejo.

BIOGRAPHICAL/CRITICAL SOURCES:

BOOKS

Dictionary of Literary Biography, Volume 113: *Modern Latin-American Fiction Writers, First Series,* Gale (Detroit, MI), 1992.*

*   *   *

MENDEZ, Miguel 1930-

PERSONAL: Born June 15, 1930, in Bisbee, AZ; son of Francisco Mendez Cardenas (a farmer and miner) and Maria Morales; married Maria Dolores Fontes;

children: Miguil Fontes, Isabel Cristina. *Education:* Attended schools in El Claro, Sonora, Mexico, for six years.

ADDRESSES: Office—Department of Spanish and Portuguese, University of Arizona, Modern Languagees, Tucson, AZ 85721.

CAREER: Writer. Went to work as an itinerant farm laborer along the Arizona-Sonora border at the age of fifteen; bricklayer and construction worker in Tucson, AZ, 1946-70; Pima Community College, Tucson, AZ, instructor in Spanish, Hispanic literature and creative writing, 1970—. Instructor in Chicano literature, University of Arizona.

MEMBER: Association of Teachers of Spanish and Portuguese.

AWARDS, HONORS: Honorary Doctor of Humanities, University of Arizona, 1984; Jose Fuentes Mares National Award of Mexican Literature, Universidad Autonoma de Ciudad Juarez, 1991; Creative Writing fellowship, Arizona Commission on the Arts, 1992.

WRITINGS:

(Contributor) Octavio I. Romano and Herminio Rios-C., editors, *El Espejo/The Mirror,* Quinto Sol, 1969.
Peregrinos de Aztlan (novel), Editorial Peregrinos, 1974, translation by David W. Foster published as *Pilgrims in Aztlan,* Bilingual Press/Editorial Bilingue, 1992.
"Los criaderos humanos y Sahuaros" (poem; title means "The Human Breeding Grounds and Saguaros"), Editorial Peregrinos, 1975.
Cuentos para ninos traviesos: Stories for Mischievous Children (short stories; bilingual edition), translations by Eva Price, Justa, 1979.
Tata Casehua y otros cuentos (short stories; bilingual edition; title means "Tata Casehua and Other Stories"), translations by Price, Leo Barrow, and Marco Portales, Justa, 1980.
Critica al poder politico, Ediciones Universal (Miami, FL), 1981.
De la vida y del folclore de la frontera (short stories; title means "From Life and Folklore along the Border"), Mexican–American Studies and Research Center, University of Arizona, 1986.
El sueno de Santa Maria de las Piedras (novel), Universidad de Guadalajara, 1986, translation by David W. Foster published as *The Dream of Santa Maria de las Piedras,* Bilingual Press/Editorial Bilingue (Tempe, AZ), 1989.

Cuentos y ensayos para reir y aprender (title means "Stories and Essays for Laughing and Learning"), 1988.
Que no mueran los suenos, Era (Mexico), 1991.
Peregrinos de Aztlan, Bilingual Press/Editorial Bilingue (Tempe, AZ), 1991, translation by David William Foster published as *Pilgrims in Aztlan,* 1992.
Los Muertos Tambien Cuentan, Universidad Autonoma de Ciudad Juarez, 1995.
Entre letras y ladrillos: autobiografia novelada, Bilingual Press/Editorial Bilingue (Tempe, AZ), 1996, translation by David William Foster published as *From Labor to Letters: A Novel Autobiography,* 1997.
Rio Santacruz, Ediciones Osuna (Armilla, Granada), 1997.

Also author of *El Hombre vibora, Pasen, lectores, pasen. Aqui se hacen imagenes,* (poems), and *Cuentos para ninos precoces* (short stories). Contributor to periodicals, including *La Palabra* and *Revista Chicano-Riquena.* The spring-fall 1981 issue of *La Palabra* is entirely devoted to Mendez' work.

SIDELIGHTS: "Chicano literature has in Miguel Mendez one of its finest and most sensitive writers," reports Salvador Rodriguez del Pino in *Chicano Writers.* Mendez has attracted the admiration of many critics with his richly poetic prose, his erudite language, and his depictions of the poor members of an uprooted society at odds with the Anglo-American culture that threatens their heritage. His first novel, 1974's *Peregrinos de Aztlan* (translated as *Pilgrims in Aztlan* and published in 1992), is considered a landmark in Chicano literature for its experimental use of Spanglish (a mixture of Spanish and English), its blending of mythology with social realism, and its attention to poor, itinerant farm workers who formed the bulk of early Mexican immigration to the United States.

Much of Mendez' work uses elements from his Spanish and Yaqui Indian heritages. The name Aztlan in *Peregrinos de Aztlan,* for instance, is taken from the mythic northern homeland of the Aztec Indians of Mexico, and is believed to have been somewhere in the southwestern United States. Loreto Maldonado, the main character of *Peregrinos de Aztlan,* who now wanders the streets of Laredo, Texas, making a living by washing cars, was once a revolutionary and served under Pancho Villa. The title character in "Tata Casehua," found in the short-story collection *Tata Casehua y otros cuentos,* is actually the hero warrior Tetabiate, and the story details his search for an heir to whom he can pass on his tribe's history. And Timoteo, a key character in Mendez' novel *El sueno de Santa Maria de las Piedras,* ventures across the United States in search of the earthly god Huachusey, apparently with success, as he is repeatedly told "What you say?" by Americans in answer to his questions about the creator of things he encounters.

Mendez also draws upon his personal past, growing up in a Mexican government farming community and later working in agriculture and construction, for his stories. "During my childhood," he told Juan Bruce-Novoa in *Chicano Authors: Inquiry by Interview,* "I heard many stories from those people who came from different places, and, like my family, were newcomers to El Claro. They would tell anecdotes about the [Mexican] Revolution, the Yaqui wars, and innumerable other themes, among which there was no lack of apparitions and superstitions. Those days were extremely dramatic. I learned about tragedy, at times in the flesh." When at the age of fifteen Mendez left Mexico to find work as an agricultural laborer in the United States, he met the exploited people who appear in his fiction—indigent workers, prostitutes, and Hispanics looking for jobs in the North, among others.

Another major component of the author's work is the oral tradition handed down by these poor people; indeed, Mendez sees their plight as one symptom of the loss of that tradition. "Familial, communal, ethnic, and national heritage, which once was preserved by word of mouth, is disappearing into silence," explains Bruce-Novoa. "At the same time, written history represents only the elite classes' vision of the past, ignoring the existence of the poor. Thus, as the poor abandon the oral preservation of their heritage and simultaneously embrace literacy, alienation and a sense of diaspora possess them. Mendez counterattacks through his writing, not only by revealing the threat to the oral tradition, but also by filling his written texts with oral tradition." Mendez' interest in reclaiming this lost tradition is evidenced in *El sueno de Santa Maria de las Piedras,* in which he "employs the narrative voice of five old Mexicans . . . in order to unfold the historical fragments of a fictitious, yet universal Mexican town in the Sonora desert between 1830 and 1987," remarks Roland Walter in *Americas Review.*

BIOGRAPHICAL/CRITICAL SOURCES:

BOOKS

Anaya, Rodolfo A., and Francisco A. Lomeli, editors, *Aztlan: Essays on the Chicano Homeland,* Academia/El Norte, 1989.

Bruce-Novoa, Juan D., *Chicano Authors: Inquiry by Interview,* University of Texas Press, 1980.

Martinez, Julio A., *Chican Scholars and Writers: A Bio-Bibliographical Directory,* Scarecrow Press, 1979.

Rodriguez del Pino, Salvador, *Interview with Miguel Mendez M.,* Center for Chicano Studies, University of California, Santa Barbara, 1976.

Tatum, Charles M. *Chicano Literature,* Twayne, 1982.

PERIODICALS

America, July 18, 1992, p. 42.
Americas Review, spring, 1990, pp. 103-112.
Bloomsbury Review, March/April, 1994, pp. 3, 5.
Booklist, December 15, 1992, p. 719.
Denver Quarterly, fall, 1981, pp. 16-22; spring, 1982, pp. 68-77.
La Palabra, spring-fall, 1981, pp. 3-17, 50-57, 67-76.
Library Journal, March 15, 1993, p. 108.
Publishers Weekly, February 8, 1993, p. 83.*

*   *   *

MEYER, Doris (L.) 1942-

PERSONAL: Born January 2, 1942, in Summit, NJ; daughter of Hans J. (an importer-exporter) and Maria L. (an editor and translator) Meyer. *Education:* Radcliffe College, B.A., (magna cum laude), 1963; University of Virginia, M.A., 1964, Ph.D., 1967. *Avocational interests:* Flying, golf, fly fishing.

ADDRESSES: Home—68 Estates Dr., Santa Fe, NM 87501.

CAREER: University of North Carolina, Wilmington, assistant professor of Spanish, 1967-69; Brooklyn College of the City University of New York, Brooklyn, NY, assistant professor, 1972-75, associate professor, 1976-79, professor of Spanish, 1980-86; Connecticut College, New London, professor of Hispanic studies and head of department, 1986-98, Weller professor emeritus of Hispanic studies, 1998—.

MEMBER: Modern Language Association of America, American Association of Teachers of Spanish and Portuguese, PEN, Latin American Studies Association, American Literary Translators Association, National Women's Studies Association, Phi Beta Kappa.

AWARDS, HONORS: Woodrow Wilson fellowship, 1964-66; American Philosophical Society grant, 1976; National Endowment for the Humanities fellowship, 1977-78.

WRITINGS:

Traditionalism in the Works of Francisco de Quevedo y Villegas, University of North Carolina Press, 1970.

Victoria Ocampo: Against the Wind and Tide, Braziller, 1979.

(Editor with Margarite Fernandez Olmos) *Contemporary Women Authors of Latin America,* two volumes, Brooklyn College Press, Volume 1: *New Translations,* Volume 2: *Introductory Essays,* both 1983.

(Editor) *Lives on the Line: The Testimony of Contemporary Latin American Authors,* University of California Press, 1988.

Reinterpreting the Spanish American Essay: Women Writers of the 19th and 20th Centuries, University of Texas Press (Austin), 1995.

Rereading the Spanish American Essay: Translations of 19th and 20th Century Women's Essays, University of Texas Press (Austin), 1995.

Contributor of articles and translations to history and Spanish studies journals; contributor to *Nimrod.*

SIDELIGHTS: Regarding her 1979 work *Victoria Ocampo: Against the Wind and Tide,* Doris Meyer commented: "I was motivated to write the book . . . through a combination of an Argentine background on my mother's side and an intense concern with bringing to the attention of North American readers the remarkable contributions of a much-overlooked South American woman, a legend in her own country, a social rebel and a feminist." Meyer knew Ocampo personally for nearly twenty years and, according to John Russell in the *New York Times,* provides an "unremittingly earnest" view of her life. "Books and the men who wrote them were what [Ocampo] most cared for in life," notes Russell. "She had the looks, the means and the gall to chase the writers of her choice, and for much of her life she did just that." The founder in 1931 of the influential literary review *Sur,* Ocampo also ran a publishing company that provided Spanish translations of such literary giants as James Joyce, Andre Malraux, William Faulkner, and Vladimir Nabokov. Russell praises Meyer's book as a "decent, serious, well-researched survey, and it is graced by a discretion now rare among biographers."

Since her book on Ocampo, Meyer has provided English-speaking readers with access to other Latin American authors, in particular women writers. In 1983, she co-edited the two-volume *Contemporary Women Authors of Latin America,* which collects previously unpublished translations by forty female writers and provides in-depth profiles of the lives and work of over a dozen. According to Sonja Karsen in *World Literature Today,* the volumes, which cover both established and little-known writers, "fill an important gap that has existed in our knowledge of Latin American literature." In 1988, Meyer edited *Lives on the Line: The Testimony of Contemporary Latin American Writers,* a collection of first-hand accounts by writers which, according to Alberto Ciria in the Toronto *Globe and Mail,* show "the artists' involvement (or lack of it) in social and political issues together with considerations about their literary experiences." Ciria comments that *Lives on the Line* is "helpful in suggesting some of the roots of [Latin American] literature, some of the problems faced by those writers in their lives as well as in their crafts, and some of the painful consequences of repression, exile and interior exile' for Latin American intellectuals."

Meyer once explained: "My retirement to New Mexico in 1998 has given me the time to do research and to write at my leisure. I have also become affiliated as a research scholar with the University of New Mexico, which has excellent collections in my field. I am thrilled with this new stage of my life."

BIOGRAPHICAL/CRITICAL SOURCES:

PERIODICALS

Globe and Mail (Toronto), June 25, 1988.
Los Angeles Times Book Review, July 17, 1988.
New York Times, August 9, 1979.
World Literature Today, winter, 1985.

*   *   *

MIRANDA, Javier
  See BIOY CASARES, Adolfo

*   *   *

MISTRAL, Gabriela
  See GODOY ALCAYAGA, Lucila

MOHR, Nicholasa 1938-

PERSONAL: Born November 1, 1938, in New York, NY; daughter of Pedro and Nicholasa (Rivera) Golpe; married Irwin Mohr (a clinical child psychologist), October 5, 1958 (deceased); children: David, Jason. *Ethnicity:* "Latino, Puerto Rican." *Education:* Attended Art Students League, 1956-58, Brooklyn Museum of Art School, 1964-66, and Pratt Center for Contemporary Printmaking, 1967-69.

ADDRESSES: Home—27 President St., Brooklyn, NY 11215. *E-mail*—noni@compuserve.com.

CAREER: Fine arts painter in New York, California, Mexico, and Puerto Rico; printmaker in New York and Mexico; Art Center of Northern New Jersey, instructor, 1970-71; MacDowell Colony, Peterborough, NH, writer-in-residence, 1972, 1974, and 1976; State University of New York at Stony Brook, lecturer in Puerto Rican studies, 1977; Rutgers University, New Brunswick, NJ, lecturer, 1985, 1986; Queens College of the City University of New York, Flushing, NJ, distinguished visiting professor, 1988-90; University of San Francisco, Irvine visiting scholar, 1990; Smithsonian Institution, visiting scholar, 1990; American International University in London, writer–in–residence at Richmond College, 1994-95; resident or visiting scholar at New York State Writers Institute, Bronx Museum of the Arts, Bronx County Historical Society, Center for American Culture Studies at Columbia University, and Writers Community, New York. Visiting lecturer in creative writing for various educator, librarian, student, and community groups, including University of Illinois Educational Alliance Program (Chicago), 1977, community schools of Cedar Rapids, IA, 1978, writers-in-residence seminar, University of Wisconsin—Oshkosh, 1978, and public schools of Bridgeport, CT, 1978. Head creative writer and co-producer of television series *Aqui y Ahora* (title means "Here and Now"). Film Video Arts, member of board of trustees, 1974-90; New York State Developmental Disabilities Planning Council, member, 1990-94; New Jersey State Council on the Arts, member; Young Filmmakers Foundation, member of board of trustees and consultant; consultant on bilingual media training for Young Filmmakers/Video Arts.

MEMBER: Authors Guild, Authors League of America, PEN American Center.

AWARDS, HONORS: Outstanding book citation (juvenile fiction), *New York Times,* 1973, Jane Addams Children's Book Award, Jane Addams Peace Association, 1974, and citation of merit for book jacket design, Society of Illustrators, 1974, all for *Nilda;* outstanding book citation (teenage fiction), *New York Times,* 1975, best book citation, *School Library Journal,* 1975, and National Book Award finalist for "most distinguished book in children's literature," 1976, all for *El Bronx Remembered: A Novella and Stories;* best book citation, *School Library Journal,* best book for young adults citation, American Library Association, and Notable Trade Book Award, joint committee of National Council for the Social Studies and Children's Book Council, all 1977, all for *In Nueva York; Nilda* was selected as one of *School Library Journal*'s "Best of the Best 1966-78"; Notable Trade Book Award, joint committee of National Council for the Social Studies and Children's Book Council, 1980, and American Book Award, Before Columbus Foundation, 1981, both for *Felita;* Yaddo fellow, 1985, 1990; commendation from the Legislature of the State of New York, 1986, for *Rituals of Survival: A Woman's Portfolio; Going Home* was selected a "parent's choice remarkable book for literature" by Parents' Choice Foundation, 1989; honorary doctorate of letters, State University of New York at Albany, 1989; Edgar Allan Poe Award, Bronx Historical Society, 1990; award from El Instituto de Escritores Latinoamericanos, Eugenio Maria de Hostos Community College, 1993; award for preserving the Latino cultural identity, Association of Hispanic Arts, 1993; Annual Achievement in Literature Award, National Hispanic Academy of Media Arts and Sciences, 1995, for *In My Own Words: Growing Up inside the Sanctuary of My Imagination;* Americas Award, children's and young adult literature-commended title, Consortium of Latin American Studies Programs, 1996, for *Old Letivia and the Mountain of Sorrows;* lifetime achievement award, National Congress of Puerto Rican Women, 1996; resident at Wurlitzer Foundation, 1996; Professional Achievement Award in the Field of Arts and Culture, Boricua College, 1997; Hispanic Heritage Award for Literature, 1997.

WRITINGS:

YOUNG ADULT FICTION

(And illustrator) *Nilda* (novel), Harper (New York City), 1973, second edition, Arte Publico (Houston), 1986.

(And illustrator) *El Bronx Remembered: A Novella and Stories,* Harper, 1975, second edition, Arte Publico, 1986.

In Nueva York (short stories), Dial (New York City), 1977, revised edition, Arte Publico, 1988.

(And illustrator) *Felita* (novel), Dial, 1979.

Going Home (novel; sequel to *Felita*), Dial, 1986.

All for the Better: A Story of El Barrio, illustrated by
    Rudy Gutierrez, Raintree (Austin, TX), 1992.
Isabel's New Mom, Macmillan (New York City), 1993.
The Magic Shell (novel), illustrated by Gutierrez, Scho-
    lastic, Inc. (New York City), 1995.
Old Letivia and the Mountain of Sorrows, Viking (New
    York City), 1993.
The Song of El Coquai, and Other Tales of Puerto Rico,
    illustrated by Antonio Martorell, Viking, 1995.
I Never Even Seen My Father (play based on a short
    story from *In Nueva York*), produced in London at
    Richmond College, 1995.

OTHER

Rituals of Survival: A Woman's Portfolio, Arte Publico,
    1985.
*In My Own Words: Growing Up inside the Sanctuary
    of My Imagination,* Simon & Schuster (New York
    City), 1994.
A Matter of Pride and Other Stories, Arte Publico,
    1997.

Also author, with Ray Blanco, of *The Artist* (screenplay)
and *Inside the Monster* (radio play), 1981. Contributor
of stories to textbooks and anthologies, including
*Kikiriki: Stories and Poems in English and Spanish for
Children,* edited by Sylvia Cavazos Pena, Arte Publico,
1981; *Woman of Her Word: Hispanic Women Write,*
edited by Evangelina Vigil, Arte Publico, 1983; *Images
and Identity: The Puerto Rican in Two World Cultures,*
edited by Adela Rodriguez de Laguna, Transaction
Books (New Brunswick, NJ), 1985; *Tun-Ta-Ca-Tun:
More Stories and Poems in English and Spanish for
Children,* edited by Cavazos Pena, Arte Publico, 1986;
Passages, Holt (New York City), 1988; *When I Was
Your Age,* Candlewick Press, 1996; and *The Ethnic
American Woman: Problems, Protests, Life-styles,* edited by Edith Blicksilver. Contributor of short stories to
*Children's Dig-est, Scholastic Magazine, Americas Re-
view,* and *Nuestro.* Member of board of contributing
editors of *Nuestro;* contributing editor, *Americas Re-
view.*

WORK IN PROGRESS: A novel for children, for
Viking.

ADAPTATIONS: Mohr's book *In My Own Words:
Growing Up inside the Sanctuary of My Imagination* was
adapted for inclusion in the television documentary, *The
Dignity of Children,* broadcast by ABC-TV in 1997.

SIDELIGHTS: Nicholasa Mohr is the author and illustrator of picture books, young adult and adult novels,
and short stories that offer what reviewers have hailed
as realistic and uncompromising portraits of life in
New York City's Puerto Rican barrio. Drawing on
memories from her own adolescence and passage to
adulthood in fashioning the characters and events that
fill her fictions, Mohr has replaced brushes, paint,
and canvas with pen and paper; from a young painter
and printmaker working throughout the United States
during the 1950s, she has developed into one of the
most critically acclaimed Hispanic writers of young
adult literature.

Mohr was born and raised in New York City, one of
seven children of a Puerto Rican couple who had moved
to the East Coast during the Great Depression. An early
talent and interest in drawing marked young Nicholasa
as a creative and imaginative child; her art also allowed
her to escape from a world that was not always pleasant.
Raised in an impoverished family that retained strong
traditional values about women's subservient role, Mohr
found herself catering to her six older brothers rather
than developing her own friendships and interests. Both
parents died by the time Mohr reached high school, and
she was left in the custody of an aunt. Continuing to
develop her talent as an artist, Mohr graduated from a
trade high school and enrolled in courses at New York's
Arts Students' League, where she became aware of the
work of Mexican muralists like Diego Rivera. A trip to
Mexico City awakened Mohr to the power of personal
and political symbolism. The works that she would produce after viewing the art of Rivera, Jose Clemente
Orozco, and Frida Kahlo were more boldly drawn, full
of expressive faces, urban images, and possessing an
almost graffiti-like texture. "In a profound way their
work spoke to me and my experiences as a Puerto Rican
woman born in New York," Mohr would later explain
in an autobiographical essay in *Something about the
Author Autobiography Series* (*SAAS*). "The impact was
to shape and form the direction of all my future work."

Such influences can be felt in *Nilda,* Mohr's first novel,
which was published in 1973. Taking place during the
early 1940s, the author portrays a Puerto Rican girl as
she grows from a child to a teenager: coping with the
poverty of her family and the prejudice of teachers and
fellow students, and attempting to gain a sense of her
own identity. Throughout the work, Mohr poses the
question: "What does it feel like being poor and belonging to a despised minority?," according to *New York
Times Book Review* contributor Marilyn Sachs. Although
Sachs finds that several books for young people have
attempted to explore this condition, "few come up to
Nilda in describing the crushing humiliations of poverty
and in peeling off the ethnic wrappings so that we can

see the human child underneath." Another article in the *New York Times Book Review* notes that 1973's *Nilda* "provides a sharp, candid portrayal of what it means to be poor and to be called 'spics,' 'animals,' 'you people'—and worse."

Mohr's subsequent story collections, 1975's *El Bronx Remembered: A Novella and Stories* and *In Nueva York,* published two years later, have afforded similar insight into the lives of Hispanics in New York City. Sachs offers this assessment of *El Bronx Remembered:* "If there is any message . . . in these stories, any underlying theme, it is that life goes on. But Nicholasa Mohr is more interested in people than in messages." The reviewer notes that the stories are without "complicated symbolism . . . , trendy obscurity of meaning . . . hopeless despair or militant ethnicity. Her people endure because they are people." Sachs adds: "Some of them suffer, some of them die, a few of them fail, but most of the time they endure."

Other novels have included *Felita* and *Going Home,* both of which chronicle events in the life of a young Puerto Rican girl as she attempts to adapt to new surroundings and new friendships. While these novels, like her other novels and short stories, feature a teen protagonist, Mohr denies that her books are written solely for younger readers. "I write for people," the author told Paul Janeczko in an interview for *From Writers to Students.* "Some of them are young and some of them are old. . . . [G]ood writing is writing that someone picks up and says, 'Okay, I want to go on with this, not because it's for a teenager or adolescent, but because the writer is saying something that I want to get involved with.'" A deeply creative individual, Mohr has found both personal and artistic fulfillment in the written word. "I feel blessed by the work I do," she explained in *SAAS,* "for it permits me to use my talents. . . . [to] recreate those deepest of personal memories as well as validate and celebrate my heritage and my future."

BIOGRAPHICAL/CRITICAL SOURCES:

BOOKS

Authors and Artists for Young Adults, Volume 8, Gale (Detroit), 1992.
Children's Literature Review, Volume 22, Gale, 1991.
Contemporary Literary Criticism, Volume 12, Gale, 1980.
Dictionary of Literary Biography, Volume 145, Gale, 1994.
Discovering Authors Modules: Multicultural Authors Module, Gale, 1996.

Notable Hispanic American Women, Gale, 1993, pp. 274-77.
Reference Guide to American Literature, third Edition, St. James Press (Detroit), 1994.
Something about the Author Autobiography Series, Volume 8, Gale, 1989.
Weiss, M. Jerry, editor, *From Writers to Students: The Pleasures and Pains of Writing,* International Reading Association, 1979, pp. 75-78.

PERIODICALS

America's Review, spring-summer, 1994, p. 179.
Best Sellers, December, 1975, p. 266.
Booklist, December 1, 1979, p.559; July, 1986, p. 1615; July, 1994, p. 1934; June 1, 1995, p. 1779; August, 1995, p. 1947.
Bulletin of the Center for Children's Books, June, 1976, p. 161; July/August, 1977, p. 178; May, 1986, p. 178.
Children's Literature, Volume 3, 1974, pp. 230-34.
English Journal, February, 1978, p. 100.
Essence, May, 1980, p.25.
Horn Book, February, 1976, p. 57; February, 1980, p. 56; September/October, 1986, p. 591.
Interracial Bulletin of Books for Children, November 4, 1976, p. 15.
Kirkus Reviews, June 15, 1994, p. 849.
Lion and the Unicorn, fall, 1978, pp. 6-15.
Newsweek, March 4, 1974.
New York Times, January 20, 1980.
New York Times Book Review, November 4, 1973, pp. 27- 28; November 10, 1974; November 16, 1975; May 22, 1977.
Publishers Weekly, July 25, 1986, p. 190; July 10, 1995, p. 56.
Revista Interamericana, Volume 9, 1979-80, pp. 543-49.
School Library Journal, April, 1977, p. 79; August, 1986, p. 105; December, 1992, pp. 35-36; May, 1993, p. 118; August, 1995, pp. 137 and 167; October, 1995, p. 138.
Vista, May 14, 1989, p. 3.

*   *   *

MORA, Pat(ricia) 1942-

PERSONAL: Born January 19, 1942, in El Paso, TX; daughter of Raul Antonio (an optician) and Estella (a homemaker; maiden name, Delgado) Mora; married William H. Burnside Jr., July 27, 1963 (divorced,

1981); married Vernon Lee Scarborough (an archaeologist), May 25, 1984; children: (first marriage) William, Elizabeth, Cecilia. *Education:* Texas Western College, B.A., 1963; University of Texas at El Paso, M.A., 1967. *Politics:* Democrat.

ADDRESSES: Agent—423 Oakview Place, Cincinnati, OH 45209.

CAREER: El Paso Independent School District, El Paso, TX, teacher, 1963-66; El Paso Community College, part-time instructor in English and communications, 1971-78; University of Texas at El Paso, part-time lecturer in English, 1979-81, assistant to vice president of academic affairs, 1981-88, director of University Museum and assistant to president, 1988-89; writer and speaker, 1989—; gives presentations and poetry readings nationally and internationally. W. K. Kellogg Foundation, consultant, 1990-91. Member of Ohio Arts Council panel, 1990; member of advisory committee for Kellogg National Fellowship program, 1991-94. Host of radio show, *Voices: The Mexican-American in Perspective,* on National Public Radio- affiliate KTEP, 1983-84.

MEMBER: International Reading Association, Poetry Society of America, Academy of American Poets, Society of Children's Book Writers, National Council of Teachers of English, Texas Institute of Letters, National Association of Bilingual Educators.

AWARDS, HONORS: Creative writing award, National Association for Chicano Studies, 1983; *New America: Women Artists and Writers of the Southwest* poetry award, 1984; Harvey L. Johnson Book Award, Southwest Council of Latin American Studies, 1984; Southwest Book awards, Border Regional Library, 1985, for *Chants,* 1987, for *Borders,* and 1994, for *A Birthday Basket for Tia;* Kellogg National fellowship, 1986-89; Leader in Education Award, El Paso Women's Employment and Education, 1987; Chicano/Hispanic Faculty and Professional Staff Association Award, University of Texas at El Paso, 1987, for outstanding contribution to the advancement of Hispanics; named to *El Paso Herald-Post* Writers Hall of Fame, 1988; National Endowment for the Arts fellowship, 1994.

WRITINGS:

POETRY

Chants, Arte Publico (Houston), 1984.
Borders, Arte Publico, 1986.
Communion, Arte Publico, 1991.

Agua Santa/Holy Water, Beacon Press (Boston), 1995.
Aunt Carmen's Book of Practical Saints, Beacon Press (Boston), 1997.

Work represented in anthologies, including *New Worlds of Literature,* Norton (New York City), and *Woman of Her Word: Hispanic Women Write.*

FOR CHILDREN

A Birthday Basket for Tia, illustrated by Cecily Lang, Macmillan (New York City), 1992.
Listen to the Desert: Oye al desierto, Clarion (New York City), 1994.
The Desert Is My Mother/El desierto es mi madre, with art by Daniel Lechon, Pinata Books (Houston), 1994.
Agua, Agua, Agua, illustrated by Jose Ortega, GoodYearBooks, 1994.
Pablo's Tree, illustrated by Lang, Macmillan, 1994.
(With Charles Ramirez Berg) *The Gift of the Poinsettia,* Pinata Books, 1995.
Confetti (poems), illustrated by Enrique Sanchez, Lee & Low (New York City), 1995.
The Race of Toad and Deer, illustrated by Maya Itzna Brooks, Orchard Books, 1995.
Uno, dos, tres/One, Two Three, illustrated by Barbara Lavallee, Clarion, 1996.
Tomas and the Library Lady, illustrated by Raul Colon, Knopf (New York City), 1997.
This Big Sky (poetry), Scholastic, Inc. (New York City), 1998.
Delicious Hulabaloo = Pachanga deliciosa, illustrated by Francisco X. Mora, Spanish translation by Alba Nora Martinez and Pat Mora, Pinata Books (Houston), 1998.
The Rainbow Tulip (picture book), Viking, in press.

OTHER

Nepantla: Essays from the Land in the Middle (nonfiction), University of New Mexico Press (Albuquerque), 1993.
House of Houses (memoir), Beacon Press (Boston), 1997.

Contributor of articles and poems to periodicals, including *The Best American Poetry, 1996, Daughters of the Fifth Sun, Prairie Schooner, Latina: Women's Voices from the Borderland, Calyx,* and *Ms.*

SIDELIGHTS: Pat Mora is acknowledged as a leader in the contemporary movement to recognize and express the many voices of the Hispanic population—and especially those of Latinas—in the United States. Her collections of poems for children and adults reflect her experiences as an American woman of Mexican heritage. By portraying her native traditions as well as the physical surroundings of the Southwest desert, Mora gives voice both to herself and her people. As a poet and an author of children's books, she is essential to the movement to understand and uphold Mexican American culture. The author herself comments in a *Horn Book* essay: "I take pride in being a Hispanic writer. I will continue to write and to struggle to say what no other writer can say in quite the same way."

Born in El Paso, Texas, Mora was raised by her parents—Estella (Delgado) and Raul Antonio Mora, an ophthalmologist—as well as by her grandmother and her mother's half-sister. She received her bachelor's degree in 1963 from Texas Western College and married soon after graduation. Earning a master's degree from the University of Texas—El Paso in 1967, Mora held teaching positions at the secondary, post-secondary, and college levels; however, after her divorce in 1981, she began to devote herself more seriously to writing. Her poetry gained rapid acclaim, winning the Creative Writing Award from the National Association for Chicano Studies in 1983, and both the *New America: Women Artists and Writers of the Southwest* Poetry Award and the Harvey L. Johnson Book Award in 1984. Mora continues to write, lecture and give readings of her work. She is also collaborating with others to have April 30th designated as Dia de los Ninos: Dia de los Libros, a national celebration of children and bilingual literacy.

Mora's first two collection of poems, *Chants* and *Borders,* are steeped in the aura of the Southwest, celebrating that region's desert landscape. Throughout these works she explores the theme of identity, especially that of woman and her connection with the various forms of the "earth mother"—the *curandera,* or healer, and the *abuelita,* the nurturing grandmother. In an essay for *The Desert Is No Lady: Southwestern Landscapes in Women's Writing and Art,* Tey Diana Rebolledo notes that in Mora's poetry collections, "Nature and the land . . . become allies of the woman hero. Keeping her in touch with her self, they are a kind of talisman that enables her to make her way through the alienations of male society, and also of the received female traditions of a limited society, whether represented by the history of Spain or Mexico."

In her third collection, *Communion,* Mora departs her beloved Southwest and relates impressions gained from her subsequent travels. She finds herself experiencing daily life in Cuba ("The Mystery"), overwhelmed by the aura of the big city ("New York: 2 a.m."), and washing at the Yamuna River in central India ("The Taj Mahal"). In these poems women's identities remain the prevalent concern as Mora explores the implicit questions: "Who am I? Who are we?" In doing so, however, she consciously avoids didacticism. "I try not to have a message when I start out," Mora insists in *This Is about Vision: Interviews with Southwestern Writers,* writing on the subject of message poetry. "I really do. If I have a message then I say to myself, 'That's great, but that's not a poem.' I like to begin with an idea, a line, an image and see where it goes. But I am stubborn enough that a lot of my deep feelings are obviously going to come in, because of the way I see the world."

In addition to verse, Mora has written several prose commentaries that have been collected and published in *Nepantla: Essays from the Land in the Middle.* These, too, address themes of what it means to be a woman and a Chicana; they synthesize the experiences of a culture attempting to grasp its identity and make its voice heard. In a *Nation* review of *Nepantla,* Ray Gonzalez observes that the work is important "because it allows a Chicana writer to present strong opinions, dreams and commitments—all of them backed by a tough voice of poetic experience." *Bloomsbury Review* contributor Mary Motian-Meadows likewise praises *Nepantla,* noting of Mora: "Her experiences as an American woman of Mexican descent are integrated into a rich mosaic of insights that include the best of both worlds."

Because the elements of the Southwest are so prevalent in her work, Mora has been labeled a "regional" writer. Although she has expanded her view to encompass women's experience in other parts of the world, the author agrees that her Southwest emphasis is very important. As many scholars point out, the experiences of the Chicana have been virtually ignored in American society; writers such as Mora empower Hispanics—especially Hispanic women—through a celebration of the native traditions which lie at the heart of their cultural identity. "For a variety of complex reasons," Mora once explained: "anthologized American literature does not reflect the ethnic diversity of the United States. I write, in part, because Hispanic perspectives need to be part of our literary heritage; I want to be part of that validation process. I also write because I am fascinated by the pleasure and power of words." That "validation process" has also been a strong incentive for Mora to produce children's literature and juvenile poetry for and about Hispanic Americans. Through a series of bilingual books and stories that feature Hispanic protagonists, she has sought to establish pride in heritage for young Chicanos. "There is particular pleasure for me in poetry, there's just no doubt about that, but I see children's books as very close to that," the author explains in *This Is about Vision.* "I have very strong feelings that Chicano kids need good children's books, well illustrated, from big publishing houses, and that is something I would really like to work at."

As for the muse that drives her, Mora relates in *This Is about Vision:* "I think one of my big reasons for writing poetry is to help people feel less lonely; that's what poetry did for me. . . . I was able to read women writers and feel less lonely, and so any time my poetry does that for somebody, that is probably my definition of success."

BIOGRAPHICAL/CRITICAL SOURCES:

BOOKS

Balassi, William, John F. Crawford, and Annie O. Eysturoy, editors, *This Is about Vision: Interviews with Southwestern Writers,* University of New Mexico Press, 1990, pp. 129-139.
Hispanic Literature Criticism, Volume 2, Gale (Detroit, MI), 1994, pp. 844-854.
Norwood, Vera, and Janice Monk, editors, *The Desert Is No Lady: Southwestern Landscapes in Women's Writing and Art,* Yale University Press (New Haven, CT), 1987, pp. 96-124.
Notable Hispanic American Women, Gale, 1993, pp. 280-282.

PERIODICALS

Bloomsbury Review, September/October, 1993, p. 5.
Horn Book, July/August, 1990, pp. 436-437; November/December, 1994, pp. 723-724.
Nation, June 7, 1993, pp. 772-774.
Publishers Weekly, December 5, 1994, p. 76.
San Jose Studies, spring, 1989, pp. 29-40.
School Library Journal, October, 1994, p. 112.

*   *   *

MORAGA, Cherrie 1952-

PERSONAL: Born September 25, 1952, in Whittier, CA; daughter of Joseph Lawrence and Elvira Moraga.

Education: Received B.A., 1974; San Francisco State University, M.A., 1980.

ADDRESSES: Home—P.O. Box 410085, San Francisco, CA 94141. *Office*—Chicano Studies Department, University of California, 3404 Dwinelle Hall, Berkeley, CA 94720.

CAREER: High school English teacher in Los Angeles, CA, mid-1970s; Kitchen Table/Women of Color Press, New York City, co-founder and administrator, 1981—; INTAR (Hispanic-American arts center), New York City, playwright-in-residence, 1984; University of California, Berkeley, part-time writing instructor, 1986—; writer.

AWARDS, HONORS: American Book Award from Before Columbus Foundation, 1986, for *This Bridge Called My Back: Writings by Radical Women of Color;* NEA Theatre Playwrights' Fellowship Fund for New American Plays Award.

WRITINGS:

(Editor with Gloria Anzaldua, and contributor) *This Bridge Called My Back: Writings by Radical Women of Color,* Persephone Press, 1981, revised bilingual edition (edited with Ana Castillo) published as *Esta puente, mi espalda: Voces de mujeres tercer-mundistas en los Estados Unidos,* Spanish translation by Castillo and Norma Alarcon, ISM Press, 1988.
Loving in the War Years: Lo que nunca paso por sus labios (poetry and essays; subtitle means "What Never Passed Her Lips"), South End Press, 1983.
(Editor with Alma Gomez and Mariana Romo-Carmona) *Cuentos: Stories by Latinas,* Kitchen Table/Women of Color Press, 1983.
Giving Up the Ghost: Teatro in Two Acts (two-act play; first produced as stage reading in Minneapolis at At the Foot of the Mountain theater, June 16, 1984; produced in Seattle at Front Room Theater, March 27, 1987; revised version produced in San Francisco at Mission Cultural Center, April 5, 1987), West End Press, 1986.
Heroes and Saints (two-act play), first produced in Los Angeles at Los Angeles Theatre Lab, 1989.
(Editor with Norma Alarcon and Ana Castillo) *The Sexuality of Latinas,* Third Woman Press, 1991.
The Last Generation: Poetry and Prose, South End Press, 1993.
Heroes and Saints and Other Plays, West End Press, 1994.

*Waiting in the Wings: Portrait of a Queer Mother-
  hood,* Firebrand Books (Ithaca, NY), 1997.

Also author of two-act plays *La extranjera,* 1985, and
Shadow of a Man, 1988.

WORK IN PROGRESS: Dreaming of Other Planets, a
collection of poems.

SIDELIGHTS: Through her writing, Cherrie Moraga
explores her identity as a Chicana, a feminist, and a
lesbian. By publicly addressing each of these aspects
of herself, noted Yvonne Yarbro-Bejarano in her *Dictionary of Literary Biography* essay, Moraga speaks
for feminists and lesbians within the Chicano culture,
and for Chicanas within the larger American culture,
who have not spoken or cannot speak for themselves;
she "has given voice and visibility in Chicano writing
to those who have been silenced." In addition to
writing her own poetry, plays, and essays, Moraga
has co-edited two collections of women's writings,
and in 1981 she helped found Kitchen Table/Women
of Color Press, which is devoted to publishing the
works of minority women.

Moraga's first collection, *Loving in the War Years:
Lo que nunca paso por sus labios,* was published in
1983. It includes the poem "For the Color of My
Mother," which explores the relationship between the
light-skinned writer and her darker-skinned Chicana
mother (the author's father is Anglo-American), and the
essay "A Long Line of Vendidas," which interprets the
sexuality of Chicanas in terms of their cultural identity.
The essay describes women's subordination within
Chicano culture and explains that women are raised to
place men's needs before their own. Chicanas—whether
heterosexual or homosexual—must resist this tendency,
Moraga writes, and must instead emphasize their own
needs. This assertion "is not separatist," according to
Yarbro-Bejarano, "but woman-centered. Chicana feminism means putting women first." The reviewer called
"A Long Line of Vendidas" "a cornerstone text in the
development of a Chicana feminist analysis of sexuality
and gender."

Moraga's 1993 work, *The Last Generation: Poetry and
Prose,* continues the author's search for a "Queer
Aztlan," the "Chicano 'imagined community' that she
proposes to reinvent from a feminist, lesbian perspective," remarks *Nation* contributor Jan Clausen. Using a
mixture of poems, letters, memoirs, and essays, Moraga
laments the possible passing of a lost Chicano culture;
examines the legacy of heterosexism and patriarchalism
that she feels has damaged the Chicano community;

and explores lesbian love and commitment. Writing in
the *Women's Review of Books,* Marie-Elise Wheat-
wind remarks that "What Moraga points to, again and
again, is the potential power of women."

Moraga's plays, like her other writings, often illustrate
Chicano themes from a feminist perspective. *Giving Up
the Ghost,* for example, which was produced and published during the mid-1980s, consists of poetic monologues spoken by two women at different points in their
lives. The characters, speaking a mixture of Spanish and
English, recall the oppressive forces that have damaged
their perceptions of themselves as women. One character, Marisa, has tried to cope with being raped—and
with society's general disrespect for women—by assuming male attitudes and characteristics. The other woman,
Amalia, has become emotionally lifeless from repressing
her feelings, which she often finds too painful. For a
time the women comfort each other by becoming lovers,
but that relationship does not last. Each woman nonetheless gains something from the relationship, as Yarbro-
Bejarano notes. Amalia once again allows herself to feel
for another person, and Marisa learns to love and respect women after allowing herself to be loved.

Although Moraga has received considerable praise for
her own writings, she probably remains best known
for editing, with Gloria Anzaldua, the 1981 anthology
*This Bridge Called My Back: Writings by Radical
Women of Color.* The collection of poetry, fiction, essays, letters, and other forms of writing addresses the
differences as well as the similarities between feminist
women, touching on such subjects as skin color, class,
and sexual identity. "From this painful probing," observed Barbara Baracks in *Voice Literary Supplement,*
"emerges mutual respect far firmer than bland generalizations of sisterhood." Sara Mandelbaum, writing in
Ms., praised the book for demonstrating that women can
more truthfully communicate and more securely unite if
they acknowledge, rather than ignore, their differences.
"This Bridge," she assessed, "marks a commitment of
women of color to their *own* feminism—a movement
based not on separatism but on coalition." Mandelbaum
concluded, *"This Bridge* not only utterly challenged me,
but it filled me with greater hope for feminism than I
had felt in a long time."

BIOGRAPHICAL/CRITICAL SOURCES:

BOOKS

Dictionary of Literary Biography, Volume 82: *Chicano
    Writers, First Series,* Gale (Detroit), 1989.
Hispanic Writers, Gale, 1991.

PERIODICALS

Ms., March, 1982.
Nation, May 9, 1994, p. 634.
Publishers Weekly, August 30, 1993, p. 88.
Voice Literary Supplement, October, 1981.
Women's Review of Books, January, 1994, p. 22.*

*   *   *

MORALES, Rafael 1919-

PERSONAL: Born July 31, 1919, in Talavera de la Reina, Spain. *Education:* University of Madrid, Licenciatura (romance philology).

ADDRESSES: Agent—Espasa-Calpe, APDO 547 Madrid 28080 Spain.

CAREER: Writer. University of Madrid, professor of literature; Juan March Foundation, Department of Literature and Philology, secretary; *Estafeta Literaria* (journal), director.

AWARDS, HONORS: Premio Nacional de Literatura, 1954, for *Cancion sobre el asfalto;* grants from the Juan March Foundation, 1957, 1971.

WRITINGS:

Poemas de toro, Hispanica/Adonais (Madrid), 1943.
El corazon y la tierra, Santaren/Halcon (Valladoid, Spain), 1946.
Los desterrados, Hispanica/Adonais, 1947.
Poemas del toro y otros versos, Aguado (Madrid), 1949.
Cancion sobre el asfalto, Poetas/Radio (Madrid), 1954.
La pintura de Juan Guillermo, Ateneo (Madrid), 1957.
Antologia y pequena historia de mis versos, Escelicer (Madrid), 1958.
Entrevistas de Clarinero, [Mexico City], 1958.
La mascara y los dientes, Espanola (Madrid), 1958.
Dardo, el caballo del bosque, Doncel (Madrid), 1961.
Granadeno, toro bravo, Nacional (Madrid), 1964.
(Editor, with others) *Literatura contemporanea espanola e hispanoamericana,* O.F.E. (Madrid), 1964.
Poesias completas, Giner (Madrid), 1967.
(Editor) *Los 100 poetas mejores de la lirica castellana,* Giner, 1967.
La rueda y el viento, Alamo (Salamanca, Spain), 1971.
Antologia poetica, Pozanco (Barcelona), 1979.
Obra poetica, Espasa-Calpe (Madrid), 1982.

Reflexiones sobre mi poesia, Escuela Universitaria (Madrid), 1982.
Granadeno, toro bravo, Akal (Madrid), 1988.
Entre tantos adioses, Rusadir (Melilla), 1993.
Prado de Serpientes, Muelle de Uribitarte Editores, 1996.

SIDELIGHTS: In *Dictionary of Literary Biography,* Paula W. Shirley called Rafael Morales "one of the most lyrical and humanistic poets of the post-civil-war era in Spain. . . . he evokes the lyricism he perceives in all things. Among contemporary Spanish poets he has been admired for his innocence and the childlike love of all people that serves as a base for his poetic explorations." Morales was born in Talavera de la Reina, Spain, in 1919, and grew up in a difficult time in Spain's history, living under the varied rule of King Alfonso XIII, the brief Republic, and the Spanish Civil War. During his studies at the University of Madrid, Morales met with several other students to read poetry together and encourage each other in their writing careers. Morales's participation in this energetic group stimulated his literary career.

Morales had always been interested in writing, completing his first poem when he was seven years old, and publishing some lyrics at age fourteen. As a teenager, he idolized poet Vicente Aleixandre, whom he met in 1936. As he grew older, however, he began to find his own voice, and to produce work that was not marked by anyone else's influence. These poems, published as the collection *Poemas del toro* (Poems of the Bull), "brought him a great deal of attention from people important in the literary world," according to Shirley.

These poems were inspired by an experience in the summer of 1940, when Morales was home from school and went to a stock sale. One bothersome bull remained on his mind, and he wrote a poem about the animal. Aleixandre, who was his mentor, encouraged him to write more sonnets, and when he did, they were eagerly received by students and other writers. Despite the fact that bulls and bullfights were written about so frequently by Spanish poets, Morales brought freshness and enthusiasm to this formerly cliched topic. Shirely quoted Jose Maria de Cossio, a historian and critic of the bullfight, who praised "the vigor of expression, the mystery and power of the subject, the fortunate realization of the poem. . . . And the focus given to such a complicated subject as seen in these notes ennobles with its novelty, originality, and depth, the poetry of bullfighting."

Morales's second collection of poems, *El corazon y la tierra* ("The Heart and the Land"), lacks the focus of his first collection, according to Shirley. In 1945, broke and needing money, he gave all the poems he had to the journal *Fantasia*. He later said that he would have thrown some of them away if he had not been so desperate, but in later editions, he still did not remove these poems. According to Shirley, he called this book "the condemned, damned book that is to suffer a long purgatory." The poems, focusing on love, landscape, and death, are full of lonely images of misty places and separated lovers. Despite this imagery, Morales is offended by critics who maintain that his work fits into the category of *tremendismo*, or the "(grotesque) emphasis on the most negative and monstrous aspects of life."

Los desterrados ("The Exiles") focuses on compassion and humanitarianism, principles illustrated by Morales's behavior during the book's production. A friend of his, Jose Luis Hidalgo, had written a book that was scheduled to be published after Morales's, but when Morales found out that Hidalgo was terminally ill, he begged the publisher to change the order of the books and produce Hidalgo's first. The publisher agreed, but Hidalgo died before he could see his work in print.

Cancion sobre el asfalto ("Song on Asphalt") has been regarded as among his best work so far, and won the Premio Nacional de Literatura for 1954. These poems mark the beginning of Morales's social awareness. Shirley quoted critic Julio Lopez, who wrote that the collection "meets completely the need to humanize the monstrous cities we live in with a spiritual kind of solution, a clear Christian humanism, of evangelical stamp, that makes men more human and sensitive, able to sympathize not only with their fellow creatures but with the meanest objects, which then become human and companions." For example, in "Cantico doloroso al cubo de la basura" ("Sorrowful Canticle to the Garbage Can"), he writes, "Tenderness became round in you, / became round, soft, and sorrowful." Shirley remarked: "The can lovingly embraces the most humble of objects—an apple peel, a dusty bit of banana. Morales's artistry exalts the humble and the forgotten."

In his preface to *Poesias completas*, Morales listed three guiding principles for his work: "the search for expressive beauty, which affects the formal aspect; the attraction of the reality of the world, which affects the themes; love, which affects the essential content, the most deep and universal sense of it all." According to Shirley, critic C.D. Ley noted that

Morales has been "one of the most read poets of his generation. His poems have been reprinted more frequently than those of any other poet after 1939." And, as Shirley wrote, Morales's work has "had a profound influence on post-civil-war Spanish poetry, placing humanity—including the humble and forgotten—once again at the center of poetic concerns."

BIOGRAPHICAL/CRITICAL SOURCES:

BOOKS

Dictionary of Literary Biography, Volume 108: *Twentieth-Century Spanish Poets,* Gale (Detroit, MI), 1991.*

*   *   *

MORENO, Dorinda 1939-

PERSONAL: Born August 8, 1939, in Half Moon Bay, CA; daughter of migrant farm workers; married; children: three.   *Education:* San Francisco State University, B.A. (women's studies); graduate studies in journalism and communications at Stanford University.

ADDRESSES: Agent—Casa Editorial, 5503 Esplanada Avenue, Santa Maria, CA 93455.

CAREER: Poet and writer. Taught courses in philosophy, history, journalism, theater writing, and Chicana studies, Napa College, Ohlone College, and San Francisco State University, 1972-77; founded and directed cultural groups such as Las Cucarachas-Mexcla Teatral and Concilio Mujeres.

WRITINGS:

(Editor) *La mujer: En pie de lucha, y la hora es ya* (title means "The Woman: On a Footing of Struggle, and the Hour Is Now"), Espina del Norte (Mexico City), 1973.

The Image of the Chicana, and the La Raza Woman, Moreno (Stanford, CA), 1975.

Lu mujer es la tierra: La tierra da vida (title means "The Woman Is the Land: The Land Gives Life"), Casa Editorial (San Francisco, CA), 1975.

Also author of *Las cucarachas.*

ADAPTATIONS: Chicano Art: A Renaissance (includes poems read by Moreno), North Hollywood, CA, Center for Cassette Studies, 1974.

SIDELIGHTS: Dorinda Moreno was born in Half Moon Bay, California, and grew up in San Francisco and Mountain View, California. She was the third oldest of eight brothers and sisters, and grew up with an extended family of another two hundred relatives. Her parents worked as migrant farm laborers until she was twelve years old, and then her father worked as a gardener in San Francisco for the next twenty-eight years. Because her parents worked so hard, Moreno took on the responsibility of helping them raise her younger brothers and sisters. Moreno's anthology, *La mujer: En pie de lucha, y la hora es ya* contains some of her short stories, which she based on her father's work experiences.

As a child, Moreno moved from school to school as her parents followed the crops, but she dreamed even then of becoming a writer. Her interests in stories, as well as in history, activism, and human development, were fueled by her aunt. This aunt suffered from tuberculosis and had had a lung removed, without anesthesia, when she was thirteen. Confined to bed, she read and told Moreno stories about female heroes such as Babe Zaharias Didrickson, Amelia Earhart, Helen Gahagan Douglass, and others.

Moreno attended various high schools, and at age twenty-nine and with three children, entered San Francisco State University, where she earned a degree in women's studies. Later she began the M.A. program in journalism and communications at Stanford University, but did not complete that degree. From 1972 to 1977 she combined teaching various courses at Napa College, Ohlone College, and San Francisco State University with founding and directing cultural groups, including Las Cucarachas-Mexcla Teatral and Concilio Mujeres. Las Cucarachas was a performing arts group that provided a forum for new Chicano writers, poets, and actors, and Concilio Mujeres was an information center for Chicanas and Latinas.

Moreno's poetry is based on her devotion to social action, and her ethnic and cultural heritage. For example, the anthology she edited, *La mujer: En pie de lucha, y la hora es ya,* includes works by several writers, including Moreno, who expose injustices against people of color. In her writing, she works to make women aware that they have been discriminated against for centuries, and that indigenous people have also suffered at the hands of European Christians. Mingling invocations of ancient goddesses with current social and political events, Moreno's poetry speaks clearly about oppression while still remaining optimistic about positive change in the future.

Lu mujer es la tierra: La tierra da vida is an autobiographical collection of prose and poetry that expresses her love for her family, particularly her mixed-race son, Andre, who she calls "Blaxican." The poems give voice to her feelings on the oppression of women, the need for family and love, and an invitation to women to become activists. She believes that change for Chicano women cannot come about until they take action. Most of Moreno's poems are in free verse, and many use "code-switching," a mixture of English and Spanish. In *Dictionary of Literary Biography,* Maria Teresa Marquez quoted her as saying, "Today I speak their languages, both English and Spanish, but still I am neither, nor do I want to be. . . . I am Chicana." Most of her stories, however, are written in English.

Assessing the impact of Moreno's life and work, Marquez said: "Moreno takes risks in shaping the cultural awareness of the Chicana experience and voice, struggling to remedy the lack of cultural support. Emerging Chicana writers who have read her work or listened to Moreno publicly read her poetry see her as a role model. . . . Although she does not write poetry anymore, Moreno's place in the development of Chicano literature is secured. She now devotes her time to writing film scripts and novels. Her commitment to the Chicana struggle remains undiminished."

BIOGRAPHICAL/CRITICAL SOURCES:

BOOKS

Dictionary of Literary Biography, Volume 122: *Chicano Writers,* Gale (Detroit, MI), 1992.*

*   *   *

MUGICA, Rafael
  See CELAYA, Gabriel

*   *   *

MURGUIA, Alejandro 1949-

PERSONAL: Born in 1949. *Education:* Attended San Francisco State University.

ADDRESSES: Home—1799 Revere Ave., San Francisco, CA 94124-2345.

CAREER: Writer.

WRITINGS:

Farewell to the Coast, Heirs Press (San Francisco, CA), 1980.
(Editor with Barbara Paschke) *Volcan: Poems from Central America; A Bilingual Anthology,* City Lights (San Francisco, CA), 1983.
Southern Front, Bilingual Press (Tempe, AZ), 1990.*

*   *   *

MURRAY, Frederic W(illiam) 1933-

PERSONAL: Born January 24, 1933, in Vancouver, British Columbia, Canada; became U.S. citizen, 1948; son of Kenneth Scrimgeour and Winnefred Annie (Williams) Murray; married Berth M. Kahn, August 23, 1959; children: Kathleen Ann, Frederic, Jr., Rebecca Jean. *Education:* University of New Mexico, B.A., 1959, Ph.D., 1968. *Religion:* Catholic. *Avocational interests:* Travel, reading ("My vocation and avocation seem to have blended into one).

ADDRESSES: Home—1405 Bugle Boy Dr., Henderson, NV 89014-6098. *Office*—Department of Foreign Languages & Literatures, Northern Illinois University, De Kalb, IL 60115. *E-mail*—fmurray33@aol.com.

CAREER: University of Maine, Orono, instructor and assistant professor of Spanish, 1962-69; Northern Illinois University, De Kalb, associate professor of Spanish-American literature, 1969-92, chair of department, 1991-95, professor of Spanish-American literature, 1992-95, Emeritus professor/department chair, 1995—. *Military service:* Reno Air National Guard, Fourth Air Force, served on active duty, 1951-52 in 131st Communications Squadron.

MEMBER: American Association of Teachers of Spanish and Portuguese, Latin American Studies Association, Midwest Modern Language Association, Modern Language Association, Academy of American Poets (member of Delegate Assembly representing Midwest region, 1990-93).

AWARDS, HONORS: NDEA Title IV Ph.D. Fellowship in Ibero-American Studies, 1959-62; first place award and honorable mention, Nevada State Literary Competition, National League of PEN Women, 1997, for two poems; second prize and three honorable mentions, Nevada Poetry Society National Contest, 1998, for four poems.

WRITINGS:

La imagen Arquetipica en la Poesia de Ramon Lopez Velarde, Department of Romance Languages, University of North Carolina at Chapel Hill, 1972.
The Aesthetics of Contemporary Spanish–American Social Protest Poetry, Edwin Mellen (Lewiston, NY), 1990.

Contributor to H. Ryan-Ranson's *Imagination, Emblems, and Expressions: Essays on Latin American, Caribbean, and Continental Culture and Identity,* Bowling Green State University Popular Press (Bowling Green, OH), 1993. Contributor to periodicals, including *Chasqui, Mairena, Cincinnati Romance Review, Inter-American Review of Bibliography, New Mexico Quarterly,* and *Hispania.*

WORK IN PROGRESS: Three poems to appear in December, 1999 issue of *Wild Word;* "writing a book of poems that intertwine Native American languages (Chinook, Lakota, Hupa, etc.) with English, thus tying together my professional training and career as a linguist/translator with my talent as a poet"; "also writing poems on sundry themes and various styles, including a series on scientific topics."

SIDELIGHTS: Frederic Murray once explained: "After having enjoyed a successful career as a professor and scholar of Spanish–American literature and culture, I now find myself (as an emeritus professor) with the luxury of time and freedom from daily travail that all writers thirst for. Now I spend my days exploring the meaning of the creative process from the standpoint of a poet. I find the perspective and processes quite different from those of a literary scholar or critic. The creative process is basically an upwelling from the subconscious of wispy thought/nebulous emotion/amorphous word-feel that is then meditated upon by a sensual, cadenced word-phrase play . . . wolfsong, windsigh, frogcall that strums the senses with sound-image-emotion-word linked meaning. The literary critic's approach, on the other hand, is all rational thought, abstract theory; in a word, right brain versus left brain: analogic versus analytic thought. Happy the person who is able to glory in both!"

BIOGRAPHICAL/CRITICAL SOURCES:

BOOKS

Directory of American Scholars, Volume 3, R. R. Bowker Company (New York), 1982.

*   *   *

NALE ROXLO, Conrado 1898-1971
(Chamico)

PERSONAL: Born February 15, 1898, in Buenos Aires, Argentina; died July 2, 1971; married Teresa Isabel de la Fuente.

CAREER: Poet, c. 1922-. *Don Goyo* (humor magazine), editor, 1925.

AWARDS, HONORS: Winner of Babel Contest, for *El Grillo;* two National Theater Prizes, for *La Cola de la Sirena* and *Una Viuda Dificil;* Sixto Randal Rios Prize, 1967, for *Las Puertas del Purgatorio.*

WRITINGS:

Veinte poemas para ser leidos en el tranvia, [Paris, France], 1922.
El grillo (poems), Babel (Buenos Aires, Argentina), 1923.
Claro desvelo (poems), Sur (Buenos Aires), 1937.
La cola de la sirena (play), Hachette (Buenos Aires), 1941, edition by R. E. Gillespie, Appleton (East Norwalk, CT), 1957.
(Under pseudonym Chamico) *Cuentos de Chamico,* Halcon (Buenos Aires), 1941.
(Under pseudonym Chamico) *El muerto profesional,* Poseidon (Buenos Aires), 1943.
Antologia apocrifa (collected articles), Hachette, 1943.
Una viuda dificil (play), 1943, Poseidon, 1944.
El pacto de cristina: El cuervo del arca (play), Losada (Buenos Aires), 1945.
(Under pseudonym Chamico) *Cuentos de Cabecera,* La Cuerda Floja (Buenos Aires), 1946.
Poemas; El grillo; Claro desvelo, Ruggero (Buenos Aires), 1951.
De Otro Cielo (poems), Ruggero, 1952.
El diario de mi amiga Cordelia, la nina hada, Abril (Buenos Aires), 1953.
El humor de los humores: Almanaque de medicina para el ano que viene, Pie de Imprenta (Buenos Aires), 1953.

Libro de quejas, La Cuerda Floja, 1953.
(Under pseudonym Chamico) *Mi pueblo,* Emece (Buenos Aires), 1953.
Cuentos y poesias, edited by Gillespie, Appleton, 1954.
La escuela de las hadas (juvenile), Abril, 1954.
Sumarios policiales, Agepe (Buenos Aires), 1955.
(Under pseudonym Chamico) *Las puertas del purgatorio* (stories), Agepe, 1956.
Teatro: Judith y las rosas, El cuervo del arca, La cola de la sirena, Una viuda dificil, El pacto de Cristina, Sudamericana, 1956.
Antologia poetica, Perrot (Buenos Aires), 1957.
Extrano accidente (novel), Sudamericana, 1960.
Amado Vilar, Ministerio de Educacion y Justicia (Buenos Aires), 1962.
Genio y figura de Alfonsina Storni, Editorial Universitaria de Buenos Aires (Buenos Aires), 1964.
Teatro breve: El pasado de Elisa, El nebli, El vacio, El reencuentro, Huemul (Buenos Aires), 1964.
El ingenioso hidalgo, Editorial Universitaria de Buenos Aires, 1965.
Una viuda dificil; Judith y las rosas, Huemul, 1965.
Nueva antologia apocrifa, Fabril (Buenos Aires), 1969.
Borrador de memorias, Plus Ultra (Buenos Aires), 1978.

Also author, under pseudonym Chamico, of self-illustrated collection *La Medicina Vista de Reojo,* 1952; also author of the collection *Poesia Completa,* 1967. Contributor to magazines and newspapers, including *Proa* and *Martin Fierro.**

*   *   *

NARANJO, Carmen 1930-

PERSONAL: Born January 30, 1930, in Cartago, Costa Rica; daughter of Sebastian Naranjo Prida (in business) and Caridad Cot Troyo. *Education:* University of Costa Rica, licentiate degree, 1953. *Religion:* Catholic.

ADDRESSES: Agent—c/o Editorial Universitaria Centroamericana, San Pedro de Montea de Oca, Calle 41 (Barrio Los Yoses), Apdo. 64, San Jose, Costa Rica.

CAREER: Costa Rican poet, novelist, essayist, educator and public servant. Served as Costa Rican ambassador to Israel, 1972-74. Has taught several writer's workshops. Costa Rican Electric Company, assistant manager, 1964; La Caja, assistant manager, secretary general; served as Costa Rican Minister of culture, youth, and sports, 1974; Association of Caribbean and Central American Writers, vice president, 1976-78; Worldwide Association of Writers and Journalists, vice president; UNICEF Early Childhood Education Program for Central America and Panama, in Guatemala, 1976-78, in Mexico, 1978-80; Costa Rica Museum of Art, director, 1980-82; Editorial Universitaria Centroamericana (Central America Universities Publishing House), San Jose, Costa Rica, director, 1982-92.

MEMBER: Order of Alfonso X El Sabio, 1977—; Academia Costarricense de la Lengua (Costa Rican Academy of Language), 1988—.

AWARDS, HONORS: Aquileo Echeverria Prize, 1967, for *Los perros no ladraron* (title means "The Dogs Will Not Bark"); Prize for the Novel, Superior Council of Central American Universities, for *Diario de una multitud;* Premio Magon de Cultura, 1986.

WRITINGS:

Cancion de la ternura, Elite (San Jose, Costa Rica), 1964.
Hacia tu isla, Artes Graficas (San Jose, Costa Rica), 1966.
Los perros no ladraron (title means "The Dogs Will Not Bark"), Costa Rica (San Jose, Costa Rica), 1966.
Misa a oscuras, Costa Rica (San Jose, Costa Rica), 1967.
Memorias de un hombre palabra, Costa Rica (San Jose, Costa Rica), 1968.
Comino al mediodia, Lehmann (San Jose, Costa Rica), 1968.
Responso por el nino Juan Manuel, Conciencia Nueva (San Jose, Costa Rica), 1971.
Idioma del invierno, Conciencia Nueva, 1971.
Hoy es un largo dia, Costa Rica, 1972.
Diario de una multitud, Editorial Universitaria Centroamericana (San Jose, Costa Rica), 1974.
Por Israel y por las paginas de la Biblia, Fotorama de Centro Amercia (San Jose, Costa Rica), 1976.
Cinco temas en busca de un pensador, Minsterio de Cultura, Juventud y Deportes (San Jose, Costa Rica), 1977.
Las relaciones publicas en las instituciones de seguridad social, Instituto Centroamericano de Administracion Publica (San Jose, Costa Rica), 1977.

Mi guerrilla, Editorial Universitaria Centroamericana (San Jose, Costa Rica), 1977.
Cultura: 1. La accion cultural en Latinoamerica. 2. Estudio sobre la planificacion cultural, Instituto Centroamericano de Administracion Publica (San Jose, Costa Rica), 1978.
Ejercicios y juegos para mi nino, UNICEF (Guatemala City, Guatemala), 1981.
La mujer y el desarrollo, Sep Diana (Mexico City), 1981.
Homenaje a don Nadie, [Costa Rica], 1981.
Mi nino de 0 a 6 anos, UNICEF, 1982.
Ondina, Editorial Universitaria Centroamericana (San Jose, Costa Rica), 1983.
Nunca huba alguna vez, translated by Linda Britt as *There Never Was a Once Upon a Time,* Latin American Literary Review Press (Pittsburgh, PA), 1989.
(With Graciela Moreno) *Estancias y dias,* [Costa Rica], 1985.
Sobrepunto, Editorial Universitaria Centroamericana (San Jose, Costa Rica), 1985.
El caso 117.720, Editorial Universitaria Centroamericana (San Jose, Costa Rica), 1987.
Otro rumbo para la rumba, Editorial Universitaria Centroamericana (San Jose, Costa Rica), 1989.
Mujer y cultura, Editorial Universitaria Centroamericana (San Jose, Costa Rica), 1989.
Ventanas y asombros, Editorial Universitaria Centroamericana (San Jose, Costa Rica), 1990.
(Contributor) *Relatos de mujeres: antologia de narradoras de Costa Rica,* Editorial Mujeres (San Jose), 1993.
En partes, Farben Grupo Editorial (San Jose), 1994.

WORK IN PROGRESS: An autobiographical novel titled *Insomnios de una adolescente que nacio vieja* (title means "Sleepless Nights of an Adolescent Who Was Born Old").

SIDELIGHTS: Carmen Naranjo's life as a Costa Rican public servant is closely linked to her work as a writer; her work in both capacities reveals the same concerns she has had as an individual. Whether expressed in her novel *Los perros no ladraron* ("The Dogs Will Not Bark"), or through one of the programs she espoused while serving as Costa Rica's Minister of Culture, Youth, and Sports, a position she held for two years, Naranja has always shown a concern for the Costa Rican middle and lower classes. One of the most recognized public figures in her native land, Naranja has been awarded numerous honors, both as a writer and for her public service. Two such examples are the 1967 Aquileo Echeverria

Prize that she received for *Los perros no ladraron,* her debut novel, and the Premio Magon de Cultura, an honor bestowed on her in 1986 for her lifelong pursuit in promotion of education and culture in Costa Rica's urban centers. For the writings she produced, Naranjo is considered, by both her fellow citizens and foreign critics alike, one of her nation's most important literary figures, and certainly one of its most well known. In all she has published seven novels, as many volumes of poetry, four books of short stories, and another four comprised of essays.

Although she is most known for her poetry, Naranjo has accomplished a great deal with her novels and short stories. Oftentimes, she has used fiction as a vehicle to criticize various aspects of the Costa Rican social milieu that she perceived to be morally wrong or unjust. In her stories, she has also employed experimental and creative narrative styles, a technique that has made hers a unique voice in the Costa Rican literary scene. Her career in the political sphere hit its pinnacle when she was appointed her country's ambassador to Israel (1972-74), an experience she chronicled in her book of essays *Por Israel por las paginas de la Biblia.*

Though she has lived the majority of her life in the Costa Rican capital of San Jose, Naranja's career has also stretched beyond the country's borders. Between 1976 and 1980 she coordinated relief efforts for the United Nations International Children's Emergency Fund (UNICEF) throughout Central America and Mexico. Her writing career has also taken her abroad, as she was invited and subsequently participated in a writer's workshop at the University of Iowa, also teaching a Latin-American literature class at that institution. To this day, Naranjo is active in Costa Rica's literary community. Since 1993 her voice has continued to be publicly heard, as she has contributed a regular column to one of Costa Rica's largest newspapers, *El Dia.* She has also fostered interest in literature by conducting *talleres,* or workshops, for those who want to pursue a writing career. And on top of all of this, Naranja continues to work on her own projects, including a novel, mostly based on her life, called *Insomnios de una adolescente que nacio vieja.*

Born in the town of Cartago in 1930, Naranjo was the third of four children of Sebastian Naranjo Prida and Caridad Cot Troyo. Though her father was a businessman, Naranjo and her three brothers were forced to work at an early age to help provide a living for the family. Naranjo's life was imperiled when she contracted a severe case of polio at the age of seven, after her family had moved to San Jose. However, the disease did force her to cutback on her work, which enabled her to begin her first year of education under the direction of a personal tutor. It was also during this time that she was introduced to numerous literary works, including those by Plato and Aristotle, which undoubtedly influenced her to choose the path in life that she did.

By the time she graduated from high school, Naranjo was an avid reader, taking in the works of William Faulkner, Emily Dickinson, Walt Whitman, and Carson McCullers. Naranjo's first writing experience, other than keeping an extensive diary, came when she began penning speeches for her father to read at the meetings of the Spanish Society, to which he was a member. Naranja attended college at the University of Costa Rica, where she studied the liberal arts, graduating in 1953. Soon thereafter, she landed a job with the Caja Costarricense del Seguro Social (Bureau of Social Security). While working for the United Nations in Venezuela, Naranjo completed her first book of poetry, *Cancion de la ternura.* This was the first time that she was away from her family for any extended period, and the book is reflective of the love she was feeling for them. Modest about her literary talents, Naranjo shelved the work, and it was not published until 1964, nearly a decade later.

Soon after returning to her homeland, Naranja enrolled into a writer's workshop, and began making a name for herself in the literary community when she published two volumes of poetry. After she wrote *Los perros no ladraron,* Naranja began reading the works of other Latin American writers, including those by Carlos Fuentes, Juan Rulfo, Jorge Luis Borges, and Octavio Paz, and she began to see herself in the same light. Her first three novels, including *Los perros no ladraron,* and followed by *Memorias de un hombre palabra* and *Camino al mediodia,* both published in 1968, all concentrate on the lives of unnamed, middle-class men as they weave their way through urban Costa Rica. Each of the novels is somewhat critical of the political environment of Costa Rica at the time, a world that was dominated by a patriarchal mentality.

With *Los perros no ladraron,* Naranja wrote a story that takes place on a typical Friday in urban Costa Rica. Middle-class in nature, the book revolves around the point of view of several characters, each of whom comes from a different segment of the country's social makeup: a junk man, a domestic servant, a professional, a madman, government worker, and an entrepreneur. Through their dealings, the reader is able to get a look at the entire Costa Rican hierarchy, from the homeless street person, who is ultimately the main character, to the upper echelon of society. It also shows the discrepancies in what each member of society is able to attain, despite that fact that each is interconnected and relies on the others in some way. The narrative style that Naranjo employs is innovative, a series of inner monologues, which represent the protagonist's inner thoughts and feelings.

Because of the success of her first three novels, Naranjo began to earn a reputation outside of her native land, ultimately leading to the invitation by the University of Iowa, which she accepted. While in Iowa, Naranja completed her next novel, *Diario de una multitud,* probably her most critically lauded effort. During this time, her political life was also on the rise. After a series of jobs in the public sector, she served as the ambassador to Israel, and wrote weekly essays that were published in various Costa Rican newspapers. Through these essays, Naranjo became a popular individual among her people. In fact, she became so popular that, after her term in Israel was up, President Daniel Oduber Quiros appointed her as Minister of Culture, Youth, and Sports, a position she held for two years. Many critics have suggested that Naranjo's notoriety as a public servant fanned the flames of her literary career, and gained her a wider audience than she probably would have otherwise had. Still, the impact of her work has been profound in her native land, as it has often shed light on many of Costa Rica's social problems. In a 1993 interview with Ardis L. Nelson, reprinted in *Reinterpreting the Spanish American Essay,* Naranja described some of the motivations behind her work. "It is as if with a pencil you can draw blood. As if in your desire to find yourself you find all humanity," Naranja told Nelson.

Critics have not missed that point. "Her work is intellectual, original, linguistically innovative, psychological, and compassionate. Her poetry is metrically free and structurally lyrical; her narrative exhibits a mixture of fantasy and reality, a preoccupation with the Spanish language, and a search for identity, both individual and cultural," Arlen O. Schade remarked in *Women Writers of Spanish America.* "The verbal style that characterizes the author, in prose as in poetry, is that of an amazing abundance of words, images, concepts, metaphors, and enumerations," asserted Aura Rosa Vargas in *Kanina.* Since the late 1970s, Naranja has lent her time to a number of projects, including a stint as the director of the Costa

Rica Museum of Art, and another in a similar position with EDUCA (Central America Universities Publishing House). She also published several more literary works, including *Nunca hubo alguna vez* in 1984, a book of short stories directed towards children, and a work that she conceived while working with the Costa Rican youth.

BIOGRAPHICAL/CRITICAL SOURCES:

BOOKS

Dictionary of Literary Biography, Volume 145: *Modern Latin-American Fiction Writers,* second series, edited by William Luis and Ann Gonzalez, Gale (Detroit, MI), 1994.
Reinterpreting the Spanish-American Essay: Studies of Nineteenth– and Twentieth–Century Women's Essays, edited by Doris Meyer, University of Texas Press (Austin), 1994.
Women Writers of Spanish America, edited by Diane E. Marting, Greenwood Press (New York City), 1987.

PERIODICALS

Kanina, July-December, 1977, pp. 33-36.*

* * *

NIOSI, Jorge 1945-

PERSONAL: Born December 8, 1945, in Buenos Aires, Argentina; son of Salvador (in business) and Emilia (Farina) Niosi; married Graciela Ducatenzeiler (a university professor), November, 1971; children: Marianne, Laurence. "Caucasian." *Education:* National University of Buenos Aires, license in sociology, 1967; Institut d'Etudes du Developpement Economique et Social, Paris, France, certificate in advanced studies in economics, 1970; Ecole Pratique, Paris, Ph.D., 1973.

ADDRESSES: Home—4052 Marlowe, Montreal, Quebec, Canada H4A 3M2. *Office*—Center for Research on the Development of Industry and Technology, University of Quebec at Montreal, Annexe Garneau, 1750 rue Saint-Andre, Montreal, Quebec, Canada H3C 3P8; fax 514-987-4166/3084.

CAREER: University of Quebec at Montreal, associate professor, 1970-74, aggregate professor, 1974-81, professor of sociology, 1981—, professor of administrative science, 1989—, director of Center for Research on the Development of Industry and Technology, 1986—. Statistics Canada, researcher, 1987-90.

MEMBER: International Sociological Association, International Management of Technology Association, European Association for Evolutionary Political Economy, Royal Society of Canada (fellow).

AWARDS, HONORS: John Porter Award, Canadian Sociological Association, 1983, for Canadian Capitalism; Fulbright fellow, 1995-96.

WRITINGS:

Los empresarios y el estado Argentino (title means "Business and the Argentine State"), Siglo XXI, 1974.
The Economy of Canada, Black Rose Books, 1978.
Canadian Capitalism, Lorimer, 1981.
Canadian Multinationals, Garamond, 1985.
The Decline of the American Economy, Black Rose Books, 1988.
La montee de l'ingenierie canadienne, Presses de l'Universite de Montreal (Montreal, QUEBEC), 1990.
Technology and National Competitiveness, McGill-Queen's University Press (Montreal), 1991.
Flexible Innovation, McGill-Queen's University Press, 1995.

WORK IN PROGRESS: A book on Canada's national system of innovation; research on Canadian technology transfer abroad.

SIDELIGHTS: Reflecting on her career, Jorge Niosi noted: "I started working on Canada with the idea of comparing it to Argentina. Both countries were similarly rich and successful fifty years ago. Why did Argentina fail when Canada succeeded? The comparison, however, never materialized.

"In Canada, I discovered that Canadian-owned large firms were much stronger and numerous than generally believed, that many of them were multinational corporations, and that their industrial base was much healthier than most of the literature had previously stated. The relative decline of American industry is not strongly affecting Canada's manufacturing industry, which is mostly based on energy- and resource-intensive strongholds like pulp and paper, metal refining, and petrochemicals. In 1982 I started studying Canadian innovation and technology. This is, and will remain, my main field of study. My main motivation for writing is pure curiosity."

*   *   *

NOGUERA, Magdalena
See CONDE, Carmen

O

OBEJAS, Achy 1956-

PERSONAL: Born Born June 28, 1956, in Havana, Cuba, daughter of Jose and Alicia Obejas. *Education:* Attended Indiana University, 1977-79; Warren Wilson College, M.F.A., 1993.

ADDRESSES: Home—1354 W. Carmen Ave., Chicago, IL 60640-2934. *Office*— Columbia College, Chicago, IL 60605.

CAREER: Writer. *Chicago Tribune,* Chicago, IL, columnist and cultural critic; Columbia College, Chicago, creative writing instructor.

MEMBER: National Association of Hispanic Journalists, National Lesbian and Gay Journalists Association.

AWARDS, HONORS: National Endowment for the Arts, poetry fellow, 1986; Illinois Arts Council completion grant; Lisagor Award (journalism), 1989; two Yaddo fellowships; four Ragsdale Foundation fellowships; Lambda Literary Award, 1997, for *Memory Mambo.*

WRITINGS:

We Came All the Way from Cuba So You Could Dress like That?, Cleis Press (Pittsburgh, PA), 1994.
Memory Mambo, Cleis, 1996.

SIDELIGHTS: Cuban-born author Achy Obejas teaches creative writing and writes newspaper columns in Chicago. She has published a collection of short stories; her first novel, 1996's *Memory Mambo,* has won awards and high critical praise.

We Came All the Way from Cuba So You Could Dress like That?, published in 1994, collects short stories, personal memoirs, and essays exploring the plight of refugees as outsiders trying to fit in. Several of her narrators are lesbians trying to figure out how to make relationships work. In "Forever," one character says of her ex-lover, "We're good lesbians: we've been painfully breaking up for two years." In "Wrecks" the narrator explains that she is due for another car crash because her lover has just left her; every time that happens, she gets into a wreck. Other characters include junkies, gay people, people with AIDS, and Cuban boat people. In "Above All, a Family Man," a married man insists to his gay lover that he is not at risk for AIDS since he is married. The title story tells the history of an immigrant Cuban family, with its fragmented memories and dreams of returning home. A *Kirkus Reviews* commentator, in a review of *We Came All the Way from Cuba* declared that Obejas has written "very accessible, sweet stories" which are "down-to-earth," and a *Booklist* reviewer asserted that Obejas's prose "moves us." Deanna Kriesel, assessing the collection in *Belles Lettres,* noted that "the subject matter is compelling and fresh."

In *Memory Mambo,* which was published in 1996, Obejas continues and deepens the story of Cuban immigrants in Chicago. Protagonist Juani Casas ponders the unreliability of memory as she tries to understand the secrets, obsessions, and true history of her family, both biological and extended. Because Juani, a twenty-four year old lesbian, walks a thin line between being "out" about her sexuality and the need to be discreet around her biological family, she allows her cousin-in-law Jimmy to tell them lies about her relationship with Gina, which ended violently. She comes to believe the lies herself and loses her ability to distinguish fact from fiction. Jimmy has a violent nature and abuses Juani's cousin Caridad, but Juani is a batterer herself, more like Jimmy than she is willing to admit. A critic for *Booklist* called the book "[r]aw, powerful and uncompromising," and a *Gay Studies* contributor deemed Obejas's writing "sharp and mordantly funny [and] . . . ultimately very moving." A *Midwest Book Review* commentator called Obejas "supremely talented," with a "gift for dialogue, character development, and insight into the human condition." Catey Sullivan, writing for *Outlines*, maintained that *Memory Mambo* stood out from other family dramas because of "the absolute immediacy and the gorgeousness of Obejas' prose."

BIOGRAPHICAL/CRITICAL SOURCES:

PERIODICALS

Belles Lettres, January, 1996, p. 55.
Booklist, October 15, 1994, p. 394; September 1, 1996, p. 63.
HUES, summer, 1997, p. 53.
Kirkus Reviews, August 15, 1994, p. 1079.
Library Journal, August 1996, p. 113.
Publishers Weekly, July 8, 1996, p. 79.

OTHER

Outlines, October, 1996, http://www.suba.com/~outlines/jacqtemp/author-o.html.*

*   *   *

ONETTI, Juan Carlos 1909-1994

PERSONAL: Born July 1, 1909, in Montevideo, Uruguay; died May 30, 1994, in Madrid, Spain; son of Carlos and Honoria (Borges) Onetti; married Dolly Muhr, November, 1955; children: Jorge, Isabel.

CAREER: Writer of novels and short stories. Worked as editor for Reuter News Agency in Montevideo, Uruguay, 1942-43, and in Buenos Aires, Argentina, 1943-46; manager of advertising firm in Montevideo, 1955-57; director of municipal libraries in Montevideo, beginning 1957.

AWARDS, HONORS: National Literature Prize of Uruguay, 1963; Ibera-American Award, William Faulkner Foundation, 1963; Casa de las Americas Prize, 1965; Italian-Latin American Institute Prize, 1972.

WRITINGS:

El pozo (also see below), Signo, 1939, enlarged and revised edition bound with *Seguido de origen de un novelista y de una generacion literaria* by Angel Rama, Editorial Alfa, 1965, second revised edition, Arca, 1973.
Tierra de nadie (novel), Editorial Losada, 1941, reprinted, Editorial Seix Barral, 1979, *No Man's Land* with translation by Peter Bush, Quartet Books, 1994.
Para esta noche (also see below), Editorial Poseidon, 1943.
La vida breve (novel), Editorial Sudamericana, 1950, reprinted, Edhasa, 1980, translation by Hortense Carpentier published as *A Brief Life,* Grossman, 1976.
Un sueno realizado y otros cuentos (also see below), Numero, 1951.
Los adioses (novel; also see below), Sur, 1954, reprinted, Bruguera, 1981.
Una tumba sin nombre, Marcha, 1959, published as *Para una tumba sin nombre* (also see below), Arca, 1959, reprinted, Editorial Seix Barral, 1982.
La cara de la desgracia (novella; also see below), Editorial Alfa, 1960.
El astillero (novel), Compania General Fabirl Editora, 1961, reprinted, Catedra, 1983, translation by Rachel Caffyn published as *The Shipyard,* Scribner, 1968.
El infierno tan temido, Editorial Asir, 1962.
Tan triste como ella (also see below), Editorial Alfa, 1963, reprinted, Lumen, 1982.
Juntacadaveres (novel), Editorial Alfa, 1964, revised edition, Arca, 1973.
Jacob y el otro [and] *Un sueno realizado y otros cuentos,* Ediciones de la Banda Oriental, 1965.
Cuentos completos, Centro Editor de America Latina, 1967, revised edition, Corregido, 1974.
Tres novelas (contains *La cara de la desgracia, Tan triste como ella,* and *Jacob y el otro*), Editorial Alfa, 1967.
Novelas cortas completas (contains *El pozo, Los adioses, La cara de la desgracia, Tan triste como ella,* and *Para una tumba sin nombre*), Monte Avila Editores, 1968.
La novia robada y otros cuentos (short stories including *La novia robada;* also see below), Centro Editor de America Latina, 1968, reprinted, Siglo Veintiuno Editores, 1983.

Los rostros del amor, Centro Editor de America Latina, 1968.

Obras completas, Aguilar, 1970.

La muerte y la nina (also see below), Corregidor, 1973.

Onetti (collection of articles and interviews), Troisi y Vaccaro, 1974.

Tiempo de abrazar y los cuentos de 1933 a 1950 (short stories), Arca, 1974.

(With Joacquin Torres-Garcia and others) *Testamento artistico,* Biblioteca de Marcha, 1974.

Requiem por Faulkner, Arca, 1975.

Tan triste como ella y otros cuentos (short stories), Lumen, 1976.

El pozo [and] *Para una tumba sin nombre,* Editorial Calicanto/Arca, 1977, second edition, Seix Barral, 1980.

Dejemos hablar al viento, Bruguera Alfaguara, 1979.

La muerte y la nina [and] La novia robada, Bruguera, 1980.

Cuentos secretos, Biblioteca de Marcha, 1986.

Presencia y otros cuentos (contains "Presencia"), Almarabu, 1986.

Cuando entonces, Editorial Sudamericana, 1988.

Goodbyes and Stories (contains *Goodbyes, A Dream Come True, Esbjerg by the Sea, The House on the Sand, The Photograph Album, Hell Most Feared, The Image of Misfortune, Sad as She, New Year's Eve,* and *The Stolen Bride*), translation by Daniel Balderston, University of Texas Press, 1990.

The Pit and Tonight (contains *El pozo* and *Para esta noche*), translated by Peter Bush, Quartet, 1991.

Body Snatcher, Random House, 1992.

Farewells & A Grave with No Name, translation by Peter Bush, Quartet Books, 1992.

Past Caring?, translation by Peter Bush, Quartet, 1995.

Editor of *Marcha,* 1939-42, and *Vea y Lea,* 1946-55.

SIDELIGHTS: Although considered by a number of critics to have been among the finest and most innovative novelists in South America, Juan Carlos Onetti was generally not well known outside of his homeland in Latin America. While praised and admired for their richness in imagination, creativity, and unique vision, Onetti's writings have also been described as fundamentally ambiguous, quite fragmentated, and often complex. As M. Ian Adams confirms in his book, *Three Authors of Alienation: Bombal, Onetti, Carpentier,* "Complexity and ambiguity are the major characteristics of Onetti's novels."

"Onetti's art is a strange aggregate of cultural characteristics and personal circumstances (some elusive, many contradictory and a few truly illuminating) none of which would really endear his writings to us were it not for the extraordinary nature of his style," states Luys A. Diez in *Nation.* Diez continues, "His prose has a genuinely hypnotic force, digressive and meandering, but quite without apparent *longueurs,* studded with linguistic quirks and poetic flights, economically terse and playfully serious; he teases the reader with alternate scenarios for a given situation to concentrate afterwards on a passing thought or a seemingly unimportant gesture."

Despite his critical recognition, few of Onetti's books have been translated into English. *The Shipyard,* though written after *A Brief Life,* was published first. It tells the story of Larsen, a shipyard worker who seeks to improve his social status by attaching himself to the shipyard owner's daughter. But he is unable to see that the society he aspires to has disintegrated, and the novel ends with his death. "Larsen moves through Onetti's pages as a figure virtually doomed to disaster," declares James Nelson Goodsell in the *Christian Science Monitor.* "Onetti is trying to evoke a picture of futility and hopelessness—a task which he performs very ably. . . . Onetti's purpose is to keep the reader absorbed, but to remain enigmatic. He succeeds admirably. [He] is a skillful writer whose prose is absorbing and demanding." And David Gallagher endorses *The Shipyard* in the *New York Times Book Review* as "a book which, for all its portentousness, few Latin American novelists have equaled."

The plot of *A Brief Life* is much more fantastical than that of *The Shipyard.* It concerns Juan Carlos Brausen, referred to as a "sort of Argentine Walter Mitty" by Emir Rodriguez Monegal in the *New York Times Book Review.* Brausen escapes from his many burdens by retreating from reality into a series of complex and often bizarre fantasy adventures. In *Review 75,* Hugo J. Verani calls *A Brief Life* "one of the richest and most complex novelistic expressions in Spanish-American fiction."

In a *Newsweek* review, Margo Jefferson writes that *A Brief Life* "is a virtuosic blend and balance of opposites: melodrama and meditation, eroticism and austerity, naturalism and artifice. . . . In Onetti's hands, the novel becomes an excursion into a labyrinth where the real and the imagined are mirror images. . . . Behind his sleight of hand is a melancholy irony—for all our efforts to escape a single life, we remain prisoners of a pattern, 'condemned to a soul, to a manner of being.'"

Because of its unique unfolding of plot, *A Brief Life* has received inevitable comparisons with the work of William Faulkner. Diez notes in the *Nation* that "much of Faulkner's rich, dark sap flows through the meandering narrative." Diez also contends that "Onetti's novelistic magic, like Faulkner's, requires a certain amount of perseverance on the reader's part." And Monegal remarks that "in *A Brief Life,* Onetti's love for Faulknerian narrative is already evident."

Several critics have expressed their high regard for Onetti's skillful use of experimental narration. Zunilda Gertel writes in *Review 75* that "Onetti's narrative does not postulate an ideology or an intellectual analysis of the ontological. Instead, the existential projection of the 'I' is shown as a revelation within the signs imposed on him by literary tradition considered as ritual, not as reconciliation." Also writing in *Review 75,* John Deredita claims that *A Brief Life* "exhaustively tests the power of fantasy and fictional imagination as a counter to the flow of time." And Verani concludes that "Onetti does not emphasis the mimetic quality of narrative. The aim of his fiction is not to reflect an existent reality, a factual order, but . . . to create an essentially fabulated reality invested with mythic significance."

Goodbyes and Stories contains the novella-length *Goodbyes* and nine other short stories. Offering praise for the title story, originally published as *Los Adioses* in 1954, Mary-Lee Sullivan writes in *Studies in Short Fiction,* "Few contemporary fiction writers have depended as heavily on the interpretative strategies of the reader as did Juan Carlos Onetti." *Goodbyes,* according to Sullivan, "is one of his most demanding texts in this regard, it is also a hallmark of the Onettian narrative in its controlled structuring of ambiguity. . . . The fact that the past 40 years of critical theorizing have failed to exhaust the responses elicited by *Goodbyes* would seem to confirm that the power of the text to draw on the unconscious projections of any given reader is inherent in its composition."

Djelal Kadir writes in *American Book Review,* "The reader coming to Onetti for the first time through the short stories in the present collection will feel the accumulating density of this author's brooding prose. How soon one succumbs either to the enchantment or to the exasperation elicited by Onetti's writing depends on one's constitution." Sullivan adds, "Onetti's is a literature of subjectivity, about how we perceive and interpret, as we are perceived and interpreted by others. Through words we are capable of transforming others and being transformed by them, as so many

fragments of perceptions and interpretations coalesce in order to create any given version of reality." In "The Image of Misfortune," one of the stories from the collection, the main character remarks on his brother's suicide, "Words are pretty, or try to be, when they point toward an explanation. From the first, all these words are useless, at odds with one another."

In *Body Snatcher,* published two years before Onetti's death in 1994, The author depicts a dissatisfied pharmacist's effort to realize his lifelong dream to own a brothel. However, after Larsen, known as the "Body Snatcher," wins his bid to establish the first bordello in his hometown, public opinion eventually turns against him and he faces opposition from the League of Decency. As David Buckley notes in the *Observer,* the novel represents Onetti's "bleak but compelling vision of people without values" and "acts of town life which offer no relief from alienation." Praising the novel in the *New York Times Book Review,* James Polk writes, Onetti "is probably the least-known giant among Latin American writers. Here he shows us what we've missed, controlling a wandering narrative with firmness and verve. Mr. Onetti clearly prefers the circular to the linear and the static to the dynamic. The result is intense and highly idiosyncratic."

BIOGRAPHICAL/CRITICAL SOURCES:

BOOKS

Adams, M. Ian, *Three Authors of Alienation: Bombal, Onetti, Carpentier,* University of Texas Press, 1975.

Contemporary Literary Criticism, Gale, Volume 7, 1977, Volume 10, 1979.

Curiel, Fernando, *Onetti: Obra y calculado infortunio,* Universidad Nacional Autonoma de Mexico, 1980.

Harss, Luis and Barbara Dohmann, *Into the Mainstream: Conversations with Latin-American Writers,* Harper, 1967.

Kadir, Djelal, *Juan Carlos Onetti,* Twayne, 1977.

Ludurer, Josefina, *Onetti: Los procesos de construccion del relato,* Sudamericana, (Buenos Aires), 1977.

Maloof, Judy, *Over Her Dead Body: The Construction of Male Subjectivity in Onetti,* P. Lang, 1995.

Milian-Silveira, Maria C., *El primer Onetti y sus contextos,* Editorial Pliegos, 1986.

Millington, Mark, *An Analysis of the Short Stories of Juan Carlos Onetti: Fictions of Desire,* E. Mellen Press, 1993.

Murray, Jack, *The Landscapes of Alienation: Ideological Subversion in Kafka, Celine, and Onetti,* Stanford University Press, 1991.

Prego, Omar and Maria Angelica Petit, *Juan Carlos Onetti o la salvacion por la escritura,* Sociedad General Espanola de Libreria (Madrid), 1981.

Ruffinelli, Jorge, editor, *Onetti* Marcha (Montevideo), 1973.

Ruffinelli, *Palabras en ordern* Crisis (Buenos Aires), 1974, pp. 69-88.

Verani, H., editor, *Juan Carlos Onetti, el escritor ante la critica,* Taurus (Madrid), 1987.

PERIODICALS

American Book Review, April, 1991, p. 17.
Camp del'Arpa, June-July, 1977.
Choice, September, 1990, p. 122.
Christian Science Monitor, October 8, 1968.
Cuadernos Hispanoamericanos, October-December, 1974.
Eco, March, 1970.
Hispania 71, May, 1988.
Library Journal, March 1, 1976.
Nation, April 3, 1976.
New Statesman, February 26, 1993.
Newsweek, February 16, 1976.
New Yorker, February 9, 1976.
New York Times Book Review, June 16, 1968; January 11, 1976; August 11, 1991, p. 6; January 10, 1993, p. 28.
Observer, November 17, 1991.
Publishers Weekly, April 20, 1990, p. 68; March 29, 1991.
Review 75, winter, 1975.
Saturday Review, January 24, 1976.
Studies in Short Fiction, summer, 1994, p. 441.

OBITUARIES:

PERIODICALS

Chicago Tribune, June 2, 1994, p. 10.
New York Times, June 1, 1994, p. B10.
Times (London), June 2, 1994, p. 19.
Washington Post, May 31, 1994, p. D7.*

*   *   *

ORTEGA y GASSET, Jose 1883-1955
(Jose Ortega y GASSET)

PERSONAL: Born May 9, 1883, in Madrid, Spain; died October 18, 1955, in Madrid, Spain; son of Jose Ortega y Munilla (a journalist and novelist) and Maria Dolores Gasset Chinchilla; married Rosa Spottorno y Topete, April 7, 1910; children: Miguel German, Jose, Soledad. *Education:* University of Madrid, licenciatura en filosofia y letras (M.A.), 1902, Ph.D., 1904; postgraduate study at universities of Leipzig, 1905, Berlin, 1906, and Marburg, 1906-07, 1911.

CAREER: Escuela Superior del Magisterio (normal school), Madrid, Spain, professor of psychology, logic, and ethics, 1908-10; University of Madrid, Madrid, professor of metaphysics, 1910-29 (resigned in protest against Spanish government), and 1930-36; representative of Province of Leon to Constitutional Parliament of Second Spanish Republic, 1931. Writer in exile in France, Netherlands, Argentina, and Portugal, beginning 1936; University of San Marcos, Lima, Peru, professor of philosophy, beginning 1941. Founder Instituto de Humanidades (Madrid), 1948; Founder or co-founder of several publications, including *Faro* (title means "Beacon"); *Europa,* 1911; monthly journal *Espana* (organ of League for Political Education), c. 1914; newspaper *El sol,* 1917; founder and co-editor of literary monthly *La Revista de Occidente,* 1923-35.

MEMBER: League for Political Education (founder, c. 1914), Group at the Service of the Republic (co-founder, 1931), Pen Club (president).

AWARDS, HONORS: Scholarship from Spanish government for postgraduate study in Germany, 1906; elected to Royal Academy of Moral and Political Sciences, 1914; Gold Medal of City of Madrid, 1936; named to Bavarian Academy of Fine Arts, 1949; honorary doctorates from universities of Marburg and Glasgow, 1951.

WRITINGS:

Meditaciones del Quijote, Residencia de Estudiantes (Madrid), 1914, reprinted, Revista de Occidente en Alianza (Madrid), 1981, translation by Evelyn Rugg and Diego Marin published as *Meditations on Quixote,* Norton, 1961.

El espectador (title means "The Spectator," Volumes 1 and 2, Renacimiento (Madrid), 1916, 1917, Volume 3, Calpe (Madrid), 1921, Volumes 4-8, Revista de Occidente, 1925-34, reprinted as one volume, Biblioteca Nueva (Madrid), 1950.

Personas, obras, cosas (title means "Persons, Works, Things," Renacimiento, 1916, published as *Mocedades* (title means "Juvenilia"), Revista de Occidente, 1973.

Espana invertebrada (title means "Invertebrate Spain," Calpe, c. 1921, reprinted, Revista de Occidente en Alianza, 1981, translation of selections by Mildred Adams published by Norton, 1937.

El tema de nuestro tiempo, Calpe, 1923, reprinted, Revista de Occidente en Alianza, 1981, translation by James Cleugh published as *The Modern Theme,* Harper, 1931.

La deshumanizacion del arte e ideas de la novela, Revista de Occidente, 1925, reprinted, Revista de Occidente en Alianza, 1984, translation by Helene Weyl published as *The Dehumanization of Art: Ideas on the Novel,* Princeton University Press, 1948.

La rebelion de las masas, Revista de Occidente, 1930, reprinted, Revista de Occidente en Alianza, 1981, translation by J. R. Carey published as *The Revolt of the Masses,* 1932, translation by Anthony Kerrigan published under the same title, with foreword by Saul Bellow, University of Notre Dame Press, 1986, reprinted under same title, Norton, 1994.

La mision de la universidad, Revista de Occidente, 1930, reprinted, Revista de Occidente en Alianza, 1982, translation by Howard Lee Nostrand published as *Mission of the University,* Norton, 1946.

La redencion de las provincias y de la decencia nacional (title means "The Redemption of the Provinces and National Decency"), Revista de Occidente, 1931, reprinted, Revista de Occidente Alianza, 1966.

Rectificacion de la Republica (title means "Rectification of the Republic"), Revista de Occidente, 1931.

Obras (title means "Works"), Espasa-Calpe (Madrid), 1932, reprinted with additions, 1943.

Pidiendo un Goethe desde dentro, Revista de Occidente, 1932, title essay translated by Willard R. Trask as "In Search of Goethe from Within" and included in *The Dehumanization of Art and Other Essays on Art, Culture, and Literature,* Princeton University Press, 1968.

Notas (title means "Notes"), Espasa-Calpe, 1938, reprinted with introduction by Julian Marias, Anaya (Salamanca), 1967.

Ensimismamiento y alteracion [and] *Meditacion de la tecnica* (title means "Self Contemplation and Alteration" [and] "Meditation on the Technical"), Espasa-Calpe Argentina, 1939, translation of *Ensimismamiento y alteracion* by Willard R. Trask published as "The Self and the Other" in *Partisan Review,* July, 1952, translation of *Meditacion de la tecnica* by W. Atkinson published as Man the Technician in *History as a*

System and Other Essays toward a Philosophy of History, Greenwood Press, 1961 (also see below).

Ideas y creencias (title means "Ideas and Beliefs"), Espasa-Calpe Argentina, 1940, reprinted, Revista de Occidente, 1942.

El libro de las misiones (title means "The Book of Missions"), Espasa-Calpe Argentina, 1940, reprinted, Espasa-Calpe (Madrid), 1959.

Historia como sistema [and] *Concordia y libertad,* Revista de Occidente, 1941; *Historia como sistema* reprinted in *Historia como sistema y otros ensayos de filosofia,* Revista de Occidente en Aliaza, 1981; translation of *Historia como sistema* by W. Atkinson published in *History as a System and Other Essays toward a Philosophy of History,* Greenwood Press, 1961; translation of *Concordia y libertad* by Helene Wehl published as *Concord and Liberty,* Norton, 1946.

Castilla y sus castillos (title means "Castile and Her Castles"), Afrodisio Aguado (Madrid), 1942, reprinted, 1952.

Teoria de Andalucia (title means "Theory of Andalucia"), Revista de Occidente, 1942.

Man and Crisis, Revista de Occidente, 1942, translation by Mildred Adams published as *Man and Crisis,* Norton, 1958, published as *Entorno a Galileo* (title means "Concerning Galileo"), Revista de Occidente en Alianza, 1982.

Two Prologues, Revista de Occidente, 1944, first prologue reprinted in *Veinte anos de caza mayor* (title means "Twenty Years of Big-Game Hunting") by Eduardo Figueroa, Plus Altra (Madrid), 1948, translation of *Veinte anos* by Howard B. Wescott published as *Meditations on Hunting,* Scribners, 1986.

Obras completas, Revista de Occidente, volumes 1 and 2, 1946, volumes 3-6, 1947, Volume 7, 1961, volumes 8 and 9, 1962, volumes 10 and 11, 1969; volumes 1-11 reprinted, and Volume 12 published, by Alianza Editorial, Revista de Occidente, 1983.

Sobre la aventura y la caza (title means "On Adventure and the Hunt"), Afrodisio Aguado, 1949.

Papeles sobre Velazquez y Goya, Revista de Occidente, 1950, translation by Alexis Brown published in *Velazquez, Goya, and the Dehumanization of Art,* Studio Vista (London), 1972.

Estudios sobre el amor (title means "Studies on Love"), Aguilar (Madrid), 1950, reprinted, Revista de Occidente en Alianza, 1981, translation by Toby Talbot published in *On Love: Aspects of a Single Theme,* Meridian Books, 1960.

El hombre y la gente, Revista de Occidente, 1957,

reprinted, Revista de Occidente an Alianza, 1981, translation by Willard R. Trask published as *Man and People,* Norton, 1963.

Meditacion de un pueblo joven (title means "Meditation on a Young Nation"), Revista de Occidente, 1958.

La idea de principio en Leibniz y la evolucion de la teoria deductiva, Revista de Occidente, 1958, reprinted by Revista de Occidente en Alianza, 1981, translation by Mildred Adams published as *The Idea of Principle in Leibniz and the Evolution of Deductive Theory,* Norton, 1971.

Prologo para alemanes (title means "Prologue for Germans"), Taurus (Madrid), 1958, reprinted, 1974, translation by Philip W. Silver published in *Phenomenology and Art,* Norton, 1975.

Idea del teatro (title means "Idea of Theatre"), Revista de Occidente, 1958, reprinted in *Ideas del teatro y de la novela,* Alianza, 1982, translation of *Idea del teatro* by Philip W. Silver published in *Phenomenology and Art* (see above).

Kant, Hegel, Dilthey, Revista de Occidente, 1958, reprinted, 1973.

Que es filosofia?, Revista de Occidente, 1958, reprinted, Revista de Occidente en Alianza, 1982, translation by Mildred Adams published as *What is Philosophy?,* Norton, 1960.

Apuntes sobre el pensamiento: su teurgia y su demiurgia (title means "Notes on Thinking: Its Creation of the World and Its Creation of God"), Revista de Occidente, 1959, reprinted, Revista de Occidente en Alianza, 1980, translation by Helene Weyl published in *Concord and Liberty* (see above).

Una interpretacion de la historia universal, Revista de Occidente, 1960, reprinted, Revista de Occidente en Alianza, 1980, translation by Mildred Adams published as *An Interpretation of Universal History,* Norton, 1973.

Meditacion de Europa (reprinted from *Obras completas,* Volume 9), Revista de Occidente, 1960.

Vives-Goethe, Revista de Occidente, 1961, reprinted, 1973.

Pasado y Porvenir para el hombre actual (title means "Past and Future for Man Today"; reprinted from *Obras completas,* Volume 9), Revista de Occidente, 1962, portions translated and published as The Past and Future of Western Thought in *Modern Age,* summer, 1958.

Mision del bibliotecario (y otros escritos afines) (title means "Mission of the Librarian [and Other Related Writings"; reprinted from *Obras completas,* Volume 5), Revista de Occidente, 1962, portions translated by H. Muller and published as Man Must Tame the Book in *Wilson Library Bulletin,* 1936.

Unas lecciones de metafisica, Alianza, 1966, reprinted, Revista de Occidente en Alianza, translation by Mildred Adams published as *Some Lessons in Metaphysics,* Norton, 1969.

Origen de la filosofia, Revista de Occidente, 1967, reprinted, Revista de Occidente en Alianza, 1981, translation by Toby Talbot published as *Some Lessons in Metaphysics,* Norton, 1967.

La razon historia, Revista de Occidente, 1979, reprinted, Revista de Occidente en Alianza, 1983, translation by Philip W. Silver published as *Historical Reason,* Norton, 1984.

Investigaciones psicologicas, Revista de Occidente Alianza, 1982, translation by Jorge Garcia-Gomez published as *Psychological Investigations,* Norton, 1987.

Que es conocimiento? (title means "What Is Knowledge?"), Revista de Occidente en Alianza, 1984.

Ensayos escogidos, Taurus (Madrid), 1997.

Contributor to numerous periodicals.

SIDELIGHTS: The significance of Jose Ortega y Gasset, whose world fame mainly stems from his controversial book *La rebelion de las masas* (*The Revolt of the Masses,* 1930) has always sparked debate. His most enthusiastic students believe that his philosophy is on a level "beyond which nothing has yet been achieved," as Julian Marias declares in *Ortega y Gasset,* while his critics see him as imprecise, inconsistent, literary rather than philosophical, and overly metaphorical in handling serious intellectual problems. Despite this critical split, Ortega y Gasset merits a place in history as both a major transitional figure between phenomenology and existentialism and as a key figure in Spanish culture. He aspired to elevate his native culture to match that of the rest of Western Europe, and in the first three decades of the twentieth century he is considered to have accomplished much toward achieving that goal.

During Ortega y Gasset's adolescence, Spain still reeled from losing its brief 1898 war with the United States. A group of writers, known today as the Generation of '98, found that Spain's humiliation could be viewed as the symptom of a deeper national disease—demoralization—and that this sense of defeatism had actually preceded colonial defeat. As a young man Ortega y Gasset considered himself a member of the Generation of '98, and he joined forces with such leading lights as Miguel de Unamuno and Antonio Machado in promoting the Europeanization of Spanish culture. The Generation of '98 was fortunate to have found a sympathizer in Ortega y Gasset. Breaking into print at an early age, he gave the group's writings ample publicity in his own articles, and he encouraged members to publish in the many magazines he founded to promote the moral and mental reform of Spanish society. Ortega y Gasset's writing style was so effective, his mode of presenting his ideas so attractive and persuasive, that, had he desired, he could have developed like his father into a brilliant journalist. Instead, in 1905 he decided to pursue postgraduate philosophy studies in Germany.

In his adolescence Ortega y Gasset had developed a passion for the works of German philosopher Friedrich Wilhelm Nietzsche, and he carried this enthusiasm with him to Germany when he went there at age twenty-two. At the University of Leipzig, where he was unable to secure admittance into classes of philology, he spent his days reading in the university library. He then went to Berlin, where he attended the public lectures of philosopher Georg Simmel. As a neo-Kantian, Simmel applied Immanuel Kant's philosophy—that knowledge is limited by perception—to an understanding of man and his relation to culture. Influenced by Nietzsche, Simmel enthralled Ortega y Gasset with his subtle ideas on life as a conflict between man—the creator of culture—and his own cultural products.

Late in 1906 Ortega y Gasset began studying at the University of Marburg under such Neo-Kantians as Hermann Cohen and Paul Natorp. From Cohen, Ortega y Gasset learned a sense of the drama associated with problems in philosophy along with the will to solve them with a system of disciplined ideas. Cohen based his own system on the discipline of modern physics, and he applied the logic of mathematics in solving philosophical problems. He believed that the mind could establish laws of conduct that would prove as valid for sciences of the spirit as Newton's laws are for the sciences of nature. Moreover, Cohen contended that the laws of nature and the laws of the spirit, when expressed in art, aroused a feeling for beauty, a sentiment valid as a law for all mankind. Cohen regarded individual life as an awareness and pursuit of the personal ideal, and he saw culture (logic, ethics, aesthetics) as the solution to the problem. But Ortega y Gasset, in considering culture, always returned to the problem of life, a self-conscious search for identity.

Through Natorp, a psychologist, Ortega y Gasset discovered the means of extending philosophy beyond neo-Kantian thought. Following the blueprint of

Cohen, who intended to crown his own structure of ideas with psychology, Natorp built a two-part psychological system, one both descriptive and genetic. The first part described psychic experience; the second traced its causes. After studying Natorp's ideas in 1912, Ortega y Gasset turned to the writings of one of Natorp's inspirations, Edmund Husserl, whose concept of psychic experience, particularly as explicated in *Logische Untersuchungen* (*Logical Investigations*), differed somewhat from Natorp's, and—as Julian Marias noted—provided the cornerstone for Ortega y Gasset's own philosophy. To the question," Who is the thinker of mathematical logic, the willer of logical ethics, the feeler of logical aesthetics?," Natorp responded, "Spirit (or mind-in-general), thinking, willing, and feeling throughout history;" and he added that psychology has the task of studying the mind-in-general. But Husserl held that the mind could be studied not only externally by psychology, but internally by phenomenology. Ortega y Gasset argued that what was real was the mind conceived as a natural object situated among other natural objects; toward these objects the mind constantly focused its attention, and from them it received endless stimuli. Thus Husserl's notion of the life-world was reflected in Ortega y Gasset's "I am myself and my circumstance," a statement that comprised both the first principle and summary of Ortega y Gasset's entire philosophy. Ortega y Gasset reached this conclusion in 1914, the same year that he reconciled his enthusiasm for Germanic culture with his loyalty to native Spain.

Inspired by the writings of Generation of 1898 leader Unamuno, Ortega y Gasset published *Meditaciones del Quijote* (*Meditations on Quixote,* 1914), which he intended as the first in a series of works noting universal values to be found in specific aspects of Spanish culture—Cervantes's view of life, the writings of Baroja and Azorin, and bullfighting, as examples. The book contained many philosophical insights, including the notion of human life as the frame of reference for all other realities; the idea of life as having nothing given to it except the problem of clarifying its own destiny; and the imperative to address this problem in view of concrete possibilities or circumstances.

Both Ortega y Gasset's conciliatory mood and the incomplete state of *Meditations* derived from his increased involvement in politics. In the fall of 1913 he founded a new political party, the League for Political Education, which he launched in a public lecture, *"Vieja y nueva politica"* ("Old and New Politics"). In his speech he claimed to live in a country of two

Spains: Official Spain which was comprised of outworn institutions, the corrupt Parliament, the established political parties, the conservative press, and the ministries, and Vital Spain, which included the creative forces in the country, especially select minorities of intellectuals and the Spanish people. Old Spain, he declared, had crippled the country. New Spain, he added, might restore it. He attributed much of Spain's cultural deficiency to its lack of outstanding individuals and inspiring projects, and he defined a healthy society as one in which select minorities encourage the masses to willingly ignore their own private interests and enthusiastically collaborate. As the League's first priority Ortega y Gasset set the formation of an elite to educate the people in creative politics. But because he offered no concrete platform or program for the League, it dissolved in less than two years.

During the 1923 to 1930 military dictatorship of Miguel Primo de Rivera, Ortega y Gasset's intellectual creativity reached its peak. Unable to partake in politics, he wrote his most famous works. In 1925 he published a five-part series of articles titled *"Hacia una antropologia filosofica"* ("Toward a Philosophical Anthropology") in which he applied phenomenologist Max Scheler's idea of a basic science centered on man and his relationship to all other beings, and completed *Les deshumanizaci n del arte e ideas de la novela* (*The Dehumanization of Art*) which is respected by critics for its insights into the experimental—what Ortega y Gasset called "dehumanizing"—art of the early twentieth century. During that same period of inspiration, he also borrowed from such thinkers as Martin Heidegger and Wilhelm Dilthey to further develop his own philosophy. The result was the explication of four basic principles, repeated in nearly every major work written by Ortega y Gasset after 1929: First, individual human life is the "root reality" to which all other realities must be referred and in which all others appear as in a framework; second, life is given to each human being as a problem to solve, as a "task" not finished beforehand, but needing to be done; third, life is a "decision" about what to do to be oneself; and fourth, life is a series of concrete possibilities from which to decide, and the possibilities, plural but not infinite in number, make up each individual's "circumstances."

The circumstances in which Ortega y Gasset unveiled his mature principles to the public represented a crowning moment of his life. This moment occurred in 1929, the year before the fall of the dictator Rivera, whose power diminished as a result of economic depression. When Rivera closed the University of Madrid, Ortega y Gasset protested by resigning as professor of metaphysics there, then rented a theater and sold tickets of admission to "What Is Philosophy?," the very course interrupted by the closure. In these lectures Ortega y Gasset expressed his four mature principles of human life and defined philosophy as universal knowledge, free of forejudgments. Because this knowledge relied on concepts, he saw philosophy as more akin to theology than to mysticism, which was unable to conceptualize union with God. He likened philosophy to sports—disciplined in accordance with internal rules requiring direct proof of every philosophical statement—and declared that life, with its four principles, is self-evident.

While teaching "What Is Philosophy?" Ortega y Gasset published parts of *The Revolt of the Masses* as separate articles. Like *Que es filosofia?*(*What Is Philosophy?*), a collection of the course lectures published in 1958, *The Revolt of the Masses* is a transitional work between anthropology and existentialism. Here Ortega y Gasset studied the character-type of the average European of his day. With every trait described, he passed judgment from the standpoint of his metaphysical principles of human life. Life was a task, a decision, and a repertory of possibilities, he declared, but the mass man was any person, whatever his social class, who performed no task and never innovated. His countertype was the select individual, ever pioneering and perfectionistic. *The Revolt of the Masses* is significant for its dire prophecies, made in the late 1920s, of what actually took place in the 1930s and 1940s. In retrospect, writes Jose Gaos in *Sobre Ortega y Gasset y otros trabajos de historia de las ideas en Espana y la America espanola,* "the prediction seems to have come true of the seriousness of the crisis, socialization, the reign of the masses—although in the face of facts like those represented by the *Duce* and the *Fuhrer,* there may be room for discussion about their susceptibility to direction from without, denied by Ortega y Gasset."

As if unmindful of his pessimism about the masses, Ortega y Gasset plunged back into politics after the fall of Primo de Rivera in January 1930. In February of 1931, Ortega y Gasset and writers Gregorio Maranon and Ramon Perez de Ayala founded the Group at the Service of the Republic, which resembled the earlier League for Political Education. The Group wanted Spain divided into ten large regions, each with its own local government, but all recognizing the sovereignty of the nation as a whole; it desired a strong central Parliament with as much authority as the executive to provide a system of checks and balances; it advocated a planned economy, designed to bring about agrarian reform; it supported a gradual but complete separation of Church and State; and it argued for a balanced budget as a first step to energetic public and private investment. On April 14, 1931, municipal elections in Madrid brought in the Second Spanish Republic, while voting out the monarchy. Surprised by the speed and peacefulness of the transition, Ortega y Gasset privately expressed uneasiness, though in his articles he hailed the simplicity with which the Republic had come into being. Less than a year later, Ortega y Gasset's political aspirations ended as the result of an escalating disagreement. Minister of Labor Gabriel Maura questioned Ortega y Gasset's elitism, which was seen as incompatible with concern for the interests of workers. As recorded in his 1931 essay "Siguer los 'problemas concretas'" ("More on 'Concrete Problems'") Ortega y Gasset merely responded with a sportive metaphor, suggesting that his service to the Republic was a form of aristocracy, which meant "fair play." In parliamentary debate over the emerging Constitution of the Republic, when his metaphorical style of speaking was attacked as false and affected, he defended its authenticity and claimed an unalienable right to practice, as he declared in *Rectificacion de la Republica* ("Rectification of the Republic"), "a poetic, philosophical, heart-felt, and merry politics." But Parliament was unresponsive to his wit and keen thought. As partisanship and extremism divided the Republic, Ortega y Gasset left politics in August 1932, and he dissolved the Group at the Service of the Republic the following October. After leaving politics, Ortega y Gasset resumed his studies of Heidegger and Dilthey.

History, Dilthey's favorite area of interest, dominated the last twenty years of Ortega y Gasset's intellectual study. He attempted to make history a scientific discipline. Ortega y Gasset's justification for treating history as a science appeared in *Historia como sistema* (*History as a System;* 1941). Here Ortega y Gasset posed an historical problem, as always: humanity by the early twentieth century had lost confidence in natural science, once a replacement for religious faith. Now he wondered what life meant. Physics could not provide an answer; neither could any sciences that used its methods. Ortega y Gasset, following Dilthey, believed that the science of history could cure this crisis of faith, for history discovered the system of beliefs that guided man in deciding among possibilities for being himself—a process that was, after all, the task of life. For Ortega y Gasset, beliefs differed from mere ideas, or views of the world that man himself manipulated with full awareness. To understand the impact of subconscious beliefs on men's lives, it was only necessary to tell the story of their lives. Thus, Ortega y Gasset maintained, the science of history was the new science on which man must pin his faith. History told man what he was and clarified the meaning of his life. History could also guide his future: Once he learned the mistakes of the past, he would avoid them afterwards in the trial-and-error process that is living.

The year after publishing *History as a System,* Ortega y Gasset made an unpopular decision, one that prompted criticism from many Spaniards: he fled Spain shortly after the outset of its civil war. Some critics, such as Pedro Cerezo Galan, felt that when Ortega y Gasset went into exile, he lost the power to speak as he had before. The books he wrote afterwards, declared Cerezo Galan in *La voluntad de aventura,* "lacked . . . the feel and breath of that circumstantial reality which blew like a clean wind throughout his best works." From 1936 to 1945 Ortega y Gasset remained outside Spain. In France, the Netherlands, Argentina, and Portugal he endured great hardships while desiring to write two long books, *Aurora de la razon historia* ("Dawn of Historical Reason") and *El hombre y la gente* (*Man and People,* 1957): In a prologue to *Ideas y creencias* ("Ideas and Beliefs", 1940), he declared, "I have suffered misery, I have suffered long sicknesses of the kind in which death is breathing down your neck, and I should say that if I have not succumbed among so much commotion, it has been because the hope of finishing those two books has sustained me when nothing else would." Ortega y Gasset wrote merely a few pages of *The Dawn of Historical Reason,* mostly repeating ideas from *History as a System.* As for *Man and People,* in its final form it was a lengthy course in sociology given in 1949 and 1950. Far more revealing about Ortega y Gasset's life and times is *La idea de principio en Leibniz y la evolucion de la teoria deductiva* (*The Idea of Principle in Leibniz and the Evolution of Deductive Theory,* 1958), the book praised by Marias in *Ortega y Gasset* as the writer's best.

The longest work he ever wrote, *The Idea of Principle in Leibniz* was left incomplete among his papers to be published after his death. Compared with its German sources—chiefly Husserl, Dilthey, and Heidegger—it is stimulating, often entertaining reading, filled with wordplay and jokes, and it shows Ortega y Gasset at his sharpest as an intellectual sportsman. Its theme is the history of the idea of principle. Ortega y Gasset began the work by translating into Spanish many notions from Heidegger's 1929 essay "Vom Weser des Grundes" ("On the Essence of Ground"), which explained how the philosophers Gottfried Wilhelm Leibniz, Kant, and Aristotle dealt with the idea of principle. Next Ortega y Gasset used his science of history to show that Aristotle, in handling principles, was inexact and "unprincipled," and he implied that Heidegger was similarly imprecise. In *The Idea of Principle in Leibniz* Ortega y Gasset also objected to Heidegger's general tone, which he found too somber and anguished for philosophy. Among the Greeks, noted Ortega y Gasset, philosophy was a game of riddle-solving. Plato, for instance, often compared philosophy to sports and games. But Heidegger, when philosophizing about anguish and nothingness, seemed to make a sport of wallowing in despair, and his gloomy view of the world struck Ortega y Gasset as too narrow. "For that reason," wrote Ortega y Gasset in *The Idea of Principle in Leibniz,* "since my first writings, against the narrowness of a 'tragic sense of life' . . . I have counterposed a 'sportive and festive sense of existence,' which my readers— naturally!—read as a mere literary phrase."

Ortega y Gasset wanted to spend his final years in Madrid, the city of his birth and of his greatest triumphs, but on his return in 1945, according to Victor Ouimette in *Jose Ortega y Gasset,* he had to face "the hostility of the Church and the mistrust felt by the government of General Franco." He did extensive lecturing abroad in Germany and made appearances in Britain and Italy as well as a single visit to the United States. Operated on for cancer on October 12, 1955, he died six days later. Controversy surrounded his death as it had so many aspects of his life. The Spanish press reported the visit to his home of the Jesuit Father Felix Garcia and the Archbishop of Saragossa. Had he converted to Catholicism at the last moment? Conservative factions contended that he had. But intimates of the philosopher, according to Guillermo Moron in *Historia politica de Jose Ortega y Gasset,* reported that he said, when the priests wanted to be admitted to confess him, "Let them allow me to die in peace."

BIOGRAPHICAL/CRITICAL SOURCES:

BOOKS

Abellan, Jose Luis, *Ortega y Gasset en la filosofia espanola: Ensayos de apreciacion,* Tecnos (Madrid), 1966.

Bayon, J., *Razon vital y dialectica en Ortega y Gasset,* Revista de Occidente, 1972.

Benitez, Jaime, *Political and Philosophical Theories of Jose Ortega y Gasset,* University of Chicago Press, 1939.

Brenan, Gerald, *The Spanish Labyrinth,* Cambridge University Press, 1960.

Cepeda Calzada, Pablo, *Las ideas politicas de Ortega y Gasset,* Alcala (Madrid), 1968.

Cerezo Galan, Pedro, *La voluntad de aventura: Aproximamiento critico al pensamiento de Ortega y Gasset,* Ariel (Barcelona), 1984.

Chamizo Dominguez, Pedro J., *Ortega y Gasset y la cultura espanola,* Cincel (Madrid), 1985.

Dilthey, Wilhelm, *Introduccion a las ciencias del espiritu,* translated by Julian Marias, 2nd edition, Revista de Occidente, 1966.

Duran, Manuel, editor and author of prologue, *Ortega y Gasset hoy,* Biblioteca Universitaria Veracruzana (Mexico), 1985.

Fernandez, Pelayo H., *La paradoja en Ortega y Gasset,* Jose Porrua Turanzas (Madrid), 1985.

Ferrater Mora, Jose, *Ortega y Gasset: An Outline of His Philosophy,* Yale University Press, 1963.

Gaete, Arturo, *El sistema maduro de Ortega y Gasset,* Compania General Fabril Editora (Buenos Aires), 1962.

Gaos, Jose, *Sobre Ortega y Gasset y otros trabajos de historia de las ideas en Espana y la America espanola,* Imprenta Universitaria (Mexico), 1957.

Garagorri, Paulino, *Introduccion a Ortega y Gasset,* Alianza (Madrid), 1970.

Garcia Astrada, Arturo, *El pensamiento de Ortega y Gasset,* Torquel (Buenos Aires), 1961.

Graham, John T., *A Pragmatist Philosophy of Life in Ortega y Gasset,* University of Missouri Press, 1994.

Graham, John T., *Theory of History in Ortega y Fasset: "The Dawn of Historical Reason,"* University of Missouri Press, 1996.

Hanneman, Bruno, contributor, *Ortega y Gasset Centennial/Centenario Ortega y Gasset,* Jose Porrua Turanzas (Madrid), 1985.

Holmes, Oliver W., *Human Reality and the Social World: Ortega y Gasset's Philosophy of History,* University of Massachusetts Press, 1975.

Kern, Iso, *Husserl und Kant,* Nijhoff (The Hague), 1964.

Lalcona, Javier F., *El idealismo politico de Ortega y Gasset,* Cuadernos para el Dialogo (Madrid), 1974.

L. Aranguren, Jose Luis, *La etica de Ortega y Gasset,* 2nd edition, Taurus (Madrid), 1959.

Larrain Acuna, Hernan, *La genesis del pensamiento de Ortega y Gasset,* Compania General Fabril Editora (Buenos Aires), 1962.

Lopez Campillo, Evelyn, *La Revista de Occidente y la formacion de minorias, 1923-1936,* Taurus (Madrid), 1972.

Lopez-Morillas, Juan, contributor, *Intelectuales y espirituales,* Revista de Occidente (Madrid), 1961.

Marias, Julian, *El lugar del peligro; Una cuestion disputada en torno a Ortega y Gasset,* Taurus (Madrid), 1958.

Marias, Julian, *Ortega y Gasset,* 2 volumes, Alianza (Madrid), 1983.

Marrero, Domingo, *El centauro: Persona y pensamiento de Ortega y Gasset,* Imprenta Soltero (Puerto Rico), 1961.

Marrero, Vicente, *Ortega y Gasset, filosofo "mondain,"* Rialp (Madrid), 1961.

McClintock, Robert, *Man and His Circumstances: Ortega y Gasset as Educator,* Teachers College Press, 1971.

Menendez Pidal, Ramon, *La Espana del Cid,* Espasa-Calpe, 1967.

Molinuevo, Jose Luis, *El idealismo de Ortega y Gasset,* Narcea (Madrid), 1984.

Moron, Guillermo, *Historia politica de Jose Ortega y Gasset,* Ediciones Oasis (Mexico), 1960.

Moron Arroyo, Ciriaco, *El sistema de Ortega y Gasset,* Alcala (Madrid), 1968.

Niedermayer, Franz, *Jose Ortega y Gasset,* Colloquium Verlag (Berlin), 1959.

Orringer, Nelson R., *Ortega y Gasset y sus fuentes germanicas,* Gredos (Madrid), 1979.

Orringer, Nelson R., *Nuevas fuentes germanicas de Que es filosofia? de Ortega y Gasset,* Consejo Superior de Investigaciones Cientificas (Madrid), 1984.

Ortega y Gasset, Jose, *The Idea of Principle in Leibniz and the Evolution of Deductive Theory,* Norton, 1971.

Ortega y Gasset, Jose, *Ideas y creencias,* Espasa-Calpe Argentina, 1940.

Ortega y Gasset, Jose, *The Modern Theme,* introduction by Jose Ferrater Mora, translated by James Cleugh, Harper, 1961.

Ortega y Gasset, Manuel, *Ninez y mocedad de Ortega y Gasset,* C.L.A.V.E. (Madrid), 1964.

Ouimette, Victor, *Jose Ortega y Gasset,* Twayne, 1982.

Paine, Stanley G., *The Spanish Revolution,* Norton, 1970.

Raley, Harold C., *Jose Ortega y Gasset: Philosopher of European Unity,* University of Alabama Press, 1971.

Rama, Carlos, *La crisis de la Espana del siglo XX,* Fondo de Cultura Economica (Mexico), 1960.

Rodriguez Huescar, Antonio, *Con Ortega y Gasset y otros escritos,* Taurus (Madrid), 1964.

Rodriguez Huescar, Antonio, *Jose Ortega y Gasset Metaphysical Innovation: A Critique and Overcoming Idealism,* State University of New York Press, 1995.

Romero, Francisco, *Ortega y Gasset y el problema de la jefetura espiritual,* Losada (Buenos Aires), 1960.

Rukser, Udo, *Bibliographia de Ortega y Gasset,* Revista de Occidente (Madrid), 1971.

Salmeron, Fernando, *Las mocedades de Ortega y Gasset,* Colegio de Mexico, 1959.

Sanchez Villasenor, Jose, *Ortega y Gasset, Existentialist: A Critical Study of His Thought and His Sources,* translated by Joseph Small, Regnery, 1949.

Silver, Philip W., *Ortega y Gasset as Phenomenologist: The Genesis of "Meditations on Quixote,"* Columbia University Press, 1978.

Spiegelberg, Herbert, *The Phenomenological Movement: A Historical Introduction,* 2nd edition, 2 volumes, Nijhoff (The Hague), 1971.

Thomas, Hugh, *The Spanish Civil War,* Harper, 1961.

Tuttle, Howard N., *The Crowd is Untruth: The Existential Critique of Mass Society in the Thought of Kierkegaard, Nietzsche, Heidegger, and Ortega y Gasset,* P. Lang, 1996.

Tuttle, Howard N., *The Dawn of Historical Reason: The Historicality of Human Existence in the Thought of Dilthey, Heidegger, and Ortega y Gasset,* P. Lang, 1994.

Twentieth-Century Literary Criticism, Volume 9, Gale, 1983.

Unamuno, Miguel de, *Obras completas,* 9 volumes, Escelicer (Madrid), 1966-71.

PERIODICALS

Aporia, number 3, 1981.

Azafea, number 1, 1985.

Comparative Criticism, number 6, 1984.

Cuadernos Salmantinos de Filosofia, number 8, 1981.

Cuenta y Razon, number 3, 1981.

Estudios, number 29, 1973.

Hispanic Review, number 47, 1979.

Journal of Aesthetics and Art Criticism, number 23, 1964.

Modern Language Notes, number 85, 1970, number 88, 1973, number 92, 1977.

Razon y Fe, June, 1941.

Revista de Occidente, number 140, 1974.

Romance Notes, number 17, 1976.*

OTERO SILVA, Miguel 1908-1985

PERSONAL: Born October 26, 1908, in Barcelona, Venezuela; died following a heart attack, August 27, 1985, in Caracas, Venezuela; son of Henrique Otero Vizcarrondo and Mercedes Silva Perez; married Mercedes Baumester de Otero; children: (from a previous marriage) two. *Education:* Attended Universidad Central de Venezuela; later earned licentiate in journalism.

CAREER: Novelist, poet, and journalist. *El Morrocoy* (Venezuelan weekly humor publication; title means "The Blue Morrocoy"), founder, 1941, staff member, 1941-46; *El Nacional* (daily newspaper), Caracas, Venezuela, founder, 1943. Venezuelan Senate, senator from Aragua state, 1958.

AWARDS, HONORS: Premio Nacional de Periodismo, 1960; Order of Andres Bello, 1967; Order of Francisco Miranda, 1967; Lenin Prize for Literature, 1980; Order of General Joaquin Crespo, 1982; D.H.C., Universidad de Merida, 1985; Cuba's Felix Varela Award, 1985.

WRITINGS:

12 Poemas Rojos (poems), [Caribe], 1933.

Agua y Cauce (poems; title means "Water and Channel"), Mexico Nuevo (Mexico City, Mexico), 1937.

Fiebre (novel; title means "Fever"), Elite (Caracas, Venezuela), 1939.

25 Poemas (title means "Twenty-Five Poems"), Elite (Caracas, Venezuela), 1942.

Casas Muertas (novel; title means "Dead Houses"), Losada (Buenos Aires, Argentina), 1955.

(With Alejandro Otero Rodriguez) *Polemica sobre Arte Abstracta* (title means "Polemic on Abstract Art"), Ministerio de Educacion (Caracas), 1957.

Elegia Coral a Andres Eloy Blanco (title means "Choral Elegy for Andres Eloy Blanco"), Vargas (Caracas), 1958.

El Cercado Ajeno: Opiniones sobre Arte y Politica, Pensamiento Vivo (Caracas), 1961.

Oficina No. 1 (novel; title means "Office Number One"), Losada (Buenos Aires), 1961.

Sinfonias Tontas, Casa del Escritor (Caracas), 1962.

La Muerte de Honorio (novel; title means "The Death of Honorio"), Losada (Buenos Aires), 1963.

Discurso de Orden Pronunciado en la Sesion Solemne del 23 de Enero de 1965, Direccion de Relaciones Publicas del Concejo Municipal (Caracas), 1965.

DMOS: Exposicion Donacion, Museu de Bellas Artes (Caracas), 1965.

La Mar Que Es el Morir (poems; title means "The Sea Which Is Death"), Arte (Caracas), 1965.

25 Cuadros de Pintores Venezolanos, Shell de Venezuela (Caracas), 1965.

Poesia hasta 1966, edited by Jose Ramon Medina, Arte (Caracas), 1966.

Umbral (poems; title means "Threshold"), Ateneo (Caracas), 1966.

Mexico y la Revolucion Mexicana: Un Escritor Venezolano en la Union Sovietica, Universidad Central de Venezuela (Caracas), 1966.

Cuando Quiero Llorar no Lloro (novel; title means "When I Wish to Cry, I Cannot"), Tiempo Nuevo (Caracas), 1970, revised edition, 1972.

Discurso de Incorporacion como Individuo de Numero, Academic Venezolana de la Lengua (Caracas), 1972.

Poesia Completa, Monte Avila (Caracas), 1972.

Un Morrocoy en el Cielo, Tiempo Nuevo (Caracas), 1972.

(With Manuel Alfredo Rodriguez) *Andres Eloy Blanco: Homenaje en el LXXVIII Aniversario de su Natalicio,* Congreso de la Republica (Caracas), 1974.

Florencia, Ciudad del Hombre, Arte (Caracas), 1974.

Ocho Palabreos, Tiempo Nuevo (Caracas), 1974.

Mitologia de una Generacion Frustrada, Universidad Central de Venezuela (Caracas), 1975.

Romeo y Julieta, Fuentes (Caracas), 1975.

Quien Fue Andres Eloy Blanco?, Ministerio de Educacion (Caracas), 1975.

Obra Humoristica Completa, Seix Barral (Barcelona, Spain), 1976.

Obra Poetica, Seix Barral (Barcelona), 1977.

Prosa Completa: Opiniones sobre Arte y Politica (title means "Complete Prose: Opinions on Art and Politics"), Seix Barral (Barcelona), 1977.

Lope de Aguirre, Principe de la Libertad (novel; title means "Lope de Aguirre, Prince of Liberty"), Seix Barral (Barcelona), 1979.

(Editor with Matilde Neruda) Pablo Neruda, *Para Nacer he Nacido* (personal anecdotes; title means "I Was Born to Be Born"), Seix Barral (Barcelona), 1981, translation by Margaret Sayers Peden published as *Passions and Impressions,* Farrar, Straus (New York City), 1983.

Ahora Que Entre Nosotros Solo Puede Haber Palabras, Aula (Montevideo, Uruguay), 1982.

Obra Escogida, Progreso (Mexico), 1982.

Un Morrocoy en el Infierno, Ateneo (Caracas), 1982.

Tiempo de Hablar, Academia Nacional de Historia (Caracas), 1983.

Discurso de Incorporacion, Academia Venezolana (Caracas), 1984.

La Piedra Que Era Cristo (novel; title means "The Rock That Was Christ"), Oveja Negra (Bogota, Colombia), 1984.

Casas Muertas, Lope de Aguirre, Ayacucho (Caracas), 1985.

La Poesia Social de Miguel Otero Silva, Ateneo (Caracas), 1985.

Semblanza de un Hombre y de un Camino, Centauro (Caracas), 1985.

Contributor to periodicals.

SIDELIGHTS: Miguel Otero Silva dedicated his life to letters, working as a journalist and newspaper editor, promoting the efforts of an entire generation of young writers, and producing a number of novels and volumes of poetry. His novels, suggested Rick McCallister in the *Dictionary of Literary Biography,* "parallel the rise and fall of the modern novel in Venezuela with the rise and climax of bourgeois democracy." His avant-garde fiction also reflects the author's unswerving determination "to create a genuine national culture rooted in sociopolitical realities and dedicated to change," McCallister asserted.

Otero Silva came of age under the dictatorship of Juan Vicente Gomez. As a university student in Caracas he joined protest movements and conspiracies against Gomez and others who were virtually giving away Venezuela's national resources to provide luxuries for the rich. As a result, he spent much of the time between 1928 and 1941 in prison or in exile. After the death of Gomez, Otero Silva wrote his first novel *Fiebre,* a fictional treatment of the failed "Revolution of 1928" that had originally landed its author in jail. An important theme of the novel, McCallister commented, "is the chasm between verisimilitude—the popular perception of reality as seen or received by society—on one hand and objective reality on the other. . . . [T]he book chronicles the folly of those who put their faith in verisimilitude . . . only to face the consequences of objective reality. . . . The revelation of so many layers of contradictions makes the work an excellent guide to Venezuelan realities of the era." This theme would recur in various forms in Otero Silva's later novels. In 1941 Otero Silva returned from abroad to enjoy the fruits of Venezuela's first democratic government, that of General Isaias Medina Angarita. The democracy

lasted only seven years, and the fruits were bittersweet. The abuses of the Gomez years had a lingering effect on the social and economic structure of the country. The decimated agrarian heritage was replaced by an industrial, petroleum-based society that lured people from the villages to the cities and oil fields, creating hope for the future but leaving behind an aura of loss and abandonment. The novel *Casas Muertas,* McCallister remarked, "mirrors the chaotic reality of Latin America in its mixture of vitality and desolation." The story of a dying town seen through the eyes of its grieving people, *Casas Muertas* is sociopolitical in nature, according to McCallister, but successful because "[t]he reader comes to know the people [first] and then condemn injustice through their eyes." This, he contended, "makes the novel more convincing than most such works."

The novel *Oficina No. 1* explores what McCallister called "the assault by the capitalist petroleum industry upon human destiny" as it follows the protagonist of *Casas Muertas* into her future. It describes the changes in her life and values that result after she abandons her old home for a new life in an oil town. The change is essential to her survival, but it is not without great cost. McCallister noted: "Once again the reader sees the conquest of dreams and popular notions of reality by objective reality."

Subsequent novels, for the most part, reflect the changes that Otero Silva observed in Venezuela as time passed: the frustrating elusiveness of social equality and justice and the failure of bourgeois democratic rule. *Lope de Aguirre, Principe de la Libertad,* for example, "presents tyranny and bourgeois democracy as two sides of the same coin with a common history," McCallister wrote. He concluded: "The importance of Otero Silva's last two novels [*Lope de Aguirre* and *La Piedra que era Cristo*] lies in taking back history in the name of the people by stripping it to its essentials, defeating verisimilitude and ideology by confronting them with objective reality."

BIOGRAPHICAL/CRITICAL SOURCES:

BOOKS

Dictionary of Literary Biography, Volume 145: *Modern Latin-American Fiction Writers, Second Series,* edited by William Luis and Ann Gonzalez, Gale (Detroit, MI), 1994.*

P-Q

PACHECO, Jose Emilio 1939-

PERSONAL: Born June 30, 1939, in Mexico City, Mexico; married; wife's name, Cristina; children: Laura Emilia, Cecilia. *Education:* Attended Universidad Nacional Autonoma de Mexico, 1957-64.

ADDRESSES: Office—c/o New Directions, 80 Eighth Ave., New York, NY 10011; and Reynosa 63, Mexico City Z.P. 11, Mexico.

CAREER: Writer, 1958—. Editorial collaborator on literary journals, including positions as co-coordinator, *Estaciones* magazine, beginning 1957; *Mexico en la Cultura* (literary supplement), contributor, 1958, editorial secretary, 1961; editorial secretary, *Revista de la Universidad de Mexico* (journal), 1959-65; and chief editor, *Siempre* (magazine), 1962-71. Lecturer at the University of Maryland and other universities in Mexico, the United States, Canada, and Great Britain.

AWARDS, HONORS: National Poetry Prize (Mexico), 1969, for poetry collection *No me preguntes como pasa el tiempo (Poemas, 1964-1968);* National Journalism Prize, 1980, for column "Inventario"; elected to the Colegio Nacional, 1985. Also winner of Magda Donato and Xavier Villaurrutia prizes; recipient of grants from the Centro Mexicano de Escritories and Guggenheim foundation; recipient of honorary degrees from the Universities of Sinaloa and Chihuahua.

WRITINGS:

POETRY

Los elementos de la noche (title means "The Elements of the Night"), Universidad Nacional Autonoma de Mexico, 1963.

El reposo del fuego (title means "The Repose of Fire"), Fondo de Cultura Economica, 1966.

No me preguntes como pasa el tiempo (Poemas, 1964-1968), J. Mortiz, 1969, translation by Alastair Reid published as *Don't Ask Me How the Time Goes By: Poems, 1964-1968,* Columbia University Press (New York City), 1978.

Arbol entre dos muros/Tree Between Two Walls, bilingual Spanish-English edition with translation by Edward Dory and Gordon Brotherston, Black Sparrow Press, 1969.

Iras y no volveras (title means "You Will Go and Not Return"), Fondo de Cultura Economica, 1973.

Islas a la deriva (title means "Islands Adrift"), Siglo Veintiuno, 1976.

Ayer es nunca jamas (anthology; title means "Yesterday Is Never Again"), Monte Avila (Caracas), 1978.

Desde entonces: Poemas 1975-1978 (title means "Since Then: Poems, 1975-1978"; includes "Jardin de ninos"), Ediciones Era, 1980.

Tarde o temprano (anthology; title means "Sooner or Later"), Fondo de Cultura Economica, 1980.

Signals from the Flames (anthology), translated by Thomas Hoeksema, edited by Yvette Miller, Latin American Literary Review Press, 1980.

Los trabajos del mar (title means "Labors of the Sea") Ediciones Era, 1983.

Fin de siglo (anthology; title means "End of the Century"), Cultura SEP, 1984.

Aproximaciones (anthology; title means "Approximations"), Editorial Penelope, 1984.

Alta traicion (anthology; title means "High Treason"), Alianza (Madrid), 1985.

Album de zoologia, Cuarto Menguante, 1985, translation published as *An Ark for the Next Millennium:*

Poems, edited by Jorge Esquinca, University of Texas Press, 1993.

Miro la tierra (title means "I Look at the Earth"; includes "Las ruinas de Mexico [Elegia del retorno]" and "Lamentaciones y alabanzas"), Ediciones Era, 1986.

Jose Emilio Pacheco: Selecciones (anthology), edited by Luis Antonio de Villena, Ediciones Jucar (Madrid), 1986.

Selected Poems (anthology), bilingual English/Spanish edition with translations by Hoeksema and others, edited by George McWhirter, New Directions, 1987.

Ciudad de la memoria: Poemas 1986-1989, Ediciones Era, 1989, English translation by Cynthia Steele and David Lauer published as *City of Memory and Other Poems,* City Lights (San Francisco), 1997.

Distant Death, Sun & Moon Press, 1993.

El Silencio de la Luna: Poemas 1985-1993, Ediciones Era, 1994.

NOVELS AND SHORT STORIES

La sangre de Medusa (short stories; title means "The Blood of Medusa"), Cuadernos del Unicornio, 1958, published as *La sangre de Medusa, y otros cuentos marginales,* Ediciones Era, 1990.

El viento distante (short stories; title means "The Distant Wind"), Ediciones Era, 1963, 2nd expanded edition, 1969.

Moriras lejos (novel; title means "You'll Die Far Away"), J. Mortiz, 1967.

El principio del placer (short stories; title means "The Pleasure Principle"), J. Mortiz, 1972.

Las batallas en el desierto (short stories), Ediciones Era, 1981, translation by Katherine Silver published as *Battles in the Desert and Other Stories,* New Directions (New York City), 1987.

EDITOR

La poesia mexicana del siglo XIX: Antologia (title means "Nineteenth-Century Mexican Poetry: An Anthology"), Empresas, 1965.

Universidad, politica y pueblo (title means "University, Politics, and the People"), Universidad Nacional Autonoma de Mexico, 1967.

Antologia del modernismo (1884-1921) (title means "Anthology of Modernism"), Universidad Nacional Autonoma de Mexico, 1970.

(Editor with Gabriel Zaid) Jose Carlos Becerra, *El otono recorre las islas (Obra poetica, 1961-1970),* Ediciones Era, 1973.

Federico Gamboa, *Diario de Federico Gamboa, 1892-1939* (title means "Diary of Federico Gamboa, 1892-1939"), Siglo Veintiuno, 1977.

Novo, Salvador, *La Vida en Mexico en el Periodo Presidencial de Miguel Aleman,* Consejo Nacional para la Cultura y las Artes, 1994.

Also editor of anthologies *Literatura ingelesa,* 1982, *Poesia moderna hispanoamericana,* 1983, and *La novela historica de folletin,* 1985; editor of Salvador Novo's *La vida en Mexico.*

OTHER

(Author of prologue) *Gimenez Botey: Escultura* (title means "Gimenez Botey: Sculpture"; text in Spanish, French, and English), Fournier, 1964.

(Contributor) *Ensayos contemporaneos sobre Jaime Torres Bodet* (title means "Contemporary Essays on Jaime Torres Bodet"), edited by Beth Miller, Universidad Nacional Autonoma de Mexico, 1976.

(Contributor) *Inframundo, the Mexico of Juan Rulfo,* Ediciones del Norte (Hanover, N.H.), 1983.

Author, with Arturo Ripstein, of screenplays *El castillo de la pureza, El Santo Oficio,* and *Foxtrot.* Author of translations into Spanish of works by Samuel Beckett, Oscar Wilde, and Tennessee Williams. Contributor of essays, articles, and criticism to literary journals; author of column "Inventario," *Proceso,* 1976—.

SIDELIGHTS: Jose Emilio Pacheco is one of Mexico's most prominent poets. His earliest verse collections, *Los elementos de la noche* ("The Elements of the Night") and *El reposo del fuego* ("The Repose of Fire") plumb metaphysical questions of time and human destruction with surrealist and symbolist imagery. In both volumes Pacheco's language is hermetic and his poetic voice bleakly prophetic as it presents a doomed world of ceaseless flux, in which man is represented as both victim and perpetrator of disaster.

Pacheco's third collection, *No me preguntes como pasa el tiempo (Don't Ask Me How the Time Goes By),* marks a shift to simpler, more direct writing and broader thematic concerns. But a dark underlying mood centered on the futility of experience in time still permeates the volume. The poet's precision, restraint, and balance, a *Times Literary Supplement* critic pointed out, "makes the sense of evil and disaster in his poems the more striking." Pacheco's diverse subjects include travel impressions and such political events as the death of South American revolutionary leader Che Guevara and the 1968 Tlatelolco student massacre in Mexico City. The poet also introduces whimsical verse meditations on animal life that reveal human foibles. Some translated verses from other poets—or "approximations," as Pacheco prefers to call them—complete the volume, which won Mexico's prestigious National Poetry Prize in 1969.

Pacheco's succeeding volumes of poetry are similarly structured. Free verse and prose poem forms predominate as the poet's technical mastery allows him to experiment with a wide variety of styles, particularly in his "approximations." Metaphysical concerns are always present, but they lie beneath reflections on social life, the natural environment, and the nature of artistic creation. For example, in "Jardin de ninos" ("Children's Garden"), a cycle of twenty poems in the collection *Desde entonces* ("Since Then"), Pacheco uses the metaphor of a child's development from the womb to adulthood to illuminate ethical and epistemological questions in the modern world. "The poems seem . . . extraordinarily powerful and effective, a remarkable statement of a generation's conscience and temper," remarked Michael J. Doudoroff in *Hispania.*

The devastating Mexico City earthquake of 1985 is Pacheco's central metaphor in *Miro la tierra* ("I Look at the Earth"). The longest work in this volume is "Las ruinas de Mexico (Elegia del retorno)" ("The Ruins of Mexico [Elegy of Return]"). Each of its five sections begins with an abstract meditation and progresses through twelve short poems to a detailed portrait of the ruined city's human suffering. "Pacheco transforms this harrowing experience into a major elegy, perhaps his most important single poem since *El reposo del fuego,*" opined Doudoroff. *Miro la tierra* also includes a group of twenty short verses titled "Lamentaciones y alabanzas" ("Laments and Praises") that mourn humankind's seemingly insoluble social and metaphysical problems but celebrate the fleeting small pleasures in life.

Intertextuality and a broad interpretation of the poetic are key features of Pacheco's work. His original poems are often replete with allusions to the work of others, and he sometimes includes "found" poems—fragments of prose texts from many sources—in his verse collections. The "approximations" that appear in Pacheco's books range from very precise and formally exact translations to extensively rewritten interpretations. Pacheco's poetic quotes, translations, and rewritings reflect his view of poetry as essentially social and transient, with no single meaning enduring through all ages and cultures and, in a sense, no

single author. Thus, one of his "approximations" in *Miro la tierra* is a translation of American poet Ezra Pound's translation of a Japanese version of an ancient Chinese poem.

In addition to his poetry, Pacheco has published a well-received historical novel, *Moriras lejos* ("You'll Die Far Away"), and several short story collections. A principal theme in these prose works is the interplay of historical myth, social injustice, and personal alienation in contemporary Mexico City. In *Battles in the Desert and Other Stories,* for instance, all seven short stories in the collection are set in Mexico City, and "all [are] centered on key-moments-in-the-life-of a narrator," commented Helene J. F. de Aguilar in *Parnassus.* The title story in this collection features a narrator who is remembering an adolescent crush he had on an older woman. Writing in the *New York Times Book Review,* Peter Sourian praised Pacheco's "sturdy, straightforward style."

BIOGRAPHICAL/CRITICAL SOURCES:

BOOKS

Forster, Merlin H., *Four Contemporary Mexican Poets: Tradition and Renewal,* Illinois University Press, 1975.
Verani, Hugo, editor, *Jose Emilio Pacheco ante la critica,* Universidad Autonoma Metropolitana, 1987.
Villena, Antonio de, *Jose Emilio Pacheco,* Jucar, 1986.

PERIODICALS

American Book Review, August/September, 1994, p. 19.
Chasqui, February-May, 1985, pp. 3-13, 15-23; November, 1990, p. 33-42.
Hispamerica, May 15, 1976; July 20, 1978.
Hispania, May, 1989, pp. 264-76.
Latin American Literary Review, Volume 3, number 5, 1974, pp. 143-46; Volume 6, number 11, 1977, pp. 36-42.
New York Times Book Review, May 24, 1987, p. 12.
Parnassus, February, 1988, p. 233.
Rocky Mountain Review of Language and Literature, Volume 38, numbers 1-2, 1984, pp. 59-64.
Studies in Short Fiction, fall, 1987, p. 448.
Times Literary Supplement, June 18, 1970; October 12, 1973.
Virginia Quarterly Review, winter, 1979.
World Literature Today, Number 4, 1977, p. 596; spring, 1979.*

PANERO, Leopoldo 1909-1962

PERSONAL: Full name, Leopoldo Panero Torbado; born October 17, 1909, in Astorga, Spain; died August 27, 1962, in Madrid, Spain; son of Moises Panero and Maxima Torbado de Panero; married Felicidad Blanc y Bergnes de las Casas (a writer). *Education:* Attended college in Valladolid, Spain; studied law at University of Madrid.

CAREER: Poet. *Humo* (weekly literary review), copublisher, 1928; *Nueva Revista,* founder; worked as an interpreter for the Spanish philosopher and writer Miguel de Unamuno in England; Spanish Institute, London, England, began as librarian, became director; toured Latin America for the Spanish government, 1949; Instituto de Cultura Hispanica, Spain, editor. *Wartime service:* Served with nationalist forces during Spanish Civil War.

AWARDS, HONORS: First prize, Floral Games, Jerez Harvest Festival, 1948, for the poem "Canto al Teleno;" Fastenrath Prize from Spanish Royal Academy and Premio Nacional de Literatura, 1949, both for *Escrito a Cada Instante;* Jose Antonio Primo de Rivera Prize, Falangists, for *Canto Personal;* annual poetry prize of the Instituto de Cultura Hispanica was named in honor of Leopoldo Panero, 1963.

WRITINGS:

(With brother Juan Panero, Luis Alonso Luengo, and Ricardo Gullon) *Guia Artistica y Sentimental de la Ciudad de Astorga* (title means "Artistic and Sentimental Guide to the City of Astorga"), [Leon, Spain], 1929.

(Editor) *Antologia de la Poesia Hispanoamericana,* two volumes, Nacional (Madrid, Spain), 1944-45.

La Estancia Vacia, Fragmentos, Escorial (Madrid), 1945.

Escrito a Cada Instante (title means "Writing at Every Moment"), Escelicer (Madrid), 1949.

Canto Personal: Carta Perdida a Pablo Neruda (title means "Personal Canto: Lost Letter to Pablo Neruda"), Cultura Hispanica (Madrid), 1953.

C. Martinez Novillo, Direccion General de Bellas Artes (Madrid), 1959.

Poesia, 1932-1960, Cultura Hispanica (Madrid), 1963.

Antologia, edited by Juan Luis Panero, Plaza y Janes (Esplugas de Llobregat, Spain), 1973.

Obras Completas: Poesias, Prosa, two volumes, edited by J. L. Panero, Nacional (Madrid), 1973.

Literary reviewer for *Blanco y Negro,* 1957-60; reviewer for *El Sol* in the 1930s. Contributor to periodicals, including *Fantasia, Noreste, Escorial,* and *Cuadernos Hispanoamericanos.* Editor, *Correo Literario.*

SIDELIGHTS: Leopoldo Panero's success as a poet emerged during the years surrounding the Spanish Civil War. It was a time when dissidence in Spanish literature was not tolerated, and experimentation with new ideas and literary styles was not safe. The political environment silenced many of Spain's leading poets, but, as Ana Maria Alfaro-Alexander reported in the *Dictionary of Literary Biography,* "Panero's quiet, insistent lyrics, which celebrate the acceptable themes of family, landscape, religion, and death, came increasingly to prominence."

Panero's work remained consistent throughout the poet's life. Alfaro-Alexander noted: "Almost all the themes he elaborates in his mature poetry originated in the pristine experience of his childhood and youth . . . the only major theme of his poetry not present in his serene childhood [is] his recurrent meditations on temporality and death." Panero spent a happy childhood in the province of Leon. As a teenager at college in Valladoid, Panero, his brother, and some of their friends began to publish a literary review and, soon afterward, Leopoldo began to write prose and then poetry. As a university student in Madrid he was drawn toward the literary circles of Spain's capital city, and he soon established another review, *Nueva Revista.* Exposed to the work of Spain's leading contemporary poets, Panero experimented with free verse, surrealism, and other modernist forms, but the flirtations were brief. At the age of twenty he was hospitalized with tuberculosis, then sought rejuvenation in the mountains of his ancestral home. There, after much rest and solitude and reading, Panero began to write the poems that, according to Alfaro-Alexander, "signal his mature work in its use of metaphor and the treatment of landscape as the subject matter of a poetic world."

The serenity of childhood and youth was shattered by the outbreak of the Spanish Civil War. By virtue of his travels abroad and the literary company he kept at home, Panero was accused of subversion and narrowly escaped prison. The war prevented the freedom of expression and placed a burden upon all facets of the Spanish cultural scene. When Panero's beloved brother died in an automobile crash in 1937, the cumulative effect of stress and grief changed the poet forever. The changes are evident in the poem

"Adolescente en Sombra," a tribute to his brother that contrasted notably with the traditional form of the elegy. Alfaro-Alexander observed: "Panero recreates his own intensely emotional experience of the childhood world shared with his brother and from which his brother's presence is inseparable. . . . Panero's attempt to retain the sensitive child's subjective, even solipsistic, perception of the world by transforming it into the never-ending symbolic universe of poetry became, from this point on, the poignant hallmark of his vision."

The end of the war brought Panero peace, marriage, and a successful career in Spain and abroad with the Spanish government. Panero's popularity had reached a new height, and the poet used the opportunity to anthologize his own work. From an eclectic body of work that reflected many poetic influences, he selected only the works that resonated with the one specific voice he wanted to call his own. The result, *Escrito a Cada Instante,* was a critical triumph. The title means "Writing at Every Moment" and defines the core of Panero's creative inspiration, as Alfaro-Alexander explained: "His life is a continuous creation, or, better, a never-ending reception of divine inspiration that then translates into poetry."

One of Panero's last poems, "Candida Puerto," is considered by some critics to be among his best. Toward the end of his life, Panero turned increasingly toward spirituality and religion. In the poem, the "shining door" of a local bakery whose bread sustains the townspeople becomes a symbol of the tabernacle door that protects the holy bread of the Eucharist, which sustains the soul. "'Candida Puerto' is a personal hymn," Alfaro-Alexander asserted, "a spiritual song in which the symbol of the bakery becomes the poet's desire to reach that [shining door]. . . . Panero seems to hear his name pronounced by the one (God) that inhabits this tabernacle."

BIOGRAPHICAL/CRITICAL SOURCES:

BOOKS

Dictionary of Literary Biography, Volume 108: *Twentieth-Century Spanish Poets, First Series,* edited by Michael L. Perna, Gale (Detroit, MI), 1991, pp. 262-69.
Ruiz-Fornells, Enrique, editor, *A Concordance to the Poetry of Leopoldo Panero,* University of Alabama Press (University, AL), 1978.*

PAREJA DIEZCANSECO, Alfredo 1908-1993
(Alfredo Pareja y Diez Canseco)

PERSONAL: Born October 12, 1908, in Guayaquil, Ecuador; died May 3, 1993; married Mercedes Cucalon Concha, 1934; children: Cecilia, Jorge, Francisco. *Avocational interests:* Reading, traveling.

CAREER: High school teacher, Guayaquil, Ecuador, 1931-34; Universidad de Guayaquil, Guayaquil, Ecuador, college instructor, beginning in 1934; Ecuadoran congressional representative, Quito, Ecuador, 1938; United Nations Relief and Rehabilitation Administration for Mexico, Central America, Argentina, Uruguay, and Paraguay, chief officer, 1945-48; University of Texas, Austin, TX, visiting professor, 1982; Ecuadoran ambassador to France, 1983-84. Universidad San Francisco de Quito, Quito, Ecuador, instructor of history; visiting professor in other Spanish-speaking nations and in the United States. Worked variously as a journalist, bookseller, businessperson, accountant, banker, salesperson, dock laborer and waiter; also worked on ships. Also known as Alfredo Pareja y Diez Canseco.

AWARDS, HONORS: Farrar Rinehart international novel contest, second prize, 1941, for *Las tres ratas;* Premio Nacional de Cultura Eugenio Espejo, Ecuador, 1979-80; degree of doctor honoris causa, University of Guayaquil, 1988.

MEMBER: Ecuadoran Academy of History of Language.

WRITINGS:

NOVELS

La casa de los locos (title means "The Insane Asylum"), Artes Ecuador (Guayaquil, Ecuador), 1929.
La senorita Ecuador (title means "Miss Ecuador"), Jouvin (Guayaquil, Ecuador), 1930.
Rio arriba (title means "Up the River"), Graficos (Guayaquil, Ecuador), 1930.
El muelle (title means "The Wharf"), Bolivar (Quito, Ecuador), 1933.
La Beldaca (title means "The Beldaca"), Ercilla (Santiago, Chile), 1935.
Baldomera, Ercilla, 1938, published with *Las pequenas estaturas,* Ayacucho (Caracas, Venezuela), 1991.
Hechos y hazanas de don Balon de Baba y su amigo Inocente Cruz (title means "Facts and Deeds from don Balon de Baba and His Friend Inocente Cruz"), Club del Libro (Buenos Aires, Argentina), 1939.

Hombres sin tiempo (title means "Men without Time"), Losada (Buenos Aires, Argentina), 1941.

Las tres ratas (title means "The Three Rats"), Losada, 1944.

La advertencia (title means "The Warning"), Losada, 1956.

El aire y los recuerdos (title means "The Air and the Memories"), Losada, 1959.

Los poderes omnimodos (title means "All-Embracing Powers"), Losada, 1964.

Las pequenas estaturas (title means "Small Statures"), Revista de Occidente (Madrid, Spain), 1970, published with *Baldomera,* Ayacucho, 1991.

La manticora (title means "The Manticora Monster"), Losada, 1974.

NONFICTION

Temario para el curso de historia politica de America Latina, Departamento de Hacienda, Servicio de Compra y Suministro (San Juan, Puerto Rico), 1923.

La dialectica en el arte: El sentido de la pintura, [Portugal], 1936.

La hoguera barbara: Vida de Eloy Alfaro (title means "The Barbarous Bonfire: A Life of Elroy Alfaro"), Compania General Editora (Mexico City, Mexico), 1944.

Breve historia del Ecuador (title means "Brief History of Ecuador"), Secretaria de Educacion Publica (Mexico City, Mexico), 1946, revised and augmented edition published as *Historia del Ecuador* (title means "History of Ecuador"; four volumes), Casa de la Cultura Ecuatoriana (Quito, Ecuador), 1954, revised and enlarged edition published as *Historia del Ecuador* (two volumes), Casa de la Cultura Ecuatoriana, 1958.

Consideraciones sobre el hecho literario ecuatoriano, Casa de la Cultura Ecuatoriana, 1948.

Vida y leyenda de Miguel de Santiago (title means "The Life and Legend of Miguel de Santiago"), Fondo de Cultura Economica (Mexico City, Mexico), 1952.

La lucha por la democracia en el Ecuador, Ruminahui (Quito, Ecuador), 1956.

Thomas Mann y el nuevo humanismo (title means "Thomas Mann and the New Humanism"), Casa de la Cultura Ecuatoriana, 1956.

El Ecuador de Eloy Alfaro, Secretaria de Educacion (Mexico City, Mexico), 1966.

Historia de la Republica, Ariel (Quito, Ecuador), 1974.

Ensayos de ensayos: Una seleccion de los aparecidos en diversas publicaciones periodicas de varios paises, Casa de la Cultura Ecuatoriana, 1986.

Notas de un viaje a China, Casa de la Cultura Ecuatoriana, 1986.

El entenao, Universidad de Guayaquil (Guayaquil, Ecuador), 1988.

El Populismo en el Ecuador, ILDIS (Quito, Ecuador), 1989.

Contributor to books, including *El duro oficio* (title means "The Hard Task"), edited by Francisco Febres Cordero, Municipio de Quito (Quito, Ecuador), 1989. Contributor to periodicals.

ADAPTATIONS: Las tres ratas was adapted into a film and produced in Argentina, 1946.

SIDELIGHTS: Critics consider novelist, historian, and diplomat Alfredo Pareja Diezcanseco one of Ecuador's greatest writers. His work has influenced writers in Ecuador and other Latin America nations as well as other writers around the world. Pareja Diezcanseco emerged as a writer in the 1930s, a period of great transition in Ecuadoran literature. He was a member of the Grupo de Guayaquil, a literary movement whose members intended to create a wholly Ecuadoran literature by eschewing European literary influence. These Ecuadoran writers strove to create literature that depicted the Ecuadoran urban centers of Quito, its capital, and Guayquil, its largest city.

Born in Guayaquil, Pareja Diezcanseco honed his craft in the 1920s and 1930s, and by the 1940s was creating renowned works of Ecuadoran literature. Several of Pareja Diezcanseco's novels take place in Guayaquil and focus on the city's class system. His novels, full of Ecuadoran history, challenge readers to face the inequalities of such a society. Pareja Diezcanseco wrote fourteen novels, beginning with *La casa de los locos* ("The Insane Asylum"), and ending with *La manticora* ("The Manticora Monster"). He also wrote a number of nonfiction works, including the biographies *La hoguera barbara: Vida de Eloy Alfaro* ("The Barbarous Bonfire: A Life of Elroy Alfaro") and *Vida y leyenda de Miguel de Santiago* ("The Life and Legend of Miguel de Santiago"), historical volumes such *Breve historia del Ecuador* ("Brief History of Ecuador") and *Historia de la Republica,* and works of literary criticism, such as *Thomas Mann y el nuevo humanismo* ("Thomas Mann and the New Humanism").

In addition to his writing career, Pareja Diezcanseco was a respected educator, historian, and public servant. Despite having little formal education, began teaching high school in Guayaquil in 1931. Three years later he moved to the university level, ultimately teaching history at the Universidad San Francisco de Quito for several years. He also served as a visiting professor at various universities in Latin America and the United States. Pareja Diezcanseco served in Ecuador's congress and in various diplomatic positions, and was appointed Ecuador's ambassador to France in 1983. For his many achievements as a writer and a public servant, the Ecuadoran government awarded Pareja Diezcanseco the Premio Nacional de Cultura Eugenio Espejo.

Pareja Diezcanseco knew from personal experience about Ecuador's laborers and their working conditions. As a child, he worked to support his large family. He held a series of odd jobs in Ecuador, then traveled to the United States as a young man and worked at various jobs in New York City. Throughout this period, he devoted his spare time to reading and educating himself. Pareja Diezcanseco attracted critical notice with the publication of his fourth novel, *El muelle* ("The Wharf,"1933). The story contains autobiographical elements, as it depicts the journey of Ecuadoran protagonist Juan Hidrovo, who heads for New York City for work and financial gain. When Hidrovo arrives in the United States, he encounters racist attitudes and continues to struggle financially. Eventually, Hidrovo returns home, only to find more problems. With this work, Pareja Diezcanseco introduces a topic he would revisit in his fiction: the exploited but talented urban poor.

His next two novels, *La Beldaca* (1935) and *Baldomera* (1938), focus on similar themes as *El muelle*. *La Beldaca* is the story of a fisherman who goes to great lengths to buy a boat, which is named *La Beldaca*. To buy it, the man has to secure a loan from a corrupt businessman, who charges the fisherman a exorbitant interest rate. *Baldomera* revolves around an actual 1922 incident in which Ecuadoran government troops killed more than a thousand protesters during a labor strike. The same year *Baldomera* was published, 1938, Pareja Diezcanseco served as a congressional representative in Ecuador. He was imprisoned for his views during a politically volatile time, but was later released.

Pareja Diezcanseco's imprisonment provided him with the inspiration and information for his next novel, *Hombres sin tiempo* ("Men without Time," 1941). It features a man who is sentenced to serve sixteen years in prison after being convicted of attempted murder and rape. He serves his time in Garcia Moreno Penitentiary, one of Ecuador's most notorious prisons. *Hombres sin tiempo* focuses on the thoughts and feelings of the protagonist, who develops a sense of self-worth during his sentence. It offers an accurate depiction of Ecuadoran prison life of the time, as it includes scenes of homosexuality and violent punishment. Ultimately, the novel addresses the need for full-scale prison reform. After writing *Las tres ratas* ("The Three Rats") in 1944, Pareja Diezcanseco did not produce another novel for over a decade. During this time, he wrote works of nonfiction and contributed pieces to periodicals.

Between 1956 and 1974, nearly all of Pareja Diezcanseco's novels, including *La advertencia* ("The Warning," 1956), *El aire y los recuerdos* ("The Air and the Memories,"1959), and *Los poderes omnimodos* ("All-Embracing Powers," 1964), revolve around Ecuadoran history. *La advertencia,* for example, describes a military coup that took place in 1925, while *El aire y los recuerdos* recounts political battles of 1932. Pareja Diezcanseco's ambitious final novel, *La manticora*, was published in 1974. *La manticora* incorporates complex narrative and dialogue structures. It is a debate between the narrator, presumably Pareja Diezcanseco, and the main character, Pablo Canelos, who seeks his own autonomy from the narrator. The novel contains much discussion about Ecuadoran history, philosophy, and politics. Its title alludes to the manticore, a mythical monster that eats human flesh, a creature Pareja Diezcanseco compares to freedom, especially the freedom of Latin American countries that have been dominated by foreign influences. Discussing *La manticora* in the *Dictionary of Literary Biography,* Michael Handelsman wrote that Pareja Diezcanseco "concludes that there are no manticores or mythical monsters to fear—or to use as an excuse for inaction." Upon completing this formidable novel, Pareja Diezcanseco suffered a heart attack that would curtail his ability to write. He remained active in promoting the arts in Ecuador until his death in 1993.

BIOGRAPHICAL/CRITICAL SOURCES:

BOOKS

Dictionary of Literary Biography, Volume 145: *Modern Latin-American Fiction Writers, Second Series,* Gale (Detroit, MI), 1994.*

PAREJA y DIEZ CANSECO, Alfredo
  See PAREJA DIEZCANSECO, Alfredo

*   *   *

PARRA, Teresa de la
  See de la PARRA, Teresa

*   *   *

PAZ, Octavio 1914-1998

PERSONAL: Born March 31, 1914, in Mexico City, Mexico; died of cancer, April 19, 1998, in Mexico City, Mexico; son of Octavio Paz (a lawyer) and Josephina Lozano; married Marie Jose Tramini, 1964; children: one daughter. *Education:* Attended National Autonomous University of Mexico, 1932-37. *Politics:* "Disillusioned leftist." *Religion:* Atheist.

CAREER: Writer. Government of Mexico, Mexican Foreign Service, posted to San Francisco, CA, and New York, NY, secretary at Mexican Embassy in Paris, beginning 1945, charge d'affaires at Mexican Embassy in Japan, beginning 1951, posted to Mexican Secretariat for External Affairs, 1953-58, Extraordinary and Plenipotentiary Minister to Mexican embassy, 1959-62, ambassador to India, 1962-68. Visiting professor of Spanish American Literature, University of Texas at Austin and University of Pittsburgh, 1968-70; Simon Bolivar Professor of Latin American Studies, 1970, and fellow of Churchill College, Cambridge University, 1970-71; Charles Eliot Norton Professor of Poetry, Harvard University, 1971-72; Professor of Comparative Literature, Harvard University, 1973-80. Regent's fellow at University of California, San Diego.

MEMBER: American Academy and Institute of Arts and Letters (honorary).

AWARDS, HONORS: Guggenheim fellowship, 1944; Grand Prix International de Poesie (Belgium), 1963; Jerusalem Prize, Critics Prize (Spain), and National Prize for Letters (Mexico), all 1977; Grand Aigle d'Or (Nice), 1979; Premio Ollin Yoliztli (Mexico), 1980; Miguel de Cervantes Prize (Spain), 1982;

Neustadt International Prize for Literature, 1982; Wilhelm Heinse Medal (West Germany), 1984; German Book Trade Peace prize, 1984; T. S. Eliot Award for Creative Writing, Ingersoll Foundation, 1987; Tocqueville Prize, 1989; Nobel Prize for Literature, 1990.

WRITINGS:

POETRY

Luna silvestre (title means "Sylvan Moon"), Fabula (Mexico City), 1933.

No pasaran!, Simbad (Mexico City), 1936.

Raiz del hombre (title means "Root of Man"; also see below), Simbad, 1937.

Bajo tu clara sombra y otros poemas sobre Espana (title means "Under Your Clear Shadow and Other Poems about Spain"; also see below), Espanolas (Valencia), 1937, revised edition, Tierra Nueva (Valencia), 1941.

Entre la piedra y la flor (title means "Between the Stone and the Flower"), Nueva Voz (Mexico City), 1938, 2nd edition, Asociacion Civica Yucatan (Mexico City), 1956.

A la orilla del mundo y Primer dia; Bajo tu clara sombra; Raiz del hombre; Noche de resurrecciones, Ars (Mexico City), 1942.

Libertad bajo palabra (title means "Freedom on Parole"), Tezontle (Mexico City), 1949.

Aguila o sol? (prose poems), Tezontle, 1951, 2nd edition, 1973, translation by Eliot Weinberger published as *Aguila o sol?/Eagle or Sun?* (bilingual edition), October House, 1970, revised translation by Weinberger published under same title, New Directions, 1976.

Semillas para un himno, Tezontle, 1954.

Piedra de sol, Tezontle, 1957, translation by Muriel Rukeyser published as *Sun Stone/Piedra de sol* (bilingual edition; also see below), New Directions, 1963, translation by Peter Miller published as *Sun-Stone,* Contact (Toronto), 1963, translation by Donald Gardner published as *Sun Stone,* Cosmos (New York City), 1969, translation by Eliot Weinberger published as *Sunstone—Piedra De Sol,* New Directions, 1991.

La estacion violenta, Fondo de Cultura Economica (Mexico City), 1958, reprinted, 1978.

Agua y viento, Ediciones Mito (Bogota), 1959.

Libertad bajo palabra: Obra poetica, 1935-1958, Fondo de Cultura Economica, 1960, revised edition, 1968.

Salamandra (1958-1961) (also see below), J. Mortiz (Mexico City), 1962, 3rd edition, 1975.

Selected Poems of Octavio Paz (bilingual edition), translation by Rukeyser, Indiana University Press, 1963.

Viento entero, Caxton (Delhi), 1965.

Blanco (also see below) J. Mortiz, 1967, 2nd edition, 1972, translation by Weinberger published under same title, The Press (New York City), 1974.

Disco visuales (four spatial poems), Era (Mexico City), 1968.

Ladera este (1962-1968) (title means "Eastern Slope (1962-1968)"; also see below), J. Mortiz, 1969, 3rd edition, 1975.

La centena (Poemas: 1935-1968), Seix Barral (Barcelona), 1969, 2nd edition, 1972.

Topoemas (six spatial poems), Era, 1971.

Vuelta (long poem), El Mendrugo (Mexico City), 1971.

Configurations (contains *Piedra de sol/Sun Stone, Blanco,* and selections from *Salamandra* and *Ladera este*), translations by G. Aroul and others, New Directions, 1971.

(With Jacques Roubaud, Edoardo Sanguinetti, and Charles Tomlinson; also author of prologue) *Renga* (collective poem written in French, Italian, English, and Spanish), J. Mortiz, 1972, translation by Tomlinson published as *Renga: A Chain of Poems,* Braziller, 1972.

Early Poems: 1935-1955, translations by Rukeyser and others, New Directions, 1973.

3 Notations/3 Rotations (contains fragments of poems by Paz), Carpenter Center for the Visual Arts, Harvard University, 1974.

Pasado en claro (long poem), Fondo de Cultura Economica, 1975, revised edition, 1978, translation included as title poem in *A Draft of Shadows and Other Poems* (also see below), New Directions, 1979.

Vuelta, Seix Barral, 1976.

(With Tomlinson) *Air Born/Hijos del aire* (sonnets written in Spanish and English), Pescador (Mexico City), 1979.

Poemas (1935-1975), Seix Barral, 1979.

A Draft of Shadows and Other Poems, edited and translated by Weinberger, with additional translations by Elizabeth Bishop and Mark Strand, New Directions, 1979.

Selected Poems (bilingual edition), translations by Tomlinson and others, Penguin, 1979.

Octavio Paz: Poemas recientes, Institucion Cultural de Cantabria de la Diputacion Provincial de Santander, 1981.

Selected Poems, edited by Weinberger, translations by G. Aroul and others, New Directions, 1984.

Cuatro chopos/The Four Poplars (bilingual edition), translation by Weinberger, Center for Edition Works (New York City), 1985.

The Collected Poems, 1957-1987: Bilingual Edition, New Editions, 1987.

One Word to the Other, Latitudes Press, 1991.

La Casa de la Presencia: Poesia e Historia, Fondo de Cultura Economica, 1994.

A Tale of Two Gardens: Poems from India, 1952-1995, edited and translated by Eliot Weinberger, Harcourt Brace (New York City), 1997.

PROSE

El laberinto de la soledad (also see below), Cuadernos Americanos, 1950, revised edition, Fondo de Cultura Economica, 1959, reprinted, 1980, translation by Lysander Kemp published as *The Labyrinth of Solitude: Life and Thought in Mexico,* Grove, 1961.

El arco y la lira: El poema; La revelacion poetica; Poesia e historia, Fondo de Cultura Economica, 1956, 2nd edition includes text of *Los signos en rotacion* (also see below), 1967, 3rd edition, 1972, translation by Ruth L. C. Simms published as *The Bow and the Lyre: The Poem, the Poetic Revelation, Poetry and History,* University of Texas Press, 1973, 2nd edition, McGraw-Hill, 1975.

Las peras del olmo, Universidad Nacional Autonoma de Mexico, 1957, revised edition, Seix Barral, 1971, 3rd edition, 1978.

Tamayo en la pintura mexicana, Universidad Nacional Autonoma de Mexico, 1959.

Cuadrivio: Dario, Lopez Velarde, Pessoa, Cernuda, J. Mortiz, 1965.

Los signos en rotacion, Sur (Buenos Aires), 1965.

Puertas al campo (also see below), Universidad Nacional Autonoma de Mexico, 1966.

Claude Levi-Strauss; o, El nuevo festin de Esopo, J. Mortiz, 1967, translation by J. S. Bernstein and Maxine Bernstein published as *Claude Levi-Strauss: An Introduction,* Cornell University Press, 1970 (published in England as *On Levi-Strauss,* Cape, 1970).

Corriente alterna, Siglo Veintiuno Editores (Mexico City), 1967, reprinted, 1980, translation by Helen R. Lane published as *Alternating Current,* Viking, 1973.

Marcel Duchamp; o, El castillo de la pureza, Era, 1968, translation by Gardner published as *Marcel Duchamp; or, The Castle of Purity,* Grossman, 1970.

Conjunciones y disjunciones, J. Mortiz, 1969, 2nd edition, 1978, translation by Lane published as *Conjunctions and Disjunctions,* Viking, 1974.

Mexico: La ultima decada, Institute of Latin American Studies, University of Texas, 1969.

Posdata (also see below) Siglo Veintiuno, 1970, translation by Kemp published as *The Other Mexico: Critique of the Pyramid,* Grove, 1972.

(With Juan Marichal) *Las cosas en su sitio: Sobre la literatura espanola del siglo XX,* Finisterre (Mexico City), 1971.

Los signos en rotacion y otros ensayos, edited and with a prologue by Carlos Fuentes, Alianza (Madrid), 1971.

Traduccion: Literatura y literalidad, Tusquets (Barcelona), 1971.

Aparencia desnuda: La obra de Marcel Duchamp, Era, 1973, new enlarged edition, 1979, translation by Rachel Phillips and Gardner published as *Marcel Duchamp: Appearance Stripped Bare,* Viking, 1978.

El signo y el garabato (contains *Puertas al campo*), J. Mortiz, 1973.

(With Julian Rios) *Solo a dos voces,* Lumen (Barcelona), 1973.

Teatro de signos/Transparencias, selection and montage by Rios, Fundamentos (Madrid), 1974.

La busqueda del comienzo: Escritos sobre el surrealismo, Fundamentos, 1974, 2nd edition, 1980.

El mono gramatico, Seix Barral, 1974, translation from the original Spanish manuscript published as *Le singe grammarien,* Skira (Geneva), 1972, translation by Lane of Spanish original published as *The Monkey Grammarian,* Seaver, 1981.

Los hijos del limo: Del romanticismo a la vanguardia, Seix Barral, 1974, translation by Phillips published as *Children of the Mire: Modern Poetry from Romanticism to the Avant-Garde,* Harvard University Press, 1974.

The Siren and the Seashell, and Other Essays on Poets and Poetry, translations by Kemp and Margaret Sayers Peden, University of Texas Press, 1976.

Xavier Villaurrutia en persona y en obra, Fondo de Cultura Economica, 1978.

El ogro filantropico: Historia y politica, 1971-1978 (also see below), J. Mortiz, 1979.

In/mediaciones, Seix Barral, 1979.

Mexico en la obra de Octavio Paz, edited by Luis Mario Schneider, Promexa (Mexico City), 1979.

El laberinto de la soledad; Posdata; Vuelta a El laberinto de la soledad, Fondo de Cultura Economica, 1981.

Sor Juana Ines de la Cruz; o, Las trampas de la fe, Seix Barral, 1982, reprinted, Fondo de Cultura Economica, 1994, translation by Peden published as *Sor Juana; or, The Traps of Faith,* Harvard University Press 1988.

(With Jacques Lassaigne) *Rufino Tamayo,* Ediciones Poligrafia (Barcelona), 1982, translation by Kenneth Lyons published under same title, Rizzoli, 1982.

(With John Golding) *Guenther Gerzo* (Spanish, English and French texts), Editions du Griffon (Switzerland), 1983.

Sombras de obras: Arte y literatura, Seix Barral, 1983.

Hombres en su siglo y otros ensayos, Seix Barral, 1984, translation by Michael Schmidt published as *On Poets and Others,* Seaver Books, 1987.

Tiempo nublado, Seix Barral, 1984, translation by Lane with three additional essays published as *On Earth, Four or Five Worlds: Reflections on Contemporary History,* Harcourt, 1985.

The Labyrinth of Solitude, The Other Mexico, Return to the Labyrinth of Solitude, Mexico and the United States, The Philanthropic Ogre, translated by Kemp, Yara Milos, and Rachel Phillips Belash, Grove, 1985.

Arbol adentro, Seix Barral, 1987, translation published as *A Tree Within,* New Directions, 1988.

Convergences: Essays on Art and Literature, translation by Lane, Harcourt, 1987.

The Other Voice: Essays on Modern Poetry, Harcourt, 1991.

Essays on Mexican Art, Harcourt, 1994.

My Life with the Wave, Lothrop, 1994.

Fundacion y Disidencia: Dominio Hispanico, Fondo de Cultura Economica, 1994.

Generaciones y Semblanzas: Dominio Mexicano, Fondo de Cultura Economica, 1994.

Los Privilegios de la Vista, Fondo de Cultura Economica, 1994.

Obras Completas de Octavio Paz, Fondo de Cultura Economica, 1994.

The Double Flame: Love and Eroticism, translated by Helen Lane, Harcourt Brace, 1995.

In Light of India, translated by Eliot Weinberger, Harcourt Brace, 1997.

An Erotic Beyond: Sade, Harcourt Brace, 1998.

EDITOR

Voces de Espana, Letras de Mexico (Mexico City), 1938.

(With others) *Laurel: Antologia de la poesia moderna en lengua espanola,* Seneca, 1941.

Antologie de la poesie mexicaine, Nagel, 1952.

Antologia poetica, Revista Panoramas (Mexico City), 1956.

(And translator with Eikichi Hayashiya) Matsuo Basho, *Sendas de Oku,* Universidad Nacional Autonoma de Mexico, 1957, 2nd edition, Seix Barral, 1970.

Anthology of Mexican Poetry, translation of Spanish manuscript by Samuel Beckett, Indiana University Press, 1958.

Tamayo en la pintura mexicana, Imprenta Universitaria (Mexico City), 1958.

Magia de la risa, Universidad Veracruzana, 1962.

Fernando Pessoa, *Antologia,* Universidad Nacional Autonoma de Mexico, 1962.

(With Pedro Zekeli) *Cuatro poetas contemporaneos de Suecia: Martinson, Lundkvist, Ekeloef, y Lindegren,* Universidad Nacional Autonoma de Mexico, 1963.

(With others and author of prologue) *Poesia en movimiento: Mexico, 1915-1966,* Siglo Veintiuno, 1966, translation edited by Mark Strand and published as *New Poetry of Mexico,* Dutton, 1970.

(With Roger Caillois) *Remedios Varo,* Era, 1966.

(And author of prologue) Xavier Villaurrutia, *Antologia,* Fondo de Cultura Economica, 1980.

Mexico: Splendors of Thirty Centuries, Metropolitan Museum of Art, 1990, translated as *Mexico: Esplendores de Treinta Siglos,* Friends of the Arts of Mexico, 1991.

CONTRIBUTOR

In Praise of Hands: Contemporary Crafts of the World, New York Graphic Society, 1974.

Avances, Fundamentos, 1978.

Democracy and Dictatorship in Latin America: A Special Publication Devoted Entirely to the Voices and Opinions of Writers from Latin America, Foundation for the Independent Study of Social Ideas (New York City), 1982.

Instante y revelacion, Fondo Nacional para Actividades Sociales, 1982.

Frustraciones de un destino: La democracia en America Latina, Libro Libre, 1985.

Weinberger, editor, *Nineteen Ways of Looking at Wang Wei: How a Chinese Poem Is Translated,* Moyer Bell, 1987.

TRANSLATOR

(And author of introduction) William Carlos Williams, *Veinte Poemas,* Era, 1973.

Versiones y diversiones (translations of poems from English, French, Portuguese, Swedish, Chinese, and Japanese), J. Mortiz, 1974.

Apollinaire, *15 Poemas,* Latitudes (Mexico City), 1979.

OTHER

La hija de Rappaccini (one-act play; based on a short story by Nathaniel Hawthorne; firLa hija de

Rappaccini (one-act play; based on a short story by Nathaniel Hawthorne; first produced in Mexico, 1956), translation by Harry Haskell published as *Rappaccini's Daughter* in *Octavio Paz: Homage to the Poet,* Kosmos (San Francisco), 1980.

(Author of introduction) Carlos Fuentes, *Cuerpos y ofrendas,* Alianza, 1972.

(Author of introduction) *Antonio Palaez: Pintor,* Secretaria de Educacion Publica (Mexico), 1975.

(Author of foreword) *A Sor Juana Anthology,* translation by Alan S. Trueblood, Harvard University Press, 1988.

(Author of introduction) James Laughlin, *Random Stories,* Moyer Bell, 1990.

(Author of introduction) Elena Poniatowska, *Massacre in Mexico,* University of Missouri Press, translation by Helen R. Lane, 1991.

In Search of the Present, Harcourt, 1991.

Al Paso, Seix Barral (Barcelona), 1992.

La llama doble: Amor y erotisma, Seix Barral (Barcelona), 1993, translation by Helen Lane published as *The Double Flame: Love and Eroticism,* Harcourt, 1995.

(Author of essay) *Nostalgia for Death / Hieroglyphs of Desire: A Critical Study of Villaurrutia,* edited by Eliot Weinberger, Copper Canyon (Port Townsend, WA), 1993.

Excursiones/Incursiones: Dominio extranjero, Fondo de Cultura Economica, 1994.

Vislumbres de la India, Seix Barral, 1995.

Contributor to numerous anthologies. Founder of literary review, *Barandal,* 1931; member of editorial board and columnist, *El Popular,* late 1930s; co-founder of *Taller,* 1938; co-founder and editor, *El Hijo Prodigo,* 1943-46; editor of *Plural,* 1971-75; founder and editor, *Vuelta,* 1976-98.

SIDELIGHTS: Often nominated for the Nobel Prize in his lifetime, Mexican author Octavio Paz continues to have a worldwide reputation as a master poet and essayist. Although Mexico figures prominently in Paz's work—one of his best-known books, *The Labyrinth of Solitude,* for example, is a comprehensive portrait of Mexican society—*Los Angeles Times* contributor Jascha Kessler called Paz "truly international." *World Literature Today's* Manuel Duran felt that Paz's "exploration of Mexican existential values permit[ted] him to open a door to an understanding of other countries and other cultures" and thus appeal to readers of diverse backgrounds. "What began as a slow, almost microscopic examination of self and of a single cultural tradition widens unexpectedly," Duran continued, "becoming universal without sacrificing its unique characteristic."

One aspect of Paz's work often mentioned by critics was his tendency to maintain elements of prose—most commonly philosophical thought—in his poetry and poetic elements in his prose. Perhaps the best example to support this claim can be found in Paz's exploration of India titled *The Monkey Grammarian,* a work which *New York Times Book Review* contributor Keith Botsford called "exceedingly curious" and described as "an extended meditation on the nature of language." In separate *World Literature Today* essays critics Jaime Alazraki and Jose Miguel Oviedo discussed the difficulty they would have assigning the book to a literary genre. "It is apparent," Alazraki noted, "that *The Monkey Grammarian* is not an essay. It is also apparent that it is not a poem, at least not in the conventional sense. It is both an essay and a poem, or perhaps neither." Oviedo similarly stated that the book "does not belong to any specific genre—although it has a bit of all of them—because it is deliberately written at the edge of genres."

According to Oviedo, *The Monkey Grammarian* is the product of Paz's long-stated quest "to produce a text which would be an intersection of poetry, narrative and essay." The fusion of opposites found in this work is an important element in nearly all Paz's literary production. In many instances both the work's structure and its content represent a blending of contradictory forces: *Renga,* for example, is written in four languages, while *Air Born/Hijos del Aire,* is written in two. According to *World Literature Today* contributor Frances Chiles, Paz strived to create in his writing "a sense of community or communion" which he found lacking in contemporary society. In his Neustadt Prize acceptance speech reprinted in *World Literature Today,* Paz attempted to explain his emphasis on contrasting thoughts: "Plurality is Universality, and Universality is the acknowledging of the admirable diversity of man and his works. . . . To acknowledge the variety of visions and sensibilities is to preserve the richness of life and thus to ensure its continuity."

Through juxtaposition of contrasting thoughts or objects Paz created a more harmonious world, one based on complementary association of opposites found in the Eastern concept of yin and yang. This aspect of Paz's thinking revealed the influence of his six-year stay in India as Mexican ambassador to that country. Grace Schulman explained Paz's proclivity for Eastern philosophy in her *Hudson Review* essay: "Although he had embraced contraries from the beginning of his writing career, [as] Mexican ambassador to India [he] found in Tantric thought and in Hindu religious life dualities that enforced his conviction that history turns on reciprocal rhythms. In *Alternating Current,* he writes that the Hindu gods, creators or destroyers according to their names and region, manifest contradiction. 'Duality,' he says, 'a basic feature of Tantrism, permeates all Hindu religious life: male and female, pure and impure, left and right. . . . In Eastern thought, these opposites can coexist; in Western philosophy, they disappear for the worst reasons: far from being resolved into a higher synthesis, they cancel each other out.'"

Critics have pointed to several repeated contrasting images that dramatically capture the essence of Paz's work. Ronald Christ, for example, commented in his *Nation* review of *Aguila o sol?/Eagle or Sun?* (the Spanish portion of which is the equivalent of the English expression "heads or tails?"): "The dual image of the Mexican coin which gives *Eagle or Sun?* its title epitomizes Paz's technique and credo, for we see that there is no question of eagle *or* sun rather of eagle *and* sun which together in their oppositeness are the same coin." Another of the poet's images which reviewers frequently have mentioned is "burnt water," an ancient Mexican concept which appears in Paz's work in both Spanish and in the Aztec original, "atl tlachinolli." Schulman maintained that "burnt water" is "the dominant image of [Paz's] poetry" and found that the image fulfills a role similar to that of the two sides of the coin in *Eagle and Sun?* She noted: "Paz sees the world burning, and knows with visionary clarity that opposites are resolved in a place beyond contraries, in a moment of pure vision: in that place, there are no frontiers between men and women, life and death." Chiles called the Aztec combination of fire and water "particularly apt in its multiple connotations as a symbol of the union of all warring contraries."

In *Sor Juana; or, The Traps of Faith,* Paz examined the literary achievement of Sor Juana Ines de la Cruz, the legendary seventeenth-century New Spain nun and poetess who produced masterful verse from a convent in Mexico City. *New York Times Book Review* contributor Frederick Luciani wrote, "Her extant works, in contrast [to documentary evidence related to her life], are of such abundance and variety, in such a range of styles, voices and manners, as to be simultaneously seductive and bewildering. With characteristic lucidity, Mr. Paz sorts through this textual morass and arrives at an admiring and sympathetic portrait, but an honest and demythologizing one, too." To understand his subject, Paz addressed the complex and turbulent civilization of colonial Mexico. "It is, after all," according to Jonathan Keates in the *Observer,* "not only the nun's tale but that of Mexico itself, the kingdom of New Spain, its imposed framework of ideal constructs eroded by mutual resentment between governors and governed and by a chronic fear of change." According to Electa Arenal in *Criticism,* "*Sor Juana; or, The Traps of Faith* is a tour de force—biography, cultural history and ideological criticism all in one. It describes the intellectual, political and religious climate of sixteenth and seventeenth-century Mexico; comments on the poet as rebel against orthodoxy, then and now; and studies the life, times, and art of a woman with whom Paz identifies and to whom he implicitly compares himself."

With *La llama doble: Amor y erotisma,* translated as *The Double Flame,* Paz provided a social and literary history of love and eroticism, comparing modern manifestations to those of earlier ages, while noting the special relationship between eroticism and poetry. "This book is a product of immense wisdom and patient observation, an approach to passion from the vantage of maturity," wrote Ilan Stavans in *Washington Post Book World.* "His ultimate thesis is that our society is plagued by erotic permissiveness, placing the stability and continuity of love in jeopardy, and that the difficult encounter between two humans attracted to each other, has lost importance, a development that he believes threatens our psychological and cultural foundations." According to Paz, "Both love and eroticism—the double flame—are fed by the original fire: sexuality."

In *The Other Voice: Essays on Modern Poetry* Paz offered a critique of contemporary poetry, including analysis of the Romantics and Symbolists and forceful objection to postmodernism and consumerism. Though noting Paz's conservative New Critic perspective, Raymond Leslie Williams wrote in *American Book Review,* "The breadth of Paz's literary repertoire in this volume, as in all his writing, is impressive. His understanding of Pound, Eliot, Apollinaire, and many other modern poets is vast." Paz emphasized the unifying power of poetry and asserted the importance of a public audience. "The volume's prevailing theme," wrote Ilan Stavans in a *Nation* review, is "poetry as a nonconformist, rebellious force of the modern age." Stavans observed, "Paz argues that while poets are elitists by nature, despite the tiny circulation of their craft it has a profound impact on society." For Paz, as John Butt wrote in the *Times Literary Supplement,* "the poem aspires to be all-encompassing, an image of what a unified theory of life might be, 'a miniature, animated cosmos' which 'unites the ten thousand things' that swirl around us."

Critics have agreed that Paz's great theme of a blended reality situates his work in the forefront of modern literature. As Christ noted: "By contraries then, by polarities and divergences converging in a rhetoric of opposites, Paz established himself as a brilliant stylist balancing the tension of East and West, art and criticism, the many and the one in the figures of his writing. Paz [wa]s thus not only a great writer: he [wa]s also an indispensable corrective to our cultural tradition and a critic in the highest sense in which he himself use[d] the word." Enrique Fernandez similarly saw Octavio Paz as a writer of enormous influence. "Not only has he left his mark on world poetry, with a multilingual cortege of acolytes," Fernandez wrote in a *Village Voice* essay, "he is a force to be reckoned with by anyone who chooses that modernist *imitaio Christi,* the Life of the Mind."

BIOGRAPHICAL/CRITICAL SOURCES:

BOOKS

Contemporary Literature Criticism, Gale, Volume 3, 1975, Volume 4, 1975, Volume 6, 1976, Volume 10, 1979, Volume 19, 1981, Volume 51, 1989, Volume 65, 1989.
Hispanic Literature Criticism, Gale, 1989.
Ivask, Ivar, *The Perpetual Present: The Poetry and Prose of Octavio Paz,* University of Oklahoma Press, 1973.
Poetry Criticism, Gale, Volume 1, 1989.
Roman, Joseph, *Octavio Paz,* Chelsea House, 1994.
Wilson, Jason, *Octavio Paz,* Twayne, 1986.

PERIODICALS

American Book Review, August-September, 1992, p. 3.
Booklist, November 15, 1991, p. 595.
Commonweal, January 27, 1989, p. 50.
Comparative Literature, fall, 1989, p. 397.
Criticism, Vol. XXXI, No. 4, p. 463.
Hudson Review, autumn, 1974.
Interview, October, 1989.
Journal of Youth Services in Libraries, summer, 1990, p. 311.
Kirkus Reviews, January 1, 1995, p. 62.
Library Journal, January, 1995, p. 79.
London Review of Books, May 18, 1989, p. 20.
Los Angeles Times, November 28, 1971.
Los Angeles Times Book Review, September 18, 1988, p. 3; April 30, 1995, p. 6.
Nation, August 2, 1975; February 17, 1992, p. 205.
New Republic, October 9, 1995, p. 40.

New Yorker, May 15, 1995, p. 93.

New York Times Book Review, December 27, 1981; December 25, 1988, p. 12.

Observer, January 15, 1989, p. 49.

Publishers Weekly, January 16, 1995, p. 444.

Small Press, winter, 1994, p. 89.

Times (London), June 8, 1989.

Times Literary Supplement, December 30, 1988-January 5, 1989, p. 1435; July 24, 1992, p. 6; August 2, 1996, p. 7.

Tribune Books (Chicago), September 11, 1988, p. 24.

Village Voice, March 19, 1985.

Washington Post Book World, July 23, 1995, p. 11.

World Literature Today, autumn, 1982; autumn, 1994, p. 795; winter, 1995, p. 111.

OBITUARIES:

PERIODICALS

Chicago Tribune, April 21, 1998, sec. 1, p. 1.

CNN Interactive (electronic), April 20, 1998.

Los Angeles Times, April 20, 1998, p. A18; April 21, 1998, p. A1.

New York Times, April 21, 1998, p. A1.

Times (London; electronic), April 21, 1998.

Washington Post, April 21, 1998, p. B6.*

*   *   *

PEREZ, Gilberto (Guillermo) 1943-

PERSONAL: Born March 20, 1943, in Havana, Cuba; son of Gilbert Perez Castilio and Edemia Guillermo; married Diane Stevenson, March 18, 1988. *Education:* Massachusetts Institute of Technology, B.S. (physics and mathematics), 1964; Princeton University, M.A. (physics), 1968.

ADDRESSES: Office—Department of Film History, Sarah Lawrence College, Bronxville, NY 10708.

CAREER: Writer, film historian, and critic. Princeton University, lecturer in film history and theory, 1972-80; Cornell University, visiting lecturer in cinema studies, 1980-81; William Paterson College, professor, 1981-82; Harvard University, professor, 1982-83; Sarah Lawrence College, professor of film history, 1983—.

AWARDS, HONORS: Museum of Modern Art, New York City, Noble Foundation Fellowship for Advanced Studies in the Visual Arts, 1970-72; Harvard University Andrew W. Mellon Faculty Fellowship in the Humanities, 1982-83.

WRITINGS:

The Material Ghost: Films and Their Medium, Johns Hopkins University Press (Baltimore, MD), 1998.

Contributor of numerous articles on film and other subjects to periodicals, including *The Hudson Review, The Nation, Raritan,* and *Yale Review.*

SIDELIGHTS: Gilberto Perez's 1998 study of films and filmmakers, *The Material Ghost,* was described by Edward W. Said, quoted on the barnesandnoble.com web site, as "a superb work of interpretation and understanding." According to the publisher, the book discusses a broad range of filmmakers, from the earliest days of the art form to the present. For Perez, the publisher notes, film is "a medium both lifelike and dreamlike, both documentary and fictional, where figures appear before us like actors on a stage and yet are removed from us like characters in a novel."

BIOGRAPHICAL/CRITICAL SOURCES:

OTHER

Barnes and Noble web site, http:/shop.barnesand noble.com/...0LHRNKKFS242k0V&isbn=0801856 736.*

*   *   *

PEREZ-REVERTE, Arturo 1951-

PERSONAL: Born 1951, in Cartagena, Spain.

ADDRESSES: Agent—c/o Harcourt Brace, 15 E. 26th St., New York, NY 10010; Alfaguara, Juan Bravo 38, 28006 Madrid, Spain.

CAREER: Writer, journalist, and television host.

WRITINGS:

El husar, Akal (Madrid), 1986.

El maestro de esgrima, Mondadori (Madrid), 1988.

La tabla de Flandes, Alfaguara (Madrid), 1990, translation by Margaret Jull Costa published as *The Flanders Panel,* Harcourt Brace (New York City), 1994.

El club Dumas, Santillana (Madrid), 1993, translation by Sona Soto published as *The Club Dumas, or, The Shadow of Richelieu,* Harcourt Brace, 1997.

La sombra del aguila, Alfaguara, 1993.

Territorio comanche: un relato, Ollero & Ramos (Madrid), 1994.

La piel del tambor (title means "The Skin of the Drum"), Santillana, 1995, translation by Sonia Soto published as *The Seville Communion,* Harcourt Brace, 1998.

Los heroes cansados (collection), foreword by Santos Sanz Villanueva, edited by Jose Belmonte Serrano, Espasa Calpe (Madrid), 1995.

Obra breve (title means "Short Works"), Alfaguara, 1995.

El capitan Alatriste, Alfaguara, 1996.

Limpieza de sangre, Alfaguara, 1997.

SIDELIGHTS: Spanish novelist Arturo Perez-Reverte may have been aided in his novelistic career by his popularity as a war correspondent and television personality, but it was his intelligence and literary acumen that allow him to remain a bestselling author in his native country. Three of his literary thrillers have been translated into English.

The Flanders Panel, published in 1994, is a translation of Perez-Reverte's 1990 novel *La tabla de Flandes.* It belongs to the genre of postmodern mysteries made popular by Italian author Umberto Eco, but in the opinion of the *Times Literary Supplement*'s Michael Eaude, "Perez-Reverte's plotting is much tighter and his narrative is more exciting." The novel's heroine, Julia, is an art restorer who discovers a murder mystery hidden in a medieval painting of a chess game. The game's moves are continued in the form of messages and events in Julia's life amid the Madrid art world; gradually, she realizes that she has become a target in the centuries-old mystery.

Eaude, praising the book with reservations about its "undistinguished" prose style and stereotyped characters, maintained that "*The Flanders Panel* is never boring." The critic commended the way Perez-Reverte worked background material, including chess moves, into the plot, and noted "a number of shocking twists." "Above all," Eaude concluded, "Perez-Reverte makes use of a vivid imagination." Plaudits also came from a reviewer for the *Observer,* who called the novel a "delightfully absorbing confection" and "ingenious hocus-pocus from start to finish." A *Publishers Weekly* contributor characterized the novel as "uneven but intriguing." That reviewer, like Eaude, faulted the characters as underdeveloped and

also argued that the mystery was solved unconvincingly and conventionally. The reviewer responded most favorably to Perez-Reverte's use of chess metaphors for human actions, and Julia's analyses of the painting, which she termed "clever and quite suspenseful."

Translated into English in 1997 as *The Club Dumas, or, The Shadow of Richelieu* was Perez-Reverte's 1993 novel, *El club Dumas.* In this work the author's proclivity for multilayered wit is given full play. The novel revolves around a rare book scout who is asked to find the last two of the three existing copies of the Renaissance work *The Book of the Nine Doors to the Kingdom of Darkness,* in which each door is represented by an illustration that is crucial to Perez-Reverte's plot. The search for this book becomes entangled with the acquisition of a manuscript of Alexandre Dumas's *The Three Musketeers,* and a trip to Paris ensues. A *Times Literary Supplement* reviewer reported, "Readers get, together with a mass of tables, diagrams, clues, decoys, and nudgings about intertextuality . . . all twenty-seven illustrations so that they can play spot-the-differences, and draw their own conclusions." The reviewer called *The Club Dumas* a "wayward and moderately enjoyable" mystery novel. *Booklist* contributor Brian Kenney labeled the novel "witty, suspenseful, and intellectually provocative."

Perez-Reverte's 1995 novel *La piel del tambor*, translated by Sonia Soto as *The Seville Communion,* was reviewed in the *Economist* in 1996. Again Perez-Reverte's work was noted for its enjoyably skillful plotting, rich use of background information (including in this case a map of Seville, Spain), and intellectual gamesmanship. The premise of the narrative is that the secret files of the Vatican have been broken into by a computer hacker, and a priest-sleuth is called in to investigate. Meanwhile another, more traditional priest, aided by a nun, is fighting a corrupt real-estate developer. *Economist* reviewer called Perez-Reverte "a master of intelligent suspense and reader-friendly action," and pointed out that this novel was "a hymn to Seville," and a work in which "postmodernistic tics do not interfere with a smoothly written, realist novel."

BIOGRAPHICAL/CRITICAL SOURCES:

PERIODICALS

Atlantic, September, 1994, p. 114.

Booklist, May 15, 1994, p. 1667; October 1, 1996, p. 292.

Books, September, 1994, p. 26; September, 1995, p. 25.

Economist, July 20, 1996, pp. 14-15.

Library Journal, June 15, 1994, p. 96; September 1, 1996, p. 211.

New York Times Book Review, June 12, 1994, p. 42; December 4, 1994, p. 69; September 22, 1996, p. 40.

Observer, July 31, 1994, p. 5B.

People Weekly, May 12, 1997, p. 30.

Publishers Weekly, May 2, 1994, p. 284; July 15, 1996, p. 23; November 18, 1996, p. 61.

Times Educational Supplement, December 29, 1995, p. 12.

Times Literary Supplement, August 12, 1994, p. 23; September 6, 1996, p. 23.*

* * *

PERI ROSSI, Cristina 1941-

PERSONAL: Born November 12, 1941, in Montevideo, Uruguay; immigrated to Barcelona, Spain, 1972. *Education:* Licenciada in comparative literature. *Politics:* Leftist.

ADDRESSES: Home—Barcelona, Spain. *Agent*—International Editors, Rambia de Cataluna 63, 3 piso, Barcelona 08007, Spain.

CAREER: Writer, 1963—. Teacher of literature in Montevideo, Uruguay; professor of comparative literature, Autonomous University of Barcelona. Writer for newspapers and magazines, including *Marcha;* exiled from Uruguay, settled in Barcelona, Spain, 1972.

AWARDS, HONORS: Arca Prize, 1968; *Marcha* Prize, 1969; Inventarios Provisionales Prize, 1973, for *Diaspora;* City of Palma de Mallorca prize, 1976; Benito Perez Galdos Prize, 1980; City of Barcelona Prize, 1991.

WRITINGS:

Viviendo (short stories), Alfa (Montevideo), 1963.

El libro de mis primos (novel), Biblioteca de Marcha (Montevideo), 1969.

Los museos abandonados (short prose), Arca (Montevideo), 1969.

Indicios panicos (poetry and short prose), Nuestra America (Montevideo), 1970.

Evohe: poemas eroticos, Giron (Montevideo), 1971.

Descripcion de un naufragio (poetry), Lumen (Barcelona), 1975.

Diaspora (poetry), Lumen, 1976.

La tarde del dinosaurio (short stories), Planeta (Barcelona), 1976.

(Editor) Homero Aridjis, *Antologia,* Lumen, 1976.

Linguistica general (poetry), Prometeo (Valencia, Spain), 1979.

La rebelion de los ninos (short stories), Monte Avila (Caracas), 1980.

El museo de los esfuerzos inutiles (short stories and essays), Seix Barral (Barcelona), 1983.

La nave de los locos (novel), Seix Barral, 1984, translation by Psiche Hughes published as *The Ship of Fools,* Readers International (London), 1989.

Una pasion prohibida, Seix Barral, 1986, translation by Mary Jane Treacy published as *A Forbidden Passion,* Cleis (Pittsburgh, PA), 1993.

Europa despues de la lluvia (poetry), Banco Exterior de Espana (Madrid), 1987.

Solitario de amor (Grijalbo (Barcelona), 1988.

Cosmoagonias, Laia (Barcelona), 1988.

Babel barbara (poetry), Angria (Caracas), 1990.

Fantasias eroticas, Temas de Hoy (Madrid), 1991.

La ultima noche de Dostoievski, Mondadori (Madrid), 1992, translation by Laura C. Dail published as *Dostoevsky's Last Night,* Picador (USA), 1995.

Aquella noche, Lumen (Barcelona), 1996.

Desastres intimos, Lumen, 1997.

SIDELIGHTS: An Uruguayan writer living in exile in Spain, Cristina Peri Rossi is the author of revolutionary poetry and prose. Her darkly humorous writings reflect a strong opposition to the inequities of class and sexual division and to the social and political repression that exist within dictatorial states. Themes of alienation, eroticism, and uncontrolled power dominate her works. "Her tales break down the logical interrelation of their parts and renounce all novelistic development and anecdotal mimesis in favor of the presentation of states of consciousness as images," wrote Hugo J. Verani in the *Dictionary of Literary Biography.* "The lyrical attitude, playful exploration of reality, metaphorical profusion, and digressive and cumulative forms are all signs of a poetic reality, a total experience intolerant of boundaries."

Peri Rossi's life as a political exile from her native Uruguay has influenced her writings. Her 1984 novel, *La nave de los locos,* translated as *The Ship of Fools,* is an unusual narrative that follows the exiled character Equis or Ecks (pronounced "X") on a never-ending journey, tracing his numerous encounters with women and his revelations about the lack of communication in the world. "The powerful sense of cultural alienation that the characters feel in the novel," explained Carol Gardner in the *Women's Review of Books,* "is clearly the product of the writer's own experience; it's a theme that recurs throughout her work written in exile." Verani agreed, calling the book "a lucid reflection on uprooting and displacement: in a troubled era, modern society subsists only fragmented and deprived of finality." "Around the image of the voyage," the *Dictionary of Literary Biography* contributor continued, "the novel presents successive stories of outcasts bereft of belongings and companions, symbolic figures in perpetual flight conscious of traveling without a fixed destination and alienated from society."

Equis is accompanied on part of his journey by fellow passengers who are equally as lost and adrift as he is. La Bella Pasajera is a woman who exists only for the pleasure of others. Vercingetorix is a political prisoner who proves unable to come to terms with his own past—he was held in a polluted cement town whose inhabitants had nearly all deserted it. Gordon, a former lunar astronaut, spends his life bemoaning the fact that he can never return to the moon. Morris is an eccentric with a passion for collecting odd objects, such as pipes and maps. "Condemned to temporariness and wandering," Verani wrote, "Equis accepts precariousness as a form of survival. The other characters . . . are denied apparent individuality and psychological development. Exiled from themselves and from the world, they surpass geographic, political, and temporal barriers."

In her fiction, Peri Rossi also strives to escape traditional forms of storytelling in order to avoid what she sees as oversimplification of her art. "All her stories," Verani declared, "maintain a heterogeneous sense of invention as they alternate spontaneously between diverse motifs, never letting any one feature dominate—a creative propensity that rules out the possibility of reducing Peri Rossi's work to mere components cut off from its diverse and complex context." In *The Ship of Fools,* for instance, "she rejects traditional narrative form," writes Gardner. "The novel's shape (or shapelessness) is a critique of structure—of those comforting artistic visions that, while giving us refuge from chaos, also confine us (both men and women) to certain 'proper' roles." Dan Bellm, writing in the *Voice Literary Supplement,* commented, "*The Ship of Fools* is a mess in the finest sense—a glorious mess, baffling and alluring." Quot-

ing from Peri Rossi's prose, the critic continued, "'We value in art the exercise of mind and emotion that can make sense of the universe without reducing its complexity.' That's hard to do, and that's what she's done."

Peri Rossi's 1992 novel *La ultima noche de Dostoievski,* translated and published in 1995 as *Dostoevsky's Last Night,* again plays with narrative expectations and modern themes. Verani commented that "the subversive potential of humor, irony, parody, and the absurd, distinctive traits of her literary practice, reaches a radical antimimetic and highly imaginative treatment" in the book. "The awareness of living at the end of a historical period . . . with its crumbling cities, unconscious fears and desires, and displaced and defamiliarized fantasies," the *Dictionary of Literary Biography* contributor added, "moves in her fourth novel toward a playful and flippant takeoff on Fyodor Dostoyevsky's fascination with gambling that generates a relentlessly ironic, postmodern vision of humanity reduced to absurdity and undermines once again the very notion of representation and the reading experience."

Dostoevsky's Last Night is the story of Jorge, a magazine journalist who has a fascination with gambling. He plays Bingo European-style—not the church-basement American game, but a casino version in which "this simple game is played with jungle ferocity," according to *New York Times Book Review* contributor Erik Burns. Like the Russian writer Feodor Dos-toevsky, Jorge rationalizes his addiction as a way of escaping the dullness of his job and his life. He says as much to his psychoanalyst Lucia, with whom he later falls in love. "For Jorge," noted *Atlanta Journal-Constitution* reviewer Candice Dyer, "gambling is the grand passion, identifying him as an artiste whose risk-worshiping temperament sets him apart from the bourgeoisie who have taken 'society's precious path.'"

Critics agree that in her depiction of Jorge's obsession Peri Rossi presents a condemnation of the emptiness of modern life. Jorge "propitiates luck," Dyer explained, "with a mysticism that those who occasionally buy lottery tickets or brandish troll dolls at the bingo hall will recognize as their lark turned inexorably self-destructive." In her protagonist's speeches, Burns stated, Peri Rossi "convey[s] all too accurately the sensation of time and money being frittered away" on both empty psychoanalysis and on games of chance. *Booklist* contributor Donna Seaman declared that "Rossi dazzles us with acute and powerfully articulate observations about chance, desire, disorder, luck, literature and how" modern society has recategorized sin as compulsion and replaced ethics with psychology.

BIOGRAPHICAL/CRITICAL SOURCES:

BOOKS

Contemporary World Writers, 2nd edition, St. James Press (Detroit), 1993.
Dictionary of Literary Biography, Volume 145: *Modern Latin-American Fiction Writers, Second Series,* Gale (Detroit), 1994.
Peri Rossi, Cristina, *The Ship of Fools,* translated by Psiche Hughes, Readers International, 1989.

PERIODICALS

Atlanta Journal-Constitution, December 24, 1995, p. K10.
Booklist, July, 1995, p. 1861.
Los Angeles Times Book Review, July 23, 1995, p. 6.
New York Times Book Review, July 30, 1995, p. 14.
Voice Literary Supplement, May, 1989.
Woman's Review of Books, July, 1989, p. 37.
World Literature Today, winter, 1990, p. 79.

*   *   *

PICON-SALAS, Mariano 1901-1965

PERSONAL: Born January 26, 1901, in Merida, Venezuela; died January 1, 1965, in Caracas, Venezuela. *Education:* Attended Universidad Central, Caracas, Venezuela, 1920; Universidad de Chile, degree in history, 1923, doctorate, 1928.

CAREER: Worked as a superintendent of education in Chile; Internado Barrios Arana, Chile, teacher, beginning in 1929; Liceo Lastarria, Chile, teacher, until 1936; Ministry of Education of Venezuela, superintendent, c. 1936; appointed Chilean *charge d'affaires* in Czechoslovakia, 1936-37; Universidad Central, Caracas, Venezuela, dean of humanities faculty, 1946-47; Venezuelan ambassador to Colombia, 1947-48; Universidad Central, teacher of humanities, 1951-58; Venezuelan ambassador to Brazil, 1958; United Nations, Paris, France, Venezuelan representative to UNESCO, until 1963; named general secretary of the cabinet of Venezuela, 1963. Indice (literary group), founding member, 1930-34; Instituto Nacional de Cultura y Bellas Artes, president, c. 1963. Visiting professor at U.S. institutions, including Columbia University, Middlebury College, Smith College, and University of California, Berkeley, between 1942 and 1944, University of Puerto Rico, 1949, and University of California, Los Angeles, 1951; University of Concepcion, lecturer, 1931.

AWARDS, HONORS: Venezuela's Premio Nacional de Literatura, 1954.

WRITINGS:

Las nuevas corrientes del arte, El Lapiz (Merida, Venezuela), 1917.
En las puertas de un mundo nuevo, Universitatis Andinensis (Merida), 1918.
Buscando el camino, Cultura Venezolana (Caracas, Venezuela), 1920.
Mundo imaginario, Nascimento (Santiago, Chile), 1927.
Hispanoamerica: Posicion critica, Universitaria (Santiago), 1931.
Odisea en tierra firme, Renacimiento (Merida), 1931.
Problemas y metodos de la historia del arte, Nascimento, 1934.
Registro de huespedes, Nascimento, 1934.
Intuicion de Chile y otros ensayos en busca de una conciencia historica, Ercilla (Santiago), 1935.
Preguntas a Europe, Zig-Zag (Santiago), 1937.
Cinco discurses sobre el pasado y el presente de la nacion Venezolana, La Torre (Caracas), 1940.
Formacion y proceso de la literatura Venezolana, Cecilio Acosta (Caracas), 1940.
Un viaje y seis retratos, Elite (Caracas), 1940.
Viaje al Amanecer, Mensage (Mexico City, Mexico), 1943.
De la conquista a la independencia: Tres siglos de historia cultural hispanoamericana, FCE (Mexico City), 1944, 3rd edition, 1958, translation by Irving A. Leonard published as *A Cultural History of Spanish America: From Conquest to Independence,* University of California Press (Berkeley, CA), 1962.
On Being Good Neighbors, translation by A. Flores, Pan American Union (Washington, DC), 1944.
Miranda, Losada (Buenos Aires), 1946.
Europa-America, Cuadernos Americanos (Mexico City), 1947.
Comprension de Venezuela, Ministerio de Educacion Nacional (Caracas), 1949, revised edition, 1955.
Pedro Claver, el santo de los esclavos, FCE, 1950.
Dependencia e independencia en la historia hispanoamericana, Cruz del Sur (Caracas), 1952.
Gusto de Mexico, Porrua y Obregon (Mexico City), 1952.

Los dias de Cipriano Castro: Historia Venezolana del 900, Garrido (Caracas), 1953.

Obras selectas, Edime (Caracas), 1953.

Simon Rodriguez, 1771-1854, Fundacion Mendoza (Caracas), 1953.

Sudamerica: Periodo colonial, Fournier (Mexico City), 1953.

Crisis, cambios, y tradicion: La crisis y el aire de nuestra cultura (novel), Edime, 1955.

Los tratos de la noche (novel), Nueva Segovia (Barquisimeto, Venezuela), 1955.

Ensayos escogidos, edited by J. Loveluck, Zig-Zag, 1958.

Las nieves de Antano: Pequena anoranza de Merida, Universidad del Zulia (Maracaibo, Venezuela), 1958.

Regreso de tres mundos: Un hombre en su generacion, FCE, 1959.

Los malos salvajes: Civilizacion y politica contemporaneas, Sudamericana (Buenos Aires), 1962, translation by H. Weinstock published as *The Ignoble Savages,* Knopf (New York City), 1965.

Obras completas, Edime, 1962.

(Author of commentary) *Promesa de Venezuela: Una seleccion fotografica de Graziano Gasparini,* Presidencia de la Republica (Caracas), 1964.

Las formas y las visiones: Ensayos sobre arts, Galeria de Arte Nacional Fundarte (Caracas), 1982.

Viejos y nuevos mundos, edited by Guillermo Sucre, Biblioteca Ayacucho (Caracas), 1983.

Biblioteca Mariano Picon-Salas, Monte Avila (Caracas), 1987.

Autobiografias, introduction by Sucre, notes and variations by Cristian Alvarez, Monte Avila, 1987.

Suma de Venezuela, introduction by Sucre, notes and variations by Alvarez, Monte Avila, 1988.

De la conquista a la independencia y otros estudios, introduction by Sucre, notes and variations by Alvarez, Monte Avila, 1990.

Paginas, edited by Sucre, Instituto de Altos Estudios de America Latina, Universidad Simon Bolivar (Caracas), 1991.

La conquista del Amanecer, edited by Jose Prats Sariol, Casa de las Americas (Havana, Cuba), 1992.

Founder, *Letras,* 1929.

BIOGRAPHICAL/CRITICAL SOURCES:

BOOKS

Stabb, Martin S., *In Quest of Identity,* University of North Carolina Press (Chapel Hill, NC), 1967.

PERIODICALS

La Torre, July-September, 1970, p. 75.*

*   *   *

PINON, Nelida   1937-

PERSONAL: Born May 3, 1937 (some sources say 1935), in Rio de Janeiro, Brazil; daughter of Lino Muinos and Olivia Carmen (Cuinas) Pinon. *Education:* Graduate of Catholic University of Rio de Janeiro, School of Journalism. *Religion:* Catholic.

ADDRESSES: Home—Av. Rodolfo Amoedo, 418 apto. 201, Barra de Tijuca, 22620 Rio de Janeiro, Brazil. *Office*—Av. Epitacio Pessoa, 4956 8 andar Lagoa, 22471-001 Rio de Janeiro Brazil. *Agent*—Agencia Carmen Balcells, Diagonal 580, 08021 Barcelona, Spain.

CAREER: Author and educator. Pontifica Universideade Catolica, Rio de Janeiro, faculty of philosophy. Taught at Federal University of Rio de Janeiro, Columbia University, New York City, Johns Hopkins University, Baltimore, MD, and University of Miami, Coral Gables, FL.

MEMBER: Brazilian Academy, Pen Club of Brazil, Brazilian Institute of Hispanic Culture, Academy Conselho Estadual de Cultura, Phi Beta Delta (Beta Theta chapter).

AWARDS, HONORS: Named One of Ten Women of the Year, Sector Literature, 1979; Manuel Bandeira medal, University of Campina Grande, 1986; Gold Golfinho award, Government of State of Rio de Janeiro and State Council of Culture, 1990; Bienale Nestle, 1991; Castelao medal, Galician Parliament, 1992; Galicia Medal.

WRITINGS:

Guia mapa de Gabriel Arcanjo, G.R.D. (Rio de Janeiro, Brazil), 1961.

Madeira Feita Cruz, G.R.D. (Rio de Janeiro), 1963.

Tempo das frutas, Alvaro (Rio de Janeiro), 1966.

Fundador, Alvaro (Rio de Janeiro), 1969.

A casa da paixao, Mario de Andrade (Rio de Janeiro), 1972.

Sala de armas, Sabia (Rio de Janeiro), 1973.

Tebas do meu coracao, Olympio (Rio de Janeiro), 1974.

A forca do destino, Record (Rio de Janeiro), 1977.

O calor das coisas, Nova Fronteira (Rio de Janeiro), 1980.

A republica dos sonhos, Alves (Rio de Janeiro), 1984, translation published as *The Republic of Dreams,* Knopf (New York City), 1989.

A doce cancao de Caetana, Guanabara (Rio de Janeiro), 1987, translation published as *Caetana's Sweet Song,* Knopf (New York City), 1992.

SIDELIGHTS: The novels and short stories of Brazilian Nelida Pinon are marked with a strong sense of feminism and eroticism, as well as the author's love of the performing arts, particularly opera. One of Brazil's most important contemporary writers of fiction, Pinon's reputation has spread beyond the borders of her native land in recent years, and many American literary critics have begun taking notice of her work. Since the publication of her first novel *Guia mapa de Gabriel Arcanjo* ("Guide Map of Gabriel Archangel") in 1961, Pinon's work has been recognized for its experimental use of both language and plot. She has been known to end some sentences in the middle of an idea or thought, while others run on for great lengths, incorporating many ideas.

Though she has a college education, having earned a degree in journalism, Pinon inherited much of her storytelling ability while learning of her Galician heritage. While her mother was born in Brazil, Pinon's father and both sets of grandparents were from Galicia, Spain, and moved to Brazil. Not only did Pinon learn the stories of the ancient homeland of her ancestors, she spent two of her formative years living there, a period the author has said was profoundly influential on her. While in Galicia, Pinon stayed at an old farm that had been owned by her family for generations, and that was near a small village where the young girl witnessed firsthand the storytelling ability of the old-timers. "It was marvelous because I integrated myself into rural life, the life of the European interior-therefore into the old way of life," Pinon told Bill Hinchberger in an interview for *Americas.* "I used to always go talk with those old men, the popular narrators, the storytellers. They taught me that there is a story to be told, that the history of man is waiting there to be narrated. No story had a final ending: It was always to be continued—because the history of man is to be continued."

This Galician influence can best be identified in her 1984 novel *Republica dos sonhos* (translated as *The Republic of Dreams*), her trademark work. Covering the successes and failures of four generations of a Brazilian family that had originated in Galicia, the novel, according to Pinon, represents "the dream of Brazil seen by immigrants from outside, [and] inside . . . a corrupted and degraded dream marked by disillusionment." In essence, the saga follows the family as it weaves its way through the course of actual historical events that have taken place in Brazil over the course of the last century. In fact, this incorporation of Brazilian history is another aspect often found in Pinon's work. In her fiction she has taken on some of Brazil's larger social problems, including the treatment of women by a patriarchal hierarchy. Though she does not claim to be a feminist, Pinon has created a host of female protagonists and characters who, in one way or another, rebel against sexist traditions. An example of such a character is Marta from the 1972 novel *A casa da paixao* ("The House of Passions"). Marta is a young girl in the midst of puberty, who, in the course of the story, discovers and then begins to embrace a sexual awakening. The story, like many of Pinon's other works, is filled with scenes of sexual intercourse and displays of erotic passion, a fact that has drawn its share of controversy throughout her career. Yet critics have overwhelmingly praised her work, both for its ingenuity and its social consciousness.

Pinon has earned a number of literary awards for her fiction, including the 1972 Mario de Andrade Prize given by the Association of Art Critics of Sao Paulo, an organization that also bestowed upon her the 1984 prize for best fictional work for *A republica dos sonhos.* A member of the prestigious Brazilian Academy of Letters since 1989, Pinon is also a teacher of literature, both in Brazil and abroad, including stints at various universities throughout the United States, where recognition for her work has steadily grown over the last decade. She is a noted lecturer, and is often asked to discuss various topics including her own literary works as well as Central American literature in general. In Brazil, she continues to be a prominent figure in the literary community, contributing editorials to leading newspapers, and participating in writer's workshops. In recent years, she has begun to write children's stories, including *The Windmill,* which was published in 1996.

Pinon was born May 3, 1937, in the city of Rio de Janeiro, and was the product of a strict Catholic upbringing. She attended a high school that was administered by German nuns and went on to study journalism at the Catholic University of Rio de Janeiro, which was run by a group of Jesuit priests. At an early age Pinon developed a strong, lifelong appreciation for ballet and opera that she has continually expressed in her fiction, such as in *A forca do destino,* a retelling of a Verdi opera, in which Pinon inserts herself as an instrumental character. Pinon was also able to immerse herself in the history of the two cultures that became so instrumental in her prose. "I am the child of two cultures," Pinon told Hinchberger. "I was a Brazilian and I spoke the Portuguese language, but at home or in my grandparents' house, where affection flowed like a river, there were only foreign presences—particularly Spanish and especially Galician. It is an intense, archaic, old world. I circulated between the Spanish-Galician language and the Portuguese language." She published *Guia mapa de Gabriel Arcanjo* in 1961, followed by her next novel, *Madeira feita cruz,* in 1963. Both works displayed Pinon's firm grasp of language, though it was at times so loaded with multiple meanings, many readers were too confused to appreciate the young writer's promise.

In 1966, after a period of literary maturation, Pinon published a volume of short stories titled *Tempo das frutas,* which was her first critical and popular success. The work introduced Pinon's tendency to feature themes such as eroticism and irony. In 1969, with Pinon's reputation on the rise, Afranio Coutinho, who was then the chair of the Department of Letters at the Federal University of Rio de Janeiro, enlisted her to conduct a workshop for literary development, the first of its kind at the university. Her success in this capacity was well noted, and for the rest of her career, she would be asked to serve in a similar capacity throughout the world. Also in 1967 Pinon published her next novel, *Fundador,* a book that has since been translated into three other languages. The book features Pinon's growing awareness of the political and social issues that plagued Brazil. Modeled after a medieval epic romance, *Fundador* is the adventurous story of a small band of radical villagers as they fight destructive and oppressive social forces deep within a symbolic forest world. Similarities can be drawn between the small group's predicament and that of various Central American countries that have struggled with dictatorial and oppressive regimes over the last half-century.

After publishing the erotic *A casa da paixao* in 1972, Pinon completed several other works, including *A forca do destino,* before beginning work on *A republica dos sonhos,* generally considered her masterpiece, and her first work to be translated into English, as *The*

Republic of Dreams, in 1989. A tribute to her Galician heritage, the novel follows the life of Madruga, who leaves Galicia at the turn-of-the-century in hopes of attaining wealth in Brazil. The story continues on into the 1980s, by which time Madruga has attained a fortune and become the patriarch of an extended family. An old man, Madruga is the only link between his Brazilian family and his native land. Having learned many Galician legends that were told to him by his grandfather Xan when he was a boy, Madruga imparts these ancient tales to his granddaughter Breta, the story's other main character. Over the course of the narrative, the story jumps back and forth through time and over continents, as Breta learns the Galician lessons. Yet just as important to the narrative is contemporary Brazilian history, which has shaped and molded the family. Colonialism is an apparent target of Pinon's derision, as she strips naked Brazil's social and political systems. In the process, she has been noted for enlightening many readers and critics.

BIOGRAPHICAL/CRITICAL SOURCES:

BOOKS

Dictionary of Literary Biography, Volume 145: *Modern Latin-American Fiction Writers, Second Series,* edited by William Luis and Ann Gonzalez, Gale Research (Detroit, MI), 1994, pp. 237-46.

PERIODICALS

Americas (English edition), February, 1997, p. 40.
New York Times, July 30, 1989, section 7, p. 22.*

*   *   *

PONCE, Mary Helen   1938-

PERSONAL: Born January 24, 1938, in Pacoima, CA; daughter of Tranquilino and Vincenta (maiden name, Solis) Ponce; married; children: Joseph, Ana, Mark, Ralph. *Ethnicity:*"Mexican-American." *Education:* California State University at Northridge, B.A., 1978, M.A. (Mexican-American studies), 1980; University of California at Los Angeles, M.A. (history), 1984; doctoral work in American Studies at University of New Mexico.

ADDRESSES: Agent—University of New Mexico Press, 1720 Lomas Blvd., N.E., Albuquerque, NM 87131-1591.

CAREER: Writer. White Memorial Medical Center Cancer Clinic, Los Angeles, community liaison; University of California at Los Angeles (UCLA), instructor of Chicano studies, 1982-87, adjunct professor, 1987-88; California State University of Northridge, teacher; University of New Mexico, Women's Studies program, adjunct faculty member, 1988-92; University of California at Santa Barbara, Chicano Studies program, adjunct faculty member, 1992—.

MEMBER: Mexican American National Women's Association, Western Association of Women Historians, and Mujeres Activas en Letras y Ciencias Sociales.

AWARDS, HONORS: Danforth Fellowship, University of California at Los Angeles.

WRITINGS:

Recuerdo: Short Stories of the Barrio, Ponce/Adame (Tujunga, CA), 1983.
Taking Control, Arte Publico Press (Houston, TX), 1987.
The Wedding, Arte Publico Press, 1989.
Hoyt Street: An Autobiography, University of New Mexico Press (Albuquerque, NM), 1993.

Also contributor of stories and essays to anthologies and literary journals.

SIDELIGHTS: Mary Helen Ponce is a prolific writer of books, articles, and short stories in both Spanish and English. She was born and grew up in the San Fernando Valley of California, in a community of Mexican immigrants, in the 1940s. In her writing she celebrates Hispanic culture of her childhood. Ponce is the youngest of seven daughters and three brothers, and says that her sisters are her main role models in life. Her sisters taught her many skills and encouraged her to succeed; one of them opened her eyes to literature by giving her a subscription to the Book of the Month Club.

Ponce married soon after she graduated from high school, and stayed home to take care of her four children until the youngest one began attending kindergarten. When he began school, she began her college education, reading and writing about her culture. Ponce believes that she would have become a writer no matter where she grew up, but that her sheltered ethnic heritage has provided her with a wealth of material to record and explore. She is especially interested in issues of biculturalism, bilingualism, and acculturation, as well as women's experience in the

era she has chosen to record. An active proponent of the value of church, family, and school, she celebrates these three aspects of life in her writing about Mexican-American culture.

As the mother of four children, Ponce worked hard to balance parenting, home life, and reading time with her schooling and writing time. She has presented her work at many campuses, including the University of California at Los Angeles, the University of New Mexico, and El Colegio de Mexico in Mexico City. A turning point in her professional career occurred in 1981 when she was invited to read her work at the Mexican–American National Women's Association meeting in Washington, D.C. This meeting, and the recognition she received there, allowed her to realize that she was indeed "a writer." In 1990 she was one of four writers invited to present their work at the New Mexico Women's History Conference. In addition to presenting at academic conferences and in academic journals, Ponce also takes her work to the community, publishing in local papers such as *La Opinion,* the largest Spanish-language newspaper in southern California.

Ponce's early work was largely autobiographical and written in the first person. Later, she wrote narratives, often with titles that began "Recuerdo" ("I Remember") that were written in the first person but that reflected the experiences of many Mexican women. Even later, when she began writing in the third person, most of her stories were based on her own experiences. As Angelina F. Veyna wrote in *Dictionary of Literary Biography,* "Ponce explains that she writes from memory and that her narratives are chiefly the result of her elaborating on situations or people with whom she has come in contact and mentally 'archived.' Much of her writing, she explains, tends to reflect her appreciation for people who are direct and honest."

In her novel, *The Wedding,* Ponce explores the experiences of a young, Mexican-American, working-class woman, Blanca, who is preparing for her wedding. Set in the San Fernando Valley in the 1940s, the book depicts her thoughts, hopes, and dreams as she prepares for this climactic event in her life, as well as all the interpersonal and family dynamics among the characters; Blanca, her friend, her godmother, and her boyfriend, as well as the rival groups to which some of the characters belong. The book ends inconclusively, with uncertainty about whether the marriage will survive, and what will become of Blanca in the future. When the book was originally published, some chapters were cut, and other parts of the book were altered. Ponce hopes eventually to publish an uncut, original version of the book.

Ponce is also working on a play based on the book, "Blanca's Wedding," and on "Mujeres Solas" ("Single Women"), a collection of narratives about elderly women told from a ten-year-old's point of view. She believes that older women should be respected and admired as survivors, but that they are often not recognized in their communities, and the collection is intended to give them this recognition.

Ponce's future plans include writing about women workers in the garment industry, as well as a biography of Fabiola Cabeza de Vaca, a New Mexican author she admires. She also plans to write more fiction based on the lives of Mexican-American and Chicano women. This focus on women, and the consideration of events and feelings common to all women, whether Mexican, Anglo, or members of some other group, is typical on Ponce. Veyna wrote of her, "Though she does not presently consider herself a feminist writer, she continues to address the historical and personal experiences of Chicana and Latina women, and she anticipates exploring a feminist perspective in future works."

BIOGRAPHICAL/CRITICAL SOURCES:

BOOKS

Dictionary of Hispanic Biography, Gale (Detroit, MI) 1993.
Dictionary of Literary Biography, Volume 122: *Chicano Writers,* Gale, 1992.

PERIODICALS

Hispanic, July, 1995, p. 82.
Nation, June 7, 1993, pp. 772-74.
School Library Journal, December, 1992, p. 36.*

* * *

PONIATOWSKA, Elena 1933-

PERSONAL: Born May 19, 1933, in Paris, France; daughter of John E. and Paula (Amor) Poniatowska; married Guillermo Haro (an astronomer); children: Emmanuel, Felipe, Paula. *Education:* Educated in Philadelphia, PA. *Religion:* Roman Catholic.

ADDRESSES: Home—Cerrada del Pedregal 79, Coyoacan, ZP 21, Mexico City, Mexico. *Office*—*Novedades,* Balderras 87, Mexico City 1, Mexico.

CAREER: Member of writing staff of *Excelsior,* 1954-55; *Novedades,* Mexico City, Mexico, staff member, 1955—. Instructor at Injuve. Founder of Editorial Siglo Veinto Uno, Cineteca Nacional, and Taller Literario. Speaker at schools and conferences; guest on radio and television programs.

MEMBER: International PEN.

AWARDS, HONORS: D.H.C. from University of Sinaloa; fellowship from Centro de Escritores, 1957; Premio de Periodismo from Turismo Frances, 1965; Premio Mazatlan, 1970, for *Hasta no verte Jesus mio;* Premio Villaurrutia, 1970, for *La noche de Tlatelolco: Testimonios de historia oral;* Premio de Periodismo from *Revista Siempre,* 1973; Premio Nacional de Periodismo, 1978.

WRITINGS:

IN ENGLISH TRANSLATION

La noche de Tlatelolco: Testimonios de historia oral, Ediciones Era, 1971, translation by Helen R. Lane published as *Massacre in Mexico,* introduction by Octavio Paz, Viking, 1975.
Querido Diego, te abraza Quiela, Ediciones Era, 1978, translation by Katherine Silver published as *Dear Diego,* Pantheon, 1986.
Until We Meet Again, translation by Magda Bogin, Pantheon, 1987.
Frida Kahlo: The Camera Seduced, Chronicle Books, 1992.
Nothing, Nobody: The Voices of the Mexico City Earthquake, Temple University Press, 1995.
Tinisima, Farrar, 1996.

IN SPANISH

Lilus Kikus, Los Presentes, 1954.
Meles y teleo: A puntes para una comedia, Panoramas, 1956.
Palabras cruzadas: Cronicas, Ediciones Era, 1961.
Todo empezo el domingo, Fondo de Cultura Economica, 1963.
Los cuentos de Lilus Kikus (title means "The Stories of Lilus Kikus"), Universidad Veracruzana, 1967.

Hasta no verte, Jesus mio (novel; title means "See You Never, Sweet Jesus"), Ediciones Era, 1969, reprinted, 1983; also known as *Until I See You, Dear Jesus.*

(Contributor) *El Primer Primero de Mayo,* Centro de Estudios Historicos del Movimiento Obrero Mexicano, 1976.

Gaby brimmer, Grijalbo, 1979.

De noche vienes (stories), Grijalbo, 1979.

Fuerte es el silencio, Eras Cronicas, 1980.

Domingo 7, Oceano, 1982.

El ultimo guajolote, Cultura, 1982.

Ay vida, no me mereces!, J. Mortiz, 1985.

Serena y alta figura, Oceano, 1986.

La Flor de Lis, Ediciones Era, 1988.

Todo Mexico, Diana, 1991.

Luz y Luna, Las Lunitas, Ediciones Era, 1994.

Author of screenplay *Hasta no verte, Jesus mio,* released by Producciones Barbachano Ponce.

OTHER

(Author of introduction) Nellie Campobello, *Cartucho and My Mother's Hands,* University of Texas Press, 1988.

(Editor with Carlos Monsivais) *EZLN: Documentos y Comunicados,* Ediciones Era, 1994.

(Translator of Sandra Cisneros's original novel into Spanish) *La casa en Mango Street,* Random House, 1994.

Work represented in anthologies, including *Antologia de cuentistas mexicanos,* Emmanuel Carballo, 1956; *Rojo de vida, y negro de muerte,* edited by Carlos Coccoli. Contributor to magazines, including *Revista Mexicana de Literatura, Siempre!, Estaciones, Abside,* and *Evergreen Review.*

SIDELIGHTS: Elena Poniatowska is a respected and well-known journalist contributing to several of Mexico's finest newspapers and periodicals as well as the author of many books of fiction and nonfiction. Born in Paris, the daughter of a Polish father and Mexican mother, Poniatowska immigrated with her family to Mexico when she was ten years old. A few years later, Poniatowska was sent to Philadelphia to attend the Convent of the Sacred Heart.

Following study at Manhattanville College on a scholarship, Poniatowska began her career as a journalist by interviewing key Mexican literary and political personalities. In 1954 she began writing for *Excelsior;* the following year she began working for *Novedades,*

an association that continues to the present. An industrious reporter for *Novedades,* she conducted an interview a day, with a production goal of three articles per week, according to Maria-Ines Lagos in the *Dictionary of Literary Biography.* She continues to produce a large volume of journalism, submitting twenty pages a week to *La Jornada* and *El Nacional* in addition to her work for *Novedades.* In a 1996 interview with *Bloomsbury Review,* Poniatowska commented, "I see myself mainly as a journalist. I always said to myself: 'When I get older. I'll have more time to write literature!'" She was also a co-founder of the Mexican film library Cineteca Nacional and the publishing house Siglo XXI.

A common thread running through Poniatowska's writing is a blending of both fiction and journalism. Several of her books are based on the correspondence of or interviews with real persons, such as the common-law wife of muralist Diego Rivera and the photographer Tina Modetti. However, Poniatowska tends to focus on the marginalized elements of Mexican society, including the poor and women. Frequently, she places females as the protagonists of her fictions, revealing their strength of character in the face of a patriarchal Mexican society. Her use of colloquial language for her characters provides a voice for the lower classes.

Poniatowska writes almost exclusively in Spanish—to date only a few of her books have been translated into English. *La noche de Tlatelolco: Testimonios de historia oral,* later translated as *Massacre in Mexico,* recounts Poniatowska's experiences in Mexico City during the 1968 student riots. J. A. Ellis explains in the *Library Journal* that Poniatowska's *Massacre in Mexico* is "the story of the continuing tragedy of Mexico. . . . The mood ranges from the early heady optimism of the students. . . to shock and despair." In a *Commonweal* review, Ronald Christ states that *Massacre in Mexico* is a "shatteringly beautiful book. . . . Recording everything she could about the incident and the events that led up to it, Poniatowska has assembled what she calls 'a collage of voices,' a brilliantly edited text whose texture is the weaving of anecdote, official history, gossip, placards, graffiti, journalism, eye-witness accounts, agonized interpretation."

Dear Diego, the translation of Poniatowska's *Querido Diego, te abraza Quiela,* is a fictionalized reconstruction of the correspondence between the internationally famed artist, Diego Rivera, and his common-law wife of seven years, Russian painter Angelina Beloff.

Written in the voice of Beloff, *Dear Diego* is a series of twelve imaginary letters describing the emotions and thoughts the young woman must have experienced after her lover leaves their home in Paris to return to his native Mexico. Although hopeful at first that Rivera will send for her and they will be reunited, Beloff eventually realizes that they will never be together again.

Barbara Probst Solomon explains the premise of this book in the *Nation*: "Elena Poniatowska's *Dear Diego* . . . is about a heated *menage a trois* between Diego Rivera, his Russian emigre common-law wife, Angelina Beloff, and the jealous third lover, art itself. Poniatowska's narrative . . . blends real documents with her own imaginative reconstruction of Angelina Beloff's relation to Diego Rivera. Exactly how much of this is Poniatowska and how much is drawn from actual documents is not made clear, and since Rivera was a real person, the reader can't help filling the gaps in this impressionistic novella with what is already known about him."

"The novella's subject is longing," writes Hayden Herrera in the *New York Times Book Review*. Herrera continues: "Angelina tries to span the ocean separating her from Diego with a bridge of words. Her mood shifts from despair to anger to nostalgic affection. We feel her growing apprehension that his absence is permanent. As we share her struggle with loneliness, poverty, and illness, we come to admire her determination to survive. . . . Although she was abandoned, she was not a loser. To be able to love as she did was a gift."

After ten years of research, Poniatowska published *Tinisima* in Spanish in 1994. In novel form, it tells the tale of Tina Modetti, an Italian artist and photographer who emigrated from Italy to San Francisco when she was seventeen. She later moved to Mexico and became the photographer Edward Weston's lover. She also had liaisons with Diego Rivera and other Mexican cultural and political contemporaries and became a communist militant. Cristina Ferreira-Pinto, in *World Literature Today,* writes: "[*Tinisima*] is a novel that certainly involves the reader. It stimulates much reflection, and the issues it addresses, through its portrayal of a woman, a country, and a time, are disturbingly contemporary."

Poniatowska examines more recent events in her oral history, *Nothing, Nobody: The Voices of the Mexico City Earthquake.* Compiled with nearly twenty other journalists, it records the inaction of the Mexican Government in the face of the tragedy and the response of the Mexican people to the earthquake.

BIOGRAPHICAL/CRITICAL SOURCES:

BOOKS

Dictionary of Literary Biography, Volume 113: *Modern Latin-American Fiction Writers, First Series,* Gale, 1992.
Jorgensen, Beth Ellen, *The Writing of Elena Poniatowska: Engaging Dialogues,* University of Texas Press, 1994.

PERIODICALS

Best Sellers, November, 1975.
Bloomsbury Review, December, 1992, p. 11; May-June, 1996, p. 9.
Booklist, October 15, 1992, p. 390; December 15, 1992, p. 719; March 15, 1993, p. 1304.
Choice, February, 1996, p. 1007.
Commonweal, January 16, 1976.
Library Journal, June 1, 1975; January, 1995, p. 77.
Nation, August 2-9, 1986.
New York Times Book Review, July 20, 1986.
Publishers Weekly, July 24, 1995, p. 59.
Washington Post Book World, February 2, 1992, p. 15; August 27, 1995.
Wilson Library Bulletin, February, 1995, p. 36.
World Literature Today, autumn, 1989, p. 658; winter, 1994, p. 90.*

*   *   *

PORCEL, Baltasar 1937-

PERSONAL: Born March 14, 1937, in Andratx, Mallorca, Spain; son of Baltasar (a sailor and farmer) and Sebastiana (a homemaker; maiden name, Pujol) Porcel; married Maria-Angels Roque (an anthropologist), July, 1972; children: Baltasar, Violant. *Ethnicity:* "Catalan." *Politics:* Democrat. *Religion:* Roman Catholic.

ADDRESSES: Home—Barcelona, Spain. *Office*—Institut Catalia de la Mediterrania, Ave. Diagonal, 407 bis, 08008 Barcelona, Spain; fax 34-4-218-4513. *Agent*—Antonia Kerrigan, Agencia Literaria Kerrigan/Miro/Calonje, Travessera de Gracia, 12 5e 2a, 08021 Barcelona, Spain.

CAREER: Institut Catalia de la Mediterrania, Barcelona, Spain.

AWARDS, HONORS: Caballos Hacia La Noche (Horses into the Night) listed among the best books of 1995 by *Publisher's Weekly* and *Critics Choice.*

WRITINGS:

Caballos Hacia La Noche, (novel), translated by John L. Getman as *Horses Into the Night,* University of Arkansas Press (Fayetteville, AR), 1995.
Dias Immortales (title means "Immortal Days"), Aims International Books, 1996.

Author of numerous novels in Spanish. Also author of a daily opinion feature, *La Vanguardia.*

WORK IN PROGRESS: A novel, *Springs and Autumns.*

SIDELIGHTS: Catalan novelist Baltasar Porcel once commented on his work. "My primary motivation for writing is a desire to interpret the world through imagination, through the strength of words, and to communicate this to people. What particularly influences my work is the world that I know about, the Mediterranean, and man in its passions. My writing process is to absorb sensations, to glimpse ideas. It is a slow elaboration of mental and emotional atmosphere, a redaction as exigent as enthusiastic. Definitively, what inspires me to write on the subjects that I choose is my relation with reality.

"In 1996 I published, in Spanish, a long book that is a historical report, through all the countries that include the Mediterranean cultures and their great creative moments from prehistory until today, with frequent lyrical incidences."

*　　*　　*

PUIG, Manuel 1932-1990

PERSONAL: Born December 28, 1932, in General Villegas, Argentina; died July 22, 1990, in Cuernavaca, Mexico; son of Baldomero (a businessperson) and Maria Elena (a chemist; maiden name, Delledonne) Puig. *Education:* Attended University of Buenos Aires, beginning 1950, and Centro Sperimentale di Cinematografia, beginning 1955; studied languages and literature at private institutes. *Religion:* None.

CAREER: Translator and Spanish and Italian teacher in London, England, and Rome, Italy, 1956-57; assistant film director in Rome and Paris, France, 1957-58; worked as a dishwasher in London and in Stockholm, Sweden, 1958-59; assistant film director in Buenos Aires, Argentina, 1960; translator of film subtitles in Rome, 1961-62; Air France, New York, City, clerk, 1963-67; writer, 1967-90. Argentina Air Force, 1953; served as translator.

AWARDS, HONORS: La traicion de Rita Hayworth was named one of the best foreign novels of 1968-69 by *Le Monde* (France); best script award, 1974, for "Boquitas pintadas," and jury prize, 1978, for "El lugar sin limites," both from San Sebastian Festival; American Library Association (ALA) Notable Book, 1979, for *The Kiss of the Spider Woman; Plays & Players* Award for most promising playwright, 1985, for *Kiss of the Spider Woman.*

WRITINGS:

La traicion de Rita Hayworth, Sudamericana (Buenos Aires), 1968, reprinted, Casa de las Americas, 1983, translation by Suzanne Jill Levine published as *Betrayed by Rita Hayworth,* Dutton, 1971, reprinted, 1987.
Boquitas pintadas, folletin (also see below), Sudamericana, 1969, translation by Levine published as *Heartbreak Tango: A Serial,* Dutton, 1973.
The Buenos Aires Affair: Novela policial, Sudamericana, 1973, translation by Levine published as *The Buenos Aires Affair: A Detective Novel,* Dutton, 1976.
El beso de la mujer arana (also see below), Seix-Barral (Barcelona), 1976, translation by Thomas Colchie published as *The Kiss of the Spider Woman,* Knopf, 1979.
Pubis angelical (also see below), Seix-Barral, 1979, translation by Elena Brunet published under same title, Vintage, 1986.
El beso de la mujer arana (play; adapted from his novel; also see below), first produced in Spain, 1981, translation by Allan Baker titled *Kiss of the Spider Woman,* first produced in London at the Bush Theatre, 1985, produced in Los Angeles at the Cast Theatre, 1987.
Eternal Curse upon the Reader of These Pages, Random House, 1982, Spanish translation by the author published as *Maldicion eterna a quien lea estas paginas,* Seix Barral, 1982.
Sangre de amor correspondido, Seix Barral, 1982, translation by Jan L. Grayson published as *Blood of Requited Love,* Vintage, 1984.

Bajo un manto de estrellas: Pieza en dos actos [and] *El beso de la mujer arana: Adaptacion escenica realizada por el autor* (plays; also see below), Seix Barral, 1983, 12th edition, French & European Publications, 1992.

Under a Mantle of Stars: A Play in Two Acts, translation by Ronald Christ, Lumen Books, 1985, revised edition, 1993, (produced in the original Spanish as *Bajo un manto de estrellas*).

La cara del villano; Recuerdo de Tijuana (play; title means "Face of the Scoundrel; Memory of Tijuana"), Seix Barral (Barcelona), 1985

(Contributor) G. W. Woodyard and Marion P. Holt, editors, *Drama Contemporary: Latin America,* PAJ Publications, 1986.

Mystery of the Rose Bouquet (play; produced at the Bush Theatre, 1987), translation by Baker, Faber, 1988 (produced in the original Spanish as *Misterio del ramo de rosas*).

Cae la noche tropical, Seix Barral, 1988, translation by Levine as *Tropical Night Falling,* Simon & Schuster, 1991.

Kiss of the Spider Woman and Two Other Plays, Norton, 1994.

Also author of screenplays for *Boquitas Pintadas,* adapted from his novel, 1974, *El lugar sin limites,* adapted from Jose Donoso's novel, 1978, and *Pubis angelical,* adapted from his 1979 novel. Contributor to various periodicals, including *Omni.*

ADAPTATIONS: The Kiss of the Spider Woman was made into a film by Brazilian director Hector Babenco in 1985 and starred Raul Julia, William Hurt (in an Oscar-winning performance), and Sonia Braga.

SIDELIGHTS: As a boy growing up in rural Argentina, novelist Manuel Puig spent countless hours in the local movie house viewing screen classics from the United States and Europe. His enchantment with films led him to spend several years pursuing a career as a director and screenwriter until he discovered that what he wanted to write was better suited to fiction; nevertheless, Puig's work is saturated with references to films and other popular phenomena.

"[But] if Puig's novels are 'pop,'" observed Jonathan Tittler in his *Narrative Irony in the Contemporary Spanish-American Novel,* it is because "he incorporates into his fiction elements of mass culture—radionovelas, comic books, glamour magazines, and in *Betrayed by Rita Hayworth,* commercial movies—in order to unveil their delightfully insidious role in shaping contemporary life." Puig echoes the design of these media, "us[ing] those forms as molds to cast his corny, bathetic material in a form displaying a witty, ironic attitude toward that material," noted Ronald Christ in *Commonweal.* Ronald Schwartz concurred with this assessment; writing in his study *Nomads, Exiles, and Emigres: The Rebirth of the Latin American Narrative, 1960-80,* the critic contended that Puig employed "the techniques of pop art to communicate a complex vision of his own world. It is [the] cinematic influence that makes *Betrayed by Rita Hayworth* and Puig's subsequent novels some of the most original contemporary Latin American narratives." In *Betrayed by Rita Hayworth,* "the idea of the novel is simple: the drama and pathos of moviegoing as a way of life in the provinces, where often people get to respond to life itself with gestures and mock programs taken over from film," described *New York Times Book Review* contributor Alexander Coleman. The story is narrated primarily through the eyes of Toto, a young boy born in the Argentinian pampas, and recounts the everyday life of his family and friends. "The novel's charm," claimed *Newsweek* writer Walter Clemons, "is in the tender gravity with which Puig records the chatter of Toto's family and neighbors. Kitchen conversations, awkwardly written letters and flowery schoolgirl diary entries . . . combine to evoke lives of humblest possibility and uncomplaining disappointment." While this description may sound gloomy, stated Coleman, nevertheless *Betrayed by Rita Hayworth* "is a screamingly funny book, with scenes of such utter bathos that only a student of final reels such as Puig could possibly have verbally recreated [it] for us." "Above all, Puig has captured the language of his characters," D. P. Gallagher reported in his *Modern Latin American Literature,* and explained: "There is no distance separating him from the voices he records, moreover, for they are the voices that he was brought up with himself, and he is able to reproduce them with perfect naturalness, and without distortion or parodic exaggeration. That is not to say that his novels are not very polished and very professional," the critic continued. "Like all the best Latin American novels. . . , they are structured deliberately as fictions. But the authenticity with which they reflect a very real environment cannot be questioned."

Puig's next novel, *Heartbreak Tango,* "in addition to doing everything that *Rita Hayworth* did (and doing it better, too) actually proclaims Puig not only a major writer but a major stylist whose medium brings you both the heartbreak *and* the tango," Christ declared in *Review 73.* Bringing together letters, diaries, newspapers, conversations, and other literary artifices,

Heartbreak Tango, as *New York Times* reviewer Christopher Lehmann-Haupt related, "reconstructs the lives of several Argentine women, most of whom have in common the experience of having once passionately loved a handsome, ne'er-do-well and doomed young man who died of tuberculosis." Mark Jay Mirsky commented in the *Washington Post Book World* that at first "I missed the bustle, noise and grotesque power of *Betrayed by Rita Hayworth.* The narrative of *Heartbreak Tango* seemed much thinner, picking out the objects and voices of its hero [and] heroines with too obvious a precision." Nevertheless, the critic admited, "as we are caught up in the story, this taut line begins to spin us around." Michael Wood, however, believed that it is this "precision" which makes *Heartbreak Tango* the better novel, as he detailed in a *New York Review of Books* article: "*Heartbreak Tango* seems to me even better than Puig's earlier *Betrayed by Rita Hayworth* because its characters' moments are clearer, and because the general implication of the montage of cliche and cheap romance and gossip is firmer." The critic added that "the balance of the new book," between irony and sentimentalism, "is virtually perfect." Gallagher presented a similar opinion in the *New York Times Book Review,* noting that "it has been said that [*Heartbreak Tango*] is a parody, but that underestimates the balance between distance and compassion that Puig achieves. His characters are camp, but they are not camped up, and their fundamental humanity cannot be denied." Despite this serious aspect, the critic remarked that *Heartbreak Tango* "is a more accessible book than its predecessor without being less significant. It is compelling, moving, instructive and very funny." "At the same time," concluded David William Foster in *Latin American Literary Review,* "no matter how 'popular' or 'proletarian' the novel may appear to be on the surface, the essential and significant inner complexity of [*Heartbreak Tango*], like that of *Betrayed by Rita Hayworth,* bespeaks the true artistic dimensions of Puig's novel."

"The appearance of Manuel Puig's new novel, *The Buenos Aires Affair,* is especial cause for celebration," Ronald De Feo asserted in the *National Review,* "not only because the book makes for fascinating reading, but also because it demonstrates that its already highly accomplished author continues to take chances and to grow as an artist." Subtitled *A Detective Novel,* the story takes place in the city and investigates a kidnapping involving two sexually deviant people. "It is not devoid of the lucid and witty observation of absurd behaviour that characterized" *Heartbreak Tango,* maintained a *Times Literary Supple-*

ment, "but it is altogether more anguished." As Toby Moore elaborated in another *Times Literary Supplement* review, "Puig's subject is the tangle made up of love and sexual desire. . . . In *The Buenos Aires Affair* the anxieties and inhibitions of the two characters are so great that they never get to a point of love; all they have is the dream of sex which obsesses and torments them." The author sets this psychological drama within the framework of a traditional thriller; "what makes Puig so fascinating," wrote *New York Times Book Review* contributor Robert Alter, is "the extraordinary inventiveness he exhibits in devising new ways to render familiar material." De Feo, however, faulted the author for being "a shade too inventive, [for] we are not always convinced that [these methods] are necessary. But," the critic added, "the book is more intense, serious, and disturbing than the other novels, and it is a welcome departure for this searching, gifted writer." And a *Times Literary Supplement* writer claimed that *The Buenos Aires Affair* "is technically even more accomplished than the previous novels, and Sr Puig is able to handle a wide variety of narrative devices in it without ever making them seem gratuitous."

Shortly after the publication of *The Buenos Aires Affair* in 1973, Puig found it more difficult to remain in Argentina; *Affair* had been banned (presumably because of its sexual content), and the political situation was becoming more restrictive. This increasingly antagonistic climate led Puig to a self-imposed exile, and is reflected in what is probably his best-known work, *The Kiss of the Spider Woman.* Set almost entirely in an Argentinian jail cell, the novel focuses on Valentin, a radical student imprisoned for political reasons, and Molina, a gay window-dresser being held on a "morals" charge, who recounts his favorite 1930s and 1940s movies as a means of passing time. "In telling the story of two cellmates, Puig strips down the narrative to a nearly filmic level—dialogue unbroken even to identify the speakers, assuming we can project them onto our own interior screens," related Carol Anshaw in the *Voice Literary Supplement.* "If this insistent use of unedited dialogue tends to make the book read a bit like a radio script, however," observed *New York Times Book Review* contributor Robert Coover, "it is Mr. Puig's fascination with old movies that largely provides [the novel's] substance and ultimately defines its plot, its shape. What we hear," the critic continued, "are the voices of two suffering men, alone and often in the dark, but what we see. . . [is] all the iconographic imagery, magic and romance of the movies." The contrast between the two men, who gradually build a friendship "makes this Argentinian odd couple both funny and affecting," Larry Rohter stated in the *Washington Post Book World*. But when Molina is released in hopes that he will lead officials to Valentin's confederates, "the plot turns from comedy to farce and Puig's wit turns mordant."

In addition to the continuous dialogue of the jail cell and surveillance report after Molina's release, *The Kiss of the Spider Woman* contains several footnotes on homosexuality whose "clumsy academic style serves to emphasize by contrast that the two prisoners' dialogue is a highly contrived storytelling device, and not the simulation of reality you may take it to be at first," commented Lehmann-Haupt. Because of this, the critic explained, the book becomes "a little too tricky, like a well-made, 19th-century play." Other reviewers, however, found *The Kiss of the Spider Woman* "far and away [Puig's] most impressive book," as Anshaw said. "It is not easy to write a book which says something hopeful about human nature and yet remains precise and unsentimental," Maggie Gee remarked in the *Times Literary Supplement*. "Puig succeeds, partly because his bleak vision of the outside world throws into relief the small private moments of hope and dignifies them, partly through his deft manipulation of form." Schwartz similarly concluded that *The Kiss of the Spider Woman* "is not the usual jumble of truncated structures from which a plot emerges but, rather, a beautifully controlled narrative that skillfully conveys basic human values, a vivid demonstration of the continuing of the genre itself."

Inspired by a stay in New York, *Eternal Curse on the Reader of These Pages* was written directly in English and, similar to *The Kiss of the Spider Woman,* is mainly comprised of an extended dialogue. Juan Jose Ramirez is an elderly Argentinian living in exile in New York and Lawrence John is the irritable, taciturn American who works part-time caring for him. But as their dialogues progress, Lehmann-Haupt notes, "it becomes increasingly difficult to tell how much is real and how much the two characters have become objects of each other's fantasy life." *Los Angeles Times Book Review* critic Charles Champlin, although he believed these dialogues constitute a technical "tour de force," questioned "whether a technical exercise, however clever, [is] the best way to get at this study of conflicting cultures and the ambiguities in the relationship." Gilbert Sorrentino similarly felt that *Eternal Curse* is "a structural failure, . . . for the conclusion, disastrously, comments on and 'explains' an otherwise richly ambivalent and mysterious text." The

critic continued in the *Washington Post Book World:* "It's too bad, because Puig *has* something, most obviously a sense that the essential elements of life, life's serious 'things,' are precisely the elements of soap opera, sit-coms, and B-movies." But Lehmann-Haupt thought *Eternal Curse* is "more austere and intellectually brittle than any of [Puig's] previous books, [and] less playful and dependent on the artifacts of American pop culture," and called the novel a "fascinating tour de force." "Puig is an artist, . . . and his portrait of two men grappling with their suffering is exceedingly moving and brilliantly done," declared William Herrick in the *New Leader*. "Stran-gely, the more space I put between the book and myself, the more tragic I find it. It sticks to the mind. Like one cursed, I cannot find peace, cannot escape from its pain."

Echoing themes of Puig's previous work, maintained *Nation* contributor Jean Franco, "politics and sexuality are inseparable in *Pubis Angelical."* Alternating the story of Ana, an Argentinian exile dying of cancer in Mexico, with her fantasies of a 1930s movie star and a futuristic "sexual soldier," *Pubis Angelical* speaks "of the political nightmares of exile, disappearance, torture and persecution," described Franco, "though as always in Puig's novels, the horror is tempered by the humor of his crazy plots and kitsch stage props." "Puig is both ruthless and touching in his presentation of Ana's muddled but sincere life," stated Jason Wilson in the *Times Literary Supplement;* "and if he is sometimes too camp, he can also be very funny." The critic elaborated: "His humour works because he refuses to settle for any single definition of woman; Ana is all feeling and intuition . . . although she is also calculating, and unfeeling about her daughter." But while Ana's advancing cancer and the problems of her dream counterparts are severe, "however seriously Puig is questioning gender assumptions and behavior his voice is never a solemn one," Nick Caistor claimed in the *New Statesman*. "The work as a whole fairly bristles with ingenuity and energy," Robert Towers wrote in the *New York Review of Books;* "the thematic parallels between the three texts seem almost inexhaustible, and one finishes the novel with a sense of having grasped only a portion of them." Nevertheless, the critic faulted *Pubis Angelical* for being "an impressive artifact rather than a fully engrossing work of fictional art." Steve Erickson likewise criticized the novel, commenting in the *New York Times Book Review* that "what's amazing about 'Pubis Angelical' is how utterly in love it is with its own artificiality." The critic added that "the novel fails most devastatingly" in the portrayals of Ana's fantasies: "There's nothing about their lives to suggest that . . . they have a reality for her." While Jay Cantor similarly believed that "it isn't till the last quarter of the book that the fantasies have sufficient, involving interest," he acknowledged in the *Los Angeles Times Book Review* that "there is an audacity to Puig's method, and an intellectual fire to Puig's marshaling of motifs that did then engage me." "In any case, whatever the whole [of the novel] amounts to, each individual part of 'Pubis Angelical' develops its own irresistible drama," countered Lehmann-Haupt. "Though it takes an exercise of the intellect to add them together, they finally contribute to what is the most richly textured and extravagant fiction [Puig] has produced so far."

In *Blood of Requited Love* Puig recounts a failed romance between a construction worker, Josemar, and the young daughter of a successful businessman in rural Brazil. The story is based largely on Puig's interviews with a real-life carpenter. As in other novels, Puig employs extended dialogue incorporating multiple voices to juxtapose reality and fantasy, and to illustrate entrapment caused by despair. Dean Flower called the novel "another dazzling *tour de force*," in the *Hudson Review,* "both a book-length dramatic monologue and a kind of philosophical inquiry into the dialectics of narrative self-invention." According to Norman Lavers in *American Book Review,* "It is the way that the novel is narrated that marks it as Puig's. For almost the first time in Puig there is a narrator, and the narrator seems almost like that chatty nineteenth-century omniscient author, except he is so unreliable—perhaps exaggerating the subjectivity of the standard authorial voice—that only the most careful reading can ferret out when he is telling the truth. However, the narrator turns out to be Josemar himself, telling his own story in the third person." Stephen Dobyns concluded in a *Times Literary Supplement* review, "This is a sad book and a very impressive one. We move from seeing Josemar as a selfish brute, to feeling sympathy and compassion; he is completely responsible for his life and he is trapped."

Tropical Night Falling, originally published two years before Puig's death in 1990, also involves the effective use of dialogue, interspersed with letters, to portray both internal and external conflict. The novel follows the conversations and correspondence of two elderly sisters in Rio who debate and attempt to disentangle the emotional lives of their family, neighbors, and the function of romance in the contemporary world. *Times Literary Supplement* contributor

John Butt praised the novel, noting that "the ending is a masterpiece of graceful bathos that is characteristic of Puig at his funniest." Peter Matthews wrote in an *Observer* review, "This spare, elegant chamber piece was Puig's last novel. . . and it must be his saddest." Butt similarly concluded, "*Tropical Night Falling* shows that this unusual and attractive voice among modern novelists was strong to the last." "Less interested in depicting things as they might be, and concerned with things as they are, Puig does not resort to make-believe," Alfred J. MacAdam asserted in *Modern Latin American Narratives: The Dreams of Reason.* "His characters are all too plausible, . . . [and their lives] simply unfold over days and years until they run their meaningless course." It is this ordinary, commonplace quality of life, however, that the author prefers to investigate, as he once told *Washington Post* interviewer Desson Howe: "I find literature the ideal medium to tell certain stories that are of special interest to me. Everyday stories with no heroics, the everyday life of the gray people." And films play such a large role in his work because of the contrast they provided to this mundane world: "I think I can understand the reality of the 1930s by means of the unreality of their films," Puig also remarked in a *Los Angeles Times* interview with Ann Marie Cunningham. "The films reflect exactly what people dreamed life could be. The relationships between people in these films are like the negative of a photograph of real life." "I can only understand realism," the author further explained to *New York Times* writer Samuel G. Freedman. "I can only approach my writing with an analytical sense. . . . I can write dreams, but I use them as part of the accumulation of detail, as counterpoint."

Because of his realistic yet inventive portrayals, contended Schwartz, "Manuel Puig is a novelist moving in the direction of political commitment in his depiction of the provincial and urban middle class of Argentina, something that has never before been attempted so successfully in Latin American letters." The critic concluded: "Clearly, Puig, thriving self-exiled from his native country, is an eclectic stylist, a consummate artist."

BIOGRAPHICAL/CRITICAL SOURCES:

BOOKS

Contemporary Literary Criticism, Gale, Volume 3, 1975, Volume 5, 1976, Volume 10, 1979, Volume 28, 1984, Volume 65, 1990.

Dictionary of Literary Biography, Volume 113: *Modern Latin-American Fiction Writers, First Series,* Gale, 1992.

Duran, Victor M., *A Marxist Reading of Fuentes, Vargas Llosa, and Puig,* University Press of America (Lanham), 1994.

Gallagher, D. P., *Modern Latin American Literature,* Oxford University Press, 1973.

MacAdam, Alfred J., *Modern Latin American Narratives: The Dreams of Reason,* University of Chicago Press, 1977.

Schwartz, Ronald, *Nomads, Exiles, and Emigres: The Rebirth of the Latin American Narrative, 1960-80,* Scarecrow Press, 1980.

Tittler, Jonathan, *Narrative Irony in the Contemporary Spanish-American Novel,* Cornell University Press, 1984.

PERIODICALS

American Book Review, May, 1985, p. 9.
Commonweal, June 24, 1977.
Hudson Review, summer, 1985, p. 307.
Latin American Literary Review, fall, 1972.
Los Angeles Times, January 30, 1987; February 3, 1987.
Los Angeles Times Book Review, June 20, 1982; December 28, 1986.
Nation, April 18, 1987.
National Review, October 29, 1976.
New Leader, June 28, 1982.
New Statesman, October 2, 1987.
Newsweek, October 25, 1971; June 28, 1982.
New York Review of Books, December 13, 1973; January 24, 1980; December 18, 1986.
New York Times, November 28, 1973; April 23, 1979; June 4, 1982; September 25, 1984; August 5, 1985; December 22, 1986; October 25, 1988.
New York Times Book Review, September 26, 1971; December 16, 1973; September 5, 1976; April 22, 1979; July 4, 1982; September 23, 1984; December 28, 1986.
Observer, July 5, 1992, p. 63.
Review 73, fall, 1973.
Times (London), August 23, 1985.
Times Literary Supplement, November 6, 1970; August 31, 1973; September 21, 1984; October 16, 1987; August 11-17, 1989, p. 877; July 3, 1992, p. 27.
Tribune Books (Chicago), April 15, 1979.
Voice Literary Supplement, April, 1987; April, 1989.
Washington Post, November 16, 1985.
Washington Post Book World, November 25, 1973; April 22, 1979; August 1, 1982.
World Literature Today, winter, 1981.*

QUINN, Anthony (Rudolph Oaxaca) 1915-

PERSONAL: Born April 21, 1915 (one source says 1916), in Chihuahua, Mexico; immigrated to United States; naturalized U.S. citizen, 1947; son of Frank (a camera operator and props handler) and Manuella (Oaxaca) Quinn; married Katherine DeMille, October 21, 1937 (divorced); married Iolanda Addolori, January 1966; children: (first marriage) Christopher, Christina, Kathleen, Valentina, Duncan, (second marriage) Francesco, Daniele, Lorenzo. *Avocational interests:* Painting, collecting books and paintings.

ADDRESSES: Agent—c/o HarperCollins, 10 East 53rd St., New York, NY 10022.

CAREER: Actor, director of motion pictures, and writer. Worked as laborer in early 1930s. Actor in motion pictures, including *The Plainsman,* 1936; *Blood and Sand,* 1941; *The Road to Morocco,* 1942; *Black Gold,* 1947; *Against All Flags,* 1952; *Viva Zapata,* 1952; *La Strada,* 1954; *Magnificent Matador,* 1955; *Ulysses,* 1955; *Lust for Life,* 1955; *The Hunchback of Notre Dame,* 1957; *The Black Orchid,* 1958; *Wild Is the Wind,* 1958; *Barabbas,* 1962; *Lawrence of Arabia,* 1962; *Requiem for a Heavyweight,* 1963; *Zorba the Greek,* 1964; *The Shoes of the Fisherman,* 1968; *The Secret of Santa Vittoria,* 1969; *R. P. M.,* 1970; *The Don Is Dead,* 1973; *Caravans,* 1978; *The Greek Tycoon,* 1978; *The Inheritance,* 1978; *Treasure Island,* 1978; *Revenge,* 1990; *Jungle Fever,* 1990; *The Last Action Hero,* 1993; *A Walk in the Clouds,* 1995. Actor in stage productions, including *Clean Beds,* 1936; *A Streetcar Named Desire,* 1950; *Borned in Texas,* 1950; *Let Me Hear the Melody,* 1951; *Zorba!,* 1983. Actor in television productions, including *Onassis: The Richest Man in the World,* 1988; *The Old Man and the Sea,* 1990; *This Can't Be Love, 1994.* Director of motion pictures, including *The Buccaneer,* 1958. Art work represented in exhibitions.

AWARDS, HONORS: Academy Award, best supporting actor, Academy of Motion Picture Arts and Sciences, 1952, for *Viva Zapata;* Academy Award, best supporting actor, 1956, for *Lust for Life;* Academy Award nomination, best actor, 1958, for *Wild Is the Wind;* Antoinette Perry Award nomination, best actor in a drama, 1961, for *Becket;* Academy Award nomination, best actor, 1965, for *Zorba the Greek;* Cecil B. DeMille Award, Hollywood Foreign Press Association, 1987, for "outstanding contribution to the world of entertainment"; Ellis Island Medal of Honor from National Ethnic Coalition of Organizations, 1990.

WRITINGS:

Thirty Three Men (play), 1937.
The Original Sin: A Self Portrait (autobiography),
   Little, Brown (Boston, MA), 1972.
(With Michael Paisner) *One Man Tango* (autobiogra-
   phy), HarperCollins (New York), 1995.

SIDELIGHTS: Anthony Quinn is a prominent actor
who has enjoyed substantial success in film and on
television and the stage during a career that spans the
greater part of the twentieth century. Quinn was born
in Mexico in 1915 and his family moved to Texas
when he was still a small child. After the family
traveled west and settled in Los Angeles, Quinn's
father found work with a film crew. Through his
father's efforts, the young Quinn won a small film
role. But after his father died in an automobile accident, Quinn concentrated on his school studies,
sculpting, and playing the saxophone. He ended his
education during the Depression and traveled throughout California, where he managed to find a range of
jobs.

In the mid-1930s Quinn returned to acting and soon
found a role in the stage production *Clean Beds.*
Around that same time Quinn also obtained a small
role in the crime drama *Parole.* On the strength of
that performance, he was cast as an Indian in film
mogul Cecil B. DeMille's production *The Plainsman.*
For the next several years Quinn honed his acting
skills in a host of ethnic roles. He appeared as an
African sheik in *The Road to Morocco,* played a
Chinese warrior in *China Sky,* and portrayed a Philippine soldier in *Back to Bataan.* In addition, he appeared on Broadway as a Greek-American congress-
man in *The Gentleman from Athens,* and he played
Polish-American Stanley Kowalski in a traveling production of Tennessee Williams' *A Streetcar Named
Desire.*

By the early 1950s Quinn was well established as a
versatile performer with a particular flair for head-
strong ethnic types. In 1952 he won an Academy
Award supporting Marlon Brando in director Elia
Kazan's *Viva Zapata,* an acclaimed drama. Four years
later he won another Academy Award, in the same
category, for his rendering of French painter Paul
Gaugin in director Vincente Minelli's *Lust for Life.*

Between playing his two award-winning roles, Quinn
traveled to Europe, where he worked regularly in the
mid-1950s. Prominent among his films from this period is *La Strada,* master filmmaker Federico Fellini's

work featuring Quinn as a crude, brutal strongman
touring Italy with his long-suffering wife. Quinn appeared in a singing role in *Cavalleria Rusticana,* an
adaptation of Mascagni's *verismo* opera, and he supported Kirk Douglas in *Ulysses,* an Italian production
adapted from Homer's epic. After returning to Hollywood, Quinn appeared in *Lust for Life* and won acclaim for his sympathetic portrayal of Quasimodo in
a 1957 production of *The Hunchback of Notre Dame.*
The next year Quinn directed *The Buccaneer,* a war
drama depicting Andrew Jackson and his ties to the
French soldier Lafayette during the War of 1812.

In the 1960s Quinn continued to work regularly in a
wide variety of roles. He played the lead in the Biblical drama *Barabbas* and won great acclaim for his
exuberant characterization of the title role in director
Michael Cacoyannis's *Zorba the Greek.* Notable
among his supporting performances from this decade
was his appearance as an Arab fighter in director
David Lean's adventure epic *Lawrence of Arabia.* In
addition, Quinn appeared as Kublai Khan in *Marco
the Magnificent.*

Quinn continued to prove his versatility and acting
stamina in ensuing decades. In the 1970s, a decade in
which Quinn reached his sixtieth year, he played in
more than fifteen films, including *Flap,* in which he
portrayed a Native American rights advocate; *The
Don Is Dead,* in which he appeared as a mob leader;
and *The Greek Tycoon,* in which he played Greek
shipping billionaire Aristotle Onassis. Quinn also
played the lead role in *Onassis: The Richest Man in
the World,* a television film broadcast in 1988. Also
notable among his television films is *The Old Man
and the Sea,* in which Quinn played the determined
fisherman of Ernest Hemingway's acclaimed tale.
And his film credits from the 1990s include *Revenge,*
a thriller starring Kevin Costner; *Jungle Fever,* Spike
Lee's drama about an interracial relationship, with
Quinn as a concerned parent; and *The Last Action
Hero,* an Arnold Scwharzenegger vehicle with Quinn
as a drug kingpin.

Although Quinn is certainly best known for his
achievements as an actor, he has also won recognition
for his efforts as a sculptor and painter, and his works
have been exhibited in the United States and Europe.
In addition, he has written two autobiographies. *The
Original Sin: A Self Portrait,* which was published in
1972, was readily acknowledged as an unusually candid celebrity biography. In it, Quinn combined recollections of his career exploits with accounts of his
experiences in psychoanalysis. The result, as Robert

Berkvist reported in the *New York Times Book Review,* is a work that is "by turns embarrassingly candid, baldly awkward, funny, tragic, moving and full of life."

More than twenty years later, Quinn published another autobiography, *One-Man Tango,* which Jonathan Yardley appraised in the *Washington Post Book World* as "an account at once good-humored and self-critical of a life that has been, on the whole, happy and robust and productive." Yardley also observed that in *One-Man Tango* Quinn "is a somewhat unorthodox memoirist not merely because he rises several flights above mere gossip," and he deemed Quinn's career "unique."

BIOGRAPHICAL/CRITICAL SOURCES:

PERIODICALS

Interview, May, 1991, pp. 129, 138.
New York Times Book Review, October 8, 1972, p. 41; November 26, 1995, p. 23.
Saturday Review, October 21, 1972, pp. 79-80.
Times Literary Supplement, May 18, 1973, p. 563.
Washington Post Book World, August 6, 1995, p. 3.*

*   *   *

QUINTANA, Leroy V. 1944-

PERSONAL: Born June 10, 1944, in Albuquerque, NM; married Yolanda Holguin (a registered nurse), 1970; children: Sandra, Elisa, Jose. *Education:* University of New Mexico, B.A., 1971; graduate study at University of Denver; New Mexico State University, M.A. (English), 1974; Western New Mexico University, M.A. (counseling), 1984. *Politics:* Democrat. *Religion:* Roman Catholic.

ADDRESSES: Home—9230-C Lake Murray Blvd., Apt. C, San Diego, CA 92119. *Office*—San Diego Mesa College, 7250 Mesa College Dr., San Diego, CA 92111.

CAREER: New Mexico State University, Las Cruces, instructor in English, beginning in 1975; El Paso Community College, El Paso, TX, instructor in English, 1975-80, coordinator of poetry series; University of New Mexico, Albuquerque, instructor in English, beginning in 1980; *Albuquerque Tribune,* Albuquerque, feature writer and sportswriter, 1981-82;

National City Family Clinic, San Diego, CA, counselor, 1984-87; San Diego Mesa College, San Diego, associate professor of English, 1988—; writer. Worked as a roofer, and as an alcoholism counselor in Albuquerque. *Military service:* U.S. Army, Airborne, 1967-69, served in Vietnam.

MEMBER: PEN, Modern Language Association.

AWARDS, HONORS: National Endowment for the Arts creative writing fellow, 1978; American Book Award for poetry from Before Columbus Foundation and El Paso Border Regional Library Association award, both 1982, both for *Sangre;* American Book Award, Before Columbus Foundation, 1993, for *The History of Home;* runner-up, Paterson Poetry prize, Paterson Poetry Center, 1994.

WRITINGS:

Hijo del Pueblo: New Mexico Poems (title means "Son of the Son of the People"), illustrations by Trini Lopez, Puerto Del Sol Press, 1976.
Sangre (title means "Blood"), Prima Agua Press, 1981.
The Reason People Don't Like Mexicans, Bilingual Review/Press, 1984.
Interrogations, Bilingual Revista Press, 1992.
Now and Then, Often, Today, 1992.
The History of Home, Burning Cities Press, 1993.
(Editor, with Virgil Suarez) *Paper Dance: Fifty-five Latino Poets,* Persea, 1995.
My Hair Turning Grey among Strangers, Bilingual Press, 1996.
Great Whirl of Exile, Curbstone Press, 1999.

Also editor of *Metaforas Verdes: Anthology of Spanish/English Poetry.* Works represented in anthologies, including *Shore Anthology of Poetry, Chicano Voices, Hispanics in the United States: An Anthology of Creative Literature,* edited by Gary D. Keller and Francisco Jimenez, Bilingual/Editorial Bilingue, 1980, and *Five Poets of Aztlan,* edited by Santiago Daydi-Tolson, Bilingual/Editorial Bilingue, 1985.

Contributor to periodicals, including *Contact/II, Latin America Literary Review, New Mexico Magazine, Poetry Texas, Revista Chicano-Riquena, Rocky Mountain Review, Southwest Heritage,* and *Voices International.* Poetry editor of *Thunderbird* (University of New Mexico literary magazine), 1970, and of *Puerto del Sol* (New Mexico State University literary magazine), 1973-74. Contributing editor to the Baleen Press, Phoenix, AZ, 1974.

WORK IN PROGRESS: Why, or Me, a Thousand Lives, poetry about grade-school chums; a novel; research on the image of the Chicano in American detective fiction.

SIDELIGHTS: "In many ways, I'm still basically a small-town New Mexico boy carrying on the oral tradition," two-time American Book Award-winning poet Leroy V. Quintana was quoted as saying in *Dictionary of Literary Biography.* Author of the collections *Hijo del Pueblo* ("Son of the People"), *Sangre* ("Blood"), and the bilingual *My Hair Turning Gray among Strangers,* Quintana was born in Albuquerque and raised by his grandparents, who told him *cuentos,* or traditional Mexican folk tales, and stories of life in the Old West. For his poems Quintana draws on Hispanic folklore for subject matter as well as spirit, and he includes many ancient storytelling devices—such as conversational structure and unreliable narrators—in his contemporary poetic form.

"I was raised by my grandparents," Quintana told *Hispanic Writers,* "and my major form of entertainment was the old *cuentos* I was told. I have always enjoyed stories—I read comic books by the hundreds, went to the movies, and recited the stanzas in the back of the catechism religiously."

After high school and a tour of duty in the U.S. Army during the Vietnam War, Quintana enrolled in the University of New Mexico, where he first wrote poems and edited *Thunderbird,* the school's literary journal. In 1976 he published his first poetry collection, *Hijo del Pueblo,* a celebration of small-town New Mexican life as seen through the eyes of a young boy. Using phrases borrowed from the storytellers—"I have been told" and "Grandfather used to say"—Quintana effectively draws the reader into his writings, which bring modern expression to such Mexican and Indian traditions as undertaking pilgrimages to the shrine of the Virgin Mary of Guadalupe and performing ritual dances. He also addresses new phenomena, including the return home of Mexican-American soldiers from foreign wars and the effects of Anglos on Hispanic culture and society. And in *"Sterling, Colorado,"* quoted by Douglas K. Benson in an article in the *Dictionary of Literary Biography,* Quintana discusses the prejudice many Hispanics suffer: "On Saturdays we would go into town / after picking potatoes all week / and the Anglos would laugh at us / and call us dirty Mexicans." But the poet also recalls that as a way of overcoming subsequent frustration his mother "loops and loops the laughter" into "yet another doilie."

Quintana's subsequent collection, *Sangre,* which follows in the same grassroots tradition, was honored with an American Book Award in 1993 In the five years since *Hijo del Pueblo* was published Quintana's poetic style had matured, and the poems of *Sangre* express the poet's greater range and vision. The New Mexican experience—particularly village life—is portrayed colorfully and effectively, and Quintana addresses contemporary issues as well: the Vietnam War, the fallibility of television heroes, the realization that the simple life of the past is gone. Indeed, in the final poem of the collection, "A Legacy," the narrator, who was educated among Anglos, longs to return to the innocence and security of the time when his grandfather told *cuentos.*

In 1994's *Interrogations,* the poet has distilled his experiences and memories about the war in Vietnam. Composed in five sections—"Preface," "How It Was Going to Be," "The Nam," "The Years After," and "Epilogue," a poetic plea for peace addressed to former president George Bush—the volume exemplifies the capacity of a human being to transcend the experience of war. Calling it a superior book, Jon Forest Glade notes in *American Book Review* that "The characters in *Interrogations* have been given genuine depth, and in a few succinct lines they emerge as sharply defined human beings, not as caricatures." In another award-winning volume, 1993's *The History of Home,* Quintana collects short poems into what *Nation* reviewer Ray Gonzalez likens to "a scrapbook of profiles created by someone who was raised in an isolated yet rich community of the fifties, painfully capturing a period of Chicano history few poets write about." And Quintana's fifth collection, *My Hair Turning Gray among Strangers,* finds the poet attempting to reconnect himself to the spiritual and emotional elements of his youth. As he told *Hispanic Writers,* "I seem to be tied to a sense of the past; my work reflects the 'sense of place' evoked by New Mexico. I hope I am worthy of portraying the land and its people well."

A licensed marriage, family, and child counselor, Quintana believes that his study of psychology has aided him in discerning human motivation, thereby helping him in his writing. In addition to his collected verse, he has also served as editor, with Virgil Suarez, of the anthology *Paper Dance: Fifty-five Latino Poets,* which assembles the work of some of the most talented Hispanic writers in the United States, including Luis J. Rodriguez, Lucha Corpi, and Julia Alvarez.

BIOGRAPHICAL/CRITICAL SOURCES:

BOOKS

Dictionary of Literary Biography, Volume 82: *Chicano Writers,* Gale, 1989.
Lomeli, Francisco A., and Donaldo W. Urioste, *Chicano Perspectives in Literature: A Critical and Annotated Bibliography,* Pajarito Publications, 1976.
Quintana, Leroy V., *Hijo del pueblo: New Mexico Poems,* Puerto del Sol Press, 1976.

PERIODICALS

American Book Review, December, 1977; April/May, 1994, p. 21.
Bilingual Review/La Revista Bilingue, number 12, 1987.
Contact/II, winter/spring, 1984-85.
Nation June 7, 1993, p. 772.
New Mexico Humanities Review, spring, 1982.
Perspectives on Contemporary Literature, number 12, 1986.
Publishers Weekly, November 27, 1995, p. 65.
School Library Journal, July 1995, p. 105.*

R

RABASSA, Gregory 1922-

PERSONAL: Born March 9, 1922, in Yonkers, NY; son of Miguel and Clara (Macfarland) Rabassa; married Roney Edelstein, July 14, 1956 (marriage ended, 1966); married Clementine C. Christos (a teacher and critic), May 29, 1966; children: Catherine, Clara. *Education:* Dartmouth College, A.B., 1945; Columbia University, M.A., 1947, Ph.D., 1954. *Politics:* Democrat. *Religion:* None.

ADDRESSES: Home—40 East 72nd St., New York, NY 10021. *Office*—Department of Romance Languages, Queens College of the City University of New York, 65-30 Kissena Blvd., Flushing, NY 11367.

CAREER: Columbia University, New York City, assistant professor, 1948-64, associate professor of Spanish and Portuguese, 1964-68; City University of New York, Queens College, Flushing, NY, and Graduate School and University Center, New York City, professor, 1968-85, distinguished professor of Romance languages and comparative literature, 1985—. Democratic committee, New York County, 1956-60. *Military service:* U.S. Army, Office of Strategic Services, 1942-45; became staff sergeant; received Croce al Merito di Guerra (Italy), and special citation from Allied Forces Headquarters, both 1945.

MEMBER: American Association of Teachers of Spanish and Portuguese, American Association of University Professors, American Literature Translators Association, Congreso Internacional de Literatura Iberoamerica, Hispanic Society of America, Latin American Studies Association, Modern Language Association of America, PEN American Center (member of executive board, 1972-77), Renaissance Society of America, Phi Beta Kappa.

AWARDS, HONORS: Fulbright-Hays fellow, Brazil, 1965-66; National Book Award for translation, 1967, for *Hopscotch;* National Book Award nomination for translation, 1971, for *One Hundred Years of Solitude,* and 1977, for *The Autumn of the Patriarch;* American PEN translation prize, 1977, for *The Autumn of the Patriarch;* National Endowment for the Humanities grant, 1980; Alexander Gode Medal, American Translators Association, 1980; Gulbenkian Award, 1981, for translation of *Avalovara;* PEN Medal for Translation, 1982; Litt.D., Dartmouth College, 1982; Professional Staff Congress/City University of New York grant, 1983; New York Governor's Arts Award, 1985; Order of San Carlos, Republic of Colombia, 1985; Guggen-heim fellow, 1988-89; Wheatland Prize for Translation, 1988; Literature Award, American Academy and Institute of Arts and Letters, 1989; Presidential Medal for Excellence, Dartmouth College, 1991; Ivan Sandrof Award, National Book Critics Circle, 1993; Literary Lion, New York Public Library, 1993; Mellon Humanities Award, Loyola University, 1995.

WRITINGS:

O Negro na ficcao brasileira (title means "The Negro in Brazilian Fiction"), Tempo Brasileiro, 1965.
(Author of introduction) *The World of Translation,* PEN American Center (New York City), 1987.
A Cloudy Day in Gray Minor (poetry), Cross-Cultural Communications (Merrick, NY), 1992.

TRANSLATOR

Julio Cortazar, *Hopscotch,* Pantheon (New York City), 1966.

Clarice Lispector, *The Apple in the Dark,* Knopf (New York City), 1967.

Miguel Asturias, *Mulata,* Delacorte (New York City), 1967, published in England as *The Mulatta and Mr. Fly,* P. Owen (London), 1967.

Mario Vargas Llosa, *The Green House,* Harper (New York City), 1969.

Juan Goytisolo, *Marks of Identity,* Grove (New York City), 1969.

Afranio Coutinho, *An Introduction to Literature in Brazil,* Columbia University Press (New York City), 1969.

Asturias, *Strong Wind,* Delacorte, 1969.

Manuel Mujica-Lainez, *Bomarzo,* Simon & Schuster (New York City), 1969.

Gabriel Garcia Marquez, *One Hundred Years of Solitude,* Harper, 1970.

Asturias, *The Green Pope,* Delacorte, 1971.

Garcia Marquez, *Leaf Storm and Other Stories,* Harper, 1972.

Cortazar, *Sixty-Two: A Model Kit,* Pantheon, 1973.

Dalton Trevisan, *The Vampire of Curitiba,* Knopf, 1973.

Asturias, *The Eyes of the Interred,* Delacorte, 1973.

Jose Lezama Lima, *Paradiso,* Farrar Straus (New York City), 1974.

Vargas Llosa, *Conversation in the Cathedral,* Harper (New York City), 1975.

Garcia Marquez, *The Autumn of the Patriarch,* Harper, 1976.

Garcia Marquez, *Innocent Erendira and Other Stories,* Harper, 1978.

Cortazar, *A Manual for Manuel,* Pantheon, 1978.

Demetrio Aguilera-Malta, *Seven Serpents and Seven Moons,* University of Texas Press (Austin), 1979.

Garcia Marquez, *In Evil Hour,* Harper, 1979.

Osman Lins, *Avalovara,* Knopf, 1980.

Cortazar, *A Change of Light and Other Stories,* Knopf, 1980.

Luis Rafael Sanchez, *Macho Camacho's Beat,* Pantheon, 1981.

Vinicius de Moraes, *The Girl from Ipanema,* Cross-Cultural Communications, 1982.

Juan Benet, *A Meditation,* Persea Books (New York City), 1983.

Cortazar, *We Love Glenda So Much and Other Tales,* Knopf, 1983.

Garcia Marquez, *Chronicle of a Death Foretold,* Knopf, 1983.

Luisa Valenzuela, *The Lizard's Tail,* Farrar, Straus 1983.

Jorge Amado, *Sea of Death,* Avon (New York City), 1984.

Cortazar, *A Certain Lucas,* Knopf, 1984.

(With B. J. Bernstein) Garcia Marquez, *Collected Stories,* Harper, 1984.

Benet, *Return to Region,* Columbia University Press, 1985.

Oswaldo Franca Jr., *The Man in the Monkey Suit,* Ballantine (New York City), 1986.

Amado, *Captains of the Sands,* Avon, 1988.

Amado, *Showdown,* Bantam (New York City), 1988.

Antonio Lobo Antunes, *Fado Alexandrino,* Grove/Weidenfield, 1990.

Jose Donoso, *Taratuta and Still Life with Pipe,* Norton (New York City), 1993.

Jorge Amado, *The War of the Saints,* Bantam, 1993.

Mario de Carvalho, *A God Strolling in the Cool of the Evening,* Louisiana State University Press (Baton Rouge), 1997.

Joachim Maria Machado de Assis, *The Posthumous Memoirs of Bras Cubas,* Oxford University Press (New York City), 1997.

Machado de Assis, *Quincas Borba,* Oxford University Press, 1998.

OTHER

Contributor of translations, articles, and reviews to numerous periodicals and professional journals, including *Atlantic, Esquire, Nation, New Yorker, New York Times Book Review, Playboy,* and *Saturday Review.* Associate editor, *Odyssey Review,* 1961-63. Latin-American editor, *Kenyon Review,* 1978—.

WORK IN PROGRESS: Translations, including *My World Is Not of This Kingdom* by Joao de Melo; *The Sirens, Too, Sang That Way,* by Irene Vilar, for Pantheon; *Fazendas,* by Fernando Tasso Fragoso Pires, for Abbeville Press.

SIDELIGHTS: Translator of over forty works, Gregory Rabassa is "a one-man conveyor belt" bringing Latin American fiction to the English-speaking world, according to Patrick Breslin in the *Washington Post Book World.* A professor of Romance languages with the City University of New York, Rabassa never intended to become a professional translator. In the early 1960s, however, he began translating short fiction as part of his work with *Odyssey Review,* a literary quarterly. Shortly after the magazine folded, Rabassa was contacted about writing an English version of Julio Cortazar's *Hopscotch.* "An editor called me up and we had lunch," Rabassa recalled to Edwin McDowell in *Americas.* "I looked through the novel, liked it and gave her a couple of sample chapters. . . . She chose me, and I went to work on it immediately in my spare time. It took about a year working in spurts, and I've been translating ever since."

Cortazar so approved of Rabassa's manuscript that he recommended his work to Gabriel Garcia Marquez, a Colombian writer. Rabassa's rendition of *One Hundred Years of Solitude,* published in 1970, gained widespread attention in the United States for both Garcia Marquez's work and that of other Latin American writers. The work also gained attention for Rabassa when Garcia Marquez, the 1982 Nobel laureate, remarked that he preferred the translation to his own work; "Rabassa's *One Hundred Years of Solitude* improved the original," the author remarked to *Time* contributor R. Z. Sheppard. Rabassa comments, however, that the work lent itself to translation because of its quality: "A very good book in its own language goes over more easily into another language than a book that's not so good," he told Jason Weiss in the *Los Angeles Times.* "Part of the quality of the well-written book is that it's easy to translate."

The Posthumous Memoirs of Bras Cubas was another "masterful translation," in the opinion of *Library Journal* reviewer Harold Augenbraum. This novel was written in 1880, "at the same moment of literary history when Henry James was writing its aesthetic opposite, *The Portrait of a Lady,*" commented Gary Amdahl, a contributor to *Nation.* Through an unexplained circumstance, the narrator of the book is able to write his memoirs—even though he is already dead. In one hundred and sixty brief chapters, the fictional author Bras Cubas muses about his life and the composition of the book. "This fictional work may lead English readers unfamiliar with Brazilian writer de Assis' work to expand their view of Western modernist and postmodernist literature," predicted Jim O'Laughlin in *Booklist.* "Rich with allusions to past literary works, its acrobatic narrator relentlessly undermines any tendency we as readers might have to immerse ourselves in the 'realistic' world of a memoir; instead, he constantly invokes us, teases us, and chastens us in our reading, often in ridiculously self-deprecating or self-congratulatory ways."

Bras Cubas is an altogether "bravura narrative performance," concluded O'Laughlin. Amdahl placed *The Posthumous Memoirs of Bras Cubas* squarely in "a long line of brilliantly odd and (relatively) outrageous works like Laurence Sterne's *Tristram Shandy* and Xavier de Maistre's *Voyage around My Room.* . . . I begin the line at Aristophanes, including the Dostoyevsky of

Notes from Underground, the Hamsun of *Hunger,* the Beckett of *Malone Dies,* and end with Donald Barthelme, Barry Hannah's incomparable *Ray* and Thomas McGuane's seriously undervalued *Panama.*"

Rabassa takes a reader's approach to his writing, almost always choosing to work with manuscripts that interest him. His translating methods also reflect this interest; in working with *Hopscotch,* "I read it as I translated it," Rabassa remarked to McDowell. "I do that with many books because it's more fun that way, and because translation should be the closest possible reading of the book." Although he commented to Weiss that translation is "lazy man's writing," he sees it as creative work in its own right. "One of the great advantages of translation," he told McDowell, "is that your plots and characters are already written, all you have to do is breathe life into them."

BIOGRAPHICAL/CRITICAL SOURCES:

PERIODICALS

Americas, July-August, 1986.
Booklist, November 15, 1997, p. 541; December 1, 1997, p. 609.
Library Journal, June 15, 1996, p. 74; November 1, 1997, p. 116; November 15, 1998, p. 96.
Los Angeles Times, August 12, 1982.
Nation, November 3, 1997, p. 64.
New Republic, May 25, 1998, p. 36.
New York Times Book Review, November 23, 1997, p. 28; February 22, 1998, p. 14.
Time, March 7, 1983.
Washington Post Book World, December 19, 1984.*

*   *   *

RAMIREZ, Sergio 1942-

PERSONAL: Born August 5, 1942, in Masatepe, Masaya, Nicaragua; son of Pedro and Luisa (maiden name: Mercado) Ram; married Gertrudis Gerrero, July 26, 1964; children: Sergio, Maria, Dora Elliane. *Education:* National Autonomous University of Nicaragua, degree in law, 1964.

ADDRESSES: Office—Fundacion Victimas de Guerra Nicaragua, Apartado Postal RP24, Managua, Nicaragua.

CAREER: Nicaraguan author and political official.

AWARDS, HONORS: Doctorate honoris causa, Central University of Equador; Premio award, Bruno Kreisky Foundation, 1988; grantee Deutscher Akademischer Austauschdienst, Berlin, 1973-1975; named Knight of the Order of Arts and Letters, French Ministry of Culture, 1993.

WRITINGS:

Nuevos cuentos, Universidad Nacional Autonoma de Nicaragua (Leon), 1963.

La narrativa centroamericana, Editorial Universitaria (San Salvador), 1970.

Tiempo de fulgor, Editorial Universitaria (Guatamala), 1970.

Mariano Fiallos: Biografia, Universidad Nacional Autonoma de Nicaragua, 1971.

De tropeles y tropelias, Editorial Universitaria de El Salvador, 1972.

Charles Atlas tambien muere, J. Mortiz (Mexico), 1976, translation by Nick Caistor published as *Stories,* Readers International (New York City), 1988.

Te dio miedo la sangre?, Monte Avila Editores, 1977, translation by Caistor published as *To Bury Our Fathers,* Readers International, 1979.

Biografia de Sandino, Ediciones Ministerio de Educacion, 1979.

Sandino siempre, Universidad Nacional Autonoma de Nicaragua, 1980, translation by R. E. Conrad published as *Sandino, the Testimony of a Nicaraguan Patriot,* Princeton University Press (Princeton, NJ), 1990.

El pensamiento vivo de Sandino, Ediciones Centauro, 1981.

El muchacho de Niquinohomo, 1981.

El alba de oro: La historia viva de Nicaragua, Siglo Veintiuno Editores, 1983.

Balcanes y volcanes y otros ensayos y trabojos, Editorial Nueva Nicaragua, 1983.

Sandino es indohispano y no tiene fronteras en America Latina, 1984.

Seguimos de frente: Escritos sobre la revolucion, Ediciones Centauro (Caracas), 1985.

Estas en Nicaragua, Muchnik (Barcelona), 1985, translation by Darwin J. Flakoll published as *You Are in Nicaragua,* Curbstone Press (Willmantic, CT), 1990.

Las armas del futuro, 1987.

Castigo divino, Mondadori, 1988.

El muchacho de Niquinohomo, Editorial Vanguardia, 1988.

La marca del zorro: Hazanas del Comandante Francisco Rivera Quintero contadas a Sergio Ramirez, Mondadori Espana, 1989.

Confesion de amor, Eddiciones Nicarao, 1991.

Clave de sol, Editorial Nueva Nicaragua, 1992.

Cuentos, [Mexico], 1994.

Hatful of Tigers: Reflections on Art, Culture, and Politics, translated by D. J. Flakoll, Curbstone Press (Willimantic, CT), 1995.

Un baile de mascaras, Aguilar, Altea, Taurus, Alfaguara (Mexico), 1995.

SIDELIGHTS: Nicaraguan Sergio Ramirez has served his homeland in two important capacities. Considered one of the most significant writers to emerge from Nicaragua in second half of the twentieth-century, Ramirez has also played a paramount role in the country's chaotic political affairs, having risen to the office of vice president in the mid-1980s. An avid adherent to the convictions of Nicaraguan patriotic hero Augusto Cesar Sandino (1895-1934), Ramirez was an instrumental player in the rise to power of the Sandinistas, a revolutionary group with socialist beliefs that overthrew the long-time dictatorship of Anastasio Somoza. The same type of motivations that fueled Ramirez's political activities are also apparent in his writings, which consist of novels and short stories, as well as several volumes of essays, some of which were devoted to the life of Sandino.

His political views permeate his work, though they do not define it. Ramirez has demonstrated a versatile ability to create character and plot, and some of his narrative techniques are innovative and experimental. His stories are populated with common, everyman-type individuals of the Nicaraguan countryside who suffer at the hands of a tyrannical government, and or foreign imperialism, a reflection of the circumstances that have plagued the country for over a century. Somoza and the United States are the biggest targets of his disdain. A perfect example of the political overtones in Ramirez's work is his renowned collection of short stories titled *Charles Atlas tambien muere* (translated as *Stories,* 1976). The work's six stories decry what Ramirez sees as the absurdity of Nicaragua's dependency on America and its economic policies. The title story is a particularly scathing denouncement of this relationship, as its main character, who has a diminutive physique, comes across an advertisement in a magazine touting the results of a physical training course taught by U.S. bodybuilder Charles Atlas. The man enrolls in the program and travels to the United States to personally meet with Atlas. However, when he gets there, he is greatly disappointed when he discovers Atlas is an aged and dying man. The obvious ramifications of the story are that the United States, which is seen in Nicaragua as a near omnipotent power, is just as mortal as any nation.

In *Te dio miedo la sangre?* (*To Bury Our Fathers,* 1977), his second novel, Ramirez writes an account of a popular uprising against the Somoza dictatorship during a period between 1930 and 1961, and that ultimately led to the formation of the National Sandinista Liberation Front, or Sandinistas for short. Although the novel is a fictional account, it is strongly based on actual Nicaraguan historical events. One of Ramirez's most complex works, the novel is a mixture of six story lines, all related by the uprising, and incorporating various narrative perspectives. All of his works have not relied on political messages, however. One example is his 1988 novel *Castigo divino* (*Divine Punishment*), a dramatic account of one of Nicaragua's most sensational crimes. The story revolves around a 1930s murder trial in the city of Leon that held the entire nation captive for years. In the fashion of a journalistic account, Ramirez interlaced known facts of the case with poetic license in creating what most critics have hailed as his most engrossing novel.

Ramirez's stature in the Nicaraguan literary community is probably unparalleled, but his influence has also reached well beyond the country's borders. He was one of the founding members of Editorial Universitaria Centroamericana (EDUCA), a publishing company based in San Jose, Costa Rica, that for many years was instrumental in providing a market for the most important writers in Central America. Also, for his continuing contributions to the field, the French Ministry of Culture named Ramirez a Knight of Arts and Letters in 1993.

Since an early age Ramirez showed an aptitude for writing. Born in the small town of Masatepe in the province of Masaya, Ramirez was an unlikely candidate to become an enemy of the Somoza regime. His father was a farmer and local politician, while his mother was a school teacher. By all accounts, Ramirez's liberal family benefited from Somoza's government. In fact, while in high school, Ramirez was the editor of its newspaper, in which he published several articles that were actually praiseworthy of Somoza. However, his outlook began to change while attending a national university in Leon. All around the city people were protesting against the dictator's policies, culminating in what became known as the mas-

sacre of El Chaparral, an event that irrevocably altered Ramirez's life. "Four students were killed and more than seventy wounded," Ramirez explained in an interview with Stephen White. "The massacre had an intense effect on the city and on the country. For me, and many others of my generation, it was the point of no return. We were deeply and decidedly shaken."

With his new convictions, Ramirez and a friend established a literary magazine called *Ventana* ("Windows"), in which he published some of his original fiction. "The magazine and the group were born with the wounds of the massacre. We were repulsed by the dictatorship and had a militant conception of literature—not socialist realism or anything like that. But from the beginning we did reject the position that had reigned in Nicaragua up to that time in terms of artistic labor: the famous story of art for art's sake; the artist's sworn aversion to political contamination," Ramirez told White. While publishing the magazine, he continued his education, ultimately graduating from law school, and then published his first collection of short stories titled *Cuentos* in 1963. However, rather than becoming a lawyer and starting his own practice, as his parents had hoped, Ramirez decided to enter the field of literature. "By that time," he said in a later interview, "I wanted to be a writer, no matter what it took." He traveled to Costa Rica where he was to found EDUCA, as well as write his first novel, *Tiempo de fulgor* ("Time of Brilliance," 1970), a work that is considered magical realism. Although not his best work, the novel showed clearly that Ramirez possessed a great deal of talent.

Ramirez continued to write, and in 1971 he published the award-winning *De tropeles y tropelias* ("Rush and Mad Rush"). In the next several years, he traveled around the globe, including stays in Berlin, Germany and in El Salvador, where he worked for the United Nations. Throughout this period, he was still producing literary works, completing *Te dio miedo la sangre?* during his time in Berlin. However, the political situation in his homeland ultimately drew him back to Central America, and he officially joined the Sandinistas in 1976, acting as a propagandist for the group. It was during this time that he completed his biographies of Sandino, as well as some books of essays that concentrated on the social and political climate of his homeland.

After the successful overthrow of Somoza's regime, Ramirez was elected as Daniel Ortega's vice-president in 1984, even though many in the country felt that the election was a farce. A powerful new political group, the Contras emerged in opposition to the Sandinista government and were supported by the United States. Political chaos once again erupted. With foreign help, democratic elections were finally held in 1990 and Ortega and Ramirez were defeated. Ramirez became the minority leader in the new National Assembly, a position he held until 1994. Since that time, he has remained an active writer. Critics, readers, and patriots alike, have all praised him for his contributions. Critic George R. McMurray concluded: "He is not only a gifted storyteller but also a sensitive spokesman for the Third World."

BIOGRAPHICAL/CRITICAL SOURCES:

BOOKS

Dictionary of Literary Biography, Volume 145: *Modern Latin-American Fiction Writers,* Gale (Detroit), 1994.
Encyclopedia of World Literature in the 20th Century, Continuum (New York City), 1993.

PERIODICALS

New Republic, April 1, 1991, p. 39.
Publishers Weekly, May 15, 1995, p. 66.*

* * *

RAMOS, Graciliano 1892-1953

PERSONAL: Born October 27, 1892, in Quebrangulo, Alagoas, Brazil; died March, 1953, in Rio de Janeiro, Brazil; son of Sebastiao Ramos (in business and farming); married Maria Augusta de Barros, c. 1914 (died 1920); married Heloisa Medeiros, c. 1920s; children: (with de Barros) four; (with Medeiros) four.

CAREER: Writer. Worked as a journalist and short story writer, Rio de Janeiro, Brazil, c. 1913-15; owner of a dry goods shop, Palmeira dos Indios, Brazil, beginning 1915; mayor of Palmeira dos Indios, c. 1920s; Director of Public Instruction, Alagoas, c. 1930s.

MEMBER: Brazilian Writers Union (president).

WRITINGS:

NOVELS

Caetes, Schmidt (Rio de Janeiro), 1933.
Sao Bernardo, [Rio de Janeiro], 1934, translated by R. L. Scott-Buccleuch, [London], 1975.
Angustia, J. Olympio (Rio de Janeiro), 1936, translation by Lewis C. Kaplan published as *Anguish,* Knopf (New York City), 1946.
Vidas secas, [Rio de Janeiro], 1936, published as *Barren Lives,* translated and with an introduction by Ralph Edward Dimmick, University of Texas Press, 1965.
(With Jorge Amado, Jose Lins do Rego, Anibal Machado, and Raquel de Queiroz) *Brandao Entre o Mar e o Amor,* [Rio de Janeiro], 1942.

SHORT STORIES

Dois Dedos, [Rio de Janeiro], 1945.
Historias Incompletas, Edicao da Livraria do Globo (Rio de Janeiro), 1946.
Insonia, J. Olympio (Rio de Janeiro), 1947.
Historias Agrestes, selected and with a preface by Ricardo Ramos, Editora Cultrix (Sao Paulo), 1960.

MEMOIRS

Infancia, J. Olympio (Rio de Janeiro), 1945, translation by Celso de Oliveira published as *Childhood,* introduction by Ashley Brown, P. Owen (London), 1979.
Memorias do carcere, four volumes, J. Olympio (Rio de Janeiro), 1953.

NONFICTION

Viagem, J. Olympio (Rio de Janeiro), 1954.
Linhas Tortas, [Sao Paulo], 1962.
Viventas das Alagoas, [Sao Paulo], 1962.
Cartas, third revised edition, [Sao Paulo], 1982.

FOR CHILDREN

A Terra dos Meninos Pelados, [Rio de Janeiro], 1939.
Historias de Alexandre, Editora Leiture (Rio de Janeiro), 1944.

Also author of "Pequena Historia da Republica" in *Senhor,* 1960.

OTHER

(Translator)Booker T. Washington, *Memorias de um Negro,* [Rio de Janeiro], 1940.
(Translator)Albert Camus, *A Peste,* [Rio de Janeiro], 1950.
Obras completas, six volumes (novels, short stories, nonfiction, and autobiography), 1961.

SIDELIGHTS: Regarded as one of the most important Brazilian novelists of the twentieth century, Graciliano Ramos was associated with the Generation of 1930, a group of Brazilian writers whose works focused on the social, economic, and political problems of the impoverished and culturally backward northeastern region of their country. At the same time there are features of Ramos's work that distinguish him from this group. Ramos's contemporaries were largely concerned with using fiction as a means for social change; their works are less devoted to artistic than political ends and are inherently optimistic with respect to the betterment of Brazilian society. In contrast, Ramos's displays a conspicuous artistry in his prose style and narrative structure, while his underlying philosophy is clearly one of pessimism regarding the human condition in general as represented by the grim destinies of his Brazilian protagonists. In addition, Ramos's novels have a psychological depth unparalleled in the more sociologically oriented works of his contemporaries. Prominent critic and scholar Morton Dauwen Zabel asserted, in a review of *Anguish* in the *Nation:* "Graciliano Ramos is notable among contemporary Brazilian writers for a severity of style, an accuracy of social and moral observation, and an intensity of tragic sensibility which derive as much from a scrupulous fidelity to native experience as from the stylists—Proust, Joyce, and more relevantly, Celine—whom his American publisher mentions as his models."

Ramos was born in Alagoas, in northeastern Brazil. His father, a merchant who became a cattle rancher, was nearly ruined financially when a severe drought caused this venture to fail. In the following years, Ramos's father worked at various occupations, necessitating several relocations for his growing family. Throughout his childhood, Ramos experienced firsthand the harsh realities of life in the *sertao* ("backlands") of Brazil. Although Ramos attended both primary and secondary schools, he strongly disliked formal schooling and was largely self-educated. Ramos's father introduced him to literature, and at an early age he began reading Brazilian and European novelists, among them Eca de Queiroz and Fyodor Dostoevsky.

This concern for Ramos's education was uncharacteristic of his father, who is portrayed in Ramos's 1945 childhood memoirs, *Infancia (Childhood)*, as stern, authoritarian, and uncommunicative, and who, along with Ramos's ill-tempered mother, mistreated Ramos. A generally unhappy childhood, marked by alienation from his parents and the hardships of the sertao, is considered the probable origin of the misanthropy and pessimism expressed in Ramos's writing. H. R. Hays, in a review of *Anguish* in the *New Republic,* remarked that "by indirect ideological allusion and by means of a single limited character [Ramos] has written an agonized indictment of life in his own country and at the same time he has created a work of literature which reflects the anguish of the entire world."

When he was twenty-one Ramos moved to Rio de Janeiro, where he had a brief, unsuccessful career as a journalist and began writing short stories. In 1915 he moved to Palmeira dos Indios and opened a dry goods shop. During the next fifteen years, he edited the town newspaper, wrote his first novel, *Caetes,* and was elected mayor. Ramos's mayoral report to the state government concerning social and political problems in Palmeira dos Indios greatly impressed the Alagoas authorities with its honesty, nonbureaucratic style, and simple, precise Portuguese. This report was published in national newspapers and came to the attention of Augusto Frederico Schmidt, a prominent poet and publisher. Schmidt learned that Ramos was the author of an unpublished novel, and under his auspices *Caetes* appeared in 1933.

During the 1930s Ramos published three more novels—*Sao Bernardo, Angustia (Anguish)* and *Vidas secas (Barren Lives)*—and associated with a small group of northeastern Brazilian novelists whose writing realistically portrayed Brazilian life and reflected the rise of a nationalist movement in Brazil. In addition, he held public-service positions, among them Director of Public Instruction in Alagoas. It was while serving in this capacity in 1936 that he was imprisoned during a political upheaval. The dictatorship in power regarded Ramos as a communist and his books as subversive; although the reasons for his incarceration are unknown, this official view of Ramos has been considered a probable cause. Upon his release from prison, he returned to Rio de Janeiro and in 1938 was appointed to another public-service position. In the following years he produced works in several genres, the most notable of which are his autobiography *Childhood* and his 1953 prison memoirs, *Memorias do carcere.*

Richard A. Mazzara, in his *Graciliano Ramos,* maintained: "In the *Memorias,* then, as in all of Graciliano Ramos' career, there are two fundamental, contradictory tendencies. . . . Graciliano the thinker and artist strives to dominate the confusion through clarity and harmony, and he imposes these controls on his creatures. The struggle between the two opposing currents is the basic theme of Graciliano's work and determines its structures. A simple, terse, clear style is the chief instrument employed by Graciliano to bring order out of chaos. If he does not succeed in every instance, it is because Graciliano's re-creation, like life, does not always succeed. If his characters do not triumph, or triumph only in a limited or ambiguous sense, it is because Graciliano's work must reflect life. Their efforts to succeed, largely through the medium placed at their disposal by the author, reflect life also."

Childhood is considered especially important as a rare personal account of life in a remote area of Brazil in the late nineteenth and early twentieth centuries, as a memoir of Ramos's gradual awakening to his artistic vocation, and as a work of verbal artistry. Serving as president of the Brazilian Writers Union, Ramos attended a literary congress in Moscow near the end of his life, and an unfinished essay about his trip, *Viagem,* was published posthumously. He died in Rio de Janeiro in 1953.

Largely episodic in structure, Ramos's novels have a psychological emphasis uncommon in other Brazilian works of the same period, subordinating plot to character studies of individuals struggling in hostile natural environments and unjust societies. In *Caetes*—a novel that examines self-interest as the determinant of ethical values—the adulterous affair of Joao Valerio, a clerk, with his employer's wife leads to the suicide of his employer. Valerio is also an aspiring novelist who has abandoned his historical novel about a local cannibalistic tribe, the Caete Indians, when he concludes that he cannot fathom the mind of a cannibal, yet ultimately he recognizes the same savagery in himself and in his society. Similarly, Paulo Honorio in *Sao Bernardo* is forced to confront his life in which he ruthlessly ascended from fieldhand to landowner and caused the suicide of his wife by falsely accusing her of infidelity.

Anguish takes place in the tormented mind of Luis da Silva, who is trapped by painful childhood memories and by the hopeless circumstances of his adult life: his meager existence, lack of purpose, and sense of failure and frustration. *Barren Lives* is the story of Fabiano and his backlander family, victims of poverty and the periodic drought, who suffer and survive many trials and humiliations. Critics have noted that despite the extreme adversity and degradation experienced by Fabiano, a sense of dignity and of hope for the future somewhat distinguishes him from the other protagonists who, in the words of Russell G. Hamilton in his essay in *Luso-Brazilian Review,* "live either in a desolate present or a ruinous past."

In addition to creating characters of psychological depth and complexity, Ramos revealed himself to be a skillful prose stylist, and critics have praised him for avoiding both the stilted, formal Portuguese traditional in Brazilian literature as well and the ungrammatical Portuguese of his contemporaries. While his novels are all distinguished by the same artistic prose style, each exhibits a different narrative approach. *Caetes* has been compared with the well-made novel of the nineteenth century, following the formalistic tradition of Gustave Flaubert and de Queiroz, while *Sao Bernardo* is written in the more vernacular style popular in the 1930s. *Anguish,* a work in which Ramos employed stream–of–consciousness technique, is a fragmented, chaotic confession notable for its eerie, dreamlike quality. *Barren Lives* is composed of disconnected sketches, each of which focuses more on character than action. Reflecting on the variety of styles and techniques in Ramos's novels, Fred P. Ellison observed, in his *Brazil's New Novel: Four Northeastern Masters:* "Using language perfectly in accord with the theme, the characters, and the locale, Ramos achieves an artistic form which is incomparable in its sobriety, elegance, and refinement."

While Ramos's novels derive their subject matter from Brazilian life, these works nonetheless attain a universality that has made Ramos one of the few Brazilian authors of his time to achieve and sustain international recognition. As Ralph Edward Dimmick stated, in his introduction to *Barren Lives,* his translation of *Vidas secas:* "By reason of the keenness of his psychological insight, of his deep feeling for the vernacular, of his unfailing sense of proportion, of his skilled craftsmanship in construction, Ramos has been able to fashion from the simplest and most unpromising of materials works which stand among the most impressive creations of modern Brazilian literature." Marie F. Sovereign, in *Luso-Brazilian Review,* remarked: "This, then, is the secret of Ramos' greatness as a writer and of his success in communicating his attitudes toward life. He has so identified himself with the underdog in human existence that he has been able poignantly to reveal the loneliness, the misunderstanding, the frustration, and the meaning-lessness which is commonly shared, to a greater or lesser degree, by all men. In so doing, he challenged his own loneliness by saying, in effect, 'This is the way I see it. Have you, the reader, not had such an experience?' At least, in the act of reaching out to unburden his own soul, Ramos eloquently speaks to ours about certain aspects of human reality."

BIOGRAPHICAL/CRITICAL SOURCES:

BOOKS

Ellison, Fred P., *Brazil's New Novel: Four Northeast-ern Masters,* University of California Press, 1954.

Martins, Wilson, *The Modernist Idea: A Critical Sur-vey of Brazilian Writing in the Twentieth Century,* translated by Jack E. Tomlins, 1970, Greenwood Press, 1979.

Mazzara, Richard A., *Graciliano Ramos,* Twayne, 1974.

Ramos, Graciliano, *Barren Lives,* translated and with an introduction by Ralph Edward Dimmick, Uni-versity of Texas Press, 1965.

PERIODICALS

Arizona Quarterly, spring, 1986, pp. 17-30.

Hispania, September, 1984, pp. 377-384.

Luso-Brazilian Review, June, 1968, pp. 86-92; sum-mer, 1970, pp. 57-63.

Modern Language Journal, February, 1967, pp. 119-120.

Nation (New York City), April 20, 1946, pp. 482-483.

New Republic, June 17, 1946, p. 876.

New York Times Book Review, March 31, 1946, p. 10.

Proceedings: Pacific Northwest Council on Foreign Languages, 28, Part 1, April 21-23, 1977; 30, Parts 1 and 2, April 19-21, 1979.

Saturday Review of Literature, April 13, 1946, p. 76.

Times Literary Supplement, January 2, 1976, p. 17.*

*   *   *

RAMOS, Luis Arturo 1947-

PERSONAL: Born November 9, 1947 in Minatitlan, Veracruz, Mexico. *Education:* University of Veracruz, M.A. (magna cum laude; Spanish literature), 1976.

ADDRESSES: Office—Department of Language and Linguistics or Chicano Studies & Research Program, University of Texas at El Paso, El Paso, TX 79968. *Agent*—c/o Joaquain Mortiz, Ave Insurgentes Sur No 1162-3, Col Del Valle, 03100, Mexico DF. *E-mail*—laramos@utep.edu.

CAREER: University of Texas at El Paso, assistant professor of languages and linguistics, member of Chicano Studies and Research Program faculty; Edi-torial Universitaria (publishing house), Universidad Veracruzana, director. Founding member of ecologi-cal group to preserve rainforests.

AWARDS, HONORS: Recipient of two national fiction prizes, Instituto Nacional de Bellas Artes/State Gov-ernment of Colima, for *Violeta-Peru* and *Este Era un Gato;* Moritz-Planeta prize finalist, for *La Casa del Ahorcado.*

WRITINGS:

SHORT STORIES

Del Tiempo y Otros Lugares, Editorial Amate (Mexico), 1979.

Los Viejos Asesinos, Premia Editora (Mexico), 1981.

Also contributor to *El Cuento Policial Mexicano,* se-lected and with and introduction by Vicente Francisco Torres, Editorial Diogenes (Mexico), 1982.

NOVELS

Violeta-Peru, University of Veracruz (Xalapa, Mexico), 1979.

Intramuros, University of Veracruz (Xalapa, Mexico), 1983, translation by Samuel A. Zimmerman pub-lished as *Within These Walls,* Latin American Literary Review Press (Pittsburgh, PA), 1997.

Este Era un Gato, Grijalbo (Mexico), 1988.

La casa del ahorcado, Joaquain Mortiz (Mexico), 1993.

OTHER

Angela de Hoyos, a Critical Look: Lo Heroico y lo Antiheroico en su Poesia (literary criticism) Pajarito Publications (Albuquerque, NM), 1979.

Junto al Paisaje, Editorial Oasis (Mexico), 1984.

Melmanias: La Ritualizacion del Universo (literary criticism), Universidad Nacional Autonoma de Mexico, 1990.

La Senora de la Fuente, Joaquin Mortiz (Mexico), 1996.

Also contributor to *Acerca de Literatura: (dialogo con tre autores Chicanos),* M & A Editions (San Antonio, TX), 1979.

SIDELIGHTS: Luis Arturo Ramos is the author of short stories and novels set in his native Mexico. *Del Tiempo y Otros Lugares* (1979), a collection of short stories by Ramos, "create[s] oppressive, uneasy atmospheres in which the dynamic of the imagination has priority over a detached perception of reality," according to Timothy A. B. Richards in *Hispania.* Ramos's first novel, *Violeta-Peru* (1979) features, according to Richards, "a proletarian Walter Mitty . . . daydreaming about what might be or might have been." Richards also wrote that Ramos's *Los Viejos Asesinos* (1983), another collection of Ramos's short stories, "focus[es] on the relativity of values and the individual perspective on reality."

In his second novel, *Intramuros* (1983), Ramos follows the lives of several immigrants who arrive in Mexico in 1939. The immigrants are Spaniards who have fled the Spanish Civil War to settle in Veracruz. From that focal point the novel carries the reader back in time to the American invasion of Veracruz in 1914 and forward to the death of Spanish dictator Francisco Franco. World events shed light on the individual characters' lives. Richards wrote of the novel, "The passing of the years is marked by reference to major events, national and international, each of which evokes strife and repression. The Falangist victory causes a wave of immigration. Differing phases of the Second World War and the Cold War, the Mexican railroad strike of 1958, the Cuban Revolution of 1959, the 1968 Tlatelolco massacre, the fall of Allende in 1973, clarify the intervening temporal progression on the large canvas." Against this backdrop of historical events, Ramos's characters live out their existence in a city first regarded as full of promise but later viewed as the dead end of their dreams. *Intramuros* was translated into English in 1997 as *Within These Walls.*

BIOGRAPHICAL/CRITICAL SOURCES:

BOOKS

Martinez, Julio A., *Chicano Scholars and Writers,* Scarecrow Press (Metuchen, NJ), 1979.

PERIODICALS

Hispania, September, 1988, pp. 531-535.

OTHER

Barnes & Noble, http://www.barnesandnoble.com (December 10, 1998).
Harbourfront Reading Series, http://www.icomm.ca/ifoa97/ramos.html (December 10, 1998).
University of Texas at El Paso, http://www.utep.edu/lgsling.faculty.htm (December 10, 1998); http://www.utep.edu/chicano/Luis.htm (December 10, 1998).*

*   *   *

RECHY, John (Francisco) 1934-

PERSONAL: Born in 1934, in El Paso, TX; son of Roberto Sixto and Guadalupe (Flores) Rechy. *Education:* Texas Western College (now University of Texas at El Paso), B.A.; attended New School for Social Research.

ADDRESSES: Home—Los Angeles, CA; and New York, NY. *Agent*—c/o Georges Borchardt Inc., 136 East 57th St., New York, NY 10022.

CAREER: Writer. Conducted writing seminars at Occidental College and University of California; presently teaches film and literature classes in the graduate school of the University of Southern California. *Military service:* U.S. Army; served in Germany.

MEMBER: National Writers Union, Authors Guild, Authors League of America, PEN, Texas Institute of Letters.

AWARDS, HONORS: Longview Foundation fiction prize, 1961, for short story "The Fabulous Wedding of Miss Destiny"; International Prix Formentor nominee, for *City of Night;* National Endowment for the Arts grant, 1976; *Los Angeles Times* Book Award nomination, 1984, for body of work.

WRITINGS:

City of Night (novel), Grove, 1963.
Numbers (novel), Grove, 1967.
This Day's Death (novel), Grove, 1969.
The Vampires (novel), Grove, 1971.

The Fourth Angel (novel), Viking, 1973.

The Sexual Outlaw: A Documentary (nonfiction), Grove, 1977.

Momma as She Was—Not as She Became (play), produced in New York City, 1978.

Rushes (novel), Grove, 1979.

Bodies and Souls (novel), Carroll & Graf, 1983.

Tigers Wild (play), first produced in New York City, at Playhouse 91, October 21, 1986.

Marilyn's Daughter (novel), Carroll & Graf, 1988.

The Miraculous Day of Amalia Gomez (novel), Arcade, 1991.

Our Lady of Babylon (novel), Arcade, 1996.

Also author of a screenplay based on his novel *City of Night* and a play based on *Rushes.*

CONTRIBUTOR

LeRoi Jones, editor, *The Moderns,* Corinth, 1963.

Robert Rubens, editor, *Voices,* M. Joseph, 1963.

Bruce Jay Friedman, editor, *Black Humor,* Bantam, 1965.

Donald M. Allen and Robert Creeley, editors, *New American Story,* Grove, 1965.

Collision Course, Random House, 1968.

Floren Harper, editor, *Scripts,* Houghton, 1973.

W. Burns Taylor, Richard Santelli, and Kathleen McGary, editors, *Passing Through,* Santay Publishers, 1974.

Susan Cahill and Michele F. Couper, editors, *Urban Reader,* Prentice-Hall, 1979.

David Madden and Peggy Bach, editors, *Rediscoveries II,* Carroll & Graf, 1988.

Also contributor to Edmundo Garcia Giron, editor, *Literatura Chicana,* Prentice-Hall, and to Carlota Cardeneste Dwyer, editor, *Chicano Voices,* 1975. Contributor of short stories, articles, and reviews to periodicals, including *Evergreen Review, Nugget, Big Table, Mother Jones, London Magazine, Los Angeles Times Book Review, New York Times Book Review, Saturday Review, Washington Post Book World, Village Voice,* and *Nation;* contributor of translations from Spanish to periodicals.

WORK IN PROGRESS: Autobiography: A Novel, and *The Coming of the Night,* a novel.

SIDELIGHTS: John Rechy's first book, *City of Night,* was "hailed as the advent of a unique voice by critics and writers as diverse as Larry McMurtry, James Baldwin, Herbert Gold, and Christopher Isherwood," declares Gregg Barrios in *Newsday.* It became a best

seller in 1963, a rare accomplishment for a first novel, and it is now regarded as a modern classic and is taught in modern literature courses. However, the book's controversial subject matter—it traced the journey of a sexual adventurer through the night life of urban America—has drawn attention away from what Rechy considers a more important aspect of his work: the structure of the novel and the craftsmanship of Rechy's art, aspects the author continues to emphasize in his more recent fiction.

Rechy draws on many aspects of his Mexican-American heritage, as well as his past, to create his own vision of art. His novels, declare Julio A. Martinez and Francisco A. Lomeli in *Chicano Literature: A Reference Guide,* "reveal the underlying power that Chicano culture can exert even on those Mexican-American writers generally considered outside the mainstream of Chicano literature." One recurring symbol Rechy uses in his novel *Rushes* is drawn from the Catholic faith he practiced in childhood; as the protagonist advances further into despair, his trip reflects the stations of the cross, the route that Jesus took through Jerusalem on his way to Calvary. "Whether Chicano literature is defined as literary work produced about Mexican-Americans or by them," state Martinez and Lomeli, "his works can be included in that category, especially since their plots usually contain some Mexican details and their themes frequently derive, at least in part, from Chicano culture." "Still, beyond these restrictive labels," Rechy once explained, "I am and always have been a LITERARY WRITER, a novelist, a creative writer who has experimented with various forms."

Much of Rechy's work concerns finding patterns in life, and reflecting those patterns in his fiction. His first novel, he tells John Farrell in the University of Southern California's faculty newsletter *Transcript,* grew out of his "desperate need to try to give order to the anarchy I had experienced." In later books, such as *Numbers, The Vampires, The Fourth Angel, The Sexual Outlaw,* and *Bodies and Souls,* Rechy has experimented not only with content, but also with the form of storytelling itself. *The Sexual Outlaw,* is an experiment with a form Rechy called a "documentary," while *Bodies and Souls* "is, I believe," noted Rechy in his *Contemporary Authors Autobiography Series* entry, "a daring novel in content and form; a grand and lasting artistic achievement."

Bodies and Souls relates the story of three runaways who have come to Los Angeles looking for answers and the realization of their dreams. However, Rechy intersperses their tale with vignettes of Los Angeles residents whose lives are as empty as those of the three young people. "The all-pervading isolation and loneliness that Mr. Rechy dramatized so effectively in his novels about homosexual night life," declares Alan Cheuse in the *New York Times Book Review,* "becomes in this . . . book a commonplace about daily life in California." Rechy told interviewer Jean Ross: "I think of it as an epic novel of Los Angeles today—an 'apocalyptic' novel. In it, through the many lives I depict, I explore what I call 'the perfection of what is called accident'—the seemingly random components that come together perfectly to create what in retrospect we name 'fate.'"

Rechy considers *Marilyn's Daughter* his "most complex and literary novel, dealing with artifice as art, the power of legend over truth." Richard Hall, writing in the *San Francisco Chronicle,* deems the novel "a marvel of literary engineering," praising its "complex plot. . . which loops and doubles back in time." Normalyn Morgan, who may or may not be Marilyn Monroe's daughter by Robert Kennedy, travels to Los Angeles after her foster mother's suicide to find out if Monroe was, in fact, her mother. Normalyn's journey of discovery leads her through a many-layered maze of deception and ambiguity—some of it laid down by Monroe herself, other parts hidden or forgotten by people whose lives intersected at one time with hers. "In her search for Monroe," explains Hall, "Normalyn comes up against one of the great, overarching symbols of American confusion." "Rechy notes that, whether [the book] succeeds on its own terms or not," states Farrell, "what the novelist intended was a truly innovative approach to narrative and a serious exploration into the origin of legends and their power over truth."

Marilyn's Daughter, says its author in *Newsday,* is "an extravagant literary creation. It deals with how one finally cannot run away from one's self." "Marilyn Monroe was a monument to self-creation, to self-consciousness," Rechy explains to Farrell. "She was artifice as art." Farrell continues: "Art, he insists, signifies only secondarily. Primarily and permanently—in all its potency to move us to exquisite vicarious experience—art *is.*"

In his next novel, *The Miraculous Day of Amalia Gomez,* Rechy relates the plight of a beautiful, twice-divorced Mexican-American woman in Los Angeles who recalls traumatic events of her life after seeing what she believes is a divine apparition in the form of a silver cross in the sky. While Amalia attempts to rationalize the religious vision, through a series of flashbacks the reader learns of her abusive childhood in El Paso, Texas, with an alcoholic father, her first marriage to a man who raped her, the death of her son in prison, and a procession of related misfortunes. Judith Freeman describes the novel in the *Los Angeles Times Book Review* as "a disturbing portrayal of one day in the life of a middle-aged Mexican-American woman who is struggling to raise her children amid the decaying and drug-ridden neighborhoods of East Los Angeles and Hollywood." Though critical of the novel's implausible denouement, Karen Brailsford writes in the *New York Times Book Review* that Rechy is "most successful in his graphic descriptions of the hellish underbelly of East Los Angeles."

Our Lady of Babylon, set in eighteenth-century Europe, describes the flight and redemption of a woman wrongly accused of killing her husband. Pursued by papal authorities, the unnamed lady finds refuge at a countryside estate with Madame Bernice, to whom she recounts her numerous incarnations as Eve, Delilah, Helen of Troy, Mary Magdalene, and Medea. Though finding fault in the novel's frequent narrative disjunctions, *Washington Post Book World* contributor Elizabeth Hand writes, "Rechy writes gracefully, and sometimes poignantly, of the fate of fallen women over the centuries."

BIOGRAPHICAL/CRITICAL SOURCES:

BOOKS

Contemporary Authors Autobiography Series, Volume 4, Gale, 1986.
Contemporary Literary Criticism, Gale, Volume 1, 1973; Volume 7, 1977; Volume 14, 1980; Volume 18, 1981.
Dictionary of Literary Biography, Volume 122: *Chicano Writers, Second Series,* Gale, 1992.
Dictionary of Literary Biography Yearbook: 1982, Gale, 1983.
Gilman, Richard, *The Confusion of Realms,* Random House, 1963, 5th edition, 1969.
Hispanic Literature Criticism, Gale, 1994.
Martinez, Julio A., and Francisco A. Lomeli, editors, *Chicano Literature: A Reference Guide,* Greenwood Press, 1985.

PERIODICALS

Booklist, June 1 & 15, 1996, p. 1677.
Chicago Review, 1973.

Library Journal, February 1, 1963; June 15, 1996,
    p. 92.
London Magazine, June, 1968.
Los Angeles Times, September 7, 1988.
Los Angeles Times Book Review, July 17, 1982; Janu-
    ary 27, 1985; October 2, 1988; September 22,
    1991, p. 3.
Nation, January 5, 1974.
Newsday, September 10, 1988.
New York Times, December 27, 1967.
New York Times Book Review, June 30, 1963; January
    14, 1968; April 3, 1977; July 17, 1977; February
    17, 1980; July 10, 1983; May 10, 1992, p. 16.
People, May 22, 1978.
Prairie Schooner, Fall, 1971.
Publishers Weekly, June 28, 1991, p. 87; May 13,
    1996, p. 58.
San Francisco Chronicle, August 7, 1988.
Saturday Review, June 8, 1963.
Times Literary Supplement, September 11, 1970.
Transcript, November 28, 1988.
Village Voice, August 22, 1977; October 3, 1977;
    March 3, 1980.
Washington Post Book World, August 12, 1973; July
    21, 1996, p. 8.*

* * *

REGO, Jose Lins do
    See do REGO, Jose Lins

* * *

RIDRUEJO (JIMENEZ), Dionisio 1912-1975

PERSONAL: Born October 12, 1912, in Burgo de
Osma, Spain; died after a heart attack, June 29, 1975,
in Madrid, Spain; son of Dionisio Ridruejo Martin (a
merchant and banker) and Segunda Jimenez Ridruejo;
married Gloria de Ros, June 26, 1944. *Education:*
Attended Universidad de Maria Cristina, beginning in
1929; attended Universidad de Madrid; earned law
degree; studied journalism at El Debate, Madrid,
Spain.

CAREER: Writer. Falange Espanola, member, beginning in 1935, served as local political officer of propaganda in Segovia, Spain, and as regional chief,
between 1936 and 1937, national propaganda officer,
1938-41; Agencia Pyresa, Rome, Italy, journalist,

1948-51; Radio Intercontinental, Spain, director,
1951. Partido Social de Accion Democratica, founder,
1957. University of Puerto Rico, teacher of Spanish
literature and civilization, c. 1962; University of
Wisconsin, Madison, teacher of Spanish literature,
1968. *Military service:* Spanish armed forces, Blue
Division, 1941-42; served in Russia; received Cruz
Roja de Merito Militar.

AWARDS, HONORS: Premio Nacional de Literatura,
1950, for *En Once Anos.*

WRITINGS:

Plural, privately printed (Segovia, Spain), 1935.
Primer Libro de Amor (poems; title means "First
    Book of Love"), Yunque (Barcelona, Spain),
    1939.
Poesia en Armas: Cuadernos de la Guerra Civil (title
    means "Poetry in Arms: Notebooks of the Civil
    War"), Jerarquia (Barcelona), 1940.
(Author of prologue) Antonio Machado, *Obras
    Completas* (title means "Complete Works"),
    Espasa-Calpe (Madrid, Spain), 1941.
Fabula de la Doncella y el Rio (poems; title means
    "Fable of the Maiden and the River"), Nacional
    (Madrid), 1943.
Sonetos a la Piedra (title means "Sonnets to Stone"),
    Nacional (Madrid), 1943.
Poesia en Armas: Cuadernos de Rusia (title means
    "Poetry in Arms: Notebooks from Russia"),
    Aguado (Madrid), 1944.
En la Soledad del Tiempo (poems; title means "In the
    Solitude of Time"), Montaner and Simon (Barce-
    lona), 1944.
Don Juan, Nacional (Madrid), 1945.
Elegias, Adonais (Madrid), 1948.
En Once Anos (poems; title means "In Eleven Years"),
    Nacional (Madrid), 1950.
Dentro del Tiempo, Arion (Barcelona), 1960, revised
    edition published as *Diario de una Tregua,* Destino
    (Barcelona), 1972.
En Algunas Ocasiones, Aguilar (Madrid), 1960.
Hasta la Fecha (poems; title means "Until Now"),
    Aguilar (Madrid), 1961.
Escrito en Espana (prose; title means "Written in
    Spain"), Losada (Buenos Aires, Argentina), 1962,
    revised edition, 1964.
Espana 1963: Examen de una Situacion (essays),
    Centro de Documentacion y Estudios (Paris,
    France), 1963.
Cuaderno Catalan, Revista de Occidente (Madrid),
    1965.
122 Poemas, Losada (Buenos Aires), 1967.

Casi en Prosa, Revista de Occidente (Madrid), 1972.

Entre Literatura y Politica, Seminarios (Madrid), 1973.

Castilla la Vieja, two volumes, Destino (Barcelona), 1973-74.

En Breve (poems; title means "Briefly"), Litoral (Malaga, Spain), 1975.

Primer Libro de Amor, Poesia en Armas, Sonetos (title means "First Book of Love, Poetry in Arms, Sonnets"), Castalia (Madrid), 1976.

Casi unas Memorias (title means "Almost Memoirs"), edited by Cesar Armando Gomez, Planeta (Barcelona), 1976.

Poesia, edited by Luis Felipe Vivanco, Alianza (Madrid), 1976.

Sombras y Bultos, Destino (Barcelona), 1977.

Los Cuadernos de Rusia (title means "The Notebooks from Russia"), edited by Gomez and Gloria de Ros, Planeta (Barcelona), 1978.

Cuadernos de Rusia, En la Soledad del Tiempo, Cancionero de Ronda, Elegia (title means "Notebooks from Russia, In the Solitude of Time, Songbook of Ronda, Elegies"), Castalia (Madrid), 1981.

Coeditor of *Boletin Informativo,* 1963.

SIDELIGHTS: Dionisio Ridruejo was a Spanish political activist who first embraced, then challenged, the turbulent regime of Francisco Franco. He is best known as the author of hundreds of poems, the most noted of which he produced between 1930 and 1950. Teresa Scott Soufas reported in the *Dictionary of Literary Biography:* "Dionisio Ridruejo led a life of crisis, surrounded by and involved in the turmoil of war, exile, court trials, and imprisonment. His life, like his poetry, reflects the reversals and contradictions characteristic of the man who at a very early age had attained positions of importance within the Falangist party only to suffer confinement and banishment after his break with the Francisco Franco regime."

These elements were not evident in the poet's earliest work. In his twenties, Ridruejo published traditional verses of love and romance. The poems in *Fabula de la doncella y el rio,* according to Soufas, "deal with a girl who is both real and symbolic, as is the river [of the title] that represents her lover. She is the eternal adolescent awaiting the arrival of love." Some critics have declared that Ridruejo's most masterful poetry is contained in this volume, which, though it includes poems first composed in the 1930s, was not published until 1943. Later poems, collected in *Primer libro de amor,* "take on a more personal and

subjective quality," Soufas noted; "[b]eneath the stylized form there runs the thread of a subjective story. . . . Evident in Ridruejo's poetry from here on is the inclination toward a thematic unity."

Throughout the 1940s Ridruejo became embroiled in the activities of Spain's Falangist party, and in a short period of time rose to the position of national propaganda officer. No sooner had he reached this peak than he began to criticize the party and its militant leader, directly if not publicly. Soufas wrote: "Filled with frustration and disappointment during this period, Ridruejo nevertheless clung to the hope and conviction of his dreams of bettering the country while, as he later explained, each day brought a new defeat for those ideals in the face of disappointing reality." In 1941 Ridruejo resigned his political position and served instead in the military campaign of the Blue Division in Russia. These events wrought changes in his poetry, which appears in the collections *Poesia en armas: cuadernos de la guerra civil* and *Poesia en armas: cuadernos de Rusia.*

Soufas dismissed the civil war poems as "ideological and propagandist in nature . . . not among the best of Ridruejo's works." She reported that the poet himself would have expunged them from later collections had they not served as a valid reflection of "his youthful idealism." The poems of the Russian campaign, on the other hand, appear to demonstrate increasing maturity and a transition from the abstractions of earlier writings toward a more concrete reality. Soufas commented that the poetry of Ridruejo's "Russian experience . . . marks an expansion of theme, for he deals with his time as a soldier. . . , recording his states of mind. . . . In this poetry Ridruejo no longer speaks of imaginary, indistinct, bucolic landscapes. . . , but instead describes vividly the settings and sights around him. . . . Death is likewise faced as a reality rather than as a mere abstract concept."

As the decade progressed Ridruejo became increasingly displeased with the Franco regime and increasingly vocal about his displeasure. As a result, he spent significant portions of the next twenty-five years under house arrest, in prison, or in exile. He continued to write but was not always permitted to publish his work at will. Soufas observed: "The poetry written just before and during Ridruejo's initial period of confinement is of a mature quality, reflecting the disillusionment and existential suffering of one who has experienced solitude and who is fully aware of the passing moments." The critic added that later work includes *Elegias,* "in which his disillusionment reaches its fullest expression. . . . The passage of time, Ridruejo's errors, and his internal rebellion against those errors are the root of the *desengano* [disillusion] that finds expression in these long poems."

Ridruejo spent his mature years, for the most part, as an exile. He lived in Paris and traveled widely. Works published in the 1960s and 1970s were often reprints or minor revisions of the seminal work of the forties and early fifties. After Ridruejo's death following a heart attack in 1975, posthumously published material reveals what Soufas called "a legacy of challenges to his compatriots."

BIOGRAPHICAL/CRITICAL SOURCES:

BOOKS

Dictionary of Literary Biography, Volume 108: *Twentieth-Century Spanish Poets, First Series,* edited by Michael L. Perna, Gale (Detroit, MI), 1991, pp. 270-80.*

*   *   *

RIOS, Alberto (Alvaro) 1952-

PERSONAL: Born September 18, 1952, in Nogales, AZ; son of Alberto Alvaro (a justice of the peace) and Agnes (a nurse; maiden name, Fogg) Rios; married Maria Guadalupe Barron (a librarian), September 8, 1979; children: Joaquin. *Education:* University of Arizona, B.A. (English literature and creative writing), 1974, B.A. (psychology), 1975, M.F.A., 1979; attended law school at the University of Arizona, 1975-76. *Politics:* "Liberal/Democrat." *Religion:* "Cultural Catholic."

ADDRESSES: Home—3038 North Pennington Dr., Chandler, AZ 85224. *Office*—Department of English, Arizona State University, Tempe, AZ 85287.

CAREER: Arizona Commission on the Arts, Phoenix, artist in Artists-in-Education Program, 1978-83, consultant, 1983—; Arizona State University, Tempe, assistant professor, 1982-85, associate professor, 1985-89, professor of English, 1989—, co-chair of Hispanic Research and Development Committee, 1983—, director, Creative Writing Program, 1986-89. Counselor and instructor in English and algebra in Med-Start Program at University of Arizona, summers, 1977-80. Writer-in-residence at Central Ari-

zona College, Coolidge, 1980-82. Board of directors, Associated Writing Programs, 1988—, secretary, 1989—; board of directors, Arizona Center for the Book, 1988—, vice chairman, 1989—. Member of National Advisory Committee to the National Artists-in-Education Program, 1980; member of grants review panel, Arizona Commission on the Arts, 1983; member, National Endowment for the Arts Poetry Panel. Judge of New York City High School Poetry Contest. Gives poetry readings, lectures, and workshops.

AWARDS, HONORS: First place in Academy of American Arts poetry contest, 1977, for "A Man Then Suddenly Stops Moving"; writer's fellowship in poetry from the Arizona Commission on the Arts, 1979; fellowship grant in creative writing from National Endowment for the Arts, 1980; Walt Whitman Award from the National Academy of American Poets, 1981, for *Whispering to Fool the Wind;* second place in *New York Times* annual fiction award competition, 1983, for "The Way Spaghetti Feels"; Western States Book Award (fiction), 1984, for *The Iguana Killer;* New Times Fiction Award, 1983; Pushcart Prize for fiction, 1986, and poetry, 1988, 1989; Chicanos Por La Causa Community Appreciation Award, 1988; received nomination for distinguished teaching award from Arizona State University.

WRITINGS:

Elk Heads on the Wall (poetry chapbook), Mango Press (San Jose, CA), 1979.
Sleeping on Fists (poetry chapbook), Dooryard Press (Story, WY), 1981.
Whispering to Fool the Wind (poetry), Sheep Meadow (New York City), 1982.
The Iguana Killer: Twelve Stories of the Heart, Blue Moon/Confluence (Lewiston, ID), 1984.
Five Indiscretions (poetry), Sheep Meadow, 1985.
The Lime Orchard Woman: Poems, Sheep Meadow, 1988.
The Warrington Poems, Pyracantha Press (Tempe, AZ), 1989.
Teodoro Luna's Two Kisses, Norton (New York City), 1990.
Pig Cookies and Other Stories, Chronicle Books (San Francisco), 1995.
The Curtain of Trees: Stories, University of New Mexico Press (Albuquerque), 1999.

Contributor of poetry, fiction, and drama to anthologies, including *Southwest: A Contemporary Anthology,* edited by Karl Kopp and Jane Kopp, Red Earth

Press, 1977; *Hispanics in the United States: An Anthology of Creative Literature,* edited by Gary D. Keller and Francisco Jimenez, Bilingual Review Press, 1980; *The Norton Anthology of Modern Poetry,* edited by Richard Ellmann, Robert O'Clair, and John Benedict, Norton, 1988; and *American Literature,* Prentice-Hall, 1990. Contributor to periodicals, including *American Poetry Review, Little Magazine, Bloomsbury Review,* and *Paris Review.* Also contributor of translations to *New Kauri* and *Poetry Pilot.* Corresponding editor, *Manoa,* 1989—; editorial board, *New Chicano Writing,* 1990—.

SIDELIGHTS: Alberto Rios has won acclaim as a writer who uses language in lyrical and unexpected ways in both his poems and short stories, which reflect his Chicano heritage and contain elements of magical realism. "Rios's poetry is a kind of magical storytelling, and his stories are a kind of magical poetry," comments Jose David Saldivar in the *Dictionary of Literary Biography.* Rios grew up in a Spanish-speaking family but was forced to speak English in school, leading him to develop a third language, "one that was all our own," as he described it. Rios once commented "I have been around other languages all my life, particularly Spanish, and have too often thought of the act of translation as simply giving something two names. But it is not so, not at all. Rather than filling out, a second name for something pushes it forward, forward and backward, and gives it another life."

Saldivar writes of Rios, "Many of his important early poems dramatize the essence of this uncanny third language." There are examples of these in the prize-winning collection *Whispering to Fool the Wind,* which contains poems that Mary Logue, writing in the *Voice Literary Supplement,* calls "written miracles" that "carry the feel of another world." These poems, she notes, are informed by his upbringing in the border town of Nogales, Arizona, "where one is neither in this country nor the other."

Saldivar explains that Rios tells stories in verse, something that many writers have been unable to do successfully. Rios, however, is able to bring to life characters such as a man who dies of anger when a seamstress refuses to give him pins with which to display his butterfly collection. "Throughout *Whispering to Fool the Wind* magical-realist events are related with the greatest of accuracy without being forced on the reader," Saldivar writes. "It is left up to readers to interpret things for themselves in a way that is most familiar to them."

Saldivar deems "Nani," about Rios's grandmother, the best poem in the collection "and one of the most remarkable poems in Chicano literature." It "captures the reality of the invented third language," he says, with lines such as "To speak, now-foreign words I used to speak, too, dribble down her mouth. . . . By the stove she does something with words and looks at me only with her back." Logue also praises the poet's unusual use of language, observing that "Rios's tongue is both foreign and familiar, but always enchanting."

In *Five Indiscretions,* "most of the poems achieve a level of excellence not far below the peak moments of [Rios's] earlier poetry," Saldivar asserts. Almost all of these poems deal with romantic and sexual relationships between men and women, with the poet taking both male and female viewpoints. This collection has "regrettably . . . not received the acclaim and attention it deserves," Saldivar opines. "The few book reviews, however, praised his ability to represent gender issues and his use of the American language."

Rios's award-winning book of short stories, *The Iguana Killer: Twelve Stories of the Heart,* contains tales "explor[ing] the luminous world of his childhood and border culture," Saldivar relates. The title story centers on a young Mexican boy who uses a baseball bat to become his country's leading iguana killer. "The Birthday of Mrs. Pineda" is about an oppressed wife who finally gets a chance to speak for herself. This and "The Way Spaghetti Feels" are, in Saldivar's estimate, "the best stories in the book"; he comments that they "border on the metafictional and magical-realist impulse in postmodern fiction."

These characteristics also are evident in *Pig Cookies and Other Stories,* set in a small Mexican town where cookies exhibit supernatural powers and life takes other surprising twists and turns. "The tales in this collection glisten with a magical sheen, at once otherworldly and real," remarks Greg Sanchez in *World Literature Today.* "Rios takes us from the realm of imagination to the concrete and back again with surprising fluidity." Rios also creates winning characters, writes a *Publishers Weekly* reviewer: "These poignant, funny tales of the rich, unsuspected lives of regular folks transcend time and place."

Indeed, while Rios's Chicano heritage informs his writing and while he is one of that culture's important voices, his work "is anything but narrow and exclusive," contends Robert McDowell in an essay for *Contemporary Poets.* Rios, McDowell says, is dedicated "to finding, declaring, and celebrating the diversity and power of community in the experience of those around him. Thus, his vision is more outward directed, less private than might at first glance be apparent." Saldivar adds that "Rios is surely one of the major vernacular voices in the postmodern age."

BIOGRAPHICAL/CRITICAL SOURCES:

BOOKS

Contemporary Poets, 6th edition, St. James Press (Detroit), 1996.
Dictionary of Literary Biography, Volume 122: *Chicano Writers, Second Series,* Gale (Detroit), 1992.

PERIODICALS

New York Times Book Review, February 9, 1986; September 17, 1995, p. 25.
Publishers Weekly, March 20, 1995, p. 54.
Voice Literary Supplement, October, 1982.
World Literature Today, spring, 1996, p. 415.*

*   *   *

RIOS, Isabella
  See LOPEZ, Diana

*   *   *

RIVERA, Jose Eustasio 1889-1928

PERSONAL: Born in 1889, in Neiva, Colombia; died in 1928, of pneumonia while on a speaking tour in the United States. *Education:* Graduated from teachers' college, Bogota, c. 1909; graduated with a law degree from National University, Bogota, c. 1917.

CAREER: Colombian lawyer, novelist, essayist, and poet. Served on government commission tracing boundary between Colombia and Venezuela, 1922.

WRITINGS:

Tierra de promision (poetry), 1921, Ancora (Bogota, Colombia), 1985.

La voragine (novel), 1924, Distribuidora Cultural (Managua, Nicaragua), 1983, translation by Earle K. James published as *The Vortex,* Putnam (New York City), 1935.
Obras completas (complete works), Montoya (Medellin, Colombia), 1963.

SIDELIGHTS: Jose Eustasio Rivera is best known as the author of *La voragine* (*The Vortex*), one of the first novels to realistically portray the South American jungle and its inhabitants. Esteemed for its evocative, lyrical prose style and the fidelity of its descriptions, *The Vortex* has also been applauded for its frank disclosure of the social injustices inflicted on Colombian peasants. Rivera's novel exerted a marked influence on South American literature, helping to inspire the trend toward the use of native themes and settings that has culminated in the internationally recognized achievements of such authors as Gabriel Garcia Marquez and Mario Vargas Llosa.

Rivera was born into a family of modest means in the southern Colombian town of Neiva. Graduating from a teachers' college in Bogota at the age of twenty, he received a law degree from the National University eight years later. Rivera subsequently established himself both as a lawyer and as a member of Bogota's intellectual community, publishing a collection of sonnets, *Tierra de promision,* in 1921.

The following year he traveled to the Colombian jungle as secretary of a congressional committee investigating a border dispute between his country and Venezuela, an experience that provided the inspiration for *The Vortex.* In particular, Rivera was impressed by the majestic beauty and destructive power of the jungle, and his sympathies were aroused by the abominable conditions to which Colombians working for the nascent rubber industry were subjected. While in the jungle, Rivera contracted beriberi, and it was during his convalescence that he wrote *The Vortex.* The novel was an immediate success, bringing Rivera international acclaim. However, his health remained poor due to the lingering effects of his disease, and in 1928 he died of pneumonia while on a speaking tour in the United States.

Displaying Rivera's literary talents as well as his keen powers of perception, *The Vortex* has been described by L. H. Titterton in the *New York Times Book Review* as an admirable combination of "stark realism . . . [and] lyrical romanticism." In the novel, Rivera sought to portray the dramatic conflict between human beings and the South American jungle, which is described by Rivera's protagonist, Arturo Cova, as a "green hell." Some critics have therefore argued that Rivera viewed the jungle as a hostile environment which inflicts physical and mental pain on its human inhabitants and evokes savage behavior.

Arturo Torres-Rioseco has written in *The Epic of Latin American Literature* that, in *The Vortex,* Rivera showed how the "forest dominates the human beings who drag themselves through its depths; how it attacks their minds and bodies, incubating fevers and insanity; how with its thousand tentacles it seizes men and transforms them into wild beasts." However, some oppose this view of *The Vortex,* most notably Richard J. Callan, who asserted in *Romance Notes* that Rivera depicted the jungle as a testing ground where an individual might yield to baser impulses but might also display heroic endurance.

The Vortex purports to be the memoirs of Cova, a young Colombian intellectual. At the beginning of the novel, he elopes with his girlfriend, Alicia, leaving Bogota to settle among the lawless cattle herders of the Colombian plains. When Alicia is subsequently abducted and taken to the jungle, Cova follows. There he meets Don Clemente Silva and Ramiro Estevanez, whose accounts of Colombian history and its impact upon life in the jungle combine with Cova's story to form the sweeping narrative of *The Vortex.* The story ends when Cova, having found Alicia and killed her abductor, disappears with her into the jungle.

While *The Vortex* has generally been applauded for its exciting plot, lyrical prose, and colorful descriptive passages, the narrative has also been criticized for what many view as a lack of coherence between Cova's accounts of his adventures and the historical accounts related by Silva, Estevanez, and other minor characters. Eduardo Neale-Silva has speculated in *PMLA* that Rivera wrote the purely fictional passages separately from the sections based on Colombian history and later attempted to fuse them. However, Seymour Menton disagrees with the widely held view that the narrative lacks coherence and has suggested that *The Vortex* is a carefully constructed allegory. According to Menton, whose essay "*La voragine:* Circling the Triangle" appeared in *Hispania* in 1976, the novel should be regarded as "a complex Christian vision of man's fall from paradise and his punishment and ultimate death in the concentric circles of hell."

The Vortex has long been appreciated as both a richly descriptive regional novel and a compelling, romantic adventure story. In addition, late-twentieth-century analyses have emphasized the psychological complexity and technical sophistication of Rivera's narrative, as well as the author's skillful allusions to classical and modern literature. Highly esteemed in Spanish-speaking countries, Rivera is also one of the few Colombian writers to have achieved international recognition.

Assessing *The Vortex* in his mid-century survey *Contemporary Spanish-American Fiction,* Jefferson Rea Spell described the novel as "rich in information about strange and little-known regions, abounding in emotion that is deeply felt, [and] endowed with a high and noble purpose. . . . In it the forest and the jungle have been masterfully interpreted. Here is a Colombia unknown before in the annals of literature."

BIOGRAPHICAL/CRITICAL SOURCES:

BOOKS

Franco, Jean, *The Modern Culture of Latin America: Society and the Artist,* Pall Mall Press, 1967.

Magnarelli, Sharon, *The Lost Rib: Female Characters in the Spanish-American Novel,* Bucknell University Press, 1985.

Spell, Jefferson Rea, *Contemporary Spanish-American Fiction,* University of North Carolina Press, 1944.

Torres-Rioseco, Arturo, *The Epic of Latin American Literature,* Oxford University Press, 1942.

PERIODICALS

Americas, March, 1965, pp. 33-38.

Bulletin of Hispanic Studies, April, 1964, pp. 101-110.

Hispania, September, 1971, pp. 470-476; September, 1976, pp. 418-434.

Nation, June 26, 1935, p. 749.

New Republic, June 19, 1935, p. 174.

New York Herald Tribune Books, April 21, 1935, p. 6.

New York Times Book Review, April 28, 1935, pp. 8, 17.

PMLA, March, 1939, pp. 316-331.

Revista de estudios hispanicos, May, 1980, pp. 39-46.

Romance Notes, autumn, 1961, pp. 13-16.

Romanic Review, December, 1948, pp. 307-318.

Saturday Review of Literature, May 11, 1935, p. 25.*

RODO, Jose Enrique 1872(?)-1917

PERSONAL: Born July 15, 1872 (some sources say 1871), in Montevideo, Uruguay; died May 1, 1917, in Palermo, Italy.

CAREER: Essayist and literary critic, c. 1909-13. *Revista Nacional de Literatura y Ciencias Sociales,* cofounder, 1895, publisher, 1895-97. Worked as university professor; served as member of Uruguay's national Chamber of Representatives, 1902-10; European correspondent for newspapers in Montevideo, Uruguay, and Buenos Aires, Argentina, 1916-17.

WRITINGS:

Motivos de Proteo (essays; originally published, 1909), translation published as *The Motives of Proteus,* Brentano's (New York City), 1928, translation by Angel Flores, with introduction by Havelock Ellis, Gordon Press (New York City), 1977.
Ariel (originally published in a pamphlet series), University of Chicago Press (Chicago, IL), 1929, translation by Margaret Sayers Peden, with foreword by James W. Symington and prologue by Carlos Fuentes, University of Texas Press (Austin, TX), 1988.

Author of *El Mirador de Prospero,* 1913; and *El Camino de Paros* (collected writings). Author of a pamphlet series, including *El Que Vendra,* 1897, *Ruben Dario,* 1899, and *Ariel,* 1900; author of the pamphlet *Liberalismo y Jacobinismo,* 1906.

BIOGRAPHICAL/CRITICAL SOURCES:

BOOKS

Encyclopedia of World Biography, 2nd edition, Volume 13, Gale (Detroit, MI), 1998.
Penco, Wilfredo, *Jose Enrique Rodo,* Arco (Montevideo, Uruguay), 1978.*

* * *

RODRIGUEZ, Richard 1944-

PERSONAL: Born July 31, 1944, in San Francisco, CA; son of Leopoldo (a dental technician) and Victoria (a clerk-typist; maiden name, Moran) Rodriguez. *Education:* Stanford University, B.A., 1967; Columbia University, M.A., 1969; graduate study at University of California, Berkeley, 1969-72, 1974-75, and Warburg Institute, London, 1972-73. *Religion:* Roman Catholic.

ADDRESSES: Agent—Georges Borchardt, Inc., 136 East 57th St., New York, NY 10022.

CAREER: Held a variety of jobs, including janitorial work and freelance writing, 1977-81; writer, 1981—; University of Chicago, Perlman lecturer, 1984; journalist and essayist for PBS series *MacNeil-Lehrer NewsHour;* Pacific News Service, editor.

AWARDS, HONORS: Fulbright fellowship, 1972-73; National Endowment for the Humanities fellowship, 1976-77; Gold Medal from the Commonwealth Club, 1982; Christopher Award, 1982, for *Hunger of Memory: The Education of Richard Rodriguez;* Anisfield-Wolf Award for Race Relations, 1982.

WRITINGS:

Hunger of Memory: The Education of Richard Rodriguez (autobiography), David R. Godine, 1982.
Days of Obligation: An Argument with My Mexican Father (autobiography), Viking Penguin, 1992.
American Soul, 1995.
King's Highway, 1999.

Writings have also appeared in *American Scholar, New Republic, Wall Street Journal, Los Angeles Times, Harper's,* and *Washington Post.*

SIDELIGHTS: In the opinion of *New York Times* critic Le Anne Schreiber, Richard Rodriguez's autobiography, *Hunger of Memory,* is an "honest and intelligent account of how education can alter a life." It also offers a negative view of bilingual education and affirmative action policies that some readers have applauded and others have decried.

Hunger of Memory details Rodriguez' journey through the U.S. educational system and his resultant loss of ethnicity. The son of Mexican-American immigrants, unable to speak English when he entered a Sacramento, California, elementary school, Rodriguez went on to earn a master's degree and was a Fulbright scholar studying English Renaissance literature in London when he abruptly decided to leave academic life. The choice was prompted by the feeling that he was "the beneficiary of truly disadvantaged Mexican-Americans." "I benefited on their backs," he told *Publishers Weekly* interviewer Patricia Holt.

The alienation from his culture began early in Rodriguez' life; as soon, in fact, as he learned the "public" language that would separate him from his family. Catholic nuns who taught Rodriguez asked that his parents speak English to him at home. When they complied, related the author in a *Newsweek* article by Jean Strouse, the sound of his "private" language, Spanish, and its "pleasing, soothing, consoling reminder of being at home" were gone. Paul Zweig observed in the *New York Times Book Review* that "son and parents alike knew that an unnamable distance had come between them." Rodriguez' parents were eventually "intimidated by what they had worked so diligently to bring about: the integration of their son into the larger world of gringo life so that he, unlike they themselves, could go far, become, one day, powerful, educated," noted the reviewer.

Rodriguez reached the goals his parents had sought for him but eventually began to fight the very policies that helped him to attain them. In ten years of college and postgraduate education, Rodriguez received assistance grounded in merit but based in part on his minority status. He left London and tried to reestablish the long-since-severed connection with his parents. He failed to recover his lost ethnicity, remaining "an academic, . . . a kind of anthropologist in the family kitchen."

His revolt against affirmative action began when he turned down several university-level teaching jobs. As Schreiber explained, "He wrote letters to all the chairmen of English departments who thought they had found the perfect answer to affirmative action in Richard Rodriguez. He declined their offers of jobs, because he could not withstand the irony of being counted a 'minority' when in fact the irreversibly successful effort of his life had been to become a fully assimilated member of the majority." Rodriguez spent the next six years writing *Hunger of Memory,* parts of which appeared in magazines before being brought together in book form.

Rodriguez' arguments against affirmative action stem from his belief, as he told *Detroit Free Press* reporter Suzanne Dolezal, that "the program has primarily benefited people who are no longer disadvantaged, . . . as I no longer was when I was at Stanford, [by] ignoring the educational problems of people who are genuinely disadvantaged, people who cannot read or write." His opposition to bilingual education is just as vocal. "To me," he declared in the *Publishers Weekly* interview, "public educators in a public schoolroom have an obligation to teach a public language. Public language isn't just English or Spanish or any other formal language. It is the language of public society, the language that people outside that public sector resist. For Mexican-Americans it is the language of *los gringos.* For Appalachian children who speak a fractured English or Black children in a ghetto, the problem is the same it seems to me. . . . My argument has always been that the imperative is to get children away from those languages that increase their sense of alienation from the public society."

Hunger of Memory was praised by several critics, especially for its discussion of the impact of language on life. Le Anne Schreiber found that "what matters most about this intensely thoughtful book is that Richard Rodriguez has given us the fruit of his long meditation upon language—his intimate understanding of how we use language to create private and public selves, his painful awareness of what we gain and lose when we gain and lose languages." Paul Zweig judged that "the chapters Mr. Rodriguez devotes to his early experiences of language are uncannily sensitive to the nuances of language learning, the childhood drama of voices, intonations." A *New Yorker* review commended Rodriguez as "a writer of unusual grace and clarity, . . . eloquent in all his reflections."

Rodriquez's 1992 book, *Days of Obligation: An Argument with My Mexican Father,* is a collection of previously published autobiographical essays. In this collection, Rodriguez returns to many of the issues he probed in *Hunger of Memory:* language, history, and the immigrant history. He also explores in detail his feelings about his Mexican and Indian heritages as well as his present-day experiences in AIDS-ravaged San Francisco. Reviewing the book in Chicago's *Tribune Books,* Rockwell Gray commented, "In these revisionary essays, Rodriguez ranges widely over issues of personal allegiance, homeland, ethnic identity, the future of Roman Catholicism and the shibboleth of 'diversity' invoked to gloss over the rifts in an increasingly fragmented American society."

Critics remarked that *Days of Obligation* lacks the intuitive, coherent structure of *Hunger of Memory* but averred that the book once again displays the author's skill in producing powerful autobiographical writing. For instance, *Washington Post Book World* critic Jonathan Yardley noted, "though the earnestness of Rodriguez's self-examination remains affecting and convincing, *Days of Obligation* . . . never states in sufficiently clear terms either the nature of the argument or the author's own line of reasoning." Though admitting that the book can be "maddeningly presumptuous and determinedly obscure," *New York Times Book Review* contributor David L. Kirp exclaimed that "In its most powerful passages, 'Days of Obligation' reveals the writer as a tightrope walker who balances pessimism and the defeat of predictable expectations against the discovery of the profoundly unanticipated." Concluded Gray, "The wrestling with his elusive and insistent past makes these sinuous ruminations worthy of inclusion in the long American tradition of spiritual autobiography."

Rodriguez once told *Hispanic Writers:* "I see myself straddling two worlds of writing: journalism and literature. There is Richard Rodriguez, the journalist—every day I spend more time reading newspapers and magazines than I do reading novels and poetry. I wander away from my desk for hours, for weeks. I want to ask questions of the stranger on the bus. I want to consider the political and social issues of the day.

"Then there is Richard Rodriguez, the writer. It takes me a very long time to write. What I try to do when I write is break down the line separating the prosaic world from the poetic word. I try to write about everyday concerns—an educational issue, say, or the problems of the unemployed—but to write about them as powerfully, as richly, as well as I can.

"My model in this marriage of journalism and literature is, of course, George Orwell. Orwell is the great modern example. He embarrasses other journalists by being more. He never let the urgency of the moment overwhelm his concern for literary art. But, in like measure, he embarrasses other writers because he had the courage to attend to voices outside the window, he was not afraid to look up from his papers. I hope I can be as brave in my life."

BIOGRAPHICAL/CRITICAL SOURCES:

PERIODICALS

America, May 22, 1982, pp. 403-04; September 23, 1995, p. 8.
American Review, fall-winter, 1988, 75-90.
American Scholar, spring, 1983, pp. 278-85, winter, 1994, p. 145.
Christian Science Monitor Monthly, March 12, 1982, pp. B1, B3.
Commentary, July, 1982, pp. 82-84.
Diacritics, fall, 1985, pp. 25-34.
Melus, spring, 1987, pp. 3-15.
New York Times Book Review, November 22, 1992, p. 42.
Reson, August-September, 1994, p. 35.
Time, January 25, 1993, p. 70.
Tribune Books (Chicago), December 13, 1992, p. 1.
Washington Post Book World, November 15, 1992, p. 3.*

* * *

ROJAS, Gonzalo 1917-

PERSONAL: Born in 1917, in Chile; son of a coal miner.

CAREER: Poet. Taught reading and writing to miners in the desert of Chile; taught at the university in Concepcion, in the 1950s; appointed Chilean cultural attache in Beijing, China, 1971; taught at universities in Venezuela and the United States, until 1981.

AWARDS, HONORS: Chile's National Prize for Literature, 1992; Spain's Reina Soffia Prize, for poetry.

WRITINGS:

La miseria del hombre (title means "The Misery of Man"), 1948.
Contra la muerte (title means "Against Death"), 1964.
Oscuro (title means "Obscure"), 1977.
Del relampago (title means "Of Lightning"), 1981, expanded edition, 1984.
Criptico y otros poemas (title means "Cryptic and Other Poems"), 1985.
El Alumbrado (title means "The Seer"), 1986.
Schizotext and Other Poems/Esquizotexto y otros poemas, translations by Russell M. Cluff and L. Howard Quackenbush, Peter Lang (New York City), 1988.
Las hermosas: Poesias de amor (anthology; title means "The Beautiful: Love Poems"), 1991.
Cinco visiones: Seleccion de poemas (title means "Five Visions: Selection of Poems"), 1992.

BIOGRAPHICAL/CRITICAL SOURCES:

BOOKS

Giordano, Enrique, editor, *Poesia y poetica de Gonzalo Rojas,* Maiten (Santiago, Chile), 1987.
May, Hilda R., *La Poesia de Gonzalo Rojas,* Hiperion (Spain), 1991.*

ROMERO, Orlando 1945-

PERSONAL: Born September 24, 1945, in Santa Fe, NM; son of Jose (a machinist) and Ruby Anne Romero; married Rebecca Lopez (a journalist), February 10, 1968 (one source says February 23, 1967); children: Carlota Bernarda, Orlando Cervantes, Enrique Alvaro. *Education:* College of Santa Fe, B.A., 1974; University of Arizona, M.L.S., 1976. *Politics:* "A determination to save blue corn, blue sky, and New Mexico's earth." *Religion:* "Humanity revealed through the contemplative mysteries of God and Nature." *Avocational interests:* "I am a voracious reader. I sculpt in wood. I tie flies and I can squander my life away in the midst of a trout stream or in a field of ripening blue corn. I also like to build with adobe bricks. And conversation, be it with a philosophical hobo or a great man of letters."

ADDRESSES: Home—Rt. 1, Box 103, Santa Fe, NM 87501. *Office*—History Library, P.O. Box 2087, Santa Fe, NM 87504-2087.

CAREER: Office of the New Mexico Secretary of State, Santa Fe, aide, 1964-67; New Mexico State Library, Santa Fe, library assistant, 1967-69, Librarian I, 1976-79, Librarian for Southwest Studies, 1979-83; New Mexico State Supreme Court Law Library, Santa Fe, library assistant, 1969-74; Director of Northern New Mexico Regional Library, 1975-76; research librarian for the Museum of New Mexico, 1983—; New Mexico History Library, Palace of the Governors, Santa Fe, director, 1983—. Consultant, guest lecturer, sculptor, and painter; work on permanent exhibit at Folk Art Museum, Santa Fe.

MEMBER: New Mexico Preservation Coalition (board member), New Mexico Historical Society (former board member), Santa Fe Historical Society (board member, 1981-86); Santa Fe Council for the Arts (chair, 1981-86); Pojoaque Valley Water Users Association (vice president, 1988); Environmental Task Force for Sante Fe (founding member).

AWARDS, HONORS: Fellowship, Graduate Library Institute for Spanish–Speaking American, 1976; fellowship in creative writing, National Endowment for the Arts, 1979; Commission for Higher Education, New Mexico Eminent Scholars Program, 1989.

WRITINGS:

Nambe—Year One (novel; excerpts first appeared in *Puerto del Sol,* 1974, and *El Grito del Sol,*

January-March, 1976), Tonatiuh International (Berkeley, CA), 1976.

(With David Larkin) *Adobe: Building and Living with Earth,* photography by Michael Greeman, Houghton (Boston), 1994.

Also author of *The Day of the Wind* (short stories). Contributor to books, including *Southwest,* edited by Karl and Jane Kopp, Red Earth (Albuquerque, NM), 1977; *A Ceremony of Brotherhood: 1680-1980,* edited by Rudolfo A. Anaya and Simon J. Ortiz, Academia (Albuquerque), 1981. Contributor of weekly column for *Santa Fe Reporter,* 1988—. Contributor of numerous articles, short stories, and poems relating to the people and history of New Mexico and the Southwest. Work has been featured in periodicals such as *El Grito del Sol, De Colores* and *El Palacio.* Romero's papers are held by the Special Collections Department at the University of New Mexico, Albuquerque, and the New Mexico History Library, Santa Fe.

SIDELIGHTS: "Through his writings, Orlando Romero recreates an image of a people whose values and customs may soon be erased, or significantly altered, by forces dedicated to progress," wrote J. Allan Englekirk in the *Dictionary of Literary Biography.* A native of New Mexico, Romero's literary efforts "attempt to preserve the past for the future," continued Englekirk, "so that succeeding generations may be exposed to those beliefs most basic to traditional Hispanic culture in the southwestern United States." Englekirk sees Romero's grandfather, Enrique, as a primary influence in the writer's approach to man and nature: "A man tied to 'los tiempos de antes' (the bygone days), [Romero's] grandfather preferred traditional methods of irrigation, cultivation, and harvest and taught Orlando the value of a slower, more philosophical pace."

Critics have identified Romero as a Chicano author, a tag that does not please him. According to Englekirk, Romero "believes that the culture of the Southwest and West is too diverse to be identified by a single phrase: 'Chicano culture—you cannot mix together people from California, Arizona, southern Colorado . . . into a homogeneous bottle of milk. Our food is different, our thinking is different—we are united politically under *chicanismo*'. . . . When asked to define his literature, he prefers to consider it 'New Mexican literature.'"

Orlando Romero once explained of his work: "What motivates my writing? Primarily, *Nambe—Year One* was the beginning of self-realization, more precisely, an autobiographical way to state the Hispano's relationship to the earth. Ritual motivates me. Ritual as in the seasons, the menstrual cycles of streams and all the life therein. Wild dogs howling at the moon and barren wombs whispering the decay of autumn. Which in essence means redefining ritual.

"What motivates my writing? Hope for mankind and the eternal dream that we can live in peace with ourselves and the earth that sustains us. It is not concrete that inspires it, or cities like Albuquerque or Phoenix or Los Angeles, but ancient people against the background of eternally blue skies and their determination to remain self-sufficient despite the cost.

"My work is regional only in the sense that spawning salmon return to their place of birth, only in the sense that all of us are part of dark, brown earth and only in the sense that I am nourished by blue corn meal and blue skies."

Romero's novel *Nambe—Year One* was released in 1976. Englekirk described the work: "*Nambe—Year One* is written in the form of an autobiography narrated by Mateo Romero, a young man in his mid thirties who resides in Nambe. The events of the text . . . follow the flow of Mateo's thoughts as he envisions his existence. Though randomly presented, no stage of his life is left unportrayed. . . . Interspersed among the happenings of Mateo's life are stories based on folklore or related to episodes in the lives of his ancestors or other inhabitants of the region." "Much of the autobiographical detail describes Mateo's love for a Gypsy woman of enchanting beauty who," continued Englekirk, "is present in his life either physically or spiritually form the start. . . . Balanced against the protagonist's affection for the Gypsy is his deep-seated emotional attachment to the land and people of his region. The conflict of interest between these to forces confounds the narrator . . . and compels him to constant self-analysis." When summarizing the reviews of *Nambe—Year One,* Englekirk said: "Critical reaction to *Nambe—Year One* has been generally favorable." Among the praises Englekirk listed were remarks on "its three-dimensional treatment of time," "Romero's compelling portrayal of Hispano-Indian life and customs in New Mexico," and the novel's "local color." Not all comments were flattering, however; criticism cited by Englekirk included complaints of "repetitive imagery and for excessive attention directed to the Gypsy."

For the 1994 publication *Adobe: Building and Living with Earth* Romero collaborated with David Larkin and photographer Michael Greeman to create what an *American Heritage* reviewer called "a coffee-table book as simple and functional as its subject—mud houses." The work presents images and information on a range of adobe structures, "treat[ing] adobe with the same awe that must have filled . . . searching settlers."

BIOGRAPHICAL/CRITICAL SOURCES:

BOOKS

Dictionary of Literary Biography, Volume 82: *Chicano Writers, First Series,* Gale, 1989.

PERIODICALS

American Heritage, May-June, 1995, p. 99.
Explorations in Ethnic Studies, July, 1978.
La Luz, October, 1977.
Latin American Literary Review, fall/winter, 1978.
New Mexican, November, 1979.
World Literature Today, summer, 1974.*

*   *   *

ROMO-CARMONA, Mariana 1952-

PERSONAL: Born August 31, 1952, in Santiago, Chile; immigrated to the United States, 1966; became a naturalized U.S. citizen; daughter of Juan Jose Romo (an artist) and Adriana Maria Carmona (an artist); companion of June Chan; children: John Christian. *Ethnicity:* "Latina." *Education:* University of Connecticut, B.A. (Latin American and Spanish literature), 1983. *Avocational interests:* Playing the guitar, modern dancing, practicing martial arts (especially karate).

ADDRESSES: Office—Master of Fine Arts Program, Goddard College, Plainfield, VT 05667. *Agent*—c/o Latina Lesbian History Project, P.O. Box 850, Knickerbocker Station, New York, NY 10002. *E-mail*—romochan@juno.com.

CAREER: Conditions: Feminist Journal, editor (with others), 1988-92; *Queer City, the Portable Lower East Side,* editor (with others), 1992; *COLORLife!,* founder (with Lidell Jackson), 1992, managing editor (with others), 1992-94; Goddard College, Plainfield, VT, associate faculty member in the Master of Fine Arts Program, 1994—; MacDowell Colony, artist-in-residence, 1997; Millay Colony for the Arts, artist-in-residence, 1998; Norcroft Foundation, artist-in-residence, 1998. Also worked as a translator, publisher, teacher, radio commentator, lecturer, human rights activist, and community organizer.

AWARDS, HONORS: Fiction Prize, Astraea National Lesbian Action Foundation, 1991; Activist Award, Men of All Colors Together/New York, 1992; Paumanok Poetry Award semifinalist, State University of New York Farmingdale, 1996; Visionary and Leadership Award, Las Buenas Amigas, 1996; Anti-Violence Project Courage Award, 1997; Honoring Our Past Award, Audre Lorde Project, 1998.

WRITINGS:

NOVELS

Living at Night, Spinsters Ink (Duluth, MN), 1997.

COLLECTIONS

(Editor with Alma Gomez and Cherrie Moraga) *Cuentos: Stories by Latinas,* Kitchen Table: Women of Color Press (New York City), 1983.
Speaking Like an Immigrant: A Collection, Latina Lesbian History Project (New York City), 1999.

Contributor to books, including *Companeras: Latina Lesbians,* edited and compiled by Juanita Ramos, Latina Lesbian History Project, 1987, second edition published by Routledge (New York City), 1994; *Beyond Gender and Geography: American Women Writers,* East-West Press (New Delhi, India), 1994; *Lesbian Travels: A Literary Companion,* Whereabouts Press (San Francisco, CA), 1998; *Mom,* Alyson Books (Los Angeles, CA), 1998; *Pillow Talk,* Alyson Books, 1998; *Queer 13,* Rob Weisbach Books (New York City), 1998; and *A Woman Like That,* Avon Books (New York City), 1999.

WORK IN PROGRESS: Lo que queda en la memoria, a novel; *Book Ends,* a collection of novellas; *The Woods at the Bottom of the World,* a children's book.

SIDELIGHTS: Mariana Romo-Carmona's novel *Living at Night* is set in Connecticut in the 1970s. It features Erica Garcia, a young Hispanic woman who leaves college due to her mother's illness. Erica finds work as a nurse's aide on the night shift in a school and residential center for developmentally delayed people. At the center, she observes the struggles of her patients to maintain their dignity despite repeated

obstacles. Meanwhile, Erica's lover, Millie, wants her to find a day job so they can spend more time together. Erica must learn to balance her personal and professional relationships and values, all while asserting her identity as a Latina woman in a predominantly white community.

Reviewing *Living at Night* in the *Library Journal,* Editha Ann Wilberton noted that although the sections dealing with Garcia's personal life "can become painfully slow," she called the sections about 1970s institutional life "disturbingly accurate" and deemed the work "a decent first novel." *Phoebe* contributor Carolyn Morell, a social worker, claimed that "*Living at Night* is disquieting as well as enlightening," praising its "rich description of life inside the training school." *Booklist* contributor Whitney Scott declared the book "engrossing," observing that "Romo-Carmona draws us into the darkly compelling world of night work." According to *Calyx: A Journal of Art and Literature by Women* contributor Bonnie Blader, *Living at Night* "is not a 'coming of age' story; it is a story of 'coming into focus,'" adding that Romo-Carmona "ties the loose ends of her plot back into the cloth of the whole, making *Living at Night* a lesson in living for its readers." Reviewing the same work in *Sojourner: The Women's Forum,* Eleanor J. Bader concluded: "Romo-Carmona is well-attuned to sight, sound, people, and place. Like a journalist hellbent on social realism, she has conjured a late-night world that is peppered with conflict and passion. A good read and an inspiring example, *Living at Night* marks an audacious fictional debut by a highly talented and original storyteller."

With others, Romo-Carmona has edited the periodicals *Conditions: Feminist Journal* and *Queer City, the Portable Lower East Side.* She helped found *COLOR Life!* with Lidell Jackson and served as the magazine's managing editor with others. Romo-Carmona has co-edited collections of short stories and poetry, including *Cuentos: Stories by Latinas* (1983). She has written *Speaking like an Immigrant: A Collection* for the Latina Lesbian History Project and has contributed to books. She has also worked as a publisher, translator, and activist in addition to her work as a faculty member at Goddard College.

BIOGRAPHICAL/CRITICAL SOURCES:

PERIODICALS

Booklist, September 15, 1997, p. 210.
Calyx, summer, 1998, pp. 110-111.

Detour, November 7-13, 1997.
Discourse, Volume 21, number 3, 1999.
Gay Community News, March 22-April 4, 1992, pp. 9, 20.
La Voz, September, 1997.
Lesbian Review of Books, winter, 1997/1998.
Library Journal, August, 1997, p. 135.
Metroline, November, 1997.
Ms., November/December, 1997.
MultiCultural Review, June, 1998.
Phoebe, fall, 1998.
Sojourner, September, 1997.
Today's Books, January 19, 1998; March 29, 1999.

* * *

RULFO, Juan 1918-1986

PERSONAL: Born May 16, 1918, in Sayula, Jalisco, Mexico; died January 7, 1986, of a heart attack in Mexico City, Mexico; married Clara Aparicio in 1947; children: Francisco, Pablo, Juan Carlos, Claudia.

CAREER: Worked as an accountant and in several clerical positions; on staff of Mexican Immigration Department, beginning 1935, processed the crews of impounded German ships during World War II; member of sales staff, B.F. Goodrich Rubber Co., 1947-54; member of Papaloapan Commission, 1955; National Institute for Indigenous Studies, Mexico City, Mexico, beginning 1962, became director of editorial department. Adviser to writers at Centro Mexicano de Escritores.

MEMBER: Centro Mexicano de Escritores (fellow).

AWARDS, HONORS: Rockefeller grants, 1953 and 1954; Guggenheim fellowship, 1968; National Prize for Letters (Mexico), 1970; Principe de Asturias award (Spain), 1983.

WRITINGS:

FICTION

El llano en llamas y otros cuentos, Fondo de Cultura Economica, 1953, translation by George D. Schade published as *The Burning Plain and Other Stories,* University of Texas Press, 1967, 2nd Spanish edition, corrected and enlarged, Fondo de Cultura Economica, 1970.

Pedro Paramo (novel), Fondo de Cultura Economica, 1955, translation by Lysander Kemp published as *Pedro Paramo: A Novel of Mexico,* Grove, 1959, translation by Margaret Sayers Peden, Grove, 1994.
El gallo de oro y otros textos para cine, Ediciones Era, 1980.
Obras, Fondo de Cultura Economica (Mexico City), 1987.

OMNIBUS VOLUMES

Obra completa, Biblioteca Ayacucho, 1977.
Antologia personal, Nueva Imagen, 1978.

CONTRIBUTOR

Aberlardo Gomez Benoit, editor, *Antologia contemporanea del cuento hispano-americano* (title means "A Contemporary Anthology of the Hispanic-American Story"), Instituto Latinoamericano de Vinculacion Cultural, 1964.
Cronicas de Latinoamericano, Editorial Jorge Alvarez, 1968.

OTHER

Juan Rulfo: Autobiografia armada, compiled by Reina Roffe, Ediciones Corregidor, 1973.
(With others) *Juan Rulfo: Homenaje nacional,* with photographs by Rulfo, Instituto Nacional de Bellas Artes (Mexico City), 1980, 2nd edition published as *Inframundo: El Mexico de Juan Rulfo,* Ediciones del Norte (Hanover, NH), 1983, translation by Jo Anne Engelbert published as *Inframundo: The Mexico of Juan Rulfo,* Ediciones del Norte, 1983.
Los Cuadernos de Juan Rulfo, edited by Yvette Jimenez de Baez, Ediciones Era, 1994.
Arquitectura de Mexico: Fotografias de Juan Rulfo, Consejo Nacional para la Cultura y las Artes, 1994.

Also author of television scripts and film adaptations, beginning 1954, and *La cordillera* (title means "The Mountain Range"), a novel. Collaborator with Juan Arreola on the review *Pan. Pedro Paramo* was made into a film in the 1960s.

SIDELIGHTS: The late Mexican novelist Juan Rulfo was part of what Alan Riding in the *New York Times Magazine* called "the contemporary Latin American literary boom." Rulfo and such writers as Jorge Luis Borges, Julio Cortazar, Gabriel Garcia Marquez, and

Carlos Fuentes wrote imaginative fiction that was made available through translation to readers in the United States during the 1950s, 1960s, and early 1970s.

Unlike his literary colleagues, who prolifically turned out stories and novels, Rulfo established his reputation with a solitary collection of stories, *El llano en llamas y otros cuentos*—translated as *The Burning Plain and Other Stories*—and one novel, *Pedro Paramo*. Two characteristics of these Latin American writers were their special affinity for innovative narrative techniques and their style of interweaving the historical with the marvelous, called magic realism; both qualities are often mentioned by reviewers of Rulfo's work. In his introduction to *The Burning Plain and Other Stories,* George D. Schade used the story "Macario"—included in the collection—as an example of Rulfo's narrative style. "In 'Macario,'" Schade observed, "the past and present mingle chaotically, and frequently the most startling associations of ideas are juxtaposed, strung together by conjunctions which help to paralyze the action and stop the flow of time in the present."

In *Into the Mainstream: Conversations with Latin-American Writers,* Luis Harss and Barbara Dohmann comment on Rulfo's story "The Man," noting the multiple points of view and foreshadowing used to heighten the reader's identification with the protagonist. The narrative devices mentioned by Schade, Harss, and Dohmann are also found in Rulfo's *Pedro Paramo,* which Schade called "a bold excursion into modern techniques of writing." Using flashbacks, interior monologues and dialogues, and atemporal time-sequences, Rulfo creates what Enrique Anderson-Imbert claimed in *Spanish-American Literature: A History* is a "story . . . told in loops, forward, backward, [and] to the sides." The narrative technique demands a lot of the reader, but the story in itself is difficult. Halfway through the novel, for example, the reader realizes that all the characters are dead; the story all along has been the remembered history of ghosts conversing from their graves. Startling as this revelation is, the mingling of death and life is typical of Mexican culture. Commenting in a *Nation* essay, Earl Shorris noted: "Everywhere in the novel, death is present: not the hidden, feared death we know in the United States but Mexican death, the death that is neither the beginning nor the end, the death that comes and goes in the round of time." Shorris observed that the constant reminders of death in Mexican life destroy "the distinction between [this] life" and the next. This hazy line between life and death accentuates the author's deliberately ambiguous delineation of scenes, narrators, and past and present time. The technical difficulties with which Rulfo confronts the reader become the framework for what Kessel Schwartz called in *A New History of Spanish-American Fiction* "an ambiguous and magical world, a kind of timeless fable of life and death" where historical facts—references to actual events in Mexican history—and fictive details are fused.

In his analysis of *Pedro Paramo* appearing in *Tradition and Renewal: Essays on Twentieth-Century Latin-American Literature and Culture,* Luis Leal observed that while Rulfo's style was experimental, it was also firmly rooted in the historical reality of Mexico. Leal wrote: "The scenes are juxtaposed, united only by the central theme and lyrical motifs. . . . The novel, a mixture of realism and fantasy . . . has been created through the use of images, which, although poetic, are structured in a language that is characteristic of the countryside." Rulfo's sparse, dry prose reflects the parched, stark Mexican landscape. Harss and Dohmann remarked: "His language is as frugal as his world, reduced almost to pure heartbeat. . . . He sings the swan song of blighted regions gangrened by age, where misery has opened wounds that burn under an eternal midday sun, where a pestilent fate has turned areas that were once rolling meadows and grasslands into fetid open graves. . . . He writes with a sharp edge, carving each word out of hard rock, like an inscription on a tombstone." According to Irving A. Leonard in the *Saturday Review,* "the bleak, harsh surroundings" Rulfo described with his "bare phrases" reflected his "pessimistic view of man's condition. Murder, incest, adultery, death overpowering life, violence in varied forms are predominant themes, unrelieved by humor or love." Although Rulfo published a collection of film scripts and worked on the manuscript for another novel, *La cordillera,* for the rest of his life, further success as a writer eluded him. While a London *Times* reporter noted that *Pedro Paramo* "will be remembered as a unique achievement," the same writer believed that Rulfo himself seemed content to be known merely as "the master who could not write a second masterpiece."

BIOGRAPHICAL/CRITICAL SOURCES:

BOOKS

Anderson-Imbert, Enrique, *Spanish-American Literature: A History, Volume II: 1910-1963,* 2nd edition, revised and updated by Elaine Malley, Wayne State University Press, 1969.

Contemporary Literary Criticism, Volume 8, Gale, 1978, Volume 80, 1994.

Dictionary of Literary Biography, Volume 113: *Modern Latin-American Fiction Writers,* Gale, 1992.

Forster, Merlin H., editor, *Tradition and Renewal: Essays on Twentieth-Century Latin American Literature and Culture,* University of Illinois Press, 1975.

Harss, Luis, and Barbara Dohmann, *Into the Mainstream: Conversations with Latin-American Writers,* Harper, 1967.

Schwartz, Kessel, *A New History of Spanish-American Fiction,* Volume II, University of Miami Press, 1971.

PERIODICALS

Christian Science Monitor, January 4, 1968.
English Journal, January, 1974.
Guardian Weekly, June 12, 1994.
Hispania, December, 1971; September, 1974; March, 1975.
Los Angeles Times, January 9, 1986.
Nation, May 15, 1982.
National Observer, March 24, 1973.
New Statesman, March 11, 1994, p. 38.

New York Herald Tribune Book Review, August 2, 1959.
New York Times Book Review, June 7, 1959; August 6, 1995, p. 19.
New York Times Magazine, March 13, 1983.
San Francisco Chronicle, August 30, 1959.
Saturday Review, June 22, 1968.
Times Literary Supplement, February 5, 1960.
Wilson Library Bulletin, February, 1995.

OBITUARIES:

PERIODICALS

New York Times, January 9, 1986.
Times (London), January 10, 1986.
Washington Post, January 11, 1986.*

*   *   *

RuPAUL
  See CHARLES, RuPaul Andre

S

SABATO, Ernesto (R.) 1911-

PERSONAL: Born June 24, 1911, in Rojas, Argentina; son of Francisco Sabato (a mill owner) and Juana Ferrari; married Matilde Kusminsky-Richter, 1936; children: Jorge Federico, Mario. *Education:* National University of La Plata, Ph.D., 1937; additional study at Joliot-Curie Laboratory (Paris), 1938, and Massachusetts Institute of Technology, 1939.

ADDRESSES: Home—1676 Santos Lugares, Buenos Aires, Argentina. *Office*—Langeri 3135, Santos Lugares, Argentina.

CAREER: National University of La Plata, La Plata, Argentina, professor of theoretical physics, 1940-43; novelist and essayist, 1943—. Guest lecturer at universities throughout the United States and Europe. Chairman of National Commission on the Disappearance of Persons (Argentina), 1983.

AWARDS, HONORS: Argentine Association for the Progress of Science fellowship in Paris, 1937; sash of honor from Argentine Writers Society and Municipal Prose prize from the City of Buenos Aires, both 1945, both for *Uno y el universo;* prize from the Institute of Foreign Relations (West Germany; now Germany), 1973; Grand Prize of Honor from the Argentine Writers Society, from Premio Consagracion Nacional (Argentina), and from Chevalier des Arts et des Lettres (France), all 1974; Prix au Meilleur Livre Etranger (Paris), 1977, for *Abaddon, el Exterminador;* Gran Cruz al Merito Civil (Spain) and Chevalier de la Legion D'Honneur (France), both 1979; Gabriela Mistral Prize from Organization of American States, 1984; Miguel de Cervantes Prize from the Spanish Ministry of Culture, 1985; Commandeur de la Legion d'Honneur (France), 1987; Jerusalem Literary Prize, Wolf Foundation, 1989.

WRITINGS:

NOVELS

El tunel, Sur, 1948, translation by Harriet de Onis published as *The Outsider,* Knopf, 1950, translation by Margaret Sayers Peden published as *The Tunnel,* Ballantine, 1988.
Sobre heroes y tumbas, Fabril, 1961, reprinted, Seix Barral, 1981, excerpt published as *Un dios desconocido: Romance de la muerte de Juan Lavalle (de "Sobre heroes y tumbas"),* A. S. Dabini, 1980, translation by Stuart M. Gross of another excerpt published as Report onReport on the Blind in *TriQuarterly,* Fall-Winter, 1968-69, translation by Helen Lane of entire in *Tri-Quarterly,* Fall-Winter, 1968-69, translation by Helen Lane of entire novel published as *On Heroes and Tombs,* David Godine, 1981.
Abaddon, el Exterminador (title means "Abaddon, The Exterminator"), Sudamericana, 1974, translation by Andrew Hurley published as *The Angel of Darkness,* Ballantine (New York City), 1991.

ESSAYS

Uno y el universo (title means "One and the Universe"), Sudamericana, 1945.
Hombres y engranajes (title means "Men and Gears"), Emece, 1951, reprinted, 1985.

Heterodoxia (title means "Heterodoxy"), Emece, 1953.

El otro rostro del peronismo: Carta abierta a Mario Amadeo (title means "The Other Face of Peronism: Open Letter to Mario Amadeo"), Lopez, 1956.

El caso Sabato: Torturas y libertad de prensa—Carta abierta al Gral. Aramburu (title means "Sabato's Case: Torture and Freedom of the Press—Open Letter to General Aramburu"), privately printed, 1956.

Tango: Discusion y clave (title means "Tango: Discussion and Key"), Losada, 1963.

El escritor y sus fantasmas (title means "The Writer and His Ghosts"), Aguilar, 1963.

Tres aproximaciones a la literatura de nuestro tiempo: Robbe-Grillet, Borges, Sartre (title means "Approaches to the Literature of Our Time . . ."; essays), Universitaria (Chile), 1968.

La convulsion politica y social de nuestro tiempo (title means "The Political and Social Upheaval of Our Time"), Edicom, 1969.

Ernesto Sabato: Claves politicas (title means "Ernesto Sabato: Political Clues"), Alonso, 1971.

La cultura en la encrucijada nacional (title means "Culture in the National Crossroads"), Ediciones de Crisis, 1973.

(With Jorge Luis Borges) *Dialogos* (title means "Dialogues"), Emece, 1976.

Apologias y rechazos (title means "Apologies and Rejections"), Seix Barral, 1979.

La robotizacion del hombre y otras paginas de ficcion y reflexion (title means "The Robotization of Man and Other Pages of Fiction and Reflection"), Centro Editorial del America Latina, 1981.

The Writer in the Catastrophe of Our Time, Council Oak Books, 1990.

Informe Sobre Ciegos, Anaya & M. Muchnik, 1994.

COLLECTIONS

Obras de ficcion (title means "Works of Fiction"; contains *El tunel* and *Sobre heroes y tumbas*), Losada, 1966.

Itinerario (title means "Itinerary"; selections from Sabato's novels and essays), Sur, 1969.

Obras: Ensayos (title means "Works: Essays"), Losada, 1970.

Paginas vivas (title means "Living Pages"), Kapelusz, 1974.

Antologia (title means "Anthology"), Libreria del Colegio, 1975.

Narrativa completa (title means "Complete Narrative"), Seix Barral, 1982.

Paginas de Ernesto Sabato (title means "Pages from Ernesto Sabato"), Celtia (Buenos Aires), 1983.

OTHER

(Editor) *Mitomagia: Los temas del misterio* (title means "Mitomagia: Themes of the Mysterious"), Ediciones Latinoamericanas, 1969.

(Author of introduction) *Testimonios: Chile, septiembre, 1973* (title means "Eyewitness Accounts: Chile, September, 1973," Jus, 1973.

(With Antonio Berni) *Cuatro hombres de pueblo,* Libreria de la Ciudad, 1979.

(Editor with Anneliese von der Lipper) *Viaje a los mundos imaginarios,* Legasa, 1983.

Contributor to *Sur* and other periodicals.

SIDELIGHTS: When one considers that Argentine novelist and essayist Ernesto Sabato published only three novels, the impact he had on Hispanic literature is remarkable: His first novel, *The Tunnel,* was a best-seller in his native land; his second work of fiction, *On Heroes and Tombs,* according to Emir Rodriguez Monegal in the *Borzoi Anthology of Latin American Literature,* "became one of the most popular contemporary novels in Latin America." *Abaddon, el Exterminador* ("Abbadon, the Exterminator"), Sabato's third novel, was similarly acclaimed and was granted France's highest literary award—the Prix au Meilleur Livre Etranger. Sabato's importance was officially recognized in 1985 when he received the first Miguel de Cervantes Prize (considered the equivalent of the Nobel in the Hispanic world) from Spain's King Juan Carlos. Harley Dean Oberhelman, in his study of the author titled *Ernest Sabato,* calls Sabato "Argentina's most discussed contemporary novelist." His appeal rests largely in his portrayals of Argentine society under the domination of military strongmen such as Juan Peron and others, with his recurrent themes of incest, blindness, insanity, and abnormal psychology reflecting the distress of the Argentine people.

Born into a large, prosperous family of Italian origin, at age thirteen Sabato left the rural community where he had grown up to attend school in the city of La Plata. The transition from familial life to life alone in a unfamiliar urban area was a disturbing one for the future writer, and Sabato found order in his otherwise turbulent world in the study of mathematics. His academic studies were briefly interrupted for a five-year period, however, when he became involved in the Argentine communist movement. Soon, upon learning of Stalinist atrocities, he lost faith in the communist cause and decided to retreat again to his academic work.

Sabato's success as a student earned him a research fellowship for study in Paris, and, while there his interest in writing was born. Deeply impressed by the surrealist movement, he secretly began writing a novel. Although his writing started to play an increasingly important role in his life, Sabato continued his scientific research and accepted a teaching position upon his return to Argentina. Nonetheless, his literary efforts continued and he became a regular contributor to the popular Argentine magazine, *Sur*. Teaching was to remain his livelihood until 1943 when a conflict with the Juan Peron government resulted in his dismissal from his posts.

Commenting on his departure from the scientific world, Sabato wrote in an autobiographical essay appearing in English translation in *Salmagundi*, "The open, public transition from physics to literature was not an easy one for me; on the contrary, it was painfully complicated. I wrestled with my demons a long time before I came to a decision in 1943—when I resolved to sequester myself, with wife and son, in a cabin in the sierras of Cordoba, far from the civilized world. It was not a rational decision. . . . But in crucial moments of my existence I have always trusted more in instinct than in ideas and have constantly been tempted to venture where reasonable people fear to tread."

While living in the cabin for a year Sabato wrote an award-winning book of essays, *Uno y el universo*, in which he condemned the moral neutrality of science. Two years later his first novel, *The Tunnel*, appeared. Profoundly influenced by psychological thought and existential in tone, the work evoked comparison to the writings of French authors Albert Camus and Jean-Paul Sartre. It is the story of an Argentine painter who recounts the events leading up to his murder of his mistress. As an exercise in self-analysis for the lonely painter, unable to communicate his thoughts and feelings, *The Tunnel* contains many of the themes found in Sabato's later work. "The almost total isolation of a man in a world dominated by science and reason," notes Oberhelman, "is the most important of these themes, but at the same time the reader sees the inability of man to communicate with others, an almost pathological obsession with blindness, and a great concern for Oedipal involvement as important secondary themes."

The landmark of Sabato's work stands to be his 1961 novel, *On Heroes and Tombs,* which appeared in an English edition in 1982. It tells the story of Martin del Castillo and his love for Alejandra Vidal Olmos.

Alejandra's father, Fernando Vidal Olmos, apparently involved in an incestuous relationship with his daughter, is another important figure in the book, along with Bruno Bassan, a childhood friend of Fernando. The work is lengthy and complex and has spawned numerous critical interpretations. "When it first appeared . . . ," writes *Newsweek* contributor Jim Miller, "Ernesto Sabato's Argentine epic was widely praised. This belated translation finally lets Americans see why. Bewitched, baroque, monumental, his novel is a stunning symphony of dissonant themes—a Gothic dirge, a hymn to hope, a tango in hell." Commenting on the novel's intricacy, John Butt observes in the *Times Literary Supplement,* "This monster novel . . . works on so many levels, leads down so many strange paths to worlds of madness, surrealistic self-analysis and self-repudiation, and overloads language so magnificently and outrageously, that the reader comes out of it with his critical nerve shot, tempted to judge it as 'great' without knowing why." Also noting the novel's multifaceted contents, Ronald Christ in his *Commonweal* review refers to it as "wild, hypnotizing, and disturbing."

On Heroes and Tombs is divided into four parts, the third being a novel-within-a-novel called "Report on the Blind." *Review* contributor William Kennedy characterizes this portion of the novel—a first-person exploration of Fernando's theories about a conspiracy of blind people who rule the world—as "a tour de force, a document which is brilliant in its excesses, a surreal journey into the depths of Fernando's personal, Boschian hells, which in their ultimate landscapes are the provinces of a 'terrible nocturnal divinity, a demoniacal specter that surely held supreme power over life and death.'" In his *Washington Post Book World* review Salman Rushdie calls this section "the book's magnificent high point and its metaphysical heart." In Sabato's hands Fernando's paranoidal ravings fuse with the rest of the novel making the work at once a cultural, philosophical, theological, and sociological study of man and his struggle with the dark side of his being. According to Oberhelman, *On Heroes and Tombs* "without a doubt is the most representative national novel of Argentina written in the twentieth century." Kennedy describes the impact of the work when he concludes: "We read Sabato and we shudder, we are endlessly surprised, we exult, we are bewildered, fearful, mesmerized. He is a writer of great talent and imagination."

Sabato's third novel, *Abbadon, el Exterminador,* was published in Spanish in 1974 and in English translation as *The Angel of Darkness* in 1991. The novel's structure is circular, with the beginning of the novel corresponding to the end of the story in chronological terms. The original Spanish title refers to a character in the Book of Revelation, and the story revolves around a writer named Ernesto Sabato who becomes a four-foot–tall bat and who may or may not be the "angel of darkness" of the title. The plot is filled with nightmarish events, political intrigue, and "a huge cast of eccentric characters from every walk of Argentine life," notes Allen Josephs in the *New York Times Book Review*. Critics note that readers unfamiliar with Sabato's previous novels will have difficulty understanding the plot, since many of the characters from the two earlier novels reappear here. Writing in the *Times Literary Supplement*, John Butt remarks that *The Angel of Darkness* is "a magnificent, haunting, often horrifying novel whose every page confronts us with some paradox central to our condition." Butt also avers that the novel is "easily as impressive" as Sabato's earlier masterpiece, *On Heroes and Tombs*. While *Spectator* reviewer Cressida Connolly feels that "Sabato's failings are all flaws of excess" and that "the vast surfeit of story strands makes the plot unmanageably bulky," she also reserves high praise for the novel by comparing it to a painting by Francis Bacon: "You may recoil at the image, but you could not fail to be awed by the technique, and you recognise at once that its true subject is the human condition." Josephs explains that "Not everyone will want to wrestle with this intransigent angel of a book, but the undaunted will encounter a truly hellish match." And Butt concludes that *The Angel of Darkness* is "a masterpiece of bitter and sophisticated irony."

In addition to his award-winning novels, Sabato has also produced numerous essay collections. Although most of these have not been translated into English, one that has is *The Writer in the Catastrophe of Our Time*. The forty essays in this collection focus on art, writing, and philosophy, revealing Sabato's continual preoccupation with the meaning and impact of artistic pursuits.

BIOGRAPHICAL/CRITICAL SOURCES:

BOOKS

Contemporary Literary Criticism, Gale, Volume 10, 1979, Volume 23, 1983.
Dictionary of Literary Biography, Volume 145: *Modern Latin-American Fiction Writers, Second Series,* Gale, 1994.
Hispanic Writers, Gale, 1991.

Oberhelman, Harley Dean, *Ernesto Sabato,* Twayne, 1970.
Rodriguez Monegal, Emir, *The Borzoi Anthology of Latin American Literature,* Knopf, 1986.

PERIODICALS

Commonweal, June 18, 1982.
Hispanofila, September, 1991.
Library Journal, July, 1990, p. 97.
London Review of Books, January 27, 1994, p. 23.
Modern Fiction Studies, Autumn, 1986.
Newsweek, September 21, 1981.
New York Times Book Review, August 28, 1988; December 29, 1991, p. 13.
Publishers Weekly, June 15, 1990, p. 64; August 9, 1991.
Review, May-August, 1981.
Review of Contemporary Fiction, fall, 1990, p. 226.
Salmagundi, Spring-Summer, 1989.
Spectator, May 30, 1992, p. 31.
Times Literary Supplement, August 13, 1982; May 29, 1992, p. 22.
Washington Post Book World, August 16, 1981.*

*   *   *

SACASTRU, Martin
See BIOY CASARES, Adolfo

*   *   *

SAENZ, Jaime 1921-1986

PERSONAL: Born October 8, 1921, in La Paz, Bolivia; died of malnutrition, August 13, 1986; married.

CAREER: Poet and novelist.

WRITINGS:

El Escalpelo (poetic prose; title means "The Scalpel"), Talleres Graficos El Progreso (La Paz, Bolivia), 1955.
Muerte por el Tacto (poems), Editora Nacional (La Paz), 1957.
Aniversario de una Vision (poems; title means "Anniversary of a Vision"), Empresa Editora Burillo (La Paz), 1960.

Visitante Profundo, Empresa Editora Burillo (La Paz), 1964.

El Frio; Muerte por el Tacto; Aniversario de una Vision (poems), Cooperativa de Artes Graficas E. Burillo (La Paz), 1967.

Recorrer Esta Distancia, Cooperativa de Artes Graficas E. Burillo (La Paz), 1973.

Obra Poetica (poems; contains *El Escalpelo, Muerte por el Tacto, Aniversario de una Vision, Visitante Profundo, El Frio,* and *Recorrer Esta Distancia*), Biblioteca del Sesquicentenario de la Republica (La Paz), 1975.

Bruckner: Las Tinieblas, Difusion (La Paz), 1978.

Felipe Delgado (novel), Difusion (La Paz), 1979.

Imagenes Pacenas, Difusion (La Paz), 1979.

Al Pasar un Cometa, Ediciones Altiplano (La Paz), 1982.

La Noche, Talleres Escuela de Artes Graficas del Colegio Don Bosco (La Paz), 1984.

Los Cuartos (novel; title means "The Rooms"), Ediciones Altiplano (La Paz), 1985.

Vidas y Muertes (autobiography; title means "Lives and Deaths"), Ediciones Huayna Potosi (La Paz), 1986.

La Piedra Iman (autobiography; title means "The Stone Magnet"), Ediciones Huayna Potosi (La Paz), 1989.

Los Papeles de Narciso Lima-Acha (novel; title means "The Papers of Narciso Lima-Acha"), Instituto Boliviano de Cultura (La Paz), 1991.

Contributor to periodicals, including *Mundo Nuevo.*

SIDELIGHTS: "Jaime Saenz is one of the most complex and interesting writers of modern Bolivia," declared Javier Sanjines C., in the *Dictionary of Literary Biography.* "Irrational and oblivious to the construction of clear and well-defined meanings, his work occupies an exceptional place in Bolivian literature." As challenging and confusing as his work might be, repelling the reader with the horrors he describes, while at the same time compelling one to explore the world and the self through unique perspectives, Saenz maintained a devoutly loyal following throughout his life. He was acclaimed as both a poet and a novelist of the grotesque.

Sanjines declared: "Like few other authors, his narrative flows from a personal poetic universe that cannot be considered separately from the writer's eccentric life." Saenz spent his life in the city of La Paz, where he immersed himself in the seamy, hedonistic company of drunks and *aparapitas,* or freeloaders. He

consumed dangerous amounts of alcohol on a regular basis, inhabiting a dark underworld in which the real, the magical, and the impossible could mingle and overlap. He haunted the city morgue, preoccupied by cadavers, death, and decay. The two autobiographical works that were published after Saenz' death reveal a nocturnal, antisocial individual whose assimilation into anything resembling a normal family was marginal at best. He married and apparently respected the institution of marriage, according to his account in *La Piedra Iman,* but his own nature and behavior negated any possibility of a lasting, loving relationship. Despite a loyal coterie of devotees and friends, whose lives he recorded in *Vidas y Muertes,* Saenz died of malnutrition at the age of sixty-four. The only positive figure in his life seems to have been his aunt Esther, who he immortalized as the protagonist of the novel *Los Cuartos.*

From this solitary and eccentric life emerged what Sanjines called "a unique and personal vision of the world, a vision in which the interplay between death and life is constantly present." He added, "For Saenz the profound essence of being is completely at odds with the material appearance of things." The physical body becomes nothing more than a vehicle for the essence of life, and the difference between the concepts of "you" and "I" become inextricably blurred. In the poetry collection *Aniversario de una Vision* the blending of "self" and "other" leads to hallucinations, what Sanjines described as "the indefinite postponement of identity," and ultimately the self-destruction of the body. In the poetic prose collection *El Escalpelo,* Saenz relates stories that expand the theme of physical anomaly and decay and its relationship to "the ambivalent feeling of the divided self," as Sanjines commented; ". . .there is a relation between his fractured ego and the constant distortions of reality" In such fiction, the critic suggested, "Saenz does not address the rationalist or the scientist in the reader but the child or the potential psychotic."

The poems and stories are forerunners of what some critics consider to be Saenz's masterpiece—the novel *Felipe Delgado.* Sanjines wrote: "Corsino Ordonez's dark cellar, lost in the cold nights of the *aparapitas* (freeloaders) of La Paz, is the privileged meeting place for Felipe Delgado, the protagonist, and his humorous, eccentric friends. Here, while they consume alcohol by the gallons, they also reflect upon the world . . . [and] Felipe Delgado carries on the search for his meaningful self" The search raises demons, horrifying apparitions, and sordid nightmares that threaten Felipe's sanity and propel him toward self-destruction. To his irrational mind, the only way to release his pure, inner essence is to destroy the physical body in which it is trapped; his weapon of choice is the alcohol in Ordonez's cellar. Sanjines observed: "*Felipe Delgado,* a novel of the ridiculous and the terrible, shocks the reader's consciousness and rationality because corporeal waste and refuse provoke cultural and individual horror and disgust symptomatic of the inability of Western culture to accept the body's materiality, limits, and mortality. . . . The pestiferous apparitions that Felipe sees and smells are things that the sane human being . . . must ignore, repress, or flatly deny."

Saenz explored similar themes in all of his writing, including the novel *Los Papeles de Narciso Lima-Acha,* which clarifies some issues that were left ambiguous in *Felipe Delgado.* For example, by representing the homosexuality of Narciso as a form of self-love in the search for identity, he makes it clear, according to Sanjines, that the achievement of love renders the object of love—the body, male or female—irrelevant.

Published after the author's death, the novel capped an intense career dedicated to the search for a deep, if highly subjective, truth. Sanjines summarized: "In his literary endeavors Saenz, the solitary scrutinizer of the night side of the city, was revered by his followers as a source of poetic knowledge. Though disquieting as his eccentricities may have been, they sustain his impressive literary production and make it impossible to forget him"

BIOGRAPHICAL/CRITICAL SOURCES:

BOOKS

Dictionary of Literary Biography, Volume 145: *Modern Latin-American Fiction Writers, Second Series,* edited by William Luis and Ann Gonzalez, Gale (Detroit, MI), 1994, pp. 278-84.*

*   *   *

SALAS, Floyd Francis 1931-

PERSONAL: Born January 24, 1931, in Walsenburg, CO; son of Edward (a restaurant owner) and Anita (a housewife; maiden name, Sanchez) Salas; married Velva Daryl Harris (a nursery school owner), January, 1948 (divorced, 1970); married Virginia Ann Staley, June 25, 1979 (divorced, 1981); children: Gregory Francis. *Education:* Attended College of Arts and Crafts, 1950-54, Oakland Junior College, 1955-56, and University of California, Berkeley, 1956-57; San Francisco State College (now University), B.A., 1963, M.A., 1965. *Politics:* Democrat. *Religion:* "Agnostic-Theist."

ADDRESSES: Home—1206 Delaware St., Berkeley, CA 94702. *Agent*—Linda Allen, 1949 Green St. No. 5, San Francisco, CA 94123.

CAREER: San Francisco State University, San Francisco, CA, lecturer in English, 1966-67, state coordinator of Poetry in the Schools, 1973-76; writer, 1967-75; Peralta College for Non-Traditional Studies, Berkeley, CA, instructor in creative writing, 1975-76; University of California, Berkeley, assistant boxing coach, 1975—, lecturer in English, 1977-78; writer, 1978-80; Foothill College, Los Altos, CA, lecturer in creative writing, 1979—. Sonoma State University, Rohnert Park, California, instructor in English, 1984—. Teacher of creative writing at correctional camp for youth, Folsom State Prison, San Quentin Prison, and private workshop classes.

AWARDS, HONORS: Rockefeller Foundation scholar at El Centro Mexicano de Escritores, 1958; Joseph Henry Jackson Award from the San Francisco Foundation, 1964, for *Tattoo the Wicked Cross;* Eugene F. Saxon fellowship, fellowship from National Endowment for the Arts, 1978; Bay Area writing project fellowship, 1984.

WRITINGS:

NOVELS

Tattoo the Wicked Cross (novel), Grove, 1967.
What Now My Love (novella), Grove, 1970.
Lay My Body on the Line (novel), Y'bird Press, 1978.
Buffalo Nickel (novel), Arte Publico Press, 1992.
State of Emergency (novel), Arte Publico Press, 1994.

EDITOR AND CONTRIBUTOR

I Write What I Want, San Francisco State University, 1974.
Word Hustlers, Word Hustlers Press, 1976.
To Build a Fire, Mark Ross Publishers, 1977.
Stories and Poems From Close to Home, Ortalda & Associates, 1986.

OTHER

Color of My Living Heart (poetry), Arte Publico Press, 1996.

Work represented in anthologies, including *California Childhood, The San Francisco Bark, Calafia, Many Californias, Short Fiction by Hispanic Writers of the United States, Forgotten Pages of American Literature,* and *Chicano Voices.* Contributor of poems, articles, and reviews to periodicals, including *Writer, Transfer, Library Journal,* and *Hyperion,* and to newspapers, including the *Los Angeles Times, San Diego Reader,* and *Oakland Tribune.*

Salas's papers are in the Floyd Salas Collection, Bancroft Library, University of California, Berkeley.

SIDELIGHTS: Floyd Francis Salas once noted of his career "Boxing and writing have been entwined throughout my life. I went to the University of California on a boxing scholarship, the very first one offered there. I found that fighting and writing complemented each other. Both require the same basic traits of character: dedication, durability, and courage, as well as the need to be spiritually pure and humble if you want to do well. I teach boxing the same way I teach writing. Both are very simple, composed of only three technical elements each. In boxing, the elements are the jab, the cross, and the hook. All punches are one of the three. In writing, the elements are description, narration, and dialogue. All writing is one or another, or a combination of them.

"Those who make a total commitment of self and devotion to the ideal of either writing or fighting become excellent by their commitment. This [belief] in commitment is rooted in two medieval models, the samurai warrior of Japan and the Knights of the Round Table of England. The only knight who could pull the sword from the stone was the knight with the purest character. Among samurai contenders, the greatest warrior was the one with the greatest character. So I teach my students in fighting and writing that the fighter or the writer with the greatest character will win the boxing match or become a successful professional writer."

Salsa also added: "Being a poet and a novelist, I have two views of the creative writing process but they are related. Substance is primary, style is secondary. There is only one thing that will make a work of writing live and this is spirit. Styles change with the fashions of the time."

"A poem exists for only one reason: to convey the feelings, the soul, of one person, the poet, to the feelings, the soul, of another person, the reader. A work of fiction exists for only one reason: to tell a story about the feelings, the soul, of one or more persons, the characters, to the feelings, the soul, of another person, the reader.

"Style is only a medium, a means to an end in both poetry and fiction. All consideration of language, of ideas, of symbols and metaphors serve only one function: to convey the soul of a living being to the souls of other living beings and in that process break us out of our isolation and oneliness, put us in touch with the universal spirit and make our lives richer and more meaningful in spite of the doom that awaits us all."

Salas described *Buffalo Nickel* as "a memoir in the form of a novel about a writer and his older, drug addict brother." The author detailed how "it took me thirty-five years to write *Buffalo Nickel,*" from its genesis as a short story based on an incident involving his brother Al through "an August day in 1966, in a hundred-year-old cabin in Big Sur . . . [when] I wrote out of my great sadness and loss, at the death of our love, which was as great as any brotherly love that ever existed. [Al] was like a father and a friend at his best, during my early teens, and like a leech and a scurrilous enemy incapable of true love after he got hooked. From that came the novel, *Gin for Xmas,* which I then sold to Grove Press the following year." But Salas was unsatisfied with the text after rereading it and withdrew the book. Later, a short story he wrote for the *California Childhood* anthology formed the groundwork upon which the final version of the novel—now called *Buffalo Nickel*—was built. "I then took all the autobiographical chapters of the novel, *Gin for Xmas,* and rewrote them in the first person . . . and told the story of my brother and me," Salas continued. "I called the book a memoir to indicate that it was a limited recounting of my past, limited to one main subject: my relationship with my brother Al."

Salas described *State of Emergency* as "about a student leader who leaves the United States when Bobby Kennedy is killed to get away from the political murders in the United States and write a novel about his own battles with the secret police and how they infiltrate the student movement. The CIA sets out to stop him, without killing him, trying to co-opt his girlfriend and keep him from writing his book as he travels in Europe and North Africa in search of love and artistic and political freedom. This leads to suffering and violence. They force him back to the United

States again, like they forced those famous political rebels of the sixties, Eldridge Cleaver and Timothy Leary, back. Yet the end of the book is a triumph of love and art over the forces of Franco and fascism. Two very famous writers are in the book by name, Norman Mailer and James Jones, though only Norman Mailer makes an actual physical appearance."

While the novel was written between 1972 and 1976, its publication was delayed, Salas explained because "there was a cold war then and pre-censorship was the order of the day. That war is over and now material like mine, about a liberal, somewhat anarchic artist fighting the military state, can be published, because the great enemy, Communism, is no longer there. A seventeen-year wait has been normal for me and it's worth it, just to see the books appear in print."

Salas's first book of verse was published in 1996. *Color of My Living Heart* includes poems focusing on the weightiness of emotions, related through "visceral metaphors," according to a *Publishers Weekly* reviewer. The reviewer noted that the poems reveal that Salas "finds that the throb of existence nearly always has a sexual component."

BIOGRAPHICAL/CRITICAL SOURCES:

BOOKS

Dictionary of Literary Biography, Volume 82: *Chicano Writers,* Gale, 1989.

PERIODICALS

Americas Review, fall-winter, 1994, p. 127.
Best Sellers, October 1, 1967.
Bookwatch, July, 1996, p. 7.
Hudson Review, winter, 1967-68.
Nation, January 18, 1993, p. 65.
Negro Digest, June, 1968.
New York Times Book Review, September 17, 1967.
Publishers Weekly, September 30, 1996, p. 20.
Time, September 8, 1967.*

*   *   *

SALINAS, Luis Omar 1937-

PERSONAL: Born June 27, 1937, in Robstown, TX; son of Rosendo and Olivia (Trevino) Salinas. *Education:* Attended Fresno State University, 1967-72.

ADDRESSES: Home—2009 Ninth St., Sanger, CA 93652.

CAREER: Poet, editor, and interpreter.

AWARDS, HONORS: California English Teachers citation, 1973; Stanley Kunitz Poetry Prize, 1980, for *Afternoon of the Unreal;* Earl Lyon Award, 1980; General Electric Foundation Award, 1983.

WRITINGS:

Crazy Gypsy: Poems (includes "Sunday . . . Dig the Empty Sounds," "Crazy Gypsy," "The Train," "Aztec Angel," "Mexico Age Four," and "Guevara"), Origenes Publications, 1970.
(Editor with Lillian Faderman) *From the Barrio: A Chicano Anthology,* Canfield Press, 1973.
(With others) *Entrance: Four Chicano Poets; Leonard Adame, Luis Omar Salinas, Gary Soto, Ernesto Trejo* (anthology), Greenfield Review Press, 1975.
I Go Dreaming Serenades (poetry), Mango, 1979.
Afternoon of the Unreal (poetry), Abramas Publications, 1980.
Prelude to Darkness (poetry), Mango, 1981.
Darkness under the Trees: Walking behind the Spanish (poetry; includes "You Are Not Here"), Chicano Studies Library Publications, University of California, 1982.
The Sadness of Days: Selected and New Poems, Arte Publico, 1987.

Also author of the poems "Many Things of Death" and "What Is Poverty." Editor of *Backwash* at Fresno State University, 1969-70. Poems have been anthologized in *Speaking for Ourselves: American Ethnic Writing,* edited by Lillian Faderman, Scott Foresman & Co., 1969; *Mexican-American Authors,* edited by Amerigo Paredes and Raymund Paredes, Houghton, 1972; *We Are Chicanos,* edited by Philip D. Ortego, Washington Square Press, 1973; *Time to Greeze! Incantations from the Third World,* edited by Janice Mirikitani and others, Glide Publications, 1974; *Settling America: The Ethnic Expression of Fourteen Contemporary Poets,* edited by David Khekdian, Macmillan, 1974; *Voices of Aztlan: Chicano Literature of Today,* edited by Dorothy E. Harth and Lewis M. Baldwin, New American Library, 1974; and *Festival de Flor y Canto: An Anthology of Chicano Literature,* edited by Alurista and others, University of Southern California Press, 1976.

Also contributor to periodicals, including *San Francisco Chronicle, Transpacific, Partisan, Bronze, Es Tiempo,* and *Revista Chicano-Riquena.*

SIDELIGHTS: Born in Texas, poet Luis Omar Salinas spent a few early years in Mexico, but from the age of nine he lived with an aunt and uncle in California. While supporting himself with a variety of jobs, Salinas attended college in California and became involved in the literary community at Fresno State University. He is best known for his surrealistic vision, which he defines in *Chicano Literature: A Reference Guide* as "the strange fullness of the unreal."

In Salinas's view, dreamlike and fantastical imagery can better convey reality and suffering as it is experienced by people than can a conventional "realistic" approach. The author's work often addresses such problems as poverty, prejudice, and the alienation that Mexican-Americans undergo in American society. In *Chicano Literature* he summarized his poetic aspirations as "somehow to come to terms with the tragic and through the tragic gain a vision which transcends this world in some way." Through his unusual observations, imagery, and metaphors, Salinas reveals common aspects of reality which have been overlooked because they are accepted as normal. "For Salinas the common or 'normal' dulls our senses and deadens our response to the tyranny of the mechanical habits of daily living. By creating 'the fullness of the unreal,' he defamiliarizes the world for us and then forces us to confront the 'true' nature of the society that surrounds us," according to a contributor to *Chicano Literature.*

BIOGRAPHICAL/CRITICAL SOURCES:

BOOKS

Martinez, Julio A. and Francisco A. Lomeli, editors, *Chicano Literature: A Reference Guide,* Greenwood Press, 1985.

*   *   *

SANCHEZ, Trinidad, Jr.

PERSONAL: Male.

ADDRESSES: Home—P.O. Box 5557, San Antonio, TX 78201.

CAREER: Writer, poet, and motivational speaker. Mission Road Development Corp., San Antonio, TX,

group monitor, 1997—. Gives readings from his works, some of which have been collected in the videotapes *Poets as Resources—Couplets: Michigan Poets on Poetry,* Network Nine Productions (Mount Clemens, MI); and *Authentic Chicano Food Is Hot!,* Mestizo Productions (Detroit, MI).

AWARDS, HONORS: Champion of Education Award, San Antonio Independent School District, 1994; recognition awards, St. Mary's University, San Antonio, TX, 1997, and Texas A & M University, 1998.

WRITINGS:

(With Trinidad V. Sanchez) *Poems by Trinidad Sanchez, Jr./Poesias de Trinidad V. Sanchez: A Collection of Poems by Father and Son,* two volumes, Renaissance Publications (Lansing, MI), 1984-85, published as *Poems by Father and Son,* two volumes, Pecan Grove Press (San Antonio, TX), 1997.
Compartiendo de la Nada, Casa de Unidad Cultural Arts and Media Center (Detroit, MI), 1989.
Authentic Chicano Food Is HOT!, Casa de Unidad Cultural Arts and Media Center, 1990.
Why Am I So Brown?, MARCH/Abrazo Press (Chicago, IL), 1991.

Work represented in anthologies, including *The XY Files: Poems on the Male Experience,* Sherman Asher Publishing (Santa Fe, NM), 1997; *The Sounds of Poetry, Spring, 1997,* Coffee Cup (Detroit), 1997; and *Narratives,* Learning Communities Network (Cleveland, OH), 1998. Contributor to magazines, including *Simple Vows: Journal for Arts.*

*   *   *

SANCHEZ-BOUDY, Jose   1927-

PERSONAL: Born October 17, 1927, in Havana, Cuba; immigrated to the United States. *Education:* Earned Ph.D.

ADDRESSES: Office—Department of Romance Languages, University of North Carolina at Greensboro, 1000 Spring Garden St., Greensboro, NC 27412.

CAREER: Served as diplomat and university teacher; practiced law in Cuba, until 1961; University of

North Carolina at Greensboro, professor of Latin American literature, Latin American civilization, and Afro-Caribbean literature.

WRITINGS:

Cuentos grise, [Barcelona, Spain], 1966.

Ritmo de sola, Bosch (Barcelona), 1967.

Poemas de otono e invierno, Bosch (Barcelona), 1967.

Las novelas de Cesar Andreu Inglesias y la problematica puertorriquena actual, Bosch (Barcelona), 1968.

Cuentos del hombre, Bosch (Barcelona), 1969.

Madame Bovary; un analisis clinico sobre neurosis y psicosis psicogena, Bosch (Barcelona), 1969.

Poemas del silencio, Bosch (Barcelona), 1969.

La tematica novelistica de Alejo Carpentier, Ediciones Universal (Miami, FL), 1969.

Baudelair (psicoanlisis e impotenicia), Ediciones Universal (Miami, FL), 1970.

Modernismo y Americanismo, Bosch (Barcelona), 1970.

La nueva novela hispanoamericana y Tres tristes tigres, Ediciones Universal (Miami, FL), 1971.

Cuentos a luna llena, Ediciones Universal (Miami, FL), 1971.

Homo sapiens: teatro del no absurdo, Universal, 1971.

Los cruzados de la aurora, Ediciones Universal (Miami, FL), 1972.

Orbus terrarum: la ciudad de Humanitas, Ediciones Universal (Miami, FL), 1974.

Cuba and Her Poets: The Poems of Jose Sanchez-Boudy, edited and translated by Woodrow W. Moore, Ediciones Universal (Miami), 1974.

Pregones, Ediciones Universal (Miami, FL), 1975.

Ache, babalu aye: retablo afrocubano, Ediciones Universal (Miami, FL), 1975.

Historia de la literatura cubana en el exilio, Ediciones Universal (Miami, FL), 1975.

La Soledad de la Playa Larga (manana, mariposa): dram en dos actos y cinco escenas, Ediciones Universal (Miami, FL), 1975.

El corredor Kresto, Ediciones Universal (Miami, FL), 1976.

El picuo, el fisto, el barrio y otras estampas cubanas, Ediciones Universal (Miami, FL), 1977.

Los sarracenos del ocaso, Ediciones Universal (Miami, FL), 1977.

Ekue abanakue ekue, Ediciones Universal (Miami, FL), 1977.

Lyendas de asucar prieta: leyendas negras: cabio silo, Ediciones Universal (Miami, FL), 1977.

Lilayando pal tu: mojito y picardia cubana: antinovel, Ediciones Universal (Miami, FL), 1978.

Niquin el cesante, Ediciones Universal (Miami, FL), c. 1978.

Diccionario de cubanismos mas usuales: como habla el cubano, Ediciones Universal (Miami, FL), 1978.

Afro-Cuban Poetry de Oshun a Yemaya: The Afro-Cuban Poetry of Jose Sanchez- Boudy in English Translation, edited and translated by Claudio Freixas, illustrated by Gaby de la Riva, Ediciones Universal (Miami, FL), 1978.

Tiempo Congelado: poemario de una isla ausente, Ediciones Universal (Miami, FL), 1979.

La rebelion de los negreos; El hombre que era dos; Tres tiros un Viernes Santo; El heroe: cuatro piezas teatrales, Ediciones Universal (Miami, FL), 1980.

Cuentos blanco y negros, Ediciones Universal (Miami, FL), 1983.

La tematica novelistica de Severo Sarduy: De donde don los cantantes, Ediciones Universal (Miami, FL), 1985.

Patrioticas: la patria no ha muerto, no, esta en el viento, Ediciones Universal (Miami, FL), 1986.

Fulastres y fulastones y otras estampas cubanas, Ediciones Universal (Miami, FL), 1987.

Poema del Parque, [Miami], 1983.

Acuara ochun de caracoles verdes, Ediciones Universal (Miami, FL), 1987.

Vida y cultura sefardita en los poemas "La Vara": del ladino al espanol, Ediciones Universal (Miami, FL), 1987.

Potaje y otro mazote de estampas Cubanas, Ediciones Universal (Miami, FL), 1988.

Mi barrio y mi esquina: a la una mi mula a las dos mi reloj, Ediciones Universal (Miami, FL), 1989.

Dewey e la crisis de la educacion en los Estados Unidos, Ediciones Universal (Miami, FL), 1989.

Dile a Catalina, Ediciones Universal (Miami, FL), 1990.

Enrique Jose Varona y Cuba, Ediciones Universal (Miami, FL), 1990.

La crisis de la civilization occidental, Ediciones Universal (Miami, FL), 1990.

Partiendo el "Jon": estampas cubanas de alla y de aqui, Ediciones Universal (Miami, FL), 1990.

La perennidad de la Consititucion de los Estados Unidos y otros ensayos, Ediciones Universal (Miami, FL), 1992.

Guante sin grasa, no coge bola!: el refranero popular cubano: los refranes del chuchero, de los estibadores, de la bodega, del amor, del gua-guero— y otros estudios, Ediciones Universal (Miami, FL), 1993.

Filosofia del cubano y de lo cubano, Ediciones Universal (Miami, FL), 1996.*

SANCHEZ-SCOTT, Milcha 1953(?)-

PERSONAL: Born in 1953 (one source says 1955), in Bali; came to the United States in 1969. *Education:* Attended University of San Diego.

ADDRESSES: Home—2080 Mount St., Los Angeles, CA 90068. *Agent*—George Lane, William Morris Agency, 1350 Avenue of the Americas, New York, NY 10019.

CAREER: Playwright.

WRITINGS:

PLAYS

Latina (produced in Los Angeles, 1980), published in *Necessary Theater: Six Plays about the Chicano Experience,* edited Jorge A. Huerta, Arte Publico Press (Houston, TX), 1989.
Dog Lady; and, The Cuban Swimmer: Two One-Act Plays (both produced in New York City, May, 1984), Theatre Communications Group (New York City), 1984.
Roosters (produced in New York City, 1987), published in *On New Ground: Contemporary Hispanic American Plays,* edited by M. Elizabeth Osborn, Theatre Communications Group, 1987.
Stone Wedding, first produced at the Los Angeles Theater Center, Los Angeles, CA, December, 1988.
Evening Star, Dramatists Play Service (New York City), 1989.
El Dorado, produced in Costa Mesa, CA, 1990.
The Old Matador, produced in Tucson, AZ, 1995.

Also author of *Carmen* (adapted from Georges Bizet's opera of the same title), first produced at the Los Angeles Theater Center.

ADAPTATIONS: Roosters was broadcast on the *American Playhouse* television series in 1988 and was adapted as a film in 1995.

SIDELIGHTS: Though Milcha Sanchez-Scott rejects labels, her bicultural, and often bilingual, plays show the influence of feminism and magic realism. "Like Horton Foote's South Texas and Faulkner's Yoknapatawpha County, Sanchez-Scott's southwestern territory has proven a rich dramatic landscape," proclaimed Howard Allen in *American Theatre.* Born in Bali of an Indonesian mother and a Columbian father, Sanchez-Scott spent her winters in Catholic schools in England and her summers in Santa Marta, Columbia, before moving with her family to La Jolla, California, as a teenager. "I feel I am an American writer who has been influenced by the places I've lived or where my parents were born," she stated in *Notable Hispanic American Women.*

Her first play, *Latina,* produced in Los Angeles in 1980, highlights the variety of Latina experience through seven women characters looking for jobs through the Felix Sanchez Domestic Agency. Even in this first effort, wrote John G. Kuhn in *Contemporary Dramatists,* "a remarkable playwriting voice made Sanchez-Scott's bilingual and bi-level dramatic visions clear, rich, and effective—even for materialistic, English-speaking audiences." In *The Cuban Swimmer,* the Suarez family in their boat is cheering on daughter Margarita as she swims in an invitational race to the island of Catalina. Margarita is initially sunk by either exhaustion or the condescending tone of the television reporter who flies in a helicopter over her head, but rises again to walk on the waters of Catalina Island through the power of her abuela's (grandmother's) prayers and invective. *Dog Lady,* another one-act play published with *The Cuban Swimmer,* features two more athletic Latina adolescents in a coming-of-age tale featuring "soaring fantasies, functional but very funny misunderstandings, and sparkling dialogue," according to Kuhn.

Evening Star is another uplifting coming-of-age tale set among impoverished Latin-American families. In this story, as the fifteen-year-old daughter of one family gives birth to a child in her neighbor's house, "little epiphanies, tendernesses, and strengths bloom like roses," Kuhn noted. *Roosters,* Sanchez-Scott's next work, is a more hard-hitting drama than its precursors. It is also arguably the playwright's most successful piece to date. Having premiered at International Art Relations (INTAR) in New York City, it played in San Francisco before being filmed for television's *American Playhouse* in 1988; *Roosters* was also made into a feature-length film starring Edward James Olmos in 1995.

Roosters centers on Gallo Morales, a cock-fight promoter who has just been released from prison, his weary, long-suffering wife, their son, who has taken over his father's place raising roosters for cock fights, and their mystical daughter Angelita, who wears cardboard angel wings. Rod Lurie called the dramatic confrontation between these characters as it plays out over the course of a single day "a shockingly cruel indictment of the modern Latino family," in his review of the film adaptation in *Los Angeles Magazine*. But Janice Arkatov, in a review of the play in the *Los Angeles Times,* remarked: "We all have to leave our parents. We all have to grow up and leave home, face the various stages of life, grow old. These people in this play are mythical, archetypal characters: mother/father, madonna/whore, son/daughter. And they are Americans." And Kuhn concluded: "The predicted cockfight between Hector and Gallo allows rightful shares of nobility to each generation, character, and way of living. Sanchez-Scott achieves this persuasively."

In *The Old Matador,* Sanchez-Scott stages another confrontation between generations in a Latino family. The title character, Enrique, dreams of returning to Spain for a chance to face a bull in the ring; his wife Margarita, cannot comprehend that kind of passion; their daughter Jesse, first seen in *Dog Lady,* dreams of escape, and Jesse's brother Cookie, loves rap music and sees an angel. The personal drama of their conflicting desires is set against the backdrop of a three-day-old rescue attempt of a lost Boy Scout in the San Jacinto Mountains. "The tension-fraught atmosphere evoked by this collision of old world and new will strike a familiar chord for those who have followed the career of playwright Milcha Sanchez-Scott," remarked Howard Allen in *American Theatre.*

BIOGRAPHICAL/CRITICAL SOURCES:

BOOKS

Contemporary Dramatists, 5th edition, St. James Press (Detroit), 1993, pp. 578-579.
Notable Hispanic American Women, Gale (Detroit), 1993, pp. 367-368.

PERIODICALS

American Theatre, January, 1995, p. 12.
Chicago Tribune, March 9, 1989, sec. 5, p. 7.
Latin–American Theater Review, spring, 1990, pp. 63-74.
Los Angeles Magazine, July, 1995, p. 106.
Los Angeles Times, June 15, 1988, p. 3; April 22, 1991, p. 1.
New Statesman, May 15, 1987, pp. 25-26.
New York Times, May 10, 1984, p. C32; March 24, 1987, p. C15; May 16, 1988, p. C13.
Time, July 11, 1988, p. 82.

SANIN CANO, Baldomero 1861-1957

PERSONAL: Born in 1861; died in 1957.

CAREER: Professor of literature, economist, minister of the Colombian treasury, journalist, and critic, beginning c. 1918.

WRITINGS:

An Elementary Spanish Grammar, Clarendon Press (Oxford, England), 1918.
A Key to An Elementary Spanish Grammar, Clarendon Press, 1920.
Spanish Reader, Clarendon Press, 1920.

Author of the autobiography *On My Life and Others.*

BIOGRAPHICAL/CRITICAL SOURCES:

BOOKS

Felde, Alberto Zum, *Indice Critico de la Literatura Hispanoamericana,* Volume I, Editorial Guarania (Mexico City, Mexico), 1954.
Mead, Robert G., Jr., *Breve Historia del Ensayo Hispanoamericano,* Ediciones de Andrea (Mexico City), 1956.
Roggiano, Alfredo, editor, *La Cultura y la Literatura Iberoamericanas,* University of California Press (Berkeley, CA), 1957.

PERIODICALS

Americas, May, 1951, p. 42.*

*   *   *

SARDUY, Severo 1937-1993

PERSONAL: Born February 25, 1937, in Camaguey, Cuba; died June, 1993, in Paris, France, of complications related to acquired immune deficiency syndrome (AIDS); son of Severo and Mercedes Sarduy. *Education:* Attended Lecole du Louvre and the University of Havana.

CAREER: Novelist, poet, essayist, and literary critic. Advisor to French publishing house Seuil; publisher of *Lunes de Revolucion.*

MEMBER: Societe des Gens de Lettres (France).

AWARDS, HONORS: Prix Medicis etranger, 1972, for *Cobra;* Guggenheim fellowship, 1975; Prix Italia; Prix Paul Gilson.

WRITINGS:

Gestos (novel; title means "Gestures"), Seix Barral (Barcelona), 1963.

De donde son los cantantes (novella), Mortiz (Mexico City), 1967, translation by Suzanne Jill Levine published in *Triple Cross* as *From Cuba with a Song,* Dutton (New York City), 1972, published separately as *From Cuba with a Song,* Sun & Moon (College Park, MD), 1994.

Escrito sobre un cuerpo: Ensayos de critica (essays), Sudamericana (Buenos Aires), 1969, translation by Carol Maier published as *Written on a Body,* Lumen Series (Brighton, MA), 1989.

Flamenco, Manus Presse (Stuttgart), 1969.

Mood Indigo, Manus Presse, 1970.

Merveilles de la nature, Pauvet (Paris), 1971.

Cobra (also see below; novel), Sudamericana, 1972, translation by Levine published under same title, Dutton, 1975.

Overdose (poetry), Inventarios Provisionales (Las Palmas, Grand Canary), 1972.

Big Bang (poetry), Tusquets Editores (Barcelona), 1974.

Barroco (essays; title means "Baroque"), Sudamericana, 1974.

Maitreya (also see below), Seix Barral, 1977, 2nd edition, 1981, translation by Levine published under same title, Ediciones del Norte (Hanover, NH), 1987.

Para la voz, Fundamentos (Madrid), 1978, translation by Philip Barnard published as *For Voice,* Latin American Literary Review (Pittsburgh), 1985.

Daiquiri, Poeticas 2 (Santa Cruz, Tenerife), 1980.

La doublure, Flammarion, 1981.

La simulacion (essays and lectures), Monte Avila (Caracas), 1982.

(With Annemieke van de Pas) *Micro-opera de Benet Rossell* (criticism), Ambit, 1984.

Colibri (novel), Argos Vergara (Barcelona), 1984.

(With others) *Antonio Saura, figura y fondo* (criticism), Edicions del Mall, 1987.

Un testigo fugaz y disfrazado (poems), Edicions del Mall (Barcelona), 1987.

El Cristo de la rue Jacob (prose), Edicions del Mall, 1987, translation by Levine published as *Christ on the Rue Jacob,* Mercury House (San Francisco), 1995.

Nueva inestabilidad, Vuelta (Mexico City), 1987.

Cocuyo, Tusquets Editores, 1990.

Pajaras de la playa, Tusquets Editores, 1993.

Epitafios, Imitacion, Aforismos, Ediciones Universal (Miami), 1994.

Cobra [and] *Maitreya,* Dalkey Archive, 1995.

Also author of *Sobre la playa* (title means "On the Beach"), 1971, *La caida* (title means "The Fall"), 1974, *Relato,* 1974, and *Los matadores de hormigas* (title means "The Ant Killers"), 1976. Contributor to periodicals, including *Tel Quel.*

SIDELIGHTS: Cuban-born Severo Sarduy was known as the author of experimental fiction which resisted the idea of literature as a reflection of the real world in favor of seeing literature as a purely linguistic phenomena. Julia A. Kushigian in the *Dictionary of Literary Biography* explained that "Sarduy's ruminations on the signifier/signified relationship in language brings him into close contact with [certain] structuralists." Writing in *World Literature Today,* Thomas E. Case found that, in his fiction, Sarduy "elaborated and expanded his complex and multifaceted literary world." In addition to his fascination with the ability of language to create its own reality, Sarduy was also fascinated with sexually ambivalent characters who are both male and female. As a critic for the *Review of Contemporary Fiction* observed, Sarduy "put the swish in the Boom explosion of Latin American literature in the sixties and seventies with his gloriously baroque fictions filled with transvestites and bizarre *mise-en-scenes.*"

Sarduy studied medicine, art, and literature in his native Cuba until 1960, when he received a government grant to study art history in Europe and left the country. He never returned. Settling in Paris, where he became associated with a number of avant-garde literary figures, Sarduy began writing novels heavily influenced by French literary models, including the *nouveau roman.* His novels contain fragmented plots, little psychological characterization, and an abundance of surface imagery depicting the human being as an object among other objects. Sarduy's writing also places a heavy emphasis on language as it both creates and changes reality, evincing the author's preoccupation with the multiple meanings of words. According to Jerome Charyn in his *New York Times Book Review* critique of *Cobra,* "Language is everything in Sarduy's book."

Review 74 contributor Roberto Gonzalez Echevarria viewed Sarduy's first two works—the 1963 *Gestos* and the 1967 *De donde son los cantantes*—as "rehearsals" for the well-received *Cobra,* which appeared in 1972. In *Gestos,* for example, the influence of the nouveau roman reveals itself in Sarduy's attention to description, as it does in the later novel. "An objective, unfastened, disinterested language dances before the eyes of the reader," the critic remarked, "except that almost all the objects described in [*Gestos*] are pictures. In other words, the novel does not produce an immediate reality but gives instead detailed descriptions of canvases by well-known painters and projects the action of the story upon them." At the bidding of words, reality again undergoes a series of metamorphoses in *De donde son los cantantes,* which was translated as *From Cuba with a Song.* Divided into three related narratives, based on the three ethnic groups which comprise Cuban society—Spanish, African, and Chinese—the novel takes a wildly parodic view of Cuban history. As a *Review of Contemporary Fiction* critic described it, the novel is a "campy parody of Cuban history." Writing in the *Washington Post,* Alan West described *From Cuba with a Song* as "an unorthodox exploration of Cuban identity." In the book, *New York Times Book Review* critic E. Rodriguez Monegal reported, "the moth-eaten image of Christ which two acolytes carry to Havana (they are also transvestites) gradually rots away in keeping with the metamorphosis of the Cuban landscape and the Spanish language."

In his third novel Sarduy concentrated most heavily on the theme of transformation. "*Cobra* is a book of changes," Michael Wood commented, "and its title indicates not its meaning but the kind of activity it is engaged in." The book's narrative presents a hero-heroine named Cobra who begins life as a female wax doll, then undergoes a sex-change operation in a mysterious Tangier abortion clinic, joins a motorcycle gang in Amsterdam that mutilates and destroys her/him in a kinky religious ceremony, and becomes, finally, an embodiment of the Hindu god of creation and destruction, Shiva. However, the real protagonist of the book, Wood suggested, may be the word "cobra" in all its possible references. At various times in the novel, cobra is the name of a snake, a motorcycle gang, a singer, a group of artists, and a form of the Spanish verb *cobrar.* "The references define the word cobra as a sort of crazy semantic crossroads, a linguistic point where unlikely meanings intersect, and it is the intersection that counts rather than the meanings themselves," Wood observed. *Review 74* contributor Robert Adams concurred, noting that the snake-like shedding of personae and meaning "positively forbids us to read [*Cobra*] in depth. . . . The book is primarily a stream of images, glittering, exotic, trite and disgusting, cosmic and squalid, grotesque and funny, strung on a set of generative puns."

Cobra was admired by such critics as Helene Cixous, who wrote in another *Review 74* article that "*Cobra* is in a class of its own, unrelated to any serious genre, whether encoded or codable, to any type except the one whose new genius it invents: a bizarre hybrid, a composite of snake, writings, rhythms, of a flight of luminous traces and a series of infinitesimal sparkling instants." A *New Yorker* critic remarked: "What is impressive is the rich vocabulary, the free-wheeling imagination, and the utter cockiness. When, in a footnote, the author addresses us as 'moronic reader,' he has a certain charm."

In the posthumously published *Christ on the Rue Jacob,* a translation of *El Cristo de la rue Jacob,* Sarduy gathered together a number of short sketches and essays on a variety of topics. As Brad Hooper explained in *Booklist,* the first section of the book contains autobiographical pieces, while the second section contains "a series of impressions of places, events, and material objects." Hooper judged *Christ on the Rue Jacob* to be "a special book of thrilling ideas excitingly expressed." The reviewer for *Publishers Weekly* found it a "truly beautiful book."

BIOGRAPHICAL/CRITICAL SOURCES:

BOOKS

Barrenechea, Ana Maria, *Textos hispanoamericanos de Sarmiento a Sarduy,* Monte Avila, 1978.
Contemporary Literary Criticism, Volume 6, Gale (Detroit), 1976.
Dictionary of Literary Biography, Volume 113: *Modern Latin-American Fiction Writers, First Series,* Gale, 1992.
Gazarian Gautier, Marie-Lise, *Interviews with Latin-American Writers,* Dalkey Archive Press, 1989.
Gonzalez Echevarria, Roberto, *Isla a su vuelo fugitiva,* Porrua (Madrid), 1983, pp. 123-44.
Gonzalez Echevarria, Roberto, *La ruta de Severo Sarduy,* Ediciones del Norte (Hanover, NH), 1987.
Goytisolo, Juan, *Disidencias,* Seix Barral, 1977, pp. 171-92.
Guerrero, Gustavo, *La estrategia neobarroca: estudio sobre el resurgimiento de la poetica barroca en la obra narrativa de Severo Sarduy,* Edicions del Mall, 1987.
Kushigian, Julia Alexis, *Orientalism in the Hispanic Literary Tradition: In Dialogue with Borges, Paz and Sarduy,* University of New Mexico Press (Albuquerque), 1991.
Mace, Marie-Anne, *Severo Sarduy,* L'Harmattan (Paris), 1992.

Mendez Rodenas, Adriana, *Severo Sarduy: El neo-barroco de la transgresion,* Universidad Nacional Autonoma de Mexico (Mexico City), 1983.

Ortega, Julio, *La contemplacion y la fiesta,* Monte Avila, 1969, pp. 205-11.

Perez, Rolando, *Severo Sarduy and the Religion of the Text,* University Press of America (Lanham, MD), 1988.

Rivero Potter, Alicia, *Autor/lector: Huidobro, Borges, Fuentes y Sarduy,* Wayne State University Press (Detroit), 1991.

Sanchez-Boudy, Jose, *La tematica novelistica de Severo Sarduy,* Ediciones Universal, 1985.

Schulman, Ivan A., *Narrativa y critica de Nuestra America,* edited by Joaquin Roy, Castalia (Madrid), 1978, pp. 387-404.

PERIODICALS

Booklist, July, 1995, p. 1854.

Choice, March, 1986, p. 1069; June, 1988, p. 1562.

Diacritics, summer, 1972, pp. 41-45.

Diario 16, June 23, 1985, pp. 4-5.

Hispamerica, No. 10, 1975, pp. 9-24.

Hispania, May, 1992, pp. 335-36, 927-37; March, 1994, p. 84.

Latin–American Literary Review, spring-summer, 1980, pp. 152-60, 161-72; fall-winter, 1983, pp. 7-13.

Linden Lane, No. 1, 1983, p. 6.

Modern Language Notes, March, 1977, pp. 269-95; March, 1994, pp. 268-82.

El Mundo, November 24, 1979, p. 15.

Mundo Nuevo, No. 2, 1966, pp. 15-26; No. 14, 1967, pp. 70-71.

Nation, June 11, 1973.

New Yorker, January 27, 1975.

New York Review of Books, March 20, 1975.

New York Times Book Review, December 24, 1972; March 9, 1975.

Papeles, No. 16, 1972, pp. 25-47.

Publishers Weekly, September 22, 1989, pp. 50-51; May 15, 1995, p. 69.

Review, winter, 1974.

Review 74, winter, 1974.

Review of Contemporary Fiction, summer, 1989, pp. 242-43; fall, 1994, p. 237.

Revista de Occidente, No. 93, 1970, pp. 315-43.

Revista Iberoamericana, April-June, 1972, pp. 333-43; July-December, 1975, pp. 569-78.

Symposium, No. 1, 1985, pp. 49-60.

Vuelta, April, 1984, pp. 14-20.

Washington Post, July 31, 1995, p. D2.

World Literature Today, autumn, 1991, pp. 676-77; summer, 1994, p. 537; spring, 1995, pp. 336-7.

OBITUARIES:

PERIODICALS

Art Press, January, 1994, pp. 49-50.*

* * *

SIERRA, Ruben 1946-

PERSONAL: Born December 6, 1946, in San Antonio, TX; son of Miguel and Elvira (a stage performer; maiden name, Escamilla) Sierra; married Elizabeth Imberg, August 12, 1989. *Education:* San Antonio College, graduated, 1967; St. Mary's University, B.A. (speech, drama, and sociology), 1970; University of Washington, Seattle, M.A. (directing), 1974. *Religion:* Roman Catholic.

ADDRESSES: Office—California Institute of Arts, 24700 McBean Pkwy., Valencia, CA, 91355.

CAREER: Playwright, educator, actor, director, producer, and entrepreneur. University of Washington, Seattle, professor of theater, 1974-79, director of Ethnic Center, 1979-89; California Institute of the Arts, Valencia, dean, 1990—; Seattle Group Theatre, artistic board of directors, 1978—. Consultant with the Ford Foundation, 1985-90, Washington Arts Commission, 1980, 1982, 1984, 1988, and the Rockefeller Foundation. *Military service:* United States Army, 1970-72.

MEMBER: Dramatists Guild, Screen Actors Guild, Actors' Equity Association, American Federation of Television and Radio Artists.

AWARDS, HONORS: Citizen Artist Award, Allied Arts of Seattle, 1985; Governor's Art Award, Washington, 1987; Citizen of Year Award, Ethnic Heritage Council, 1989; *Seattle Weekly* awards, best theatre director, 1987, 1988.

WRITINGS:

PLAYS

La Raza Pura, or Racial, Racial, St. Mary's University (San Antonio, TX), 1968.

The Conquering Father, Downstage Theatre (San Antonio, TX), 1972.

La capirotada de los espejos, Teatro del Piojo (Seattle, WA), 1973.

Manolo (three acts), Teatro Quetzalcoatl (Seattle, WA), 1975; revised, California State University, Northridge, 1982.

The Millionaire y el Pobrecito, Public Theatre (Los Angeles, CA), 1979.

Articuss and the Angel, Group Theatre (Seattle), 1983.

I Am Celso (adapted by Sierra and Jorge Huerta from Leo Romero's *Celso*), University of California (Los Angeles), 1985.

Say, Can You See, Group Theatre, April 28, 1988.

SIDELIGHTS: Using a blend of wit, humor, and stark realism, Chicano playwright Ruben Sierra has written a collection of plays that have exposed some of the injustices that have plagued his people. Also a noted director, actor and educator, Sierra has been active in the theatrical community for the better part of three decades. Not only have Sierra's plays concentrated on the plight of the Chicano people, but he has also been instrumental in bringing the theatre into their communities, where he has sparked an interest and helped many of them to become active in drama themselves. Growing up in San Antonio, Texas, Sierra became aware of the disparity that existed between the Anglo communities and that of the Latinos, who were mostly relegated to impoverished barrios where drug and alcohol abuse was widespread.

The subject matter of Sierra's plays often reflect this inequality, as is the case with his first production, 1968's *La Raza Pura, or Racial, Racial,* a biting tale that features an interracial love affair between an Anglo girl and a Chicano. Despite his matter-of-fact approach, Sierra often employs comedy and satire to soften the blow of the intense social consciousness of his plays. Sierra's motto, as related by Arthur Ramirez in *Dictionary of Literary Biography,* is: "We don't have to take ourselves seriously, but we can be serious about what we're doing." In the early 1970s, following a stint in the army, Sierra moved to Seattle, Washington, where he continued to create socially relevant productions, as well as becoming one of that city's leading proponents of the theater. *Seattle Post-Intelligencer* drama critic O. Casey Corr, quoted by Bob Marvel in *Voz,* once referred to Sierra as the "social conscience of Seattle theater, and possibly its single-most important figure." Sierra also earned several honors for his work, including the 1985 Citizen Artist Award that was presented to him by Allied Arts of Seattle. During his lengthy career, Sierra has traveled throughout the United States, as well as to Mexico, and is undoubtedly one of the most prominent and unique voices in contemporary Chicano theater.

Although *La Raza Pura, or Racial, Racial* was his first play, Sierra affected audiences and critics alike with what was viewed as the production's honesty, freshness, and experimentation. Made up of twenty-five scenes, the play incorporates slides, film and music, and uses a total of thirty-four actors. In addition, several plot lines are developed, all related to various aspects of racial conflict and racial prejudice. The play hinges on the relationship between the interracial couple, a subject that was very controversial in 1968 San Antonio. *La Raza Pura's* prevailing message is that the concept of racial purity is a mythical notion. On its opening night, the play met with an overwhelmingly strong response from the audience, which was multiracial itself. Critics offered generally favorable responses to the play. "The total integration of plot and character, which is the mainstay of an effective play, is, ironically, lacking in this play on racial integration. Nonetheless, *La Raza Pura* is important for its inventive use of multimedia, and for the creativity of each of its scenes," wrote Jorge Huerta in *Revista Chicano-Riquena.* Tom Nickell, reviewing the play for the *San Antonio News,* maintained that the play went "from painfully funny to painfully melodramatic; yet even the near-maudlin moments succeed by dint of the irresistible force of a youthful sincerity."

Manolo, a three-act play, focuses on the addiction of a Chicano Vietnam veteran, who, after the war, comes home to his run-down barrio. Though he went through a treatment program at a army hospital and seemingly has beaten his heroin addiction, Manolo relapses into the habit after his mother dies and the local drug dealer is able to convince him to start using again. In the play, Sierra tries to demonstrate that drug addiction can destroy even the best-intentioned of men, and that individual responsibility is sometimes more difficult than it may seem. Sierra took the play on the road, touring through the states of Texas and Colorado, oftentimes playing in barrio communities. Another of Sierra's successful plays is 1985's *I Am Celso,* the story of a barrio alcoholic who is also a street poet and storyteller. To all those who will listen, Celso, who lives in an adobe hut, recounts his many adventures, some in which he takes other forms, such as a priest or a skeleton. He has even created his own religion, which he calls "the Gospel of the Holy Grape." "*I Am Celso* makes the playgoer more aware of the fascinating diversity of life—and grateful for the awareness. Not many evenings in the theatre accomplish that. *I Am Celso* and Ruben Sierra do," declared Wayne Johnson in the *Seattle Times*.

BIOGRAPHICAL/CRITICAL SOURCES:

BOOKS

Dictionary of Literary Biography, Volume 122: *Chicano Writers, Second Series,* edited by Francisco A. Lomeli and Carl R. Shirley, Gale (Detroit, MI), 1992.

PERIODICALS

Revista Chicano-Riquena, summer, 1977.
San Antonio News, October 28, 1969.
Seattle Times, June 7, 1985.
Voz, January-February, 1982, pp. 10-13.*

*   *   *

SINAN, Rogelio
   See ALBA, Bernardo Dominguez

*   *   *

SKARMETA, Antonio 1940-

PERSONAL: Born November 7, 1940, in Antofagasta, Chile; son of Antonio and Magdalena (Vranicic) Skarmeta; married Cecilia Boisier (a painter), 1964 (divorced); children: Beltran, Gabriel. *Education:* Attended University of Chile; Columbia University, M.A..

ADDRESSES: Home—Chile. *Agent*—Carmen Balcells, Diagonal 580, Barcelona 08021, Spain.

CAREER: University of Chile, Santiago, professor of contemporary Latin American literature, early 1970s; German Academy of Film and Television, West Berlin, West Germany (now Berlin, Germany), professor of screenwriting, 1978-81; freelance writer and filmmaker, 1981—; creator and host of *El Show de los Libros* (late-night television series), 1992—; La Batea (Chilean restaurant), West Berlin, former music director. Worked as a journalist and book translator in Chile; visiting professor at colleges and universities in Europe and the United States; film director in West Germany. Director of film *Ardiente paciencia.*

MEMBER: International PEN.

AWARDS, HONORS: Premio Casa de las Americas from the government of Cuba, 1969, for short story collection *Desnudo en el tejado;* first prizes from the Biarritz, France, and Huelva, Spain, film festivals, both 1983, for film *Ardiente paciencia;* Guggenheim fellowship, 1986.

WRITINGS:

SHORT STORIES

El entusiasmo, ZigZag (Santiago, Chile), 1967.
Desnudo en el tejado, Sudamericana (Buenos Aires, Argentina), 1969.
Tiro libre, Siglo Veintiuno (Buenos Aires), 1973.
No paso nada y otros relatos, Pehuen, 1985.
Uno a uno: cuentos completos, Sudamericana, 1969.

NOVELS

El ciclista del San Cristobal, Quimantu (Santiago, Chile), 1973.
Novios y solitarios, Losada (Buenos Aires, Argentina), 1975.
Sone que la nieve ardia, Planeta (Barcelona), 1975, translation by Malcolm Coad published as *I Dreamt the Snow Was Burning,* Readers International (London), 1985.
Chileno!, translated from the Spanish by Hortense Carpentier, Morrow, 1979.
La insurreccion, Ediciones del Norte (Hanover, NH), 1982, translation by Paula Sharp published as *The Insurrection,* Ediciones del Norte, 1983.
Ardiente paciencia, Ediciones del Norte, 1985, translation by Katherine Silver published as *Burning Patience,* Pantheon (New York City), 1987.
Love-Fifteen, translation by Jonathan Tittler, Latin American Literary Review Press, 1996.

EDITOR

Joven narrativa despues del golpe: Antologia, American Hispanist (Clear Creek, IN), 1976.
Poesia joven de Chile, Federlese (Munich, Germany), 1985.
Santiago Pena Capital, Documentas (Santiago, Chile), 1991.

OTHER

(Translator with Cecilia Boisier) Elizabeth Bowen, *La casa en Paris,* ZigZag, 1969.

No paso nada, Pomaire (Barcelona), 1980.

Arduente paciencia (play), produced in Berlin at the Bat Theatre, June 1983.

Match Ball, Sudamericana (Buenos Aires), 1989.

Watch Where the Wolf Is Going, translation by Donald L. Schmidt and Federico Cordovez, Readers International, 1991.

Musica ligera, Grijalbo, 1994.

Author of screenplay for the film *La Victoria,* directed by Peter Lilienthal in 1973 but never released. Also author of the screenplays *Es herrscht Ruhe im Land, La insurreccion, Ardiente paciencia,* and *Dry Manhattan* (in pre-production at Chile's Roos Films, c. 1998). Author of radio plays and song lyrics.

Contributor to books, including *Cronicas de Chile,* edited by Rodrigo Quijada, J. Alvarez (Buenos Aires), 1973; *Del cuerpo a las palabras: La narrativa de Antonio Skarmeta,* edited by Raul Silva Castro, LAR (Madrid), 1983; *Mas alla del Boom,* 2nd edition, edited by David Vinas, Folios (Buenos Aires), 1984; *Enciclopedia labor,* Labor (Barcelona), 1984. Work also represented in anthologies, including *Tres cuentistas: Rene Marques, Antonio Skarmeta, Luis Britto Garcia,* Casa de las Americas, 1979. Contributor of articles and essays to newspapers, magazines, and literary journals, including *Revista de Literatura Hispanoamericana* and *Review.*

ADAPTATIONS: Ardiente paciencia was adapted as a film released by Miramax as *Il Postino,* staring Massimo Troisi and directed by Michael Radford.

WORK IN PROGRESS: a novel; a screenplay adaptation of Isabel Allende's "Eva Luna," to be directed by Michael Radford.

SIDELIGHTS: Antonio Skarmeta is a leading figure of the so-called "postboom generation" of Latin American novelists, whose writings reflect the political and social disturbance in the region during the past two decades. A Chilean who fled to Europe when a bloody military coup toppled socialist President Salvador Allende in 1973, Skarmeta is best known as a novelist, but he has also written short stories, screenplays, radio plays, and literary criticism. Skarmeta's fiction reflects "the crisis, the conflict and the search for identity" experienced by a whole generation of young South American intellectuals driven from their native lands by the repressive governments of the 1970s, critic Malva E. Filer observed in *World Literature Today.* Thematically, the author himself has noted, his work and that of his generation is rooted in concrete everydayness and shows greater interest in building a bond of shared experience with the reader than in exploring the mythic and transcendental questions that animate the writings of such "boom" figures as Julio Cortazar and Gabriel Garcia Marquez.

Skarmeta once commented that his second novel, *Sone que la nieve ardia* (translated as *I Dreamt the Snow Was Burning*) tries to express the mood of youths living in Chile during the early 1970s. *Chileno!,* which was published in English in 1979, draws on the author's personal experience as an exile in West Berlin to tell the story of a sixteen-year-old Chilean boy living as a political refugee in the West German city. The political setting for *La insurreccion (The Insurrection)* is the Sandinista-led popular rebellion against the Anastasio Somoza dictatorship in the city of Leon, Nicaragua, in 1978. Using straight narrative as well as letters, poems, and other literary devices to tell the story, *La insurreccion* traces the revolution's course through the personal lives of a humble local family. Fast-paced and cinematic in its vivid imagery, the story was made into a prize-winning film written by Skarmeta and directed by Peter Lilienthal.

The author returns to a Chilean setting in *Ardiente paciencia,* translated as *Burning Patience,* one of his most popular novels among English readers. Skarmeta described his book as a chronicle of "the warm but volatile friendship between Chile's great poet Pablo Neruda and a young postman who uses Neruda's poetry to seduce the girl he loves." The novel also reflects on the nature of language and poetry, yielding comically flowery conversations between Neruda and his young apprentice. "The whole book," observed *Village Voice* critic Enrique Fernandez, "in fact, is written in a mock epic tone, bursting with hyperbole, that is both a parody of and homage to Neruda's poetry." *Burning Patience* "is a witty and imaginative meditation on the relationship between literature and reality, and a wry, affectionate depiction of youthful passion," added Jonathan Yardley in the *Washington Post.*

Skarmeta also penned the screenplay for a film version of *Burning Patience* that won first prize at two European film festivals. Another screenplay adaptation of *Ardiente paciencia* was released by Miramax as *Il Postino,* staring Massimo Troisi and directed by Michael Radford. Known in the United States as *The Postman,* this second film "is really about the power of poetry to transform lives," maintained Joseph Cunneen in the *National Catholic Reporter.* "[S]et in 1952 Italy," recounted Cunneen, *The Postman* tells of how "the Italian government [responds] to popular protests against deporting the visiting Chilean poet Pablo Neruda . . . [and] offers [Neruda] and his mistress a splendid villa on a small island south of Naples. The islanders, mostly illiterate, normally don't need much postal service, but Neruda's celebrity makes it necessary to hire someone to deliver his mail. The simple plot consists in the slowly growing relationship between Mario and the poet." Viewers of *The Postman,* warned a *Publishers Weekly* contributor, will not find "the intimacy and conscience of the film" when they read Skarmeta's 1996 novel *Love-Fifteen.* The critic referred to *Love-Fifteen* as merely "a vapid, lusty little intrigue illustrating the soulless lives of the very rich and famous."

Beginning in 1992, Skarmeta hosted a late-night television series he created. As Hans Ehrmann reported in *Variety* Skarmeta described his popular, award-winning show, *El Show de los Libros*: "From the beginning I realized that an academic approach to books and literature would be hopeless. So, I developed a show in which each program was centered on a specific subject, linking literature with, for example, sports in one week, the telephone in another, horses, the moon, postmen, whorehouses and schools. This I illustrated with film clips, popular period music, interviews, plus dramatizations of pertinent scenes from novels or short stories."

BIOGRAPHICAL/CRITICAL SOURCES:

BOOKS

Alegria, Fernando, and Jorge Ruffinelli, editors, *Paradise Lost or Gained,* Arte Publico, 1990.
Dictionary of Literary Biography, Volume 145: *Modern Latin-American Fiction Writers, Second Series,* Gale, 1994.
Meyer, Doris, editor, *Lives on the Line: The Testimony of Contemporary Latin American Authors,* University of California Press, 1988.
Silva Caceres, Raul, *Del cuerpo a las palabras: La narrativa de Antonio Skarmeta,* Literatura Americana Reunida (Madrid), 1983.

PERIODICALS

Hispania, September, 1986.
Los Angeles Times Book Review, May 3, 1987.
National Catholic Reporter, August 11, 1995.
New Orleans Review, fall, 1980.
New Republic, July 3, 1995.
New York Times Book Review, May 3, 1987.

Publishers Weekly, September 23, 1996.
Times Literary Supplement, April 15, 1988.
Variety, March 23, 1998.
Village Voice, July 28, 1987.
Washington Post, April 15, 1987.
World Literature Today, summer, 1983; summer, 1984; summer, 1986.*

*   *   *

SOLORZANO, Carlos 1922-

PERSONAL: Born May 1, 1922, in San Marcos, Guatemala; imigrated to Mexico in 1939; married Beatrice Caso, September 3, 1946; children: one son (deceased), two daughters. *Education:* National University of Mexico, B.A., 1939, M.A., 1944, Ph.D., 1946.

ADDRESSES: Home—Condor 199, Col. Alpes Tlacopac, 01010 DF, Mexico.

CAREER: Playwright, novelist, editor, and essayist. National University of Mexico, artistic director of the university theatre, 1952-62, professor, 1960-85, professor emeritus, 1985—. director of National Theatre, 1977-82. Visiting lecturer at numerous universities in Mexico and abroad.

MEMBER: International PEN, Hispanic Society of America (corresponding member), Playwrights and Composers Society, Spanish Royal Academy of Language (corresponding member), Latin American Community of Writers Society.

AWARDS, HONORS: Rockefeller fellowship, 1948-50.

WRITINGS:

PLAYS; UNLESS OTHERWISE NOTED

Del sentimiento de lo plastico en la obra de Unamuno (nonfiction), [Mexico City], 1944.
Dona Beatriz, la sin ventura (produced in 1952), published in *Cuadernos americanos,* no. 59, 1951, published in *Teatros guatemalteco contemporaneo,* Aguilar (Madrid), 1964.
El hechicero: tragedia en tres actos (produced in 1952), Ediciones Cuadernos Americanos (Mexico City), 1955.

Las manos de Dios (produced in Mexico City, 1956), B. Costa-Amic, 1957, reprinted, Center for Curriculum Development, 1971, translation by W. Keith Leonard and Marlo T. Soria published as *The Hands of God,* Hiram College, 1968.

Mea Culpa (produced in 1956), published in *Teatro Breve,* 1977.

El crucificado (produced 1958), published in *Tres actos,* 1959, translated as *The Crucifixion* in *The Orgy: Modern One-Act Plays from Latin America,* edited by Gerardo Luzuriaga and Robert S. Rudder, University of California Press (Berkeley), 1974.

Los fantoches (produced in 1958), published in *Tres Actos,* 1959, and in *Teatro,* 1972.

Cruce de vias (produced in 1959), published in *Tres actos,* 1959, and in *Teatro breve,* 1977, translation published as *Crossroads* in *Selected Latin American One-Act Plays,* edited by Francesca Colecchia and Julio Matas, University of Pittsburgh Press (Pittsburgh, PA), 1973.

Tres actos, El Unicornio, 1959.

El sueno del angel (produced in 1960), published in *Teatro,* 1972.

Teatro latinoamericano del siglo XX, Nueva Vision (Buenos Aires), 1961, revised edition, Macmillan (New York City), 1963.

(Editor) *Teatro guatemalteco contemporaneo,* Aguilar (Madrid), 1964.

(Editor) *El teatro hispanoamericano contemporaneo,* 2 volumes, Fondo de Cultura Economica (Mexico City), 1964, reprinted, 1981.

El zapato (produced in 1966), published in *Cosmos* 2, 1966.

El visitante (play), produced in 1966.

(Editor) *Teatro breve hispanoamericano contemporaneo,* Aguilar, 1970.

Las celdas (novel), J. Mortiz, 1971.

Teatro (collection, includes *Les fantoches; El crucificado; Las manos de Dios;* and *El sueno del angel*), Editorial Universitaria Centroamericana (San Jose, Costa Rica), 1972.

(Editor and author of introduction) *El teatro actual latinoamericano,* De Andrea (Mexico City), 1972.

Testimonios teatrales de Mexico (nonfiction), Universidad Nacional Autonoma de Mexico (Mexico City), 1973.

Los falsos demonios (novel, based on his own play), J. Mortiz, 1973.

Teatro breve (collection, includes *El zapato; Cruce de vias; El sueno del angel; Mea culpa; El crucificado;* and *Los fantoches*), J. Mortiz, 1977.

Crossroads, and Other Plays, translated and edited by Francesca Colecchia, Associated University Presses, 1993.

Also author of *Espejo de novelas,* 1945; *Unamuno y el existencialismo,* 1946; *Novelas de Unamuno,* 1948; work has been included in numerous anthologies, including *Uno, dos, tres: tres dramas mexicanos en un acto,* edited by Jeanine Gaucher-Shultz and Alfredo O. Morales, Odyssey Press, 1971, and *Teatro centroamericano contemporaneo,* del Pulgarcito, 1977. Contributor to journals and magazines.

SIDELIGHTS: Carlos Solorzano is a playwright, editor, and educator whose efforts have been influential in the growing recognition of Latin American theatre in the second half of the twentieth century. In particular, as artistic director of Teatro Universitario in Mexico in the 1950s, and as a professor of dramatic art at the National Autonomous University of Mexico from the 1960s through the 1980s, "he actively and passionately promoted the theatre through histories, anthologies, articles, lectures, and festivals," according to George Woodyard writing in *Contemporary World Writers.* As a playwright, Solorzano was signally influenced by the philosophy of the existentialists, and his plays of the 1950s are considered classic expressions of the existentialist philosophy in art.

Born into one of Guatemala's oldest families, Solorzano moved to Mexico at the age of seventeen, attending the National Autonomous University of Mexico throughout the 1940s. From 1948 until 1950 he studied theatre at the Sorbonne in Paris, funded by a Rockefeller Fellowship, where he met such pivotal cultural figures as Albert Camus and adopted both the existentialist philosophy and its proponents' penchant for creating symbolic art. Woodyard commented: "Solorzano's theatre is a reflection of his existentialist approach to contemporary situations. His anguished characters strive to establish meaningful communication and relationships within a world of alienation." The 1950s was Solorzano's period of greatest artistic creativity, seeing the production of his plays *Dona Beatriz, la sin ventura* ("The Unfortunate") in 1952, *El hechicero* ("The Sorcerer") in 1954, and *Las manos de Dios* (*The Hands of God*) in 1956. Later, he wrote several influential works of criticism on Latin American theatre, including *Teatro latinoamericano del siglo XX* (title means "Latin American Theatre in the Twentieth Century") in 1961 and *Testimonios teatrales de Mexico* in 1973. Solorzano stopped publishing in the 1970s. His writings, though no longer in fashion, are nevertheless widely known and respected throughout the Latin–American theatre world.

Woodyard sees Solorzano's three major plays as explorations of the existentialist idea of freedom of choice. Thus, in *The Hands of God,* which Woodyard dubs Solorzano's "masterwork," the Devil dares a young woman to steal jewels from the Church in order to bribe her imprisoned brother's way to freedom. "While attacking both Church and State for keeping people enslaved in a state of ignorance, Solorzano dramatizes the plight of the individual who must make decisions that are critical for his or her own self-realization," wrote Woodyard. The play was an instant success when it premiered in 1956 and quickly became a classic of existentialist theatre.

BIOGRAPHICAL/CRITICAL SOURCES:

BOOKS

Contemporary World Writers, 2nd edition, St. James Press (Detroit), 1993, pp. 488-489.
Foster, David William, *Mexican Literature: A Bibliography of Secondary Sources,* Scarecrow Press (Metuchen, NJ), 1992.
International Dictionary of Theatre-2: Playwrights, St. James Press, 1994, pp. 904-905.

PERIODICALS

Booklist, February 1, 1973, p. 513; September 15, 1996, p. 227.
Chasqui, vol. 1, no. 1, 1972.
Comunidad Latinoamericano de Escritores Boletin, March, 1970.
Latin American Theatre Review, vol. 4, no. 2, 1971; vol. 9, 1976; vol. 17, no. 2, 1984; vol. 25, no. 1, 1991.
Modern Drama, vol. 7, 1968-69.
World Literature Today, spring, 1996, p. 371.

* * *

SOTO, Gary 1952-

PERSONAL: Born April 12, 1952, in Fresno, CA; son of Manuel and Angie (Trevino) Soto; married Carolyn Sadako Oda, May 24, 1975; children: Mariko Heidi. *Education:* California State University, Fresno, B.A., 1974; University of California, Irvine, M.F.A., 1976. *Avocational interests:* Karate, reading, Aztec dancing, travel.

ADDRESSES: Home—43 The Crescent, Berkeley, CA 94708.

CAREER: University of California, Berkeley, assistant professor 1979-85; associate professor of English and ethnic studies, 1985-92, part-time senior lecturer in English department, 1992-93; University of Cincinnati, Elliston Poet, 1988; Wayne State University, Martin Luther King/Cesar Chavez/Rosa Parks Visiting Professor of English, 1990; full-time writer, 1993—.

AWARDS, HONORS: Academy of American Poets Prize, 1975; *Discovery/Nation* prize, 1975; United States Award, International Poetry Forum, 1976, for *The Elements of San Joaquin;* Bess Hokin Prize from *Poetry,* 1978; Guggenheim fellowship, 1979-80; National Endowment for the Arts fellowships, 1981 and 1991; creative writing fellowship, National Education Association, 1982; Levinson Award, *Poetry,* 1984; American Book Award, Before Columbus Foundation, 1985, for *Living up the Street;* California Arts Council fellowship, 1989; Best Book for Young Adults citation, American Library Association, 1990, Beatty Award, California Library Association, 1991, and Reading Magic Award, *Parenting* magazine, all for *Baseball in April, and Other Stories;* George G. Stone Center Recognition of Merit, Claremont Graduate School, 1993; Carnegie Medal, 1993; National Book Award and *Los Angeles Times* Book Prize nominations, both 1995, both for *New and Selected Poems.*

WRITINGS:

The Elements of San Joaquin (poems), University of Pittsburgh Press (Pittsburgh), 1977.
The Tale of Sunlight (poems), University of Pittsburgh Press, 1978.
Fathers Is a Pillow Tied to a Broom, Slow Loris (Pittsburgh), 1980.
Where Sparrows Work Hard (poems), University of Pittsburgh Press, 1981.
Black Hair (poems), University of Pittsburgh Press, 1985.
Living up the Street: Narrative Recollections (prose memoirs), Strawberry Hill (San Francisco, CA), 1985.
Small Faces (prose memoirs), Arte Publico (Houston, TX), 1986.
The Cat's Meow, illustrated by Carolyn Soto, Strawberry Hill, 1987.
Lesser Evils: Ten Quartets (memoirs and essays), Arte Publico, 1988.
(Editor) *California Childhood: Recollections and Stories of the Golden State,* Creative Arts Book Company (Berkeley, CA), 1988.

A Fire in My Hands (poems), Scholastic (New York City), 1990.

A Summer Life (autobiography), University Press of New England (Hanover, NH), 1990.

Baseball in April and Other Stories (short stories), Harcourt (San Diego, CA), 1990.

Who Will Know Us? (poems), Chronicle Books (San Francisco, CA), 1990.

Home Course in Religion (poems), Chronicle Books, 1991.

Taking Sides, Harcourt, 1991.

Neighborhood Odes, Harcourt, 1992.

Pacific Crossing, Harcourt, 1992.

The Skirt, Delacorte (New York City), 1992.

Too Many Tamales (picture book), Putnam (New York City), 1992.

(Editor) *Pieces of the Heart: New Chicano Fiction,* Chronicle Books, 1993.

Local News (short stories), Harcourt, 1993.

The Pool Party, Delacorte, 1993 (also see below).

Crazy Weekend, Scholastic Inc., 1994.

Jesse, Harcourt, 1994.

Boys at Work, Delacorte, 1995.

Canto Familiar/Familiar Song (poetry), Harcourt, 1995.

The Cat's Meow, Scholastic Inc., 1995.

Chato's Kitchen, Putnam, 1995.

(Editor) *Everyday Seductions,* Ploughshare Press (Sea Bright, NJ), 1995.

New and Selected Poems, Chronicle Books, 1995.

Summer on Wheels, Scholastic Inc., 1995.

The Old Man and His Door, Putnam, 1996.

Snapshots of the Wedding, Putnam, 1996.

Off and Running (juvenile), illustrated by Eric Velasquez, Delacorte (New York City), 1996.

Buried Onions, Harcourt (San Diego), 1997.

Novio Boy (play), Harcourt, 1997.

Junior College: Poems, Chronicle Books (San Francisco), 1997.

Petty Crimes, Harcourt, 1998.

Big Bushy Mustache, Knopf (New York City), 1998.

Chato's Surprise Pachanga, Putnam, 1998.

Chato and the Party Animals, Putnam, 1999.

Nerdlandia: A Play, PaperStar (New York City), 1999.

My Little Car, Putnam, 2000.

SHORT FILMS

The Bike, Gary Soto Productions, 1991.

The Pool Party, Gary Soto Productions, 1993.

Novio Boy, Gary Soto Productions, 1994.

SIDELIGHTS: Gary Soto is an American poet and prose writer influenced by his working-class Mexican-American background. Born in Fresno, California, in the agricultural San Joaquin Valley, he worked as a laborer during his childhood. In his writing, as Raymund Paredes noted in the *Rocky Mountain Review,* "Soto establishes his acute sense of ethnicity and, simultaneously, his belief that certain emotions, values, and experiences transcend ethnic boundaries and allegiances." Many critics have echoed the assessment of Patricia De La Fuente in *Revista Chicano-Requena* that Soto displays an "exceptionally high level of linguistic sophistication."

In his first volume of poetry, *The Elements of San Joaquin,* Soto offers a grim portrait of Mexican-American life. His poems depict the violence of urban life, the exhausting labor of rural life, and the futility of trying to recapture the innocence of childhood. In the book *Chicano Poetry* Juan Bruce-Novoa likened Soto's poetic vision to T. S. Eliot's bleak portrait of the modern world, *The Waste Land.* Soto uses wind-swept dust as a dominant image, and he also introduces such elements as rape, unflushed toilets, a drowned baby, and, as Bruce-Novoa quotes him, "men/ Whose arms/ Were bracelets/ Of burns." Soto's skill with the figurative language of poetry has been noted by reviewers throughout his career, and in *Western American Literature* Jerry Bradley praised the metaphors in *San Joaquin* as "evocative, enlightening, and haunting." Though unsettled by the negativism of the collection, Bruce-Novoa felt the work "convinces because of its well-wrought structure, the craft, the coherence of its totality." Moreover, he thought, because it brings such a vivid portrait of poverty to the reading public, *San Joaquin* is "a social as well as a literary achievement."

Many critics have also observed that Soto's writing transcends social commentary. Bruce-Novoa said that one reason why the author's work has "great significance within Chicano literature" is because it represents "a definite shift toward a more personal, less politically motivated poetry." As Alan Williamson suggested in *Poetry,* Soto avoids either idealizing the poor for their oppression or encouraging their violent defiance. Instead, he focuses on the human suffering that poverty engenders. When Peter Cooley reviewed Soto's second volume of poetry, *The Tale of Sunlight,* in *Parnassus,* he praised the author's ability to temper the bleakness of *San Joaquin* with "imaginative expansiveness." The poems in *Sunlight,* many of which focus on a child named Molina or on the owner of a

Hispanic bar, display both the frustrations of poverty and what Williamson called "a vein of consolatory fantasy which passes beyond escapism into a pure imaginative generosity toward life." Williamson cited as an example "the poem in which an uncle's gray hair is seen as a visitation of magical butterflies."

In the poems in *Black Hair,* Soto focuses on his friends and family. He portrays fondly the times he shared with his buddies as an adolescent and the more recent moments he has spent with his young daughter. Some critics, such as David Wojahn in *Poetry,* argued that Soto was moving away from his strengths as a writer. While acknowledging that "by limiting his responses to a naive aplomb, Soto enables himself to write with a freshness that is at times arresting," Wojahn considered the work "a disappointment." He praised *San Joaquin* and *Tale of Sunlight* as "thematically urgent . . . and ambitious in their scope" and said that "compared to them, *Black Hair* is a distinctly minor achievement." Others, such as Ellen Lesser in *Voice Literary Supplement,* were charmed by Soto's poetic tone, "the quality of the voice, the immediate, human presence that breathes through the lines." Lesser contended that Soto's celebration of innocence and sentiment is shaded with a knowledge of "the larger, often threatening world." In the *Christian Science Monitor,* Tom D'Evelyn hailed Soto's ability to go beyond the circumstances of his own life and write of "something higher," concluding, "Somehow Gary Soto has become not an important Chicano poet but an important American poet. More power to him."

When Soto discusses American racial tensions in the prose collections *Living up the Street: Narrative Recollections* and *Small Faces,* he uses vignettes drawn from his own childhood. One vignette shows the anger the author felt upon realizing that his brown-skinned brother would never be considered an attractive child by conventional American standards. Another shows Soto's surprise at discovering that, contrary to his family's advice to marry a Mexican, he was falling in love with a woman of Japanese ancestry. In these deliberately small-scale recollections, as Paredes noted, "it is a measure of Soto's skill that he so effectively invigorates and sharpens our understanding of the commonplace." With these volumes Soto acquired a solid reputation as a prose writer as well as a poet; *Living up the Street* earned him an American Book Award.

Soto's autobiographical prose continued with *Lesser Evils: Ten Quartets* and *A Summer Life.* The first of

these, as Soto explained in an unpublished 1988 interview, reflects the author's experience with Catholicism—in the same interview Soto declared himself a reconciled Catholic. *A Summer Life* consists of thirty-nine short essays. According to Ernesto Trejo in the *Los Angeles Times Book Review,* these pieces "make up a compelling biography" of Soto's youth. As he had done in previous works, Soto here "holds the past up to memory's probing flashlight, turns it around ever so carefully, and finds in the smallest of incidents the occasion for literature." Writing in the *Americas Review,* Hector Torres compared *A Summer Life* with Soto's earlier autobiographical texts and asserted that the later book "moves with greater stylistic elegance and richer thematic coherence."

During the early 1990s Soto turned his attentions in a new direction: children's literature. A first volume of short stories for young readers, *Baseball in April and Other Stories,* was published in 1990. The eleven tales depict Mexican-American boys and girls as they enter adolescence in Hispanic California neighborhoods. In the *New York Times Book Review,* Roberto Gonzalez Echevarria called the stories "sensitive and economical." Echevarria praised Soto: "Because he stays within the teenagers' universe . . . he manages to convey all the social change and stress without bathos or didacticism. In fact, his stories are moving, yet humorous and entertaining." In the *Americas Review,* Torres suggested that *Baseball in April* was "the kind of work that could be used to teach high school and junior high school English classes."

One of Soto's juvenile characters, a boy named Lincoln Mendoza, appears as a protagonist in two works: *Taking Sides* and *Pacific Crossing.* As a Mexican-American eighth-grader in *Taking Sides,* Lincoln is confronted with challenges and insecurities when he and his mother move from San Francisco's Mission District to a predominantly Anglo suburb. He works to keep his heritage intact in his new environment. *Pacific Crossing* finds Lincoln and one of his friends facing cultural challenges in another context: they embark on a voyage to Japan as exchange students. Writing in the *Multicultural Review,* Osbelia Juarez Rocha called *Pacific Crossing* "cleverly crafted" and "entertaining."

Soto has also written poetry for younger readers, most notably the volumes *A Fire in My Hands* and *Neighborhood Odes,* both of which focus on growing up in the Mexican neighborhoods of California's Central Valley. Soto has ventured as well into the arena of children's picture books. *Too Many Tamales* depicts the story of Maria, a young girl who misplaces her mother's wedding ring in tamale dough while helping to prepare a Christmastime feast. Maria—with her cousins' help—embarks on a futile effort to recover the ring by consuming vast quantities of tamales. *Chato's Kitchen* introduces a cat whose efforts to entice the local "ratoncitos"—little mice—lead him to prepare abundant portions of fajitas, frijoles, enchiladas, and other foods.

In a 1989 volume of the *Dictionary of Literary Biography,* Hector Torres declared: "Soto's consistent attention to the craft of writing and his sensitivity to his subject matter have earned him an indisputable place in American and Chicano literature." Torres noted that critical response to Soto's work has been "overwhelmingly positive." He attributed that respect and admiration to Soto's ability to represent his experience "in a manner that shows his talent at creating poetry and prose that, through simple and direct diction, expresses the particulars of everyday life and simultaneously contains glimpses of the universal."

BIOGRAPHICAL/CRITICAL SOURCES:

BOOKS

Bruce-Novoa, Juan, *Chicano Poetry: A Response to Chaos,* University of Texas Press (Austin), 1982.
Children's Literature Review, Volume 38, Gale, 1996.
Contemporary Literary Criticism, Gale, Volume 32, 1985; Volume 80, 1994.
Dictionary of Literary Biography, Volume 82: *Chicano Writers,* Gale, 1989.
Hispanic Literature Criticism, Gale, 1994.

PERIODICALS

American Book Review, July-August, 1982.
Americas Review, spring, 1991, pp. 111-15.
Christian Science Monitor, March 6, 1985.
Denver Quarterly, summer, 1982.
Los Angeles Times Book Review, August 5, 1990, pp. 1, 9.
Multicultural Review, June 1993, pp. 76, 78.
Nation, June 7, 1993, pp. 772-74.
NEA Today, November, 1992, p. 9.
New York Times Book Review, May 20, 1990, p. 45.
Parnassus, fall-winter, 1979.

Poetry, March, 1980, June, 1985.
Publishers Weekly, March 23, 1992, p. 74; April 12, 1993, p. 64; August 16, 1993, p. 103; February 6, 1995, pp. 84-85.
Revista Chicano-Riquena, summer, 1983.
Rocky Mountain Review, Volume 41, numbers 1-2, 1987.
San Francisco Review of Books, summer, 1986.
Voice Literary Supplement, September, 1985.
Western American Literature, spring, 1979.*

*   *   *

SUAREZ LYNCH, B.
See BIOY CASARES, Adolfo

*   *   *

SUASSUNA, Ariano Vilar 1927-

PERSONAL: Born in 1927. *Education:* Studied law.

CAREER: Playwright. Pernambuco Student Theater, Brazil founder, 1946.

WRITINGS:

Auto da compadecida (play), 1956, translation published as *The Rogue's Trial,* University of California Press (Berkeley, CA), 1963.
Uma mulher vestida de sol (play; title means "A Woman Dressed in the Sun"), 1947.
O santo e a porca (play; title means "The Saint and the Pig"), 1957.
Romance d'a Pedra do Reino (historical novel; title means "Romance of the Kingdom's Stone"), 1971.
A pena e a lei, 1971.
Farsa da boa preguica, 1974.
Ferros do Cariri: uma heraldica sertaneja, Guariba Editora de Arte, 1974.
O Movimento Armorial, Editoria Univerestaria, 1974.
Historia do rei degolado nas caatingas do sertao (historical novel; title means "Story of the King Beheaded in the Sagebrush of the Backlands"), 1977.
Fernando e Isaura, Edicoes Bagaco, 1994.

BIOGRAPHICAL/CRITICAL SOURCES:

BOOKS

Dinneen, Mark, *Listening to the People's Voice: Erudite and Popular Literature in North East Brazil,* Kegan Paul International (New York City), 1996.
Dineen, Mark, *The Relationship between Erudite Literature and Popular Culture in the North East of Brazil: Ariano Suassuna and Armorial Art,* Latin American Studies, University of Glasgow (Glasgow, Scotland), 1990.

PERIODICALS

Hispania, March, 1961, pp. 282-84.*

T-U

TEJA, Jesus F(rancisco) de la 1956-

PERSONAL: Born July 17, 1956, in Cienfuegos, Cuba; became U.S. citizen; son of Francisco and Julia Maria (maiden name, Irimia; present surname, Castellano) de la Teja; married Magdalena Hernandez (a college dean), August 6, 1983; children: Eduardo, Julia. *Education:* Seton Hall University, B.A., 1979, M.A., 1981; University of Texas at Austin, Ph.D., 1988. *Politics:* Independent. *Religion:* Roman Catholic. *Avocational interests:* Music appreciation, travel, light home remodeling.

ADDRESSES: Home—Austin, TX. *Office*—Department of History, Southwest Texas State University, San Marcos, TX 78666; fax 512-245-3043. *E-mail*—JD10@swt.edu.

CAREER: Texas General Land Office, Austin, assistant archivist, 1985-89, archivist, 1989-90, director of archives and records, 1990-91, managing editor of *The Land Commissioners of Texas: 150 Years of the General Land Office,* 1986, and *Guide to Spanish and Mexican Land Grants in South Texas,* 1988; Southwest Texas State University, San Marcos, assistant professor, 1991-96, associate professor of history, 1996—. Austin Community College, adjunct instructor, 1988-90; Institute of Texas Studies, instructor, 1992, 1994; guest speaker at University of Texas at Austin, 1985, 1989, Victoria College and Texas Southern University, 1992, St. Mary's University and University of California, San Diego, 1993; and University of Texas at Arlington, 1995. Appeared in the videotape documentary *The Texas Revolution: From Anahuac to San Jacinto,* produced by Forest Glen Television Productions, Inc., 1989, the television documentary *The Alamo,* broadcast by The History Channel, 1996, and *America's Hispanic Heritage: Deep Roots, Continuing Enrichment,* a radio series produced by Media Works, 1996; expert witness in Texas District Court on land tenure patterns and land grant history. Catholic Archives of Texas, member of advisory committee, 1989—; Texas Conservation Fund, member of board of directors, 1991—; City of Austin, member of Library Commission, 1994—; Castlewood-Oak Valley Neighborhood Association, president, 1994—. South Austin Optimists Little League, coach, 1993-94.

MEMBER: Conference on Latin American History, Western History Association, Southwest Council on Latin American Studies (life member), Society of Southwest Archivists, Texas State Historical Association (life member), Texas Catholic Historical Society.

AWARDS, HONORS: Grant from John D. and Catherine T. MacArthur Foundation, 1991-92; Sons of the Republic of Texas, Summerfield G. Roberts Award, 1991, for *A Revolution Remembered,* and Presidio La Bahia Award, 1995, for *San Antonio de Bexar;* Citation, San Antonio Conservation Society, 1995, for *San Antonio de Bexar.*

WRITINGS:

(Editor and contributor) *A Revolution Remembered: The Memoirs and Selected Correspondence of Juan N. Seguin,* State House Press (Austin, TX), 1991.
(Technical editor) *Society of Southwest Archivists Guide to Archival and Manuscript Repositories,* Society of Southwest Archivists, 1993.
San Antonio de Bexar: A Community on New Spain's Northern Frontier, University of New Mexico Press (Albuquerque, NM), 1995.

The Settlement of Texas, Part I: *The Native Americans,* Part II: *The Hispanics and the Americans* (documentary videotape series), W. S. Benson and Co., 1996.

Working Texas: From Ranchers and Roughnecks to Sodbusters and Spacemen (documentary videotape), W. S. Benson and Co., 1996.

Contributor to books, including *Hispanic Texas: A Historical Guide,* edited by Helen Simons and Cathryn Hoyt, University of Texas Press (Austin), 1992; *Tejano Journey, 1770-1860,* edited by Gerald E. Poyo, University of Texas Press, 1996; and *Myths, Misdeeds, and Misunderstandings: The Roots of Conflict in United States-Mexico Relations,* edited by Jaime E. Rodriguez O. and Kathryn Vincent, Scholarly Resources (Wilmington, DE), 1997. Contributor of articles, translations, and reviews to periodicals, including *Locus: An Historical Journal of Regional Perspectives, East Texas Historical Journal, Historia Mexicana,* and *Gulf Coast Historical Review.* Member of editorial advisory board, *Southwestern Historical Quarterly,* 1996—; advisory editor, *New Handbook of Texas,* 1989-96.

WORK IN PROGRESS: "Spanish Colonial Texas," to be included in a survey on the demographic, economic, and social history of the Spanish North American borderlands; research on the history of the annual trade fair held at Saltillo, Mexico, from the eighteenth through the nineteenth centuries.

*   *   *

TELLES, Lygia Fagundes 1923-

PERSONAL: Born April 19, 1923 (some sources cite 1924), in Sao Paulo, Brazil; married Gofredo da Silva Telles (divorced, 1961); married Paulo Emilio Salles Gomes (writer and film critic; died, 1977). *Education:* Educated at various institutions; obtained degrees in physical education and law.

ADDRESSES: Office—c/o Livaria Jose Olympio Editora, CP 9018, 22251 Rio de Janeiro RJ, Brazil.

CAREER: Lawyer and author; president of Brazilian Cinematheque.

AWARDS, HONORS: Afonso Arinos prize, 1949; Instituto Nacional do Livro prize, 1958; Boa Leitura Prize, 1961; Cannes Prix International des Femmes,

1969, for short story "Before the Green Masquerade"; Guimaraes Roas prize, 1972; Coelho Neto prize, Brazilian Academy of Letters, Sao Paulo Association of Art Critics fiction prize, and Jabuti Prize, Association of Brazilian Publishers, all 1973, all for *As menias;* Pedro Nava award, 1989; elected to Brazilian Academy of Letters.

WRITINGS:

FICTION

Porao e sobrado (short stories), [Sao Paulo], 1938.

Praia viva (short stories; title means "Living Beach"), Martins (Sao Paulo), 1943.

O cacto vermelho (short stories; title means "Red Cactus"), Merito (Rio de Janeiro), 1949.

Ciranda de pedra (novel; title means "Stone Screen"), Nova Fronteira (Rio de Janeiro), 1954, fifth edition, Olympio (Rio de Janeiro), 1976, translation by M. Neves published as *The Marble Dance,* Avon (New York City), 1986.

Historias do desencontro (short stories; title means "Stories of the Conflict"), Olympio, 1958.

Historias escolhidas, Boa Leitura (Sao Paulo), 1961.

Verao no aquario (novel; title means "Summer in the Aquarium"), Martins, 1963, fourth edition, Olympio, 1976.

O jardim selvagem (short stories; title means "Savage Garden"), Martins, 1965.

Antes do baile verde (short stories; title means "Before the Green Masquerade"), Bloch (Rio de Janeiro), 1970, third edition, Olympio, 1975.

Seleta. Organizaco estudos e notas da professora Nelly Novais Coelho, Olympio, 1971.

As menias (novel), Olympio, 1973, eighth edition, 1976, translation by Margaret A. Neves published as *The Girl in the Photograph,* Avon, 1982.

Seminario dos ratos (title means "Rat Seminar"), Olympio, 1977, translation by M. Neves published as *Tigrela and Other Stories,* Avon, 1986.

Filhos prodigos (short stories; title means "Prodigal Sons"), Cultura (Sao Paulo), 1978.

A disciplina do amor: fragmentos (title means "The Discipline of Love"), Nova Fronteira, 1980.

Misterios: ficcoes, Nova Fronteira, 1981.

Os melhores contos, edited by Eduardo Portella, Global (Sao Paulo), 1984.

Diez contos escolhidos, Horizonte (Brasilia), 1984.

Venha ver o por-do-sol y outros contos, Atica (Sao Paolo), 1988.

As horas nuas, Nova Fronteira, 1989.

A Estrutura da bolha de sabao: contos, 1991.

A noite escura e mais eu: contos, 1995.

Also author of *Os mortos,* 1963, and *A confissao de Leontina,* 1964.

SIDELIGHTS: Writer Lygia Fagundes Telles finished her first fiction in 1938, when she was just fifteen years old; five decades later she was still impressing critics and audiences alike with her sometimes surrealistic examinations of her native Brazil's middle and upper classes. "Her efforts as a writer have brought her to the forefront of contemporary Brazilian fiction," writes Jon M. Tolman of Telles in a *Review* article. "Indeed, she has won virtually every major literary prize in Brazil and her writings have found their way into high school and college curricula around the country."

A consistent best-selling author in Brazil, Telles's best-known translated work is the novel *The Girl in the Photograph,* published in the United States in 1982, nine years after its original Brazilian release. A densely layered tale of three school friends from the 1960s who embody the various roles of women in contemporary Brazil—from Marxist revolutionary to bourgeois idealist—*Photograph* is a work whose plot several critics have likened to Jacqueline Susann's *Valley of the Dolls* as seen through the stream-of-consciousness mind of James Joyce's Molly Bloom.

Indeed, some critics found *Photograph* slow going: The narration, "sometimes buried in subordinate clauses deep within pages-long interior monologues," according to a *Los Angeles Times Book Review* contributor, "is hard for this Philistine mind to follow." William Kennedy, reviewing Telles's novel in the *Washington Post Book World,* elaborates: "The internal monologue is a tool, but only a genius can use it to the degree Fagundes Telles uses it. It becomes repetitive and obvious here, an unpleasant thing to say about a writer of her quality." *Newsweek's* Jim Miller, comparing Telles's work to those of two other contemporary Brazilian novelists, sees "puzzling, pungent, often starkly political" images in the books. While he found *Photograph* "the most naturalistic and least edgy" of the three Brazilian novels he read, Miller adds that "in all three, there's a sense of fierce urgency, a readiness to try almost anything, as if the raw material of history had sabotaged the comforts of conventional narrative."

BIOGRAPHICAL/CRITICAL SOURCES:

BOOKS

Contemporary World Writers, St. James Press (Detroit, MI), 1993.

Monteiro, Leonardo, editor, *Lygia Fagundes Telles* (selected works and criticism), Abril Educacao (Sao Paulo), 1980.

PERIODICALS

Los Angeles Times Book Review, August 1, 1982, p. 8.
Modern Language Studies, Volume 19, number 1, 1989.
Newsweek, July 12, 1982, p. 71.
New York Times Book Review, May 4, 1986.
Review, September 1981; Volume 36, 1986.
Washington Post Book World, August 1, 1982, p. 1.
World Literature Today, spring, 1978, p. 276.*

*   *   *

THURLO, Aimee
(Aimee Duvall, Aimee Martell, pseudonyms)

PERSONAL: Born in Cuba; married David Thurlo (a writer).

ADDRESSES: Home—P.O. Box 2747, Corrales, NM 87048. *Agent*—c/o Forge, 175 Fifth Ave., New York, NY 10010. *E-mail*—72640.2437@compuserve.com.

CAREER: Full-time writer, with husband David Thurlo, of romance and mystery novels.

AWARDS, HONORS: Nominated for Career Achievement Award, *Romantic Times Magazine,* 1997.

WRITINGS:

ROMANCE NOVELS; WITH HUSBAND, DAVID THURLO (NOT CREDITED)

Ariel's Desire ("Dell Candlelight Ecstasy" series, #509), Harlequin (New York City), 1987.
The Right Combination ("Harlequin Super" series, #312), Harlequin (New York City), 1988.
Expiration Date ("Harlequin Intrigue" series, #109), Harlequin (New York City), 1989.
Black Mesa ("Harlequin Intrigue" series, #131), Harlequin (New York City), 1990.
Suitable For Framing ("Harlequin Intrigue" series, #141), Harlequin (New York City), 1990.
Strangers Who Linger ("Harlequin Intrigue" series, #162), Harlequin (New York City), 1991.

Night Wind ("Harlequin Intrigue" series, #175), Harlequin (New York City), 1991.

Breach Of Faith ("Harlequin Intrigue" series, #200). Harlequin (New York City), 1992.

Shadow Of the Wolf ("Harlequin Intrigue" series, #217), Harlequin (New York City), 1993.

Spirit Warrior ("Harlequin Intrigue" series, #246), Harlequin (New York City), 1993.

Timewalker ("Harlequin Intrigue" series, #275), Harlequin (New York City), 1994.

Bearing Gifts ("Harlequin Intrigue" series, #304), Harlequin (New York City), 1994.

Fatal Charm ("Harlequin Intrigue" series, #337), Harlequin (New York City), 1995.

Cisco's Woman (Harlequin Intrigue—"Renegade Lawman" series), Harlequin (New York City), 1996.

ROMANCE NOVELS; "FOUR WINDS" TRILOGY; WITH DAVID THURLO (NOT CREDITED)

Her Destiny, Harlequin (New York City), 1997.
Her Hope, Harlequin (New York City), 1997.
Her Shadow, Harlequin (New York City), 1997.

ROMANCE NOVELS UNDER PSEUDONYM AIMEE MARTEL; WITH DAVID THURLO (NOT CREDITED)

Secrets Not Shared ("Leisure" series), Harlequin (New York City), 1981.

The Fires Within ("Silhouette Desire" series, #136), Harlequin (New York City), 1984.

Hero At Large ("Silhouette Desire" series, #249), Harlequin (New York City), 1984.

Redhawk's Heart ("Harlequin Intrigue" series), Harlequin, 1999;

Redhawk's Return ("Harlequin Intrigue" series), Harlequin, 1999.

ROMANCE NOVELS UNDER PSEUDONYM AIMEE DUVALL; WITH DAVID THURLO (NOT CREDITED)

Too Near the Sun ("Second Chance at Love" series, #56), Harlequin (New York City), 1982.

Halfway There ("Second Chance at Love" series, #67), Harlequin (New York City), 1982.

Lover in Blue ("Second Chance at Love" series, #84), Harlequin (New York City), 1982.

The Loving Touch ("Second Chance at Love" series, #159), Harlequin (New York City), 1983.

After the Rain ("Second Chance at Love" series, #179), Harlequin (New York City), 1984.

One More Tomorrow ("Second Chance at Love" series, #211), Harlequin (New York City), 1984.

Brief Encounters ("Second Chance at Love" series, #252), Harlequin (New York City), 1985.

Spring Madness ("Second Chance at Love" series, #299), Harlequin (New York City), 1985.

Kid at Heart ("Second Chance at Love" series, #348), Harlequin (New York City), 1986.

Made for Each Other ("Second Chance at Love" series, #392), Harlequin (New York City), 1987.

To Tame a Heart ("Pageant Romance" series), Harlequin (New York City), 1988.

Wings Of Angels ("Pageant Romance" series), Harlequin (New York City), 1989.

MYSTERY NOVELS; WITH DAVID THURLO

Second Shadow, Forge (New York City), 1993.

Blackening Song ("Ella Clah" series), Forge (New York City), 1995.

Death Walker ("Ella Clah" series), Forge (New York City), 1996.

Bad Medicine ("Ella Clah" series), Forge (New York City), 1997.

Enemy Way ("Ella Clah" series), Forge (New York City), 1998.

OTHER

Contributor to periodicals, including *National Enquirer, Grit,* and *Popular Mechanics*.

WORK IN PROGRESS: More romance novels

SIDELIGHTS: Aimee Thurlo has been married to her husband, David, for nearly thirty years and they have been writing together for almost as long. The couple began their writing partnership with articles for periodicals such as *Grit, Popular Mechanics,* and the *National Enquirer,* but soon branched out into fiction. Together the Thurlos have written more than thirty novels which have been published in over twenty countries and repeatedly made both Waldenbooks' and B. Dalton's bestseller lists.

Born in Cuba, Thurlo has lived in New Mexico for almost thirty years. Her husband, David, was raised in Shiprock, New Mexico, on the Navajo Indian Reservation, which he left after seventeen years to complete his education at the University of New Mexico. The couple spent years honing their talents writing romance and romantic intrigue novels under Thurlo's name and the pseudonyms Aimee Martel and Aimee Duvall and have produced such works as *Strangers Who Linger, Expiration Date,* and *To Tame a Heart.*

In the early 1990s the Thurlos took a new direction with their writing. They decided to pool their resources and use their knowledge of genre fiction and Navajo traditions to produce unique mysteries set on the Shiprock Reservation.

The Thurlo's first Shiprock novel, *Second Shadow,* combines mystery and romantic elements. Irene Pobikan, a Tewa Indian and an architect, receives her first commission—to renovate the Mendoza hacienda—because of her extensive experience with adobe buildings from the Pueblo. The Mendozas have a history of mistreating the people of her tribe, and tight deadlines force both architect and construction crew to live on the isolated Mendoza property. No sooner does she begin construction, however, than a series of mysterious accidents occurs. When Irene discovers a twenty-year-old corpse on the site and becomes aware of a hostile prowler, she turns to her Tewa beliefs and calls on her guardian spirit, the mountain lion, for protection and help. In the meantime, she finds herself falling for Raul Mendoza despite the fact that his alcoholic brother Gene is determined to sabotage her hard work. Also present in the novel is Raul's beautiful but mildly retarded sister, Elena, who has an important secret she cannot share. Although a *Publishers Weekly* reviewer found the novel's "cliffhanger" chapter endings too formulaic, *Library Journal* reviewer Marion F. Gallivan praised the plotting, noting that the suspense "builds effectively to the finale."

Inspired by mystery novelist Tony Hillerman's enthusiasm and buoyed by the initial success of *Second Shadow,* the Thurlos then developed a mystery series set in the Southwest that features Ella Clah, a Navajo FBI agent who combines modern investigative techniques with traditional Native American beliefs to solve mysteries. In the first novel of the series, *Blackening Song,* Ella is called from Los Angeles to return to the Shiprock Reservation, which she had left at age eighteen. Her father, a Christian minister, has been found murdered and mutilated in a way that suggests a ritual killing. Ella's brother Clifford, a *hataali,* or traditional medicine man, has fled and is now a prime suspect. Before the murder Clifford, a traditionalist, had argued vehemently with his father over the construction of a Christian church on the reservation. With the FBI investigation being conducted by an Anglo whose difficult history with the Navajo community, Ella finds that she must act as liaison between the bureau, the tribe, and the tribal police.

Teaming up with Wilson Joe, a college professor who is Clifford's closest friend and staunchest defender,

Ella finds her brother, who tells her that their father was murdered by Navajo witches called "skinwalkers," members of a religious cult that practices black magic. Rumors about the skinwalkers abound on the reservation, and when ghostly coyotes are spotted before three men are found murdered in a manner similar to that of Ella's father, Ella is forced to reconsider the traditional beliefs she abandoned years ago. A *Publishers Weekly* reviewer commented, "Contrasting the high-tech and hyperrational methods of the FBI with the ritual world of the Navajo . . . , the Thurlos ratchet up a lot of suspense. Throw away logic and enjoy." A *Library Journal* critic observed that "the action moves swiftly in this well-written mystery." A *Kirkus Reviews* critic, while commenting that the characters are "thinly sketched," commented, "The real pleasure here is in the complex depiction of cultural conflict and assimilation."

In *Death Walker,* the second in the Ella Clah series, Ella joins the Navajo tribal police force as a special investigator. The case she faces threatens the cultural traditions of the Navajo people, who revere their elders as "living treasures," those who embody the tribe's heritage and collective wisdom. After tribal historian Kee Dodge is clubbed to death and apparently symbolic religious artifacts are left near his body, one elder after another is similarly slain, and Ella must face the likely possibility that the malignant skinwalkers are preying upon the tribe again. While dealing with a minimal staff, threats directed at her family, and the skewed mind of the psychopathic killer, Ella draws both on her FBI experience and her intuition to solve the crimes. She is aided by her young cousin, Justine Goodluck, who joins the investigation as Ella's assistant. A reviewer for the *Armchair Detective* praised the "grittily convincing atmosphere and landscapes" and noted that the female characters in *Death Walker* are "particularly well drawn." A *School Library Journal* reviewer also praised the Thurlos' use of landscape and description and approved of the way "characters develop into unique individuals with talents, strengths, weaknesses, and idiosyncrasies." This reviewer called *Death Walker* "a fast-paced, intriguing novel."

Bad Medicine, the third novel in the Ella Clah series, begins with two seemingly unrelated homicides. On her way to investigate the fatal clubbing of Navajo–rights activist Stanley Bitah, Ella attends to a report of a drunk driver fatality. The problem is that Angelina Yellowhair was not drunk at all; she had been fatally poisoned even before her car crashed, and Ella finds herself pulled in many directions as she struggles to focus on both murders. Suspects in Bitah's murder include fellow coal miners who may resent his ties to the Navajo Justice Church, as well as the members of the Brotherhood, a white supremacist group, and the Fierce Ones, composed of residents of the Navajo reservation. However, the suspects must go temporarily uninvestigated because State Senator James Yellowhair, the father of Angelina, is pressuring Ella and tribal medical examiner Carolyn Roanhorse to overlook forensic evidence of drugs in Angelina's body and halt their investigation.

While Ella struggles to balance her cases, Angelina's tissue samples and poisoned organs disappear. Infections soon break out among Dr. Roanhorse's patients, and the medical examiner's credibility, career, and home come under attack. Stories on the reservation suggest that the examiner has been contaminated by the *chindi,* earthbound spirits of the dead, and that Dr. Roanhorse is spreading this contamination to the people. Ella must prove Dr. Roanhorse's innocence before her friend is murdered. A *Kirkus Reviews* critic found *Bad Medicine* "overstuffed" and "too much of a good thing," and added "trying to sort out the suspects and subplots is like wandering for hours" in a museum "filled with fascinating exhibits."

In *Enemy Way,* the fourth Ella Clah mystery, the Navajo Police force continues to be strained to the limit. Gang violence, drunk driving, and the murder of a loved one of an old friend create headaches for Ella as her investigative skills are needed everywhere at once. When her mother is seriously injured in a car accident, Ella takes on family responsibilities that threaten her career just at a time when her old enemies, the skinwalkers, make their presence known once again. A *Publishers Weekly* said of *Enemy Way,* "In a world out of balance, Ella strives to find the harmony between work and family, tradition and modernity. She herself remains an intriguing bundle of contrasts."

BIOGRAPHICAL/CRITICAL SOURCES:

BOOKS

Heising, Willetta L., editor, *Detecting Women 2,* Purple Moon Press (Dearborn, MI), 1996.
Reginald, Robert, *Science Fiction & Fantasy Literature, 1975-1991,* Gale (Detroit, MI), 1992.

PERIODICALS

Armchair Detective, summer, 1996, pp. 361-362.

Kirkus Reviews, May 1, 1995, p. 216; October 1, 1997.
Library Journal, October 15, 1993, p. 91; July, 1995, p. 124.
Publishers Weekly, April 5, 1991, p. 140; October 4, 1993, p. 65; May 1, 1995, p. 46; April 22, 1996, p. 62; August 25, 1997, pp. 48-49; July 27, 1998, p. 57.
School Library Journal, March, 1997, pp. 216-217.

OTHER

Amazon.com, http://www.amazon.com (August 16, 1998).
Aimee and David Thurlo page, http://www.primenet. com/~callie/authors/thurlo.htm (December 16, 1998).
Aimee and David Thurlo, Authors of the Ella Clah Mystery Series, http://www.comet.net/writersm/ thurlo/home.htm (September 4, 1997).
Daphne's Dream (A Bookstore) - Aimee Thurlo Page, http://www.mindspring.com/~driordan/authors/ thurlo.htm (December 17, 1998).
My Unicorn—Aimee Thurlo Bibliography, http:// www.myunicorn.com/bib110\bib11050.html (December 17, 1998).
Ultimate Mystery Fiction Web Guide, http://www. magicdragon.com/UltimateMystery/authorsT. html#Th (December 16, 1998).*

*   *   *

TORRES, Daniel 1958-

PERSONAL: Born August 20, 1958, in Teresa de Cofrentes, Valencia, Spain; son of Francisco Torres (a doctor) and Maria Perez; children: Carlos, Javier. *Education:* Studied fine art at the University of Valencia, 1975-80.

ADDRESSES: Home—Paseo San Juan 22, 08010 Barcelona, Spain. *Agent*—Norma Editorial, Passeig de Sant Joan 22, 08010 Barcelona, Spain. *E-mail*—norma @norma-ed.es.

CAREER: Writer and illustrator.

WRITINGS:

SELF-ILLUSTRATED;

Opium, Norma (Barcelona, Spain), 1983.

Las aventuras siderales de Roco Vargas, Norma, 1984.

El misterio de Susurro, Norma, 1985.

Saxxon, Norma, 1986.

Del asesinato al Olimpo, Norma, 1986.

La Estrella lejana, Norma, 1987.

Sabotaje, Norma, 1988.

Triton, Norma, 1989.

El octavo dia, Norma, 1992.

Textura humana: historias cortas 1988-1992, Norma, 1995.

Cabronerias, o, Historias de tres cuerpos, 1995.

El octavo dia II, Norma, 1996.

Tom, Norma (Barcelona, Spain), 1996, translation by Julie Simmons-Lynch, Viking, 1996.

ILLUSTRATOR

David Gerrold, *Chess with a Dragon,* Walker, 1987.

WORK IN PROGRESS: Tom in LA and *The Angel of Notre-Dame.*

SIDELIGHTS: Born in Valencia, Spain, Daniel Torres is an author and illustrator of children's books. With an educational background in fine arts, Torres has been praised for his illustrations, which *New York Times Book Review* critic Karla Kuskin described as "proficiently drawn and painted . . . with amusing attention to detail."

Torres once explained: "For me, to make an illustration is to tell a little story with just one image, so that the reader will be seduced as much by the moment the drawing represents as by the 'before' and the 'after' of that instant. If we study the works of the masters, Rackham [Arthur], Rockwell [Norman], Wyeth [N. C.], Dulac [Edmund], etc., we will see that their mastery of technique is the vehicle they have used to catch the reader with the scene, so that he or she will be able to imagine things that are only suggested in the image. To attain that fascination is the most attractive aspect in this job. I try to find it every time I place myself in front of a white sheet of paper.

"When I was a child I read the story of a boy who kept a dragon inside a shoe box: the fact that nobody believed him didn't make his dragon less real. *Tom* tells the adventures of a dinosaur who visits New York. Somehow, Tom is a descendant of my childhood's dragon. For me, he is more real than many people I know, and I try [to ensure], when telling his adventures, that all those who meet him get to believe that they have a dragon in a shoe box."

Tom, is Torres' attempt to bring a dragon—or rather a dinosaur—to life. Tom, the main character, is a dinosaur who travels around the world on his own island. When Tom arrives in New York, he decides to brave the city traffic and crowds to find a job. He tries several careers, but none of them have the right fit for a Jurassic giant. The art critic father of a newfound friend then suggests a career as an artist, inspiring Tom to use his artistic flair for creating footprints to become a huge success. Ilene Cooper of *Booklist* called the story a "clever tale of a friendly dino who tries to make it in the Big Apple," while Roger Sutton of *Bulletin of the Center for Children's Books* was less enthused, labeling *Tom* a "small formulaic story." Torres' detailed illustrations, however, were the subject of frequent praise. Karla Kuskin, in the *New York Times Book Review,* waxed poetic when writing of the "city and sky . . . suffused in soft blues." Emphasizing the role of "the pictures [that] amaze and astonish," a *Kirkus Reviews* critic asserted, "this is a book for the eyes."

BIOGRAPHICAL/CRITICAL SOURCES:

PERIODICALS

Booklist, March 15, 1996, p. 1269.

Bulletin of the Center for Children's Books, March, 1996, p. 245.

Kirkus Reviews, March 15, 1996, p. 453.

New York Times Book Review, May 19, 1996, p. 32.

Publishers Weekly, June 12, 1987, pp. 85-86.

School Library Journal, September, 1987, p. 196.

*   *   *

TREJO, Ernesto 1950-1991

PERSONAL: Born March 4, 1950, in Fresnillo, Mexico; died in 1991. *Education:* California State University, Fresno, B.A. and M.A.; University of Iowa, M.F.A., 1976.

CAREER: Poet. Government economist in Mexico City, Mexico, beginning in 1976; California State University, Fresno, part-time teacher of Spanish and English, 1983; Fresno City College, Fresno, teacher of writing and literature classes, 1985-90. Gave readings of his works.

WRITINGS:

POETRY

The Day of Vendors, Calavera (Fresno, CA), 1977.

Instrucciones y Senales (title means "Instructions and Signals"), Maquina Electrica (Mexico City, Mexico), 1977.

Los Nombres Propios (title means "Proper Names"), Latitudes (Mexico City), 1978.

El Dia entre las Hojas (title means "The Day among the Leaves"), Fondo de Cultura Economica (Mexico City), 1984.

(Editor with Jon Veinberg, and contributor) *Piecework: Nineteen Fresno Poets,* Silver Skates (Albany, CA), 1987.

Entering a Life, Arte Publico (Houston, TX), 1990.

Work represented in anthologies, including *Entrance: Four Chicano Poets,* edited by Leonard Adame, Greenfield Review Press (Greenfield Center, NY), 1975; *California Poetry Anthology,* Second Coming (San Francisco, CA), 1976; *Asamblea de Poetas,* edited by Gabriel Zaid, Siglo Veintiuno (Mexico City), 1980; *Palabra Nueva: Dos Decadas de Poesia en Mexico,* edited by Sandro Cohen, Premia (Mexico City), 1981; *Antologia de la Poesia Erotica,* Federacion Editorial Mexicana (Mexico City), 1982; *Parvada: Poetas Jovenes de Baja California,* Universidad Autonomas de Baja California (Mexicali, Mexico), 1985; *500 Anos de Poesia en el Valle de Mexico,* edited by Aurora Marya Saavedra, Extemporaneos Ediciones Especiales (Mexico City), 1986; and *Mexico/Estados Unidos—Mexican/American Border Writing,* edited by Jose Manuel DiBella, Sergio Gomez Montero, and Harry Polkinhorn, Direccion de Asuntos Culturales/Institute for Regional Studies of the Californias (San Diego, CA), 1987. Contributor to periodicals, including *Nation, Partisan Review, Antioch Review, Vuelta, Backwash,* and *Kayak.*

TRANSLATOR

Tristan Solarte, *The Rule of Three,* International Writing Program, University of Iowa (Iowa City), 1976.

Gary Soto, *Como Arbustos de Niebla,* Latitudes, 1980.

(And editor, with Philip Levine) *Tarumba: The Selected Poems of Jaime Sabines,* Twin Peaks (San Francisco), 1987.

SIDELIGHTS: Ernesto Trejo earned acclaim from notable fellow poets in both Mexico and the United States. One of his admirers, Christopher Buckley, wrote in the *Dictionary of Literary Biography* that "whether in Spanish or in English, Trejo celebrates the imagination and its power to breathe a sense of expanded consciousness into the objects and events of the world. He employs inventive language and imagery, yet he is never overtaken by abstraction or the temptations of style for its own sake."

One of the distinctive features of Trejo's poetry is the elevation of the simple and the ordinary into the magical or unexpected. An example is the poem "This Is What Happened," from the collection *The Day of the Vendors,* which begins with the simple story of a driver whose attempt to avoid an animal in the road results in a car accident. When the poem is retold from the creature's point of view, however, the story changes dramatically and takes on a magical and somewhat unnerving tone.

Trejo composed poems in both Spanish and English with equal success. In his Spanish collections, Buckley asserted, Trejo exhibits a "concern with writing poetry . . . that is free of the rhetorical style of early modern Mexican poetry." His work, the critic noted, "demonstrates a fine balance between imagination and startling imagery [as in *Instrucciones y Senales*], and the personal and poignant tone of narrative [as in *Los Nombres Propios*]." Using both styles in various combinations, the poems in *El Dia entre las Hojas* "dissect appearance and reality and those fleeting moments made accessible only through the power of memory," according to Buckley. They "filter the illogical and ungenerous details of life and offer a reality that, while not always desirable, is compassionate in its awareness."

Similar features run through Trejo's English collections. Buckley observed that he "makes the emotions and ideas of his poems accessible to the reader even though Trejo is working at the edge of the surreal image-making process. . . . He makes us take a second and third look at the world around us and at ourselves." Trejo's first chapbook, *The Day of the Vendors,* was published while he was working as an economist in Mexico City, but the work attracted favorable attention from United States critics, as did the poems in the earlier anthology, *Entrance: Four Chicano Poets.*

The full-length collection *Entering a Life* contains both old and new poems, some of which are personal or autobiographical in nature. Even the story-poems that are rooted in family events display the inventiveness and twists of imagination that characterize all of his work, and each poem grows from the kernel of human emotion at its core. "Trejo pulls out all the possibilities to get at the uncertainty in our lives," Buckley declared, "but always he shows in his speculation great compassion, for all the outcomes are possible and real. . . . Even in the marvelous and somewhat surreal 'E.' poems. . . , we can tell that the poet's inventiveness is firmly anchored in the real world where often it is only imagination and song that lift us above our suffering and allow us to cherish our lives."

BIOGRAPHICAL/CRITICAL SOURCES:

BOOKS

Dictionary of Literary Biography, Volume 122: *Chicano Writers, Second Series,* edited by Francisco A. Lomeli and Carl R. Shirley, Gale (Detroit, MI), 1992, pp. 272-76.*

*   *   *

TRISTAN
  See GOMEZ DE LA SERNA, Ramon

*   *   *

ULIBARRI, Sabine R(eyes) 1919-

PERSONAL: Born September 21, 1919, in Santa Fe, NM; married Connie Limon, 1942; one child. *Education:* University of New Mexico, B.A., 1947, M.A., 1949; University of California, Los Angeles, Ph.D., 1959.

ADDRESSES: Home—1402 Dakota N.E., Albuquerque, NM 87110.

CAREER: Writer and educator. Teacher in Rio Arriba County, NM, schools, 1938-40; El Rito Normal School, El Rito, NM, teacher, 1940-42; University of New Mexico, Albuquerque, associate professor, 1947-68, professor of Spanish beginning in 1968; retired; chair of modern and classical languages department, 1971-80. Consultant, D.C. Heath-Louis de Rochemont project for teaching Spanish on television, 1962; directed National Defense Education Act (NDEA) Language Institute, Quito, Ecuador, 1963-64; director of

University of New Mexico Andean Study Center, Quito, 1968. *Military service:* U.S. Air Force, 1942-45; flew thirty-five combat missions as a gunner; received Distinguished Flying Cross and Air Medal four times.

MEMBER: Modern Language Association of America, American Association of Teachers of Spanish and Portuguese (vice president, 1968; president, 1969), Rocky Mountain Modern Language Association.

AWARDS, HONORS: Named distinguished citizen of Quito, Ecuador, 1964; member of Academia Norteamericana de la Lengua Espanola, 1978; Governor's Award for Excellence in Literature, 1988; Distinguished Alumni Award and Regents' Medal of Merit, University of New Mexico, 1989; Hispanic Heritage Award, 1989.

WRITINGS:

Spanish for the First Grade, Department of Modern and Classical Languages and College of Education, University of New Mexico, 1957.

El mundo poetico de Juan Ramon; estudio estilistico de la lengua poetica y de los simbolos, Edhigar (Madrid, Spain), 1962.

Fun Learning Elementary Spanish, [Albuquerque], Volume I, 1963, Volume II, 1965.

Tierra Amarilla: Cuentos de Nuevo Mexico, Casa de Cultura (Quito, Ecuador), 1964, English translation by Thelma Campbell Nason, with illustrations by Kercheville, published as *Tierra Amarilla: Stories of New Mexico,* University of New Mexico Press, 1971.

Al cielo se sube a pie (poetry), Alfaguara (Madrid), 1966.

Amor y Ecuador (poetry), Jose Porrua Turanzas (Madrid), 1966.

(Compiler, editor, translator, author of introduction, and contributor) *La fragua sin fuego/No Fire for the Forge* (stories and poems; parallel text in English and Spanish), translation by Flora V. Orozco and others, San Marcos Press (Cerrillos, NM), 1971.

El alma de la raza, University of New Mexico Minority Group Cultural Awareness Center, 1971.

Mi abuela fumaba puros y otros cuentos de Tierra Amarilla/My Grandma Smoked Cigars and Other Stories of Tierra Amarilla (parallel text in English and Spanish), illustrations by Dennis Martinez, Quinto Sol Publications (Berkeley), 1977.

Primeros encuentros/First Encounters (parallel text in English and Spanish), Editorial Bilingue/Bilingual Press (Ypsilanti, MI), 1982.

El gobernador Glu Glu, Editorial Bilingue/Bilingual Press, 1988.

El condor, and Other Stories (parallel text in English and Spanish), Arte Publico Press (Houston, TX), 1989.

Kissing Cousins: 1000 Words Common to Spanish and English, FOG Publications, 1991.

Flow of the River: Corre el Rio, Hispanic Culture Foundation, 1992.

Suenos/Dreams, University of Texas-Pan American Press, 1994.

Sabine R. Ulibarri: Critical Essays, edited by Maria Duke dos Santos and Patricia De la Fuente, University of New Mexico Press, 1995.

Mayhem Was Our Business/Memorias de un veterano, Bilingual Press, Hispanic Research Center, Arizona State University (Tempe, AZ), 1996.

SIDELIGHTS: Sabine R. Ulibarri is a celebrated Chicano writer best known for short stories in the *costumbrismo* literary tradition. These works combine elements of the oral folktale and local color, depicting the history, manners, and language of the New Mexican Chicano community familiar to Ulibarri from his childhood. Ulibarri was born in New Mexico. He attended the University of New Mexico, Georgetown University, and the University of California at Los Angeles. He later taught Spanish at the University of New Mexico and chaired the modern and classical languages department from 1971 until 1980.

Ulibarri has written and spoken in support of the Chicano Movement since its inception in the 1960s, and his works display wide knowledge of and concern for the distinctive culture of New Mexico's native Spanish-speaking population. Ulibarri has written poetry since childhood, and *Al cielo se sube a pie,* a collection of fifty short poems, was published in Mexico in 1961 and later in Spain. *Amor y Ecuador,* a second poetry collection, appeared in 1966.

Ulibarri is best known, however, for his short stories. The collections *Tierra Amarilla: Cuentos de Nuevo Mexico* (1964; *Tierra Amarilla: Stories of New Mexico/Cuentos de Nuevo Mexico*) and *Mi abuela fumaba puros y otros cuentos de Tierra Amarilla/My Grandmother Smoked Cigars, and Other Tales of Tierra Amarilla* (1977) contain some of his best-known works. Set for the most part in the Tierra Amarilla region of New Mexico where Ulibarri was born, these stories depict the people, mores, and language of the area with insight and compassion. Although Ulibarri's prose features realistic and naturalistic detail, particularly of landscape and behavior,

commentators note that a poetic sensibility informs his fiction. In some stories that antedate these collections, such as those collected in *El condor, and Other Stories* (1989), Ulibarri combines the *costumbrismo* tradition with elements of magical realism, in which fantastic elements are presented objectively to obscure distinctions between illusion and reality. Many of his story collections, including *Primeros encuentros/First Encounters* (1982), *Gobernador Glu Glu y otros cuentos/Governor Glu Glu, and Other Stories* (1988), *Corre el rio/Flow of the River* (1992), *El condor,* and *The Best of Sabine R. Ulibarri* (1993), have been published in bilingual editions in both Spanish and English.

Ulibarri's more recent introduction of elements of magical realism into his fiction has not been enthusiastically received; Juan Bruce-Novoa proposed giving this "interesting, if not altogether successful, synthesis of New Mexican oral tradition and mainstream magical realism" the designation "magical regionalism." Ulibarri is, however, largely commended for his facility as a costumbrista. The bilingual publication of much of Ulibarri's short fiction makes him one of the most widely read and accessible Chicano authors in the United States. Donald W. Urioste has written that Ulibarri's stories "transcend the superficially picturesque and quaint intent of *costumbrismo* to present larger, more universal lessons about life and human conduct."

BIOGRAPHICAL/CRITICAL SOURCES:

BOOKS

Contemporary Literary Criticism, Volume 83, Gale, 1994.

Dictionary of Literary Biography, Volume 82: *Chicano Writers, First Series,* Gale, 1989.

Lomeli, Francisco A. and Donald W. Urioste, *Chicano Perspectives in Literature: A Critical and Annotated Bibliography,* Pajarito Publications (Albuquerque), 1976.

Martinez, Julio A. and Francisco A. Lomeli, editors, *Chicano Literature: A Reference Guide,* Greenwood Press, 1985.

Meier, Matt S., *Mexican American Biographies: A Historical Dictionary, 1836-1987,* Greenwood Press, 1988.

PERIODICALS

English Journal, November, 1982.

Southwestern American Literature, spring, 1972.

Western American Literature, fall, 1989, pp. 279-80.
World Literature Today, summer, 1978.*

*   *   *

UMPIERRE (HERRERA), Luz Maria 1947-

PERSONAL: Born October 15, 1947, in Santurce, Puerto Rico; daughter of Eduardo (an executive with the motor vehicle department of Puerto Rico) and Providencia (a telephone operator for Chase Manhattan Bank; maiden name, Herrera) Umpierre. *Education:* Universidad del Sagrado Corazon, B.A., 1970; Bryn Mawr College, M.A., 1976, Ph.D., 1978; postdoctoral studies at University of Kansas, 1981-82.

ADDRESSES: Office—Department of Foreign Languages and Literature, SUNY, Brockport Tower, Building 103A, Brockport, NY 14420.

CAREER: Academia Maria Reina, Rio Piedras, PR, instructor in Spanish and head of Spanish department, 1971-74; Haverford College, Haverford, PA, instructor in Spanish, 1975- 76; Rutgers, the State University of New Jersey, New Brunswick, NJ, assistant professor, 1978-84, associate professor, department of Spanish and Portuguese, 1984-89; Western Kentucky University, Bowling Green, professor and chair, Modern Languages and Intercultural Studies, 1989—91; SUNY, Brockport, professor and chair, 1991—. Director of Spanish House, Bryn Mawr College, 1974-77. Visiting lecturer, Immaculata College, 1978—. Guest writer at several colleges and universities in the United States; lecturer and/or chair at numerous Latin American and women's literature conferences in the United States. Conducts poetry readings. Consultant to National Endowment for the Humanities. Secretary for New Jersey Voters for Civil Liberties. Speaker at March on Washington for Gay and Lesbian Rights; has made guest appearances on radio programs.

MEMBER: Modern Language Association (Ethnic Studies representative, Delegate Assembly, 1985-87), American Association of Teachers of Spanish and Portuguese, Feministas Unidas, National Organization of Women, Phi Sigma Iota.

AWARDS, HONORS: First prize for essay, Chase Manhattan Bank, 1976; first prize for poetry, International Publications, 1977; National Research Council/ Ford Foundation fellowship, 1981-82; grants from

Rutgers University, 1981, 1985, and 1986; Coalition of Lesbians/Gays in New Jersey Lifetime Achievement Award, 1990.

WRITINGS:

Una puertorriquena en Penna, Masters (San Juan), 1979.
En el pais de las maravillas, Third Woman Press (Indiana University), 1982.
Nuevas aproximaciones criticas a la literatura puertorriquena contemporanea, Cultural (Puerto Rico), 1983.
Ideologia y novela en Puerto Rico, Playor (Spain), 1983.
. . . Y otras desgracias / And Other Misfortunes . . . , Third Woman Press, 1985.
The Margarita Poems, Third Woman Press, 1987.
(Contributor) Elizabeth and Timothy Rogers, editors, *In Retrospect: Essays on Latin American Literature,* Spanish Literature Publications, 1987.

Poems represented in anthologies. Translator, with Nancy Gray Diaz, of Rosario Ferre's "Opprobium." Contributor to *Bibliographical Dictionary of Hispanic Literature in the United States* and *Encyclopedia of World Literature—20th Century.* Contributor of articles and reviews to numerous journals and other periodicals in the United States and Latin America, including *Revista Chicano-Riquena, Gay Studies Newsletter, Plural, Latin–American Theatre Review, Hispanic Journal, Revista de Estudios Hispanicos, Sojourner, Hispania, Third Woman,* and *Bilingual Review-Revista Bilingue;* contributor of poems to journals and newspapers, including *El Mundo.* Associate editor, Third Woman Press, 1982—; reader and consultant, *Latin–American Theater Review,* 1983—, *Revista Chicano-Riquena,* 1984—, and *National Women Studies Association Journal,* 1987.

WORK IN PROGRESS: A book of essays on lesbian and gay writing; a book of poems on "women who have had an impact on me but who have died"; research on gay and lesbian literature.

SIDELIGHTS: Luz Maria Umpierre stated: "Most of my writings rise from my condition as a lesbian and Puerto Rican woman in the United States. My poetry books deal with the alienation I have felt in the U.S.A. I also want the literature of my country, Puerto Rico, to be better known and to this effect I have devoted many of my research pieces to it. I am also interested in women writers and have made a serious commitment to myself since 1982 to write mostly on women."

BIOGRAPHICAL/CRITICAL SOURCES:

OTHER

Puerto Rican Writers in the U.S.A. (film), Zydnia Nazario, 1988.

*   *   *

UNAMUNO (y JUGO), Miguel de 1864-1936

PERSONAL: Born September 29, 1864, in Bilbao, Spain; died December 31, 1936, in Salamanca, Spain; married Concepcion Lizarraga Ecenarro, 1891; children: ten. Attended Colegio de San Nicolas and Instituto Vizacaino, Bilbao, Spain; University of Madrid, Ph.D., 1884.

CAREER: Educator, poet, novelist, and playwright. University of Salamanca, Salamanca, Spain, professor of Greek, 1891-1924, 1930-34, and rector, 1901-1914, 1934-36; exiled to Canary Islands, 1924, and lived and wrote in France, 1924-30; placed under house arrest for criticism of Franco government, 1936. Cortes (Spanish parliament) deputy from Salamanca; president, Council for Public Education. Taylor lecturer, Oxford University.

AWARDS, HONORS: Cross of the Order of Alfonso XII, 1905; honorary doctorate, University of Grenoble, 1934.

WRITINGS:

FICTION

Paz en la guerra, F. Fe, 1897, translation by Allen Lacy and Martin Nozick with Anthony Kerrigan published as *Peace in War* [Volume 1 of *Obras selectas (Selected Works,)*], edited by Kerrigan, Princeton University Press, 1983.

Amor y pedogogia, 1902, Espasa-Calpe, 1934, translation by Michael Vande Berg published as *Love and Pedagogy,* P. Lang, 1996.

El espejo de la muerte (also see below), 1913, Compania Ibero-americana de Publicaciones, 1930.

Niebla, 1914, Renacimiento, 1928, translation by Warner Fite published as *Mist,* Knopf, 1928.

Abel Sanchez: Una historia de pasion, Renacimiento, 1917, translation published as *Abel Sanchez,* edited by Angel del Rio and Amelia de del Rio, Holt, 1947, reprinted, Catedra, 1995.

Tres novelas ejemplares y un prologo, Espasa-Calpe, 1920, translation by Angel Flores published as *Three Exemplary Novels and a Prologue,* A. & C. Boni, 1930.

La tia Tula (also see below), Renacimiento, 1921.

San Manuel Bueno, martir, y tres historias mas (also see below), Espasa-Calpe, 1933, translation by Francisco de Segovia and Jean Perez published in bilingual edition as *San Manuel Bueno, martir,* Harrap, 1957.

Cuentos (stories), edited by Eleanor Krane Paucker, Minotauro, 1961.

Ver con los ojos y otros relatos novelescos (stories), Espasa-Calpe, 1973.

San Manuel Bueno, martir [and] *La novela de don Sandalio, jugador de ajedrez* (title means "The Novel of Don Sandalio, Chessplayer"; also see below), edited with introduction and notes by C. A. Longhurst, Manchester University Press, 1984.

Also author of *Tulio Montalban y Julio Macedo,* 1920.

PLAYS

El otro, misterio en tres jornadas y un epilogo (title means "The Other"; also see below), Espasa-Calpe, 1932.

El hermano Juan; o, El mundo es teatro, Espasa-Calpe, 1934.

La esfinge (also see below), 1934, Alfil, 1960.

Soledad (also see below), Espasa-Calpe, 1957.

El pasado que vuelve, edited by Manuel Garcia Blanco, Alfil, 1960.

Also author of *La venda* (also see below), *La princesa,* [and] *Dona Lambra,* 1913, *Fedra* (also see below), 1924, *Sombras de sueno,* 1931, *Raquel encadenada* (also see below), 1933, *La difunta,* 1959, and *Medea* (also see below).

POETRY

Poesias, J. Rojas, 1907.

Rosario de sonetos liricos, Imprenta Espanola, 1911.

El Cristo de Velazquez, Calpe, 1920, translation by Eleanor L. Turnbull published as *The Christ of Velazquez,* Johns Hopkins University Press, 1951.

Teresa: Rimas de un poeta desconocido presentadas y presentado por Miguel de Unamuno (also known as "Teresa: Rhymes of an Unknown Poet Presented by Miguel de Unamuno,") Renacimiento, 1923.

De Fuerteventura a Paris: Diario intimo de confinamiento y destierro vertido en sonetas (verse and prose), Excelsior, 1925.

Poems, translation by Turnbull, Johns Hopkins Press, 1952.

Cancionero: Diario poetico, edited by Federico de Onis, Losada, 1953.

Cincuenta poesias ineditas (previously unpublished work), edited by Garcia Blanco, Papeles de Son Armadans, 1958.

Poemas de los pueblos de Espana, selected by Garcia Blanco, Anaya, 1961.

Poesias escogidas, selected by Guillermo de Torre, Losada, 1965.

The Last Poems of Miguel de Unamuno, translation by Edita Mas-Lopez, Fairleigh Dickinson University Press, 1974.

Also author of *Rimas de dentro,* 1923.

ESSAYS

En torno al casticismo, F. Fe, 1902.

Vida de Don Quijote y Sancho, F. Fe, 1905, translation by Homer P. Earle published as *The Life of Don Quixote and Sancho,* Knopf, 1927.

Mi religion y otros ensayos breves, 1910, Espasa-Calpe, 1942, translation by Stuart Gross published as *Perplexities and Paradoxes,* Philosophical Library, 1945.

Soliloquios y conversaciones, 1911, Espasa-Calpe, 1942.

Del sentimiento tragico de la vida en los hombres y en los pueblos, 1913, Renacimiento, 1928, translation by J. E. Crawford Flitch published as *The Tragic Sense of Life in Men and in Peoples,* Macmillan, 1926.

La agonia del cristianismo, 1925, Renacimiento, 1931, translation by Pierre Loving published as *The Agony of Christianity,* Payson & Clark, 1928, translation by Kurt F. Reinhardt published as *The Agony of Christianity,* Ungar, 1960.

Essays and Soliloquies, translation and introduction by Flitch, Knopf, 1925.

Como se hace una novela (title means "How to Make a Novel;" also see below), Alba, 1927.

Dos articulos y dos discursos, Historia Nueva, 1930.

Algunas consideraciones sobre la literatura hispano-americana, Espasa-Calpe, 1947.

Visiones y comentarios, Espasa-Calpe, 1949.

Espana y los espanoles (also see below), edited with

notes by Garcia Blanco, Aguado, 1955.

Inquietudes y meditaciones, prologue and notes by Garcia Blanco, Aguado, 1957.

La vida literaria, Espasa-Calpe, 1967.

El gaucho Martin Fierro, Americalee, 1967.

Also author of *Tres ensayos,* 1900, and *El porvenir de Espana,* with Angel Ganivet, 1912 (also see below).

JOURNALISTIC PIECES

Pensamiento politico, edited by Elias Diaz, Tecnos, 1965.

Desde el mirador de la guerra, edited by Louis Urrutia, Centre de Recherches Hispaniques (Paris), 1970.

Discursos y articulos, Escelicer, 1971.

En torno a las artes: Del teatro, el cine, las bellas artes, la politica y las letras, Espasa-Calpe, 1976.

Escritos socialistas: Articulos ineditos sobre el socialismo, 1894-1922, edited by Pedro Ribas, Ayuso, 1976.

Articulos olvidados sobre Espana y la primera guerra mundial, edited by Christopher Cobb, Tamesis, 1976.

Cronica politica espanola (1915-1923), edited by Vicente Gonzalez Martin, Almar, 1977.

Republica espanola y Espana republicana, edited by Gonzalez Martin, Almar, 1979.

Unamuno: Articulos y discursos sobre Canarias, edited by Francisco Navarro Artiles, Cabildo Insular de Fuerteventura, 1980.

Ensueno de una patria: Periodismo republicano, 1931-36 (political), Pre-Textos, 1984.

Articulos en "La Nacion" de Buenos Aires, 1919-1924, Ediciones Universidad de Salamanca, 1994.

Unamuno y el socialismo: articulos recuperados (1886-1928), Comares, 1997.

De patriotismo espiritual: articulos en "La nacion" de Buenos Aires, 1901-1914, Ediciones Universidad de Salamanca, 1997.

LETTERS

(With Juan Maragall) *Epistolario,* Edimar, 1951, revised edition, Distribuidora Catalonia, 1976.

(With Juan Zorrilla de San Martin) *Correspondencia,* [Montevideo], 1955.

Trece cartas ineditas de Miguel de Unamuno a Alberto Nin Frias, La Mandragora, 1962.

Cartas ineditas, compiled by Sergio Fernandez Larrain, Zig-Zag, 1965.

(With Alonso Quesada) *Epistolario,* edited by Lazaro Santana, Museo Canario, 1970.

Cartas 1903-1933, compiled by Carmen de Zulueta, Aguilar, 1972.

Unamuno "agitador de espiritus" y Giner: Correspondencia inedita, edited by D. Gomez Molleda, Narcea, 1976.

(With Leopoldo Gutierrez Abascal and Juan de la Encina) *Cartas intimas: Epistolario entre Miguel de Unamuno y los hermanos Gutierrez Abascal,* edited with notes by Javier Gonzalez de Durana, Equzki, 1986.

(With Jose Ortega y Gasset) *Epistolario completo Ortega-Unamuno,* edited by Laureano Robles Carcedo with Antonio Ramos Gascon, El Arquero, 1987.

AUTOBIOGRAPHY

Recuerdos de ninez y de mocedad, V. Suarez, 1908, selected and edited by William Atkinson, Longmans, Green, 1929.

En el destierro (recuerdos y esperanzas), selected and annotated by Garcia Blanco, Pegaso, 1957.

Mi vida y otros recuerdos personales, complied by Garcia Blanco, Losada, 1959.

Diario intimo (also see below), edited by P. Felix Garcia, Escelicer, 1970.

De mi vida, Espasa-Calpe, 1979.

OMNIBUS VOLUMES IN ENGLISH

Abel Sanchez and Other Stories, translated by Kerrigan, Regnery, 1956, revised edition, with an introduction by Mario J. Valdes, Regnery (Washington, D.C.), 1996.

Our Lord Don Quixote and Sancho with Related Essays [Volume 3 of *Obras selectas (Selected Works)*], translated and edited by Kerrigan, Princeton University Press, 1967.

The Tragic Sense of Life in Men and Nations [Volume 4 of *Obras selectas (Selected Works)*], translated and edited by Kerrigan, Princeton University Press, 1972.

The Agony of Christianity and Essays on Faith [Volume 5 of *Obras selectas (Selected Works)*], translated and edited by Kerrigan, Princeton University Press, 1974.

Novela/Nivola [Volume 6 of *Obras selectas (Selected Works)*; includes "How to Make a Novel"], translated and edited by Kerrigan, Princeton University Press, 1976.

Ficciones: Four Stories and a Play [Volume 7 of *Obras selectas (Selected Works)*; includes *The Other, Tia Tula,* and *The Novel of Don Sandalio, Chessplayer*), translated and edited by Kerrigan, Princeton University Press, 1976.

The Private World: Selections from the Diario Intimo and Selected Letters [Volume 2 of *Obras selectas (Selected Works)*], translated by Kerrigan, Lacy, and Nozick, edited by Kerrigan, Princeton University Press, 1984.

Miguel de Unamuno's Political Writings, 1918-1924, Mellen Press, 1996.

ANTHOLOGIES AND OMNIBUS VOLUMES IN SPANISH

Ensayos (essays), seven volumes, Fortanet, 1916-18, revised edition, two volumes, Aguilar, 1942.

Ensayos y sentencias de Unamuno, edited with introduction and notes by Wilfred A. Beardsley, Macmillan, 1932.

Prosa diversa, selected by J. L. Gili, Oxford University Press, 1939.

Antologia poetica (poetry), edited by Luis Felipe Vivanco, Escorial, 1942.

Antologia poetica (poetry), edited by Jose Maria de Cossio, Espasa-Calpe, 1946.

Obras selectas (selected works), Pleyade, 1946.

De esto y de aquello, edited by Garcia Blanco, Sudamericana, 1950.

Obras completas (collected works), Aguado, 1950-51.

Teatro: Fedra. Soledad. Raquel encadenada. Medea. (plays), edited by Garcia Blanco, Juventud, 1954.

Obras completas (collected works), ten volumes, edited by Garcia Blanco, Aguado, 1958-61, reprinted, Turner, 1995.

Teatro completo, edited by Garcia Blanco, Aguilar, 1959.

Antologia, edited by Luis Gonzalez Seara, Doncel, 1960.

Antologia, Fondo de Cultura Economica, 1964.

El espejo de la muerte, y otros relatos novelescos, Juventud, 1965.

Cancionero: Antologia (poetry), selected by Ramos Gascon, Taurus, 1966.

Unamuno: Sus mejores paginas, edited by Philip Metzidakis, Prentice-Hall, 1966.

Obras completas, Volume 1: *Paisajes y ensayos,* Volume 2: *Novelas,* Volume 3: *Nuevos ensayos,* Volume 4: *La raza y la lengua,* Volume 5: *Teatro completo y monodialogos,* Volume 6: *Poesia,* Volume 7: *Meditaciones y ensayos espirituales,* Las Americas, 1966-69.

La agonia del cristianismo, Mi religion, y otros ensayos (collected essays), Las Americas, 1967.

Tres nivolas de Unamuno (novels), edited by Demetrios Basdekis, Prentice-Hall, 1971.

El porvenir de Espana y los espanoles (contains *El porvenir de Espana* and *Espana y los espanoles*), Espasa-Calpe, 1972.

Novela (novels), edited by Eugenio de Bustos Tovar, Noguer, 1976.

Antologia poetica (poetry), edited by Jose Maria Valverde, Alianza, 1977.

Antologia poetica (poetry), edited by Mercedes Santos Moray, Editorial Arte y Literatura, 1979.

Jubilacion de don Miguel de Unamuno: Cuaderno de la Magdalena y otros papeles (papers), Libreria Estudio, 1980.

Unamuno multiple: Antologia, edited by Amelia de del Rio, University of Puerto Rico, 1981.

La esfinge; La venda; Fedra (plays), edited by Jose Paulino, Castalia, 1987.

Poesia completa, Alianza, 1987—.

Nuevo Mundo, Editorial Trotta, 1994.

Works also published in multiple editions.

OTHER

Paisajes (travel), 1902, Aguado, 1950.

De mi pais (travel), F. Fe, 1903.

Por tierras de Portugal y de Espana (travel), V. Prieto, 1911.

Contra esto y aquello, Renacimiento, 1912.

(Editor) *Simon Bolivar, libertador de la America del Sur, por los mas grandes escritores americanos,* Renacimiento, 1914, reprinted with prologue by Manuel Trujillo as *Bolivar,* Biblioteca Ayacucho, 1983.

Andanzas y visiones espanolas (travel), Renacimiento, 1922.

Romancero del destierro, Alba, 1928.

La ciudad de Henoc: Comentario 1933, Seneca, 1941.

Cuenca iberica (lenguaje y paisaje), Seneca, 1943.

El caballero de la triste figura, Espasa-Calpe, 1944.

Almas de jovenes, Espasa-Calpe, 1944.

La dignidad humana, Espasa-Calpe, 1944.

Paisajes del alma, Revista de Occidente, 1944.

La enormidad de Espana, Seneca, 1945.

Madrid, Aguado, 1950.

Mi Salamanca, selected by Mario Grande Ramos, Escuelas Graficas de la Santa Casa de Misericordia, 1950.

(With Ruben Dario) *Don Jose Lazaro, 1862-1947,* edited by Antonio R. Rodriguez Monino, Castalia, 1951.

Viejos y jovenes, Espasa-Calpe, 1956.

Autodialogos, Aguilar, 1959.

Escritos de toros, Union de Bibliofilos Taurinos, 1964.

Mi bochito, selected by Garcia Blanco, Libreria Arturo, 1965.

La raza vasca y el vascuence: En torno a la lengua espanola, Espasa-Calpe, 1968.

(Translator) Arthur Schopenhauer, *Sobre la voluntad en la naturaleza,* Alianza, 1970.

Solitana (bilingual edition), edited by Pablo Bilbao and Emilia Doyaga, Washington Irving, 1970.

Libros y autores espanoles contemporaneos, Espasa-Calpe, 1972.

Monodialogos, Espasa-Calpe, 1972.

Gramatica y glosario del Poema del Cid, edited by Barbara D. Huntley and Pilar Liria, Espasa-Calpe, 1977.

La muerte de Ramirez y las olvidadas memorias del general Anacleto Medina, A. Pena Lillo, 1980.

Also translator of *Etica de las prisiones, Exceso de legislacion, De las leyes en general,* by Herbert Spencer, three volumes, 1895, *Historia de la economica politica,* by J. K. Ingram, c. 1895, and *Historia de las literaturas castellana y portuguesa,* by Ferdinand J. Wolf, two volumes, 1895-96.

ADAPTATIONS: Julio de Hoyos adapted one of the novellas from *Tres novelas ejemplares, Nada menos que todo un hombre,* into a drama titled *Todo un hombre.*

SIDELIGHTS: "At his death in 1936," Arthur A. Cohen claimed in the *New York Times Book Review,* "Miguel de Unamuno was the most influential thinker in Spain, more renowned than his younger contemporary [Jose] Ortega y Gasset and regarded by his own aficionados as the greatest stylist in the Spanish language since Cervantes." Author of fiction, drama, poetry, philosophical essays, and a variety of nonfiction, Unamuno "dug deeper into the national spirit than any of his contemporaries, a generation whose collective project was the exploration of Spanishness," Enrique Fernandez proposed in the *Voice Literary Supplement.* "Quixote incarnate, he lived out his nationality to its logical philosophical conclusions. . . . The soul-searching of the first Spanish moderns, who would be called the generation of 1898, found its fullest expression in Unamuno. In poems, plays, novels, and essays," the critic continued, Unamuno questioned "Spanishness, modernity, science, politics, philosophy, faith, God, everything." The foremost questions for Unamuno were often existential, exploring issues of death, mortality, and faith. "Written all over [Unamuno] are the passions and yearnings of a sincere religious searcher," Paul Ilie commented in *Unamuno: An Existential View of Self and Society.*

"[He] is, at the same time, clouded by the doubts and anguish of a rational mind too sophisticated for the simple faith of ordinary men." These religious doubts led to several turbulent spiritual crises, from which Unamuno "developed the dominant convictions of his later life," as Howard T. Young described in *The Victorious Expression: A Study of Four Contemporary Spanish Poets:* "to struggle for the sake of struggle, to believe in the need to believe, even if he himself could not believe. His paradoxes symbolize a lasting insecurity." Indeed, as Frances Wyers noted in *Miguel de Unamuno: The Contrary Self,* Unamuno's work was marked by paradox, "a persistent contrariness, an almost desperate need to set up oppositions and then collapse them into a single entity, to take sides and then switch, to deny and then deny the denial or to assert that what was denied was really affirmed. . . . Unamuno's paradoxes are the result of an unexamined, almost frantic, effort to tie together opposing aspirations." In searching for resolutions to his doubts, Unamuno brought a profound passion to his writing, an intensity which informs all his work. "On whatever page we open one of his writings we find an identical atmosphere, a permanent and invariable note, forced into use with equal passion . . . throughout all of his volumes and all of his life," Julian Marias stated in his study *Miguel de Unamuno.*

This repetition of atmosphere and theme reflected the author's foremost concern: "Man in his entirety, man who goes from his birth to his death, with his flesh, his life, his personality, and above all his desire never to die completely," as Marias defined it. "It is living, suffering man who interests Unamuno, not the abstraction humanity," A. Dobson said in a *Modern Languages* essay. "What makes man authentically human is his fear of death, and for Unamuno, the preservation of the individual's personality is his supreme task." "The evolution of [Unamuno's] thought was marked by three books or great essays, more professions of faith than philosophical treatises:" *The Life of Don Quixote and Sancho, The Tragic Sense of Life in Men and Peoples,* and *The Agony of Christianity,* as Arturo and Ilsa Barea catalogued in their book *Unamuno.* In these works, Unamuno fought what *Nation* contributor Mark Van Doren referred to as "the windmills of despair," an emotion inspired by his knowledge of his own mortality. Nevertheless, the critic added, "Unamuno fights because he knows there is not a chance in the world to win. He has tasted the glory of absurdity. He has decided to hope what he cannot believe. He has discovered grounds for faith in the very fact that there are no grounds." Thus it was this "continuous struggle with death,"

according to Cohen, that for Unamuno "makes [life] worth living. . . . Any means by which a man subverts the kingdom of death is a triumph for life and, in Unamuno's clever logic, for eternity." This conflict between faith and reason, between "the truth thought and the truth felt," Salvador de Madariaga remarked in *The Genius of Spain,* became the primary focus of Unamuno's meditations. "It is because *The Tragic Sense of Life* is the most direct expression of [Unamuno's conflict] that this book is his masterpiece." In this essay, Angel and Amelia de del Rio recounted in the introduction to *Abel Sanchez,* "Unamuno analyzes what he calls the tragic essence of modern civilization, resulting from the longing for knowledge which, guided by reason, has destroyed man's faith in God and in immortality, a faith necessary for his emotional life. Hence, modern humanity, incapable of solving the problem, is forced to struggle in uncertainty, and at the same time to strive after truth, a struggle and agony inherently tragic."

In a style that would characterize all Unamuno's essays, the Bareas asserted, *The Tragic Sense of Life* "was not meant as an orderly philosophical treatise on the human condition, but as one man's record of his thoughts on life and death, confessed before his fellow-mortals with all the passionate sincerity of which that man was capable." The work "is the greatest of the many monologues Unamuno wrote," the critics continued. "Every bit of reasoning in it springs from his intimate spiritual needs; nothing is 'objective.' This is as he meant it to be, and he argues at the very beginning of the book that this subjectivity is the only truthful approach possible." The result, as Van Doren described it, was "modern Catholicism's richest, most passionate, most brilliant statement of the grounds that exist for faith in immortality, now that reason and science have done their worst."

In *The Life of Don Quixote and Sancho* Unamuno brought a new approach to the literary essay. As Demetrios Basdekis summarized in his *Miguel de Unamuno,* "it is literary criticism which is not quite a critical essay; it is a novelizing of a particular novel and a theory of the novel in general; it is creative prose which is not quite prose fiction, although it sometimes borders on this." In arguing that the character of Don Quixote surpassed his creator—that Cervantes was unaware of his own work's implications—Unamuno "set forth the essential premise of all his intellectual criticism: madness is reality, and historical objectivity is madness," Cohen stated. Thus, "the chivalric vocation and undertakings of Don Quixote, continuously pragmatized by his sympathetic squire [Sancho Panza], are treated by Unamuno as the ultimate pilgrimage." "Don Quixote became in the eyes of Unamuno a prophet, a divinely inspired figure preaching the doctrine of quixotism, which is the doctrine of immortality through mundane glory, salvation through high-minded battle against the mean reality of the world," Young postulated. "Turning Cervantine irony into the tragic irony of life, Unamuno exalted Don Quixote as a stirring figure struggling against human fate." "Unamuno's *The Life of Don Quixote and Sancho,*" concluded Basdekis, "is a major theoretical doctrine; in turn it is a huge step toward his 'novel of extreme situations' entitled *Mist.*" "As a novelist, Unamuno was often ahead of his time, especially in his denial of the usual boundaries between life and art," Allen Lacy maintained in a *Nation* article. Novels such as *Mist, Abel Sanchez,* and *San Manuel Bueno, martir,* are "very fresh even in the 1960s," said Lacy, "especially for [their] improvisatory technique. His sense of the novel as a vehicle of serious play, as a comic metaphysic, has strong affinities to the best work of Jorge Luis Borges and John Barth."

Proposing a new form which he called a "nivola," Unamuno attempted a spontaneous creation that would give its characters their own existence. "With the guiding principle of the nonreality of the material world in view, the *nivolas* eliminate all externals, particularly settings and character descriptions," in order to focus on individual personalities, L. Livingstone noted in *Hispania.* "The destruction of form in the *nivola* . . . gives it an other-worldliness, a timelessness and freedom from spatial dimensions, that reproduce the author's hunger for immortality." As Jose Ferrater Mora explained in *Unamuno: A Philosophy of Tragedy,* the author "emphasized that the characters he depicted—or more exactly, in whose innards he poked about—were truly intimate because of what they revealed of themselves. With the 'soul of their soul' laid bare, Unamuno held, they were indistinguishable from truly existing beings."

This theory is exemplified in several works, especially the last chapter of *Mist,* in which, Carlos Blanco Aguinaga related in *Modern Language Notes,* "the conventions of Fiction, and therefore of existence, are broken." Wanting to discuss the possibility of suicide, protagonist Augusto Perez travels to Salamanca to speak to Unamuno, whom he knows as a learned philosopher—only to learn that he is a fictional character subject to the whims of his creator and thus unable to commit suicide. Augusto returns to his home and soon dies after a strangely compulsive

bout of overeating, leaving the reader to wonder whether Unamuno or Augusto willed the death. *Mist* "abounds in ingenious conceptions and paradoxes," the del Rios observed, resting "on an idea that is eminently paradoxical, as Unamuno's ideas regularly are." Despite his success as an essayist and novelist, Unamuno "maintained that he would be best remembered by his poetry," the Bareas reported. "His rough-tongued poems with their blend of fervour and contemplation brought indeed a new note into Spanish lyrical poetry at the turn of the century, but their poetic form was never strong enough to absorb the sentiments and thoughts that inspired them."

As Young outlined, Unamuno believed that "ideas—and, consequently, feelings, for in Unamuno the two could never be separated—take precedence over all other considerations. What the poet says is more important than how he says it; meter, rhyme, and pattern are secondary to content and emotion." As a result, much of Unamuno's poetry tended to be prosaic and "inelegant," as Young termed it; thus, it is a "pleasant surprise" to discover "the Miltonic flow of *The Christ of Velazquez,* and the subdued sadness of his later sonnets." The former work, a book-length poem, "is Unamuno's major accomplishment in poetry," Basdekis remarked, a "blank verse hymn . . . liberally sprinkled with paraphrase and quotations from the Old and New Testaments." Inspired by seventeenth-century Spanish painter Diego Velazquez's masterpiece depicting Christ's crucifixion, Unamuno's poem reflects his usual focus by "sing[ing] in resounding tones of the Incarnation, Death, and Resurrection of Jesus, and derives from these beliefs his hope of escaping total death," Martin Nozick suggested in his study *Miguel de Unamuno.* "Free of the mesh of doctrine and philosophy, he is carried away by pure love, by a fundamental devotion to Gospel whose meanings he deepens, embroiders, and personalizes." Despite the length of the poem, Madariaga stated, it "easily maintains [a] lofty level throughout, and if he had written nothing else Unamuno would still remain as having given to Spanish letters the noblest and most sustained lyrical flight in the language. It abounds in passages of ample beauty, and often strikes a note of primitive strength in the true Old Testament style." *The Christ of Velazquez,* concluded Nozick, is "a major work of unflagging vitality and resonances, a Cantata to the Son of God on the Cross, made up of wave upon wave of Whitmanesque rhythms, or what Unamuno himself called 'a sort of rhythmoid, dense prose.'" The intense emotions Unamuno brought to *The Christ of Velazquez* and his other works have led critics to observe a poetic sense in all his writing. "For Unamuno, a poem or novel (and he holds that a novel is but a poem) is the out-pouring of a man's passion, the overflow of the heart which cannot help itself and lets go," Madariaga proposed.

The Bareas similarly commented that "Unamuno's true poetic creation was the personality he projected into all his work; his 'agony,' his ceaseless struggle with himself and the universe, was the core of every one of his novels and stories, poems and essays." "His style, rather than the clear, orderly style of a philosopher, is always that of a poet, impassioned, full of images, sometimes difficult because of the abundance of allusions, paradoxes, digressions, parentheses, exclamations, and ingenious plays upon words and ideas," the del Rios maintained. Ferrater Mora similarly declared that in analyzing Unamuno's work, "it must always be kept in mind that a poetic *elan* breathes within it, that the written word is meant to be only a shadow of the creative voice. . . . Unamuno wanted to dissolve all 'genres,' all classifications, to fuse all 'genres' together in the deathless fountain of poetry. For Unamuno the only 'literary form' was the poem, and the numerous, perhaps infinite, forms that the poem adopts."

The author's poetic emphasis and concern with human mortality have led many critics to characterize his work as distinctively Spanish. Calling Unamuno "the greatest literary figure of Spain [of his time]," Madariaga asserted that the author "is head and shoulders above [his contemporaries] in the highness of his purpose and in the earnestness and loyalty with which, Quixote-like, he has served all through his life. . . . Unamuno, by the cross which he has chosen to bear, incarnates the spirit of modern Spain," the critic continued. "His eternal conflict between faith and reason, between life and thought, between spirit and intellect, between heaven and civilization, is the conflict of Spain herself." Cohen likewise noted a unique Spanish temperament in the author's work; "the principal debate, the argument that undergirds all of Unamuno's life and thought and gives to it a power most peculiarly Spanish and most thoroughly universal . . . is Unamuno's contest with death." The critic elaborated, stating that "Spain, a culture which has stylized violence, is overwhelmed with death and committed to resurrection." "In the last analysis, it is useless to attempt to define the subject matter, the ideas, and the substance of Unamuno's writing," the del Rios suggested, "because his combined work, his life, and his personality, have for root and impulse a

dynamic or dialectical contraction whose import Unamuno formulated again and again."

The critics added that Unamuno's "metaphysical concepts of desperation, anguish, and agony . . . are, for him, the essence of the Spanish spirit, composed of dissonances, with its perpetual conflict between the ideal and reality, between heaven and earth, between its Sancho Panza-like sense of the immediate and its quixotic yearning for immortality." "[It was] for Unamuno, a figure who transcends the notion of generations and who speaks, at one and the same time, as both modern and universal man, to synthesize and spell out in his poetry, essays and, especially, in his 'nivolas' the dilemma of the individual 'of flesh and bones,' as he was found of saying, alienated both psychologically and metaphysically in the twentieth century," J. F. Tull contended in the *Humanities Association Bulletin*. "Though he ravaged all genres," Fernandez remarked, "Unamuno is hard to classify as a writer—if he even *is* a writer." His fiction and poetry, "though powerful, is more philosophical than lyrical," the critic continued, and his philosophical writings "are emotional and personal" rather than logical or theoretical. "Too writerly to be a philosopher, too philosophical to be an artist," Fernandez concluded, "Unamuno is, as he deserves to be, a category unto himself."

BIOGRAPHICAL/CRITICAL SOURCES:

BOOKS

Barea, Arturo and Ilsa Barea, *Unamuno,* translated by I. Barea, Bowes & Bowes, 1952.

Basdekis, Demetrios, *Unamuno and Spanish Literature,* University of California Press, 1967.

Basdekis, Demetrios, *Miguel de Unamuno,* Columbia University Press, 1969.

Bleiberg, Herman and E. Inman Fox, editors, *Spanish Thought and Letters in the Twentieth Century: Miguel de Unamuno: 1864-1964,* Vanderbilt University Press, 1966.

Ferrater Mora, Jose, *Unamuno: A Philosophy of Tragedy,* translated by Philip Silver, University of California Press, 1962.

Ilie, Paul, *Unamuno: An Existential View of Self and Society,* University of Wisconsin Press, 1967.

Lacy, Allen, *Miguel de Unamuno: The Rhetoric of Existence,* Mouton & Co., 1967.

Lopez, Julio, *Unamuno,* Jucar, 1985.

Madariaga, Salvador de, *The Genius of Spain, and Other Essays on Spanish Contemporary Literature,* Oxford University Press, 1923.

Marias, Julian, *Miguel de Unamuno,* translated by Frances M. Lopez-Morillas, Harvard University Press, 1966.

Nozick, Martin, *Miguel de Unamuno,* Twayne, 1971.

Rubia Barcia, Jose, and M. A. Zeitlin, editors, *Unamuno: Creator and Creation,* University of California Press, 1967.

Rudd, Margaret Thomas, *The Lone Heretic: A Biography of Miguel de Unamuno y Jugo,* University of Texas Press, 1963.

Tibbetts, Orlando L., *The Man of Salamanca,* Rutledge Books, 1996.

Twentieth-Century Literary Criticism, Gale, Volume 2, 1979, Volume 9, 1983.

Unamuno, Miguel de, *Abel Sanchez,* edited by Angel del Rio and Amelia de del Rio, Holt, 1947..

Wyers, Frances, *Miguel de Unamuno: The Contrary Self,* Tamesis, 1976.

Young, Howard T., *The Victorious Expression: A Study of Four Contemporary Spanish Poets,* University of Wisconsin Press, 1964.

PERIODICALS

Hispania, December, 1941.

Humanities Association Bulletin, winter, 1970.

Modern Language Notes, Volume 79, number 2, 1964.

Modern Languages, June, 1973.

Nation, May 17, 1922, June 24, 1968.

New York Times Book Review, December 16, 1973.

Voice Literary Supplement, May, 1987.*

V-Z

VALENTE, Jose Angel 1929-

PERSONAL: Born April 25, 1929, in Orense, Galicia, Spain. *Education:* University of Santiago de Compostela; University of Madrid, licentiate diploma (romance philology), 1953; Oxford University, M.A.

ADDRESSES: Agent—Ambit Serveis Editorials, Consell de Cent, 282, Barcelona 08007 Spain.

CAREER: Poet. Oxford University, lecturer.

AWARDS, HONORS: Adonais literary prize, 1955, for *A modo de esperanza;* Critica prize, 1960, for *Poemas a Lazaro.*

WRITINGS:

A modo de esperanza, Rialp/Adonais (Madrid), 1955.
Poemas a Lazaro, Indice (Madrid), 1960.
Sobre el lugar del canto, Literaturasa/Colliure (Barcelona), 1963.
La memoria y los signos, Revista de Occidente (Madrid), 1966.
Siete representaciones, Bardo (Barcelona), 1967.
Breve son, Ciencia Nueva/Bardo (Madrid), 1968.
Presentacion y memorial para un monumento, Poesia para Todos (Madrid), 1970.
El inocente, Mortiz (Mexico City), 1970.
Las palabras de la tribu, Siglo Veintiuno (Madrid), 1971.
Punto cero, Seix Barral (Barcelona), 1972.
El fin de la edad de plata, Seix Barral (Madrid), 1973.
Numero trece, Inventarios Provisionales (Las Palmas, Gran Canario, Spain), 1973.
Ensayo sobre Miguel de Molinos, Seix Barral, 1974.

Interior con figuras, Seix Barral, 1976.
Material memoria, Gaya Ciencia (Barcelona), 1979.
Siete cantigas de alen, Castro (Sada, La Coruna, Spain), 1981.
Tres lecciones de tinieblas, Gaya Ciencia, 1981.
La piedra y el centro, Taurus (Madrid), 1982.
Mandorla, Catedra (Madrid), 1982.
Poesia y poemas, Narcea (Madrid), 1983.
El fulgor, Catedra, 1984.
Entrada en materia, Catedra, 1985.
El inocente; seguido de Treinta y siete fragmentos, Orbis (Barcelona), 1985.
Fin de siglo y formas de la modernidad, Instituto de Estudios Almerienses, 1987.
Al dios del lugar, Tusquets (Barcelona), 1989.
Cantigas de alen, Ambit Serveis Editorials, 1989.
Obra poetica 2 vols., edited by Andres Sanchez Roybana, Ambit Serveis (Barcelona), 1990.
Variaciones sobre el pajara y la red, precedido de, La piedra y el centro, Tusquets, 1991.
No amanece el cantor, Tusquets Editores, 1992.
Material memoria (1979-1989), Alianza Editorial (Madrid), 1992.
Las palabras de la tribu, Tusquets Editores, 1994.
El fin de la edad de plata; seguido de Nueve enunciaciones, Tusquets Editores, 1995.

Has translated the poetry of Gerard Manley Hopkins, Constantino Cafavis, and Eugenio Montale.

SIDELIGHTS: Jose Angel Valente was born in 1929, and is one of a group of noted Spanish poets who became known in the late 1950s and early 1960s. This group also includes Claudio Rodriguez, Carlos Sahagun, Francisco Brines, and Eladio Cabanero. Their work does not fit into any well-defined school of poetry, and even among this group, there are no obvious shared themes or techniques. What these writers have in common is a belief that the act of writing poetry involves the creation of a new reality that did not exist before the writing of the poem.

Valente is fascinated with this process of poetic exploration and discovery. He is also intrigued with the paradox that, although language is used to express reality, it is limited, and its limitations may actually prevent one from expressing true reality. In *Dictionary of Literary Biography,* Margeret H. Persin wrote that according to Valente, "the poet must continue in his task, in spite of the inherent ambiguities, inconsistencies, and imperfect approximations that language entails. It is within the context of these difficulties that the reader's role becomes paramount. Both poet and reader must approach the language of poetry as a starting point: poet, word, idea, and reader all participate in the ongoing process of the creative act."

Although Valente's poetry is deeply philosophical, it is not removed from everyday life. Valente merges his philosophical thoughts with details of daily life, politics, family relationships, and other personal and historical events. For example, in his first book, *A modo de esperanza* ("In the Manner of Hope"), the poet considers death and loss and discusses their social, existential, and metaphysical meaning, but he also describes events and scenes from daily life, which anchor the more abstract musings.

As Persin noted, "Valente favors simple, uncluttered verse, devoid for the most part of rhetorical devices. But because of the philosophical basis from which he begins, the simplest of terms, descriptions, and evocations of common experience often take on symbolic or allegorical overtones. Thus his poetry is more conceptual than emotive, more suggestive than descriptive. He is a product of his age: his art reveals the society that produced it. He is not a political ideologue; rather, he wishes to know reality through his art and make it comprehensible to others in the same terms."

BIOGRAPHICAL/CRITICAL SOURCES:

BOOKS

Christie, C. R., *Poetry and Doubt in the Work of Jose Angel Valente and Guillermo Carnero,* E. Mellen Press (Lewiston, NY), 1996.
Dictionary of Literary Biography, Volume 108: *Twentieth-Century Spanish Poets,* Gale Detroit, MI), 1991.*

VALENZUELA, Luisa 1938-

PERSONAL: Born November 26, 1938, in Buenos Aires, Argentina; came to the United States, 1979; returned to Buenos Aires, 1989; daughter of Pablo Francisco Valenzuela (a physician) and Luisa Mercedes Levinson (a writer); married Theodore Marjak, 1958 (divorced); children: Anna-Lisa. *Education:* University of Buenos Aires, B.A. *Avocational interests:* Masks, ceremonies, travel.

ADDRESSES: Home—Artilleros 2130, 1428 Buenos Aires, Argentina.

CAREER: La Nacion, Buenos Aires, Argentina, editor of Sunday supplement, 1964-69; writer, lecturer and freelance journalist in the United States, Mexico, France, and Spain, 1970-73; freelance writer for magazines and newspapers in Buenos Aires, 1973-79; Columbia University, New York City, writer-in-residence, 1979-80, taught in Writing Division, 1980-83; New York University, New York City, visiting professor, 1984-89. New York Institute for the Humanities, fellow.

MEMBER: PEN, Fund for Free Expression (member of Freedom to Write Committee), Academy of Arts and Sciences (Puerto Rico).

AWARDS, HONORS: Awards from Fondo Nacional de las Artes, 1966 and 1973, and Instituto Nacional de Cinematografia, 1973, for script based on *Hay que sonreir;* Fulbright fellowship, Iowa International Writers' Program, 1969; Guggenheim fellowship, 1983; honorary doctorate, Knox College, 1991; Machado de Assis Medal, Brazilian Academy of Letters, 1997.

WRITINGS:

Hay que sonreir (novel), Americalee (Buenos Aires, Argentina), 1966.
Los hereticos (short stories), Paidos (Buenos Aires), 1967.
El gato eficaz (novel; portions have appeared in periodicals in English translation under title "Cat-O-Nine-Deaths"), J. Mortiz (Mexico City, Mexico), 1972.
Aqui pasan cosas raras (short stories), Ediciones de la Flor (Buenos Aires), 1976.
Clara: Thirteen Short Stories and a Novel (contains translations of *Hay que sonreir,* published as *Clara,* and stories from *Los hereticos*), translated by Hortense Carpentier and J. Jorge Castello, Harcourt (San Diego, CA), 1976.

Como en la guerra (novel), Sudamericana (Buenos Aires), 1977, translation by Helen Lane published as *He Who Searches,* Dalkey Archive Press, 1987.

Strange Things Happen Here: Twenty-Six Short Stories and a Novel (contains *He Who Searches* and translation of *Aqui pasan cosas raras*), translated by Lane, Harcourt, 1979.

Libro que no muerde (title means "Book That Doesn't Bite"; includes stories from *Aqui pasan cosas raras* and *Los hereticos*) , Universidad Nacional Autonoma de Mexico (Mexico City), 1980.

Cambio de armas (short stories), Ediciones del Norte (Hanover, NH), 1982, translation by Deborah Bonner published as *Other Weapons,* Ediciones del Norte/Persea Books (New York City), 1985.

Cola de largartija (novel), Bruguera (Buenos Aires), 1983, translation by Gregory Rabassa published as *The Lizard's Tail,* Farrar, Straus (New York City), 1983.

Donde viven las aguilas (short stories), Celtia (Buenos Aires), 1983, translation published as *Up among the Eagles,* North Point Press (Berkeley, CA), 1988.

Open Door (short stories), translated by Carpentier and others, North Point Press, 1989.

Novela negra con argentinos (novel), Ediciones del Norte, 1990.

Realidad nacional desde la cama (novel), [Buenos Aires], 1990, translation published as *Bedside Manners,* Serpent's Tail (New York City), 1995.

(With Argentines) *Black Novel,* Simon & Schuster (New York City), 1992.

The Censors: A Bilingual Selection of Stories (short stories) Curbstone, 1992.

Simetrias (short stories), Sudamerica, 1993, translation published as *Simetries,* Serpent's Tail, 1998.

Author of the script for a film adaptation of *Hay que sonreir.* Contributor to *La Nacion* and *Crisis;* contributor to U.S. periodicals, including *Vogue* and *Village Voice.*

SIDELIGHTS: "Luisa Valenzuela's writing belongs to that class of contemporary works Umberto Eco has called 'open works,'" Patricia Rubio observes in *Salmagundi.* "In them the harmonious representation of reality, supported by logic and syllogism, is replaced by a more ample and complex vision in which the laws of causality cease to operate in a linear fashion. The ordered *Weltanschauung* of the standard realist narrative . . . disintegrates in the face of desire, cruelty, the instinctual, the magical, the fantastic, the

sickly." Noting the magical and the fantastic elements in the Argentine novelist and short-story writer's work, critics often describe her fiction—with its mixture of the fantastic and the real—as belonging to that popular Latin American school of writing called magic realism. Not content with this characterization, Valenzuela is quoted by *Time* contributor R. Z. Sheppard as saying, "Magical realism was a beautiful resting place, but the thing is to go forward." She has forged into new fictive territory: her work is much more bizarre, erotic, and violent than that of magic realism's best-known proponents, such as Gabriel Garcia Marquez and Julio Cortazar. As one of the few Latin-American women writers to achieve widespread recognition in the United States, Valenzuela also distinguishes herself from other contemporary Latin American writers by bringing a decidedly feminist slant to the male-dominated world of Hispanic literature.

As Rubio points out, Valenzuela's work—with the exception of *Hay que sonreir,* her first novel (published in English translation as *Clara),* and *The Heretics,* her first collection of short stories—is highly experimental. Constantly shifting points of view, extensive use of metaphors, and word play have become her trademark. In her fiction the form of the work as well as the words used to write it are equal candidates for renewal. *Hispania* contributors Dorothy S. Mull and Elsa B. de Angulo observe that Valenzuela's linguistic experimentations include "efforts to distort language, to 'break open' individual words to examine how they function, to expose their hidden facets as a watchmaker might probe and polish the jewels in a timepiece." In the *Voice Literary Supplement* Brett Harvey notes, "Valenzuela plays with words, turns them inside out, weaves them into sensuous webs. She uses them as weapons, talismans to ward off danger and name the unnameable."

An effort to name the unnameable seems to be a strong motivating force behind Valenzuela's fiction, in this case the unnameable being the surreal reality of Argentine politics. Emily Hicks finds politics such an important facet of Valenzuela's novella, *He Who Searches,* that the critic writes in a *Review of Contemporary Fiction* essay, "The reader of this text will not be able to understand it without considering the current political situation in Argentina." Valenzuela has herself admitted the political content of her work. For example, in an interview with Evelyn Picon Garfield in the *Review of Contemporary Fiction,* Valenzuela notes that the reason she wrote her most popular novel, *The Lizard's Tail,* was for "only one purpose:

to try to understand." Valenzuela explained that it is almost impossible for her to comprehend how the Argentine people allowed themselves to become victims of the harsh military regimes that dominated their country for such a long time. In a similar conversation with Barbara Case for *Ms.*, Valenzuela reveals that the magic found in her work is paradoxically the result of the reality the writer discovered in her native land. "Everything is so weird now and it becomes more and more strange," Valenzuela explained. "We thought we had this very civilized, integrated, cosmopolitan country, and suddenly we realized we were dealing with magic. It's been discovered that a minister in Isabel Peron's cabinet was in real life a witch doctor and had books published on witchcraft. Argentinians were caught in a trap of believing ourselves to be European while ignoring all our Latin American reality."

The Lizard's Tail has been described as a *roman a clef* based on the life of the cabinet minister Valenzuela mentioned in her interview with Case. Jose Lopez Rega, Peron's Minister of Social Welfare, appears in the novel as the Sorcerer, a man who has three testicles. He refers to this third testicle as his sister "Estrella" and dreams of having a child with her. "Of course this character," Case observes, "renounces women since he already has one built in—his own 'trinity of the crotch.' But in this unique parody of Latin machismo, his third testicle, Estrella, exists in the Sorcerer to restrain him. When he gets too feisty, Estrella contracts with pain and leaves him doubled up on the floor." Through the use of first-person monologues—described as the Sorcerer's novel or diary—and additional first- and third-person narrations, Valenzuela tells the story of the Sorcerer's rise to power, his fall, his plans to return to power, and his death. Other characters include the Sorcerer's mother (whom he boils and drinks), the Generalissimo, the Dead Woman Eva, and Valenzuela herself.

The work seems to contain everything that readers have come to expect in Valenzuela's fiction: magic, power, political commentary, circular time, female/male conflicts, and violence. However, some critics believe Valenzuela tries to cover too much in the work. *New York Times Book Review* contributor Allen Josephs states, "Her attempt at virtuosity tends to undermine the novel. In order to convince the reader of the Sorcerer's madness and narcissistic depravity, she resorts to surrealism, hyperbole and self-indulgent prose. The parody becomes increasingly self-conscious as the novel proceeds." Reviewer Herbert Gold also criticizes the novel, writing in the *Los Angeles*

Times Book Review, "She is trying for intelligence and trying for magic; but the novelist here points to herself too much. . . . She broods about making magic too much to be able to make the magic. She wants to be wild; that's not the same as wildness."

Other critics praise the novel, seeing it as an important work of Latin American fiction. In *Review of Contemporary Fiction* Marie-Lise Gazarian Gautier calls *The Lizard's Tail* "one of the most fascinating novels written in recent years by a Latin American." Harvey refers to it as "a gorgeously surreal allegory of Argentine politics." In her *Review* essay on the work, critic and translator Edith Grossman finds the novel "remarkable" and notes that in it "Valenzuela reaffirms the powerful significance of language and the value of the artful word as legitimate modes of understanding the dark enigmas of brutality and violence."

Valenzuela's criticism of Argentine politics is often coupled with her equally harsh look at the fate of women in such a society. In her *World Literature Today* essay on the writer, Sharon Magnarelli finds Valenzuela "always subtly political and/or feminist." Magnarelli detects a link between Valenzuela's wordplay and her portrayal of women in her fiction, believing that the Argentine's "work is clearly an attempt to free language and women from the shackles of society." Valenzuela's novel, *Hay que sonreir,* deals with Clara, a young woman who comes to Buenos Aires from the provinces and turns to prostitution in order to support herself. In the novel one sees the beginnings of Valenzuela's characteristic experimentation with form: the story is told through first and third person narrations alternating between past and present tenses. The book also contains a clear statement of the writer's feminist concerns. "One of the main themes of the text," Magnarelli notes, "is unquestionably contemporary woman's plight with the social expectations that she will be passive, silent, industrious (but only in areas of minor import), possessed by a male (be he father, husband, or pimp) and that she will continue to smile (*hay que sonreir* ["one has to smile" in English]) in spite of the exploitation or violence perpetrated against her."

Critics also comment on the female protagonists of the stories in Valenzuela's collection, *Other Weapons,* five narratives dealing with male/female relationships. While many Argentine writers have focused attention on the larger social and economic ramifications of their country's continually violent political situation, Valenzuela, as both *Voice Literary Supplement* contributor Brett Harvey and *Review* contributor

Mary Lusky Friedman comment, reveals how the stress of living in a repressive society undermines interpersonal ties between individuals in that society. *"Other Weapons* is a book that testifies to the difficulty of forging, in politically distressed times, sustaining personal relationships," Friedman observes. "The failures of intimacy that Valenzuela depicts are the quieter casualties of Argentina's recent crisis." In Valenzuela's work, as Valerie Gladstone points out in the *New York Times Book Review,* "Political absurdity is matched only by the absurdity of human relations."

BIOGRAPHICAL/CRITICAL SOURCES:

BOOKS

Contemporary Literary Criticism, Volume 31, Gale (Detroit, MI), 1985.

Cordones-Cook, Juanamaria, *Poetica de la trasgresion en la novelistica de Luisa Valenzuela,* Peter Lang, 1991.

Diaz, Gwendolyn, and Maria Ines Lagos Pope, editors, *La palabra en vilo: Narrative de Luisa Valenzuela,* Ediciones Cuarto Propio (Chile), 1996.

Dictionary of Literary Biography, Volume 113: *Modern Latin-American Fiction Writers,* Gale, 1992.

Garfield, Evelyn Picon, *Women's Voices from Latin America,* Wayne State University Press (Detroit), 1985.

Gautier, Marie-Lise Gazarian, *Interviews with Latin American Writers,* Dalkey Archive Press, 1989.

Kaminsky, Amy, *The Image of the Prostitute in Modern Literature,* 1984.

Magnarelli, Sharon, *Reflections/Refractions: Reading Luisa Valenzuela,* Peter Lang (New York City), 1988.

Martinez, Z. Nelly, *El silencio que habla: Aproximacion a la obra de Luisa Valenzuela,* Ediciones Corregidor (Buenos Aires), 1994.

Minc, Rose S., editor, *El Cono Sur: Dinamica y dimensiones de su literatura: A Symposium,* Montclair State College (Upper Montclair, NJ), 1985.

Pinto, Magdalena Garcia, *Historias Intimas: Conversaciones con diez escritoras latinoamericanos,* Ediciones del Norte, 1988.

Reference Guide to Short Fiction, St. James Press, 1993.

Short Story Criticism, Volume 14, Gale, 1986.

Valis, Noel, and Maier, Carol, Editors, *In the Feminine Mode: Essays on Hispanic Women Writers,* Associated University Presses, 1990.

PERIODICALS

Cuadernos Americanos, Volume 247, number 2, 1983.

Hispamerica, 46-67, 1987.

Hispania, May, 1986.

Insula: Revista de Letras y Ciencias Humanas, 35, 1980.

Kentucky Romance Quarterly, 1986.

Letras Femeninas, spring, 1984.

Library Journal, May 15, 1992; December, 1995, p. 135.

Los Angeles Times Book Review, September 11, 1983.

Ms., October, 1983.

Nation, March 6, 1995, p. 316.

New Statesman, July 10, 1992.

New York Times Book Review, July 1, 1979; October 2, 1983; October 30, 1988.

Publishers Weekly, November 21, 1994; March 9, 1992.

Review, January-May, 1984; July-December, 1985.

Review of Contemporary Fiction, fall, 1986.

Revista Canadiense de Estudios Hispanicos, 4, 1979.

Revista Iberoamericana, 132-133, 1985.

Romance Quarterly, 1986.

Salmagundi, spring-summer, 1989.

Time, March 7, 1983.

Voice Literary Supplement, December, 1985.

World Literature Today, winter, 1984; autumn, 1995.

*   *   *

VALLE, Victor Manuel 1950-

PERSONAL: Born November 10, 1950, in Whittier, CA; son of a dairy worker; married Maria Lau; children: Lucina, Alejandra. *Education:* California State University, Long Beach, B.A. (anthropology; cum laude), 1974, M.A. (comparative literature), 1978; Northwestern University, Medill School of Journalism, M.S.J., 1981.

ADDRESSES: Agent—New Press, 450 West 41st St., New York, NY 10036

CAREER: Poet, journalist, and translator. *Los Angeles Times,* staff writer.

AWARDS, HONORS: Third Irvine Chicago Prize for poetry, 1977, for *Illegal;* Artist-in-residence grant, California Arts Council.

WRITINGS:

Illegal [Los Angeles], 1977.

La educacion universitaria en El Salvador: un espejo roto en los 1980s, 1991.

Calendar of Souls, Wheel of Fire, Pacific Writers Press, 1991.

Siembra de vientos: El Salvador 1960-69, 1993.

(With Mary Lau Valle) *Recipe of Memory: Five Generations of Mexican Cuisine,* New Press (New York City), 1995.

Also contributor of numerous poems, nonfiction, and translations to many anthologies and periodicals. Associate editor, *Somos* magazine; literary editor, *Chismearte* magazine.

SIDELIGHTS: Victor Manuel Valle was born and raised in Whittier, California, in a family of dairy workers of Mexican descent; many of them were political exiles from Mexico and had been followers of Pancho Villa. According to Enrique R. Lamadrid in *Dictionary of Literary Biography,* Valle said that he had "a rather mundane public life and education. However, privately, I learned to raise mockingbirds, gorreones [sparrows], pigeons, crows, lizards, deer, and about 13 dogs. . . . The oral tradition of my grandparents and aunts provided me with insight and knowledge on Mexican history. Before my grandfather Alfredo died, my grandma Matilde wrote all his memoirs of *la Revolucion* down. I'll be rewriting them sometime in the future."

Valle is a poet, translator, editor, activist, and investigative reporter. Much of his work is inspired by his family background and childhood experiences. Although he began as a poet, more recently his journalistic pieces have taken much of his time. Because he has translated the work of many other writers, he is deeply familiar with contemporary Latin American literature, which gives him a wider perspective than many other writers. In addition to writing poetry and nonfiction and translating, Valle has produced a video program, *A Choice of Colors,* about gangs and graffiti, as well as a radio program, *Nicaragua: Lucha de las Americas* (Nicaragua: Struggle of the Americas). He has worked as associate editor of *Somos* magazine and as literary editor of *Chismearte* magazine. He has also run a creative-writing workshop for Latino writers in Los Angeles.

Although Valle's poems have appeared in several literary magazines, such as *New, Tin Tan,* and *Rara Avis,* Lamadrid noted that "he is comparatively underpublished as a poet, considering the special qualities of his work." His first book, *Illegal,* which was originally published in a limited underground edition, established his reputation as a poet; it later won the third Irvine Chicago Prize for poetry. Lamadrid wrote that "Valle's poems explore the links and contradictions between the deeply personal and the historical, opposite poles of experience that are usually alienated or dichotomized in most American poetry. In Valle's poetry they reach a powerful synthesis, as he is able to perceive the workings of history in the most insignificant everyday aspects of his life and in those of the people around him." Valle's poems are easily understood and accessible, despite their depth. He is committed to his belief that poetry and writing are empowering, and participated in the National Endowment for the Humanities Poetry in the Schools program, teaching students at a junior high school that they are poets, too.

BIOGRAPHICAL/CRITICAL SOURCES:

BOOKS

Dictionary of Literary Biography, Volume 122: *Chicano Writers,* Gale (Detroit, MI), 1992.

PERIODICALS

Publishers Weekly, October 16, 1995, p. 58.*

*   *   *

VALLE-INCLAN, Ramon (Maria) del 1866-1936

PERSONAL: Born Ramon Jose Simon del Valle y Pena; born October 28, 1866, in Villaneuva de Arosa, Galicia, Spain; died of bladder cancer, January 5, 1936, in Santiago de Compostela, Spain; son of Ramon del Valle-Inclan Bermudez (a poet and journalist) and Dolores de la Pena y Montenegro del Valle-Inclan; married Josefina Angela Blanco (an actress), August 24, 1907 (divorced, 1932); six children (second son drowned). *Education:* Studied law at Instituto de Santiago de Compostela, 1887-89.

CAREER: Playwright, novelist, poet, short story writer, and essayist, wrote for Spanish newspapers *Globo* and *Diario de Pontevedra,* 1880s; wrote for Mexican newspapers *Correo Espanol* and *Universal,* early 1890s; professor of ethics at Madrid School of Fine Arts, beginning 1916; served as correspondent on the Western Front during World War I for the Spanish paper *El Imparcial;* named by Spanish Republic as Director of the Spanish School of Fine Arts at Rome, Italy; elected president of the Madrid Atheneum, 1932.

AWARDS, HONORS: Named by Spanish Republic as Curator of the Artistic Patrimony.

WRITINGS:

Femeninas: Seis historias amorosas (short stories; title means "Females"), Landin (Pontevedra), 1895.

Epitalamio: Historia de amores (novella; title means "Epithalamium"), Marzo (Madrid), 1897.

Cenizas (play; title means "Ashes"; first produced in Madrid, 1899), Rodriguez y Perma (Madrid), 1899.

(Translator) Jose Maria Eca de Queiros, *El crimen del padre Amaro,* Maucci (Barcelona), 1901.

(Translator) Paul Alexis, *Las chicas del amigo Lefevre,* Pueblo (Valencia), 1902.

(Translator) Eca de Queiros, *La reliquia,* Maucci, 1902.

(Author of prologue) Almagro San Martin, *Sombras de vida,* Marzo, 1902.

Sonata de otono: Memorias del marques de Bradomin (novel), Perez (Madrid), 1902, translation by May Heywood Broun and Thomas Walsh published in *The Pleasant Memoirs of the Marquis de Bradomin: Four Sonatas,* Harcourt (New York), 1924.

Corte de amor: Florilegio de honestas y nobles damas, Marzo, 1903.

Jardin umbrio (short stories; title means "Shady Garden"), Rodriguez Serra (Madrid), 1903.

Sonata de estio: Memorias del marques de Bradomin (novel), Marzo, 1903, translation by Heywood Broun and Walsh published in *The Pleasant Memoirs of the Marquis de Bradomin: Four Sonatas,* Harcourt, 1924.

Flor de santidad: Historia milenaria (novel; title means "Flower of Holiness"), Marzo, 1904.

(Translator) Eca de Queiros, *El primo Basilio,* Maucci, 1904.

Sonata de primavera: Memorias del marques de Bradomin (novel), Marzo, 1904, translation by Heywood Broun and Walsh published in *The Pleasant Memoirs of the Marquis de Bradomin: Four Sonatas,* Harcourt, 1924.

Sonata de invierno: Memorias del marques de Bradomin (novel), Archivos, Bibliotecas y Museos (Madrid), 1905, translation by Heywood Broun and Walsh published in *The Pleasant Memoirs of the Marquis de Bradomin: Four Sonatas,* Harcourt, 1924.

Jardin novelesco: Historias de santos, de almas en pena, de duendes y de ladrones, Archivos, Bibliotecas y Museos, 1905, enlarged edition, Maucci, 1908.

Aguila de blason: Comedia barbara dividida en cinco jornadas (play; title means "The Emblazoned Eagle"), Granada (Barcelona), 1907.

Aromas de leyenda: Versos en loor de un santo ermitano (poetry; title means "Aromas of Legend"; includes "Flor de la tarde" [title means "Afternoon Flower"] and "No digas de dolor" [title means "Do Not Talk about Pain"]), Villavicencio (Madrid), 1907.

El marques de Bradomin: Coloquios romanticos, Pueyo (Madrid), 1907.

Historias perversas, Maucci (Barcelona), 1907.

(Translator) Matilda Serao, *Flor de pasion,* Maucci, 1907.

Romance de lobos: Comedia barbara dividida en cinco jornadas (play; title means "Ballad of Wolves"), Pueyo (Madrid), 1908.

El yermo de las almas: Episodios de la vida intima (title means "The Desert of Souls"), Balganon & Moreno (Madrid), 1908.

Los cruzados de la causa (novel), Balganon & Moreno, 1908.

El resplandor de la hoguera (novel), Pueyo, 1909.

Gerifaltes de antano (novel), Suarez (Madrid), 1909.

La guerra carlista (title means "The Carlist War"; includes *Los cruzados de la causa, El resplando de la hoguera,* and *Gerifaltes de antano,*), Suarez, 1909.

Cofre de sandalo, Suarez, 1909.

Una tertulia de antano, Cuento Semanal (Madrid), 1909.

Cuento de abril: Escenas rimadas en una manera extravagante, Pueyo, 1910.

Las mieles del rosal, Alemana (Madrid), 1911.

Voces de gesta: Tragedia pastoril (play), Alemana, 1912.

Obras completas, 19 volumes, edited by Perlado Paez, Renacimiento (Madrid), 1912-28.

La marquesa Rosalinda: Farsa sentimental y grotesca (play; title means "The Marchioness Rosalinda"), Alemana, 1913.

El embrujado: Tragedia de tierras de Salnes, Perlado & Paez (Madrid), 1913.

La cabeza del dragon (play), Perlado & Paez, 1913, translation by Heywood Broun published as *The Dragon's Head,* R. G. Badger (Boston), 1919; published as *Farsa infantil de la cabeza del dragon* in *Tablado de marionetas.*

La lampara maravillosa: Ejercicios espirituales (essays; title means "The Marvelous Lamp: Spiritual Exercises"), Helenica (Madrid), 1916, translation by Robert Lima published as *The Lamp of Marvels: Spiritual Exercises,* Lindisfarne Press (West Stockbridge, MA), 1986.

Eulalia, Novela Corta (Madrid), 1917.

La media noche: Vision estelar de un momento de guerra (essays; title means "Midnight: Starry Vision of a Moment of War"), Clasica Espanola (Madrid), 1917.

Rosita, Novela Corta (Madrid), 1917.

Mi hermana Antonia, Blass (Madrid), 1918.

Cuentos, estetica y poemas, edited by Guillermo Jimenez, Cultura (Mexico City), 1919, translation by Robert Lima published as *Autobiography, Aesthetics, Aphorisms,* 1966.

La pipa de kif (poetry; title means "The Hashish Pipe"; includes "Aleluya" [title means "Hallelujah"], "La tienda del herbolario" [title means "The Herbalist Shop"], "Rosa de sanatorio" [title means "The Sanatorium Rose"], "Fin de carnaval" [title means "The End of Carnival"], and "El crimen de Mendinica"), Sociedad General Espanola de Libreria (Madrid), 1919.

Divinas palabras (play; title means "Divine Words"), Yagues (Madrid), 1920, translation, Heinemann/ National Theatre (London), 1977.

Farsa de la enamorada del rey: Dividida en tres jornadas (title means "Farce of the King's Sweetheart"), Sociedad General Espanola de Libreria (Madrid), 1920, published as *Farsa italiana de la enamorada del rey* in *Tablado de marionetas.*

El pasajero: Claves liricas (poetry; title means "The Passenger"; includes "Rosa del sol" [title means "Sun Rose"], "Rosa metrica" [title means "Metric Rose"], "Rosa hiperbole" [title means "Hyperbole Rose"], "Rosa matinal" [title means "Morning Rose"], "Rosa de caminante" [title means "The Traveler's Rose"], "Rosa de turbulos" [title means "Rose of Trouble"], "Alegoria" [title means "Allegory"], "Rosa vespertina" [title means "Evening Rose"], "Rosa de zoroastro" [title means "Zoroaster Rose"], "Rosa gnostica" [title means "Gnostic Rose"], "Rosa de Job" [title means "Job's Rose"], and "Karma"), Yagues, 1920.

Zacarias el cruzado, Artistica Saez Hermanos (Madrid), 1920.

Farsa y licencia de la reina castiza (play; title means "Farce and License of the Chaste Queen"), Artes de la Ilustracion (Madrid), 1922.

Cara de plata: Comedia barbara (play; title means "Silver Countenance"), Renacimiento (Madrid), 1923.

The Pleasant Memoirs of the Marquis de Bradomin: Four Sonatas (novels; includes *Sonata de otono, Sonata de estio, Sonata de primavera,* and *Sonata de invierno*), translation by May Heywood Broun and Thomas Walsh, Harcourt, 1924.

"La rosa de papel" y "La cabeza del Bautista": Novelas macabras (includes "La rosa de papel" [also known as "The Paper Rose Sacrilege"]), Prensa Grafica (Madrid), 1924.

(Author of prologue) Victoriano Garcia Marti, *De la felicidad (Eternas inquietudes),* Mundo Latino (Madrid), 1924.

Luces de Bohemia: Esperpento (play; title means "Lights of Bohemia"; also see below), Cervantina (Madrid), 1924, translation by Anthony N. Zahareas and Gerald Gillespie published as *Lights of Bohemia,* University of Pennsylvania Press (University Park), 1969.

Opera omnia, Rivadeneyra (Madrid), 1924-33.

Cartel de ferias: Cromos isabelinos, Prensa Grafica, 1925.

Los cuernos de don Friolera: Esperpento (play; title means "The Horns of Don Friolera"), Cervantina, 1925.

Ecos de Asmodeo, Novela Mundial (Madrid), 1926.

El terno del difunto, Novela Mundial, 1926.

Las galas del difunto (title means "The Corpse's Regalia"), Rivadeneyra (Madrid), 1926.

Ligazon: Auto para siluetas, Novela Mundial, 1926.

Tablado de marionetas (plays; includes *Farsa italiana de la enamorada del rey, Farsa infantil de la cabeza del dragon,* and *Farsa y licencia de la reina castiza*), Rivadeneyra, 1926, published as *Tablado de marionetas para educacion de principes,* Espasa-Calpe (Madrid), 1961.

Tirano Banderas (novel), Rivadeneyra, 1926, published as *Tirano Banderas: Novela de Tierra caliente,* Espasa-Calpe (Buenos Aires), 1937; translation by Margarita Pavitt published as *The Tyrant (Tirano Banderas): A Novel of Warm Lands,* Holt (New York), 1929.

(Author of prologue) Ricardo Baroja, *El Pedogree,* Caro Ragio (Madrid), 1926.

La corte de los milagros: El ruedo iberico (novel), Rivadeneyra, 1927.

Estampas isabelinas: La rosa de oro, Novela Mundial, 1927.

La hija del capitan (play), Novela Mundial, 1927.

Retablo de la avaricia: La lujuria y la muerte, Rivadeneyra, 1927.

Fin de un revolucionario: Aleluyas de la Gloriosa, Moderna (Madrid), 1928.

Las reales antecameras, Atlantida (Madrid), 1928.

Teatrillo de enredo, Moderna, 1928.

Viva mi dueno: El ruedo iberico (novel), Rivadeneyra, 1928.

Otra castiza de Samaria, Novela de Hoy (Madrid), 1929.

(Author of prologue) S. J. Sender, *El problema religioso en Mexico,* Cenit (Madrid), 1929.

Claves liricas: "Aromas de leyenda," "El pasajero," "La pipa de Kif" (poetry), Rivadeneyra, 1930.

Martes de carnaval: Esperpentos (title means "Shrove Tuesday"; contains *Las galas del difunto, Los cuernos de don Friolera,* and *La hija del capitan*), Rivadeneyra, 1930.

Flores de almendro, Bergua, 1936.

Opera lirica (contains *Voces de gesta* and *Cuento de abril*), Rua Nueva (Madrid), 1943.

Obras completas de Don Ramon del Valle-Inclan, 2 volumes, Rivadeneyra, 1944.

Publicaciones periodisticas anteriores a 1895, edited by William L. Fichter, Colegio de Mexico (Mexico City), 1952.

Baza de espadas, AHR (Barcelona), 1958, published as *Baza de espadas: Fin de un revolucionario,* Elliot's Books, 1993.

Obras escogidas, prologue by Gaspar Gomez de la Serna, Aguilar (Madrid), 1958.

Teatro selecto, Escelicer (Madrid), 1969.

Divinas Palabras (also see below) [and] *Luces de Bohemia,* Las Americas (Long Island City, NY), 1972.

El trueno dorado, Nostromo (Madrid), 1975.

Divinas Palabras = Divine Words: A Village Tragicomedy, English version by Trader Faulkner, Heinemann/National Theatre (London), 1977.

Articulos completos y otras paginas olvidadas, Istmo (Madrid), 1987.

Savage Acts: Four Plays, translated by Robert Lima, Estreno (University Park, PA), 1993.

Plays, translated and introduced by Maria Delgado, Methuen Drama (London), 1993.

Also author of *La cara de Dios* (novel), 1900, and *Sacrilegio* (play), produced 1924.

SIDELIGHTS: An acknowledged master of prose style, Ramon del Valle-Inclan was one of the great modernizers of twentieth-century Spanish drama. He invented a new genre: the *esperpento,* in which all the elements of drama are satirically distorted to create Goyaesque images of horror and comedy. Conveying a sense of dehumanization and senseless struggle in an irrational world, the esperpentos are now seen as the forerunners of Absurdist works such as those of Samuel Beckett and Eugene Ionesco. Valle-Inclan's literary work is not, however, limited to his dramas.

In addition to his esperpentos, he is also known for his novels, particularly the *Sonatas,* elegantly styled, fictive memoirs of the rakish Marquis de Bradomin.

Valle-Inclan was born to a family of disinherited aristocrats at Villaneuva de Arosa, in the Spanish region of Galicia, and spent his youth in this rugged land of primitive customs. Educated in Pontevedra, he studied law briefly at the University of Santiago de Compostela, where he also began to write poetry and prose. Although in his youth he identified with the Carlists—a conservative, aristocratic political group—throughout his life he moved progressively to the left, eventually denouncing the monarchy, the military, and the church. Often described as restless and eager for adventure, he left for Mexico in 1890, claiming that he went there because "it was the only country whose name is written with an X." He worked as a journalist in America for three years, then returned to Galicia. After publishing his first book, *Femeninas: Seis historias amorosas,* in 1895, he traveled to Madrid and began to participate in the capital's literary circles.

In Madrid Valle-Inclan led an eccentric, bohemian existence. He made up fantastic stories about his past and started many exotic rumors about himself. He wore his hair loose and flowing past his shoulders, his beard down to his chest, and usually sported a long, black cloak and broad-brimmed hat. He created a scandal by marrying a noted actress, having six children with her, and then leaving her and taking their offspring with him. A cafe brawl with literary critic Manuel Bueno led to an infected arm injury and an eventual amputation. The author reportedly refused to take any anaesthetic and calmly watched the operation.

By the turn of the century, Valle-Inclan had begun work on his *Sonatas,* the series of four novels that brought him fame in the early twentieth century. He recorded his impressions of World War I in *La media noche: Vision estelar de un momento de guerra* (1917), a collection of essays written while he served as a newspaper correspondent on the Western Front. Following the war, Valle-Inclan wrote his first esperpento, *Luces de bohemia* (1924; *Lights of Bohemia*), and also composed dramas and novels, wherein he incorporated the satirical and grotesque elements of the *esperpento* form. He began his *El ruedo iberico* cycle, a projected series of nine novels, in the late 1920s, but finished only two of the works—*La corte de los milagros: El ruedo iberico* (1927) and *Viva mi dueno: El ruedo iberico* (1928)—before his death in 1936.

Valle-Inclan's literary development is generally divided into two periods. The first, extending from 1895 until World War I, is characterized by a fin-de-siecle decadence reminiscent of Barbey d'Aurevilly and Gabriel D'Annunzio. In *Femeninas,* a collection of love stories, Valle-Inclan employed an exquisite, romantic style while treating erotic themes. Similarly, in the *Sonata de otono: Memorias del Marques de Bradomin* (1902) he projected an overtly romantic portrait of himself as the Marquis de Bradomin. Also in this period, Valle-Inclan wrote the novel *Flor de santidad* (1904)—the story of an innocent country girl who believes she is impregnated by Jesus after a sexual encounter with a wayfaring rogue—and the first of two dramas known collectively as the *comedias barbaras, Aguila de blason* (1907) and *Romance de lobos* (1908), which draw on the traditions and folklore of his native Galicia. His *La guerra carlista* trilogy (1908-09), historical novels of the Carlist Wars in Spain, marks a first departure from the eroticism of his earlier works.

Following World War I, a drastic change took place in Valle-Inclan's writing. In 1916 he outlined his new aesthetic theory in *La lampara maravillosa: Ejercicios espirituales.* Discarding the Decadents' notion of the artist as one who finds pleasure in beauty, Valle-Inclan now expressed a disillusioned vision, which he hoped would achieve an objective view of reality and allow things to, in the words of Manuel Salas, "reveal their flaws and imperfections, their absurdities and dissonances." In *Lights of Bohemia* and the esperpentos that followed—*Los cuernos de don Friolera* (1925), *La hija del capitan* (1927), and *Las galas del difunto* (1930)—Valle-Inclan pursued this aesthetic, producing serio-comic distortions of reality. These later dramas focus on society and its conventions and deal with contemporary life, satirizing institutionalized vice, militarism, political corruption, and human frailty—all of which aligned Valle-Inclan more closely with the socially progressive Generation of 1898. His novels continue in the same spirit, as in *Tirano Banderas: Novela de Tierra caliente* (1926, *The Tyrant*), the story of a rebellion in the fictional Latin American state of Tierra Caliente wherein he analyzes the failures of Spanish society; or, the first novels of the *El reudo iberico* cycle which indict Isabella II's government.

Valle-Inclan's oeuvre has been discussed by critics largely in terms of temporal divisions. His early works, especially the *Sonatas,* won him popularity, though many critics disparaged their eroticism and the cruelty found in them. Reaction to his later writing was likewise mixed. Some scholars objected to the grotesqueness of his esperpentos and the severity of the political satire in his later writings; however, his contemporaries, including the writer Jose Martinez Ruiz and the philosopher Jose Ortega y Gasset, admired Valle-Inclan for his adept, innovative style and unique use of language. His work was largely forgotten for many years because it was banned by the Franco regime; none of his plays were performed in Spain for twenty-five years, nor could any critical studies about his writing be published.

"Post-Franco abolition of the censorship has spurred rediscovery of Valle-Inclan's theatre and critical re-evaluation of his work, resulting in an outpouring of articles, monographs, and translations," noted Janet Perez in *Reference Guide to World Literature.* Calling him "a genius long unrecognized because his radical originality was decades ahead of his time," Perez ranked Valle-Inclan as one of Spain's "most profoundly innovative dramatists and . . . almost unquestionably the most significant writer for Spanish theatre since Calderon." Manuel Salas deemed Valle-Inclan "a musician with words, a sovereign artist, a master stylist."

BIOGRAPHICAL/CRITICAL SOURCES:

BOOKS

Andrews, Jean, *Spanish Reactions to the Anglo-Irish Literary Revival in the Early Twentieth Century: The Stone by the Elixir,* Edwin Mellen Press (Lewiston, NY), 1991.

Bano, Jose Severa, *Ramon del Valle-Inclan,* Jucar (Madrid), 1983.

Bell, Aubrey F. G., *Contemporary Spanish Literature,* Knopf (New York City), 1925.

Sleiberg, German, and E. Inman Gox, editors, *Spanish Thought and Letters in the Twentieth Century: An International Symposium Held at Vanderbilt University to Commemorate the Centenary of the Birth of Miguel de Unamuno, 1864-1964,* Vander-bilt University Press (Nashville, TN), 1966, pp. 201-206.

Boyd, Ernest, *Studies from Ten Literatures,* Scribner (New York City), 1925, pp. 87-95.

de Madariaga, Salvador, *Genius of Spain and other Essays on Spanish Contemporary Literature,* Oxford University Press (London), 1923.

Diaz-Plaja, Guillermo, *Las esteticas de Valle-Inclan,* Gredos (Madrid), 1965.

Dictionary of Literary Biography, Volume 134: *Twentieth-Century Spanish Poets, Second Series,* Gale (Detroit), 1994.

Drake, William A., *Contemporary European Writers*, John Day, 1928, pp. 130-137.

Edwards, Gwynne, *Dramatists in Perspective: Spanish Theatre in the Twentieth Century*, St. Martin's Press (New York City), 1985, pp. 36-74.

Glaze, Linda S., *Critical Analysis of Valle-Inclan's Rudeo Iberico*, Ediciones Universal (Miami), 1984.

Guerrero, Obdulia, *Valle-Inclan y el novecientos*, Magisterio Espanol (Madrid), 1977.

Gullon, Ricardo, editor, *Valle-Inclan: Centennial Studies*, University of Texas, 1968.

Hispanic Literature Criticism, Volume 2, Gale (Detroit), 1994.

Lado, Maria Dolores, *Las guerras carlistas y el reinado isabelino en la obra de Ramon del Valle-Inclan*, University of Florida Press (Gainesville), 1966.

Larson, Everette E., *Ramon Maria del Valle-Inclan: A Bibliography*, Library of Congress (Washington, DC), 1986.

Lima, Robert, *An Annotated Bibliography of Ramon del Valle-Inclan*, Pennsylvania State University Libraries (University Park, PA), 1972.

Lima, Robert, *Ramon del Valle-Inclan*, Columbia University Press (New York City), 1972.

Lima, Robert, *Valle-Inclan: Autobiography, Aesthetics, Aphorisms*, Limited Centennial Edition, 1966.

Lima, Robert, *Valle-Inclan: The Theatre of His Life*, University of Missouri Press (Columbia), 1988.

Litvak, Lily, *A Dream of Arcadia: Anti-Industrialism in Spanish Literature, 1895-1905*, University of Texas Press, 1975.

Lyon, John, *The Theatre of Valle-Inclan*, Cambridge University Press (New York City), 1983.

Maier, Carol and Roberta L. Salper, eds., *Ramon Maria del Valle-Inclan: Questions of Gender*, Bucknell University Press (Lewisburg, PA), 1994.

Marval-McNair, Nora de, editor, *Selected Proceedings of the Singularidad y trascendencia Conference, held at Hofstra University, November 6, 7, 8, 1986: A Semicentennial Tribute to Miguel de Unamuno, Ramon del Valle-Inclan, and Federico Garcia Lorca*, Society of Spanish and Spanish-American Studies (Boulder, CO), 1990.

Reference Guide to World Literature, Volume 2, St. James Press (Detroit), 1995.

Rubia, Jose Barcia, *A Biobibliography and Iconography of Valle Inclan, 1866-1936*, University of California Press (Berkeley), 1960.

Salinas, Pedro, *Literatura espanola del siglo XX*, Alianza (Madrid), 1970.

Sinclair, Alison, *Valle-Inclan's Ruedo Iberico: A Popular View of Revolution*, Tamesis Books (London), 1977.

Smith, Verity, *Ramon del Valle-Inclan*, Twayne (New York City), 1973.

Smith, Verity, *Valle-Inclan-Tirano Banderas*, Grant & Cutler (London), 1971.

Tolman, Rosco N., *Dominant Themes in the Sonatas of Valle-Inclan*, Playor (Madrid), 1973.

Townsel, A. Sylviane, *Don Juan Revisitado: Donjuanismo en Zorrilla y en Valle-Inclan*, P. Lang (New York City), 1997.

Twentieth-Century Literary Criticism, Volume 5, Gale, 1981.

Tucker, Peggy Lynne, *Time and History in Valle-Inclan's Historical Novels and Tirano Banderas*, Albatros Hispanofila Ediciones (Valencia), 1980.

Valle-Inclan, Ramon del, *Sontata de Primavera*, edited and with an introduction by Manuel Salas, Dryden (Hinsdale, IL), 1941.

Vila, Xavier, *Valle-Inclan and the Theatre: Innovation in La Cabeza del Dragon, El Embrujado, And La Marquesa Rosalinda*, Bucknell University Press, 1994.

Warren, L. A., *Modern Spanish Literature: A Comprehensive Survey of the Novelists, Poets, Dramatists and Essayists from the Eighteenth Century to the Present, Volume 1*, Brentano's, 1929, pp. 256-272.

Young, Robert Baker, *La guerra carlista de Valle Inclan: variantes en las refuniciones de la obra*, [Mexico], 1958.

Zahareas, Anthony N., editor, *Ramon del Valle-Inclan: His Life and Works*, Las Americas (New York City), 1968.

PERIODICALS

Bulletin of Hispanic Studies, Volume 33, 1956, pp. 152-64; July, 1962, pp. 78-89, 177-87; Volume 46, number 2, 1969, pp. 132-152.

Drama Critique, spring, 1966, pp. 69-78.

Drama Survey, spring-summer, 1967, pp. 3-23.

Educational Theatre Journal, December, 1967, pp. 455-466.

Hispania, May, 1961, pp. 266-268; September, 1974, p. 600.

Hispanic Review, January, 1961, pp. 120-133.

International P.E.N. Bulletin of Selected Books, Volume 21, number 1, 1970, pp. 108-112.

Modern Language Quarterly, September, 1964, pp. 330-337.

Papers of the Modern Language Association, March, 1967, pp. 128-135.

Revista de estudios hispanicos, January, 1972, pp. 33-93; January, 1974, pp. 33-93.*

VALLEJO, Boris 1941-

PERSONAL: Born January 8, 1941, in Lima, Peru; imigrated to the United States, 1964; son of a lawyer; married Doris Maier (a writer), 1967; children: Dorian, Maya. *Education:* Escuela Nacional de Bellas Artes, graduate, 1959; also studied pre-medicine for two years. *Avocational interests:* Playing the violin.

ADDRESSES: Agent—c/o Alaska Momma, Inc., 303 5th Ave., New York, NY 10016.

CAREER: Freelance artist. During the mid-1960s, worked in the advertising department for a store chain in Hartford, CT, then New York City; worked as a freelance artist of fashion art, Christmas cards, and comic books. Work has been licensed for merchandising on many products, including calendars, posters, jigsaw puzzles, greeting cards, figurines, T-shirts, board games, beer steins, skateboards, belt buckles, jewelry, metal buttons, bookmarkers, bookplates, trading cards, plastic beverageware, masks, mirrors, bedding, and computer programs.

Exhibitor at Museo Nacional de Arte, Lima, Peru; Harvard Club, New York City; Society of Illustrators, New York City; Delaware Art Museum, Wilmington, DE; Brandywine Fantasy Gallery, Kenilworth, IL; Pendragon Gallery, Anapolis, MD; Robin Hutchins Gallery, Maplewood, NJ; Leo Burnett Agency, Chicago, IL; and Feria Internacional, Barcelona, Spain.

AWARDS, HONORS: Gold Medal, Escuela Nacional de Bellas Artes, 1959; first prize, Feria Internacional del Pacifico, 1960; first prize, Campaign of Social Awareness (Lima, Peru), 1962; first prize, Bienal del Pacifico, 1963; first prize, Festival de las Artes, 1963; Best Fantasy Artist of the Year, San Diego Fantasy and Science Fiction Convention, 1978; Best Mystery Cover of the Year, 1979; Hugo Award nomination, 1980, for best science–fiction artist of the year; Best Cover Artist of the Year, Toutain Publishing (Barcelona, Spain), 1984 and 1986.

WRITINGS:

Fantasy Art Techniques, Arco Publishing (New York City), 1985.
Bodies: His Photographic Art, Thunder's Mouth Press (New York City), 1997.

ART COLLECTIONS

The Fantastic Art of Boris Vallejo, introduction by Lester del Rey, Ballantine (New York City), 1978.
Mirage, text by D. Vallejo, Ballantine, 1986.
The Boris Vallejo Portfolio, Paper Tiger/Dragon's World, 1994.
Boris Vallejo's 3D Magic, Paper Tiger, 1995.

Work also collected in *Boris I,* Anaconda; *Boris II,* Anaconda; *A Guide to Fantasy,* Dragon's World; *Diva,* Zoom Press (France); *Fantasy,* Volksverlag (Germany); and *Boris Vallejo Fantasztikus Vilaga,* Konyvtar (Hungary).

ILLUSTRATOR

Doris Vallejo, *The Boy Who Saved the Stars* (juvenile), O'Quinn Studios, 1978.
D. Vallejo, *Enchantment* (short stories), Ballantine, 1984.
Larry Niven, *Achilles' Choice,* Tor, 1991.
D. Vallejo, *Ladies: Retold Stories of Goddesses and Heroines,* ROC, 1992.

SIDELIGHTS: "The elements of a fantasy illustration need make no pretence of imitating life such as they must in, say, an illustration for a gothic, a mystery, or a novel," asserted fantasy artist Boris Vallejo in *Fantasy Art Techniques.* "Fantasy engages the imagination to a much larger extent; the creatures portrayed may come partly or entirely from your head. And yet, to be successful, the scenes from your imagination must be convincing enough for a viewer to be willing to go along with you: to willingly suspend his disbelief and say, *'Yes, this could work.'"*

Vallejo has become well known in the art world. Reproductions of his fantastic paintings of well-muscled barbarians, sexy heroines, and bizarre beasts are especially hard to avoid if one reads fantasy or science–fiction novels, though his work can also be found on the covers of mysteries, gothic romances, mainstream novels, and even on boxes for fantasy computer games, all with the telltale signature "Boris" in the corner. Enthusiasts of Vallejo's imaginative visions can purchase Boris Vallejo calendars and art book collections, as well as hundreds of merchandising items. Because of the commercialism surrounding Vallejo's art, many critics are slow to take the artist's work seriously. As Lester del Rey pointed out in his introduction to *The Fantastic Art of Boris Vallejo,* however, "the self-styled cognoscenti . . . forget that much of the greatest art of all time was produced on commercial assignment."

The son of a lawyer, Vallejo was born into an affluent home in Lima, Peru, on January 8, 1941. From an early age, Vallejo had a keen interest in art that was encouraged by his father. "When I was about ten," the artist remembered in *The Guide to Fantasy Art Techniques,* "my father bought me a set of about fifty 8 x 10 inch prints of famous paintings, beautifully reproduced in full colour on fine-grain canvas-like paper. . . . I treasured those prints. They were all Old Masters such as Vermeer, Rembrandt, Van Gogh, Da Vinci and so on. I spent several years copying these paintings. My basic training in art was as a fine artist—I liked classical painters best. My favourites were two Spanish painters—Murillo and Velasquez. I considered their work to be the highest standard of painting."

But painting was not Vallejo's only interest. For seven years he studied to become a concert violinist, but he decided that a career as a doctor might be a more practical pursuit than either music or art. However, at the age of fourteen—and still assuming that he would eventually become a physician—Vallejo began to study art formally at the Escuela Nacional de Bellas Artes on a full scholarship he received after winning a national competition. The youngest student ever to be admitted to that institution, young Vallejo was placed even further ahead of his peers when he began his studies of figure drawing at the second year level. Two years later, in 1957, he enrolled in a pre-med program while continuing to hone his art technique.

Medical school did not last long, though, and in 1959 Vallejo gave it up to pursue art full time. That same year, he became the youngest student to win the Gold Medal for best student of the year at his art school. One reason Vallejo decided to abandon medicine was that he was offered a job drawing instruction sheet diagrams—suddenly, it actually seemed possible to earn a living as an artist. Another opportunity came the artist's way in 1963, when Vallejo was offered a scholarship sponsored by the Italian embassy for art study in Florence. For many young artists, such a chance was a once-in-a-lifetime break, but Vallejo chose to pass up the scholarship so he could imigrate to the United States.

In 1964 Vallejo—who didn't as yet speak English—arrived in New York City to become a professional artist. With eighty dollars in his pocket and no friends, family, or business connections, the young artist had to find a job quickly before he ended up on the streets. Fortunately, he met some of his fellow countrymen in a restaurant one day, and they provided him with a room in the Bronx for only ten dollars a week. It was also one of these new friends who located an employer willing to hire Vallejo as an advertising artist. Moving to Hartford, Connecticut, Vallejo worked for the company—a large chain store—for half a year before returning to New York City. It was here that he first met his future wife, Doris Maier.

Vallejo didn't want to stay in advertising forever, and the desire to do something more creative caused him to leave a steady paycheck behind for the uncertain life of a freelance artist. Accepting assignments from wherever they came, Vallejo worked under tight deadlines, drawing everything from Christmas cards to fashion designs. "I had already been working professionally for several years when I began to direct my efforts toward fantasy art," Vallejo recalled in *Fantasy Art Techniques.* "I had tried children's book illustration, mystery, men's magazines, and so on. But something jelled when I became aware of fantasy illustration." There was one major influence behind Vallejo's attraction to fantasy art. Ever since his first sessions drawing nude models at art school, Vallejo had been fascinated with the physical form of living creatures, whether they be human or animal. As a body builder, Vallejo was particularly interested in creating images of perfect human shapes. "I am interested in what I can do with a figure, and how well I can do it, how close to perfection I can come," the artist said. "And, by 'perfection' I don't mean how true to life but, rather, how true to a personal mental image or vision. I strive not only to copy life but also in a sense, to enhance it." The fantasy genre, where humans are often heroic and larger-than-life and monsters pose challenging anatomy problems, fit Vallejo's passions perfectly.

Vallejo was first exposed to the possibilities of fantasy art by reading comic books. His interest piqued by the illustrations he saw in these magazines, Vallejo copied the comic-book style as well as he could and, in 1971, submitted the results to Marvel Comics. To his amazement, the publisher accepted his paintings immediately, and it was not long before his illustrations were in great demand. When Vallejo decided to take the next step by taking his painting to book publishers, however, he was rejected several times. Chris Evans explained in *The Guide to Fantasy Art Techniques* that Vallejo later realized these rejections were the result of his "not being objective enough about his work. He believes that the artist has to cultivate an awareness of his shortcomings before he can begin to improve and produce professional work."

In *Fantasy Art Techniques,* Vallejo related how, after completing a few assignments for comic books, his confidence had grown—only to be knocked back down again when he attended his first Society of Illustrators show in New York City: "Since the annual show is supposed to contain the best that has been done in illustration for the given year, I was eager to see how my opinion of my work stacked up against the facts. The show was truly an eye opener—it made me realize how far I still had to go. I was disturbed for about a week, but after that I was simply determined to improve. As such, the show was not just a humbling experience for me but an inspiration and an impetus toward growth."

Resolving to break into the paperback market, Vallejo fine-tuned his technique during the mid-1970s and then took some of his comic illustrations to Ballantine Books. As del Rey recalled, "I remember the session we held at Ballantine Books when Boris first left his portfolio. I hardly had time to arrive at the office of my wife Judy-Lynn, who edits all the science fiction, before she urged me toward the art department. There Ian Summers, who was then Art Director, spread out half a dozen paintings to fill the room. 'Will you look at those backgrounds!' he called over his shoulder. 'Look at the detail—the depth.' Such enthusiasm in a busy art department is unusual, to say the least." Ballantine quickly agreed to pay Vallejo for several cover illustrations. In a matter of months, the artist's skills were in great demand, and in 1978 he won the best fantasy artist of the year award at the San Diego Fantasy and Science Fiction Convention.

It was through Ballantine that Vallejo created the book covers that would gain him a large circle of fantasy art fans. Already known for his depictions of Conan the Barbarian for Marvel Comics, he was selected to do the covers for Ballantine's reissue of seven of the "Gor" novels by John Norman and all of Edgar Rice Burroughs's "Tarzan" books; Vallejo also received attention for his work on the "Doc Savage" series. Of the artist's renditions for the Burroughs stories, del Rey judged that the "result was the finest series of paintings of the exploits of Edgar Rice Burroughs' ape-man ever to appear. The series won such instant acclaim that Ballantine Books then issued the first fully-illustrated Tarzan calendar, with many of the cover illustrations from the books and a splen-

did centerfold showing La of Opar, especially drawn for the calendar. Fans of Tarzan had long requested such a calendar, but the proper material for it simply wasn't in existence. Now it exists, through the artistry of Boris Vallejo."

Vallejo's paintings not only helped sell fantasy and science fiction novels to readers who had never picked up such books before; fans who already owned Tarzan, Conan, and Gor books were buying reprints simply for their new jacket illustrations. "There is an old saying," Vallejo commented in *Fantasy Art Techniques,* "that one shouldn't judge a book by its cover. But often enough a book is bought precisely because of its cover." The artist's talents had finally found a niche.

Although Vallejo has also painted covers for gothics, romances, westerns, mysteries, and science fiction novels, his fame mostly rests on his fantasy work, and it is these paintings that have also caused him the most grief from his critics (a number of whom have discredited the artist for his tendency to portray his subjects with little or no clothing). Vallejo, as one *Washington Post Book World* critic reported, "gets a bit irascible when he hears [his paintings] called 'soft-porn.'" And it's not only art critics, but also Vallejo's publishers who have censored his creations. "He's . . . learned to live with the frustrations of having cover-art returned to him with brass brassieres or G-strings added to cover up the more delicate parts of his female anatomies," commented Evans. As a response to those who would prefer that Vallejo keep his art a little more tame, the artist produced a collection of uncensored paintings titled *Mirage.*

To help him paint his heroes and damsels, Vallejo first used professional models, "but now I find I get a more spontaneous and natural feeling if I work with non-professional people," he said in *The Guide to Fantasy Art Techniques.* Among these non-professionals are his friends, his wife Doris, and himself. Professional models are expensive to employ, and having them pose for long periods of time—even if the model is a friend or spouse—can be a tiresome experience for both model and artist. As a result, Vallejo usually uses photographs. "Today, ninety-nine percent of all illustrators work from photographs," he remarked in *Fantasy Art Techniques.* "It saves time and money. Students have asked me if this isn't cheating. First of all, you have to define what cheating is in the context of any given project. It is not as though specific rules are set down for the production of an illustration, and if you don't follow them, you are cheating. You must do whatever facilitates the process of getting the painting finished. This is especially important when you have to deal with deadlines." Whenever his students persist in their arguments by saying the Old Masters never used photographs, Vallejo logically argues that "I'm quite sure that if cameras had been available to the Old Masters, many of them would have preferred working from photographs rather than having the model shifting and moving and falling asleep, or whatever."

This doesn't mean, however, that an artist should reproduce exactly what he sees in a photograph. When it comes to painting a monster, Vallejo obviously has to improvise. But even when portraying humans and more conventional animals such as horses, "I rarely attempt to do a portrait or achieve a faithful likeness of my model," he revealed, later adding that "I sacrifice authenticity to achieve effect." Referring to one painting he did of a mounted warrior woman, the artist confessed, "I exaggerated an action and altered anatomy to heighten the sense of drama and movement." At the same time, he strives not to have his characters look like comic book heroes, with their dramatic and over-exaggerated poses. "He is also," Evans further noted, "at pains to avoid the photographic strangeness of frozen action, aiming for a more graceful, classical movement."

Vallejo wrote in *Fantasy Art Techniques* that knowing when and when not to break the rules is a decision best left to a fully trained artist. There is more than one way to achieve this goal. "More or less 'self-taught' artists will often discount the value of formal study. On the one hand I agree that the experience of painting itself is the most effective teacher. . . . On the other hand, nothing can take the place of being part of a learning community of your peers," he said, asserting later, "I did go to art school. I did become well acquainted with established methods and rules. I did study and copy the paintings of the Old Masters." A combination of formal and informal study worked well for Vallejo, but it was the informal training that was the most valuable. "One of his friends was a talented artist himself," reported Evans, "and Vallejo believes that he learned more from being coached by him than from formal classes at art school."

Because of his respect for the older techniques he learned in art school, Vallejo prefers to use oils when he paints, rather than the acrylics most commercial artists prefer. Acrylics are usually used because they dry much faster than oils, but Vallejo is able to achieve what del Rey called "a much wider range of tones and a feeling of what I can only describe as

transparency that makes the painting seem deeper and more alive." The artist does this by adding coats of gesso, acrylic, and oil paint before beginning the actual painting. The combination of this base and the oil paints results in the effect that del Rey and so many others admire.

When Vallejo completes a painting, the final touch is to apply "one or two coats of retouch varnish to even out the colours," as he related in *Fantasy Art Techniques*. This will not preserve a work of art as well as adding a heavy varnish coat, but Vallejo is somewhat ambivalent about saving his art for posterity. His works are meant for commercial reproduction, so he is not too concerned about their immortality (though in his contracts he requests that his original paintings be returned to him after copies have been made). "Maybe I should be more interested in posterity, but I'm not at this time," he said. On the other hand, Vallejo switched from using ordinary illustration board to a higher quality, acid-free board that will keep his works from deteriorating. In *The Guide to Fantasy Art Techniques* he said, "Formerly I used to feel that if a painting lasted as long as I did, that was fine. But now I feel that if I really put myself into a painting I would like it to last as long as possible." Whether or not his paintings endure for future generations, Vallejo remains unique among fantasy artists because, as del Rey attested, "the vision of Boris is one that can penetrate to our deepest wishdreams and give them the full visualization that makes them seem real and alive."

BIOGRAPHICAL/CRITICAL SOURCES:

BOOKS

Dean, Martyn, editor, *The Guide to Fantasy Art Techniques,* text by Chris Evans, Arco Publishing, 1984.
Vallejo, Boris, *The Fantastic Art of Boris Vallejo,* introduction by Lester del Rey, Ballantine, 1978.
Vallejo, Boris, *Fantasy Art Techniques,* Arco Publishing, 1985.
Weinberg, Robert, *Biographical Dictionary of Science Fiction and Fantasy Artists,* Greenwood Press, 1988.

PERIODICALS

Booklist, February 15, 1986, p. 845.
Locus, July, 1994, pp. 23-25, 64-65.
Publishers Weekly, September 25, 1995, p. 42.
School Library Journal, May, 1986, p. 117.

Science Fiction Chronicle, April, 1986, p. 41; December, 1995, p. 61.

Science Fiction Review, fall, 1986, p. 16.

Washington Post Book World, October 24, 1982, p. 15.*

* * *

VALVERDE, Jose Maria 1926-

PERSONAL: Born January 26, 1926, in Valencia de Alcantara, Spain; married Pilar Hedy Gefaell, 1952; children: two. *Education:* University of Madrid, Ph.D., 1952. *Religion:* Catholic.

ADDRESSES: Office—Universidad de Extremadura, Plaza de Caldereros, 10071 Caceres Spain. *E-mail*—valverde@ba.unex.es.

CAREER: Writer. Spanish Institute of the University of Rome, teacher, 1949- 55; University of Barcelona, teacher (aesthetics), 1955-67, 1977—; University of Trent, Ontario, professor of Spanish, then chair of Spanish department, 1968-77. Taught for a semester at the University of Virginia.

AWARDS, HONORS: Jose Antonio Primo de Rivera National Prize for Literature, 1949, for *La espera;* Premio de la Critica, 1962, for *Poesias reunidas.*

WRITINGS:

Hombre de Dios: Salmos, elegias y oraciones, Instituto Nacional de Ensenanza Ramiru de Maeztu (Madrid), 1945.

La espera, Cultura Hispanica (Madrid), 1949.

Estudios sobre la palabra poetica, Rialp (Madrid), 1952.

Versos del domingo, Barna (Madrid), 1954.

Guillermo de Humboldt y la filosfia del lenguaje, Gredos (Madrid), 1955.

Storia della lettertura spagnola, Radio Italiana (Turin), 1955.

Il Don Chisciotte di Cervantes, Radio Italiana, 1955.

Cortas a un cura esceptico en materia de arte moderna, Seix Barral (Barcelona), 1959.

(With Martin de Ricquer) *Historia de la literatura universal,* 3 vols., Noquer (Barcelona), 1957-59; Volume 4: *La literatura de Hispanoamerica,* Planeta (Barcelona), 1977.

Poesias reunidas, hasta 1960, Giner (Madrid), 1961.

Breve historia de la literatura espanola, Guadarrama (Madrid), 1969.

El profesor de espanol, Ediciones Universitarias (Valparaiso, Chile), 1971.

Ensenanzas de la edad, Seix Barral (Barcelona), 1971.

Azorin, Planeta, 1972.

Antonio Machado, Siglo XXI (Madrid), 1975.

Ser de palabra y otros poemas, Seix Barral, 1976.

(With Martin de Ricquer) *La literatura de Hispanoamerica,* Planeta (Barcelona), 1977.

Antologia poetica, Alianza Editorial (Madrid), 1977.

Joyce, Dopesa (Barcelona), 1978.

Antologia de sus versos, Catedra (Madrid), 1978.

Vida y muerte de las ideas: pequena historia del pensamiento universal, Planeta (Barcelona), 1980.

El barroco: una vision de conjunto, Montesinos (Barcelona), 1980.

Breve historia de la litteratura espanola, Guadarrama, 1980.

La literatura: que era y que es, Montesinos, 1983.

Historia de la literatura universal: con textos antologicos y resumenes argumentales, Planeta (Barcelona), 1984.

(With Damaso Santos) *Antologia de la poesia espanola e hispanoamericana,* Anthropos (Barcelona), 1986.

Viena, fin del imperio, Planeta (Barcelona), 1990.

Poesias reunidas, 1945-1990, Editorial Lumen (Barcelona), 1990.

Las claves de la crisis del siglo XVII, 1600-1680, Planeta (Barcelona), 1991.

(Contributor) J. Martinez Ruiz, *Articulos anarquistas,* Editorial Lumen (Barcelona), 1992.

El arte del articulo, 1949-1993, Universitat de Barcelona Publicacions (Barcelona), 1994.

Also contributor of numerous poems to anthologies and literary periodicals; contributor of translations of authors including Thomas Merton, Rainer Maria Rilke, Charles Dickens, Wulfgang von Goethe, William Shakespeare, Herman Melville, Bertholdt Brecht, James Joyce, Friedrich Holderlin, Christian Morgen-stern, and T. S. Eliot, as well as the Bible.

SIDELIGHTS: Jose Maria Valverde was born in 1926 in Valencia de Alcantara, Spain, near the Portuguese border, and grew up in Madrid. His father was an avid reader, and Valverde first read poetry in his father's library. When he was thirteen years old he began to write, and when he was seventeen his first published poem appeared. In the same year, when he was a student at the University of Madrid, Valverde sent a collection of his poems to Jose Garcia Nieto, the editor of *Garcilaso.* Nieto was impressed, and began publishing the poems. Later, the poems would be collected in Valverde's first book, *Hombre de Dios* ("Man of God").

Valverde is a devout Catholic, and his religious beliefs are prominent in his work. In *Dictionary of Literary Biography,* Michael Perna wrote that when his first book appeared, Valverde was recognized "as a sincere new poet in search of God. Many of these poems present his Christian childhood as a happy state without fears or doubts, and they invoke his past faith as they include meditations on his own death, the meaning of existence, and the value of unattractive and unhappy people around him."

Valverde's second book, *La espera* ("The Waiting") won the Jose Antonio Primo de Rivera National Prize for Literature in 1949. After winning this award, he taught at the Spanish Institute of the University of Rome until 1955, lectured on Spanish literature for Radio Italiana, and worked on his doctorate at the University of Madrid. During this time he also wrote a novel and a play, both which remain unpublished.

In *Versos del domingo* (Sunday Verses), Valverde celebrates the pleasures of life in Italy, and presents his view that poetry can be done on relaxed Sunday afternoons without interfering with the weekly work routine. Valverde, who had married Pilar Hedy Gefaell in 1952, apparently had many relaxed and happy Sunday afternoons with his family, and simple family pleasures appear in poems, such as "Montes de azul" ("Mountains of Blue"), which is a dialogue between nature and a baby from the time of its birth. As Perna wrote, "The thirst for eternity, dominant in his earlier books, no longer prevents his enjoyment of the ordinary pleasures so dear to the Italians among whom he lives."

Valverde's focus on daily life in his poetry is paralleled by his existential and religious views, described by Perna: "Valverde concludes that his search for salvation must lead through the things of this world, as he submits to the ordinariness of life by the humility of using a clear, simple style in his verse. Just as the great mysteries are inherent in daily routine, his deepest poetic insights require a sincere, if prosaic, language." Valverde returned to Spain in 1955 and taught aesthetics at the University of Barcelona. This work led to years of scholarly and critical work on Spanish and European literature, as well as collaborations and translations with many prominent poets.

Valverde's *Poesias reunidas* evoked very different responses among readers. Some felt that he was a safe, religious writer, no threat to conservative interests. Others saw him as a questioning, wide-awake seeker. These different opinions mirrored the political situation in Spain in the mid-1960s, when students and others were rebelling against dictator Francisco Franco. Some professors who sided with the students were dismissed, and although Valverde was not dismissed, his friend Aranguren was, so Valverde resigned in solidarity with him. For some time after that, he had to meet students secretly, since he was not allowed to teach, and eventually he left Spain and taught for a semester at the University of Virginia. After this he went to the University of Trent, Ontario, in 1968, where he eventually became chair of the Spanish department.

In 1977, after Franco's death and the reappointment of the professors who had been fired twelve years before, Valverde returned to the University of Barcelona. He has continued to write, teach, and translate.

BIOGRAPHICAL/CRITICAL SOURCES:

BOOKS

Dictionary of Literary Biography, Volume 108: *Twentieth-Century Spanish Poets,* Gale Research (Detroit, MI), 1991.*

*   *   *

VARDERI, Alejandro   1960-

PERSONAL: Born January 17, 1960, in Caracas, Venezuela; immigrated to the United States, 1985; son of Ramon and Juana Varderi; married Raun Gay Norquist, February 14, 1994. *Education:* Universidad Central, Venezuela, B.A., 1984; University of Illinois at Urbana—Champaign, M.A., 1988; New York University, Ph.D., 1995.

ADDRESSES: Office—BMCC of CUNY, 199 Chambers St., New York, NY 10007-1097; Department of Modern Languages, Borough of Manhattan Community College of the City University of New York, New York, NY 10007. *E-mail*— AXVBM@CUN YVM.CUNY.EDU.

CAREER: Gilard Accounting Office, Caracas, Venezuela, accounting assistant, 1978-79; Association Internationale des Etudiants en Sciences Economiques et Commerciales (International Association of Students in Business and Economics), Caracas, financial director, 1978-80; La MetropoLitana Insurance Co., Caracas, economist, 1979-80; State Foundation for the Arts, Caracas, publications director, 1984-85; University of Illinois, instructor in Spanish, 1985-88; New York University, New York City, instructor in Spanish, 1988—; Borough of Manhattan Community College, associate professor of modern languages, 1998—. Columbia University, lecturer at Barnard College, 1998. *El Nacional* (newspaper), Caracas, journalist, 1978-85; *El Universal* (newspaper), Caracas, journalist, 1985—. Oxigeno Publishing House, founding associate editor, 1980-87; Pantheon Books, editorial assistant, 1988-90.

MEMBER: Associacion Internacional de Hispanistas, North American Catalan Society, Modern Language Association of America, Instituto Literario y Cultural Hispanico, Latin-American Studies Association, Latin-American Writers Institute.

AWARDS, HONORS: Latino Recognition Award Literary, University of Illinois, 1986, 1988; "Letras de Oro" Award, University of Miami, 1987, for a novel; Spanish Department Fellowship, University of Illinois, 1988; *Disurso Literario* Award, Rice Univerity, 1988; Graduate School of ArrtsSenior Teaching Fellowship, New York University, 1991-92; Pennfield Fellowship, New York University, 1993; Research awards, PSC-CUNY, 1996, 1998; BMCC Faculty Development Grant, 1997.

WRITINGS:

Cuerpo plural, 1978.
Ritos civicos, 1980.
Ettedgui: Arte-informacion para la comunidad, 1986.
Anotaciones sobre el amor y el deseo, 1986.
Nuevos narradores del Distrito Federal, 1986.
Para repetir una mujer, 1987.
Yo, el otro, 1993.
Severo Sarduy y Pedro Almodovar: Del barroco al kitsch en la narrativa y el cine postmodernos, 1996.
Anatomia de una seduccion: Reescrituras de lo femenino, 1996.
Amantes y reverentes, 1999.

Contributor to periodicals. Founding associate editor of *La gaveta ilustrada,* 1977-81, *Linea plural,* 1986-88, and *Enclave,* 1991; consulting editor, *Imagen,* 1984-85; *Bajo Palabra,* 1993-95; *Verbigracia,* 1997-99.

WORK IN PROGRESS: Origen Final, a novel, publication expected in 2001; *From Sublime to Kitsch in Spanish-American Narrative and Film,* publication expected in 2002.

SIDELIGHTS: Alejandro Varderi once explained of his work: "The purpose of my writing is to persevere in the fight against intolerance toward minorities in today's world. A world where our perception has become extremely clouded by greed, consumerism, and the exposure to high technology. A world threatening us with an existence solely experienced on the surface of things, in an oblique and vicarious way."

*   *   *

VARGAS LLOSA, (Jorge) Mario (Pedro) 1936-

PERSONAL: Born March 28, 1936, in Arequipa, Peru; son of Ernesto Vargas Maldonaldo and Dora Llosa Ureta; married Julia Urquidi, 1955 (divorced); married Patricia Llosa, 1965; children: (second marriage) Alvaro, Gonzalo, Morgana. *Education:* Attended University of San Marcos; University of Madrid, Ph.D., 1959. *Politics:* Liberal. *Religion:* Agnostic. *Avocational interests:* Movies, jogging, football.

ADDRESSES: Office—Agencia Carmen Balcells, Diagonal 580, 08021 Barcelona, Spain, *Agent*—c/o PEN, 7 Duke Street, London, SW3, England.

CAREER: Writer. Journalist with *La Industria,* Piura, Peru, and with Radio Panamericana and *La Cronica,* both in Lima, Peru, during 1950s; worked in Paris, France, as a journalist with Agence France-Presse, as a broadcaster with the radio-television network ORTF, and as a language teacher; University of London, Queen Mary College and Kings College, London, England, faculty member, 1966-68; Washington State University, Seattle, writer-in-residence, 1968; University of Puerto Rico, Puerto Rico, visiting professor, 1969; *Libre,* Paris, co-founder, 1971; Columbia University, New York City, Edward Laroque Tinker Visiting Professor, 1975; former fellow, Woodrow Wilson Center, Washington, DC; former host of Peruvian television program *The Tower of Babel*; Peruvian presidential candidate, Liberty Movement, 1990.

MEMBER: PEN (president 1976-79), Academy Peruana de la Lengua.

AWARDS, HONORS: Premio Leopoldo Alas, 1959, for *Los jefes;* Premio Biblioteca Breve, 1962, for *La ciudad y los perros;* Premio de la Critica Espanola, 1963, for *La ciudad y los perros,* and 1967, for *La casa verde;* Premio Nacional de la Novela, 1967, for *La casa verde;* Premio Internacional Literatura Romulo Gallegos, 1967, for *La casa verde;* Ritz Paris Hemingway Award, 1985, for *The War of the End of the World;* Principe de Asturias Prize for Letters, 1986; Cervantes prize for literature, 1994; Jerusalem prize, 1995.

WRITINGS:

FICTION

Los jefes (story collection; title means "The Leaders"), Rocas (Barcelona), 1959, translation by Ronald Christ and Gregory Kolovakos published in *The Cubs and Other Stories,* Harper, 1979

La ciudad y los perros (novel), Seix Barral (Barcelona), 1963, translation by Lysander Kemp published as *The Time of the Hero,* Grove (New York City), 1966.

La casa verde (novel), Seix Barral, 1966, translation by Gregory Rabassa published as *The Green House,* Harper (New York City), 1968.

Los cachorros (novella; title means "The Cubs"), Lumen (Barcelona), 1967.

Conversacion en la catedral (novel), two volumes, Seix Barral, 1969, translation by Rabassa published as *Conversation in the Cathedral,* Harper, 1975.

Los cachorros; Los jefes, Peisa (Lima), 1973.

Pantaleon y las visitadoras (novel), Seix Barral, 1973, translation by Christ and Kolovakos published as *Captain Pantoja and the Special Service,* Harper, 1978.

La tia Julia y el escribidor (novel), Seix Barral, 1977, translation by Lane published as *Aunt Julia and the Scriptwriter,* Farrar, Straus (New York City), 1982.

The Cubs and Other Stories (includes *The Leaders* and *The Cubs*), translations by Ronald Christ and Gregory Kolovakos, Harper, 1979.

La guerra del fin del mundo (novel), Seix Barral, 1981, translation by Lane published as *The War of the End of the World,* Farrar, Straus, 1984.

Historia de Mayta (novel), Seix Barral, 1985, translation by Alfred MacAdam published as *The Real Life of Alejandro Mayta,* Farrar, Straus, 1986.

Quien mato a Palomino Molero? (novel), Seix Barral, 1986, translation by MacAdam published as *Who Killed Palomino Molero?,* Farrar, Straus, 1987.

El hablador (novel), Seix Barral, 1987, translation by Lane published as *The Storyteller,* Farrar, Straus, 1989.

Elogio de la madrastra (novel), Tusquets (Barcelona), 1988, translation by Lane published as *In Praise of the Stepmother,* Farrar, Straus, 1990.

Lituma en los Andes (novel), Planeta (Barcelona), 1993, translation by Edith Grossman published as *Death in the Andes,* Farrar, Straus, 1996.

PLAYS

La senorita de Tacna (first produced as *Senorita from Tacna* in New York City, 1983; produced as *The Young Lady from Tacna* in Los Angeles, 1985), Seix Barral, 1981, translation by David Graham-Young published as *The Young Lady from Tacna* in *Mario Vargas Llosa: Three Plays* (also see below).

Kathie y el hipopotamo: Comedia en dos actos (play; translation by Kerry McKenny and Anthony Oliver-Smith produced as *Kathie and the Hippopotamus* in Edinburgh, Scotland, 1986), Seix Barral, 1983, translation by Graham-Young published in *Mario Vargas Llosa: Three Plays* (also see below).

La chunga (play; translation by Joanne Pottlitzer first produced in New York City, 1986), Seix Barral, 1986, translation by Graham-Young published in *Mario Vargas Llosa: Three Plays* (also see below).

Mario Vargas Llosa: Three Plays (contains *The Young Lady from Tacna, Kathie and the Hippopotamus,* and *La chunga*), Hill & Wang (New York City), 1990.

El senor de los balcones (play; title means "Lord of the Balconies "), Seix Barral, 1993.

Also author of *Le Huida* (title means "The Escape"), produced in Piura, Peru.

OTHER

La novela, Fundacion de Cultura Universitaria (Montevideo), 1968.

(With Gabriel Garcia Marquez) *La novela en America Latina,* Milla Batres (Lima), 1968.

(Editor with G. Brotherston) *Seven Stories from Spanish America,* Elsevier Science, 1968.

Antologia minima de M. Vargas Llosa, Tiempo Contemporaneo (Buenos Aires), 1969.

Letra de batalla per "Tirant lo Blanc," Edicions 62, 1969, published as *Carta de batalla por Tirant lo Blanc,* Seix Barral, 1991.

(With Oscar Collazos and Julio Cortazar) *Literatura en la revolucion y revolucion en la literatura,* Siglo Veintiuno (Mexico City), 1970.

Los cachorros; El desafio; Dia domingo, Salvat (Barcelona), 1970.

Dia domingo, Amadis (Buenos Aires), 1971.

Garcia Marquez: Historia de un deicidio (title means "Garcia Marquez: The Story of a Deicide"), Seix Barral, 1971.

La historia secreta de una novela, Tusquets, 1971.

(With Martin de Riquer) *El combate imaginario: Las cartas de batalla de Joanot Martorell,* Seix Barral, 1972.

(With Angel Rama) *Garcia Marquez y la problematica de la novela,* Corregidor-Marcha (Buenos Aires), 1973.

Obras escogidas: Novelas y cuentos, Aguilar (Madrid), 1973.

La orgia perpetua: Flaubert y "Madame Bovary," Seix Barral, 1975, translation by Helen Lane published as *The Perpetual Orgy: Flaubert and "Madame Bovary,"* Farrar, Straus, 1986.

Conversacion en la catedral; La orgia perpetua; Pantaleon y las visitadoras, Aguilar, 1978.

Jose Maria Arguedas, entre sapos y halcones, Ediciones Cultura Hispanica del Centro Iberoamericano de Cooperacion (Madrid), 1978.

La utopia arcaica, Centre of Latin American Studies, University of Cambridge (Cambridge, England), 1978.

The Genesis and Evolution of "Pantaleon y las visitadoras," City College (New York City), 1979.

Art, Authenticity and Latin American Culture, Wilson Center (Washington, DC), 1981.

Entre Sartre y Camus, Huracan (Rio Piedras, Puerto Rico), 1981.

Contra viento y marea (journalism; title means "Against All Odds"), three volumes, Seix Barral, 1983-90.

La cultura de la libertad, la libertad de la cultura, Fundacion Eduardo Frei (Santiago, Chile), 1985.

El debate, Universidad del Pacifico, Centro de Investigacion (Lima), 1990.

La verdad de las mentiras (essays; title means "The Truth of Lies"), Seix Barral, 1990.

A Writer's Reality, Syracuse University Press (Syracuse, NY), 1991.

El pez en el agua: Memorias, Seix Barral, 1993, translated by Lane as *A Fish in the Water: A Memoir,* Farrar, Straus, 1994.

Desafios a la Libertad, Aguilar, 1994.

Ojos bonitos, cuadros feos, Peisa, 1996.

Los cuadernos de don Rigoberto, Alfaguara, 1997.

Making Waves, edited and translated by John King, Farrar, Straus & Giroux, 1997.

Una historia no oficial, Editorial Espasa Calpe, 1997.

(With Paul Bowles) *Claudio Bravo: Paintings and Drawings,* Abbeville Press (New York City), 1997.

Contributor to *The Eye of the Heart,* 1973; contributor to periodicals, including *Commentary, Harper's, National Review, New Perspectives Quarterly, New York Times Book Review, New York Times Magazine, UNESCO Courier,* and *World Press Review.* Selected works have been recorded by the Library of Congress Archive of Recorded Poetry and Literature.

ADAPTATIONS: The Cubs was filmed in 1971; *Captain Pantoja and the Special Service* was filmed in 1976 (Vargas Llosa directed the film, which was banned in Peru); *Aunt Julia and the Scriptwriter* was adapted as a television series in Peru, as a screenplay written by William Boyd and directed by Jon Amiel in 1989, and as a motion picture titled *Tune in Tomorrow,* c. 1990.

SIDELIGHTS: Peruvian writer Mario Vargas Llosa often draws from his personal experiences to write of the injustices and corruption of contemporary Latin America. At one time an admirer of communist Cuba, since the early 1970s Vargas Llosa has been opposed to tyrannies of both the political left and right. He now advocates democracy, a free market, and individual liberty, and he cautions against extreme or violent political action, instead calling for peaceful democratic reforms. In 1989 he was chosen to be the presidential candidate of Fredemo, a political coalition in Peru; though at one point he held a large lead in election polls, in the end he lost the election to Alberto Fujimori. Through his novels—marked by complex structures and an innovative merging of dialogue and description in an attempt to recreate the actual feeling of life—Vargas Llosa has established himself as one of the most important of contemporary writers in the Spanish language. His novels, a London *Times* writer comments, "are among the finest coming out of Latin America."

As a young man, Vargas Llosa spent two years at the Leoncio Prado Military Academy. Sent there by his father, who had discovered that his son wrote poetry and was therefore fearful for the boy's masculinity, Vargas Llosa found the school, with its "restrictions, the military discipline and the brutal, bullying atmosphere, unbearable," he writes in the *New York Times Magazine.* His years at the school inspired his first novel, *The Time of the Hero* (first published in Spanish as *La ciudad y los perros*). The book is, R. Z.

Sheppard states in *Time,* "a brutal slab of naturalism about life and violent death." The novel's success was ensured when the school's officials objected to Vargas Llosa's portrayal of their institution. "One thousand copies were ceremoniously burned in the patio of the school and several generals attacked it bitterly. One of them said that the book was the work of a 'degenerate mind,' and another, who was more imaginative, claimed that I had undoubtedly been paid by Ecuador to undermine the prestige of the Peruvian Army," Vargas Llosa recalls in his *New York Times Magazine* article.

Vargas Llosa wrote *The Time of the Hero* after leaving Peru for Europe in 1958, when he was twenty-two. In embracing Europe and entering into self-imposed exile from his native land, Vargas Llosa was following in the footsteps of numerous Latin American writers, including Jorge Luis Borges, Julio Cortazar, and Carlos Fuentes. Vargas Llosa was to stay in Europe for thirty years, returning to Peru in the late 1980s after the country had slipped into political chaos and economic impoverishment—conditions that prompted Vargas Llosa's decision to seek the presidency of Peru. During his three decades in Europe, Vargas Llosa became an internationally celebrated author.

Though Vargas Llosa had attracted widespread attention with his first novel, it was his second novel that cemented his status as a major novelist. In the award-winning *La casa verde (The Green House)*, Vargas Llosa draws upon another period from his childhood for inspiration. For several years his family lived in the Peruvian jungle town of Piura, and his memories of the gaudy local brothel, known to everyone as the Green House, form the basis of his novel. The book's several stories are interwoven in a nonlinear narrative revolving around the brothel and the family that owns it, the military that runs the town, a dealer in stolen rubber in the nearby jungle, and a prostitute who was raised in a convent. "Scenes overlap, different times and places overrun each other . . . echoes precede voices, and disembodied consciences dissolve almost before they can be identified," Luis Harss and Barbara Dohmann write in *Into the Mainstream: Conversations with Latin-American Writers.* Gregory Rabassa, writing in *World Literature Today,* notes that the novel's title "is the connective theme that links the primitive world of the jungle to the primal lusts of 'civilization' which are enclosed by the green walls of the whorehouse." Rabassa sees, too, that Vargas Llosa's narrative style "has not reduced time to a device of measurement or location, a practical

tool, but has conjoined it with space, so that the characters carry their space with them too . . . inseparable from their time." Harss and Dohmann find that *The Green House* "is probably the most accomplished work of fiction ever to come out of Latin America. It has sweep, beauty, imaginative scope, and a sustained eruptive power that carries the reader from first page to last like a fish in a bloodstream."

With *Conversacion en la catedral (Conversation in the Cathedral)* Vargas Llosa widened his scope. Whereas in previous novels he had sought to recreate the repression and corruption of a particular place, in *Conversation in the Cathedral* he attempts to provide a panoramic view of his native country. As John M. Kirk states in *International Fiction Review,* this novel "presents a wider, more encompassing view of Peruvian society. [Vargas Llosa's] gaze extends further afield in a determined effort to incorporate as many representative regions of Peru as possible." Set during the dictatorship of Manuel Odria in the late 1940s and 1950s, the society depicted in the novel "is one of corruption in virtually all the shapes and spheres you can imagine," Wolfgang A. Luchting writes in the *Review of the Center for Inter-American Relations.* Penny Leroux, in a review of the book for *Nation,* calls it "one of the most scathing denunciations ever written on the corruption and immorality of Latin America's ruling classes."

The nonlinear writing of *Conversation in the Cathedral* is seen by several critics to be the culmination of Vargas Llosa's narrative experimentation. Writing in the *Review of the Center for Inter-American Relations,* Ronald Christ calls the novel "a masterpiece of montage" and "a massive assault on simultaneity." Christ argues that Vargas Llosa links fragments of prose together to achieve a montage effect that "promotes a linking of actions and words, speech and description, image and image, point of view and point of view." Kirk explains that in *Conversation in the Cathedral,* Vargas Llosa is "attempting the ambitious and obviously impossible plan of conveying to the reader all aspects of the reality of [Peruvian] society, of writing the 'total' novel." By interweaving five different narratives, Vargas Llosa forces the reader to study the text closely, making the reader an "accomplice of the writer [which] undoubtedly helps the reader to a more profound understanding of the work." Kirk concludes that *Conversation in the Cathedral* is "both a perfect showcase for all the structural techniques and thematic obsessions found in [Vargas Llosa's] other work, as well as being the true culmination of his personal anguish for Peru."

Speaking of these early novels in *Modern Latin American Literature,* D. P. Gallagher argues that one intention of their complex nonlinear structures is to "re-enact the complexity of the situations described in them." By juxtaposing unrelated elements, cutting off dialogue at critical moments, and breaking the narration, Vargas Llosa suggests the disparate geological conditions of Peru, recreates the difficulties involved in living in that country, and re-enacts "the very nature of conversation and of communication in general, particularly in a society devoted to the concealment of truth and to the flaunting of deceptive images," Gallagher believes. Ronald de Feo points out in the *New Republic* that these early novels all explore "with a near-savage seriousness and single-mindedness themes of social and political corruption." But in *Pantaleon y las visitadoras (Captain Pantoja and the Special Service),* "a new unexpected element entered Vargas Llosa's work: an unrestrained sense of humor," de Feo reports.

A farcical novel involving a military officer's assignment to provide prostitutes for troops in the Peruvian jungle, *Captain Pantoja and the Special Service* is "told through an artful combination of dry military dispatches, juicy personal letters, verbose radio rhetoric, and lurid sensationalist news reports," Gene Bell-Villada writes in *Commonweal.* Vargas Llosa also mixes conversations from different places and times, as he did in previous novels. And like these earlier works, *Captain Pantoja and the Special Service* "sniffs out corruption in high places, but it also presents something of a break, Vargas Llosa here shedding his high seriousness and adopting a humorous ribald tone," Bell-Villada concludes. The novel's satirical attack is aimed not at the military, a *Times Literary Supplement* reviewer writes, but at "any institution which channels instincts into a socially acceptable ritual. The humor of the narrative derives less from this serious underlying motive, however, than from the various linguistic codes into which people channel the darker forces."

The humorous tone of *Captain Pantoja and the Special Service* is also found in *La tia Julia y el escribidor (Aunt Julia and the Scriptwriter).* The novel concerns two characters based on people in Vargas Llosa's own life: his first wife, Julia, who was his aunt by marriage, and a writer of radio soap opera who Vargas Llosa names Pedro Camacho in the novel. The eighteen year old narrator, Mario, has a love affair with the thirty-two year old Julia. Their story is interrupted in alternate chapters by Camacho's wildly complicated soap opera scripts. As Camacho goes mad, his daily scripts for ten different soap operas become more and more entangled, with characters from one serial appearing in others and all of his plots converging into a single unlikely story. The scripts display "fissures through which are revealed secret obsessions, aversions and perversions that allow us to view his soap operas as the story of his disturbed mind," Jose Miguel Oviedo writes in *World Literature Today.* "The result," explains Nicholas Shakespeare in the *Times Literary Supplement,* "is that Camacho ends up in an asylum, while Mario concludes his real-life soap opera by running off to marry Aunt Julia."

Although *Aunt Julia and the Scriptwriter* is as humorous as the previous novel, *Captain Pantoja and the Special Service,* "it has a thematic richness and density the other book lacked," de Feo believes. This richness is found in the novel's exploration of the writer's life and of the relationship between a creative work and its inspiration. In the contrasting of soap opera plots with the real-life romance of Mario and Julia, the novel raises questions about the distinctions between fiction and fact. In a review for *New York,* Carolyn Clay calls *Aunt Julia and the Scriptwriter* "a treatise on the art of writing, on the relationship of stimuli to imagination." It is, de Feo observes, "a multilayered, high-spirited, and in the end terribly affecting text about the interplay of fiction and reality, the transformation of life into art, and life seen and sometimes even lived as fiction."

In *The War of the End of the World,* Vargas Llosa for the first time sets his story outside of his native Peru. He turns instead to Brazil of the nineteenth century and bases his story on an apocalyptic religious movement that gained momentum towards the end of the century. Convinced that the year 1900 marked the end of the world, these zealots, led by a man named the Counselor, set up the community of Canudos. Because of the Counselor's continued denunciations of the Brazilian government, which he called the "antichrist" for its legal separation of church and state, the national government sent in troops to break up this religious community. The first military assault was repulsed, as were the second and third, but the fourth expedition involved a force of some 4,000 soldiers. They laid waste to the entire area and killed nearly 40,000 people.

Vargas Llosa told Wendy Smith in *Publishers Weekly* that he was drawn to write of this bloody episode because he felt the fanaticism of both sides in this conflict was exemplary of present-day Latin America.

"Fanaticism is the root of violence in Latin America," he explained. In the Brazilian war, he believes, is a microcosm of Latin America. "Canudos presents a limited situation in which you can see clearly. Everything is there: a society in which on the one hand people are living a very old-fashioned life and have an archaic way of thinking, and on the other hand progressives want to impose modernism on society with guns. This creates a total lack of communication, of dialogue, and when there is no communication, war or repression or upheaval comes immediately," he told Smith. In an article for the *Washington Post,* Vargas Llosa explained to Curt Suplee that "in the history of the Canudos war you could really see something that has been happening in Latin American history over the 19th and 20th centuries—the total lack of communication between two sections of a society which kill each other fighting *ghosts,* no? Fighting fictional enemies who are invented out of fanaticism. This kind of reciprocal incapacity of understanding is probably the main problem we have to overcome in Latin America."

Not only is *The War of the End of the World* set in the nineteenth century, but its length and approach are also of that time. A writer for the London *Times* calls it "a massive novel in the 19th century tradition: massive in content, in its ambitions, in its technical achievement." Gordon Brotherston of the *Times Literary Supplement* describes the book as being "on the grand scale of the nineteenth century," while Salman Rushdie of *New Republic* similarly defines the novel as "a modern tragedy on the grand scale." Richard Locke of the *Washington Post Book World* believes that *The War of the End of the World* "overshadows the majority of novels published here in the past few years. Indeed, it makes most recent American fiction seem very small, very private, very gray, and very timid."

Vargas Llosa's political perspective in *The War of the End of the World* shows a marked change from his earlier works. He does not attack a corrupt society in this novel. Instead he treats both sides in the Canudos war ironically. The novel ends with a character from either side locked in a fight to the death. As Rushdie observes, "this image would seem to crystallize Vargas Llosa's political vision." This condemnation of both sides in the Canudos conflict reflects Vargas Llosa's view of the contemporary Latin American scene, where rightist dictatorships often battle communist guerrillas. Suplee describes Vargas Llosa as "a humanist who reviles with equal vigor tyrannies of the right or left (is there really a difference, he asks, between 'good tortures and bad tortures'?)."

Although his political views have changed during the course of his career, taking him from a leftist supporter of communist Cuba to a strong advocate of democracy, Vargas Llosa's abhorrence of dictatorship, violence, and corruption has remained constant. And he sees Latin American intellectuals as part of a continuing cycle of "repression, chaos, and subversion," he told Philip Bennett in the *Washington Post.* Many of these intellectuals, Vargas Llosa explained further, "are seduced by rigidly dogmatic stands. Although they are not accustomed to pick up a rifle or throw bombs from their studies, they foment and defend the violence." Speaking of the ongoing conflict in Peru between the government and a Maoist guerrilla movement, the Shining Path, Vargas Llosa clarified to Suplee that "the struggle between the guerrillas and the armed forces is really a settling of accounts between privileged sectors of society, and the peasant masses are used cynically and brutally by those who say they want to 'liberate' them."

Vargas Llosa believes that a Latin American writer is obligated to speak out on political matters. "If you're a writer in a country like Peru," he told Suplee, "you're a privileged person because you know how to read and write, you have an audience, you are respected. It is a moral obligation of a writer in Latin America to be involved in civic activities." This belief led Vargas Llosa in 1987 to speak out when the Peruvian government proposed to nationalize the country's banks. His protest quickly led to a mass movement in opposition to the plan, and the government was forced to back down. Vargas Llosa's supporters went on to create Fredemo, a political party calling for democracy, a free market, and individual liberty. Together with two other political parties, Fredemo established a coalition group called the Liberty Movement. In June of 1989 Vargas Llosa was chosen to be the coalition's presidential candidate for Peru's 1990 elections. Visiting small rural towns, the urban strongholds of his Marxist opponents, and the jungle villages of the country's Indians, Vargas Llosa campaigned on what he believes is Peru's foremost problem: "We have to defend democracy against the military and against the extreme Left." Opinion polls in late summer of 1988 showed him to be the leading contender for the presidency, with a 44–to–19 percent lead over his nearest opponent. By the time of the election, however, Vargas Llosa's lead had eroded, and he ended up losing the election to Alberto Fujimori.

Vargas Llosa chronicles his experience as a presidential candidate in *A Fish in the Water*. In addition to discussing the campaign, however, the author also offers a memoir of his early years in Peru. Notes Rockwell Gray in Chicago's *Tribune Books,* "One string of alternating chapters in the book ends with the young writer's departure for France in 1958; the other recreates the exhausting and dangerous [presidential] campaign that carried him to every corner of Peru." Alan Riding in the *New York Times Book Review* adds that the book "serves as [Vargas Llosa's] mea culpa: he explains why the aspiring writer of the 1950's became a politician in the late 1980's and why, in the end, this was a terrible mistake." Vargas Llosa's account of his childhood and young adulthood includes his ambivalent relationship with his father, whom he met for the first time at age eleven and toward whom he had an intense dislike. Mark Falcoff, writing in the *Times Literary Supplement,* declares, "The pages of this book dealing with the father-son relationship are among the most violent and passionate Vargas Llosa has ever written." The author also covers his years at a military prep school and his university years in Lima.

In discussing his failed presidential campaign in *A Fish in the Water,* Vargas Llosa portrays the political backstabbing, unavoidable compromises, and character attacks that characterized the campaign against Fujimori. He also writes about his alienation from the majority of Peruvians: as a white, wealthy, educated, expatriate intellectual, he had little in common with poor Peruvians of Indian descent, many of whom do not speak Spanish. Comments Riding, "Tall, white and well dressed, he invariably looked out of place." Falcoff exclaims that "the chapters dealing with the presidential campaign suggest an impressive knowledge of Peruvian society at all levels and in the several regions, particularly the needs of its humblest groups." Gray, however, remarks that "Much of this book is engaging and informative, but it becomes at times slack, even gossipy, and assumes an interest in the nuances of Peruvian political and literary life shared by very few American readers."

After losing the campaign, Vargas Llosa returned to Europe—this time to Spain, where he assumed Spanish citizenship. However, his first novel after running for president, *Death in the Andes,* is set in his homeland amid the modern political and social strife evidenced by the rebellion of the Shining Path guerilla movement. In part a murder mystery, the novel follows Corporal Lituma as he ventures from his home in Peru's coastal region to a mountain village to investigate the disappearance of three men. In addition to the story line of the missing men, Vargas Llosa intersperses tales of violence committed by the Shining Path as well as a romantic story involving Tomas Carreno, Lituma's guide and partner. Critics praised Vargas Llosa's skill in creating a technically ambitious novel, although some reviewers remarked that the author failed to integrate the various plot lines into a coherent story line. *New York Times Book Review* contributor Madison Smartt Bell, for instance, comments that "Amid this multiplicity of plot potential, the reader may share Lituma's difficulty in finding any central focus, or even in identifying a single continuous thread." Similarly, Rockwell Gray, again writing in Chicago's *Tribune Books,* avers that "for all the author's adroit weaving of shifts in viewpoint, voice and time—his attempt to grasp Peru's dilemma from many angles—this technically interesting novel is not on a par with his best work." In contrast, *Washington Post Book World* contributor Marie Arana-Ward writes, "This is well-knit social criticism as trenchant as any by Balzac or Flaubert—an ingenious patchwork of the conflicting mythologies that have shaped the New World psyche since the big bang of Columbus's first step on shore." And Bell admits, "The individual vignettes are often brilliant."

"A major figure in contemporary Latin American letters," as Locke explains, and "the man whom many describe as the national conscience of his native Peru," as George de Lama writes in the *Chicago Tribune,* Vargas Llosa is usually ranked with Jorge Luis Borges, Gabriel Garcia Marquez, and other writers of what has been called the Latin American "Boom" of the 1960s. His body of work set in his native Peru, Suzanne Jill Levine writes in the *New York Times Book Review,* is "one of the largest narrative efforts in contemporary Latin American letters. . . . [He] has begun a complete inventory of the political, social, economic and cultural reality of Peru. . . . Very deliberately, Vargas Llosa has chosen to be his country's conscience." But Vargas Llosa warns that a writer's role is limited. "Even great writers can be totally blind on political matters and can put their prestige and their imagination and fantasy at the service of a policy, which, if it materialized, would be destruction of what they do," Sheppard quotes Vargas Llosa as telling a PEN conference. "To be in the situation of Poland is no better than to be in the situation of Chile. I feel perplexed by these questions. I want to fight for societies where perplexity is still permitted."

BIOGRAPHICAL/CRITICAL SOURCES:

BOOKS

Booker, M. Keith, *Vargas Llosa among the Postmodernists,* University Press of Florida, 1994.

Cano Gaviria, Ricardo, *El buitre y el ave fenix: Conversaciones con Mario Vargas Llosa,* Anagrama (Barcelona), 1972.

Contemporary Literary Criticism, Volume 3, 1975, Volume 6, 1976, Volume 9, 1978, Volume 10, 1979, Volume 15, 1980, Volume 31, 1985, Volume 42, 1987, Volume 85, 1995.

Dictionary of Literary Biography, Volume 145: *Modern Latin-American Fiction Writers,* second series, Gale, 1994.

Feal, Rosemary Geisdorfer, *Novel Lives: The Fictional Autobiographies of Guillermo Cabrera Infante and Mario Vargas Llosa,* University of North Carolina Press, 1986.

Gallagher, D. P., *Modern Latin American Literature,* Oxford University Press, 1973.

Gerdes, Dick, *Mario Vargas Llosa,* Twayne (Boston), 1985.

Harss, Luis, and Barbara Dohmann, *Into the Mainstream: Conversations with Latin-American Writers,* Harper, 1967.

Hispanic Literature Criticism, Gale, 1994.

Lewis, Marvin A., *From Lime to Leticia: The Peruvian Novels of Mario Vargas Llosa,* University Press of America (Lanham, MD), 1983.

A Marxist Reading of Fuentes, Vargas Llosa, and Puig, University Press of America, 1994.

Moses, Michael Valdez, *The Novel and the Globalization of Culture,* Oxford University Press, 1995.

Oviedo, Jose Miguel, editor, *Mario Vargas Llosa: El escritor y la critica,* Taurus (Madrid), 1981.

Oviedo, *Mario Vargas Llosa: La invencion de una realidad,* Seix Barral, 1982.

Pereira, Antonio, *La concepcion literaria de Mario Vargas Llosa,* Universidad Nacional Autonoma de Mexico (Mexico City), 1981.

Rodriguez Elizondo, Jose, *Vargas Llosa: Historia de un doble parricidio,* La Noria (Santiago, Chile), 1993.

Rossmann, Charles, and Alan Warren Friedman, editors, *Mario Vargas Llosa: A Collection of Critical Essays,* University of Texas Press, 1978.

Standish, Peter, *Vargas Llosa: La ciudad y los perros,* Grant & Cutler (London), 1983.

Williams, Raymond Leslie, *Mario Vargas Llosa,* Ungar, 1986.

PERIODICALS

Americas, March-April, 1989, p. 22; March-April, 1995, p. 62.

Bookletter, April 28, 1975.

Bulletin of Bibliography, December, 1986.

Chicago Tribune, January 3, 1989; June 23, 1989; August 3, 1989.

Commonweal, June 8, 1979.

Esquire, April, 1990, p. 103.

Harper's, June, 1987, p. 15.

Hispamerica, Volume 63, 1992, pp. 33-41.

Hispania, March, 1976.

Hudson Review, winter, 1976.

International Fiction Review, January, 1977.

Interview, September, 1988, p. 86.

Latin American Literary Review, Volume 11, number 22, 1983, p. 15-25; January-June, 1987, pp. 121-31, 201-06.

Library Journal, March 15, 1994, p. 116; May 1, 1994, p. 114.

Los Angeles Times, May 20, 1985; December 18, 1988.

Los Angeles Times Book Review, February 2, 1986.

Maclean's, April 9, 1990, p. 32.

Modern Language Notes, March, 1990, pp. 351-66.

Mother Jones, January, 1989, p. 22.

Nation, November 22, 1975; February 12, 1996, p. 28.

National Review, December 10, 1982; May 16, 1994, p. 65; April 17, 1995, p. 53.

New Leader, March 17, 1975; November 15, 1982.

New Perspectives Quarterly, fall, 1993, p. 53.

New Republic, August 16-23, 1982; October 8, 1984, pp. 25-27; June 8, 1987, p. 54; February 12, 1990, p. 20.

Newsweek, February 10, 1986; April 9, 1990, p. 33; October 1, 1990, p. 67.

New York, August 23, 1982.

New Yorker, February 24, 1986, pp. 98; 101-04; August 24, 1987, p. 83; December 25, 1989, p. 103; October 1, 1990, pp. 107-10; April 15, 1996, p. 84.

New York Review of Books, March 20, 1975; January 24, 1980; July 16, 1987, p. 35; October 11, 1990, p. 17; May 26, 1994, p. 19; May 9, 1996, p. 16.

New York Times, March 30, 1985; January 8, 1986; February 9, 1986; February 12, 1986; September 10, 1989.

New York Times Book Review, March 23, 1975; April 9, 1978; September 23, 1979; August 1, 1982; December 2, 1984; February 2, 1986; May 31, 1987, p. 13; October 29, 1989, p. 1; October 14, 1990, p. 11; March 10, 1991, p. 13; May 15, 1994, p. 10; February 18, 1996, p. 7.

New York Times Magazine, November 20, 1983; November 5, 1989, p. 44.

Paris Review, fall, 1990, pp. 47-72.

Partisan Review, Volume 46, number 4, 1979.

People, April 9, 1990, p. 71.

PMLA, Volume 106, number 1, 1991, pp. 46-59.

Publishers Weekly, October 5, 1984; November 20, 1995, p. 65.

Review of the Center for Inter-American Relations, spring, 1975.

Saturday Review, January 11, 1975.

Spectator, May 14, 1983.

Time, February 17, 1975; August 9, 1982; January 27, 1986; March 10, 1986; July 27, 1987 p. 64; September 7, 1987; November 13, 1989, p. 110; April 9, 1990, p. 56; October 22, 1990, p. 89; June 13, 1994, p. 75; February 12, 1996, p. 75.

Times (London); May 13, 1985; August 5, 1986.

Times Literary Supplement, October 12, 1973; May 20, 1983; March 8, 1985; May 17, 1985; July 1, 1988; June 17, 1994, p. 11.

Tribune Books (Chicago), October 7, 1979; January 12, 1986. October 29, 1989; September 11, 1994, p. 7; March 3, 1996, p. 6.

U.S. News and World Report, May 9, 1988, p. 69; November 5, 1990, p. 15.

Utne Reader, July-August, 1994, p. 96.

Vital Speeches, October 1, 1992, p. 755.

Vogue, October, 1990, p. 254.

Washington Post, August 29, 1983; October 1, 1984; March 26, 1989.

Washington Post Book World, August 26, 1984; February 9, 1986; May 22, 1994, p. 5; February 25, 1996, p. 1.

World Literature Today, winter, 1978 (special issue on Vargas Llosa); spring, 1978.

OTHER

Sklodowska, Elzbieta, *An Interview with Mario Vargas Llosa,* American Audio Prose Library, 1994.*

*   *   *

VEGA (YUNQUE), Ed(gardo) 1936-

PERSONAL: Born May 20, 1936, in Ponce, Puerto Rico; son of Alberto Vega Lebron (a Baptist minister) and Abigail Yunque Martinez; married Patricia Schumacher (a systems analyst), December 31, 1961; children: Suzanne, Alyson, Matthew, Timothy. *Education:* Attended Santa Monica College; New York University, B.A., 1963. *Religion:* Buddhist.

ADDRESSES: Office—S. Bergholz Literary Services, 17 West 10th St., Suite 5, New York, NY 10011.

CAREER: Block Communities, Inc., training director, 1964-66; Addiction Services Agency, New York City, director, 1966-68; Young Adults University Settlement, director, 1968-69; Hunter College of the City University of New York, New York City, lecturer, beginning in 1969; Hostos Community College of the City University of New York, Bronx, NY, assistant professor; State University of New York College at Old Westbury, assistant professor; College of Staten Island of the City University of New York, New York City, assistant professor, until 1977; freelance writer, 1982—. Latin American Writers Institute, member of advisory board; Ollantay Center for the Arts, chairperson of literary board; Latea Theater, chairperson; Clemente Soto Velez Cultural and Educational Center, president; also worked with Aspira of New Jersey. *Military service:* U.S. Air Force, 1954-58; became airman first class.

MEMBER: International PEN, Authors Guild.

AWARDS, HONORS: Grants from National Endowment for the Arts, 1989, and New York Foundation for the Arts, 1990.

WRITINGS:

The Comeback (novel), Arte Publico (Houston, TX), 1985.

Mendoza's Dreams (stories), Arte Publico, 1987.

Casualty Report, Arte Publico, 1991.

(Author of foreword) Joy L. DeJesus, editor, *Growing Up Puerto Rican: An Anthology,* Morrow (New York City), 1997.

Work represented in anthologies, including *Hispanics in the United States: An Anthology of Creative Literature,* edited by Gary D. Keller and Francisco Jiminez, Bilingual Press (Ypsilanti, MI), 1980; and *A Decade of Hispanic Literature,* edited by Nicolas Kanellos, Arte Publico, 1982. Contributor to periodicals, including *Nuestro, Revista Chicano-Riquena, Maize, Americas Review,* and *Portable Lower East Side.*

BIOGRAPHICAL/CRITICAL SOURCES:

PERIODICALS

American Book Review, November-December, 1984, pp. 16-17.

Kirkus Reviews, February 15, 1987.

Pawn Review, Volume VII, number 3, 1983, pp. 95-100.

San Francisco Chronicle, May 17, 1987.

Short Story Review 4, fall, 1987, p. 12.

Vista, March 12, 1989, p. 4.*

* * *

VEGA, Jose Luis 1948-

PERSONAL: Born June 18, 1948, in Santurce, PR; son of Jose Vega Serrano (in business) and Aida Esther Colon (a homemaker); married Catalina Vincens Salas (a psychologist), October 13, 1956. *Education:* University of Puerto Rico, doctorate, 1983.

ADDRESSES: Home—Box 23058, U.P.R., San Juan, Puerto Rico 00931. *Office*—University of Puerto Rico, Box 23058, San Juan, Puerto Rico 00931. *E-mail*—jlvega@prtc.net.

CAREER: High school teacher in Puerto Rico, beginning in 1968; University of Puerto Rico, Rio Piedras, teacher of Hispanic American literature and poetry, director of Hispanic Studies Department, 1998-99, dean of College of Humanities, 1999—; Spanish Language Academy of Puerto Rico, director, 1999—. *Ventana* (poetry magazine), copublisher, beginning in 1972; *Cariban* (literary magazine), copublisher, beginning in 1984.

AWARDS, HONORS: National Prize, International PEN, 1983, for *La naranja entera;* prize, Instituto de Literatura Puertorriquena, 1990, for *Bajo los efectos de la poesia.*

WRITINGS:

Comienzo del canto (poems), Yaurel (Rio Piedras, PR), 1967.

Las natas de los Parpados/Suite erotica (poems), Ventana (Rio Piedras), 1974.

Signos vitales (poems), Cultural (Rio Piedras), 1974.

La naranja entera (poems), Antillana (Rio Piedras), 1983.

Cesar Vallejo en "Trilce" (literary criticism), Editorial de la Universidad de Puerto Rico (Rio Piedras), 1983.

Editor, *Reunion de espejos: Antologia del cuento Puertorriqueno actual* (stories), Cultural, 1983.

Tiempo de bolero (poems), Cultural, 1985.

Bajo los efectos de la poesia (poems), Editorial de la Universidad de Puerto Rico, 1989.

Solo de pasion (poems), Editorial Universidad de Puerto Rico, 1996.

Also author of *Techo a dos aguas* (essays and poems), Editorial Plaza Mayor (Rio Piedus). Contributor of essays and reviews to periodicals.

WORK IN PROGRESS: Cola de cometa/Antologia Personal 1967-1999, selected poems, publication expected in Spain in 2000.

* * *

VELASQUEZ, Gloria (Louise) 1949-

PERSONAL: Born December 21, 1949, in Loveland, CO; daughter of John E. (a migrant farm worker) and Frances (a migrant farm worker) Velasquez; divorced; children: Brandi Lynn Trevino, Robert John Velasquez Trevino. *Education:* University of Northern Colorado, B.A. (Chicano and Spanish studies), 1978; Stanford University, M.A., 1980, Ph.D. (Spanish literature), 1985. *Politics:* Democrat. *Religion:* Catholic and Dine. *Avocational interests:* Playing the guitar; lead singer in own rock band.

ADDRESSES: Home—980 San Adriano Court, San Luis Obispo, CA, 93405.

CAREER: Author and educator. Hewlett Packard, secretary, 1966-67; California Polytechnic State University, professor, 1985—. Member, Canto Al Pueblo board, 1979, Koger Kamp Foundation, 1992-93. UNC Ambassador, 1992—.

MEMBER: PEN.

AWARDS, HONORS: Stanford University, Premiere, Prix in Poetry, 1979; Stanford University, Deu Xieue, Prix in Poetry, 1979; University of Northern Colorado-Greeley, honored alumni, 1987, Hall of Fame, 1989; 11th Chicano Literary Prize, short story, University of California—Irvine, 1985.

WRITINGS:

Juanita Fights the School Board, Pinata Books (Houston, TX), 1994.

Maya's Divided World, Pinata Books (Houston, TX), 1995.

Tommy Stands Alone, Pinata Books (Houston, TX), 1995.

I Used to be a Superwoman (poetry), Arte Publico Press (Houston, TX), 1997.

Rina's Family Secret, Arte Publico Press, 1998.

SIDELIGHTS: In her work, Chicana poet and novelist Gloria Velasquez has often touched on the themes that have influenced her life. Born to parents who were migrant farm workers, Velasquez spent a good deal of her childhood travelling between Colorado and Texas. Like many other Latino-Americans, the family lived an existence of poverty, knowing little stability in the search to make ends meet. Much of her poetry and short fiction reflects this reality, and shows a deep yearning to change an environment that allows such widespread disparity. She also expresses a strong feminist viewpoint, rebelling against the domination of the Chicana in modern-day society. Though much of her early work was poetry, Velasquez has recently written several young-adult novels, four of which make up the "Roosevelt High School" series, beginning with *Juanita Fights the School Board* (1994). Each of these novels incorporates the topics that the author feels most strongly about, as well as emphasizing Chicano/Latino characters, something very rare in the young-adult genre.

Velasquez was born in 1949 in Loveland, Colorado, where she attended her first years of school. In the course of her family moving from one place to another, she was to attend another school in Texas, before her parents finally settled the family in Johnstown, Colorado. In Johnstown, Velasquez' parents were able to find other work outside of the farm industry, and it was here that she graduated from Roosevelt High School, a place that would become the model for her young-adult series that she was to write much later in her life. After high school, Velasquez worked as a secretary for Hewlett-Packard and attended night classes at a local college. It was during these classes that the future author began to develop her craft. She showed so much promise that she won a fellowship from the University of Northern Colorado, where she was able to study full-time, double majoring in Chicano and Spanish studies. After earning her B.A. at the University of Northern Colorado, Velasquez moved on to Stanford University where she won several literary awards and ultimately attained a Ph.D. in Spanish literature. During her graduate work she wrote a groundbreaking dissertation entitled "Cultural Ambivalence in Early Chicana Prose Fiction," a work that concentrated on the writings of female early Chicano

authors of the twentieth-century, as well as setting the tone for the themes that were to become prevalent in her prose.

In the "Roosevelt High School" series, Velasquez has addresses many of the issues that have plagued the Chicano/Latino community for years. Alcoholism, single mothers and divorce, lack of self—identity, and violence are just some of the themes that she tackles in a manner young readers will be able identify with. One of the reasons that the series is so notable is because Velasquez writes about Chicano characters, a rarity in the U.S. publishing industry. In addition to *Juanita Fights the School Board,* the series also includes *Maya's Divided World* (1995), *Tommy Stands Alone* (1995), and *Rina's Family Secret* (1998). The series features several recurring characters, the most prominent of which is Sandra Martinez, a guidance counselor at Roosevelt. Throughout the series, Ms. Martinez gives assistance to the children, helping them cope with their problems and providing a listening ear whenever the they need to talk. Velasquez also uses Martinez to develop subplots in some of the stories. In *Maya's Divided World,* for instance, Martinez's life has many parallels with that of Maya, the book's main character.

Maya's Divided World is the tale of a girl whose seemingly charmed life comes unraveled because of problems at home. When the story begins, Maya is introduced as the perfect student who is good looking, has wealthy parents, and is the envy of her classmates. Then one day, Maya's parents separate and file for a divorce. The breakup is a tremendous blow to Maya. Her school work begins to suffer, and she isolates herself from all of her best friends, unable to face them for fear that they will find out about the divorce. Finally, Maya's best friend persuades her into having a talk with Ms. Martinez, who helps the girl cope with her problems. Velasquez uses multiple first-person narratives throughout the book, providing multi-faceted viewpoints of Maya's predicament. Jeanne Triner of *Booklist* enthused about the use of Chicano characters and felt that Velasquez did "a nice job of giving readers a window into the culture and providing some positive role models."

Tommy Stands Alone, the next book in the series, also dealt with a sensitive issue. The main character in the story, Tommy, who is also a Chicano student at Roosevelt, is a homosexual. To all of his friends and classmates, Tommy, a friend of Maya's, seems just like everybody else. He desperately tries to conceal his sexual identity. But when a friend discovers a note in his pocket that was written by a well-known gay boy, everyone soon knows Tommy's secret. Alienated and hurt, Tommy turns to alcohol and even attempts suicide in the hopes that it will ease his pain. Ms. Martinez again intercedes, and counsels the young man. Critic Merri Monks of *Booklist* called *Tommy Stands Alone* an "engaging story."

The last volume of the series, *Rina's Family Secret,* features a girl named Rina whose father is an alcoholic and physically abusive, both to her mother and to her and her siblings. When Rina's father, in a night of rage, stabs her mother with a knife, Rina decides that she can no longer tolerate her father's abusive ways, nor her mother's passivity to it, and moves in with her grandmother. Ms. Martinez, who shares a common past with Rina, again plays a large role in helping the Puerto Rican student with her dilemma. *Rina's Family Secret* was warmly received by some critics. Debbie Carton of *Booklist* called it "a believable portrait of a multiethnic high-school community" that "realistically captures the emotions and actions of the teenagers who are part of it."

Velasquez is also the author of a 1997 collection of poetry titled *I Used to be a Superwoman.* The collection, which includes such poems as "Advice," "America," "Chicana," "Days Gone By in Orange County," and "From Good Morning, Vietnam to Good Morning, Mom," treats such themes as the Chicano Movement in America, calling for an end to poverty and discrimination, and urging readers to take up the fight for justice.

Velasquez once commented: "Born and raised in poverty, I truly believe that when you are born with nothing you have everything. It is this gift from the Divine spirits that I share in my writing with the world, with our youth, with society."

BIOGRAPHICAL/CRITICAL SOURCES:

BOOKS

Day, Frances, *Latina and Latino Voices in Literature,* Heinemann, 1997, pp. 169-175.
Dictionary of Literary Biography, Volume 122: *Chicano Writers, Second Series,* edited by Francisco A. Lomeli and Carl R. Shirley, Gale (Detroit, MI), 1992.

PERIODICALS

Booklist, March 1, 1995, p. 1236; October 15, 1995, p. 397; August, 1998, p. 1992.

Kirkus Reviews, June 15, 1998.
School Library Journal, April, 1995, p. 158; November, 1995, p. 124; October, 1998, p. 147.
Wilson Library Bulletin, April, 1995, p. 114.

*   *   *

VERISSIMO, Erico (Lopes)   1905-1975

PERSONAL: Born December 17, 1905, in Cruz Alta, Rio Grande do Sul, Brazil; died November 28, 1975; son of Sebastiao Verissimo da Fonseca (a pharmacist) and Abigail Lopes Verissimo (a seamstress); married Mafalda Volpe, July 15, 1931; children: Clarissa, Luis Fernando.

CAREER: Writer. Worked in a dry-goods store, Cruz Alta, Rio Grande do Sul, Brazil, mid-1920s, and as a pharmacist in Cruz Alta, until 1930; caricaturist and short-story writer for two newspapers in Porto Alegre, Brazil; *Revista do Globo* (later expanded to become Editora Globo publishing house), Porto Alegre, translator and editor, c. 1932-40; Pan American Union (now the Organization of American States), Washington, DC, director of Department of Cultural Affairs, 1953-56. Host of children's radio show *Amigo Velho,* Porto Alegre, late 1930s; lecturer at several U.S. universities at the invitation of the U.S. Department of State, 1941-46.

AWARDS, HONORS: Honorary doctorate in letters, Mills College, 1944; Juca Pato Prize as Brazilian intellectual of the year, 1967.

WRITINGS:

FOR ADULTS

Fantoches (title means "Puppets"), Globo (Porto Alegre, Brazil), 1932.
Clarissa, Globo (Porto Alegre), 1933.
Caminhos cruzados, Globo (Porto Alegre), 1935, translated by L. C. Kaplan as *Crossroads,* Macmillan (New York), 1943, republished as *Crossroads and Destinies,* Arco (London), 1956.
Musica ao longe (title means "Distant Music"), Nacional (Sao Paulo, Brazil), 1935.
Um lugar ao sol (title means "A Place in the Sun"), Globo (Porto Alegre), 1936.
Olhai os lirios do campo, Globo (Porto Alegre), 1938, translated by Jean Neel Karnoff as *Consider the Lilies of the Field,* Macmillan (New York), 1947.

Saga, Globo (Porto Alegre), 1940.

Gato preto em campo de neve (title means "Black Cat in a Field of Snow"), Globo (Porto Alegre), 1941.

Viagem atraves da literatura americana, Instituto Brasil-Estados Unidos (Rio de Janeiro, Brazil), 1941.

As maos do meu filho, Meridiano (Porto Alegre), 1942.

O resto e silencio, Globo (Porto Alegre), 1943, translated by Kaplan as *The Rest Is Silence,* Macmillan (New York), 1946.

Brazilian Literature: An Outline, Macmillan (New York), 1945.

A volta do gato preto (title means "The Return of the Black Cat"), Globo (Porto Alegre), 1947.

Ana Terra, Associados (Porto Alegre), 1949.

Um certo Capitao Rodrigo (title means "A Certain Captain Rodrigo"), Globo (Porto Alegre), 1949.

O tempo e o vento: O continente, Globo (Porto Alegre), 1949, translated by Linton Lomas Barrett as *Time and the Wind,* Macmillan (New York), 1951, revised and enlarged as *O tempo e o vento: O continente; O retrato,* 2 volumes, Globo (Porto Alegre), 1951, revised and enlarged as *O tempo e o vento: O continente; O retrato; O arquipelago,* 3 volumes, Globo (Porto Alegre), 1962.

Lembranca de Porto Alegre, Globo (Rio de Janeiro), 1954, translated by Iris Strohschoen as *Souvenir of Porto Alegre,* Globo (Rio de Janeiro), 1960.

Noite, Globo (Rio de Janeiro), 1954, translated by Barrett as *Night,* Macmillan (New York), 1956.

Gente e bichos: Historias infantis, Globo (Porto Alegre), 1956.

Mexico: Historia duma viagem, Globo (Porto Alegre), 1957, translated by Barrett as *Mexico,* Orion (New York), 1960.

O ataque (title means "Attack"), Globo (Porto Alegre), 1959.

O senhor embaixador, Globo (Porto Alegre), 1965, translated by Barrett and Marie McDavid Barrett as *His Excellency, the Ambassador,* Macmillan (New York), 1967.

Ficcao completa, five volumes, Aguilar (Rio de Janeiro), 1966-67.

O prisioneiro (title means "The Prisoner"), Globo (Porto Alegre), 1967.

Israel em abril (title means "Israel in April"), Globo (Porto Alegre), 1969.

Incidente em Antares (title means "Incident in Antares"), Globo (Porto Alegre), 1971.

Um certo Henrique Bertaso, Globo (Porto Alegre), 1972.

Rio Grande do Sul, Brunner (Sao Paulo), 1973.

Solo de clarineta: Memorias (title means "Clarinet Solo: Memoirs"), part one, Globo (Porto Alegre), 1973, part two, Globo (Porto Alegre), 1976.

Artistas gauchos, Sociedade Israelita Riograndense (Porto Alegre), 1975.

Contos, Globo (Porto Alegre), 1978.

Historias infantis de Erico Verissimo, RBS (Porto Alegre), 1978.

Galeria fosca, Globo (Rio de Janeiro), 1987.

Contributor of short stories to the periodical *Madrugada.*

FOR CHILDREN

A vida de Joana d'Arc (title means "The Life of Joan of Arc"), Globo (Porto Alegre), 1935.

As aventuras do aviao vermelho (title means "The Adventures of the Red Airplane"), Globo (Porto Alegre), 1936.

Meu ABC (title means "My ABCs"), Globo (Porto Alegre), 1936.

Rosa Maria no castelo encantado (title means "Rosemary in the Enchanted Castle"), Globo (Porto Alegre), 1936.

Os tres porquinhos pobres (title means "The Three Poor Little Pigs"), Globo (Porto Alegre), 1936.

As aventuras de Tibicuera, que sao tambem as aventuras do Brasil (title means "The Adventures of Tibicuera"), Globo (Porto Alegre), 1937.

O urso com musica na barriga (title means "The Bear with Music in Its Tummy"), Globo (Porto Alegre), 1938.

Aventuras no mundo da higiene (title means "Adventures in the World of Hygiene"), Globo (Porto Alegre), 1939.

Outra vez os tres porquinhos (title means "The Three Little Pigs Again"), Globo (Porto Alegre), 1939.

Viagem a aurora do mundo (title means "Voyage to the Dawn of the World"), Globo (Porto Alegre), 1939.

A vida do elefante Basilio (title means "The Life of Basil the Elephant"), Globo (Porto Alegre), 1939.

TRANSLATIONS

John Steinbeck, *Ratos e homens,* Globo (Porto Alegre), 1940.

James Hilton, *Adeus, Mr. Chips,* Globo (Porto Alegre), 1941.

Robert Nathan, *O retrato de Jennie,* Meridiano (Porto Alegre), 1942.

Hilton, *Nao estamos sos,* Globo (Porto Alegre), 1943.
Aldous Huxley, *Contraponto,* Globo (Porto Alegre), 1943.

ADAPTATIONS: O tempo e o vento was produced as a television serial in Brazil in the 1980s.

SIDELIGHTS: Even after his death in 1975, Erico Lopes Verissimo remained one of Brazil's most highly regarded writers of popular fiction. Over the course of a career that spanned more than five decades, Verissimo authored dozens of titles ranging from allegorical fables for children to sweeping sagas of historical fiction. One of his country's most successful literary figures of the twentieth century, Verissimo also enjoyed acclaim at an international level as a result of foreign translations of many of his novels.

Verissimo was born Erico Lopes Verissimo in December of 1905 in the city of Cruz Alta, located in Brazil's Rio Grande do Sul province, its southernmost state. He suffered the loss of his father, a pharmacist, when he was just a small child; his mother, Abigail Lopes Verissimo, worked as a seamstress to support them. As an adolescent, he was sent to a boarding school in Porto Alegre, the main city of Rio Grande do Sul, but he returned to Cruz Alta to work as a store clerk before launching his own business as a pharmacist. Verissimo, however, was far more interested in the arts than sciences, and because of his own love of literature, music, and intellectual currents, his pharmacy became a gathering place for local prog-ressives and Cruz Altans interested in English literature.

Verissimo began writing as a young man, and his first short story, "Ladrao de gado" ("Cattle Thief"), was accepted for publication in Porto Alegre's leading newspaper in 1929. A year later he closed his pharmacy, and in 1931 he married Mafalda Volpe and moved to Porto Alegre. There he worked as a caricaturist and short-story writer for a pair of newspapers and enjoyed a small success with the publication of his first collection of short stories, *Fantoches* ("Puppets"), in 1932. *Revista do Globo,* a Porto Alegre publication, hired him as an editor, and in this job he also translated novels and detective fiction from English, French, and Spanish into Brazilian Portuguese. One of his translations was the 1928 Aldous Huxley novel, *Point Counter Point,* published as *Contraponto* in 1943. Verissimo was greatly influenced by the unusual narrative structure that Huxley used, and its stamp is found upon two of his own novels written around this time, *Caminhos cruzados* and *O resto e silencio.*

Revista do Globo would eventually expand to become one of Brazil's major publishing houses, Editora Globo, and though he left his editorial position with the firm by the early 1940s, Verissimo continued to enjoy a long professional relationship with the company, which issued nearly all of his works in Brazil, including his first novel, *Clarissa,* in 1933. The coming-of-age story of a contemporary young woman in Brazil, *Clarissa* would be the first of several of Verissimo's novels featuring this affluent, urban teenager, her boyfriend, and other assorted characters. A sequel of sorts, *Caminhos cruzados*—a work first published in English translation as *Crossroads* in 1943—introduced Professor Clarimundo, and an adult couple, Fernanda and Noel. As the teenagers step into the wider world, the professor provides an adult perspective on their actions and motives; the events of the era feature into the plot as well, especially with the departure of Clarissa's thoughtful cousin, Vasco, to fight in the Spanish Civil War. *Musica ao longe* ("Distant Music"), *Um lugar ao sol* ("A Place in the Sun"), and 1940's *Saga* round out the "Clarissa" cycle. "The five-work series," wrote Mary L. Daniel in a *Dictionary of Literary Biography* essay on Verissimo, "is presented in a flowing, accessible prose style that created an enthusiastic public for these works and the author's later novels." Verissimo even named his own daughter, born in 1935, after his famous protagonist. His other child, Luis Fernando, would also achieve notoriety; like his father, Luis became a well-regarded fiction writer in Brazil.

For a time during the 1930s, concurrent with the *Clarissa* novels, Verissimo also wrote books for children. Between 1935 and 1939 he and Globo enjoyed great success with titles such as *A vida de Joana d'Arc* ("The Life of Joan of Arc"), *Rosa Maria no castelo encantado* ("Rosemary in the Enchanted Castle"), *O urso com musica na barriga* ("The Bear with Music in Its Tummy"), *Aventuras no mundo da higiene* ("Adventures in the World of Hygiene"), and *A vida do elefante Basilio* ("The Life of Basil the Elephant"), among several others. "The author's pedagogical purpose, communicated in charmingly attractive narrative style and graphic illustrations, was so successful that a children's radio series, *Amigo Velho* ("Old Friend") hosted by Verissimo was carried by the major station in Porto Alegre," noted Daniel.

Verissimo's reputation as a serious novelist was cemented, however, in 1938 with the success of *Olhai os lirios do campo,* a work translated into English nine years later and published in the United States as

Consider the Lilies of the Field. The novel follows physician Eugenio Fontes and the personal and professional dramas that occur in his world; a wider, socially conscious perspective is also woven into the narrative structure through the doctor's concern for the poor of his city and their lack of access to health care. As Daniel wrote in her *Dictionary of Literary Biography* essay, "the density of psychological penetration of this novel, couched in an easily flowing style characterized by ample use of the historic present, takes precedence over the panoramic views and gallery of socio-economic types that predominated in Verissimo's earlier novels; the focus is now on dramas of conscience."

Another novel from this period, the 1943 work *O resto e silencio,* also consolidated Verissimo's reputation as both a popular Brazilian writer and a well-regarded novelist in English translation. Published in the United States as *The Rest Is Silence* in 1946, the work—drawing upon the style of the Huxley *Point Counter Point* novel—uses multiple narratives to sketch the events of one dramatic twenty–six hour period in Porto Alegre that begins with the suicidal fall of a woman on the Roman Catholic holy day of Good Friday. All of the characters witness the death—two businessmen and their wives, a newsboy, a city council official, a writer (the thwarted love interest that may have caused the woman to jump), a reporter, and the conductor of an orchestra. Their lives all intersect because of their presence at the suicide, and, as *Dictionary of Literary Biography* essayist Daniel wrote, "as more encounters occur, the characters are seen as complementary pieces in a meaningful puzzle, as though they had always been searching for each other but only at this point have been able to make contact as a result of yet another unknown person's tragedy." At the close of *O resto e silencio,* all gather for the Saturday evening orchestra performance; as they listen to the conductor's choice of a Beethoven symphony for the eve of Easter Sunday, "the music speaks of hope and strength in the midst of turmoil and courage in the face of trials," remarked Daniel.

In 1949 the first installment in Verissimo's weighty cycle of historical fiction appeared to enthusiastic sales. The work, published in several different textual configurations but referred to by a collective title, *O tempo e o vento,* would also appear in English translation. *O tempo e o vento: O continente* ("Time and the Wind: The Continent") was the first of the books, a novel that focuses on the history of Verissimo's home state, Rio Grande do Sul, roughly between 1745 to 1895. It recounts external events and the region's

political, economic, and social evolution—tied in to that of larger Brazil—through two family groups, the Terras and the Cambaras clans. "*O continente* is frontier literature at its best," asserted Daniel in her *Dictionary of Literary Biography* essay, "and serves as the undisputed masterpiece of historical regionalism dealing with southern Brazil and surrounding territory."

Verissimo continued his *O tempo e o vento* cycle with the 1951 publication *O retrato* ("The Portrait"), presenting the historical events and generational shifts that beset the next age of Terra and Cambaras characters from 1909 to 1915. The subsequent three decades are finished off in *O arquipelago* ("The Archipelago"), which did not appear until 1962. Bringing Brazil, Rio Grande do Sul, and the clans up to the year 1945, *O arquipelago* incorporates several real-life figures from Brazilian politics and culture. "From the solid image of the eighteenth- and nineteenth-century continent with its robust expectation of expansion and growth to the fragmentation of the mid-twentieth-century archipelago, the trilogy reflects Verissimo's increasing pessimism regarding human relations in general and Brazilian socio-economic and political life in particular," asserted Daniel in *Dictionary of Literary Biography.* During the 1960s several sections of *O tempo e o vento* were published independently, and its popularity continued into the 1980s with its serialization for Brazilian television.

Verissimo had, with the favorable international reception of *Olhai os lirios do campo* and *O resto e silencio,* already become a well-known literary figure in both Brazil and abroad during the 1940s. He made academic tours of American universities at the invitation of the U.S. Department of State during the 1940s, and in 1953 he arrived in Washington, D.C., for a more permanent stay after being offered the directorship of the Department of Cultural Affairs at the Pan American Union (now the Organization of American States). He lived in the United States for three years and used his Washington experiences as a sometimes unwilling participant in the complex politesse of international diplomacy as the basis for a later novel.

Published in 1965, *O senhor embaixador*—issued in translation in the United States as *His Excellency, the Ambassador* in 1967—is set in Washington and features a cast of characters drawn from the international diplomatic corps. The storyline is centered on the actions of an ambassador from the fictional "Republic of Sacramento," whose tale is recounted through the narrative voice of an American journalist. Vying factions, closed-door intrigues, and fear over the growing Western involvement in the war in Southeast Asia—and America's penchant for foreign intervention on a larger scale—move the plot forward, and in the end the ambassador returns home and is shot by a firing squad. Daniel, writing in *Dictionary of Literary Biography,* called *O senhor embaixador* "Verissimo's thinly veiled commentary upon the state of affairs in the nations of the Western hemisphere and the fundamental inhumanity of even the most sophisticated members of officialdom."

Another work with a similarly dire outlook was Verissimo's 1967 novel *O prisioneiro* ("The Prisoner"). Set in Vietnam, the book features characters that do not have names, only military titles, and behind the tale of military discipline and wartime conduct is Verissimo's commentary on the way in which such necessities often override basic moral concerns. The novel, wrote Daniel, "is a kind of antiwar parable, an accessible and perhaps deceptively simple plea for human rights in the international context of deep-seated racism, ethnic zeal, and paranoia by an author moved by humanitarian rather than political motives."

Though by this point in his career Verissimo was one of the most successful of modern Brazilian novelists, he was not hesitant to explore new literary veins and push his writing further toward experimentation. His final novel, *Incidente em Antares* ("Incident in Antares"), appeared in 1971. Elements of magical realism, at the time a fresh new current in Latin–American literature that had begun with Gabriel Garcia Marquez's *Cien anos de soledad* (*One Hundred Years of Solitude*) in 1967, found their way into this work of Verissimo's. Antares, like Garcia Marquez's creation of Macondo, is a fictional city and apotheosis of southern Brazil and the Rio Grande do Sul region. The story's action occurs on the eve of a 1964 revolution: seven citizens die, but their bodies remain unburied because of a gravediggers' strike. The "incident" involves a unionization of sorts among the deceased characters, who assemble at the town's bandstand to address the populace. The dead represent several strata of Brazilian society, all of whom find a common bond only in their death. Observed Daniel in her *Dictionary of Literary Biography* essay, "Verissimo has a message, or rather an appeal, in his last novel not radically different from the one that remained constant throughout earlier works: it is within the power of human beings to make or break their society, to weave or tear the sociocultural fabric of family, local, regional, national, and international life."

Verissimo's first volume of his memoirs, *Solo de clarineta: Memorias* ("Clarinet Solo: Memoirs"), was published in 1973. He died in November of 1975, a few weeks before his seventieth birthday. A second volume of his memoirs was published posthumously in 1976.

BIOGRAPHICAL/CRITICAL SOURCES:

BOOKS

Dictionary of Literary Biography, Volume 145: *Modern Latin-American Fiction Writers,* Second Series, edited by William Luis and Ann Gonzalez, Gale, 1994, pp. 335-343.*

*   *   *

VIGIL, Angel   1947-

PERSONAL: Born September 15, 1947, in Albuquerque, NM. *Education:* University of Kansas, B.A.

ADDRESSES: E-mail—avigil1@uswest.net.

CAREER: Writer, c. 1994—. Colorado Academy, Denver, director of drama and chairperson of Department of Fine and Performing Arts. Director of more than a hundred dramatic productions for schools, communities, and professional theaters. Colorado Council on the Arts, featured storyteller for the folk arts collection "Do Not Pass Me By: A Celebration of Colorado Folklife."

AWARDS, HONORS: Named Master Folk Artist and Heritage Artist in Traditional Hispanic Storytelling.

WRITINGS:

(Reteller) *The Corn Woman: Stories and Legends of the Hispanic Southwest/La mujer del maiz: Cuentos y leyendas del sudoeste hispano,* translated by Jennifer Audrey Lowell and Juan Francisco Marin, Libraries Unlimited (Englewood, CO), 1994.
Teatro! Hispanic Plays for Young People, Teacher Ideas Press (Englewood), 1996.
Una linda raza: Cultural and Artistic Traditions of the Hispanic Southwest, Fulcrum Publishing, (Golden, CO), 1998.

Co-author of the play *Cuentos.*

WORK IN PROGRESS: The Eagle in the Sun, Traditional Stories from Mexico, for Libraries Unlimited, publication expected in 2000.

* * *

VIGIL-PINON, Evangelina 1949-

PERSONAL: Born November 29, 1949, in San Antonio, TX; daughter of a shoe repairman; married Mark Anthony Pinon (a musician/artist) February 14, 1983; children: Marc Antony. *Ethnicity:* "Hispanic." *Education:* Prairie View A & M University, 1968-70; University of Houston B.A. (English), 1974; graduate studies, University of Texas, San Antonio, 1977.

ADDRESSES: Office—Arte Publico Press, University of Houston, 4800 Calhoun-2L, Houston, TX 77004.

CAREER: Poet. Worked in Houston, San Antonio, and Galveston, TX as an arts administrator, 1976-82; Harlandale Independent School District and Texas Commission for the Arts, writer-in-residence, 1977-78; Galveston Cultural Arts Center, poet-in-residence, 1981; University of Houston, guest lecturer (English), 1982; National College of District Attorneys, paralegal/training program administrator, early 1980s; Arte Publico Press, editor.

AWARDS, HONORS: First Place, National Literary Competition, Coordinating Council of Literary Magazines, 1976; Fellowship for Creative Writers, National Endowment for the Arts, 1979-80; American Book Award, Before Columbus Foundation, 1983.

WRITINGS:

Nade y Nade (title means "Deeper and Deeper") M & A Editions (San Antonio, TX), 1978.
Thirty An' Seen a Lot (poems), Arte Publico Press (Houston, TX), 1985.
The Computer Is Down (poems), Arte Publico Press, 1987.
(Translator) Tomas Rivera, *Y no se lo trago la tierra (And the Earth Did Not Devour Him),* Arte Publico Press (Houston, TX), 1987.
(Editor) *Woman of Her Word: Hispanic Woman Write,* Arte Publico Press, 1987.
(Editor with Julian Olivares) *Decade II: An Anniversary Anthology,* Arte Publico Press, 1993.

Also contributor to numerous anthologies and literary periodicals. Also wrote and directed *Night Vigil* (videotape), De Colores Productions (Houston, TX), 1984.

SIDELIGHTS: Evangelina Vigil-Pinon, the second child in a family of ten children, grew up speaking both Spanish and English. Her mother's family came from Mexico to San Antonio, Texas, in the early 1900s, and her father's family came from the area of Seguin, Texas. In her later childhood, she lived with her maternal grandmother's extended family and heard her great-uncle tell many stories about life in Mexico and the United States at the turn of the century. According to Elaine Dorough Johnson in the *Dictionary of Literary Biography,* "from her maternal grandmother she learned 'to observe and listen for words of wisdom which come only with experience.'" Her great-uncle, who was a father figure to her during her teenage years, gave her a sense of responsibility and discipline. From her mother, an avid reader, she received a lifelong love of books.

Even as a small child, Vigil-Pinon was sensitively aware of her environment; she recalls wandering in a rose garden, savoring the flowers' fragrance and the distant music of a neighbor's radio. She was talented in art, and in sixth grade was one of only two grade school students who attended the Inman Christian Center, a private art school in San Antonio. According to Johnson, she recalled, "The art studio was a wonderful place—I loved the smell of paints and inks and art supplies all around, the students' canvasses on easels. . . . My teacher's name was Mrs. Burk. She was the most inspiring teacher I've ever known."

Like her father, a shoe repairman who played the guitar and sang to friends and family, Vigil-Pinon loved music. She sang with the radio and in the school choir, and formed a neighborhood combo with her cousins. In high school, she told Johnson, "Music became central to my existence. But then music had really been in the center of my soul, nurtured by the culture of San Antonio, where people 'live' music." She wrote her first poem when she was eight years old (winning third place in a newspaper poetry contest), and her love of music and words intertwined as she grew older; she wrote down the lyrics of her favorite songs, filling in the lines she didn't know with her own words. Poetry, she told Johnson, is "the rhythm of time, the ticking of clocks, hearts beating. To me poetry is music. It is that song in our heart. Life is the dance to that music." She still sings, write songs, and performs on the classical guitar, with her husband, a musician.

Vigil-Pinon might have become a professional artist or musician if she had not been encouraged to pursue secretarial science in high school. She then received a scholarship to study business administration at Prairie View A & M University, a small, mostly African American school in Houston, Texas. This exposure to her African American classmates—learning about their history, pride, faith, and music—increased her awareness of her own Hispanic identity.

In her junior year, Vigil-Pinon transferred to the University of Houston, where she changed her major from business to English with a minor in political science. Although she studied classical writers as well as counterculture poets, she told Johnson that the writers who influenced her most were African Americans, particularly Frederick Douglass, James Baldwin, Nikki Giovanni, and Ntozake Shange. She told Johnson, "Spirituality is central to Black culture, and rhythm and music are very much a manifestation and symbol of this in Black poetry—as is the ritual of song and dance in Native American works. Similarly, in the heart of Hispanic culture, one finds song, music and dance combined in an enduring ritual." Vigil-Pinon worked to convince the University of Houston to establish a Mexican-American studies program, and in her final year of school, the program was established.

In 1976 Vigil-Pinon moved back to San Antonio, where she worked with the Mexican-American Cultural Center, the Artists' Alliance of San Antonio, and the Texas Institute for Educational Development. She also taught composition and American literature at the Universidad Jacinto Trevino, and was writer-in-residence for the Harlandale Independent School District and the Texas Commission of the Arts. In 1979-80, she used a grant from the National Endowment for the Arts to travel to Central America and the Caribbean, where she learned a great deal about culture and politics.

In San Antonio she also took graduate courses and studied Mexican American, Native American, and African American writers, who inspired her own writing. She also read widely in Spanish. In 1978 Vigil-Pinon decided to devote more time to her writing; most of the poems in her collection *Thirty an' Seen a Lot* were written between 1976 and 1979, and *Nade y Nade* was published in 1978. *Nade y Nade* is a collection of thirty poems on the topics of sadness, the passage of time, self-knowledge, and communication with others. Johnson wrote, "In spite of the weighty sound of these themes, the poems in this volume are neither ponderous not bitter in tone. In

fact many are characterized by gentleness and a contemplative spirit." The poems often combine Spanish and English and accurately portray Hispanic dialogue, but their subjects are universal.

Thirty an' Seen a Lot is a collection of poems written during a six-year period in Houston, San Antonio, and Galveston, where Vigil-Pinon moved in 1981. The poems praise simple pleasures, celebrate the wisdom passed down by elders in the barrio, portray Hispanic culture, and show her relationship with nature. Vigil-Pinon loved living in Galveston, on the coast of the Gulf of Mexico, and told Johnson, "If there is one single element that has inspired me the most to write, it has to be the ocean, the sea, the surf, beaches and breezy umbrella skies."

She returned to Houston in 1982. She had been employed as a poet-in-residence at the Galveston Cultural Arts Center, and as a guest lecturer at the University of Houston Department of English, but these jobs were not financially rewarding. She told Johnson, "realizing that I was getting nowhere financially through my usual employment as writer-in-residence and other temporary employment situations in the field of arts administration, I decided to find a stable, full-time position. By chance I came upon a position in victim/witness assistance and management." She still works in this field as a paralegal and training-program administrator for the National College of District Attorneys.

In 1983 Vigil-Pinon married Mark Anthony Pinon. She told Johnson that married life gave her less time to write, but she did not mind this, saying, "Ensconced in a warm, loving relationship, I don't feel the solitude and sense of isolation which I experienced in my younger years. The transformation has been from the single, carefree writer, to the full-time professional, and mother and wife. . . . Yet, the creative process never remains the same, so I don't long for the inspirational elements of my past."

BIOGRAPHICAL/CRITICAL SOURCES:

BOOKS

Dictionary of Literary Biography, Volume 122: *Chicano Writers,* Gale (Detroit, MI), 1992.
Garcia, Juan A., Theresa Cordova and Juan R. Garcia, editors, *The Chicano Struggle: Analysis of Past and Present Efforts,* Bilingual Press (Binghamton, NY), 1984.*

VILLASENOR, Edmund
    See VILLASENOR, Victor E(dmundo)

*   *   *

VILLASENOR, Victor
    See VILLASENOR, Victor E(dmundo)

*   *   *

VILLASENOR, Victor E(dmundo) 1940-
    (Edmund Villasenor, Victor Villasenor)

PERSONAL: Born May 11, 1940, in Carlsbad, CA; son of Salvadore (in business) and Lupe (Gomez) Villasenor; married Barbara Bloch, December 29, 1974; children: David Cuauhtemoc, Joseph. *Education:* Attended University of San Diego and Santa Clara University.

ADDRESSES: Home—1302 Stewart St., Oceanside, CA 92054.

CAREER: Construction worker in California, 1965-70; journalist and writer, 1970—. *Military service:* U.S. Army.

AWARDS, HONORS: Named to the top "100 Influentials" by the Hispanic Business Association.

WRITINGS:

(Under name Edmund Villasenor) *Macho!* (novel), Bantam, 1973.
(Under name Victor Villasenor) *Jury: The People vs. Juan Corona* (nonfiction), Little, Brown, 1977.
The Ballad of Gregorio Cortez (screenplay; based on the novel *With His Pistol in His Hands* by Americo Paredes), Embassy Pictures, 1983.
Rain of Gold (nonfiction), Arte Publico (Houston, TX), 1991, published as *Lluvia de Oro,* Delta, 1996.
Walking Stars (short stories), Arte Publico, 1994.
Wild Steps of Heaven (nonfiction), Delacorte, 1996.
Authentic Family-Style Mexican Cooking (historical narrative), 1997.

Contributor to periodicals, including *Aztlan.*

SIDELIGHTS: Author and journalist Victor E. Villasenor has attained recognition well beyond his small and somewhat insular Chicano literary community. The author of novels, a collection of short fiction, and several works of nonfiction, Villasenor has been hailed, along with other Latino writers such as Julia Alvarez, Oscar Hijuelos, and Sandra Cisneros, for "offer[ing] insight into the mixture of economic opportunity and discrimination that Latinos encounter in the United States," according to Susan Miler in *Newsweek.*

Villasenor was born in the barrio of Carlsbad, California, and grew up on a ranch nearby. Both his parents, immigrants from Mexico, were poorly educated; he grew up in a house where there were no books. "When I started school, I spoke more Spanish than English," Villasenor recalled. "I was a D student and every year of school made me feel more stupid and confused—many of these feelings had to do with being Chicano. In my junior year of high school, I told my parents I had to quit school or I would go crazy. Finally, they allowed me to quit. I was eighteen years old. I felt free, I felt wonderful, but I didn't know what to do with my freedom."

"I worked on the ranch, I worked in the fields—I was making money and it felt great. But then that fall when the other kids went back to school and the illegal workers went back to Mexico, I didn't know what to do with my life. An older cousin got me into college on a temporary basis if I finished high school. It was the University of San Diego and it was just getting started and was not yet accredited. On this campus I found out that books were not punishment, and if I couldn't remember dates I wasn't necessarily stupid. I flunked English of course (because I only had the reading ability of a fifth grader) and every other course except for philosophy and theology."

"The shock of my life came that year when a teacher told me I was very bright. But still I felt like I was going crazy. I was beginning to realize that I was ashamed of being Mexican. So I boxed. I fought with such a rage of confusion that I was undefeated."

"The following summer for the first time in my life I began to drink and discover my sexuality and feel wonderful and yet terrible from guilt. My parents sent me to Mexico where I fell in with some hip people. I was introduced to Mexican art, Mexican history, and I read my first book, Homer's *Iliad,* as well as *Tender Is the Night* by F. Scott Fitzgerald, and *The Little Prince.* I began having all-night talks with an older woman. I felt good about myself. I wanted to stay in Mexico and never return to the United States where I felt ashamed of being Mexican. But my parents came for me and after weeks of arguments I agreed to go back home for awhile."

"I found myself feeling like a bombshell—ready to explode, prepared to kill anyone who made me feel ashamed. I was reading a copy of James Joyce's *Portrait of the Artist as a Young Man,* given to me by the woman in Mexico, when it hit me: I would write. Instead of killing or bashing people's brains out, I would change their minds. I would write good books that reach out and touch people, and I would influence the world. I got a dictionary and a high school English grammar book, and I built a desk and began to read books eight months out of the year. I'd go to bookstores and buy ten books at a time, read them, dissect them, and then reassemble them. Then for four months of the year I'd support myself in construction."

Only then did Villasenor begin to write. "I wrote for ten years," he remembered, "completing nine novels and sixty-five short stories and receiving more than 260 rejections before I sold my first book, *Macho!*" Villasenor's first novel benefited from being published at the height of a powerful migrant farmworkers' organizing campaign in California in 1973. The novel recounts a year in the life of Roberto Garcia, a young Tarascan Indian from the state of Michoacan, Mexico, who migrates illegally to California in 1963 to work in the fields. Villasenor describes Garcia's intense culture shock in abandoning his isolated, tradition-bound village for the rich but lonely and frightening land of the North. The victim of exploitation and discrimination in the United States, Garcia finally decides to go back to his village and resume working his family's small farm. But he returns a changed man who can no longer accept without question the traditional Mexican social code, particularly the *machista* demand that he take blood vengeance against the villager who murdered his father. Thus, Garcia's adventure reflects the Chicano's transcultural experience—the melding of features from both the Spanish-Mexican and North American societies.

Villasenor has since written several full-length works of nonfiction, as well as a collection of short stories about his parent's childhoods in Mexico titled *Walking Stars: Stories of Magic and Power,* which Cathi Dunn MacRae praised in *Wilson Library Bulletin* as "buoyant tales of extraordinary triumph [that] demonstrate the powerful 'magic of your God-given soul.'" His 1992 work *Rain of Gold* and its sequel, 1995's *Wild Steps of Heaven,* focus on the experiences of the author's parents as they made their way from Mexico to California. *Rain of Gold* is a nonfiction account, but Villasenor had a hard

time finding a publisher willing to accept the book in its non-novel format. Finally, he was able to link up with Texas-based Arte Publico, which released the book in a limited edition and has since sold the paperback rights due to its popularity.

Rain of Gold recounts the years surrounding Villasenor's parents' marriage, which took place in California in 1929. Recalling the stories of relatives who had been drawn into the violence of the Mexican Revolution of 1910, "the life [Villasenor's parents]' families led before that cataclysm and their eventual settlement in the United States is one of survival and wonder," according to Tom Miller, reviewing the book in the *New York Times Book Review.* From life in impoverished, war-torn Mexico to the arduous crossing from Juarez to the United States, during which time they were forced to live in camps in primitive conditions, where food was almost non-existent and violence was born of desperation, to the opportunities as well as prejudices they would encounter upon reaching the "promised land," Villasenor's book features "keenly drawn" characters and provides a revealing portrait of turn-of-the-century social and political life south of the border, according to Miller.

The saga of Villasenor's family continues in the second volume of a proposed trilogy, *Wild Steps of Heaven.* In this volume, the author goes back in time to the days of his grandfather's youth. Young Jose Villasenor lives with his parents and thirteen siblings on a ranch in the highlands of Los Altos de Jalisco, Mexico. Looked upon with disdain by his proud, Spanish-born father, who favors his blue-eyed children over those exhibiting his wife's Indian blood, Jose eventually bests his father by taming a horse thought to be untamable. Unfortunately, his success angers his father to the point that Jose is banished from the family home. With nowhere else to go, he becomes involved in the revolution and returns home a hero after uncovering the corruption of a colonel and prohibiting the federal officer's attempts to further injure the common people. Retaliation by the colonel follows, against not only Jose but his entire village. At this point his mother gathers together what is left of her family and attempts the trip north that serves as the subject of *Rain of Gold.* While some critics suggested that *Wild Steps of Heaven* contained too many stylistic flourishes and was too ambitious in scope, others found it intriguing. A *Kirkus* reviewer likened the work to "a Latin American *Roots,*" while Greg Burkman in *Booklist* called it "tightly wrought."

While most of Villasenor's works focus on the history of his own family, he has also joined his writing talent with his skills as an investigative journalist. In the early 1970s, while he was waiting for *Macho!* to be published, he read about Juan Corona's arrest for twenty-five murders. "Immediately I thought, Another Mexican being arrested. Hell, no man could kill twenty-five people. He must be innocent. So I talked to my publisher and he told me to look into it and write a short letter about what kind of book I thought I could write. They commissioned me to do the book. I spent the next three years investigating and writing about the Corona case."

Villasenor's *Jury: The People vs. Juan Corona* is a nonfiction account of the trial of Juan Corona, a California labor contractor who was convicted in 1973 of murdering twenty-five derelicts and drifters. After covering the trial as a journalist, Villasenor decided to write a book focusing on the jury's agonizing struggle to reach a fair verdict in one of the worst mass murder cases in U.S. history. By exhaustively interviewing all of the jurors over a period of months, Villasenor was able to reconstruct the details of eight days of emotionally charged deliberations that led the jury from an original majority favoring acquittal to a unanimous verdict of guilty.

Villasenor's examination of the highly complicated and controversial case offers provocative insights into the workings of the U.S. jury system. The author questions the system, quoting a Corona juror agonizing over whether a man's life should rest in the hands of twelve ordinary people seemingly ill-equipped by education or training to sort out a tangled skein of law and evidence. Based on the Corona trial, Villasenor determines that the system does indeed work: in the crucible of unrestricted deliberations, a jury will rise to the solemn challenge of judging and render its verdict with integrity and good faith. In light of the Corona jury members' obvious human frailties, Villasenor nevertheless concludes in *Jury,* "In becoming close to all the jurors and their families, I regained a respect and admiration for my fellow man."

BIOGRAPHICAL/CRITICAL SOURCES:

BOOKS

Villasenor, Victor, *Rain of Gold,* Arte Publico, 1991.

PERIODICALS

Booklist, April 1, 1996, p. 1344.
Christian Science Monitor, October 13, 1977.
English Journal, January 1974.

Examiner and Chronicle (San Francisco), November 6, 1973.
La Gente, April 1974.
Hispanic, August 1991; January/February 1995, p. 124.
Kirkus Reviews, December 15, 1995, p. 1760.
Library Journal, July 1994, p. 80.
Newsweek, April 20, 1992, pp. 78-79.
New York Times Book Review, May 1, 1977; September 8, 1991, p. 20; February 25, 1996, p. 26.
Publishers Weekly, September 12, 1994, p. 92; December 11, 1995, pp. 64-65.
School Library Journal, November 1994, p. 129.
Washington Post Book World, September 8, 1991.
Wilson Library Bulletin, April 1995, p. 114.*

*   *   *

VILLEGAS DE MAGNON, Leonor   1876-1955

PERSONAL: Born June 12, 1876, in Nuevo Lared, Tamaulipas, Mexico; died April 17, 1955; daughter of Joaquin Villegas (a rancher, miner, and importer/exporter) and Valeriana Rubio; married Adolfo Magnon (a steamship agent), January 10, 1901; children: Leonor, Joaquin, Adolfo. *Education:* Trained at various boarding schools and convents; studied education at Mount St. Ursula's Convent in New York.

CAREER: Political activist and writer, c. 1910-48.

WRITINGS:

The Rebel, edited by Claire Lomas, Arte Publico Press (Houston, TX), 1994.

SIDELIGHTS: Leonor Villegas de Magnon was born in Nuevo Laredo, Tamaulipas, Mexico, just a few days after Porfirio Diaz, who would be dictator of Mexico for thirty–four years, took control of Mexico City. When soldiers searching for hidden revolutionaries searched the area, they heard the newborn girl crying, and thought she was a hidden rebel fighter. As a result, her father affectionately nicknamed her "La Rebelde," a name she proudly used later as the title for her autobiography. The name was appropriate, as she later opposed the Diaz government, rebelled against the aristocratic class system, and fought the traditional view of women in Mexican society.

Villegas de Magnon grew up in a wealthy family: her father, Joaquin Villegas, who came from Spain, was a rancher and mine owner, and ran an import/export business. Her mother, Valerian Rubio, came from a rich family. Villegas de Magnon and her siblings, Leopoldo, Lorenzo, and Lina, were raised in a privileged, aristocratic setting on their family rancheria, but their world was abruptly altered when their mother died at a young age and their father remarried. Their stepmother, Heloise Monsalvatge, urged their father to move to Laredo, Texas, and then sent the children to boarding schools.

Villegas de Magnon attended the Ursuline Convent in San Antonia from 1882 through 1885, and then transferred to the Academy of the Holy Cross in Austin, Texas until 1889. After this, Heloise sent all four of the siblings to New York City, where Villegas de Magnon entered Mount St. Ursula's Convent. She considered becoming a nun, and studied education, but after graduating in 1895, with honors, she went back to Laredo.

On January 10, 1901, she married Adolfo Magnon, a U.S. citizen. They moved to Mexico City, where he worked for several steamship companies. Her lifestyle during this time was, like that of her childhood, steeped in luxury and ease, but she saw poor people all around her and was troubled by their fate. She and her husband had three children, Leonor, Joaquin, and Adolfo. After their births, Villegas de Magnon became involved with revolutionaries who supported Francisco Madero, a leader who opposed Diaz. She began writing insurgent articles against the Diaz dictatorship, which she signed with her original family name of Villegas.

In 1910, Villegas de Magnon took her children to visit her father, who was terminally ill, and found that most of his property had been taken by the Mexican government as punishment for her revolutionary writings. Soon after this, the revolution broke out, and she was separated from her husband. She threw herself more deeply into the revolutionary cause, becoming a member of the Revolutionary Council. She wrote more articles on the revolutionary movement and provided housing for political exiles. When Madero finally took over the government in 1911, she opened a bilingual school and founded an organization called Union, Progreso y Caridad ("Union, Progress and Charity"). The organization encouraged women to extend their influence beyond the home to society, and use their abilities and influence to educate children, beautify the city, promote charity work, and hold cultural and social events.

In January of 1911, when the revolutionary forces attacked Nuevo Laredo, Villegas de Magnon used her inheritance to found and finance the Cruz Blanca ("White Cross"), a medical relief group for wounded soldiers. Soon after this, she recruited women and men from the border area to travel with the Constitutionalist forces from El Paso, Texas, to Mexico City; after the revolution, they returned to Laredo and their normal lives. Villegas de Magnon worked at her bilingual school as well as for the State Democratic Executive Committee, Women's Division, of Texas.

In 1940, with her money gone, Villegas de Magnon went to Mexico City to look for a job with the Mexican Veterans' Administration. She joined the Women's International Club, and after years of lobbying, she and other women were officially recognized as veterans of the revolution. In 1946, as part of the Mexican land redistribution program, she agreed to work her own piece of land in Rancherias Camargo, Tamaulipas, but the program was a failure. In two years she had exhausted all her credit and money, and she returned to Laredo.

She began writing her autobiography, *El Rebelde,* because she wanted to "do justice to those worthy nurses and brave women who so patriotically defended their country." The autobiography is written in the third person, and romanticizes the revolution and her own life. For example, she writes that several incidents foretold her dramatic life as a revolutionary: her birthdate on the eve of the revolution, her nickname, and a burn on her right hand that was identical to that of Venustiano Carranza, who was president of Mexico from 1915 to 1920. She presents herself as a sensitive, lonely orphan who was a brave, bold woman who was devoted to her duty and her country. She was not successful in having the Spanish version of the autobiography published, so she wrote a longer English version titled *The Lady Was a Rebel,* but was also unable to find a publisher.

Both the Spanish and English versions of the book describe the idyllic, pastoral life of her childhood on her father's hacienda, and the transition from that life to the insecure one with her Americanized stepmother, and her experiences in the boarding schools. After this, both books present diary entries describing the work of the Cruz Blanca and the work of its members as nurses and doctors, but also as spies, informers, reporters, propagandists, printers, telegraph operators, and railroad engineers. Villegas de Magnon also tells the stories of several brave women, including Maria de Jesus Gonzalez, who worked as a messenger, then as a spy, and who, dressed as a man, eventually became a colonel. Many other anecdotes present Villegas de Magnon as La Rebelde, a resourceful and shrewd revolutionary.

Although Villegas de Magnon wrote the book in order to preserve the memory of the revolutionaries, the autobiography, and the stories it contains, was nearly lost. Many years after her death, however, editor Claire Lomas visited her family and received drafts of both versions, as well as scrapbooks, letters, and albums. From these, Lomas began reconstructing the book, now titled *The Rebel.* "Neither Villegas de Magnon's aristocratic background nor her humanitarian or rebellious deed have allowed her to overcome limitations imposed by gender," explained Lomas in an essay from *Dictionary of Literary Biography.* "Restoration of autobiographicalnarratives such as hers will allow us better to understand links within our cultural heritage which take into account class, ethnic/national, gender, and spatial considerations."

BIOGRAPHICAL/CRITICAL SOURCES:

BOOKS

Dictionary of Literary Biography, Volume 122: *Chicano Writers,* Gale (Detroit, MI), 1992.*

*   *   *

VIRAMONTES, Helena Maria 1954-

PERSONAL: Born February 26, 1954, in East Los Angeles, CA; daughter of a construction worker and a homemaker; children: two. *Education:* Immaculate Heart College, B.A., 1975; attended University of California at Irvine.

ADDRESSES: Agent—c/o Dutton/Signet, 375 Hudson St., New York, NY 10014.

CAREER: Fiction writer. Co-founder of Southern California Latino Writers and Film Makers group; teaches at Cornell University.

AWARDS, HONORS: Statement Magazine first prize for fiction, California State University, for the short stories "Requiem for the Poor, 1977, and "The Broken Web," 1978; first prize for fiction, University of California at Irvine Chicano Literary Contest, for the short story "Birthday," 1979; National Endowment for the Arts fellowship, 1989.

WRITINGS:

The Moths and Other Stories, Arte Publico Press (Houston, TX), 1985.
Under the Feet of Jesus, Dutton (New York City), 1995.

NONFICTION

(Co-editor, with Maria Herrera-Sobek) *Chicana Creativity and Criticism: Charting New Frontiers in American Literature,* Arte Publico Press (Houston, TX), 1988.
(Co-editor, with Maria Herrera-Sobek) *Chicana (w)rites: On Word and Film,* Third Woman Press (Berkeley, CA), 1995.

OTHER

Works represented in anthologies, including *Cuentos: Short Stories by Latinas,* Kitchen Table/Women of Color Press, 1983; *Woman of Her Word,* edited by Evangelina Vigil, Arte Publico Press (Houston, TX), 1984; *Breaking Boundaries: Latina Writings and Critical Readings,* edited by Asuncion Horno-Delgado, Eliana Ortego, Nina M. Scott, and Nancy Saporta Sternbach, University of Massachusetts Press (Amherst, MA), 1989; and *New Chicana/Chicano Writing,* edited by Charles M. Tatum, University of Arizona Press (Tuscon, AZ), 1992. Contributor of short stories to periodicals, including *XhismeArte, Hispanic Link, America's 2001, Pearl,* and *Blue Mesa Review;* adapted one of her stories for film, 1991.

WORK IN PROGRESS: Their Dogs Came with Them, a novella about interracial violence in Los Angeles.

SIDELIGHTS: A Chicana writer whose work addresses social issues, Helena Maria Viramontes "believes that writing can bring about social change," related Kayann Short in her interview with the author in the *Bloomsbury Review.* The stories in her debut collection, *The Moth and Other Stories,* many of which were published previously in small magazines, are set mostly in Los Angeles, and present everyday incidents of oppression—economic, racial, and sexist—in the lives of ordinary, often Chicana, women of all ages. "Viramontes' relentlessly serious stories," a *Kirkus Reviews* critic remarked, "are really a series of poignant vignettes, slices of Latina life. Were she to lighten up a bit and sacrifice ideology for artistry, she might become [an] important new voice." *Village Voice* book reviewer Laurie Stone found most of the stories in *Moth* "tense, direct, and powerfully imagined," but also noted that in some stories "her characters sink under rhetorical points about the condition of women."

Viramontes's novel, *Under the Feet of Jesus,* is narrated by a young female migrant worker, Estrella, who rebels against her rural community's racial and sexual restrictions, and offers a Chicana perspective on corporate agricultural practices. "If they read the book, and if they think about the piscadores when they eat their salad, that would bring me great satisfaction as a writer," Viramontes told Short. *Booklist* reviewer Gilbert Taylor praised *Under the Feet of Jesus* noting that "in Viramontes' hands the canvas . . . teems with color." A *Kirkus Reviews* contributor wrote that her novel is "a compelling debut with prose that sometimes stumbles but more often soars in describing human suffering and faith." Sonia Saldivar-Hull, writing in the *Dictionary of Literary Biography,* assessed Viramontes's literary contributions thusly: "Her groundbreaking narrative strategies, combined with her sociopolitical focus, situate her at the forefront of an emerging Chicana literary tradition that redefines Chicano literature and feminist theory."

BIOGRAPHICAL/CRITICAL SOURCES:

BOOKS

Dictionary of Literary Biography, Volume 122: *Chicano Writers,* Gale (Detroit, MI), 1992.
Notable Hispanic American Women, Gale (Detroit, MI), 1993.

PERIODICALS

Bloomsbury Review, January/February, 1996.
Booklist, April 15, 1995, pp. 1481-1482.
Kirkus Reviews, October 1, 1985, p. 1046; February 15, 1995, pp. 180-181.
Publishers Weekly, March 20, 1995, pp. 42-43.
Village Voice, April 15, 1986, p. 55.
Washington Post Book World, May 14, 1995, p. 4.*

*   *   *

VIVANCO, Luis Felipe   1907-1975

PERSONAL: Born August 22, 1907, in El Escorial, Spain; died November 21, 1975 of a heart attack; son

of Rosario (maiden name, Bergamin) Vivanco; married Maria Luisa Gefaell (a musician and children's book writer), 1945; children: Juan, Soledad, Franco. *Education:* University of Madrid, Ph.D. (architecture), 1932. *Religion:* Catholic.

CAREER: Poet and architect, 1936-75.

AWARDS, HONORS: Premio de Fastenrath by the Spanish Real Academia, 1957, for *Introduccion a la poesia espanola contemporanea;* Critics' Award, 1974, for *Los caminos (1945-1965).*

WRITINGS:

Cantos de primavera, Heroe (Madrid), 1936.
(Editor with Luis Rosales) *Poesia heroica del imperio,* Jerargvia (Madrid), 1940.
Tiempo de dolor, Aguirre (Madrid), 1940.
(Editor) *Antologia poetica: Miguel de Unamumo,* Escorial (Madrid), 1942.
Continuacion de la vida, Gallades (Madrid), 1949.
Alberto Sartorius, Escuela de Altamira (Santander, Spain), 1951.
Primera bienal hispanoamericana de arte, Aguado (Madrid), 1952.
El Escorial, Noguer (Barcelona), 1953, translation by John Forrester published as *The Escorial,* Editorial Noguer (Barcelona, Spain), 1956.
Angel Ferrante: Estudio, Gallades (Madrid), 1954.
El descampado, Papeles de Son Armadans (Madrid), 1957.
Introduccion a la poesia espanola contemporanea, Guadarrama (Madrid), 1957.
Memoria de la plata, Rialp (Madrid), 1958.
Lecciones para el hijo, Aguilar (Madrid), 1961.
Los ojos de Toledo: Leyenda autobiografica, Barna (Barcelona), 1963.
Moratin y la ilustracion magica, Taurus (Madrid), 1972.
Los caminos (1945-1965), Cultura Hispanica (Madrid), 1974, translation published as *The Roads,* 1974.
Prosas propicias, Plaza & Janes (Esplugas de Llobregat, Spain), 1976.
Antologia poetica, edited by Jose Maria Valverde, Alianza (Madrid), 1976.
Azorin, Fundacion (Madrid), 1979.
Diario, 1945-1975, Taurus (Madrid), 1983.

Also translator of works by poets Rainer Maria Rilke and Paul Claudel.

SIDELIGHTS: Luis Felipe Vivanco was a well-known Spanish poet of the Generation of 1936. Known for his lyric and philosophic poetry, he experienced disruption in his life as well as in his work when the Spanish Civil War broke out. Vivanco was born on August 22, 1907, the oldest of five children in a wealthy, well-educated Catholic family. His mother, who was very close to him, encouraged him in his two careers as architect and poet, as well as instilling her strong religious beliefs in him. He was educated at Marianist (Catholic) schools. When he was fourteen, his father was transferred to Toledo, Spain, where Vivanco was handicapped by his deep shyness, his unusually strong connection to his parents, and his dreamy nature. Vivanco attended the University of Madrid and began studying architecture there; he received his Ph.D. in architecture in 1932. During his education, he also drew and went to museums to feed his interest in art. He later worked for his uncle's architectural firm for several years. He attempted to study philosophy at the university, but did not complete a degree because of the interruption of the Spanish Civil War; after the war he discontinued his studies because he believed the quality of the faculty had declined. His politics were leftist during this time, in conflict with his family's conservative views. He was not reconciled with them until 1936, when an emotional crisis as well as disenchantment with leftist leaders led him to believe that government should be more authoritarian.

Although Vivanco worked as an architect, his true love was poetry. He began writing verse during his studies at the university, but later destroyed most of his work from that time. Some poems have survived, although in a reworked form, in *Memoria de la plata* ("Silver Memory"). The poems in this book are based on a summer in the late 1920s, when the writer Rafael Alberti spent the summer with him at his family's home in El Escorial. Vivanco's mother did not approve of their friendship and would not allow Alberti to sleep in the house, so he had to sleep out in the fields, and obtain her permission to come inside in the morning to shave, eat, and visit Vivanco. Vivanco was friends with most of the well-known poets of his time and described their work and its background in *Introduccion a la poesia espanola contemporanea*. He also translated works of other poets into Spanish, particularly those of Rainer Maria Rilke and Paul Claudel.

In 1936 Vivanco's father decided that certain leftist politicos were a threat to his family's safety, and he and Vivanco sought refuge in an embassy. The family as a whole took the side of the dictator Franco and his rightist Falangist government, and Vivanco wrote political material for the Falangists. He also wrote for the government-approved journal *El Escorial*. Despite his conservative politics, however, he did not support discrimination against those who had opposed Franco, and in general saw people as individuals rather than as members of one party or another. In 1945 he married Maria Luisa Gefaell, a talented musician who had converted from Judaism to Catholicism. They had three children: Juan, Soledad, and Franco. Vivanco's marriage began a period of stability and creativity, during which he withdrew from his political connections to pursue a more contemplative artistic life. From 1949 to 1951 he was a member of the Escuela de Altamira, a group of artists in all fields. At meetings of the group he presented papers on architecture, art, and literature, and these make clear that if he had been allowed to, he would have produced interesting innovations in architecture as well as in poetry.

Vivanco's work generally focused on personal, rather than social or political, experience. This personal focus may be a result of his introspective, introverted temperament, but also was influence by the repressive political regime in Spain at that time. "In this time of retreat into poetry, family, and self, which was never so complete as to exclude numerous friendships and even considerable responsibilities within the world of literature and art," wrote *Dictionary of Literary Biography* contributor Clark Colahan, "there were moments of discouragement and a sense of isolation." If Vivanco had not lived under an oppressive regime, the validity of his writings would not have been questioned. One notable feature of his work is a continuing search for integrity and authority. He sought to find a deeper philosophic and spiritual meaning beyond the surface of life, and in his youth was fascinated by the writings of the mystics San Juan de la Cruz and Saint Teresa. In his poetry he explores his experiences of exaltation, loss, or frustration as he attempts to draw closer to God through experiences of beauty, nature, or love.

Vivanco's poetry is intensely imagistic, and does not make much use of plot, characters, or systematic frameworks. He placed a special emphasis on the dreaming state as the source of insight and enlightenment. This idea was consistent with the time in which he lived, when artists were becoming aware of the concept of the unconscious mind, and espousing their belief that it was the primary influence on human behavior. Vivanco combined this concept with his belief that God is the ultimate reality that poetry can reveal: poetry is a mystical quest toward union with God, through dreamlike states of insight and enlightenment. "His work," said Colahan, "can also stand on its own for its intensity, its technical variety and quality, and its reflection of the spiritual trajectory over sixty years of a poet whose underlying attitudes evolved, by and large, like those of his countrymen."

BIOGRAPHICAL/CRITICAL SOURCES:

BOOKS

Dictionary of Literary Biography, Volume 108: *Twentieth-Century Spanish Poets,* Gale (Detroit, MI), 1991.*

*   *   *

WERNER, Flora
    See GONZALEZ (MANDRI), Flora

*   *   *

WOOD, Stephanie 1954-

PERSONAL: Born May 26, 1954, in Santa Rosa, CA; married Robert Haskett, June 21, 1980; children: Jeffrey, Alexis. *Education:* University of California, Santz Cruz, B.A. (with honors), 1977; University of California, Los Angeles, M.A., 1979, Ph.D., 1984.

ADDRESSES: Home—2085 University St., Eugene, OR 97403-1541. *Office*—Department of History, Box 1288, University of Oregon, Eugene, OR 97403-1288; fax 541-346-4895. *E-mail*—swood@darkwing. uoregon.edu.

CAREER: University of Maine at Orono, assistant professor of Latin American and U.S. history, 1984-89; University of Oregon, Eugene, adjunct assistant professor of Latin American history, 1988—. Meridian Productions, director of research for the videotape documentary, *The Sixth Sun: Mayan Uprising in Chiapas,* broadcast on television by Public Broadcasting Service (PBS), 1996; consultant for other videotape documentaries, including *Columbus and the Age of Discovery,* PBS, 1991, *The Last Zapatista,* PBS, 1996, and the series *Sleeping Kings.*

AWARDS, HONORS: Fulbright fellow in Mexico, 1981-82; American Council of Learned Societies, grants, 1987 and 1988, fellowship, 1996-97.

WRITINGS:

(Contributor) Arij Ouweneel and Simon Miller, editors, *The Indian Community of Colonial Mexico: Fifteen Essays on Land Tenure, Corporate Organizations, Ideology, and Village Politics,* Center for Latin American Research and Documentation (Amsterdam, Netherlands), 1990.
(Editor with Susan Schroeder and husband, Robert Haskett, and contributor) *Indian Women of Early Mexico,* University of Oklahoma Press (Norman, OK), 1997.
(Editor with Xavier Noguez Ramirez, and contributor) *De Tlacuilos y Escribanos: Estudios sobre Documentos Indigenas Coloniales del Centro de Mexico,* El Colegio Mexiquense (Toluca, Mexico), 1998.
(Contributor) Matthew Restall and Susan Kellogg, editors, *Dead Giveaways: Indigenous Testaments of Colonial Spanish America,* University of Utah Press (Salt Lake City, UT), in press.

Contributor of articles and reviews to academic journals, including *Estudios de Cultura Nahuatl, Americas,* and *Ethnohistory.*

WORK IN PROGRESS: Transcending Conquest: Indigenous Views of the Spanish in Colonial Mexico.

*   *   *

YANEZ, Jose Donoso
    See DONOSO, Jose

*   *   *

ZAMORA, Bernice (B. Ortiz) 1938-

PERSONAL: Born January 20, 1938, in Aguilar, CO; father was a coal miner, farmer, and automobile painter; mother worked for an optical company (maiden name, Valdez); married to husband named Zamora (divorced, 1974); children: Rhonda, Katherine. *Education:* University of Southern Colorado, B.A.; Colorado State University, M.A., 1972; Stanford University, Ph.D., 1986; attended Marquette University, 1973.

CAREER: Poet. Instructor of Chicano studies, University of California, Berkeley.

MEMBER: Modern Language Association, Bay Area Chicano Poets/Chicano Writers' Union, Ancient Mystical Order Rosae Crucis.

WRITINGS:

(With Jose Antonio Burciaga) *Restless Serpents* (poems), Disenos Literarios (Menlo Park, CA), 1976.

(Editor with Jose Armas) *Flor y Canto IV and V: An Anthology of Chicano Literature,* Pajarito (Albuquerque, NM), 1980.

Releasing Serpents (poems), Bilingual Press/Editorial Bilingue (Ypsilanti, MI), 1994.

Contributor to anthologies, including *Calafia: The California Poetry,* edited by Ishmael Reed, 1979, and *Chicanos: Antologia historica y literaria,* 1980. Contributor to *Caracol, De Colores, Mango, Atisbos,* and *Revista Chicano-Riquena.* Editor, *De Colores,* 1979; guest editor, *El Fuego de Aztlan.* A collection of Bernice Zamora's papers is housed at the Mexican American Collections at Stanford University.

WORK IN PROGRESS: A play; a novel; a book on La Malinche, the Aztec mistress of Hernan Cortes, the conqueror of Mexico.

SIDELIGHTS: "Bernice Zamora's considerable reputation as a poet rests largely on one book, *Restless Serpents,*" writes Nancy Vogeley in *Dictionary of Literary Biography.* "Zamora's poetry in *Restless Serpents* explores such topics as Chicano cultural traditions, the experience of women in that culture, language, and the power of poetry."

Zamora was born in a small village in the coal-mining region of Colorado. Her parents spoke Spanish at home and adhered to the practices and traditions of Roman Catholicism and Chicano culture. Yet, once she began school, Zamora was encouraged to confine herself to the English language—something she came to resent in her adult years. In an interview with Juan Bruce-Novoa, published in *Chicano Authors: Inquiry by Interview,* she described her reading material during her formative years: "Sunday missals, Catechisms, and biographies of saints. . . . My favorite saints were St. Teresa the mystic and St. Thomas Aquinas, the latter because he was presented in the children's literature as an outcast and a dullard who, after pleading to God for guidance, became the teacher of his teachers." Zamora was an excellent student. After high school graduation, she married and began a family, then returned to college in the mid-1960s to earn an undergraduate degree in English. Some time later, after her marriage ended, she returned to school at Stanford University, where she earned a doctorate in 1986.

Restless Serpents, published in 1976, contained poems by Zamora and Jose Antonio Burciaga, and is considered a seminal work of Chicano poetry. Many critics praised Zamora's contributions to the volume for their lyricism, beauty, power, and the complexity of the thoughts and feelings behind the poems. Like the serpents of the title, "Zamora's poetry fascinates," Bruce-Novoa writes in *Latin American Literary Review.* "Inscrutable signs of life and death in beautiful form, capable of demonic possession; gods of mysterious, lost worlds, only accessible to us in the surface of the images they themselves are. They demand and deserve attention . . . but they carry a venomous bite. However, doesn't the fascination of life stem from the perverse intensity of the play of the deadly unknown dangers in the spaces we find most seductive?"

The clarification of relationships is an important element of Zamora's writing, including the reinterpretation of sexual relationships. "The primary determinant of Zamora's poems in *Restless Serpents* is sex," writes Marta Ester Sanchez in *Contemporary Chicana Poetry: A Critical Approach to an Emerging Literature.* Sanchez continues that *Restless Serpents* "represent[s] attempts to redefine sexual relationships between men and women as well as relationships between a text and its literary source." Sanchez emphasizes that "if there is a fundamental loyalty marking Zamora's poetic consciousness, it is to her female voice, to her identity as a woman."

Zamora does not see herself as a traditional feminist, however. She told Bruce-Novoa for *Chicano Authors: Inquiry by Interview:* "It would be a mistake . . . to call [Chicana writers] feminist writers. To be a purely feminist writer is to ignore the issue of race—racial discrimination, division, and deprivation—these are entirely overlooked by the feminists." She continued, "besides, our relationship with our men is far different than that of the feminist with her man. These are the affinities we share with Blacks as I have discussed them with those Black writers I know." And Vogeley recounts that "although Zamora admits a feminist message in her poetry, she says her primary anger is directed against oppression in all forms."

Zamora sees Chicanos as connected with other nonwhite races, especially in their literature: "An oral tradition is one important affinity we share with Native Americans and Blacks; another is our penchant for integrating our religious and spiritual symbols with our arts; and most important is our similar experience of resistance to cultural suppression," she told Bruce-Novoa. She continued: "The common ground we have with Blacks is, of course, our respective oral traditions and our heavy reliance on internal rhythms for expression. We may write in English, but we rarely write in iambic pentameter." Zamora also told Bruce-Novoa that "the rhythmic expressions in poetry, the humor and poignancy . . . the experimentation and extension of our oral tradition in the novel," are among the strengths of Chicano writing. She believes that its weaknesses "lie in our critical writings. We have yet to learn to separate the cultural qualities from the societal and academic ones in order to restructure a balanced approach."

BIOGRAPHICAL/CRITICAL SOURCES:

BOOKS

Binder, Wolfgang, editor, *Partial Autobiographies: Interviews with Twenty Chicano Poets,* Verlag Palm and Enke (Erlangen, West Germany), 1985, pp. 221-229.

Bruce-Novoa, Juan, *Chicano Authors: Inquiry by Interview,* University of Texas Press (Austin), 1980.

Bruce-Novoa, Juan, *Chicano Poetry: A Response to Chaos,* University of Texas Press, 1982.

Contemporary Literary Criticism, Volume 89, Gale (Detroit), 1996.

Dictionary of Literary Biography, Volume 82: *Chicano Writers: First Series,* Gale, 1989.

Candelaria, Cordelia, *Chicano Poetry: A Critical Introduction,* Greenwood Press (Westport, CT), 1986, pp. 146-156.

Magill, Frank N., *Masterpieces of Latino Literature,* HarperCollins (New York City), 1994.

Modern Chicano Writers: A Collection of Critical Essays, Joseph Sommers and Tomas Ybarra-Frausta, editors, Prentice-Hall (Englewood Cliffs, NJ), 1979.

Sanchez, Marta Ester, *Contemporary Chicana Poetry: A Critical Approach to an Emerging Literature,* University of California Press (Berkeley), 1985.

PERIODICALS

American Book Review, October, 1979, p. 20.
Confluencia, spring, 1986, pp. 10-17.
De colores, Number 3, 1978, pp. 42-52.
El fuego de Aztlan, summer, 1977, p. 4.

Imagine, summer, 1985, pp. 26-39.
Latin American Literary Review, spring-summer, 1977, pp. 152-154.
MELUS, fall, 1980, pp. 55-68; winter, 1980, pp. 102-104.
Nation, January 31, 1994, pp. 131-133.
Nuestro, March, 1986, pp. 35-39.
Publishers Weekly, November 22, 1993, p. 59.
Revista Chicano-Riquena, autumn, 1978, p. 64-73.
Revista Iberoamericana, July-December, 1985, pp. 565-573.
Third Woman, Volume 2, number 1, 1984, pp. 75-102.

OTHER

Rodriguez del Pino, Salvador, *Interview with Bernice Zamora* (videotape), Center for Chicano Studies, University of California (Santa Barbara), 1977.*

*　　*　　*

ZELLER, Ludwig 1927-

PERSONAL: Born February 1, 1927, in Rio Loa, Chile; immigrated to Canada, 1971; son of Guillermo and Rosa Elvira (Ocampo) Zeller; married Susana Wald (an artist); children: Harald, Beatriz, Alejo, Javier. *Education:* Attended University of Chile.

ADDRESSES: Home—Toronto, Ontario, Canada.

CAREER: Poet and artist, c. 1975—. Chilean Ministry of Education, visual consultant and artist, 1953-68. Oasis Publications, Toronto, Ontario, co-founder and publisher. Work represented in exhibitions, including a retrospective at Hamilton Art Gallery, 1979.

WRITINGS:

Exodo y otras soledades, 1957.
Del manantial, 1961.
A Aloyse, 1964.
Las reglas del juego, 1968.
Mujer en sueno (title means "Woman in Dream"), 1975.
(Illustrator, with collages) Enrique Gomez-Correa, *Mother-Darkness,* English version by wife, Susanna Wald, Oasis (Toronto, Ontario), 1975.
When the Animal Rises from the Deep, the Head Explodes, 1976.

Wanderers in the Mandala (poems and collages), 1978.

Alphacollage, 1979.

In the Country of the Antipodes: Poems, 1964-1979, edited and partially translated by S. Wald, and A. F. Moritz, Mosaic Press (Oakville, Ontario), 1979.

(Illustrator with S. Wald) Moritz, *Black Orchid,* Dreadnaught (Toronto), 1981.

50 Collages, 1981.

(With S. Wald) *Espejismos/Mirages* (collages), Hounslow (Toronto), 1983.

A Perfumed Camel Never Does the Tango (aphorisms), 1985.

The Marble Head and Other Poems, 1987.

Ludwig Zeller, A Celebration, 1987.

Salvar la poesia quemar las naves, 1988.

The Ghost's Tattoos, 1989.

To Saw the Beloved to Pieces Only When Necessary, 1990.

(Illustrator, with collages) Robin Skelton, *A Devious Dictionary,* Cacanadadada Press (Vancouver, British Columbia), 1991.

Zeller Free Dream/Zeller sueno libre, 1992.

Totem Women/Mujeres en el Totem, Exile Editions (Toronto), 1993.

Echoes of the Storm: An Anthology of Spanish-American Poetry, 1993.

Aserrar a la amada cuando es necesario, 1994.

Los engranajes del encantamiento, 1996.

Also author of *Los placeres de edipo, Circe's Mirrors,* and *Visions and Wounds.**

Hispanic Writers
Cumulative Author Index

(Numeral appearing below refers to edition in
which the author's most recent entry appears.)

Hispanic Writers
Cumulative Nationality Index

(Authors are listed alphabetically under country of origin
and/or their country of citizenship. Numeral refers to edition
in which the author's most recent entry appears.)

Cervantes, Lorna Dee **1**
Chacon, Eusebio **1**
Charles, Rupaul Andre **2**
Chavez, Denise (Elia) **2**
Chavez, John R(ichard) **1**
Chavez, Manuel **1**
Cisneros, Sandra **2**
Collignon, Rick **2**
Cruz, Gilbert R(alph) **1**
Cruz, Ricardo Cortez **2**
Cumpian, Carlos **2**
de las Casas, Walter **2**
De Leon, Nephtali **2**
DeSena, Carmine **2**
Diaz Valcarcel, Emilio **1**
Duran, Roberto (Tinoco) **2**
Espinosa, Aurelio M(acedonio) Jr. **1**
Espinosa, Aurelio M(acedonio) **1**
Fornes, Maria Irene **1**
Frohock, Fred M(anuel) **2**
Gamboa, Reymundo **2**
Gamboa (T., Jr.), Harry Jr. **2**
Garcia, Cristina **2**
Garcia, Guy D. **2**
Garcia, Lionel G. **1**
Garcia, Richard A. **2**
Garza, Roberto J(esus) **1**
Geigel Polanco, Vicente **1**
Gilbert, Fabiola **2**
Gonzales, Rebecca **2**
Gonzales, Sylvia Alicia **1**
Gonzalez, Alexander G. **2**
Gonzalez, Genaro **2**
Gonzalez, Ray **2**
Gonzalez-Crussi, F(rank) **2**
Gracia, Jorge J(esus) E(miliano) **2**
Herrera, Juan Felipe **1**
Hijuelos, Oscar **2**
Hinojosa, Gilberto Miguel **2**
Hinojosa(-Smith), Rolando (R.) **2**
Huerta, Jorge A(lfonso) **1**
Islas, Arturo **1**
Kanellos, Nicolas **1**
Keller, Gary D. **1**
Lizardi, Joseph **2**
LoMonaco, Palmyra **2**
Lopez, Diana **2**
Luis, William **2**
Marques, Rene **2**
Martinez, Elizabeth Coonrod **2**
Martinez, Max(imiano) **1**
Mendez, Miguel **2**
Meyer, Doris (L.) **2**
Mohr, Nicholasa **2**
Mora, Pat(ricia) **2**
Moraga, Cherrie **2**
Morales, Alejandro **1**
Moreno, Dorinda **2**
Morton, Carlos **1**
Murguia, Alejandro **2**
Nava, Julian **1**
Ortego y Gasca, Philip D. **1**
Pacheco, Henry L(uis) **1**
Paredes, Americo **1**
Ponce, Mary Helen **2**
Portillo Trambley, Estela **1**
Quintana, Leroy V. **2**
Quirarte, Jacinto **1**
Rabassa, Gregory **2**
Ramirez, Susan E(lizabeth) **1**
Ramirez de Arellano, Diana (T. Clotilde) **1**
Rechy, John (Francisco) **2**
Rios, Alberto (Alvaro) **2**

Rivera, Geraldo (Miguel) **1**
Rivera, Tomas **1**
Rodriguez, Richard **2**
Rodriguez-Alcala, Hugo (Rosendo) **1**
Romero, Orlando **2**
Rosales, Francisco A(rturo) **1**
Ruiz, Ramon Eduardo **1**
Sagel, Jim **1**
Salinas, Luis Omar **2**
Samora, Julian **1**
Sanchez, Ricardo **1**
Sanchez, Thomas **1**
Sanchez, Trinidad Jr. **2**
Sanchez-Korrol, Virginia **1**
Seltzer, Chester E. **1**
Sierra, Ruben **2**
Silva, Beverly **1**
Soto, Gary **2**
Soto, Shirlene A(nn) **1**
Souza, Raymond D(ale) **1**
Tafolla, (Mary) Carmen **1**
Thomas, Piri **1**
Ulibarri, Sabine R(eyes) **2**
Urista, Alberto H. **1**
Valdez, Luis (Miguel) **1**
Valle, Victor Manuel **2**
Vasquez, Richard **1**
Velasquez, Gloria (Louise) **2**
Velez-Ibanez, Carlos G(uillermo) **1**
Vigil, Angel **2**
Vigil-Pinon, Evangelina **2**
Villanueva, Alma Luz **1**
Villanueva, Tino **1**
Villarreal, Jose Antonio **1**
Villasenor, Victor E(dmundo) **2**
Viramontes, Helena Maria **2**
Wood, Stephanie **2**
Yglesias, Jose **1**
Zamora, Bernice (B. Ortiz) **2**

URUGUAY

Agustini, Delmira **2**
Benedetti, Mario **2**
Galeano, Eduardo (Hughes) **1**
Ibarbourou, Juana de **1**
Martinez Moreno, Carlos **1**
Onetti, Juan Carlos **2**
Peri Rossi, Cristina **2**
Quiroga, Horacio (Sylvestre) **1**
Rein, Mercedes **1**
Rodo, Jose Enrique **2**
Rodriguez Monegal, Emir **1**
Sanchez, Florencio **1**

VENEZUELA

Caballero, Manuel **1**
Gallegos (Freire), Romulo **1**
Otero Silva, Miguel **2**
Picon Salas, Mariano **2**
Varderi, Alejandro **2**